Annotated Teacher's Edition

Prentice Hall
WRITING and GRAMMAR
Communication in Action

About the Authors

Joyce Armstrong Carroll, Ed.D., has taught every grade level in her forty years in the profession. She is a consultant in all aspects of the language arts. She has written extensively on reading, writing, literature, and teacher training and has received numerous awards for her professional service.

Edward E. Wilson, a former editor of *English in Texas,* is a writing, reading, and literature consultant for school districts nationwide. He has collaborated on several works, including an anthology of poetry.

Gary Forlini has taught high-school language arts and has served as a writing consultant. He has authored several text-books, including Prentice Hall's *Grammar and Composition.*

Prentice Hall

Grade 9 ISBN: 0-13-043350-0
Grade 10 ISBN: 0-13-043351-9
Grade 11 ISBN: 0-13-043352-7
Grade 12 ISBN: 0-13-043353-5

1 2 3 4 5 6 7 8 9 10
04 03 02 01 00

Prentice Hall is pleased to introduce...

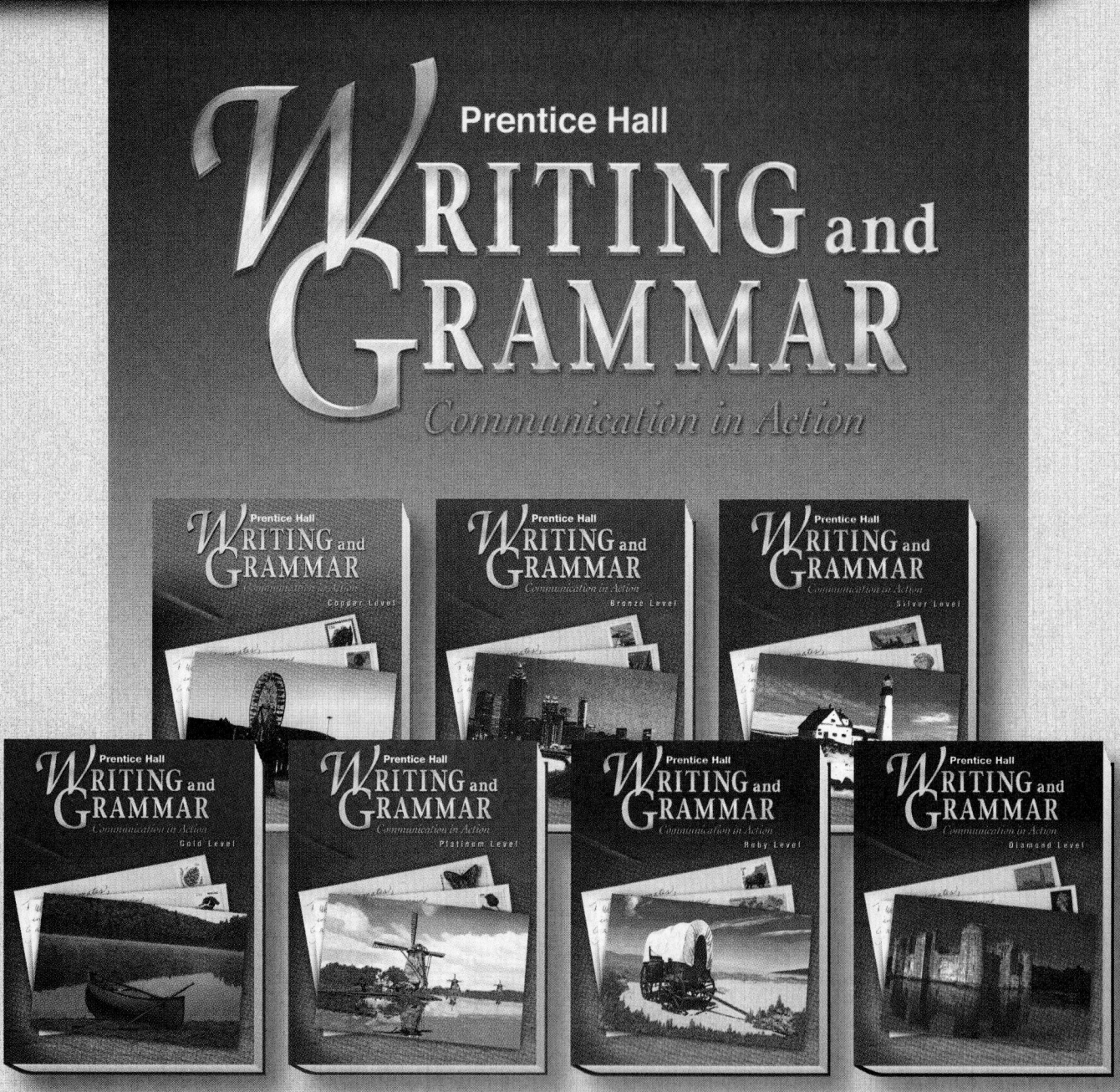

...*Prentice Hall Writing and Grammar: Communication in Action,*
a brand-new program that uses real-world connections and engaging links
to develop writing, grammar, and communication skills.

Put students' words into action!

Only Prentice Hall features ...

- More grammar exercises—including a unique **Hands-on Grammar** feature—than any other program!

- Unique hands-on strategies for every stage of the writing process, especially revision!

- Extensive standardized test preparation support, including a **Standardized Test Preparation Workshop** at the end of every chapter!

- Relevant connections—including real student models; high-interest thematic grammar exercises; and real-world skills instruction—for the twenty-first century!

Writing

Unique hands-on strategies for every stage of the writing process–especially revision!

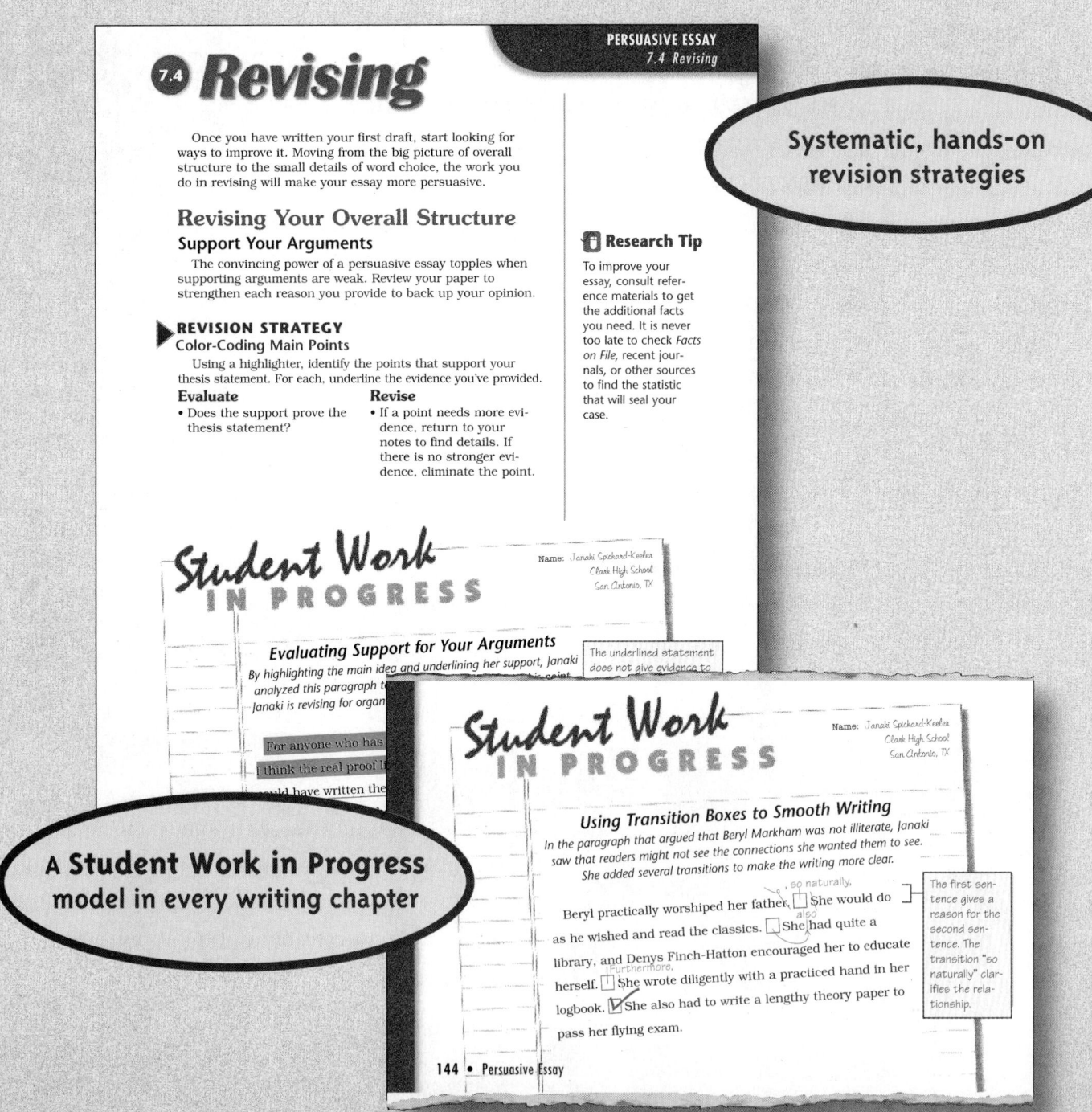

Systematic, hands-on revision strategies

A Student Work in Progress model in every writing chapter

PERSUASIVE ESSAY
7.4 Revising

7.4 Revising

Once you have written your first draft, start looking for ways to improve it. Moving from the big picture of overall structure to the small details of word choice, the work you do in revising will make your essay more persuasive.

Revising Your Overall Structure
Support Your Arguments

The convincing power of a persuasive essay topples when supporting arguments are weak. Review your paper to strengthen each reason you provide to back up your opinion.

▶ **REVISION STRATEGY**
Color-Coding Main Points

Using a highlighter, identify the points that support your thesis statement. For each, underline the evidence you've provided.

Evaluate
- Does the support prove the thesis statement?

Revise
- If a point needs more evidence, return to your notes to find details. If there is no stronger evidence, eliminate the point.

Research Tip

To improve your essay, consult reference materials to get the additional facts you need. It is never too late to check *Facts on File*, recent journals, or other sources to find the statistic that will seal your case.

Student Work IN PROGRESS

Name: Janaki Spichard-Keeler
Clark High School
San Antonio, TX

Evaluating Support for Your Arguments

By highlighting the main idea and underlining her support, Janaki analyzed this paragraph t...
Janaki is revising for organ...

For anyone who has ...
I think the real proof l...
...uld have written the...

The underlined statement does not give evidence to ...

Student Work IN PROGRESS

Name: Janaki Spichard-Keeler
Clark High School
San Antonio, TX

Using Transition Boxes to Smooth Writing

In the paragraph that argued that Beryl Markham was not illiterate, Janaki saw that readers might not see the connections she wanted them to see. She added several transitions to make the writing more clear.

Beryl practically worshiped her father. ☐ , so naturally, She would do as he wished and read the classics. ☐ also She had quite a library, and Denys Finch-Hatton encouraged her to educate herself. ☐ Furthermore, She wrote diligently with a practiced hand in her logbook. ☑ She also had to write a lengthy theory paper to pass her flying exam.

The first sentence gives a reason for the second sentence. The transition "so naturally" clarifies the relationship.

Grammar in Your Writing
Using the Conventions for Writing Titles

As you proofread, make sure you have used the conventions for writing titles. Long works are set off by underlining or italics. In addition to the titles of novels and plays, other titles that are italicized include the names of newspapers, magazines, movies, paintings, and sculptures.

Enclose short works in quotation marks. In addition to the titles of poems and short stories, other titles that are enclosed in quotation marks are essays, articles, and songs.

Titles of books: *West With the Night* by Beryl Markham
Titles of short stories: "A Day's Wait" by Ernest Hemingway
Titles of long poems: *Paradise Lost* by John Milton
Titles of short poems: "The Bells" by Edgar Allan Poe

Find It in Your Reading Find three titles in the completed student essay on pp. 130–133. Explain the conventions used for writing the titles.

Find It in Your Writing As you proofread your persuasive essay, check that you have written all titles correctly.

For more on writing titles correctly, see Chapter 29.

*Two **Grammar in Your Writing** features in every chapter*

Writers in ACTION

Although you may not have heard of Victorian writer Edward Bulwer-Lytton, his words have become a motto for the power of persuasion. Since the nineteenth century, people have quoted his famous line:

"The pen is mightier than the sword."

***Writers in Action** provides useful tips from established writers.*

TOPIC BANK

If you're having trouble coming up with your own topic, consider these possibilities:

1. **Editorial About Violence on Television** Television networks have come under attack for the violence that is telecast on the news and in dramas. Write an editorial in which you criticize or defend a network's programming choices.

2. **Persuasive Essay on Equal Funding for Girls' Sports** Schools and colleges budget large amounts of money for traditionally male sports. In some states, football receives more funding than field hockey. In a persuasive essay, argue for or against this financial situation.

Responding to Fine Art

3. This painting, *The Pond*, might inspire you to find the beauty of your community's natural spaces. Write a persuasive essay on an action that impacts the local environment. For example, you might evaluate the effect of mandatory recycling programs or weigh the results of the increased building of shopping malls and housing.

Pond, 1985, Adele Alsop, courtesy of Schmidt Bingham Gallery, NYC

Responding to Literature

4. Read "The Cask of Amontillado" by Edgar Allan Poe. As a lawyer, write a persuasive essay in which you either defend or prosecute Montresor for his actions. You can find this story in *Prentice Hall Literature: Timeless Voices, Timeless Themes*, Gold.

☑ Cooperative Writing Opportunity

5. **Persuasive Brochure on Volunteerism** With a group, split the task of researching volunteer work. Each group member can research a different aspect of the topic; for example, one might report on the benefits to the volunteer, while another could focus on the benefits to others. Together, create a pamphlet on the values of volunteering.

Prewriting • 135

*Topic Bank includes **Responding to Fine Art** and **Responding to Literature***

Grammar

More grammar exercises–including a unique **Hands-on Grammar** feature–than any other program!

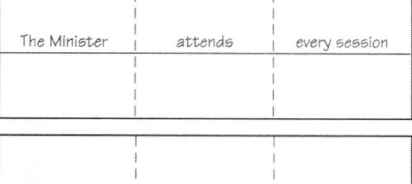

Hands-on Grammar

Subject-Verb Agreement Color Match

Cut three strips of paper of equal length. Draw a blue line across the center of one. Draw a red line across the center of the other. Fold the strip into thirds, as shown in the illustration. The_____ tence with a singular subject, a singular verb _____ across the blue line. Write the subject in the _____ second, and the remaining words in the _____ sentence on the strip with the red line, _____ plural verb form. Next, cut each strip on _____ up the parts of the sentence. You will find th_____ color match between a singular subject and a plur_____

The Minister	attends	every session

The Ministers	attend	every session

Hands-on Grammar

GRAMMAR EXERCISES 24–29

Exercise 24 Correcting Errors in Pronoun-Antecedent Agreement In the following sentences, most of the pronouns do not agree with their antecedents. Identify pronouns that do not agree. Then, write the correct form. If the sentence is correct, write C.

1. Anyone who has e-mail probably corresponds with their friends often.
2. Both Marissa and Tashina check their mailboxes every day.
3. Neither likes to open their mailbox to find that no one has written to them.
4. However, each of the girls always has messages waiting for them.
5. One feature of an e-mail program is their ability to store messages.

Exercise 25 Correcting Special Problems in Pronoun-Antecedent Agreement Rewrite the following paragraph, correcting the errors in pronoun and antecedent agreement. Not all sen-

Exercise 26 Revision Practice: Pronoun Antecedent Agreement Revise the following paragraph, correcting errors in pronoun and antecedent agreement.

(1) There are homes in America in which they don't watch much TV. (2) Instead, each family member spends their time on other activities. (3) This is much better for you. (4) One health expert reports that when someone stares at TV, they don't use their imagination. (5) National TV-Turnoff Week is sponsored by TV-Free America, and millions of Americans participate in it.

Exercise 27 Find It in Your Reading Reread the excerpt from Bill Gates's *The Road Ahead* on page 589. Find at least three personal pronouns, and write them down along with their antecedents.

Exercise 28 Find It in Your Writing Select a writing sample from your portfolio. On your draft, draw a circle around each pronoun and underline its antecedent. Finally, check to be sure that the pronouns and the antecedents agree.

More grammar practice than any other program

25 AGREEMENT
Chapter Review

_____he marchers come the ringmaster into the center ring to introduce the acts. (5) Often there's acts going on in all three rings simultaneously. (6) The funniest act are the clowns. (7) In they come, running and tumbling, each wearing their own silly costume. (8) Sounds of laughter from the audience fills the big top. (9) One of the most breathtaking acts are the trapeze artists. (10) Flying through the air, he or she catches each other with amazing precision.

591

Chapter 25 *Chapter Review*

GRAMMAR EXERCISES 30–36

Exercise 30 Choosing Verbs That Agree With Subjects Choose the verb that agrees with the subject in each sentence.

1. (Do, Does) your group of friends enjoy movies?
2. One of my favorite old films (is, are) *The Wizard of Oz.*
3. *The Wizard of Oz,* as well as *Return to Oz,* (was, were) based on a novel by Frank Baum.
4. Very popular today (is, are) action films.
5. Almost every one of them (features, feature) dazzling special effects.
6. Sophisticated electronics (has, have) made the visual effects possible.
7. Acoustics (is, are) the science that has given us the frighteningly realistic sound effects.
8. *Tarzan and the Amazons* (was, were) made with simple special effects in 1945.
9. Back then, only a small percentage of films (was, were) shot in color.
10. Black and white (was, were) more common.

Exercise 31 Revising for Subject-Verb Agreement Rewrite each sentence, revising it according to the instructions given in brackets. Change the verb form as needed. Not all verbs will change.

1. After the regular baseball season comes the long-awaited event. [Change *event* to *championship games.*]
2. The World Series contests bring baseball fever to its highest pitch. [Delete *contests.*]
3. The cheering crowd is a thrilling sight. [Change *crowd* to *fans.*]
4. Excited indeed is every baseball lover

across the country. [Change *every baseball lover* to *all baseball lovers.*]
5. The early part of the series starts the buildup to the final game. [Change *part* to *games.*]
6. The maximum number of series games is seven. [Change the word order, making *seven* the subject of the sentence.]
7. However, there have been series won in only four or five games. [Insert *some* before *series.*]
8. Both teams try hard to come out on top. [Change *Both teams* to *Each team.*]
9. Donald Honig's book *The October Heroes* describes great World Series games. [Delete *Donald Honig's book.*]
10. A Web site giving baseball statistics is located at www.baseballstats.com. [Delete *A Web site giving.*]

Exercise 32 Revising for Pronoun-Antecedent Agreement Revise the following paragraph, correcting all errors in pronoun and antecedent agreement.

(1) In the Hawaiian Islands, they have some of the best scuba diving in the world. (2) If yourself and your friends want a truly exciting experience, you should try it. (3) Each of the diving sites around the island of Oahu has their own special attractions. (4) The guides always take the divers to the places they like best. (5) A person diving in Maunalua Bay, for example, will see exotic fish that they won't see anywhere else. (6) A reef on the south shore contains a shipwreck, but a diver must be experienced to explore it. (7) Anyone who sees the orange cup corals at Ulua Cave won't believe their eyes. (8) Some divers might think that an occasional shark or octopus is dangerous, but usually they're not. (9) All the instruc-

Hawaiian Islands, we'd jump at the chance.

Exercise 33 Revising Sentences to Eliminate Errors in Agreement Revise the following sentences, correcting any errors in agreement. Not every sentence has an error.

1. The U.S. communications industry conveys information in their various forms.
2. In addition to TV and radio, you have publishing and the Internet.
3. Either television or the Internet are the source of news for most people, although both newspapers and radio are still important.
4. Each of the recent technological advances help provide information even faster.
5. However, often the advances mean that you have to buy expensive new equipment to access it.
6. Not all bits of information is beneficial.
7. For example, everyone must guard themselves against false advertising.
8. Almost every qualified person can find work in the communications industry.
9. However, they must have the right training.
10. *Cybercareers* (Massie and Morris), along with other books on communications jobs, are available in bookstores.

Exercise 34 Revising a Paragraph to Eliminate Errors in Agreement Revise the following paragraph, correcting all errors in agreement.

(1) Almost every child has fun at the circus. (2) They burst with excitement when the sounds of the opening pageant begins. (3) As the elephants, horseback riders, and other performers parade around the ring, you hear the rousing music play. (4) After

Exercise 35 Writing Application Write a paragraph about either an aspect of your local or state government or a technological advance that interests you. Make sure that all your verbs agree with their subjects and that your pronouns agree with their antecedents.

Exercise 36 CUMULATIVE REVIEW Sentence Errors Revise the following paragraphs, correcting sentence errors and errors in verb and pronoun usage and agreement. Note that a numbered section may have one error, several errors, or no error.

(1) If one asks whomever has visited New York what they think of the statue in the harbor, the answer might be "Awesome." (2) Originally called Liberty Enlightening the World, it is now knowed as the Statue of Liberty. (3) It was a gift from France to we the American people. (4) The statue symbolizing freedom. (5) She holds a torch in her right hand. (6) In her left hand, she carries a book inscribed "July 4, 1776." (7) Broken chains symbolizing the defeat of tyranny lies at her feet. (8) The Statue of Liberty one of the largest statues in the world. (9) Its builded of copper sheets riveted to an iron frame. (10) Amazingly, 306 feet 8 inches are it's height from the base to the torch.

> **Grammar in Literature** feature provides point-of-use models from quality literature.

Chapter
25 Agreement

> **Visual appeal and high-interest thematic content make grammar relevant.**

When you speak, you automatically use words that agree with other words. You might say, for example, "She *speaks* faster than they *speak*." You know you must add an *-s* to *speak* when the subject is *she* to make the verb agree with the subject.

Agreement is the match—the "fit"—between words or grammatical forms. Because grammatical agreement is not always obvious, you need to study some sentences more closely than others. In this chapter, you will learn to make a verb agree with its subject and to make a pronoun agree with its antecedent.

▲ **Critical View**
Which parts of this picture would you name with plural nouns? Which parts would you name with singular nouns? **[Analyze]**

Assessment

Extensive standardized test preparation support, including a **Standardized Test Preparation Workshop** at the end of every chapter

Standardized Test Preparation Workshop

Standard English Usage: Subject-Verb Agreement

Knowledge of the rules of subject-verb agreement is one of the skills most frequently tested on standardized tests. When checking a test sentence for errors, first identify the subject. Next, identify the type of subject: singular, plural, or compound. Then, apply the rules of agreement to make sure that the verb in the sentence agrees with the subject.

The following questions will give you practice with different formats used for items that test knowledge of subject-verb agreement.

Test Tip

If you are having trouble with a sentence revision, eliminate any answer choices in which the subject and verb clearly do not agree.

Sample Test Item	Answers and Explanations
Identify which underlined words and phrases in the following sentence contain an error. Neither Zach nor Tim are interested in (A) (B) (C) attending Sunday's concert at the arena. (D) No error (E)	The correct answer is *C*. To arrive at this answer, identify the subject of the sentence (whom the sentence is about). The subject is *Zach nor Tim*. It is a compound subject made up of two singular subjects joined by nor. Such a subject takes a singular verb, in this case, *is*.
Choose the revised version of the following sentence that eliminates all errors in grammar, usage, and mechanics. Neither Zach nor Tim are interested in attending Sunday's concert at the arena. A Neither Zach nor Tim is interested in B C D	The correct answer is *A*. To arrive at this answer, identify the subject of the sentence (whom the sentence is about). The subject is *Zach nor Tim*. It is a compound subject made up of two singular subjects joined by *nor*. Such a subject takes a singular verb, in this case, *is*.

▶ Practice 1 Identify which underlined words and phrases in each of the following sentences contain an error.

1. Evergreen trees never loses all their
   (A)   (B)
   leaves at one time but remain
              (C)
   green throughout the year. No error
              (D)   (E)

2. Like all evergreens, a pine or fir tree
   (A)   (B)
   reproduce by means of seeds
   (C)
   contained in its cones. No error
   (D)   (E)

3. Insects, such as the bee, avoid
   (A)   (B)
   the sticky sap of the evergreen.
   (C)   (D)
   No error
   (E)

4. Neither pine trees nor fir trees
   (A)   (B)
   thrives in a desert climate. No error
   (C)   (D)   (E)

5. Beyond those buildings is a
   (A)   (B)
   dense forest filled with evergreen
   (C)   (D)
   trees. No error
   (E)

▶ Practice 2 Choose the revised version of each numbered sentence that eliminates all errors in grammar, usage, and mechanics.

1 The jack pine release its seeds when heated in a fire, and this help renew the forest.

A The jack pines releases its seeds when heated by fire, and this helps renew the forest.

B The jack pine releases its seeds when heated by fire, and this help renew the forest.

C The jack pine release its seeds when heated by fire, and this help renews the forest.

D The jack pine releases its seeds when heated by fire, and this renew the forest.

2 The Douglas fir, th... other types of climates, s...
F The ...

G ...

594 •

Standardized Test Preparation Workshop

Responding to Persuasive Writing Prompts

The writing prompts on many standardized tests are designed to measure your opinions. You will be evaluated on your ability to do the following:

- Define and state your thesis clearly.
- Provide organized supporting arguments for your main point.
- Use language and details that are likely to influence the audience specified in the prompt.
- Elaborate your arguments effectively through the use of striking examples, anecdotes, facts, and other details.
- Use correct grammar, spelling, and punctuation.

When writing for a timed test, plan to devote a specified amount of time to prewriting, drafting, revising, and proofreading.

Below are examples of persuasive writing prompts. Use the suggestions on the opposite page to help you respond. The clocks next to each stage show a suggested percentage of time to devote to the stage.

Test Tip

- Analyze prompts before responding. Underline key instructional phrases and words in the prompt, such as *choose one*, *argue*, *support*, and *explain*.

Sample Writing Situations

Most schools hold regular classes for an average of 180 days each year. In 1983, a study recommended extending the school year to between 200 and 220 days. Some schools have lengthened the school year. Others have not. Choose one of the following prompts, and respond to it:

Write a letter to the school board in which you argue for or against an extended school year. Persuade the members of the board to adopt your opinion. Be sure to support your position with convincing reasons and to explain your reasons in detail.

Write an editorial for the school newspaper in which you urge students to either support or protest an extended school year. Be sure to support your choice with convincing reasons and to explain your reasons in detail.

154 • Persuasive Essay

Prewriting

Allow about one quarter of your time for prewriting.

Identify the Issue and the Audience Whether you have several options or a single assigned topic, you must quickly determine what the purpose of your response will be—what issue or action are you being asked to defend or oppose? Then, look for the words that identify your audience. Each prompt on the previous page has a different audience. The first prompt addresses an audience of adults on the school board. The second addresses an audience of students. You may choose one prompt or another based on the audience you feel best able to influence.

Analyze the Issue Although you probably already have an opinion on the issue, examining your reasons will help you gather details for your persuasive response. Examine your reasons by making a T-chart. See p. 138 to review how to use a T-chart.

Drafting

Allow approximately half of your time for drafting.

Organize Your Arguments Create an outline or a list of points you want to include. Use numbers or an outline to prioritize the list, beginning with the least important and moving to the most important. Next to each item on the list, write sentences that incorporate the details on your T-chart.

Elaborate You probably won't have time to copy your paper twice, so plan to include your elaboration in the first draft. Look over the list of points that support your opinion. For at least three of the points, think of an anecdote, a statistic, or a fact that illustrates the reason or point. Choose details that will influence your specific audience. Write these next to the points they illustrate so that you remember to include them as you write.

Put It on Paper Write your response on your test paper. Begin with a statement of your opinion. Pause occasionally to review your outline or list. Make sure that you continue to follow the logical sequence you have set up and that you are including all your points. Write your response neatly.

Revising, Editing, and Proofreading

Allow about one quarter of your time to revise, edit, and proofread your paper.

Clean It Up Review your persuasive response. Neatly cross out any details that will not influence your audience. Check for errors in spelling. If you are unsure of the spelling of a word, consider replacing it with one you know better. If you are crossing out or erasing, do so neatly.

Standardized Test Preparation Workshop • 155

Standardized Test Preparation Workshops

**Writing
Grammar
Reading
Vocabulary**

Diagnostic Test

Directions: Write all answers on a separate sheet of paper.

Skill Check A. Choose the verb in parentheses that agrees with th[e] subject in each of the following sentences.

1. In most democracies, the people (enjoys, enjoy) basic rights.
2. Freedom of speech, along with other ideals, (is, are) treasured.
3. Neither dictatorships nor most monarchies (grants, grant) broad freedoms to their people.
4. In some countries, either secret police or the military (enforces, enforce) the law.
5. The people and their government (needs, need) to work together for the common good.
6. Dear to the hearts of many (is, are) the concept of liberty.
7. Today in the world, there (is, are) [...]
8. Among the changes (is, are) a strug[...]
9. Collapsing communist government[...] changes.
10. A group of Russians (wants, want) [...]
11. Politics (is, are) difficult in many f[...]
12. Each of the countries (deals, deal) [...]
13. Roger Manser's *Failed Transitions* [...] in the Eastern European economy [...]
14. Fifty years (was, were) a long time [...]
15. More than half the world's populat[...]

Skill Check B. Choose the pronoun i[...] with the antecedent in each of the [...]

16. Many say our culture takes (its, th[...]
17. The development of democracy has [...] people around the world conduct (l[...]
18. Neither Thomas Jefferson nor Benj[...] judged the impact (his, their) work [...]
19. Every person enjoying democracy t[...] her, their) opportunities to America [...]
20. Each of us should be grateful for (h[...]

Skill Check C. Revise the following se[...] in pronoun reference.

21. Even in a corrupt democracy, the g[...] progress.
22. Officials may demand bribes from ordinary citizens in exchange for basic services. This practice makes them rich.
23. When opposing forces unseat a corrupt leader, most citizens are relieved. Then, they have a big job ahead.
24. In the newspaper article, it said that a free election was held.

---

will be most useful to you in future writing projects?

www.phsch[...]
phschool.com

Rubric for Self-Assessment

Use these criteria to evaluate your comparison-and-contrast essay.

	Score 4	Score 3	Score 2	Score 1
Audience and Purpose	Clearly provides a reason for a comparison-contrast analysis	Adequately provides a reason for a comparison-contrast analysis	Provides a reason for a comparison-contrast analysis	Does not provide a reason for a comparison-contrast analysis
Organization	Clearly presents information in a consistent organization best suited to the topic	Presents information using an organization suited to the topic	Chooses an organization not suited to comparison and contrast	Shows a lack of organizational strategy
Elaboration	Elaborates most ideas with facts, details, or examples; links all information to comparison and contrast	Elaborates many ideas with facts, details, or examples; links most information to comparison and contrast	Does not elaborate all ideas; does not link some details to comparison and contrast	Does not provide facts or examples to support a comparison and contrast
Use of Language	Demonstrates excellent sentence and vocabulary variety; includes very few mechanical errors	Demonstrates adequate sentence and vocabulary variety; includes few mechanical errors	Demonstrates repetitive use of sentence structure and vocabulary; includes many mechanical errors	Demonstrates poor use of language; generates confusion; includes many mechanical errors

2 • Comparison-and-Contrast Essay

Peer Review

Say Back

In a small group, share your revised draft. Read your persuasive essay twice, asking readers to listen the first time and respond the second time. Use these questions as a starting point for group discussion:

1. What is the most persuasive point?
2. About which point would a reader want to know more?

After you've heard from your classmates, consider using their suggestions to improve your draft.

Diagnostic Tests before each grammar chapter

Writing Rubics included in every chapter

Peer Reviews for students to work together

Relevance

Relevant connections–including real student models; high-interest thematic grammar exercises; and real-world skills instruction–for the twenty-first century!

7.7 Student Work IN PROGRESS

FINAL DRAFT

◄ Critical
What quali
this picture
that Beryl M
was a risk-tak
[Connect]

Who Wrote West With the Night?

Janaki Spickard-Keeler
Clark High School
San Antonio, Texas

For years, no one even knew the question existed. For years, too, no one even knew that the book existed. After a brief period of success, reaching *The New York Times* bestseller list, the book faded into obscurity with the onset of World War II. It was rediscovered in the 1980's by George Gutekunst while he read through some of Ernest Hemingway's letters. In a letter to Maxwell Perkins, Hemingway wrote: "Did you read Beryl Markham's book, *West With the Night*? I knew her fairly well in Africa and never

Janaki's research provided a compelling quotation to invite readers' interest.

148 • Persuasive Essay

> **An authentic student model in every writing chapter tracks all the stages of the writing process.**

PERSUASIVE ESSAY
7.6 Publishing and Presenting

7.6 Publishing and Presenting

Building Your Portfolio

Sharing your essay may prove powerful—your ideas could change a law, inspire a turnaround in people's habits, or provoke readers to see an idea in a new way. Consider these ideas for publishing and presenting your work:

1. **Encourage Action** Sponsor a read-aloud of several persuasive essays. As a group, choose one of the issues on which to act. Discuss ways to begin the process of making a change for the better—and then get started!

2. **Mail Your Essay** Invite a local, state, or federal elected official to act on the issue your essay addresses. Use government directories to find the address of the most appropriate official. Save a copy of the letter and any response you receive in your portfolio.

Reflecting on Your Writing

Take a moment to jot down your ideas about the persuasive writing experience. Save a copy of your ideas in your portfolio. These questions might direct your reflection:

• What have you learned about your topic?
• Which writing strategy might you recommend to a friend?

🖥 **Internet Tip**

To see model essays scored with this rubric, go to
www.phwg.phschool.com

Rubric for Self-Assessment

Use the following criteria to evaluate your persuasive essay:

	Score 4	Score 3	Score 2	Score 1
Audience and Purpose	Demonstrates highly effective word choice; clearly states focus on persuasive task	Demonstrates good word choice; states focus on persuasive task	Shows some good word choices; minimally states focus on persuasive task	Shows lack of attention to persuasive task
Organization	Uses clear, consistent organizational strategy	Uses clear organizational strategy with occasional inconsistencies	Uses inconsistent organizational strategy; presentation is not logical	Demonstrates lack of organizational strategy
Elaboration	Provides convincing, well-elaborated reasons to support the position	Provides two or more moderately elaborated reasons to support the writer's position	Provides several reasons but few are elaborated; only one elaborated reason	Provides no specific reasons or does not elaborate
Use of Language	Incorporates many transitions to create clarity of expression; includes very few mechanical errors	Incorporates some transitions to help flow of ideas; includes few mechanical errors	Incorporates few transitions; does not connect ideas well; includes many mechanical errors	Does not connect ideas; includes many mechanical errors

Publishing and Presenting • 147

> **Publishing and Presenting** sections show students that writing and accurate use of language are relevant to their lives now and in the future.

Model From Literature

Nevada Barr, a writer of mystery novels, uses the national parks as the setting of many of her stories. Drawing on the writer's experiences as a park ranger, this essay asserts the benefits of the national park system for all citizens.

Reading Writing Connection

Reading Strategy: Interpret Connotation Be alert to a word's **connotation**—the way a specific word can make you feel. As you read, take special notice of the emotional power of the words Barr chooses. You'll see that effective persuasion can turn on the wise use of one word over another.

We Can Go Home Again

Nevada Barr

When I was asked to write an article on why it is important to preserve our national parks, I was a tad shocked. The question seemed unanswerable in its outrageousness—as if I had been asked why is it important to inhale after exhaling, why is it important to drink plenty of liquids when hiking in the desert, why is it important for the sun to rise in the morning?

To those few wretched souls who have been locked away in a box on the moon for the past 50 years and so did not know this, what could be said? I didn't know where to begin. Should I dwell on the gifts these places bestow: the microbes in Lechuguilla Cave that might prove invaluable to the medical community; the clean water and air; the wealth of plant and animal life? Maybe I should

130 • Persuasive Essay

Connections to literature, writing, and grammar help students apply grammar in their writing and see literary applications of writing and grammar techniques.

GRAMMAR IN LITERATURE

from The Road Ahead
Bill Gates

Bill Gates uses both the masculine and feminine pronouns (his or her) *to refer to the indefinite antecedent* anybody.

Before the invention of writing 5,000 years ago, the only form of communication was the spoken word and the listener had to be in the presence of the speaker or miss his message. Once the message could be written, it could be stored and read later by *anybody*, at *his* or *her* convenience. I'm writing these words at home on a summer evening, but I have no idea where or when you'll read them. One of the benefits of the communications revolution will bring to all of us is more control over our schedules.

In the preceding example, there is no antecedent for the pronoun *they*. The sentence can be corrected by replacing *they* with a noun or a personal pronoun that agrees with the antecedent *program*.

Grammar in Your Writing
Punctuating Adverb Clauses

You may find that in your essay you have used many adverb clauses. Adverb clauses show the relationship between ideas by telling *where, when, how, why, to what extent,* or *under what condition.*

Time relationship (when): After the book was published

Cause-and-effect relationship (why): Because so many people like the book

Opposing relationship (under what condition): Although many thought it was well-written

All adverb clauses contain a subject and a verb and begin with a subordinating conjunction.

Common Subordinating Conjunctions That Introduce Adverb Clauses

after	although	as
because	before	if
since	unless	until
when	whenever	where
wherever	whether	while

When an adverb clause introduces a sentence, use a comma to separate it from the rest of the sentence. Note, however, that it is usually not necessary to use a comma before an adverb clause at the end of a sentence.

Introductory adverb clause
After the book was published, critics came forward to question its source.

Adverb clause at the end of a sentence
Hemingway praised the writer because he thought she was talented.

Find It in Your Reading Review "We Can Go Home Again" by Nevada Barr on pages 130–133 of this chapter. Identify two sentences that contain introductory adverb clauses.

Find It in Your Writing Review your draft to identify three adverb clauses. Be sure that you have placed a comma after those that start sentences. If you cannot identify three adverb clauses, challenge yourself to add at least one more to your writing. You may like the improvement you've made.

For more on adverb clauses, see Chapter 21.

Media and Technology Skills

Recognizing Persuasive Techniques

Activity: Find Persuasion in Television Programs

Television entertains and informs, but often it also persuades. Even programs that seem to be simply entertainment carry subtle messages that influence the way you look at the world. Learn to view television programs critically, and evaluate what you see and hear.

Think About It News shows, documentaries, sportscasts, sitcoms, weekly dramas, talk shows, and awards programs are just some of the types of programs offered on television. News programs and documentaries may influence you by lingering on one image or by using words with strong connotations, such as *generous* and *risky*. Sports announcers interject their opinions as they narrate the action of a game. The way the plot of a sitcom turns out carries a message. Talk-show hosts share their opinions, and awards programs place a value on performance. Think about other ways that television programs persuade or influence your perceptions.

Watch It Choose a television program that you enjoy watching. Watch an episode with a notebook and pencil nearby, taking notes on a chart like the one below:

What Is Shown	What I Think
1.	
2.	
3.	

Analyze It Review your notes, and read the boxed side column on this page. Identify the techniques used in the program to influence your perceptions and responses.

Techniques Used to Influence Viewer Response

In a News Program or Documentary
• Focusing on an image
• Comments by the newscaster
• Using words with connotations

In a Sportscast
• Comments by the announcer
• Shots of crowd reaction
• Close-ups on the winning or losing team

In Sitcoms and Dramas
• Plot events in which characters are rewarded or punished
• Portraying certain types of ch...cool o...
• M...

In A...
• Who...
• Shots o... and candid "b... the scenes" shots

Media and Technology Skills workshops teach students relevant, real-world media skills essential for success in the twenty-first century.

Media and Technology Skills • 153

TEACH

 **Interest GRABBER** Write the following sentences on the board, asking students if they can provide the missing pronoun.

Eric or Elaine will bring ___ laptop.

(Students may recognize the problem: neither his nor her ___ solution w___ indef___

---

crow

bicycle

hallway   it

Steven   he

cameras   they

Step-by-Step Teaching Guide

1. Explain to students this basic principle of pronoun and antecedent agreement: a pronoun must always agree with its antecedent in number and gender. For example, if the antecedent is feminine and singular (*Ms. Jones*), the pronoun used to replace it must also be feminine and singular (*she, her, hers, or herself*).

2. Have each student write down two feminine nouns, two masculine nouns, and two neuter nouns. They may be either singular or plural. Then have them trade lists with a partner and write a sentence for each noun. Each sentence must include the noun and a pronoun to replace it.

   Ms. Jones is known for her challenging math tests.

continued

50

 Section 26.2

Pronoun and Antecedent Agreement

Antecedents are the nouns (or the words that take the place of nouns) for which pronouns stand. The word *antecedent* comes from a Latin word meaning "to go before." In English, an antecedent usually precedes its pronoun. This ___ion will explain how pronouns agree with their ___

___en ___ ___nd Antecedents

___un and antecedent agreement is ___ ___er rules:

___ pronoun must agree with its ___nder. ■

___ of a noun or pronoun indicates ___lural.

___d nouns also indicate one of three gen-___eminine, or neuter. Nouns referring to ___ as *uncle* and *boy*, are masculine. Nouns referring ___es, such as *actress* and *mother*, are feminine. Nouns that do not refer to either males or females, such as *stone* and *freedom*, are neuter. Only pronouns in the third-person singular indicate gender.

GENDER OF THIRD-PERSON SINGULAR PRONOUNS		
Masculine	Feminine	Neuter
he, him, his, himself	she, her, hers, herself	it, its, itself

In the following example, the pronoun and antecedent agree completely. Both the antecedent *Charlene* and the pronoun *her* are singular, third person, and feminine.

EXAMPLE: **Charlene** accessed **her** friend's home page.

Agreement in Number Making personal pronouns agree with their antecedents in number is usually a problem only when the antecedent is a compound.

▶**KEY CONCEPT** Use a singular personal pronoun to refer to two or more singular antecedents joined by *or* or *nor*. ■

EXAMPLE: Neither **Keith nor Rob** remembers **his** password.

50 • Agreement

Theme: Technology and Communications

In this section, you will learn about pronoun and antecedent agreement. The example sentences are about communications and technology.

▶**KEY CONCEPT** Use a ___ two or more antecedents ___

EXAMPLE: **Gene and R___**

Agreement in Perso___ agreement between perso___ and their antecedents oft___ shift in person.

▶**KEY CONCEPT** When ___ pronoun-antecedent agree___ not to shift person. ■

SHIFT IN PERSON: **Becca** ___
                 program ___
                 you n___
                 in com___

CORRECT: **Becca** ___
              gramm___
              she n___
              in com___

Note about generic mas___ nouns: Historically, a ma___ (*he, his, him, himself*) has ___ refer to a singular antece___ der is not specified. Such ___ culine pronoun is said to ___ meaning it covers both th___ feminine genders. Today, ___ writers prefer to use both ___ and feminine pronouns (*h___ her, his or her, himself or ___ of the generic masculine ___ using both forms become ___ best to rewrite the senten___

▶**KEY CONCEPT** When ___ masculine and feminine ___

EXAMPLES: A **student** s___ secret.
          Students s▶

⏱ **TIME AND RESOURCE MANAGER**

Resources
Print: Grammar Exercise Workbook, Exercises 00–00
          Grammar Exercises on Transparencies
Technology: Grammar CD-ROM Gold 26.2 Test Program

In-Depth Coverage	Accelerated Pace
• Work through all key concepts, pp. 50-55	• Assign pp. 50-55, for independent student
• Assign and review Exercise1-3	
• Read and discuss ___ ___57	

☑ **ONG___**

If students have difficulty ___ review the following to as___

In the Text
Nouns and Pronouns, pp. ___

T-12

An outstanding collection of program resources to teach students that writing and grammar go together for successful communication—on tests AND in the real world!

TEACHING RESOURCES

Writing

Writing Support Activity Book
Topic Bank for Heterogeneous Classes
Support for Research Writing
Writing in the Content Areas and in the Workplace

Grammar, Usage, and Mechanics

Grammar Exercise Workbook, Teacher's Edition
Daily Language Practice
Hands-on Grammar Activity Book, Teacher's Edition

Academic and Workplace Skills

Academic and Workplace Skills Activity Book, Teacher's Edition
Vocabulary and Spelling Practice Book, Teacher's Edition
Reading Support Practice Book, Teacher's Edition

Assessment

Standardized Test Preparation Workbook, Teacher's Edition
Writing Assessment and Portfolio Management
Formal Assessment/Assessment Resources Software CD-ROM

Professional Resources

How to Manage Instruction in the Block
How to Assess Student Work
Putting Patterns to Work
Kick Off for Success: Organizing for School
Hearing All Sides: Resolving Conflict

Transparency Samples

Transparencies Sampler

ADDITIONAL ANCILLARIES

Workbooks

Hands-on Grammar Activity Book
Writing Support Activity Book
Grammar Exercise Workbook
Reading Support Practice Book
Vocabulary and Spelling Workbook
Academic and Workplace Skills Workbook
Standardized Test Preparation Workbook

Transparencies

Writing Support Transparencies
Daily Language Practice Transparencies
Grammar Exercises Answers on Transparencies
Scoring Rubrics on Transparencies

Technology

Writing Lab CD-ROM
Language Lab CD-ROM
Interactive Writing and Grammar Web site
Resource Pro CD-ROM (including Assessment Resources Software)
Writers at Work Videotape

Spanish Support
Extra Grammar and Writing Exercises
Basic Skills Intervention Kit
Multi-Genre Research Writing

26.2 PRONOUN AND ANTECEDENT AGREEMENT

rsonal pronoun to refer to
und. ■

hecked **their** e-mail.

in
uns
a

ith
e care

g
course
egree
nce.

g pro-
rse
egree
nce.

ronoun
d to
e gen-
e mas-
e and
many
line
im or
tead
n
l, it is

not specified, u
r rewrite the se
o **his or her** pa

their passwords a

Step-by-Step Teaching Guide continued

3. When they finish, have students give their sentences to their partners. Then, have them underline the pronoun and antecedent in each of the six sentences. If any of the pronouns do not agree in number and gender with their antecedents, have them make corrections so that they do.

Critical Viewing

Analyze Students may readily identify several technologies that have increased the convenience, frequency, and speed with which people communicate: e-mail, cell phones, video technology.

Language Highlight

The historical custom of using *his* and *him* for antecedents of unspecified gender is common to many languages besides English. Modern writers are becoming less comfortable with this custom but are well aware of the awkwardness of the *his* or *her* solution, especially when it is used repeatedly. The "gender-neutral
y in

Pronoun and Antecedent Agreement • 51

Time Savers show you how to use program resources, such as answers on transparencies, to make teaching easier.

SESSMENT SYSTEM: Prerequisite Skills

un and antecedent agreement, you may find it necessary to
ge of prerequisite knowledge.

Print Resources	Technology
Grammar Exercise Workbook Exercises 00-00	Grammar CD-ROM Gold Level

⏱ **TIME SAVERS!**

Answers on Transparency
Use Transparency 1 to have students correct one another's exercises.

Interactive CD-ROM
tudents complete the
The Auto

Ongoing Assessment System makes it easy to diagnose students' skill levels, monitor their progress, reinforce and reteach as necessary, and assess mastery.

Correlation to the Six Traits Analytic Model

Chapter	Ideas	Organization	Voice	Word Choice	Sentence Fluency	Conventions
1 The Writer in You			p. 3			
2 A Walk Through the Writing Process						
2.1	pp. 16–19	p. 20				
2.2	p. 22	p. 21				
2.3		pp. 23–4		p. 25		
2.4						p. 26
Spot/Hum.	p. 28					
3 Paragraphs and Compositions						
3.1	pp. 33–6					
3.2	p. 37	pp. 38–9				
3.3			pp. 42–3	pp. 42–3	p. 42	
Spot/Hum.	p. 44					
4 Narration: Autobiography						
4.1	pp. 50–3	pp. 50–3				
4.2	pp. 54–7					
4.3	pp. 58–9	p. 58				
4.4	pp. 60–1			pp. 63–4	p. 62	
4.5						p. 65
4.7	pp. 67–9	pp. 68–9				
Spot/Hum.	p. 70					
5 Narration: Short Story						
5.1	pp. 76–7	pp. 76–7				
5.2	pp. 78–81					
5.3	pp. 82–3		p. 82			
5.4	pp. 84–5	p. 84		pp. 85–6, p. 88	p. 86	p. 87
5.5						p. 89
5.7	pp. 91–5	pp. 91–5				
Spot/Hum.	p. 96					
6 Description						
6.1	pp. 102–05	pp. 102–05		pp. 102–05		
6.2	pp. 106–09					
6.3	p. 111	p. 110				
6.4	pp. 112–13	p. 112		p. 116		pp. 114–15
6.5						p. 118
6.7	pp. 120–1, p. 123	pp. 120–1, p. 123		pp. 121–3		
Spot/Hum.	p. 124					
7 Persuasion: Persuasive Essay						
7.1	pp. 130–3	pp. 130–3		pp. 130–3		
7.2	pp. 134–8					
7.3	pp. 139–140	pp. 139–140		p. 140		
7.4	pp. 141–2	pp. 141–2, p.145		p. 145	p. 144	p. 143
7.5						p. 146
7.7	pp. 147–51	pp. 147–51				
Spot/Hum.	p. 152					
8. Persuasion: Advertisement						
8.1	p. 158					
8.2	pp. 159–62					
8.3	p. 163	p. 163				
8.4	p. 164			pp. 165–6	p. 165	
8.5						p. 167
8.7	pp. 169–70	pp. 169–71		p. 71		
Spot/Hum.	p. 172					
9 Exposition: Comparison and Contrast						
9.1	pp. 178–9	pp. 178–9		pp. 178–9		
9.2	pp. 180–3					
9.3	p. 185	p. 184				
9.4	p. 187	pp. 186–7		p. 188, p. 190		pp. 188–9
9.5						p. 191
9.7	pp. 193–7	pp. 193–7				
Spot/Hum.	p. 198					

Chapter	Ideas	Organization	Voice	Word Choice	Sentence Fluency	Conventions
10 Exposition: Comparison and Contrast						
10.1	pp. 204–05					
10.2	pp. 206–09	p. 209				
10.3	p. 211	p. 210				
10.4	pp. 212–13	pp. 212–13				
10.5				p. 216	p. 214	p. 215
						p. 217
10.7	pp. 219–21	pp. 219–21		p. 223		
Spot/Hum.	p. 224	p. 223				
11 Exposition: Problem and Solution						
11.1	pp. 230–1	pp. 230–1				
11.2	pp. 232–5					
11.3	p. 237	p. 236				
11.4	p. 238			p. 240	p. 239	p. 239
11.5						p. 241
11.7	pp. 243–5	pp. 243–5				
Spot/Hum.	p. 246					
12 Research						
12.1	pp. 252–5	pp. 252–5				pp. 252–5
12.2	pp. 256–60	p. 260				
12.3	p. 261, p. 263	pp. 261–3				
12.4	p. 264	p. 265		p. 267	p. 266	p. 266
12.5						pp. 268–9
12.7	pp. 271–5	pp. 271–5				pp. 271–5
Spot/Hum.	p. 276					
13 Response to Literature						
13.1	pp. 282–5	pp. 282–5	pp. 282–5	pp. 282–5		
13.2	pp. 286–90					
13.3	p. 292	p. 291				
13.4	pp. 293–4			pp. 295–6		pp. 295–6
13.5						p. 298
13.7	pp. 300–03	pp. 300–03	pp. 300–03	pp. 300–03	pp. 300–03	
Spot/Hum.	p. 304					
14 Writing for Assessment						
14.1	pp. 310–11			pp. 310–11		
14.2	p. 313	p. 312				
14.3	pp. 314–15	p. 314		p. 315		
14.4						p. 316
14.6	pp. 318–19	pp. 318–19				
Spot/Hum.	p. 320					
15 Workplace Writing						
15.1	p. 327	p. 326				
15.2	pp. 328–9	pp. 328–9				
Spot/Hum.	p. 334					
16 Nouns and Pronouns						
16.1						pp. 342–5
16.2						pp. 346–57
17 Nouns and Pronouns						
17.1				p. 362		pp. 362–5
17.2						pp. 366–9
17.3						pp. 370–5
18 Adjectives and Adverbs						
18.1				p. 380		pp. 380–9
18.2						pp. 390–7
18.3						
19 Prepositions, Conjunctions and Interjections						
19.1						pp. 402–07
19.2						pp. 408–15

Correlation to the Six Traits Analytic Model

Chapter	Ideas	Organization	Voice	Word Choice	Sentence Fluency	Conventions
20 Basic Sentence Parts 20.1 20.2 20.3						pp. 422–7 pp. 428–33 pp. 433–45
21 Phrases and Clauses 21.1 21.2						pp. 450–67 pp. 468–87
22 Effective Sentences 22.1 22.2 22.3 22.4					pp. 495–9 pp. 500–03	pp. 492–4 pp. 504–19
23 Verb Usage 23.1 23.2						pp. 526–539 pp. 540–7
24 Pronoun Usage 24.1 24.2						pp. 552–8 pp. 559–63
25 Agreement 25.1 25.2						pp. 572–83 pp. 584–93
26 Using Modifiers 26.1 26.2					p. 606	pp. 598–603 pp. 604–11
27 Miscellaneous Problems in Usage 27.1 27.2						pp. 616–19 pp. 620–31
28 Capitalization						pp. 638–50
29 Punctuation 29.1 29.2 29.3 29.4 29.5 29.6						pp. 654–57 pp. 658–73 pp. 674–83 pp. 684–97 pp. 698–711 pp. 712–27
Sentence Diagraming Workshop						pp. 728–41
30 Speaking Listening, Viewing and Representing 30.1	p. 746, p. 748	p. 747		p. 747		
31 Vocabulary and Spelling 31.1 31.2 31.3 31.4				pp. 767–71 pp. 772–4 pp. 775–8		pp. 779–87
32 Reading Skills 32.1 32.2 32.3	pp. 798–802 p. 805	pp. 796–7 pp. 798–800 p. 805	p. 805	p. 803 pp. 806–7		p. 806
33 Study, Reference, and Test-Taking Skills						
34 Workplace Skills and Competencies						

Prentice Hall

WRITING and GRAMMAR

Communication in Action

Gold Level

Gold Level

Prentice
Hall

Upper Saddle River, New Jersey
Needham, Massachusetts
Glenview, Illinois

Writing and Grammar
Communication in Action

Copper
Bronze
Silver
Gold
Platinum
Ruby
Diamond

Program Authors

The program authors guided the direction and philosophy of *Prentice Hall Writing and Grammar: Communication in Action*. Working with the development team, they contributed to the pedagogical integrity of the program and to its relevance to today's teachers and students.

Joyce Armstrong Carroll

In her forty-year career, Joyce Armstrong Carroll, Ed.D., has taught on every grade level from primary to graduate school. In the past twenty years, she has trained teachers in the teaching of writing. A nationally known consultant, she has served as president of TCTE and on NCTE's Commission on Composition. More than fifty of her articles have appeared in journals such as *Curriculum Review, English Journal, Media & Methods, Southwest Philosophical Studies, Ohio English Journal, English in Texas*, and the *Florida English Journal*. With Edward E. Wilson, Dr. Carroll co-authored *Acts of Teaching: How to Teach Writing* and co-edited *Poetry After Lunch: Poems to Read Aloud*. Beyond her direct involvement with the writing pedagogy presented in this series, Dr. Carroll guided the development of the Hands-on Grammar feature. She co-directs the New Jersey Writing Project in Texas.

Edward E. Wilson

A former editor of *English in Texas*, Edward E. Wilson has served as a high-school English teacher and a writing consultant in school districts nationwide. Wilson has served on the Texas Teacher Professional Practices Commission and on NCTE's Commission on Composition. With Dr. Carroll, he co-wrote *Acts of Teaching: How to Teach Writing* and co-edited the award-winning *Poetry After Lunch: Poems to Read Aloud*. In addition to his direct involvement with the writing pedagogy presented in this series, Wilson provided inspiration for the Spotlight on Humanities feature. Wilson's poetry appears in Paul Janeczko's anthology *The Music of What Happens*. Wilson co-directs the New Jersey Writing Project in Texas.

Gary Forlini

Gary Forlini, a nationally known education consultant, directed the development of the grammar, usage, and mechanics instruction and exercises in this series. After teaching in the Pelham, New York, schools for many years, he established an educational research agency that provides information for product developers, media companies, and arts organizations, as well as private-sector corporations and foundations. Forlini has written numerous industry reports on elementary, secondary, and post-secondary markets.

National Advisory Panel

The teachers and administrators serving on the National Advisory Panel provided ongoing input to the development of *Prentice Hall Writing and Grammar: Communication in Action*. Their valuable insights ensure that the perspectives of teachers and students throughout the country are represented within the instruction in this series.

Dr. Pauline Bigby-Jenkins
Coordinator for Secondary English
   Language Arts
Ann Arbor Public Schools
Ann Arbor, Michigan

Lee Bromberger
English Department Chairperson
Mukwonago High School
Mukwonago, Wisconsin

Mary Chapman
Teacher of English
Free State High School
Lawrence, Kansas

Jim Deatheridge
Language Arts Department
   Chairperson
Richland High School
Richland, Washington

Luis Dovalina
Teacher of English
La Joya High School
La Joya, Texas

JoAnn Giardino
Teacher of English
Centennial High School
Columbus, Ohio

Susan Goldberg
Teacher of English
Westlake Middle School
Thornwood, New York

Jean Hicks
Director, Louisville Writing Project
University of Louisville
Louisville, Kentucky

Karen Hurley
Teacher of Language Arts
Terry Meridian Middle School
Indianapolis, Kentucky

Karen Lopez
Teacher of English
Hart High School
Newhall, California

Marianne Minshall
Teacher of Reading and Language Arts
Westmore Middle School
Columbus, Ohio

Nancy Monroe
English Department Chairperson
Bolton High School
Alexander, Louisiana

Ken Spurlock
Assistant Principal
Boone County High School
Florence, Kentucky

Dr. Debi Sulzer
Senior Administrator for Instruction
Orange City Public Schools
Orlando, Florida

Cynthia Katz Tyroff
Staff Development Specialist
   and Teacher of English
Northside Independent School District
San Antonio, Texas

Holly Ward
Teacher of Language Arts
Campbell Middle School
Daytona Beach, Florida

Grammar Review Team

The following teachers reviewed the grammar instruction in this series to ensure accuracy, clarity, and pedagogy.

Kathy Hamilton
Paul Hertzog
Daren Hoisington
Beverly Ladd

Dianna Louise Lund
Karen Lopez
Sean O'Brien

CONTENTS IN BRIEF

Chapters 1–15

Part 1: Writing 1

Chapter 1 The Writer in You 2

2 A Walk Through
the Writing Process 14

3 Paragraphs and Compositions . . . 32

4 Narration:
Autobiographical Writing 48

5 Narration: Short Story 74

6 Description. 100

7 Persuasion: Persuasive Essay . . . 128

8 Persuasion: Advertisement 156

9 Exposition:
Comparison-and-Contrast Essay . 176

10 Exposition:
Cause-and-Effect Essay 202

11 Exposition:
Problem-and-Solution Essay 228

12 Research: Research Paper 250

13 Response to Literature. 280

14 Writing for Assessment 308

15 Workplace Writing. 324

Chapters 16–29

Part 2: Grammar, Usage, and Mechanics 338

Chapter 16 Nouns and Pronouns 340
        17 Verbs 360
        18 Adjectives and Adverbs 378
        19 Prepositions, Conjunctions,
           and Interjections 400
        20 Basic Sentence Parts 420
        21 Phrases and Clauses 448
        22 Effective Sentences 490
        23 Verb Usage 524
        24 Pronoun Usage 550
        25 Agreement 570
        26 Using Modifiers 596
        27 Miscellaneous Problems in Usage . 614
        28 Capitalization 636
        29 Punctuation 652

Chapters 30–34

Part 3: Academic and Workplace Skills .. 742

Chapter 30 Speaking, Listening, Viewing,
           and Representing 744
        31 Vocabulary and Spelling 766
        32 Reading Skills 790
        33 Study, Reference,
           and Test-Taking Skills 812
        34 Workplace Skills
           and Competencies 834

Resources

Citing Sources and Preparing Manuscript 848
Penmanship Reference 848
Internet Research Handbook 855
Commonly Overused Words 860
Commonly Misspelled Words 862
Abbreviations Guide 864
Proofreading Symbols Reference 868
Student Publications 869
Glossary 870
Index 878

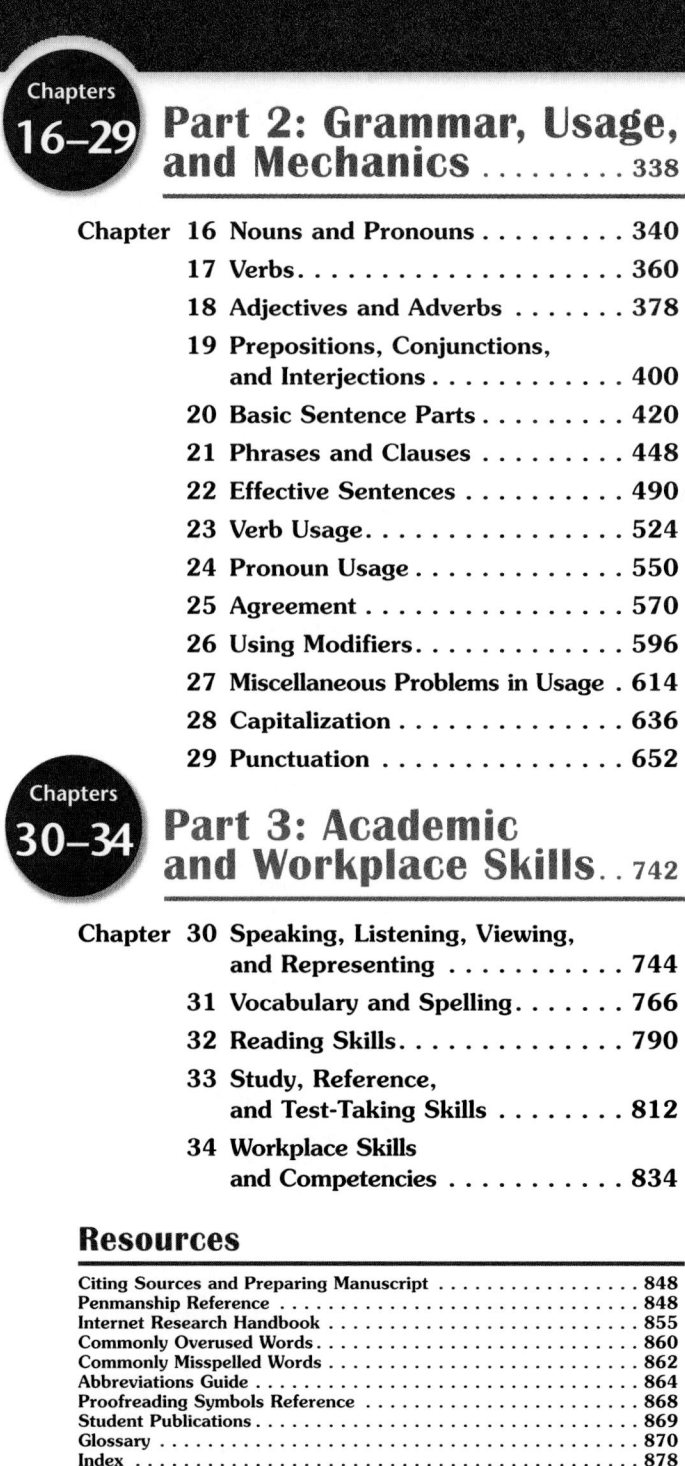

Contents in Brief • **vii**

CONTENTS
PART 1: WRITING

Chapter 1 The Writer in You 2

Writing in Everyday Life 2
Why Write? 3
What Are the Qualities of Good Writing? 3
Developing Your Writing Life 4
Reflecting on Your Writing 8
Writers in Action 9

Chapter 2 A Walk Through the Writing Process 14

Types of Writing 14
The Process of Writing 15
A Guided Tour 15
2.1 What Is Prewriting? 16
2.2 What Is Drafting? 21
2.3 What Is Revising? 23
2.4 What Are Editing and Proofreading? 26
2.5 What Are Publishing and Presenting? 27

Chapter 3 Paragraphs and Compositions
Structure and Style 32

3.1 Writing Effective Paragraphs 33
Main Idea and Topic Sentence 33
Writing a Topic Sentence 34
Writing Supporting Sentences 35
Placing Your Topic Sentence 36
3.2 Paragraphs in Essays and Other Compositions . 37
Unity and Coherence 37
Creating Coherence 38
The Parts of a Composition 39
Types of Paragraphs 40
3.3 Paragraph Style 42
Developing Style 42
Using Formal and Informal English 42

INTEGRATED SKILLS

▶ **Spotlight on the Humanities**
Analyzing How Meaning Is Communicated Through the Arts 10
▶ **Media and Technology Skills**
Using a Variety of Technologies
Introduction to Technology . 11
▶ **Standardized Test Preparation Workshop**
Writing for Standardized Tests 12

INTEGRATED SKILLS

▶ **Spotlight on the Humanities**
Exploring Themes Across Cultures
Focus on Art: Maxfield Parrish 28
▶ **Media and Technology Skills**
Using Technology for Writing
Activity: Building an Electronic Portfolio 29
▶ **Standardized Test Preparation Workshop**
Using the Writing Process to Respond to Writing Prompts 30

INTEGRATED SKILLS

▶ **Spotlight on the Humanities**
Recognizing Themes
Focus on Theater: *A Raisin in the Sun* 44
▶ **Media and Technology Skills**
Exploring Technology Use . 45
▶ **Standardized Test Preparation Workshop**
Strategy, Organization, and Style 46

Chapter 4 Narration

Autobiographical Writing 48

4.1 Model From Literature
"The Shadowland of Dreams" by Alex Haley 50

4.2 Prewriting
Choosing Your Topic 54
    Song List 54
    Blueprinting 54
    Topic Bank 55
Narrowing Your Topic 56
    Use Invisible Writing to Narrow a Topic 56
Considering Your Audience and Purpose 56
    Identify Your Audience 56
    Refine Your Purpose 56
Gathering Details 57
    Make a Timeline 57

4.3 Drafting
Shaping Your Writing 58
    Identify Your Main Point 58
    Organize to Convey Your Main Point 58
Providing Elaboration 59
    Use Thought Shots to Elaborate 59

4.4 Revising
Revising Your Overall Structure 60
    Revision Strategy: Color-Coding to Improve Unity . . 60
Revising Your Paragraphs 61
    Revision Strategy: Exploding the Moment 61
Revising Your Sentences 62
    Revision Strategy: Combining Sentences
    to Vary Sentence Length 62
Revising Your Word Choice 63
    Revision Strategy: Circling Action Verbs 63
Peer Review 64
    Revision Strategy: Color-Coding Word Choice
    and Clichés 64

4.5 Editing and Proofreading
Focusing on Punctuation 65

4.6 Publishing and Presenting
Building Your Portfolio 66
Reflecting on Your Writing 66
    ☑ Rubric for Self-Assessment 66

Connected Assignment: Firsthand Biography 69

Student Work
IN PROGRESS

Featured Work:
"Cedar Avenue Recycling:
The Rise and Fall
of a Family Business"
by Sara Holman
Towson High School
Towson, Maryland

Using a Blueprint to
Choose a Topic 54
Using a Timeline to Gather
Details 57
Elaborating With Thought
Shots 59
Exploding the Moment . . . 61
Evaluating Action Verbs . . 63
Using Peer Revision to
Evaluate Word Choice 64
Final Draft 67

INTEGRATED SKILLS

▶ **Grammar in Your Writing**
Relative Pronouns 62
Using an Exclamation Point
to Show Emotion 65

▶ **Spotlight on the Humanities**
Examining Ideas Represented
in Various Art Forms
Focus on Film: *Citizen Kane.* 70

▶ **Media and Technology Skills**
Using a Video Camera to
Communicate Specific Messages
Activity: Creating a Video
Postcard 71

▶ **Standardized Test
Preparation Workshop**
Responding to Narrative
Writing Prompts 72

Chapter 5 Narration

Short Story 74

5.1 Model From Literature
"The Appalachian Trail" by Bruce Eason 76

5.2 Prewriting
Choosing Your Topic 78
Sentence Starters. 78
List and Itemize Interests 78
Topic Bank 79
Narrowing Your Topic 80
Summarize the Plot 80
Considering Your Audience and Purpose 80
Consider Your Audience 80
Refine Your Purpose 80
Gathering Details 81
Know the Elements of Storytelling 81

5.3 Drafting
Shaping Your Writing 82
Choose a Narrator 82
Providing Elaboration 83
Show, Don't Tell 83

5.4 Revising
Revising Your Overall Structure 84
Revision Strategy: Using Chutes and Ladders
to Track Conflict 84
Revising Your Paragraphs 85
Revision Strategy: Reading With a Partner 85
Revising Your Sentences 86
Revision Strategy: Highlighting Verbs 86
Revising Your Word Choice 88
Revision Strategy: Circling Vague Nouns 88
Peer Review 88
Pointing 88

5.5 Editing and Proofreading
Focusing on Punctuation 89

5.6 Publishing and Presenting
Building Your Portfolio 90
Reflecting on Your Writing 90
☑ **Rubric for Self-Assessment** 90
Connected Assignment: Drama 94

Student Work
IN PROGRESS

Featured Work:
"A Stranger's Lesson"
by David Friggle
Columbia High School
Maplewood, New Jersey

Listing and Itemizing
to Find a Topic 78
Gathering Details About
Characters 81
Using Elaboration
to Show Instead of Tell . . . 83
Reviewing Conflict With
Chutes and Ladders 84
Highlighting Verbs
to Identify Active Voice . . . 86
Final Draft 91

INTEGRATED SKILLS

▶ **Grammar in Your Writing**
Active vs. Passive Voice . . . 87
Punctuating Dialogue
Correctly 89
▶ **Spotlight on the Humanities**
Recognize Shared
Characteristics of Cultures
Focus on Myth: *Pyramus
and Thisbe* 96
▶ **Media and Technology Skills**
Using Technology to Respond
to Literature
Activity: Producing a Video
Adaptation of a Short
Story 97
▶ **Standardized Test
Preparation Workshop**
Responding to Questions
About Short Stories 98

Chapter 6

Description 100

6.1 Model From Literature
"See Ya' at the Subway" by Edwina Armstrong 102

6.2 Prewriting
Choosing Your Topic 106
   Observation 106
   Trigger Words and Objects 106
   Topic Bank 107
Narrowing Your Topic 108
   Using an Index-Card Camera 108
Considering Your Audience and Purpose 108
   Identify Your Audience 108
   Refine Your Purpose 108
Gathering Details 109
   Cubing to Gather Details 109

6.3 Drafting
Shaping Your Writing 110
   Choose an Organization That Suits Your Topic 110
Providing Elaboration 111
   Add Figurative Language 111

6.4 Revising
Revising Your Overall Structure 112
   Revision Strategy: Color-Coding to Highlight
   Your Main Impression 112
Revising Your Paragraphs 113
   Revision Strategy: Building Snapshots 113
Revising Your Sentences 114
   Revision Strategy: Color-Coding to Identify Run-ons 114
Revising Your Word Choice 116
   Revision Strategy: Circling Verbs to Enliven Writing . 116
Peer Review 117
   Encourage Specific Peer Review 117

6.5 Editing and Proofreading
Focusing on Agreement 118

6.6 Publishing and Presenting
Building Your Portfolio 119
Reflecting on Your Writing 119
  ☑ **Rubric for Self-Assessment** 119
Connected Assignment: Poem 122

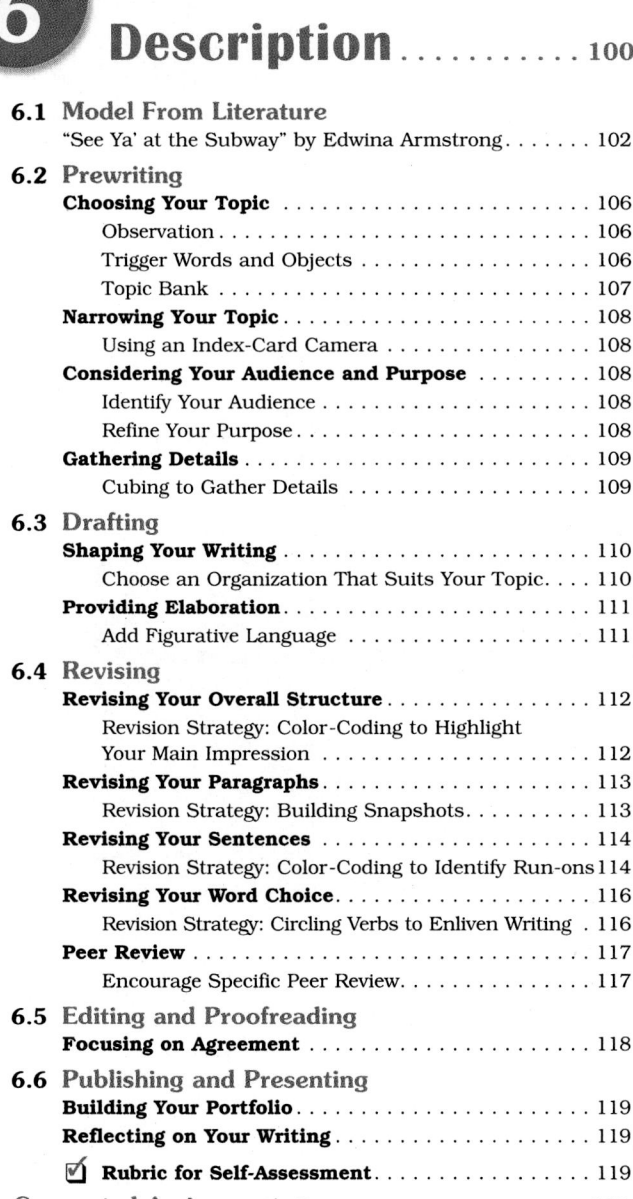

Student Work
IN PROGRESS

Featured Work:
"My 'Sister'"
by Allison Lutes
Butler Traditional High School
Louisville, Kentucky

Using Trigger Words to
Choose a Topic 106
Cubing to Gather Details . 109
Creating a General
Impression Through
Organization 110
Building Snapshots for
Revision 113
Bracketing to Identify
Run-on Sentences 114
Circling Verbs to
Evaluate Word Choice . . 116
Final Draft 120

INTEGRATED SKILLS

▶ **Grammar in Your Writing**
Semicolons 115
Making Verbs Agree With
Indefinite Pronouns 118
▶ **Spotlight on the Humanities**
Examining Relationships
Among Art Forms
Focus on Dance:
Ballets Russes 124
▶ **Media and Technology Skills**
Examining Media's Power to
Construct a Perception of
Reality
Activity: Compare Photos to
Text in Magazines 125
▶ **Standardized Test
Preparation Workshop**
Analyzing Strategy,
Organization, and Style . . 126

Contents • xi

Chapter 7 Persuasion

Persuasive Essay 128

7.1 Model From Literature
"We Can Go Home Again" by Nevada Barr 130

7.2 Prewriting
  Choosing Your Topic 134
    Hot Topics 134
    Discussion Group 134
    Notebook Review 134
    Topic Bank 135
  Narrowing Your Topic 136
    Use Looping to Narrow a Topic 136
  Considering Your Audience and Purpose 137
    Analyze Your Audience 137
  Gathering Evidence 138
    Conduct Research 138

7.3 Drafting
  Shaping Your Writing 139
    Develop a Thesis Statement 139
    Organize to Emphasize the Strongest Support 139
  Providing Elaboration 140
    Use a Variety of Elaboration Methods 140

7.4 Revising
  Revising Your Overall Structure 141
    Revision Strategy: Color-Coding Main Points 141
  Revising Your Paragraphs 142
    Revision Strategy: Finding a Place to Address the
    Opposition 142
  Revising Your Sentences 144
    Revision Strategy: Using Transition Boxes 144
  Revising Your Word Choice 145
    Revision Strategy: Reading Aloud 145
  Peer Review 145
    Say Back 145

7.5 Editing and Proofreading
  Focusing on Fact Checking 146

7.6 Publishing and Presenting
  Building Your Portfolio 147
  Reflecting on Your Writing 147
  ☑ **Rubric for Self-Assessment** 147

Connected Assignment: Editorial 151

Student Work
IN PROGRESS

Featured Work:
"Who Wrote *West
With the Night?*"
by Janaki Spickard-Keeler
Clark High School
San Antonio, Texas

Looping 136
Organizing Research
With a T-Chart 138
Evaluating Support
for Your Arguments 141
Addressing the Critics . . . 142
Using Transition Boxes
to Smooth Writing 144
Final Draft **148**

INTEGRATED SKILLS

▶ **Grammar in Your Writing**
Punctuating Adverb
Clauses 143
Using the Conventions
for Writing Titles 146
▶ **Spotlight on the Humanities**
Evaluating Artistic
Performances
Focus on Dance: Vernon
and Irene Castle 152
▶ **Media and Technology Skills**
Recognizing Persuasive
Techniques
Activity: Find Persuasion in
Television Programs 153
▶ **Standardized Test
Preparation Workshop**
Responding to Persuasive
Writing Prompts 154

Chapter

8

Persuasion
Advertisement 156

8.1 Model From Literature
Advertisement for Michigan Opera Theater 158

8.2 Prewriting
Choosing Your Topic 159
    Products and Services Schedules 159
    Classroom Interest Poll. 159
    Topic Bank 159
Narrowing Your Topic 160
    Narrow a Topic With Cubing. 160
Considering Your Audience and Purpose 161
    Match Your Audience With Your Purpose. 161
Gathering Details 162
    Make a Link to Audience and Angle. 162

8.3 Drafting
Shaping Your Writing 163
    Organize to Persuade 163
Providing Elaboration 163
    Include the Facts 163

8.4 Revising
Revising Your Overall Structure 164
    Revision Strategy: Circling Main Ideas
    to Improve the Layout 164
Revising Your Paragraphs and Sentences 165
    Revision Strategy: Shortening Your Sentences 165
Revising Your Word Choice 166
    Revision Strategy: Color-Coding to Improve
    Word Choice 166
Peer Review 166
    Focus Groups 166

8.5 Editing and Proofreading
Focusing on Spelling 167

8.6 Publishing and Presenting
Building Your Portfolio 168
Reflecting on Your Writing 168
   ☑ **Rubric for Self-Assessment** 168

Connected Assignment: Product Packaging 170

Student Work
IN PROGRESS

Featured Work:
   "Pets Complete the
    Family Picture"
   by Caitlin Mahoney
   Darien High School
   Darien, Connecticut

Matching Your Audience With
Your Purpose 161
Linking Audience, Angle, and
Details 162
Shortening Sentences . . . 165
Using Color-Coding to
Improve Word Choice . . . 166
Final Draft. 169

INTEGRATED
SKILLS

▶ **Grammar in Your Writing**
Using Abbreviations. 167
▶ **Spotlight on the Humanities**
Evaluating the Persuasive
Techniques of Art Forms

Focus on Photography:
Gordon Parks 172
▶ **Media and Technology Skills**
Using Print Technology to
Extend a Meaning

Activity: Creating an
Advertisement on a Word
Processor 173
▶ **Standardized Test
Preparation Workshop**
Analyzing Persuasive
Texts. 174

Chapter 9

Exposition: *Comparison-and-Contrast Essay* 176

9.1 Model From Literature
"Digital Video Daze" by Joshua Quittner 178

9.2 Prewriting
Choosing Your Topic 180
   Finding Related Pairs 180
   Listing and Itemizing 180
   Topic Bank 181
Narrowing Your Topic 182
Considering Your Audience and Purpose 182
   Identify Your Audience 182
   Specify Your Purpose 182
Gathering Details 183
   Identify Points of Comparison 183

9.3 Drafting
Shaping Your Writing 184
   Organize to Show Comparisons and Contrasts 184
Providing Elaboration 185
   Support Generalizations With Specifics 185

9.4 Revising
Revising Your Overall Structure 186
   Revision Strategy: Improving Your Lead 186
Revising Your Paragraphs 187
   Revision Strategy: Refining or Adding
   Connecting Sentences 187
Revising Your Sentences 188
   Revision Strategy: Listing Verbs to Evaluate
   the Use of Tense 188
Revising Your Word Choice 190
   Revision Strategy: Identifying Repeated Words 190
Peer Review 190
   Showing 190

9.5 Editing and Proofreading
Focusing on Grammar 191

9.6 Publishing and Presenting
Building Your Portfolio 192
Reflecting on Your Writing 192
   ☑ **Rubric for Self-Assessment** 192

Connected Assignment: Consumer Report 196

Student Work
IN PROGRESS

Featured Work:
"Working Out Possibilities"
by Elizabeth Dunbar, Maggie
McCray, Cassie McKinstry,
and Emily Szeszycki,
with additional reporting by
Liz Humston
Staff of *the little hawk*
City High School
Iowa City, Iowa

Listing and Itemizing. . . . 180
Identifying Points of
Comparison 183
Planning a Subject-by-Subject
Organization. 184
Improving Your Lead. . . . 186
Evaluating Verb Tense . . 188
Final Draft. 193

INTEGRATED SKILLS

▶ **Grammar in Your Writing**
Six Tenses of Verbs 189
Degrees of Comparison . . 191

▶ **Spotlight on the Humanities**
Analyzing Ideas Represented
in Art
Focus on Art: Giotto. 198

▶ **Media and Technology Skills**
Comparing Media Coverage
Activity: Analyze News
Coverage 199

▶ **Standardized Test
Preparation Workshop**
Using Comparison-and-
Contrast Skills to Respond
to Writing Prompts. 200

Chapter 10 Exposition
Cause-and-Effect Essay 202

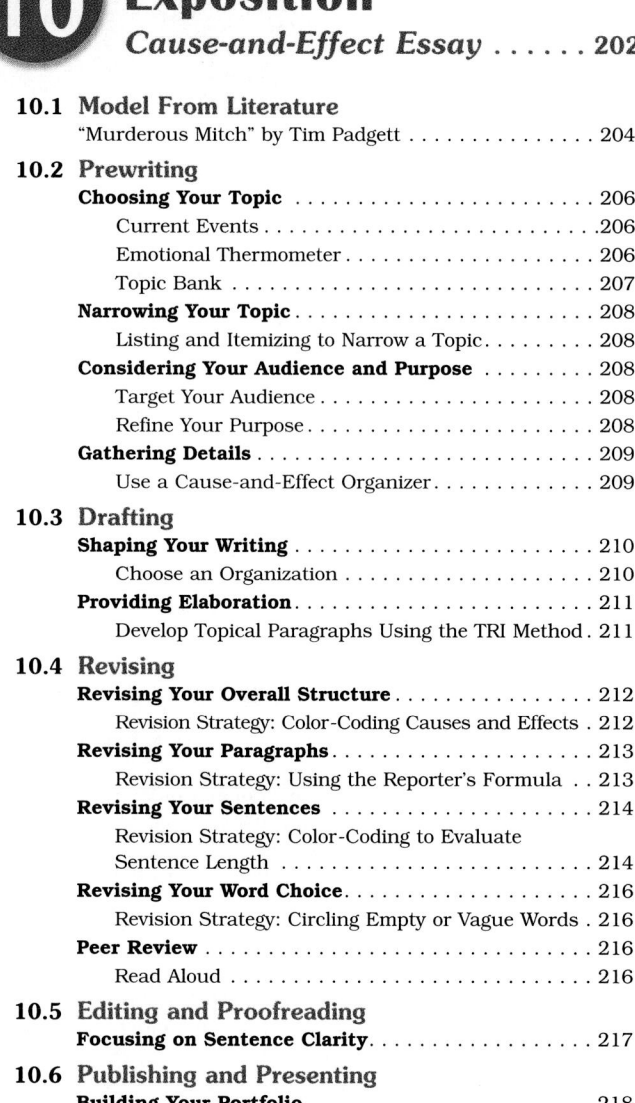

10.1 Model From Literature
"Murderous Mitch" by Tim Padgett 204

10.2 Prewriting
Choosing Your Topic 206
    Current Events 206
    Emotional Thermometer 206
    Topic Bank 207
Narrowing Your Topic 208
    Listing and Itemizing to Narrow a Topic. 208
Considering Your Audience and Purpose 208
    Target Your Audience 208
    Refine Your Purpose 208
Gathering Details 209
    Use a Cause-and-Effect Organizer 209

10.3 Drafting
Shaping Your Writing 210
    Choose an Organization 210
Providing Elaboration 211
    Develop Topical Paragraphs Using the TRI Method . 211

10.4 Revising
Revising Your Overall Structure 212
    Revision Strategy: Color-Coding Causes and Effects . 212
Revising Your Paragraphs 213
    Revision Strategy: Using the Reporter's Formula . . 213
Revising Your Sentences 214
    Revision Strategy: Color-Coding to Evaluate
    Sentence Length 214
Revising Your Word Choice 216
    Revision Strategy: Circling Empty or Vague Words . 216
Peer Review 216
    Read Aloud 216

10.5 Editing and Proofreading
Focusing on Sentence Clarity 217

10.6 Publishing and Presenting
Building Your Portfolio 218
Reflecting on Your Writing 218
    ☑ **Rubric for Self-Assessment** 218

Connected Assignment: Documentary. 222

Student Work
IN PROGRESS

Featured Work:
"The Music of the Soul" by
Sonia Reimann
Athens High School
Athens, Texas

Using an Emotional
Thermometer 206

Using a Cause-and-Effect
Organizer 209

Developing Topical
Paragraphs. 211

Highlighting Sentences
to Evaluate Structure . . . 212

Color-Coding Short
Sentences. 214

Evaluating Empty or
Vague Words 216

Final Draft. 219

INTEGRATED SKILLS

▶ **Grammar in Your Writing**
Using Appositive Phrases
to Combine Sentences . . . 215

Placement of Adverbs. . . . 217

▶ **Spotlight on the Humanities**
Examining Styles of Art
Across Cultures

Focus on Theater:
Commedia dell'Arte 224

▶ **Media and Technology Skills**
Analyzing Special Effects
With Technology

Activity: Compare Special
Effects in Movies 225

▶ **Standardized Test
Preparation Workshop**
Using Cause-and-Effect
Skills to Respond to
Writing Prompts 226

Contents • xv

Chapter 11 Exposition

Problem-and-Solution Essay. . 228

11.1 Model From Literature
from *Dinosaurs Rediscovered* by Don Lessem 230

11.2 Prewriting
Choosing Your Topic 232
    Newspaper Scan 232
    Sentence Starters. 232
    Topic Bank 233
Narrowing Your Topic 234
    Use a Target Diagram. 234
Considering Your Audience and Purpose 234
    Identify Your Audience 234
    State Your Purpose 234
Gathering Details 235
    Record Details on a T-Chart 235

11.3 Drafting
Shaping Your Writing 236
    Choose an Appropriate Organization 236
Providing Elaboration 237
    Use Examples and Anecdotes 237
    Pointing to Supports 237

11.4 Revising
Revising Your Overall Structure 238
    Revision Strategy: Highlighting Topic Sentences. . . 238
Revising Your Paragraphs 238
    Revision Strategy: Color-Coding to Eliminate
    Generalizations 238
Revising Your Sentences 239
    Revision Strategy: Color-Coding to Identify
    Sentences to Combine 239
Revising Your Word Choice 240
    Revision Strategy: Circling Suspect Words 240
Peer Review 240
    Read Aloud 240

11.5 Editing and Proofreading
Focusing on Semicolons 241

11.6 Publishing and Presenting
Building Your Portfolio 242
Reflecting on Your Writing 242
    ☑ Rubric for Self-Assessment 242

Connected Assignment: Question-and-Answer Column . . 245

Student Work
IN PROGRESS

Featured Work:
"Safety and Progress"
by Michael C. Mahoney
St. Stephen's School
Hickory, North Carolina

Using Sentence Starters . 232
Gathering Details With
a T-Chart 235
Point to Supports 237
Supporting
Generalizations. 238
Refining Word Choice . . . 240
Final Draft 243

INTEGRATED SKILLS

▶ **Grammar in Your Writing**
Creating Complex
Sentences 239
Punctuating Compound
Sentences With Commas
and Semicolons 241

▶ **Spotlight on the Humanities**
Examining Culture and Ideas
Represented in Art
Focus on Dance:
Alvin Ailey 246

▶ **Media and Technology Skills**
Using Word-Processing
Technology
Activity: Trouble-shooting . 247

▶ **Standardized Test
Preparation Workshop**
Using Problem-and-Solution
Skills to Respond to
Writing Prompts 248

Chapter

12 Research

Research Paper 250

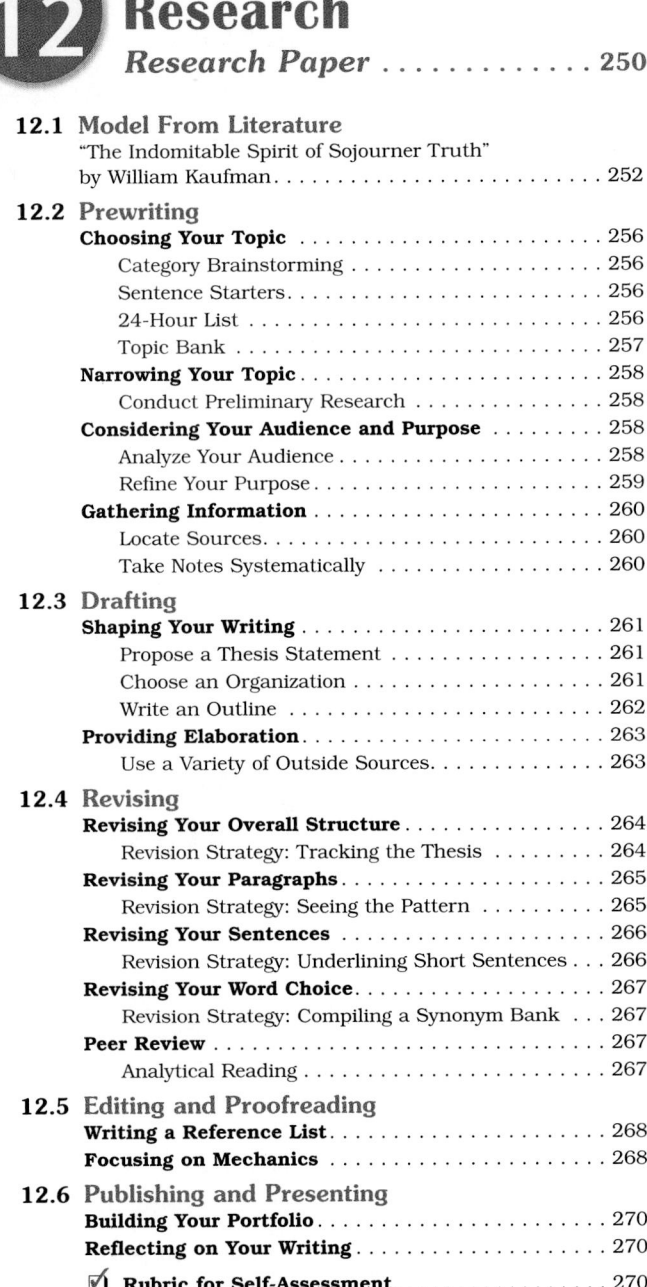

12.1 Model From Literature
"The Indomitable Spirit of Sojourner Truth"
by William Kaufman. 252

12.2 Prewriting
Choosing Your Topic 256
    Category Brainstorming 256
    Sentence Starters. 256
    24-Hour List 256
    Topic Bank 257
Narrowing Your Topic. 258
    Conduct Preliminary Research 258
Considering Your Audience and Purpose 258
    Analyze Your Audience. 258
    Refine Your Purpose. 259
Gathering Information 260
    Locate Sources. 260
    Take Notes Systematically 260

12.3 Drafting
Shaping Your Writing 261
    Propose a Thesis Statement 261
    Choose an Organization 261
    Write an Outline 262
Providing Elaboration. 263
    Use a Variety of Outside Sources. 263

12.4 Revising
Revising Your Overall Structure. 264
    Revision Strategy: Tracking the Thesis 264
Revising Your Paragraphs. 265
    Revision Strategy: Seeing the Pattern 265
Revising Your Sentences 266
    Revision Strategy: Underlining Short Sentences . . . 266
Revising Your Word Choice. 267
    Revision Strategy: Compiling a Synonym Bank . . . 267
Peer Review 267
    Analytical Reading 267

12.5 Editing and Proofreading
Writing a Reference List. 268
Focusing on Mechanics 268

12.6 Publishing and Presenting
Building Your Portfolio. 270
Reflecting on Your Writing. 270
☑ **Rubric for Self-Assessment**. 270

Connected Assignment: Documented Essay 275

IN PROGRESS

Featured Work:
"Tracking the Success of
Bubble Gum"
by Angelika Klien
Sunnyslope High School
Phoenix, Arizona

Creating a 24-Hour List . 256
Using Purpose to Direct
Research 259
Creating a Roman
Numeral Outline. 262
Seeing the Paragraph
Patterns. 265
Final Draft. 271

INTEGRATED SKILLS

▶ **Grammar in Your Writing**
Semicolons 266
Conventions for
Documentation 269
▶ **Spotlight on the Humanities**
Examining Ideas as
Represented in Various Media
Focus on Film: *Field of
Dreams* 276
▶ **Media and Technology Skills**
Using Video Technology to
Communicate Specific
Messages
Activity: Producing a
Documentary. 277
▶ **Standardized Test
Preparation Workshop**
Revising and Editing 278

Chapter 13 Response to Literature 280

13.1 Model From Literature
"Lederer's 'Miracle' Is His Well of Wit and Wisdom With
Words" Review by Charles Harrington Elster 282

13.2 Prewriting
Choosing Your Topic 286
Class Book Awards 286
Sentence Starters......................... 286
Topic Bank 287
Narrowing Your Topic.................... 288
Use Hexagonal Writing to Narrow a Topic 288
Considering Your Audience and Purpose 289
Analyze Your Audience..................... 289
Analyze Your Purpose...................... 289
Gathering Details 290
Find Details to Support Your Position 290

13.3 Drafting
Shaping Your Writing..................... 291
Develop a Thesis Statement 291
Organize to Support Your Ideas 291
Providing Elaboration..................... 292
Include References to Support Your Thesis 292

13.4 Revising
Revising Your Overall Structure............... 293
Revision Strategy: Identifying Contradictory
Information 293
Revising Your Paragraphs.................... 294
Revision Strategy: Highlighting Topic Sentences... 294
Revising Your Sentences 295
Revision Strategy: Circling Subjects and Verbs.... 295
Revising Your Word Choice.................. 296
Revision Strategy: Bracketing Modifiers......... 296
Peer Review 297
Plus and Minus Scoring 297

13.5 Editing and Proofreading
Focusing on Spelling 298

13.6 Publishing and Presenting
Building Your Portfolio...................... 299
Reflecting on Your Writing................... 299
☑ **Rubric for Self-Assessment**................ 299

Connected Assignment: Movie Review 303

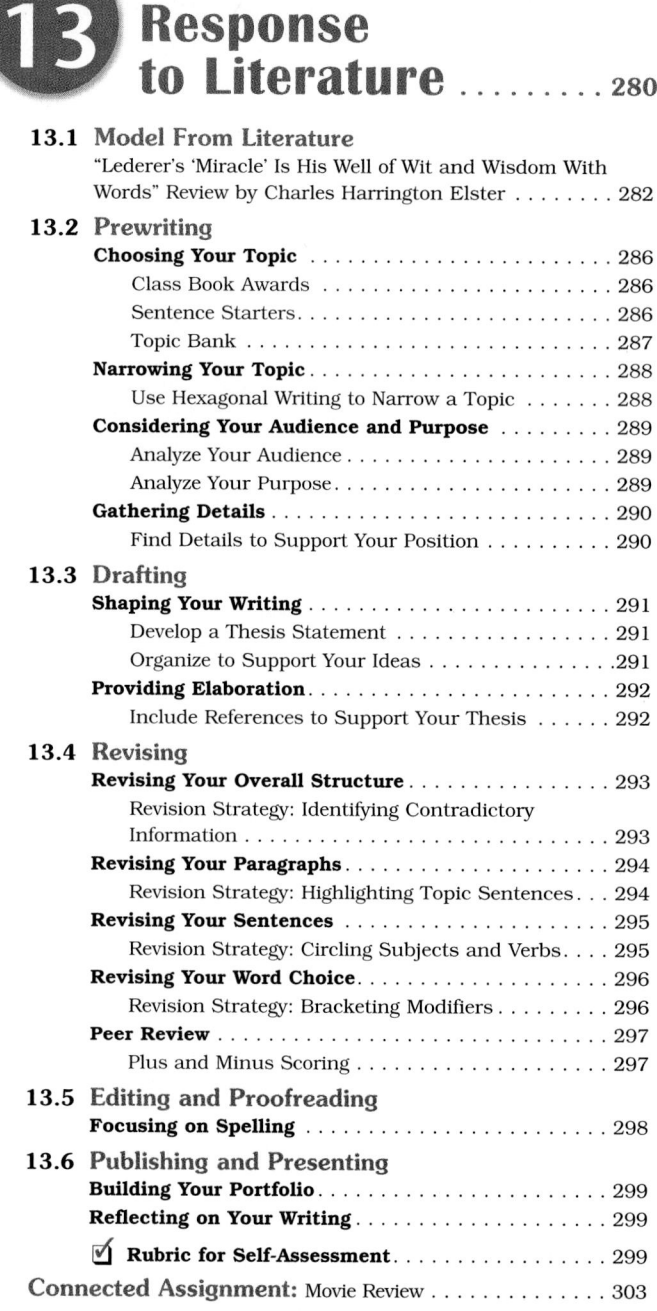

Student Work
IN PROGRESS

Featured Work:
"The Poetic Power of
'The Raven' "
by Andrea Montgomery
Omaha Northwest High School
Omaha, Nebraska

Using Sentence Starters
to Find a Topic 286
Using Hexagonal Writing
to Narrow a Topic 288
Using Index Cards to
Gather Supporting Details 290
Incorporating References
From the Text......... 292
Highlighting Topic
Sentences............ 294
Color-Coding Modifiers . . 296
Final Draft.......... 300

INTEGRATED
SKILLS

▶ **Grammar in Your Writing**
Agreement in Inverted
Sentences 295
Avoiding Common
Homophone Errors 298
▶ **Spotlight on the Humanities**
Analyzing Themes in Various
Art Forms
Focus on Art: Grace Albee 304
▶ **Media and Technology Skills**
Comparing Your Responses
to Others'
Activity: Evaluating Movie
Ads and Reviews 305
▶ **Standardized Test
Preparation Workshop**
Responding to Literature-
Based Prompts 306

Chapter 14 Writing for Assessment 308

14.1 Prewriting
    Choosing Your Topic 310
        Consider What You Know 310
        Pinpoint Your Strengths 310
        Draft a Single Sentence 310
        Topic Bank 310
    Narrowing Your Response 311
        Circle Key Words to Identify Your Purpose 311

14.2 Drafting
    Shaping Your Writing 312
        Find a Focus 312
        Plan a Structure 312
    Providing Elaboration 313
        Support Your Thesis With Specifics 313

14.3 Revising
    Revising Your Overall Structure 314
        Revision Strategy: Reviewing the Question
        Against Your Answer 314
    Revising Your Paragraphs 314
        Revision Strategy: Checking the Introduction
        Against the Conclusion 314
    Revising Your Sentences 315
        Revision Strategy: Deleting Irrelevant Ideas 315
    Revising Your Word Choice 315
        Revision Strategy: Evaluating Informal Language . . 315

14.4 Editing and Proofreading
    Focusing on Eliminating Errors 316

14.5 Publishing and Presenting
    Building Your Portfolio 317
    Reflecting on Your Writing 317
    ☑ **Rubric for Self-Assessment** 317

Connected Assignment: Open-Book Test 319

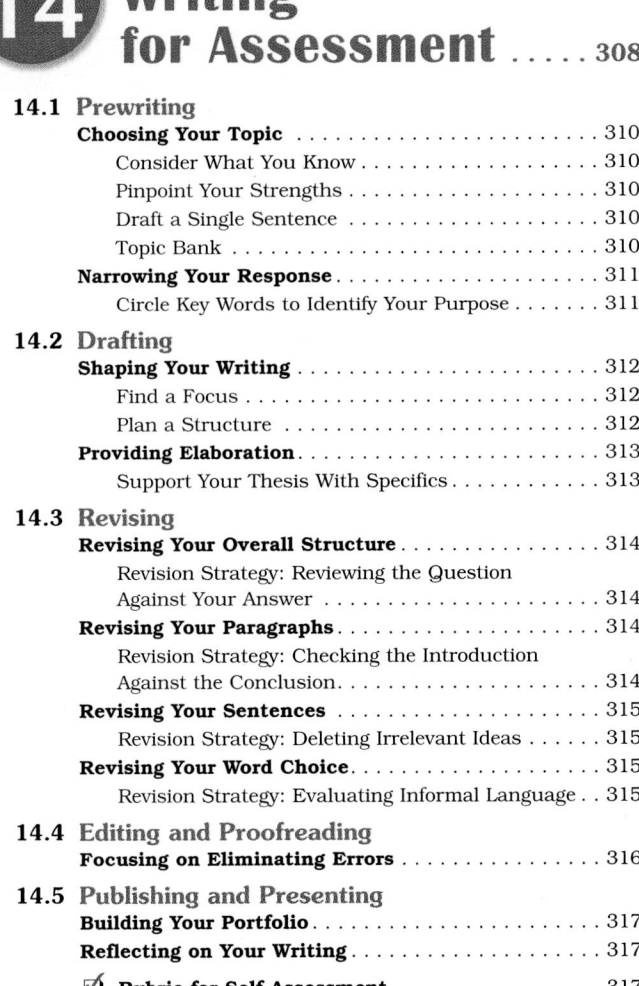

Student Work
IN PROGRESS

Featured Work:
"The Lesson of
'The Scarlet Ibis'"
by Megan Holbrook
Buena High School
Ventura, California

Circling Key Words in
Questions 311
Including Details to
Support a Thesis 313
Final Draft 318

INTEGRATED SKILLS

▶ **Grammar in Your Writing**
  Homophones 316
▶ **Spotlight on the Humanities**
  Analyzing Ideas as Represented
  in Various Art Forms
  Focus on Theater: *Annie* . . 320
▶ **Media and Technology Skills**
  Using Technology to Respond
  to a Variety of Test Formats
  Activity: Practice With
  Computerized Test Banks . 321
▶ **Standardized Test
  Preparation Workshop**
  Analyzing Mechanical
  Errors 322

Contents • xix

Chapter

15 Workplace Writing 324

15.1 Business Letter

What Is a Business Letter? 326

    Model Business Letter 326

Topic Bank 327

15.2 Meeting Minutes

What Are Meeting Minutes? 328

    Model Meeting Minutes......................328

Topic Bank 329

15.3 Forms and Applications

What Are Forms and Applications? 330

    Model Form: Fax (Facsimile) Cover Sheet........330

    Model Application.........................331

Connected Assignment: Phone Messages 332

INTEGRATED SKILLS

▶ **Spotlight on the Humanities**
Examining Ideas Represented
in a Variety of Arts

Focus on Music: Peter Ilich
Tchaikovsky 334

▶ **Media and Technology Skills**
Using Technology for Aspects
of Writing

Activity: Using Word
Processing to Create Effective
Error-Free Writing 335

▶ **Standardized Test
Preparation Workshop**
Applying Verb Usage
Rules 335

PART 2: GRAMMAR, USAGE, AND MECHANICS

Chapter 16

Nouns and Pronouns 340

▶ **Diagnostic Test**. 341

16.1 Nouns 342

Compound Nouns 343

Common and Proper Nouns 344

▶ **Section Review**. 345

16.2 Pronouns. 346

Antecedents of Pronouns 346

Personal Pronouns 348

Reflexive and Intensive Pronouns 349

Demonstrative, Relative, and Interrogative
Pronouns. 350

Indefinite Pronouns 353

▶ **Hands-on Grammar**. 354

▶ **Section Review**. 355

▶ **Chapter Review** 356

▶ **Standardized Test Preparation Workshop** . 358

Chapter 17

Verbs 360

▶ **Diagnostic Test**. 361

17.1 Action Verbs 362

Transitive and Intransitive Verbs. 363

▶ **Hands-on Grammar**. 364

▶ **Section Review**. 365

17.2 Linking Verbs 366

Forms of *Be*. 366

Other Linking Verbs 367

Linking Verb or Action Verb?. 368

▶ **Section Review**. 369

17.3 Helping Verbs 370

Recognizing Helping Verbs 370

Finding Helping Verbs in Sentences. 372

▶ **Section Review**. 373

▶ **Chapter Review** 374

▶ **Standardized Test Preparation Workshop** . 376

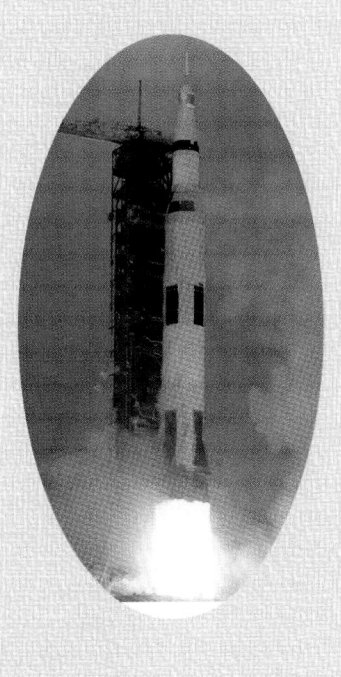

Contents • **xxi**

Chapter 18

Adjectives and Adverbs 378

- ▶ **Diagnostic Test** 379
- **18.1** Adjectives 380
  - ▶ **Hands-on Grammar** 388
  - ▶ **Section Review** 389
- **18.2** Adverbs 390
  - ▶ **Section Review** 395
  - ▶ **Chapter Review** 396
  - ▶ **Standardized Test Preparation Workshop** . 398

Chapter 19

Prepositions, Conjunctions, and Interjections 400

- ▶ **Diagnostic Test** 401
- **19.1** Prepositions 402
  - ▶ **Hands-on Grammar** 406
  - ▶ **Section Review** 407
- **19.2** Conjunctions and Interjections 408
  - ▶ **Section Review** 413
  - ▶ **Chapter Review** 414
  - ▶ **Standardized Test Preparation Workshop** . 416

- ▶ **Cumulative Review: Parts of Speech** ... 418

Chapter 20

Basic Sentence Parts 420

- ▶ **Diagnostic Test** 421
- **20.1** Complete Subjects and Predicates 422
  - ▶ **Hands-on Grammar** 426
  - ▶ **Section Review** 427
- **20.2** Hard-to-Find Subjects 428
  - ▶ **Section Review** 433
- **20.3** Complements 434
  - Direct Objects 434
  - Indirect Objects 437
  - Subject Complements 439
  - The Objective Complement 441
  - ▶ **Section Review** 442
  - ▶ **Chapter Review** 444
  - ▶ **Standardized Test Preparation Workshop** . 446

Chapter 21

Phrases and Clauses 448

▶ **Diagnostic Test**. 449

21.1 Phrases 450

▶ **Hands-on Grammar**. 466

▶ **Section Review** 467

21.2 Clauses 468

Independent and Subordinate Clauses 468

Adjective Clauses 469

Adverb Clauses 474

Noun Clauses 480

Sentences Classified by Structure 482

▶ **Section Review**. 485

▶ **Chapter Review** 486

▶ **Standardized Test Preparation Workshop** . 488

Chapter 22

Effective Sentences 490

▶ **Diagnostic Test**. 491

22.1 Classifying the Four Functions
of a Sentence 492

▶ **Section Review**. 494

22.2 Sentence Combining. 495

▶ **Section Review**. 499

22.3 Varying Sentences. 500

▶ **Section Review**. 503

22.4 Avoiding Sentence Errors. 504

▶ **Hands-on Grammar**. 516

▶ **Section Review** 517

▶ **Chapter Review** 518

▶ **Standardized Test Preparation Workshop** . 520

▶ Cumulative Review:
Phrases, Clauses, Sentences 522

Contents • xxiii

Chapter 23

Verb Usage 524

▶ Diagnostic Test 525
23.1 Verb Tenses 526
▶ Section Review 538
23.2 Active and Passive Voice 540
▶ Hands-on Grammar 544
▶ Section Review 545
▶ Chapter Review 546
▶ Standardized Test Preparation Workshop . 548

Chapter 24

Pronoun Usage 550

▶ Diagnostic Test 551
24.1 Identifying Case 552
▶ Section Review 558
24.2 Special Problems With Pronouns 559
▶ Hands-on Grammar 564
▶ Section Review 565
▶ Chapter Review 566
▶ Standardized Test Preparation Workshop . 568

Chapter 25

Agreement 570

▶ Diagnostic Test 571
25.1 Subject and Verb Agreement 572
▶ Hands-on Grammar 581
▶ Section Review 582
25.2 Pronoun and Antecedent Agreement . . . 584
▶ Section Review 591
▶ Chapter Review 592
▶ Standardized Test Preparation Workshop . 594

Chapter 26

Using Modifiers 596

▶ Diagnostic Test 597
26.1 Degrees of Comparison 598
▶ Section Review 603
26.2 Making Clear Comparisons 604
▶ Hands-on Grammar 608
▶ Section Review 609
▶ Chapter Review 610
▶ Standardized Test Preparation Workshop . 612

xxiv • Contents

Chapter 27

Miscellaneous Problems in Usage 614

▶ **Diagnostic Test**..................... 615
27.1 Negative Sentences................. 616
▶ **Section Review** 619
27.2 Common Usage Problems 620
▶ **Hands-on Grammar**................. 628
▶ **Section Review** 629
▶ **Chapter Review** 630
▶ **Standardized Test Preparation Workshop** . 632

▶ **Cumulative Review: Usage**............ 634

Chapter 28

Capitalization 636

▶ **Diagnostic Test**..................... 637
   Capitalizing Words in Sentences......... 638
   Capitalizing Proper Nouns 640
   Capitalizing Proper Adjectives 645
   Capitalizing Titles 646
▶ **Hands-on Grammar**.................. 644
▶ **Chapter Review** 649
▶ **Standardized Test Preparation Workshop** . 651

Chapter 29

Punctuation.................... 652

▶ **Diagnostic Test**..................... 653
29.1 End Marks....................... 654
▶ **Section Review** 657
29.2 Commas......................... 658
▶ **Hands-on Grammar**................. 672
▶ **Section Review**.................... 673
29.3 The Semicolon and the Colon 674
▶ **Section Review**.................... 683
29.4 Quotation Marks With Direct Quotations . 684
▶ **Section Review** 697
29.5 Dashes, Parentheses, and Hyphens.... 698
▶ **Section Review** 711
29.6 Apostrophes 712
▶ **Section Review** 721
▶ **Chapter Review** 722
▶ **Standardized Test Preparation Workshop** . 724

▶ **Cumulative Review: Mechanics**........ 726

▶ **Sentence Diagraming Workshop**....... 728

Contents • **xxv**

Chapter 30

Speaking, Listening, Viewing, and Representing ... 744

30.1 Speaking and Listening Skills 745
Speaking in a Group Discussion 745
Giving a Speech 746
Using Critical Listening 749

30.2 Viewing Skills 752
Interpreting Maps and Graphs 752
Viewing Information Media Critically 755
Viewing Fine Art Critically 757

30.3 Representing Skills 758
Creating Visual Representations 758
Using Formatting 760
Working With Multimedia 761
Creating a Flip Chart 762
Performing or Interpreting 763
▶ **Standardized Test Preparation Workshop** . 764

Chapter 31

Vocabulary and Spelling 766

31.1 Developing Your Vocabulary 767
Listening, Discussing, and Reading 767
Recognizing Contest Clues 768
Denotation and Connotation 770
Recognizing Related Words 770
Using Related Words in Analogies 771

31.2 Studying Words Systematically 772
Using a Dictionary and a Thesaurus 772
Remembering New Vocabulary 773

31.3 Studying Word Parts and Origins 775
Using Prefixes 775
Recognizing Roots 776
Using Suffixes 777
Exploring Etymologies (Word Origins) 778

31.4 Improving Your Spelling 779
Keeping a Spelling Notebook 779
Using Memory Aids 780
Following Spelling Rules 781
Understanding Rules and Exceptions 786
Proofreading Carefully 787
▶ **Standardized Test Preparation Workshop** . 788

Chapter 32

Reading Skills...................790

32.1 Reading Methods and Tools..........791
32.2 Reading Nonfiction Critically.........798
32.3 Reading Literary Writing 804
32.4 Reading From Varied Sources 808
▶ **Standardized Test Preparation Workshop**. 810

Chapter 33

Study, Reference, and Test-Taking Skills........812

33.1 Basic Study Skills.................813
33.2 Reference Skills 816
33.3 Test-Taking Skills 827
▶ **Standardized Test Preparation Workshop**. 832

Chapter 34

Workplace Skills and Competencies.............834

Working With People.................835
Learn to Communicate One on One.......835
Learning Teamwork 837
Moving Toward Your Goals 839
Solving Problems and Thinking Creatively . . 840
Managing Time 842
Managing Money 843
Applying Math Skills 844
Applying Computer Skills 845
▶ **Standardized Test Preparation Workshop**. 846

Resources

Citing Sources and Preparing Manuscript 848
Penmanship Reference 848
Internet Research Handbook 855
Commonly Overused Words 860
Commonly Misspelled Words 862
Abbreviations Guide 864
Proofreading Symbols Reference 868
Student Publications 869
Glossary 870
Index 878

▶ *Lesson Objectives*

1. To understand writing as a recursive process and to develop ownership of their own writing processes.

2. To write in a variety of forms, including narrative, descriptive, persuasive, expository, and literary texts, and to develop skills in writing for assessment.

3. To analyze works of literature and student drafts as models and examples of specific writing strategies.

4. To develop voice and adjust their writing to various audiences and purposes.

5. To develop research skills and to use writing as a tool for learning.

6. To apply specific prewriting strategies for generating and narrowing writing topics.

7. To use graphic organizers and other methods for organizing and supporting ideas in drafting.

8. To approach revision in a systematic way in terms of overall structure, paragraphs, sentences, and word choice.

9. To edit and proofread drafts to ensure appropriate usage and accuracy in spelling and the conventions and mechanics of written English.

10. To understand rubrics and to use them to evaluate their own writing and the writing of others.

PART

1

Writing

Benjamin Comfort (detail), Percy Ives, Detroit Historical Museum

Responding to Fine Art

Benjamin Comfort by Percy Ives (1931–)

Use this artwork to start a discussion about the process of writing.

1. Have students examine the painting on pages xxiv–1. You might use the following questions to prompt discussion:

   What do you think the man in this painting is doing? In what time period do you think this man lives? What details from the painting can you use to support your response?

   What do you think the man is writing?

2. The background that is visible through the windows of the painting is as much a focal point as the man sitting at his desk. Ask students to discuss the relationship of the "outside world" to the writing process.

Time and Resource Manager

In-Depth Lesson Plan

	LESSON FOCUS	PRINT AND MEDIA RESOURCES
DAY 1	**Introduction to Writing** Students learn the qualities of good writing and methods for generating ideas and executing writing (pp. 2–5).	
DAY 2	**Introduction to Writing (continued)** Students learn about how to organize themselves to begin writing, working with others, publishing their work and careers in writing (pp. 6–13).	

Accelerated Lesson Plan

	LESSON FOCUS	PRINT AND MEDIA RESOURCES
DAY 1	**Introduction to Writing** Students learn the qualities of good writing and how to gather ideas, write, and publish their work (pp. 2–13).	

Options for Adapting Lesson Plans

HOMEWORK

Have students complete any stage of the lesson for homework.

TECHNOLOGY

Students can complete any stage of the lesson on computer. Have them print out their completed work.

FEATURES

Extend coverage with Spotlight on the Humanities (p. 10), Media and Technology Skills (p. 11), and the Standardized Test Preparation Workshop (p. 12).

INTEGRATED SKILLS COVERAGE

Real-World Connection
SE p. 9

Viewing and Representing
Critical Viewing, SE pp. 2, 4, 5, 6, 7, 10

ASSESSMENT SUPPORT

Standardized Test Preparation SE p. 12; ATE p. 12

MEETING INDIVIDUAL NEEDS

ESL Students ATE p. 8
Less Advanced Students ATE pp. 11, 13
More Advanced Students ATE p. 13

BLOCK SCHEDULING

Pacing Suggestions
For 90-minute Blocks
• Have students read and discuss the chapter in a single period.

Resources for Varying Instruction
• *Writers at Work* **Videotape** Show The Writer in You segment in class.

Professional Development Support
• *How to Manage Instruction in the Block* This Teaching Resource provides management and activity suggestions.

MEDIA AND TECHNOLOGY

For the Student
• *Writing Lab* **CD-ROM**

For the Teacher
• *Writers at Work* **Videotape**, The Writer in You
• *Resource Pro* **CD-ROM**

WRITING AND GRAMMAR WEBSITE

The Interactive Writing and Grammar Website provides a wide array of support for students, teachers, and parents. Writing support includes:

• Interactive revision checkers
• Scoring rubrics with complete models

phwg.phschool.com

▶ *Lesson Objectives*

1. To understand the importance of using writing to communicate, to express oneself, and to remember facts and details.

2. To develop ways of keeping track of ideas for writing.

3. To develop different approaches to writing.

4. To organize the environment in a way conducive to writing.

5. To discover ways to work with others on writing projects.

6. To find ways to publish one's writing.

7. To learn about the techniques of professional writers.

8. To reflect upon and evaluate one's writing.

▲ **Critical Viewing**
What kind of writing might the students in the photograph be doing?
[Speculate]

Critical Viewing

Speculate Students may say the students are writing a research report.

One of the biggest mistakes that some people make when they think about writing is to consider writing to be a chore. The truth is that writing isn't a chore: It's an opportunity. It is an opportunity to express your ideas, to open up your imagination, to persuade others to agree with your point of view.

Writing in Everyday Life

Writing is already an important part of your everyday life. If you have access to computers, you most likely exchange e-mail messages with friends. You probably also write notes and cards to friends and family members to say thank you or to celebrate a special occasion. In addition, you may keep a journal in which you jot down private thoughts and feelings. As a student, you also do a substantial amount of writing—papers, stories, essay tests. The various types of writing you do every day give you an opportunity to capture and share your feelings and to demonstrate what you know.

⏱ TIME AND RESOURCE MANAGER

Resources
Print: Writing Support Transparency 1-A; Writing Support Activity Book 1-1

• Cover pp. 2–9 in class.
• Discuss examples of writing that you or students have done.

Why Write?

Developing your writing skills will not only help you to express yourself more effectively, it will also help you achieve success in life. Being a strong writer will help you do well in school and it will serve you well in a wide range of occupations—from law and medicine to nursing and auto mechanics.

What Are the Qualities of Good Writing?

Ideas Sometimes the hardest part of writing is coming up with ideas. However, there are ideas for writing all around you—you just may not recognize them. Most of the things that interest you—sports, music, clothes—are a source of an unlimited number of writing ideas. Starting with an idea that interests you makes it more likely that you will produce a good piece of writing. It is important, however, to consider whether potential readers will also find the idea interesting. Even the best pieces of writing won't succeed if the audience is uninterested.

Organization Once you have the ideas for a piece of writing, you must decide how to arrange them. Good writing has a clear and consistent organization that suits the topic. For example, if you are telling a story, you will probably want to arrange your details chronologically, or in the order in which they occurred.

Voice Voice refers to all of the distinctive qualities of your writing—from the type of language you use and the way you put together sentences and paragraphs to the ideas you like to write about and the attitude you convey to readers.

Word Choice Not surprisingly, word choice is a key element of good writing. By choosing words that convey your meaning as precisely as possible and capture your attitude toward your subject, you will help to ensure that readers understand your points and will increase the likelihood that you can sway them to accept your viewpoint.

Sentence Fluency In a piece of good writing, sentences seem to flow seamlessly from one to another. Transitions make it clear how one sentence connects to the next. A variety of lengths, structures, and openers helps to create a rhythm that engages readers.

Conventions Finally, it is essential for a piece of writing to follow the conventions of English grammar, usage, and mechanics. Errors in these areas will distract readers.

Writers in ACTION

Writing is not limited to the nation's classrooms and newsrooms, as this quotation from Larry Cataldo, an auto mechanic proves:

"People would be surprised by how important writing is to my job. Without a clearly written work order, I wouldn't know what to look for when I inspect a car. And if I didn't write careful notes about what the problem was, what the repair was, and what procedure I had used, customers wouldn't have a clear understanding of what work had been done and why."

Learn More

To learn about strategies to help you develop writing that has these qualities, see Chapter 2, "A Walk Through the Writing Process," p. 14.

The Writer in You • 3

Teaching Resources: Writing Support Transparency 1-A; Writing Support Activity Book 1-1

1. **Notebook.** Ask students what they could have recently recorded in their notebook if they had been keeping one.

2. **Writer's Journal.** Ask for ideas of small objects that might be placed in a writer's journal to spur writing. (concert or movie tickets, trip souvenirs, maps, invitations)

3. **Learning Log.** Point out that learning does not occur only in school. Everyone is learning things everywhere, all the time. Even if we are sure that we will remember something, it is still wise to write it down. Display the transparency to model the learning log for students. Give students copies of the blank organizer and have them write one entry as practice.

Critical Viewing

Speculate Students may say she is writing a journal entry.

Developing Your Writing Life

There isn't just one correct way to approach the writing you do. Instead, writers experiment with different routines and approaches to writing until they find one that works for them. Following are some suggestions to help you develop your own writing routine:

Keep Track of Your Ideas

A great idea is only great if you remember it. Keep track of your thoughts and observations.

Notebook Take a tip from many professional writers and keep a small notebook with you at all times. In it, record thoughts, ideas, snippets of overheard conversation (great for helping you write realistic dialogue), and anything else that grabs your interest throughout the day. If coming up with a topic ever presents a problem, your notebook may contain the solution.

Writer's Journal Like a notebook, a writer's journal can be a great source of writing ideas. The writing in a writer's journal is writing you do for yourself alone, so this is a place where you can experiment with different writing styles or just let your ideas flow without stopping to edit yourself. A writer's journal is also a place where you can keep drawings, clippings, or other mementos that might inspire future writing projects.

Learning Log Often, writing about something can help you understand it. This is one of the benefits of keeping a learning log. A learning log is a place to record information you have learned—anything from methods for solving equations to a new technique for stopping on in-line skates. Writing something in a learning log that you want to remember might inspire you to conduct further research on the same topic, to turn it into a larger writing project.

▼ **Critical Viewing** What type of writing do you imagine that this girl is doing? Why? **[Speculate]**

Learning Log October 26, 1999		
What I Learned	Where I Learned It	Connections I Make
Not every number is something you count with. Some numbers are like a vanishing point that a series of numbers gets closer and closer to but never reaches.	Math class	This idea reminds me of what happened to the crew of the Space Cat on last week's episode—they got closer and closer to the center of the black hole but never reached it.
When putting a new string on a guitar, always start winding the string at the bottom of the peg and wind up.	Kevin next door	My strings used to buzz a lot before I tried this—I wonder if it will help.

Keep Track of Your Writing and Reading

Writing Portfolio Keeping a writing portfolio can also help you develop as a writer. Looking over your old work can remind you which writing strategies have worked well for you and which have not. A portfolio is a place where you save your written work and also monitor your progress as a writer. In a portfolio you can collect finished pieces as well as the notes and drafts you developed during the writing process. If you work on a computer, you might keep a portfolio disk instead of—or as well as—a paper portfolio.

Reader's Journal You can learn from other writers by keeping a journal in which you jot down quotations that you particularly like. Review these before you write; they may inspire you. Also, by familiarizing yourself with writing that has impressed you, you will develop an ear for effective style.

Try Different Approaches

Just as you have your own tastes, likes, and dislikes, you will find that you will develop a unique approach to writing. Following are suggestions to help you find your own approach:

Getting Started There are many different ways of getting started on a piece of writing. You may find that simply sitting quietly and gathering your thoughts is your first step. In contrast, you may discover that sitting in front of a blank computer screen is the best way to begin.

Finding Ideas If you keep a learning log or journal (see page 4), you may turn to its pages to find inspiration for your writing. You might also look to the media as a valuable source for writing topics.

Writing a Draft Once you have assembled ideas and research, you might like to write a draft—on-line or by hand—in one continuous burst of writing. Another good method is to work out a few ideas, leave your writing for a while, and then come back to it.

Improving Your Work You might like to improve your sentences and paragraphs as you write, erasing or crossing out and rewriting before you have finished a draft. Alternatively, you may work best by improving a finished draft. Collaborate with a peer reviewer to revise and edit your work.

Experiment

Don't be afraid to try new strategies from time to time. As you develop as a writer, pay attention to the techniques that work best for you so that you can develop the most effective writing process.

▼ **Critical Viewing** Compare and contrast the setting in which this girl is writing with a more formal setting—such as a classroom. **[Compare]**

Keep Track of Your Writing and Reading

1. **Writing Portfolio.** If students already have a portfolio, ask them what kinds of writing it contains. If not, have students suggest written work that they might want to keep in a portfolio.
2. **Reader's Journal.** Ask students what they have read recently that is worth recording in a reader's journal.
3. Stress that ideas they put in a notebook or journal can be private. No one else ever has to see it. So they should not hesitate to include their deepest feelings—joys and sadness, fears, and hopes and dreams.

Try Different Approaches

1. Remind students that they have all used the writing process. Ask which of the approaches they find the easiest and hardest. Some students have many ideas but have difficulty organizing them. Others never can think of a topic, but if one is assigned, then they can easily write about it.
2. Invite students to share other strategies for writing that they have heard about.
3. Emphasize that students will have many opportunities to write with a partner or group of classmates, who can help one another with the parts of writing they find difficult.

Critical Viewing

Compare Some students may say that they enjoy writing in a setting like the one shown because it is quiet and peaceful. Others may say being outside is too distracting.

1. **Choose the Right Spot.** Invite students to suggest their own comfortable places for writing. The right spot is different for everyone. Harry sprawls on the bed with the cat. Barry sits at his desk with everything arranged just so. Carry needs absolute quiet. Mary likes soft music in the background.

2. **Come Prepared.** With students, brainstorm for a list of reference materials that are helpful to have on hand. (dictionary, encyclopedia, atlas, thesaurus, style manual, magazines for writing ideas)

3. **Budget Your Time.** Discuss with students the calendar one student set up for completing a research assignment. Ask them if they would allot more or less time to each of the steps.

Critical Viewing

Evaluate Students may say that the student did select a good place because no one else is around to disturb him.

Planning to Write

In your everyday life, you do certain types of writing with barely a thought. For example, when you leave a quick note in a friend's locker telling where and when to meet you after school, you don't have to agonize over every word. There are, however, circumstances in which the act of writing can be anxiety-provoking. Writing a complex research paper, taking an essay test, or drafting an important letter can all be daunting tasks—but you can make things easier for yourself by organizing your writing life. Here are some ideas:

Organize Your Environment

Writing requires more than a pen and paper. You also need uninterrupted stretches of time to think through ideas, write a draft, and review what you have written. You need to find and create an environment that encourages your writing process.

Choose the Right Spot Choose a spot where interruptions will be minimal and where you find it easy to concentrate. Some writers prefer a quiet library. Some prefer to work in their own room with music playing in the background. Make sure that you can work effectively in whatever place and conditions you choose.

Come Prepared Make sure that you have readily available all the materials that you need, such as reference works, pens, paper, and your own notes. Having to stop to get more paper in the middle of an exciting thought can be a frustrating experience.

Budget Your Time Writing under the pressure of a deadline can get your creative juices flowing. It can also make you sloppy and force you to settle for undeveloped ideas. To create a comfortable pace for writing, chart a schedule for your work. Using a calendar, divide up the time you have been given for the assignment. Estimate the amount of time it will take to complete each stage of the writing process, and assign yourself mini-deadlines. As you work through the writing process, use these mini-deadlines to keep a good working pace. If one stage takes more or less time than you expected, you can adjust the deadlines for remaining stages.

▲ Critical Viewing
Do you think that this student has selected a good place to write? Why or why not?
[Evaluate]

October

Sunday	Monday	Tuesday	Wednesday	Thursday	Friday	Saturda
		Start Research **1**	**2**	Finish Research **3**	Write Outline **4**	**5**
6	**7**	Finish First Draft **8**	**9**	Finish Revising **10**	Finish Proof-reading **11**	**12**
13	DUE DATE **14**	**15**	**16**	**17**	**18**	**19**

Working With Others

If you think of writing as a solitary activity, think again. Working with others can be a key part of the writing process.

Group Brainstorming Brainstorming is a great way to work with others to generate writing topics. Gather in a group and freely suggest ideas. Let one idea lead to another. Do not stop to ask whether the ideas connect with one another or whether they are good or not. Take notes to keep track of the ideas that come up. When you review your notes, you may find writing ideas you would not have discovered on your own.

Collaborative and Cooperative Writing Professional writers often work together to produce a piece of work. You can do the same thing. In collaborative writing, you and one or more classmates work together on a piece of writing or a project that includes writing. Each group member takes an assigned role, such as interviewing certain people or writing a particular section of the complete product. The group then works together to assemble the individual pieces into a completed project. In cooperative writing, which is less structured than collaborative writing, you may work together with other students throughout all the stages of an assignment.

Peer Reviewers During the revision process, it's often useful to ask another person to help you catch mistakes or weaknesses. A peer reviewer can also point out strengths in your writing that can be further developed.

▼ Critical Viewing
Do you think these students are brainstorming, drafting, or reviewing a draft? Why? **[Analyze]**

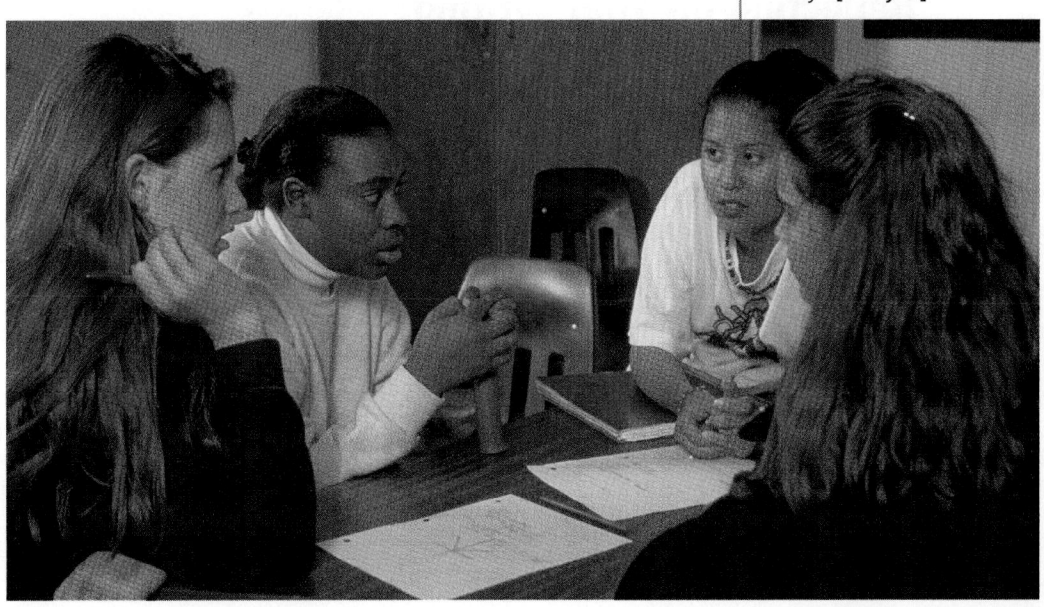

The Writer in You • 7

Step-by-Step Teaching Guide

Working With Others

1. **Group Brainstorming.** To demonstrate the power of brainstorming, ask students to brainstorm for one of these topics:

   a theme for a school celebration

   a book to read aloud in class

   After the brainstorming session, ask students what they think its benefits are. (more ideas in less time, more points of view, ideas sparking other ideas)

2. **Collaborative and Cooperative Writing.** Suggest a topic to students, such as snowboarding, and ask for their ideas on how to divide the research among group members. (how to snowboard, its history, kinds of equipment)

3. **Peer Reviewers.** Ask students why they might be more willing to have a classmate review their writing, rather than a teacher or other adult.

Integrating Speaking and Listening Skills

Remind students that when they work with others, they need to set and follow guidelines for speaking and listening. One guideline is for speakers to phrase their suggestions and questions about a peer's writing in positive terms.

Critical Viewing

Analyze Students' responses will vary, but make sure they support their responses with details from the photo.

Publishing or Presenting Your Work

1. Ask students for suggestions of other places they might get their work published. (local newspaper, school or community newsletter)

2. Tell students that publishing simply means sharing. They can "publish" the work by reading it aloud, acting it out as a skit, posting it on a bulletin board, e-mailing it to a friend, or designing a cover and making a minibook.

Real-World Connection

Ask students to suggest jobs that do not require writing. For each job, challenge the whole class to think of how the job *does* require writing. For the obvious example of alligator wrestler, point out that alligators get *very* hungry. If the wrestler's order for alligator chow lists the wrong brand or the wrong amount, well . . .

Customize for *ESL Students*

Students learning English may be aware of professions that require translation skills. Examples are court and medical personnel. Ask them to tell how being able to write as well as speak more than one language could be a job asset.

Reflecting on Your Writing

Students may want to display what they consider their best written work and to explain how they accomplished it.

Publishing or Presenting Your Work

Few experiences can be as rewarding as knowing that your work has found its audience. Look for opportunities to publish your writing, whether it is through a student Web site or submission to a magazine contest. Here are a few places that publish student work:

Periodicals

- Merlyn's Pen: The National Magazine of Student Writing, P.O. Box 1058, East Greenwich, RI 02818
- Skipping Stones, P.O. Box 3939, Eugene, OR 97403

On-line Publications

- Kid Pub http://en-garde.com/kidpub
- MidLink Magazine/www.cs.ucf.edu/~Midlink/

Contests

- Annual Poetry Contest, National Federation of State Poetry Societies, 3520 State Route 56, Mechanicsburg, OH 43044
- Paul A. Witty Outstanding Literature Award, International Reading Association, Special Interest Group for Reading for Gifted and Creative Students, c/o Texas Christian University, P.O. Box 32925, Fort Worth, TX 76129

Reflecting on Your Writing

To continue to improve as a writer, it is important to take time to reflect after you complete a piece of writing. Ask yourself what worked well and what you could have done better. At this time, take a moment to think about the various kinds of writing you have done in the past. Consider the kinds of writing you have found rewarding. Then, think about things you would like to change or improve in your writing. Here are some questions to direct your reflection:

- Of which written pieces are you most proud? What might they have in common?

- With which pieces have you been least satisfied? What might they have in common?

- What aspect of your writing would you like to improve the most?

Take some time to share your responses with a partner, and then jot down your ideas in a writer's journal.

Writers in Action

Careers in Writing, Writing in Careers

For some people, writing is more than a communication tool—it is a career. There are a multitude of professionals who earn their living by writing: novelists, television scriptwriters, movie screenwriters, songwriters, speech writers, and advertising copywriters all fall under this category.

There are also many professionals who are not technically writers but for whom writing is an indispensable part of their daily workday. The ability to write a strong and well-organized letter, a persuasive proposal, or a clear, concise summary is useful, if not mandatory, in many lines of work.

Meet the Professionals

In the chapters that follow, you'll meet professionals who use different types of writing on the job. These "Writers in Action" include:

Anne McCaffrey, a science-fiction and fantasy writer, uses vivid, descriptive details to transport readers to fantastic lands filled with dragons and other imaginary creatures.

Isabel Allende, an internationally acclaimed novelist, writes enchanting stories and novels that have entertained millions of readers.

Gene Bryan Johnson, a public-radio journalist, writes and presents reports on current events to keep his listeners informed.

Larry Weitzman, a publicist and sports writer, creates films, proposals, and public-service announcements to build enthusiasm about the sport of basketball.

Ellen Harkins Wheat, an art historian and biographer, conducts extensive research about noted people, such as painter Jacob Lawrence.

Lawrence Chua, a book reviewer, helps guide the public in deciding which books to read.

Grant Moran, an animation scriptwriter, writes imaginative scripts for various cartoons.

Glo Simon, a pediatric intensive-care nurse, records careful observations about her patients and compiles summaries of their care and treatment.

Reading insights about writing from these professionals may help you to imagine ways you might someday use writing.

Writers at Work Videotape

You can view these Writers at Work demonstrating their writing process in the *Writer's at Work* videos.

Ellen Harkins Wheat

Glo Simon

Real-World Connection

In addition to professionals who earn their living by writing, there is a multitude of other professionals who require writing skills—doctors, nurses, teachers, and lawyers. Encourage students to name other professions that require good writing skills.

Lesson Objectives

1. To listen and respond appropriately to presentations and performances.
2. To evaluate artistic performances in media presentations.
3. To analyze ideas as represented in various media.
4. To recognize how visual and sound techniques convey messages in media.
5. To examine the effect of media on constructing a perception of reality.
6. To write an essay.

Step-by-Step Teaching Guide

Analyzing How Meaning Is Communicated Through the Arts

1. Choose one of the Spotlight elements for class discussion, or have students work individually or in groups on the element of their choice. Give students the initiative to find examples of the various media.

2. Display a selection of fine art or lead students to on-line or local gallery exhibits. Discuss and have students identify many different types of fine art.

3. Invite students to brainstorm applications for photography. Challenge interested students to share favorite photographs and explain their reactions.

4. Review recent theatrical productions at your school or in your community. Show students a play on videotape. What do they think are the pluses and minuses of this media?

5. Invite students' ideas about effective recent films. Were these adapted from books or other original media? What made them successful films?

6. Hold a class music festival in which students can share their favorite music. (Remind them to share only music appropriate to school discussion.) What makes music so captivating?

7. Talk with students about the many kinds of dance people

Spotlight on the Humanities

Analyzing How Meaning Is Communicated Through the Arts
Introducing the Spotlight on the Humanities

Overview In addition to writing, you can express yourself through many other media. Following are some you might consider:

- **Fine Art** creates meaning through color, line, texture, and subject. Paintings, sketches, sculpture, and collage can convey literal or abstract ideas.

- **Photography** uses still images to create meaning. While a photograph captures still images on film, photographers express ideas through subject, composition, and lighting.

- **Theater** is designed to be performed by actors on a stage. Using props, scenery, sound effects, and lighting, drama brings a story to life. In some cases, music, songs, and dance are incorporated into the story line.

- **Film** captures sound and motion. Like dramatic theater, most films tell stories and use settings, costumes, and characterization. A filmmaker can create a unique point of view using camera angles, lighting, and sound techniques.

- **Music** uses sound to create meaning. Whether presented as an oboe solo, an operatic aria, or a symphony, music can create moods or present variations on a theme.

- **Dance** creates meaning through organized movement. It can be performed by a single person, a pair, or large groups.

Introducing the Spotlights on the Humanities In the Spotlight on the Humanities features, you will discover how all art is connected—layer upon layer—and how the inspiration that moved the hearts and minds of creative artists in the past continues to touch artists of today.

Writing Activity: Exploring Inspiration
In a brief piece of writing, explain what *inspiration* is and discuss the different ways in which inspiration is reflected in various art forms.

▲ **Critical Viewing**
What can you tell about the style of this artist's work based on this photograph? **[Analyze]**

enjoy, from traditional dances to contemporary popular dances. How does dance speak to basic human needs?

Viewing and Representing

Activity Invite interested students to create performance art that conveys the essential meaning of their essay. Tell them to include words in the performance, either as signage or with song or monologue.

Critical Viewing

Analyze Students' responses will vary. Make sure they support their responses with details from the photograph.

Media and Technology Skills

Using a Variety of Technologies

Introduction to Technology

Computers offer valuable writing tools—tools that can help you communicate, express yourself creatively, research subjects of interest, and expand publication options. To harness these technology tools, get to know the features your computer offers.

Learn About It Check out these basic computer tools:

- **Internet** Search engines can help you find on-line information, books, articles, videos, and chat sites. Use Bookmarks to return quickly to favorite search engines or Web pages. Publish final writing products on your school's Web site or another appropriate site.

- **Word Processor** Use word-processing software at every stage of the writing process. Draft initial ideas, reposition and edit text, experiment with the way your document looks, and revise until you are satisfied.

- **E-mail** To send e-mail, select Messages from the menu bar and then choose New Message to bring up a blank letter form. Enter the e-mail address of your recipient, and type your message. Then, choose and activate the Send function.

- **Desktop Publishing** Create professional-looking newspapers, invitations, and brochures using desktop publishing software.

Reflect on It Think about the various ways you can use computers to help you in your writing projects this year. Capture your ideas in a graphic organizer like this one.

```
My Writing Goal: _____
Ideas for Using Computers

Internet: _____
         _____
         _____

Word Processor: _____
                _____

E-mail: _____
        _____
        _____

Desktop Publishing: _____
                    _____
                    _____
```

Ways to Use Computers

Internet
- Scan on-line publications with index functions.
- Obtain up-to-the-minute news from on-line news services.
- Access ever-changing statistics and facts in on-line encyclopedias.

Word Processor
- Use formatting tools to change the way your documents look.
- Organize your writing in logically labeled files for easy access.
- Spot and correct errors with spell and grammar checkers.

E-mail
- Communicate around the world or down the hall.
- Reach multiple recipients quickly.

Desktop Publishing
- Create video postcards.
- Develop print ads, class newspapers, and documentaries.

Media and Technology Skills • 11

▶ Lesson Objectives
1. To use a variety of technologies to communicate specific messages.
2. To use a range of techniques to plan and create media text.
3. To use technology for aspects of creating, revising, editing, and publishing.
4. To compile information in systematic ways using available technology.

Step-by-Step Teaching Guide

Using a Variety of Technologies

Teaching Resources: Writing Support Transparency 1-B; Writing Support Activity Book 1-2

1. Discuss the suggested ways to use computers and challenge students to add to the list.

2. Ask students to share ways that they use computers, whether for communication or entertainment. List some of these on the chalkboard for students to consider as they complete the activity.

3. Display the transparency and clarify its use with students.

4. Give students copies of the blank organizer and encourage them to note their ideas about technology use in it. Invite volunteers to exchange organizers and share ideas. Suggest that students keep the organizer and add to it as the year continues.

Customize for *Less Advanced Students*

If students are unfamiliar with basic computer functions, work with them individually or in small groups to demonstrate the listed functions. As you model each function, give some examples of how to use it on a mock writing assignment.

1. To write in a style appropriate to audience and purpose.
2. To use prewriting strategies to generate ideas, develop voice, and plan.
3. To organize ideas to ensure logical progression and support for ideas.
4. To demonstrate control over grammatical elements.
5. To produce legible work that shows accurate spelling and correct use of punctuation and capitalization conventions.

Step-by-Step Teaching Guide

Writing for Standardized Tests

1. Emphasize with students the importance of understanding and following directions on standardized tests. Students should pay careful attention to the prompt and to any related text. They should then focus their response carefully on the prompt.

2. Acknowledge with students the challenges of writing in a timed situation. Students should be realistic about how much they can accomplish in the given time. Encourage them to practice timed test taking as much as possible to gain comfort with planning and writing under time limitations.

3. Explain that test examiners understand the constraints of timed writing. Students should not expect to fully edit and revise their work. They should, however, spend a significant portion of time on planning to minimize the need for editing and revising.

4. Encourage students to use scrap paper and pencil for prewriting plans. These notes can be very brief as they will not be evaluated.

Standardized Test Preparation Workshop

Writing for Standardized Tests

In this chapter, you have learned about many of the situations in which you will write, both in school and outside of school. One other situation in which you will be called on to write is when you take various standardized tests. The writing prompts on standardized tests assess your ability to present information clearly and to build and support an argument. Following are some of the things that scorers will look for when they evaluate your writing:

- Have you responded directly to the prompt and completed all of the activities or processes that the prompt includes?
- Have you introduced a main idea in your introductory paragraph and developed that idea in a series of body paragraphs that each focus on a single subtopic?
- Have you used a logical and consistent organization?
- Have you offered thorough supporting evidence to back up your key points?
- Have you used precise language that clearly conveys your intended meaning?
- Have you made sure that all of your sentences contribute to your main points?
- Have you used correct spelling, capitalization, punctuation, grammar, usage, and sentence structure?

The process of writing for a test can be divided into stages. Plan to use a specific amount of time for prewriting, drafting, revising, and proofreading. Following is an example of one type of writing prompt you might find on a test. Use the suggestions on the next page to help you respond. The clocks next to each stage show a plan for organizing your time.

Test Tip

Watch the clock. Try to keep within the time limits suggested so you can complete your essay and revise it.

Sample Writing Situation

> Writer Rudolfo Anaya has said: "I am shaping what I believe of the world, and I believe that vision to be worthy of sharing with you. . . ."

> Write an essay in which you explain the meaning of Anaya's statement and discuss how you might be able to apply this statement to yourself as you develop as a writer.

◈ TEST-TAKING TIP

Some writers find it difficult to get started. In a test situation, such hesitation can cost students critical minutes. Encourage them to quickly draft a second paragraph on scrap paper. Chances are that once they have the second paragraph, the first paragraph will come more easily. Another option is to leave a blank page for the first paragraph. Finally, students might try to write a one-sentence response to the prompt. This single sentence is probably a good topic sentence for an opening paragraph.

Ask students to suggest a single sentence response to the sample prompt.

Sample Prompt: Like Anaya, I can use my writing to describe and convey my vision of the world.

Prewriting

Allow close to one quarter of your time for prewriting.

Analyze the Prompt Look carefully at Anaya's quotation and at the prompt that follows it. Jot down the key words in both the quotation and the prompt. Then, think about what Anaya is saying. What does he mean when he says that he is "shaping what [he believes] of the world"? Once you feel confident that you understand the quotation, jot down notes about how you could apply his observation to yourself.

Organize Details Next, review your notes, and decide on the best way to organize your information. You may find that the best method is to start by explaining the quotation and to follow with one or more paragraphs connecting it to yourself.

Drafting

Allow almost half of your time for drafting.

Present the details you have gathered in a logical and coherent way, using an introduction, body paragraphs, and a conclusion.

Write an Introduction In your introduction, state the main point of your essay. The main point should include both an interpretation of the quotation and a brief statement about how it relates to you.

Develop Supporting Paragraphs Develop body paragraphs that each focus on a single subtopic. Each paragraph should include a topic sentence and other sentences that support the idea presented in the topic sentence. Avoid including sentences in a paragraph that do not relate to the topic sentence.

End With a Strong Conclusion End your essay by restating your main point and making one or more additional observations that will make an impression on the readers who will score your work.

Revising, Editing, and Proofreading

Allow just over a quarter of your time for revising and proofreading.

Check Your Organization Review your essay to ensure that you have used a consistent organization throughout your essay. If you have strayed from your planned organization, rearrange some of your information. Mark your changes clearly.

Add Transitions to Connect Ideas Look for places where you can add transitions to connect your ideas.

Make Corrections Check for errors in spelling, grammar, and punctuation. When making changes, place a line through text that you want to eliminate and place it in brackets. Use a caret [^] to indicate places where you would like to add words.

Time and Resource Manager

In-Depth Lesson Plan

	LESSON FOCUS	PRINT AND MEDIA RESOURCES
DAY 1	**Introduction to the Writing Process** Students get overview of writing process (pp. 14–15).	
DAY 2	**Prewriting** Students walk through process of choosing and narrowing a topic, considering their audience and purpose, and gathering details (pp. 16–20).	**Teaching Resources** *Writing Support Transparencies, 2-A–D;* *Writing Support Activity Book, 2-1–3*
DAY 3	**Drafting** Students review model drafts and strategies for drafting (pp. 21–22).	*Writing Support Transparencies, 2-E*
DAY 4	**Revising** Students review strategies for revising their drafts (pp. 23–25).	*Writing Support Transparencies, 2-F*
DAY 5	**Editing and Proofreading; Publishing and Presenting** Students learn how to check their work for accuracy and correctness and present their final drafts (pp. 26–27).	*Writing Support Transparencies, 2-G*

Accelerated Lesson Plan

	LESSON FOCUS	PRINT AND MEDIA RESOURCES
DAY 1	**Drafting** Students review an introduction to the writing process and the prewriting and drafting stages (pp. 14–22).	**Teaching Resources** *Writing Support Transparencies 2-A–E;* *Writing Support Activity Book 2-1–3*
DAY 2	**Revising to Presenting** Students familiarize themselves with the revising, editing and proofreading, and publishing and presenting stages of the writing process (pp. 23–27).	*Writing Support Transparencies 2-F–G*

Options for Adapting Lesson Plans

HOMEWORK

Have students complete any stage of the lesson for homework.

TECHNOLOGY

Students can complete any stage of the lesson on computer. Have them print out their completed work.

FEATURES

Extend coverage with Spotlight on the Humanities (p. 28), Media and Technology Skills (p. 29), and the Standardized Test Preparation Workshop (p. 30).

INTEGRATED SKILLS COVERAGE

Vocabulary
Integrating Vocabulary Skills ATE p. 22

Workplace Skills
Integrating Workplace Skills ATE p. 26

Technology
Integrating Technology Skills ATE p. 26

Real-World Connection
ATE pp. 16, 21

Viewing and Representing
Critical Viewing, SE pp. 14, 28
Viewing and Representing ATE p. 28

ASSESSMENT SUPPORT

Standardized Test Preparation SE p.30; ATE p. 30

Standardized Preparation Workbook, pp. 3–4

Scoring Rubrics on Transparency, Ch. 2

Formal Assessment, Ch. 2

Writing Assessment and Portfolio Management

MEETING INDIVIDUAL NEEDS

More Advanced Students ATE p. 31

ESL Students ATE p. 31

Visual/Spatial Learners ATE pp. 17, 29

Verbal/Linguistic Learners ATE p. 20

BLOCK SCHEDULING

Pacing Suggestions
For 90-minute Blocks
• Have students complete the Prewriting and Drafting stages in a single period.
• Focus one class period on Revising and Editing and Publishing and Presenting. Allow at least 30 minutes for peer revision.

Resources for Varying Instruction
• *Writing Lab* **CD-ROM** If your students have access to hardware, a 90-minute block provides an ideal opportunity for students to work on computer.

Professional Development Support
• *How to Manage Instruction in the Block* This Teaching Resource provides management and activity suggestions.

MEDIA AND TECHNOLOGY

For the Student
• *Writing Lab* **CD-ROM**

For the Teacher
• *Resource Pro* **CD-ROM**

WRITING AND GRAMMAR WEBSITE

The Interactive Writing and Grammar Website provides a wide array of support for students, teachers, and parents. Writing support includes:

• Interactive revision checkers
• Scoring rubrics with complete models

phwg.phschool.com

Chapter
2
A Walk Through
the Writing Process

Lesson Objectives

1. To distinguish between categories of writing: reflexive and extensive.

2. To distinguish among modes of writing: narration, description, persuasion, exposition, research writing, response to literature, writing for assessment, and workplace writing.

3. To preview the steps of the writing process: prewriting, drafting, revising, editing and proofreading, and publishing and presenting.

4. To practice sample strategies for choosing and narrowing a topic, considering audience and purpose, gathering and organizing information, and shaping writing.

Critical Viewing

Support Students may say that libraries provide books and other resources as well as help from librarians and other professionals.

Writing is a process that begins with the exploration of ideas and ends with the presentation of a final draft. The steps of the writing process can help you make your finished product the best it can be.

▲ **Critical Viewing**
Identify two ways in which libraries support effective writing. [Support]

Types of Writing

Often, the types of writing are grouped into **modes** according to form and purpose. The chart at right shows the writing modes you will encounter in this book.

Writing can also be classified as *reflexive* or *extensive*. **Reflexive writing** refers to writing for which you choose the subject and the form. Often, reflexive writing is written for the writer alone and is not shared with an outside audience. **Extensive writing,** on the other hand, is writing for which you are given a subject or a range of subjects. Writing extensively results in sharing your writing with an audience—often your teacher.

The Modes	of Writing
Narration	Research Writing
Description	Response to Literature
Persuasion	Writing for Assessment
Exposition	Workplace Writing

⏱ TIME AND RESOURCE MANAGER

In-Depth Coverage	Accelerated Pace
• Cover pp. 14–15 in class. • Discuss examples of writing you or students know about or bring to class.	• Assign pp. 14–15 for independent student review.

The Process of Writing

These are the stages of the writing process:

- **Prewriting** is the stage in which you explore possible topics, choose a topic, and then gather details you can include in your writing.
- **Drafting** involves putting ideas down on paper in a rough format.
- **Revising** is the stage in which you rework your rough draft to improve both its form and its content.
- **Editing and proofreading** are the stages in which you polish your writing, fixing errors in grammar, spelling, and mechanics.
- **Publishing and presenting** are the sharing of your writing.

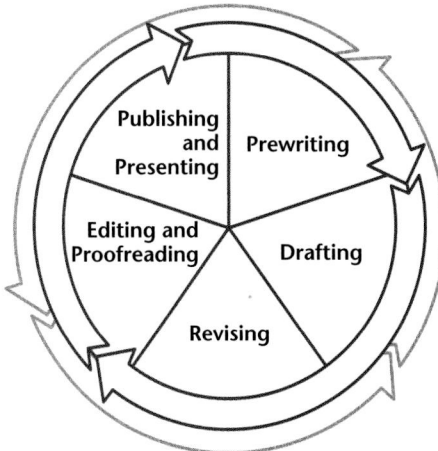

Although it may appear to be the case, these stages do not form a linear sequence. As a writer, you may find yourself skipping stages or returning to earlier stages. For example, you may begin drafting and find that you need to go back to do more research for more material with which to work. In another case, you may plunge right into drafting a story without taking time to jot down your ideas.

A Guided Tour

Use this chapter as a guided tour of the stages of the writing process. Learn about the steps of the process, and experiment with the sample strategies that are presented. In the chapters that follow, you will learn about many other strategies that you can use for each stage of the process.

Interest GRABBER Invite students to tell about guided tours they have taken, such as a tour of a factory, a historical site, a museum, a national park, or a zoo. (If no student has taken a tour, give your own example.) Explain that such tours are meant to introduce visitors to the site and give them basic information so they can enjoy and learn from further exploration on their own.

Activate Prior Knowledge

Ask students when they themselves have acted as guides, for example, showing visiting relatives around their town or city, or a new student around their school. Tell them they will now be on the other side as they are guided through the writing process.

TEACH

Step-by-Step Teaching Guide

Prewriting: Writing With Invisible Ink

1. The writing process should be familiar to students, no matter what school(s) they have attended previously. Explain that in this chapter they will review the steps and learn some tips and procedures to make the process easier.

2. Provide each student with a piece of carbon paper to place carbon-side down (the dark, shiny side) on a blank sheet of paper. Using lined paper as the top sheet may result in more legible carbon copies. Students using a computer can write at the keyboard with the monitor turned off or darkened.

3. The point of the Invisible Ink activity is to allow students' ideas to flow freely onto paper, without their inner "critic" being able to see the ideas and censor them.

Real-World Connection

For students, much of their world is school and homework. Stress that the writing process can also help them write reports for history and science classes. They can also use it when writing a play for the Drama Club, an editorial for the school paper, or any other writing they do for school or on their own.

2.1 What Is Prewriting?

Even experienced writers can feel challenged when faced with a blank sheet of paper. Prewriting acts as a preparation for writing by helping to flex and stretch your creative muscles, just as athletes' warm-up activities help prepare them for a meet or competition. Prewriting serves as a mental warm-up. It consists of activities and strategies to help you get started.

Choosing Your Topic

Obviously, you can't create a piece of writing if you don't have a topic. If a topic hasn't been assigned to you and if one doesn't immediately spring to mind, there are a variety of strategies you can use to generate possible topics. Following is one such strategy:

SAMPLE STRATEGY

When you can't see the words you are entering, you won't be tempted to edit your thoughts as you enter them.

Writing With Invisible Ink Turn off your computer monitor, and begin writing about the events of a typical day. Let one idea flow freely into the next. When you have written freely for approximately ten minutes, turn the monitor back on. Review what you have written, and see whether any of the ideas might make a good topic. If you are unable to work on a computer, you can write using a pen with no ink on a piece of paper placed over carbon paper with a clean sheet of paper underneath.

 Write with monitor turned off.

 Turn on monitor to reveal what you have written.

Today I rode the bus to school. My friend Marissa told me that . . .

Learn More

For additional prewriting strategies suited to specific writing tasks, see Chapters 4–15.

16 • A Walk Through the Writing Process

TIME AND RESOURCE MANAGER

Resources
Print: Writing Support Transparencies 2-A–D; Writing Support Activity Book 2-1-3

In-Depth Coverage	Accelerated Pace
• Cover pp. 16–20 in class. • Have students complete a planning web, audience profile, and hexagonal.	• Assign pp. 16–20 for independent student review.

Narrowing Your Topic

Even the most interesting topic won't lead to an effective piece of writing if the topic is too broad. For example, if you chose "sports" as your topic, you might not be able to cover it thoroughly unless you wrote a whole series of books. However, if you narrowed this topic to focus on the impact of rule changes in basketball, you would have a topic just right for a short paper. Following is one strategy you can use to narrow a topic:

SAMPLE STRATEGY

Using a Planning Web or Cluster Diagram Draw a diagram, beginning with a central circle with extending lines. Write your central thought, topic, or story title in the center circle. Draw additional circles around the central circle and use lines to connect them to the central circle. In each of these circles, jot down thoughts that the central subject or topic inspires. Each of the circles may generate new circles of its own or may serve as a natural stopping point—it's up to you. In this example, the writer narrowed the broad topic "Soccer" to "Loss Against Burton High."

SAMPLE PLANNING WEB

Prewriting: Using a Planning Web or Cluster Diagram

Teaching Resources: Writing Support Transparency 2-A; Writing Support Activity Book 2-1

1. Display the transparency. Invite them to discuss the connections the student made among topics.

2. Give students copies of the blank organizer. Have students start with a topic they like from the Invisible Ink activity, circle it, and surround it with other circled topics linked by lines.

3. Encourage students to let their ideas flow freely, without worrying about coming up with a "perfect" topic.

4. Have students look over their completed planning webs to see if they have a narrower topic they like.

Customize for
Visual/Spatial Learners

Visual learners will benefit greatly from organizing their ideas in a web or cluster diagram. You may want to have such students work with less visually-inclined students to help show them how to organize their ideas in a web or diagram.

Prewriting: Considering Your Audience and Purpose

Teaching Resources: Writing Support Transparency 2-B; Writing Support Activity Book 2-2

1. Display the transparency to show students some of the questions they should ask themselves when considering their audiences.

2. Have students brainstorm for audiences for their writing—for example, teachers, classmates, other classes, parents, younger children, and readers of a community newspaper.

3. Ask students to choose a topic suggested by their planning web and to answer the questions about two or three possible audiences for their writing.

4. Give students copies of the blank organizer to complete.

5. If students need help with this exercise, give them this example and encourage them to add information of their own:

Topic: Soccer

Audience #1: First graders
Audience #2: Parents

• What does the audience already know? Audience #1 may know something about the rules of the game from watching older brothers or sisters play. Audience #2 may or may not have seen a soccer game.

• What do they need to know? Audience #1 may need to know more about the rules and history of soccer. Audience #2 may need some of the same information.

• What details will interest or influence the audience? Audience #1 might like to know why many kids love the game. Audience #2 may be interested in how kids benefit from playing the game.

• What is the purpose of writing for this audience? For Audience #1, the purpose might be to encourage more children to join soccer teams. For Audience #2, the purpose could be to encourage raising money for soccer equipment.

Considering Your Audience and Purpose

Before you begin writing your first draft, it is important to identify your audience; these are the people or person who will read your work. Next, consider your purpose; this is the goal you wish to accomplish through your writing. Both your audience and purpose will affect your use of language and choice of details.

Considering Your Audience Identify who will read your work. Think about what your audience does and does not know about your topic, and consider the type of language that would suit them. For instance, if you are writing a children's story, your language and descriptions should be simple and clear. On the other hand, if you are writing a personal essay for a college application, you should use much more sophisticated language and include details about yourself that might appeal to a college admissions board.

To help you identify the needs of your audience and keep these needs in mind as you write, develop an audience profile on a note card. Use the one below as a model. Refer back to your audience profile as you develop and draft your paper.

Audience Profile		
Age: Children	(Teenagers)	Adults
Appropriate Language: Very Informal	(Informal)	Formal
Audience Knowledge of Topic: _____		
What Will Interest the Audience Most: _____		

Considering Your Purpose Next, identify what you want to accomplish through your writing. For example, you may want to influence readers to accept your point of view, or you may simply want to entertain and amuse your audience. Keep your purpose in mind as you develop your paper, and use language and details that will help you achieve this purpose.

2.3 *What Is Revising?*

Using a Systematic Approach

Once you've finished writing, revise your work carefully. In this book, you will learn a systematic revision process called **ratiocination** (rash´ ē äs ə nā´shen). The word *ratiocination* refers to logical thinking. As a revision approach, the word refers to applying logic to the way you look at your work by color-coding items for analysis. Begin by looking at your overall structure, and then look at your paragraphs, sentences, and words. At each stage, use a process of color-coding and marking clues in your work to help you revise.

Revising Your Overall Structure

Start by examining the soundness of your structure, or overall organization. Your ideas should flow logically from beginning to end. You may strengthen the structure by reordering paragraphs or by adding information to fill in gaps.

Writers in ACTION

Edgar Allan Poe's detective stories featured C. Auguste Dupin, an amateur detective who was a master of ratiocination skills. In "The Murders in the Rue Morgue," Dupin made an analytical study of a crime scene to solve the crime.

SAMPLE STRATEGY

▶ **REVISION STRATEGY**
Highlight to Frame Your Writing

To view the structure of your writing, highlight the statement of the main point of your paper and the key sentence in your conclusion. Then, in a second color highlight the main idea of each paragraph. Evaluate whether the progression of your writing is sound, or logical, and rearrange or add information as needed. With the details stripped from the example at right, you can analyze the structure of the essay.

EVALUATING STRUCTURE

On the whole, the advantages of having a part-time job outweigh the disadvantages.

Working may take time away from study and extracurricular activities. . . .

While working at a job, a student learns what it means to have responsibilities, which is excellent preparation for the future. . . .

Another advantage is the salary, which the student can use for various worthwhile purposes, such as class trips or a college fund. . . .

Despite the time commitment and scheduling issues, a part-time job is a valuable experience for a student.

What Is Revising? • **23**

1. Point out how the model uses one color for the introductory and concluding main idea, and another for the details that elaborate on that idea.

2. Students can choose something from their portfolios and use different colors to highlight main idea(s) and details

---

⏱ TIME AND RESOURCE MANAGER

Resources
Print: Writing Support Transparency 2-F

In-Depth Coverage	Accelerated Pace
• Cover pp. 23–25 in class. • Review the sample strategies with students.	• Assign pp. 23–25 for independent student review.

23

Step-by-Step Teaching Guide

Revising: Color-Coding to Check Connections

Teaching Resources: Writing Support Transparency 2-F

1. Display the transparency.
2. Have volunteers read each relationship in the chart.
3. Tell students that using the transitional words will help their readers better understand the connections between ideas.

Step-by-Step Teaching Guide

Listing Sentence Starters to Vary Sentence Beginnings

Tell students that readers will get bored if there is not enough sentence variety in their writing.

Revising Your Paragraphs

Next, examine each paragraph in your writing. Consider the way each sentence contributes to the point of the paragraph. As you evaluate your draft, rewrite or eliminate any sentences that are not effective. Try the strategy below:

SAMPLE STRATEGY

▶ **REVISION STRATEGY**
Color-Coding to Check Connections

Go through each paragraph, and circle the places in which you introduce a specific example, a cause, an effect, a comparison, or a contrast. Use different symbols to identify each of these relationships. Then, evaluate whether each idea follows logically from the one before it. Add transitional words or phrases to make connections more clear. This chart suggests symbols for color-coding and provides effective transitions for each relationship.

IDENTIFYING RELATIONSHIPS		
Relationship	**Symbol**	**Transitionals**
Comparison	●	both, all, similarly, moreover, and, too
Contrast	■	although, but, however, yet, nevertheless, instead
Example	▼	for instance, for example
Cause and Effect	➡	because, as a result, consequently, since, so

Revising Your Sentences

When you study the sentences in your draft, check to see that they flow smoothly from one to the next. Look to see that you have avoided the pattern of beginning most of your sentences in the same way.

SAMPLE STRATEGY

▶ **REVISION STRATEGY**
Listing Sentence Starters to Vary Sentence Beginnings

Make a list of the first word in each sentence of your draft. Review your list, and eliminate repetition by rearranging the word order or adding introductory material to begin each sentence in a different way.

24 • A Walk Through the Writing Process

ⓠ Learn More

To learn specific strategies for varying your sentences, see Chapter 22, Writing Effective Sentences.

Revising Your Word Choice

The final step in the process of revising your work is to analyze your choice of words. Make sure that each word conveys the exact meaning you intended. Also, look for the repetition of words, and make revisions to reduce the number of the most commonly repeated words.

SAMPLE STRATEGY

▶ **REVISION STRATEGY**
Circling Repeated Words

Go through your writing, and circle any nouns, verbs, adjectives, or adverbs that you have used more than once. Then, evaluate each of these repeated words to decide whether you should replace it with a synonym.

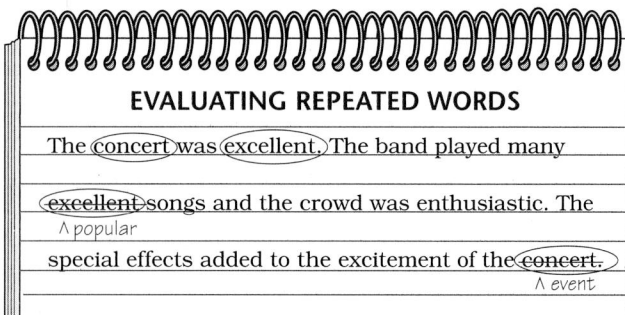

EVALUATING REPEATED WORDS

The (concert) was (excellent.) The band played many

(excellent) songs and the crowd was enthusiastic. The
  ∧ popular

special effects added to the excitement of the (concert.)
                                              ∧ event

Peer Review

After you've finished revising your draft, work with one or more classmates to get a fresh perspective on your writing.

Focus Your Peer Reviewer To get the most specific feedback possible, focus on one element or provide questions that lead to suggestions for improvement. Look at the sample questions at right.

Evaluate the Peer Responses Weigh the responses of your peer reviewer, and determine which suggestions you want to incorporate in your draft. Ask your peer reviewer for clarification of any points that seem unclear.

FOCUSING PEER REVIEW

- Which parts were most confusing to you?
- Where did I leave out details?
- Where was I repetitive?

▶ **APPLYING THE REVISION STRATEGIES**

Choose a piece of writing that you did last year or one you've written recently. Go through the piece, using each of the revision strategies described on the preceding pages. Then, write an explanation of how the strategies helped you make additional improvements to your work.

What Is Revising? • 25

Revising: Circling Repeated Words

1. Explain to students that using precise, colorful words will help make their writing more appealing to readers.
2. Remind students about the importance of using a thesaurus to help them revise their word choice.

Revising: Use Peer Revision Strategies

1. Discuss with students why it is important, when reviewing a classmate's work, to balance positive and negative comments. Ask what their responses would be if a peer reviewer simply said, "It's boring. You should start over again."
2. Read aloud the following peer reviewer comments. Ask students which are helpful and which are not. Have them give reasons for their choices.

   It's disorganized.

   Putting the second paragraph at the end could make your writing flow better.

   It's too long.

   Deleting these sentences would tighten up the construction.

   Your word choices are wrong.

   Can you think of a more precise word for this one?

3. Remind students that a peer reviewer's comments are merely suggestions, and the writer can choose to follow these suggestions or not.

Editing and Proofreading: Proofreading Symbols

Teaching Resources: Writing Support Transparency 2-G

1. Display the transparency and go over each proofreading symbol.

2. Write the following help wanted ad on the chalkboard and ask students how they would react if they read it in a newspaper.

   Experienced Poofreader Neded. Must be able to catch mispellings and incorret grammer. Atention to detals critcal.

3. Ask volunteers to come to the chalkboard and correct the ad.

Integrating Technology Skills

Remind students that the spellcheck function on computers questions only words it does not recognize. Ask why spell checking would not catch the errors in this sentence: Now is thee time fur all awl good pebble two comb to the aide of there partly.

Integrating Workplace Skills

Many jobs require good writing skills. Checking one's work for grammatical errors is of utmost importance. Writing that contains mistakes and errors is not only difficult to read, but reflects poorly on the writer.

2.4 # What Are Editing and Proofreading?

Don't let errors in grammar, usage, mechanics, and spelling ruin the impact of your writing. Carefully proofread your work to identify and correct these types of errors.

Focusing on Proofreading

In each of the chapters that follows, you will find a specific proofreading focus—an area on which to place extra attention. Address the suggested element; however, you should always take care to find and eliminate *all* types of errors. Here are the broad categories you should address:

- Spelling
- Grammar
- Usage
- Mechanics
- Accuracy
- Legibility

Using Proofreading Symbols As you proofread your paper, use the symbols below to mark corrections. If you are working on a computer, enter the changes, and print out a clean final copy. If you are not working on a computer, mark the corrections as neatly as possible before turning in your paper.

PROOFREADING SYMBOLS

∧	insert letters or words here	⌿	make this letter lowercase
#	insert space here	b	capitalize this letter
∽	switch the order of two letters or words	⌢	link inserted material
¶	begin a new paragraph		

▶ **APPLYING THE EDITING AND PROOFREADING STRATEGIES**

Write a one-paragraph composition on a topic that interests you. For the purposes of a proofreading exercise, intentionally include a variety of different types of errors in your work. Then, exchange papers with a classmate. Using the proofreading symbols above, identify and mark the necessary corrections.

Technology Tip

Don't make the mistake of thinking that a spell-check feature on a computer will catch all of your spelling errors. Doing a spell check is a great first step, but you still need to carefully proofread your work.

⏱ TIME AND RESOURCE MANAGER	

Resources
Print: Writing Support Transparency 2-G

In-Depth Coverage	Accelerated Pace
• Cover pp. 26–27 in class. • Go over the proofreading symbols on p. 26 with students.	• Assign pp. 26–27 for independent student review.

2.5 What Are Publishing and Presenting?

Moving Forward

This walk through the writing process gives you a preview of the strategies and techniques that you can incorporate into your writing process. Chapters 4–15 will provide more specific instruction focused on the modes of writing, offering you effective strategies for improving your writing.

Building Your Portfolio Save your finished writing products in a folder, file, box, or other safe and organized container. Your portfolio will serve as a record of your development and growth as a writer. To see this change, you may want to compare recent work with writing that you completed some time ago. Your portfolio can also act as a resource for future writing: In a section of your portfolio, keep partly completed pieces of writing, writing ideas, clippings, and photos that inspire you.

Reflecting on Your Writing Every time you complete a piece of writing, you are presented with a learning experience, a chance to learn something about yourself, something about your topic, and something about your writing process. Questions at the end of each writing chapter will help you think about what you have learned and how you have learned it. To help you learn from your experiences, add your reflections to your portfolio.

Assessing Your Writing In each chapter, you'll find a rubric, or set of criteria, on which your work can be evaluated. Refer to the rubric throughout the writing process to be certain you are addressing the key issues.

▶ APPLYING THE PUBLISHING AND PRESENTING STRATEGIES

1. Choose a prewriting strategy you used in this introduction to the writing process. Put your prewriting ideas in your portfolio to be worked into a fully developed piece of writing at a later time.
2. Start your reflection by answering these questions:

   • Which of the strategies or activities did you find most useful or usable? Explain.

   • What are your strengths as a writer?

Publishing and Presenting

1. Publishing means sharing. Here are some ways students can publish their work.

   • Read it to their class or another class

   • Publish it in the school newspaper

   • Post it on a classroom or library bulletin board

   • E-mail it to friends and relatives

   • Illustrate it, design a cover, and make a book

   • Combine it with classmates' writing into a longer book

   • Present a reader's theater

   • Rewrite it as a play, with sets and costumes, and present it to an audience.

2. Ask students to suggest other ways to publish their work.

3. Invite students to create their own "guided tour" of the writing process. They can do this in the form of a flowchart, a map, a diagram, or another format. Adding visual symbols of each step of the process could help them understand and remember those steps.

Lesson Objectives

1. To read world literature, including classic and contemporary works.
2. To recognize shared characteristics of cultures through media.
3. To evaluate media presentations.
4. To analyze ideas as represented in various media.
5. To write a journal entry.

Exploring Themes Across Cultures

1. Choose one of the Spotlight elements for class discussion, or have students work individually or in groups on the element of their choice. Give students the initiative to find the necessary book, pictures, and audiorecordings.

2. Interested students may use library and electronic sources to research Maxfield Parrish's work and its impact on the communication and fine art worlds. Invite students to generate a critique of a Parrish painting.

3. Ask students who have seen *Sleeping Beauty* to describe its basic story elements—plot, characters, and setting. Show a videotaped performance. Then discuss how, if at all, Tchaikovsky's music helps advance the story or support its mood.

4. Lead a mini-literature festival of *Sleeping Beauty* retellings. Have students locate several versions, present these in dramatic readings, and then compare and contrast the versions.

Spotlight on the Humanities

Exploring Themes Across Cultures

Focus on Art: Maxfield Parrish

Like writing, painting and other fine arts involve a process of development. One artist whose work illustrates this process is Maxfield Parrish. Inspired to become an artist when he was visiting Europe as a teenager, Parrish (1870–1966) created illustrations for children's books and fairy tales, like *Sleeping Beauty*, at the turn of the nineteenth century. While in Europe, he studied the paintings of the classical masters and developed a painting technique using layers of thin oil and varnish over stretched paper. Parrish, a master craftsman, used photography to measure proportions for his oil paintings. His work graced the covers of American magazines for more than forty years.

Study for Old King Cole, Maxfield Parrish

▲ Critical Viewing How does Parrish's illustration of Old King Cole create a setting for the fairy tale? [Analyze]

Dance Connection One of the most famous ballets of all time is Peter Tchaikovsky's *Sleeping Beauty*, which is also based upon a fairy tale. The ballet is filled with magical fairies, a prince and princess, and characters from other fairy tales at the final wedding—including Puss-n-Boots, Little Red Riding Hood, and the Wolf.

Literature Connection Several versions of the Sleeping Beauty story have evolved through the ages, with the best-known tale being that written by the Brothers Grimm. Their original name for Sleeping Beauty was Briar Rose. The origins of the Sleeping Beauty story may go back to an Arthurian romance printed in 1528. Instead of the hero being a prince, he was a king. In the Perrault version of the story, the prince does not kiss the sleeping princess; she wakes up as he kneels beside her.

Writing Process Writing Activity: Inspirational Writers Just as Maxfield Parrish was inspired by the great European master painters, think of a time when a song, movie, photograph, or story inspired you. Write a journal entry describing the work you admire and what you learned from the artist or writer as a result of the work.

Viewing and Representing

Activities Urge students to add visuals to their journal entries, perhaps photocopied from the books or other media viewed during the Spotlight. Students might also add their own sketches to the journal entry. Invite volunteers to share their entries with the class.

Critical Viewing

Analyze Students responses will vary, but make sure they support their responses with details from the painting.

Media and Technology Skills

Using Technology for Writing
Activity: Building an Electronic Portfolio

Computers generally allow you to store your writing products. That way, you can work through the stages of the writing process at your own pace, accessing your computer files as you progress. Develop organizational systems, and you'll soon be locating files quickly and easily.

Learn About It Think of building your electronic portfolio just as you might use a traditional filing system. Then, use the tools outlined below to put your portfolio into place.

- **Build a Structure** Group your files into general categories, such as word processing, games, and accounting. Then, break down your work within these categories, making folders and subfolders for each. Continue making folders inside of folders as you need them.

- **Track Your Progress** To see the development of a writing project from inspiration through revision to final draft. Consider a system that allows you to name a file and then use the Save As function to track the versions. For example, the first draft of an essay might be "innovations". The next versions could be "innovations.2" and "innovations.3".

Sort It List all your school assignments from the last two weeks. Then, sort them into logical groups to build an effective structure. Jot down your ideas in a chart like the one shown here.

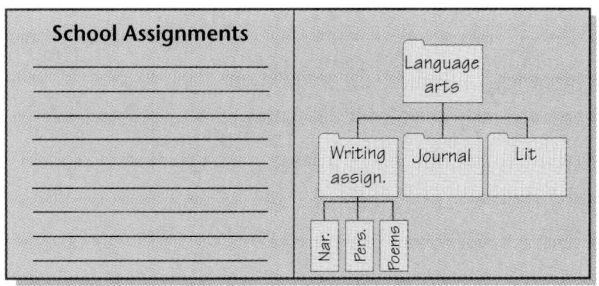

Apply It Using your organization plan, generate and organize some actual files on a personal or school computer. After a week, reflect and comment on how well your electronic portfolio works.

Lesson Objectives
1. To use technology for aspects of creating, revising, and publishing.
2. To organize and convert information into different forms.
3. To use a variety of forms and technologies.
4. To compile information in systematic ways using available technology.

Step-by-Step Teaching Guide

Using Technology for Writing

Teaching Resources: Writing Support Transparency 2-H; Writing Support Activity Book 2-4

1. If possible, conduct the lesson with student access to computers. Failing this, use diagrams or charts from computer manuals as a model to sketch likely screens on the chalkboard for reference.
2. Emphasize to students that in many ways organizing and storing information on a computer is not all that different from applying these processes to printed documents, hobby collections, or any other materials. Review the organizing and storing tips with students. Discuss how these could be applied to any media or collection of material.
3. Display the transparency and invite volunteers to explain its use. Clarify as necessary.
4. Give students copies of the blank organizer for students to complete. Have them exchange completed organizers with a partner. Ask partners to comment on the organization and make suggestions. After students complete their hands-on file organization, return with them to the organizing and storing tips. Invite additions or changes.

Customize for
Visual/Spatial Learners

Acknowledge with students that many computer functions are difficult to describe with words. Invite students to assist you in creating accompanying explanatory charts and diagrams. Challenge them to suggest visuals that will explain the storing and organizing concepts with limited text.

1. To write in a style appropriate to audience and purpose.
2. To use prewriting strategies to generate ideas, develop voice, and plan.
3. To develop drafts by organizing and reorganizing content and refining style.
4. To demonstrate control over grammatical elements.
5. To produce legible work that shows accurate spelling and correct use of punctuation and capitalization conventions.

Step-by-Step Teaching Guide

Using the Writing Process to Respond to Prompts

1. Clarify for students the key difference between standardized test writing and other writing assignments—time limitation. Students must learn to budget time according to their own writing process. Encourage them to begin with the pacing suggested here but to quickly explore adjustments.

2. Encourage students to use outlining as they plan for timed test writing. Well-organized outlines will save important time as students work through the writing process.

3. Remind students that they must produce legible writing although examiners expect some corrections. Reassure students that it is better to make corrections than omit these out of concern for neatness. Still, students must write clearly— neither too small nor too large.

4. Suggest that students can prepare for timed test writing by expanding their vocabularies. This way they'll have access to many word choices when writing. If students are unsure of a word's spelling, for example, they can choose a synonym that they can confidently spell.

Standardized Test Preparation Workshop

Using The Writing Process to Respond to Prompts

Your writing skills on standardized tests are often measured by requiring you to respond to a given prompt. You can apply what you have learned about the writing process to the writing that you do on standardized tests. However, you will need to be careful about the way you budget your time for each stage of the process.

Following are some of the criteria on which your writing for standardized tests will be evaluated:

- using a logical, consistent organization
- clearly stating the main point of your paper
- supporting your key points with facts, examples, and other types of details
- linking your ideas with transitions
- following the conventions of spelling, grammar, usage, and mechanics

Following is an example of one type of writing prompt that you might find on a standardized test.

Use the suggestions on the following page to help you respond. The clocks next to each stage show a suggested plan for organizing.

Sample Writing Situation

Your high school has received a donation to be used to install either a pool on campus or an air-conditioning system in the classrooms. Decide which you think would be best for your school, and describe your choice in a letter to the school board. Support your argument with convincing reasons. Be sure to explain your reasons in detail.

30 • A Walk Through the Writing Process

TEST-TAKING TIP

Tell students that transition words often make the difference between a coherent and logically presented argument and a series of seemingly unconnected pieces of information. Encourage students to familiarize themselves with transition words used to show *cause and effect, comparison and contrast, sequence of events,* and *order of importance.* Ask students to give some examples of each type of transition word. Which might be most useful in responding to the sample prompt?

Examples: therefore, because, since, so; also, like, similarly, in contrast to, instead, but; first, second, next, then, last; most importantly, least significantly

Sample Prompt: order of importance and/or comparison and contrast

Prewriting

Allow about one quarter of your time for prewriting.

Gather Details Using a T-Chart Draw a large *T* on your paper. On the top, write your choice of a pool or air conditioning. In the left column, list all the reasons the school should support your choice. On the right side, list reasons that people may not support your views. Address opposing viewpoints in your letter to strengthen your own position.

Consider Your Audience Since you will be writing a letter to the school board, use formal language and avoid all use of slang. Remember that your purpose is to persuade your audience. Include information that may be new to them and will support your position.

Drafting

Allow approximately half of your time for drafting.

Organize Your Arguments As you draft your letter, organize information in a logical manner. Begin with an introduction that states your preference for either air conditioning or a pool. In the next paragraph, list important points that support your choice. The following paragraph should address any weaknesses and your attempt to refute them. The final body paragraph should summarize your strongest support for your choice. Finally, write a conclusion that summarizes your ideas.

Elaborate The most important part of your letter will be the strong, persuasive details that you include to make your choice convincing. Find points that you can expand upon by providing additional descriptive details. Focus on points that strongly support your position.

Revising, Editing, and Proofreading

Allow about one quarter of your time to revise, edit, and proofread your paper.

Add Transitions Check your paper for places to add transitions that will clarify relationships between details. For example, *first, second,* and *next* indicate order of importance; *as a result* and *because* indicate a cause-and-effect relationship. Using transitions will help make ideas flow smoothly and logically.

Correct Errors Revise your draft, and neatly correct any mistakes you see.

Customize for
ESL Students

You may want to let students practice timed test writing in their first language before transitioning them to English timed writing. Once students are working in English, urge them to take extra care in reading prompts to be certain they understand the question.

Customize for
More Advanced Students

Give students copies of their own test writing or use samples from this and other sources. Challenge students to improve the writing in a specified amount of time. You might designate their focus, such as details, transition, or opening or closing statements.

Time and Resource Manager

In-Depth Lesson Plan

	LESSON FOCUS	PRINT AND MEDIA RESOURCES
DAY 1	**Writing Effective Paragraphs** Students learn and apply concepts of writing topic and supporting sentences (pp. 32–36).	
DAY 2	**Paragraphs and Compositions** Students learn and apply concepts about unity, coherence, and the parts of a composition (pp. 37–41).	
DAY 3	**Writing Style** Students learn and apply concepts about writing style (pp. 42–43).	

Accelerated Lesson Plan

	LESSON FOCUS	PRINT AND MEDIA RESOURCES
DAY 1	**Writing Effective Paragraphs** Students learn and apply concepts of writing topic and supporting sentences (pp. 32–36).	
DAY 2	**Paragraphs, Compositions and Writing Style** Students learn and apply concepts about unity, coherence, the parts of a composition, and writing style (pp. 37–43).	

Options for Adapting Lesson Plans

HOMEWORK
Have students complete any stage of the lesson for homework.

TECHNOLOGY
Students can complete any stage of the lesson on computer. Have them print out their completed work.

FEATURES
Extend coverage with Writing Models (pp. 33, 40), Spotlight on the Humanities (p. 44), Media and Technology Skills (p. 45), and the Standardized Test Preparation Workshop (p. 46).

INTEGRATED SKILLS COVERAGE

Writing Models
SE pp. 33, 40

Vocabulary
Integrating Vocabulary Skills ATE p. 43

Technology
Technology Tip ATE p. 38

Viewing and Representing
Critical Viewing, SE pp. 32, 35, 37, 43, 44
Viewing and Representing ATE p. 44

ASSESSMENT SUPPORT

Standardized Test Preparation SE p. 46; ATE p. 46
Standardized Test Preparation Workbook, pp. 5–6
Scoring Rubrics on Transparency, Ch. 3
Formal Assessment, Ch. 3
Writing Assessment and Portfolio Management

MEETING INDIVIDUAL NEEDS

Less Advanced Students ATE p. 37; See also Ongoing
Assessments ATE pp. 34, 38, 43
ESL Students ATE p. 34
Gifted/Talented Students ATE p. 43

BLOCK SCHEDULING

Pacing Suggestions
For 90-minute Blocks
• Have students complete the Prewriting and Drafting stages in a single period.
• Focus one class period on Revising and Editing and Publishing and Presenting. Allow at least 30 minutes for peer revision.

Resources for Varying Instruction
• *Writing Lab* CD-ROM If your students have access to hardware, a 90-minute block provides an ideal opportunity for students to work on computer.

Professional Development Support
• *How to Manage Instruction in the Block* This Teaching Resource provides management and activity suggestions.

MEDIA AND TECHNOLOGY

For the Student
• *Writing Lab* CD-ROM

For the Teacher
• *Resource Pro* CD-ROM

WRITING AND GRAMMAR WEBSITE

The Interactive Writing and Grammar Website provides a wide array of support for students, teachers, and parents. Writing support includes:

• Interactive revision checkers
• Scoring rubrics with complete models

phwg.phschool.com

LITERATURE CONNECTIONS

Related selections from *Prentice Hall Literature: Timeless Voices, Timeless Themes,* Gold:
from *Silent Spring,* Rachel Carson, SE p. 33
from *Arthur Ashe Remembered,* John McPhee, SE p. 33
from "An Entomological Study of Apartment 4A," Patricia Volk, SE p. 40

▶ *Lesson Objectives*

1. To understand the characteristics of a paragraph.
2. To identify paragraphs' stated topic sentences and implied main ideas.
3. To write topic sentences for paragraphs.
4. To write supporting sentences that include facts, examples, and details.
5. To build paragraphs by using topic, restatement, and illustration.
6. To revise paragraphs to achieve unity and coherence.
7. To distinguish between topical paragraphs and functional paragraphs.
8. To use sentence variety, diction, and tone to create personal paragraph style.
9. To use formal and informal English appropriately in paragraphs.

Critical Viewing

Connect Students may say that to prepare a meal well, you have to follow important steps, just as you do when writing an effective paragraph.

Chapter 3 Paragraphs and Compositions
Structure and Style

▲ **Critical Viewing** In what way do the items on this table fit together to create a whole? [Connect]

What Are Paragraphs and Compositions?

A **paragraph** consists of a group of sentences that share a common topic and work together as a unit of expression. A new paragraph is indicated by visual clues, such as an indentation or an extra space between lines of text. When you write, your organization and meaning will determine how you insert these breaks.

In a **composition,** paragraphs are organized around a main idea. Each paragraph supports, develops, or explains the main idea of the whole work. Essays, speeches, autobiographical narratives, and research reports are just a few of the types of compositions.

32 • Paragraphs and Compositions

⏱ TIME AND RESOURCE MANAGER	
In-Depth Coverage	**Accelerated Pace**
• Cover pp. 32–37 in class. • Show video of "Writing Effective Paragraphs." • Discuss examples of paragraphs and have your students bring some to class.	• Discuss topic and supporting sentences. • Assign pp. 32–37 for independent reading.

3.1 *Writing Effective Paragraphs*

Main Idea and Topic Sentence

Most paragraphs develop one main idea. This main idea is usually stated in the paragraph's **topic sentence.** The remaining sentences of the paragraph support, explain, develop, or illustrate the topic sentence.

When the main idea of a paragraph is not directly stated, all the sentences in the paragraph work together to support the **implied main idea.** In a paragraph that has an implied main idea, the reader infers the point of the paragraph based on the details that are provided.

WRITING MODELS

from Silent Spring
Rachel Carson

There was once a town in the heart of America where all life seemed to live in harmony with its surroundings. The town lay in the midst of a checkerboard of prosperous farms, with fields of grain and hillsides of orchards where, in spring, white clouds of bloom drifted above the green fields. In autumn, oak and maple and birch set up a blaze of color that flamed and flickered across a backdrop of pines. Then foxes barked in the hills and deer silently crossed the fields, half hidden in the mists of the fall mornings.

> In this passage, the stated topic sentence is shown in blue italics.

from Arthur Ashe Remembered
John McPhee

His mother was tall, with long soft hair and a face that was gentle and thin. She read a lot. She read a lot to him. His father said of her, "She was just like Arthur Junior. She never argued. She was quiet, easygoing, kindhearted."

> In this passage, all the sentences work together to suggest the unstated main idea that Arthur Ashe's mother was a beautiful person—personally and physically.

Writing Effective Paragraphs • 33

More About the Writers

Rachel Carson (1907–1964) was a marine biologist and an author. Her 1962 book, *Silent Spring,* was one of the first alerts to the American public about the dangers of pollution. It began the environmental movement. Because Carson combined accurate scientific observation with lyrical description, her work appealed to scientists and the general public.

John McPhee has been a prolific and versatile journalist. He is a former editor for *Time* and has also written for many other publications. Currently McPhee is a staff writer for *The New Yorker.*

PREPARE and ENGAGE

Interest GRABBER Display the following paragraph on an overhead projector or read it aloud.

Pigs are mammals. They have a long snout, a short-legged body, bristly hide, and a short tail. A famous pig from literature is Wilbur, in Charlotte's Web. Pigs were introduced to the Americas by Columbus in 1493. They are valuable for their meat and fat, and their hide is used for gloves and footballs. Babe was a pig in a movie.

Ask students if it is a good paragraph. That is, does it have a main idea? Are the ideas organized? Does it make sense? (It is all about pigs, but Wilbur and Babe are irrelevant.)

Activate Prior Knowledge

Have students look at the first page of Ralph Helfer's "Fly Away" (*Prentice Hall Literature: Timeless Voices, Timeless Themes,* Gold). Without reading the whole page, ask why new paragraphs begin where they do. (Students should recognize a new paragraph each time the speaker changes. In the second column, they should note that the new paragraphs show a change in idea or time.)

TEACH

Step-by-Step Teaching Guide

Main Idea and Topic Sentence

1. Ask students why they think a paragraph's main idea is important to identify. (Possible answer: It is important to know what you are reading about and what points the writer is trying to make.)

2. Read the excerpts aloud.

3. After each reading, ask students to discuss the excerpts. You can use questions such as these to prompt discussion:
   - What is the main idea?
   - What are some details that support or describe the main idea?
   - How does the opening of Carson's paragraph resemble stories you have read?
   - Might McPhee's paragraph seem to come from the beginning or end of his text?

Writing Topic Sentences

1. Remind students that every paragraph is about something. That is its topic. Sometimes it is stated directly, as in Exercise 1.

2. Other times the topic is implied—not stated directly—as in Exercise 2. Implied ideas are harder to determine. Students must read carefully and think about what the sentences have in common.

Answer Key

Exercise 1

First sentence: I was six when my mother taught me the art of invisible strength.

Exercise 2

Possible main idea: Things happen to people that are so important that they never forget them, and the experiences affect their whole life.

Exercise 3

Answers will vary. Topic sentences should be explicit. Samples are given.

1. I play soccer after school because it is fun and good exercise.
2. I like Jaime because he has a great sense of humor.
3. I don't like swimming because I am afraid I'll sink to the bottom of the pool.
4. My backpack contains everything—I haven't cleaned it out in two weeks.
5. I take the bus at Oak Street to school.

Customize for
ESL Students

It may help students who share the same home language to work together on the exercises in this chapter.

3.1

> **Exercise 1** Identifying a Stated Topic Sentence Identify the stated topic sentence in this paragraph from Amy Tan's "Rules of the Game."

I was six when my mother taught me the art of invisible strength. It was a strategy for winning arguments, respect from others, and eventually, though neither of us knew it at the time, chess games.

> **Exercise 2** Identifying an Implied Main Idea Identify the implied main idea in the following paragraph from "Children in the Woods" by Barry Lopez.

I have never forgotten the texture of this incident. Whenever I recall it I am moved not so much by any sense of my young self but by a sense of responsibility toward children, knowing how acutely I was affected in that moment by that woman's words. The effect, for all I know, has lasted a lifetime.

Writing a Topic Sentence

Each topic sentence presents a main point within your whole piece of writing. You may often develop topic sentences in the planning stages of your writing, before you actually write your paragraphs. As you revise your work, you may want to rework some of these sentences.

To write a topic sentence, review the details you will include in your writing. Look for groups of details that have something in common. For each group, make a statement that expresses the idea or quality that these details have in common. Use this statement as the topic sentence of a paragraph that includes the grouped details.

> **Exercise 3** Writing a Topic Sentence Write a topic sentence for a paragraph about each of the following topics.
> 1. Why you do or don't participate in an after-school club or activity
> 2. Which aspect of your best friend's personality you find most appealing
> 3. The reasons you do or do not enjoy a particular sports activity
> 4. The contents of your backpack
> 5. How you get to and from school each day

34 • Structure and Style

☑ ONGOING ASSESSMENT: Monitor and Reinforce

If students have difficulty identifying and writing topic sentences, try one of the following options.

Option 1 Before students actually write their paragraphs, have them respond to this question: "How can I summarize my ideas in a single sentence?" The answer to this question can serve as their topic sentence.	**Option 2** After students have read a paragraph, have them write a single sentence that describes what the paragraph is about. They can then look for the sentence containing the same information. This will be the topic sentence.

Writing Supporting Sentences

Your topic sentence, whether stated or implied, will direct the remaining sentences in the paragraph. These other sentences should give enough information to support, explain, or develop the topic sentence completely.

You can support or develop the main idea by using one or more of the following strategies:

Use Facts Facts are statements that can be verified. They support your key idea by providing concrete evidence or proof.

TOPIC SENTENCE:	Antarctica has the most hostile environment on Earth for humans.
SUPPORTING FACTS:	Not a tree or bush grows there. No human beings are native to the land. The only permanent inhabitants of Antarctica—such as seals, penguins, and a few other birds—must feed in the sea.

Use Statistics A statistic is a fact, usually stated using numbers.

TOPIC SENTENCE:	The children's zoo is very busy on Saturdays.
SUPPORTING STATISTIC:	Surveys reveal that the zoo receives 70 percent of its visitors on weekends.

Use Examples, Illustrations, or Instances An example, illustration, or instance is a specific thing, person, or event that demonstrates a point.

TOPIC SENTENCE:	Seals are very popular zoo attractions.
ILLUSTRATION:	Last weekend, spectators lined up twenty minutes in advance to view the seals' afternoon feeding.

Use Details Details are the specifics of your writing. They make your point or main idea clear by showing how all the pieces fit together.

TOPIC SENTENCE:	Families like to watch the seals being fed.
DETAILS:	Adults and children gasp with awe, clap excitedly, and cheer happily as the seals bark, catch the fish, and perform tricks.

▶ **Exercise 4** Writing Supporting Sentences Write two supporting sentences for each of the following topic sentences.
1. Exercise and a balanced diet contribute to good health.
2. Competitive athletes work hard to achieve their goals.
3. Space exploration may result in new lifestyle options.

▼ **Critical Viewing**
What details would you use to support the statement that these seals are healthy? [**Support**]

Writing Supporting Sentences

1. Go over the examples of different kinds of support.
2. Explain that writers can combine strategies. Use the first topic sentence ("Antarctica has . . . ") as an example. The writer could go on to include statistics, such as the average temperature. Then he or she could give an example, such as a quotation from someone who has visited Antarctica.
3. Just as students use different types of sentences to add interest and variety to their writing, they also can use different kinds of details.

Answer Key

▶ **Exercise 4**

Students may not be able to write supporting sentences off the top of their head. They can use classroom resources to find statistics and details. Or they can simply tell what kind of information they would include. For sentence 2, students might want to find statistics of how long certain athletes practice. For sentence 3, they might want to give examples of food and equipment used in space exploration that have become part of daily life.

Critical Viewing

Support Students may mention the seals' weight and other aspects of their physical appearance.

Placing Your Topic Sentence

1. Most students instinctively place the topic sentence—a declarative sentence—at the beginning of every paragraph.

2. Read aloud the following simple paragraph, to show how a topic sentence can come at the end.

   It was warm, and the sun was shining. My sister and I grabbed our bathing suits and got on our bikes. All day long we swam in the ocean, made sand castles, and lay in the sun. Our noses got sunburned! Going to the beach is our favorite thing to do.

3. Students may fear that they will forget their topic if they do not begin the paragraph with it. They can write it in pencil in the margin as a reminder.

Answer Key

Exercise 5

Revisions will vary. Sample is given.

Topic Sentence: The force of a hurricane is frightening and devastating.

   The force of a hurricane is frightening and devastating. The winds of a hurricane swirl at 75 miles per hour or more, causing great destruction. Strong winds, for example, tear down trees and buildings. If the hurricane hits near the shore, flood waters make roads impassable and damage property.

3.1

Placing Your Topic Sentence

The topic sentence presenting your main idea can be located at any point in the paragraph. You may place it at the beginning, in the middle, or at the end of the paragraph; or you may leave it unstated. When the topic sentence comes at the beginning of a paragraph, it gives a preview of and direction to the sentences that come after it. Placed at the end of the paragraph, the topic sentence may draw a conclusion or function as a summary. When you leave the topic sentence unstated, the reader can synthesize the information you have presented.

Topic, Restatement, Illustration With the TRI pattern (Topic, Restatement, Illustration) you "build" a paragraph with the following elements:

TOPIC SENTENCE: You state your key idea.

RESTATEMANT: You interpret your key idea—put it into other words.

ILLUSTRATION: You support your key idea with an illustration or an example.

T   Dragons were often associated with royalty. According to legend, when Uther, father of King

R   Arthur of the Round Table, saw a flaming dragon in the skies, his advisors said this meant he would one

I   day be king. Once Uther became king, he had a golden dragon made to carry with him, and he took the name Pendragon.

Once you have identified the basic elements of your paragraph, experiment with variations of the TRI pattern, such as TIR, TRI, or ITR, until you are satisfied with the effect.

 Exercise 5 **Placing a Topic Sentence** Identify the topic sentence that expresses the main idea of the following group of sentences. Then, use two variations of the TRI pattern to organize the sentences. Use transitions and, if necessary, additional sentences. Choose the arrangement you think is most effective.
   1. The winds of a hurricane swirl at 75 miles per hour or more.
   2. The force of a hurricane is frightening and devastating.
   3. Strong winds tear down trees and buildings.
   4. Flood waters make roads impassable and damage property.
   5. Hurricanes cause great destruction.

36 • Structure and Style

STANDARDIZED TEST PREPARATION WORKSHOP

Topic Sentences Standardized tests often measure students' ability to identify topic sentences. Share the following paragraph with students and ask them to choose the number of the sentence that is the topic sentence:

   (1) It is hard to identify some plants. (2) Poison ivy usually resembles a vine, but if it grows near a bush it may take on a bushlike appearance. (3) Dandelions normally grow fairly tall. (4) But if you keep mowing them they adapt and survive by growing shorter.

The correct choice is sentence 1. The other sentences provide details that support this main idea.

3.2 *Paragraphs in Essays and Other Compositions*

Unity and Coherence

Maintain Unity

Unity in a paragraph or composition means that all the parts are related to a single key idea. In a unified composition, the main idea of each paragraph is clearly connected to the main idea or **thesis statement** of the composition. In a paragraph that has unity, all the sentences either develop, support, or explain the stated or implied topic sentence.

In the following paragraph, one sentence is marked for deletion because it interferes with the unity of the paragraph.

WRITING MODEL

Some of the domestic cat's features resemble those of all felines. For instance, a cat's whiskers help it gauge spaces through which it may fit, and its night vision is powerful, as with most other felines. ~~Artists have portrayed the domestic cat in many different ways through the ages.~~ Its playfulness as a kitten and hunting habits mimic those of feline counterparts in the wild.

▲ **Critical Viewing**
What statement communicates your overall impression of this cat? **[Describe]**

▶ **Exercise 6** **Revising for Unity** On a separate sheet of paper, copy the following paragraphs. Mark for deletion any sentences that interfere with the unity of the paragraphs.

Reactions to poison ivy vary. Some people seem to be immune to it, although the immunity may not continue throughout a lifetime. Usually, those who are allergic to poison ivy develop an itchy skin rash when they come into physical contact with the vine. The smoke from burning poison ivy vines can also carry the poison. For many people, the severity of the rash diminishes with each exposure.

Runners and hikers may contract poison ivy on their legs as they brush past the weed. The leaves of this plant are quite distinctive. Children often get rashes on their hands and faces while playing outdoors.

Paragraphs in Essays and Other Compositions • 37

Maintain Unity

1. Refer students to the pig paragraph in the Interest Grabber. It is a good example of lack of unity. Wilbur and Babe are famous pigs, but they have nothing to do with what pigs look like and how they are useful.

2. In the model, the sentence about cats in art is disruptive in the same way. It may be relevant to an essay on cats—it just doesn't belong in this paragraph.

Answer Key

▶ **Exercise 6**

Reactions to poison ivy vary. Some people seem to be immune to it, although the immunity may not continue throughout a lifetime. Usually, those who are allergic to poison ivy develop an itchy skin rash when they come into physical contact with the vine. ~~The smoke from burning poison ivy vines can also carry the poison.~~ For many people, the severity of the rash diminishes with each exposure.

Runners and hikers may contract poison ivy on their legs as they brush past the weed. ~~The leaves of this plant are quite distinctive.~~ Children often get rashes on their hands and faces while playing outdoors.

Customize for
Less Advanced Students

Provide highlighting pens in many colors. Students can mark their topic sentences in one color and their supporting details in another color. Or they can highlight facts in pink, statistics in green, examples in blue, and so on.

Critical Viewing

Describe Student answers will vary but may indicate that the cat looks self-assured and unaffected by humans.

⏱ TIME AND RESOURCE MANAGER

In-Depth Coverage	Accelerated Pace
• Cover pp. 37–41 in class. • Read the Writing Models on pages 37 and 40. • Assign and review Exercises 6–10.	• Assign pp. 37–41 for independent student review.

Construct Coherence

1. Transitions help both the writer and the reader follow a piece of writing.

2. Transitional words and phrases can serve several purposes. They can show time order (first, next, then, finally). They can show cause and effect (so, therefore, as a result). They can indicate comparison and contrast (but, however, also, like).

Answer Key

Exercise 7

Revisions will vary.

Technology Tip

Revising is easy on the computer. Students can highlight a sentence, then drag it to a new location (and they can drag it back if they change their mind). They can use the cross-out function to cross out a sentence they think they want to delete but are not positive yet. Let students experiment with dragging, copying, pasting, crossing out, and other revision techniques.

3.2

Construct Coherence

Coherence means that ideas are organized in a logical order and in a way that allows readers to see the connections and understand the flow of ideas.

When you write your draft, arrange the order of the sentences of each paragraph so that one leads logically to the next. Choose an organization for your paragraphs, and use it consistently throughout the composition. Indicate the connections between ideas by using transitional words and phrases.

TRANSITIONAL WORDS AND PHRASES
To Show Comparison, Contrast, and Development

again	however	like
along with	in contrast	namely
also	in fact	next
although	instead of	similarly
as a result	for example	than
as in	for instance	therefore
both	furthermore	together
consequently	in addition	too
finally	in conclusion	

To Show Time

after	first	next
at last	last	now
before	later	soon
finally	meanwhile	then

To Show Location

above	beneath	inside
ahead	beyond	near
behind	in back of	next to
below	in front of	outside

To Show Importance

another	furthermore	next
even greater	moreover	one
finally	most important	second
first	most significantly	third

Exercise 7 Revising for Coherence On a separate sheet of paper, revise the following paragraph to construct coherence. If necessary, reorder sentences and add transitions.

Many people find the microwave a useful tool to solve the problems presented by the lengthy meal preparation times demanded by traditional cooking. America is a country always on the move. Many American citizens no longer have or want to take the time to cook a full meal. Microwave cooking can provide a quick, tasty, nutritious meal.

38 • Structure and Style

☑ ONGOING ASSESSMENT: Monitor and Reinforce

If students have difficulty creating coherence, try the following option.

Have students carefully read the paragraph in question, looking for relationships between the sentences. Have them note any relationship they find. Then they can use appropriate transitional words and phrases to indicate these relationships.

The Parts of a Composition

To compose means "to put together." In a written composition, sentences and paragraphs are put together and organized to develop a single focus. No matter what type of organization is used, most compositions have three main sections or parts: an *introduction,* a *body,* and a *conclusion.*

Introduction

The **introduction** of a composition does what its name suggests: It introduces the focus of the composition, usually in a sentence called the **thesis statement.** In addition, the introduction usually captures readers' interest with a strong **lead.** An attention-getting lead may be an interesting quotation, a surprising statement, or a unique observation.

Body Paragraphs

The **body** paragraphs of a composition develop the thesis statement. They provide supporting facts, details, and examples. The paragraphs in the body are organized in a logical order, such as time order, order of importance, or spatial order.

Conclusion

The **conclusion** brings a composition to a close. Usually in the conclusion, the thesis statement is restated and the support is summarized. An effective conclusion also ends with a striking image or thought that will stick in readers' minds.

> **Exercise 8** **Planning a Composition** On a separate sheet of paper, outline the parts of a persuasive composition on an issue of importance to you. Write a thesis statement and a possible lead. Then, plan the topic sentences for each of several body paragraphs. (Although you may not have specific facts and statistics at hand, you can plan the points you will try to support.) Finally, restate your thesis statement in a way that you could use in a conclusion.

 **Learn More**

For more information about organizing paragraphs, see pages 33–35.

Step-by-Step Teaching Guide

The Parts of a Composition

1. Review with students the three major parts of a composition.
2. Bring in examples of short compositions, or have students find examples, and work with the class to identify these three parts.

Answer Key

Exercise 8

Answers will vary.

Types of Paragraphs

1. Tell students that they can distinguish between these two major types of paragraphs by remembering a topical paragraph consists of information about a *topic,* while functional paragraphs serve a *function.*

2. Review the different kinds of functional paragraphs.

3. Have a volunteer read aloud the excerpt.

4. Ask students how the first paragraph captures their interest. Do they agree that the second paragraph creates emphasis?

5. Point out that Patricia Volk could have written about a bug expert in a different way. For example: *Louis Sorkin is an expert on insects. People often come to him for advice. He examines two flies . . .* Her readers would be bored if she had told just the facts. Instead, she put a "human face" on the bug man, and we want to know more about him and his work.

3.2

Types of Paragraphs

Topical Paragraphs

A **topical paragraph** is a group of sentences that contains one main sentence or idea and several sentences that support or develop that key idea. Most paragraphs are topical paragraphs, but many compositions also include functional paragraphs.

Functional Paragraphs

Functional paragraphs serve a specific purpose. Although they may not have a topic sentence, they are unified and coherent because the sentences (if there is more than one sentence) all follow a logical order and are clearly connected. Functional paragraphs can be used for the following purposes:

To Create Emphasis A very short paragraph of one or two sentences lends weight to what is being said because it breaks the reader's rhythm.

WRITING MODEL

from An Entomological Study of Apartment 4A
Patricia Volk

The phone rings. It rings all day. Louis Sorkin is the 911 of insect emergencies. If you open your safe and bugs fly in your face or you need to know whether New Mexican centipedes produce cyanide, Sorkin's your man.

He studies two flies I found on the bathroom windowsill. There's no masking his disgust.

> The short, direct second paragraph following the longer, more conversational paragraph emphasizes Louis Sorkin's reaction.

To Indicate Dialogue One of the conventions of written dialogue is that a new paragraph begins each time the speaker changes.

To Make a Transition A short paragraph can help readers move between the main ideas in two topical paragraphs.

Paragraph Blocks

Sometimes, a key idea requires an amount of support or development that is too extensive for a single paragraph. Therefore, you may occasionally use several paragraphs to develop a single idea. These paragraphs function as a "block." Each paragraph within the block contributes support to the key idea or topic sentence. By dividing the development of the ideas into chunks, you make your ideas clear and accessible.

Topic sentence: Recycling is one of the most beneficial ways to reduce waste.

Paragraph 1	It's economical	**B**
Paragraph 2	It's more economical than reducing consumption	**L O**
Paragraph 3	It creates new jobs	**C K**

> **Exercise 9** Identifying Functional Paragraphs Skim a book review or some other piece of persuasive writing to find examples of functional paragraphs that create emphasis, indicate dialogue, and make transitions. Explain to a partner how these paragraphs work within the longer piece of writing.

> **Exercise 10** Analyzing Types of Paragraphs Photocopy a newspaper or magazine article. Analyze each type of paragraph and identify its type. Draw a box around topical paragraphs. Underline any stated topic sentences. Write implied topic sentences in the margin of the article, next to the paragraph. Put a red star next to functional paragraphs that arouse or sustain interest, a blue star next to dialogue, and a yellow star next to paragraphs that create emphasis. Then, mark paragraph blocks with a brace: [ ]. Discuss with a partner why each paragraph type is or is not an effective choice.

Paragraph Blocks

1. Tell students that there is no single rule to govern paragraph length. However, it is always a good idea to keep paragraphs short. This helps the reader follow a writer's train of thought more easily.

2. Paragraph blocks can be seen as separate subtopics. Each paragraph is still connected to the others by the larger topic.

Answer Key

> **Exercise 9**

Responses will vary.

> **Exercise 10**

Remind students that topical paragraphs explain the topic and that functional paragraphs create emphasis, indicate dialogue, or make transitions. Students can share their accounts with a partner and discuss how the accounts are paragraphed.

1. Remind students of purposes for writing: to persuade, to describe, to explain, to entertain. A writer's purpose has an effect on his or her choice of sentence type, diction, and tone.

2. Refer students to the literature models in this chapter.

   • Rachel Carson's purpose (page 33) is to describe a situation. She uses long sentences and vivid nouns, verbs, and adjectives. Her tone could be described as literary, even as poetic.

   • John McPhee's purpose (page 33) is to describe the physical characteristics and personal qualities of an individual. To create his admiring tone, the author uses a long introductory sentence that describes the woman's physical features, followed by short sentences to describe her actions. A comparison relates the mother to the son, and the final sentence summarizes her inner qualities. The simple diction emphasizes the simple qualities that made her a person to be admired.

   • Patricia Volk's purpose (page 40) is to explain and entertain. Her tone is funny, but she manages to explain what a bug expert does all day long.

Answer Key

Exercise 11

Encourage volunteers to read their paragraphs aloud. Students can comment on how successful the writers were in capturing the style of their model.

3.3 Writing Style

You can express your personal style in any number of ways: through clothing, hairstyle, movie preferences, choices in friends, and so on. Just as your style may be apparent in the people and things you identify with, so your style is reflected in your writing. Your writing style may be affected by a number of elements.

$$\left.\begin{array}{l} \text{sentence variety} \\ \\ \text{diction} \\ \\ \text{tone} \end{array}\right\} \text{Paragraph Style}$$

Sentence Variety The variety of outfits in your closet may reflect different aspects of your style and the various ways you perceive yourself. You may choose to project one image on a certain occasion and an entirely different image on another. You have options in your writing style as well. When you write a paragraph, you choose from a variety of sentence types, lengths, and structures. Vary your sentences to express your style.

Diction The overall effect, or style, of a paragraph is affected by the words you choose. You can achieve an eccentric or off-beat style by using words with unusual or unexpected connotations or associations, or you can use words with formal or scholarly connotations if you want to assume a traditional or authoritative stance. The sounds of words can also contribute to the style of a paragraph.

Tone Tone is your attitude toward your subject. You may feel any number of ways about your subject—passionately opinionated, amused, saddened, or objective. If you are writing a letter of reference, your paragraphs will have a businesslike, formal tone. If you are e-mailing your sister or brother about a comical family event, your paragraphs will probably have a lighthearted, informal tone.

▶ **Exercise 11** Identifying Paragraph Style Read the two Models From Literature on page 33. Study the sentence lengths and structures, the word choice, and the tone of each paragraph. Discuss with a partner how the styles of the two paragraphs are similar and different. Then, write a paragraph of your own, modeled on the style of the paragraphs you read.

⏱ TIME AND RESOURCE MANAGER

In-Depth Coverage	Accelerated Pace
• Cover pp. 42–45 in class. • Assign and review Exercises 11–12. • Read Standardized Test Preparation Workshop, pp. 46–47.	• Assign pp. 42–45 for independent student review. • Cover pp. 46–47 in class.

Formal and Informal English

Standard English can be either formal or informal. Informal English is used when you want to achieve a conversational tone in your writing and for casual writing. Formal English is used to address subjects in a serious way.

Use the Conventions of Formal English

Formal English is appropriate for research projects, essays, speeches, business letters, and most of your school assignments. When writing in formal English, you should observe the following conventions:

• Do not use slang.
• Avoid contractions.
• Use standard English and grammar.

Use Informal English

Informal English is conversational in tone. It is appropriate for friendly letters, humorous writing, casual notes, some narratives, and much dialogue. When using informal English, you can:

• Use contractions.
• Use slang and popular expressions.

FORMAL ENGLISH: Please contact me at your earliest convenience if I can be of any further assistance.

INFORMAL ENGLISH: Feel free to give me a call whenever you've got a moment.

▼ Critical Viewing
Do you think this girl is using formal or informal English? Explain. [Deduce]

▶ **Exercise 12** Using Formal and Informal English On a separate sheet of paper, rewrite the following sentences. Use formal English for those written in informal English. Use informal English for those written in formal English.
1. This awesome song really rules.
2. The facts to which the reporter referred were of unquestionable veracity.
3. It was such a bummer when the storm ended the concert early.
4. The enthusiastic English teacher gratefully acknowledged her students' efforts and thanked them effusively.
5. Park yourself over there and grab yourself some grub.

Writing Style • 43

☑ ONGOING ASSESSMENT: Monitor and Reinforce

If students have difficulty knowing when to use formal and informal English, try the following option.

Tell students that their purpose for writing and their intended audience will often dictate the formality of the language they use. Provide students with the following situations and ask them to determine if informal or formal English would be appropriate:

• a letter to the school principal (formal)
• an e-mail to a friend (informal)
• a note to a parent (informal)
• a speech to a community organization (formal)

43

Lesson Objectives

1. To recognize themes in works of art.
2. To keep a journal of quotations to use in compositions.

Step-by-Step Teaching Guide

Recognizing Themes

1. Choose one of the Spotlight elements for class discussion, or have students work individually or in groups on the element of their choice. Give students the initiative to find the necessary books and videos.

2. Interested students may want to read the entire play and research more about the development and critical reception of the play.

3. Encourage students to find more examples of Hughes's poetry. Have students research more information about Hughes's life and work.

4. Interested students can watch the film versions of Hansberry's play. Encourage students to research the critical and popular reception of these works.

Viewing and Representing

Activity Tell students that they may want to organize the quotations in their journals by topic. This will help them find quotations to use for specific purposes in the future.

Critical Viewing

Speculate Students might say that the man is saying something the woman finds hard to believe.

Spotlight on the Humanities

Recognizing Themes

Focus on Theater: *A Raisin in the Sun*

Effective paragraphs are formed by taking interesting ideas and phrases and combining them into captivating sentences. Written in 1959, playwright Lorraine Hansberry's *A Raisin in the Sun* was the first drama by a black woman to be produced on Broadway. Set in Chicago, the play tells the story of a black chauffeur, Walter Lee, who dreams of finding a better life for his family. Through a series of events involving stolen money in a business scheme and a neighborhood that does not want a black family on their block, Walter learns the true meaning of dignity. *A Raisin in the Sun* won the New York Drama Critics' Circle Award.

▲ **Critical Viewing** Why might the woman in this picture look skeptical? **[Speculate]**

Literature Connection The title for the drama *A Raisin in the Sun* comes from a poem by author Langston Hughes (1902–1967) entitled "Dream Deferred." Hughes's first book of poems was published in 1926, and he continued to write about the poor and homeless black people who went through the Great Depression. Hughes lived in New York City's Harlem in a period of great creativity known as the Harlem Renaissance. Jazz, dance, the blues, and literary forms blossomed.

Film Connection In 1961, actor Sidney Poitier starred in a film version of *A Raisin in the Sun*. Now considered a classic, the film also starred Claudia McNeil, who played Lena in the original 1959 stage version. McNeil later played Lena in a musical version of the play entitled *Raisin*, originally produced in 1973. In 1981, McNeil starred in another revival.

Writing Activity: Start a Quotations Log

Lorraine Hansberry used a quotation from a Langston Hughes poem as the title of her play. Quotations can also be used effectively in the titles, introductions, or conclusions of compositions. Begin keeping a journal of quotations that you might use in compositions. After each quotation, write a few words of your own that reflect on the quotation. You might begin looking for quotations in the poetry of Langston Hughes. As you encounter meaningful quotations in books, movies, and speeches, add them to your log.

Media and Technology Skills

Lesson Objectives

1. To explore different forms of technological communication.
2. To conduct a class survey on technology use.

Exploring Technology Use

Activity: Technology Survey

Recently, several networks have moved television studios to glass-enclosed, ground-floor spaces that allow crowds of passersby to achieve a new form of the American Dream: appearing on national television, if only for a few moments. The ratings spike this generates shows that even watching ordinary people like themselves getting on TV offers a vicarious thrill for millions of ordinary viewers. The mass media—television, radio, and the Internet—have become a powerful force in our lives.

Think About It The oldest form of mass communication—the printing press—is less than six hundred years old. Electronic forms of communication like the telephone, radio, television, and computer date back a hundred years or less; home computers and the Internet have become popular only in the last two decades. When you look at the math of time, 99 percent of our civilized history was untouched by devices that seem as necessary and natural a part of our environment as air and water.

Analyze It To see just how large a role these communication technologies play in your everyday life, conduct a class survey of technology use. Prepare a survey sheet and, with your teacher's permission, distribute it to classmates. The sample at right shows how you can set up the questions. Develop questions about how much time the different technologies are used and for what purpose. Use the varieties of communication technology listed in the box as categories for your questions.

Evaluate It Collect and tally the results of your survey. Based on the results, draw conclusions about which types of technology are most used for information gathering and which are most used for entertainment. Share your results with classmates, and use them as a basis for a group discussion on technology use.

Varieties of Communication Technology

Print
- Books
- Magazines
- Newspapers
- Paper Mail
- Facsimile

Electronic
- E-Mail
- Radio
- CD
- Audiotape
- Videotape
- Telephone
- Movies
- Television
- Internet

How much time do you think you spend each day using the following media?

	Less than 1 hour	1–2 hours	3–4 hours	more than 4 hours
Radio	○	○	○	○
Television	○	○	○	○
Computer	○	○	○	○
Telephone	○	○	○	○

Which technology do you most use for information gathering?

Radio	Television	Computer	Telephone
○	○	○	○

Step-by-Step Teaching Guide

Exploring Technology Use

1. Review with students the different forms of communication technology.
2. Encourage students to add questions to the sample survey sheet. Have students make sure that their surveys cover all necessary areas of technology use.
3. As an extension, you may want to have students create graphs or charts to visually display their data.

Media and Technology Skills • 45

Step-by-Step Teaching Guide

Strategy, Organization, and Style

1. Have a volunteer read aloud the three types of questions students may encounter.

2. Have students identify the skills they have learned in this chapter that would be helpful to answer each type of question.

3. Encourage students to take notes in the margin or to highlight the passages as they read, noting any areas that might need revision. Students should also take notes to identify the writer's point of view, tone, and diction. They can refer to these notes when answering the questions.

Standardized Test Preparation Workshop

Strategy, Organization, and Style

Standardized tests frequently measure your knowledge of writing skills. In these types of tests, items include a passage in which part of a sentence is marked for your analysis. You will be asked to analyze strategy, organization, sequence of sentences, and style within a passage. The following are three types of questions that you may encounter:

- Strategy questions ask whether a given revision is appropriate in the context of the passage.

- Organization questions ask you to choose the most logical sequence of ideas or to decide whether a sentence should be added, deleted, or moved.

- Style questions focus on your ability to identify the writer's point of view or evaluate the use of language for an intended audience.

The sample test items that follow will give you practice in answering these types of questions.

Test Tips

- Pay attention to language that sounds awkward, because you may be noticing part of the text that needs revision.
- Notice whether you are following the logic of the passage you are reading. If it is confusing, consider how it could be rewritten to make more sense to you.

Sample Test Item	Answer and Explanation

Directions: Read the passage, and then answer the questions that follow.
 	
¹Before I knew it, I had created a huge snow man. ²Once outside, I picked up the fresh snow and started to roll it into a ball. ³After seeing the snow outside my window, I could not wait to go outside.
 	
1 Choose the best sequence to make the passage the most logical.
 	
  A 1, 2, 3
  B 2, 3, 1
  C 3, 2, 1
  D 3, 1, 2
	The correct answer is C. This sequence begins with the narrator seeing the snow, then the character is out in the snow, and it ends with the narrator's completion of a snow man.

✎ TEST-TAKING TIP

Many organization questions require students to choose the most logical sequence of ideas. Students need to pay careful attention to any transitional words or phrases that will help them determine the best sequence of ideas. For example, in the sample test item, students should see that words and phrases such as *Before I knew it, Once outside,* and *After seeing the snow* give clues as to the most logical sequence of these sentences.

▶ **Practice 1** **Directions:** Read the passage, and then answer the questions that follow. Choose the letter of the best answer.

¹Known as the "horseless carriage," automobiles were not completely welcomed, by Americans when they were first invented. ²An automobile was considered dangerous by some, not to mention that the noise of a backfiring engine could scare a horse off the road. ³In time, attitudes toward automobiles started to change. People began to realize the opportunities and freedom the automobile could provide. ⁴The ability to go farther in a shorter amount of time became invaluable. ⁵As cars became more acceptable and affordable, the number of people buying cars increased. ⁶Only 8,000 Americans owned cars in 1900 as opposed to 4.5 million Americans who owned automobiles in 1917.

⁷Fortunately, in 1913, a man named Henry Ford had introduced the asssembly line, a method of production in which workers add parts to a product as it moves along on a belt. ⁸With the assembly line, cars could be produced in large quantities quickly and cheaply. ⁹Over time, convertible cars would become very popular with some people. ¹⁰Ford's assembly line enabled America to keep up with the new demand for cars.

1 Suppose the writer wanted to say more about the production of automobiles in the passage. Which of the following additions is most suitable?

A Over the last century, cars have become extremely advanced and now travel at great speeds.

B As the assembly belt moved, one group of workers would put seats into the car frame, the next group would add the roof, and so on, until the car was complete.

C Many people continued to prefer using horses to cars because horses did not require gasoline.

D Before long, traffic in cities would become a common problem.

2 Which of the following draws attention away from the main idea?

F Part 5

G Part 7

H Part 8

J Part 9

3 Which of the following best identifies the author's purpose?

A To persuade

B To entertain

C To inform

D To criticize

4 Choose the best sequence for the first three sentences in paragraph 1.

F 1, 2, 3

G 2, 3, 1

H 3, 2, 1

J 1, 3, 2

5 Suppose the author wanted to say more about the popularity of cars. Which of the following additions is most suitable?

A Another challenge for people was learning how to drive an automobile.

B In the meantime, another means of travel, the airplane, was being developed.

C With a car, visiting friends and family who lived farther away became more feasible.

D It was one of the greatest inventions in American history.

▶ **Practice 1**

1. B
2. J
3. C
4. F
5. C

In-Depth Lesson Plan

	LESSON FOCUS	PRINT AND MEDIA RESOURCES
DAY 1	**Introduction to Autobiography** Students learn key elements of autobiographical writing and analyze the Model From Literature (pp. 48–53).	*Writers at Work* **Videotape**, Narration *Writing Lab* **CD-ROM**, Narration
DAY 2	**Prewriting** Students choose and narrow a topic, consider their audience and purpose, and gather information (pp. 54–57).	**Teaching Resources** *Writing Support Transparencies*, 4-A–D; *Writing Support Activity Book*, 4–1
DAY 3	**Drafting** Students organize their ideas and write their first drafts (pp. 58–59).	**Teaching Resources** *Writing Support Activity Book* *Writers at Work* **Videotape**
DAY 4	**Revising** Students revise their drafts in terms of overall structure, paragraphs, sentences, and word choice (pp. 60–64).	**Teaching Resources** *Writing Support Transparencies*, 4C–G; *Writing Lab* **CD-ROM**, Narration
DAY 5	**Editing and Proofreading; Publishing and Presenting** Students check their work for accuracy and correctness and present their final drafts (pp. 65–66).	**Teaching Resources** Scoring Rubrics on Transparency, Chapter 4; *Formal Assessment*, Chapter 4 *Writing Lab* **CD-ROM**, Narration

Accelerated Lesson Plan

	LESSON FOCUS	PRINT AND MEDIA RESOURCES
DAY 1	**Drafting** Students review characteristics for autobiographical writing, select topics, and write drafts (pp. 48–59).	**Teaching Resources** *Writing Support Transparencies*, 4-A–D; *Writing Support Activity Book*, 4–1 *Writers at Work* **Videotape**, Narration *Writing Lab* **CD-ROM**, Narration
DAY 2	**Revising to Presenting** Students work individually or with peers to revise, edit, and proofread their work for presentation (pp. 60–66).	**Teaching Resources** *Writing Support Transparencies*, 4-E–G; Scoring Rubrics on Transparency, Chapter 4; *Formal Assessment*, Chapter 4

Options for Adapting Lesson Plans

HOMEWORK

Have students complete any stage of the lesson for homework.

TECHNOLOGY

Students can complete any stage of the lesson on computer. Have them print out their completed work.

FEATURES

Extend coverage with Connected Assignment (p. 69), Spotlight on the Humanities (p. 70), Media and Technology Skills (p. 71), and the Standardized Test Preparation Workshop (p. 72).

INTEGRATED SKILLS COVERAGE

Integrating Grammar
Relative Pronouns, SE p. 62
Exclamation Mark, SE p. 65

Reading/Writing Connection
Reading Strategy, SE p. 50
Writing Application, SE p. 53

Speaking and Listening
Integrate Speaking and Listening Skills ATE p. 55

Language
Language Highlight ATE pp. 52, 64

Vocabulary
Integrating Vocabulary Skills ATE p. 67

Technology
Integrating Technology Skills ATE p. 53

Real-World Connection
ATE p. 68

Social Studies Skills
Integrating Social Studies Skills ATE p. 57

Viewing and Representing
Critical Viewing, SE pp. 48, 50, 53, 56, 67, 69, 70
Viewing and Representing ATE p. 70

MEETING INDIVIDUAL NEEDS

Less Advanced Students ATE pp. 59; See also Ongoing Assessments ATE pp. 49, 53, 61, 62, 64

More Advanced Students ATE p. 73

ESL Students ATE pp. 54, 63

Verbal/Linguistic Learners ATE p. 61

Interpersonal Learners ATE pp. 54, 71

BLOCK SCHEDULING

Pacing Suggestions
For 90-minute Blocks
• Have students complete the Prewriting and Drafting stages in a single period.
• Focus one class period on Revising and Editing and Publishing and Presenting. Allow at least 30 minutes for peer revision.

Resources for Varying Instruction
• *Writing Lab* CD-ROM If your students have access to hardware, a 90-minute block provides an ideal opportunity for students to work on computer.
• *Writers at Work* Videotape Show the Autobiographical writing segment in class.

Professional Development Support
• *How to Manage Instruction in the Block* This Teaching Resource provides management and activity suggestions.

ASSESSMENT SUPPORT

Standardized Test Preparation SE p. 72; ATE p. 72
Standardized Test Preparation Workshop, pp. 7–8
Scoring Rubrics on Transparency, Ch. 4
Formal Assessment, Ch. 4
Writing Assessment and Portfolio Management

MEDIA AND TECHNOLOGY

For the Student
• *Writing Lab* CD-ROM, Narration

For the Teacher
• *Writers at Work* Videotape, Narration
• *Resource Pro* CD-ROM

WRITING AND GRAMMAR WEBSITE

The Interactive Writing and Grammar Website provides a wide array of support for students, teachers, and parents. Writing support includes:
• Interactive revision checkers
• Scoring rubrics with complete models

phwg.phschool.com

LITERATURE CONNECTIONS

Related selections from *Prentice Hall Literature: Timeless Voices, Timeless Themes,* Gold:
"Rosa Parks: My Story," SE p. 53

Lesson Objectives

1. To define and identify different types of autobiographical writing.

2. To use prewriting strategies to generate ideas, develop voice, and plan.

3. To develop drafts, alone and collaboratively, by organizing and reorganizing content and by refining style to suit occasion, audience, and purpose.

4. To produce legible work that shows accurate spelling and correct use of the conventions of punctuation such as italics and ellipses.

5. To demonstrate control over grammatical elements such as subject-verb agreement, pronoun-antecedent agreement, verb forms, and parallelism.

6. To evaluate writing for both mechanics and content; and respond productively to peer review of his/her own work.

7. To read to be entertained, to appreciate a writer's craft, to be informed, to take action, and to discover models to use in his/her own writing.

8. To describe how meanings are communicated through elements of design, including shape, line, color, and texture.

Critical Viewing

Evaluate Students' responses will vary.

Chapter 4 Narration
Autobiographical Writing

▲ Critical Viewing
What good memories of your family can provide the source for an interesting narration? **[Evaluate]**

Autobiography in Everyday Life

At first glance, the word *autobiography* may seem a suitable writing form only for famous people with great accomplishments. However, when you take a closer look at this form, you'll realize that you don't have to be famous to have an interesting life story. The humorous anecdotes relatives tell about your antics as a child, an account of your participation in a championship game, the story about the way you met your best friend—these, too, are "life stories," or autobiographical narratives. In fact, each individual life unfolds like a story. Whenever you retell a part of your life story, you are sharing an autobiographical narrative.

Resources
Technology: Writers at Work videotape

In-Depth Coverage	Accelerated Pace
• Cover pp. 48–53 in class. • Show Narration: Autobiography section of the Writers at Work videotape.	• Assign pp. 48–53 for independent student review. • Discuss definitions and types of autobiographical essays in class.

What Is Autobiographical Writing?

When you write an **autobiography,** you are telling a story from your own life. Effective autobiographical writing includes

- a series of events involving the writer as a main character.
- a conflict or event that changed the writer's viewpoint.
- details about people and places.
- an insight based on the events narrated.
- a logical organization.

To preview the criteria on which your autobiographical writing will be judged, see the Rubric for Self-Assessment on page 66.

Types of Autobiographical Writing

Each type of autobiographical writing has a name that reflects its unique purpose:

- **Autobiographical sketches** often include information about the writer's life and his or her personal qualities.
- **Memoirs** focus on the writer's relationship with a particular person, place, or animal.
- **Reflective essays, personal essays, or autobiographical incidents** share a personal experience and include the writer's reflections on the significance of the experience.
- **Anecdotes** are brief, usually humorous accounts of a single event.

Writers in
ACTION

Isabel Allende is a Chilean writer who began her writing career as a journalist. She frequently draws on her own experience when writing:

"Memory always betrays me. That's why I write—to preserve memory."

PREVIEW

Student Work
IN PROGRESS

In this chapter, you will follow the work of Sara Holman, a student at Towson High School, in Towson, Maryland. Sara recounts her activities as a nine-year-old entrepreneur. As you will see, she used prewriting, drafting, and revising techniques to develop her autobiographical piece. You can read the completed draft at the end of this chapter.

Autobiographical Writing • **49**

PREPARE AND ENGAGE

Interest GRABBER Write the word *autobiography* on the board. Underline each part of the word (auto, bio, graphy) and ask students what each of these parts means (auto=self, bio=life, graphy=writing). Students will see that an autobiography is the story of someone's life written or told by himself or herself.

Activate Prior Knowledge

Ask students to name some autobiographies they have read recently and to tell what they liked about these life stories. Ask them what draws them to autobiographies. Have them discuss the special features autobiographies have that biographies do not.

More About the Author

Born in 1942, Isabel Allende is one of the first female Latin American writers to win popular recognition. Many of her books, including *House of the Spirits*, *The Stories of Eva Luna*, and *Paula*, draw on her own experiences. Her style derives from the techniques of magical realism popularized by Jorge Louis Borges and Gabriel Garciá Márquez.

ONGOING ASSESSMENT: Diagnose

Use one of the following options to diagnose students' current level of proficiency in autobiographical writing.

Option 1 Have each student select the strongest example of his or her autobiographical writing from the previous year. Ask students to review their writing critically and to write a short paragraph on the strengths and weaknesses of their writing. Review these critical paragraphs with each student to determine the areas in which they will need extra support.	**Option 2** Ask students to select an event from their lives that would make a good subject for an autobiographical anecdote. Have them include details about the event. If students have difficulty with this exercise, you may need to devote more time to the prewriting phase of the process.

Reading\Writing Connection

Reading: Distinguish Between Fact and Opinion

Briefly review the definitions of *fact* and *opinion* and have students look for examples of each as they read "The Shadowland of Dreams." You might ask students to divide a piece of paper into two columns and record facts in one column and opinions in the other. Discuss students' reactions to opinions about writing and about dreams.

Teaching from the Model

You can use this model from literature as an aid in showing students how to find a topic. Point out that Haley writes about a dream and the decisions and struggles he encounters in order to achieve that dream. Have students brainstorm for a list of times they've had to struggle to accomplish a goal. What did they learn from these struggles. What lessons might be interesting or valuable for a reader?

Step-by-Step Teaching Guide

Engage Students Through Literature

1. Read Haley's essay aloud in class, or have students read it together in small groups. Use the margin notes to guide and inform the students.

2. Model the practice of pausing to pay attention to details. If you are reading the text aloud, pause at the word *typewriter* at the bottom of page 4: *Typewriter. I don't know exactly when this piece was written, but here is clue that it's before the computer/word processor era, which means it's probably before the mid-1980s.*

continued

Critical Viewing

Evaluate Students should say that the photograph of Washington Square Park is an appropriate illustration for Haley's writing because it is located in Greenwich Village, the neighborhood in New York City where Haley lived.

4.1 Model From Literature

Alex Haley's book Roots: The Saga of an American Family *was an immediate bestseller. Within two years of its publication, it had won 271 awards. Haley's success, however, did not happen overnight. He had worked for many years and made many sacrifices to achieve his dream. In the following autobiographical narrative, Haley shares an incident that marked a choice, a turning point, in his life as a writer.*

Reading Strategy: Distinguish Between Fact and Opinion
When you read nonfiction, recognize both fact and opinion. Determine which ideas are **facts**—statements that can be proven true—and which are **opinions**—statements that can be supported, but not proven. As you read "The Shadowland of Dreams," distinguish between the facts of Haley's life and the opinions he formed based on those facts.

▲ **Critical Viewing** This photograph shows Washington Square Park, a New York City landmark. Why is it an appropriate illustration for Alex Haley's writing? [Evaluate]

The Shadowland of Dreams

Alex Haley

Many a young person tells me he wants to be a writer. I always encourage such people, but I also explain that there's a big difference between "being a writer" and writing. In most cases these individuals are dreaming of wealth and fame, not the long hours alone at a typewriter. "You've got to want to *write*," I say to them, "not want to be a *writer*."

The narrative opens with one of the writer's main points—writing requires sacrifice and dedication.

50 • Autobiographical Writing

The reality is that writing is a lonely, private and poor-paying affair. For every writer kissed by fortune there are thousands more whose longing is never requited. Even those who succeed often know long periods of neglect and poverty. I did.

When I left a 20-year career in the Coast Guard to become a freelance writer, I had no prospects at all. What I did have was a friend in New York City, George Sims, with whom I'd grown up in Henning, Tennessee. George found me my home, a cleaned-out storage room in the Greenwich Village apartment building where he worked as superintendent. It didn't even matter that it was cold and had no bathroom. I immediately bought a used manual typewriter and felt like a genuine writer.

After a year or so, however, I still hadn't gotten a break and began to doubt myself. It was so hard to sell a story that I barely made enough to eat. But I knew I wanted to write. I had dreamed about it for years. I wasn't going to be one of those people who die wondering, *What if?* I would keep putting my dream to the test— even though it meant living with uncertainty and fear of failure. This is the Shadowland of hope, and anyone with a dream must learn to live there.

Then one day I got a call that changed my life. It wasn't an agent or editor offering a big contract. It was the opposite—a kind of siren call tempting me to give up my dream. On the phone was an old acquaintance from the Coast Guard, now stationed in San Francisco. He had once lent me a few bucks and liked to egg me about it. "When am I going to get that $15, Alex?" he teased.

"Next time I make a sale."

"I have a better idea," he said. "We need a new public-information assistant out here, and we're paying $6000 a year. If you want it, you can have it."

Six thousand a year! That was real money in 1960. I could get a nice apartment, a used car, pay off debts and maybe save a little something. What's more, I could write on the side.

As the dollars were dancing in my head, something cleared my senses. From deep inside a bull-headed resolution welled up. I had dreamed of being a writer—full time. And that's what I was going to be. "Thanks, but no," I heard myself saying. "I'm going to stick it out and write."

Afterward, as I paced around my little room, I started to feel like a fool. Reaching into my cupboard—an orange crate nailed to the wall—I pulled out all that was there: two cans of sardines. Plunging my hands into my pockets, I came up with 18 cents. I took the cans and coins and jammed them into a crumpled paper

---

After setting up the situation, the writer will support his point by telling a true story in which he is the main character.

The contrast between the writer's expectations and the reality of his situation provides the conflict that drives the narrative.

Haley makes an artful link to the title of the essay. Here, he describes the "Shadowland" of hope.

Dialogue adds variety to the writing and reveals the writer's decision at a turning point in his life.

Details about Haley's thoughts and feelings help readers understand the significance of events.

---

3. After reading the first paragraph, have students predict what the essay will be about. Elicit that since it is an autobiographical essay, it probably will be about the writer's own experience with the contrast he sets up in the first paragraph: wanting to be a writer versus actually writing.

4. Discuss the struggles that Haley endures while pursuing his dream.

5. Discuss the meaning of the essay's title. What exactly is the "Shadowland of Dreams"? What images does it conjure up? Why is it such an important place to the author?

continued

More About the Author

Alex Haley (1921–1992) achieved fame as the author of *Roots: The Saga of an American Family* (1976). Haley's work won both the Pulitzer Prize and the National Book Award. His book and the popular television miniseries that followed are credited with awakening a national interest in genealogy. However, *Roots* was not Haley's first significant work. A decade earlier he rose to prominence as Malcolm X's collaborator in *The Autobiography of Malcolm X*, one of the truly historic works of the era.

6. Ask students to consider the author's tone and what it contributes to the writing. Elicit that the matter-of-fact tone contrasts well with the tough times he is describing. Discuss how a self-pitying tone or a casual, light-hearted tone might have lessened the impact of Haley's message.

7. Discuss how the introduction of other people adds to the essay. Haley is no longer talking only about himself, so the essay becomes more universal.

8. Ask students what relevance Haley's essay has for them. Do they have dreams? Are they prepared to live in the "Shadowland"?

9. Haley's piece is more than a fine example of autobiographical writing. The example of *Roots* shows that every family, and every person, has a past filled with interesting stories. Ask whether anyone they know has ever lived in the "Shadowland" in order to achieve a dream. Have willing students share these stories.

Language Highlight

Similes A *simile* is a type of figurative language in which a writer compares two unlike things using the word *like* or *as*. Similes can add depth to a piece of writing by encouraging the reader to look at an event or experience in a different light. Alex Haley provides a striking example of a simile on this page when he compares his thoughts to birds flying south.

4.1

bag. *There, Alex,* I said to myself. *There's everything you've made of yourself so far.* I'm not sure I've ever felt so low.

I wish I could say things started getting better right away. But they didn't. Thank goodness I had George to help me over the rough spots.

Through him I met other struggling artists like Joe Delaney, a veteran painter from Knoxville, Tennessee. Often Joe lacked food money, so he'd visit a neighborhood butcher who would give him big bones with morsels of meat and a grocer who would hand him some wilted vegetables. That's all Joe needed to make down-home soup.

Another Village neighbor was a handsome young singer who ran a struggling restaurant. Rumor had it that if a customer ordered steak the singer would dash to a supermarket across the street to buy one. His name was Harry Belafonte.

People like Delaney and Belafonte became role models for me. I learned that you had to make sacrifices and live creatively to keep working at your dream. That's what living in the Shadowland is all about.

As I absorbed the lesson, I gradually began to sell my articles. I was writing about what many people were talking about then: civil rights, black Americans and Africa. Soon, like birds flying south, my thoughts were drawn back to my childhood. In the silence of my room, I heard the voices of Grandma, Cousin Georgia, Aunt Plus, Aunt Liz and Aunt Till as they told stories about our family and slavery.

There were stories that black Americans had tended to avoid before, and so I mostly kept them to myself. But one day at lunch with editors of *Reader's Digest* I told these stories of my grandmother and aunts and cousins; and I said that I had a dream to trace my family's history to the first African brought to these shores in chains. I left that lunch with a contract that would help support my research and writing for nine years.

It was a long, slow climb out of the shadows. Yet in 1976, 17 years after I left the Coast Guard, *Roots* was published. Instantly I had the kind of fame and success that few writers ever experience. The shadows had turned into dazzling limelight.

For the first time I had money and open doors everywhere. The phone rang all the time with new friends and new deals. I packed up and moved to Los Angeles, where I could help in the making of

Here, the writer elaborates by giving details about people, places, and feelings. This added information helps build the significance of Haley's struggle.

The series of events is organized in chronological order.

Details about the writer's thoughts and feelings show the impact of the change in his situation.

Haley revisits the "shadow" references, building the contrast he wants to emphasize.

the *Roots* TV mini-series. It was a confusing, exhilarating time, and in a sense I was blinded by the light of my success.

Then one day, while unpacking, I came across a box filled with things I had owned years before in the Village. Inside was a brown paper bag.

I opened it, and there were two corroded sardine cans, a nickel, a dime and three pennies. Suddenly the past came flooding in like a riptide. I could picture myself once again huddled over the type-writer in that cold, bleak, one-room apartment. And I said to myself, *The things in this bag are part of my roots too. I can't ever forget that.*

I sent them out to be framed in Lucite. I keep that clear plastic case where I can see it every day. I can see it now above my office desk in Knoxville, along with the Pulitzer Prize; a portrait of nine Emmys awarded the television production of *Roots;* and the Spingarn medal—the NAACP's highest honor. I'd be hard pressed to say which means the most to me. But only one reminds me of the courage and persistence it takes to stay the course in the Shadowland.

It's a lesson anyone with a dream should learn.

Writing Application:
Including Fact and Opinion
As you draft your autobio-graphical narrative, use a combination of factual details about incidents and the opinions you formed about those facts.

LITERATURE

To see another narra-tive about someone whose courage led to the realization of a dream, read "Rosa Parks: My Story." You can find it in *Prentice Hall Literature: Timeless Voices, Timeless Themes,* Gold.

After he begins to taste success, the writer returns to a box that reminds him—and his readers —of his past.

The writer concludes by stating the signifi-cance of his experi-ence and making his main point.

▶ **Critical Viewing** What relevance does Haley assign to sardines like the ones shown here? **[Connect]**

Sardines and Olives, Francis Livingston, Jerry Leff Associates, Inc.

Model From Literature • 53

Prewriting: Choosing Your Topic

Teaching Resources: Writing Support Transparency, 4-A

1. Model the Song List strategy by recalling a song and a memory that goes with it. Since students are listing their memories and associations, encourage them to freewrite as they work.

2. Display the transparency. Review the Blueprinting method and lead students through the Student Work in Progress. Visual and spatial learners might find this strategy especially useful.

3. Remind students that sometimes things are so familiar that they begin to feel unremarkable or boring. One person, for example, may see nothing unusual about dinnertime with his family. However, a friend who experiences just one meal with that family might find the experience especially entertaining or instructive.

4. Encourage students to suggest other methods to use. As students identify topics, ask them to share the method they used to select the topic.

Customize for *Interpersonal Learners*

Another strategy for choosing a topic is based on talk shows. Working in pairs, have one student interview the other about influential people or events in his or her life. Students might recall interesting stories and details once they start talking.

Customize for *ESL Students*

Suggest that students write about a memorable or rewarding experience involving their learning a new language.

4.2 Prewriting

Choosing Your Topic

Your life is full of stories, so you may have trouble choosing only one! On the other hand, you might think you have no experiences interesting enough to write about. Either way, the following strategies will help you select or discover a topic:

Strategies for Generating Topics

1. **Song List** Make a list of your favorite songs. For each, record the memories each song inspires. Review your list, and choose one of the ideas to develop as your topic.

2. **Blueprinting** Draw a blueprint of someplace you remember. It can be a home, park, camp, or any place you value. Label each room or area. Then, jot down words and phrases you associate with these areas. Choose one of your ideas as the topic of your narrative.

Writing Lab CD-ROM

For more help finding a topic, explore the activities and suggestions in the Choosing a Topic section of the Narration lesson.

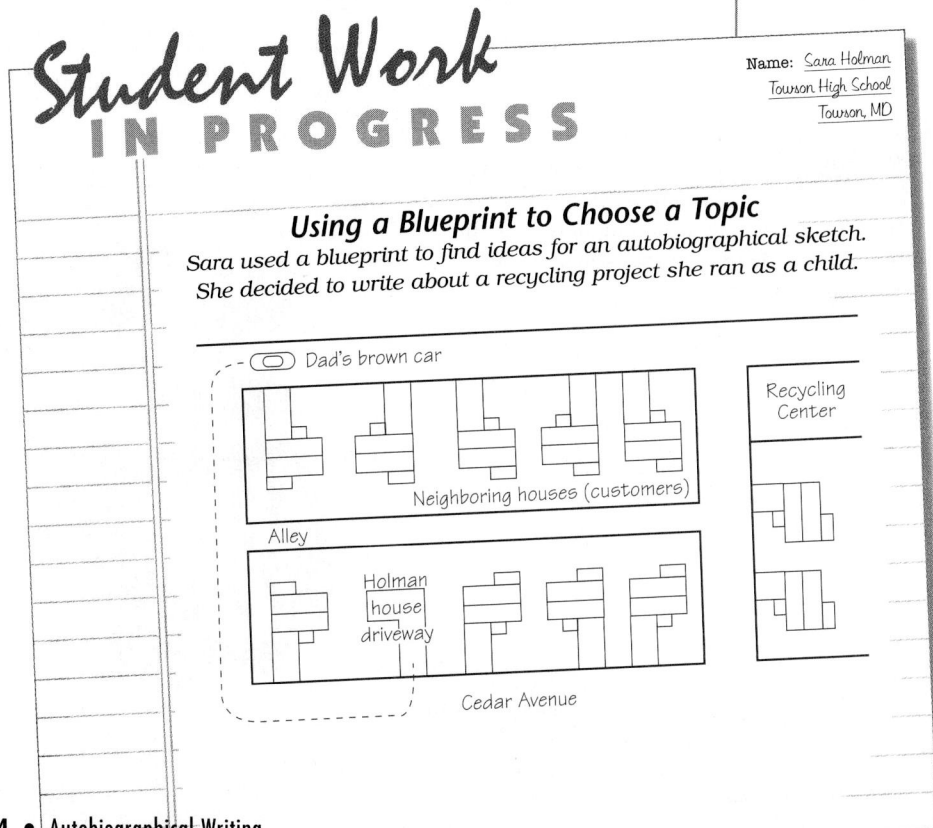

Student Work IN PROGRESS

Name: Sara Holman
Towson High School
Towson, MD

Using a Blueprint to Choose a Topic

Sara used a blueprint to find ideas for an autobiographical sketch. She decided to write about a recycling project she ran as a child.

Dad's brown car

Neighboring houses (customers)

Alley

Holman house driveway

Cedar Avenue

Recycling Center

54 • Autobiographical Writing

⏱ TIME AND RESOURCE MANAGER

Resources
Print: Writing Support Transparency, 4A–C
Technology: Writing Lab CD-ROM, Narration; Writing Support Activity Book, 4–1

In-Depth Coverage	Accelerated Pace
• Cover pp. 54–57 in class. • Work through Song List and Blueprinting activity with the class. Use the Blueprinting Transparency on page 54 in Writing Support Transparencies. • Use the Responding to Fine Art transparency to generate additional topics. • Do the timeline activity in class.	• Discuss strategies for generating topics. • Have students work independently to choose and narrow their topics. • Have students work with partners to focus on audience, purpose, and gathering details.

TOPIC BANK

If you are having trouble choosing a topic, consider these possibilities:

1. **Account of a Competition** Recall some particularly exciting competition that you witnessed or in which you participated. Write an autobiographical narrative that focuses on your reactions to the outcome of the competition.

2. **Anecdote About a Humorous Experience** Tell the story of a humorous mix-up or misunderstanding that you have experienced. In addition to details showing what happened, include your thoughts and feelings about the event.

Responding to Fine Art

Travelling Carnival, John Sloan, National Museum of American Art

3. *Travelling Carnival* may remind you of summer adventures or weekends of fun. In an autobiographical essay, describe an event this painting brings to mind. Like the artist, capture the excitement and atmosphere of your experience.

Responding to Literature

4. In Robert Frost's poem, "The Road Not Taken," the speaker reflects on an important decision. Read the poem, and use a quotation from it to inspire an essay about a time that you chose to follow an unusual or unexpected path. You can find this poem in *Prentice Hall Literature: Timeless Voices, Timeless Themes,* Gold.

☑ Cooperative Writing Opportunity

5. **Group Autobiography** Work with a group to tell the narrative of a shared experience, such as a field trip or other school event. Some members can create a timeline of the events, others can interview one another for eyewitness accounts, and some can create pictures and captions to highlight the important moments of the experience.

Prewriting • 55

Prewriting: Narrowing Your Topic; Considering Your Audience and Purpose

1. Discuss why it is important to narrow topics. Ask students which is a more realistic assignment to tackle, an essay entitled "The Story of My Life" or "A Ninth Grader's Important Choice"? Have students defend their choices.

2. Explain to students that the purpose of Invisible Writing is to turn off the editor or judge in our minds. Without viewing what they write, they are more likely to sneak past the judgmental part of their minds that dismisses ideas before they have had a chance to form.

3. After students have worked through the Invisible Writing activity, have them review their work with an open mind, circling nuggets of ideas that could be worked into an autobiographical essay.

4. Discuss with students several reasons for considering their audience. Beyond the general reasons stated in the text, having a specific person in mind can be a useful tool in freeing up their narrative voice. Students can write as if they are telling the story to that person, which can help keep the language immediate and fresh.

5. Ask students the following question to help them consider the purpose of their essays. Beyond the classroom assignment, why are you writing? Some possible reasons: to tell a story, to understand an event in their lives, to amuse, to instruct. Tell students that their writing will be more engaging and convincing if it has a meaningful purpose.

Critical Viewing

Connect Students may suggest that informal language would best suit an audience of peers.

Narrowing Your Topic

An autobiographical narrative is like putting a moment of your life under a magnifying glass. By enlarging a single moment or event, you make visible the unique qualities of the event that might otherwise go unseen. Narrow your topic so that you can describe and analyze it effectively. One way to narrow your topic is to use "invisible writing."

Use Invisible Writing to Narrow a Topic

If you can't see what you are writing as you write, you are more likely to write freely and continuously, concentrating on your ideas. Use the following steps to complete an invisible-writing exercise.

1. To prepare to write, slip a piece of carbon paper between two sheets of lined paper. Use a pen with the cap on or an empty ballpoint pen. Alternatively, start a new writing file on a word processor and turn the monitor off.

2. Write freely and continuously about your general topic for five minutes. Allow your thoughts to wander within the limits of the general topic, and note whatever ideas come to mind.

3. When you are finished, reveal what you have written. Review your notes, and circle key ideas that interest you.

4. Narrow your topic by choosing one moment, event, or detail that was most memorable or significant. Use this as the focus of your autobiographical writing.

Considering Your Audience and Purpose

Identify Your Audience Your audience is the person or people who will read your work. Their expectations and knowledge should influence your writing. For example, if you are sharing a story with your grandparents, you may need to define some terms they may not know, but you won't necessarily need to describe your family in full detail.

Refine Your Purpose Your purpose is your reason for writing. Look at these specific purposes and suggestions. Then, consider your goal for writing, and include language and ideas to achieve it.

- **To entertain** Include descriptions of situations or events that were especially funny.

- **To reflect** Focus on an event that is completed, and include information about how you have changed as a result of your experiences.

▼ Critical Viewing If you were writing for an audience of your peers, what level of language might you use to address them? [Connect]

56 • Autobiographical Writing

☑ **ONGOING ASSESSMENT: Monitor and Reinforce**

If students have difficulty narrowing their topics, try the following option.

In addition to the invisible writing strategy, students can create concept webs to help them narrow their topics. Have students write the general topic in the center oval of their webs.

Then have them identify ideas related to this general topic and record them in the outer ovals. Students can then choose one or two of these details as the focus for their writing.

Gathering Details

Once you have chosen an incident on which to focus, gather details to bring the experience to life. Consider reviewing photographs or journals to gather details for your writing. You may even want to talk to relatives or friends to learn more about the events or experiences you'll narrate. To help focus your work, examine your topic by making a timeline of key events.

Make a Timeline

Create a detailed record of events by making a timeline. Write down the first event or incident related to the subject of your narrative. Record each event in the relative order each occurred.

Writing Lab CD-ROM

To help find the appropriate words to describe your setting, use the Setting Profile and the Sensory Word Bins in the Narration lesson.

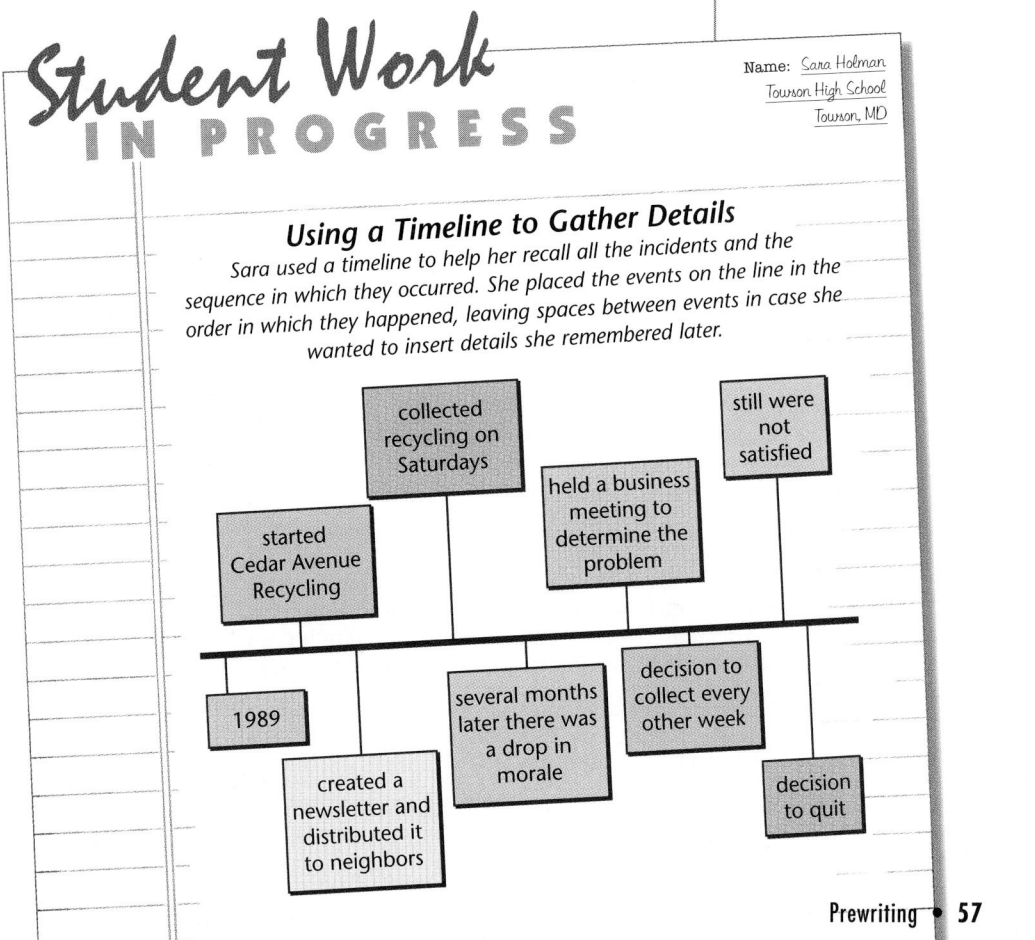

Student Work
IN PROGRESS

Name: *Sara Holman*
Towson High School
Towson, MD

Using a Timeline to Gather Details
Sara used a timeline to help her recall all the incidents and the sequence in which they occurred. She placed the events on the line in the order in which they happened, leaving spaces between events in case she wanted to insert details she remembered later.

- collected recycling on Saturdays
- still were not satisfied
- held a business meeting to determine the problem
- started Cedar Avenue Recycling
- 1989
- several months later there was a drop in morale
- decision to collect every other week
- created a newsletter and distributed it to neighbors
- decision to quit

Prewriting • 57

Step-by-Step Teaching Guide

Prewriting: Gathering Details
Teaching Resources: Writing Support Transparency 4C; Writing Support Activity Book 4-1

1. Discuss why details such as the taste of a meal or the scent of a house can play an important role in autobiographical writing.

2. Discuss with students that the events in a story do not need to be told in chronological order but that writers need to know the sequence of events before they begin to write.

3. Review with students the Student Work in Progress and display the transparency as an example of using a timeline to gather details.

4. Give students copies of the blank organizer for them to use in gathering details.

Integrating Social Studies Skills

Suggest that students use social studies books to find examples of timelines and other graphic organizers, as well as to learn more about providing contexts for events in a story.

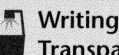 **TIME SAVERS!**

Writing Support Transparencies
Use the transparencies for Chapter 4 to teach these strategies.

Writing Support Activity Book
Use the graphic organizers for Chapter 4 to facilitate these strategies.

Drafting: Shaping Your Writing

1. Review the chain of events as presented on this page: conflict, rising action, climax, and conclusion.

2. Ask students to identify the conflict, rising action, climax, and conclusion in "The Shadowland of Dreams."

   • conflict: his decision to move to New York and become a writer

   • rising action: the people he meets, his background in the Coast Guard

   • climax: his decision to turn down a secure job and his taking stock of his life

   • conclusion: selling *Roots*; looking at the case on his wall

3. After reviewing Haley's essay, ask students to look at their topic not just as a chronology of events but as a story that must build in drama. Have them identify the conflict, rising action, climax, and conclusion in their own stories.

4.3 Drafting

Once you've done all your prewriting work, use the drafting stage to give shape to the details. Arrange the details you have gathered into a logical order that leads up to the turning point of your narrative—the moment of decision or insight.

Shaping Your Writing

Identify Your Main Point

Identify the turning point around which your details will be organized. To help you identify your turning point, think about why your topic experience is memorable or significant to you. It may be that you learned something from the experience or that the experience changed the way you look at life. Ask yourself the questions that follow. Then, use your answers to help you recognize the moment that moves your narrative forward.

• **What have I learned?**

• **What do I want my audience to understand?**

Once you have identified the main point of your narrative, begin organizing details to communicate it.

Organize to Convey Your Main Point

You will probably want to organize the events of your narrative in chronological, or time, order. While you may want to include many episodes of your experience, remember that not every event is of equal importance. As you review the details you have gathered, look for the following narrative elements to include in your draft:

Conflict Identify the problem that set the events in motion. Introduce the conflict at the beginning of your narrative. Provide details and comments that show the event as the root of the narrative.

Rising Action Several events will probably occur between the introduction of your narrative and the climax, or most significant moment. These events should build on one another to create tension in the narrative. Organize them in chronological order to give your readers a context for understanding the conflict or insight that is at the heart of your narrative.

Climax The turning point in your narrative, the climax, is the moment in which you make a decision or a realization that changes your outlook or your situation.

Conclusion After the climax of the narrative, include a reflection that provides insight about your experience.

Writing Lab CD-ROM

Use the Audio-Annotated Literary Models that show different ways to organize a narrative. You can find them in the Narration lesson.

Learn More

For more instruction on the elements of storytelling, see Chapter 5.

⏱ TIME AND RESOURCE MANAGER

Resources
Print: Writing Support Transparency 4-D
Technology: Writing Lab CD-ROM, Narration

In-Depth Coverage	Accelerated Pace
• Cover pp. 58–59. • Work through organizing events with students. • Have students write their draft in class. • Use the transparency to demonstrate the technique of using thought shots to elaborate. **Option** Have students work independently or in small groups using the Writing Lab CD-ROM.	• Have students review pp. 58–59 independently, then write their first drafts. • Respond to individual drafting issues as needed.

Providing Elaboration

As you draft your narrative, elaborate to help readers understand the significance of your experience. Provide details of what you thought and felt to allow readers to see the experience from your perspective.

Use Thought Shots to Elaborate

Cut from colored paper several "thought shot" balloons like the one shown on this page. After you complete each episode in your draft, slide a balloon down your draft as you look for places to add details about your reactions or thoughts. When you find a place, write the details on the balloon and tape or clip it in the margin where you want to make an addition. To strengthen your writing, include the ideas in your next draft.

☞ Challenge

Whenever possible, provide sensory details that appeal to the five senses. This will enrich your writing and help your readers experience the events you are narrating.

Student Work
IN PROGRESS

Name: *Sara Holman*
Towson High School
Towson, MD

Elaborating With Thought Shots
Sara intensifies the conflict by providing more information about what her narrator was thinking.

However, as time passed, company morale began to drop drastically. I called an executive meeting. We gathered on the driveway and sat in a circle. Will spoke first: "I hate this junk. We have to work really hard, and we only get paid ten cents a bag! That's nothing! I need time to work on my new invention—a hovering skateboard—and this is getting me nowhere."

> When I heard these comments, I realized I felt the same way. When was I going to finish my friendship bracelet?

Next, Jane shared her opinion: "I hate it, too. Every single Saturday, I have to do all this work. I just wanna play. I never even have time to play house with you, Sara."

I gave an executive order. We stopped going every Saturday, and, instead . . .

Drafting • 59

If you observe that students are having trouble providing significant or pertinent details for their narratives, try the following strategy.

Have students work in pairs to examine each other's draft. Students should read their partner's draft, indicating points in which more details would be beneficial.

Step-by-Step Teaching Guide

Drafting: Providing Elaboration

Teaching Resources: Writing Support Transparency 4-D

1. Use the transparency to show students how "thought shots" look in practice. Point out why Sara added the thought shots where she did.

2. See that students understand that the thought shots technique allows them to focus on the structure of their narrative; they can add detail later through elaboration. Have them look at each event, asking how they can add *physical* detail: look, taste, feel, smell, sound; and *emotional* detail: How did it feel? Were they happy, sad, confused, excited, numb?

Customize for
Less Advanced Students

Help students compile a list of adjectives that can be used to express each sense: *sight, sound, taste, touch, smell.* Have students work in small groups. Each group can focus on one sense and share their list of adjectives, which they can then use in their thought shots.

Elaboration Tip

In autobiographical writing there should be a balance between physical and emotional details. Too many physical details make a story seem like a vocabulary exercise. Too many emotional details get the reader lost inside the narrator's mind at the cost of the setting of the narrative. Remind students to try to create a balance in their details so the reader will have a good sense of both the story's plot and the narrator's feelings.

⏱ TIME SAVERS!

Writing Support Transparencies
Use the transparencies for Chapter 4 to teach these strategies.

Revising: Focus on Unity

1. Discuss with students that the first challenge in revising is getting sufficient distance from their writing. Sometimes, merely putting away their writing for an afternoon will help them return to their work with fresh eyes.

2. To help students identify unnecessary events in their work, ask them to recall a time when they read or listened to a story full of unnecessary details. Have them describe what effect that had on them. Then ask them what the speaker or writer could have cut to make the story more appealing.

3. Remind students that it is important to clarify relationships between events, people, and details in narratives. What is readily apparent to writers, as participants in their own narratives, might not be so apparent to readers. Have students give their essays to a classmate, asking them to draw question marks near details that need clarification.

4. Color coding events to determine their relationship to the turning point is a useful method for creating unity. Encourage students to go through their entire draft, color coding every detail and event. Mention that some details may not directly relate to the turning point, but they add humor, color, pathos, or some other characteristic to the narrative. Still, students should examine these exceptions carefully, making sure they add something of value to the narrative.

Revision Tip

It is possible that a student's autobiographical narrative describes something that happened only to him or her. It is more likely, however, that others were involved, even if only in bit parts. Suggest that students show their drafts to the other people involved. They may remember details that the writer forgot.

4.4 Revising

Revision is your chance to polish your writing. As you revise, take a fresh look at your narrative. Add details that convey your ideas more effectively. Begin revising by evaluating the overall structure of your narrative.

Revising Your Overall Structure
Focus on Unity

When you check the unity of your writing, you analyze the way all the details fit together to present one idea. Here are two ways to create unity in your narrative:

Cut Unnecessary Events The significance of the experience you are relating may be lost if you include every event that occurred. Review your draft, and eliminate any events that do not contribute to developing the main point.

Establish Relationships As a participant in the action of your narrative, you know how one event was related to another. Your readers may need some clarification. Look for places where you have moved from one event to another or one time period to another. Add explanations and transitions to clarify relationships between events.

▶ **REVISION STRATEGY**
Color-Coding to Improve Unity

Draw a box around the climax or turning point in your narrative. Then, use yellow to underline causes of the event, red to underline effects of the event, and green to highlight details that build the background, context, or tension. Then, evaluate any remaining details to see whether they should be eliminated or clarified. Use these tips to guide your revision:

Evaluate	Revise
• Does any unmarked text add to the narrative?	• Find ways to incorporate additional details to clarify the relationship of the event to the turning point.
• Do all the marked passages flow smoothly in a logical order?	• Consider reordering some passages to improve the writing.

Challenge

Take a tip from filmmakers who show only scenes or actions that add to their stories. For example, you may never see a film's main character actually working at a job unless the filmmaker can tie it to the story in a meaningful way.

⏱ TIME AND RESOURCE MANAGER

Resources
Print: Writing Support Transparencies 4-E–G
Technology: Writing Lab CD-ROM, Narration

In-Depth Coverage	Accelerated Pace
• Cover pp. 60–64. • Work through Revising with the entire class. • Use the relevant transparencies to demonstrate strategies for exploding a moment, revising word choice, and evaluating word choice. **Option** Divide the class into groups for peer review activity (p. 64).	• Assign students review pp. 60–64 independently. • Have students revise their essays independently.

Revising Your Paragraphs
Build Interest by Adding Information

Your narrative focuses on a single event or incident. To enrich each paragraph of your draft, add details that build the significance of the experience you narrate. You can do this in a number of ways:

- Add adjectives to make a word picture more vivid.
- Add dialogue to bring a scene to life.
- Add personal insights to show what you were thinking.

▶ **REVISION STRATEGY**
Exploding a Moment

Read your draft, and identify the most significant moments in the narrative. Consider paragraphs that describe conflict or episodes that build tension. For each, use a small piece of paper to expand your presentation of the moment. Jot down details to show *what*, *where*, *when*, *how*, or *why* something happened. Then, incorporate your ideas into the revised draft.

Student Work
IN PROGRESS

Name: Sara Holman
Towson High School
Towson, MD

Exploding a Moment

Sara added details to her narrative by identifying critical moments. She found an uncomfortable moment between her brother and herself. The details she added make the struggle more obvious.

"Let's go, Will! We still have five more houses!" My younger

brother and junior partner responded to my urging. *by sticking out his tongue*

He and I were not getting along too well. *because we were doing hard work*

Several months earlier, Will and I had started Cedar Avenue

Recycling.

Revising • 61

Step-by-Step Teaching Guide

Revising: Revising Your Paragraphs

Teaching Resources: Writing Support Transparency 4-E

1. Discuss with students that all events and characters in a narrative are not equal and often do not deserve the same amount of detail. Remind them to prioritize the events and people in their writing. Then they can develop the more important events and people in greater detail.

2. Display the transparency. Explain that without the addition of these details, many readers would be left wondering why Sara and her brother were not getting along. Adding these details helps clarify potentially confusing situations for readers.

3. Help students use the strategy first to identify the critical events, and then to add details. Remind students that the main idea with this strategy is to expand upon important moments in their writing.

Customize for *Verbal/Linguistic Learners*

Good writing sounds right. Let partners read their drafts aloud to one another. Then have them the discuss the places that do not "sound" right. Do they need more details? Should they be rephrased? Warn students about colloquialisms, slang, and incorrect usage, but encourage them to use their ears as a test for writing that sounds right.

✓ ONGOING ASSESSMENT: Monitor and Reinforce

If students have difficulty cutting unnecessary events or establishing relationships between paragraphs as they revise, try one of the following options.

Option 1 Have students highlight each event in their drafts. Encourage students to ask themselves how each event contributes to the overall narrative. If students have difficulty coming up with reasons, suggest that they omit the event.

Option 2 Encourage students to use a timeline, like the one they used to gather details, to map out the events in their drafts. If students find that some events do not follow each other logically, suggest that they add transitions to make the connections more clear or that they reorder the events.

⏱ TIME SAVERS!

Writing Support Transparencies
Use the transparencies for Chapter 4 to teach these strategies.

Step-by-Step Teaching Guide

Revising: Vary Sentence Length

1. Write the following example on the chalkboard and ask students to comment on how it reads:

   I went to the store. I needed to get a gift for Karla. I wanted to get something that would surprise her.

2. Ask students to suggest how to rewrite the sentences so they are varied in length and not as choppy. Elicit something like the following:

   I went to the store to get a gift for Karla. I wanted to get something that would surprise her.

3. Point out that the goal is to avoid a series of short declarative sentences that result in a monotonous rhythm.

Step-by-Step Teaching Guide

Grammar in Your Writing: Relative Pronouns

1. Explain to students that using relative pronouns to form subordinate clauses is one strategy for combining sentences.

2. Review the examples given. Read them aloud and point out to students the varied rhythm that results from using the relative pronoun to combine sentences.

3. Write the following example on the chalkboard and ask students to use relative pronouns to combine the sentences.

   We are going to the party. Suki is having it for Tomas. (We are going to the party <u>that</u> Suki is having for Tomas.)

Find It in Your Reading

There are numerous sentences in "The Shadowland of Dreams" in which the author uses relative pronouns. Since his piece is about people, it is not surprising that *who* is the relative pronoun used most. Help students identify whether the relative pronoun informs a noun or acts as one.

Find It in Your Writing

Check students' work, asking them to explain why they chose the sentence combining strategy they did.

Revising Your Sentences
Vary Sentence Length

To improve your writing, consider revising not only what you say, but how you say it. One way to improve your writing style is to eliminate a string of short, choppy sentences by combining some of them.

▶ **REVISION STRATEGY**
Combining Sentences to Vary Sentence Length

Bracket any short sentences in your draft that only provide more information about a noun or pronoun in a nearby sentence. Combine these sentences with the ones they support.

SHORT SENTENCES:	It was a great day. I'll never forget it.
COMBINED:	It was a great day that I will never forget.

Grammar in Your Writing
Relative Pronouns

A **relative pronoun** begins a subordinate clause and connects it to another idea in the sentence. The relative pronouns are *who, whom, whose, which,* and *that.*

You can combine two sentences by inserting *who, which,* or *that* in place of the subject of one sentence. Then, insert the new subordinate clause into the other sentence to modify its subject. Look at these examples.

Two Sentences: Janice sometimes teases me. She is older than I am.
Combined: Janice, who is older than I am, sometimes teases me.

You can also combine sentences by inserting *that* or *who* at the beginning of one sentence. Use the resulting clause as a noun in the other sentence.

Two Sentences: Paul sometimes forgets us. It doesn't bother me.
Combined: That Paul sometimes forgets us doesn't bother me.

Find It in Your Reading Read "The Shadowland of Dreams" on pages 50–53. Find two sentences that contain relative pronouns. Identify whether the clause introduced by the relative pronoun gives more information about a noun or acts as a noun.

Find It in Your Writing Look through your draft to find places where you have used relative pronouns. Challenge yourself to combine sentences by including at least three relative pronouns in your final draft.

For more information on using relative pronouns, see Chapter 16.

☑ ONGOING ASSESSMENT: Prerequisite Skills

If students have difficulty with pronouns, you may find it helpful to refer them to the following materials to assure coverage of prerequisite knowledge.

In the Textbook	Print Resources	Technology
Pronouns, pp. 346–355	Grammar Exercise Workbook, pp. 5–12	Language Lab CD-ROM, Nouns and Pronouns, On-Line Exercise Bank, Section 16.2

Revising Your Word Choice

Make Verbs Work for You

Strong verbs work to build vivid pictures in the minds of your readers. Use precise action verbs to communicate exactly what is happening in your narrative. Choose the most vivid action verb for your meaning. Look at these examples.

VAGUE: Urgency *moved* through us.

VIVID: Urgency *flashed* through us.

VAGUE: She *turned* the pages, looking for the coupon.

VIVID: She *flipped* the pages, looking for the coupon.

▶ REVISION STRATEGY
Circling Action Verbs

To circle the action verbs in your draft, ignore *being* verbs such as *am, is, are, was, were, be, being,* and *been.* Evaluate each circled verb to decide whether a more vivid verb might be better suited to your needs.

🅠 Learn More

For more about the difference between action and linking verbs, see Chapter 17.

Student Work IN PROGRESS

Name: Sara Holman
Towson High School
Towson, MD

Evaluating Action Verbs

In the paragraph that described how Sara and her siblings conducted their recycling business, Sara replaced vague verbs with action verbs to better convey the feeling she wanted.

Our business was fairly simple. Every Saturday morning, we ~~went with~~ *pulled* our wagon from house to house and ~~gathered~~ *collected* recycling for a mere ten cents a bag. Then, we ~~put~~ *hauled* the bags into our big brown van and Dad ~~brought~~ *drove* them to a nearby recycling center.

At first, ~~putting~~ *loading* these bags of pickle jars, milk jugs, and soup cans into our red wagon was fun.

Step-by Step-Teaching Guide

Revising: Revising Your Word Choice

Teaching Resources: Writing Support Transparency 4-F

1. Action verbs make the difference between lively writing and "just-the-facts" writing. Review with students the example on the page. Discuss the fact that *flashed* provides more action and vividness than *moved.*

2. Discuss with students that action verbs tend to be very specific. For example, *flashed* is a specific kind of movement. Remind students that highly charged action verbs such as *flash, charge, storm,* and *plow* need to be used judiciously. The sentence *He slashed through the line, bowled over the linebacker, and stormed into the end zone* suffers from too many highly charged action verbs.

3. Display the transparency. Have students discuss how Sara's revisions improve her draft.

4. Have students review their drafts, circling all action verbs. Have them give reasons why they changed to more vivid verbs.

5. Have some students read their changes in class and discuss if or how the changes improved the writing.

Customize for
ESL Students

Students learning English may have difficulty coming up with more vivid verbs. Ask them to think of synonyms in their native languages for the verbs they circled. Then have them use a bilingual dictionary to find some English equivalents of these words.

🔹 STANDARDIZED TEST PREPARATION WORKSHOP

Verbs Standardized test questions may ask students to choose the action verb that best completes the sentence. Have students review the following sentence and choose the most appropriate, vivid action verb that best completes it:

The seated soldier _____ attention when the general walked into the room.

Choose the word or group of words that best complete the sentence.

A came to   C snapped to

B stood at   D moved to

All four choices make sense in the sentence, and all have similar meanings. But only item **C** allows the reader to visualize the action.

⏲ TIME SAVERS!

 Writing Support Transparencies
Use the transparencies for Chapter 4 to teach these strategies.

Revising: Peer Review

Teaching Resources: Writing Support Transparency 4-G

1. Display the transparency to show students the process of evaluating word choice.

2. Before setting up the peer review pairs, remind students to comment first on the essay's strengths before reviewing ways it could be improved. Urge students to be polite but honest when giving suggestions for improvement.

3. Tell students that errors in grammar, punctuation, and spelling likely will be caught in the proofreading stage. Ask them to focus their attention now on content.

4. Peer review conferences can yield general points that can be helpful to the entire class. Ask students to take notes during their conferences. Later, ask students to volunteer points they think might help their classmates.

Language Highlight

Clichés A cliché is a phrase or expression that has been worn out by long use. *Cliché* comes from a French word meaning "a block of printing type." Once the type was formed into a block, it could be used over and over again in the printing process.

4.4

Peer Review

Having a peer review your work will help you identify problems in your writing that you may be too close to catch. After you have done a thorough revision on your draft, ask a peer to read it with a critical eye. To focus the review, ask your reader to identify vague words or clichés that don't communicate an idea in an interesting way.

▶ **REVISION STRATEGY**
Color-Coding Word Choice and Clichés

Make a photocopy of your draft, and give it to a peer reviewer. Ask your reader to mark imprecise words with a check and to box any clichés or overused expressions. When your peer reviewer has finished marking your writing, meet to discuss the problems the reviewer found. Consider these tips:

- Work together to share ideas about how a cliché might be replaced with a fresher expression.

- Brainstorm to list words that might be more precise than the ones you have chosen.

Consider your reviewers suggestions, but use your own judgment as you revise your draft.

Writing Lab CD-ROM

For more tips on peer reviews, see the checklist of peer revision strategies. You can find it in the Narration lesson.

Student Work **IN PROGRESS**

Name: Sara Holman
Towson High School
Towson, MD

Using Peer Revision to Evaluate Word Choice
After a peer reviewer checked vague words and boxed clichés and overused expressions, Sara used the evaluation to revise her draft.

At first, loading these bags of pickle jars, milk jugs, and soup cans into our ca̶r̶t̶ was fun. *red wagon*

However, we were soon down in the dumps again. Anxious to *as time passed, company morale began to drop drastically.* determine the cause of this problem, I gathered the troops. *called an executive meeting.*

We gathered on the driveway and sat in a circle.

 **Writing Support Transparencies**
Use the transparencies for Chapter 4 to teach these strategies.

✓ **ONGOING ASSESSMENT: Monitor and Reinforce**

If students have difficulty identifying vague words or clichés in their writing, try the following strategy.

Have students form groups and take turns reading aloud their drafts. Group members should listen for words and phrases that might need revision. Then, the students should provide the reader with viable alternatives.

4.5 Editing and Proofreading

Once you have completed revising the content of your narrative, check your draft for spelling, grammar, punctuation, and capitalization. Strive to make your final draft error-free.

Focusing on Punctuation

As you proofread, pay special attention to whether you have punctuated your sentences correctly. Look at these specific punctuation problem areas:

- **End punctuation** Check the end of each sentence to see that you have chosen the correct mark.
- **Dialogue** Review the conventions for punctuating dialogue, and confirm that you have used them correctly in your writing.
- **Commas** While a comma can create a necessary pause, it is also frequently misused. Review your draft to see whether you have inserted commas only where necessary.

⊘ Learn More

Check the rules for punctuating dialogue. You can find them in Chapter 29.

Grammar in Your Writing
Using an Exclamation Mark to Show Emotion

An **exclamation mark** can be used to signal a strong emotion or force. It can also indicate that words are spoken loudly or with intensity. Whether the emotion is enthusiasm, anger, or surprise, an exclamation mark puts power behind the words. Weigh your interpretations of these two sentences:

I found it under the sink.   I found it under the sink!

Use exclamation marks sparingly. Too many of these marks in your writing will diminish their effectiveness.

Find It in Your Reading Find an example of a sentence in "The Shadowland of Dreams," on pages 50–53, that Alex Haley has punctuated with an exclamation mark. Discuss with a partner what emotion is expressed and why it is being expressed with intensity.

Find It in Your Writing Look through your narrative to see whether there is a sentence or two that could be more effectively punctuated with an exclamation mark than with a period.

For more on end punctuation, see Chapter 29.

Editing and Proofreading • 65

⏱ **TIME AND RESOURCE MANAGER**

Resources
Print: Scoring Rubrics on Transparency, Chapter 4; Writing Assessment: Scoring Rubric and Scoring Models for Autobiographical Writing
Technology: Writing Lab CD-ROM, Narration

In-Depth Coverage	Accelerated Pace
• Cover pp. 65–68 in class. • Analyze in class the Final Draft on pp. 67–68. • Have students edit and proofread their essays in class.	• Assign pp. 65–68 for independent review. • Have students independently edit and proofread their essays. • Respond to individual editing issues as needed.

Step-by-Step Teaching Guide

Editing and Proofreading: Focusing on Punctuation

1. Some students may regard errors in punctuation, spelling, and grammar as unimportant. Impress upon students that these mistakes can distract the reader. Also, readers may assume that a writer who spells badly thinks badly too. A writer whose work is filled with punctuation or spelling errors is less credible than one who takes the time to present a polished final product.

2. Have students proofread their work. Have them take special care to check the punctuation of dialogue.

Step-by-Step Teaching Guide

Grammar in Your Writing: Exclamation Marks

1. Discuss with students that too many exclamations can make a piece of writing resemble a comic book. Their impact is reduced when they are not used judiciously. Also, they can take away from an autobiographical piece whose tone is intended to be serious.

2. Students may protest that some dialogue, reflecting reality, consists mostly of exclamations. If that is the case, show students how they can vary dialogue from direct expressions to third-person paraphrasing.

   "This poster is so cool!" screamed Janice.

   Janice screamed that the poster was cool.

Find It in Your Reading

Haley uses an exclamation point in the following sentence: *Six Thousand a year!*

Find It in Your Writing

Have students review their writing. Exclamation points might be useful in the more dramatic or emotional parts of their essays.

65

Publishing and Presenting: Building Your Portfolio

1. Have students discuss additional ways they might share their work; for example, publishing a classroom magazine, using a video camera to tape students reading their work, e-mailing it to the people mentioned in the narrative, or displaying it on a classroom or hall bulletin board.

2. Have students work in small groups to share their reflections about their writing before holding a general class discussion. Discuss with students how writing about an event or experience can change how they feel about it or remember it. Ask students to consider how the careful use of language can make even the most everyday events memorable and meaningful.

ASSESS

Teaching Resources: Scoring Rubrics on Transparency 4; Formal Assessment, Chapter 4

1. Display the Scoring Rubrics transparency and review the criteria in class.

2. Before students proceed with self-assessment, you may wish to review the Final Draft of the Student Work in Progress on pages 67–68. Have students score the Final Draft in one or more of the rubric categories. For example, how would students score the essay in terms of audience and purpose?

3. In addition to student self-assessment, you may wish to use the following assessment options:

   • score student essays yourself, using the rubric and scoring models from Writing Assessment.

   • review the Standardized Test Preparation Workshop on pages 72–73 and have students respond to a narrative writing prompt within a time limit.

   • administer the Chapter 4 test from Formal Assessment in Teaching Resources to assess students' grasp of concepts presented.

4.6 Publishing and Presenting

Consider sharing your autobiographical writing with a large or small audience. The following suggestions offer two ideas for presenting your work to others:

Building Your Portfolio

1. **Submit It to Your School Newspaper or Magazine** Talk to the editor or a faculty advisor to find out what the requirements are for submitting work. Review and revise your narrative as necessary to meet these requirements. Then, submit your work.

2. **Send an Audiotape** Record a reading of your narrative on audiotape and add music to enhance the ideas. Then, send the tape to a friend or relative who lives far from you.

Reflecting on Your Writing

Reflect on your writing process by answering the following questions in your notebook or writing journal:

• How is writing about yourself different from other kinds of writing you've done?

• In what ways did writing about an event or experience change your view of it?

Rubric for Self-Assessment

Use the following criteria to evaluate your autobiographical writing:

	Score 4	Score 3	Score 2	Score 1
Audience and Purpose	Contains details that engage the audience; provides a clear insight about an experience	Contains details appropriate for an audience; addresses a clear reason for writing	Contains few details that appeal to an audience; gives a reason for writing	Is not written for a specific audience or purpose
Organization	Organizes events to relate an interesting narrative	Presents clear sequence of events	Presents a confusing sequence of events	Presents no logical order of events
Elaboration	Contains rich details that shape vivid characters; clearly elaborates an insight	Contains details that develop character and describe setting; elaborates an insight	Contains characters and setting; provides a context for the experience	Contains few or no details to develop characters or setting; does not set experience in context
Use of Language	Uses an excellent variety of sentence beginnings; contains no errors in grammar, punctuation, or spelling	Uses a good variety of sentence beginnings; contains few errors in grammar, punctuation, and spelling	Introduces some variety in sentence beginnings; contains some errors in grammar, punctuation, and spelling	Uses monotonous pattern of sentence beginnings; has many errors in grammar, punctuation, and spelling

66 • Autobiographical Writing

☑ ONGOING ASSESSMENT: Assess Mastery

Use one of the following options to assess final drafts of students' autobiographical writing.

Self-Assessment Ask students to score their essay using the rubric provided. then have students write a paragraph reflecting on the most valuable strategy they learned in completing this essay.	**Teacher Assessment** Use the rubric and the scoring models provided in Writing Assessment, Autobiographical Writing, to score students' work.

4.7 Student Work
IN PROGRESS

FINAL DRAFT

◄ **Critical Viewing**
According to the essay, what are the benefits and drawbacks of running a recycling business? **[Interpret]**

Cedar Avenue Recycling: The Rise and Fall of a Family Business

Sara Holman
Towson High School
Towson, Maryland

The year was 1989. The relatively new field of environmental science was growing exponentially, providing countless business opportunities for one eager and determined entrepreneur. Being the risk-taker that I was, I leapt at the chance to enter the business arena, taking aim at the Fortune 500. I was nine years old.

"Let's go, Will! We still have five more houses!" My younger brother and junior partner responded to my urging by sticking out his tongue and deliberately walking more slowly. He and I were not getting along too well because, at the moment, we were sharing a less than enjoyable task.

In mock-business style, Sara introduces herself as the main character.

Teaching From the Final Draft

1. Have Sara's final draft read. You can either read it aloud or have students read it together in small groups.

2. As students read the final draft, have them use the margin notes to guide their reading. See that students identify the organizational structure: Sara builds from a conflict to a turning point to a conclusion.

continued

Critical Viewing

Interpret Students may suggest that although running a recycling business provides business experience, it takes too much time and yields little profit.

Integrating Vocabulary Skills

Have students discuss business-related jargon, such as *entrepreneur, risk-taker, Fortune 500,* or *business arena,* from the first paragraph of Sara's essay. Ask students to discuss any other examples they have heard of on TV, in newspapers, or in magazines.

67

3. Review the essay with students. Point out the use of irony in the introduction, with such phrases as *environmental science* and *Fortune 500*. Show how Sara keeps up the tone with references to *company morale* and *executive order*.

4. Ask students what they think of the essay. Do they find that the humor and irony add to or detract from it? Why? Regardless, they should understand how Sara successfully organizes her narrative to build toward the turning point.

Real-World Connection

You can use Sara's narrative as a springboard to a discussion about goals. The missing ingredient in Sara's business was the absence of realistic goals. Discuss with students the importance of goals in maintaining any enterprise. If they are not sure why you are doing something, they are more likely to give up at the first sign of trouble or conflict. Real goals get people through the hard times by keeping them focused and giving a reason for the effort.

4.7

Several months earlier, Will and I had started Cedar Avenue Recycling. I was president, and he and my sister, Jane, were employees.

Our business was fairly simple. Every Saturday morning, we pulled our wagon from house to house and collected recycling for a mere ten cents a bag. Then, we hauled the bags into our big brown van and Dad drove them to a nearby recycling center.

At first, loading these bags of pickle jars, milk jugs, and soup cans into our red wagon was fun. However, as time passed, company morale began to drop drastically. Anxious to determine the cause of this problem, I called an executive meeting. We gathered on the driveway and sat in a circle. Will spoke first: "I hate this junk. We have to work really hard, and we only get paid ten cents a bag! That's nothing! I need time to work on my new invention—a hovering skateboard—and this is getting me nowhere."

Next, Jane shared her opinion: "I hate it, too. Every single Saturday, I have to do all this work. I just wanna play. I never even have time to play house with you, Sara."

Upon hearing these comments, I realized that I felt the same. When was I going to finish that friendship bracelet I was working on? How would I earn enough money for a set of the color-changing markers that were all the rage among my fifth-grade classmates?

With these questions floating in my mind, I gave an executive order. We stopped going every Saturday, and, instead, our collections took place every other week. Also, our price of ten cents per bag doubled to twenty cents per bag. Feeling better, we all skipped off to our various activities for the remainder of the day.

The next Saturday, I realized with dread that it was collection day. Will, Jane, and I trudged off to our task, grumbling about an inconsiderate neighbor who had failed to sort the green glass from the clear. Even though we made twice our usual profit, all of us were unhappy when we finished. Will and Jane had fought the whole time, and the day was nearly over. Pondering these facts, I wondered why we still weren't satisfied.

Perhaps it was because our prices, even doubled, were not enough to yield us more than one or two dollars per person. Maybe we just didn't get along. However, I began to suspect that it was something else. I decided that none of us really wanted to spend the time this job required. After another executive meeting, my employees and I decided officially to close Cedar Avenue Recycling. Although I never did get to buy color-changing markers, my most precious resource—time—was once again at my disposal. The Fortune 500 would just have to wait.

68 • Autobiographical Writing

Here, Sara includes details about the other significant people who shared the experience she is narrating.

Sara uses dialogue to reveal the conflict that develops in her family.

Details of Sara's thoughts and feelings show how the experience caused conflict in her mind, too.

The decision Sara makes at this turning point indicates that her experience has changed her outlook.

Sara concludes with a statement that captures the insight she gained from the experience.

Connected Assignment *Firsthand Biography*

In an autobiography, the writer tells his or her own life story. In contrast, the writer of a biography tells the story of someone else's life. A **firsthand biography** combines the writer's personal observations from an interaction or knowledge of the subject with objective information gathered through research to create an engaging narrative. Because the writer knows the subject, a firsthand biography takes on a more intimate tone than a formal biography does.

The following writing process steps will help you write a firsthand biography of someone you know.

Prewriting Choose your subject by thinking about the people in your life. Consider the people who have been special to you, and decide whose life or personality would be interesting to address.

Once you've chosen your biography subject, focus on a moment that especially captures his or her spirit or that particularly impresses you. Complete a timeline like the one shown here to gather details about a specific period in your subject's life. Use the timeline to spark ideas and observations about your subject's behavior, appearance, and attitude.

Initiating Event

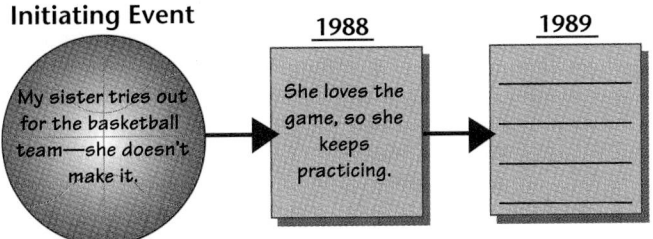

1988 She loves the game, so she keeps practicing.

1989

My sister tries out for the basketball team—she doesn't make it.

▲ **Critical Viewing**
How would your own interactions with a person change the way you describe them to others? **[Analyze]**

Drafting Refer to your notes as you draft your biography. Try to balance objective facts with personally observed data as you include details that bring your subject to life. Keep your relationship with the subject clear by writing in the first person and using possessive phrases such as *my friend*.

Revising and Editing As you review your biography, look for places where you could elaborate your own interpretations and impressions. Check that you've maintained first-person narration throughout. Replace overused verbs with more precise and engaging language.

Publishing and Presenting After you have completed your firsthand biography, put the essay and selected photographs together in a booklet to share with classmates or your subject.

Connected Assignment: Firsthand Biography • **69**

Lesson Objectives

1. To write a firsthand biography appropriate to audience and purpose.
2. To use prewriting strategies to generate ideas.
3. To develop a draft by organizing content and refining style.
4. To publish a firsthand biography in book form with photographs.

Step-by-Step Teaching Guide

Firsthand Biography

Teaching Resources: Writing Support Transparency 4-H; Writing Support Activity Book 4-2

1. Remind students that their biographies will be a blend of their own personal knowledge of the subject and factual information about this person. Students should try to think of an event from this person's life that they will be able to address in a short essay.
2. Suggest that students review strategies from Chapter 4.
3. Display the transparency to show students how one person used a time line to organize his or her ideas.
4. Give students copies of the blank organizer for them to use in gathering details and organizing these details as they begin their drafts.

Critical Viewing

Analyze Students may say that interacting with a person provides you with firsthand knowledge of what that person is like.

Lesson Objectives

1. To evaluate media presentations.
2. To analyze ideas as represented in various art forms.
3. To write a movie proposal.

Step-by-Step Teaching Guide

Examining Ideas Represented in Various Art Forms

1. Choose one of the Spotlight elements for class discussion, or have students work individually or in groups on the element of their choice. Give students the initiative to find the necessary videotapes, books, and pictures.

2. Have interested students research the troubled history of the making of Welles's film. There are also a few documentaries and TV movies that have been made about this subject.

3. Interested students can read Campbell's work, as well as research other literary works that deal with the myth of the hero. Encourage students to present their findings to the class.

4. Have students use the library and the Internet to search for photographs of and information regarding the Hearst Castle. A number of documentary films have also been made about this spectacular home.

Viewing and Representing

Activity Remind students to keep their audience and purpose in mind when writing their proposals. Encourage students to focus on aspects of their subject's life that would appeal to audiences.

Critical Viewing

Respond Students may mention the fact that the figure is looking down upon the viewer from a higher spot, as well as the larger-than-life feeling created by his image in the poster in the background.

Spotlight on the Humanities

Examining Ideas Represented in Various Art Forms

Focus on Film: *Citizen Kane*

A popular form of contemporary storytelling is filmmaking. Nominated for nine Academy Awards, the 1941 film *Citizen Kane* remains one of the treasures of American motion pictures. Directed by and starring Orson Welles, the film tells the story of Charles Foster Kane, a newspaper tycoon. Through flashbacks, a reporter interviews the people in Kane's life in an attempt to understand the man. The film explores the meaning of success, the values society embraces in heroes, and the myths behind our cultural icons. Many believe *Citizen Kane* is the best film ever made. It is widely thought to be based on the life of millionaire William Randolph Hearst.

▲ **Critical Viewing** How does this film still from *Citizen Kane* make the subject appear important? **[Respond]**

Literature Connection *Citizen Kane* suggests that wealth is one factor that creates an American hero. Assumptions like this sparked American thinker Joseph Campbell (1904–1987) to study the concept of the hero. In 1949, he published *The Hero with a Thousand Faces*, addressing the "myth of the hero" and explaining that all cultures share a pattern of heroic journey. According to Campbell, this single pattern appears in their myths.

Design Connection William Randolph Hearst—the man who many believe was the inspiration for *Citizen Kane*—lived like a hero in a mansion that blended several architectural styles. The Hearst Castle was filled with tapestries, art, furniture, statues, and other architectural items imported to the site from many parts of the world. This lavish compound took more than twenty-five years to complete and has become one of the most popular tourist attractions in California.

Autobiographical Writing Activity: Movie Proposal
Interview someone you admire—your mom, a teacher, a friend, a grandparent—about their life, hopes, and dreams. Then, in a memo to a movie producer, explain why your subject would make a great topic for a feature film.

Media and Technology Skills

Using a Video Camera to Communicate Specific Messages

Activity: Generating a Video Postcard

While writing a letter is one way to communicate your experiences with friends, you might enjoy sharing the news of your daily life with a video postcard. Use a video camera to capture daily experiences or special moments visually. Once you master this technology, you'll find endless ways to connect with the people in your life.

Learn About It Plan your postcard the same way you would a written letter. Decide who will receive your finished product, and focus on events they'd like to share. Capitalize on the visual nature of video to blend action images with sound and narration. For example, video lets you show events as they occur rather than just telling about them afterward. However, what you see and hear as you film is what your viewer will get, so make it engaging; avoid pitfalls that will result in poor sound quality or bad pictures.

Plan It If you want to script your video postcard, sketch out your scene ideas on a storyboard chart like this one. In each box, jot down the pictures or footage to include. Then, note ideas for narration to explain and link the scenes.

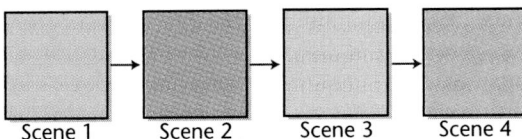

Alternatively, you may choose to create a more spontaneous videotape. In that case, identify and list a few elements or scenes you will want to include. Then, use these ideas to guide the filming.

Tape It Study the taping techniques in the boxed side column on this page. Then, use a video camera to film your postcard. View your final product before you send it.

Steps to Great Videos

Technical Tips
- Read camera directions to familiarize yourself with special features such as zoom.
- Check for tape, and rewind if necessary.
- Use a new tape if possible, and carry a backup.
- Test tape for both visual images and sound.
- Check batteries.

Taping Tips
- Consider showing still images such as maps to orient viewers to your movements within the postcard.
- Vary images to include interviews, action scenes, and long shots that establish location.
- Use narration to link scenes as you fade from one section to another.

Lesson Objectives

1. To create a video postcard.
2. To examine the effect of media to construct a perception of reality.
3. To recognize how visual techniques convey messages in media.

Step-by-Step Teaching Guide

Using a Video Camera to Communicate Specific Messages

Teaching Resources: Writing Support Transparency 4-I; Writing Support Activity Book 4-3

1. Review the technical and taping tips with students. If any of the students in the class are familiar with video technology, you may want to have them assist you in teaching the rest of the class.

2. Display the transparency and talk with students about how to map out their video postcards.

3. Give students copies of the blank organizer, encouraging them to use it to map out the scenes they wish to shoot.

4. Remind students that there may often be differences between what they think they are shooting and what the footage looks like. Before students begin shooting their postcards, have them spend time familiarizing themselves with the features of the video camera. Encourage them to shoot some test scenes first.

Customize for
Interpersonal Learners

You may want to divide the class into small groups. Each member of the group can be responsible for a different task in the production of each member's postcard. One student can operate the camera, another student can direct the cameraperson, and so on.

71

Lesson Objectives

1. To respond to a narrative writing prompt.
2. To use recursive writing processes to generate ideas, develop a draft, and then revise, edit, and proofread.

Responding to Narrative Writing Prompts

1. Have students review the criteria by which their responses will be evaluated. Remind students to keep these criteria in mind as they draft their responses.

2. Have a volunteer read aloud the writing prompt to the class. Ask students to identify the form their writing will take, the audience for their writing, and their purpose for writing. Remind them to keep these factors in mind when responding to the prompt. Students should see that their writing will take the form of a narrative essay that will involve both narrative and persuasive forms of writing and that will be written for an audience of a school board.

Standardized Test Preparation Workshop

Responding to Narrative Writing Prompts

Some sections of standardized tests measure your ability to write using narrative elements and techniques. Your writing will be evaluated according to these criteria:

- Vary word and sentence choice for the purpose and audience named in the response.
- Choose a method of organization that suits your topic.
- Use appropriate transitions to make the connections among your ideas clear to readers.
- Elaborate your experience through the effective use of description, characterization, and other details.
- Use correct grammar, spelling, and punctuation.

When writing for a timed test, plan to devote a specified amount of time to prewriting, drafting, revising, and proofreading.

Following is an example of a narrative writing prompt. Use the suggestions on the following page to help you respond. The clocks next to each stage show a suggested percentage of time to devote to each stage.

Sample Writing Situation

> Whether you volunteer to clean up the environment, help an elderly relative, or raise money for school functions, you are involved in enriching your community. Volunteering is such a central part of everyday life that many schools are incorporating it into the curriculum as coursework that must be performed before graduation. Decide whether you support a plan to make volunteerism a graduation requirement.

Test Tips

- Before drafting your narrative, make sure that the details you have gathered support your response to the prompt. If not, eliminate them.
- Even if a prompt asks you to describe a personal experience, keep your audience and purpose in mind. Avoid topics or details that may not be appropriate for the writing situation.

◇ TEST-TAKING TIP

Remind students that one important key to effective writing is good, solid organization. Students should make outlines to help them organize their thoughts before they draft their responses. Students should remember to support each of their main points, since they want to be as persuasive as possible in trying to get the school board to mandate or not mandate volunteerism. Suggest that students use some of the writing strategies they have learned in this chapter to help them with all of the stages in the writing process.

Challenge students to write a brief description of how their responses would be different if the audience for their essays was a group of their peers.

Prewriting

Allow about one quarter of your time for prewriting.

Gather Details Begin to gather information from your personal experiences with community service to use in your writing.

- If you have volunteer experience, list people, places, and events in your experience that you may want to use as support.
- If you have no experience with community service, make a list to identify the reasons that have kept you from it, or jot down the opportunities you would want to pursue if you could.

Drafting

Allow approximately half of your time for drafting.

Plan an Organization You may choose to organize events of your experience in chronological order. Frame your narrative with an introduction and conclusion that present your opinion about volunteerism.

Use Persuasive Language Because the writing prompt asks you to take a position, use persuasive language to convey your opinion. Words like *best* and *rewarding* can support a positive response. Words like *wasteful* and *awful* convey a negative one. Whatever language you use, support your opinion with facts.

Elaborate With Personal Experience To effectively support your view of community service and the schools, include details that elaborate on your own experiences. Whether or not you have done community work, elaborate your ideas with specific examples that support your position on making volunteerism part of the curriculum.

Revising, Editing, and Proofreading

Allow about one quarter of your time to revise, edit, and proofread your paper.

Check Unity Review your draft to see that all paragraphs and details contribute to your main idea. Delete information that does not support your writing goal.
In some cases, the addition of a transitional word, phrase, or sentence may improve the unity of your work.

Make Corrections Read your response for errors in spelling, grammar, and punctuation. When making changes, delete text with a single line and use a caret [^] to indicate the places you want to insert material.

5 Time and Resource Manager

In-Depth Lesson Plan

		LESSON FOCUS	PRINT AND MEDIA RESOURCES
DAY 1		**Introduction to Narrative Short Stories** Students learn key elements of short stories and analyze the Model From Literature (pp. 74–77).	*Writers at Work* **Videotape**, Narration *Writing Lab* **CD-ROM**, Narration
DAY 2		**Prewriting** Students choose and narrow a topic, consider their audience and purpose, and gather information (pp. 78–81).	**Teaching Resources** *Writing Support Transparencies*, 5-A–C; *Writing Support Activity Book*, 5-1
DAY 3		**Drafting** Students organize their ideas and write their first drafts (pp. 82–83).	**Teaching Resources** *Writing Support Transparencies*, 5-D
DAY 4		**Revising** Students revise their drafts in terms of overall structure, paragraphs, sentences, and word choice (pp. 84–88).	**Teaching Resources** *Writing Support Transparencies*, 5-E–F; *Writing Support Activity Book*, 5-2
DAY 5		**Editing and Proofreading; Publishing and Presenting** Students check their work for accuracy and correctness and present their final drafts (pp. 89–90).	**Teaching Resources** *Scoring Rubrics on Transparency*, Chapter 5; Writing Assessment: Scoring Rubrics and Scoring Models for Short Story

Accelerated Lesson Plan

		LESSON FOCUS	PRINT AND MEDIA RESOURCES
DAY 1		**Drafting** Students review characteristics for short story writing, select topics, and write drafts (pp. 74–83).	**Teaching Resources** *Writing Support Transparencies*, 5-A–D; *Writing Support Activity Book*, 5-1–2 *Writing Lab* **CD-ROM**, Narration *Writers at Work* **Videotape**, Narration
DAY 2		**Revising to Presenting** Students work individually or with peers to revise, edit, and proofread their work for presentation (pp. 84–90).	**Teaching Resources** *Writing Support Transparencies*, 5-E–F; *Writing Support Activity Book*, 5-2; *Scoring Rubrics on Transparency*, Chapter 5; Writing Assessment: Scoring Rubrics and Scoring Models for Short Story

Options for Adapting Lesson Plans

HOMEWORK

Have students complete any stage of the lesson for homework.

TECHNOLOGY

Students can complete any stage of the lesson on computer. Have them print out their completed work.

FEATURES

Extend coverage with Connected Assignment (p. 94), Spotlight on the Humanities (p. 96), and the Standardized Test Preparation Workshop (p. 98).

INTEGRATED SKILLS COVERAGE

Integrating Grammar
Active vs. Passive Voice, SE p. 87
Punctuating Dialogue, SE p. 89

Reading/Writing Connection
Reading Strategy, SE p. 76
Writing Strategy, SE p. 77

Reading
Responding to Literature, SE pp. 77, 79

Real-World Connection
ATE p. 84

Viewing and Representing
Critical Viewing, SE pp. 74, 76, 85, 91, 93, 94, 96
Integrating Representing Skills, SE p. 84

BLOCK SCHEDULING

Pacing Suggestions
For 90-minute Blocks
- Have students complete the Prewriting and Drafting stages in a single period.
- Focus one class period on Revising and Editing and Publishing and Presenting. Allow at least 30 minutes for peer revision.

Resources for Varying Instruction
- *Writing Lab* **CD-ROM** If your students have access to hardware, a 90-minute block provides an ideal opportunity for students to work on computer.
- *Writers at Work* **Videotape** Show the Short Story segment in class.

Professional Development Support
- *How to Manage Instruction in the Block* This Teaching Resource provides management and activity suggestions.

ASSESSMENT SUPPORT

Standardized Test Preparation SE p. 98; ATE p. 98

Standardized Test Preparation Workshop, pp. 9–10

Scoring Rubrics on Transparency, Ch. 5

Formal Assessment, Ch. 5

Writing Assessment and Portfolio Management

MEDIA AND TECHNOLOGY

For the Student
- *Writing Lab* **CD-ROM**, Narration

For the Teacher
- *Writers at Work* **Videotape**, Narration
- *Resource Pro* **CD-ROM**

MEETING INDIVIDUAL NEEDS

Less Advanced Students ATE pp. 86, 95, 99; See also Ongoing Assessments ATE pp. 75, 79, 81, 83, 85, 87, 90

More Advanced Students ATE pp. 82, 99

ESL Students ATE p. 77

Bodily/Kinesthetic Learners ATE pp. 83, 95

Visual/Spatial Learners ATE p. 97

WRITING AND GRAMMAR WEBSITE

The Interactive Writing and Grammar Website provides a wide array of support for students, teachers, and parents. Writing support includes:

- Interactive revision checkers
- Scoring rubrics with complete models

phwg.phschool.com

LITERATURE CONNECTIONS

Related selections from *Prentice Hall Literature: Timeless Voices, Timeless Themes*, Gold:
"Uncle Marcos," Isabel Allende, SE p. 77
"I Have a Dream," Martin Luther King, Jr., SE p. 79

Lesson Objectives

1. To understand the characteristics of narrative short story writing.

2. To choose and narrow a short story topic.

3. To consider audience and purpose in developing a short story.

4. To apply strategies for gathering details.

5. To draft a short story with a first- or third-person narrator and sentences that "show" rather than "tell."

6. To evaluate and revise the short story draft to strengthen the conflict.

7. To analyze the paragraphs and ensure that the dialogue sounds realistic.

8. To rewrite passive voice sentences in the active voice.

9. To use replace vague nouns with more specific ones.

10. To edit, proofread, and publish a short story.

Critical Viewing

Hypothesize Students may say that the photo would inspire a story about an athlete.

5 Narration
Short Story

▲ Critical Viewing
What kind of story
might be inspired by
this sculpture?
[Hypothesize]

Stories in Everyday Life

Narratives are stories—something you hear and tell every day. Some are true: They're a way to share the events of your latest experiences, and they're a way to reveal the events in the world. These stories are **nonfiction.** But not all stories have to be true. When the stories are made up, they are called *fiction,* and they can take on a life all their own. You see, hear, and imagine fictional stories when you watch television sit-coms, read novels, or daydream about becoming a movie star. One kind of imaginative narration is the **short story**—a written piece of fiction that follows specific rules and has its own unique characteristics.

74 • Narration

Resources
Technology: Writers at Work videotape

In-Depth Coverage	Accelerated Pace
• Cover pp. 74–75 in class. • Show Short Story section of the Writers at Work video. • Read literature excerpt (pp. 76–77) in class and use it to review short story elements with students. • Discuss short stories students enjoy or have read in class.	• Discuss the elements of the short story and the different types of short story in class. • Assign Model from Literature for independent reading.

Providing Elaboration

Plan the flow of your story, and then fill in details to create a complete picture for your reader. Remember that you are constructing a specific effect. Choosing what to tell and what not to tell is an important ingredient of good storytelling.

Show, Don't Tell

If you find yourself writing sentences that simply tell readers what you want them to think, challenge yourself to be a better storyteller. To do this, provide the instances that will make the writing speak for itself. Use characters' actions, details of setting, and dialogue to show readers what you want them to see.

Follow up "telling" sentences with "showing" ones. Look at this example:

TELLING:	My four-year-old brother Jake loves me.
SHOWING WITH INSTANCES:	For instance, when I come home from school, my four-year-old brother, Jake, runs out of the house, hugs me, and gives me a kiss.

🌼 **Grammar and Style Tip**

While you want to make the world of your story vivid, be especially careful not to bog down your writing with too many adjectives and adverbs. Keep the action of your story moving, and add description with the nouns and verbs you use.

Student Work IN PROGRESS

Name: David Friggle
Columbia High School
Maplewood, NJ

Using Elaboration to Show Instead of Tell

By adding examples of the confusion the narrator felt, David shows his audience more about the character and the conflict.

The initial shock of being told about a death quickly subsided, to be replaced with confusion.

PROVIDE INSTANCES

Who was Great-Uncle Paul? Was he nice? Had I ever met him? Why don't I remember him? Should I remember him? Thoughts of my great-uncle Paul stayed in my mind until I was asleep.

Drafting • 83

Step-by-Step Teaching Guide

Drafting: Providing Elaboration; Show, Don't Tell
Teaching Resources: Writing Support Transparency 5-D

1. Remind students of the indirect characterization used in "The Appalachian Trail." Point out that this is a good example of "showing." Here, the writer allows the characters' words and actions to speak for themselves.

2. Display the transparency. Ask students to suggest other ways that David could *show* the transition from shock to confusion felt by the narrator. (Possible response: description of the narrator's actions: "My face froze when I heard the words 'he's dead.' Then, as the tension slipped away, questions began to enter my mind.")

Customize for Bodily/Kinesthetic Learners

Have partners explore the different ways a writer can show rather than tell. Write the following "tell" sentence on the chalkboard:

Harrison was disappointed at his friend for breaking his new snowboard.

Have one student brainstorm for and model ways that Harrison might act, things that he might say, body movements he might perform, and facial expressions he might produce. Have him or her ask the partner to create sentences for the words spoken and the actions performed. Have students exchange roles and continue the activity with additional "tell" sentences.

☑ **ONGOING ASSESSMENT: Monitor and Reinforce**

Students sometimes have problems recognizing effective "showing" sentences. If you think this is the case with your students, try the following strategy.

Have students work in pairs. Each student writes down his or her best "showing" sentences on note cards or self-sticking notes and asks the other student to place them in order of strongest to weakest. Students can then discuss the effectiveness of their "showing" sentences before continuing to draft.

⏱ **TIME SAVERS!**

 Writing Support Transparencies
Use the transparencies for Chapter 5 to teach these strategies.

Revising: Track the Conflict

Teaching Resources: Writing Support Transparency 5-E; Writing Support Activity Book 5-2

1. Display the transparency and give students copies of the blank organizer. As students look at the Chutes and Ladders diagram, focus their attention on the ladder. Point out that readers need "steps" to bring them up to the climax. If there haven't been enough events to heighten interest or suspense, the climax will lack impact.

2. Model using the Chutes and Ladder diagram by recalling stories the class has read recently. Draw a diagram on the chalkboard. Ask students to fill in the events that go on the various points of the diagram.

3. Suggest that students revise their drafts to include at least three events in the "ladder" portions of their stories.

Real-World Connection

Emphasize that the ability to tell a story is an important on-the-job skill in many professions, not only in obvious fields such as journalism. Advertisers and marketers have to "tell the story" of products in direct mail and print and broadcast advertisements. Lawyers tell stories to judges and juries. In fact, any employee who must produce a presentation is, in effect, telling a story.

Integrating Representing Skills

To help students further examine the overall structure of their narratives, encourage them to create plot diagrams that illustrate the sequence of events. Students should be able to list events from their drafts for each point on the diagrams—Introduction, Rising Action, Climax, Falling Action, Resolution. If not, they may need to add additional events.

5.4 Revising

Review your draft to find ways to improve your writing. Focus on the plot, the dialogue, and the language you have chosen. Use the strategies that follow to revise your story.

Revising Your Overall Structure
Track the Conflict

The higher you climb to the top of a slide, the greater the anticipation of the ride becomes. Use a chutes-and-ladders diagram to think of your story's conflict in the same way.

▶ **REVISION STRATEGY**
Using Chutes and Ladders

Write the events that build the conflict of your story on a diagram like the one shown here. Put the climax of the story—the highest point of interest or suspense of your story—at the top of the slide. Review your diagram, and consider adding more events to your draft to make the conflict stronger.

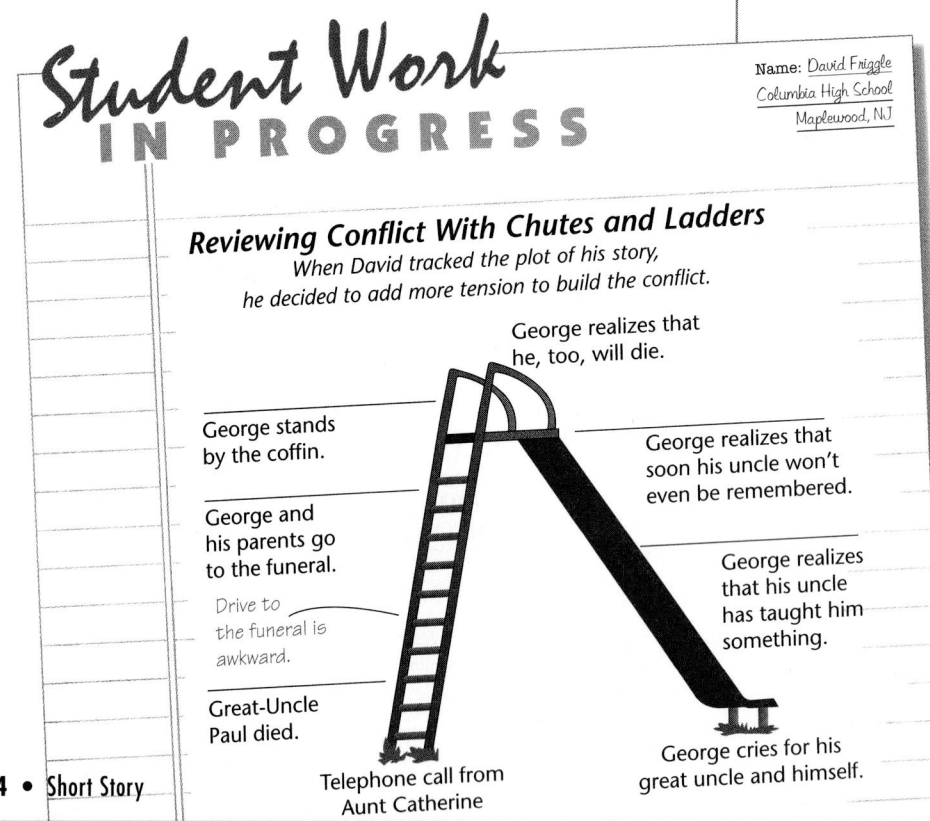

Student Work
IN PROGRESS

Name: David Friggle
Columbia High School
Maplewood, NJ

Reviewing Conflict With Chutes and Ladders
When David tracked the plot of his story, he decided to add more tension to build the conflict.

George realizes that he, too, will die.

George stands by the coffin.

George and his parents go to the funeral.

Drive to the funeral is awkward.

Great-Uncle Paul died.

Telephone call from Aunt Catherine

George realizes that soon his uncle won't even be remembered.

George realizes that his uncle has taught him something.

George cries for his great uncle and himself.

84 • Short Story

⏱ TIME AND RESOURCE MANAGER

Resources
Print: Writing Support Transparencies 5-E–F; Writing Support Activity Book 5-2
Technology: Writing Lab CD-ROM, Narration

In-Depth Coverage	Accelerated Pace
• Cover pp. 84–88 in class. • Use the relevant transparencies for demonstrating each revision strategy: using chutes and ladders, writing realistic dialogue, highlighting verbs, and circling vague nouns.	• Ask students to review the revision strategies on pp. 84–88. • Have students work independently to revise their short story drafts.

Revising Your Paragraphs

Make Dialogue Sound Realistic

Dialogue gives credibility to your characters and your story. To hone your skill at writing authentic dialogue, listen to the speech habits of friends and family. Broaden your study by noticing the variety of speech patterns you hear in school, in stores, and at restaurants. Then, apply the conversational habits you've overheard to your story's dialogue to make your characters sound more real.

▶ **REVISION STRATEGY**
Reading With a Partner

Ask a partner to read your dialogue aloud with you. Jot down dialogue that sounds stiff or unnatural. Later, you can make the words your characters say sound more realistic.

▲ **Critical Viewing**
What emotions might the dialogue between these children convey?
[Hypothesize]

REVISING FORCED DIALOGUE

Forced Dialogue

"Mother, please write a note for school," Sam asked, looking down at the ground.

"I'd be happy to write that for you," she said.

"Thank you so much," Sam said, handing her a sheet of paper. His eagerness raised her suspicion.

"By the way, what is this for?"

☑ Change formal language to informal words when appropriate.

☑ Have characters interrupt each other or speak in half-uttered sentences.

☑ Insert interjections that show character.

Realistic Dialogue

"Mom, could you write me a note for school?" Sam asked.

"Sure, I'd be..." but Sam was jumping ahead of her.

"Thanks!" he said, handing her a sheet of paper. His eagerness raised her suspicion.

"What is this for, anyway?"

Revising • 85

☑ **ONGOING ASSESSMENT: Monitor and Reinforce**

If you find that students have difficulty identifying passages in their drafts that need more realistic dialogue, use the following strategy.

As a variation of the "Reading With a Partner" strategy, students should listen to their dialogue being read by someone else. If dialogue does not sound as conversational as the writer intended, it should be marked. As students revise their dialogue to make it sound less forced and more realistic, tell them to concentrate on applying conversational habits they have overheard.

Revising: Use the Active Voice

Teaching Resources: Writing Support Transparency 5-F

1. If students are unfamiliar with the difference between active voice and passive voice, you may want to review the Grammar in Your Writing activity on the next page before introducing the revision strategy.

2. Write the following sentence pairs on the chalkboard:

   The village was destroyed by bulldozers.

   Bulldozers destroyed the village.

   Freedom for all the hostages was sought by the negotiators.

   The negotiators sought freedom for all the hostages.

   Have students comment on which sentence in each pair is more dynamic.

3. Explain that even in stories that take place in the past, there was action going on at the time. So the active voice is almost always preferable.

4. Display the transparency and ask students how David improved his writing.

Customize for
Less Advanced Students

Help students recognize passive voice constructions. Point out that passive voice sentences use helping verbs such as *was, will be,* and *had been.* Ask students to look for helping verbs in their drafts. After they find sentences containing helping verbs, students should ask themselves whether the subject is performing the action, or whether the action is being performed on the subject.

5.4

Revising Your Sentences
Use the Active Voice

To create dynamic sentences in which your characters are acting instead of being acted upon, choose the active voice. Its opposite, the passive voice, can make your characters and actions dull and slow. Using the active voice helps you create characters that act on their emotions and shape their own lives.

ACTIVE VOICE: Daniel *caught* the ball
PASSIVE VOICE: The ball *was caught* by Daniel.

▶ **REVISION STRATEGY**
Highlighting Verbs

Read each sentence in your draft, focusing on the action performed in each case. As you analyze your writing, identify whether each sentence is written in the active or passive voice. Using a highlighter, mark all the passive verbs in your essay. Evaluate each use of the passive voice, weighing whether changing the sentence to active voice could make the writing more interesting or direct. Challenge yourself to change some of your passive-voice verbs to active-voice ones.

Student Work
IN PROGRESS

Name: David Friggle
Columbia High School
Maplewood, NJ

Highlighting Verbs to Identify the Active Voice

In his first draft, David used the passive voice often. To make the writing more lively, he changed passive to active. In these examples, he recast the sentences.

Our house is old, and you can half hear when ⟨someone talks⟩ a joke is told downstairs. You may not hear the joke, but you know someone told one. But there was no laughter from my mom, nor was there any idle chatter. In muffled voices,
⟨The muffled voices spoke of seriousness, gloom, and worry.⟩
seriousness, gloom, and worry were mentioned. Someone had died, I was sure of it.

86 • Short Story

◆ STANDARDIZED TEST PREPARATION WORKSHOP

Grammar and Usage To identify the correct word for completing a sentence, a student may have to decide whether the subject of the sentence is receiving or performing the action of the verb. Show the following example to students:

After a tremendous senior season, the high school athlete _____ a scholarship at Oklahoma State University.

Choose the word or group of words that best complete the sentence.

A offered   C was offered

B will offer   D had offers

The correct answer is item **C**. The athlete receives, rather than performs, the action of the verb.

Grammar in Your Writing
Active vs. Passive Voice

Two different voices of verbs are used to show how an action is performed. In sentences written in the **active voice,** the subject performs the action. In sentences written in the **passive voice,** the action of the sentence is performed on the subject.

Active voice: The musician turns the page.

> (*Musician*, the subject of the sentence, performs the action of the sentence, *turns*.)

Passive voice: The page is turned by the musician.

> (*Page*, the subject of the sentence, has the action of the sentence, *turn*, performed upon it.)

Use the active voice

- to emphasize the actor:

  The conductor inspires his orchestra.

  The violists harmonize with the violins.

- to create vibrant writing:

  The audience applauds his efforts.

  The symphony hall brims with excitement.

Use the passive voice

- to emphasize the action:

  The budget was slashed by the board in the latest meeting.

  Each day, newspapers are delivered to these homes.

- to draw attention away from the performer of the action or to indicate action even when the performer is unknown:

  The funds will be lost for years.

  The decision has been called disastrous.

Find It in Your Reading Read "The Appalachian Trail" on pages 76–77. Identify three uses of the active voice. For each, demonstrate how the subject of the sentence performs the action. Notice that the writer avoids the passive voice.

Find It in Your Writing Review your short story, and identify all of the places where you have used the passive voice. Unless you have a specific reason for using it, change the passive voice to the active voice.

For more on active and passive voices, see Chapter 23.

Grammar in Your Writing: Active vs. Passive Voice

1. Begin by having students identify the subject and the verb in several sentences.

2. When introducing passive voice sentences, explain that the subject doesn't always perform the action of a sentence. In the first passive voice example, the action is performed by the *musician*, the object of the preposition

3. Ask students to brainstorm for other examples that are appropriate for the passive voice. Get students started by discussing the following example:

   > *For the third time in a row, the Saturday game had to be canceled, this time because of rain.*

   Here, the passive voice emphasizes the action of cancellation, not the performer of the action, the rain.

4. Encourage students to scan stories from *Timeless Voices, Timeless Themes* to find examples of passive voice construction and see why they are used. Point out that unless they have a specific reason for using the passive voice, students should revise their passive voice sentences into active ones.

Find It in Your Reading

Have students share their examples with the class.

Find It in Your Writing

Make sure students can support with reasons their uses of the passive voice.

⏱ TIME SAVERS!

 Writing Support Transparencies
Use the transparencies for Chapter 5 to teach these strategies.

Revising: Analyze Nouns

1. To demonstrate how specific nouns can be more effective that adjectives and adverbs, write the following sentences on the chalkboard. The first sentence is from "The Appalachian Trail."

   She tells me that it is her <u>ambition</u> to walk the Appalachian Trail.

   She tells me that she has a <u>strong need</u> to walk the Appalachian Trail.

   She tells me that she <u>really wants</u> to walk the Appalachian Trail.

2. Discuss the other ways the author could have written the sentence. Guide students to see that the use of the precise noun *ambition* results in a stronger sentence.

3. After students have circled the vague nouns in their drafts, encourage them to use a dictionary and thesaurus to help find more precise replacements.

4. Invite students to share both their original sentences and replacements with a partner. Have partners comment on the revised sentences.

Revising: Peer Review

Before they read, encourage students to develop a brief list of questions for their peer reviewers to answer after the second reading. For example:
- Which character do you find most well developed? Why?
- Are there any aspects of the plot that you find unclear? Explain.
- What change would you make to this story if you were revising it?

5.4

Revising Your Word Choice

Analyze Nouns

You can often get more mileage out of a specific noun than you can from several adjectives. By reviewing the nouns you have chosen and finding more precise ones, you can make your writing more efficient,m so that it communicates exactly what you want to say.

VAGUE NOUN: Yellow and blue *papers* covered the desk.
PRECISE NOUNS: *Bills* and *advertisements* covered the desk.

▶ **REVISION STRATEGY**
Circling Vague Nouns

When you choose specific nouns, you make your writing concrete and clear. This will help readers picture exactly what you had in mind. Review your draft to find vague nouns that do not suggest clear images. Where you can, replace these words with precise nouns. Look at these examples:

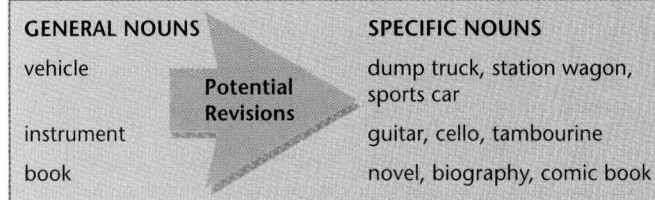

GENERAL NOUNS	SPECIFIC NOUNS
vehicle	dump truck, station wagon, sports car
instrument	guitar, cello, tambourine
book	novel, biography, comic book

(Potential Revisions)

Peer Review

Pointing

In a small group, read your story two times. The first time, ask people just to listen. The second time, ask each person to point out a specific passage he or she especially liked.

This strategy will help you identify the successful parts of your draft. For example, you may learn that you have conveyed a setting effectively or that a you developed the conflict in your narrative successfully. You may wish to extend the discussion by asking reviewers for suggestions about improving the sections that need attention.

▶ **Speaking and Listening Tip**

To get the most of your peer review, resist the urge to interrupt your partner or to finish the sentence. When you are truly listening, be patient enough to hear what your reviewer has to say.

5.5 **Editing and Proofreading**

To make your writing error-free, check spelling, punctuation, and grammar before you write your final draft. The primary purpose of using correct mechanics, including punctuation, in your writing is to make your short story easy to follow.

Focusing on Punctuation

Punctuation, especially the end marks of sentences, helps to convey emotion to the reader. Check your draft to see that you have chosen the right end marks.

Periods identify the ends of most sentences.
Question marks identify the ends of questions.
Exclamation points indicate the ends of sentences that show strong emotion.

Grammar in Your Writing
Punctuating Dialogue Correctly

The conventions of punctuating dialogue help readers to follow a conversation even when it involves several people. Enclose each speaker's words in quotation marks. Follow these rules when punctuating dialogue:

• **Dialogue that ends the sentence:** Introduce the quotation mark with a comma, and put the ending punctuation inside the quotation marks.

Mary said, "I have to go now."

• **Dialogue that begins the sentence:** Use a comma inside the quotation marks unless a question mark or exclamation point is needed to make sense of the speaker's words.

"I'll be late for this appointment if I don't leave now," said Mary.
"So go already!" her brother shouted.

• **Dialogue that is interrupted by tag words:** Use commas to set off the two parts of the quotation.

"Steven," she said, glaring at him, "we can't leave until you're ready!"

Find It in Your Reading Read "The Appalachian Trail" on pages 76–77. Find examples of the three conventions of dialogue shown here.

Find It in Your Writing As you proofread your short story, double-check the punctuation of any dialogue you have used.

For more on punctuating dialogue, see Chapter 29.

Editing and Proofreading • 89

Step-by-Step Teaching Guide

Editing and Proofreading

1. Encourage students to circle all the end marks in their short stories. Then students can reread each sentence to make sure it is punctuated correctly.

2. Suggest that students save exclamation points for punctuating dialogue. Point out that these marks lose their emphatic power if used too often.

Step-by-Step Teaching Guide

Grammar in Your Writing: Punctuating Dialogue Correctly

1. Emphasize that checking for errors in punctuating dialogue is especially important when editing short stories, since they often contain extensive dialogue.

2. Have students note that the first word between two parts of a quotation is not capitalized, even if it follows an end mark.

   "I know!" her brother insisted. "You told me already."

3. Emphasize that end punctuation at the end of a quotation goes inside the quotation mark.

4. Point out that indirect quotations do not require quotation marks.

   Ricky had told her that he wasn't going to be back until six.

Find It in Your Reading

Students should be able to find examples throughout the model.

Find It in Your Writing

Have students exchange their short stories with partners to make sure they have punctuated dialogue correctly.

⏱ TIME AND RESOURCE MANAGER

Resources
Print: Scoring Rubrics on Transparency, Chapter 5; Writing Assessment: Scoring Rubric and Scoring Models for Short Story
Technology: Writing Lab CD-ROM, Narration

In-Depth Coverage	Accelerated Pace
• Review p. 89 in class. • Distribute and review the Proofreading Checklist. • Give step-by-step coverage to Publishing and Presenting (p. 90). • Analyze in class the Final Draft on pp. 91–93. • Students can edit and proofread their short stories in class.	• Assign pp. 89–93 for independent review. • Students can independently edit and proofread their short stories. • Respond to individual editing issues as needed.

Integrating Grammar Skills

Explain to students the following points about dialogue and paragraphs:

• Begin a new paragraph each time the speaker changes.
• If a speaker's dialogue continues past the end of a paragraph, do not place a closing quotation mark at the paragraph's end. A beginning quotation mark should appear at the start of the new paragraph.

Publishing and Presenting

1. Encourage students to title their stories if they haven't already done so. Students may want to consider a key piece of dialogue from the story or a phrase related to the conflict or theme. Whatever they choose, the title should engage the reader's interest or provide a clue about what the reader will encounter in the story.

2. For the Author's Forum activity, suggest that students rehearse their readings. They may even want to tape-record practice readings for relistening as they work to develop the most effective delivery possible.

ASSESS

Assessment

Teaching Resources: Scoring Rubrics on Transparency 5; Formal Assessment, Chapter 5

1. Display the Scoring Rubric transparency and review the criteria in class.

2. Before students proceed with self-assessment, you may wish to review the Final Draft of the Student Work in Progress on pages 91–93. Have students score the Final Draft in one or more of the rubric categories. For example, how would students score the short story in terms of audience and purpose?

3. In addition to student self-assessment, you may wish to use the following assessment options:

   • score student short stories yourself, using the rubric and scoring models from Writing Assessment.

   • review the Standardized Test Preparation Workshop on pages 98–99 and have students respond to a writing prompt based on a short story within a time limit.

   • administer the Chapter 5 Test from Formal Assessment in Teaching Resources to assess students' grasp of concepts presented.

90

5.6 # Publishing and Presenting

Building Your Portfolio

When you have finalized your draft, share your short story with others. Here are some suggestions:

1. **Illustrate Your Story** An illustrated presentation of your short story can give your writing a polished and professional look. Create several illustrations that help express the mood of your story, choose the correct placement, and bind the work together.

2. **Create an Author's Forum** Invite classmates to share their short stories with the rest of the class. Following a reading, you may want to encourage a discussion of the story and the techniques the writer used.

Reflecting on Your Writing

After you have finished writing your short story, jot down your ideas about the process. Use these questions to get started:

• How did writing a short story enhance your understanding of techniques used by the writers of short stories you read?

• Which element of the short story did you find easiest to elaborate? Which was the most difficult? Explain.

Internet Tip

To see model essays scored with this rubric, go to **www.phwg. phschool.com**

Rubric for Self-Assessment

Use these criteria to evaluate your short story.

	Score 4	Score 3	Score 2	Score 1
Audience and Purpose	Presents details targeted at a unique audience; successfully narrates the events of a story	Presents details suited to an audience; narrates the events of a story	Presents few details suited to an audience; some ideas conflict with narration of story	Supports no purpose; is not written for a specific audience
Organization	Presents events that create a clear narrative; writes from a consistent point of view	Presents sequence of events; told from a specific point of view	Presents a confusing sequence of events; contains inconsistent points of view	Presents no logical order; writes from an inconsistent point of
Elaboration	Contains details that provide insight into character; contains dialogue that reveals characters and furthers the plot	Contains details and dialogue that develops characters	Contains characters and setting; contains some dialogue	Contains few or no details to develop characters or setting; no dialogue provided
Use of Language	Uses fresh word choice and tone to reveal story's setting and character; contains no errors in grammar, punctuation, or spelling	Uses interesting and fresh word choices; contains few errors in grammar, punctuation, and spelling	Uses clichés and trite expressions; contains some errors in grammar, punctuation, and spelling	Uses uninspired word choices; has many errors in grammar, punctuation, and spelling

90 • Short Story

✓ ONGOING ASSESSMENT: Assess Mastery

Use one of the following options to assess final drafts of students' short stories.

Self Assessment Ask students to score their short story using the rubric provided. Then have students write a single paragraph reflecting on the most valuable thing they learned in completing this short story.	Teacher Assessment You may wish to use the rubric and the scoring models provided in Writing Assessment, Narration: Short Story to score students' work.

Student Work IN PROGRESS

5.7

FINAL DRAFT

◄ **Critical Viewing**
How does this photograph combine with the story's title to set a mood?
[Respond]

A Stranger's Lesson

David Friggle
Columbia High School
Maplewood, New Jersey

That Friday night started out normally. I was watching television when a jarring ring broke into the studio audience's laughter. Normally, I can wait out a phone call until the answering machine or one of my parents picks it up. This time, however, my resistance gave out first, and I picked it up, slightly annoyed.

"Hello?" *This had better be good*, I thought to myself, as I muted the television.

"Hi, John?" The woman on the phone mistook me for my father, which led me to believe she was either a co-worker of his or a distant relative who'd not seen me for quite some time.

"No, this is George. Who's speaking?"

The opening paragraph provides the story's contemporary setting.

David chose to use a first-person narrator to bring the reader closer to the character's thoughts and emotions.

Step-by-Step Teaching Guide

Teaching from Final Draft

1. Help students recognize the elements that make "A Stranger's Lesson" an interesting and suspenseful short story.

   • The setting is introduced in the opening paragraph—the narrator's living room on a Friday night.

   • The story shows rather than tells with vivid details such as *forced smiles*, *jittery hands*, and *nervous tapping of feet*.

   • The story makes extensive use of realistic-sounding dialogue to create effective characterization.

   • Precise word choice, such as *muted the television* and *studio audience's laughter*, contributes to strong sentences.

   • The story gradually builds through a series of events before reaching its climax, the moment when the narrator reaches the coffin.

   • The theme, that life is frail and fleeting, is thoughtfully expressed in the closing paragraphs.

2. Ask students to share their responses to David's final draft. If they were revising this story, what—if anything—would they change? Why?

Critical Viewing

Respond Students may say it creates a dark, eerie, or somber mood.

Teaching from the Model

Have students note how the choice of a first-person narrator contributes to the impact of the story. Ask if the scene in which the narrator stands in front of the coffin would have the same effect if it were told from the third-person point of view.

5.1

"Georgie? That's you? I can't believe it! You sound just like your father! You've grown so much since the last time I saw you!"

"Really? Thanks. Yeah, it's George. Who's this?"

She suddenly took on a more serious tone.

"This is your Aunt Catherine, dear. May I talk to your mother?"

"Sure, just hold on a sec. MOM!"

"YES?"

"Aunt Catherine on the phone!"

There was a pause, then some footsteps, then a click on the line. Suddenly, my mother's voice came on, "Thanks, George, you can hang up now."

Our house is old, and you can half hear when someone talks downstairs. You may not hear the joke, but you know someone told one. But there was no laughter from my mom, nor was there any idle chatter. The muffled voices spoke of seriousness, gloom, and worry. Someone had died, I was sure of it.

The click of the phone hanging up led to a hushed conversation between my mom and dad in the living room. Then, as if on cue, I was called down to talk.

I asked what was wrong. My mom searched for words, her mouth moving as if to start saying every phrase she pondered, before finally telling me that my great-uncle Paul had died.

The initial shock of being told about a death quickly subsided, to be replaced with confusion. Who was Great-Uncle Paul? Was he nice? Had I ever met him? Why don't I remember him? *Should* I remember him? Thoughts of my great-uncle Paul stayed in my mind until I was asleep. The funeral was Saturday. At least the mystery would be solved soon.

The car ride to the funeral home was awkward. My parents' obvious grief and my persistent curiosity were offset by the saccharine voice of "Cousin Brucie," the oldies station's morning disc jockey. For an hour and a half, Cousin Brucie was the only one in the car who was talking. Herman's Hermits and Derek and the Dominos didn't seem to excite the same exuberance in my family as it did in Brucie.

The funeral service was no better. The generally uncomfortable mood during the car trip was evident tenfold at the funeral. Pop music was replaced by forced smiles, but jittery hands, nervous tapping of feet, and conversation without mention of my great-uncle Paul challenged the validity of any of the smiles. At least Cousin Brucie was genuinely excited about his silly asides.

Sitting in the corner, I felt like a complete stranger. Everyone seemed to know who I was, however. Cousins of uncles and

92 • Short Story

Dialogue establishes two of his characters: the narrator and his aunt.

By showing the character's reaction before revealing the conflict, the writer adds tension to the plot.

The conflict of the story is announced: There has been a death in the family.

To develop the conflict, the writer contrasts the enthusiasm of the radio disc jockey with the mood of the characters in the car.

Details like "forced smiles," and "jittery hands" convey the mood of the situation.

sisters-in-law of aunts all came over to me in an effort to "cheer me up." Half of them told me that if I thought high school was good, I'd love college, and the other half made some sort of weird joke when I told them I fenced in my spare time. I did my part by putting on a happy face and answering everything politely, but the whole time I wondered who was being comforted.

After a while, it was time for everyone to pay their respects. Although I had no idea what to do when I got there, I went up because I didn't know what else to do. There were several pictures of Great-Uncle Paul, in various stages of his life. He looked like my mother's side of the family, but besides that, there was nothing I recognized about him.

Standing in front of a coffin next to mourning people makes one think, and think I did. I thought about the impact he left on so many people. I thought about how I should have known him, how I should have remembered him, and how I no longer had a chance for any of that.

Suddenly, I stopped thinking about him as Great-Uncle Paul and started thinking of him as Paul Horenburg. Paul Horenburg, who told jokes to friends at work, who laughed, who fell in love, who cried on occasion, who got angry, and just a few days earlier, died. I realized that although Paul Horenburg had died, the world didn't. In days, weeks, months, or possibly years, the mourning would stop, and everyone would go back to their normal lives. Memories of Paul Horenburg would crop up occasionally, as co-workers remembered funny stories he had told, or as friends looked back on evenings they had spent with him, or when his family remembered the helpful advice he had given them in times of trouble. Then, I finally realized that he had taught me something, too.

And on that Saturday, I cried for a man I didn't know.

The narrator faces the climax of the story when he approaches the coffin.

The narrator shares his thoughts to show how his attitude and feelings have shifted, leading to the resolution in the last paragraph.

The events of the story illustrate a generalization about life and death. The narrator— and the reader—take a second look at the importance of living fully, despite life's fragility.

◄ Critical Viewing
How does this photograph convey hope and despair, the two emotions developed in the story? **[Support]**

Integrating Grammar Skills

Indirect Quotation Have students note the difference in punctuation between the direct and indirect quotations in the story. Direct quotations such as *"Aunt Catherine on the phone!"* are enclosed in quotation marks. Indirect quotations such as *I asked what was wrong* and *finally telling me that my great Uncle Paul had died* are not enclosed in quotation marks.

Critical Viewing

Support Students may suggest that the photo conveys despair through the barren tree. Others may say the sunlight expresses a sense of hope.

Lesson Objectives

1. To write a dramatic script appropriate to audience and purpose.
2. To use prewriting strategies to generate ideas, develop voice, and plan.
3. To use writing processes to develop and revise drafts.
4. To publish a dramatic script through performance to an audience.

Step-by-Step Teaching Guide

Drama

Teaching Resources: Writing Support Transparency 5-G

1. Review what students know about drama and how scripts are used to generate performances. If possible, show students several examples of dramatic scripts and allow them to familiarize themselves with features of this format.

2. Suggest that students review strategies from Chapter 5.

3. If students need additional help finding a topic, organize them into groups to brainstorm. Students might share conflicts they've experienced or witnessed.

4. Display the transparency and clarify its use. Confirm that students understand the diagram and emphasize that stage directions are written from the actors' perspective. In other words, *stage right* is to the actors' right not the audience's right.

5. Encourage and assist students in readying their drama for production and performance. If time allows, make this a class Drama Festival to share with the school community.

Critical Viewing

Analyze Students should say they suggest a soda shop, possibly in the 1950s.

Connected Assignment
Drama

Just like a short story, **drama** tells stories about characters and the conflicts or problems they face. The difference is that in drama, the story is performed by actors on a stage or in a studio. Audiences learn the story through the characters' dialogue, their movements, and their setting. In drama, there is little or no descriptive narration. Brief stage directions can indicate characters' emotions or identify gestures, but dialogue does the majority of the storytelling.

In this model, notice how the playwright provides stage directions in brackets to indicate action. Stage directions can also indicate staging, such as the entrance or exit of characters, or provide emotion cues to show actors how to present their lines.

▲ **Critical Viewing**
What specific setting do the clothing and props in this photograph suggest? **[Analyze]**

MODEL

from **The Dancers**
Horton Foote

[He goes back to reading the menu.]

WAITRESS. If it's all the same to you, I'd rather not make a sandwich. I'm closing my doors in ten minutes.

HORACE. Oh. Well, what would you like to make?

WAITRESS. Any kind of ice cream or soft drinks. *[She looks up at the ice cream menu.]* Coffee is all gone.

HORACE. How about a chocolate ice cream soda?

WAITRESS. OK. Coming up. *[She starts to mix the soda. She talks as she works.]* Going to the dance?

HORACE. No.

Write your own short drama. Use the writing process skills on the next page to help you create characters and a problem for them to face.

Prewriting To choose a topic for your drama, think of a problem you or someone you know recently faced, scan local newspapers for human-interest issues in the community, or imagine a problem that may confront a society of the future. In a sentence, identify the conflict you will present.

To develop the drama, name your characters and list details about each, including descriptions of appearances and personalities. Then, map out the events leading the characters to the story's climax. Explain the obstacles that intensify the conflict, plan the story's climax, and decide what might happen to the characters after the climax.

To imagine the stage, sketch a stage plan like the one shown here. Identify the settings you'll use, and indicate the necessary furniture.

SAMPLE STAGE PLAN

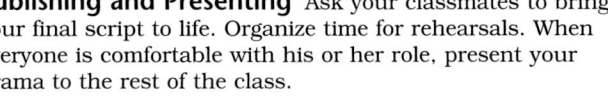

Shelves and products · Drugstore · Stanley Living Room · Couch · Counter and stools

Drafting As you draft your drama, try to hear the characters speak. They should use words and sentences that fit their personalities, ages, and backgrounds while revealing their feelings and thoughts. Speaking the dialogue aloud may help you hear it. Make use of script format, with stage directions that help readers picture the scene. Use stage directions to tell what the scene looks like, what props are involved, and what sound effects you want to include. They should also describe how and where characters move.

Revising and Editing Ask a few friends to read your script aloud in character. As you listen, note your reactions. Then, use your responses to their reading to help you revise; for example:

- Make sure your readers can visualize each character from the information you've provided. If necessary, add details to stage directions or to the character's dialogue to make his or her personality more clear.

- Confirm that each character's speech quirks remain consistent throughout—if a character pauses frequently while speaking, consider continuing this pattern throughout the script.

Publishing and Presenting Ask your classmates to bring your final script to life. Organize time for rehearsals. When everyone is comfortable with his or her role, present your drama to the rest of the class.

Connected Assignment: Drama • 95

Customize for
Kinesthetic Learners

Urge students to take advantage of the opportunity in this project to work kinesthetically. You might assign these students to staging and prop work, helping peers plan each play's arrangements.

Customize for
Less Advanced Students

Pair these students with a more advanced partner who can lead the way through the multi-step process. Students will work on their own individual dramas but consult with each other on the sequence and substance of the steps.

Lesson Objectives

1. To recognize distinctive and shared characteristics of cultures.

2. To evaluate media presentations.

3. To analyze ideas as represented in various media.

4. To compare and contrast media adaptations of the same story.

5. To retell a myth.

Step-by-Step Teaching Guide

Recognize Shared Characteristics of Cultures

1. Choose one of the Spotlight elements for class discussion, or have students work individually or in groups on the element of their choice. Give students the initiative to find the necessary books or videotapes.

2. Have interested students research additional information about Ovid and *The Metamorphoses*. Then invite them to read aloud from the climactic scene in *Pyramus and Thisbe*.

3. Show a video of a theatrical version of *Romeo and Juliet* and of Zefferelli's film version. Invite students to compare and contrast the two treatments. Ask students if they think these performances would appeal to contemporary viewers.

4. Have students listen to the soundtrack from *West Side Story* or view a video of the show or film Ask students to critique the music and dancing.

Spotlight on the Humanities

Recognize Shared Characteristics of Cultures

Focus on Myth: *Pyramus and Thisbe*

Certain classic stories contain a universal quality that moves readers enough to ensure that the plots will be passed down through generations. In fact, a story whose plot may be familiar to you first appeared when it was introduced by the Roman poet Ovid (43 B.C.?–A.D. 17) nearly two thousand years ago. Ovid introduced the mythical story of Pyramus and Thisbe in his work *The Metamorphoses*. In the myth, Pyramus and Thisbe fall in love, but their love is forbidden by their parents. One night Thisbe is to meet Pyramus at a nearby tomb, but she is frightened, by a lioness. Fleeing, she drops her veil, which the lioness smears with blood. Pyramus arrives and finds the veil; then, believing that Thisbe is dead, he takes his own life. When Thisbe returns, she finds Pyramus and, heartbroken, takes her life.

Engraving from 19th-century English edition of William Shakespeare's Romeo and Juliet (Act V, scene 3)

▲ **Critical Viewing** What details of this engraving suggest the scene takes place in a tomb? **[Support]**

Theater and Film Connection The story of Pyramus and Thisbe is retold in many dramas. Here are some of the most well-known:

- Shakespeare's *Romeo and Juliet* (c. 1596) features two young lovers who experience a similar fate to that of Pyramus and Thisbe. This story of star-crossed lovers was brought to the screen in 1968 by Italian film director Franco Zefferelli in the now classic, visually stunning film *Romeo and Juliet*.

- *West Side Story* (1957), a musical version of this tale, was produced on Broadway. Leonard Bernstein composed the music, Stephen Sondheim wrote the lyrics, and the two young lovers featured in the play meet on the streets of New York City. A 1961 film version of *West Side Story* won the Academy Award for Best Picture, as well as nine other Oscars, including Best Director.

Narrative Writing Activity: Story in a Modern Setting

West Side Story presents an ageless tale in a modern setting. Use the musical to inspire a contemporary retelling of another myth you know. After you develop a draft, share your story and discuss what makes the plot vital in today's world.

Viewing and Representing

Activity Allow interested students to work with peers to develop a dramatic reading of their story. Students need not wear costumes, but should use vocal intonation and body language to convey mood.

Critical Viewing

Support Students may mention the darkness and the position of the woman.

Media and Technology Skills

Using Technology to Respond to Literature

Activity: Producing a Video Adaptation of a Short Story

On paper, short stories invite readers to imagine the characters in the theater of the mind. Video technology gives you a tool to interpret stories dramatically. Choose a short story you have written or a classic one you enjoy, and develop your own video interpretation.

Learn About It You can create a script using the short story as an inspiration. Identify logical scene breaks, develop stage directions, and write dialogue in script format. You can use stage directions to provide details about character movements, speech styles, and emotions.

Plan It Before you film, take the time to consider locations, camera angles, and the specific flow of events in your film.

- Scout locations or create props for an on-stage performance.

- Highlight places in the script to use zoom, fade, and other special video features for optimum effect.

- Storyboard your adaptation so that you and your actors know exactly what to expect.

Rehearse It Run through several rehearsals before you begin recording. Remember that unless you have editing technology, you'll be recording the performance in sequence with very limited cutting or pasting capacity. You can halt the performance to rewind the tape if a disaster occurs (an actor falls off the stage, for example).

Track It As you rehearse, note the issues listed in the sidebar, and use a checklist like the one shown here to monitor your progress. When you feel you're ready, film your video.

Recording Checklist

- Check lighting by taping and viewing a short segment.
- Prepare tape-recorded sound effects in advance, and check the equipment.
- Walk actors through their movements to anticipate and solve problems.
- Mark scripts with timing and special effects cues for stage manager's use.
- Verify function of all equipment. Check that camera operators know how to use their equipment.
- Gather supplies, such as tapes and batteries.
- Correctly position props and costumes.

Recording Checklist

	Problem	Solution	Corrected (Yes/No)
Lighting			
Special Effects			
Actors			
Script (dialogue pacing, etc.)			
Recording Equipment			
Supplies (tapes, batteries, etc.)			
Props and Costumes			

Media and Technology Skills • 97

► Lesson Objectives

1. To use verbal and nonverbal strategies in presenting oral messages.
2. To use various forms and technologies to communicate messages.
3. To use a range of techniques to plan and create a media text.
4. To create media products to engage specific audiences.

Step-by-Step Teaching Guide

Using Technology for Literary Response

Teaching Resources: Writing Support Transparency 5-H; Writing Support Activity Book 5-3

1. Discuss the definition of a video adaptation. Urge students to choose a story they know well.
2. Review the recording checklist and invite students with videotaping experience to add tips of their own.
3. Brainstorm as a class for additional planning and rehearsing techniques or shortcuts.
4. Using the transparency and a student-suggested mock scene, demonstrate the rehearsal process. Allow volunteers to practice completing the checklist form.
5. Give students copies of the blank organizer and instruct them to use these to monitor rehearsal progress. Invite participating students to contribute comments to the rehearsal monitoring.

Customize for *Visual/Spatial Learners*

Some students may wish to storyboard their video adaptation. Provide these students with mural paper in rolls and instruct them to draw or describe each scene. They might also use photographs or magazine cuttings to indicate a scene's setting.

Lesson Objectives

1. To write in a style appropriate to audience and purpose.

2. To use prewriting strategies to generate ideas.

3. To analyze strategies that writers use.

4. To develop drafts by organizing content and refining style.

5. To demonstrate control over grammatical elements.

Step-by-Step Teaching Guide

Responding to Questions About Short Stories

1. Emphasize to students that they cannot memorize all the possible short stories a test might address. This increases the need to understand basic short story elements. Students should rely on this knowledge and their own analysis rather than specific reading preparation.

2. Urge students to read and understand the test question *before* reading any linked literary material. This will enable them to use time efficiently by focusing reading on the appropriate issues.

3. Stress with students the importance of thorough prewriting. Once they begin drafting, students will have little time or space to change directions. Prewriting need not be elaborate, just well-considered.

4. Remind students to follow their prewriting notes in a coherent manner. If they've planned well, these notes will lead the way.

5. Provide frequent practice opportunities for timed writing. Begin with longer time periods and gradually shorten the time to challenge students' organization skills.

Standardized Test Preparation Workshop

Responding to Questions About Short Stories

On some standardized tests, a story will be provided in a test booklet for you to read and analyze. In other cases, you may be asked about a piece of literature you are expected to know. Learning how the elements of a short story work together will help you write about short stories in test situations.

As you read or remember the story that is the focus of a test question, think about the way separate features combine to create an effect. Consider the following narrative elements:

- Plot is the sequence of events that catches your interest and takes you through the story.s

- Characters are the people, animals, or other beings that take part in the story's action.

- Setting is the time and place in which the story occurs.

- Theme is the message about life that the story conveys.

When writing for a timed test, plan to devote a specified amount of time to prewriting, drafting, revising, editing, and proofreading.

Following is an example of a writing prompt based on the short story, "The Appalachian Trail." Read the story on pages 76–77, and then write a short response to this question:

Sample Writing Situation

> The outcome of the conversation in "The Appalachian Trail" is not at all what the narrator—or the reader—anticipated. In an essay, explain how the writer led readers to expect another outcome. Use details and information from the story to support your answer.

Test Tip

Before you write, devote your full attention to reading the story. If you scan quickly instead of concentrating fully, you may miss important elements of the writing.

98 • Short Story

🔷 TEST-TAKING TIP

Graphic organizers can be especially useful in timed writing situations. Suggest that students familiarize themselves with a range of standard prewriting graphic organizers. This will enable them to prewrite quickly and efficiently. Tell students to sketch organizers on scrap paper and complete them with brief words or phrases. They might want to practice using the T-chart organizer suggested in the lesson. As students show their T-charts, discuss any confusions. Then invite students to offer alternative self-generated organizers for the sample prompt. Emphasize that test takers may use any organizer they wish—these will not be evaluated—but should be able to generate an organizer that suits the prompt question.

Prewriting

Allow about one quarter of your time for prewriting.

Identify the Issue While you may have several reactions to the story presented in the prompt, the question asks you to focus your writing on one element. Review the question to be certain you know what you should address in your essay.

Gather Information to Support a Response To best explain the contrast between the expected response and the surprise ending of "The Appalachian Trail," clarify both outcomes. Create a rough T-chart, noting information on one side about the story's actual ending and on the other, jotting down ideas related to the anticipated ending. Review the story to find details and clues that support either outcome.

Drafting

Allow approximately half of your time for drafting.

Organize Your Arguments Create an outline or a list of points you want to include. Use numbers to prioritize the list, beginning with least important and moving to most important. Next to each item on the list, write sentences that incorporate the details on your T-chart.

Elaborate You probably won't have time to copy your paper twice, so plan to include your elaboration in the first draft. Look over the list of points that support your opinion. For at least three of the points, find a statement from the story that illustrates your idea. Choose details that will influence your specific audience. Write these next to the points they illustrate, so that you remember to include them as you write.

Put It on Paper Write your response on your test paper. Begin with a statement that summarizes your response and states the main idea of your essay. As you draft, pause occasionally to review your prewriting notes and to make sure you continue to follow the logical sequence you have planned. Write your response neatly.

Revising, Editing, and Proofreading

Allow about one quarter of your time to revise, edit, and proofread your paper.

Clean It Up Review your essay before you turn in your paper. Check that each paragraph contributes to the main idea, and look for ways to add transitions that make your organization clear to your readers. Next, look for errors. If you are unsure of the spelling of a word, consider replacing it with one you know better. If you are crossing out or erasing, do so neatly.

Customize for
Less Advanced Students

Point out the clock icons to students and explain that these will help test takers budget time effectively. As students gain test-taking experience, they may adjust these times to suit individual pacing.

Customize for
More Advanced Students

Tell students that interest-catching essay openers and powerful essay closers can positively effect test results. Give students regular practice in generating these clearly but vividly stated essay elements. You might offer topics or prompts and have students generate only opening and closing statements.

In-Depth Lesson Plan

	LESSON FOCUS	PRINT AND MEDIA RESOURCES
DAY 1	**Introduction to Descriptive Essays** Students learn key elements of descriptive essays and analyze the Model From Literature (pp. 100–105).	*Writers at Work* **Videotape,** Description Writing Lab CD-ROM, Description
DAY 2	**Prewriting** Students choose and narrow a topic, consider their audience and purpose, and gather information (pp. 106–109).	**Teaching Resources** *Writing Support Transparencies* 6-A–C; *Writing Support Activity Book* 6-1
DAY 3	**Drafting** Students organize their ideas and write their first drafts (pp. 110–111).	**Teaching Resources** *Writing Support Transparency* 6-D
DAY 4	**Revising** Students revise their drafts in terms of overall structure, paragraphs, sentences, and word choice (pp. 112–117).	**Teaching Resources** *Writing Support Transparencies* 6-E–G;
DAY 5	**Editing and Proofreading; Publishing and Presenting** Students check their work for accuracy and correctness and present their final drafts (pp. 118–119).	**Teaching Resources** *Scoring Rubrics on Transparency,* Chapter 6; *Formal Assessment,* Chapter 6

Accelerated Lesson Plan

	LESSON FOCUS	PRINT AND MEDIA RESOURCES
DAY 1	**Printing and Drafting** Students review characteristics for descriptive writing, select topics, and write drafts.	*Writers at Work* **Videotape,** Description *Writing Lab* **CD-ROM,** Description **Teaching Resources** *Writing Support Transparency* 6-D; *Writing Support Activity Book* 6-1
DAY 2	**Revising to Presenting** Students work individually or with peers to revise, edit, and proofread their work for presentation.	**Teaching Resources** *Writing Support Transparencies* 6-E–G; *Scoring Rubrics on Transparency,* Chapter 6; *Formal Assessment,* Chapter 6

Options for Adapting Lesson Plans

HOMEWORK

Have students complete any stage of the lesson for homework.

TECHNOLOGY

Students can complete any stage of the lesson on computer. Have them print out their completed work.

FEATURES

Extend coverage with Connected Assignment (p. 122), Spotlight on the Humanities (p. 124), Media and Technology Skills (p. 125), and the Standardized Test Preparation Workshop (p. 126).

INTEGRATED SKILLS COVERAGE

Integrating Grammar
Semicolons, SE p. 115
Indefinite Pronoun-Verb Agreement, SE p. 118

Reading/Writing Connection
Reading Strategy, SE p. 102
Writing Application, SE p. 105

Reading
Responding to Literature, SE p. 107

Speaking and Listening
Integrating Speaking and Listening ATE p. 112

Spelling
Integrating Spelling Skills ATE p. 118

Workplace Skills
Integrating Workplace Skills ATE p. 119

Real-World Connection
ATE p. 100

Viewing and Representing
Critical Viewing, SE pp. 100, 105, 108, 112, 120, 122, 124
Viewing and Representing ATE p. 124

ASSESSMENT SUPPORT

Standardized Test Preparation SE p. 126; ATE p. 126
Standardized Test Preparation Workbook, pp. 11–12
Scoring Rubrics on Transparency, Ch. 6
Formal Assessment, Ch. 6
Writing Assessment and Portfolio Management

MEETING INDIVIDUAL NEEDS

Less Advanced Students ATE pp. 123, 125, 127; See also
Ongoing Assessments ATE pp. 101, 108, 115, 119
More Advanced Students ATE pp. 121, 127
ESL Students ATE pp. 111, 116
Bodily/Kinesthetic Learners ATE p. 110
Musical/Rhythmic Learners ATE p. 123

BLOCK SCHEDULING

Pacing Suggestions
For 90-minute Blocks
• Have students complete the Prewriting and Drafting stages in a single period.
• Focus one class period on Revising and Editing and Publishing and Presenting. Allow at least 30 minutes for peer revision.

Resources for Varying Instruction
• *Writing Lab* CD-ROM If your students have access to hardware, a 90-minute block provides an ideal opportunity for students to work on computer.
• *Writers at Work* videotape Show the Description segment in class.

Professional Development Support
• *How to Manage Instruction in the Block* This Teaching Resource provides management and activity suggestions.

MEDIA AND TECHNOLOGY

For the Student
• *Writing Lab* CD-ROM, Description

For the Teacher
• *Writers at Work* videotape, Description
• *Resource Pro* CD-ROM

WRITING AND GRAMMAR WEBSITE

The Interactive Writing and Grammar Website provides a wide array of support for students, teachers, and parents. Writing support includes:

• Interactive revision checkers
• Scoring rubrics with complete models

phwg.phschool.com

LITERATURE CONNECTIONS

Related selections from *Prentice Hall Literature: Timeless Voices, Timeless Themes,* Gold:
"A Celebration of Grandfathers," Rudolfo Anaya, SE p. 105
"The Secret Life of Walter Mitty," James Thurber, SE p. 107

Lesson Objectives

1. To understand the characteristics of descriptive writing.
2. To choose and narrow a descriptive writing topic.
3. To consider audience and purpose in developing a writing topic.
4. To apply strategies for gathering and organizing details.
5. To draft a description with a self-selected organizational structure and examples of figurative language.
6. To evaluate and revise the overall structure of a description draft.
7. To analyze the structure of paragraphs.
8. To examine sentences to eliminate run-ons.
9. To use precise verb choices to strengthen writing style.
10. To edit, proofread, and publish a piece of descriptive writing.

Critical Viewing

Describe Students may mention the city landscape and skyscrapers, sounds of traffic, and so on.

Real-World Connection

The ability to describe things accurately is an important everyday workplace skill. Drafting an in-house manual, preparing a presentation on a product or service, and writing a memo about what happened at a meeting all require descriptive ability. Employers cite writing skills as the area in which their employees need the most improvement.

Chapter 6 Description

▲ Critical Viewing
This is a photograph of the Seattle skyline at sunset. How would you describe the scene? **[Describe]**

Description in Everyday Life

Every time you share a meaningful experience, tell someone the details of a beautiful sight, or explain why you enjoyed a book or movie, you use description. Similarly, whether you sit down to write a poem about clouds, a song about love, a historical essay about the Civil War, or a scientific report about cell structure, you use description. Without even realizing it, you probably use description—both in speaking and in writing —many times a day.

100 • Description

⏱ TIME AND RESOURCE MANAGER

Resources
Technology: Writers at Work videotape, Description

In-Depth Coverage	Accelerated Pace
• Cover pp. 100–105 in class. • Read literature excerpt (pp. 102–105) in class and use it to brainstorm for description ideas with students. • Discuss examples of descriptive writing students know about or have read in class.	• Discuss definitions and types of descriptive writing in class. • Assign Model From Literature for independent reading.

What Is Description?

Our senses enable us to experience the world around us. We can see a beautiful sunset or hear the roar of a wave crashing against the shoreline. We can smell the spicy aroma of oven-fresh pizza, and we can taste the refreshing tang of lemonade. **Description** is writing through which we can share these sensations with others. Effective description includes

- sensory details that convey sights, sounds, smells, tastes, and physical sensation.
- vivid language that brings a subject into focus.
- figurative language that compares its subject with other objects.
- a logical organization.

To see the criteria against which your descriptive writing may be evaluated, preview the Rubric for Self-Assessment on page 119.

Types of Descriptive Writing

Many forms of writing include description. Other forms are purely descriptive. These forms include the following:

- A **description of a person, place, or thing** may focus on the physical appearance or the significance of the subject.
- A **description of an idea** uses concrete images to show an abstract, complicated, or otherwise intangible concept.
- An **observation** objectively describes an event that the writer has witnessed.
- A **remembrance** of a person, place, or thing uses vivid details to capture a memorable part of the writer's past.
- A **vignette,** also known as a "picture painted with words," captures a specific moment in the life of the writer.

PREVIEW
Student Work
IN PROGRESS

In this chapter, you'll see the work of Allison Lutes, a student at Butler Traditional High School in Louisville, Kentucky. Allison used prewriting, drafting, and revising strategies to write "My 'Sister,'" a description of a treasured friend.

Writers in ACTION

Science-fiction writers use description to create pictures of imaginary creatures and far-off planets. In her science-fiction literature Anne McCaffrey develops her descriptions by placing herself in her imaginary settings:

"You, the author, have to be where your story is taking place. You have to be there, in it. And if you are there, in it, for the duration of the story, that comes across."

Interest GRABBER Ask students to recall a moment when they saw something so unusual or incredible that it caused them to stop in their tracks. What caused them to stop and stare? Allow students a few moments to write down two or three sentences about the person, place, thing, or event. Ask volunteers to share their descriptions with the class. Explain to students that they will be learning more about the importance of description in this chapter.

Activate Prior Knowledge

Ask students if they ever call friends on the phone and say, "I've got to tell you what happened" or "You wouldn't believe what I saw." Have students discuss how they use words to help the listener visualize the experience being described. Tell them that descriptions help people share our experiences.

More About the Writer

For more than thirty years, Anne McCaffrey has been thrilling fans of science fiction and fantasy with her novels about Pern, a world inhabited by dragons and their human riders. McCaffrey, who along with Ursula K. LeGuin, was one of the first women to succeed in the male-dominated genre of science fiction, lives and writes in Ireland. Few writers have been as successful as McCaffrey in using their descriptive abilities to create a vivid and complete fictional universe.

☑ ONGOING ASSESSMENT: Diagnose

Use one of the following options to diagnose students' current level of proficiency in descriptive writing.

Option 1 Ask each student to select the strongest example of his or her descriptive writing from last year. Hold conferences in which you review each student's sample. Use the conferences to determine which students will need extra support in developing a short story.	**Option 2** Ask students to write a list of types of descriptive writing. If students have difficulty completing this exercise, you will need to devote more time to the prewriting phase of the process.

Reading\Writing Connection

Reading: Author's Purpose

Before students begin reading, review these three common purposes for writing: to inform, to entertain, or to persuade. Point out that within those broad categories, there are also more specific aims. For example, a writer might want to create a positive or negative impression of the specific places, people, or events he or she is describing. Discuss the kinds of details and language a writer might use to achieve various purposes.

Teaching from the Model

As students read "See Ya' at The Subway," encourage them to focus on the descriptive details the author uses to build a vivid portrait of both a specific place and a period of time. Point out that Armstrong doesn't merely describe the physical details of the high school hangout, she brings to life the words, actions, and routines of the people who inhabited it.

Step-by-Step Teaching Guide

Engage Students Through Literature

1. Read Armstrong's remembrance aloud, or have students take turns reading sections of the text.

2. Have students discuss the different descriptive aspects of the work. Use questions such as the following as discussion prompts:

   • What are some details that focus on the physical description of the luncheonette? (Possible response: "four booth, eight stool, one jukebox, one pin-ball machine ice cream parlor . . .")

   • What are some details that appeal to the reader's different senses? (Possible responses: hearing: specific song titles; taste: "ice cream sundae")

3. Ask students to evaluate the effectiveness of the writer's description. Do they have a clear mental picture of the luncheonette and the people who used to hang out there?

 **Model From Literature**

In this remembrance, Edwina Armstrong looks back fondly to bygone days. Armstrong uses descriptive language to bring her readers through the doors of the high-school hangout she once owned and into another time.

Reading Writing Connection

Reading Strategy: Identify and Evaluate an Author's Purpose The writer includes a particular set of details to create a specific image of her luncheonette. As you read, note the types of details she presents. Use this information to identify her purpose, and then use your own response to her writing to decide whether she is successful.

▲ **Critical Viewing**
What words would you use to describe these teenagers? [Describe]

See Ya' at The Subway...

Edwina Armstrong

We named it "Armstrong's Luncheonette." The high school kids nicknamed it "The Subway." They won.

Situated in the lower part of our homestead, this longer-than-it-was-wide, four booth, eight stool, one jukebox, one pin-ball machine ice cream parlor combined the flavor of the forties and fifties so uniquely that it became the hangout for the nearby high school crowd.

We opened "The Subway" during the final throes of the second World War, a period when Frank Sinatra was fast becoming the teen-age idol of the "Bobby Sock" era.

Adults frequented "Armstrong's," but "The Subway" belonged to the kids. Jammed like ice cream in those famous tulip-shaped glasses, they crammed into every inch of space available at "The Subway" after football games, basketball games, plays, dances, most anything important. Those late to arrive, waited patiently out-

The writer provides concrete details like "jukebox" and "pinball machine" to show readers the inside of the luncheonette.

Comparing crowds of kids to scoops of ice cream provides a vivid use of figurative language and allows readers to see the subject in a new way.

102 • Description

Critical Viewing

Describe Students may say the teenagers look happy and curious. They also look like teenagers from an earlier time.

sideor on the three steps leading down and into the world they called their own.

The only periods of quiet in "The Subway" were during school hours. After school and early into the evening, there was a steady flow of teenagers coming in and out of "The Subway." With a "Hi Ed" to my husband and a "Hi Mrs. A." to me, they first checked themselves out in the elongated mirror that ran the length of the soda fountain. The fellows gave their hair a fast do with the ever-ready comb whipped out of a back pocket. The girls adjusted the dickie collars on their sweaters and smudged on more lipstick.

Next they checked out friends by squeezing into a booth to chat with one another. The friend might be well into eating a "Bomber Special," our huge ice cream concoction immortalizing the high school logo, or munching the much touted twenty-five cent Armstrong hamburger (complete with all the trimmings), or sipping a five or ten cent cola made with real syrup (maybe with a dash of cherry or lime or some other flavor for no extra charge).

Then they checked out the jukebox—doing jitterbugs with their white bobby socked, black and white saddled feet in their minds since there was no space to dance. They vocalized "Bell bottom trousers, coat of navy blue . . ." in dreamy voices and wore out their favorites like "When the Lights Go on Again All Over the World," as they thought of that soldier or sailor coming home. Then as now music spoke to them.

One senior played, "It's The Talk of the Town" so much after his girl broke up with him that we bought another record so we could stand hearing it without the scratches.

From the forties into the beginning of the sixties, we heard "Ed, when are ya gonna get the new Tommy Dorsey?" "Ed, when are ya gonna get the new Chubby Checkers?" "Ed, the Platters made a new one."

They plunked their nickels (six plays for a quarter) for songs like "Sentimental Journey," "Shoo Fly Pie and Apple Pan Dowdy," "Give Me Five Minutes More," "Don't Sit Under the Apple Tree With Anyone Else But Me," . . . or Bill Haley and his Comets, "Rock Around the Clock."

Hitting the top of our all-time charts was Elvis Presley's "Hound Dog" which found adults (who once liked Spike Jones and his City Slickers) shaking their heads wondering what this generation was up to.

Then they (mostly boys) checked out the nickel pin-ball machine. "Ed, when are ya gonna get a new machine? This one doesn't give enough free games!" The skilled players could win free games, maneuvering the machine for a long time. They usually didn't

The next nine paragraphs use a chronological order to show readers the step-by-step routines of her customers.

Details about specific foods, like the "Bomber Special," appeal to the sense of taste. The prices may inspire either a feeling of nostalgia or disbelief.

Note that these old 78's and 45's were made of vinyl and literally wore out.

Precise details, such as song titles and artists, help place the description firmly in a different time.

Visual/Spatial Learners
To help students appreciate the wealth of visual detail provided in Armstrong's description, suggest that they sketch a floor plan of the luncheonette and fill it in with the images described by the writer. Students could begin by drawing a "longer-than-it-was wide" rectangle and adding in four booths, eight stools, a jukebox, and a pin-ball machine. Then students could draw the steps in front of the diner and the crowds waiting outside. They can continue to embellish the portrait by drawing the numerous other visual details the writer provides. Have students compare their drawings.

Teaching from the Model

Encourage students to use Armstrong's work as a possible jumping-off point for generating topics. Ask: *Is there a place that fulfills a similar role in your life to the one that "The Subway" did for Edwina Armstrong?* You might also suggest that students brainstorm for a place from their past—a park, a playhouse, or the apartment of a friend—that holds special significance to them and could serve as the subject of their description.

complain. But neophytes to the technology of pin-ball, tilted their game on the first try. True to adolescence, they blamed it on the floor, on the machine's legs, on unevenness, on bad luck—never on themselves.

Finally they checked out the billboard. It hung in the far back of the store and was plastered with pictures of athletes, newspaper clippings, score cards, posters, snapshots. Kids collected around that like bees around honey, giggling, whispering, and rubbernecking to catch "the latest."

We were firm but fair with a certain affection for our teenage customers. In turn, the kids, while sometimes mischievous, never in all those years vandalized "The Subway." We had no writing on the walls, no carving in the knotty pine, no graffiti on the outside trim.

Even with our set of rules, they respected us and the place. We allowed no off-color language. . . . And if on occasion (usually while challenged by the pin-ball machine) some boy would slip up, Ed would quickly admonish with "Watch your language!" and the kid obeyed, followed by a sigh but no sass.

Fellows were not allowed to put their arms around girls when sitting in the booths, however we did allow courting couples on a date to share one ice cream sundae.

Absolutely no loitering was allowed at "The Subway" during school hours. Some hooky players really tested us with all kinds of innovative and creative excuses but we were adamant about our rule.

Writing back in time, I remember the year we had the front (and only) large window professionally converted into a miniature football field, goal posts and all. Carved plywood figures of the first-string players were positioned on the field with their names boldly printed at the base. Cheerleaders, bedecked with pompoms, stood on the sidelines cheering those Bombers to victory. We tacked a large scorecard on the wall inside the window and wrote the scores in weekly. The kids loved it! And we treated each football player to a "Bomber Special" when they won a game. In memory, the winning was special, and we were glad to make the winners feel that specialness.

I remember what a grand event Valentine's Day was those days. We stocked the back counter with displays of heart-shaped candy boxes, big and small, gaudy with bows, satin roses, and velvet. While we didn't have a formal "lay away plan," many a gal received many a box of chocolates that had been paid out with ten and twenty-five cent payments over the weeks before the fourteenth of February.

The details that show the writer's relationship with her customers reveal the author's purpose: She wants to convey a rosy impression of her experiences.

By writing about a past experience, the writer attaches significance and perspective to her subject.

Adjectives like "gaudy" and "satin" complete the descriptions of the candy boxes.

"Mrs. A., I'm buying this one for Teresa. Think she'll like it?"
"This one's for Mom."

"Ed, do you think Anne would like the big white one with the red roses?"

In confidence, they would tell us who the lucky girl would be. We never asked; we listened, but sometimes the kids surprised us.

"I'm buying that purple one for the decoration. Gonna hang it from the rear view mirror of my hot rod."

Dialogue adds depth to the description.

A small memory is of the grammar school kids disembarking from their school bus in front of "The Subway." They trooped in for their daily free drink of water. "It's the best water there is," one first grader proclaimed in an earnest toothless lisp. Ed, tickled by this toothless little tyke asked, "What did you say?"

"Iss tha bess walther thure iss." And Ed would throw me a sideways smile.

I will always remember J. She came in alone, sat at the counter, and ordered one whole dill pickle. While the others smacked their lips over ice cream or candy, she'd chew on her pickle undisturbed and obviously enjoying every bite of it. I liked her.

As drive-ins opened, ice cream parlors closed. Kids, moving with the times, no longer borrowed Dad's car; they had their own. Outdoor movies, frozen custard, rock 'n' roll, and miniskirts replaced neighborhood meeting places, "Bomber Specials," big bands, and poodle skirts. "The Subway" had served its purpose during it's moment in time. We saw it was time to close.

I reminisce often about those times with nostalgic twinges, smiles, chuckles, and sometimes even a tear—but isn't that what memories are made of? I will always "See ya' at the Subway!"

▲ **Critical Viewing** What details in this photograph are reflected in the essay? **[Connect]**

The addition of the writer's reflections on a time gone by transforms a piece of descriptive writing into a remembrance.

Reading Writing Connection

Writing Application: Supporting Your Purpose *By adding only details that supported her general impression about the luncheonette, the author achieved a specific* **purpose**—*to reflect nostalgically on her luncheonette. When you write, include only specific details that will support your general impression of the subject.*

L̲I̲TERATURE

For another example of descriptive writing, read Rudolfo Anaya's "A Celebration of Grandfathers." You can find this descriptive essay in *Prentice Hall Literature: Timeless Voices, Timeless Themes,* Gold.

Connections with Literature

In "A Celebration of Grandfathers," Rudolfo Anaya describes his remembrances of the old people he knew in his childhood and the place of honor they held within Latino culture. As does Armstrong in "See Ya' at The Subway," Anaya paints a rosy portrait of a period from the past. Encourage students to read Anaya's essay and compare it to Armstrong's reminiscence. Which work do they find more compelling? Why?

Critical Viewing

Connect Students might mention things like the pin-ball machine, stools, and bobby socks.

Prewriting: Observation

1. Use the following activity as a warm-up to help students improve their ability to take descriptive notes. Have partners each record their independent observations on the same subject: the interior of the classroom, the view from the window, or the like. Then have partners compare notes. What kind of details did each include?

2. As an alternative to carrying a notepad, students might use a small tape recorder. Students can record their spoken notes and observations for later review.

3. Point out that this technique is used to generate topic ideas. Students might return to the site of the observation to record further notes after the topic is chosen.

Prewriting: Trigger Words and Objects

Teaching Resources: Writing Support Transparency 6-A

1. Display the transparency.

2. Before dividing students into groups, model the process with the class. Have students say a trigger word or hold up an object. Say the words or phrases that come to mind. Then say a trigger word to the class and have students jot down their responses. Ask several volunteers to share the words, phrases, or sentences they wrote.

3. To help get students started, provide each group with a few sample trigger words on index cards: *fall, icy, danger, festival,* and *resilience.*

4. Encourage students to follow up on their initial responses to the triggers. For example, if a trigger word evoked a memory of a person, students can freewrite for a few minutes on what they remember about that person.

6.2 *Prewriting*

Choosing Your Topic

When choosing a topic for a description, consider people, places, things, and experiences that strike you as memorable, important, or special. Your enthusiasm for your topic will shine through in your writing. Use one of the following strategies to choose a topic:

Strategies for Generating Topics

1. **Observation** For a few days, carry a note pad with you. Be alert to the sights, sounds, smells, tastes, and textures you encounter. Wherever you go, jot down notes about the interesting people, places, and things that you see. Then, review your notes, and select a topic for your description.

2. **Trigger Words and Objects** A single word or object can trigger a flood of ideas. For example words like, *friendship* or *fire* may remind you of people or places or evoke an emotion in you. Objects, like a leaf or a blue ribbon, may be equally suggestive. Working with a group, take turns calling out trigger words or holding up trigger objects. As each person takes a turn, jot down whatever comes to mind. When the activity is finished, review your notes and choose a topic.

Writing Lab CD-ROM

For more help finding a topic, explore the activities and suggestions in the Choosing a Topic section of the Description lesson.

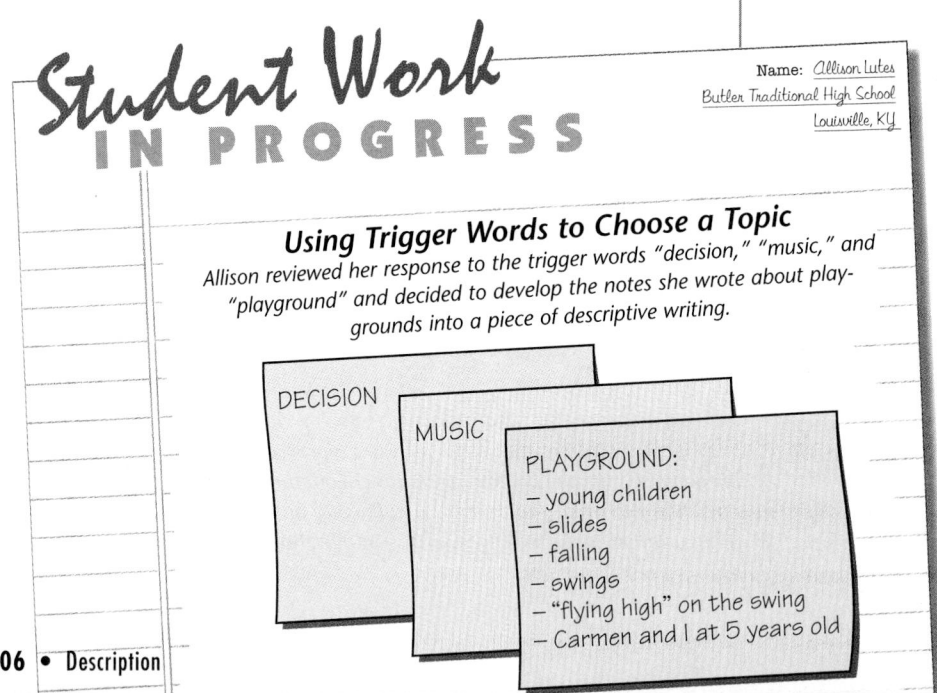

Student Work
IN PROGRESS

Name: *Allison Lutes*
Butler Traditional High School
Louisville, KY

Using Trigger Words to Choose a Topic

Allison reviewed her response to the trigger words "decision," "music," and "playground" and decided to develop the notes she wrote about playgrounds into a piece of descriptive writing.

DECISION

MUSIC

PLAYGROUND:
– young children
– slides
– falling
– swings
– "flying high" on the swing
– Carmen and I at 5 years old

106 • Description

⏱ TIME AND RESOURCE MANAGER

Resources
Print: Writing Support Transparencies 6-A–C; Writing Support Activity Book 6-1
Technology: Writing Lab CD-ROM, Description

In-Depth Coverage	Accelerated Pace
• Cover pp. 106–109 in class. • Guide students through the Strategies for Generating Topics. • Have students use the Index-Card Camera technique to narrow their topics. **Option** Have students work individually or in groups with the Writing Lab CD-ROM.	• Discuss strategies for generating topics. • Have students work independently to choose and narrow their topics. • Have students submit final topic ideas for your review.

TOPIC BANK

1. **Description of Freedom** A dictionary can define freedom, but the concept may be harder to convey. Using concrete images and examples, describe what the concept of freedom means to you.

2. **Description of a Sports Event** Radio announcers have the special skills needed to capture the action at a sports event in words. Write a description of a championship game so readers can envision all the action.

Responding to Fine Art

3. Vincent van Gogh painted this picture of his bedroom at Arles, France. Write a description of the room as he portrayed it, or use your reaction to this painting as a springboard for an idea of your own. For example, you might describe a room you'd like to call your own.

Responding to Literature

4. In his short story "The Secret Life of Walter Mitty," James Thurber uses descriptive language to convey the excitement the title character conjures up in his daydreams. Read this story to see how a comic writer makes use of descriptive language. Use Thurber's writing as a model and describe another daydream Mitty might have had. You can find this story in *Prentice Hall Literature: Timeless Voices, Timeless Themes,* Gold.

Bedroom of van Gogh at Arles Vincent van Gogh
Musee d'Orsay, Paris, France

☑ Cooperative Writing Opportunity

5. **Travel Brochure** Work with a group to write a travel brochure about a place that is real or imagined. One student can write a profile of the area's geographic features; another can write about its key places; others can draw maps or create or gather pictures. When you have completed all of these tasks, work together to assemble the pieces into a finished brochure.

Prewriting • 107

Responding to Fine Art

Bedroom of van Gogh at Arles, by Vincent van Gogh

Teaching Resources: Writing Support Transparency 6-B

You can use this artwork as a starting point to help students generate topic ideas for a description.

1. Display the transparency. Have students discuss their responses to the painting. You can use questions such as these as prompts:
   - What adjectives would you use to describe the scene in the painting?
   - Judging from his bedroom, what was most important to van Gogh?
   - If van Gogh had described his bedroom in words, rather than paint, how might his description read?

2. Ask students to brainstorm for description ideas suggested by this work of art. Here are some possibilities: a description of your favorite room; a description of your favorite place; a description of a place or thing that says something about who your are.

Responding to Literature

In Thurber's most famous story, a powerless proofreader escapes his mundane life by slipping into a daydream world. In his dreams, Mitty is the hero, wielding the power over those who dominate his everyday existence. Reading Thurber's colorful description of Mitty's fantasy life may help students generate their own topic ideas for describing a make-believe place. Encourage students to go beyond the real world and write a description that fully utilizes the power of their imaginations.

Spotlight on the Humanities

For additional topics, refer students to the Spotlight on the Humanities on page 124.

107

Narrowing Your Topic

Once you have chosen a topic, ask yourself whether you can cover it thoroughly in a brief description. A topic such as "the desert" is too broad. To make the job more manageable, you might whittle "the desert" down to "cactus." Here is a technique you might use to narrow your topic:

Use an Index-Card Camera

1. Find or create a picture of your topic or, if possible, look at the actual person, place, or thing.
2. Study the picture or actual subject as it is, noting as many sensory details as possible.
3. Cut a small hole in the center of an index card.
4. Use your "index-card camera" to zoom in on a smaller aspect of your subject. Let the camera help you to focus on details that you may have overlooked.
5. Choose one of the specific details you saw with your "camera" to use as the specific topic of your description.

▼ **Critical Viewing** What other topics related to this desert scene might the writer have focused on using the index-card camera? **[Make a Judgment]**

Considering Your Audience and Purpose

Identifying Your Audience Before you write, consider your audience. The knowledge level and interests of your readers may direct the vocabulary you use or the depth and complexity of your description.

Refining Your Purpose While your writing will be descriptive, you probably have another purpose in mind. For example, you may write to inform your readers about a place they've never been. Once you clarify your purpose, use details and language that will help you achieve it.

Writing Lab CD-ROM

Use the Interactive Audience Profile to record information about your audience's age, interest, and familiarity with your subject. You can find it in the toolkit.

108 • Description

Gathering Details

To create a vivid picture of your subject, use precise, concrete details. Using the strategy of cubing will help you gather as many details as you can.

Cubing to Gather Details

Cubing is a technique that helps you gather details by exploring your subject from a variety of angles. Draw a cube, or build one using a piece of paper. Then, use each of the six sides of the cube to jot down notes from these specific "angles":

Describe your topic. Note relevant sights, sounds, smells, textures, and tastes.

Associate it. Jot down words or experiences that your subject suggests to you.

Apply it. Note the ways in which your subject can be used.

Analyze it. Break your subject into parts. Then, consider how these parts work together.

Compare or contrast it. Identify examples of other items or ideas that are similar to your subject.

Argue for or against it. Take a position.

 **Internet Tip**

Depending on your topic, you may find it helpful to conduct research to gather details. If you're describing a well-known person, place, thing, or event, use the Internet to learn more about your subject.

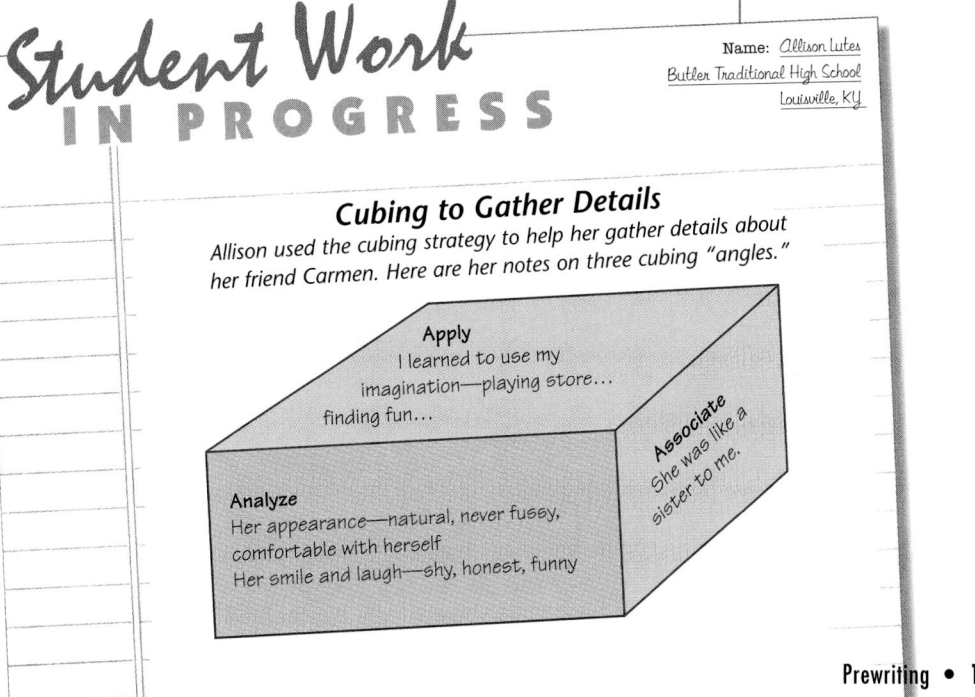

Student Work IN PROGRESS

Name: *Allison Lutes*
Butler Traditional High School
Louisville, KY

Cubing to Gather Details
Allison used the cubing strategy to help her gather details about her friend Carmen. Here are her notes on three cubing "angles."

Apply
I learned to use my imagination—playing store... finding fun...

Associate
She was like a sister to me.

Analyze
Her appearance—natural, never fussy, comfortable with herself
Her smile and laugh—shy, honest, funny

Prewriting: Cubing to Gather Details

Teaching Resources: Writing Support Transparency 6-C; Writing Support Activity Book 6-1

1. Display the transparency. Model the strategy by applying the cubing technique to an everyday object. Elicit responses for each "angle." For example:
   - This eraser—how would you describe it to someone who has never seen one before? (gray, rectangular, and so on)
   - What does it remind you of? (It is the shape of a brick or a mop head.)
   - How do you use it? (You rub it back and forth across the chalkboard.)
   - How would you separate it into parts? (One half is made of wood, the other of molded fiber.)
   - What other objects does it remind you of? (It is similar in form and purpose to a mop head.)
   - Do you like erasers? Why or why not? (No, they create a cloud of dust when they are used; yes, they make your mistakes go away.)

2. Give students copies of the blank organizer to help them gather details about their topics.

 **TIME SAVERS!**

 Writing Support Transparencies
Use the transparencies for Chapter 6 to teach these strategies.

 Writing Support Activity Book
Use the graphic organizers for Chapter 6 to facilitate these strategies.

Drafting: Choose an Organization That Suits Your Topic

Teaching Resources: Writing Support Transparency 6-D

1. Review the patterns for spatial organization and order of importance. Then display the transparency to see how Allison organized her ideas.

2. Point out that an organizational method that suits one particular topic might be less appropriate for another. A description of an event, for an example, might be best suited for time order, or chronological, organization.

3. Encourage students to experiment with different organizational methods.

Customize for
Bodily/Kinesthetic Learners

Suggest that students write down each of the details they have gathered on separate index cards. Then students can try different methods of organization, one at a time, by manipulating the index cards into different organizational structures.

Drafting Tip

Suggest that students not spend too much time and effort worrying about spelling, punctuation, or sentence construction while creating their first drafts. Errors in these areas can be corrected during the revising and editing stages.

6.3 Drafting

Shaping Your Writing

Once you have all the details you need, choose an organizational plan to present them. Here are two organizational patterns you might use:

Choose an Organization That Suits Your Topic

Spatial Organization For a physical description of a person, place, or thing, use spatial order. Describe your topic from top to bottom, left to right, front to back, or outward from the most prominent feature. To keep your order clear, use such transitional words and phrases as *to the left* and *above*.

Order of Importance To describe an idea, grab your readers' interest with your second most important point. Then, address your less important points, and build to your strongest. To use this type of order, place a number next to each of the details you'll use, so you can plan the order in which you will present them. Follow this list as you draft.

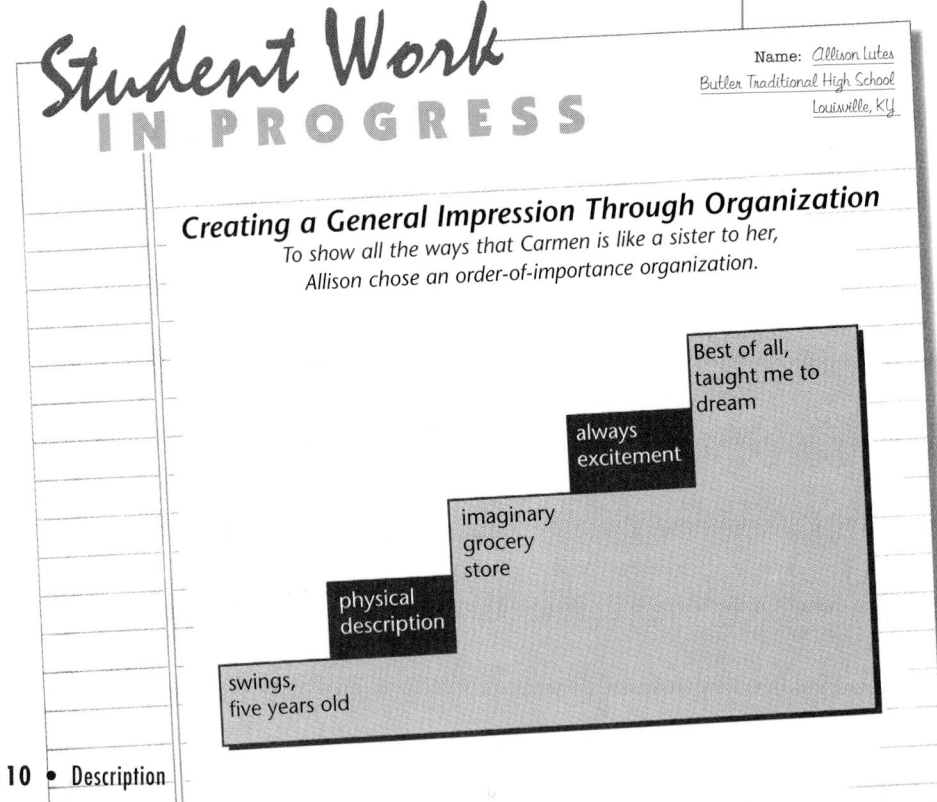

Student Work
IN PROGRESS

Name: Allison Lutes
Butler Traditional High School
Louisville, KY

Creating a General Impression Through Organization
To show all the ways that Carmen is like a sister to her, Allison chose an order-of-importance organization.

- swings, five years old
- physical description
- imaginary grocery store
- always excitement
- Best of all, taught me to dream

110 • Description

⏱ TIME AND RESOURCE MANAGER

Resources
Print: Writing Support Transparency 6-D
Technology: Writing Lab CD-ROM, Description

In-Depth Coverage	Accelerated Pace
• Cover pp. 110–111 in class. • Work through both organizational strategies with the entire class. • Have students draft their essays in class. • Review simile and metaphor with students. **Option** Have students work individually or in small groups with the Writing Lab CD-ROM.	• Have students review pp. 110–111 independently, then write the first draft of their descriptions. • Respond to individual drafting issues as needed.

Providing Elaboration

As you draft your description, focus on providing vivid sensory details—details appealing to one or more of the five senses. These will create a strong picture of your subject in the minds of your readers.

Add Figurative Language

In addition to sensory details that describe your topic exactly as it appears, use figurative language to capture your readers' interest. Figurative language is not meant to be taken literally; instead, it builds comparisons and helps suggest new ways of looking at an object. Two types of figurative language you might use are similes and metaphors.

Simile A *simile* compares one thing to another using the word *like* or *as*. The example below stresses the force of a storm's wind by comparing it to a power saw.

EXAMPLE: During the storm, the wind tore through branches *like* a power saw.

Metaphor A *metaphor* compares two unlike things by setting them up as equals. It describes one object as if it were another. This example calls hefty tree trunks matchsticks to convey the power of the storm.

EXAMPLE: Tree trunks *were* matchsticks as they snapped in the hurricane-force winds.

Collaborative Writing Tip

Work with a partner to build your experience with figurative language. Discuss both types of comparisons, and suggest specific ones that your partner might use to elaborate his or her draft with sharp and creative details.

▼ Critical Viewing
What other similes or metaphors might you use to describe this storm? **[Describe]**

Drafting • 111

Step-by-Step Teaching Guide

Drafting: Add Figurative Language

1. Remind students that figurative language is not meant literally. It is used to create imaginative images and help the reader see things in new ways.

2. Emphasize that both similes and metaphors draw comparisons between unlike things. Use the simile in the fourth paragraph of the Model From Literature as an example. Kids jammed into "The Subway" are compared to scoops of ice cream jammed into glasses.

3. Have students review the details they have gathered for their descriptions. Ask them to develop a simile and a metaphor to describe two of these details. Ask volunteers to read their similes and metaphors to the class.

Customize for ESL Students

Understanding figurative language can be especially challenging. Help students understand the comparisons expressed in the examples on the page. Focus their attention on the second example. Ask: *What are the qualities of a matchstick? What would happen to matchsticks in a strong wind?* (They are small, weak, light, easily broken; they would fly away.) Then work with students to create similes and metaphors based on the details they've collected for their drafts.

Critical Viewing

Describe Students' responses will vary. Make sure their similes use *like* or *as*.

111

Revising: Revising Your Overall Structure

1. Have students review their purposes for writing. They should ask themselves what impression they want their audience to take away from the description.

2. Explain the process of color-coding to highlight the main impression. If students have difficulty finding main impressions to highlight, they may want to revise their paragraphs by adding generalizations.

3. Suggest that students make a list of main impressions for each paragraph after they have color-coded them. Students can examine this list to see if each paragraph supports their overall purpose for writing.

Integrating Speaking and Listening Skills

Partners can take turns reading aloud paragraphs of their drafts. The listener should focus on identifying the main impression that the writer wants to convey. Students can consider the comments of their partners while revising their paragraphs.

Critical Viewing

Analyze Students' responses will vary. Encourage them to support their responses using details from the image.

6.4 Revising

Once you have completed a first draft, review your description by polishing its overall structure, analyzing its paragraphs, studying its sentences, and evaluating the word choice.

Revising Your Overall Structure
Analyze the General Impression

Remember that the purpose of descriptive writing is to paint a picture of your subject with words. To achieve this goal, your paper should convey a single impression of your subject. All of your paragraphs should contribute to that impression; your first or last paragraph should include a statement that sums up the impression.

▶ **REVISION STRATEGY**
Color-Coding to Highlight Your Main Impression

Use different-colored highlighters to mark words that reveal the main impression of each paragraph. Then, evaluate your draft using these questions as a guide:

Evaluate
- Does each paragraph contribute to a general impression? What is that impression?

- Have you included a generalization that expresses the overall impression you want to create?

Revise
- Eliminate paragraphs that are irrelevant or distracting, or revise them so they *do* contribute.

- Look carefully at your last sentence, and consider revising it or adding another sentence.

◀ **Critical Viewing**
What is the main impression you get from looking at this train station? **[Analyze]**

112 • Description

⏱ TIME AND RESOURCE MANAGER

Resources
Print: Writing Support Transparencies 6-E–G
Technology: Writing Lab CD-ROM, Description

In-Depth Coverage	Accelerated Pace
• Cover pp. 112–117 in class. • Use the relevant transparencies for demonstrating each revision strategy: build snapshots and color-coding to eliminate run-ons. **Option** Have students work individually or in groups with the Writing Lab CD-ROM, focusing on revision activities and tools.	• Ask students to review the revision strategies on pp. 112–117. • Have students work independently to revise their descriptions.

Revising Your Paragraphs

Add Details to Strengthen Your Description

Details in writing are like close-ups in a movie. To make your description precise, review each paragraph and identify places where the picture is fuzzy. Using the "snapshot" strategy can bring your description into focus.

▶ **REVISION STRATEGY**
Building Snapshots

Cut self-sticking notes into little bursts the shape of a camera's flash. Then, review your draft. Whenever you come to a place where you would like to add more detail, attach a note to your paper. Jot down a word or phrase that captures the detail you'd like to add. Use your notes to guide your revision.

Student Work
IN PROGRESS

Name: *Allison Lutes*
Butler Traditional High School
Louisville, KY

Building Snapshots for Revision

Here's how Allison used the snapshot technique to analyze one paragraph in her descriptive essay. She built these ideas into her writing.

Laughing

The swings sat side by side—one of our favorite places to play.

The wind blew our long hair back when we tried to see who

5 years old

could go the highest. We were the best of friends; we could

swing forever and never tire of each other's company. When

bare feet

our feet finally hit the ground, it was only because we had to go

in. Even then, we took our time, digging in the dirt with our

toes and running zigzags.

Cool grass

Revising • 113

Revising: Color-Coding to Identify Run-ons

Teaching Resources: Writing Support Transparency 6-F

1. Discuss run-on sentences and the three strategies for revising them. Display the transparency to show students how Allison identified run-on sentences in her draft.

2. Have students note that inserting a comma *without* a conjunction is not one of the listed strategies. Doing so creates another type of run-on, the comma splice sentence, shown in the example below:

   The apple is sweet, the skin is smooth.

3. Students can easily identify comma splice run-ons. If each half of a sentence divided by only a comma can stand alone, the sentence is a comma splice run-on.

4. After color-coding their drafts, students should examine them for each type of run-on. Suggest that they pay particular attention to longer sentences and sentences that contain more than one idea.

6.4

Revising Your Sentences
Eliminate Run-ons

As you add more descriptive details to your draft, be on the lookout for run-on sentences. A run-on sentence is two or more complete sentences written as if they were a single sentence. To revise a run-on sentence, consider one of these three strategies:

REVISING RUN-ON SENTENCES

EXAMPLE SENTENCE: The apple is sweet the skin is smooth.	
Strategy	**Example**
Add a comma and a conjunction.	The apple is sweet, and the skin is smooth.
Add a semicolon	The apple is sweet; the skin is smooth.
Split the run-on into two or more sentences.	The apple is sweet. The skin is smooth.

▶ **REVISION STRATEGY**
Color-Coding to Identify Run-ons

Using alternate colors for every other sentence, bracket the beginning and end of every sentence in your draft. Review each sentence to analyze its construction. Revise any run-on sentences you find.

Student Work
IN PROGRESS

Name: *Allison Lutes*
Butler Traditional High School
Louisville, KY

Bracketing to Identify Run-on Sentences

[It] was her Pop, and he screamed when he found out about all the food we had [taken.] [He] wanted us to give it back, but we explained to him that it didn't work that [way.] [If] he wanted the food back, he would have to [pay.] [After] all, we were running a [business.] [Her] Pop finally gave in, he would give us fifty cents if we returned all of the [food.] [We] agreed, because we had had our [fun.]

114 • Description

⏱ TIME SAVERS!

Writing Support Transparencies
Use the transparencies for Chapter 6 to teach these strategies.

🔧 STANDARDIZED TEST PREPARATION WORKSHOP

Grammar and Usage Many standardized tests require students to identify run-on sentences and to choose a correctly written replacement. Show the following example to students:

The two men enjoyed scuba diving together they had traveled to the Caribbean and Red seas.

Choose the best way to rewrite the sentence.

A The two men enjoyed scuba diving together, they had traveled to the Caribbean and Red Seas.

B The two men enjoyed scuba diving together. They had traveled to the Caribbean and Red seas.

C The two men enjoyed scuba diving together and they had traveled to the Caribbean and Red seas.

D Correct as is.

The correct answer is item **B**. Item A is a comma splice. Item C is missing a comma between the two independent clauses. Item D, the original, is a run-on.

Grammar in Your Writing
Semicolons

Semicolons can create compound sentences by connecting two simple sentences. Semicolons can indicate a strong connection between ideas or they can indicate a direct contrast.

To show a strong connection:

The fans jumped to their feet in anticipation of a win; the game was on the line.

To show a direct contrast:

The fans jumped to their feet in hopes of a win; the pitcher dug in his heels.

When the relationship between clauses is not clear, add a transition or a conjunctive adverb to clarify the sentence. Place the phrase immediately after the semicolon.

Transitional Words and Phrases

as a result	for example	on the other hand
at this time	for instance	second
first	in fact	that is

Example: They cheered for the home team; **in fact,** they clapped until their hands were sore.

Conjunctive Adverbs

also	furthermore	instead
besides	however	otherwise
consequently	indeed	therefore

Example: Fans had high hopes of victory; however, the championship was lost.

Find It in Your Reading Read "See Ya' at the Subway" on pages 102–105, and identify any sentences that include semicolons. For each, indicate whether a transitional expression or an adverb makes the connection clear.

Find It in Your Writing Review your draft, looking for places where you can use semicolons to join two simple sentences. Consider whether you need transitions or conjunctive adverbs to make the relationship between clauses clear.

For more on semicolons, see Chapter 29.

Revising • 115

ONGOING ASSESSMENT: Prerequisite Skills

If students have difficulty understanding semicolon usage, you may find it helpful to review the following to assure coverage of prerequisite knowledge.

In the Textbook	Print Resources	Technology
Punctuation, pp. 686–694	Grammar Exercise Workbook, pp. 179–180	Language Lab CD-ROM, Capitalization and Punctuation; On-Line Exercise Bank, Section 29.3

Step-by-Step Teaching Guide

Grammar In Your Writing: Semicolons

1. Remind students that a clause is a group of words that contains a subject and a verb. A simple sentence is a main clause that stands alone.
2. Emphasize that a semicolon does not indicate the relationship between clauses. Therefore, a semicolon should be used only when the relationship between clauses is obvious.
3. Write the following sentences on the chalkboard. Ask students to add a transition or conjunctive adverb to clarify the relationship between clauses:

   He ran furiously for the bus stop; the bus was already pulling away. (Possible response: however)

   The training took longer than expected; Jonathan was late getting home. (Possible response: as a result)

Find It in Your Reading

As a class, identify all the semicolons in the model.

Find It in Your Writing

Have students exchange drafts to check each other's revisions.

Integrating Grammar Skills

Point out that a third use of the semicolon is to separate items in a series when the items themselves already contain commas. Write the following example on the chalkboard:

Famous river cities include Kansas City, located on the Missouri River; St. Louis, located on the Mississippi River; and Memphis, also located on the Mississippi.

115

Revising: Use Precise Verbs

Teaching Resources: Writing Support Transparency 6-G

1. Point out some of the precise verbs used by Edwina Armstrong in "See Ya' at The Subway" such as those used to describe the action of the school kids who *disembark, troop in,* and *proclaim.*

2. Display the transparency to model for students the strategy of circling verbs.

3. Before students circle the verbs in their drafts, have them warm up with more practice finding substitutes for vague or general verbs. Have students suggest more precise verbs to replace the ones that follow:

   walk *(amble, stroll, saunter, bound)*

   see, look *(spy, stare, witness, observe)*

   take *(grab, seize, grasp)*

Customize for
ESL Students

Students learning English may have a limited verb vocabulary. For this stage of the revision process, consider pairing ESL students with native English speakers. Have the partners work together to identify precise verbs that express exactly the meaning that the ESL student wants to convey. For example, the partner could help to describe and demonstrate the various shades of meaning expressed in the synonyms for *walk* listed above.

⏱ **TIME SAVERS!**

 Writing Support Transparencies
Use the transparencies for Chapter 6 to teach these strategies.

6.4

Revising Your Word Choice
Use Precise Verbs

As you revise, put some punch into your writing style. Find tired, vague, weak verbs and throw them away. Replace them with precise, vivid verbs that express exactly the meaning that you want to convey to your readers. Here are some examples:

Throw These Out:	Replace Them With:
• go	• race, creep, streak, tumble
• say	• whisper, yell, suggest, demand
• think	• imagine, brainstorm, agonize, worry, anticipate, plan, wonder

▶ **REVISION STRATEGY**
Circling Verbs to Enliven Writing

Read through your paper, and circle the verbs you've used. As you review the circled words, analyze each one to decide whether it seems vague. Consult a thesaurus to tap the variety of words that may suit your needs. Then, consider replacing some of the verbs you've circled with words that more precisely convey the action you intended.

**Writing Lab
CD-ROM**

In addition to replacing vague verbs, strengthen your use of adjectives. Use the vague-adjectives revision checker to help you do so.

Student Work
IN PROGRESS

Name: *Allison Lutes*
Butler Traditional High School
Louisville, KY

Circling Verbs to Evaluate Word Choice
In this passage, Allison has circled dull verbs and inserted replacements to make the description stronger.

The two of us, sneaky thieves on a mission, waited until

                                              sneaked
the coast was clear and then ~~went~~ down to the kitchen.
loaded our arms with
We ~~took~~ as much as we could carry, taking foods like

oranges and peanuts and other things that wouldn't spoil

                          ran
quickly, and ~~went~~ back up to her room.

116 • Description

Peer Review

Once you have polished and improved your draft, enlist the help of a classmate. At this stage in the writing process, you have become so familiar with your piece of writing that you really need the assistance of a fresh pair of eyes. Take turns being those "fresh eyes" for each other, reviewing and commenting on each other's work.

Encourage Specific Peer Review

Ask Open-Ended Questions Avoid questions that can be answered with a yes or no response. Instead, probe with questions that ask what, how, or when.

YES/NO QUESTION:	Did you like my introduction?
OPEN-ENDED QUESTION:	What did you like best about my introduction?
	How could I improve it?
	When did you know for sure what I was describing?

Direct Your Peer's Attention Instead of asking a reviewer to comment on your whole draft, limit your peer's response. Ask questions that direct peers to comment on specific elements of your writing.

VAGUE QUESTION:	Did you like this draft?
DIRECT QUESTION:	Which comparison worked best?
	Was there any comparison that I should improve or delete?

Ask Follow-up Questions Use a peer's response as a springboard for a discussion. In this sample conversation, the writer asks follow-up questions to direct the revision.

SAMPLE PEER REVIEW DIALOGUE

Writer: What did you like best about the part that describes the arcade?

Reviewer: I could really see the bright lights.

Writer: Which words conveyed that?

Reviewer: "Dazzling" and "blinking" let me see what you were describing.

Writer: I was also trying to show the noise. Did you get that?

Reviewer: Not really. There isn't any description of the noise. Maybe you should add some there.

Revising: Peer Review

1. Before beginning the peer review activity, remind students to provide positive feedback by commenting on the strongest parts of the drafts as well as parts that could be strengthened.

2. Guide students in drafting open-ended questions to ask their peer reviewers. Here are some examples:
   - What is the strongest part of the description?
   - What impression of the description's subject does it seem like I am trying to stress?
   - Are there any parts of the description that seem unclear?
   - What aspects could use further elaboration?

Revision Tip

Have students recall their purposes for writing and the intended audience for their description and record them on an index card. Suggest that students periodically refer to the card as a guide to help them revise their drafts.

Editing and Proofreading

1. Provide students with an example of a sentence in which the subject and the verb are separated by prepositional phrases.

   Conditions <u>for the launch</u> were perfect.

2. Discuss other confusing subject-verb situations.

   Subject following verb: There ~~is~~ are also several other items on the agenda.

   Compound subject joined by *and*: Jerry and Latrice ~~relies~~ rely on him.

   Subject and verb separated by an intervening expression: Bolivia, as well as its neighbors, ~~have~~ has a wealth of mineral resources.

Grammar in Your Writing

1. With indefinite pronouns that can be singular or plural, it is important to analyze the words that they refer to.

2. List on the chalkboard several indefinite pronouns that can be either singular or plural. Challenge students to write two sentences for each pronoun, one in which it takes a singular verb and one in which it takes a plural verb.

Find It in Your Reading

Examples include *anything*.

Find It in Your Writing

Have students share examples of their revisions with the class.

Integrating Spelling Skills

Reinforce that the indefinite pronouns *something*, *anybody*, and *everyone* are each one word. Only the indefinite pronoun *no one* is two words. Have students check their work for errors such as *any body* or *some thing*.

6.5 Editing and Proofreading

While you want your description to convey an impression, prevent distractions by correcting mistakes in your final draft. Carefully check your writing to catch and correct errors in grammar, spelling, punctuation, and capitalization.

Focusing on Agreement

As you proofread, focus your attention on subject-verb agreement. Identify the subject and verb in each sentence, and double-check that they agree.

Grammar in Your Writing

Making Verbs Agree with Indefinite Pronouns

Indefinite pronouns often refer to people, places or things, without specifying which ones. Here are some common indefinite pronouns:

Common Indefinite Pronouns

Singular		Plural	Singular or Plural
anybody	nobody	both	all
anything	no one	few	any
everybody	nothing	many	more
everyone	someone	several	most

- Singular indefinite pronouns take singular verbs; plural indefinite pronouns take plural verbs.

  Singular: **Anybody** in the club **is** allowed to attend the meeting.

  Plural: **Both** of us **want** to hear the report.

- When an indefinite pronoun can be singular or plural, study the sentence. Use the antecedent, the pronoun's reference, to make the agreement choice.

  Singular: **More** of the money **is** spent in December. (refers to singular *money*)

  Plural: **More** of the gifts **are** bought at that time. (refers to plural *gifts*)

Find It in Your Reading   Read "See Ya' at the Subway" on pages 102–105. Identify any indefinite pronouns used as subjects. For each, identify whether the verb it takes is singular or plural.

Find It in Your Writing   Review your draft to correct any agreement errors involving indefinite pronouns.

For more help with subject-verb agreement, see Chapter 25.

⏱ TIME AND RESOURCE MANAGER

Resources
Print: Scoring Rubrics on Transparency, Chapter 6; Writing Assessment: Scoring Rubric and Scoring Models for Description
Technology: Writing Lab CD-ROM, Description

In-Depth Coverage	Accelerated Pace
• Review pp. 118–121 in class. • Distribute and review the Proofreading Checklist. • Give step-by-step coverage to Publishing and Presenting (p. 119). • Analyze in class the Final Draft on pp. 120–121. • Students edit and proofread their descriptions in class.	• Assign pp. 118–121 for independent review. • Students can independently edit and proofread their essays. • Respond to individual editing issues as needed.

6.6 Publishing and Presenting

Building Your Portfolio

There are numerous ways in which to share your descriptive writing. Consider these strategies:

1. **Prepare an Oral Presentation** Descriptive writing that is rich in sensory detail is well suited to reading aloud. Gather props, illustrations, or music to enhance your reading. Then, share your description with an audience.

2. **Create an Illustrated Anthology** Put several descriptions in a collection. Include at least one illustration or photograph with each piece of writing. Create a cover and a table of contents, and invite others to share your anthology.

Reflecting on Your Writing

Consider the experience of writing your descriptive paper. Use these questions to inspire a written reflection. Keep a copy of your reflection, along with a copy of your essay, in your portfolio.

- How did your view of your subject change or grow as a result of your writing about it?

- What did you find most enjoyable about this kind of writing?

 **Internet Tip**

To see model essays scored with this rubric, go to **www.phwg. phschool.com**

Rubric for Self-Assessment

Use these criteria to evaluate your descriptive writing.

	Score 4	Score 3	Score 2	Score 1
Audience and Purpose	Contains details that work together to create a single, dominant impression of the topic	Creates through use of details a dominant impression of the topic	Contains extraneous details that detract from main impression	Contains details that are unfocused and create no dominant impression
Organization	Demonstrates clear organization well-suited to the topic	Demonstrates clear organization	Demonstrates inconsistent organization	Presents information randomly
Elaboration	Contains creative use of figurative language, creating interesting comparisons	Contains figurative language that creates comparisons	Contains figurative language, but the comparisons are not fresh	Contains no figurative language
Use of Language	Contains sensory language that appeals to the five senses; contains no errors in grammar, punctuation, or spelling	Contains some sensory language; contains few errors in grammar, punctuation, and spelling	Contains some sensory language, but it appeals to only one or two of the senses; contains some errors in grammar, punctuation, and spelling	Contains no sensory language; contains many errors in grammar, punctuation, and spelling

Publishing and Presenting • 119

✓ ONGOING ASSESSMENT: Assess Mastery

Use one of the following options to assess final drafts of students' descriptive writing.

Self Assessment Ask students to score their essay using the rubric provided. Then have students write a single paragraph reflecting on the most valuable thing they learned in completing this essay.

Teacher Assessment You may wish to use the rubric and the scoring models provided in Writing Assessment, Description, to score students' work.

Publishing and Presenting

1. Have students recall the intended audiences for their work. Ask them to consider ways to present their work to those audiences.

2. For the anthology activity, encourage students to work together with classmates who wrote on similar topics or themes.

Integrating Workplace Skills

Ask interested students to contact professionals in various fields and to obtain samples of the types of descriptive writing they need to perform in the workplace. Have students present these samples to the class.

ASSESS

Assessment

Teaching Resources: Scoring Rubrics on Transparency 6; Formal Assessment, Chapter 6

1. Display the Scoring Rubric transparency and review the criteria in class.

2. Before students proceed with self-assessment, you may wish to review the Final Draft of the Student Work in Progress on pages 120–121. Have students score the Final Draft in one or more of the rubric categories. For example, how would students score the piece in terms of audience and purpose?

3. In addition to student self-assessment, you may wish to use the following assessment options.

   - score student essays yourself, using the rubric and scoring models from Writing Assessment.

   - review the Standardized Test Preparation Workshop on pages 126–127 and have students practice taking a multiple-choice test related to the analysis of a written passage.

   - administer the Chapter 5 Test from Formal Assessment in Teaching Resources to assess students' grasp of concepts presented.

Teaching from the Final Draft

1. Help students recognize the ways in which "My 'Sister'" incorporates key elements of descriptive writing.

   • The topic—memories of a childhood friend—is well chosen.

   • The title introduces the subject of the description and illustrates her importance to the writer.

   • The impression that Allison wants to stress is clearly stated in the last sentence of the first paragraph: Carmen and Allison were inseparable friends.

   • The description is strengthened by the use of figurative language and precise verbs.

   • The work is composed of cohesive paragraphs, each of which describes a different aspect of Carmen or her relationship with Allison.

   • The conclusion ties past and present together by explaining where the relationship stands today.

2. Have students discuss their responses to the final draft. Ask: *If you were peer reviewing Allison's work, what suggestions would you make to her? What would you say are the strongest aspects of her work?*

Critical Viewing

Infer Most students will describe the two girls in the photograph as being very close friends.

6.7 *Student Work*
IN PROGRESS

FINAL DRAFT

My "Sister"

Allison Lutes
Butler Traditional High School
Louisville, Kentucky

The swings sat side by side—one of our favorite places to play. We laughed as the wind blew our long hair back when we tried to see who could go the highest. As five-year-olds we were the best of friends; we could swing forever and never tire of each other's company. When our bare feet finally hit the ground, it was only because we had to go in. Even then, we took our time, digging in the dirt with our toes and running zigzags through the cool summer grass. Carmen and I were inseparable.

I remember Carmen as always being taller than I, although she was only of average height. Carmen's hair was long, dark, and beautiful. She was so proud of it that she usually let it be natural, rarely feeling the need to run a brush through it. Her skin was the color of roasted almonds, and her eyes were as dark as night. Her nose, she always complained, was too big, but I know she would never really want to change it. Carmen held her lips tight to conceal her overbite, but I knew it was there and didn't care. Her giggling, shy and suppressed, was unforgettable. Her face told more than she knew it did; her eyes told her thoughts, and she always got this shy smile on her round face when she was nervous. The clothes she wore were mostly hand-me-downs,

120 • Description

▲ **Critical Viewing**
What might be the relationship between these two girls?
[Infer]

The opening introduces Allison's childhood friendship with Carmen by presenting a memory rich with sensory details.

All of the sentences of this paragraph work together to present a physical description of Carmen.

faded and worn with age. This suited Carmen just fine. She was the kind of person who didn't really care how she looked or what people thought about her. She just enjoyed being herself.

On summer days when we were bored, we would sit in Carmen's room and try to think of something fun to do. Having our own grocery store was my idea, and Carmen was really enthusiastic about it, as she was about everything that was out of the ordinary. The two of us, sneaky thieves on a mission, waited until the coast was clear and then sneaked down to the kitchen. We loaded our arms with as much as we could carry, taking foods like oranges and peanuts and other things that wouldn't spoil quickly, and ran back up to her room. We set the food on her dresser and proudly hung up a sign to show that our grocery store was open. Then we waited, giggling nervously while we wondered who would find out first that the food was missing and come to buy it back. It was her Pop, and he screamed when he found out about all the food we had taken. He wanted us to give it back, but we explained to him that it didn't work that way. If he wanted the food back, he would have to pay. After all, we were running a business. Her Pop finally gave in; he would give us fifty cents if we returned all of the food. We agreed, because we had had our fun.

Carmen and I rarely shared a dull moment. We were always going on adventures and playing games. We lived in our own world in which we, as sisters, could do anything we wanted. We loved to wrap up in blankets and sit beneath umbrellas on her front porch during thunderstorms. Even though we were both terrified, we enjoyed weathering the storm together. Afterward, we would pack our bags and hike around the world, over the mountains in my yard and the prairies in hers.

More than anything, Carmen taught me how to dream. As best friends, we weathered many storms. Many times, our only way to get away from our problems was to dream. Carmen showed me how to turn everything in life into an adventure. This ability helps me to be strong even under the most demanding circumstances.

I still see Carmen—maybe a few times a year, if I'm lucky. We have both moved away from the neighborhood where we first met and became friends. I've found that our friendship is still deeply rooted in the past and all the time we spent together, because we don't see each other enough to base it on the present. We no longer share the secrets, stories, and summer days that we once did, but she will always be a part of my life. I spent so much of my life with her, and I know that because of that we will forever share a bond. Though she is no longer my best friend, she will always be my sister.

By comparing her friend and herself to "sneaky thieves on a mission," Allison uses figurative language that lets readers see the lighthearted conspiracy the young girls carried out.

The transitional phrase "More than anything" reveals Allison's organizational plan. She has saved the most important detail for last.

1. To write a poem appropriate to audience and purpose.

2. To use prewriting strategies to generate ideas.

3. To develop drafts by organizing content and refining style.

4. To publish a poem in an oral reading.

Step-by-Step Teaching Guide

Poem

Teaching Resources: Writing Support Transparency 6-H; Writing Support Activity Book 6-2

1. Use the model poem and others students suggest to familiarize the class with various poetic modes and conventions. Discuss descriptive language in the examples to confirm students' understanding.

2. Suggest that students review strategies from Chapter 6.

3. Display the transparency and invite student participation in completing it for a class-selected mood. Use variety in students' suggestions to point out the many different ways to achieve and support a mood.

4. Give students copies of the blank organizer and encourage them to complete it as a mood guide prior to writing.

5. Encourage students to share their poems in an oral reading and if they wish to submit poems to a school or local literary magazine. If you wish, have students generate such a magazine as a class project.

Connected Assignment
Poem

Like descriptive writing, **poetry** uses descriptive language to convey meaning. Both poets and descriptive prose writers choose words carefully for the images and emotions they suggest. They select precise language to conjure up a vivid and specific picture in the minds of the readers. Of course, descriptive prose usually falls within a larger written piece, but poetry may present description alone. Poems also uses formats that experiment with verbal structures such as rhythm, rhyme, and repetition.

In "Primer Lesson," the poet Carl Sandburg writes about the way we speak to others. By comparing "proud words" to people wearing hard boots, the poet conveys the danger of using angry words that march away from you.

▲ **Critical Viewing**
If you were to write a poem about the experience of riding on a bus, what details might you include? **[Describe]**

MODEL

Primer Lesson
by Carl Sandburg

Look out how you use proud words.
When you let proud words go, it is
        not easy to call them back.
They wear long boots, hard boots; they
        walk off proud; they can't hear you
        calling—
Look out how you use proud words.

Write your own poem, using the writing process suggestions outlined on the next page.

122 • Description

Critical Viewing

Describe Students may mention the other passengers, the noises, and the sights outside the bus.

Prewriting Take a three-step approach to the prewriting process. First, choose a topic. Sort through personal photographs, look at magazines, or take a walk outside to brainstorm for topic ideas. If you can't find a topic, consider the possibilities below:

- A seasonal moment that is especially vivid: the harvest, a snowfall, the calm of a moonlit summer evening
- An emotionally strong moment: a sports win or loss, frustration with a computer, a joke among friends
- A person with a unique personality: an enthusiastic cheerleading coach, a lonely neighbor, your best friend

Second, consider the poetic forms you can use. You may want to flip through a poetry anthology to find models of poetry styles you like. For example, you may want to try a rhyming poem, one written with a specific line count, or one that has no rules for format.

Third, gather sensory images and specific words to use in your poem. On an index card like the one shown here, list details, words, and ideas that will help you create a particular mood.

Topic: Room during an exam	
Mood: silent intensity	
-scratch of pens	-light streaming
-focused work	through window
-adrenaline	-door as a sentry
-shuffling papers	-desks in rows

Drafting Use the rules of your chosen format to organize your poem. In a poem, you can't waste a single word, so try to make every word support the mood you want. Choose specific nouns and vivid verbs along with colorful sensory language. Use a thesaurus—possibly in your word-processing software— and a rhyming dictionary, if necessary, to find words that fit your structure and your ideas.

Revising and Editing Review the rules of your poetic form, and then make sure your poem reflects them consistently. For example, don't create rhyme in one stanza and use free verse in another, unless that is a deliberate poetic choice. Invite a classmate to read your poem and describe its mood. Adjust language as necessary to achieve the effect you want.

Publishing and Presenting Share your poetry in a small group. After each writer reads, discuss the experience of hearing the poetry aloud.

Connected Assignment: Poem • 123

Customize for
Musical/Rhythmic Learners

Pair students to work orally. Encourage pairs to explore the sounds of different words and discuss how these contribute to establishing a mood. Discuss sound techniques such as alliteration and onomatopoeia.

Customize for
Less Advanced Students

In conversation, help students select a topic and mood. You might ask them to describe a memorable moment of the previous day or week as a idea-prompter. Use question and answer to help students focus on the mood of that moment. Ask: How did you feel? What ways did you move your body? What color would you link to this moment?

Lesson Objectives

1. To evaluate media presentations.
2. To analyze ideas as represented in various media.
3. To recognize how visual and sound techniques convey messages in media.
4. To write an essay.

Step-by-Step Teaching Guide

Examining Relationships Among Art Forms

1. Choose one of the Spotlight elements for class discussion, or have students work individually or in groups on the element of their choice. Give students the initiative to find the necessary audiotapes, videotapes, books, and pictures.

2. Have interested students research Diaghilev's Ballet Russes. Invite them to display photographs of the production sets and share excerpts from critical reviews. Discuss why this group of artists made such an impact on audiences.

3. Direct students to on-line gallery sources to view examples of Picasso's various "periods." Have students discuss the moods each "period" conveys and describes.

4. Play an audio recording of Stravinsky's music. Invite students to demonstrate their reactions through movement. What images does the music evoke for them?

5. Have students research recent creative movements and staging approaches in the ballet field. How are these influenced by the Ballet Russes?

Viewing and Representing

Activity Invite interested students to create exhibits to accompany their essays. They might use photocopies or display books on stands. Students can use their essay to deliver an exhibit "tour."

Spotlight on the Humanities

Examining Relationships Among Art Forms

Focus on Dance: Ballets Russes

In 1909, Russian ballet impresario Sergei Diaghilev (1872–1929) established the Ballets Russes. The company's lavish productions under Diaghilev and choreographer Michel Fokine had an incomparable impact on the ballet world by challenging the expectations of ballet audiences. Ballets Russes combined music, drama, painting, and dance to convey emotion and story lines. Diaghilev brought together painters like Henri Matisse and Pablo Picasso to design production sets. Of the dancers in the company, Vaslav Nijinsky and Anna Pavlova were the most famous.

Art Connection The Spaniard Pablo Picasso (1881–1973) created the set and costume design for Sergei Diaghilev's ballet *Parade* in 1917. Picasso, considered one of the most famous artists of the twentieth century, worked in many different styles. Most importantly, he helped develop the painting style known as Cubism. However, Picasso also had a "blue period," stretching from 1901 to 1904, during which he expressed his unhappiness and disillusionment by painting images of social outcasts in the color blue. In contrast, Picasso's "rose period" of 1904 to 1906 during which, resulted in paintings of pinks and grays. Most often, his art of this period portrayed circus clowns and acrobats. In addition to paintings, Picasso's legacy includes sculpture, ceramics, and prints.

Music Connection The Russian composer Igor Stravinsky (1882–1971) wrote several of his best-known works for Diaghilev's Ballets Russes, including *The Firebird* (1910), *Pétrouchka* (1911), and *Le Sacre du Printemps* (1913). Inspired by the French composer Claude Debussy, Stravinsky's music became known for its irregular rhythms and use of scales and chords. This style was termed *neoclassicism*.

Descriptive Writing Activity: Art or Music in Words

Listen to a piece of music by Stravinsky, or study one of Picasso's Cubist paintings. In an essay, introduce your topic to your readers. Describe the music or art in language that conveys the mood or impression of the work.

124 • Description

Costume du Chinois pour Parade, 1917, Pablo Picasso, Lauros-Giraudon

▲ **Critical Viewing** How does this ballet costume, designed by artist Pablo Picasso, contrast with more traditional dance costumes? **[Contrast]**

Critical Viewing

Contrast Students might say the costume is more colorful and less form-fitting than traditional dance costumes.

Media and Technology Skills

Lesson Objectives

1. To evaluate the credibility of information sources and determine the writer's motives.
2. To examine the effect of media to construct a perception of reality.
3. To recognize how visual techniques convey messages in media.
4. To compare and contrast media coverage of the same subject.

Examining Media's Power to Construct a Perception of Reality

Activity: Compare Photos to Text in Magazines

You may know and trust the expression, "The camera never lies." However, depending on its use, the camera can lie more effectively than the pen. For example, by touching up an unwanted blemish, by selecting or cropping images, or even by staging events, a photographer can create false images that leave a much more vivid and lasting impression than words can.

Think About It Even the most reputable and seemingly objective journalists and journals can have a persuasive agenda that is often more clearly expressed in photographs than in paragraphs. For example, a magazine that features pictures of beautifully decorated cakes and elaborately decorated homes can also include articles on weight loss, budgeting money, family time, and baking secrets. This conflict between the articles and the photographs sends a very strong mixed message. In fact, the more prominent the photograph, the greater is this potential for manipulation of readers' perceptions. Therefore, the covers of magazines are an especially important area for critical viewing.

Study It Using your library's magazine collection find two cover stories in weekly newsmagazines. First, locate a photograph that presents a flattering portrait of a subject. Consider locating an actor, artist, businessperson, activist, athlete, or politician. Then, find a cover photo that presents a critical portrait. For this image, look for a politician in crisis, a world leader at odds with the United States, a celebrity in a scandal, or an advocate for an unpopular cause. Use the chart below to compare each image with the article it promotes.

Topic:	
Image Suggests:	Facts in Article Suggest:

Analyze and Compare It In your view, explain which form of communication—the picture or the accompanying story—creates the more vivid and lasting impression of the subject.

Techniques for Evaluating News Images

- Be aware of your first reaction to the photograph. Then, try to determine what created that impression.
- Look at the subject's setting. A photograph of someone sitting alone may send a different message from a photograph of that same person in a group.
- Study the subject's facial expression or the expressions of other people in the photograph.
- Analyze body language to consider whether the subject conveys comfort, guilt, or some other message.

Step-by-Step Teaching Guide

Examining Media's Power to Construct a Perception of Reality

Teaching Resources: Writing Support Transparency 6-I; Writing Support Activity Book 6-3

1. Review the techniques students can use to evaluate news images. Discuss any additional methods students have used successfully.
2. Invite students to model the listed techniques on an example you supply. Talk as a class about the demonstrations. What works? What doesn't work?
3. Display the transparency and talk with students about how to compare different media. Reinforce the modeling done in Step 2 by noting its results in the transparency chart.
4. Give students copies of the blank organizer, encouraging them to use it to track their comparative process. Before students proceed, review with them how to locate the necessary materials through library or classroom search facilities.
5. Have students discuss their emotional reactions to their media examples. What emotions did each convey? What techniques were used to send these emotional messages?

Customize for
Less Advanced Students

Students may need additional practice at interpreting visual images or at comprehending news text. Identify areas of weakness and work individually or in small groups to clarify confusions.

Lesson Objectives

1. To evaluate writing for both mechanics and content.
2. To analyze strategies that writers use.
3. To analyze text structures.
4. To analyze characteristics of text, including its structure, word choices, and intended audience.

Step-by-Step Teaching Guide

Teaching Resources:

1. Explain to students that some standardized test questions require students to complete several different tasks or choose from task options. Encourage students to identify all the necessary tasks and choices before beginning. With such test sections, reading the directions carefully and accurately becomes even more critical than usual.

2. Urge students to take neatness very seriously when completing multiple choice test questions. The material may be very straightforward in some cases but text examiners will not appreciate the test-takers' command of the subject if answers are messy or illegible.

3. Review with students how to read a passage with numbered lines. Clarify that test questions may refer to these numbered lines.

4. Provide regular experience with multiple choice formats by including these on your own classroom exams.

Standardized Test Preparation Workshop

Analyzing Strategy, Organization, and Style

Standardized tests often measure your knowledge of writing skills. Using a multiple-choice format, tests provide passages for your analysis. Questions may cover the writer's strategy, the organization of the information, the sequence of sentences, the writer's diction, or the overall style of the passage. The following are three types of questions that you may encounter:

- **Strategy questions** require you to determine whether a specific revision is appropriate in the context of the passage.
- **Organization questions** ask you to analyze the sequence of ideas, to decide where additional information might best be placed, or to identify material that should be eliminated from the passage.
- **Style questions** test your ability to identify the writer's point of view or to evaluate the use of language for an intended audience.

The sample test items that follow will give you practice in answering these types of questions.

Test Tip

Read the passage through at least once before answering questions. Understanding the main ideas and noticing structural flaws on your own may help you revise the passage correctly.

Sample Test Item	Answer and Explanation

Directions: Read the passage, and then answer the question that follows.
 	
1 Although the weather forecast called for
2 snow, no one predicted the accumulation
3 that would develop over a short period of
4 time. Cars were left stranded, drivers skid-
5 ded across busy intersections, and schools
6 were closed, as the city dug out from the
7 surprise blizzard.
 	
1. What correction would make the passage more informative?
 	
  A   provide the amount of snow
  B   delete reference to school closings
  C   change "Although" to "As soon as"
  D   provide the amount of snow
	The correct answer is *D*. Providing the precise amount of snowfall would explain the city's reaction to the snow. The other choices would not improve the informative nature of the passage.

126 • Description

🖊 TEST-TAKING TIP

Suggest that students become familiar with the three types of questions discussed in this lesson. Remind them, however, that the questions may not be so designated on an actual test. Students will have to recognize the question type from its structure and wording. Tell students to look in the sample questions here for hints linked to the definitions given for each question type. Ask them then to label each question as a strategy, organization, or style question.

Strategy: 3

Organization: 1, 2, 6

Style: 4, 5

▶ **Practice 1** **Directions:** Read the passage, and then answer the questions that follow. Choose the letter of the **BEST** answer.

1 After receiving a large inheritance from
2 the neighbor who helped him with his
3 own homework, Robbins decided to
4 fund the center. He found a location
5 downtown, bought furniture and books,
6 and invited friends and other members
7 of the community to donate their time
8 to his project.

9 If you set your mind to it, you can make
10 a difference in someone else's life. This
11 is the philosophy behind "Books, Bites,
12 and Beyond," a storefront volunteer
13 center that provides a warm place for
14 the youth of the city. Founded by
15 Jasper Robbins, the center includes a
16 well-appointed library, a welcoming
17 cup of hot chocolate, and the friendship
18 of the volunteers who staff the facility
19 for six hours after school each day.

20 To complete the "Beyond" part of the
21 center's slogan, Robbins invites com-
22 munity leaders to speak on topics that
23 can help kids plan their own futures.
24 Recently, a veterinarian spoke about
25 the importance of a commitment to
26 school. Veterinary practices can be large
27 or small. Other community figures—
28 including small-business owners,
29 bakers, and journalists—have visited the
30 store to share their insights about life
31 beyond school.

1 Which of the following is the **BEST** order for the paragraphs?
A 1, 2, 3
B 3, 2, 1
C 1, 3, 2
D 2, 1, 3

2 Which of the following changes would be **BEST** to make the sequence of ideas in the first paragraph clearer?
A Insert the phrase "twenty-five years ago" before the comma in 30.
B Add the transition "although" to the beginning of the sentence that starts on line 4.
C Identify the location of the center.
D Name the people who worked with Robbins.

3 If the author wanted to include more information about helping kids plan their futures, which of the following would be an appropriate addition?
A The young people do not show an interest in the speaking series.
B Homework helpers are available daily.
C The center offers after-school snacks and computers for the use of the students.
D After an introduction, these meetings turn into question-and-answer sessions.

4 Which **BEST** identifies the author's purpose?
A to evaluate
B to entertain
C to criticize
D to inform

5 Which of the following draws attention away from the main focus?
A discussion of bakers
B discussion of community leaders
C discussion of sizes of veterinary practices
D discussion of library holdings

6 Where would specific information about the volunteers **BEST** fit?
A after line 31
B after line 23
C after line 9
D after line 19

Answer Key

Practice 1
1. D
2. A
3. D
4. D
5. C
6. D

Customize for
More Advanced Students

Challenge students to write brief explanations telling why each test item alternative is either incorrect or correct. Explain that by justifying each answer choice, students will gain insight into their own reasoning processes. Discuss whether any students have fallen into faulty reasoning and help students fine-tune their analytic approach.

In-Depth Lesson Plan

	LESSON FOCUS	PRINT AND MEDIA RESOURCES
DAY 1	**Introduction to Persuasive Essays** Students learn key elements of persuasive essays and analyze the Model From Literature (pp. 128–133).	*Writers at Work* **Videotape**, Persuasion *Writing Lab* **CD-ROM**, Persuasion
DAY 2	**Prewriting** Students choose and narrow a topic, consider their audience and purpose and gather information (pp. 134–138).	**Teaching Resources** *Writing Support Transparencies, 7-A–E; Writing Support Activity Book, 7-1*
DAY 3	**Drafting** Students organize their ideas and write their first drafts (pp. 139–140).	**Teaching Resources** *Writing Support Transparencies, 7-F; Writing Support Activity Book, 7-4*
DAY 4	**Revising** Students revise their drafts in terms of overall structure, paragraphs, sentences and word choice (pp. 141–145).	**Teaching Resources** *Writing Support Transparencies, 7-G–I*
DAY 5	**Editing and Proofreading; Publishing and Presenting** Students check their work for accuracy and correctness and present their final drafts (pp. 146–147).	**Teaching Resources** *Scoring Rubrics on Transparency,* Chapter 7; Writing Assessment: Scoring Rubrics and Scoring Models for Persuasion

Accelerated Lesson Plan

	LESSON FOCUS	PRINT AND MEDIA RESOURCES
DAY 1	**Drafting** Students review characteristics for persuasive writing, select topics and write drafts.	*Writing Lab* **CD-ROM**, Persuasion *Writers at Work* **Videotape**, Persuasion **Teaching Resources** *Writing Support Transparencies, 7-A–F; Writing Support Activity Book, 7-4*
DAY 2	**Revising to Presenting** Students work individually or with peers to revise, edit and proofread their work for presentation.	**Teaching Resources** *Writing Support Transparencies, 7-G–I; Scoring Rubrics on Transparency,* Chapter 7; Writing Assessment: Scoring Rubrics and Scoring Models for Persuasion

Options for Adapting Lesson Plans

HOMEWORK

Have students complete any stage of the lesson for homework.

TECHNOLOGY

Students can complete any stage of the lesson on computer. Have them print out their completed work.

FEATURES

Extend coverage with Connected Assignment (p. 151), Spotlight on the Humanities (p. 152), Media and Technology Skills (p. 153) and the Standardized Test Preparation Workshop (p. 154).

INTEGRATED SKILLS COVERAGE

Integrating Grammar
Punctuating Adverb Clauses, SE p. 143
Formatting Titles, SE p. 146

Reading/Writing Connection
Reading Strategy, SE p. 130
Writing Application, SE p. 133

Reading
Responding to Literature, SE p. 135
Find It In Your Reading, SE pp. 143, 146

Viewing and Representing
Critical Viewing, SE pp. 128, 130, 133, 139, 145, 148, 151, 152
Evaluating Artistic Performance, SE p. 152
Recognizing Persuasive Techniques, SE p. 153

Speaking and Listening
ATE p. 142

Real-World Connection
ATE p. 137

ASSESSMENT SUPPORT

Standardized Test Preparation SE p. 154; ATE p. 144

Texas Test Preparation Workshop, pp. 13–14

Scoring Rubrics on Transparency, Ch. 7

Formal Assessment, Ch. 7

Writing Assessment and Portfolio Management

MEETING INDIVIDUAL NEEDS

Less Advanced Students ATE p. 155; See also Ongoing Assessments ATE pp. 129, 130, 135, 137, 138, 140, 142, 143, 145, 155
More Advanced Students ATE pp. 132, 155
ESL Students ATE pp. 132, 144
Logical/Mathematical Learners ATE p. 140

BLOCK SCHEDULING

Pacing Suggestions
For 90-minute Blocks
• Have students complete the Prewriting and Drafting stages in a single period.
• Focus one class period on Revising and Editing and Publishing and Presenting. Allow at least 30 minutes for peer revision.

Resources for Varying Instruction
• *Writing Lab* **CD-ROM** If your students have access to hardware, a 90-minute block provides an ideal opportunity for students to work on computer.
• *Writers at Work* **Videotape** Show the Persuasion segment in class.

Professional Development Support
• *How to Manage Instruction in the Block* This Teaching Resource provides management and activity suggestions.

MEDIA AND TECHNOLOGY

For the Student
• *Writing Lab* **CD-ROM**, Persuasion

For the Teacher
• *Writers at Work* **Videotape**, Persuasion
• *Resource Pro* **CD-ROM**

WRITING AND GRAMMAR WEBSITE

The Interactive Writing and Grammar Website provides a wide array of support for students, teachers, and parents. Writing support includes:

• Interactive revision checkers
• Scoring rubrics with complete models

phwg.phschool.com

LITERATURE CONNECTIONS

Related selections from *Prentice Hall Literature: Timeless Voices, Timeless Themes*, Gold:
from *Silent Spring*, Rachel Carson, SE p. 133
"The Cask of Amontillado," Edgar Allan Poe, SE p. 135

▶ *Lesson Objectives*

1. To write a persuasive essay appropriate to audience and purpose.
2. To read to appreciate the writer's craft and to discover models for writing.
3. To use prewriting strategies to generate ideas and plan.
4. To research self-selected topics using texts and technical resources.
5. To represent information in a variety of ways, including graphics.
6. To develop drafts by organizing content to suit purpose.
7. To edit and proofread to ensure standard English usage and grammar.
8. To evaluate writing for both mechanics and content.
9. To refine selected work for publication.

Critical Viewing

Analyze Students may note that the scene represented is a trial in session and that most people in the painting seem focused on the speaker and have attentive facial expressions. Some people seem to be taking notes.

Chapter 7 Persuasion
Persuasive Essay

Trial by Jury, 1985, Adele Alsop, courtesy of Schmidt Bingham Gallery, NYC

Persuasion in Everyday Life

Whenever you argue with a friend over which movie to see or debate the merits of one musical group over another, you're using persuasive skills. **Persuasion** is writing or speaking that attempts to convince others to accept a position or take a desired action. Effective persuasion can decide a defendant's fate in a trial, lead to a change in government leadership, or even end a war.

▲ Critical Viewing
What clues in this painting indicate that the man standing in the center is speaking persuasively?
[Analyze]

⏱ TIME AND RESOURCE MANAGER

Resources
Technology: Writers at Work videotape, Persuasion

In-Depth Coverage	Accelerated Pace
• Cover pp. 128–129 in class. • Show Persuasion section of the Writers at Work videotape. • Read the Model from Literature (pp. 130–133) in class, and use it to demonstrate key techniques of persuasion.	• Discuss definitions and types of persuasive essays in class. • Assign Model from Literature for independent reading.

What Is a Persuasive Essay?

A **persuasive essay** is a short piece of writing that presents a position and aims to convince readers to accept that position or take action. An effective persuasive essay

- addresses an issue of concern or importance to the writer.
- addresses an issue that is arguable and has at least two sides.
- presents a position that is supported with relevant facts, examples, or personal experience.
- addresses the knowledge level, experiences, and concerns of the intended audience.

To see the criteria on which your final persuasive essay may be judged, preview the Rubric for Self-Assessment on page 147.

Types of Persuasion

From the note you write to ask a friend a favor to the formal proposals that nonprofit agencies write to secure million-dollar grants, persuasion takes many forms. Several types of persuasive writing are similar to the persuasive essay. These specialized types of persuasion have names that reflect their unique purposes:

- **Editorials** are published by the editors of a newspaper to offer their opinions about a current event.

- **Position papers** are prepared to influence policy on current issues.

- **Persuasive speeches** are presented aloud to an audience.

Writers in ACTION

Although you may not have heard of Victorian writer Edward Bulwer-Lytton, his words have become a motto for the power of persuasion. Since the nineteenth century, people have quoted his famous line:

"The pen is mightier than the sword."

PREVIEW Student Work IN PROGRESS

In this chapter, you'll follow the work of Janaki Spickard-Keeler, a student at Clark High School in San Antonio, Texas. In her essay, Janaki addresses the controversy over the autobiography of pilot and adventurer Beryl Markham. As you'll see, she used prewriting, drafting, and revising techniques to develop her persuasive essay "Who Wrote *West With the Night*?" You can read her complete, final draft at the end of the chapter.

Persuasive Essay • 129

Reading\Writing Connection

Reading: Interpret Connotation

Point out to students that many words have a connotation, that is, specific feelings or values associated with them. For example, *clever* and *shrewd* both mean "ingenious and quick-witted"; however, *shrewd* has the somewhat negative connotation of being artful or tricky. Writers choose words with specific connotations to evoke an attitude or feeling in the reader.

As students read this essay by Nevada Barr, have them discuss the connotative effect of these words:

- Paragraph 2: *wretched, gifts, treasures*
- Paragraph 3: *snug*
- Paragraph 5: *home, usurping, tread*

Step-by-Step Teaching Guide

Engage Students Through Literature

1. Have students read this example of a persuasive essay.

2. Ask a student to summarize the writer's main point.

3. Then ask for students' responses to the essay. Were they persuaded by the writers' supporting arguments?

4. Ask students to brainstorm for ideas for possible persuasive topics based on ideas in or responses to this essay.
   - We should preserve the historical sites in our town.
   - Because national parks are overused, the government should regulate the number of visitors.

Critical Viewing

Analyze Students may mention the grandeur of the trees and the sheer beauty of the park.

 # Model From Literature

Nevada Barr, a writer of mystery novels, uses the national parks as the setting of many of her stories. Drawing on the writer's experiences as a park ranger, this essay asserts the benefits of the national park system for all citizens.

Reading Writing Connection

Reading Strategy: Interpret Connotation Be alert to a word's **connotation**—the way a specific word can make you feel. As you read, take special notice of the emotional power of the words Barr chooses. You'll see that effective persuasion can turn on the wise use of one word over another.

▲ Critical Viewing If you were to write a persuasive essay to promote the national parks, what details from this photograph could you include? **[Analyze]**

The introduction compares the issue of preserving parkland to the essential practice of breathing. This comparison stresses the level of importance Barr places on her topic.

We Can Go Home Again

Nevada Barr

When I was asked to write an article on why it is important to preserve our national parks, I was a tad shocked. The question seemed unanswerable in its outrageousness—as if I had been asked why is it important to inhale after exhaling, why is it important to drink plenty of liquids when hiking in the desert, why is it important for the sun to rise in the morning?

To those few wretched souls who have been locked away in a box on the moon for the past 50 years and so did not know this, what could be said? I didn't know where to begin. Should I dwell on the gifts these places bestow: the microbes in Lechuguilla Cave that might prove invaluable to the medical community; the clean water and air; the wealth of plant and animal life? Maybe I should

130 • Persuasive Essay

☑ ONGOING ASSESSMENT: Monitor and Reinforce

After previewing the Model From Literature, you may anticipate that some students may have difficulty with some proper names and other words. Use one of the following options.

Option 1 If students read the model independently, have them list any unfamiliar words they encounter. Then go over pronunciations and definitions in class.	**Option 2** If you read the model to the class, take time to define unfamiliar words as they are encountered. Words such as *microbes, usurping, crystalline,* and *viscerally* may need definition.

focus on the sheer beauty of the parks, or the historical treasures that preserve our story as humans.

Though I know of these things, this is not what speaks to me on a deeper level. Right now, snug in my little house, near the supermarket and the video store, microbes hold little interest for me, and from here, I cannot see the Grand Tetons or hear the water in the Virgin River Gorge. So I crawled into my easy chair, invited my dogs to sit on my lap (an invitation they take for granted whether I make it or not), and let the Why of the national parks sink into my bones.

It came to me that I would leave microbes and watersheds to the experts. What I want to talk about is home.

Most of us have had the experience of not being able to go home again. Returning to our childhood haunts to find a gas station where the orchard once was, a concrete culvert usurping the creek where we built forts out of sticker-weeds and brush. There is a terrible sense of loss, of seeing who we were in our innocence and our youth being wiped away, replaced with things that have no heart, no intrinsic human worth. The parks, as near as we can make them, are places we have decided to take out of time. The Anasazi ruins in Mesa Verde, the Civil War battlefields in Virginia, the sunken ships of Isle Royale, the mud pots in Lassen, the meadows of Yosemite—each a place where we stopped the clock, preserving it as it was, as it is, and as it can be. Making them places that will not disappear under the tread of progress.

The parks, in every imaginable way, are our home. America is one of the only countries in the world that saw the magnificence of our chunk of the Earth and had the wherewithal to begin setting aside places that speak to us as a nation and a people. Places that will remain unchanged. Places we can go home to, places our children and grandchildren and their grandchildren can go home to, and find a sense of who we are still in our innocence and youth. Even if we choose never to go, we know it is there, that nobody slunk in and trashed it while we were growing up or getting old or making a living. Nobody turned the meadow where we hunted for four-leaf clovers into a trailer park. Nobody dammed up the river where we skipped rocks or cut down the trees we picnicked under the day we decided to get married.

Barr explains her writing process. By showing that her ideas came through deep reflection, she gives them more value.

References to Mesa Verde, Virginia, and Yosemite offer background to educate an audience that may not know many national parks or the features of a park.

The writer presents her position succinctly: The parks in every imaginable way are our home. In her essay, she'll attempt to persuade readers of the value of the parks.

Barr makes an emotional appeal to her audience by addressing common childhood experiences like skipping rocks.

Model From Literature • 131

Teaching From the Model

Have students examine the structure of Barr's essay and arguments. Have them look closely at her opening and closing, for example. What technique does she use to get readers' attention? (She expresses shock at the issue, as if preservation is taken for granted.) How does she conclude? (She succinctly states, almost with a little sarcasm, an alternative to preservation.) Students might go on to examine each point she makes.

More About the Writer

A former National Park Ranger, Nevada Barr is best known for her mystery novels. As this article suggests, Barr is deeply devoted to environmental issues, and she uses the beauty and history of numerous National Parks as the setting for her stories. Anna Pigeon, a fictional park ranger, is featured in several of Barr's novels. Readers of these books enjoy the protagonist's strength, bravery and respect for wildlife and the environment. In a recent mystery, *Liberty Falling*, Barr moves Anna Pigeon away from her usual wilderness setting to the urban parks of Liberty and Ellis Islands in New York City.

Customize for
ESL Students

Students may be unfamiliar with some of Barr's literary and popular culture references; you may find it necessary to explain some of them. For example, *Wind in the Willows* by Kenneth Grahame and *Peter Pan* by James M. Barrie are classic fantasy stories. Pogo was the title character in a comic strip that had its setting in a swamp.

Customize for
More Advanced Students

Ask students to locate on a map each of the national parks that Barr mentions. You may also wish to ask students to prepare a brief profile of a national park that they have visited or that they know about. Students might also search the Internet for photographs of the park sites.

We can't stop time, but if we can slow it down enough, we can form those wonderful memories. I have vivid memories of my first experience in the misty cathedrals of the redwood forests. At seven, I discovered the towering trunks filled my visions. On the soft padded carpet of damp-smelling needles I could track the illusive and magical beings from *Wind in the Willows* and *Peter Pan.*

That visit painted my backdrop for stories and books for years. Now here's the interesting part. My next visit, 20 some-odd years later, held the same magic for me. Redwood trees really are the tallest living thing, and the padded carpet does have a wonderful damp and mysterious smell. The redwood forests will always be a part of who I am, what I feel, and how I look at life. Part of my scrapbook of life.

The parks are our home of the magic. For ten years, I have written about them, finding mystery in each park, always different. In the northern forest the Windigo can still ride the night skies; in the south, Pogo wanders among the mangrove roots. Not all the wildlife to be preserved are readily apparent to the eye.

I've seen a winter day, shortly after sunup, at the South Rim of the Grand Canyon, with crystalline blue skies, the sun pouring into the canyon, its low angle lighting the underside of storm clouds flowing off the North Rim into the depths, like the greatest Niagara imaginable. I will never forget it and, as long as the canyon is preserved, the possibility exists that I shall see it again.

The parks are the home of beauty, the incredible sights that are unique to America, that were the stuff of legend and the tall tales two centuries ago—tales so incredible they were laughed at and wondered over: Yosemite, Yellowstone, Lassen. Unbelievable. And true. . . .

On Isle Royale I searched for wolves. In six months I found spoor and fur, scat and moose bones with bite marks. I saw wolf tracks in the sand along the lake's edge, and I heard them howl at night. Never, not once, did I see a wolf, though I feel sure that they saw me. But I dreamed of wolves and wrote stories of wolves and I studied and spoke to the visitors about wolves, of their monogamy, family values, courage, endurance. Because they let me live in their home for half a year, I could know the wolves, celebrate the wolf-like parts of myself, without ever laying eyes on one.

Our parks are the home of our wildness, our pioneer spirit. Seeing them we know we can do much, go far, withstand the harshest punishment. We know we can make it; we can survive and thrive and flourish.

132 • Persuasive Essay

The writer explains how parks are our "home" because they create a lifetime of memories.

The writer suggests that parks are the "home" of magic.

In the essay, the writer provides several ideas to support her position. She cites and develops the parks' beauty, their history, and their ability to embody the national character.

In describing how parks are "home" to our wildness, the writer takes advantage of the patriotic connotations of pioneer. The word pioneer suggests brave exploration, leadership, and survival.

The parks embody not only who we are as individuals, but who we are as a people. At Appomattox Courthouse I have seen the stub of the pencil that General Grant used to write the terms of surrender for the Army of Northern Virginia, thus ending America's greatest struggle and setting the tone for healing. This chewed piece of wood and lead made it real to me. I know the reality viscerally. I saw it. In the cannon balls we fired in the bloodiest of our wars, the one we fought against each other, I knew the pain and the destruction and was reminded that we can stand whole and strong as a nation if we stand undivided and dedicated to the creed that all people are created equal.

National parks are the home of our history, dyed in our blood, warmed by our hopes, inspired by our accomplishments.

Memories of who we were, knowledge of who we are, and dreams of who we can hope to become.

Unless, of course, we sell them for a quick buck.

Writing Application: Use Connotations
By choosing words that have emotional power, Barr lets her language make the case for her. As you write, select words that have emotional impact for your readers. They will strengthen your power to persuade.

▼ **Critical Viewing**
What might the author find most appealing about the Grand Canyon? [Synthesize]

Barr's vivid and suggestive words, such as "healing" and "undivided," make strong use of the power of language to persuade.

In her last support for the thesis that states "The parks are our home," the writer links the national parks with the nation's history.

LITERATURE

For another example of persuasive writing on an environmental topic, see the excerpt from *Silent Spring* in Prentice Hall *Literature: Timeless Voices, Timeless Themes,* Gold.

Model From Literature • **133**

Responding to Literature

If students read the excerpt from *Silent Spring,* suggest that they compare and contrast Rachel Carson's and Nevada Barr's ideas about how natural resources are being used in this country. What differences in mood and feeling do they notice in the two works?

Reading\Writing Connection
Writing Application: Use Connotations

Have students review word choices that Barr made that are effective. Remind them of the importance of word connotations in their own writing. For practice in understanding the effect of words' connotations, have them discuss the differences in attitude or effect of the words in these groups:

1. *dark, dim, shadowy*
2. *pretend, fake*
3. *mistake, blunder*

(Students may note that *dark* is more intense than *dim* and that *shadowy* carries a suggestion of mystery or threat. *Fake* suggests a greater measure of falsity or trickery than *pretend*; *blunder* implies a more serious or less excusable error than *mistake*.)

Critical Viewing

Synthesize Students may say that the writer would find the austere, dramatic natural beauty of the Grand Canyon most appealing.

Prewriting: Hot Topics

Teaching Resources: Writing Support Transparency 7-A; Writing Support Activity Book 7-1

1. To introduce the concept of "hot" topics—topics about which people hold strong opinions, you might have students informally voice opinions about topics that you provide, such as a school dress code, raising or lowering the driving age, etc.

2. Display the Hot Topics Transparency. Be sure that students see that these topics have two sides.

3. Have students fill in the blank organizer with their own "hot topics." Remind them that a good topic presents a possible argument to make from more than one point of view. Recent newspapers or magazines may also be used to generate topics.

Prewriting: Discussion Group

1. You may wish to have students engage in discussion in smaller groups. Suggest that each group assign a member to note down topics as they come up in discussion.

2. If one or more students are interested in writing on the same topic, encourage them to modify the topic slightly to allow two approaches.

Prewriting: Notebook Review

1. Have students volunteer ideas that have been presented or discussed in their other classes.

2. Encourage students to get out their notes from other classes for the review. You may wish to provide highlighting markers for students to use in this activity.

7.2 Prewriting

Choosing Your Topic

To write an effective persuasive essay, consider issues that have more than one side and select one that touches your life. Use these strategies to select a topic you'd like to develop:

Strategies for Generating Topics

1. **Hot Topics** Whether a sports hero gets into trouble off the field or a new bill is being introduced in Congress, the day's news often sparks controversy. Watch television, scan newspapers, or listen carefully to the hot issues your friends and family are discussing right now. In a chart like the one below, identify the two sides of several controversial topics, and then decide whether you feel strongly enough to present either argument.

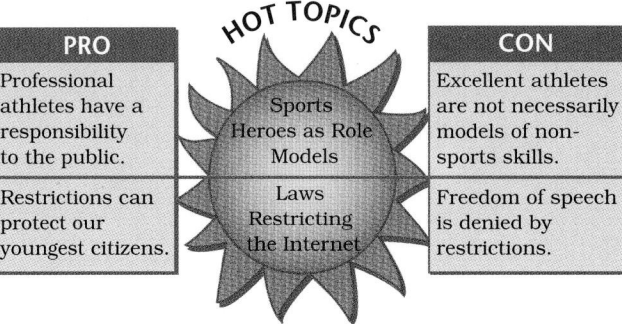

2. **Discussion Group** Meet with a group of students or residents of your community to find out what issues these people find most important. With the group, jot down a list of topics, noting those that create the most controversy or disagreement. You may decide that one of these ideas can lead to a strong persuasive writing topic.

3. **Notebook Review** Use your own classroom experiences to help you find a topic. Skim through the notebooks you keep for various subject areas. Most likely, you will come across topics you have debated in social studies or science classes, or you may be reminded of literature you have read that you would like to urge others to read. Use a highlighter to mark any topics about which you have strong opinions. Then, review the highlighted sections to choose the topic that means the most to you.

134 • Persuasive Essay

Writing Lab CD-ROM

For more help finding a topic, explore the activities and topic suggestions in the Choosing a Topic Section of the Persuasion lesson.

⏱ TIME AND RESOURCE MANAGER

Resources
Print: Topic Bank 7; Writing Support Transparencies 7-A–E; Writing Support Activity Book, 7-1–3
Technology: Writing Lab CD-ROM, Persuasion

In-Depth Coverage	Accelerated Pace
• Cover pp. 134–138 in class. • Guide students through the Strategies for Generating Topics. • Have students use the looping technique to narrow their topics. • Have students complete T-charts to gather and organize research details.	• In class, discuss how to identify a good persuasive essay topic. • Have students list possible topics. • Ask students to submit topic proposals for your review.

TOPIC BANK

If you're having trouble coming up with your own topic, consider these possibilities:

1. **Editorial About Violence on Television** Television networks have come under attack for the violence that is telecast on the news and in dramas. Write an editorial in which you criticize or defend a network's programming choices.

2. **Persuasive Essay on Equal Funding for Girls' Sports** Schools and colleges budget large amounts of money for traditionally male sports. In some states, football receives more funding than field hockey. In a persuasive essay, argue for or against this financial situation.

Responding to Fine Art

The Pond, 1985, Adele Alsop, courtesy of Schmidt Bingham Gallery, NYC

3. This painting, *The Pond*, might inspire you to find the beauty of your community's natural spaces. Write a persuasive essay on an action that impacts the local environment. For example, you might evaluate the effect of mandatory recycling programs or weigh the results of the increased building of shopping malls and housing.

Responding to Literature

4. Read "The Cask of Amontillado" by Edgar Allan Poe. As a lawyer, write a persuasive essay in which you either defend or prosecute Montresor for his actions. You can find this story in *Prentice Hall Literature: Timeless Voices, Timeless Themes*, Gold.

☑Cooperative Writing Opportunity

5. **Persuasive Brochure on Volunteerism** With a group, split the task of researching volunteer work. Each group member can research a different aspect of the topic; for example, one might report on the benefits to the volunteer, while another could focus on the benefits to others. Together, create a pamphlet on the values of volunteering.

Prewriting • 135

Responding to Fine Art
The Pond, 1985, by Adele Alsop
Teaching Resources: Writing Support Transparency 7-B

Adele Alsop resides and works in Utah. Her paintings give a vivid sense of the American landscape.

1. Display the transparency and ask students what the painting suggests to them.

2. Ask students to brainstorm for possible persuasive essay topics suggested by this work of art. Here are some possibilities:
   • Editorial about vanishing wetlands
   • Persuasive speech on the dumping of toxic waste
   • Position paper on the increasing need for housing projects

Responding to Literature
Poe's "The Cask of Amontillado" is a short story about murder and revenge. Students might write a persuasive essay on whether or not Montresor should be found innocent by reason of insanity.

Spotlight on the Humanities
For additional topic suggestions, refer students to the Spotlight on the Humanities on page 152.

☑ ONGOING ASSESSMENT: Monitor and Reinforce

If you observe that some students are having difficulty coming up with a topic, use one of the following options.

Option 1 Suggest that students choose an idea from the Topic Bank on this page. If many students have difficulty, work with the whole class on one idea selected from the Topic Bank or one suggested by students.	**Option 2** If Topic Bank ideas seem too difficult, suggest that students try one of the assignments from the Topic Bank in the Teaching Resources.

⏱ TIME SAVERS!

◗ **Writing Support Transparencies**
Use the transparencies for Chapter 7 to facilitate teaching of Hot Topics and other strategies.

📖 **Writing Support Activity Book**
Blank graphic organizers will help students apply Hot Topics and other strategies in this chapter.

135

Prewriting: Use Looping to Narrow a Topic

Teaching Resources: Writing Support Transparency 7-C

1. Display the transparency of the Student Work in Progress. Help students see Janaki's looping process: After Janaki wrote freely for a few minutes, she went back and circled one idea, autobiography. She then wrote only on this idea for a few minutes. From her writing on autobiography, she identified another idea, which she decided to use as her narrowed topic.

2. Point out to students that Janaki identified the contested authorship of *West with the Night* as a narrow enough idea, one that she could use as a topic for persuasion.

3. You may wish to demonstrate the looping strategy on the board, to illustrate how writing further about ideas helps to narrow and focus a topic.

7.2

Narrowing Your Topic

Once you've chosen a topic, consider all the points you will have to make in order to convince your readers. For example, if you plan to argue that animals should be protected from harm, you'll have to identify all the hazards animals face. That might take hundreds of pages to do well. In contrast, a narrowed topic such as "Additives in Dog Food Can Harm Your Pet's Bones" focuses your writing. Limiting your topic to one specific issue or problem enables you to cover your topic thoroughly. Looping is one strategy to narrow your topic.

Use Looping to Narrow a Topic

These are the steps of looping. First, write freely on your topic for about five minutes. Read what you have written, and circle the most important idea. Write for five minutes on that idea. Continue this process until you come to a topic that is narrow enough to address in your persuasive writing.

Student Work
IN PROGRESS

Name: *Janaki Spickard-Keeler*
Clark High School
San Antonio, TX

Looping

Here is how Janaki used looping to narrow a broad topic:

Broad topic: The controversy surrounding Beryl Markham's autobiography

I've studied the life of Beryl Markham, a pilot, adventurer, and writer. Markham may be known for her aviation feats. She may be best known because of her autobiography, *West With the Night.* Markham was a horse trainer and a breeder.

Autobiography: *West With the Night* is an exciting and gripping book that Hemingway called "wonderful."

I was surprised to learn that some people have questioned whether Beryl Markham wrote it! How could they make such a claim? She describes things that no one else could have known!

Narrowed topic: Beryl Markham is the only person who could have written *West With the Night.*

Considering Your Audience and Purpose

Your purpose in writing a persuasive essay is to convince readers to accept your position or to take action. A knowledge of your audience will be a critical element in achieving your purpose.

Analyze Your Audience

The interest, concerns, and attitude your readers bring to your subject should help direct the approach you take. For example, if you were to write a persuasive essay to promote exercise, you'd want to address the characteristics of your audience. This chart shows the arguments you might use to persuade specific groups of people:

Writing Lab CD-ROM

To help identify your audience and shape your argument appropriately, use the Audience Profile activity in the Persuasion lesson.

TOPIC: EXERCISE IS BENEFICIAL

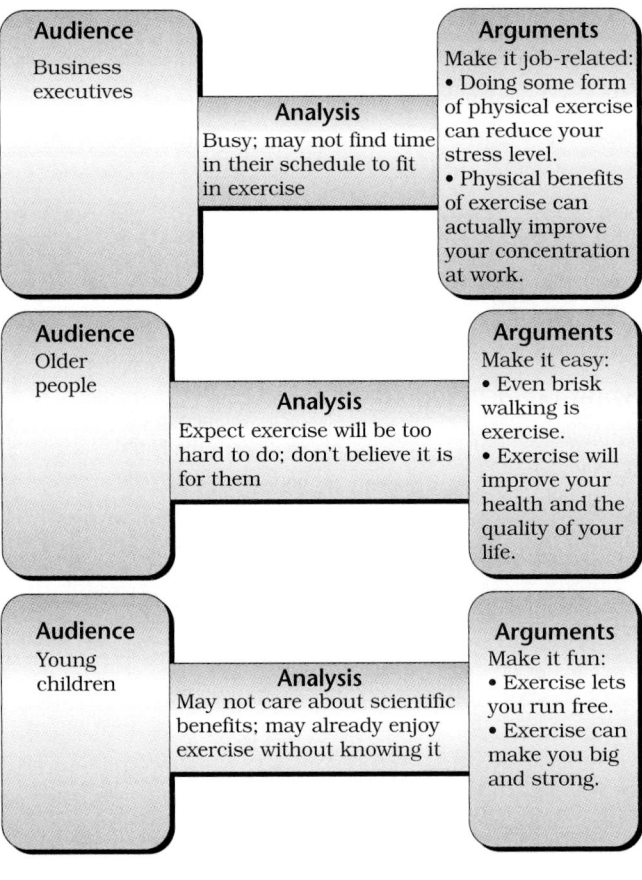

Audience	Analysis	Arguments
Business executives	Busy; may not find time in their schedule to fit in exercise	Make it job-related: • Doing some form of physical exercise can reduce your stress level. • Physical benefits of exercise can actually improve your concentration at work.
Older people	Expect exercise will be too hard to do; don't believe it is for them	Make it easy: • Even brisk walking is exercise. • Exercise will improve your health and the quality of your life.
Young children	May not care about scientific benefits; may already enjoy exercise without knowing it	Make it fun: • Exercise lets you run free. • Exercise can make you big and strong.

Prewriting • 137

Prewriting: Analyze Your Audience

Teaching Resources: Writing Support Transparency 7-D; Writing Support Activity Book, 7-2

1. Display Transparency 7-D to draw students' attention to the audience analysis chart on this page. Have them note how the arguments appeal to the needs or concerns of each audience.

2. Give students a blank copy of this audience analysis chart. Have students jot down the kinds of people they hope their essays will reach: parents, friends, the general public, legislators?

3. Then have them speculate about some of the concerns these people might have about the proposed topic. What arguments might they use to address these concerns?

Real-World Connection

Explain that in the business world, "know your audience" translates to "know your customer." Success in business is closely tied to understanding customer needs and interests. Many businesses develop information that enables them to categorize their customers by age, gender, income groups, interests, and hobbies. Businesses can then prepare catalogs, mailings, and other communications aimed at specific customers.

☑ ONGOING ASSESSMENT: Monitor and Reinforce

If you observe that students lapse into the habit of always writing for their teacher, try one of the following options.

Option 1 Suggest that students write for a very specific audience of one—a relative, a friend, or a much younger person.	**Option 2** Have students write a brief profile of their intended audience, including their level of education, skills, interests, and background knowledge of the topic.

Prewriting: Complete a T-Chart

Teaching Resources: Writing Support Transparency 7-E; Writing Support Activity Book 7-3

- You might schedule library time for students to collect data for their persuasive essays.

- Display the transparency to show students how to organize their researched information with a T-chart. Then give them a blank copy of a T-chart. They should write their position across the top of the chart. Then they can write the evidence that supports their position on one side of the chart and the evidence against it on the other side.

- This arrangement allows them to evaluate the strength of their own argument and to see any opposing arguments that they must rebut.

7.2

Gathering Evidence

To write a strong persuasive essay, you must back up your claim with convincing proof. In order to do this, you need to gather as much evidence as you can. Consider these strategies for collecting supporting information that will prove your point to your audience:

Conduct Research

To collect facts, statistics, and examples, use reliable resources: books by experts, accounts of people with experience, and primary sources such as letters and speeches. Keep bibliographic information such as title, author, and date of publication to include in your final draft. As you research, you may discover details that support an opposing position. Take notes on both sides of the argument using a T-chart.

Complete a T-Chart Write your position across the top of a sheet of paper. Then, fold the paper in half to create two columns. In one column, jot down facts and ideas that support your position. In the other column, note evidence that might be used to argue against your idea. Begin thinking about how you can answer these opposing arguments.

Student Work IN PROGRESS

Name: Janaki Spickard-Keeler
Clark High School
San Antonio, TX

Organizing Research With a T-Chart

Janaki consulted several sources to support her argument that Beryl Markham had been the sole author of West With the Night. She used a T-chart to establish evidence for both sides of the issue.

Position: Beryl Markham did write *West With the Night*.

Evidence Markham didn't write WWTW	Evidence she did write it
Claims of illiteracy	She was well read.
Father's role in her education	She had a large library.

✓ ONGOING ASSESSMENT: Monitor and Reinforce

If you observe that students are having difficulty completing their T-charts, try one of the following options.

Option 1 Suggest that four students work on the same topic, with two students gathering evidence for each side of the issue. Students can then pool their research to complete the assignment.	**Option 2** Taking an example from the Topic Bank, give students a demonstration of how you would explore both sides of an issue using a T-chart.

7.3 Drafting

Shaping Your Writing

Develop a Thesis Statement

An effective persuasive essay is built around a clearly worded **thesis statement,** a statement of the position you will prove.

SAMPLE THESIS STATEMENTS

New drivers should be required to log 100 hours with a licensed driver before obtaining a driver's license.

Any drivers who can pass a road test should receive a driver's license no matter how long they have been practicing.

As you begin drafting, introduce your topic and state your thesis. Then, in the body of your essay, provide the arguments that support and prove your thesis statement. Your arguments may consist of facts, reasons, and other examples that support your position.

Organize to Emphasize the Strongest Support

Every point in your essay should support your thesis statement. Some details provide stronger support than others. Organize your essay so that you use your strongest support to its best advantage. Consider the following suggestions:

- Save your best reason for last to finish with power.
- Use your second-best argument to get off to a strong start.
- Organize the remaining facts and details in ascending order of importance as you build toward your most powerful reason.
- Before you deliver the strongest argument, acknowledge the opposition. Show and argue against a conflicting side of the issue.

Writing Lab CD-ROM

To help you organize your argument, use the Note Cards activity in the Persuasion lesson.

▼ **Critical Viewing**
What statement about Beryl Markham could you support using details from this picture? **[Support]**

Beryl Markham, pilot and adventurer

Drafting • **139**

⏱ TIME AND RESOURCE MANAGER

Resources
Print: Writing Support Transparency 7-F; Writing Support Activity Book 7–4
Technology: Writing Lab CD-ROM, Persuasion

In-Depth Coverage	Accelerated Pace
• Cover pp. 139–140 in class. • Guide students through the development of their thesis statements. • Have students complete the elaboration chart as they prepare their first draft.	• Assign pp. 139–140 for independent student review. • Ask students to submit thesis statements before beginning to write. • Students write their first drafts.

Step-by-Step Teaching Guide

Drafting: Develop a Thesis Statement

1. Remind students that their thesis statement sums up the point about which they are trying to persuade their audience. Their position statements may already function adequately as thesis statements, but, if not, students may need to work on developing a strong thesis statement.

2. Give students the following guidelines for a suitable and effective thesis statement:
   - The thesis statement must be specific and clear, and it must make a point about the topic.
   - If students are stating an opinion, it should be based on a logical idea rather than a feeling or a personal preference.

3. Work with students to develop models of sound thesis statements that are specific, clear, and make a point that will be proved in the essay. For example, volunteering could be presented in this way:
   - Volunteering benefits both the volunteer and the recipient.

4. Remind students that they can develop a working thesis statement, which they may adjust later to be sure that it covers all their points.

Step-by-Step Teaching Guide

Drafting: Organize to Emphasize Strongest Support

1. Suggest that students look at the evidence in their T-charts. Help them determine which are the most, next, and least powerful arguments, and order them accordingly.

2. Remind them to look at the evidence against their position so that they can acknowledge it and provide a counterargument.

Critical Viewing

Analyze Students may say that the photo suggests that Markham was a confident, secure person, who seemed fully able to have written the book attributed to her.

Drafting: Providing Elaboration

Teaching Resources: Writing Support Transparency 7-F; Writing Support Activity Book 7-4

1. Display the Elaboration Methods transparency. Point out to students the house-shaped organizer, where each argument is a pillar supporting the roof, or thesis statement. Indicate that students must include enough details and arguments (elaboration) to offer solid support for the thesis.

2. This elaboration organizer shows three types of elaboration. Let students know that other types of elaboration are also valid, such as facts, examples, and quotations from authorities on the subject.

3. Hand out copies of the blank organizer. Have students fill it in with their support. They may include other types of elaboration than the ones shown. If they find that their support is weak, they must find additional evidence—more personal experience, or another comparison or statistic—to the plan for their essays.

Customize for
Logical-Mathematical Learners

Suggest that students invert the relationship between supporting details and thesis statements as shown on the chart. Point out that if the supporting material does not match well with the thesis statement, it may indicate that the statement itself should be revised to better reflect their research findings.

7.3

Providing Elaboration

As you draft, build a strong case for your position by thoroughly developing each of your supporting arguments. Use a variety of methods to elaborate on each argument. For example, as the chart below demonstrates, you can use personal experiences, comparisons, and statistics.

USE A VARIETY OF ELABORATION METHODS

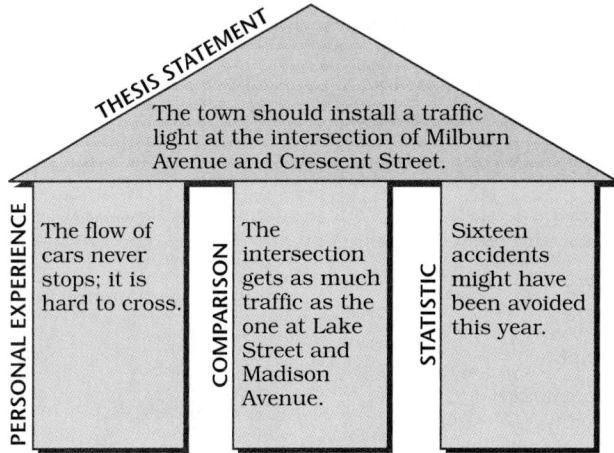

The following are some other strategies you can use to elaborate on your main point.

Describe the Situation Use sensory language to help your readers see the conditions you address. For example, to convince readers that the food in a certain restaurant is fantastic, describe the best entree you were served.

Show a Contrast Explain how your subject is different from another one. For example, to argue that toddlers need to use specialized car restraints, show how small children's safety needs are different from those of adults.

Provide an Anecdote Share a story that proves your point. For example, to support the position that a healthy diet is worth the effort, show how following a food plan changed one person's life.

☑ ONGOING ASSESSMENT: Monitor and Reinforce

If you observe that students are having trouble recognizing the strengths and weaknesses of their evidence, try the following strategy.

Have students work in pairs. Each student writes down his or her supporting points on note cards or self-sticking notes and asks the other student to place them in order of strongest to weakest.	Students can then discuss the effectiveness of their arrangements of supporting points before continuing to draft.

7.4 *Revising*

Once you have written your first draft, start looking for ways to improve it. Moving from the big picture of overall structure to the small details of word choice, the work you do in revising will make your essay more persuasive.

Revising Your Overall Structure
Support Your Arguments

The convincing power of a persuasive essay topples when supporting arguments are weak. Review your paper to strengthen each reason you provide to back up your opinion.

▶ **REVISION STRATEGY**
Color-Coding Main Points

Using a highlighter, identify the points that support your thesis statement. For each, underline the evidence you've provided.

Evaluate
• Does the support prove the thesis statement?

Revise
• If a point needs more evidence, return to your notes to find details. If there is no stronger evidence, eliminate the point.

🗋 Research Tip

To improve your essay, consult reference materials to get the additional facts you need. It is never too late to check *Facts on File,* recent journals, or other sources to find the statistic that will seal your case.

Student Work
IN PROGRESS

Name: Janaki Spickard-Keeler
Clark High School
San Antonio, TX

Evaluating Support for Your Arguments

By highlighting the main idea and underlining her support, Janaki analyzed this paragraph to evaluate her evidence. At this point, Janaki is revising for organization, rather than grammar or style.

For anyone who has read *West With the Night,* I think the real proof lies in the actual work. No one could have written the story without having been there. You'd have to have lived it to write like that. No matter what analysts say, the soul of the story is Beryl's.

The underlined statement does not give evidence to support the claim. The main point needs more evidence to support it.

To strengthen this point of her essay, Janaki decided to add a specific example of Markham's writing. See the final draft on pages 148–149.

Revising • 141

⏱ TIME AND RESOURCE MANAGER

Resources
Print: Writing Support Transparencies 7-G–I
Technology: Writing Lab CD-ROM, Persuasion

In-Depth Coverage	Accelerated Pace
• Cover pp. 141–145 in class. • Guide students through each of the revision strategies: color coding main points, addressing opposition, and using transition boxes • Review Grammar in Your Writing, p. 143	• Assign pp. 141–145 for independent student review. • Have students work in pairs to apply peer review strategies. • Students revise their drafts in response to peer review.

Revising: Finding a Place to Address the Opposition

Teaching Resources: Writing Support Transparency 7-H

1. Refer students to their T-charts (p. 138) where they listed evidence against their position.

2. Ask them to find the strongest piece of evidence against their position and come up with an argument against it.

3. Using the transparency, demonstrate how to find the best place to address an opposing point. Have students discuss the effect of inserting the opposing point in each paragraph of the student work.

4. Then have them discuss the effect of the student writer's actual placement.

5. Give students sticky notes to use for this purpose on their own drafts.

Integrating Speaking and Listening Skills

Politicians or other figures who frequently engage in public debates can demonstrate the benefits of addressing one's critics. Encourage students to watch a political talk show or debate on television. Have them choose one participant and focus on the way in which he or she addresses questions from opponents. Does he or she ignore the questions? Dismiss them as unimportant? Dwell too much on them? Take them seriously and give thoughtful rebuttals? Ask students to consider how this skill affects the speaker's overall performance.

7.4

Revising Your Paragraphs
Address the Critics

Give your essay greater credibility by showing another side of the argument. Identify an opposing point by thinking like your critics. First, imagine what your opponent might say to challenge your ideas. Then, list a few ideas, and choose one you can answer with a strong rebuttal. Finally, to find a place to insert this opposing argument and rebuttal effectively, analyze your essay at the paragraph level.

▶ **REVISION STRATEGY**
Finding a Place to Address the Opposition

Using self-sticking notes, write the opposing argument you will refute. Move this note down the margin of your essay, stopping at each paragraph to judge where the information would best fit. Once you decide on the best placement, write the idea out fully and incorporate it into your essay. Then, address the contrast between the opposition and your thesis. You may have to add a sentence or two to smooth out the connection.

Student Work
IN PROGRESS

Name: Janaki Spickard-Keeler
Clark High School
San Antonio, TX

Addressing the Critics

Janaki reviewed the main point of each paragraph. She decided to introduce the opposing view into the paragraph that contains her thesis.

First paragraph: For years, no one even knew the question existed. . . .

Second paragraph: Readers were thrilled with the book; it was an instant success. . . .

People claim Raoul's notes were on the manuscript.

Third paragraph: It is my opinion that Beryl Markham—and no one else—wrote her autobiography. . . .

142 • Persuasive Essay

☑ ONGOING ASSESSMENT: Monitor and Reinforce

If you observe that students are having difficulty dealing with opposing viewpoints, use one of the following options.

Option 1 Suggest that students ask themselves two questions: What is the best evidence *against* my position? Why doesn't this evidence cause me to change my mind? The answers to these questions can help students structure their responses to opposing viewpoints.	**Option 2** Remind students of the power of the first and last positions in a paper. Usually it is best not to begin or conclude a persuasive argument with the opposing viewpoint.

Grammar in Your Writing
Punctuating Adverb Clauses

You may find that in your essay you have used many adverb clauses. Adverb clauses show the relationship between ideas by telling *where, when, how, why, to what extent,* or *under what condition.*

Time relationship (when): After the book was published

Cause-and-effect relationship (why): Because so many people like the book

Opposing relationship (under what condition): Although many thought it was well-written

All adverb clauses contain a subject and a verb and begin with a subordinating conjunction.

Common Subordinating Conjunctions That Introduce Adverb Clauses

after	although	as
because	before	if
since	unless	until
when	whenever	where
wherever	whether	while

When an adverb clause introduces a sentence, use a comma to separate it from the rest of the sentence. Note, however, that it is usually not necessary to use a comma before an adverb clause at the end of a sentence.

Introductory adverb clause
After the book was published, critics came forward to question its source.

Adverb clause at the end of a sentence
Hemingway praised the writer because he thought she was talented.

Find It in Your Reading Review "We Can Go Home Again" by Nevada Barr on pages 130–133 of this chapter. Identify two sentences that contain introductory adverb clauses.

Find It in Your Writing Review your draft to identify three adverb clauses. Be sure that you have placed a comma after those that start sentences. If you cannot identify three adverb clauses, challenge yourself to add at least one more to your writing. You may like the improvement you've made.

For more on adverb clauses, see Chapter 21.

☑ ONGOING ASSESSMENT SYSTEM

Prerequisite Skills If students have difficulty with adverb clauses, you may find it helpful to refer them to the following materials to assure coverage of requisite skills.

In the Textbook	Print Resources	Technology
Phrases and Clauses, pp. 478–495	Grammar Exercise Workbook, pp. 81–82	On-Line Exercise Bank, Section 21.2

Grammar in Your Writing: Punctuating Adverb Clauses

1. Review adverb clauses. If necessary, direct students to Section 21.2 in Chapter 21, "Phrases and Clauses."

2. Point out that an adverb clause can often move its position in a sentence without affecting meaning. Give these examples:
   After the book was published, the author became famous.
   The author became famous *after the book was published.*
   Because so many people like the book, it is on the best-seller list.
   The book is on the best-seller list *because so many people like it.*

3. Tell students that only when an adverb clause begins a sentence do they need a comma to separate it from the rest of the sentence.

Find It in Your Reading

Students can find the following adverb clauses:

Paragraph 1: When I was asked to write an article on why it is important to preserve national parks

Paragraph 3: Though I know of these things

Paragraph 6: Even if we choose never to go

Paragraph 12: Because they let me live in their home for half a year

Paragraph 17: Unless, of course, we sell them for a quick buck.

Find It in Your Writing

Have students share examples from their writing with the class.

Integrating Grammar Skills

Point out that adverb clauses can be useful tools for varying sentence structure because they often provide a clear way to combine sentences.

- **Two sentences:** Bill Bradley was a basketball star. He became a United States Senator.
- **Combined:** Bill Bradley was a basketball star *before* he became a United States Senator.

Revising: Using Transition Boxes

Teaching Resources: Writing Support Transparency 7-1

1. Tell students that transitional words and phrases in their writing are important on two counts: They enable readers to see the connections between ideas, and they make the writing flow smoothly.

2. Use the transparency to model the strategy of using transition boxes to determine whether or not transitions are needed.

3. As students apply this strategy to their own drafts, refer them to the chart on the opposite page as a resource for possible transitions.

4. You might also have students work in pairs and read their partner's paper looking for needed transitions. A partner can be more objective than the writer.

Customize for
More Advanced Students

After they complete the "transition boxes" activity on page 144, have students look over all of the transition words they used. Ask them to evaluate whether they used any transition words too frequently, and have them make some sensible changes to create more variety in their essays.

Customize for
ESL Students

Review the transition chart on page 145 with students. Work with the class to create sentences using one transition from each column on the chart. Have students copy the four sentences in their notebooks as examples.

7.4

Revising Your Sentences
Use Transitions

Minor revisions to sentences can make a big difference. Look at each sentence to see whether rearranging or adding words will make your meaning more clear to your readers. Use transitions to clarify or reinforce the connections between ideas.

▶ **REVISION STRATEGY**
Using Transition Boxes

You may want to try this strategy with one paragraph:

1. Draw a box between the end punctuation of one sentence and the first word of the next sentence.
2. Identify the relationship that connects the sentences on either side of the box.
3. Evaluate your writing as it exists. Place a check in the box if the relationship between the sentences it connects is clear.
4. If the relationship is not clear, add a transition. (Use the chart on the next page as a reference.) Place the new word or phrase at the point where the box is located. As an alternative, you might draw a line from the box to a space where the transition makes the most sense.

Challenge yourself to apply this strategy to other paragraphs in your essay.

Writing Lab
CD-ROM

Use the Transition Word Bin in the Persuasion lesson to help improve your sentences.

Student Work
IN PROGRESS

Name: Janaki Spickard-Keeler
Clark High School
San Antonio, TX

Using Transition Boxes to Smooth Writing

In the paragraph that argued that Beryl Markham was not illiterate, Janaki saw that readers might not see the connections she wanted them to see. She added several transitions to make the writing more clear.

Beryl practically worshiped her father. ☐ She would do ⎤ , so naturally,

as he wished and read the classics. ☐ She had quite a   also

library, and Denys Finch-Hatton encouraged her to educate

herself. ☐ She wrote diligently with a practiced hand in her   Furthermore,

logbook. ☑ She also had to write a lengthy theory paper to

pass her flying exam.

> The first sentence gives a reason for the second sentence. The transition "so naturally" clarifies the relationship.

144 • Persuasive Essay

⬩ STANDARDIZED TEST PREPARATION WORKSHOP

Choosing Appropriate Transitions Many standardized tests require students to identify the appropriate words or phrases for inclusion in sentences. Use the following sample test item to give students practice in this skill.

Read the passages below and decide which one correctly uses transition words:

A The pilot switched on the intercom. *Accordingly* he addressed the passengers.

B The pilot switched on the intercom. *As well* he addressed the passengers.

C The pilot switched on the intercom. *Then* he addressed the passengers.

Item **C** is correct because the pilot must switch on the intercom before he can address the passengers, and *then* shows this temporal relationship.

TRANSITIONS THAT INDICATE LOGICAL RELATIONSHIPS			
Point to a Reason	Identify a Single Conclusion	Show a Contrast	Signal a Sequence
since, because, if	therefore, consequently, as a result, thus, hence, accordingly, so, then, in conclusion	although, even though, however, despite, yet, but, on the other hand, in contrast, except for	first, second, then, next, finally, before, after, later, soon, daily, recently, when

Revising Your Word Choice

Use Persuasive Language

The words you choose can influence the readers' reactions to your argument. If you maintain a polite tone, you can use language that points readers in the direction you want them to go.

When you want to sharpen criticism: Use words like *unfounded, shameful,* and *implausible.*

When you want to polish a recommendation: Add words like *superior* and *wise.*

When you want to defend your ideas: Include words like *obvious, clear,* and *evident.*

▶ **REVISION STRATEGY**
Reading Aloud

Read your draft aloud, as if it were a speech. Mark the ideas or sentences that you would want to stress to a crowd. Then, go back into your draft, adding the forceful words you need.

Peer Review

Say Back

In a small group, share your revised draft. Read your persuasive essay twice, asking readers to listen the first time and respond the second time. Use these questions as a starting point for group discussion:
1. What is the most persuasive point?
2. About which point would a reader want to know more?

After you've heard from your classmates, consider using their suggestions to improve your draft.

▲ **Critical Viewing**
In what ways might a peer conference like the one shown here help you fine-tune your persuasive essay? **[Hypothesize]**

Revising • 145

Revising: Use Persuasive Language

1. Have students review the examples on this page of persuasive words used to create specific effects. Then, before students go into their drafts to examine their word choices, ask them to state or write down the effect they want their essay to achieve.

2. As they review their own word choices, they can assess whether or not these words help them achieve the desired effect.

3. Have students read their drafts aloud, listening for the effect the draft would have on an audience. If they feel it does not have the desired effect, they can go back and add appropriate forceful words.

Revising: Peer Review

1. Before students engage in peer review, you may wish to allow them to photocopy and distribute their essays to group members.

2. Remind students that in their peer review groups, each writer will read his or her draft aloud twice before other group members respond, or "say back." The first reading gives listeners an overview of the whole paper and its order. On the second reading, peers will have a context for their comments. Peer reviewers might suggest specific strategies for improving the essay under discussion, such as transition boxes on page 144 or addressing the critics on page 142.

☑ **ONGOING ASSESSMENT: Monitor and Reinforce**

If students have difficulty choosing persuasive language, you may find it necessary to review the following to assure coverage of prerequisite knowledge.

As a variation of the "read aloud" strategy, students should listen to their draft being read by someone else. If particular statements do not sound as persuasive as the writer intended, they should be marked. As students revise these key statements to make them more forceful, tell them to concentrate first on verbs, then on adjectives.

Critical Viewing

Hypothesize Students may say that persuasive essays lend themselves extremely well to peer conferences; the best way to tell if an essay is persuasive is to share it with a reader and discuss whether and why he or she was persuaded.

Editing and Proofreading

1. Let students know that an important part of their proofreading is checking for accuracy. Any facts that they include, such as names, dates, statistics, or direct quotations, must be checked for accuracy. If they include direct quotations, not only must the quotation be accurate, but students must give the source as well.

2. You might wish to give students time in the library for fact-checking.

Grammar in Your Writing: Using the Conventions for Writing Titles

1. Give students this general rule of thumb for punctuating titles: Titles of short works, such as poems, stories, episodes of a television program, or articles in a newspaper, are usually put in quotation marks. Short works often fit into or are part of a longer work. The title of the longer work is in italics (or underlined). For example, short stories and poems are often part of a book. The title of the book is italicized. Television episodes are part of a series. The series title is italicized. Newspaper articles are found in a newspaper. The name of the newspaper is italicized.

2. For punctuating other types of titles, refer students to Chapter 29 in this book.

Find It in Your Reading

the *New York Times*: Titles of periodicals are italicized.

West With the Night: Titles of novels, biographies, and autobiographies are italicized.

The Splendid Outcast: Titles of short story collections (books) are italicized.

Find It in Your Writing

Have students exchange drafts with partners to check each other's work.

7.5 # Editing and Proofreading

Errors in persuasive writing can lessen your power to persuade. To make your writing error-free, check spelling, punctuation, and grammar before you create your final draft.

Focusing on Fact-Checking

Be sure you have included accurate information. Compare your draft to research notes you made, or consult reference materials to confirm details you have cited. Double-check the following kinds of details, and make corrections when necessary:

Names and dates Confirm the spelling of people's names. Make sure that the dates you cite are accurate.

Statistics Be on the lookout for numbers that may have been mistakenly transposed. For example, you may have copied 56,513 instead of 53,516 in your draft.

Quotations Check the wording of any quotations you include.

Grammar in Your Writing
Using the Conventions for Writing Titles

As you proofread, make sure you have used the conventions for writing titles. Long works are set off by underlining or italics. In addition to the titles of novels and plays, other titles that are italicized include the names of newspapers, magazines, movies, paintings, and sculptures.

Enclose short works in quotation marks. In addition to the titles of poems and short stories, other titles that are enclosed in quotation marks are essays, articles, and songs.

Titles of books:	*West With the Night* by Beryl Markham
Titles of short stories:	"A Day's Wait" by Ernest Hemingway
Titles of long poems:	*Paradise Lost* by John Milton
Titles of short poems:	"The Bells" by Edgar Allan Poe

Find It in Your Reading Find three titles in the completed student essay on pp. 130–133. Explain the conventions used for writing the titles.

Find It in Your Writing As you proofread your persuasive essay, check that you have written all titles correctly.

For more on writing titles correctly, see Chapter 29.

146 • Persuasive Essay

⏱ TIME AND RESOURCE MANAGER

Resources
Print: Scoring Rubrics on Transparency, Chapter 7; Writing Assessment: Scoring Rubric and Scoring Models for Persuasive Essay; Formal Assessment, Chapter 7
Technology: Writing Lab CD-ROM, Persuasion

In-Depth Coverage	Accelerated Pace
• Cover pp. 146–150 in class. • Have students edit and proofread their essays in class. • Review Rubric for Self-Assessment in class. • Have students present their final drafts.	• Assign pp. 146–150 for independent student review. • Have students edit and proofread their essays as homework • Have students present their final drafts.

7.6 Publishing and Presenting

Building Your Portfolio

Sharing your essay may prove powerful—your ideas could change a law, inspire a turnaround in people's habits, or provoke readers to see an idea in a new way. Consider these ideas for publishing and presenting your work:

1. **Encourage Action** Sponsor a read-aloud of several persuasive essays. As a group, choose one of the issues on which to act. Discuss ways to begin the process of making a change for the better—and then get started!

2. **Mail Your Essay** Invite a local, state, or federal elected official to act on the issue your essay addresses. Use government directories to find the address of the most appropriate official. Save a copy of the letter and any response you receive in your portfolio.

Reflecting on Your Writing

Take a moment to jot down your ideas about the persuasive writing experience. Save a copy of your ideas in your portfolio. These questions might direct your reflection:

- What have you learned about your topic?
- Which writing strategy might you recommend to a friend?

Internet Tip

To see model essays scored with this rubric, go to
www.phwg.phschool.com

Rubric for Self-Assessment

Use the following criteria to evaluate your persuasive essay:

	Score 4	Score 3	Score 2	Score 1
Audience and Purpose	Demonstrates highly effective word choice; clearly states focus on persuasive task	Demonstrates good word choice; states focus on persuasive task	Shows some good word choices; minimally states focus on persuasive task	Shows lack of attention to persuasive task
Organization	Uses clear, consistent organizational strategy	Uses clear organizational strategy with occasional inconsistencies	Uses inconsistent organizational strategy; presentation is not logical	Demonstrates lack of organizational strategy
Elaboration	Provides convincing, well-elaborated reasons to support the position	Provides two or more moderately elaborated reasons to support the writer's position	Provides several reasons but few are elaborated; only one elaborated reason	Provides no specific reasons or does not elaborate
Use of Language	Incorporates many transitions to create clarity of expression; includes very few mechanical errors	Incorporates some transitions to help flow of ideas; includes few mechanical errors	Incorporates few transitions; does not connect ideas well; includes many mechanical errors	Does not connect ideas; includes many mechanical errors

Publishing and Presenting • 147

☑ ONGOING ASSESSMENT: Assess Mastery

Use one of the following options to assess final drafts of students' persuasive essays.

Self-Assessment Ask students to score their essay using the rubric provided. Then have students write a paragraph reflecting on the most valuable strategy they learned in completing this essay.	**Teacher Assessment** Use the rubric and the scoring models provided in Writing Assessment, Persuasive Essay to score students' work.

Step-by-Step Teaching Guide

Publishing and Presenting

1. Ask students to recall their audience analysis activity from page 137. Encourage students to find ways to bring their writing to the attention of their chosen readership.

2. Remind students that most community action involves persuasive writing. Fund-raising for charities, campaigning for votes, petitioning for change require persuasion.

ASSESS

Step-by-Step Teaching Guide

Assessment

Teaching Resources: Scoring Rubrics on Transparency, 7; Formal Assessment, Chapter 7

1. Display the Scoring Rubric transparency and review the criteria in class.

2. Before students proceed with self-assessment, you may wish to review the final draft of the Student Work in Progress on pages 148–150. Have students score the final draft in one or more of the rubric categories. For example, how would students score the essay in terms of audience and purpose?

3. In addition to student self-assessment, you may wish to use the following assessment options.

   - score student essays yourself, using the rubric and scoring models from Writing Assessment in Teaching Resources.

   - review the Standardized Test Preparation Workshop on pages 154–155 and have students respond to a persuasive writing prompt within a time limit.

   - administer the Chapter 7 Test from Formal Assessment in Teaching Resources to assess students' grasp of concepts presented.

147

Teaching From the Final Draft

1. Have students read Janaki's final draft, or read it aloud yourself.

2. Review the following elements of a good persuasive paper.

   - The topic and implied audience are well chosen.
   - The introduction describes the topic clearly.
   - The introduction closes with a strong thesis statement.
   - The body of the essay addresses the issues point by point.
   - Each point is well supported with reasons or examples.
   - Transitions are used to connect ideas and show the sequence of the argument.
   - Word choice is vivid and persuasive.
   - The essay is edited and proofread to avoid errors of fact, grammar, or punctuation.

3. Ask students to review the essay in terms of the elements above. Students might then use these points as a checklist when revising their own essays or when doing peer reviews.

Critical Viewing

Connect Students may say that the wind in her hair and the confident expression on her face make Beryl Markham seem excited for the risks and challenges that pilots can face.

7.7 *Student Work*
IN PROGRESS

FINAL DRAFT

◄ **Critical Viewing**
What qualities in this picture suggest that Beryl Markham was a risk-taker? **[Connect]**

Who Wrote West With the Night?

Janaki Spickard-Keeler
Clark High School
San Antonio, Texas

For years, no one even knew the question existed. For years, too, no one even knew that the book existed. After a brief period of success, reaching *The New York Times* bestseller list, the book faded into obscurity with the onset of World War II. It was rediscovered in the 1980's by George Gutekunst while he read through some of Ernest Hemingway's letters. In a letter to Maxwell Perkins, Hemingway wrote: "Did you read Beryl Markham's book, *West With the Night*? I knew her fairly well in Africa and never

Janaki's research provided a compelling quotation to invite readers' interest.

would have suspected that she could and would put pen to paper except to write in her flyer's logbook. As it is, she has written so well, and marvelously well, that I was completely ashamed of myself as a writer. I felt that I was simply a carpenter with words, picking up whatever was furnished on the job and nailing them together and sometimes making an okay pig pen. But (she) can write rings around all of us who consider ourselves as writers. The only parts of it that I know about personally, on account of having been there at the time and heard the other people's stories, are absolutely true. . . . I wish you would get it and read it because it is really a . . . wonderful book." [Ernest Hemingway, "To Maxwell Perkins" 27 Aug 1942, *Ernest Hemingway: Selected Letters 1917–1961.* Ed. Carlos Baker. New York: Scribner, 1981. 541]

Readers were thrilled with the book; it was an instant success. They were even more thrilled to discover that Beryl Markham was still alive, living in Africa. It was then, however, that other people started stepping forward with other sides to the story. They claimed that Beryl's third husband, Hollywood writer Raoul Schumacher, was the real author of the book. In a foreword for her memoir, Beryl wrote: "I wish to express my gratitude to Raoul Schumacher for his constant encouragement and his assistance in the preparations for this book." That was all she wrote; nothing more.

Some people claimed that Beryl was illiterate, having had a spotty education. Others pointed out that if she could write so well, she should have published more. Suspicion rose when Raoul's handwriting was found on some pages of the original manuscript. The issue has been one of controversy ever since. It is my personal opinion that Beryl Markham—and no one else— wrote her autobiography.

First of all, the claim that Beryl was illiterate is utterly ridiculous. Her education had been spotty, of course, but she did go to boarding school for three years, and her father was an advocate of great literature. Beryl practically worshiped her father, so naturally she would do as he wished and read the classics. She also had quite a library, and Denys Finch-Hatton encouraged her to educate herself. Furthermore, she wrote diligently with a practiced hand in her logbook. She also had to write a lengthy theory paper to pass her flying exam. In the last years of her life, she suffered from a cataract in her eye that prevented her from reading, but she always kept her books and maps.

As to why she didn't write anything else, the people claiming this didn't look far enough, because she did. While she was married to Raoul, she wrote several short stories for magazines. After

Janaki recognizes that her readers may not know much about her subject. The background she provides here lends importance to the thesis statement she will present.

This paragraph identifies the issues the paper will address and closes with a forceful thesis statement.

To address the opposition, Janaki provides several explanations that refute the claim that Markham was illiterate.

Teaching From the Final Draft

Students may question the placement of the thesis in the essay (at the end of the third paragraph). To demonstrate the necessity of Janaki's thorough introduction, ask students how readers might react if the thesis statement was the first sentence of the essay. (Students may agree that readers need an explanatory introduction to the authorship question.) Suggest that students test the location of thesis statements in their own essays to ensure the most effective placement.

her death, these stories were compiled in a collection under the title *The Splendid Outcast*. In my opinion, I think Beryl found writing a chore. She enjoyed the product, but not the work. So after she left Raoul, her third husband, she left behind that era of her life. She was never one to stay in one place for long, both literally and figuratively.

By Beryl's own admission, her husband Raoul had helped out with the writing. After all, he was the professional author; naturally, she would ask him for help. Still, she always maintained that although he helped to edit and work out how to end it, she wrote most of it while in the Bahamas, and he never visited her in the Bahamas.

Janaki turns another opposing argument to her advantage.

For anyone who has read *West With the Night*, however, I think the real proof lies in the actual work. No one, no matter who they were, could possibly have written the story without having been there. It is simply not possible. You'd have to have lived it to write even remotely like that. It was by far the best thing Beryl ever wrote. No matter what analysts or anyone else ever says, the soul of the story is Beryl's, as this example demonstrates:

The opening line of this paragraph shows the "best-for-last" plan in action.

> I realize that the heavy drone of the plane has been, until this moment, complete and comforting silence. It is the actual silence following the last splutter of the engine that stuns me. I can't feel any fear; I can't feel anything. I can only observe with a kind of stupid disinterest that my hands are violently active and know that, while they move, I am being hypnotized by the needle of my altimeter. (Beryl Markham, *West With the Night*. New York: Farrar, Straus and Giroux. 285)

Here, Janaki elaborates with an example of the writing she defends.

In this single paragraph, she conveys her thoughts, wonders about her fears, and shares her amazed observations. No one could have written so vividly, so beautifully, so poetically about the experience of flying solo into the night. Even among those who actually have flown alone in a cockpit, you'd only find someone who could tell it the way she did once in a lifetime.

To sum up: Beryl was not illiterate, and she did write more than just her one autobiography. Furthermore, she acknowledged that Raoul helped out, but she always held that she was the actual author. Anyone who had read *West With the Night* will know that only she, Beryl Clutterbuck Markham, could possibly have written it.

A strong conclusion reviews the evidence presented and leaves no doubt about the writer's opinion.

Connected Assignment *Editorial*

Persuasive essays can be written to answer exam questions or to convince customers to consider products or services. An editorial, however, usually appears in a newspaper or magazine or is delivered orally as a part of a newscast. In an editorial, as in a persuasive essay, the writer presents a position about a topic and then provides supporting facts and examples.

Write an editorial about an issue that interests, moves, or angers you. Refer to these writing process tips as you work:

Prewriting First, choose an issue that concerns you: Consider your reaction to a controversial event affecting your school, community, state, or region. Then, identify your own views about what should be done, and list the reasons you feel this way. Use a chart like this one to gather facts or details that you need to support each reason.

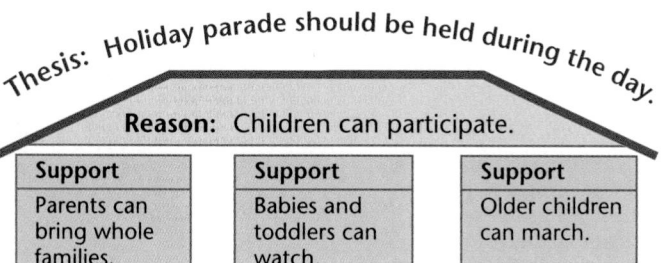

Thesis: Holiday parade should be held during the day.

Reason: Children can participate.

Support	Support	Support
Parents can bring whole families.	Babies and toddlers can watch.	Older children can march.

Drafting State your view in the opening paragraph. Then, organize your reasons for the strongest impact. Back up each reason with facts. As you draft, think about the emotions you want your audience to feel. Choose your words carefully to evoke these emotions. End with a strong conclusion that restates your viewpoint and calls for action.

Revising/Editing Have a classmate or family member read your editorial and summarize your position. If you haven't explained your ideas clearly enough, revise to clean up wordy sentences, add words to show cause-and-effect relationships, and use more precise verbs. Proofread to correct errors.

Publishing/Presenting To share your thoughts with a wider audience, send your editorial as a letter to the editor of your school, local, or regional newspaper.

▲ **Critical Viewing**
Why is a newspaper an effective place to publish an editorial or an essay of opinion? **[Analyze]**

Lesson Objectives

1. To write an editorial.
2. To organize material to ensure support for ideas.
3. To use writing processes to develop and revise drafts.
4. To publish an editorial to an audience.

Step-by-Step Teaching Guide

Editorial

Teaching Resource: Writing Support Transparency 7-J; Writing Support Activity Book 7-5

1. Bring sample editorials to class, or suggest students find them in the school or local newspaper. Review several examples with students.
2. To help students find a topic, suggest that they use the Hot Topics strategy on p. 134.
3. Display the transparency and use it to demonstrate how a thesis must be supported by reasons backed with supporting details.
4. Give students copies of the blank organizer, asking them to use it to support their own viewpoints.
5. Encourage students to refine their editorials for publication in school or local newspapers.

Critical Viewing

Analyze Students may note that newspapers are published regularly to a large audience. Most papers have pages dedicated to editorials and publish readers' reactions to encourage the interchange of opinions.

151

Step-by-Step Teaching Guide

Evaluating Artistic Performances

1. Choose one of the Spotlight elements for class discussion, or have students work individually or in groups on the element of their choice. Give students the initiative to find the necessary books, videotapes, or pictures.

2. Interested students may research additional information about the Castles and the development of ballroom dancing as performance.

3. Show a dance number from a film featuring Fred Astaire and Ginger Rogers. What mood or feeling does the dance number create?

4. Have students research recent films that include or focus on dancing. Ask students to compare and contrast the newer films with the Astaire-Rogers films.

Viewing and Representing

Activity Give interested students the opportunity to make class presentations of their reviews, showing sequences from the film to illustrate their points.

Critical Viewing

Contrast Students may mention clothing, hairstyle, and formal pose create an impression that the photograph was taken in the early part of the twentieth century.

Spotlight on the Humanities

Evaluating Artistic Performances

Focus on Dance: Vernon and Irene Castle

Making an evaluation is often the first step in writing persuasively. You can evaluate just about anything in the humanities—from movies to fine art to dancing. Ballroom dancing, a formalized, glamourous form of social dancing, became popular when a husband-and-wife team glided onto the scene in the early twentieth century. Vernon Castle (1887–1918) and Irene Castle (1893–1969) were best known for performing the turkey trot and one-step, which became known as the "Castle Walk." Together, they wrote a book called *Modern Dancing* in 1914, and Irene later wrote *My Memories of Vernon Castle* in 1918 and *Castles in the Air* in 1958. Their legacy lives on in film and theater.

Film Connection A generation after the Castles graced the dance floor, the famous dance team of Fred Astaire and Ginger Rogers immortalized them on film. In 1939, Astaire and Rogers starred in *The Story of Vernon and Irene Castle*. Irene Castle herself was a technical advisor on the film, re-creating the Castle's original steps for the graceful duo of Astaire and Rogers.

Theater Connection The choreographer Michael Bennett produced, directed, and choreographed the musical *Ballroom*, which appeared on Broadway in the 1978–1979 season. *Ballroom*, starring Dorothy Loudon and Vincent Gardenia, was a story of a couple who meet on the dance floor. Nominated for eight Tony Awards, it won Bennett his sixth Tony honor.

Persuasive Writing Activity: Evaluation Watch *The Story of Vernon and Irene Castle* with Fred Astaire and Ginger Rogers. As you enjoy the film, note the dance sequences. Write a review to share your reactions to the movie with classmates. In your review, evaluate whether the dance sections make the film more or less enjoyable.

▲ **Critical Viewing** What details of this photograph of the Castles suggest that it was taken in the early part of the twentieth century? **[Contrast]**

Media and Technology Skills

Recognizing Persuasive Techniques

Activity: Find Persuasion in Television Programs

Television entertains and informs, but often it also persuades. Even programs that seem to be simply entertainment carry subtle messages that influence the way you look at the world. Learn to view television programs critically, and evaluate what you see and hear.

Think About It News shows, documentaries, sportscasts, sitcoms, weekly dramas, talk shows, and awards programs are just some of the types of programs offered on television. News programs and documentaries may influence you by lingering on one image or by using words with strong connotations, such as *generous* and *risky*. Sports announcers interject their opinions as they narrate the action of a game. The way the plot of a sitcom turns out carries a message. Talk-show hosts share their opinions, and awards programs place a value on performance. Think about other ways that television programs persuade or influence your perceptions.

Watch It Choose a television program that you enjoy watching. Watch an episode with a notebook and pencil nearby, taking notes on a chart like the one below:

What Is Shown	What I Think
1.	
2.	
3.	

Analyze It Review your notes, and read the boxed side column on this page. Identify the techniques used in the program to influence your perceptions and responses.

Techniques Used to Influence Viewer Response

In a News Program or Documentary
- Focusing on an image
- Comments by the newscaster
- Using words with connotations

In a Sportscast
- Comments by the announcer
- Shots of crowd reaction
- Close-ups on the winning or losing team

In Sitcoms and Dramas
- Plot events in which characters are rewarded or punished
- Portraying certain types of characters as cool or popular
- Music and lighting

In Talk Shows
- Choice of guests
- Host reactions and comments

In Award Shows
- Who wins
- Shots of crowd reaction and candid "behind the scenes" shots

---

▶ Lesson Objectives

1. To evaluate and critique the persuasive techniques of media messages.
2. To recognize how visual and sound techniques convey messages in media.
3. To examine the effect of media on one's perception of reality.

Step-by-Step Teaching Guide

Recognizing Persuasive Techniques

Teaching Resources: Writing Support Transparency 7-K; Writing Support Activity Book, 7-6

1. Review the type of techniques used to persuade people in different kinds of programs.
2. Ask students to supply other means used in television shows to influence viewers. Before students view their television programs, you might have the class brainstorm more such techniques for which students may watch.
3. Using the transparency, you might walk students through an example.
4. Have students use the blank organizer to take notes as they watch a program. After they watch their programs, have students discuss the persuasive techniques they saw. Which techniques on the list were the most and least effective, and why? Did they see any techniques that were not on the list?

Customize for
Logical/Mathematical Learners

Have students collect data from classmates and make a bar graph that shows which persuasive techniques were most and least common. They can make a separate graph for each type of television program, or a combined graph that reflects the persuasive techniques used in all types of programs. When they finish, have them share results with the class.

Lesson Objectives

1. To write in a style appropriate to audience and purpose.
2. To use prewriting strategies to generate ideas.
3. To organize ideas to ensure logical progression and adequate support.
4. To demonstrate control over grammatical elements.

Step-by-Step Teaching Guide

Persuasive Writing Prompts

1. Emphasize to students that their key to success in most standardized essay tests is for them to address the question being asked. Students should read the questions carefully, and confine their answers to the topic area indicated.

2. Remind students that preliminary drafting for persuasive essays need not be extensive. Often it is enough to jot down several key words to help students remember their main points.

3. Reassure students that while neatness counts, examiners understand that time constraints prevent most standardized tests of this kind from being perfect finished products.

4. Assign a writing prompt for completion within a class period (or a shorter interval that corresponds to the time allowance for your state or local writing assessments).

Standardized Test Preparation Workshop

Responding to Persuasive Writing Prompts

The writing prompts on many standardized tests are designed to measure your opinions. You will be evaluated on your ability to do the following:

- Define and state your thesis clearly.
- Provide organized supporting arguments for your main point.
- Use language and details that are likely to influence the audience specified in the prompt.
- Elaborate your arguments effectively through the use of striking examples, anecdotes, facts, and other details.
- Use correct grammar, spelling, and punctuation.

When writing for a timed test, plan to devote a specified amount of time to prewriting, drafting, revising, and proof-reading.

Below are examples of persuasive writing prompts. Use the suggestions on the opposite page to help you respond. The clocks next to each stage show a suggested percentage of time to devote to the stage.

Test Tip

- Analyze prompts before responding. Underline key instructional phrases and words in the prompt, such as *choose one, argue, support,* and *explain.*

Sample Writing Situations

> Most schools hold regular classes for an average of 180 days each year. In 1983, a study recommended extending the school year to between 200 and 220 days. Some schools have lengthened the school year. Others have not. Choose one of the following prompts, and respond to it:
>
> Write a letter to the school board in which you argue for or against an extended school year. Persuade the members of the board to adopt your opinion. Be sure to support your position with convincing reasons and to explain your reasons in detail.
>
> Write an editorial for the school newspaper in which you urge students to either support or protest an extended school year. Be sure to support your choice with convincing reasons and to explain your reasons in detail.

154 • Persuasive Essay

🖋 TEST-TAKING TIP

A clear understanding of the writing prompt is the first step to success on a written test. Tell students to make sure to identify the exact words in the prompt that specify audience, purpose, topic, and form. They might find it useful to mark these words in the prompt before they begin to plan their response.   Ask students to pick out the key words in the prompts in the Sample Writing Prompts on this page. Then discuss why each word is so important.

Prompt 1: letter, school board, extended school year, persuade, reasons

Prompt 2: editorial, school newspaper, students, support or protest, extended school year, reasons

Prewriting

Allow about one quarter of your time for prewriting.

Identify the Issue and the Audience Whether you have several options or a single assigned topic, you must quickly determine what the purpose of your response will be—what issue or action are you being asked to defend or oppose? Then, look for the words that identify your audience. Each prompt on the previous page has a different audience. The first prompt addresses an audience of adults on the school board. The second addresses an audience of students. You may choose one prompt or another based on the audience you feel best able to influence.

Analyze the Issue Although you probably already have an opinion on the issue, examining your reasons will help you gather details for your persuasive response. Examine your reasons by making a T-chart. See p. 138 to review how to use a T-chart.

Drafting

Allow approximately half of your time for drafting.

Organize Your Arguments Create an outline or a list of points you want to include. Use numbers or an outline to prioritize the list, beginning with the least important and moving to the most important. Next to each item on the list, write sentences that incorporate the details on your T-chart.

Elaborate You probably won't have time to copy your paper twice, so plan to include your elaboration in the first draft. Look over the list of points that support your opinion. For at least three of the points, think of an anecdote, a statistic, or a fact that illustrates the reason or point. Choose details that will influence your specific audience. Write these next to the points they illustrate so that you remember to include them as you write.

Put It on Paper Write your response on your test paper. Begin with a statement of your opinion. Pause occasionally to review your outline or list. Make sure that you continue to follow the logical sequence you have set up and that you are including all your points. Write your response neatly.

Revising, Editing, and Proofreading

Allow about one quarter of your time to revise, edit, and proofread your paper.

Clean It Up Review your persuasive response. Neatly cross out any details that will not influence your audience. Check for errors in spelling. If you are unsure of the spelling of a word, consider replacing it with one you know better. If you are crossing out or erasing, do so neatly.

Time and Resource Manager

In-Depth Lesson Plan

	LESSON FOCUS	PRINT AND MEDIA RESOURCES
DAY 1	**Introduction to Advertisement** Students learn key elements of persuasion and advertisements and analyze the Model From Literature (pp. 156–158).	*Writers at Work* **Videotape** *Writing Lab* **CD-ROM**, Persuasion
DAY 2	**Prewriting** Students choose and narrow a topic, consider their audience and purpose and gather information (pp. 159–162).	**Teaching Resources** *Writing Support Transparencies* 8-A–C;
DAY 3	**Drafting** Students organize their ideas and write their first drafts (p. 163).	
DAY 4	**Revising** Students revise their drafts in terms of overall structure, paragraphs, sentences and word choice (pp. 164–166).	**Teaching Resources** *Writing Support Transparencies* 8-D–F
DAY 5	**Editing and Proofreading; Publishing and Presenting** Students check their work for accuracy and correctness and present their final drafts (pp. 167–168)	**Teaching Resources** *Scoring Rubrics on Transparency*, Chapter 8; *Formal Assessment*, Chapter 8

Accelerated Lesson Plan

	LESSON FOCUS	PRINT AND MEDIA RESOURCES
DAY 1	**Drafting** Students review characteristics for cause-and-effect writing, select topics and write drafts.	*Writers at Work* **Videotape** *Writing Lab* **CD-ROM**, Persuasion **Teaching Resources** *Writing Support Transparencies* 8-A–C
DAY 2	**Revising to Presenting** Students work individually or with peers to revise, edit and proofread their work for presentation.	**Teaching Resources** *Writing Support Transparencies* 8-D–F; *Scoring Rubrics on Transparency*, Chapter 8; *Formal Assessment*, Chapter 8

Options for Adapting Lesson Plans

HOMEWORK

Have students complete any stage of the lesson for homework.

TECHNOLOGY

Students can complete any stage of the lesson on computer. Have them print out their completed work.

FEATURES

Extend coverage with Connected Assignment (p. 170), Spotlight on the Humanities (p. 172), Media and Technology Skills (p. 173) and the Standardized Test Preparation Workshop (p. 174).

INTEGRATED SKILLS COVERAGE

Reading/Writing Connection
SE p. 158

Technology
Integrating Technology Skills
ATE pp. 159, 166

Real-World Connection
ATE p. 162

Viewing and Representing
Critical Viewing SE pp. 156, 163, 169, 170, 172
Viewing and Representing ATE p. 172

ASSESSMENT SUPPORT

Standardized Test Preparation SE p.174; ATE p. 174
Standardized Test Preparation Workbook, pp. 15–16
Scoring Rubrics on Transparency, Ch. 8
Formal Assessment, Ch. 8
Writing Assessment and Portfolio Management

MEETING INDIVIDUAL NEEDS

Less Advanced Student ATE p. 164; See also Ongoing
Assessments ATE pp. 157, 160, 165, 168
More Advanced Students ATE p. 161
Musical Learners ATE p. 163

BLOCK SCHEDULING

Pacing Suggestions
For 90-minute Blocks
• Have students complete the Prewriting and Drafting stages in a single period.
• Focus one class period on Revising and Editing and Publishing and Presenting. Allow at least 30 minutes for peer revision.

Resources for Varying Instruction
• *Writing Lab* **CD-ROM** If your students have access to hardware, a 90-minute block provides an ideal opportunity for students to work on computer.
• *Writers at Work* **Videotape** Show the Persuasion segment in class

Professional Development Support
• *How to Manage Instruction in the Block* This Teaching Resource provides management and activity suggestions.

MEDIA AND TECHNOLOGY

For the Student
• *Writing Lab* **CD–ROM**, Persuasion

For the Teacher
• *Writers at Work* **Videotape**, Persuasion
• *Resource Pro* **CD-ROM**

WRITING AND GRAMMAR WEBSITE

The Interactive Writing and Grammar Website provides a wide array of support for students, teachers and parents. Writing support includes:
• Interactive revision checkers
• Scoring rubrics with complete models

phwg.phschool.com

LITERATURE CONNECTIONS

Related selections from *Prentice Hall Literature: Timeless Voices, Timeless Themes,* Gold:
Analyzing Real-World Texts, SE p. 158
"The Birds," Daphne du Maurier, SE p. 159

▶ Lesson Objectives

1. To identify and evaluate different types of advertisements.
2. To create an advertisement.
3. To identify and practice strategies for choosing and narrowing a topic.
4. To learn strategies for revising structure.
5. To learn how to use correct abbreviations.
6. To publish an advertisement.

Critical Viewing

Analyze Students may say that it presents reading as an exciting activity.

Persuasion
Advertisement

◀ **Critical Viewing**
How does this artwork convey enthusiasm for reading? [Analyze]

Artwork copyright 2000 by Phil Yeh, www.ideaship.com

Advertisements in Everyday Life

You are bombarded by advertisements every day—on television and radio, on billboards, in magazines and newspapers, on the walls of buses and trains, and on the Internet. Advertisers do their best to get you to read, hear, and be persuaded by their messages. If you've ever accepted a free food sample or allowed yourself to be spritzed with a new fragrance in a department store, you know that advertising can go beyond words and images to address even the senses of taste and smell. As a form of persuasion, advertisements must convince; however, they have a more focused purpose: to encourage consumers to buy products or services.

156 • Persuasion

⏱ TIME AND RESOURCE MANAGER

Resources
Technology: Writers at Work videotape

In-Depth Coverage	Accelerated Pace
• Cover pp. 156–158 in class. • Show the Persuasion section of the Writers at Work videotape. • Read and analyze the model advertisement on p. 158 in class and use it to discuss the use of design elements in advertisements. • Discuss advertisements that you or students have read and seen.	• Discuss definitions and types of advertisements in class. • Assign Model from Literature for independent reading.

What Is an Advertisement?

An **advertisement** is produced by a company or an organization to persuade an audience to buy a product or service, accept an idea, or support a cause. Advertisements in print form appear in newspapers, magazines, or on billboards. Ad writers can create audio or visual commercials presented on radio, television, or the Internet. An effective advertisement may include

- a memorable slogan to grab the audience's attention.
- a call to action that encourages the readers to do something.
- details that provide practical information, such as price, location, date, or time.
- a deliberate use of layout, images, or print styles.

To see the criteria by which your final advertisement may be judged, preview the Rubric for Self-Assessment on page 168.

Writers in ACTION

Rosser Reeves, a successful advertising professional, encourages new advertising writers to find the element of a product that creates good feelings and to capitalize on that. Reeves coined the phrase, "Sell the sizzle, not the steak."

Types of Advertisements

From a flyer announcing a school musical to a campaign for the presidency of the United States, advertising takes many forms. Here are a few of the most common types of advertising:

- **Political campaigns** use print ads, posters, and television spots to educate and persuade voters about a candidate.
- **Infomercials** mix a talk-show or news format with persuasive techniques to promote a product or service.
- **Product packaging** takes advantage of the container or wrapping of a product to persuade consumers to buy it.
- **Public-service announcements** provide persuasive information to educate audiences about issues of social concern.

PREVIEW Student Work IN PROGRESS

In this chapter, you'll follow the work of Caitlin Mahoney, a student at Darien High School in Darien, Connecticut. Caitlin used prewriting, drafting, and revising techniques to create a flyer. Her interest in animal adoption inspired her ad for the Doggy Palace Animal Shelter. Her final advertisement appears at the end of this chapter.

Advertisement • 157

✓ ONGOING ASSESSMENT: Diagnose

Use one of the following options to diagnose students' current level of proficiency in persuasive writing.

Option 1 Ask each student to select the strongest example of his or her persuasive writing from last year. Hold conferences to review each student's sample and determine which students will need extra support in developing an advertisement.	**Option 2** Ask students to write a sentence persuading a friend to help them with a community service project. Then have them list three reasons or items of evidence that support that sentence. If students have difficulty completing this exercise, you will need to devote more time to the gathering evidence and elaboration phases of the writing process.

Discuss how each element of the design has a role in delivering the message of the ad. Even such elements as type style and size carry a message. Some are dignified and somber, others lively and jazzy. Size can be used to assign varying elements of importance to print information. Color has deep and subtle influences on perception.

Step-by-Step Teaching Guide

Engage Students Through Literature

1. Have student read aloud the margin notes to identify the ad's major elements.

2. Remind students that this ad is sent to people's homes. Ask them how it differs from the kinds of ads they might see on TV. (This ad specifically targets opera-goers. Ads on TV do not target audiences in the same way. For example, you may be watching TV and see an ad for a new car, even though you don't want a car or already own one. The opera ad is geared specifically for people who like opera.)

3. Discuss with students how successful they think this ad is.

8.1 Model From Literature

Like most theater companies, the Michigan Opera plans a season by identifying several productions it will present in a given year. The advertisement below, sent to homes before the first curtain, announces the operas to be performed in one season.

Incorporate Design Elements As you finalize your advertisement, use color, lines, or fonts to communicate your ideas.

LITERATURE

For another example of a print ad, see the advertisement for an automobile in the Analyzing Real-World Texts section of *Prentice Hall Literature: Timeless Voices, Timeless Themes*, Gold.

The logo at the top identifies the company that sponsored the ad.

The ad's memorable slogan "Think. Feel. See an Opera." echoes the quotation printed in a large type size. It targets a specific audience and appeals to a perceived desire to live life fully.

Details such as prices, ticket-office phone numbers, and the opera's address are essential to ticket sales. These practical details are printed on the reverse side of the mailer.

8.2 *Prewriting*

Choosing Your Topic

To write a convincing advertisement, choose a product, service, or event that you would like to promote. Use these strategies to generate a topic you'd like to develop:

Strategies for Generating Topics

1. **Products and Services Schedule** In a chart, break your day into logical segments, such as before, during, and after school. For each block of time, make a list of the products and services that you use every day. Review your chart to find a topic for your advertisement.

2. **Classroom Interest Poll** Survey your classmates to find out what products and services they buy. Develop a questionnaire or conduct a group discussion to identify the brand names of on-line services, magazines, musical groups, clothing, or stores they enjoy. Review the results of your poll, and choose a topic for your advertisement.

Writing Lab CD-ROM

For more help finding a topic, explore the activities and suggestions in the Choosing a Topic section of the Persuasion lesson.

TOPIC BANK

Consider these suggestions for more topic ideas:

1. **Advertisement for an Invented Product** Imagine a product that would make your life more manageable or interesting. Develop the concept, and then devise an advertisement that introduces your idea to consumers.

Responding to Literature

2. **Public-Service Announcement** After reading "The Birds," by Daphne du Maurier, write a public-service announcement based on the events of the story. You can find "The Birds" in *Prentice Hall Literature: Timeless Voices, Timeless Themes*, Gold.

☑ **Cooperative Writing Opportunity**

3. **Ad Campaign** With a group, decide upon a product or service to promote with a series of advertisements. Develop individual ads to appeal to specific audiences. For example, one writer can create an ad for teenagers; another can design one for families; and a third can make the product appealing to businesses.

Step-by-Step Teaching Guide

Prewriting: Choosing Your Topic

1. Students will probably have plenty of ideas for this assignment. Review the two strategies suggested in the text. A third alternative is simply to ask students what product or service they would like to focus on, reminding them that it does not have to be a product or service they personally use.

2. You may want to exclude certain categories such as alcohol and tobacco for product ads. If students want to do public service ads around those products, that is something you may want to encourage.

3. Have students review the Topic Bank for additional suggestions on selecting a topic.

Integrating Technology Skills

Students may want to think about designing an Internet banner ad. Have them go on-line and look at banner ads on product Web sites.

Responding to Literature

"The Birds" is du Maurier's chilling account of nature gone awry. When students have completed their announcements, encourage volunteers to present them to the class.

Spotlight on the Humanities

For additional topic suggestions, refer students to the Spotlight on the Humanities on page 172.

⏱ TIME AND RESOURCE MANAGER

Resources
Print: Writing Support Transparencies 8-A–C
Technology: Writing Lab CD-ROM, Persuasion

In-Depth Coverage	Accelerated Pace
• Work through the Choosing a Topic strategies with the class (p. 159). • Work through Cubing with the class (p. 160). • Use the transparency to work through Matching Audience with Purpose. **Option** Have students work independently or in small groups with the Writing Lab CD-ROM.	• Discuss strategies for generating topics. • Have students work independently to choose and narrow their topics. • Have students work with partners to focus on audience, purpose, and gathering details.

Prewriting: Narrowing Your Topic

Teaching Resources: Writing Support Transparency 8-A

1. Good ads are not simply the result of a bright idea. Ad makers are careful to choose just the right angle to make the ad effective.

2. Display the transparency. Introduce the cubing process and walk students through it, pointing out the examples of each step. Ask students to suggest additional details for each step.

3. Advertisers do this cubing process before identifying their audience and purpose. Advertisers spend huge amounts of money on market research before they produce an ad.

Customize for
Less Advanced Students

Students may have difficulty visualizing the three-dimensionality of the cube. To assist students in "seeing" all six sides, display a cube or construct one out of paper for students to use as they apply the strategy.

8.2

Narrowing Your Topic

The topic of your advertisement should be the product or service you've identified. However, you will need to find an angle that makes your product appealing. Use the cubing strategy to study your topic and narrow the focus of your advertisement.

Narrow a Topic With Cubing

Cubing allows you to look at your topic from six angles:

1. **Describe It** Explain the physical attributes of your topic.
2. **Associate It** Show how your topic may remind your audience of something else.
3. **Apply It** Tell how your topic can be used.
4. **Analyze It** Separate your topic into smaller parts.
5. **Compare and Contrast It** Explain how other products are similar to and different from yours.
6. **Argue for It** Traditionally, in cubing, you promote or reject an idea. However, narrow this cubing angle to collect only positive ideas for promoting your topic.

After you've studied your product or service from each angle, review your list. Circle the elements of the product or service that you will address in your advertisement.

Speaking and Listening Tip

To help identify those features of your topic that need more focus, do the cubing exercise with a group. As you address each angle, ask group members if you have provided a clear explanation.

CUBING TO NARROW AN AD'S FOCUS

Product: Pack and Go Radio

Describe:
(credit card size)
AM-FM radio; available in 8 colors

Associate:
like other high-tech gadgets; something a spy might use

Apply:
take news or music with you anywhere

Analyze:
digital tuner; clock feature; built-in antenna and speakers

Compare and contrast:
(provides stereo-quality sound;)
smaller than any home stereo

Argue for or against:
convenient; modern

Narrowed focus: size and quality

Writing Support Transparency
Use the transparencies for Chapter 8 to teach these strategies.

✓ ONGOING ASSESSMENT: Monitor and Reinforce

If some students are having difficulty using cubing to narrow their topic, use one of the following options.

Option 1 Use a well-organized print ad to illustrate each step of the process.	**Option 2** Have students work in small groups to pool their resources. The aim is for them to narrow the topic, even if they use the cubing process incompletely.

Considering Your Audience and Purpose

Generally, advertisements serve a predictable purpose: to show a product, service, or idea in a positive light and therefore encourage readers to take actions such as buying, voting, or participating. However, specific sales techniques will appeal to some audiences and not to others. Consider the audience you want to reach with your ad, and then devise an appeal that will move that group.

Match Your Audience With Your Purpose

A knowledge of your audience will be a critical element in achieving your purpose. Identify your target audience, list what you know about the people you want to reach, and then decide on the best way to appeal to them.

**Writing Lab
CD-ROM**

To gather information about your target audience, use the Audience Profile activity in the Persuasion lesson.

Prewriting: Matching Your Audience and Purpose

Teaching Resources: Writing Support Transparency 8-B

1. Discuss how identifying your audience is especially important for advertising. For many years, advertisers designed ads that they hoped would appeal to the widest possible audience. Then advertisers determined that they could be more successful by designing different ads for different audiences.

2. Display the transparency. Review Caitlin's work in progress. Ask students how effectively they think she targets her audience and purpose to the topic.

**Customizing for
*More Advanced Students***

Explain to students that an ad's target audience is also known as its *demographic*. Have students research how companies and advertising agencies study the demographics for particular products and ads.

Student Work
IN PROGRESS

Name: Caitlin Mahoney
Darien High School
Darien, CT

Matching Your Audience With Your Purpose

Before drafting her ad, Caitlin made a list of benefits that might persuade her audience to adopt a pet. Then, she chose a specific angle.

Angle: Pets complete the family picture

Audience: Families
  Both old and young members
  Varied interests
  Want to spend quality time together
  Parents may want value or affordability
  Kids may prefer animals that are active and fun
  Looking for ways to bring the family together and create
  memories

Prewriting • 161

Prewriting: Gathering Details

Teaching Resources: Writing Support Transparency 8-C

1. This is the critical linkage for a successful ad. See that students understand the necessity of the closest alignment possible between the angle and the audience.

2. Display the transparency. Use it to walk students through linking audience and angle. Have students examine how Caitlin linked dog ownership with families.

3. Ask students to consider lifestyle, finances, and interests in connecting their product to their audience.

Real-World Connection

Have students look in newspapers and magazines for outstanding ads. Help them analyze how the ads link audience and angle by listing the details the ads use.

8.2

Gathering Details

To write a strong advertisement, back up your pitch with details that will help convince your audience of the merits of your service, product, or cause.

Make a Link to Audience and Angle

Use a knowledge of your audience to gather details that will be persuasive. Jot down ideas that will help you prove that the product is suitable for your audience's needs, lifestyle, financial situation, and interests. Look at these suggestions:

Lifestyles If the people in your target audience lead hectic lives, show how your product or service is convenient, time-saving, or relaxing. If your readers want to add excitement to their lives, show how your product can help them do that.

Finances If you are trying to reach an audience of people who keep to a strict budget or those who want to save money, emphasize the cost and value of your product. If money is not a concern, you may choose not to address this issue.

Interests Some audiences are impressed by status—the prestige or importance that owning an item may bring them. Others are more concerned with the way a product can help their business, improve their health, or help them achieve some other goal. Gather information to address these specific interests of your target audience.

♈ Challenge

Consult the professionals by scanning newspapers and magazines to find effective ads. Consider applying the techniques you see by using them in your own advertisement.

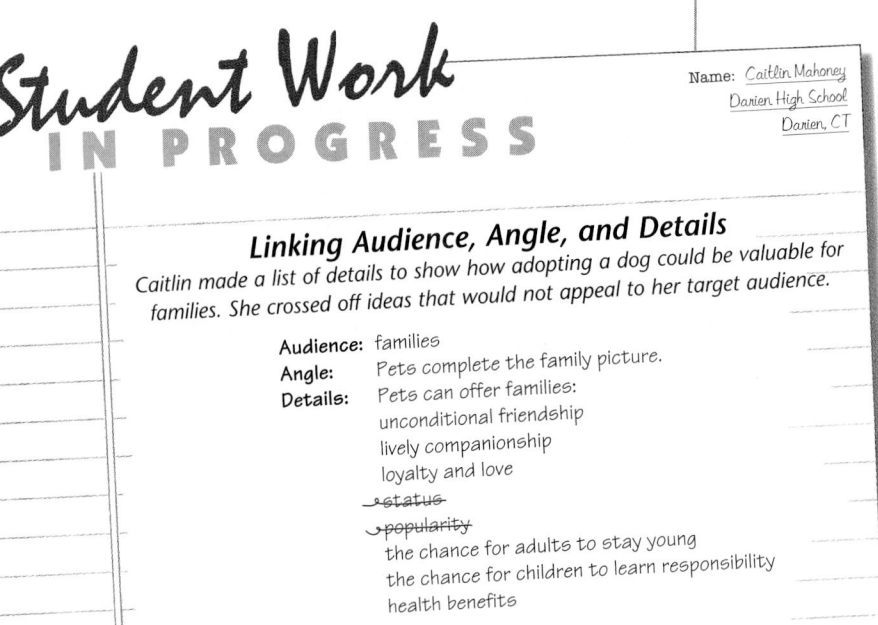

Student Work IN PROGRESS

Name: *Caitlin Mahoney*
Darien High School
Darien, CT

Linking Audience, Angle, and Details

Caitlin made a list of details to show how adopting a dog could be valuable for families. She crossed off ideas that would not appeal to her target audience.

Audience: families
Angle: Pets complete the family picture.
Details: Pets can offer families:
unconditional friendship
lively companionship
loyalty and love
~~status~~
~~popularity~~
the chance for adults to stay young
the chance for children to learn responsibility
health benefits

162 • Advertisement

⏱ TIME SAVERS!

📖 **Writing Support Transparency**
Use the transparencies for Chapter 8 to teach these strategies.

162

8.3 Drafting

Shaping Your Writing

Organize to Persuade

Although the number of words in an advertisement is drastically fewer than the count for a fully developed essay, your words must communicate your ideas and persuade your audience. Be sure your writing addresses each of these features:

- **Slogan** An effective ad is based on a catchy and memorable message. Write a short phrase or sentence that announces your main idea. Make a play on words or use rhyme to encourage your audience to learn more about your product or service.

- **Images** Pictures can often say more than words. If possible, find an appropriate photograph or illustration for your advertisement.

- **Supporting Information** Include supporting details to appeal to your target audience. Somewhere on your ad, provide information about where your readers can learn more.

Providing Elaboration

Include the Facts

While your slogan presents the strongest selling point of your product or service, it is also important to include details to answer the readers' basic questions. As you write your advertisement, include factual information, such as what the product is, what it does, why it is useful, and where to get it.

Grammar and Style Tip

Use alliteration, the repetition of initial consonant sounds, to make your slogan more memorable. For example, one restaurant chain launched a successful campaign with the phrase "Food, folks, and fun."

◄ Critical Viewing In your opinion, what is the most important information on this political advertisement? Why? [Evaluate]

Drafting • 163

Step-by-Step Teaching Guide

Drafting: Organize to Persuade; Include the Facts

1. Ask students to recall some memorable advertising slogans. Successful slogans, perhaps just from the sheer repetition, become part of our culture. Be sure to share some older memories of your own.

2. Give students some elements to work with in their slogan:

   Short and punchy phrases, not long sentences

   Alliteration

   Question (*Did somebody say . . . ?*)

   Exclamation

   Superlatives

   Parallel structure (*good food, good times*)

3. Ask students if they agree with the saying that "a picture is worth a thousand words." Remind them that the images they show do not need to be directly of or about the product. If their ad is featuring life style or interest issues, they may want show something that they want customers to associate with the product.

4. See that students work at finding supporting information that links to the slogan and the product.

Customize for
Musical Learners

Most television ads use background music, or the ad itself is a song. Students should think now about including music when they present their ad (page 168). They can have a tape-recording of some existing music to go with their print ad, or they may want to perform it themselves.

Critical Viewing

Evaluate Students may mention the candidate's name and the office for which he is running.

TIME AND RESOURCE MANAGER

Resources
Technology: Writing Lab CD-ROM, Persuasion

In-Depth Coverage	Accelerated Pace
• Work through the exercises on organizing to persuade and providing elaboration in class. • Have students write their advertisement drafts in class. **Option** Have students work independently or in small groups with the Writing Lab CD-ROM.	• Have students review p. 163 independently, then write their own advertisement drafts. • Respond to individual drafting issues as needed.

Revising: Review the Visual Layout

Teaching Resources: Writing Support Transparency 8-D

1. Display the transparency and review the sample illustration to show students one possibility for designing their ads. Tell students, however, that the design of their ad should be influenced by their messages and their audiences.

2. Since students will be revising their ads, make sure they either have multiple photocopies of their illustrations, or have them lightly tape the material to a piece of poster board so it can be safely removed and moved around.

3. Have students circle their main ideas and then be sure they are featured to their best advantage on their layout.

4. You may want to have students work in small groups so they can benefit from peer feedback.

5. Remind students to align their tone and message with the design. A public service ad raising funds to fight a disease would not work if it featured loud, splashy colors and a humorous approach.

Customize for
Less Advanced Students

You may need to work individually with students to help them identify their main ideas. Refer them back to the earlier activities about establishing their audience and angle. These are the main ideas they need to display prominently in their ad.

8.4 Revising

Revising Your Overall Structure
Review the Visual Layout

After you've completed your first draft, look for ways to make your advertisement visually appealing to your audience. Try several layouts, and choose the one that seems most logical. To make your organization more obvious, identify the main ideas your ad presents.

▶ **REVISION STRATEGY**
Circling Main Ideas to Improve the Layout

Review the first draft of your advertisement, and circle the ideas you want to convey most. To make these items stand out, evaluate their placement on the page. Decide whether a different font, size, or color would make the ideas more visible. Alternatively, consider adding bullets to call more attention to the key points. The illustration below offers one potential layout for your advertisement.

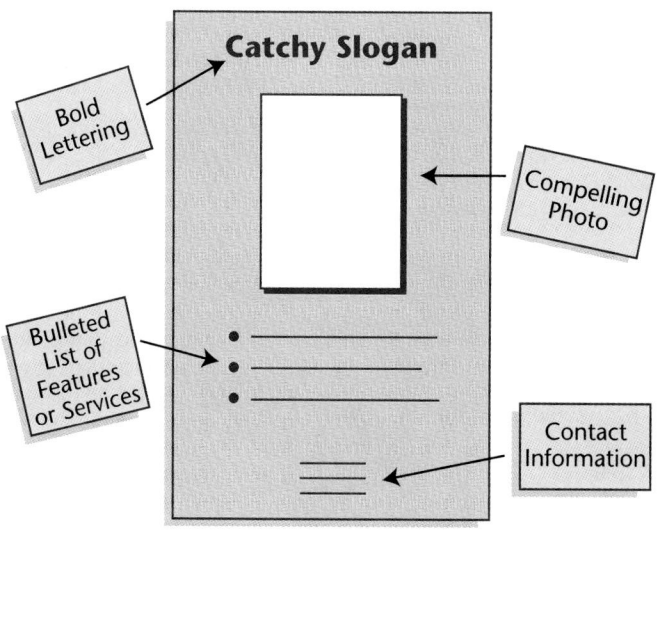

🕐 Learn More

To learn more about visual layout techniques, review the Media and Technology Skills lesson on page 173. Use what you learn to experiment with fonts, borders, and other features available on your word processor.

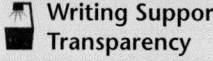 **Writing Support Transparency**
Use the transparencies for Chapter 8 to teach these strategies.

🕐 TIME AND RESOURCE MANAGER

Resources
Print: Writing Support Transparencies 8-D–F
Technology: Writing Lab CD-ROM, Persuasion

In-Depth Coverage	Accelerated Pace
• Work through revising strategy with entire class. • Use the relevant transparencies for shortening sentences and improving word choice. **Option** Divide the class into groups for peer review.	• Assign students to review pp. 164–166 independently. • Have students revise their advertisements independently.

Revising Your Paragraphs and Sentences

Improve Sentence Power

To make their point quickly and effectively, advertisements depend on short, punchy sentences or phrases. Review your draft, and replace long, wordy sentences with leaner, more powerful ones.

▶ **REVISION STRATEGY**
Shortening Your Sentences

Look at the length of the sentences in your draft in an effort to shorten each one. Revise complicated sentences by limiting many of them to a single subject, its verb, and any modifiers.

To address your audience directly, change declarative sentences to imperative ones. Look at this example:

DECLARATIVE: We advise you to compare our prices.

IMPERATIVE: Compare our prices.

Student Work
IN PROGRESS

Name: *Caitlin Mahoney*
Darien High School
Darien, CT

Shortening Sentences

To get directly to the point and add authority to her writing, Caitlin reduced wordiness by shortening many sentences in her final draft.

- ~~You'll find~~ a dog is a lively companion and a loyal friend to adults and children.

- ~~All our customers report~~ a dog will love you unconditionally for the rest of your lives together.

Revising • 165

Step-by-Step Teaching Guide

Revising: Shortening Sentences

Teaching Resources: Writing Support Transparency 8-E

1. Discuss how the rules for advertising are often the opposite of the rules for good expository writing. In writing an essay, it is important to avoid too many short sentences. In advertising, short and punchy rule. Ads get only a glimpse. If they don't immediately attract people's attention, they are ignored. A picture, good layout, punchy slogan—these are what get an ad an extended look.

2. Display the transparency and have students examine how Caitlin shortened and punched up her sentences.

3. One way to punch up writing is to drop the subject and verb and use imperative sentences in which the subject (you) is understood. Write the following additional examples on the chalkboard:

   We're sure you'll enjoy our great service. → *Great Service!*

   We have eight showrooms of fine furniture. → *8 Rooms of Fine Furniture!*

✓ **ONGOING ASSESSMENT: Monitor and Reinforce**

If some students are having difficulty shortening sentences, use one of the following options.

Option 1 For action sentences, tell students to focus on the verb, since there will be no subject. Urge them to choose strong active verbs such as *compare, enjoy, drive.*	**Option 2** For sentences that are about product features and services, show students how to drop both the subject and verb.

165

Revising: Word Choice

Teaching Resources: Writing Support Transparency 8-F

1. In advertising everything matters. Every ad is competing with hundreds of other ads. Successful ads need to give people a reason to look. Once they are "hooked," every word and image matters.

2. Remind students of two important things to consider in the language of their ads. First, the tone of their language must match the message of their ad. Second, they should consider word choice. Discuss how *nice* pales before *exciting* or *alluring*. Urge students to make each word count.

3. Have students study the language in newspaper and magazine ads for ideas.

4. Display the transparency to demonstrate how Caitlin used color-coding to help her identify words that needed replacing.

5. Have students review each other's ads in groups. Remind students of the importance of delivering feedback in a supportive, respectful manner.

Integrating Technology Skills

Have students use the thesaurus on their word processor programs to search for synonyms.

8.4

Revising Your Word Choice
Choose Words With Positive Connotations

Because people respond to the connotations or emotional meanings of words, advertising professionals know the importance of a precise label. While the words *satisfying*, *filling*, or *hearty* may seem similar, their connotations may appeal to one audience but alienate another. To reach your audience, review the words you've used in your draft.

▶ **REVISION STRATEGY**
Color-Coding to Improve Word Choice

Use a highlighter to identify words that you'd like to make more persuasive. Besides indicating dull words, mark words that are overused. To make your ad more persuasive, replace the words you've identified with more powerful ones. Use a thesaurus to spark your revision choices.

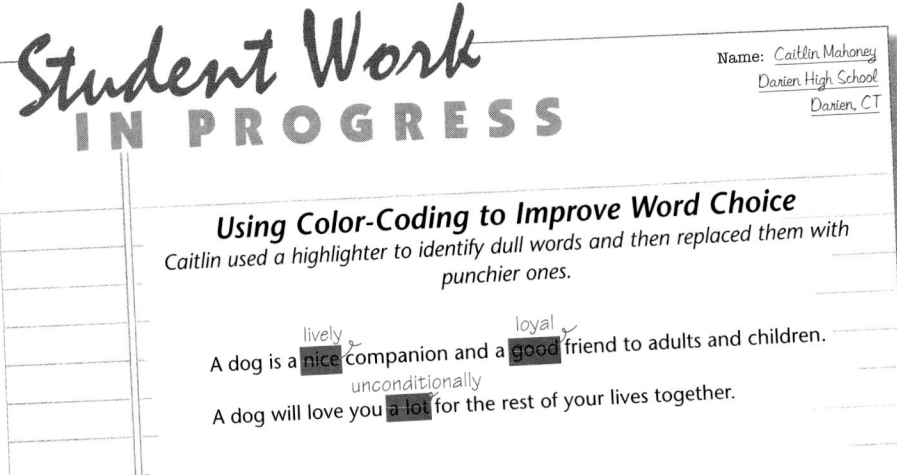

Student Work
IN PROGRESS

Name: Caitlin Mahoney
Darien High School
Darien, CT

Using Color-Coding to Improve Word Choice
Caitlin used a highlighter to identify dull words and then replaced them with punchier ones.

A dog is a ~~nice~~ *lively* companion and a ~~good~~ *loyal* friend to adults and children.
A dog will love you ~~a lot~~ *unconditionally* for the rest of your lives together.

Peer Review
Focus Groups

Before advertisements hit the pages of a magazine or the airwaves, they are tested to be sure they communicate the intended message. After a group previews your ad, use feedback to make final revisions to your work. Ask these questions to get specific responses:

• What do you think the product or service is?

• Would you buy the product or use the service based on this advertisement?

166 • Advertisement

🔆 Research Tip

To find the exact words to convey an idea to your audience, consult a thesaurus.

8.5 Editing and Proofreading

Review your writing carefully for errors. Be sure to check spelling, punctuation, and grammar before creating your final draft.

Focusing on Spelling

Unless they are intended to grab your audience's attention, errors in spelling will detract from the persuasive power of your ad. Be especially careful to spell place names and product names correctly.

Grammar in Your Writing
Using Abbreviations

An abbreviation is a shortened form of a word or a phrase. It usually consists of the first several letters of a word or the first letter of each word in a longer phrase.

Titles The most common abbreviations are the social terms *Mr.* and *Mrs.* Note these abbreviations for government leaders:

President	Pres.	Senator	Sen.	Representative	Rep.
Governor	Gov.	Treasurer	Treas.	Ambassador	Amb.

Time The abbreviations that distinguish between morning and evening can be written in three styles, as shown below. Choose one format for consistency.

A.M., a.m., am : ante meridiem, before noon

P.M., p.m., pm : post meridiem, after noon

Months of the Year Most months of the year are abbreviated to their first three letters.

January	Jan.	February	Feb.	March	Mar.
April	Apr.	May	May	June	June
July	July	August	Aug.	September	Sept.
October	Oct.	November	Nov.	December	Dec.

Find It in Your Reading As you review professional advertisements, notice the use of abbreviations to convey information.

Find It in Your Writing Circle words you have abbreviated in your ad. Double-check these to be sure you have followed standard conventions.

For more on abbreviations, see the Abbreviation Guide on pages 866–869.

Editing and Proofreading • 167

Publishing and Presenting

1. Have students present their ads to the class, describing what they think are the best aspects. For example: "I used red type for my headline so it would really stand out. I think the picture of the product is effective."

2. Students who designed public service ads may want to post them in school hallways, the library, and the cafeteria.

3. Have students use the rubric for self-assessment to review their advertisements.

ASSESS

Assessment

Teaching Resources: Scoring Rubrics on Transparency, 8; Formal Assessment, Chapter 8

1. Display the Scoring Rubric transparency and review the criteria in class.

2. Before students proceed with self-assessment, you may wish to review the Final Draft of the Student Work in Progress on page 169. Have students score the Final Draft in one or more of the rubric categories. For example, how would students score the essay in terms of audience and purpose?

3. In addition to student self-assessment, you may wish to use the following assessment options.

   • Score student essays yourself, using the rubric and scoring models from Writing Assessment.

   • Review the Standardized Test Preparation Workshop on pages 174–175 and have students respond to multiple-choice questions within a time limit.

   • Administer the Chapter 8 Test from Formal Assessment in Teaching Resources to assess students' grasp of concepts presented.

8.6 Publishing and Presenting

Building Your Portfolio

Advertising is meant to convince others to buy your product or service, support your cause, or attend your event. Try these ideas for presenting your work:

1. **Bulletin Board** Make a display to share the creative talents of your class. Next to each ad, include a few words from the writer that explain the ideas behind the work.

2. **Mail Your Ad** If your advertisement is for a product or service that exists, share your work with the company. You should be able to locate an address on the product's packaging, through library resources, or on the Internet.

Reflecting on Your Writing

Reflect on the experience of writing an advertisement. Use these questions to direct a written reflection. Include your ideas in your portfolio.

• How did the purpose of your advertisement become clear as you began to create it?

• How is drafting an advertisement different from creating other types of writing?

Internet Tip

To see a model essay scored with this rubric, go to **www.phwg. phschool.com**

Rubric for Self-Assessment

Use the following criteria to evaluate your advertisement:

	Score 4	Score 3	Score 2	Score 1
Audience and Purpose	Presents effective slogan; clearly addresses specific audience	Presents good slogan; addresses specific audience	Presents slogan; minimally addresses specific audience	Does not present slogan; shows lack of attention to specific audience
Organization	Uses layout and design elements to convey clear, consistent organizational strategy	Uses layout and design elements to convey clear organizational strategy with few inconsistencies	Uses inconsistent layout and design strategy; creates illogical presentation	Demonstrates lack of organizational strategy; creates random presentation through layout and design elements
Elaboration	Successfully combines words and images to provide convincing, unified support for a position	Combines words and images to provide unified support for a position	Includes some words or images that detract from a position	Uses words and images that do not support a position
Use of Language	Successfully communicates an idea through clever use of language; includes very few mechanical errors	Conveys an idea through adequate use of language; includes few mechanical errors	Misuses language and lessens impact of ideas; includes many mechanical errors	Demonstrates poor use of language and confuses meaning; includes many mechanical errors

168 • Advertisement

✓ ONGOING ASSESSMENT: Assess Mastery

Use one of the following options to assess final drafts of students' advertisements.

Self-Assessment Ask students to score their ad using the rubric provided. Then have students write a paragraph reflecting on the most valuable thing they learned in completing the advertisement.	**Teacher Assessment** You may want to use the rubric and scoring models provided in the Writing Assessment to score the advertisement.

FINAL DRAFT

Caitlin Mahoney
Darien High School
Darien, Connecticut

Pets Complete the Family Picture

Why adopt a dog?

🐾 A dog is a lively companion and a loyal friend to adults and children.

🐾 A dog will love you unconditionally for the rest of your lives together.

🐾 Caring for a dog and playing with a dog can keep adults young and help teach children responsibility.

🐾 Our dogs need good homes.

🐾 Doggy Palace Animal Shelter needs your support.

What will you find here?

🐾 A puppy or an adult dog that will fit happily into your household

🐾 Pets in many colors, sizes, breeds, and barks

When and where?

Monday, Sept. 23 – Friday, Sept. 27   3 P.M. – 9 P.M.
Saturday, Sept. 28 – Sunday, Sept. 29   9 A.M. – 9 P.M.

Doggy Palace Animal Shelter

11 Peters Street

Trentville

Caitlin made her headline bigger than the other text and centered it to grab the attention of readers more effectively.

◀ **Critical Viewing**
How does the photograph convey positive feelings about pets? **[Analyze]**

Caitlin uses bold subheads and icons to call out main points.

Details beneath each main point provide more information aimed at a specific audience.

At the end of the advertisement, Caitlin includes practical information such as dates and times.

Teaching from the Final Draft

1. Review the final draft of Caitlin's ad. Help students see how she has created an effective ad by covering the following issues:
   - Start with the slogan. It is effectively tied to the picture.
   - Organization: complete and tidy—why, what, and when
   - Graphic: the pawprint bullets cleverly reinforce the message
   - Text: vivid language—*lively, loyal, unconditional*
   - Layout: clean, aligned
   - Humor: *Pets in many colors, sizes, breeds, and barks*

2. After analyzing the ad, ask students if they can think of any improvements they would suggest to Caitlin.

3. Ask students to consider how the ad affects them. Does it make them want to support the Doggy Palace Animal Shelter in some way?

Critical Viewing

Analyze Students may say that it portrays pets as affectionate and cute members of the family.

Lesson Objectives

1. To write product packaging appropriate to audience and purpose.
2. To use writing strategies to develop, draft, revise, and edit product packaging.

Critical Viewing

Analyze Students may say that designers put text on these products to give consumers information about their products.

Product Packaging

Teaching Resources: Writing Support Transparency 8-G; Writing Support Activity Book 8-1

1. Have students follow the same process they did in making the advertisement.

2. In the prewriting stage, students first need to choose a topic. Ask them to brainstorm for products to add to those listed.

3. Remind students that audience and angle are important. Even if the product is for kids, discuss that it also has to appeal to the adult who will probably purchase it.

4. Urge students to look at the displays of cereal, toothpaste, and other products at a local store. They should think about which stood out or appealed to them, and which did not.

continued

Connected Assignment
Product Packaging

When you buy a product because the label says it's good for your health or when you choose something because the box says it's easy to install, you're responding to product packaging. **Product packaging** includes all the writing on a product's label or the bag, box, or container that holds the product. Generally, this packaging includes a broad range of information—from the brand name to rebates, sale offers, or nutritional content. Like all forms of advertisement, product packaging is persuasive. In addition to informing you about the product it contains, packaging also seeks to persuade you to buy that product.

One way to become a better reader of product packaging is to become a copywriter yourself. The following writing process suggestions can help.

Prewriting In preparation for writing the copy for a product, consider the items your family and friends use every day. Choose a topic from among these possibilities:

- Cereal box
- Toothpaste tube
- Child's toy or game
- CD-ROM
- Vitamins
- Microwaveable meal

Once you've chosen a product, study a few models in your home or at a store. Notice the many different kinds of information these boxes contain and the way color, images, and text sizes work together to convey an idea.

Choose or invent a brand name. Then, develop an eye-catching design to present it. Identify the audience you want to attract and a focus for your appeal. To gather the details you'll need to create effective packaging for your product, jot down ideas for communicating a positive message about your product. Use a chart like the one on the next page to list the reasons people should buy your product. For each reason you list, note the methods you'll use.

▲ **Critical Viewing** Why do you think the designers of milk containers and cereal boxes put text and information on these products? **[Analyze]**

GATHERING DETAILS

Main Idea

Buy Crunchy Flakes

Reasons	It's healthy	It tastes good	It's fun
Ways to Show	Nutrition chart	Appealing picture	Game involving cereal mascot
	Headline	Quotations from satisfied customers	Reference to Web site with related activities
	Picture of jogger	Poll results comparing it with leading competitor	Picture or cartoon of people enjoying cereal as part of their fun

Drafting If possible, work on a computer and experiment with type styles and layouts. Otherwise, sketch your packaging, and plan as many sides as necessary. For example, a cereal box has six panels; a bag of dried fruit two; and a shampoo bottle may have one label that wraps from back to front. Get an idea of how much text will fit on each segment before you start writing. Choose action verbs, concrete nouns, and vivid adjectives with positive connotations, but avoid making false promises.

Revising and Editing With product packaging, design counts as much as text. Keep this in mind as you review your work. To strike a balance between format and content, add or delete text and reorganize graphic images until you are pleased with the result.

Publishing and Presenting Set up a display in your classroom to show the product packages you and your classmates have created.

Writing Lab CD-ROM

Use the Vague Adjectives Revision Checker to help you identify words that may not sell your products effectively. You can find this tool in the Persuasion lesson.

5. Display the transparency and examine the Crunchy Flakes example. Point out how the main idea is supported by three distinct reasons, each supported by details. Give students copies of the blank organizer for them to use as they gather details.

6. Students can use graphic software to design their packages. Remind them to pay attention to organization, short, punchy language, and eye-catching design.

7. Have students display their product packages.

Step-by-Step Teaching Guide

Evaluating the Persuasive Techniques of Art Forms

1. Choose one of the Spotlight elements for class discussion, or have students work individually or in groups on the element of their choice. Give students the initiative to find the necessary books, recordings, and pictures.

2. Gordon Parks's photos tell stories of America's people—often the poor, dispossessed, forgotten, and ignored. Interested students can bring in examples of Parks's work, discussing what each image means to them and how it communicates this message.

3. Have students research the life and music of Guthrie, considered one of the giants of the folk-protest song movement.

4. Encourage interested students to examine the novel (or one of the filmed versions) in greater depth, as well as Dorothea Lang's photos of Dust Bowl farmers.

Viewing and Representing

Activity Encourage students to look for images that speak a great deal about a subject without requiring words. Have them examine the ways in which these images communicate their messages.

Critical Viewing

Respond Students may say that the photograph is an ironic portrait of the American Dream.

Spotlight on the Humanities

Evaluating the Persuasive Techniques of Art Forms
Focus on Photography: Gordon Parks

One of the keys to successful advertising is captivating photographs and images that hook an audience. Despite glamourous assignments such as his jobs as fashion photographer and staff photographer for *Life* magazine, some of Gordon Parks's (1912–   ) most lasting work created a visual history of America's poor. Working for the Farm Security Administration, a New Deal agency, Parks let his camera serve as a form of social protest. By illuminating the faces of those who became victims of the Depression, Parks created a legacy of that time period. He also created relationships with his subjects and helped many of them well after he had taken their picture.

Music Connection Woody Guthrie (1912–1967) brought to music what Gordon Parks brought to photography. After the dust storms of the 1930's hit the plains of the United States, Guthrie wrote hundreds of songs about the victims of the storms and the migrants moving west. As a young child in Pampa, Texas, Guthrie read every book in his town's small library. His first book of songs, called *Hard Hitting Songs for Hard Hit People*, was finally published in 1967. Writer John Steinbeck, also known for his descriptions of migrant farmers, wrote the introduction to Guthrie's book.

Literature Connection John Steinbeck (1902–1968) won the Pulitzer Prize for Literature in 1939 and the Nobel Prize for Literature in 1962. His most famous novel, *The Grapes of Wrath*, focuses on the Joads, a family of Dust Bowl farmers forced to become migrants in the late 1930's.

Persuasive Writing Activity: Photography Analysis
As Parks's images reveal the devastation and dignity of the working class during the Depression, current images of today's troubles may also convey a persuasive message. Scan current newspapers or magazines to find several photographs that you find especially powerful. Then, create a photo essay in which you include persuasive captions for a series of photographs.

▲ **Critical Viewing**
Study this photograph by Gordon Parks. What message do the flag, the mop and broom, and the woman's expression convey to you? **[Respond]**

Media and Technology Skills

Lesson Objectives

1. To study the formatting and graphics features of computer software.
2. To explore designs for an advertisement.

Using Print Technology to Extend a Meaning

Activity: Creating an Advertisement on a Word Processor

With the availability of animation and a wide variety of font styles, computer tools have changed the world of advertising. You can try the techniques of the professionals just by using the special graphics features of your word-processing programs. With these tools in hand, creating an advertisement on a computer is almost like having a personal design department at your fingertips. Apply graphics and layout features to experiment with your ad's appearance and enhance its impact.

Learn About It Study the formatting and graphics sections of your program manuals. Work first with word-processing tools to develop your ad's text, focusing on catchy language that your reader will remember. To find just the right word, take advantage of the program's built-in thesaurus feature. Then, experiment with text, design, and graphics features. Scan the options under Format, Font, Table, and Drawing menus for specifics. Think about how the ad looks on the screen, but remember that elaborate graphics are only effective if images are clear and text remains legible. Import pictures, charts, and other images from linked programs or on-line sources.

Design It Using a word-processing program, explore different versions of an advertisement. Use one you have already written or create a new one for this purpose. Consider the options listed in the sidebar, and record your decisions in a chart like the one shown here. Print out your completed ad, and explain your graphics and design choices to a partner.

Features to Consider

- Borders
- Shading
- Patterns
- Special typefaces
- Type effects, such as boldfacing, italicizing, and shadowing
- Colors in graphics, text, or background
- Symbols, dingbats, and icons
- Clip art
- Drawings imported, scanned, or created with built-in functions.

	What I Tried	What I Selected
Fonts		
Point size		
Shading		
Borders		
Image		

Media and Technology Skills • **173**

Analyzing Persuasive Texts

1. Carefully review with students the techniques they can use to evaluate persuasive ads.

2. Encourage students to highlight and identify any of these elements as they read. They can use their notes to help answer the questions.

3. Tell students that another helpful strategy involves skimming the questions first before they read the given ad. This will focus their attention and give them a specific purpose for evaluating the ads.

Standardized Test Preparation Workshop

Analyzing Persuasive Texts

An informed consumer is able to evaluate the information given in persuasive writing. Standardized tests often measure your ability to evaluate persuasive writing objectively. Use the following techniques to help you evaluate advertisements.

- Search for facts; be wary of opinions stated as fact.
- Check for missing information or vague statements.
- Recognize oversimplifications, such as overgeneralizations, loaded language, questionable cause-and-effect statements, either-or arguments, or bandwagon appeals.
- Look for proof of the argument or claim.

The following sample test item will give you practice with these types of questions.

Test Tips
- If one choice is much longer or much shorter than all the others, consider it carefully. It may be the correct choice.
- As you read the test passage, note your initial reactions. Very often, your first response is right.

Sample Test Item	Answers and Explanations
Directions: Read the passage, and then choose the best answer to each question. Hopewell's Herbals Vitamin Supplements: The all-new, all-natural, fast-working powerhouse preferred by Olympic athletes. Not available in stores. Call 1-800-555-FIT2. At only $29.95, supplies are limited, so call now! 1 The clause *supplies are limited* is an example of which of the following persuasive techniques? A Unsupported claim B Bandwagon appeal C Questionable cause and effect D None of the above	The correct answer is *B*. By suggesting that many people will be ordering the product, the line implies that those who do not act quickly will be left out.
2 What important information is missing from this advertisement? A Product brand name B Where to buy the product C The amount provided D All of the above	The correct answer is *C*. The writers of the ad do not indicate the quantity provided for $29.95.

174 • Advertisement

TEST-TAKING TIP

Explain to students to be careful of questions in which "none/all of the above" is a choice. They should read each choice more than once; if any of the choices are not correct, students can immediately eliminate two of the choices—the "incorrect" choice and "none/all of the above." For example, in item 2 of Practice 1, students may be tempted to choose "All of the above." However, item H is not important information, so students can eliminate items H and J. This leaves items F and G, but information on how to reach the company is more important, so the correct choice is item **G**.

Practice 1

1. C
2. G
3. B
4. J
5. A
6. J
7. C
8. J

> **Practice 1** **Directions:** Carefully read the passage. Choose the letter that best answers each question.

We all know that America's health-care system is comparatively poor among industrialized nations. Would it surprise you to learn that we are also behind in our savings? Compare the working families in Japan, who may save thousands each year, to the multitudes of American families who have no savings at all. The only sure way to plan your financial future is to take charge of your money. <u>When it comes to your future, don't be foolish—be in the financial major leagues.</u> Invest on-line with our experienced staff of experts. Log on to our convenient Web site today to see how you can become one of the smart ones: one of the wealthy ones.

1 Which passage is an example of an opinion stated as a fact?
A When it comes to your future, don't be foolish . . .
B Compare the working families in Japan . . .
C We all know America's health-care system is comparatively poor among industrialized nations.
D All of the above

2 What important information is missing from this advertisement?
F The type of investment being advertised
G How to reach the company
H The number of individuals employed by this company
J All of the above

3 The underlined passage in the advertisement is an example of which type of persuasive technique?
A Unsupported fact
B Emotional appeal
C Circular reasoning
D None of the above

4 The author indicates that the financial service advertised is—
F endorsed by professional sports
G created by a Japanese investment firm
H insured by the government
J accessible through the Internet

5 Which type of appeal is exemplified by the following statement: Compare the working families in Japan, who may save thousands each year, to the multitudes of American families who have no savings at all?
A Overgeneralization
B Either-or argument
C Bandwagon appeal
D Vague statement

6 It is clear that the author of the advertisement intends to persuade the reader to—
F save money
G invest in bonds
H move to Japan
J invest with a specific company

7 Which of the following makes an appeal to the competitive nature of the readers?
A log on to our convenient Web site
B save thousands each year
C one of the smart ones: one of the wealthy ones
D none of the above

8 You can tell the advertisement—
F is for a disreputable company
G is written to deceive the reader
H contains lies
J none of the above

Time and Resource Manager

In-Depth Lesson Plan

	LESSON FOCUS	PRINT AND MEDIA RESOURCES
DAY 1	**Introduction to Comparison and Contrast** Students learn key elements of comparison and contrast and analyze the Model From Literature (pp. 176–179).	*Writers at Work* **Videotape,** Exposition *Writing Lab* **CD-ROM,** Exposition
DAY 2	**Prewriting** Students choose and narrow a topic, consider their audience and purpose, and gather information (pp. 180–183).	**Teaching Resources** *Writing Support Transparencies* 9-A–D; *Writing Support Activity Book* 9–1
DAY 3	**Drafting** Students organize their ideas and write their first drafts (pp. 184–185).	**Teaching Resources** *Writing Support Transparencies* 9-E
DAY 4	**Revising** Students revise their drafts in terms of overall structure, paragraphs, sentences, and word choice (pp. 186–190).	**Teaching Resources** *Writing Support Transparencies* 9-F–G
DAY 5	**Editing and Proofreading; Publishing and Presenting** Students check their work for accuracy and correctness and present their final drafts (pp. 191–192)	**Teaching Resources** *Scoring Rubrics on Transparency,* Chapter 9; *Formal Assessment,* Chapter 9

Accelerated Lesson Plan

	LESSON FOCUS	PRINT AND MEDIA RESOURCES
DAY 1	**Drafting** Students review characteristics for cause-and-effect writing, select topics, and write drafts.	*Writers at Work* **Videotape,** Exposition *Writing Lab* **CD-ROM,** Exposition **Teaching Resources** *Writing Support Transparencies,* 9-A–E; *Writing Support Activity Book,* 9-1
DAY 2	**Revising to Presenting** Students work individually or with peers to revise, edit and proofread their work for presentation.	**Teaching Resources** *Writing Support Transparencies,* 9F–G; *Scoring Rubrics on Transparency,* Chapter 9, *Formal Assessment,* Chapter 9

Options for Adapting Lesson Plans

HOMEWORK

Have students complete any stage of the lesson for homework.

TECHNOLOGY

Students can complete any stage of the lesson on computer. Have them print out their completed work.

FEATURES

Extend coverage with Connected Assignment (p. 196), Spotlight on the Humanities (p. 198), Media and Technology Skills (p. 199) and the Standardized Test Preparation Workshop (p. 200).

INTEGRATED SKILLS COVERAGE

Integrating Grammar
Verb Tenses SE p. 189
Degrees of Comparison SE p. 191

Reading/Writing Connection
Reading Strategy SE p. 178
Writing Application SE p. 179

Language Highlight
ATE p. 179

Spelling
Integrating Spelling Skills ATE p. 191

Workplace Skills
Integrating Workplace Skills ATE p. 183

Technology
Integrating Technology Skills ATE pp. 182, 197

Real-World Connection
ATE p. 188, 195

Viewing and Representing
Critical Viewing SE pp. 176, 178, 185, 187, 190, 193, 195, 196, 198
Viewing and Representing ATE p. 198

ASSESSMENT SUPPORT

Standardized Test Preparation SE p. 200; ATE p. 200

Standardized Test Preparation Workbook, pp. 17–18

Scoring Rubrics on Transparency, Ch. 9

Formal Assessment, Ch. 9

Writing Assessment and Portfolio Management

MEETING INDIVIDUAL NEEDS

Less Advanced Students ATE pp. 189; See also Ongoing Assessment ATE pp. 177, 181, 183, 187, 192

ESL Students ATE pp. 180, 193

Visual/Spatial Learners ATE p. 184

BLOCK SCHEDULING

Pacing Suggestions
For 90-minute Blocks
- Have students complete the Prewriting and Drafting stages in a single period.
- Focus one class period on Revising and Editing and Publishing and Presenting. Allow at least 30 minutes for peer revision.

Resources for Varying Instruction
- *Writing Lab* **CD-ROM** If your students have access to hardware, a 90-minute block provides an ideal opportunity for students to work on computer.
- *Writers at Work* **Videotape** Show the Exposition segment in class.

Professional Development Support
- *How to Manage Instruction in the Block* This Teaching Resource provides management and activity suggestions.

MEDIA AND TECHNOLOGY

For the Student
- *Writing Lab* **CD-ROM**, Exposition

For the Teacher
- *Writers at Work* **Videotape**, Expositon
- *Resource Pro* **CD-ROM**

WRITING AND GRAMMAR WEBSITE

The Interactive Writing and Grammar Website provides a wide array of support for students, teachers and parents. Writing support includes:

- Interactive revision checkers
- Scoring rubrics with complete models

phwg.phschool.com

LITERATURE CONNECTIONS

Related selections from *Prentice Hall Literature: Timeless Voices, Timeless Themes,* Gold:

"The Rules of the Game," Amy Tan, SE p. 179

Romeo and Juliet, William Shakespeare, SE p. 181

Lesson Objectives

1. To recognize the elements of an effective comparison-and-contrast essay.
2. To learn strategies for generating and narrowing a topic for a comparison-and-contrast essay.
3. To learn strategies for organizing a comparison-and-contrast essay.
4. To recognize strategies for revising an essay's overall structure as well as its paragraphs, sentences, and word choice.
5. To edit and proofread a draft, focusing on grammar and usage errors.
6. To practice using photos and technology during the publishing and presenting stage of the writing process.

Critical Viewing

Evaluate Students may suggest the marbles' types, sizes, or colors.

▲ **Critical Viewing** What would make these marbles a good subject for a comparison-and-contrast essay? **[Evaluate]**

Comparisons and Contrasts in Everyday Life

When you make a decision about whether to try skiing instead of snowboarding, whether to wear a pair of jeans or a pair of corduroys, or whether to have a chicken sandwich instead of a salad for lunch, you are using comparison-and-contrast skills. Although choosing the contents of a meal or selecting the day's wardrobe may not have lasting consequences, you will also apply comparison-and-contrast analysis to more important decisions: what career to pursue, where to live, whom to elect to office. In each case, you consider two or more options that are similar in some ways and different in others. In the end, you use the skills of comparison and contrast to weigh all factors and make a decision.

176 • Exposition

⏲ TIME AND RESOURCE MANAGER

Resources
Technology: Writers at Work videotape

In-Depth Coverage	Accelerated Pace
• Go over pp. 176–177 in class. • Show the Comparison-and-Contrast section of the Writers at Work videotape. • Read through the Model From Literature (pp.178–179) in class.	• Have students review pp. 176–179 independently.

What Is a Comparison-and-Contrast Essay?

A **comparison-and-contrast essay** addresses two or more subjects to show their similarities and differences. It may describe or explain, reveal strengths as well as weaknesses, or persuade a reader to value one subject over another. An effective comparison-and-contrast essay

- identifies similarities and differences between two or more things, people, places, or ideas.
- provides factual details about each subject.
- identifies a purpose for comparison and contrast.
- addresses each subject equally by presenting information in one of two organizations: subject by subject or point by point.

To preview the criteria by which your final comparison-and-contrast essay may be evaluated, see the Rubric for Self-Assessment on page 192.

Types of Comparison-and-Contrast Essays

The comparison-and-contrast format is suitable for a wide range of topics. Following are some common types of comparison-and-contrast essays:

- **Essays on historic figures or events** ("The Visions of Martin Luther King, Jr., and Nelson Mandela")
- **Comparison and contrast in the humanities** ("Monet's Impressionism vs. Seurat's Pointillism")
- **Reports on consumer goods** ("This Year's New Cars")

PREVIEW Student Work IN PROGRESS

In this chapter, you will read the work of several students at City High School in Iowa City, Iowa. As you'll see, they used techniques of the writing process to write "Working Out Possibilities," a comparison-and-contrast article published in *the little hawk*, the school newspaper.

Writers in ACTION

Carl Sagan, an astronomer who made the galaxies accessible to millions, valued discovery. Just as uncovering hidden stars takes research, good comparison and contrast may take some study, but the acquired insight is worth the effort. As Sagan explained, a bold revelation has value:

"When you make the finding yourself—even if you're the last person on Earth to see the light—you'll never forget it."

Interest GRABBER Identify two students who are friends and who don't mind having attention drawn to them. Have these students sit or stand together in front of the class. Ask the class to give examples of how the two students are alike. When the class has run out of examples, ask the two students if they have anything to add. Point out that the class has just *compared* the two students. Repeat the process, this time asking for examples of how the students are different. Point out that in this step, the class *contrasted* the two students.

Activate Prior Knowledge

Ask students to share situations in which they have used comparison and contrast to make decisions. (Possible answers: choosing which shirt to buy, which movie or TV show to watch, or which after-school activity to participate in)

More About the Writer

Carl Sagan's unquenchable thirst for discovery drove him to explore life's most puzzling mystery—the origin of life on Earth. Another of Sagan's quests helped establish the scientific field of exobiology—the search for extraterrestrial life. Sagan conveyed his findings to other scientists through well-written reports and journals. He also caught the imagination of everyday people through his exciting science fiction stories, books, and TV show *Cosmos*.

☑ ONGOING ASSESSMENT: Diagnose

Use one of the following strategies to diagnose students' current level of proficiency in comparison-and-contrast writing.

Option 1 Ask each student to select the strongest example of his or her comparison-and-contrast writing from last year. Hold conferences to review each student's sample and determine which students will need extra support.

Option 2 Ask students to choose two movies that they have recently seen. Have them list details about each movie that they could use to compare and contrast the two films. If students have difficulty with this exercise, you may need to devote more time to the gathering details phase of the writing process.

Reading Strategy: Identify Writer's Audience

As students read "Digital Video Daze," ask them to keep track of clues that help reveal whom Quittner is writing for. Students may note these clues on paper, then share them in later discussion. (Possible clues: paragraph 1, the target audience is more familiar with VCRs than DVD players; paragraph 2, the audience would probably be confused if they encountered a Divx player in a store)

Step-by-Step Teaching Guide

Engage Students Through Literature

1. Have volunteers read the article aloud to the class.

2. Lead a discussion based on these questions.

   • Who is the audience? (people who may not know much about DVD players and know less about Divx technology)

   • How does the writer "reassure" the audience that they can understand the new technology? (He uses friendly words such as *kludgy;* he addresses the reader directly, using *You've* and *Let's see;* he begins with VCRs, a technology his readers are familiar with.)

   • What technique does the writer use to "teach" his audience about the new technology? (He begins with the familiar—VCRs— then moves to the unfamiliar— DVD and Divx; he points out details about how DVD and Divx work, including advantages and disadvantages.)

Critical Viewing

Contrast Students may mention the performance or ease-of-use of CD-ROMS.

9.1 Model From Literature

Joshua Quittner writes a weekly column about technology for a national newsmagazine. In this article, he compares and contrasts the latest technology for watching movies at home.

Reading | Writing Connection

Reading Strategy: Identify the Writer's Audience Because magazines address a variety of subjects and knowledge levels, you may not be the target audience for some of the articles you read. As you read "Digital Video Daze," identify the specialized language Quittner uses and note whether he defines these specific terms. Use your analysis to determine the audience Quittner probably intends to reach.

Digital Video Daze

Joshua Quittner

You've probably heard about DVD, the digital video format that allows full-length movies to be squeezed onto CDs. But chances are you don't own a DVD player—yet. Only around 700,000 people have bought one in the year since they were introduced. So what hope is there for the even newer (and curiously kludgy) format known as Divx?

The first Divx (pronounced "div-ex," it stands for digital video express) players began shipping to retail stores nationwide this month. Since Divx can run the old DVD disks while performing other amazing digital tricks, I suspect the new format is going to cause some confusion among the folks who are supposed to be trading in their VCRs for digital video decks this holiday season. Let's see if we can fine-tune the picture.

First, why would anyone want to get rid of his old reliable videotape player? For the same reasons that music lovers upgraded from record players to audio CDs: superior quality, compact storage and the ability to hop quickly to a precise spot in the programming. I've been trying out a DVD, and am surprised that the picture really does look twice as good as those blurry images

▲ **Critical Viewing** What makes the CD-ROM technology shown here different from earlier technologies such as videotape? **[Contrast]**

Quittner defines his terms for an audience he expects does not know the formats for watching films at home.

In the second paragraph, Quittner sets a purpose for his comparison and contrast: he promises to "fine-tune" the picture by eliminating the confusion over these new technologies.

my half-as-expensive, suddenly depressing VCR has been grinding out. That's because VHS recorders typically display movies at about 240 lines of resolution; digital video paints the screen with 500 lines. It's one of those situations in which you don't realize how unsatisfying a thing is until you've got something better to compare it with. And by then, of course, you're ruined. DVD decks, I should note, are available for as little as $399, or for even less as add-on drives for computers.

I like being able to jump to any spot in a video. Many digital movies are broken up into "chapters," making them easier to watch piecemeal (a plus for anyone with an infant in the house). Some DVDs allow you to change camera angles and make the picture window horizontal, like a movie theater's, or square, to fill the TV screen.

While a Divx deck can run DVDs, it also plays its own disks. Divx decks plug into the TV, just like DVD drives. But they plug into the phone line too. When you first set up your deck, you must establish an account with Divx central—your machine calls a toll-free number, and you key in credit-card information. (The player automatically calls headquarters once or twice a month in the middle of the night, which I find creepy.) You see, rather than simply renting Divx disks, you buy them outright, for $4.50, and never return them to the store. You don't have to view them right away, but once you put one in your deck, you have 48 hours tops to watch it (as many times as you want). Then the movie locks. Want to see it later? That will cost $3.25 for another 48 hours. You can buy perpetual viewing rights for $20. It's all done via that phone rigmarole.

Josh Dare, a Divx spokesman, admits that the format won't appeal to everyone. Market research showed that people who prefer staying home and watching a video to going out for a movie and dinner were especially receptive to the endless viewing possibilities of Divx. "Think of it this way: you've got a video collection you're starting for $4.50 a movie," says Dare. Me? I'd rather go out for dinner.

Writing Application: Address Your Audience As you draft your comparison-and-contrast essay, address your audience's knowledge level by defining terms your reader may not know.

By referring to VHS, a format audiences may know, the writer introduces a comfort level from which to start his comparison. Here, he compares VHS to DVD and asserts that the DVD image quality is better.

The writer defines and elaborates the advances of the new technology.

Once the reader understands the new technology, Quittner uses it to describe the newer technology. In this paragraph, Quittner first shows similarities between Divx and DVD. Then, he shows the differences.

The conclusion of the essay reveals the writer's choice but allows the readers to make their own decisions.

⎿ITERATURE

To see how comparison and contrast can enrich characterization, read Amy Tan's "The Rules of the Game." You can find the story in *Prentice Hall Literature: Timeless Voices, Timeless Themes*, Gold.

Language Highlight

Puns A pun is the use of a word so that it suggests more than one meaning. *Daze* in the title implies that many people are confused by digital video. It also sounds like *days*, and that is the pun. Nowadays, digital videos are on people's minds.

Responding to Literature

After students read "The Rules of the Game," ask them these questions:

- How does Mrs. Jong's attitude toward the chess set compare with her children's? (She didn't want a cast-off and slightly damaged gift; the children wanted to play with the chess set even if it wasn't brand new.)

- While Mrs. Jong is making dumplings by hand in the old-fashioned way, what contrasting activity is going on around her? (The children are playing chess, a new and unfamiliar family activity.)

- What is one way Waverly and her mother are alike? (They both like to have power by withholding information.)

Reading\Writing Connection
Writing: Address Your Audience

Explain to students the importance of addressing your audience in your writing. Readers should be made to feel that the writer is speaking to them; otherwise readers will lose interest or have difficulty following the writer's train of thought.

More About the Author

Joshua Quittner is a well-known expert on technology. As a gifted writer, he transforms complicated technological concepts into clear language that nonprofessionals can easily understand. Quittner also writes novels that inspire everyday people to catch his excitement about technology.

1. A comparison-and-contrast essay focuses on pairs of things—facts, ideas, or concepts that are related in some way. The pairs can be either very similar or very different.

2. Ask students to come up with an opposite or very different topic for each of the following concepts.

winter	(summer)
swimming	(flying)
reading	(writing)
running	(walking)
dog	(cat)
rock concert	(violin solo)

3. Ask students to come up with a similar topic for each of the following concepts.

movie star	(TV star)
tennis shoes	(hiking boots)
hamburgers	(tacos)
backpack	(sport bag)
drama class	(English class)
football coach	(team captain)

4. Display the transparency to illustrate one way to get comparison-and-contrast ideas.

Customize for ESL Students

Students may want to compare and contrast something from the country of their birth with something in America.

9.2 Prewriting

Choosing Your Topic

There is virtually no limit to the kinds of topics you can address in a comparison-and-contrast essay. Choose two or more subjects that invite comparison because they are related in some way or because they are aspects of the same subject. Use the following strategies to choose a topic:

Strategies for Generating a Topic

1. **Finding Related Pairs** Explore possible topics in terms of clear opposites (*spring–autumn*), clear similarities (*marching band–symphonic band)*, or close relationships (*photographs–videotape*). Start with names of people, places, objects, or ideas. Then, note a related subject that comes to mind. As you create the list, be aware of the relationships that interest you, and then choose one to develop.

2. **Listing and Itemizing** To find a topic that is relevant to your life, make a list of subjects that interest you. For example, you might list sports, music, celebrities, and current events. For each, itemize by brainstorming for a list of comparison-and-contrast pairs that the subject suggests. Review your work to choose a topic you'd like to develop.

Writing Lab CD-ROM

For more help finding a topic, explore the activities and suggestions in the Choosing a Topic section of the Exposition lesson.

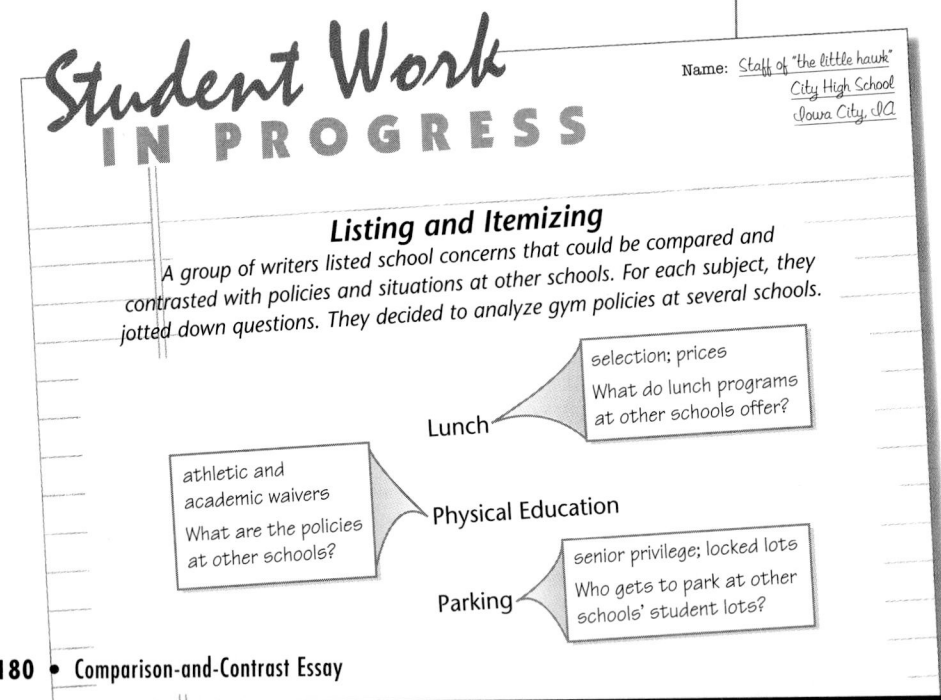

Student Work IN PROGRESS

Name: Staff of "the little hawk" City High School Iowa City, IA

Listing and Itemizing

A group of writers listed school concerns that could be compared and contrasted with policies and situations at other schools. For each subject, they jotted down questions. They decided to analyze gym policies at several schools.

Lunch — selection; prices / What do lunch programs at other schools offer?

athletic and academic waivers / What are the policies at other schools? — Physical Education

Parking — senior privilege; locked lots / Who gets to park at other schools' student lots?

180 • Comparison-and-Contrast Essay

⏱ TIME SAVERS!

📕 **Writing Support Transparencies**
Use the Transparencies for Chapter 9 to teach these strategies.

⏱ TIME AND RESOURCE MANAGER

Resources
Print: Writing Support Transparencies 9-A–D; Writing Support Activity Book 9-1
Technology: Writing Lab CD-ROM, Exposition

In-Depth Coverage	Accelerated Pace
• Work through the Step-by-Step Teaching Guides on pp. 180–183. • Point out how narrowing a topic reduces a broad topic to a manageable size for an essay. • Review the chart on p. 183.	• Have students read pp. 180–183 independently. • Have students identify a topic, audience, purpose, and points of comparison for an essay they will write.

TOPIC BANK

If you are having difficulty finding a topic, consider the following ideas:

1. **Regions of the United States** The national landscape contains a remarkable variety of habitats and climates, ranging from the frigid wilderness of northern Alaska to the tropical bamboo forests of Hawaii. Choose two regions of the United States to compare and contrast.

2. **Famous Athletes** When each was still at the top of his or her game, Michael Jordan retired from basketball, Wayne Gretzsky ended his professional hockey career, and Steffi Graf retired from tennis. Write an essay to compare and contrast the positive and negative aspects of a planned early retirement from professional sports.

Love in Ice, Veronica Ruiz de Velasco, Courtesy of the artist

Responding to Fine Art

3. Although dance is common in most cultures, dance styles can vary according to generation, region, and even purpose. Let "Love in Ice" inspire your own comparison and contrast of dance. In an essay, discuss the similarities of at least two dance styles.

Responding to Literature

4. In Shakespeare's *Romeo and Juliet*, the playwright tells a love story in contrasts. Using the Capulets and the Montagues as your subjects, compare and contrast the two families at the center of the feud. You can find the play in *Prentice Hall Literature: Timeless Voices, Timeless Themes*, Gold.

☑ Cooperative Writing Opportunity

5. **Comparison of Exercise Programs** With a group, compare and contrast the exercise plans your classmates follow. One student can study the benefits of team sports; another can report on the benefits of aerobic exercise; a third can research the results of weight training. Share your findings with the class.

Prewriting • 181

Step-by-Step Teaching Guide

Responding to Fine Art

Love in Ice by Veronica Ruiz de Velasco

Teaching Resources: Writing Support Transparency 9-B

1. Display the transparency.
2. Lead the class in brainstorming a list of various dance styles. (clogging, ballet, modern dance, tap) Write the brainstorm list on the board.
3. Ask students to select a "pair" of dance styles about which to write a comparison-and-contrast essay.

Responding to Literature

Underneath all the contrasts between the Capulets and the Montagues is one important similarity: Both families love their child.

Spotlight on the Humanities

For additional topic suggestions, refer students to the Spotlight on the Humanities on page 198.

☑ ONGOING ASSESSMENT: Monitor and Reinforce

The following strategies might be helpful for students who have difficulty choosing a topic for a comparison-and-contrast essay.

Option 1 Look for a personal connection. Choose a topic that interests you because you either already know or are curious about it. All good writing has an "emotional core" that stems from the writer's own interest in the subject.	**Option 2** Think small. You may be tempted to choose a topic that is broad because it has so much information to offer. But sorting out all that information can be an overwhelming job. Instead, think small and choose a narrow topic.

181

**Narrowing Your Topic;
Considering Your Audience
and Purpose**

*Teaching Resources: Writing Support
Transparency 9-C; Writing Support
Activity Book 9-1*

1. Have partners come up with five
   topics that interest each of them.
   They can help each other identify
   opposite topics and similar topics
   in each category, then choose a
   pair of topics they would most like
   to write about.

2. Display the transparency. Review
   the chart with students, pointing
   out how the purposes change
   with the audiences.

3. Give students copies of the blank
   organizer and have them fill in the
   Topic category with the topic they
   selected in step 1.

4. Have students list two or three
   potential audiences and match
   each with an appropriate
   purpose. Ask students to select
   one audience and corresponding
   purpose for their essay.

Integrating Technology Skills

Have students conduct a keyword
search on the Internet for a broad
topic that interests them, such as
rock music. Then have them browse
through the matches to find
narrower topics that relate to the
broader keyword.

9.2

Narrowing Your Topic

Once you've chosen a topic, consider how much information
you'll need to present in order to develop all points of comparison and contrast. Some topics are so broad that they cannot
easily be managed in an essay. For example, a useful comparison and contrast of New York City and Paris might require
hundreds of pages. However, by narrowing the focus to
address a specific topic—such as museums, tourist attractions, or transit systems—you could present an effective
comparison-and-contrast essay.

Considering Your Audience and Purpose

Identify Your Audience

Take a moment to think about the people you expect to read
your comparison-and-contrast essay. Your intended audience
will direct the types of information you include—from the level
of vocabulary you choose to the level of detail or analysis you
pursue. For example, as the chart at the bottom of this page
suggests, your audience may even direct your purpose.

Specify Your Purpose

To identify a purpose for your essay, consider what kind of
insight you want your readers to gain. Look at these options:

- **To persuade:** If you want your readers to accept your opinion that one subject is better or more desirable than the
  other, your purpose will be to persuade.

- **To explain:** If you want your readers to understand something about the subjects, your purpose will be to explain.

Consider your topic, your audience, and your purpose to
arrive at a framework for the direction your writing will take.

Topic: The Internet vs. The Library	
Audience	**Purpose**
All readers	To **describe** the similarities and differences
Older adults who prefer to use a library	To **persuade** readers that the Internet is a more convenient research tool
Children and readers who aren't familiar with the Internet	To **explain** how each works, what each can do, and how they are similar and different

**Writing Lab
CD-ROM**

To help define your
specific purpose in
writing a comparison-
and-contrast essay,
use the interactive
examples of writing
purposes. You can
find them in the
Exposition lesson.

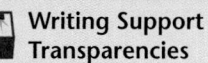
**Writing Support
Transparencies**
Use the Transparencies for
Chapter 9 to teach these
strategies.

**Writing Support
Activity Book**
Use the graphic organizers for
Chapter 9 to facilitate these
strategies.

Gathering Details

To make your writing detailed and concrete, include facts, examples, descriptions, and other information that will show the similarities and differences between your subjects. You might need to tap your own personal experiences, find out about the experiences of your friends, or conduct more extensive research. To make this information collecting easier, use your preliminary findings to identify a limited number of comparisons to pursue.

Identifying Points of Comparison As you generate the details to use in your comparison-and-contrast essay, look at the ideas you've collected, and then consider the main elements you will discuss in your draft. Here are some examples:

TOPIC: Paper Bags vs. Plastic Bags at the Grocery Store

POINTS OF COMPARISON: Convenience, durability, effects on the environment

TOPIC: Action Movies vs. Romantic Comedies

POINTS OF COMPARISON: Story lines, insight into life, special effects

Once you identify the main points of comparison, use this information to guide further detail gathering.

Research Tip

If you need to consult reference material, gather details for each one of your subjects separately.

Identifying Points of Comparison

Teaching Resources: Writing Support Transparency 9-D

1. Have partners brainstorm points of comparison for their selected topics. They can help each other pare down their brainstorm lists to three key points of comparison.

2. Display the transparency and have students examine how the chart identifies the key facts for each point of comparison and for each subject. Have students create similar graphic organizers for their own points of comparison.

Integrating Workplace Skills

People who review movies, books, and restaurants all use comparisons and contrasts. So do travel writers. All these people use specific facts and examples, so that their readers can make informed choices and decisions.

Student Work IN PROGRESS

Name: Staff of "the little hawk" City High School Iowa City, IA

Identifying Points of Comparison

The staff of the little hawk found that in some schools, athletes or those who carried a heavy academic load were sometimes excused from taking gym. The writers chose three schools to compare and generated this chart to help them gather details about this situation.

	Physical Education Requirement	Academic Waivers	Athletic Waivers
City High	Gym class once every three days	no	yes
Solon	One credit of PE each year	yes	no
CR Washington	One class of PE every other day	juniors and seniors only	yes

Prewriting • 183

Drafting: Organize to Show Comparisons and Contrasts

Teaching Resources: Writing Support Transparency 9-E

1. Explain to students that subject-by-subject and point-by-point organizations include the same information in different forms.

2. Display the transparency to show students how the writers used subject-by-subject organization to arrange their information.

3. On the board, "translate" the subject-by-subject organization into a point-by-point outline.

   I. Intro
   II. Requirements
      A. City High
      B. Solon
      C. CR Washington
   II. Waivers
      A. City High
      B. Solon
      C. CR Washington
   II. Strengths and Weaknesses
      A. City High
      B. Solon
      C. CR Washington

4. Have each student create either point-by-point or subject-by-subject outlines for their topics.

Customize for
Visual/Spatial Learners

Rather than using an outline, students may prefer to write each point on an index card, then move the cards around until they are in an order that makes sense.

9.3 Drafting

Shaping Your Writing
Organize to Show Comparisons and Contrasts

Once you have identified points of comparison and contrast, you have done a large part of the organization of your ideas. Next, think about the order in which you want to present your details. Consider these options:

- **Subject-by-Subject Organization** When you use this organization, you compare your subjects as complete units. First, discuss all the features of one subject, and then discuss all the features of the other. While this format allows you to focus on one subject at a time, be careful to address the same features and to devote equal time to each subject.

- **Point-by-Point Organization** This organization allows you to move between your subjects as you discuss points of comparison. First, compare one element of both subjects, and then address another element of both subjects, until you have addressed all the features. This method allows you to sharpen your points of comparison and contrast. It also makes it easier to address each feature for both subjects.

Writing Lab CD-ROM

For more instruction on organizing your essay, see the audio-annotated models of comparison-and-contrast organization. You can find them in the Exposition lesson.

Name: Staff of "the little hawk"
City High School
Iowa City, IA

Planning a Subject-by-Subject Organization
The writers arranged their information using a subject-by-subject organization. This plan allows readers to understand each school's program as a whole.

City High
   A. Requirements
   B. Waivers—academic and athletic
   C. Program's strengths or weaknesses

Solon
   A. Requirements
   B. Waivers—academic and athletic
   C. Program's strengths or weaknesses

CR Washington
   A. Requirements
   B. Waivers—academic and athletic
   C. Program's strengths or weaknesses

184 • Comparison-and-Contrast Essay

 **Writing Support Transparencies**
Use the Transparencies for Chapter 9 to teach these strategies.

⏱ TIME AND RESOURCE MANAGER

Resources
Print: Writing Support Transparency 9-E
Technology: Writing Lab CD-ROM, Exposition

In-Depth Coverage	Accelerated Pace
• Go over pp. 184–185 in class. • Work through the Step-by-Step Teaching Guides on pp. 184–185. • Make sure that students have correctly completed step 3 on p. 184.	• Have students review pp. 184–185 independently. • Have students create either a subject-by-subject or point-by-point outline for the essay topic they chose on p. 183.

Providing Elaboration

Whether your purpose in comparing and contrasting two subjects is to describe, to persuade, or to explain, provide enough detail to fully develop your points of comparison and contrast. It is not enough to say that cereal is a more nutritious meal than buttered toast. A good writer supports this conclusion with facts.

Support Generalizations With Specifics

Don't point out differences and similarities without including facts or information to back up your assertions. For example, if you were comparing and contrasting classical music and popular music, you'd need to do more than just state conclusions you've drawn. Include support that develops each point you make.

In this example, the writer supports a generalization by showing how it applies to a specific piece of music.

▲▼ **Critical Viewing**
What points of comparison do these photographs emphasize?
[Compare and Contrast]

GENERALIZATION: With some attention, listeners can usually identify a main musical theme and its variations in classical music.

SUPPORT: For example, Pachelbel's *Canon* takes an eight-note phrase and, through harmony and variation, develops it into a complex composition.

In the next example, the writer offers a generalization to comment on the prevalence of popular music as a soundtrack to life. To elaborate on this idea, a supporting sentence identifies several instances in which music provides such a soundtrack.

GENERALIZATION: In contrast, popular music forms a soundtrack in our lives, and in some cases, we may not even be listening.

SUPPORT: Popular music can be heard as we drive to work, shop in a store, watch a movie, or eat dinner in a restaurant.

Drafting: Providing Elaboration

1. Write this generalization on the chalkboard:

   Teenagers would rather stay up late and sleep in than go to bed early and get up early.

2. Ask students to supply some facts or examples that support this generalization. (Possible answers: Most teenagers choose the up-late/ sleep-in schedule on the weekends and during vacations; research has shown that teenagers' "biological clock" is set to the up-late/sleep-in schedule; in a survey in this class, most students preferred the up-late/sleep-in schedule.)

3. Elaboration can include opinions— as long as the opinions are supported. An essay that compares cats and dogs might conclude that dogs make better pets, an opinion. This is all right if there is support, such as: when you get home, a dog runs to you and licks your face; a dog is always glad to play catch; when you walk a dog, you meet other dog owners.

Critical Viewing

Compare and Contrast Students may mention the type of music being performed as well as the level of formality of each performance, including the dress of the performers.

✏️ STANDARDIZED TEST PREPARATION WORKSHOP

Distinguishing Between Fact and Opinion
Standardized tests often require students to distinguish between facts and opinions. Ask students which of the following statements is an opinion:

A I counted 50 businesses that participated in the career fair.

B Each career fair participant offered free printed information.

C I thought the printed information was extremely informative.

D It took us only 45 minutes to clean up after the career fair.

Item **C** is the opinion. The other choices are facts that can be supported with evidence.

Revising: Improve Your Lead

Teaching Resources: Writing Support Transparency 9-F

1. Tell students that the introduction to a comparison-and-contrast essay should include two key points: the main idea the essay conveys and the reason(s) the analysis is valuable to readers.

2. An introduction also contains a lead, the first few sentences of the paragraph. The lead should grab readers' attention with a compelling quotation, an eye-opening statistic, a personal anecdote, or another strategy.

3. Display the transparency and ask students how they think the writers improved their lead.

4. Have students write their leads (anonymously) on index cards. Collect the cards and read them aloud. Ask the class to comment and make suggestions for improvement.

9.4 Revising

After you complete your first draft, review your structure, analyze your paragraphs, study your sentences, and evaluate your word choices. This revision will strengthen your writing.

Revising Your Overall Structure

Frame Your Findings: Revive Your Introduction

Your comparison-and-contrast essay should include at least two subjects, their similarities and differences, and your reasons for writing about them. To make your purpose clear to readers, take advantage of the opportunities your introduction presents. This opening paragraph should introduce the main idea you want to convey about the comparison and contrast, and it should also prove to readers that the analysis is valid.

▶ **REVISION STRATEGY**
Improving Your Lead

Your lead, the first several sentences of your introduction, should set the stage for your comparison by presenting your subject in an interesting light. Journalists often use quotations, statistics, or descriptions to show readers the relevance or importance of the story that will follow. Review the lead you've written. Borrowing from news writers, brainstorm for ideas that will perk up your lead. Jot down several different suggestions, and then choose the one that you like best.

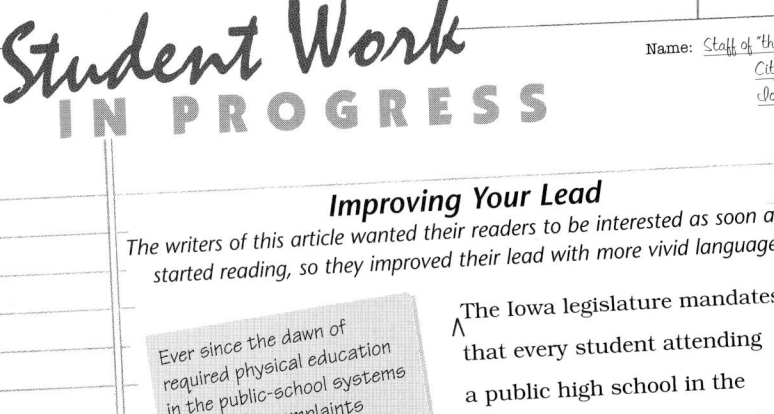

Student Work
IN PROGRESS

Name: Staff of "the little hawk"
City High School
Iowa City, IA

Improving Your Lead

The writers of this article wanted their readers to be interested as soon as they started reading, so they improved their lead with more vivid language.

Ever since the dawn of required physical education in the public-school systems of America, complaints about nine-minute runs have echoed throughout locker rooms across the country. CHS is no different.

The Iowa legislature mandates that every student attending a public high school in the state must complete at least one fifty-minute physical education class per week for every term enrolled.

186 • Comparison-and-Contrast Essay

⏱ **TIME AND RESOURCE MANAGER**

Resources
Print: Writing Support Transparencies 9-F–G
Technology: Writing Lab CD-ROM, Exposition

In-Depth Coverage	Accelerated Pace
• Follow the Step-by-Step Teaching Guides on pp. 186–190. • Work through Grammar in Your Writing on page 189. • Monitor the peer review activity to make sure students share comments in a positive and encouraging manner.	• Have students read pp. 186–190 independently. • Have students revise their introductions, paragraphs, and check their use of verb tenses in their drafts.

Revising Your Paragraphs

Make Comparisons and Contrasts Clear

Once you confirm your overall structure, focus on individual paragraphs. Whether you use a subject-by-subject organization or a point-by-point plan, each body paragraph should be unified: All of the sentences should work together to develop a single main idea.

Point-by-Point Body Paragraphs These paragraphs offer a convenient place to show comparisons and contrasts. As you move from a discussion of one subject to the other, use transitional words that make the similarities and differences clear.

EXAMPLE: *In terms of size*, the parrot is larger than the parakeet.

Subject-by-Subject Body Paragraphs Your points of comparison will be spread into separate paragraphs when you use a subject-by-subject organization. To remind readers of the connections and contrasts you want to show, use comparative or superlative forms of modifiers. In some cases, readers may not get the full elaboration until a later paragraph, but words like *cleaner, more powerful,* or *most expensive* will guide them through your analysis.

EXAMPLE: The parrot is *more friendly, more social, and more colorful* than the parakeet.

▶ REVISION STRATEGY

Refining or Adding Connecting Sentences

Review each body paragraph to be sure that you lead the reader to see the comparisons and contrasts that you draw. Identify the places where you address each subject: Use one color to underline every instance in which you refer to one subject, and use a second color to underline every reference to the other subject. To evaluate your writing in places where the colors meet, judge the connection between the two subjects. Add transitional words or phrases to make the shift more clear.

- **Transitions that show similarities:** *all, similarly, both, in the same way, equally*

- **Transitions that show differences:** *on the other hand, in contrast, however*

- **Comparative modifiers to compare two items:** *richer, busier, brighter, more confusing, more colorful*

- **Superlative modifiers to compare three or more items:** *richest, busiest, brightest, most confusing, most colorful*

▲ Critical Viewing
If you were to compare this parrot to a bird common in your region, what points of comparison might you emphasize? **[Analyze]**

Revising: Make Comparisons and Contrasts Clear; Refining or Adding Connecting Sentences

1. Have students highlight the main idea in each paragraph, which entails making sure each paragraph has an identifiable main idea. (If the paragraph has two main ideas, then it should be broken into two paragraphs.) Then have students underline the supporting details.

2. Next have students identify points of comparison and contrast. They should be more or less equal. Ten comparisons and two contrasts is unbalanced.

3. Post a list of useful transition words and phrases.

   Comparison
   as
   in the same way
   either . . . or
   neither . . . nor
   similarly
   likewise
   also

   Contrast
   yet
   unlike
   on the contrary
   but
   instead
   on the one hand
   on the other hand
   however
   in contrast

Critical Viewing

Analyze Students' responses will vary depending on the birds common in their region.

☑ ONGOING ASSESSMENT: Monitor and Reinforce

If students have difficulty adding transitional and modifying words or phrases to express relationships between ideas in their writing, try the following option.

Have students carefully read through their drafts, highlighting related ideas in each paragraph in similar colors. Remind students that these relationships will not only involve similarities, but differences. Once students have identified the nature of each relationship, have them use an appropriate transition or modifying word or phrase to make this relationship clear.

Revising: Evaluate Use of Verb Tense

Teaching Resources: Writing Support Transparency 9-G

1. Display the transparency. Ask students why they think the writers changed the tenses of the chosen verbs.

2. Students' essays may contain more than one tense. Two different tenses can even appear in the same sentences. If the Student Work in Progress were comparing PE last year and this year, it would be fine to say: *Last year students were required to take two credits, but this year they take only one credit.*

3. Have students underline all the verbs in their essays, then go back and make sure they are correct and that any verb changes are not confusing.

Real-World Connection

To illustrate the importance of correct tenses, give students this scenario. You want to spend time with your friends. Your mother asks if you have done your homework. Which answer will enable you to leave the house? I did my homework. I am doing my homework. I will do my homework.

Writing Support Transparencies
Use the Transparencies for Chapter 9 to teach these strategies.

Revising Your Sentences

To review your essay at the sentence level, review the verb tense used most in your draft. Revise any unnecessary changes in verb tense.

Make Verb Tense Work for You

The tense of a verb expresses time by showing when events happened in a sequence. Unless you want to show action in the past, present, or future, the verb tense of your writing should be consistent. For example, if you are writing about two subjects that still exist, use the present tense exclusively. On the other hand, if you discuss an event that happened in the past or compare items in different time periods, you may need to make use of the past tense. Evaluate the verbs in your draft to avoid unnecessary shifts in verb tense.

▶ **REVISION STRATEGY**
Listing Verbs to Evaluate the Use of Tense

Skim through your draft to find all the verbs, and write them on a narrow strip of paper. As you read each sentence, confirm that the verb tenses you've chosen make sense. Review your list to identify verb shifts, and make sure that any verb shifts you see are necessary to indicate a time shift. Make revisions as necessary.

Language Lab CD-ROM

For more on the six tenses of verbs, see the Principal Parts of Verbs lesson and the Verb Tense lesson.

Student Work
IN PROGRESS

Name: Staff of "the little hawk"
City High School
Iowa City, IA

Evaluating Verb Tense

By making a list of the verbs they used, the writers were able to see how they could change some verb tenses for more consistency in their writing.

> are required

> is
> has been
> can choose
> have chosen

Students at Solon are required to take one credit of PE each year, or one-half credit of PE each semester. Since the school's calendar
is
has-been based on quarters and semesters,
can choose
students have-chosen whether to take one semester of PE every other day or one quarter of PE every day.

188 • Comparison-and-Contrast Essay

Grammar in Your Writing
Six Tenses of Verbs

The **verb tenses** express time and clarify the sequence of events. The basic forms of the six tenses show the time of an action or condition in the present, past, or future. Each verb form shows when an action happens and whether it is still happening. Use the following as a guide to the correct use of the six tenses of verbs.

Present indicates an action that happens regularly or states a general truth:

I take my dog Squeegee for a walk every morning.

Past indicates an action that has already happened:

We walked earlier than usual yesterday.

Future indicates an action that will happen:

We will walk on the beach this summer.

Present perfect indicates an action that happened at some indefinite time in the past or an action that happened in the past and is still happening now:

We have walked here almost every day for two years.

Past perfect indicates an action that was completed before another action in the past.

We had walked around the corner when Squeegee started to bark.

Future perfect indicates an action that will have been completed before another:

We will have walked two hundred miles before I need new shoes.

Find It in Your Reading Review "Digital Video Daze," by Joshua Quittner on pages 178–179. Look for examples of at least four verb tenses. Note the way in which these verb tenses indicate how an action relates in time to other actions being discussed.

Find It in Your Writing As you revise your draft, identify any shifts in verb tense. Make sure that each one is correct and necessary.

To learn more about verbs, see Chapter 17.

Revising • 189

Grammar in Your Writing: Six Tenses of Verbs

Ask students to identify the verb tenses in the following sentences. They can refer to page 189 for help.

I <u>bought</u> my favorite sneakers when I was a freshman. (past)

I <u>have worn</u> them to school every day since then. (present perfect)

I <u>had decided</u> the shoes were getting too shabby to wear when my mom insisted I buy new ones. (past perfect)

Today I <u>am shopping</u> for new sneakers. (present)

Don't tell my mom, but I <u>will wear</u> my old sneakers on graduation day. (future)

Then I <u>will have worn</u> my favorite shoes throughout my entire high school career! (future perfect)

Find It in Your Reading

Sample answers: *You've probably heard:* present perfect; *allows:* present; *were introduced:* past; *is going to cause:* future. Ask students if any of the changes are incorrect and to discuss why Quittner's verb tenses can change without detracting from his message (The lively verbs fit Quittner's conversational and very peppy style).

Find It in Your Writing

Have students be prepared to explain why their shifts in verb tense are necessary.

Customize for
Less Advanced Students

The perfect tenses cause the most confusion. In the example on the page, how can *have walked* be <u>present</u> perfect? *Walked* is a past-tense verb. (Similarly for the future perfect *will have walked*.) Good question! The clue is <u>have walked</u>—*have* is present tense (as opposed to <u>had</u> walked in the past perfect). Students have to look at the whole verb phrase, not just the one *-ed* word.

Revising Your Word Choice

1. Before students read the page, write the repetitive word example on the board. Ask students to suggest revisions. Then have students compare their revisions to the revised example on the page.

2. Remind students that they can use a thesaurus to find synonyms for most words. They will not find *Ferris wheel* there, though; for some words they will have to rely on their imagination.

3. Have students share their paragraphs and revisions in small groups. Students should read their revisions aloud, asking their peers to take notes on any aspects of the paragraph that still need work.

Revision Tip

Remind students that peer reviews offer two forms of support to writers. First, of course, the reviewers' critique of the work helps the writer see where to revise and polish. Second, peer reviewers can offer the writer encouragement, pointing out instances of especially good word choice, the writer's skill in "hooking" the audience, and so on.

Critical Viewing

Evaluate Students may say that a roller coaster would make a good subject for comparison.

Revising Your Word Choice
Vary Word Use

In your essay, you move back and forth between two subjects, frequently naming your subjects and points of comparison for clarity. While you want to communicate clearly, avoid repeating the same words over and over. For variety, use synonyms, words that are similar in meaning, or pronouns, such as *it* or *they*, to break up repetition. Look at this example:

REPETITIVE WORD: At amusement parks, I enjoy the *Ferris wheel* most. I go to the *Ferris wheel* first. The *Ferris wheel* offers fantastic bird's-eye views, and the *Ferris wheel* is slow enough that I don't feel sick.

REVISED: At amusement parks, I enjoy the *Ferris wheel* most. I go to *that ride* first. *This giant hoop* offers fantastic bird's-eye views, and *it* goes slowly enough that I don't feel sick.

▶ **REVISION STRATEGY**
Identifying Repeated Words

As you review your draft, create a color-coding system to identify words that you've used frequently. Use one color to circle your first point of comparison, a second color to circle your second point of comparison, and two other colors to circle the names of your main subjects. Using the colors you assigned, underline pronouns or synonyms you've used to create variety. Evaluate each word you've identified by studying your draft one color at a time. If you have used a highlighted word frequently without using any synonyms or pronouns, challenge yourself to introduce at least two synonyms and one pronoun.

▲ Critical Viewing
What other amusement park attraction might make a good subject for comparison and contrast with the Ferris wheel? **[Evaluate]**

Peer Review

Once you've finished revising your essay on your own, ask a small group of classmates to provide feedback on it. Peer reviewers can give objective opinions about whether your points of comparison and contrast are clear.

Showing

Read your essay twice to the group. During your first reading, have your classmates simply listen. Ask your peers to complete two lists as you read your draft again. Reviewers can jot down one list of similarities they feel you've communicated or shown effectively and a second list of differences that you made clear. Use their lists—and any discussion the reading generates—to decide whether you have done your job effectively.

9.5 Editing and Proofreading

Errors in spelling, punctuation, and grammar can distract your readers from the content of your essay. Carefully proofread your essay so that it is error-free.

Focusing on Grammar

As you proofread your paper, look closely at the grammar of words you have chosen. Use these guidelines to help you:

- **Pronoun reference** Wherever you used a pronoun—such as *he*, *she*, *it*, *they*, or *them*—check the clarity of the reference.
- **Degrees of comparison** Be sure that you have used the correct form when comparing two items. For further instruction, review the box below.

⊘ Learn More

For more on pronoun and antecedent agreement, see Chapter 25.

Grammar in Your Writing
Degrees of Comparison

Most modifiers have a *positive* form, a *comparative* form for comparing two items, and a *superlative* form for comparing more than two items.

ADJECTIVES

Positive	Comparative	Superlative
tall	taller	tallest
eager	more eager	most eager
good	better	best

ADVERBS

Positive	Comparative	Superlative
early	earlier	earliest
eagerly	more eagerly	most eagerly
well	better	best

When in doubt about forming a comparison, check a dictionary. If no acceptable *-er* or *-est* forms are listed, use *more* and *most*.

Find It in Your Reading Review "Digital Video Daze" by Joshua Quittner on pages 178–179. Find two examples of modifiers that demonstrate a degree of comparison.

Find It in Your Writing Identify at least two modifiers that show a degree of comparison in your essay. If you have not used two, challenge yourself to add one. In all cases, check that you have used the correct form.

To learn more about degrees of comparison, see Chapter 26.

• 191

Step-by-Step Teaching Guide

Editing and Proofreading: Pronoun Reference

1. A pronoun can refer to an antecedent in a previous sentence. Pronouns and antecedents do not have to be close to each other, as long as the connection is clear to the reader.

2. Clarity is the key. Use the following sentence to illustrate a confusing pronoun. Does *they* refer to the girls or to their books?

   If the girls go out in the rain with their books, they may get wet.

Step-by-Step Teaching Guide

Grammar in Your Writing: Degrees of Comparison

1. Most one- and two-syllable modifiers take *-er* and *-est*.

2. Modifiers of three or more syllables always take *more* and *most*.

3. All adverbs, no matter how many (or few) syllables, take *more* and *most*.

4. *Less* and *least*, the opposites of *more* and *most*, also can be added to modifiers.

5. Add *bad, worse,* and *worst* to the list of adjectives.

Find It in Your Reading

Examples include *even newer . . . format* and *you've got something better.*

Find It in Your Writing

Remind students to determine the number of items being compared in order to decide which degree the modifier should take.

Integrating Spelling Skills

Remind students that if a modifier ends in *y*, the *y* changes to *i* before *-er* or *-est* is added: *happy, happier, happiest.*

⏱ TIME AND RESOURCE MANAGER

Resources
Print: Scoring Rubrics on Transparency, Chapter 9; Writing Assessment: Scoring Rubrics and Scoring Models for Comparison-and-Contrast Essay
Technology: Writing Lab CD-ROM, Exposition

In-Depth Coverage	Accelerated Pace
• Review pp. 191–192 in class. • Have students edit and proofread their essays. • Analyze the final draft on p. 193 in class.	• Assign pp. 191–195 for independent student review. • Have students independently edit and proofread their essays.

Publishing and Presenting

1. Talk about how visuals can enhance a piece of writing. They can accentuate particular points, express an essay's main message through a different medium, help keep a reader's attention, clarify complicated concepts through graphs and charts, and so on.

2. Brainstorm places students can find visuals to accompany their writing. These may include the writer's original art, another student's original art, photos, clip art and other computer graphics, color blocks.

3. Help students identify sources that could publish their writing (school newspaper, writing contests, Web sites, letters to the editor).

ASSESS

Assessment

Teaching Resources: Scoring Rubrics on Transparency 9; Formal Assessment, Chapter 9

1. Display the Scoring Rubric transparency and review the criteria in class.

2. Before students proceed with self-assessment, you may wish to review the Final Draft of the Student Work in Progress on pages 193–195. Have students score the Final Draft in one or more of the rubric categories. For example, how would students score the essay in terms of audience and purpose?

3. In addition to student self-assessment, you may wish to use the following assessment options.

   • score student essays yourself, using the rubric and scoring models from Writing Assessment.

   • review the Standardized Test Preparation Workshop on pages 200–201 and have students respond to a writing prompt within a time limit.

   • administer the Chapter 9 Test from Formal Assessment in Teaching Resources to assess students' grasp of concepts presented.

9.6 Publishing and Presenting

Building Your Portfolio

Sharing your comparison-and-contrast essay with others can give them a fresh insight into your subject. Consider the following suggestions for publishing and presenting:

1. **Make a Photo Montage** Using images that stress the comparisons and contrasts your essay develops, create a poster that combines your essay with the photographs or illustrations that support your ideas.

2. **Publish Your Essay On-line** Share your comparison-and-contrast essay with others who are interested in your subject by posting it on your school Web site. To reach a wider audience, consider other sites on the Web that may reach people who could benefit from your analysis.

Reflecting on Your Writing

Think about the experience of writing your essay. Use the questions that follow to help you get started. Then, jot down your ideas, and add your reflection to your writing portfolio.

• Did you start to look differently at your subjects?

• Which strategy for prewriting, drafting, revising, or editing helped you the most?

🖥 Internet Tip

To see model essays scored with this rubric, go to **www.phwg. phschool.com**

Rubric for Self-Assessment

Use the following criteria for evaluating your comparison-and-contrast essay:

	Score 4	Score 3	Score 2	Score 1
Audience and Purpose	Clearly provides a reason for a comparison-and-contrast analysis	Adequately provides a reason for a comparison-and-contrast analysis	Provides a reason for a comparison-and-contrast analysis	Does not provide a reason for a comparison-and-contrast analysis
Organization	Successfully presents information in a consistent organization best suited to the topic	Presents information using an organization suited to the topic	Chooses an organization not suited to comparison and contrast	Shows a lack of organizational strategy
Elaboration	Elaborates several ideas with facts, details, or examples; links all information to comparison and contrast	Elaborates most ideas with facts, details, or examples; links most information to comparison and contrast	Does not elaborate all ideas; does not link some details to comparison and contrast	Does not provide facts or examples to support a comparison and contrast
Use of Language	Demonstrates excellent sentence and vocabulary variety; includes very few mechanical errors	Demonstrates adequate sentence and vocabulary variety; includes few mechanical errors	Demonstrates repetitive use of sentence structure and vocabulary; includes many mechanical errors	Demonstrates poor use of language; generates confusion; includes many mechanical errors

192 • Comparison-and-Contrast Essay

☑ ONGOING ASSESSMENT: Assess Mastery

Use one of the following options to assess final drafts of students' comparison-and-contrast essays.

Self-Assessment Ask students to score their essay using the rubric provided. Then have students write a paragraph reflecting on the most valuable strategy they learned in completing this essay.	**Teacher Assessment** Use the rubric and the scoring models provided in Writing Assessment, Comparison-and-Contrast Essay, to score students' work.

9.7 Student Work IN PROGRESS

FINAL DRAFT

◀ Critical Viewing
How does this gym class compare with the ones you attend? [Relate]

Working Out Possibilities

Elizabeth Dunbar, Maggie McCray, Cassie McKinstry, and Emily Szeszycki, with additional reporting by Liz Humston

Staff *of* the little hawk
City High School
Iowa City, Iowa

Ever since the dawn of required physical education in the public-school systems of America, complaints about nine-minute runs and stinky sweat pants have echoed throughout locker rooms across the country. CHS is no different. The Iowa legislature mandates that every student attending a public high school in the state must complete at least one fifty-minute physical

In the introductory paragraph, precise details like "nine-minute runs" and "locker rooms" invite readers to relate to the subject of high-school gym classes.

Student Work in Progress • 193

Step-by-Step Teaching Guide

Teaching From the Final Draft

1. Have students read "Working out Possibilities" silently, or have volunteers read it aloud.

continued

Customize for *ESL Students*

This is not an easy article; students need to understand all the vocabulary, concepts, and comparisons/contrasts. Students can work in a reading group to help each other with the hard words and ideas.

Critical Viewing

Relate Students' responses will vary. They may say that the class shown in the photograph is more professional.

2. Lead a discussion based on the following questions.

- What words or phrases caught your interest in the article's first paragraph? (Likely answers: *nine-minute runs, stinky sweatpants, locker rooms*)

- What organizational style does this comparison-and-contrast essay follow? (subject-by-subject)

- What are the three points of comparison the writers use for each school in the article? (requirements, waivers, and strengths and weaknesses of the program)

- Who is this article's audience? (students, teachers, and parents who read the school newspaper)

- Why does this article have no conclusion? (It follows the journalistic style of putting main ideas first—in the introductory paragraph)

- Which school's system would you prefer? Why?

9.7

education class per week for every term enrolled. If students wish to graduate early, they are not required to make up the PE credits that they will be missing by doing so.

Despite these low state requirements, many Iowa high schools, including CHS, require their students to take (and pass) more gym classes than necessary in order to graduate. But even though the schools in IC and surrounding cities all require more than the minimum, their methods of acquiring the credits differ greatly.

City High

CHS's graduation requirement of gym class (55 minutes) once every three days, with the exception of an athletic waiver, including one trimester of Health PE, exceeds those of the state.

Even with the extra 50 minutes a week, PE instructor Diane Delozier thinks the students need more gym time. "Because gym is only once every three days, we see no consistency in a student's performance," Delozier said. "There's no chance for improvement. The student comes back after two days and is struggling to do the activities."

However, Delozier does think that CHS has advantages over other schools. The juniors and seniors get to choose what units they do, unlike those in some other schools. Also, CHS has some units that other schools don't offer, such as rappelling, CPR, social dancing, and cross-country skiing.

Academic waivers have also come up in discussion among CHS students. "I think they're a great idea," Clare Martin, '00, said. "It seems ridiculous that we need to take four years of PE and only two years of math and science."

Delozier, however, disagrees. "It's not the same thing. It's an issue of activity versus intellect," Delozier said. "Students won't get a workout with a good GPA."

Solon

Students at Solon are required to take one credit of PE each year, or one-half credit of PE each semester. Since the school's calendar is based on quarters and semesters, students can choose whether to take one semester of PE every other day or one quarter of PE every day.

Instead of rewarding athletes with PE waivers, Solon High School has a different waiver system. If students are taking so many classes that they don't have room in their schedule for PE, they can get a waiver. Students can waive one half credit each year, but they must take the other half credit.

Not only is Solon's scheduling of PE flexible, but students can also choose what kind of PE class they want to take. The two specialized classes are conditioning class, which includes training

194 • Comparison-and-Contrast Essay

The final sentence of the introduction explains that each school has a different gym requirement. Next, the writers use a subject-by-subject, or school-by-school, analysis set off by subheads.

First, the writers discuss their own school, addressing three points of comparison: requirements, academic and athletic waivers, and the strengths or weaknesses of the school's program.

Second, the writers discuss Solon High School, addressing the same three points of comparison.

and weight lifting; and aerobics, which includes stunts and tumbling. Students also have the option of taking a normal PE class that is separated by grade and includes various units.

If senior Kurt Kruckeberg could change something about the PE system, he would want the option of athletic waivers. A lot of people have pushed for waivers, but nothing has really happened. However, Solon is expecting some new administrators, and the issue of athletic waivers might come up again. "I think [waivers] would be very helpful," Kruckeberg said. "I have a lot of friends who get frustrated because they have to take PE in addition to weight lifting and practicing outside of school."

CR Washington

CR Washington runs on a trimester system, and PE classes meet every other day. Students at Washington are allowed one athletic PE waiver each year. Juniors and seniors are also allowed one academic waiver each year. If a student's schedule is completely full, he or she does not have to take PE for that trimester. Jim Rusick, the head of the school's athletic department, feels that the program has advantages and disadvantages.

"It rewards students who are working hard," Rusick said. "But it also allows the kids who might really need the strength and physical activity to slip through the cracks."

Some students are able to avoid physical education for an entire year if they are especially involved. Senior Erika Fry is one of those students. "I haven't had PE for the last two years, and I think it's great," Fry said. "I play golf, and I have a full schedule, so I am really glad I have that option."

Although students at Washington may not be seasoned social dancers like the students at CHS, the student body seems to have a positive attitude about it.

"Of course, some people complain, some always will," Rusick said. "But I think that most students are satisfied with how much PE they have to take."

Shorter paragraphs and direct quotations are part of the format for newspaper articles.

An analysis of the third school follows the established format by presenting the same three points of comparison.

Following journalistic style, which calls for main ideas at the start of articles, this article has no formal concluding paragraph. However, the story's title and the text of the article suggest the writers' conclusion: City High might learn from the experience of the other schools.

◀ **Critical Viewing** Identify two points of contrast to guide an analysis of the two photographs accompanying this article. **[Analyze]**

Step-by-Step Teaching Guide

Consumer Report

Teaching Resources: Writing Support Transparency 9-H; Writing Support Activity Book 9-2

1. Bring in some newspaper or magazine articles that present information to consumers on particular products or services. As students look through the articles, point out that the articles identify similarities and differences between products as well as evaluate the products' effectiveness.

2. Have students select a product to evaluate, and then choose two examples of the product, such as different brands or different models of the same brand.

continued

Critical Viewing

Relate Students may say that a consumer report will help you make an educated decision when buying a product by comparing features, prices, and capabilities of products.

Connected Assignment
Consumer Report

Comparisons and contrasts can be helpful to people as they decide which car to buy, which hair dryer has the best safety features, and which toy or CD-ROM is most appropriate for a specific age level. **Consumer reports** present information about related products or services, often evaluating or ranking them according to specific categories. These reports identify similarities and differences among several items, providing facts and examples to support the comparisons or contrasts they present. Because they contain evaluations, consumer reports may also make use of persuasive writing elements.

Using the steps outlined below, write a consumer report on a product or service that interests you.

Prewriting Chat with classmates about the products and services you each use most often. Exchange opinions about these products and services, and draft a list of the products you'd like to evaluate. If you're having trouble finding a product to discuss, consider these possibilities:

- educational value of video games
- service at neighborhood restaurants
- magazines aimed at specific audiences
- disposable cameras
- fruit juices aimed at the athletic market
- latest bicycle models
- Internet search engines
- radio stations

Once you've selected a subject, choose at least two examples for your report. Identify your points of comparison by choosing several criteria or categories in which you'll make comparisons and contrasts. Consider broad areas, such as price, convenience, quality, and durability. Then, create a chart to gather details for your consumer report. In the chart on the next page, two stores are rated according to three criteria: prices, convenience, and level of service.

▲ Critical Viewing
How can a consumer report help you choose a safe small appliance such as a hair dryer? **[Relate]**

196 • Comparison-and-Contrast Essay

	Prices	Convenience	Level of Service
Store #1	- Variety of prices	Close to two major highways	Friendly environment
Store #2	- Reasonable prices; frequent sales	Five miles from a major highway	Understaffed

Drafting Use these tips to guide you as you draft your consumer report:

- Start with an introduction to explain the value of the product or service you address. This is a great chance to use an anecdotal lead, showing readers the trouble they could avoid by making an informed decision before a purchase.

- To make your comparisons clear, include a chart to summarize your findings. Create a grading system, and then elaborate your ideas in the body of your report.

- Decide whether to use a point-by-point organization, addressing each comparison point individually, or a subject-by-subject plan, in which you describe each product as a whole. In either case, present each criterion or category and explain how each example performs.

- For each category that you discuss, mention specific details, such as brand names, materials, or nutritional content.

Revising and Editing Review your draft against your prewriting work. Check that you've discussed all categories as they apply to each example. Then, be sure that the order of these elements is clear. To help readers see the comparisons you are drawing, use comparative or superlative adjectives and adverbs—such as *best, faster,* and *most economical.*

Publishing and Presenting When your consumer report is complete, work with several of your classmates to create a booklet to share with family and friends.

 Internet Tip

Many new Web sites offer consumer reports for potential on-line shoppers. Locate such resources on-line, and use what you find as a model for your own product analysis.

Step-by-Step Teaching Guide continued

3. Display the transparency to provide students with an example of how to gather details for their reports.

4. Give students copies of the blank organizer. Tell them to choose three criteria to compare their products.

5. Have students decide whether to use point-by-point or subject-by-subject organization. They might consider using a chart or other visual to clarify or summarize the findings.

6. Have students check their drafts for transitions, verb tenses, and use of comparative modifiers. They can ask two or three other students to review the report, then make additional revisions based on their comments.

7. Students can either publish the report by posting it on a bulletin board or Web site, or present it to the class.

Customize for
Less Advanced Students

Invite these students to work in pairs or groups of three to complete their report. Point out that the article "Working out Possibilities" was written by several students as a team.

Integrating Technology Skills

Have students conduct key word searches to research information on the products they're writing about. They may also want to look for Web sites that provide product reviews for consumers, such as Consumer's Union, as well as the Web sites of companies that manufacture the products.

Lesson Objectives

1. To analyze how ideas are represented in different art forms.
2. To write a comparison-and-contrast essay about two paintings.

Step-by-Step Teaching Guide

Analyzing Ideas Represented in Art

1. Choose one of the Spotlight elements for class discussion, or have students work individually or in groups on the element of their choice. Allow students to take the initiative to find the necessary books and pictures.

2. Students interested in the work of Giotto should research the work of other Italian painters to get a sense of how Giotto's work departed from the norm of his time.

3. Students may want to read excerpts from the *Divine Comedy*. You may wish to select the excerpts for them.

4. Interested students can research to find out more about the role of music in the Protestant Church.

Viewing and Representing

Activity Encourage students to choose paintings that offer elements of comparison, and not just contrast. For example, students can choose paintings from different centuries that have the same subject matter.

Critical Viewing

Respond Students may describe the emotion as pious or solemn.

Analyzing Ideas Represented in Art

Focus on Art: Giotto

Part of the excitement of studying art is comparing and contrasting the work of one artist with that of his or her contemporaries. Creating a major change in the way art depicted life, Giotto di Bondone (c. 1266–c. 1337) was an Italian painter whose emergence may have sparked the Renaissance in Italy. Giotto's influence on the art world signaled a critical shift in how human figures were portrayed in painting: The artist brought a humanity and expression to his paintings that other art did not convey. Giotto's images of people seemed to exude vibrance and personality, in contrast to the wooden, emotionless figures created by earlier medieval artists.

Literature Connection As a citizen of Florence, Italy, the writer Dante Alighieri (1265–1321) was a contemporary of Giotto. Dante is best known as the author of the *Divine Comedy*. Written in the strict rhythmic form known as pentameter, this masterpiece has become one of the pillars of world literature. In the *Divine Comedy*, Dante referred to Giotto when describing the fleeting nature of fame. Naming one of Giotto's teachers, Dante wrote, "Cimabue once thought that he held the field of painting, and now Giotto has the praise, so much so that the other's fame is obscured." Clearly, Dante saw that Giotto's innovations were critically important to the evolution of painting.

Music Connection Martin Luther (1483–1546), of Germany, changed music as much as Giotto altered the field of painting. Not only did Martin Luther translate the Bible into German as part of the Protestant Reformation, he established congregational singing in church as an integral part of the worship service. Luther believed that music presented within the church service should be brought to the level of an art form.

Comparison-and-Contrast Activity: Art Review

Choose two paintings that were produced in different centuries. In a comparison-and-contrast essay, discuss the style, texture, and use of light and shadow in both pieces. In your writing, address similarities between the two paintings, as well as differences.

St. John the Evangelist, Apse Mosaic, Pisa Duomo, Cimabue

▲ Critical Viewing How would you describe the emotion conveyed in this church mosaic by Giotto's mentor, Cimabue? [Respond]

Media and Technology Skills

Comparing Media Coverage
Activity: Analyze News Coverage

News that now reaches us in seconds used to take weeks or even months to arrive, depending on the distance it had to travel. Now, with the Internet and twenty-four hour cable news networks, it's hard to escape the constant flow of instant information even if we choose to do so.

Think About It To sift through the information available on television news, divide your viewing into local and national newscasts. You'll find that the local news usually emphasizes regional events. In contrast, the national news focuses on national and international news. In addition to content, you'll see a contrast in format and tone that distinguishes these newscasts.

Watch It Choose a five-day stretch to analyze television newscasts. Watch the entire broadcast of your local news each night as well as one of the three major network news shows. Use a chart like the one below to take notes on these two key areas:

• **Differences in the tone of the broadcasts** Note the sets, the appearance of the anchors, and the interaction among reporters.

• **Kinds of stories reported** Compare the major stories and note the types of stories that traditionally end the broadcast. As you watch, note the approximate time devoted to each story.

Checklists for Comparing Local and National TV News		
	Local TV News	**National TV News**
Set description		
Each night's top three stories	1. 2. 3.	1. 2. 3.

Analyze It After a week of viewing, evaluate your findings. Compare the quantity and quality of coverage in each of the following areas: foreign news, domestic politics, health, crime, sports, entertainment, and weather. Note which broadcast, local or national, more accurately reflects your experience of the world. Then explain which you would turn to first to make informed judgments as a voter and citizen.

News Sources
Television
• Nightly network news
• Weeknight public television network news
• Sunday morning network news commentary programs
• Twenty-four hour cable news networks
• Local nightly newscasts

Radio
• Local all-news commercial radio stations
• Public radio network news shows
• Hourly local and/or network newscasts on music or talk stations

Computer
• Web pages of network news organizations
• Web pages of local and national newspapers
• Newsgroups

Print
• Local daily newspapers
• National daily newspapers (e.g., *USA Today, The New York Times* national edition, *The Christian Science Monitor*)
• National weekly newsmagazines

Step-by-Step Teaching Guide

Comparing Media Coverage

Teaching Resources: Writing Support Transparency 9-I; Writing Support Activity Book 9-3

1. Review the various news sources students can examine and compare.
2. If possible, bring in a few recorded news broadcasts to show to students.
3. Display the transparency and walk students through an example based on the taped broadcasts.
4. As students watch a week's worth of programming, encourage them to evaluate how different networks cover the same stories.
5. Give students copies of the blank organizer for them to record their ideas as they watch the newscasts.

1. To respond to a writing prompt in a comparison-and-contrast format.
2. To use writing strategies to generate and elaborate on ideas.
3. To revise and edit one's writing for clarity and organization of ideas.
4. To demonstrate control over grammatical elements.

Step-by-Step Teaching Guide

Using Comparison-and-Contrast to Respond to a Writing Prompt

1. Review with students the criteria by which their responses will be evaluated.
2. Have a volunteer read aloud the sample writing prompt.
3. Ask students to identify the audience and purpose for writing. (The audience is readers of the school newspaper; the purpose for writing is to express a position on the school dress code.)
4. As students begin responding, remind them to use the strategies they learned in this chapter.

Standardized Test Preparation Workshop

Using Comparison-and-Contrast to Respond to a Writing Prompt

Some writing prompts on standardized tests will ask you to structure your response using a comparison-and-contrast format. For example, you may need to show the positive and negative aspects of a position, evaluate two provided options, or generate your own items for comparison. Whatever the exact assignment, these prompts measure your ability to recognize and analyze similarities and differences between two ideas. You will be evaluated on your ability to:

- select or recognize appropriate elements for comparison-and-contrast
- choose an appropriate structure to compare and contrast parallel elements
- elaborate with specific details that stress the relationship between the two options
- choose language that highlights the comparisons and contrasts you've made
- use the conventions of grammar, usage, and mechanics correctly

Below is an example of a comparison-and-contrast prompt that could appear on a standardized test. Generate a response, considering the tips on the following page for help. Use the clocks next to each stage as time-planning guides.

Test Tips

- In writing a comparison-and-contrast for a test, think carefully about the specified audience. Compare and contrast features of concern to that audience.
- As you plan to write your response, circle all terms that may need definition. Then, when you draft, be sure to explain these terms.

Sample Writing Situation

As a result of recent conflicts arising from student wardrobe choices, the principal of your school is proposing a radical change in the school dress code. If implemented, students' wardrobes will be restricted to business dress in dark colors. Consider your position concerning this issue. Write a letter to the school newspaper, stating your position and supporting it by comparing and contrasting the current dress code with the proposed dress code.

200 • Comparison-and-Contrast Essay

✎ TEST-TAKING TIP

Tell students that a Venn diagram is a most useful tool for organizing ideas in a comparison-and-contrast format. Remind students that each circle represents the topics being compared. The overlapping section will contain similarities between the topics and the remaining section of each circle will contain the differences. Encourage students to use Venn diagrams to help them organize their ideas for their responses.

Prewriting

Allow about one quarter of your time for prewriting.

Focus on Your Audience and Purpose Use a comparison-and-contrast chart or a Venn diagram to quickly jot down ways that the old and new dress codes are similar and different. As you review your organizer, remember that your goal is to persuade the principal to choose the dress code you prefer. Circle details that will convince a school principal. For example, a reason that focuses on how one dress code will affect the school's image will be more effective than one about how it will affect your personal life.

Drafting

Allow about half of your time for drafting.

Choose a Structure Review your notes to plan an organization of your essay. You may want to use a subject-by-subject approach, addressing your school's current dress policy first and analyzing the proposed dress code next. Alternatively, use a point-by-point plan, addressing specific features as they apply to each dress policy. Once you select a structure, sketch a brief outline, listing the reasons and examples you will cite.

Make the Case Following your outline, present your main ideas and supporting details. Add specific details and examples to make your reasons convincing. Strengthen your argument by acknowledging weaknesses in your preferred option and strengths in the alternative option. Then, secure your argument by explaining why you believe in the preferred option *despite* these acknowledged strengths and weaknesses.

Be Consistent Readers will find any holes in your argument. Make sure you devote equal time and address similar features for each dress code.

Revising, Editing, and Proofreading

Allow about one quarter of your time for revising, editing, and proofreading.

Clarify Read your draft to be sure you make the jump between options smooth. Also, add comparison-and-contrast linking words, such as *similarly* or *on the other hand*, to clarify your analysis. Insert new text neatly.

Check and Check Again Read your essay through quickly. You may notice many errors. Use proofreader's marks and conventions to neatly correct misspellings and missing capital letters or end marks. If time allows, also check for common grammatical errors, such as subject-verb agreement and changes in tense or number.

Chapter 10 Time and Resource Manager

In-Depth Lesson Plan

	LESSON FOCUS	PRINT AND MEDIA RESOURCES
DAY 1	**Introduction to Cause-and-Effect Essays** Students learn key elements of cause-and-effect essays and analyze the Model From Literature (pp. 202–205).	*Writers at Work* **Videotape,** Exposition *Writing Lab* **CD-ROM,** Exposition
DAY 2	**Prewriting** Students choose and narrow a topic, consider their audience and purpose, and gather information (pp. 206–209).	**Teaching Resources** *Writing Support Transparencies* 10-A–C; *Writing Support Activity Book* 10-1
DAY 3	**Drafting** Students organize their ideas and write their first drafts (pp. 210–211).	**Teaching Resources** *Writing Support Transparency* 10-D
DAY 4	**Revising** Students revise their drafts in terms of overall structure, paragraphs, sentences, and word choice (pp.212–216).	**Teaching Resources** *Writing Support Transparencies* 10-E–G
DAY 5	**Editing and Proofreading; Publishing and Presenting** Students check their work for accuracy and correctness and present their final drafts (pp. 217–218).	**Teaching Resources** *Scoring Rubrics on Transparency,* Chapter 10; *Formal Assessment,* Chapter 10

Accelerated Lesson Plan

	LESSON FOCUS	PRINT AND MEDIA RESOURCES
DAY 1	**Drafting** Students review characteristics for cause-and-effect writing, select topics, and write drafts.	*Writers at Work* **Videotape,** Exposition *Writing Lab* **CD-ROM,** Exposition **Teaching Resources** *Writing Support Transparencies* 10-A–D
DAY 2	**Revising to Presenting** Students work individually or with peers to revise, edit, and proofread their work for presentation.	**Teaching Resources** *Writing Support Transparencies* 10-E–G; *Scoring Rubrics on Transparency,* Chapter 10; *Formal Assessment,* Chapter 10

Options for Adapting Lesson Plans

HOMEWORK

Have students complete any stage of the lesson for homework.

TECHNOLOGY

Students can complete any stage of the lesson on computer. Have them print out their completed work.

FEATURES

Extend coverage with Connected Assignment (p. 222), Spotlight on the Humanities (p. 224), Media and Technology Skills (p. 225), and the Standardized Test Preparation Workshop (p. 226).

INTEGRATED SKILLS COVERAGE

Integrating Grammar
Using Appositive Phrases, SE p. 215
Placement of Adverbs, SE p. 217

Reading/Writing Connection
Reading Strategy, SE p. 204
Writing Application, SE p. 205

Technology
Integrating Technology Skills ATE p. 206

Real-World Connection
ATE p. 213

Viewing and Representing
Critical Viewing, SE pp. 202, 204, 213, 219, 221, 222, 224
Viewing and Representing ATE p. 224

ASSESSMENT SUPPORT

Standardized Test Preparation SE p. 226; ATE p. 214
Standardized Test Preparation Workbook, pp. 19–20
Scoring Rubrics on Transparency, Ch. 10
Formal Assessment, Ch. 10
Writing Assessment and Portfolio Management

MEETING INDIVIDUAL NEEDS

Less Advanced Students ATE pp. 209, 212, 223, 227; See also
Ongoing Assessments ATE pp. 203, 205, 207, 208, 211, 213, 215, 218, 219
ESL Students ATE pp. 208, 227
Visual Spatial Learners ATE p. 210
Verbal Linguistic Learners ATE pp. 214, 225
Logical/Mathematical Learners ATE p. 223
Bodily/Kinesthetic Learners ATE p. 206
Gifted/Talented Students ATE p. 214

BLOCK SCHEDULING

Pacing Suggestions
For 90-minute Blocks
• Have students complete the Prewriting and Drafting stages in a single period.
• Focus one class period on Revising and Editing and Publishing and Presenting. Allow at least 30 minutes for peer revision.

Resources for Varying Instruction
• *Writing Lab* CD-ROM If your students have access to hardware, a 90-minute block provides an ideal opportunity for students to work on computer.
• *Writers at Work* videotape Show the Exposition segment in class.

Professional Development Support
• *How to Manage Instruction in the Block* This Teaching Resource provides management and activity suggestions.

MEDIA AND TECHNOLOGY

For the Student
• *Writing Lab* CD-ROM, Exposition

For the Teacher
• *Writers at Work* Videotape, Exposition
• *Resource Pro* CD-ROM

WRITING AND GRAMMAR WEBSITE

The Interactive Writing and Grammar Website provides a wide array of support for students, teachers, and parents. Writing support includes:

• Interactive revision checkers
• Scoring rubrics with complete models

phwg.phschool.com

LITERATURE CONNECTIONS

Related selections from *Prentice Hall Literature: Timeless Voices, Timeless Themes,* Gold:
"The Interlopers," Saki, SE p. 205
"Georgia O'Keefe," Joan Didion, SE p. 207

▶ *Lesson Objectives*

1. To write in a variety of forms using effective word choice, structure, and sentence forms.

2. To write in a voice and style appropriate to audience and purpose.

3. To use prewriting strategies to generate ideas, develop voice, and plan.

4. To develop drafts by organizing and reorganizing content and refining style to suit occasion, audience, and purpose.

5. To demonstrate control over grammatical elements.

6. To use writing to discover, organize, and support what is known and what needs to be learned about a topic.

7. To evaluate writing for both mechanics and content.

Critical Viewing

Analyze Students may say humankind's curiousity about space, the desire to learn about effects of space travel on the body, and the desire to colonize other planets.

Chapter 10 Exposition
Cause-and-Effect Essay

▲ **Critical Viewing**
What are three causes that led to the development of the space shuttle program? **[Analyze]**

Cause-and-Effect Analysis in Everyday Life

From the time we were young children, we began analyzing causes and effects. What causes the sun to rise every morning? Why does it snow? Why are the days shorter in the winter than they are in the summer? As we grow older, our questions often become more complex or more focused on specific areas of interest. We might consider what enables a rocket to be propelled into space, examine the effects of increased traffic on busy city streets, or look for a reason that a popular rock band decided to break up. Examining all of these types of causes and effects helps us better understand and appreciate our world, and it can even help us shape the directions of our lives.

202 • Exposition

⏱ TIME AND RESOURCE MANAGER

Resources
Technology: Writers at Work videotape

In-Depth Coverage	Accelerated Pace
• Cover pp. 202–205 in class. • Show the Exposition: Cause-and-Effect section of the Writers at Work videotape. • Read the literature excerpt, pp. 204–205, in class and use it to discuss the order of causes and effects in cause-and-effect writing. • Discuss examples of cause-and-effect writing that you or your students have read in or out of class or seen on TV.	• Discuss definitions and types of cause-and-effect essays in class. • Assign Model from Literature for independent reading.

What Is a Cause-and-Effect Essay?

Expository writing is writing that informs or explains. A **cause-and-effect essay** is a specific type of expository writing that focuses on an action or a series of actions that cause other actions or results. A good cause-and-effect essay features

- an introduction that presents a general statement about how one event or situation causes another.

- an analysis of the features or aspects of the **cause,** the event or condition that produces a specific result.

- an explanation of the **effect,** the outcome or result.

- facts, statistics, and other types of details to support the conclusions about both the causes and the effects.

- a clear and consistent organization.

To see the criteria upon which your cause-and-effect essay may be judged, preview the Rubric for Self-Assessment on page 218.

Types of Cause-and-Effect Essays

Cause-and-effect writing is suitable for subjects in a variety of fields. Following are some specific types of cause-and-effect essays you may encounter:

- **Lab reports** give causes and effects in a science experiment.

- **History papers** explain relationships among events.

- **Health articles** discuss connections among factors influencing well-being; for example, links among diet, heredity, behavior, and lifestyle.

Writers in ACTION

Writer Henry David Thoreau conducted an experiment to test cause-and-effect relationships on a large scale. He built a cabin himself and lived there in solitude for two years. In his book Walden, *he wrote:*

"I went to the woods because I wished to live deliberately, to front only the essential facts of life, and see if I could not learn what it had to teach, and not, when I came to die, discover that I had not lived."

PREVIEW Student Work IN PROGRESS

In this chapter, you can follow the development of an essay written by Sonia Reimann of Athens High School in Athens, Texas. Sonia used the stages of the writing process to explore the beneficial effects of laughter. You can see her final draft at the end of the chapter.

Cause-and-Effect Essay • **203**

PREPARE and ENGAGE

Interest GRABBER Toss a soft object in a high arc to a student (who has been alerted first). Then ask the class to describe both what happened and why it happened. (Your arm propelled the object out and up, and gravity brought it down.)

Activate Prior Knowledge

Ask students to explain something they did that turned out well and provide reasons why the action resulted as it did.

More About the Author

Henry David Thoreau (1817–1862) was an American poet, philosopher, and essayist who is most well known for having lived according to the philosophy of Transcendentalism, which he recorded in *Walden.*

☑ ONGOING ASSESSMENT: Diagnose

Use one of the following options to diagnose students' current level of proficiency in expository cause-and-effect writing.

Option 1 Ask each student to select the strongest example of his or her cause-and-effect writing from last year. Hold conferences to review each student's sample. Use the conferences to determine which students will need extra support in developing a cause-and-effect essay.	**Option 2** Ask students to tell you about something they did that changed something—made people react in a certain way or resulted in a task being done or something being built or accomplished.

Reading: Identifying the Main Idea

The key to reading expository writing is being able to understand the writer's main idea. The main idea is what a paragraph is about. The rest consists of supporting ideas, illustrations, and contrasting examples.

Teaching From the Model

Use the essay as an example of cause and effect writing. It vividly describes the effect of a killer storm on thousands of people in Central America.

Step-by-Step Teaching Guide

Engage Students Through Literature

1. Read the essay aloud or have a volunteer read it.

2. Use questions such as the following to prompt discussion of the essay:

   • What area of the world did Hurricane Mitch destroy? (much of Central America)

   • Why was it particularly unfortunate for this region? (The region was poor and the people had little to begin with. They had no resources to replace what they lost.)

   • What is the future for the area? (continued poverty and hardship)

   • Who were the worst hurt? (children)

3. Ask students to explain some of the effects of Hurricane Mitch. (mudslides, floods, destruction of crops and homes, malnutrition, disease, death)

Critical Viewing

Evaluate Students may say that a map enables the reader to envision the location being described.

 **Model From Literature**

In the the following article from the November 16, 1998, issue of TIME *magazine, reporter Tim Padgett describes the powerful, devastating effects of the torrential rains that were part of the storm system named Hurricane Mitch.*

Reading **Writing** **Connection**

Reading Strategy:
Identify the Main Idea
As you read, look for sentences that reveal the main idea or point that the writer is trying to make. Then, notice how the details that follow support the main idea.

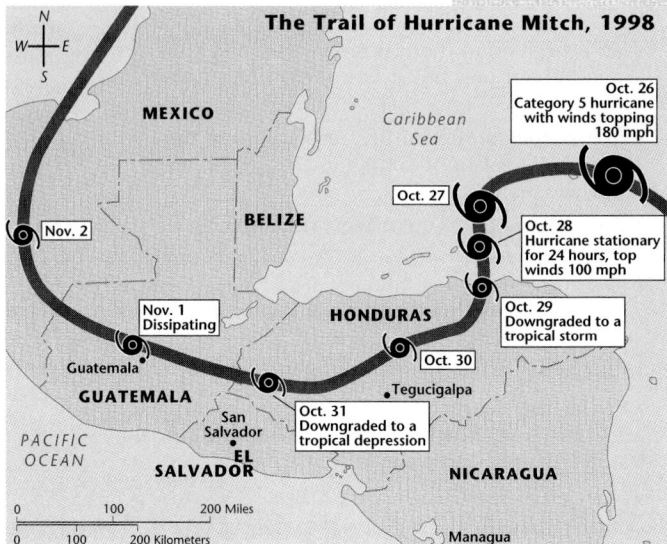

The Trail of Hurricane Mitch, 1998

Oct. 26
Category 5 hurricane with winds topping 180 mph

Oct. 27

Oct. 28
Hurricane stationary for 24 hours, top winds 100 mph

Oct. 29
Downgraded to a tropical storm

Oct. 30

Oct. 31
Downgraded to a tropical depression

Nov. 1
Dissipating

Nov. 2

MEXICO · Caribbean Sea · BELIZE · HONDURAS · Guatemala · Tegucigalpa · GUATEMALA · San Salvador · PACIFIC OCEAN · EL SALVADOR · NICARAGUA · Managua

0   100   200 Miles
0   100   200 Kilometers

▲ **Critical Viewing**
In what ways can a map help a writer communicate more effectively with an audience? **[Evaluate]**

In the introduction, the author names the worst effects of the storm: the widespread death and the destruction of homes. The article will identify and develop several other effects: destruction of the landscape, flooding, and billions of dollars in damage.

Murderous Mitch

Tim Padgett

Tragedy is numbingly routine in Central America. Poverty, earthquakes and civil wars have savaged the region for most of this century. Still, the Dantesque calamity that hit the isthmus last week may have taken suffering to a new plateau. As many as 10,000 people were estimated dead in the battered countries of Nicaragua and Honduras, while some 2 million were left homeless, in the wake of the relentless rains of Hurricane Mitch. In all, the storm caused a staggering $3 billion in damage—more than half the combined Nicaraguan and Honduran gross domestic products.

204 • **Cause-and-Effect Essay**

In Nicaragua alone, where 3,800 were thought dead, much of the landscape looks as barren as the moon. Starving, sallow-skinned children, many suffering cholera from the fetid waters that destroyed their homes, begged for food on the crumbled, mud-slick roads between Managua and the flooded northern sierras.

For towns like the once thriving community of Posoltega, nestled on rich soil beneath the Casitas Volcano in Nicaragua's mountainous northwest, Mitch was the apocalypse. Close to noon on Oct. 30, after the hurricane had dumped three days of rain into Casitas's crater, the mountainside burst with what villagers described as the angry roar of a jetliner. It hurled mud, water and rock into Posoltega's rooftops, "a terrible, towering wall that just fell out of the clouds," says Santo Díaz, 24. Díaz gathered his elderly father, mother, sister and two brothers to escape—but the avalanche claimed them. . . .

In Honduras, Mitch spawned the worst floods in 200 years. The waters may have killed more than 5,000 people and left 11,000 missing. As Vice President William Handel helicoptered over the deluged Ulúa River valley, he saw three people trapped on a patch of high ground, waving frantically. The waters rose so fast that the chopper couldn't land—and Handel, just yards away, watched them drown. . . .

As the gravity of the disaster reached around the world, close to $100 million in aid poured in. But Central America's development, which lagged far behind the rest of the world before the hurricane, has been set back decades.

Many if not most of Mitch's victims were youngsters—including not only those who drowned but also those whose malnourished bodies were no match for the deadly septic infections set free in the waters. Says Charles Compton, local head of Plan International relief organization: "We have to keep starvation and infection from claiming as many victims as the hurricane did." When the final tally is in, the assertions of a staggering toll may well be borne out. Those whom the flood waters did not kill face the problems of isolation, starvation, disease and neglect—the normal stuff of tragedy in Central America, made hundreds of times worse by Mitch's murderous rains.

Writing Application: Develop a Main Idea When you write your cause-and-effect essay, take care to clearly state your main idea. Then, to strengthen your writing, support this idea with facts and details.

In the next three paragraphs, details and firsthand accounts add impact to the description of the hurricane's effects.

Statistics make the the overall magnitude of the storm's effect more clear.

In the conclusion, Padgett describes the secondary effects of the storm. This broadens the scope of the disaster.

⸁ITERATURE

Many writers turn the cause-and-effect relationship into the spark for storytelling. For example, read Saki's story "The Interlopers," which examines the results of a struggle for a plot of land. You can find the story in *Prentice Hall Literature: Timeless Voices, Timeless Themes,* Gold.

Model From Literature • 205

More About the Author
Tim Padgett writes extensively for TIME magazine and is the magazine's Latin American Bureau Chief.

Responding to Literature
Have students keep a list of the cause-and-effect relationships as they read Saki's story.

☑ **ONGOING ASSESSMENT: Monitor and Reinforce**

After previewing the Model from Literature, you may anticipate some students may have difficulty with some proper names and other words. Use one of the following options.

Option 1 If students read the model independently, have them list any unfamiliar words they encounter. Then go over pronunciations and definitions in class.	**Option 2** If you or a prepared student read the model aloud in class, take time to define unfamiliar words as they are encountered. Words such as *Dantesque, isthmus, plateau,* and *septic* may need definition.

Prewriting: Current Events

1. The activities listed here are designed to stimulate students' thinking about a topic. In getting students to think of topics for a cause-and-effect essay, the operative words are *why?* and *what?*

2. Current events are a good place to start. Have students look through newspapers, newsmagazines, and Web sites for events that interest them. Encourage them to use current events to inquire about past events as well.

3. Have small groups brainstorm for other topics. Some areas they could explore are scientific phenomena, family or group social dynamics, adventures and misadventures.

Integrating Technology Skills

Have students go on-line to find news sites and other information they could use to formulate a topic for the cause-and-effect essay.

Prewriting: Emotional Thermometer

Teaching Resources: Writing Support Transparency 10-A

1. Use the transparency to go over the activity of drawing an emotional thermometer.

2. Review Sonia's choices in using the emotional thermometer.

3. The thermometer is only one tool for exploring topics. If some students feel uncomfortable writing about their feelings, they can consider more objective topics.

Customize for *Bodily/Kinesthetic Learners*

Suggest that students recall some group activity and remember what happened, who did what, causing what effect. With the memories in mind have them act out the events and then record their memories in an outline form.

206

10.2 Prewriting

Choosing Your Topic

A successful cause-and-effect essay begins with a topic involving two events that are clearly linked. One of the events must be a cause of the other. However, if the causes and effects are too obvious, readers may not be interested. Here are some methods you can use to generate potential topics:

1. **Current Events** Scan newspapers or magazines for headlines that interest you. Jot them down in the center column of a three-column chart. To the left of each of the headlines, write causes; to the right, list possible effects. Then, review this chart to choose a topic to develop.

2. **Emotional Thermometer** In a sketch of a thermometer, list the different intensities of various emotions, from least to most intense. To the left of each emotion, list an event that might cause it; to the right, list an effect this emotion can produce. Review your work to choose an interesting topic for a cause-and-effect essay.

Writing Lab CD-ROM

For more help choosing a topic, explore the activities and suggestions in the Choosing a Topic section of the Exposition lesson.

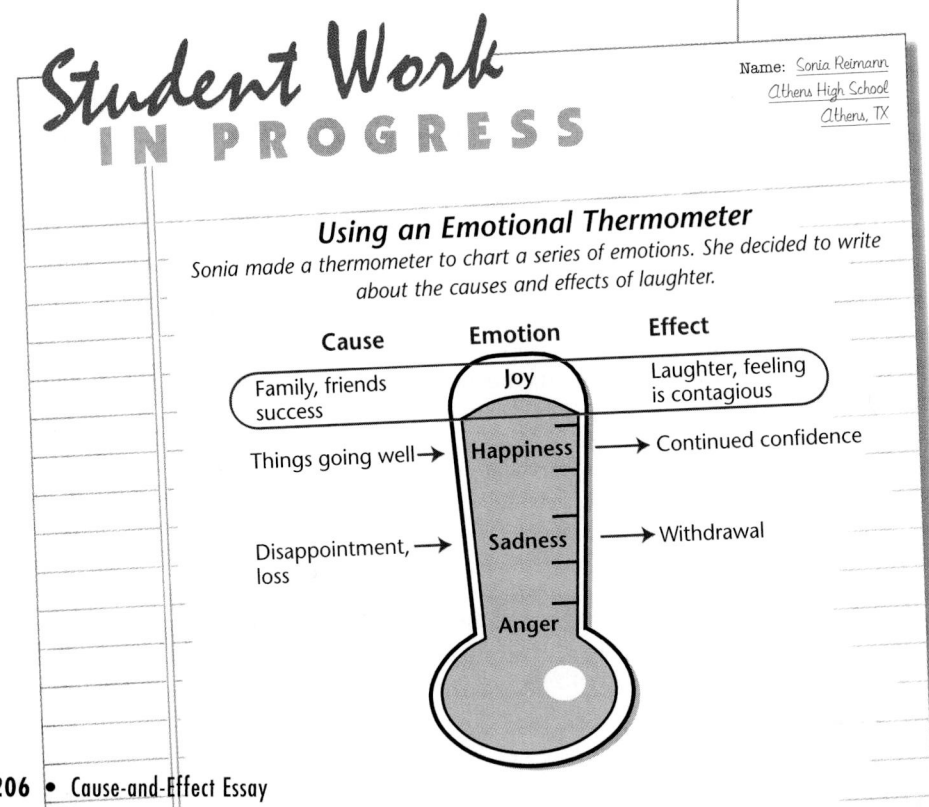

Student Work **IN PROGRESS**

Name: Sonia Reimann
Athens High School
Athens, TX

Using an Emotional Thermometer

Sonia made a thermometer to chart a series of emotions. She decided to write about the causes and effects of laughter.

Cause	Emotion	Effect
Family, friends success	Joy	Laughter, feeling is contagious
Things going well →	Happiness	→ Continued confidence
Disappointment, loss →	Sadness	→ Withdrawal
	Anger	

206 • Cause-and-Effect Essay

⏱ TIME AND RESOURCE MANAGER

Resources
Print: Writing Support Transparency 10-A–C, Writing Support Activity Book 10-1
Technology: Writing Lab CD-ROM, Exposition

In-Depth Coverage	Accelerated Pace
• Cover pp. 206–209 in class. • Work through the Current Events and Emotional Thermometer strategies with the class (p. 206). • Do the Using a Cause-and-Effect Organizer activity in class.	• Discuss strategies for generating topics. • Have students work independently to choose and narrow their topics. • Have students work with partners to focus on audience, purpose, and gathering details.

TOPIC BANK

If you have difficulty developing a topic on your own, consider one of these suggestions:

1. **Essay About Year-Round Schools** Year-round schools have effects on students, parents, and teachers. Learn more about the causes and effects of this school schedule, and write an essay to share your findings.

2. **Report on the Effects of Technology** Choose a technological development, such as the spread of cellular phones or the availability of the Internet. In an essay, examine the causes and effects of this development.

Responding to Fine Art
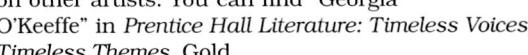

3. Use the painting *Two Lane Road Cut* to spark your own investigation of the construction of a road in your area. In a cause-and-effect essay, explain why the road was built and how the road has changed your community.

Responding to Literature

4. Read "Georgia O'Keeffe" by Joan Didion. Use the piece as the starting point for an essay about the impact of O'Keeffe's work on other artists. You can find "Georgia O'Keeffe" in *Prentice Hall Literature: Timeless Voices, Timeless Themes*, Gold.

Two Lane Road Cut, Woody Gwyn, Courtesy of the artist

☑ Cooperative Writing Opportunity

5. **Survey on the Causes and Effects of Extracurricular Activities** With a group, survey students in your school to learn more about extracurricular activities. Together, devise and use a questionnaire to gather information. Then, split the task of evaluating the results. One writer can analyze the factors influencing students' choices. Another group member can study the effects of the extracurricular involvement. Present your findings to school officials or classmates.

Responding to Fine Art
Two Lane Road Cut by Woody Gwyn
Teaching Resources: Writing Support Transparency 10-B

Display the transparency and have students discuss possible topics generated by the painting.

Responding to Literature

In addition to discussing O'Keeffe's impact on other artists, students may also want to explore the effects of other artists on O'Keeffe.

Spotlight on the Humanities

For additional topic suggestions, refer students to the Spotlight on the Humanities on page 224.

☑ ONGOING ASSESSMENT: Monitor and Reinforce

If some students are having difficulty coming up with a topic, use one of the following options.

Option 1 Suggest that students choose an idea from the Topic Bank. If many students have difficulty, work with them around one topic, modeling the process for them.	**Option 2** If the Topic Bank ideas seem too complex, suggest that students try one of the assignments from the Topic Bank for Heterogeneous Classes in the Teaching Resources.

⏱ TIME SAVERS!

 Writing Support Transparencies
Use the transparencies for Chapter 10 to teach these strategies.

Prewriting: Narrowing Your Topic; Considering Your Audience and Purpose

1. Discuss the importance of narrowing the topic to the right size. Too broad a topic cannot be covered in a short essay. Too narrow a topic leaves the writer with too little to say.

2. Direct students to the Listing activity to narrow their topic. Have them look for subtopics that are rich in causes and effects.

3. Ask students to consider the importance of targeting their audience. Writing for "everybody" is vague and not really true. Depending on the amount of background and explanation they include, they are either ignoring or boring a part of the audience.

4. Use the Model from Literature as an illustration of multiple purposes. Padgett explained the devastation caused by Hurricane Mitch. He described the effects of the hurricane. Finally, he activated readers' feelings of compassion and sadness by describing the effects on real people.

Customize for
ESL Students

Cause-and-effect writing has its own logical structure. Be sure that students are comfortable with the terminology and that they know they are to be writing about things that happen (effects) as a result of certain causes.

10.2

Narrowing Your Topic

You can't produce an effective essay if your subject is too broad to analyze. For example, a topic such as the civil rights movement might captivate readers, but there are too many causes and effects of this movement to address in a short essay. A narrowed focus—like the causes and effects of the March on Washington—might be a more manageable topic for a short paper. Use listing and itemizing to narrow your topic.

Listing and Itemizing to Narrow a Topic

1. Break your subject into subtopics.
2. Itemize each subtopic by identifying causes and effects.
3. Review your list of subtopics and their associated causes and effects, and choose the one you would like to pursue in your cause-and-effect essay.

Considering Your Audience and Purpose

Target Your Audience

Shaping your writing to appeal to your audience is one of the keys to successful writing. To define your audience and target your writing to their needs and interests, prepare an audience profile using the questions shown below. Then, keep these answers in mind as you draft and revise.

AUDIENCE PROFILE
1. **Readers** Who will read your work?
2. **Knowledge Level** How much do your readers already know?
3. **Language** What type of language will best suit your audience?
4. **Interests** What will interest your audience most about your topic?

Refine Your Purpose

The general purpose of a cause-and-effect essay is to explain. However, you might have a more specific purpose in mind, such as to convince readers to take action or to encourage a change. Once you've clarified your purpose, consider how it will affect your choice of language and details.

 Research Tip

Before narrowing your topic, read more about the general subject you've chosen. As you complete a preliminary study, you may identify a narrow topic that suits the scope of your writing and your interests.

☑ ONGOING ASSESSMENT: Monitor and Reinforce

If students consider you the teacher their audience, use one of the following options.

Option 1 Have students select a specific person as their audience, someone other than you. This will get them focused away from you and will also affect the level of detail, language, and formality that they include.	**Option 2** Have students identify a purpose for writing that has nothing to do with impressing you.

Gathering Details

Once you've focused your topic and defined your audience and purpose, you may want to plunge right in to writing your first draft. However, you will probably find it easier to write if you take some time to collect facts, statistics, examples, descriptions, and other details that you can use to clearly illustrate the causes and effects you plan to describe. It's not enough simply to say that one event or situation causes another, you have to show *how*.

Use a Cause-and-Effect Organizer

You may want to use an organizer such as the one below to record causes and effects. Write your topic in the center. List causes above it and effects below it. If you know your topic well, you will find it easy to fill in the organizer. If you don't, you may want to do some research to gather the details you'll need.

**Writing Lab
CD-ROM**

You can find a cause-and-effect organizer in the Exposition lesson.

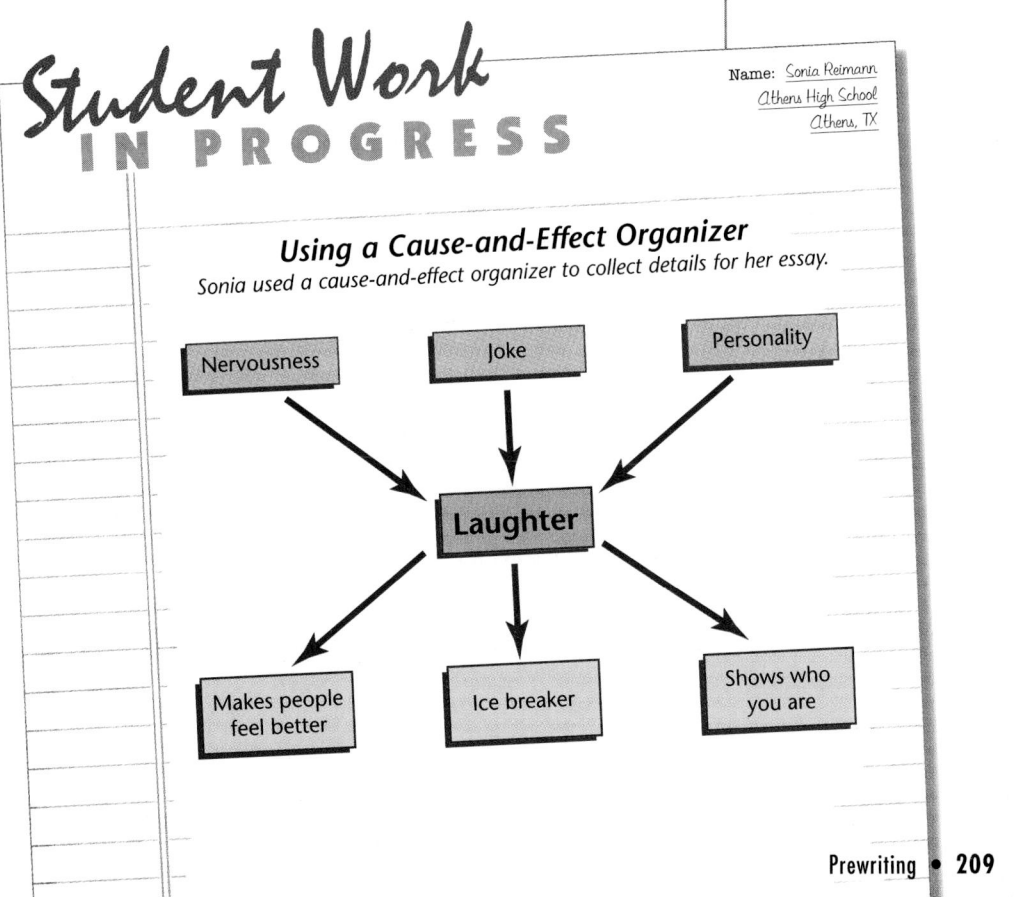

Student Work IN PROGRESS

Name: *Sonia Reimann*
Athens High School
Athens, TX

Using a Cause-and-Effect Organizer
Sonia used a cause-and-effect organizer to collect details for her essay.

Nervousness →
Joke ↓
Personality →
Laughter
→ Makes people feel better
↓ Ice breaker
→ Shows who you are

Prewriting • 209

Step-by-Step Teaching Guide

Prewriting: Using a Cause-and-Effect Organizer

Teaching Resources: Writing Support Transparency 10-C; Writing Support Activity Book 10-1

1. Begin the activity by having students list all the details associated with their topic. Tell them to not worry yet which are causes and which are effects.

2. Display the transparency. Examine Sonia's cause-and-effect organizer and how she grouped causes and effects above and below the topic.

3. Use the transparency to model the process with the following topic:

   Causes
   Desire to get good grades
   Fear of messing up
   Like to be organized

   Topic
   Study and homework plan

   Effects
   Improved grades
   Pride
   More relaxed, less worry

4. Give students copies of the blank organizer to help them gather details.

Customize for *Less Advanced Students*

Students may need assistance in differentiating causes from effects. Help them understand that causes are the reasons you do things; effects are what happens as a result of the action you do or do not take. A cause comes first; the effect/result follows.

 TIME SAVERS!

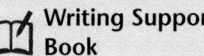

Writing Support Transparencies
Use the transparencies for Chapter 10 to teach these strategies.

Writing Support Activity Book
Use the graphic organizers for Chapter 10 to facilitate these strategies.

Drafting: Choose an Organization

1. Every essay needs an organizational structure. Two useful structures for cause-and-effect essays are chronological order and order of importance.

2. Review the example of chronological order. Ask students how many of them have a topic that deals with events over time. Suggest that this organizational structure will work well for them.

3. Review the example of order of importance. Ask students if they have a topic in which there are several different causes varying in order of importance. Suggest that this organizational structure will work well for them.

4. Point out how each organizational structure helps students give the correct emphasis to the most important events and effects.

Customize for
Visual/Spatial Learners

Students may be helped in using either organizational structure by sketching a story board of the process. Have them use sticky notes to sketch each event or effect from the story board and then arrange the notes in the proper order.

10.3 Drafting

Shaping Your Writing
Choose an Organization

As you prepare to write your first draft, you should have an organization in mind. Following are two of the possible methods for organizing your essay:

Chronological Order If you describe causes and effects that happen over time, arrange them in the order in which they happened. For example, this type of organization might be appropriate for analyzing the development of a new policy.

EVENT 1 (CAUSE)   Color films become the industry standard in Hollywood.

EVENT 2 (CAUSE/EFFECT) Interest develops in colorizing old films.

EVENT 3 (CAUSE/EFFECT) Controversy over this technique builds.

EVENT 4 (CAUSE/EFFECT) Film critics and moviegoers boycott.

EVENT 5 (EFFECT)   New policies over colorizing emerge.

Order of Importance You can also organize your essay in a sequence based on the relative importance of each idea, event, or situation you are presenting. Begin with your least important point, and work toward your most important point. This type of organization is especially effective when you are presenting a series of effects of a single event. For example, you might use this organization to present the effects of a tornado.

ORDER OF IMPORTANCE

Least Important Effect: The power was out for three days.

Many houses were damaged by flying debris.

A fire started by downed power lines caused more severe damage to several houses.

Most Important Effect: One block of houses was completely destroyed.

210 • Cause-and-Effect Essay

⏱ TIME AND RESOURCE MANAGER

Resources
Print: Writing Support Transparency 10-D
Technology: Writing Lab CD-ROM, Exposition

In-Depth Coverage	Accelerated Pace
• Cover pp. 210–211 in class. • Work through the exercises on chronological order and order of importance with the entire class. • Have students write their own cause-and-effect essay drafts in class.	• Have students review pp. 210–211 independently, then write their own cause and effect essay drafts. • Respond to individual drafting issues as needed.

Providing Elaboration

As you draft your essay, illustrate each cause and effect through layers of supporting facts, details, examples, and other types of illustrations. In your opening paragraph, introduce your topic, and illustrate why it is important. Follow with a series of topical paragraphs—body paragraphs focusing on a single subpoint of your main topic.

Develop Topical Paragraphs Using the TRI Method

To develop your topical paragraphs fully, try the TRI method. To use this strategy, follow these steps:
1. Write a sentence stating your topic; label it (T).
2. Write a sentence restating your topic; label it (R).
3. Illustrate your point through details, facts, examples, or personal experience; label this section (I). The illustration part of the paragraph may include several sentences.

Once you feel comfortable with the TRI pattern, you can vary the elements to suit the information you address. Consider a TIR or ITR approach when it would work best.

 Internet Tip

Search the Internet for more information about your topic. If you are looking for a phrase on an Internet search engine, put parentheses around the phrase when you type it in the search window.

Student Work IN PROGRESS

Name: Sonia Reimann
Athens High School
Athens, TX

Developing Topical Paragraphs

Sonia developed her opening paragraph using TIR, a variation of the TRI pattern. As you can see below, she began by stating the topic. She followed by illustrating how the message affected her, and then she restated the topic in the final sentence.

[T-topic] Laughter can break the tension of some very serious moments.

[I-illustrate] On one specific occasion I was ending a visit to Switzerland. I was saying goodbye to my cousin Martin and his family. My aunt gave me a big hug and the sadness began to build. Next was Martin. The tears in my eyes threatened to burst out at any moment. But Martin did something that made me burst with laughter, not tears. He pulled a huge polka-dot handkerchief out and started dabbing my eyes. [R-restatement] Adding laughter changed the scene completely.

Drafting • 211

1. Discuss with students the "second-chance" theory. Students' drafts are not finished products. Even professional writers often spend more time on revising than they do on the original draft.

2. Examine Sonia's work in progress for how she uses color-coding to revise her draft.

3. Use the transparency to further examine the revision strategy of color-coding causes and effects.

Customizing for
Less Advanced Students

Suggest that students work with partners. Each reads the other's draft, marking what he or she thinks is the main point of each paragraph. If the reader doesn't find the right sentences, partners can work together to clarify the writing.

10.4 Revising

Revising Your Overall Structure

When a soccer player misses a game-tying goal, he or she usually doesn't get a second chance to score. As a writer, you do have a "second chance" to correct your work and find ways to improve it. This occurs during revision. Take advantage of the opportunity by evaluating your draft carefully.

Clarify Cause-and-Effect Relationships

First, review your entire draft, focusing specifically on the causes and effects you have presented. Check to see that the relationship between the causes and effects is clear. Highlighting these key elements of your draft will help you see the connections you've made.

▶ **REVISION STRATEGY**
Color-Coding Causes and Effects

With two highlighters, use one color to mark phrases that present causes and another to mark those that discuss effects. Evaluate the connections between the two. You may need to add details to strengthen the connections, use transitional words or phrases to make the link clear, or eliminate the causes or effects that do not support your main point.

Writing Lab
CD-ROM

Use the Revision Checker for transition words to identify places where your writing could be revised for clarity. Find this tool in the Exposition lesson.

Student Work
IN PROGRESS

Name: Sonia Reimann
Athens High School
Athens, TX

Highlighting Sentences to Evaluate Structure

Sonia used highlighting to evaluate the structure of her essay. She added transitional words and phrases to clarify the cause and effect she discussed.

so that
We used his trademark laughter we could get through the pain. . . .

Because
I began remembering the powerful effect Martin's laughter had on me

I started talking about all the crazy things he had said and done. . . .

212 • Cause-and-Effect Essay

Writing Support Transparencies
Use the transparencies for Chapter 10 to teach these strategies.

⏱ TIME AND RESOURCE MANAGER

Resources
Print: Writing Support Transparencies 10-E–G
Technology: Writing Lab CD-ROM, Exposition

In-Depth Coverage	Accelerated Pace
• Cover pp. 212–216 in class. • Work through the revision strategy with the entire class. • Use the relevant transparencies for coding causes and effects. • Divide the class into groups for peer review activity.	• Assign students to review pp. 212–216 independently. • Have students revise their cause-and-effect essays independently.

Revising Your Paragraphs

Add Details to Show Cause and Effect

Once you're confident that the relationships among your causes and effects are clear, analyze each paragraph to see that you have provided a thorough set of facts, details, statistics, examples, or other types of support to illustrate each cause and effect. To identify places to add support for your ideas, use this strategy perfected by professional journalists:

▶ **REVISION STRATEGY**
Using the Reporter's Formula

Journalists use the five *W*'s to get all the facts into an effective news story. Reporters double-check to be sure they have provided information to tell *who, what, when, where,* or *why* an event happened. You can use this strategy to identify the details you want to add in order to strengthen cause-and-effect connections you've established. Review your paragraphs, and answer the questions shown below. If you cannot answer some of these questions fully, add the information that will provide the answer.

▲ **Critical Viewing**
What is the effect of having a standard set of questions ready before conducting an interview? **[Evaluate]**

Reporter's Formula	
Who	are the people involved or affected?
What	were the specific reasons it happened? What evidence is there to support this conclusion?
When	did the events take place or the situation develop? When did it start, and when did it end?
Where	did the events take place? Where was the impact greatest?
Why	did it happen?

Revising: Using the Reporter's Formula

1. Review how the 5 W's can contribute useful details for students to include in their essays. First, see that they understand that appropriate details are one of the keys to interesting writing.

2. Read the following passages to students to illustrate the power of good details:

   Who: Joey was the kid who started the joke, but he got the idea from Mikey, who is well known for his sense of humor.

   What: Ms. Henderson was helpful in getting Mr. Jackson out of the room so we could set up the surprise party.

   Why: Mr. Jackson is such a giving teacher. We thought it would be nice to show our appreciation.

Real-World Connection

Have students read newspaper or magazine articles or news articles and underline the 5 W's. These should appear in the first paragraph or soon after that.

Critical Viewing

Evaluate Students may say that it helps to make sure that all the important details are covered.

Revising • 213

☑ **ONGOING ASSESSMENT: Monitor and Reinforce**

If some students are having difficulty using the 5 W's to add details showing cause and effect, use the following option.

Have students work in pairs. Each student should interview his or her partner, asking each of the 5 W questions and recording the answers.

Revising: Color Coding to Evaluate Sentence Length

Teaching Resources: Writing Support Transparency 10-F

1. Good writing, like good songs, needs rhythm. One way to establish that rhythm is to vary sentence length. Nothing numbs the reader like a series of short, choppy sentences one after the other.

2. Do point out the Grammar and Style Tip about the use of short declarative sentences for dramatic effect. After a series of longer, varied sentences, these make a dramatic point, as the example, "He wept," amply demonstrates.

3. Display the transparency. Examine how Sonia color-coded short sentences.

4. Use the transparency to further help students practice the technique of counting words and combining sentences.

Customize for
Gifted/Talented Students

Have students read an excerpt from Steinbeck's *Of Mice and Men* and try to imitate his style of using short sentences mixed with longer descriptive ones to produce an effect of heightened details against a backdrop of rich description.

Customize for
Verbal/Linguistic Learners

Once students have counted the words in each sentence, have them identify sentences for combining. Then have them read each pair of highlighted sentences aloud, playing with connective words. If necessary, students can do the exercise in pairs so the partner can suggest connectives as well as write down the new sentences dictated by the author.

10.4

Revising Your Sentences
Combine Short Sentences

Good writing not only provides the information that readers need, but it also has a rhythm that keeps readers engaged. One way to create a rhythm in your writing is to vary the length of your sentences. As you revise, look for places to combine short sentences and establish greater sentence variety. This will eliminate choppiness and build an interesting rhythm. Use color-coding to analyze the length of your sentences.

▶ **REVISION STRATEGY**
Color-Coding to Evaluate Sentence Length

Count the number of words in every sentence in your essay. Write the number of words in the margin beside each sentence. When you're done, scan the numbers you've recorded and highlight the sentences you'd like to revise. If you discover that you have many sentences with fewer than ten words, look for places where you can combine short sentences to create longer sentences. Consider these tips:
• Add transitional words or phrases to show clearer connections among the ideas you address.
• Combine two sentences using subordinating clauses that start with conjunctions such as *after, although, despite, if,* and *whenever.*
• Use coordinating conjunctions such as *and, but, or, nor, for, so,* and *yet.*

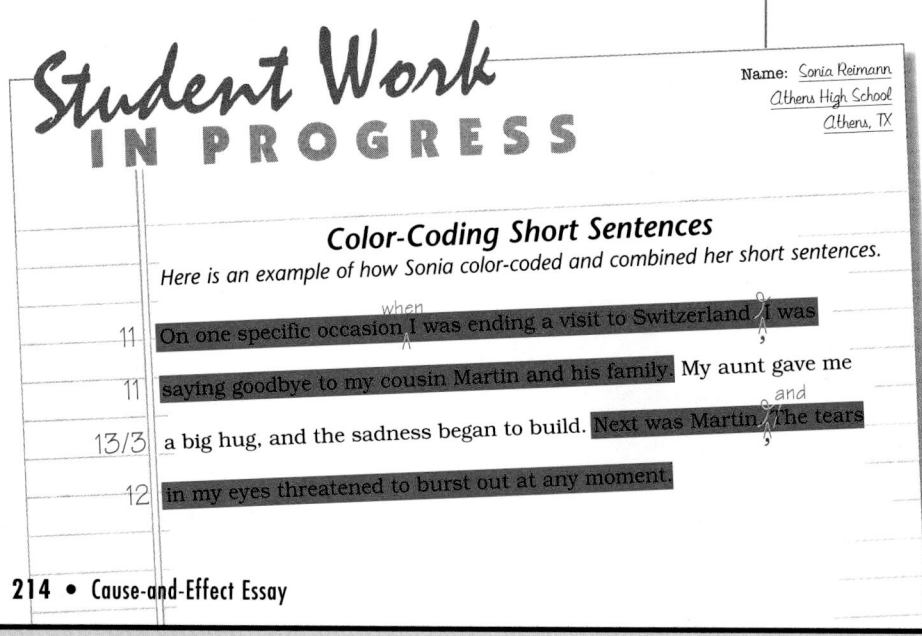

Color-Coding Short Sentences
Here is an example of how Sonia color-coded and combined her short sentences.

Name: Sonia Reimann
Athens High School
Athens, TX

11 — On one specific occasion I was ending a visit to Switzerland. I was
   (when)

11 — saying goodbye to my cousin Martin and his family. My aunt gave me

13/3 — a big hug, and the sadness began to build. Next was Martin. The tears
   (and)

12 — in my eyes threatened to burst out at any moment.

214 • Cause-and-Effect Essay

Grammar and Style Tip

Short sentences can be used occasionally for a dramatic effect. For instance, if you are describing a person who has experienced a tragic event, you might end the description with a short sentence, such as "He collapsed."

⬥ STANDARD TEST PREPARATION WORKSHOP

Appositive Phrases Standardized test questions may require students to recognize appositive phrases in sentences. Write the following examples on the chalkboard and ask students to select the one containing an appositive phrase:

A In the first half, the quarterback was brilliant.

B Jake, the quarterback, made a bad error in the third quarter.

C The quarterback and defensive end played like all-stars.

D None of the above

Item **B** contains the appositive phrase "the quarterback." The beginning of choice A is not an appositive; it is a prepositional phrase.

Grammar in Your Writing

Using Appositive Phrases to Combine Sentences

An **appositive** is a noun or a pronoun placed near another noun or pronoun to identify, rename, or explain it. An **appositive phrase** is an appositive accompanied by other words that modify it.

An appositive phrase functions as a unit, renaming or amplifying the word that precedes it. Appositive phrases are a useful tool for combining sentences. Look at the following examples.

Individual Sentences:	My little brother is a rascal if there ever was one. He's always getting into trouble.
Combined Sentence:	My little brother, a rascal if there ever was one, is always getting into trouble.
Individual Sentences:	Advance planning is essential. It is the most effective means of avoiding the problem.
Combined Sentence:	Advance planning, the most effective means of avoiding the problem, is essential.
Individual Sentences:	I've devised a more organized schedule. My plan will make life easier for me.
Combined Sentence:	To make my life easier, I've devised a plan, a more organized schedule.
Individual Sentences:	The dramatic series won many awards. It also attracts heavy viewer ratings.
Combined Sentence:	The dramatic series, winner of many awards, also attracts heavy viewer ratings.
Individual Sentences:	Paulson is the committee leader. Paulson spoke to a group of reporters about the progress of the job.
Combined Sentence:	Paulson, the committee leader, spoke to a group of reporters about the progress of the job.

Find It in Your Reading Review "Murderous Mitch" on pages 204–205. Identify one appositive phrases that it includes. Then, explain how this appositive phrase adds useful information to the sentence in which it appears.

Find It in Your Writing Combine at least three pairs of short sentences in your draft by using appositive phrases.

For more on appositive phrases, see Chapter 21. For more on combining sentences, see Chapter 22.

Grammar in Your Writing: Using Appositive Phrases to Combine Sentences

1. The function of appositives is to rename the noun the phrase modifies. Write the following additional examples on the chalkboard and have students identify the appositive and the noun modified:

    Freddy, the I'll-get-to-it-later kid, astounded everyone when he handed in his essay three days early.

    San Francisco, my favorite city, has the world's most crooked street.

2. Write the following examples on the chalkboard and ask students to form appositive phrases by renaming the noun to be modified. Then have them write sentences including the appositives.

    our goalie (Our goalie, the best goalie in the league, saved two goals.)

    the homework assignment (The homework assignment, a reading project, was difficult.)

Find It in Your Reading

Students can find the following appositive phrase in paragraph 6: local head of Plan International Relief Organization.

Find It in Your Writing

Have students exchange papers with a partner and see if the partner can offer any more suggestions for combining short sentences.

ONGOING ASSESSMENT: Monitor and Reinforce

If some students are having difficulty using appositive phrases to vary sentence length, use one of the following options.

Option 1 Have students choose one subject noun in each paragraph and write an appositive phrase to rename it.	**Option 2** Have students work in pairs to suggest using appositive phrases as a way of combining sentences.

Revising: Circling Empty or Vague Words

Teaching Resource: Writing Support Transparency 10-G

1. Remind students of the difference between conversational speech patterns and the language requirements of a formal essay. "Talking out" an essay can be a useful technique for generating a draft. Editing out inappropriate language and constructions is a vital part of the revision process.

2. Review how Sonia circled vague and empty words. Use the transparency to demonstrate the technique.

3. Have students reread their drafts, searching for empty or vague words. Remind them of the necessity of stepping back from their work and looking at it with a critical eye. Otherwise they are likely to miss many of the vague and empty words they wrote in the first place.

10.4

Revising Your Word Choice
Delete or Replace Empty and Vague Words

Empty and vague words—such as *really, very, somewhat, thing, good, bad, nice,* and *awful*—do not add to your analysis. Review your draft to identify such language in your writing.

▶**REVISION STRATEGY**
Circling Empty or Vague Words

Circle empty or vague words that you find in your writing. Evaluate each word you've marked. Delete those that do not add to the draft, and replace the others with more precise language.

Student Work
IN PROGRESS

Name: Sonia Reimann
Athens High School
Athens, TX

Evaluating Empty or Vague Words
Sonia circled weak words, deleting some and replacing others.

Laughter is ⊘like a symbol that can instantly join people and solidify

⊘real friendships. I became a friend of a girl named Krystle not

because she possessed the ⊘good qualities of honesty, reliability, and

kindness that I normally seek in friends, but because she had an even

rarer
⊘better quality—she could ⊘really make me laugh.

Peer Review
Read Aloud

When you've finished revising on your own, work with a group to make additional revisions. When you read your work aloud to a group, your peers may notice some points you have missed. After you have read your essay twice, choose one of the following points for discussion.

• Is the relationship between cause and effect clear to you?

• Do I need more examples to illustrate any causes or effects? What types of examples would be helpful?

Use feedback from your peers to make further revisions of your draft.

10.5 Editing and Proofreading

Before you create your final draft, correct errors in spelling, punctuation, and grammar.

Focusing on Sentence Clarity

To ensure that your sentences are clear, check that the subjects agree with the verbs, that modifiers are properly placed, and that your punctuation is correct.

- **Subject-Verb Agreement** Find the subject-verb combinations in each sentence, and make sure that you use the form of the verb that agrees with the subject.

- **Punctuation** Check to make sure that you have the right punctuation in the right places. Pay close attention to opening punctuation, such as parentheses or quotation marks, and make sure that each is followed by the related closing punctuation.

- **Placement of Modifiers** In most cases, adverbs and adjectives should be placed next to the words they modify. Check your essay, and make corrections where necessary.

⊚ Technology Tip

If you are using the spell-check function on a computer, enter frequently used proper names in the custom dictionary. This way, the correctly spelled name will not be identified as a misspelled word.

Grammar in Your Writing
Placement of Adverbs

Adverbs modify verbs, adjectives, or other adverbs. The placement of adverbs can change the meaning of a sentence. In the following sentences, the location of the adverbs *only* and *usually* affects the meaning.

She learned **only** yesterday that she was hired.
She learned yesterday that **only** she was hired.

She was **usually** cheerful on Monday mornings but not on Tuesdays.
She was cheerful on Monday mornings but **usually** not on Tuesdays.

Find It in Your Reading Rewrite this sentence from "Murderous Mitch" by moving the adverb *just*. Explain how the meaning is altered.

It was "a terrible, towering wall that just fell out of the clouds."

Find It in Your Writing Check all of the adverbs in your essay to make sure that they are placed in a way that makes your intended meaning clear.

Editing and Proofreading

1. Have students use one color to mark the subject and verb in each sentence. They should be especially alert for compound subjects and/or verbs.

2. Students can use another color to mark adjectives and adverbs. Then they can locate the words they modify and move some modifiers if necessary.

Grammar in Your Writing: Placement of Adverbs

Even when the placement of an adverb does not affect the meaning of a sentence, it should be next to or near the word it modifies. Here is a common example of an adverb that is too far away from the verb: *Have students <u>read</u> James Thurber's humorous story "The Secret Life of Walter Mitty" <u>aloud</u>.* The sentence would be greatly improved if it read, *Have students read aloud . . .*

⏱ TIME AND RESOURCE MANAGER

Resources
Print: Scoring Rubrics on Transparency, Chapter 10; Writing Assessment: Scoring Rubric and Scoring Model for Cause-and-Effect Essay

In-Depth Coverage	Accelerated Pace
• Cover pp. 217–221 in class. • Review p. 217 in class, including Grammar in Your Writing. • Have students edit and proofread their essays in class. • Review Rubric for Self-Assessment in class. • Students present their final drafts.	• Assign pp. 217–221 for independent review. • Have students independently edit and proofread their essays. • Respond to individual editing issues as needed.

Publishing and Presenting

1. Ask students to think back to the audience they identified for their essay. Help them think of ways to present their essays to that audience, either in person or via mail or e-mail.

2. Have students complete the Reflecting on Your Writing exercise and encourage volunteers to share their reflections with the class.

3. Have students use the rubric to self-assess their cause-and-effect essay.

Assessment

Teaching Resources: Scoring Rubrics on Transparency 9; Formal Assessment, Chapter 9

1. Display the Scoring Rubric transparency and review the criteria in class.

2. Before students proceed with self-assessment, you may wish to review the Final Draft of the Student Work in Progress on pages 219–221. Have students score the Final Draft in one or more of the rubric categories. For example, how would students score the piece in terms of audience and purpose?

3. In addition to student self-assessment, you may wish to use the following assessment options.

   • Score student essays yourself, using the rubric and scoring models from Writing Assessment.

   • Review the Standardized Test Preparation Workshop on pages 226–227 and have students respond to a writing prompt within a time limit.

   • Administer the Chapter 9 Test from Formal Assessment in Teaching Resources to assess students' grasp of concepts presented.

10.6 Publishing and Presenting

Building Your Portfolio

Once you've completed your final draft, think about the best ways to share it with others. Consider these ideas:

1. **Post It on the Web** If your school has its own Web site, consider using it to publish your complete essay. Another possibility is to search the Web for sites related to your topic. See if one of these sites would be interested in posting your essay.

2. **Create a Class Anthology** Others in your school—including students studying how to write cause-and-effect essays—might benefit from a class anthology of cause-and-effect essays. Work with classmates to assemble your essays into a booklet: design a cover; prepare a title page, and table of contents; and choose illustrations.

Reflecting on Your Writing

Take some time to reflect on the experience of writing your essay by answering these questions:

• What would you say are the most effective ways to establish cause and effect?

• Which process skill will help you most in future writing?

Internet Tip

To see model essays scored with this rubric, go to **www.phwg. phschool.com**

Rubric for Self-Assessment

Use these criteria to evaluate your cause-and effect-essay.

	Score 4	Score 3	Score 2	Score 1
Audience and Purpose	Consistently targets an audience through word choice and details; clearly identifies purpose in thesis statement	Targets an audience through most word choice and details; identifies purpose in thesis statement	Misses a target audience by including a wide range of word choice and details; presents no clear purpose	Addresses no specific audience or purpose
Organization	Presents a clear, consistent organizational strategy to show cause and effect	Presents a clear organizational strategy with occasional inconsistencies; shows cause and effect	Presents an inconsistent organizational strategy; creates illogical presentation of causes and effects	Demonstrates a lack of organizational strategy; creates a confusing presentation
Elaboration	Successfully links causes with effects; fully elaborates connections among ideas	Links causes with effects; elaborates connections among most ideas	Links some causes with some effects; elaborates connections among most ideas	Develops and elaborates no links between causes and effects
Use of Language	Chooses clear transitions to convey ideas; presents very few mechanical errors	Chooses transitions to convey ideas; presents few mechanical errors	Misses some opportunities for transitions to convey ideas; presents many mechanical errors	Demonstrates poor use of language; presents many mechanical errors

218 • Cause-and-Effect Essay

☑ ONGOING ASSESSMENT: Assess Mastery

Use one of the following options to assess final drafts of students' cause and effect essays.

Self-Assessment Ask students to score their essay using the rubric provided. Then have students write a paragraph reflecting on the most valuable thing they learned in completing this essay.	**Teacher Assessment** You may want to use the rubric and scoring models provided in the Writing Assessment, Cause-and-Effect Essay, to score the cause and effect essays.

10.7 Student Work
IN PROGRESS

FINAL DRAFT

◀ Critical Viewing
In what ways do friendship and laughter make your daily experiences more pleasant? [Connect]

The Music of the Soul

Sonia Reimann
Athens High School
Athens, Texas

One year at the State Fair of Texas, I received a free sample of chocolate. Inside the wrapper, there was a brief note: "Take time to laugh; it's the music of the soul." I hung this chocolate wrapper on a bulletin board above the bed in my room where it remains today. As I scurry through my busy life, sometimes I briefly glance up at

To capture her reader's attention, Sonia begins her essay with a vivid description of an event in her life. She also uses the paragraph to state her thesis.

Critical Viewing
Connect Students may say that they help to ease the stress in our lives.

Step-by-Step Teaching Guide

Teaching from the Final Draft

1. Read aloud Sonia's final draft or have volunteers read it.

2. Point out the strength of Sonia's opening two paragraphs. First, she states her thesis clearly. It comes with the added bonus— the colorful detail that it was included in a free sample of chocolate. Next, Sonia provides an example in the paragraph about her friend Krystle. Note also the use of a dash and short direct quotes to vary the sentence structure and rhythm.

continued

219

3. Review how Sonia follows the lighthearted example of Krystle with the more serious example of her Swiss relatives and the death of Martin. Note the cause and effect relationship she establishes using her thesis statement as a counterweight against the tragedy of Martin's death.

continued

10.7

the note and reflect on this message. When you stop to think about it, the powerful effects of laughter might surprise you.

Laughter is a symbol that can instantly join people and solidify friendships. I became a friend of a girl named Krystle not because she possessed the qualities of honesty, reliability, and kindness that I normally seek in friends, but because she had an even rarer quality—she could make me laugh. One day she and I were walking in the mall, window-shopping and running out of conversation. At that point of our friendship, I wasn't sure whether we would be good friends. Suddenly, I saw her picking up a plastic ball in a toy store, dribbling the ball across the floor, and saying, "Come on. Let's play catch!" No one else may have seen the humor in this incident, but I could not control my laughter. Krystle's ability to make me laugh is what makes her special to me. We've been close friends ever since. In this case, laughter cemented a friendship.

Laughter can break the tension of some very serious moments. My immediate family and I live in Texas, but the rest of my relatives live in Switzerland, so I hardly ever get a chance to see them. On one specific occasion when I was ending a visit to Switzerland, I was saying goodbye to my cousin Martin and his family. My aunt gave me a big hug, and the sadness began to build. Next was Martin, and the tears in my eyes threatened to burst out at any moment. But Martin did something that made me burst with laughter, not tears. He pulled a huge polka-dot handkerchief out of his pocket and began dabbing my eyes. Adding laughter changed the scene completely. Martin did things like this all the time—making the unexpected joke, pointing out the ridiculous while everyone else saw the serious, creating laughter where there was none.

Later, tragedy struck. Martin died last May, unexpectedly, at the youthful age of twenty-two. We used his trademark laughter so that we could get through the pain of this terrible loss. I remember my father telling us about his death. My sisters, my mother, and I were weeping. It was a painful moment filled with sorrow. After a short time, however, I thought about Martin's laughter. Because I began remembering the powerful effect Martin's laughter had on me, I started talking about all the crazy things he had said and done. We all began to laugh. My family joined in with more stories about Martin, and, in this way, a sorrowful scene became an on-the-spot, uplifting remembrance of Martin's unique personality.

220 • Cause-and-Effect Essay

In this paragraph, Sonia uses an adaptation of the TRI format. Here, she states her topic, provides an illustration, and then restates her main idea. The paragraph, therefore, follows the TIR format.

In each of the body paragraphs, Sonia uses a chronological order to express the relationship of cause and effect.

Sonia shows how Martin's laughter and sense of fun helped his family accept the tragedy. She develops this cause-and-effect connection with details from shared experiences.

Besides changing the tone of some awkward moments, laughter can lighten the mood of a stressful and ordinary day. Some days, I come home from school feeling the pressure of homework or tests or even papers looming on the school horizon. I know many adults get caught up in the same kind of thinking; they may spend free moments thinking about money troubles or work troubles or just hoping to pull themselves out of exhaustion. This mindset doesn't correct itself easily, either. To help myself turn it around, I visit my neighbor. Her children are young and adorable. When I watch her one-year-old laughing over the repetition of climbing in and out of a toy tunnel, I realize that dwelling on my own troubles may not be the right focus. Laughing with children makes me remember what it was like being younger myself. A child's special gifts, curiosity and playfulness, often make me laugh regardless of my previous mood. Maybe this is why the laughter of a child is the most beautiful sound in the world.

You may not always take the time to laugh, but when you take a moment to stop and reflect, you will probably see that humor can help you to cope with many difficult situations, such as major exams, first dates, or even the loss of a loved one. So my chocolate fortune proves truer than I may have previously thought. In the end, there is nothing like a good laugh.

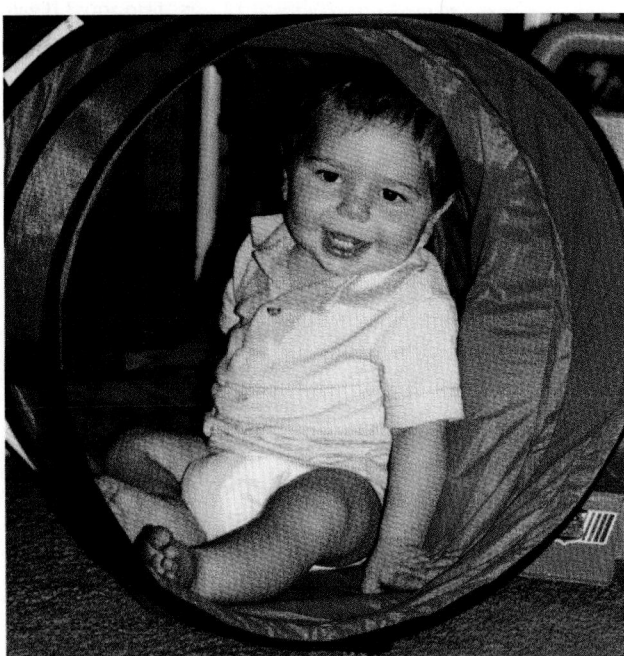

In this paragraph, Sonia discusses laughter's power to reduce stress.

Sonia wraps up her essay by restating her thesis and providing a list of familiar events that broadens her discussion of the effects of laughter.

◀ Critical Viewing
Does your first response to this picture support or refute Sonia's ideas?
[Connect]

4. Point out how well Sonia reinforces her thesis statement with her closing.

5. Ask students for their overall opinion of the essay. Elicit that the thesis statement and two extended examples of Krystle and Martin are excellent illustrations of the point and, additionally, contrast with each other.

6. Ask students to analyze the next-to-last paragraph (the example of laughter and small children). Does it work as well as the previous two examples? One could argue that it is a more clichéd observation, but whether it works depends on the reader.

Critical Viewing

Connect Most students will say that their response supports Sonia's ideas.

Connected Assignment
Documentary

Sometimes, the most effective way to show a cause-and-effect relationship is through pictures. Filmmakers create documentaries to bring these relationships to life for viewers. A **documentary** is a film that contains factual information about a specific topic or person. Like other planned media, documentaries start with a script containing stage and camera directions, prop and setting information, and spoken dialogue. Look at this example, noting the convention for including directions and narration:

▲ **Critical Viewing**
In what ways would a photograph like this one improve a documentary about field trips? **[Evaluate]**

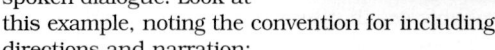

MODEL

[Footage of students on a large ship for field day.]

NARRATOR (Voice-Over): The excitement these children are feeling is obvious, but the learning that's occurring is what might surprise you. . . .

[WIDE SHOT of the same students back in the classroom.]

TEACHER: We find that field trips are an invaluable part of our learning. When we return from a trip, we process our experiences through discussions, study, journal writing, projects, and essay writing. . . .

[PHASE INTO a chart showing test scores.]

NARRATOR (Voice-Over): The rise in test scores is enough to convince administrators that field trips will continue to be a key part of the school curriculum.

Use the writing process steps suggested here to write a documentary script about a topic that interests you.

Prewriting To be sure you are inspired by your topic, choose a subject you'd like to study. Think about recent events in the news, changes at your school, or the life of a well-known person. Look for a topic that is suited to a cause-and-effect treatment.

Research your topic by conducting interviews, reading letters, or locating additional documents that can give you insight into the subject. Organize your findings to emphasize cause and effect. You can map out these links on a cause-and-effect chart like the one shown here, adding boxes for additional causes or effects as necessary. In each box, list the video or images you'll include, and note a few vivid adjectives about the mood its content suggests.

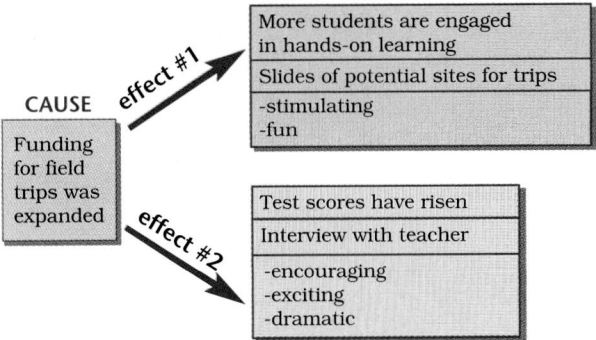

Drafting Review the format used for television or film scripts, and follow conventions for stage directions and dialogue. Draft your script in the sequence you will want to show it, using stage directions to indicate the visuals you will use. Consider these tips:

- Use narration to tie the many visual images together.

- Include cause-and-effect transition words and phrases, such as *because*, *therefore*, and *as a result*.

- Choose visual images that will emphasize the cause-and-effect link and generate the emotional responses you desire from viewers.

Revising and Editing Read your script aloud as another classmate displays each visual. Note the spots where the cause-and-effect links are unclear, where evidence seems weak, or where a section is too long. After this rehearsal, make the necessary changes.

Publishing When your script is complete, videotape your documentary. Before investing too much time, check that the equipment you are using works. When you've finished videotaping, present the documentary to your entire class.

Learn More

For more on video-taping techniques, see Media and Technology Skills on page 277.

Customize for
Less Advanced Students

You might organize students in cooperative groups and help them divide up the tasks of this assignment. Some students can research, while others write dialogue. Students with strong visual skills can plan staging and develop props or sets. Students can take turns narrating or assign a single particularly articulate student to this task.

Customize for
Logical/Mathematical Learners

Assign these students to the technical crew. Invite them to circulate among their peers, fielding questions about the technical aspects of documentary production. Remind students to answer questions in layman's language.

Lesson Objectives

1. To evaluate artistic performances in media presentations.

2. To analyze ideas as represented in various media.

3. To recognize how visual and sound techniques convey messages in media.

4. To test media impact and analyze the response, using data-gathering techniques.

5. To write a commentary on a political cartoon.

Step-by-Step Teaching Guide

Commedia dell'Arte

1. Choose one of the Spotlight elements for class discussion, or have students work individually or in groups on the element of their choice. Give students the initiative to find the necessary books, videotapes, and cartoons.

2. Interested students may research to find examples of Commedia dell'Arte performances and roles in both Roman and Renaissance times. Invite them to focus on the humor, the characters, or the staging.

3. Show scenes from at least two Marx Brothers films. Ask students to develop and then administer a rating form that asks viewers to identify influences of Commedia dell'Arte in the scenes.

4. Have students gather examples of contemporary political cartoons. (You may want to provide careful guidance on the sources for these.) Then display some examples of Daumier's cartoons. Discuss similarities and differences.

5. Ask students to suggest popular contemporary comedians whose work reflects influences of the artists discussed in this Spotlight.

Spotlight on the Humanities

Examining Styles of Art Across Cultures

Focus on Theater: Commedia dell'Arte

In the art world, one artist's work can influence the work of many future artists. For example, commedia dell'arte still has influence on today's comedy. With roots dating back to 62 B.C. in Rome, commedia dell'arte was a form of theater that emerged around 1545 in Italy during the Renaissance. Mime, improvised dialogue, acrobatics, and tumbling were all part of this theater form that soon spread throughout Europe. Commedia dell'arte consisted of four principal players who wore masks: Pantalone, Dottore, Harlequin, and Brighella. Each principal character had a specific costume and position, and the performers used jokes, slapstick, and satire to entertain their audience. The four principal players were surrounded by supporting characters who acted within several stock scenarios.

Film Connection The satirical and comic antics of the four principal players of the commedia dell'arte eventually led to the development of vaudeville and later found expression in the work of groups like the legendary Marx Brothers. In 1924, the Marx Brothers began doing musical revues and by 1929 they were making feature films. Their wisecracking, satirical humor led the group to make such films as *Animal Crackers* (1930), *Duck Soup* (1933), and *A Night at the Opera* (1935).

Art Connection Through satirical observations and emphasis on the middle class, French lithographer Honoré Daumier (1808–1879) brought to printmaking what commedia dell'arte brought to the theater. Lithography was invented in Germany in 1798, and Daumier became an early champion of this art form. He was one of the top caricaturists of the nineteenth century, targeting mostly politicians and lawyers in his work.

Cause-and-Effect Writing Activity: The Power of Satire
Today's popular comedians often rely on satire to make a point about a political candidate or public event. Find a political cartoon, and explain how you think its comedy might influence political figures and their actions.

▲ **Critical Viewing**
What elements of costume and expression make this photograph of the Marx Brothers funny? **[Respond]**

Viewing and Representing

Activity Give students the opportunity to create their own political cartoon commenting on a current issue. If you wish, assist them in sending their cartoon to an appropriate audience.

Critical Viewing

Respond Students may say that the open mouths and rolled up eyes add humor to the photograph, along with the hats and baggy coat.

Media and Technology Skills

Analyzing Special-Effects Technology
Activity: Compare Special Effects in Movies

It's almost impossible to go to a contemporary major Hollywood film today without seeing special-effects technology at work—and not only in the usual hungry dinosaurs, menacing asteroids, or quirky space aliens. Instead, you can see the results of technology in computer-generated rainstorms, animated gobs of sticky goo, and talking toys.

Think About It The latest installment of a blockbuster space adventure featured so many computer-generated creatures that many critics began to wonder whether virtual characters might eventually displace real people in feature films. Others worry that the core skills of storytelling—development of plot, character, and theme—are drowning in a tidal wave of spectacular audiovisual effects that dazzle the eye and ear but barely touch the mind.

Watch It In the theater or on a VCR, watch two major Hollywood movies released in the last five years. Choose one action-adventure or science-fiction film and one drama or comedy. As you watch each film, keep a log of any special effects—audio or visual—that you notice. Use a chart like the one shown here:

Special Effects Used	Film A	Film B
Music		
Digital sound technology		
Sound effects		
Computer-generated scenes		
Computer-generated characters		
Animation		
Editing		
Color alteration		

Analyze and Evaluate It Compare the use of special effects in the two films. Note which film used more special effects and which one used them more effectively. Then, make a full evaluation of each film by deciding which was stronger in the basic elements of storytelling and which left a more lasting impression on you.

Media and Technology Skills • 225

Special Effects in Movies

- Music
- Digital sound technology
- Sound effects
- Computer-generated backgrounds and events
- Computer-generated creatures and characters
- Animation
- Editing
- Color alteration

Lesson Objectives

1. To describe how meanings are communicated through elements of design.
2. To recognize how visual and sound techniques or design convey messages.
3. To examine the effect of media on one's perception of reality.

Step-by-Step Teaching Guide

Analyzing Special Effects

Teaching Resources: Writing Support Transparency 10-I; Writing Support Activity Book 10-3

1. Enjoy a class discussion about students' favorite movie special effects. Challenge students to explain how the effects were created.
2. Review the Special Effects in Movies list and ask students to match these categories to the examples discussed in Step 1.
3. Before students watch their films, confirm that they understand and can identify examples of each type of special effect.
4. Using the examples students supplied in Step 1 and the transparency, walk students through the special effects chart.
5. Give students copies of the blank organizer to take notes as they view the films. After viewing, pair students to confirm accurate analysis of the special effects types and discuss reactions to story elements.

Customize for
Verbal/Linguistic Learners

Remind students to focus their evaluations on story telling elements, not on the quality of the special effects. They should note the special effects as they view but need not rate these.

225

1. To write in a style appropriate to audience and purpose.
2. To use prewriting strategies to generate ideas and develop voice.
3. To develop and revise drafts by organizing content and refining style.

Step-by-Step Teaching Guide

Cause-and-Effect Writing Prompts

1. Review the bulleted criteria with students. Emphasize the importance of internalizing these criteria and explain they are fairly standard criteria that can be applied to most writing prompts. Test-takers who address these criteria have an increased chance of success.

2. Urge students to use graphic organizers efficiently when prewriting, jotting down only brief words or phrases.

3. Discuss with students the role of quick decision-making when writing for tests. For example, students may need to choose an organization for material. Several options may be appropriate but students should not waste time debating. A brief mental review of each organization is sufficient. Test examiners will evaluate how well the *chosen* organization was developed.

4. Remind students that neatness does count, but that they should never waste valuable content time. Urge them to be realistic about how perfectly neat a timed essay can be.

5. Provide regular practice with timed writing so that students gain comfort.

Standardized Test Preparation Workshop

Using Cause-and-Effect Skills to Respond to Writing Prompts

Some writing prompts on standardized tests measure your ability to show the relationships between causes and their effects. Your writing will be evaluated according to your ability to do the following:

- Respond directly to the prompt.
- Make your writing thoughtful and interesting.
- Organize ideas so they are clear and easy to follow.
- Develop your ideas thoroughly by using appropriate details and precise language.
- Write a focused response in which each sentence contributes to your composition as a whole.
- Communicate effectively by using the proper conventions of language, including spelling, capitalization, punctuation, grammar, and usage.

When writing for a timed test, plan to devote a specified amount of time to prewriting, drafting, revising, and proofreading.

The following is an example of one type of writing prompt you might find on a standardized test. Use the suggestions on the following page to help you respond. The clocks next to each stage show a suggested amount of time to devote to each stage.

Test Tips

- When writing about plot, be careful not to retell the story instead of responding to the prompt.
- Be aware of the specific audience you are asked to address. You may need to define specific terms or explain complex concepts that would be unfamiliar to your readers.

Sample Prompt

William Shakespeare's famous play *The Tragedy of Romeo and Juliet* traces the chain of events that leads to tragedy. What actions and factors cause a fatal conflict? In a letter aimed at the character of your choice, select a single important cause. Using details to support your answer, explain how this cause influences the character's behaviors, thoughts, and actions and eventually leads to the tragic ending of the play.

226 • Cause-and-Effect Essay

🔶 TEST-TAKING TIP

Well-chosen supporting detail is a critical element of a successful written test response. Time is limited so no effort should be wasted on gathering or explaining information that is not directly pertinent to the prompt. Direct students to the prompt language for guidance on necessary details. They might want to mark the words that indicate the kind of support required. Ask students to identify key words in the sample prompt that state or imply the types of supporting material required. What kind of details are required to answer this prompt?

Sample prompt: chain of events, leads to, actions lead to, single important cause, cause influences

Details should be events, actions, emotions, etc. that *influence* plot.

Prewriting

Allow close to one quarter of your time for prewriting.

Create an Audience Profile When writing for a test, address the audience named in the prompt. This prompt requires you to choose a specific character from the play. Take a few minutes to complete an audience profile for the character of your choice. Consider what this character knows about the actions of the play, what level of formality may be necessary, and what details will most effectively appeal to your reader. Use the profile to keep your audience in mind as you draft.

Use a Cause-and-Effect Organizer Using a cause-and-effect organizer, gather details for your response. List your topic in the center, causes above it, and effects below it. You can see an example of a cause-and-effect organizer on page 209.

Drafting

Allow almost half of your time for drafting.

Choose an Organization When writing a cause-and-effect essay, choose an appropriate organization, such as *chronological order* or *order of importance.*
When using chronological order, arrange details in the order that they happened. When using order of importance organization, list details from least to most important or most to least important.

Elaborate Using the Reporter's Formula Show how the cause you identified had deadly consequences. As you draft, include specifics that will help your reader understand your points. Be sure each point is developed enough to answer the five *W* questions: *Who? What? Where? When?* and *Why?*

Connect Ideas Use transitional words that indicate the logical connections between ideas. For example, the phrases *as a result* and *consequently* show relationships between causes and effects.

Revising, Editing, and Proofreading

Allow almost one quarter of your time to revise and edit. Use the last few minutes to proofread your work.

Make Corrections Review your response for errors. Delete any details that do not support your purpose or are inappropriate for your audience. Eliminate language that is vague, and replace it with precise, strong words.

Proofread Your Response Read your response to check for errors in spelling, grammar, and punctuation. When making changes. draw a line through text that you want to eliminate. Use a caret [^] to indicate the places you want to insert words.

Customize for
Less Advanced Students

For those students who may find timed writing anxiety-producing, you may want to begin with writing assignments they have already addressed in untimed situations.

Customize for
ESL Students

Talk with students about cause-and-effect prompts as a category. Use simple physical examples such as dropping a book to create noise to clarify cause and effect. Discuss and familiarize students with cause-and-effect signal words. This will help them recognize and understand the general goals of cause-and-effect prompts—even if they are struggling with the prompt's remaining vocabulary.

In-Depth Lesson Plan

	LESSON FOCUS	PRINT AND MEDIA RESOURCES
DAY 1	**Introduction to Problem-and-Solution Essays** Students learn key elements of problem-and-solution essays and analyze the Model From Literature (pp. 228–231).	*Writers at Work* **Videotape,** Exposition *Writing Lab* **CD-ROM,** Exposition
DAY 2	**Prewriting** Students choose and narrow a topic, consider their audience and purpose, and gather information (pp. 232–235).	**Teaching Resources** *Writing Support Transparencies,* 11-A–D; *Writing Support Activity Book,* 11-1–2
DAY 3	**Drafting** Students organize their ideas and write their first drafts (pp. 236–237).	**Teaching Resources** *Writing Support Transparency,* 11-E
DAY 4	**Revising** Students revise their drafts in terms of overall structure, paragraphs, sentences, and word choice (pp. 238–240).	**Teaching Resources** *Writing Support Transparencies,* 11-F–G; *Writing Support Activity Book,* 9-2
DAY 5	**Editing and Proofreading; Publishing and Presenting** Students check their work for accuracy and correctness and present their final drafts (pp. 241–244).	**Teaching Resources** *Scoring Rubrics on Transparency,* Chapter 11; *Formal Assessment,* Ch. 11

Accelerated Lesson Plan

	LESSON FOCUS	PRINT AND MEDIA RESOURCES
DAY 1	**Drafting** Students review characteristics for problem-and-solution essay writing, select topics, and write drafts (pp. 228–237).	*Writers at Work* **Videotape,** Exposition *Writing Lab* **CD-ROM,** Exposition **Teaching Resources** *Writing Support Transparencies,* 11-A-E; *Writing Support Activity Book,* 11-1–2
DAY 2	**Revising to Presenting** Students work individually or with peers to revise, edit, and proofread their work for presentation (pp. 238–244).	**Teaching Resources** *Writing Support Transparencies,* 11-F–G; *Scoring Rubrics on Transparency,* Chapter 11; *Formal Assessment,* Ch. 11

Options for Adapting Lesson Plans

HOMEWORK

Have students complete any stage of the lesson for homework.

TECHNOLOGY

Students can complete any stage of the lesson on computer. Have them print out their completed work.

FEATURES

Extend coverage with Connected Assignment (p. 245), Spotlight on the Humanities (p. 246), Media and Technology Skills (p. 247), and the Standardized Test Preparation Workshop (pp. 248–249).

INTEGRATED SKILLS COVERAGE

Integrating Grammar
Creating Complex Sentences, SE p. 239
Punctuating Compound Sentences, SE p. 241

Reading/Writing Connection
Reading Strategy, SE p. 230
Writing Application, SE p. 231

Speaking and Listening
Integrating Speaking Skills ATE p. 241

Workplace Skills
Integrating Workplace Skills ATE pp. 229, 231

Real-World Connection
ATE p. 244

Viewing and Representing
Critical Viewing, SE pp. 228, 230, 243, 245, 246

ASSESSMENT SUPPORT

Standardized Test Preparation SE p. 248; ATE p. 240

Texas Test Preparation Workshop, pp. 21–22

Scoring Rubrics on Transparency, Ch. 11

Formal Assessment, Ch. 11

Writing Assessment and Portfolio Management

MEETING INDIVIDUAL NEEDS

Less Advanced Students ATE pp. 236, 249; See also Ongoing
Assessments ATE pp. 231, 233, 237, 239, 242

More Advanced Students ATE p. 237

ESL Students ATE p. 234

BLOCK SCHEDULING

Pacing Suggestions
For 90-minute Blocks
• Have students complete the Prewriting and Drafting stages in a single period.
• Focus one class period on Revising and Editing and Publishing and Presenting. Allow at least 30 minutes for peer revision.

Resources for Varying Instruction
• *Writing Lab* CD-ROM If your students have access to hardware, a 90-minute block provides an ideal opportunity for students to work on computer.
• *Writers at Work* Videotape Show the Exposition segment in class.

Professional Development Support
• *How to Manage Instruction in the Block* This Teaching Resource provides management and activity suggestions.

MEDIA AND TECHNOLOGY

For the Student
• *Writing Lab* CD-ROM, Exposition

For the Teacher
• *Writers at Work* Videotape, Exposition
• *Resource Pro* CD-ROM

WRITING AND GRAMMAR WEBSITE

The Interactive Writing and Grammar Website provides a wide array of support for students, teachers, and parents. Writing support includes:

• Interactive revision checkers
• Scoring rubrics with complete models

phwg.phschool.com

LITERATURE CONNECTIONS

Related selections from *Prentice Hall Literature: Timeless Voices, Timeless Themes,* Gold:

"Go Deep to the Sewer," Bill Cosby, SE p. 231

"Checkouts," Cynthia Rylant, SE p. 233

Lesson Objectives

1. To write a problem-and-solution essay using effective word choice and structure, with a clear thesis and adequate support.

2. To write in a style appropriate to audience and purpose.

3. To identify and organize support to ensure coherence.

4. To use prewriting strategies to generate and refine topics.

5. To develop drafts by reorganizing content to suit audience and purpose.

6. To draft and proofread an essay for appropriateness of organization.

7. To use technology to create, revise, edit, and publish.

8. To use writing to discover, organize and support what is known and needs to be known about a topic.

9. To use compound and complex sentences, and use appropriately punctuated independent and dependent clauses.

10. To produce an error-free essay in the final draft.

Critical Viewing

Analyze Students may say that, by definition, volunteers do not require wages. This ensures that the homes these volunteers build will be affordable to low-income families.

▲ **Critical Viewing**
How do volunteer groups that build low-cost housing provide a unique solution to a problem? **[Analyze]**

Problem-and-Solution Analysis in Everyday Life

During the course of a day, you encounter problem-and-solution analyses in many forms: On radio and television, newscasters report trouble around the world and then share the innovative ways people are working to fix them; advice columnists offer suggestions for problems ranging from grape-juice stains to bankruptcy; and bookstore shelves are full of books on managing time, improving memory, and living a healthier life. While some problems affect individuals and others affect whole communities or countries, each of these is an example of problem-and-solution thinking in action.

228 • Exposition

⏱ TIME AND RESOURCE MANAGER

Resources
Technology: Writers at Work videotape

In-Depth Coverage	Accelerated Pace
• Cover pp. 228–231 in class. • Show the Exposition section of the Writers at Work videotape. • Read literature excerpt (pp. 230–231) in class and use it to brainstorm problem-and-solution essay ideas with students. • Discuss examples of problem-and-solution essays you or students bring to class (advice columns, proposals, formal letters).	• Assign pp. 228–231 for independent student review. • Discuss definitions and types of problem-and-solution essays in class. • Assign Model From Literature for independent reading.

What Is a Problem-and-Solution Essay?

A **problem-and-solution essay** is a piece of writing that identifies and explains a problem and then offers a possible solution. An effective problem-and-solution essay includes

- a statement of a problem that is focused enough to be fully developed and supported in an essay.
- a suggested solution.
- facts, statistics, and details that illustrate the problem and how it can be solved.
- a logical organization.

To see the criteria on which your final problem-and-solution essay may be judged, preview the Rubric for Self-Assessment on page 242.

Types of Problem-and-Solution Writing

Solutions to problems can be presented in a variety of written formats. In addition to essays, the following types of writing can address problems and offer solutions:

- **Formal letters** are sometimes used to offer solutions to public problems. Usually, they are addressed to the person or group with the power to implement a solution.
- **Advice columns** offer solutions to specific problems faced by individuals.
- **Memos and proposals** are used to formally suggest solutions to problems faced by businesses or organizations.

Writers in ACTION

As a public radio journalist, Gene Bryant Johnson reports on the issues that trouble our times. He analyzes problems that face the country and reports on solutions people have undertaken. Johnson says solutions to most problems are within sight:

"The ideas . . . are all around you. Everything that happens in your neighborhood and in your community has a reason and it has an effect. So pay attention."

PREVIEW Student Work IN PROGRESS

In this chapter, you will follow the development of an essay by Michael C. Mahoney of St. Stephen's School in Hickory, North Carolina. He suggests a solution to the problems caused by increased traffic in his community. You will see how Michael used prewriting, drafting, and revising to develop his essay "Safety and Progress." At the end of this chapter, you can read Michael's completed draft.

PREPARE and ENGAGE

Interest GRABBER Ask students to imagine that they have the money and resources to solve any problem in the world. What problem would they choose to solve? What would they need to solve it?

Activate Prior Knowledge

Ask students to remember the last time they had a problem. As a whole class, discuss some of the problems students faced and how they solved them. Ask students to think about how effective their solution was and whether there were other ways they could have solved the problem. Would a different solution have led to a better result? Why or why not?

Integrating Workplace Skills

Ask students to name jobs that require problem-and-solution writing. Have them determine what types of writing these jobs might require. For example, a medical researcher might have to write a grant proposal in which he or she identifies a medical problem and a possible solution in order to get funding.

☑ ONGOING ASSESSMENT: Diagnose

Use one of the following options to diagnose students' current level of proficiency in problem-and-solution writing.

Option 1 Ask each student to select the strongest example of his or her problem-and-solution essay from last year. Hold conferences in which you review each student's sample. Use the conferences to determine which students will need extra support in developing skills for problem-and-solution writing.	**Option 2** Ask students to write an advice column. Have each student think of a problem common to his or her peers and write a solution for it. If students have difficulty completing this exercise, you will need to devote more time on the process of organizing and evaluating information.

Reading: Identify Support

After students read the first paragraph of Lessem's essay, ask them what they think his purpose is. (Most students will say to inform.) After they finish reading the essay, ask the same question. (to inform and to persuade)

Teaching from the Model

You can use this Model from Literature as one way to illustrate the many uses of the problem-and-solution essay. Ask students to guess, based on the title, what problem might be the focus of this essay. Point out that problem-and-solution essay topics might come from students' own lives or from subjects that are of particular interest to them. Ask when it might be useful to be able to write a problem-and-solution essay themselves.

Step-by-Step Teaching Guide

Engage Students Through Literature

1. Build background for the text by generating a classroom discussion about scientific research. Ask students how researchers learn about dinosaurs. How is such research paid for?

2. Ask students to read the essay one paragraph at a time, using the margin notes to focus their thinking. After each paragraph, ask students what aspects of the problem Lessem describes, or what examples he offers to help readers understand the problem.

3. Ask what solution Lessem proposes. Are students convinced that his solution is a good one? Why or why not?

4. Ask students to brainstorm for a list of other topics that they could use for a problem-and-solution essay.

11.1 Model From Literature

In the introduction to his book, scientist Don Lessem invites readers to educate themselves about one of the major problems faced by scientists who study dinosaurs—funding for research.

Reading Writing Connection

Reading Strategy: Identify Support The ideas a writer presents must be supported. In a problem-and-solution essay, the issues must be explained so that readers understand the situation. As you read, look for the facts that Lessem uses to support his position.

from *Dinosaurs Rediscovered*

Don Lessem

For all its splendid achievements, dinosaur science is in a parlous state. Cutbacks in the already modest government and private support for so-called "soft sciences" jeopardize the research, and the jobs, of several dinosaur researchers in a field of but a few dozen scientists. The difficulties of making a living as a paleontologist have discouraged many promising and committed young researchers, such as Jill Peterson, who found conditions so grim that she could make a better living as a schoolteacher.

Digging dinosaurs takes money. A single element of a dinosaur skeleton, a sauropod pelvis to take the most extreme example, can be six feet long, tons in weight. To dig it out, a crew has to be brought to a field site, most likely in a spot that is difficult to reach.

Reaching remote places is expensive. If and when paleontologists find something of scientific value in the short season that weather, finances, and university schedules allow, that something must be hauled to a laboratory. There, months, sometimes years, of labor by professional preparers are needed to free the fossil from its surrounding rock matrix. Most dinosaur researchers do their own preparation work in the winter, as few museums and universities can afford the paid help.

Lots of expenses, yes, but not huge sums. The total annual expenditure on dinosaur research in the United States and

230 • Problem-and-Solution Essay

▲ Critical Viewing According to the essay, what can make digging at field sites expensive? **[Analyze]**

In the opening paragraph, the writer introduces the problem: The costs of pursuing dinosaur science challenge the future of the field.

In three paragraphs, the writer proves the problem by outlining the costs of researching dinosaurs.

Critical Viewing

Analyze Students may say that large crews must be transported to the site and paid to dig out rocks containing fossils. Then professional preparers are hired to free the fossils from the rocks.

Canada combined is scarcely $600,000, by Peter Dodson's 1989 estimate. And that is quadruple the figure from a 1980 study by Canadian paleontologist Dale Russell.

That a realm of scientific endeavor should be so woefully underfunded is disgraceful, even if typical for many of the low-tech disciplines. Why do dinosaurs matter? As the most successful animals in the history of life on land, they offer particular insights into modes and pace of evolution. For the young they are a special case of fantasy turned safely real, and in that reality a uniquely appealing introduction to scientific inquiry. For me and many of us, dinosaurs and dinosaur explorations are a source of wonderment and pleasure. They are as important as any endeavor to understand the world as it once was.

But there is a special, shameful irony about the lack of money for dinosaur research, for Dinomania is all around us. Dinosaurs have lately graced, to use the term lightly, toilet paper, ravioli, checkers, and innumerable T-shirts. They are the subjects of prime-time TV shows, documentaries, feature films, Saturday morning cartoons. . . .

Much of this dino-merchandise features inaccurate images of dinosaurs, such as the British Museum's plastic dinosaur replicas ("These are not toys," read their advertisements), which feature a sail-finned Dimetrodon, that creature of a far earlier age . . . than dinosaurs.

Unlike Ninja Turtles, dinosaurs aren't trademarked. They don't earn royalties and ancillary income from every tie-in that uses their name or their likeness. But those who made Dinomania possible, the scientists who supply the information that is used and abused so widely, could use a piece of the action and a chance to improve dinosaur products.

Along with many of the leading dinosaur scientists and artists, I've formed The Dinosaur Society, a nonprofit organization, to further dinosaur research and education. The Dinosaur Society funds international research projects and provides a timely, accurate source of information in the form of regular publications for children and adult members of our organization. All of us are volunteering our services, and several are donating a portion of their income from commercial endeavors to this effort.

 **Writing Application: Provide Support** As he outlined the problem in his essay, Don Lessem provided statistics, facts, and comparisons to support his ideas. For your essay to be most effective, include the necessary elaboration to explain your suggestion.

Statistics illustrate the extent of the problem.

The writer raises and answers a key question: Why do dinosaurs matter? Lessem elaborates on the scientific value of research.

To build the argument that dinosaur research and education is important, the writer makes an appeal to his audience: The public has a growing interest in dinosaurs and the information they are getting may be wrong.

The writer concludes with the solution he has put into action. His solution, an organization, calls attention to the financial and educational problems the essay has addressed. Lessem's book further develops this solution.

To see how a comedy writer implements the characteristics of problem-and-solution writing, read Bill Cosby's essay "Go Deep to the Sewer." You can find the essay in *Prentice Hall Literature: Timeless Voices, Timeless Themes,* Gold.

Model From Literature • 231

Integrating Workplace Skills

The author of this essay works with The Dinosaur Society as a volunteer. He uses this problem-and-solution essay to highlight a problem that exists in his work with dinosaurs: lack of funding. Tell students that people often use problem-and-solution writing in the workplace in the form of proposals and letters. The ability to solve problems and convince others that the solutions are good ones is an important skill in all jobs.

Responding to Literature

Ask students to evaluate how they think genre affects the way in which the characteristics of problem-and-solution writing are used.

☑ ONGOING ASSESSMENT: Monitor and Reinforce

After previewing the Model from Literature, you may anticipate some students may have difficulty with some proper names and other words. Use one of the following options.

Option 1 If students read the model independently, have them list any unfamiliar words they encounter. Then go over pronunciations and definitions as a class.	**Option 2** If you or a prepared student read the model aloud in class, take time to define unfamiliar words as they are encountered. Words such as *paleontologist, jeopardize,* and *ancillary* may need definition.

Prewriting

Step-by-Step Teaching Guide

Prewriting: Newspaper Scan

1. Have groups scan a variety of newspapers or news magazines to find possible essay topics. Have groups brainstorm for a list of possible topics.

2. Remind students that the problems they choose must have realistic solutions. There may be a solution to how to live on Mars, but no one—yet—knows what it is.

3. Create a list of potential topics on the chalkboard and evaluate student topics to determine whether they have possible solutions.

Step-by-Step Teaching Guide

Prewriting: Sentence Starters

Teaching Resources: Writing Support Transparency 11-A

1. Have students fill in the blanks in the sentence stubs shown as examples. Display the transparency and have students think of different endings for the stubs in the Student Work in Progress.

2. Ask students to look over their responses and choose the problem they identified that both interests them the most and that best meets the criteria for a problem-and-solution essay topic.

3. Ask students to freewrite for ten minutes on the topic they chose.

4. Have partners share their ideas to evaluate the viability of their topic. Instruct partners to try to decide whether the topic chosen is interesting, can be adequately explained, and has a realistic solution.

5. Encourage some pairs to share their topics with the class.

Choosing Your Topic

When you select a topic for a problem-and-solution essay, be sure to choose one for which you can offer a realistic solution.

Strategies for Generating Topics

1. **Newspaper Scan** Look through a newspaper for stories about community problems. List problems for which you can imagine a practical solution. Choose one as the topic of your essay.

2. **Sentence Starters** Using the sentence starters on this page, complete each sentence and jot down a few ideas to complete your thoughts. Then, review your writing to choose one of the problems as the topic for your essay.

One thing that really annoys me is ___?___.

The biggest problem people my age face is ___?___.

A problem I'd like to see solved in my town or city is ___?___.

Writing Lab CD-ROM

For more help finding a topic, explore the activities and suggestions in the Choosing a Topic section of the Exposition lesson.

Student Work
IN PROGRESS

Name: Michael C. Mahoney
St. Stephen's School
Hickory, NC

Using Sentence Starters

Michael used a sentence-starters exercise to find a problem-and-solution essay topic. After completing each sentence starter and talking with family members and neighbors, Michael decided to write his essay on the topic of sidewalks as an investment in community safety.

Life would be better in my community if . . . we recycled.

The biggest problem my town faces is . . . litter.

✓ Our neighborhood would be a better place to live if ~~everyone~~ . . . adults and children were safe from traffic.

A problem I'd like to solve in my school is . . . long lines in the cafeteria.

Most students would like to see a change in . . . the after-school activities offered.

⏱ TIME AND RESOURCE MANAGER

Resources
Print: Writing Support Transparency 11-A–D, Writing Support Activity Book 11-1–2
Technology: Writing Lab CD-ROM, Exposition

In-Depth Coverage	Accelerated Pace
• Cover pp. 232–235 in class. • Work through the Strategies for Generating Topics with the class (p. 232). • Use the Responding to Fine Art transparency to generate additional topics.	• In class, discuss how to create and choose a problem-and-solution essay topic. • Have students work independently to choose and narrow their topic. • Have partners focus on audience, purpose, and gathering details.

TOPIC BANK

If you have trouble coming up with a topic on your own, consider one of these suggestions:

1. **Essay on School Spirit** Take a look around your school for evidence of student interest in clubs, sports, and school pride. Use your school as the problem or the solution, and write an essay offering advice to any school suffering from a lack of school spirit.

2. **Essay on Recycling Participation** Most communities encourage residents to recycle. Some communities have laws requiring citizens to recycle because people might otherwise not take the trouble to do so. Write an essay in which you suggest a solution to the problem of a lack of participation in voluntary recycling.

Responding to Fine Art

3. While *Gust of Wind at Ejiri, in the Province of Suruga* shows one way to react to dangerous weather conditions, a more practical approach to rain, flood, or strong winds may be more successful. In an essay, advise others about preparing for dangerous weather.

Responding to Literature

4. Cynthia Rylant's story "Checkouts" tells of a girl who moves to another town. Read the story. Then, in a problem-and-solution essay, suggest methods for overcoming the loneliness such a move presents. You can find this story in *Prentice Hall Literature: Timeless Voices, Timeless Themes*, Gold.

Gust of Wind at Ejiri, in the province of Suruga. From the series The Thirty-six Views of Fuji, Hokusai, Metropolitan Museum of Art

☑ Cooperative Writing Opportunity

5. **Study-Habit Flyers** With a group, create flyers that provide solutions to common study-habit problems. Some group members can interview classmates to identify study problems, others can outline solutions, and others can organize and design the layout of the flyer.

Prewriting • 233

Step-by-Step Teaching Guide

Responding to Fine Art

Gust of Wind at Ejiri, in the Province of Suruga

Teaching Resources: Writing Support Transparency 11-B

1. Display the transparency and ask students what the artwork means to them.
2. Have groups brainstorm for possible problem-and-solution essay topics this piece of art brings to mind.
3. Ask students to put an asterisk next to the problems they have listed for which they can think of a realistic solution.
4. Have several groups share their answers with the class.

Responding to Literature

Cynthia Rylant's story is about a boy and a girl who fall in love at first sight, but never meet. As students read this story of missed opportunities, have them pay attention to the characters' problems and the solutions to these problems. The story may help students generate topics for their own essays.

Spotlight on the Humanities

For additional topic suggestions, refer students to Spotlight on the Humanities on page 246.

☑ **ONGOING ASSESSMENT: Monitor and Reinforce**

If you observe that some students are having difficulty coming up with a topic, use one of the following options.

Option 1 Suggest that students choose an idea from the Topic Bank. If many students have difficulty, work with the whole class on one idea selected from the Topic Bank or from ideas suggested by students.	**Option 2** If Topic Bank ideas seem too difficult, suggest that students try one of the assignments from the Topic Bank for Heterogeneous Classes in the Teaching Resources.

⏱ **TIME SAVERS!**

 **Writing Support Transparencies**
Use the transparencies for Chapter 11 to teach these strategies.

Prewriting: Narrowing Your Topic

Teaching Resources: Writing Support Transparency 11-C; Writing Support Activity Book 11-1

1. Ask students to choose a topic that is narrow enough to explain thoroughly.

2. Display the transparency and point out that the topic of environmental pollution is too broad. To illustrate this, ask students to think of other kinds of environmental pollution.

3. Explain that creating a target for their topic will help them to be sure they can adequately explain and develop support for it in their paper. Create a sample target on the chalkboard using an example such as drug abuse. Ask students to help you to narrow this topic. For example, students might say that they could focus on teen drug abuse, and then teen drug abuse in their community.

4. Hand out copies of the blank organizer. Ask students to focus their topics by answering one of the following questions: *What part of this topic affects me and my friends? What part of this topic interests me the most?*

Considering Your Audience and Purpose

1. Instruct students to think about the solutions they will propose for their problems. Ask students to jot down the answers to the questions, *Whom do I expect to act on my solution? Who has the ability to implement my suggestions?*

2. The answer to these questions reveals the essay's audience. The audience consists of the people students want to hear their message.

3. Ask students to answer some questions about their audience to help them determine how their audience will influence the choices they make in writing their essay.

11.2

Narrowing Your Topic

After you have selected a problem that needs attention, be sure that it is not too complicated to cover in your essay. Focus your topic so that you can propose realistic solutions. Completing a target diagram may help you narrow a topic.

Use a Target Diagram

Use a target diagram, like the one below, to narrow a broad topic. In the outer circle, write your general topic. Then, to narrow your topic, consider what part of your topic affects you. In the second circle, identify a single aspect of the broad topic. To complete the diagram, challenge yourself to write an even narrower topic in the center of the target.

NARROWING A TOPIC WITH A TARGET DIAGRAM

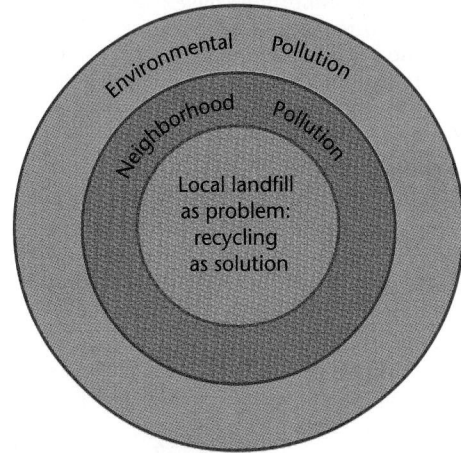

Environmental Pollution
Neighborhood Pollution
Local landfill as problem: recycling as solution

Considering Your Audience and Purpose

Identify Your Audience

When you write a problem-and-solution essay, keep a specific audience in mind: readers who have the ability to implement your suggestions. Use details and vocabulary that will appeal to that audience.

State Your Purpose

You may want to direct your readers to take action, change their behavior, or think about your topic in a new way. State your purpose in a single sentence, and use this purpose to direct your writing.

Writing Lab CD-ROM

To help you identify an audience and tailor your appeals for action, use the Audience Profile activity.

Customize for
ESL Students

Students from different countries or cultures may want to write about a problem that affects them directly. A good topic for them might be the problems of an "ESL kid." They probably have very useful and practical suggestions.

Gathering Details

Once you have identified your audience, gather the details that you'll need to write your problem-and-solution essay.

Analyzing the Problem Take the time to jot down information that will clarify the problem. Define the issue, explain why it happens, note who it affects, and collect any other information that will help readers see the trouble.

Seeing the Solution Before you write, gather as much information as you can about the solution you suggest. Note the costs involved, outline the steps that must be taken, consider complications that might arise, and note the benefits of your ideas.

Record Details on a T-Chart

To collect the information you'll need, complete a T-chart like the one shown here. For each solution you propose, write a benefit that will appeal to your audience.

Student Work
IN PROGRESS

Name: Michael C. Mahoney
St. Stephen's School
Hickory, NC

Gathering Details With a T-Chart

Michael used a T-chart to make sure he could show the benefits of each part of his suggested solution.

Problem: Wide Roads Are a Danger to Pedestrians, Bike Riders, and Children

SOLUTIONS	BENEFITS
Build sidewalks	Serve as buffer between families' yards and road
	Give pedestrians a safe place to walk
Add bike lanes	Promote safe bike traffic
	Enable bikers to travel in safety away from pedestrians
Install railings and dividers	Further ensure that traffic is kept at a safe distance

Prewriting • 235

Step-by-Step Teaching Guide

Prewriting: Record Details on a T-Chart

Teaching Resources: Writing Support Transparency 11-D; Writing Support Activity Book 11-2

1. Now that students have identified their audience and purpose, they can begin to determine the kinds of information they will need to include in their essays. Remind students to keep their audience and purpose in mind as they begin gathering details.

2. In their essays, students will need to provide a clear and detailed summary of the steps involved in their proposed solutions and an analysis of why each step is necessary.

3. Display the transparency and explain that this format provides a clear way to record and organize the details they will include in their essay.

4. Hand out copies of the blank organizer. Have students write the solutions they propose on the chart. Next, they can write why these solutions are beneficial.

5. Have partners share the information in their T-Charts. They should explain whom their intended audience is and why they think each of their solutions will appeal to that audience.

6. Encourage partners to give each other feedback about the effect they think their partner's identified benefits will have on the intended audience.

⏱ TIME SAVERS!

📄 **Writing Support Transparencies**
Use the transparencies for Chapter 11 to teach these strategies.

📖 **Writing Support Activity Book**
Use the graphic organizers for Chapter 11 to facilitate these strategies.

Drafting: Choose an Appropriate Organization

1. The way students organize their ideas in their problem and solution essay can help create audience interest and expectations.

2. Direct students' attention to the sample outline and discuss the logic reflected by the organization.

3. Ask students to write their own outline, including more specific details.

4. Instruct students to list the actions they think will be necessary to accomplish their solution.

5. Remind students that, as they develop their ideas, they may need to modify their outlines by adding or removing information.

Customize for
Less Advanced Students

Students may have difficulty "seeing" the organization of each approach. Encourage them to use a graphic organizer, such as a flow chart, to help them visualize the methods of organization.

11.3 Drafting

Shaping Your Writing

Your problem-and-solution essay must clearly identify and develop two ideas: It must establish the problem and develop a workable solution. To best address this unique form of expository writing, choose an organization that allows you to show the connection between the ideas.

Choose an Appropriate Organization

Review the two approaches presented below. Then, take a look at your prewriting work to decide on the best organization plan.

Point-by-Point Plan To show that your solution addresses a many-sided problem, use a point-by-point organization that explains each part of a problem and its solution in turn. Use this organization if you can break the problem you address into several components.

Point-by-Point Organization

Problem: High-school students have no time.
Solution: They should make an effort to change.

Problem 1: School workload has increased.
Solution 1: Students should set aside time each day.

Problem 2: They have too many commitments.
Solution 2: Setting priorities will help reduce commitments.

Block Plan A block plan allows you to develop the problem fully and then address your solution. This organization is especially useful if you want to outline the steps of your solution.

Block Organization

Problem: Teenagers often want more spending money than they have.
Solution: Get a handle on your finances.

Problem: A student's life can be expensive.
• movies and entertainment
• clothing
• food
Solution: Establish a plan for informed spending.
• make a budget
• find activities that are inexpensive

---

236 • Problem-and-Solution Essay

⏱ TIME AND RESOURCE MANAGER

Resources
Print: Writing Support Transparency 11-E
Technology: Writing Lab CD-ROM, Exposition

In-Depth Coverage	Accelerated Pace
• Cover pp. 236–237. • Work through the organization strategies with the entire class. • Have students write their own problem-and-solution essay draft in class. • Help provide elaboration through examples and anecdotes as they write.	• Have students review pp. 236–237 independently, then write their own problem-and-solution essay draft. • Respond to individual drafting issues as needed.

Providing Elaboration

Unless you are an expert yourself, your proposed solution will not make instant believers of your readers. You must demonstrate—with facts, statistics, examples, anecdotes, testimonials, or personal experiences—that your solution is both workable and likely to be the best one proposed. This may require some research on your part to locate data that will support your solution.

Using Examples and Anecdotes Depending on your topic, you can draw examples from case studies or personal experiences. Examples help your readers to see vivid and powerful depictions of the problem, as well as the proposed solution. Such examples can help you persuade your readers to agree with you.

Pointing to Supports Look for places where an example or anecdote would help you clarify your point or help persuade your readers. If you don't have such material available as you draft, indicate an idea in your draft. Later, go in search of these details, and add them to your essay.

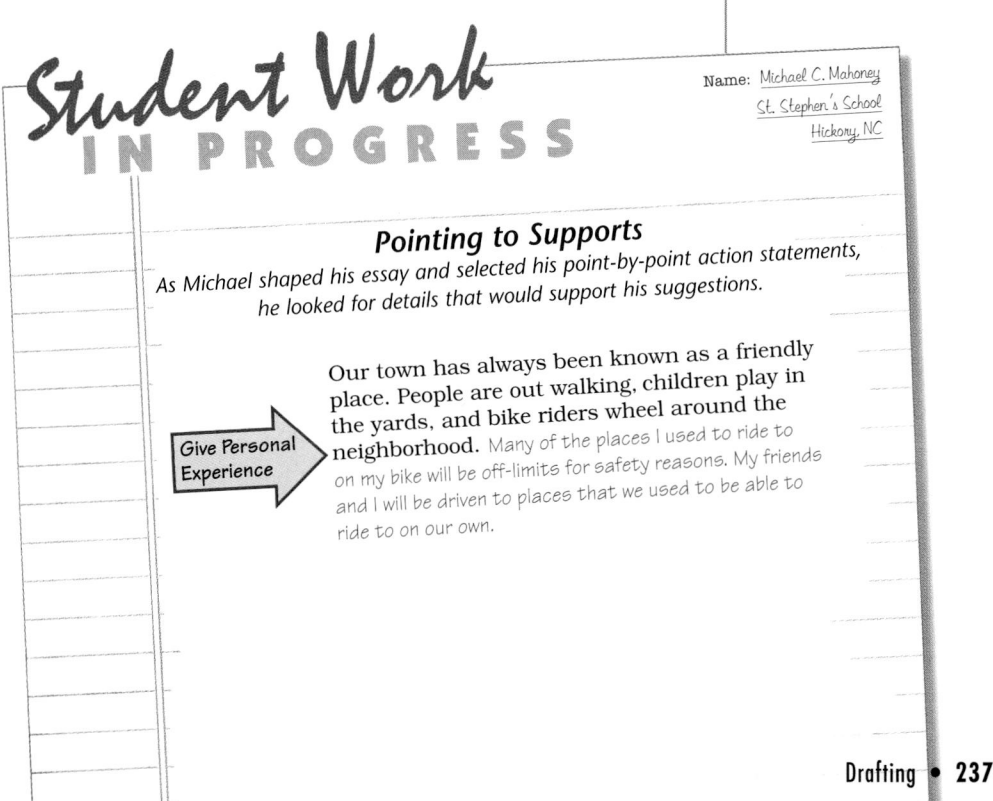

Student Work IN PROGRESS

Name: Michael C. Mahoney
St. Stephen's School
Hickory, NC

Pointing to Supports

As Michael shaped his essay and selected his point-by-point action statements, he looked for details that would support his suggestions.

Our town has always been known as a friendly place. People are out walking, children play in the yards, and bike riders wheel around the neighborhood.

Give Personal Experience → Many of the places I used to ride to on my bike will be off-limits for safety reasons. My friends and I will be driven to places that we used to be able to ride to on our own.

Drafting • 237

Drafting: Providing Elaboration

Teaching Resources: Writing Support Transparency 11-E

1. A successful problem-and-solution essay convinces the audience of the seriousness of the problem *and* the validity of the proposed solution(s). In order to accomplish this, students will need support.

2. Display the transparency. Point out that Michael has found ideas in his essay that he wants to support more adequately by providing specific examples.

3. Ask students how this additional support affects them as readers. (Students should say that the examples make the writer's ideas clearer and more convincing.)

4. Instruct students to read their own works in progress to identify places where they too need to add support for their ideas. Have students mark these places and indicate in the margins what kind of information—example, fact, or statistic—would best support the idea.

Customize for *More Advanced Students*

Advanced learners should be able to evaluate the effectiveness of the different kinds of support possible in a problem-and-solution essay. For example, they should be able to identify the advantages that facts and statistics can have over personal experiences. Encourage students to do library research on their topics and to provide more objective support for their proposed solutions.

📋 ONGOING ASSESSMENT: Monitor and Reinforce

Students often make the mistake of inadequately supporting their main point. To help them understand what kind of material they will need to illustrate the problem addressed in their essays and its possible solutions, try the following strategies.

Option 1 Ask students to remember the last time they solved a problem. How did they arrive at their solution? What kinds of options did they consider before arriving at the solution? Looking back on that situation now, do they still feel that they came up with the best solution? Why or why not?

Option 2 Have students make a list of several problems from around the world and match this list with solutions they have heard about or that they would suggest. Help them understand the correspondence between a particular problem and a realistic solution.

⏱ TIME SAVERS!

 **Writing Support Transparencies**
Use the transparencies for Chapter 11 to teach these strategies.

Revising: Highlighting Topic Sentences

1. Remind students that each paragraph in their essay should have a clear main idea, often stated in a topic sentence, that is supported and developed throughout that paragraph.

2. Have students highlight the topic sentence in each paragraph of their essays. If a paragraph does not have a topic sentence, ask students to write one in the margin and highlight it.

3. Have students create a descriptive outline that includes only the main idea in each paragraph. Instruct students to analyze their outlines to determine if the ideas are ordered logically.

4. Have partners share their outlines. Ask students to give each other feedback about organization.

Revising: Color-Coding to Eliminate Generalizations

Teaching Resources: Writing Support Transparency 11-F

1. Display the transparency and ask students how Michael's revision adds support.

2. Instruct students to check the focus of their essays first by reading each paragraph to determine whether all of the ideas included connect to and support the main idea in the topic sentence. Have students eliminate ideas that are not relevant.

3. Next, ask students to underline in one color all sentences that restate or expand on the main idea and underline in another color all sentences that give facts or details that support or develop the idea.

4. Have students look at the colors on their papers. They should have a balance. If the colors are unbalanced, students can repeat the process of looking for places where they could add support for their generalizations.

11.4 Revising

Revising Your Overall Structure

Be sure that your paragraphs make sense in the order in which you have arranged them. The main point of one paragraph should lead logically to the main point of the next.

▶ **REVISION STRATEGY**
Highlighting Topic Sentences

To evaluate the order of your ideas, highlight the topic sentence of each paragraph. Review your paragraph order, assigning numbers to show a revised order if necessary.

Revising Your Paragraphs

Look at your paragraphs to be sure that the details support or explain the main idea.

▶ **REVISION STRATEGY**
Color-Coding to Eliminate Generalizations

Look back at the main idea you highlighted in each paragraph. In blue, underline sentences that restate the idea. In red, underline sentences that support or develop the idea. If you have more sentences underlined in blue than in red, you are probably making generalizations without supporting them.

Name: Michael C. Mahoney
St. Stephen's School
Hickory, NC

Supporting Generalizations

In this paragraph, Michael discovered that he was restating the problem several times without providing concrete support. He added details to support his main idea.

Building new roads without sidewalks will make our town more like a highway attraction, where people are always enclosed by their cars. New roads will cause more traffic to come to my neighborhood. The additional traffic will create the potential for more accidents, injuries, and deaths. Many of the places I used ride to on my bike will be off-limits for safety reasons.

238 • Problem-and-Solution Essay

⏱ TIME AND RESOURCE MANAGER

Resources
Print: Writing Support Transparency 11-F–G
Technology: Writing Lab CD-ROM, Exposition

In-Depth Coverage	Accelerated Pace
• Cover pp. 238–240. • Work through topic sentence strategy with the entire class. • Help students review their own drafts for generalizations (p. 238), sentence variety (p. 239), and word choice (p. 240). • Divide the class into groups for the peer review activity (p. 240).	• Assign students pp. 238–240 for independent review. • Have students revise their problem-and-solution essays independently.

Revising Your Sentences

Combine for Sentence Variety

A series of short, choppy sentences may prevent your readers from seeing the connections between your ideas. Whenever possible, vary your sentence structure by combining two or more short sentences into one longer sentence. One way to combine sentences is to create a complex sentence.

▶**REVISION STRATEGY**
Color-Coding to Identify Sentences to Combine

Reread your essay. In red, bracket each sentence that is made up of a single independent clause. If ideas in two consecutive simple sentences are related, consider combining them in a complex sentence.

**Writing Lab
CD-ROM**

Use the revision checker to analyze your sentence length. You can find it in the Toolkit.

Grammar in Your Writing
Creating Complex Sentences

A **complex sentence** includes one independent clause and one subordinate clause linked by a subordinate conjunction.

Common Subordinate Conjunctions

after	because	since	when
although	before	so that	whenever
as	even though	unless	whether
as soon as	if	until	while

When combining two independent clauses, look for a relationship between the ideas and use a subordinating conjunction to create a complex sentence.

To show a time relationship: After she read the newspaper, she told her friends about the candidate's speech.

To show cause and effect: We'll need to get an early start if the weather is bad.

To show a contrast: Although he was disappointed, he knew he had done his best.

Use a comma to separate an introductory subordinate clause from the rest of a sentence. Do not use a comma to separate a subordinate clause at the end of a sentence.

Find It in Your Reading Find an example of a complex sentence in the excerpt from "Dinosaurs Rediscovered," on pages 230–231. Identify the relationship between the two clauses.

Find It in Your Writing Find any complex sentences you have used. If you cannot find any complex sentences, challenge yourself to create one.

To learn more about combining sentences, see Chapter 22.

Grammar in Your Writing: Creating Complex Sentences

1. Use simple examples to illustrate simple and compound sentences.

   Simple:

   Hank is smart.

   Hank and Frank are smart.

   Hank and Frank are smart and funny.

   Compound:

   Hank is smart, and so is Frank.

   Hank is smart, but Frank isn't.

   Hank is smart; Frank is smart too.

2. Students can also use complex sentences: a subordinate clause plus an independent clause.

   On Tuesdays, Frank is funny.

   Frank is funny, but not as funny as Hank.

3. Stress that using a mixture of sentence types makes writing more lively and interesting.

Find It in Your Reading

An example of a compound sentence is "Most dinosaur researchers do their own preparation work in the winter, as few museums and universities can afford the paid help." The two simple sentences are "Most dinosaur researchers do their own preparation work in the winter" and "Few museums and universities can afford the paid help."

Find It in Your Writing

Have students be sure that they punctuated their sentences correctly.

If students have difficulty with compound sentences, you may find it helpful to review the following to assure coverage of prerequisite knowledge.

In the Textbook	Print Resources	Technology
Phrases and Clauses, pp. 478–495	Grammar Exercise Workbook, pp. 91–92	On-Line Exercise Bank, Section 21.2

 TIME SAVERS!

▇ **Writing Support Transparencies**

Use the transparencies for Chapter 11 to teach these strategies.

Revising: Circling Suspect Words

Teaching Resources: Writing Support Transparency 11-G

1. Explain to students that they will need to look at their drafts through the eyes of their intended audience.

2. Display the transparency to show students how Michael refined his word choice.

3. Have students apply the strategy to their own drafts.

Revising: Peer Review

1. Ask students to tell when and how a classmate has helped them write better or more effectively. Simply being told that a peer doesn't understand something or disagrees can help a writer sharpen the focus or add more convincing details. Even the reviewers can get ideas from reading a friend's work and can practice the skill of evaluating writing, which they can later apply to their own writing.

2. Before students begin reviewing each other's work, model the process with a sample draft that students comment on together. Read the essay aloud and ask students to comment on what stood out for them. Discuss the strengths of the essay and model appropriate respectful comments in the context of the discussion.

⏱ TIME SAVERS!

▌ Writing Support Transparencies

Use the transparencies for Chapter 11 to teach these strategies.

240

11.4

Revising Your Word Choice
Choose Words That Fit Your Audience

Your intended audience has the power to implement the solution you suggest. Evaluate your word choice to make sure that you are using the right level of language for your readers.

▶ REVISION STRATEGY
Circling Suspect Words

Review your draft as if you were a member of the audience you intend to reach. Circle words that such readers may not understand, terms that may need to be defined, or vocabulary that seems too low for your readers. To improve your writing, consider revising the words you've circled.

Student Work
IN PROGRESS

Name: Michael C. Mahoney
St. Stephen's School
Hickory, NC

Refining Word Choice

Michael circled and revised words in his draft that were inappropriate for an audience of his classmates.

aspect
Another (part) of the problem is that many of the (older people) senior citizens in our town, who often walk for exercise, will not feel safe on the shoulder of a busy street with traffic flying by ∧! at 40 mph A sidewalk with a divider between the street and walking area would (help) protect the walkers and allow them to continue their exercise.

Peer Review
Read Aloud

Read your draft to a group of classmates. Ask them to consider these questions as they listen to you read:

• What did you want to know more about?

• Where did you need the connections to be shown more clearly?

Use your reviewers' responses to begin a discussion about your work. Then, make any revisions you feel would improve your writing.

🔍 STANDARDIZED TEST PREPARATION WORKSHOP

Revising and Editing Standardized tests often measure students' ability to choose the best revision to a given passage. Share the following sample test item with students:

Many important people believe that computers are important for education.

Which letter is the best revision to this sentence?

A Many experts believe that computers are an important educational tool.

B Many important people argue that computers can help students.

C Computers are an important part of education.

D Correct as is.

The best revision to the original sentence is **A**. It retains the original meaning of the sentence, but replaces vague words with more detailed ones to make the sentence more convincing.

11.5 Editing and Proofreading

Once you have revised your essay for content, review your draft to correct spelling, punctuation, and grammatical errors.

Focusing on Semicolons

Check your draft to make sure that you have used semicolons correctly. They can be used for the following purposes:

- **To separate independent clauses that are related:**
  We hoped for rain; the storm followed immediately.

- **To separate items in a series when the items are lengthy or complicated:**
  I expect to hear from Steven and Joe in St. Louis; Peter and Mariah in Moscow; and Sam in Altoona, Pennsylvania.

Grammar in Your Writing
Punctuating Compound Sentences
With Commas and Semicolons

Compound sentences are composed of two independent clauses. They can be punctuated in one of two ways: with a comma or with a semicolon.

- A **comma** must be followed by a coordinating conjunction such as *and, but, or, for,* or *nor.*

  INCORRECT: We want improvement, we can't agree about the solution.
  CORRECT: We want improvement, **but** we can't agree about the solution.

- A **semicolon** can be used alone to join independent clauses in a compound sentence. It may or may not be followed by a coordinating conjunction.

  CORRECT: We want improvement; **however,** we can't agree about the solution.

Find It in Your Reading Find an example of a compound sentence in "Dinosaurs Rediscovered" on pages 230–231. Rewrite the sentence using a semicolon.

Find It in Your Writing Check to make sure that you have correctly punctuated the compound sentences in your problem-and-solution essay.

For more on punctuating compound sentences, see Chapter 29.

Editing and Proofreading • 241

241

Publishing and Presenting

1. Students can do some research to determine who could put their ideas into action. Not every problem needs to be solved by the president of the United States or even their town's mayor. There are people in local government in charge of parks, unwanted kittens, and almost anything else students can think of.

2. The school librarian can help students find organizations with specific missions, such as the Audubon Society (it is not only birds!), the Nature Conservancy, Amnesty International, UNICEF, and thousands of others.

ASSESS

Assessment

Teaching Resources: Scoring Rubrics on Transparency 11; Formal Assessment, Chapter 11

1. Display the Scoring Rubric transparency and review the criteria in class.

2. Before students proceed with self-assessment, you may wish to review the Final Draft of the Student Work in Progress on pages 243–244. Have students score the Final Draft in one or more of the rubric categories. For example, how would students score the piece in terms of audience and purpose?

3. In addition to student self-assessment, you may wish to use the following assessment options.

   • Score student essays yourself, using the rubric and scoring models from Writing Assessment.

   • Review the Standardized Test Preparation Workshop on pages 248–249 and have students respond to a writing prompt within a time limit.

   • Administer the Chapter 11 Test from Formal Assessment in Teaching Resources to assess students' grasp of concepts presented.

11.6 Publishing and Presenting

Building Your Portfolio

To make the best use of your problem-and-solution essay, share it with people who can help you make a difference. Consider these ideas:

1. **Send a Letter** If your essay addresses a public problem, send it to someone who can put your suggestions into action. Send your essay to the appropriate government official, agency, or group. Save a copy of your letter in your portfolio, along with any reply you receive.

2. **Create a Solutions Handbook** If your essay addresses a problem faced by individuals—such as managing study time—make copies available for others to read. Ask readers for feedback on your ideas.

Reflecting on Your Writing

Reflect on what you've learned by answering these questions in a written response. Add your reflections to your portfolio.

• What have I learned about the problem that I addressed?

• In what ways is a problem-and-solution essay similar to and different from other types of writing?

Internet Tip

To see model essays scored with this rubric, go to www. phwg.phschool.com

Rubric for Self-Assessment

Use the following criteria to evaluate your problem-and-solution essay:

	Score 4	Score 3	Score 2	Score 1
Audience and Purpose	Contains language and details to successfully engage audience; clearly identifies problem and proposes solution	Contains language and details appropriate for audience and identifies problem and solution	Contains some language and details not suited for audience; contains some details not related to problem or solution	Contains language and details that are not geared for a particular audience; has an unclear purpose
Organization	Presents information clearly in an organization suited to topic consistently, logically, and effectively	Presents most information according to an appropriate organization	Presents several details that detract from main organization	Demonstrates lack of organization
Elaboration	Clearly explains problem; presents a well-elaborated, realistic solution	Has a solution that is supported with details	Presents solution; contains few details to support it	Presents unclear solution; offers no details to support it
Use of Language	Includes wide variety of sentence styles; contains no errors in grammar, punctuation, or spelling	Contains some variety of sentence styles; contains few errors in grammar, punctuation, and spelling	Contains little variety of sentence style; contains some errors in grammar, punctuation, and spelling	Contains no sentence variety; contains many errors in grammar, punctuation, and spelling

242 • Problem-and-Solution Essay

☑ ONGOING ASSESSMENT: Assess Mastery

Use one of the following options to assess final drafts of students' essays.

Self-Assessment Ask students to score their essay using the rubric provided. Then have students write a single paragraph reflecting on the most valuable thing they learned in completing this essay.	**Teacher Assessment** You may wish to use the rubric and the scoring models provided in Writing Assessment, Ruby Level, to score the essays.

11.7 Student Work
IN PROGRESS

FINAL DRAFT

Safety and Progress

Michael C. Mahoney
St. Stephen's School
Hickory, North Carolina

Many people enjoy being able to jump in their cars and quickly get from one place to another. New and faster roads help people achieve this goal. Although these roads make life more convenient in some ways, they also create some problems. The increased traffic and speed of cars on bigger roads with higher speed limits create a danger for walkers, bike riders, and small children. There is a solution—sidewalks. Sidewalks, especially sidewalks with railings or dividers, would create a safe avenue for people who want to get around without a car.

Our town has always been known as a friendly place. People are out walking, children play in the yards, and bike riders wheel

▲ Critical Viewing
How do sidewalks help the flow of motor, pedestrian, and bicycle traffic on the street shown here? **[Infer]**

After a brief explanation of the problem, Michael offers his solution: Sidewalks can ease traffic dangers to pedestrians.

Critical Viewing

Infer Students may say that they allow slower moving pedestrians to walk safely out of the path of faster moving cars and bicycles.

Step-by-Step Teaching Guide

Teaching From the Final Draft

1. Help students see that "Safety and Progress" incorporates key elements of the problem-and-solution essay.

   • The problem is clear and stated right away in the first paragraph.

   • The writer uses detailed examples to develop the essay and avoids generalizations.

   • Each paragraph develops the problem point by point, and the solution—building more sidewalks—is presented as a good solution for a number of different reasons.

   • Finally, a short conclusion restates the main problem and summarizes why finding a solution is so important.

2. Ask students if they think that the care with which the essay has been constructed contributes to their understanding of the central problem presented in the essay.

3. Explain that this is one of the reasons that it is important to write carefully—to help readers understand clearly the relationships between a problem and its solutions. Not only must there be enough information, it also must be presented in a way that highlights the importance of solving the problem.

4. Ask students if there are any changes they would recommend for this essay, to make it flow better or fine-tune the connections between the problem and the solutions presented. How might they apply these suggestions to their own writing?

243

Real-World Connection

If students have become absorbed by the problem they wrote about—or a problem a classmate wrote about—encourage them to get more information. Using the Internet or library resources, they can find the names of organizations devoted to these problems. Suggest that they send a letter or an e-mail to relevant organizations, asking for details on their work. Students may decide to do volunteer work for the organization after school or during the summer. They may even want to focus their high school and college studies so they can have a career in this field.

around the neighborhood. Building new roads without sidewalks will make our town more like a highway attraction, where people are always enclosed by their cars. New roads will cause more traffic to come to my neighborhood. The additional traffic will create the potential for more accidents, injuries, and deaths. Many of the places I used to ride to on my bike will be off-limits for safety reasons. My friends and I will be driven to places that we used to be able to ride to on our own. If the new roads were built with sidewalks, we could continue to ride our bikes safely around town.

Another aspect of the problem is that many of the senior citizens in our town, who often walk for exercise, will not feel safe on the shoulder of a busy street with traffic flying by at 40 mph! A sidewalk with a divider between the street and walking area would protect the walkers and allow them to continue their exercise. Sidewalks with dividers would also protect the young children in our neighborhoods. Kids should be able to play in their front yards, but if there is a road right at the end of the front yard, they might get hurt because they are so close to the street. If there is a sidewalk, it will make a safety zone between the yard and the street.

Statistics show that the number of accidents involving pedestrians is significantly lower in neighborhoods with sidewalks. Nearby towns have been adding sidewalks to the existing roads and planning sidewalks for the new roads. Our town would also benefit from such a plan. It is true that construction would cost some time and money, but we are obviously willing to put money into the roads, so we should be willing to put money into the sidewalks. After all, isn't safety as important as progress? Also, a safer neighborhood means that more people will be willing to move into our town. More people moving in means a better economy. The money, mess, and noise of the construction involved in the process of installing the sidewalks would be a small price to pay for the benefits in the end.

Building these sidewalks can solve the safety problem created by new roads. This solution will be worth the money and time, because it will make this a better community and make people happier. Even though it will add costs to the road program, the outcome will make the town prosper. Traffic will not be a problem for bikers and walkers anymore, children can play in their front yards more safely, and there will be fewer accidents involving pedestrians. Building sidewalks with the new roads means that safety and progress can exist together.

Michael elaborates by providing details and examples that show how increased traffic will affect his town.

The essay is organized according to a point-by-point plan, addressing components of the problem and their solutions.

Michael includes benefits that will appeal to his audience.

The proposed solution allows progress to continue while promoting safety.

Michael indicates the cost and time his solution requires but suggests that the investment would be worth the effort.

Michael concludes by reinforcing his supporting arguments.

Connected Assignment

Question-and-Answer Column

When your running shoes wear out unevenly, you can ask for help at the local shoe store or you can write to an expert at a specialty magazine. These experts offer printed or electronically transmitted problem-and-solution essays in a question-and-answer format. Like a traditional problem-and-solution essay, a **question-and-answer column** includes a clearly explained problem, proposes a solution, and explains how the solution would work.

To write a question-and-answer column, use the writing process tips outlined here:

Prewriting Identify an area of your expertise. For example, you may know a great deal about computers or getting along with friends. Announce your area of expertise, and invite a group of classmates to write questions.

When you receive a question you'd like to answer, use a problem-and-solution organizer like the one shown here to focus your thoughts. Jot down as many solutions as you can imagine. Later, you can decide which ones to develop in your response.

Problem	Solution
Want to find a unique holiday gift without spending lots of money	• Offer services like babysitting or laundry • Put together a memory book • Bake cookies, and include the recipe with the batch

Drafting First, draft the question so that it provides a clear explanation of the problem. Next, draft your answer. Offer one or more possible solutions, explaining how each idea you suggest will solve the problem. You may need to provide direction about implementing the solution you offer. In both question and answer, use polite, formal language.

Revising and Editing Share your draft with a classmate, and discuss whether the problem is sufficiently explained. Ask your partner to tell you whether the solutions are realistic and helpful. If necessary, add details to clarify the problem or suggested solutions.

Publishing and Presenting Get together with classmates to create a question-and-answer bulletin board. Invite other students to submit questions for your response.

▲ **Critical Viewing** Why do you think people put creative energy into choosing the gifts they give? **[Hypothesize]**

Lesson Objectives

1. To write a sample question-and-answer column appropriate to audience and purpose.
2. To use recursive writing processes.

Step-by-Step Teaching Guide

Question-and-Answer Column

Teaching Resources: Writing Support Transparency 11-H; Writing Support Activity Book 11-3

1. Ask students to discuss advice columns with which they are familiar. Have students focus on the kinds of questions and answers these columns provide.
2. Suggest that students review the strategies from Chapter 11.
3. Once students have identified their areas of expertise, display the transparency to show students how to organize their ideas.
4. Give students copies of the blank organizer to complete.
5. Make sure students share their drafts with a classmate to ensure that the answers they provide are helpful.

Critical Viewing

Hypothesize Students may say that people put creative energy in choosing gifts because they want to please the people who are receiving the gifts.

Spotlight on the Humanities

Examining Culture and Ideas Represented in Art

Focus on Dance: Alvin Ailey

Problem: In 1958, there was no dance troupe that conveyed African American culture through dance. *Solution:* Alvin Ailey (1931–1989) worked to become one of America's most important choreographers. After studying with legendary dancers Martha Graham and Charles Weidman, Ailey created his own dance company, the American Dance Theater. Ailey wanted to ensure the preservation and uniqueness of African American cultural expression. He choreographed a sequence of ballets to the music of Duke Ellington and worked with such companies as the Joffrey Ballet and the American Ballet Theatre. Combining the best of African-influenced dance, jazz, and modern dance, Ailey earned international praise for his work.

▲ Critical Viewing
What words can you use to describe the dance shown here? [Describe]

Music Connection Born Edward Kennedy Ellington, Duke Ellington (1899–1974) was one of America's foremost jazz musicians. Beginning as a jazz pianist in 1916, Ellington formed his own orchestra, playing the nightclubs of Harlem and later writing works of jazz of increasing complexity. His work—including *Liberian Suite* (1947), *Harlem* (1951), and *Night Creatures* (1955)—is presented concert-style all over the world.

Photography Connection Modern dance inspired a new area of photography and dance called Environmental Dance Photography. Using outdoor space as the background for dancers, Environmental Dance Photography focuses on choreography and images for film rather than for a live audience. For example, famous dancer Isadora Duncan was photographed in New York's Central Park, as well as at the Parthenon in Greece. Edward Steichen, John Lindquist, and Harry Ellis were photographers involved in this type of art.

Problem-and-Solution Writing Activity: Proposal

Use Ailey as an inspiration for starting your own club or group. Consider starting a photography club, a hiking team, or another group to pursue your unique interests. Whatever your idea, write a proposal to your school board and explain how your new group can improve student life.

Media and Technology Skills

Lesson Objectives

1. To familiarize oneself with troubleshooting basics and help features of a computer.
2. To set goals for learning a new computer application.

Using Word-Processing Technology

Activity: Trouble-shooting

The last thing you need when you're writing is a problem with your computer. However, if you familiarize yourself with trouble-shooting basics and electronic Help options, the solution can be closer than you think. Whenever you are faced with a computer glitch, solve the immediate difficulty and remember what you learned so you can head off future problems.

Learn About It When you face a problem, consult these basic avenues for assistance:

- **Manuals** Most computer programs come with on-line manuals or printed manuals. It may help to scan the index or lists of frequently asked questions. Also, use a text editor to look at Read Me files in your software's folder.

- **On-Screen Help** Many programs have on-screen help features that can trouble-shoot problems as you work. Activate these programs under Help or by clicking on a specific icon. Drop-down labels also identify function icons, and balloon help (turned on under Help) explains how to use different features. You can deactivate features like balloon help when you are concentrating on your writing.

Try It Choose an application you do not know well. Identify a task to complete with the program. Then, use two or more help methods to figure out how to accomplish your goal. In a chart like the one shown here, note the types of help you used and the information provided. Finally, write brief directions for other program users.

Where could you find help to solve the following problems?			
	Manual	Computer Help	Not Found
Printing a file	☐	☐	☐
Finding a file	☐	☐	☐
Changing a font	☐	☐	☐

Basic Trouble-shooting

- Close all applications except the one you need. This frees up memory and removes system conflicts.
- Confirm that the mouse, keyboard, and monitor are connected to the computer and that the system is plugged into an electrical outlet.
- Check that memory is sufficient.
- Turn off all external devices (printers, etc.) and shut down your computer for 5 seconds. Then, restart.
- Connect to the Internet before activating browser or e-mail programs.

Solving More Complex Problems

- If you cannot solve your problem, telephone or e-mail tech-support staff. Find numbers and addresses in Read Me files, printed manuals, or at Web sites.

Step-by-Step Teaching Guide

Using Word-Processing Technology

Teaching Resources: Writing Support Transparency 11-I; Writing Support Activity Book 11-4

1. Because students may have varying levels of familiarity with computers, you may want to have more knowledgeable students assist with setting up this activity.
2. Encourage students to choose useful applications about which they would like to learn more.
3. Display the transparency and guide students through the chart.
4. Give students copies of the blank organizer to use as they complete the activity.

Media and Technology Skills • 247

Lesson Objectives

- To respond to writing prompts using problem-and-solution skills.

Using Problem-and-Solution Skills

1. Guide students through the criteria by which their esssays will be evaluated.

2. Point out the Test Tip to students. Explain that a problem-and-solution esssay will have more power if it contains a few concrete details than if it loses focus in trying to incorporate too much information.

3. Have a volunteer read aloud the sample writing situation. Ask the class to identify the audience and purpose for writing. Remind students to keep these two elements in mind while drafting their responses.

Standardized Test Preparation Workshop

Using Problem-and-Solution Skills to Respond to Writing Prompts

Standardized test prompts often measure your ability to clearly state a problem and offer several solutions. Your response will be evaluated on the following criteria:

- clearly stating your problem, varying word and sentence choice for the purpose and audience named in the response
- choosing a method of organization that allows you to present your solution in a meaningful and coherent sequence, such as block or point-by-point organization
- using appropriate transitions to clarify the flow of ideas
- elaborating your solution by anticipating and answering reader's questions with descriptions, facts, and other details
- using correct grammar, spelling, and punctuation

When writing for a timed test, plan to devote a specific amount of time to prewriting, drafting, revising, and proof-reading.

Following is an example of an expository writing prompt that uses problem-and-solution writing skills. Follow the strategies on the next page to help you respond. The clocks next to each stage show a suggested amount of time to devote to each one.

Test Tip

When writing a problem-and-solution response, remember that using a few specific, relevant details is better than overloading your reader with numerous bits of vague and distracting information.

Sample Writing Situation

Raising money for extracurricular activities often presents a problem for high-school students. For example, while a Spanish club's trip to Spain or the marching band's involvement in a nationally televised parade can be rewarding, raising enough money for these trips can be a daunting task.

Choose an activity that you believe your school should help sponsor. Write a letter to your principal in which you clearly state the problem you are facing and offer possible solutions for fund-raising for the activity. Use details to support your response.

◈ TEST-TAKING TIP

Remind students to set aside an adequate amount of time to revise, edit, and proofread their essays. Although a majority of their time should be spent drafting the essay, students should not forget that their essays will be evaluated on the basis of grammar, usage, and mechanics. A well-thought out essay will not be as impressive if it contains numerous errors in grammar and spelling, for example.

Prewriting

Allow close to one fourth of your time for prewriting.

Focus Your Response There may be several solutions to any given problem. Use a cluster diagram to help you come up with potential solutions. In the center circle, write the problem—raising money for a school-sponsored activity—and in the surrounding circles list possible solutions. Then, review the solutions, and choose those that are most reasonable and would be agreeable to your audience.

Gather Details After you have focused on certain solutions, gather supporting details. On a piece of scrap paper, list the steps or details of your solution. For each, jot down details, facts, or examples to help you support your ideas. Refer to your chart when you draft your writing.

Anticipate Objections Before you begin to draft, note possible objections or questions that the principal may have about your solution. Plan to incorporate the information that would answer these questions in your response.

Drafting

Allow almost half of your time for drafting.

Introduce the Problem Begin your essay by making the problem clear. Start with a bold statement, situation, or question. Next, identify your subject. Then, grab the principal's attention with a bold statement, statistic, or question.

Organize Your Solution Choose a method of organization that most strongly presents your argument. Consider first developing the problem completely and then presenting the steps of your solution. Alternatively, using a point-by-point approach, you could develop one facet of the problem and offer a solution before addressing another part of the problem.

Revising, Editing, and Proofreading

Allow almost one fourth of your time for revising, editing and proofreading your work.

Review Your Information Refer to your list of possible objections, checking that you have answered each one. Neatly cross out details that are distracting or that do not support your purpose.

Proofread Your Work Use the last few minutes to check your writing for errors in spelling, grammar, and punctuation. Add words or phrases neatly in the space above the text, using a caret [^] to indicate the exact placement.

In-Depth Lesson Plan

	LESSON FOCUS	PRINT AND MEDIA RESOURCES
DAY 1	**Introduction to Writing a Research Paper** Students learn key elements of research papers and analyze the Model From Literature (pp. 250–255).	*Writers at Work* Videotape *Writing Lab* CD-ROM, Research
DAY 2	**Prewriting** Students choose and narrow a topic, consider their audience and purpose, and gather information (pp. 256–260).	**Teaching Resources** *Writing Support Transparencies,* 12-A–C
DAY 3	**Drafting** Students organize their ideas and write their first drafts (pp. 261–263).	**Teaching Resources** *Writing Support Transparencies,* 12-D
DAY 4	**Revising** Students revise their drafts in terms of overall structure, paragraphs, sentences, and word choice (pp. 264–267).	**Teaching Resources** *Writing Support Transparencies,* 12-E
DAY 5	**Editing and Proofreading; Publishing and Presenting** Students check their work for accuracy and correctness and present their final drafts (pp. 268–270).	**Teaching Resources** *Scoring Rubrics on Transparency,* Chapter 12; *Formal Assessment,* Chapter 12

Accelerated Lesson Plan

	LESSON FOCUS	PRINT AND MEDIA RESOURCES
DAY 1	**Drafting** Students review characteristics for research writing, select topics, and write drafts (pp. 250–263).	*Writers at Work* Videotape **Teaching Resources** *Writing Support Transparencies,* 12-A–D; *Writing Lab* CD-ROM, Research
DAY 2	**Revising to Presenting** Students work individually or with peers to revise, edit and proofread their work for presentation (pp. 264–270).	**Teaching Resources** *Writing Support Transparencies,* 12-E; *Scoring Rubrics on Transparency,* Chapter 12; *Formal Assessment,* Chapter 12

Options for Adapting Lesson Plans

HOMEWORK

Have students complete any stage of the lesson for homework.

TECHNOLOGY

Students can complete any stage of the lesson on computer. Have them print out their completed work.

FEATURES

Extend coverage with Connected Assignment (p. 275), Spotlight on the Humanities (p. 276), Media and Technology Skills (p. 277), and the Standardized Test Preparation Workshop (p. 278).

INTEGRATED SKILLS COVERAGE TEKS CORRELATIONS

Integrating Grammar
Semicolons, SE p. 266
Conventions for Documentation, SE p. 269

Reading/Writing Connection
Reading Strategy, SE p. 252
Writing Application, SE p. 255

Reading
Integrating Reading Skills ATE p. 265

Spelling
Integrating Spelling Skills ATE, p. 268

Technology
Integrating Technology Skills ATE p. 267

Viewing and Representing
Critical Viewing, SE pp. 250, 252, 263, 264, 267, 271, 273, 274, 275, 276
Viewing and Representing ATE p. 276

ASSESSMENT SUPPORT

Standardized Test Preparation SE p. 278; ATE p. 278
Standardized Test Preparation Workshop, pp. 23–24
Scoring Rubrics on Transparency, Ch. 12
Formal Assessment, Ch. 12
Writing Assessment and Portfolio Management

MEETING INDIVIDUAL NEEDS

Less Advanced Students ATE pp. 253, 260; See also Ongoing Assessments ATE pp. 252, 257, 259, 262, 263, 266, 269, 270,
More Advanced Students ATE p. 258
ESL Students ATE p. 253
Visual/Spatial Learners ATE p. 262
Verbal/Linguistic Learners ATE p. 262
Logical/Mathematical Learners ATE pp. 261, 277

BLOCK SCHEDULING

Pacing Suggestions
For 90-minute Blocks
- Have students complete the Prewriting and Drafting stages in a single period.
- Focus one class period on Revising and Editing and Publishing and Presenting. Allow at least 30 minutes for peer revision.

Resources for Varying Instruction
- *Writing Lab* CD-ROM If your students have access to hardware, a 90-minute block provides an ideal opportunity for students to work on computer.
- *Writers at Work* Videotape Show the Research segment in class.

Professional Development Support
- *How to Manage Instruction in the Block* This Teaching Resource provides management and activity suggestions.

MEDIA AND TECHNOLOGY

For the Student
- *Writing Lab* CD-ROM, Research

For the Teacher
- *Writers at Work* Videotape, Research
- *Resource Pro* CD-ROM

WRITING AND GRAMMAR WEBSITE

The Interactive Writing and Grammar Website provides a wide array of support for students, teachers, and parents. Writing support includes:
- Interactive revision checkers
- Scoring rubrics with complete models

phwg.phschool.com

LITERATURE CONNECTIONS

Related selections from *Prentice Hall Literature: Timeless Voices, Timeless Themes,* Gold:

"A Celebration of Grandfathers," Rudolfo A. Anaya, SE p. 257

► *Lesson Objectives*

1. To identify and define a research report.
2. To utilize strategies for choosing a topic.
3. To identify and practice strategies for narrowing a topic.
4. To identify audience and purpose.
5. To locate sources to gather support.
6. To shape writing through a thesis statement and organizational strategy.
7. To elaborate using outside sources.
8. To evaluate paragraph patterns.
9. To use semicolons to combine sentences to make connections.
10. To use synonyms for language variety.
11. To review conventions for documentation.
12. To publish and present a research report.
13. To use rubric to assess own work.
14. To read and evaluate student work in progress.

Critical Viewing

Hypothesize Students may mention standard reference books such as encyclopedias and earth science texts, as well as geographical resources—globes, maps, atlases. Educational videos and the websites of selected universities and government agencies (the U.S. Geological Survey, for instance) might also furnish relevant information.

Chapter 12 Research
Research Paper

Icebergs, Frederic Edwin Church

▲ **Critical Viewing**
What resources could you consult to learn more about the terrain featured in this painting?
[Hypothesize]

Research in Everyday Life

Your curiosity often directs your informal research—whether you are learning more about a specific breed of puppy by talking to a veterinarian, following your favorite actor's career by watching his biography on television, or scanning books, library resources, or the Internet to understand a weather pattern or to follow up on a science experiment. When your search becomes a more formal pursuit, skills in research and organization allow you to gather information by consulting sources outside your own experiences and to share your findings with others. In the process, research helps you become an expert and provides you with information to help others understand more about the subject you have studied.

⏱ TIME AND RESOURCE MANAGER

Resources
Technology: Writers at Work videotape

In-Depth Coverage	Accelerated Pace
• Cover pp. 250–251 in class. • Show Writing a Research Report section of Writers at Work videotape. • Discuss different types of research papers.	• Assign pp. 250–251 for independent student review. • Discuss definitions and types of research papers.

What Is a Research Paper?

A **research paper** is a formal, written presentation of your findings on a topic based on information you have gathered from several sources. Effective research writing has

- a clearly stated thesis statement.
- factual support from a variety of outside sources, including direct quotations whose sources are credited.
- a clear organizational strategy.
- a bibliography or a works-cited list that provides a complete listing of research sources.

To preview the criteria upon which your research paper may be evaluated, see the Rubric for Self-Assessment on page 270.

Types of Research Papers

Like the range of subjects suited to research, research writing comes in a variety of forms. Following are some of the types of research writing you will encounter:

- **Lab reports** record the purposes, processes, and results of an experiment.
- **Annotated bibliographies** help researchers by providing a list of sources related to a topic. In addition to source information such as title, author, and publication date, the researcher provides evaluations of the material.
- **Documented essays** are short versions of research papers. Because they include only a limited number of research sources, these essays provide full documentation parenthetically within the text.
- **Documentaries** use video, photographs, personal interviews, and narration to present the results of research.

Writers in ACTION

A collector of African American folklore, the writer Zora Neale Hurston (1891–1960) documented the cultural heritage of the American South. By gathering stories and retelling them, Hurston combined research techniques and writing skills to share the legacy of the oral tradition. Of her work, Hurston has said her personal interest fueled her success:

"Research is formalized curiosity. It is poking and prying with a purpose."

PREVIEW
Student Work
IN PROGRESS

In this chapter, you will follow the work of Angelika Klien, a student at Sunnyslope High School in Phoenix, Arizona. As you will see, she used writing process strategies to develop her research essay on the history and uses of bubble gum.

Reading Strategy: Evaluate the Writer's Ideas

Students need to employ critical thinking strategies: asking questions about and evaluating what they read or hear. Remind them of the dangers of simply accepting or rejecting a writer's ideas without critical thinking. Readers can begin by checking a writer's credentials, asking where his or her knowledge or authority on the topic comes from. Also, does the writer back up statements and opinions? How plausible are the writer's ideas? Do they pass a common sense test?

Teaching From the Model

You can use this Model From Literature to show students what a research report looks like, how it is structured, how a thesis statement is used, and how the author cites sources for facts.

Engage Students Through Literature

1. Examine the opening paragraph and point out the comparison the author sets up between the heroes of the antislavery and the modern civil rights movements.

continued

Critical Viewing

Support Students may mention the subject's skirt, blouse, shawl, or cap, as well as the quality of the photographic image.

12.1 Model From Literature

As a voice for freedom, Sojourner Truth faced firsthand the oppression of slavery and discrimination against women. In a preface to her autobiography, Narrative of Sojourner Truth, *William Kaufman used research to explain the context and importance of Truth's contributions.*

Reading → Writing Connection

Reading Strategy: Evaluate the Writer's Ideas Facts can often be interpreted in more than one way. For example, a writer may claim that a leader's beliefs or actions prove one generalization, whereas another writer might use the same evidence to draw a different conclusion. As you read this essay, evaluate whether the writer has wisely interpreted the information his research provides.

▲ **Critical Viewing** What details of this image tell you the subject, Sojourner Truth, lived in an earlier time period than the present? **[Support]**

The Indomitable Spirit of Sojourner Truth

William Kaufman

If we marvel at the power of will and vision that allowed post-slavery freedom fighters like Rosa Parks and Martin Luther King to defy the oppressive burden of history, to stand and inspire thousands of followers to do likewise, we can barely imagine the herculean force of character summoned by slaves such as Nat Turner, Frederick Douglass, Harriet Tubman, and Sojourner Truth in throwing off the crushing weight of outright bondage.

Narrative of Sojourner Truth is the record of one such small miracle of indomitability, one that eventually gathered enough force to touch a broad public in the antislavery, temperance, and women's rights movements. Originally named Isabella Baumfree, Sojourner Truth was born into slavery in 1797 in Ulster County,

Kaufman presents his thesis: Sojourner Truth was a miracle of indomitability. In the essay, Kaufman will use research to prove his position.

252 • Research Paper

☑ ONGOING ASSESSMENT: Diagnose

Use one of the following options to diagnose students' current level of proficiency in writing a research report.

Option 1 Ask each student to select the strongest example of his or her research report writing from last year. Hold conferences to review each student's sample. Use the conferences to determine which students will need extra support in developing a research report.	**Option 2** Ask students to write a list of questions they would ask before reading a research report. Review their list of questions for completeness and see that students understand the need to use various sources to find information that answers these questions.

New York, on the estate of a Dutch family, the Hardenberghs (she grew up speaking no English, only the Dutch she acquired from her masters). In 1808 she was sold to John Neely, an English-speaking master who frequently beat her because of her imperfect understanding of his English commands. Isabella's prayers for deliverance were answered when she was sold to Martin Scriver. In 1810 she was purchased for seventy pounds by John Dumont, on whose estate she spent the next sixteen years cooking, cleaning, weaving, and working the fields. (Truth 17) Strong in body as well as spirit, the tireless, six-foot Isabella discharged her duties with such thoroughness and skill that Dumont commented that his "Bell" was "better to me than a *man*—for she will do a good family's washing in the night, and be ready in the morning to go into the field, where she will do as much at raking and binding as my best hands." (Washington iv)

The year 1826 was a pivotal one for Isabella, thrusting her out of bondage and into her calling as a preacher-activist. That year New York passed a law emancipating all slaves in the state beginning in 1827. When Dumont reneged on his promise to free Isabella early, she seized her own freedom, fleeing the Dumont estate in 1826 with her youngest child and finding refuge and employment in the household of a Quaker couple, the Van Wagenens, whose name she took. In the summer of 1827, during Pinkster time (an annual religious festival observed by African-Dutch slaves), Isabella claimed to have undergone a religious epiphany that set her on her evangelical path; she joined the Methodist Church and the Zion African Church and began preaching at local congregations. Ranging the moral imperatives of her faith against the machinery of oppression, she launched her career as an activist by successfully suing for the return of her son Peter, who had been sold into slavery across state lines in violation of New York State law.

In 1829 Isabella moved to New York City, where she spent the ensuing decade working as a domestic and pursuing her religious interests. Beguiled by the preachings of the self-proclaimed prophet Matthias, in 1832 Isabella joined his Zion Hill sect, which dissolved in 1835 amid suspicions of foul play in the sudden demise of Matthias's patron, Elijah Pierson. (Stetson 69)

Emerging from profound grief over the death of her son Peter in 1843, Isabella felt a renewed summons to spread God's word as an itinerant preacher. She changed her name to Sojourner Truth, packed her worldly estate into a pillowcase, and ventured out from New York City on her evangelical odyssey. That year illness

Facts are organized chronologically, beginning with the subject's birth and moving through the key dates and events in her life.

To indicate the sources of his information, Kaufman includes parenthetical citations. These shortened references direct readers to full bibliographic information provided at the end of the essay.

According to a style set by the Modern Language Association (MLA), references include authors surname and page number.

Model From Literature • 253

Step-by-Step Teaching Guide continued

2. Identify the important people mentioned in the first paragraph. Rosa Parks refused to give up her seat on a segregated bus in Montgomery, Alabama, in 1955. The protest that resulted from her arrest, led by the Rev. Martin Luther King, is considered the beginning of the civil rights movement. Nat Turner led an ill-fated slave rebellion in Virginia in 1831. Frederick Douglass was an escaped slave and leader of the abolitionist movement. Harriet Tubman served as the most famous "conductor" on the Underground Railroad, leading hundreds of escaped slaves to freedom in the North.

3. Point out the quotations and citations the author uses. Ask students how these contribute to the authority of the essay.

continued

Customize for
ESL and Less Advanced Students

The words *deliverance, bondage, reneged, epiphany, imperatives, ensuing, beguiled, demise, convalescence, utopian,* and others may be challenging to students. Encourage students to use dictionaries, context clues, and the meanings of common roots, prefixes, and suffixes to figure out the words' meanings. Also have them keep a vocabulary notebook in which they record unfamiliar words. At regular intervals, have students look up the words and write down the definitions.

4. Point out the indented long quotes on the page and remind students of the rules for long quotes.

5. Ask students how the inclusion of exact words of speakers from a meeting in 1851 adds weight to the essay.

continued

12.1

led her to a convalescence at a utopian community in Northampton, Massachusetts, where her meetings with William Lloyd Garrison and Frederick Douglass inspired her to join them on the abolitionist lecture circuit. Seizing her audiences with her powerful oratory, she became a major attraction with her impassioned advocacy of black freedom, women's rights, and temperance. As her renown grew, a sympathetic white woman, Olive Gilbert, helped the illiterate Sojourner to record her remarkable life in writing in the *Narrative of Sojourner Truth*, which first appeared in 1850 and was reprinted with supplementary materials in 1878, 1881, and 1884.

Her greatest oratorical triumph occurred at a women's rights convention in 1851. Many of the women there contested her right to address the convention, fearing that press attention to a former slave would alienate public support for their cause. Nevertheless, the chair of the meeting, Mrs. Frances D. Gage, was steadfast under fire. In her own words,

> I rose and announced "Sojourner Truth," and begged the audience to keep silence for a few moments. The tumult subsided at once, and every eye was fixed on this almost Amazon form, which stood nearly six feet high, head erect, and eye piercing the upper air, like one in a dream. At her first word, there was a profound hush. She spoke in deep tones, which, though not loud, reached every ear in the house, and way through the throng and the doors and windows. (Painter 167)

Here, in part, are the words Sojourner Truth spoke that day:

> Nobody eber help me into carriages, or ober mud puddles, or gives me any best place [and raising herself to her full height and her voice to a pitch like rolling thunder, she asked] and ar'n't I a woman? Look at me! Look at my arm! [And she bared her right arm to the shoulder, showing her tremendous muscular power.] I have plowed, and planted, and gathered into barns, and no man could head me—and ar'n't I a woman? I could work as much and eat as much as a man (when I could get it), and bear de lash as well—and ar'n't I a woman? (Painter 168)

The hecklers were utterly disarmed. In Gage's words, "She had taken us up in her strong arms and carried us safely over the slough of difficulty, turning the whole tide in our favor. I have never in my life seen anything like the magical influence that

The writer reports specific names, places, and dates identified through research.

To build his argument of praise for Sojourner Truth, the writer includes facts and details to show her accomplishments.

To introduce the quotation to follow, Kaufman provides context, explaining the setting for Gage's courageous remarks.

When providing a lengthy quotation, Kaufman sets the exact words apart from the rest of the text.

Shorter quotations are incorporated into the essay's paragraphs. For each quotation, Kaufman shows the relevance of the information.

subdued the mobbish spirit of the day and turned the jibes and sneers of an excited crowd into notes of respect and admiration."

During the Civil War Sojourner Truth busied herself nursing wounded soldiers and collecting food and clothing. Her growing national reputation resulted in a tribute, titled "The Libyan Sybil," by Harriet Beecher Stowe in the *Atlantic Monthly* in 1863. In October 1864 Lincoln invited her to the White House. During her stay in Washington, D.C., she became one of the first "freedom riders," mounting a successful challenge to segregation on streetcars. In the postwar years her focus shifted to guiding Southern blacks to the West in an effort to create a domain of black self-determination. She moved to Battle Creek, Michigan, where she died on November 26, 1883.

Although Sojourner Truth's life fascinates as personal drama, it is even more compelling as a moral and spiritual odyssey. In heartening contrast to our own "culture of complaint," in which the idea of human solidarity seems lost, Sojourner Truth grew to understand that her personal quest for freedom was meaningful only as a moment in a larger struggle against the burden of injustice. Her book, her testament, shows how one resilient spirit can serve as a lever that helps to lift a whole world of oppression.

Kaufman's work demonstrates research in a variety of sources.

The conclusion provides a restatement of the thesis and makes the writer's research relevant by building a bridge to the modern world.

Works Cited

Painter, Nell Irvin. *Sojourner Truth: A Life, a Symbol*. New York: W. W. Norton, 1996.

Stetson, Erlene, and Linda David. *Glorying in Tribulation: The Lifework of Sojourner Truth*. East Lansing: Michigan State University Press, 1994.

Truth, Sojourner. *Narrative of Sojourner Truth*. Ed. Margaret Washington. New York: Vintage Books, 1993.

Washington, Margaret. Introduction. *Narrative of Sojourner Truth*. by Sojourner Truth. New York: Vintage Books, 1993.

A works-cited list at the end of the essay provides full bibliographic information for each reference mentioned in the text.

Reading Writing Connection

Writing Application: Support Your Main Ideas As you write your research paper, make your analysis clear and convincing to readers by showing logical connections among ideas.

6. Ask students to discuss their overall impressions of the essay, paying particular attention to how successfully the author supported his thesis.

7. Examine the list of works cited and compare the different types of sources the author used.

Reading\Writing Connection
Writing: Support Your Main Ideas

Have students identify two or three of Kaufman's main ideas and explain how the writer indicates the logical connections among them. Ask students how they might show the connections among main ideas in a research paper about the life, work, and legacy of Edgar Degas.

Prewriting: Choosing Your Topic

Teaching Resources: Writing Support Transparency 12-A

1. Work through the brainstorming activity. Remind students of the cardinal rule of brainstorming: no judgments. Encourage them to generate a list of topics and then to go back over the list looking for ways to narrow these topics.

2. Encourage students to do the sentence starters activity as a way of exploring their individual curiosities and interests.

3. The 24-hour list is a way for students to use their activities as a source for potential research topics. You can examine Angelika's list as a sample of the activity. Use the transparency to work through the activity with students.

12.2 Prewriting

Choosing Your Topic

When you set out to write a research paper, choose a topic that will hold your interest for the extended amount of time you will devote to it. Beyond this commitment to a topic, be sure there are enough sources of information available. To find a subject, consider one of the following strategies:

1. **Category Brainstorming** Identify a general area of interest, and brainstorm for a list of narrower categories. For example, from the general area of science, you might identify the categories of inventions, technology, and researchers. Within each of these categories, you can narrow your list even further. Review your brainstorming list to choose a topic you'd like to research.

2. **Sentence Starters** Finish one of the following sentence starters to begin generating ideas. Write for five minutes, elaborating on the idea your completed sentence starter presented. Review what you have written to see if you have identified a suitable research topic.

   I wonder why ___?___

   I'd like to learn more about ___?___

3. **24-Hour List** List the activities, ideas, and items that you encounter during a 24-hour period. Generate a research question that each point on your list suggests. As you jot down ideas, be open to the research possibilities your curiosity generates. Choose one to develop into a research paper.

Writing Lab CD-ROM

For more help finding a topic, explore the activities and suggestions in the Choosing a Topic section of the Research Writing lesson.

Student Work IN PROGRESS

Name: *Angelika Klien*
Sunnyslope High School
Phoenix, AZ

Creating a 24-Hour List

Angelika noted her activities over the course of a day. For each point she jotted down, she suggested a potential research question. This list provided her with the inspiration for her research paper on bubble gum.

10 A.M. Go to math class: How has geometry affected architecture?

3 P.M. Chew bubble gum on the way home: How did this product get invented?

5 P.M. Volunteer at community center: Why are community centers necessary?

7 P.M. On the telephone to friends: How have the telephone and the Internet changed business?

256 • Research Paper

⏱ TIME SAVERS!

Writing Support Transparencies

Use the transparencies for Chapter 12 to teach these strategies.

⏱ TIME AND RESOURCE MANAGER

Resources
Print: Writing Support Transparencies 12-A–C
Technology: Writing Lab CD-ROM, Research

In-Depth Coverage	Accelerated Pace
• Work through the Category Brainstorming and Sentence Starters strategies with the class (p. 256). • Use the Responding to Fine Arts Transparency to generate additional topics. • Do the 24-Hour List strategy in class. **Option** Have students work independently or in small groups with the Writing Lab CD-ROM.	• Discuss strategies for generating topics. • Have students work independently to choose and narrow their topics. • Have students work with partners to focus on audience, purpose, and gathering details.

TOPIC BANK

If you are having trouble finding a topic for your research paper, consider these suggestions:

1. **Report on Television Accuracy** Television combines fact with fiction to create entertaining stories. For example, television dramas set in hospitals contain realistic medical jargon; courtroom dramas incorporate elements of the modern court system. Choose a television drama, and conduct research to identify the elements of the show that are based in reality. In a report, evaluate the program's accuracy.

2. **Amazing Achievement Report** Focus on a historic event that amazed the public in its time. For example, research Lindbergh's famous flight across the Atlantic or investigate the *Titanic*'s maiden voyage. In a paper, explain how the event generated excitement or interest.

Responding to Fine Art

3. *Three Studies of a Dancer in Fourth Position* reveals the artist's attention to research and detail. Learn more about Edgar Degas and his work. In a paper, report on his life, work, and legacy. Alternatively, research the fundamentals of ballet, including arm and leg positions.

Three Studies of a Dancer in Fourth Position, c. 1879/80 (detail), Edgar Degas, Art Institute of Chicago

Responding to Literature

4. Read "A Celebration of Grandfathers" by Rudolfo A. Anaya. Use his ideas about older people in today's society as inspiration for your writing. Research the work of an older person who has made a significant contribution to society. You can find Anaya's essay in *Prentice Hall Literature: Timeless Voices, Timeless Themes*, Gold.

☑ Cooperative Writing Opportunity

5. **Technology Update** With a small group, brainstorm to identify the major technological advances of recent years. Consider inventions that affect medicine, communication, and transportation. Assign each group member one innovation to research. Combine your reports into an anthology.

Prewriting • **257**

☑ ONGOING ASSESSMENT: Monitor and Reinforce

If some students are having difficulty coming up with a topic, use one of the following options.

Option 1 Suggest that students choose an idea from the Topic Bank. If many students have difficulty, work with them around one topic, modeling the process for them.	**Option 2** If Topic Bank ideas seem too complex, suggest that students try one of the assignments from the Topic Bank for Heterogeneous Classes in the Teaching Resources.

Narrowing Your Topic
Conduct Preliminary Research

Before you finalize the topic you'd like to explore, conduct preliminary research to assess the amount of material available to you. Use your general idea as a starting point, and surf the Web or browse through relevant books, magazines, and indexes at the library. As you conduct this preliminary research, jot down the names, ideas, and events that appear most often. Use this information to narrow your focus.

For example, you might have started your research with the topic of the best educational programs on television. After some early research, you may have discovered that many articles address children's educational programs and that one series is analyzed frequently. Limiting your topic to a discussion of this series allows you to research your original interest while effectively narrowing the research and writing required.

Considering Your Audience and Purpose
Analyze Your Audience

The degree of your audience's familiarity with your topic helps you determine the level of research to conduct and the level of information to include. For example, if your audience is unfamiliar with your topic, the ideas you address should be described in general terms and any special terminology should be defined or modified. When you write for an expert audience, use terminology more freely, defining only those terms you feel your readers may not know. This chart illustrates how an audience's knowledge level should direct your research goal and help refine your topic.

Matching Audience's Knowledge With Research Goals		
Audience	Research Goal	Sample Topic
Novices	Discuss the topic in a general, nontechnical way	Types of fish
General Audiences	Give some background, and define all the special terms used	Specific needs and habits of one species
Experts	Report the results of your research	Effect of a new environment on a group of migrating fish

Refine Your Purpose

Your purpose shapes the details you choose to include in your essay and directs the points or arguments you choose to emphasize. Here are three common purposes for research writing, along with suggestions for meeting these goals:

- **To Persuade** Include support from acknowledged authorities. Provide details that will convince your readers to accept your position.
- **To Honor** Use vocabulary that offers a positive impression and captures the best qualities of the topic.
- **To Show Cause and Effect** Include evidence that establishes logical connections among the causes and effects you identify.

Match Your Purpose With Your Research

To get the most out of the time you spend researching, consider creating a list of the types of information you will need to achieve your purpose. As you find facts or details that address each item, check them off your list.

Student Work
IN PROGRESS

Name: *Angelika Klien*
Sunnyslope High School
Phoenix, AZ

Using Purpose to Direct Research

Angelika's purpose is to entertain her audience with interesting facts about her topic. To guide her research, she identifies several questions that may lead to interesting results. Checks indicate the information she has found in the initial stages of her research.

Purpose: To entertain by providing a lightheated look at bubble gum.

✓ Is there evidence for the early use of gum chewing?

✓ Who invented bubble gum?

What are the ingredients in bubble gum?

Are there unusual uses for bubble gum?

✓ Are there unusual facts about bubble gum?

Prewriting • 259

Step-by-Step Teaching Guide

Prewriting: Refining Your Purpose

Teaching Resources: Writing Support Transparency 12-C

1. Review the three purposes detailed in the text. Explore additional purposes such as the following.
   - To entertain
   - To explore in order to satisfy curiosity
   - To provoke discussion
   - To introduce unfamiliar topics
   - To inform

2. Discuss some of the challenges and opportunities that relate to the research process. For instance, if people had all the time in the world, they wouldn't need to direct their research: they could just follow their curiosity. However, few people have that luxury. Explain how students can use their purpose to direct their research by outlining questions or avenues to pursue.

3. Display the transparency. Examine Angelika's work in progress, pointing out how she uses her purpose to specify five questions, then narrows them down to three. Use the transparency to teach the process further.

ONGOING ASSESSMENT: Monitor and Reinforce

If some students are having difficulty using purpose to direct their research, use one of the following options.

Option 1 After they identify their audience and purpose, have students ask, "What would this audience want to know about the topic?" and "What is my specific purpose?"	**Option 2** Have partners help each other to identify audience and purpose and to write specific questions to pursue in research.

TIME SAVERS!

Writing Support Transparencies
Use the transparencies for Chapter 12 to teach these strategies.

Prewriting: Gathering Information

1. Good researchers use detective skills and start by identifying the best sources of information. Who are the authorities in the field? Where is information located?

2. Offer students the following scenario. You are researching the accomplishments of Robert Peary, the first man to reach the North Pole. In reading about Peary, you come across a reference to Matthew Henson, Peary's African American assistant. You check the copyright date of the book; it was published in 1962. You check more recent sources because you are still curious about Henson. In later sources you find that Henson was more than Peary's assistant. In fact, he deserves major credit for the success of the expedition. Remind students that good detective work yields good information.

3. Stress the importance of taking good notes, especially when dealing with noncirculating library reference sources. Remind students that it is virtually impossible to remember every detail from a source, no matter how indelible an impression it makes.

4. In the note-taking process, it is important for students to follow two procedures. First, they need to put verbatim words in quotation marks to avoid using them without attribution in their essays. Second, they need to note all sources and gather complete bibliographical information.

Customize for
Less Advanced Students

Students may need some assistance in the note-taking process. Show them some simple approaches: not writing complete sentences, using abbreviations for long words (*gov.* for government, *const.* for Constitution), and organizing notes according to purpose questions.

12.2

Gathering Information

Consult a variety of library sources, including books, encyclopedias, magazines, and newspapers. You can also find a wide range of information on the Internet.

Locate Sources

You can find sources of specific information through a card catalog, an on-line search, or these more complex resources:

Indexes: Locate magazine or newspaper articles by consulting the *Readers' Guide to Periodical Literature.*

Databases: Access databases of information to find appropriate sources; for example, the Modern Language Association database that indexes articles on topics within the humanities.

Take Notes Systematically

As you locate information, take notes efficiently. This will help when you draft your paper and create a reference list.

Source Cards For each source, create a single card to note the information you'll need. Note the title, author, publisher, and city and date of publication. Assign a number to each source; then, use this number to link note cards to source cards.

Note Cards Use note cards to record specific items of information. Place only one item on a card, and include a categorizing label to identify the contents. When copying a direct quotation, record the words accurately. In addition to any notes, indicate page numbers on which you found the information.

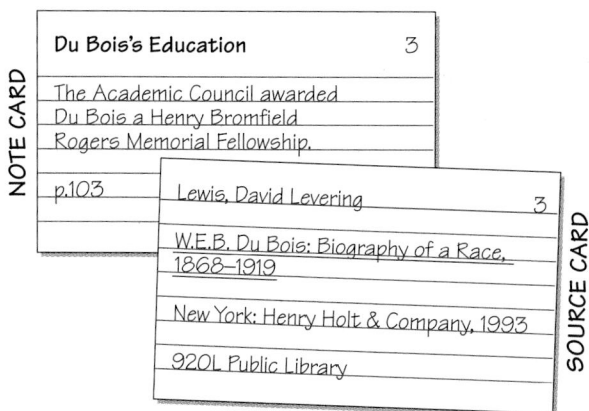

High-Tech Options Print out information you find on-line or photocopy articles that address your topic. Include bibliographical information for later use.

Learn More

For more information on specialized reference material, see Chapter 33.

12.3 Drafting

Shaping Your Writing

When you have gathered enough information for your research paper, think about organizing it. Begin with a proposal for a thesis statement.

Propose a Thesis Statement

An effective thesis statement expresses an idea that can be supported by research. To propose your thesis statement, review your research notes and look for one idea that can be supported by a majority of the information you have found in your research. Confirm that the thesis is narrow enough to address the ideas you will present. Then, use this thesis to guide your draft. If you find your ideas shifting as you write, be prepared to revise the sentence.

Sample Thesis Statement

- Spain offers a variety of pleasant activities for vacationers.
- The roots of the Northern Ireland conflict date back many centuries.
- During the first year of its life, a baby shows an amazing ability to learn.

Choose an Organization

Use your thesis statement, your audience, and your purpose as a basis for choosing an organizational strategy. Consider these options:

Types of Organization	Sample Topics
Chronological Order • Presents events in the order in which they occur • Ideal for reporting the history of a subject	Explaining the events leading up to the election of a president
Order of Importance • Presents details in order of increasing or decreasing importance • Ideal for writing persuasively or to build an argument	Analyzing the elements of laboratory safety
Comparison and Contrast • Presents similarities and differences • Ideal for addressing two or more subjects	Discussing the themes of two works by the same author

 **Challenge**

You may choose to organize your paper using *inductive reasoning*. With this strategy, you cite specific examples and build to the generalization they illustrate. In contrast, a paper organized according to *deductive reasoning* starts with a general claim and concludes with a specific statement.

Drafting: Shaping Your Writing

1. A thesis statement is the core of a research paper. Students need to be thinking about their thesis statements all during the research process. Moreover, they should be mindful of the direction their research is taking them, rather than just compiling data blindly.

2. Assist students in devising a thesis statement and organizational plan.

3. Go over the types of organization featured on the chart. Be sure students see how audience, organization, and thesis statement are connected.

Customize for
Logical/Mathematical Learners

Help students use their sense of logic to identify an organizational plan for their essays. Help them understand that a logical organization to the essay does two things: it makes it easier for the reader to follow what the writer is saying, and it heightens the writer's credibility in the reader's eyes.

Drafting • 261

⊘ TIME AND RESOURCE MANAGER

Resources
Print: Writing Support Transparency 12-D
Technology: Writing Lab CD-ROM, Research

In-Depth Coverage	Accelerated Pace
• Discuss identifying a thesis statement and an organizational plan. • Work through the exercise on a formal outline with the entire class, using the transparency. • Have students elaborate using outside sources and graphics. **Option** Have students work independently or in small groups with the Writing Lab CD-ROM.	• Have students review pp. 261–263 independently before writing their own research report drafts. • Respond to individual drafting issues as needed.

Drafting: Write an Outline

Teaching Resources: Writing Support Transparency 12-D

1. Show students how the structure of roman numerals, capital letters, and Arabic numbers show the distinctions among main ideas, subideas, and supporting details. Stress that most writers, amateur or professional, use some kind of outline for structuring their work in advance.

2. Display the transparency. Use Angelika's outline to help students choose a form and execute their outlines.

Customize for
Verbal/Linguistic Learners

Students might benefit from talking through their main ideas and supporting details. Have students work in pairs, with one student working as scribe, writing down the other student's spoken ideas.

Customize for
Visual/Spatial Learners

Students may benefit from sketching a story board of the drafting process. They might use self-stick notes to sketch each section of the story board and then use the notes to make a formal outline.

12.3

Write an Outline

Roman Numeral Outline When you have decided how you want to organize your information, prepare an outline to guide your drafting. Give each of your subtopics a Roman numeral, each of your major pieces of supporting information a capital letter, and each smaller detail an Arabic number. Refer to the sample outline on this page as a model for your work.

Sentence Outline To begin developing the tone of your writing and deciding on the way you will present your ideas, you might want to create a sentence outline. Write complete sentences for each topic and subtopic you'll address. You can use this skeletal essay as the basis for your draft.

Student Work
IN PROGRESS

Name: *Angelika Klien*
Sunnyslope High School,
Phoenix, AZ

Creating a Roman Numeral Outline
Angelika planned her essay using a chronological organization. Her outline helped her organize the key ideas she presents.

Thesis Statement: Bubble gum is big business in the United States.

I. Introduction —The prevalence of bubble gum

II. History of Gum Chewing
   A. Archaeological Evidence
   B. Invention
      1. Fleer Corporation
      2. Walter Deimer
      3. William J. White

III. Manufacture and Promotion of Commercial Gum
   A. Manufacturing—Ingredients and Process
   B. Promotion

IV. Funny Facts
   A. Other Uses
   B. Bubble Gum Alley

V. Snappy Summary and Conclusion

📝 Writing Support Transparencies
Use the transparencies for Chapter 12 to teach these strategies.

☑ ONGOING ASSESSMENT: Monitor and Reinforce

If some students are having difficulty creating an outline, use one of the following options.

Option 1 Help students identify the main ideas of their paper. If they have used their purpose to direct research, the main ideas could be identified as each of the questions they sought to answer in their research.	**Option 2** Remind students that an outline is a tool to get and keep them organized in the drafting process. Encourage students having difficulty to mix and match formal and sentence outline approaches to find one that works for them.

Providing Elaboration
Use a Variety of Outside Sources

Although the voice of your writing should integrate all the ideas you are reporting, support your ideas with the statistics, facts, examples, and quotations you have found through research. Consider these options:

Make Direct Reference to Sources You can use one of these three methods to incorporate the information you've learned through research.

- **Direct Quotation** When using a writer's exact words, enclose the entire statement in quotation marks. If you delete words from a lengthy sentence for clarity, be sure your editing does not change the intention of the quotation. Remember to show your deletions by the insertion of ellipses, or three dots.
- **Paraphrase** This technique involves restating a writer's specific ideas in your own words. You can paraphrase a sentence or a paragraph to convey the mood or intensity of the writer's description or ideas.
- **Summary** You can include the material you found through research by summarizing or reporting key ideas.

Incorporate Visuals To make your topic more understandable, consider including a visual representation, like the one shown here, when appropriate. For example:

- **Charts** can summarize information.
- **Graphs** can show comparisons and contrasts or indicate growth or decline over time.
- **Maps** can illustrate a variety of topics, including geography, war zones, and population.

Integrate References by Framing
Whenever you include information gathered through research, smooth your writing by providing a context for the material you use. First, introduce the material. Then, present the quotation or visual. Finally, complete the frame by explaining how the material supports the point you are making.

Prepare to Credit Sources

When you include a direct quotation, present an idea that is not your own, or provide a fact that is available in only one source, you must include documentation. As you draft, circle all ideas and words that are not your own. At this stage, for each circled item, use parentheses to note the author's last name and the page numbers of material used. Later, you can use these notes to create formal citations.

🖱 Research Tip
Avoid the temptation to present someone else's work as your own. When using another writer's words, quote the author directly. If you summarize or rephrase, be sure the words are your own and give the author credit.

Access to Media

	USA	Japan
Newspaper circulation per 1,000	230	578
Radios per 1,000	2,076	906
Television sets per 1,000	741	611

Source: *Europa World Yearbook; World Factbook*

▲ **Critical Viewing**
How could this chart help demonstrate a contrast between two countries' media access? **[Analyze]**

Drafting • 263

Drafting: Providing Elaboration

1. First, make sure that students understand the reason for using sources. Their opinions, though interesting, do not carry the authority of established sources in a given field. (Of course, someday *they* may be the experts, and ninth graders will use *their* work as source material.)

2. Paraphrasing and summarizing are specialized skills with which students may need some help. See that students can rewrite ideas in their own words. In summarizing, they should include the main idea and maybe one or two details, leaving out other details and transitional phrases.

3. Encourage students to use visuals. The first challenge is identifying where visuals will aid their presentations. Maps or how-to diagrams are often helpful; tables and graphs are useful when data are being compared or measured.

4. Framing is a useful transitional device. Successful research papers need more than good data. They need also a skillful narrative voice that presents and interprets information and provides graceful transitions.

5. Insist that students credit all sources during the drafting process. Point out that it is crucial to cite every source now, because when students look back in the revision stage, they may forget which words are their own and which are others'.

Critical Viewing

Analyze Students may say that the chart provides figures on the two countries' access to media, which helps demonstrate the contrast.

✓ ONGOING ASSESSMENT: Monitor and Reinforce

If some students are having difficulty paraphrasing and summarizing, use one of the following options.

Option 1 Work with students in pairs or small groups, having them paraphrase and summarize each other's remarks.	**Option 2** Write a short paragraph from the text on the board. Help students summarize it in one or two sentences.

263

1. If students followed their outlines during the drafting process, there is less likelihood of a discrepancy between their thesis statements and conclusion. Of course, students' enthusiasm during the drafting process may have caused them to vary slightly off course.

2. Have students check carefully the progression of their thesis statements through their essays. One method is for a student to write the thesis statement on an index card and use the card as a guide, reading sentence-by-sentence and paragraph-by-paragraph to check for consistent elaboration and development of the thesis statement.

Critical Viewing

Hypothesize Students may say that if you found a point that required further elaboration, you might have to go back to do more research.

12.4 Revising

Finishing the first draft of your research paper is an achievement. Take the time now to polish your work, creating a final draft that reflects the amount of time and commitment you have already devoted to this writing. Review your draft several times, focusing on a different element of the writing each time.

Revising Your Overall Structure
Refine Your Thesis Statement

In the process of drafting your paper, you may have learned something new, changed your interpretation of your subject, or developed a slightly different focus from the one you had planned. To avoid presenting a research paper that does not support your thesis statement, review your draft to be sure that all the details fit together to present a unified idea.

▶ **REVISION STRATEGY**
Tracking the Thesis From Introduction to Conclusion

Review your draft, identifying the organizational skeleton you originally planned. Highlight the thesis statement in which you first present the main idea of your paper. As you read through the body of your paper, highlight the topic sentences of each topical paragraph. Finally, highlight the thesis as restated in your conclusion. Looking only at what you have marked, evaluate the clarity of your paper. Use these tips to guide your revision:

Evaluate

- Does the thesis statement presented in the introduction match the idea presented in the conclusion?

- Is the sequence of main ideas logical?

Revise

- If not, locate the point in your paper where the writing changed course. Revise your thesis or your conclusion to reflect the body of your paper. You may need to adjust the body paragraphs to correct the conflict.

- Consider reordering paragraphs or adding transitional words, phrases, or sentences that will make the sequence logical.

▲ **Critical Viewing**
In what situation might revising your paper send you back to do more research? **[Hypothesize]**

🌐 **Learn More**

For more instruction on topical paragraphs, those that develop a topic sentence, see Chapter 3.

⏱ TIME AND RESOURCE MANAGER

Resources
Print: Writing Support Transparency 12-E
Technology: Writing Lab CD-ROM, Research

In-Depth Coverage	Accelerated Pace
• Work through Revising strategy with entire class. • Work through Grammar in Your Writing (p. 266). **Option** Divide the class into groups for peer review activity. **Option** Have students work independently or in small groups with the Writing Lab CD-ROM, focusing on revision activities and tools.	• Assign students to review pp. 264–267 independently. • Have students revise their research reports independently.

Revising Your Paragraphs

Evaluate Your Paragraph Patterns

Because research often addresses complex subjects, you may have included a majority of long topical paragraphs in the body of your draft. This could make the writing seem dense and complicated. Consider adding functional paragraphs that increase readability and maintain reader interest.

Introduce Functional Paragraphs Short, functional paragraphs can create variety in the body of your draft by summarizing data, emphasizing points, or presenting special effects. Review your essay to decide whether a functional paragraph will improve the flow of ideas.

▶ **REVISION STRATEGY**
Seeing the Pattern

Using self-sticking notes, indicate the subject of each topical paragraph in your essay. Wherever you see a series of long topical paragraphs, consider inserting a functional paragraph to break the pattern. These paragraphs give your readers a chance to interpret the material you've presented, review what you've said, or anticipate your next point.

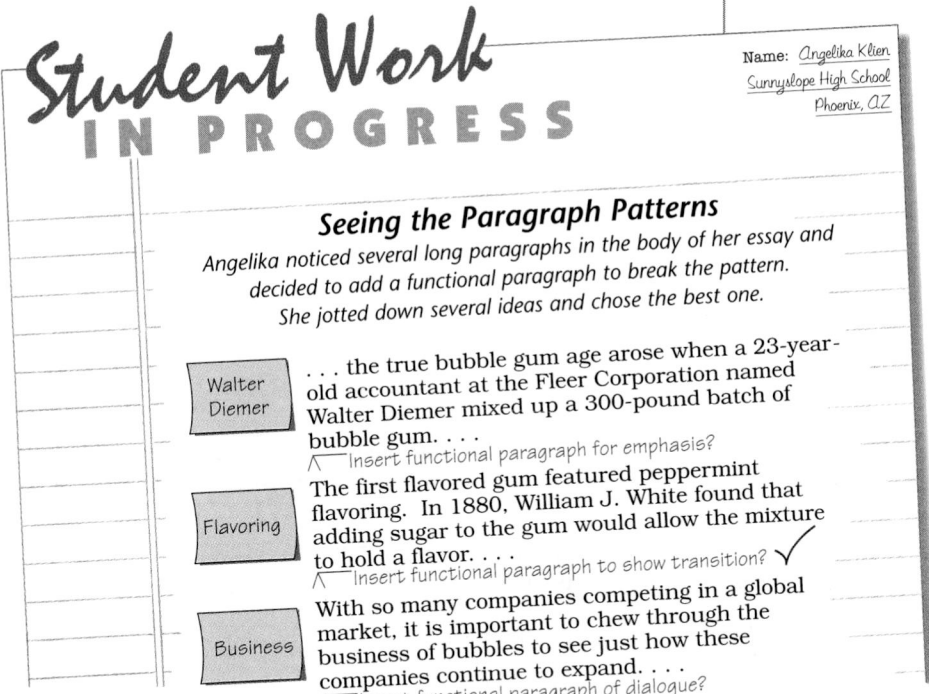

Student Work
IN PROGRESS

Name: Angelika Klien
Sunnyslope High School
Phoenix, AZ

Seeing the Paragraph Patterns

Angelika noticed several long paragraphs in the body of her essay and decided to add a functional paragraph to break the pattern. She jotted down several ideas and chose the best one.

Walter Diemer
... the true bubble gum age arose when a 23-year-old accountant at the Fleer Corporation named Walter Diemer mixed up a 300-pound batch of bubble gum. . . .
⌃ Insert functional paragraph for emphasis?

Flavoring
The first flavored gum featured peppermint flavoring. In 1880, William J. White found that adding sugar to the gum would allow the mixture to hold a flavor. . . .
⌃ Insert functional paragraph to show transition? ✓

Business
With so many companies competing in a global market, it is important to chew through the business of bubbles to see just how these companies continue to expand. . . .
⌃ Insert functional paragraph of dialogue?

Revising • 265

Step-by-Step Teaching Guide

Revising: Revising Your Paragraphs

Teaching Resources: Writing Support Transparency 12-E

1. In research papers, paragraphs serve various purposes. Often big, dense paragraphs present information, whereas other paragraphs are needed to introduce, summarize, and analyze information. Still others could compare and contrast ideas or facts, establish causes and effects, or arrange details in different sequences.

2. Display the transparency. Use Angelika's work in progress to teach students how to identify and mark the topics of each paragraph in their drafts.

Integrating Reading Skills

Have students read articles in news magazines or on Websites in order to practice identifying the functions of paragraphs.

⏱ **TIME SAVERS!**

📰 **Writing Support Transparencies**
Use the transparencies for Chapter 12 to teach these strategies.

Step-by-Step Teaching Guide

Revising: Revising Your Sentences

1. Discuss the importance of varying sentences to create an interesting style that engages the reader and avoids monotony.

2. Review the use of conjunctions to combine sentences to show sequence, cause and effect, and comparison and contrasts.

3. Have students use the revision strategy to identify short sentences that could be combined with conjunctions.

Step-by-Step Teaching Guide

Grammar in Your Writing: Semicolons

1. When connecting statements with a semicolon, one must be sure that the two independent clauses are related.

2. Write the following examples on the board to illustrate the correct and incorrect use of related clauses connected by a semicolon.

   Incorrect: The goalie made a great save; we went camping last summer.

   Correct: The goalie made a great save; the crowd went wild.

Find It in Your Reading

You can find such a sentence in the second paragraph on page 253 ("In the summer of 1827 . . .") The relationship is both sequential and cause and effect. Isabella has a religious epiphany and joins the churches and begins preaching.

Find It in Your Writing

Have students carefully review their drafts to make sure they have used semicolons correctly. If they have not used any, encourage them to combine sentences with semicolons.

12.4

Revising Your Sentences
Combine Sentences to Make Connections

In many cases, you can join simple sentences by using coordinating conjunctions such as *and, but, for, or, so,* and *yet* or subordinating conjunctions such as *after, because, until,* and *wherever.* To strengthen your writing, combine short sentences into longer ones that show these relationships between ideas.

SEQUENCE OF EVENTS: *Once* he learned skills, he found a job.

CAUSE AND EFFECT: He was offered many other positions *because* he was so qualified.

COMPARISON AND CONTRAST: She expected him to be happy with the offer; *however,* he was not.

▶ **REVISION STRATEGY**
Underlining Short Sentences

Review your draft, and underline sentences of eight words or less. If you see two or three short sentences in a row, challenge yourself to combine them into a compound one by clarifying the relationship between ideas.

Grammar in Your Writing
Semicolons

Semicolons can create compound sentences by linking clauses that otherwise stand as separate sentences. The semicolon emphasizes the close connection between ideas.

   Example: The game was critical; fans streamed into the stadium.

To create a compound sentence using a semicolon, use the punctuation mark to separate main clauses. If you are introducing a transition such as *however, finally, consequently,* or *therefore,* place the word immediately after the semicolon and separate the transition from the second main clause with a comma.

   Example: The game was critical; **consequently,** fans streamed into the stadium.

Find It in Your Reading Review "The Indomitable Spirit of Sojourner Truth" on pages 252–255. Identify one compound sentence created with a semicolon. Explain the relationship between the two main clauses.

Find It in Your Writing Strive to use the semicolon construction correctly at least twice in your final draft.

For more on semicolons, see Chapter 29.

266 • Research Paper

☑ ONGOING ASSESSMENT: Prerequisite Skills

Refer students to the following resources to ensure coverage of prerequisite skills.

In the Textbook	Print Resources	Technology
Punctuation, pp. 674–683	Grammar Exercise Workbook, pp. 179–180	Language Lab CD-ROM, Capitalization and Punctuation; On-Line Exercise Bank, Section 29.3

Revising Your Word Choice

Examine Language Variety

Except for the specific terminology associated with your topic, avoid using the same word over and over. Increase language variety with pronouns, synonyms, and specific proper nouns like names of people and places.

▶ REVISION STRATEGY
Compiling a Synonym Bank

Identify words that are key to your topic, and review your writing to find words that you have repeated. Circle them as you go. Using a thesaurus, generate a list of possible synonyms, and substitute them as appropriate. Look at these examples:

SYNONYM BANKS

technology	theory	Woodrow Wilson
innovation, invention, product, brainchild	belief, policy, system, position, idea	president, government official, leader

Peer Review

Analytical Reading

In a research paper, it is especially important to document information that comes from someone else. Ask a small group of classmates to read a draft that indicates which statements or ideas you plan to cite with formal documentation. Ask each reader to evaluate your writing according to these questions:

1. Do I provide enough evidence of research?
2. Do you see enough variety of sources?
3. Which quotation is best integrated into the writing? Do any need better framing?
4. Do you see more statements of facts, ideas, or discoveries that should be referenced?

When appropriate, incorporate your reviewer's ideas into your final revision.

🔧 Grammar and Style Tip

Although you should try to avoid repetition of key words in your draft, do not substitute another word unless you are certain its meaning is appropriate.

▼ Critical Viewing
How can a peer review group like the one shown here help you fine-tune your research paper? **[Analyze]**

Revising • 267

Step-by-Step Teaching Guide

Revising: Peer Review

1. Read students the following passage:

   People flocked to the game because this game was the game that both teams had been waiting for. This game would decide who was the better team.

   Ask students to respond to the repeated use of the word *game* and to suggest some alternative words. *(contest, match)*

2. Have students highlight repeated words in their essays and find synonyms they can use as replacements.

3. Remind students of the purpose of peer review: to help one's partner write a better report. Suggest that students make sure they have found items to praise before they offer any feedback.

4. Remind students that errors in grammar and punctuation can be fixed during the editing and proofreading stage. Ask them to focus their attention during the peer review activity.

Integrating Technology Skills

Check to see that students know how to use the thesaurus on the word processor. If some do not, use peer tutoring to ensure that all students become proficient with this tool.

Critical Viewing

Analyze Students may mention the ability of peers' fresh eyes to see small errors and inconsistencies in one's own writing.

🔷 STANDARD TEST PREPARATION WORKSHOP

Vocabulary Standardized test questions may require students to identify synonyms for words. Write the following on the board and ask students to choose the correct synonym for the underlined word.

The two candidates were worthy <u>adversaries</u>.

A politicians   C opposites

B opponents   D debaters

Students should choose item **B**. *Opponents* and *adversaries* are synonyms.

Editing and Proofreading

1. Editing and proofreading is detailed work, and it is important that students understand the paramount importance of eliminating all errors in their reports. If William Kaufman had misspelled words, or if his subjects and verbs didn't agree, readers might assume that they could not trust his facts or conclusions.

2. See that students understand the importance of compiling a correct and complete list of reference sources. A research paper is a special form of writing in which the citations and listing of sources is an important component.

3. If time and resources permit, allow students to consult the style manuals cited in the text.

4. Have students check their use of mechanics throughout their reports.

Integrating Spelling Skills

Explain to students the importance of double- or even triple-checking spelling as they compile their lists of works cited. Remind students that they will be using author and publisher names that may not be commonly known, and the only way to avoid spelling errors is to copy them carefully and then to recheck for errors.

12.5 Editing and Proofreading

By the time you've arrived at the point of editing and proof-reading, you may have completed the hardest work of your research paper. With researching, organizing, drafting, and revising behind you, you can focus on the final touches.

Writing a Reference List

Whether you use a bibliography or a works-cited list, your paper should document your sources of information. A works-cited page provides information on each source you reference in your paper. In contrast, a bibliography offers a complete list of your research sources. In both cases, items are arranged alphabetically by author or, for works with no known author, by title. Identify the format your teacher requires, review your source cards, and create your reference list.

Consult Style Manuals

For consistency within the community of scholars who publish their research, conventions for documentation are set by several organizations.

Papers on literature and the arts often follow the format of the Modern Language Association (MLA) stylebook or *The Chicago Manual of Style* (CMS). Papers on scientific or social science topics usually follow the style developed by the American Psychological Association (APA).

Before you draft your reference list, identify the format your teacher requires. Then, consult models of that style, and make sure that each entry is complete and that it is properly punctuated.

Focusing on Mechanics

Take the time to review your research paper for misspelled words, problems with punctuation, and other errors in mechanics. Pay special attention to these conventions for including quoted material:

- When quoting a few words or part of a sentence, make sure the quoted material fits grammatically with the rest of the sentence.

- When providing a quotation of three lines of more, set it off from your writing by indenting the text on both the right and the left. When you present a quotation this way, do not use quotation marks.

Learn More

To double-check your knowledge of mechanics issues, see the chapters on capitalization and punctuation.

268 • Research Paper

⏰ TIME AND RESOURCE MANAGER

Resources
Print: Scoring Rubrics on Transparency, Chapter 12; Writing Assessment: Scoring Rubric and Scoring Models for Research Report
Technology: Writing Lab CD-ROM, Research

In-Depth Coverage	Accelerated Pace
• Review pp. 268–274 in class. • Have students edit and proofread their essays in class. • Give step-by-step coverage to Publishing and Presenting, p. 270. • Analyze in class the Final Draft on pp. 271–274.	• Assign pp. 268–274 for independent review. • Have students edit and proofread their essays independently. • Respond to individual editing issues as needed.

Grammar in Your Writing
Conventions for Documentation

To credit sources within a research paper, include direct documentation in the form of footnotes, endnotes, or internal citations. At the end of your paper, provide a reference list giving complete bibliographic information.

Bibliographic Form Present your sources in a standardized format. Include authors' names, source titles, places of publication, publishers, and the dates of publication. For on-line references, indicate the date on which you accessed the site. The following examples are in MLA format:

For a book with one author:
Wolfe, Tom. *The Right Stuff.* New York: Bantam Books, 1979.

For a book with more than one author:
Aaron, Hank, with Lonnie Wheeler. *I Had a Hammer: The Hank Aaron Story.* New York: HarperCollins, 1991.

For an article:
Quittner, Joshua. "Digital Video Daze." *Time.* 2 Nov. 1998: 112.

For an on-line source:
"Half Past Autumn: Newshour Transcript" *Online Newshour.* 19 Oct. 1999. <http://www.pbs.org/newshour/bb/entertainment/jan–june98/gordon_1/>

Footnotes and Endnotes When using footnotes or endnotes to provide internal citation, include full details about the source and cite the page number. Indicate a citation by placing a number at the end of a passage. Place footnote documentation at the bottom of the page on which the number appears; place endnote documentation on a page preceding the reference list.

First footnote or endnote for a book:

1. Tom Wolfe, *The Right Stuff* (New York: Bantam Books, 1979), 61.

Subsequent footnotes or endnotes citing same source:

2. Wolfe 92.

Parenthetical Citations To cite parenthetically, include the source information in parentheses immediately after the quoted material. This information, along with your reference list, directs readers to your source.

In her analysis of heroic behavior, Lewis suggests, "If you look inside yourself, you might find a hero waiting" (Lewis 90).

Find It in Your Reading and Writing Review the MLA documentation presented in William Kaufman's essay on pages 252–255. As you finalize your paper, make the format of your documentation consistent with one style.

For a complete discussion of documentation styles, see the Handbook for Citing Sources and Manuscript Preparation.

Grammar in Your Writing: Conventions for Documentation

1. Point out that the purpose of documentation is to enable a reader to locate the citation in the source noted.

2. Encourage students to recognize that standards of credibility and integrity are important issues relating to documentation. If a reader cannot locate a citation, what does this say about the author's accuracy? Every citation needs to be stated (and checked) carefully. If necessary, point out that padding a list of citations is both dishonest and unethical.

3. To encourage accuracy, have students work with partners and check each other's citations.

Find It in Your Reading and Writing

Encourage students to look for other documentation in other research reports to help them familiarize themselves with proper documentation.

☑ ONGOING ASSESSMENT: Monitor and Reinforce

If some students are having difficulty with the conventions for documentation, use one of the following options.

Option 1 Lead students through the information on bibliographic form and have them identify each component: author, source title, place of publication, publisher, and date.	**Option 2** Show students examples of correctly footnoted material and have them copy the form as they document their own papers.

Publishing and Presenting

1. Have students practice before giving a presentation. If resources are available, have them use an overhead projector to display graphics. In any case, encourage students to add visual displays to their presentations.

2. Have students complete the Reflecting on Your Writing exercise, and encourage volunteers to share their reflections with the class.

3. Have students use the rubric to evaluate their own writing.

ASSESS

Assessment

Teaching Resources: Scoring Rubrics on Transparency 12; Formal Assessment, Chapter 12

1. Display the Scoring Rubric transparency and review the criteria with the class.

2. Before students proceed with self-assessment, you might review the Final Draft of the Student Work In Progress on pages 271–274. Invite students to score the Final Draft in one or more of the rubric categories. For example, how would they rate the essay's elaboration?

3. In addition to student self-assessment, you may wish to use the following assessment options.

   • Score student essays yourself, using the rubric and scoring models from Writing Assessment.

   • Review the Standardized Test Preparation Workshop on pages 278–279 and have students respond to multiple-choice questions within a time limit.

   • Administer the Chapter 12 Test from Formal Assessment in Teaching Resources to assess students' grasp of concepts presented.

12.6 # Publishing and Presenting

Now that you have finished your research paper, share what you have learned with others. Here are some suggestions for publishing or presenting your work:

1. **Publish On-line** If your school has a Web site, post your paper on the school Web page. You might choose to group research papers with similar topics or arrange for the creation of links to Web sites you used as resources.

2. **Organize a Panel Discussion** If several of your classmates have written on a similar topic, plan a panel to compare and contrast your findings. Speakers can summarize their research before opening the discussion to questions and observations from the audience.

Reflecting on Your Writing

Reflect on the experience of writing a research essay. Add your thoughts, along with a copy of your research paper, to your portfolio. Use these questions to direct your reflection:

• How did writing a research paper affect your appreciation, understanding, or opinion of your topic?

• What were the best and worst parts of this experience?

🖥 Internet Tip

To see model essays scored with this rubric, go to **www.phwg. phscool.com**

Rubric for Self-Assessment

Use these criteria to evaluate your research paper.

	Score 4	Score 3	Score 2	Score 1
Audience and Purpose	Focuses on a clearly stated thesis; gives complete citations	Focuses on a clearly stated thesis; gives citations	Focuses mainly on the chosen topic; gives some citations	Presents information without a focus; gives few or no citations
Organization	Presents information in logical order, emphasizing details of central importance	Presents information in logical order	Presents information logically, but organization is inconsistent	Presents information in a scattered, disorganized manner
Elaboration	Draws clear conclusions from information gathered from multiple sources	Draws conclusions from information gathered several sources	Explains and interprets some information; cites some sources	Presents information with no interpretation or synthesis; cites few sources
Use of Language	Shows overall clarity and fluency; contains few mechanical errors; consistently uses conventions for citation	Shows good sentence variety; contains some errors in spelling, punctuation, or usage; demonstrates minor errors in documentation style	Uses awkward or overly simple sentence structures; contains many mechanical errors; demonstrates several errors in documentation style	Contains incomplete thoughts and mechanical errors that make the writing confusing; does not follow conventional documentation format

---

☑ ONGOING ASSESSMENT: Assess Mastery

Use one of the following options to assess final drafts of students' research reports.

Self-Assessment Ask students to score their essays using the rubric provided. Then have students write a paragraph reflecting on the most valuable thing they learned in completing this essay.	**Teacher Assessment** You may want to use the rubric and scoring models provided in the Writing Assessment, Gold Level, to score the research reports.

12.7 Student Work IN PROGRESS

FINAL DRAFT

Tracking the Success of Bubble Gum

**Angelika Klien,
Sunnyslope High School
Phoenix, Arizona**

◄ Critical Viewing
Why is bubble gum an appropriate item for a vending machine? [Analyze]

We sit on it, step on it, buy it, blow it, snap it, pop it, and chew it: bubble gum—that messy pink wonder that seems to be everywhere. We chew it to keep hydrated while running; we buy it for the baseball cards that are included in the package; we chomp to the rhythm of our favorite music. We challenge our friends to bubble-blowing contests if we're feeling silly; we snap it if we're angry. In fact, we may not give too much thought to this integral piece of teenage life, but it is part of our daily routines.

Bubble gum is a major part of life in the United States. Let us unwrap the beginnings of bubble gum, chew on the business of bubbles, and pop in on some of bubble gum's best uses.

Although it might be hard to believe, scientists have found evidence of a chewing gum habit as early as 9,000 years ago. In 1993, archaeologists uncovered a 9,000-year-old wad of resin bearing human tooth marks, proving the existence of caveman chewers (Gustaitis 30). The chewing habit has continued throughout the centuries and around the world.

The beginnings of chewing gum in the United States are clouded by legend. Some sources say that Mexican dictator Santa Anna brought gum to the United States in the 1870's (Tuleja 64). However, bubble gum had entered the record books slightly

A cleverly worded lead presents the topic of bubble gum and Angelika's enthusiasm for her subject.

In the second paragraph of her introduction, Angelika reels her reader in by providing the thesis statement and an overview of the information she will include in her paper.

CLOSE

Step-by-Step Teaching Guide

Teaching From the Final Draft

1. Read the essay aloud or have it read by volunteers.

2. Point out the use of parallel construction and strong active voice that gives Angelika's opening paragraph so much energy.

3. Also note the way Angelika uses a semicolon to connect sentences. Help students see that the clauses contrast with one another.

continued

Critical Viewing

Analyze Students might mention the product's attractive appearance and relative lack of expense.

271

4. Use the margin notes to guide discussion of the essay.

5. Point out Angelika's continued use of lively and topical verbs in the second paragraph thesis statement. Have students note not only the verbs, but also the effect of the verbs on them as readers. Engaging, catchy writing makes us want to read on.

6. Note the functional paragraph and the use of contrast to distinguish bubble gum from fads like the hula hoop, yo-yo, and sock hop.

continued

12.7

earlier. According to one source, "In 1906 the Fleer Corporation unveiled the first bubble gum ever" (Wardlaw 47). Mr. Fleer himself gave it the tongue-twisting name Blibber-Blubber. The gum had mixed success. It tasted terrific and bubbled beautifully, but the bubbles would explode without warning and sometimes stuck to people's faces.

According to Lee Wardlaw, a modern-day bubble gum reporter, the true bubble gum age arose when a 23-year-old accountant at the Fleer Corporation named Walter Diemer mixed up a 300-pound batch of bubble gum (Wardlaw 49). He had been experimenting with batches of bubbly brew at home for over a year; a few days before Christmas in 1928, Diemer succeeded in creating the perfect bubble gum. "Pink food coloring was the only kind on hand, so he grabbed a bottle and dumped the bright liquid into the monstrous vat" (Wardlaw 49). This spontaneous decision started a trend that has continued to this day.

The first flavored gum featured peppermint flavoring. In 1880, William J. White found that adding sugar to the gum would allow the mixture to hold a flavor. In the century to follow White's work, gum manufacturers would take his ideas to create the wide variety of flavors available today (Warner Lambert Company Web site).

The Hula Hoop and the sock hop had their day. Even the yo-yo is not as popular as it was when first introduced. However, unlike some of these other popular items that come and go, bubble gum would prove it was not a fad. Today, there are more than 550 companies in 93 countries producing enough bubble gum to keep everyone happily chewing (Wardlaw 72).

With so many companies competing in a global market, it is important to chew through the business of bubbles to see just how these companies continue to expand. To brew up a pot of bubbly requires an enormous number of ingredients and a complicated manufacturing process. The basic ingredients are the same in all gums—sugar, gum base, corn syrup, softeners, flavoring, and coloring. It is the quality of the ingredients and the amounts in which they are used that make the difference between great gum and gross gum.

Mixing a batch of gum is an elaborate and precise process that takes anywhere from three to five days to complete. The ingredients are refined and mixed together at different intervals and temperatures until the right consistency is achieved. The gum is cooled a little and kneaded for hours. It is then formed to the desired dimensions

272 • Research Paper

For each fact Angelika located through research, she cites her source parenthetically. Readers can find full bibliographical information in the works-cited list at the end of her paper.

To develop the history of bubble gum, Angelika devotes one paragraph to an inventor and one to the introduction of flavorings.

A functional paragraph about popular fads makes the transition from the early days of mass-market bubble gum development to her next topic: the business of making and marketing the gum.

before being packaged and shipped out (Hendrickson 143–144).

Of course, manufacturing is just the beginning of the bubble. According to the National Association of Chewing Gum Manufacturers, William Wrigley, Jr., can be credited with using advertisements to sell gum. In the early 1900's, Wrigley used newspaper ads to build the popularity of his product (National Association of Chewing Gum Manufacturers Web site). Since then, promotional gimmicks and giveaways have become a big part of business. Some manufacturers have used comic strips to tickle your funny bone while tempting you toward bubble gum; others have provided baseball cards.

But bubble gum is useful for more than business or bubbling.

The U.S. military had learned just how valuable chewing gum could be during World War I. It freshened and cleansed the mouth when toothbrushes were unavailable. It quenched thirst when water was scarce. Most importantly, it relaxed soldiers during tense moments of fighting, increased their morale, and kept them alert—all of which helped save lives (Wardlaw 58).

So bubble gum has proved useful in time of war. This quotation explains why chewing gum was part of every soldier's gear in World War II.

Any product good enough for the government to distribute to soldiers has got to be good enough for the nation's artists and for popular, impromptu sculpture. Clearly, the medium of choice for most artists is more long-lasting and less sugar-based. However, although gum may never replace paint or marble as a medium for fine art, a sort of monument has been erected in California to honor bubble gum. There, in the town of San Luis Obispo, there is a six-foot-wide alley, the walls of which are covered with chewed bubble gum, in some spots up to ten wads thick (Wardlaw 130). Bubble Gum Alley was started in

Angelika supports her paper with information from a variety of sources, including books, magazine articles, and Web sites.

Before providing an extended quotation, Angelika explains the value of the material she chose to include. After the indented quotation, she transitions back to her own ideas.

◄ Critical Viewing
What link does the writer make to connect war with bubble gum? **[Identify]**

Monument of Iwo Jima, raising of the Flag

7. Follow the organizational structure Angelika uses on this page. Assist students in identifying the topic of each of the three paragraphs on the page. (In order they are: marketing, use in military, use in art.)

8. Discuss the effect of Angelika's quotation about the military use of chewing gum. It both exceeds our expectations and at the same time seems to defeat itself by claiming an importance that is hard to believe. Extend discussion to the idea that sometimes it is good to let the topic speak for itself and not try to give it more importance than it really deserves.

continued

Critical Viewing

Identify Students should mention that the writer discusses how bubble gum was used by soldiers during World Wars I and II.

9. Ask students for their overall impressions of the essay. How would they describe its strengths and weaknesses? How would they judge its value as a research report? Does it also have value as entertainment?

10. If necessary, point out the strengths of the draft: its lively style, strong organization, strong narrative voice, informative details, good thesis statement and conclusion, and varied sources cited in the correct form.

Critical Viewing

Identify Students may mention the invention of other types of gum or other uses for gum.

12.7

the 1960's. Since then, this Great Wall of Gum has become a tourist attraction and has been featured on the late-night TV shows of Johnny Carson, David Letterman, and Conan O'Brien.

Considering the rave reviews this alley has received, we may soon see bubble gum blowing into the art world after all.

We have sat, stepped, bought, blown, snapped, popped, and chewed on bubble gum's history, the business of bubbles, and bubble gum's other uses. When one takes into account the important role America has played in the creation and development of bubble gum, it is no wonder that North American children spend half a billion dollars on gum each year (National Association of Chewing Gum Manufacturers Web site).

But gum chewing is not just an American phenomenon. Today, there are bubble maniacs in more than one hundred countries around the world. We can all breathe easier knowing that wherever we travel, there is a good chance that we will come home with a gummy glob on the bottoms of our shoes. And we have Walter Diemer to thank for that.

While paraphrasing the story of a specific work of "bubble gum art," Angelika includes her own interpretation of the potential uses of bubble gum in the future.

◄ **Critical Viewing** What factors might cause the success or failure of bubblegum in the coming years? **[Identify]**

In her conclusion, Angelika restates her thesis and draws a conclusion about the reasons for the success of bubble gum.

Works Cited

Gustaitis, Joseph. "The Sticky History of Chewing Gum." *American History* Oct 1998: 30–38.

Hendrickson, Robert. *The Great American Chewing Gum Book.* Radnor, PA: Chilton Book Company, 1976.

National Association of Chewing Gum Manufacturers Web site. 19 Dec. 1999 <http: www.nacgm.org/consumer/funfacts.html>

Tuleja, Tad. *The New York Public Library Book of Popular Americana.* New York: The Stonesong Press, 1994.

Wardlaw, Lee. *Bubblemania.* New York: Aladdin Paperbacks, 1997.

Warner Lambert Company Web Site, 22 Nov. 1999 <http://www.gum-mints.com/historyofgum.html>

A works-cited list created in MLA format provides publishing information about each source referenced in the research paper.

Connected Assignment *Documented Essay*

Like a traditional research paper, a **documented essay** presents a thesis that is supported by evidence. The difference in these two research products is in the length of the writing and in the number of sources consulted. In a documented essay, writers refer to a limited number of sources. They cite researched information and include quotations from books, interviews, or electronic sources, using full citation information parenthetically rather than providing a works-cited list. A documented essay can also be slightly less formal in tone.

Follow the writing process steps below to develop your own documented essay:

Prewriting As with any research paper, choose a topic that interests you, so that you'll want to devote the necessary time to it. For ideas, flip through magazines, scan on-line news services, or chat with friends. Consider a more contemporary topic than you might choose for a research paper.

Develop a thesis statement to focus your research. Identify candidates for interview or experts on the subject you are researching; their quotations will lend your essay a more personal tone. As you collect information, devise a note-card system for recording facts and sources. This will help later with your referencing. Look at these sample note cards.

Topic: Trends related to teens who go to school and work

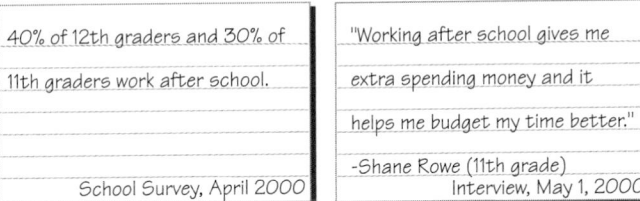

40% of 12th graders and 30% of 11th graders work after school.

School Survey, April 2000

"Working after school gives me extra spending money and it helps me budget my time better."
-Shane Rowe (11th grade) Interview, May 1, 2000

Drafting Choose an organization that fits your ideas, and draft an outline to help plan your writing. For an essay about a current trend, you might use a pro-and-con organization to present opposing views about the topic. Refer frequently to your note cards for evidence to support your ideas.

Revising and Editing To improve the tone and readability of your essay, replace wordy explanations with livelier examples or direct quotations.

Publishing and Presenting When the final draft of your documented essay is complete, submit it to your school newspaper or class magazine.

▲ Critical Viewing Who might you interview to learn more about students who hold after-school jobs? **[Apply]**

Connected Assignment: Documented Essay • 275

Lesson Objectives
1. To write a documented essay appropriate to audience and purpose.
2. To use writing to formulate questions, refine topics, and clarify ideas.
3. To compile information from primary and secondary sources in systematic ways.
4. To compile written ideas and representations into reports and draw conclusions.
5. To publish a documented essay to an audience.

Step-by-Step Teaching Guide

Documented Essay
1. Bring examples of documented essays to class. You might find these in magazines among the news and feature articles.
2. Suggest that students review strategies from Chapter 12. In particular, identify strategies that can help students finalize a topic and thesis statement.
3. Explain how students can complete their own note cards. Discuss the kinds of information included in the sample cards in order to help students focus their own note taking.
4. Direct students to the publication requirements for the school newspaper or class magazine. Encourage students to refine their essays to meet these requirements.

Critical Viewing
Apply Students may suggest job counselors at schools or local youth groups, potential employers of students, advertising sales representatives for want-ads, or students who have held (or hope to hold) after-school jobs.

275

Lesson Objectives

1. To evaluate media presentations.
2. To analyze relationships and ideas as represented in various media.
3. To deconstruct media to get the main idea of the message's content.
4. To write a research report.

Step-by-Step Teaching Guide

Examining Ideas in Media

1. Choose one of the Spotlight elements for class discussion, or have students work individually or in groups on the element of their choice. Give students the initiative to find the necessary videotapes, books, and pictures.

2. Show a videotape of *Field of Dreams*. Ask students to analyze how the film blends historical fact, realistic fiction, and fantastic elements. Invite them to develop a system to identify the three different elements in the film as they watch it.

3. Interested students might read reviews of *Da* and if possible, view the play on videotape. Have students exchange ideas about father-son relationships.

4. If students view the Conlon photograph of Ty Cobb, ask if they agree that it is the greatest baseball action shot. Why or why not?

Viewing and Representing

Activity Invite students to present their report as a feature story on a weekend sports television show. Students should augment their orally delivered text with photos and film clips.

Critical Viewing

Analyze Students may say that by placing the figure all alone in an open space, the director suggests that he is isolated.

Spotlight on the Humanities

Examining Ideas as Represented in Various Media

Spotlight on Film: *Field of Dreams*

Combining fantasy with research-based facts is an intriguing and challenging combination for a motion picture producer. The 1989 film *Field of Dreams* successfully mixed these two elements, telling the story of an Iowa farmer who builds a baseball field in a cornfield because he hears a voice tell him to do it. The field becomes a place where people are given a second chance; in fact, it creates the setting for the ghosts of a scandalized baseball team to play again. Because of the redesigned field, the farmer also achieves a reconciliation with his father.

Theater Connection Hugh Leonard's play *Da* is another drama that explores reconciliation between an estranged father and son. When it opened on Broadway in 1978, *Da* starred Barnard Hughes as the father of successful New York playwright Charlie. In the drama, Da has died. As Charlie remembers specific incidents in their lives, Da reappears onstage through memory. Father and son come to grips with the loss and love in their lives.

Photography Connection As a game, baseball inspires storytellers and artists alike. Charles M. Conlon photographed many major-league baseball players. Between 1904 and 1942, he was considered the greatest baseball photographer of his day. His photograph of Ty Cobb stealing third base at the New York Yankees' old Hilltop Park grounds is considered the greatest baseball action photo.

Research Report Writing Activity: Report on the Chicago Black Sox Scandal

Research the events surrounding Shoeless Joe Jackson and the 1919 Chicago Black Sox scandal. Identify the conflict, the players, and the outcome. Consider using *Field of Dreams* as a starting point, but find the true story in reference books and other library sources.

▲ Critical Viewing
How did the director of *Field of Dreams* use the visual impression shown here to communicate the idea of isolation? **[Analyze]**

Media and Technology Skills

Using Video Technology to Communicate Specific Messages

Activity: Producing a Documentary

Video technology enables you to convey your ideas to an audience and transform research material into a lively presentation by communicating through visual images, music, and sound effects. In addition to reporting research findings in a video format, you can use a camera's special features to create effects that enhance your work.

Learn About It The heart of a successful documentary is a vibrant script that blends many different media. Writers approach the process from one of two directions—either using an outline of a final written research product or building a documentary from raw research material. Either way, like other forms of exposition, documentaries focus on a single main idea.

- **Take Advantage of the Format** To create your own documentary, strive to combine words and sounds to illustrate your main idea. Develop your script scene by scene, planning the images your viewers will see. Use a chart like the one shown here to organize your material. Try to use visual and audio components to convey mood. Then, add music and sound effects, apply fade-out or zoom features, and include dramatic voice-over narration.

```
                    Main Message

   New Visuals  | Existing Documents | Sound Effects & Music
```

- **Respect Your Limitations** Unless you have access to editing technology through a video studio or on your computer, you'll have to shoot your documentary in sequence. You can view the tape as you record, however, and rewind to reshoot as necessary.

Tape It Put your ideas into action by filming your script. Then, share your finished product with classmates.

Video Techniques to Consider

Visuals
- Long shots to establish setting
- Maps with tracing lines to show routes covered
- Primary documents, such as letters, diaries, and still photos
- Step-by-step images of a process to explain or show cause and effect
- Close-ups of interview subjects

Sound Effects/Music
- Live sounds that show both action and mood
- Reaction sounds such as laughter or crying
- Familiar or evocative music to support mood
- Silence to signal dramatic shifts

Step-by-Step Teaching Guide

Using Video Technology to Communicate Specific Messages

Teaching Resources: Writing Support Transparency 12-F; Writing Support Activity Book 12-1

1. Review and discuss the listed video techniques.
2. As a class, identify additional techniques students feel are effective. Have students exchange information about how to apply these techniques.
3. Set up peer review groups to help students focus their main message. Peer reviewers can ask questions and generate comments to narrow topics to a single statement.
4. Display the transparency and model its use for students.
5. Give students copies of the blank organizer and have them use it to flesh out their main idea and organize their research.
6. After students complete their planning and researching, have them reassemble in-peer groups to discuss proposed components.

Customize for
Logical/Mathematical Learners

Students may wish to list scenes in chronological order prior to videotaping. This will enable them to see and experiment with different sequences until they find a logical progression of images and ideas.

Lesson Objectives

1. To proofread writing for appropriateness of organization, content, and conventions.
2. To analyze drafts by organizing and reorganizing content.
3. To evaluate writing for both mechanics and content.
4. To demonstrate control over grammatical elements.

Step-by-Step Teaching Guide

Revising and Editing

1. Stress with students the importance of accuracy and care when completing multiple-choice questions. Answers indicated in a messy or unclear fashion may be graded incorrectly or not at all.
2. Test-takers must read each question carefully to clearly understand it before answering. Remind students to answer only the question being asked.
3. Discuss the heading "Revising and Editing." Clarify with students that test-takers are not graded on the quality of the original passage, but rather on their improvement of the passage using one of the offered alternatives.
4. Talk with students about time management strategies for multiple-choice tests. Students should calculate the available time and allow about one-tenth to read the directions and passage. Then they should divide up the questions equally according to the available time, leaving about five minutes at the end to check answers.

Standardized Test Preparation Workshop

Revising and Editing

One of the most important steps in writing a research paper is revising and editing. Standardized tests often measure your ability to complete such a task by presenting prewritten passages and asking you to choose the best revisions. These methods can help you address these questions:

- Pay attention to words or phrases that should be further clarified.
- Note facts or details that do not connect to the rest of the information being presented.
- Identify errors in mechanics, grammar, and spelling.

The following sample test item will give you practice with questions on revising and editing.

Sample Test Item	Answers and Explanations

Directions: Read the passage, and then answer the questions that follow.
 	
[1] To many, Shakespeare's dramatic story of *The Tragedy of Romeo and Juliet* presents tragic lovers who represent the essence of romantic love for many people. [2] Since it was written hundreds of years ago, it has relevance to today's audiences.
 	
1 What is the best change, if any, to make in Part 2?
 	
  A. Change <u>since</u> to <u>although</u>.
 	
  B. Change <u>since</u> to <u>when</u>.
 	
  C. Change <u>since</u> to <u>after</u>.
 	
  D. Make no change.
	The correct answer is *A*. The transition *although* shows the contrast between the date the play was written and the play's modern relevance.

🖉 TEST-TAKING TIP

Tell students that successful time management must include provisions for "problem" questions. Students should skip over any difficult questions in order to complete the maximum number of questions. If time remains, they can return to challenging questions and apply familiar strategies. For example, they can check the question wording for clues (such as "the best change") that might clarify the kind of answer being sought. Then they can rule out answer alternatives that seem incorrect. Finally, if students are still unsure, it is worthwhile on a multiple-choice test to hazard a guess. After all, students get no points for an uncompleted question but may guess correctly some of the time.

Answer Key

1. D
2. C
3. A
4. D
5. C
6. C
7. A

▶ **Practice 1** **Directions:** Read the passage, and then answer the questions that follow. Choose the letter of the best answer.

¹ As a young man, William Shakespeare went to London, where he wrote and acted in plays. ² *The Tragedy of Romeo and Juliet* was produced in a public theater. ³ Public theaters in Elizabethan England were built around roofless courtyards; without artificial light. ⁴ Performances, therefore, were given only during daylight hours. ⁵ Circling the surrounding area of the courtyard were three levels of galleries with benches where wealthier playgoers sat. ⁶ Less wealthy spectators, called groundlings, stood and watched a play from the courtyard, which was called the pit. ⁷ The actors on stage portrayed stories of love, war, and conspiracy. ⁸ The groundlings often got rowdy and could be disruptive.

1 What is the best change, if any, to make in Part 2?

A. Change *and* to *And*.

B. Change was produced to is produced.

C. Change public theater to Public Theater.

D. Make no change.

2 Which of these sentences would best fit before Part 1?

A. Shakespeare's genius transformed a story of star-crossed lovers into the most famous love story the world has ever known.

B. Considered one of the greatest playwrights, William Shakespeare wrote thirty-seven plays.

C. William Shakespeare was born in Stratford-on-Avon in England.

D. William Shakespeare worked in a theater with no scenery.

3 Which of the following changes is needed in the passage?

A. Part 3: delete a semicolon

B. Part 4: delete therefore

C. Part 5: change courtyard to Courtyard

D. Part 7: add a comma after actors

4 Which transition would best fit at the start of Part 6?

A Similarly

B. Luckily

C. Nevertheless

D. In contrast

5 At the beginning of which part would the words "Like most of his plays" best fit?

A Part 7

B. Part 4

C. Part 2

D. Part 6

6 Which information draws attention away from the main idea?

A. Part 5

B. Part 6

C. Part 7

D. Part 8

7 Which of the following sentences would best elaborate the ideas presented in the passage?

A. The stage was a platform that extended into the pit.

B. Acting companies were made up of boys and men.

C. Actors wore elaborate clothing.

D. Scholars disagree about the dimensions of the original Globe theater.

In-Depth Lesson Plan

	LESSON FOCUS	PRINT AND MEDIA RESOURCES
DAY 1	**Introduction to Response to Literature** Students learn key elements of responding to literature and analyze the Model From Literature (pp. 280–285).	*Writers at Work* **Videotape,** Response to Literature; *Writing Lab* **CD-ROM,** Response to Literature
DAY 2	**Prewriting** Students choose and narrow a topic, consider their audience and purpose and gather information (pp. 286–290).	**Teaching Resources** *Writing Support Transparencies* 13-A–D; *Writing Support Activity Book* 13–1
DAY 3	**Drafting** Students organize their ideas and write their first drafts (pp. 291–292).	**Teaching Resources** *Writing Support Transparency* 13-E
DAY 4	**Revising** Students revise their drafts in terms of overall structure, paragraphs, sentences and word choice (pp. 293–297).	**Teaching Resources** *Writing Support Transparencies* 13-F–H; *Writing Support Activity Book* 13–2
DAY 5	**Editing and Proofreading; Publishing and Presenting** Students check their work for accuracy and correctness and present their final drafts (pp. 298–299).	**Teaching Resources** *Scoring Rubrics on Transparency,* Chapter 13; *Formal Assessment,* Chapter 13

Accelerated Lesson Plan

	LESSON FOCUS	PRINT AND MEDIA RESOURCES
DAY 1	**Drafting** Students review characteristics for cause-and-effect writing, select topics and write drafts.	**Teaching Resources** *Writing Support Transparency* 13-E *Writing Lab* **CD-ROM,** Response to LIterature
DAY 2	**Revising to Presenting** Students work individually or with peers to revise, edit and proofread their work for presentation.	**Teaching Resources** *Writing Support Transparencies* 13-F–H; *Scoring Rubrics on Transparency,* Chapter 13; *Writing Support Activity Book* 13-2; *Formal Assessment,* Chapter 13 *Writing Lab* **CD-ROM,** Response to Literature

Options for Adapting Lesson Plans

HOMEWORK

Have students complete any stage of the lesson for homework.

TECHNOLOGY

Students can complete any stage of the lesson on computer. Have them print out their completed work.

FEATURES

Extend coverage with Connected Assignment (p. 303), Spotlight on the Humanities (p. 304), Media and Technology Skills (p. 305), and the Standardized Test Preparation Workshop (p. 306).

INTEGRATED SKILLS COVERAGE

Integrating Grammar
Agreement in Inverted Sentences, SE p. 295
Common Homonym Errors, SE p. 298

Reading/Writing Connection
Reading Strategy, SE p. 282
Writing Application, SE p. 285

Vocabulary
Integrating Vocabulary Skills ATE p. 284

Language
Language Highlight ATE p. 284

Real-World Connection
ATE p. 292

Viewing and Representing
Critical Viewing, SE pp. 280, 282, 285, 291, 297, 300, 302, 303, 304
Viewing and Representing ATE p. 304

ASSESSMENT SUPPORT

Standardized Test Preparation SE p. 306; ATE p. 297

Standardized Test Preparation Workshop, pp. 25–26

Scoring Rubrics on Transparency, Ch. 13

Formal Assessment, Ch. 13

Writing Assessment and Portfolio Management

MEETING INDIVIDUAL NEEDS

Less Advanced Students ATE pp. 283, 288, 307; See also Ongoing Assessments ATE pp. 281, 283, 287, 289, 292, 295, 296, 299

ESL Students ATE pp. 285, 286, 307

Gifted/Talented Students ATE p. 301

BLOCK SCHEDULING

Pacing Suggestions
For 90-minute Blocks
• Have students complete the Prewriting and Drafting stages in a single period.
• Focus one class period on Revising and Editing and Publishing and Presenting. Allow at least 30 minutes for peer revision.

Resources for Varying Instruction
• *Writing Lab* **CD-ROM** If your students have access to hardware, a 90-minute block provides an ideal opportunity for students to work on computer.
• *Writers at Work* **Videotape** Show the Response to Literature segment in class.

Professional Development Support
• *How to Manage Instruction in the Block* This Teaching Resource provides management and activity suggestions.

MEDIA AND TECHNOLOGY

For the Student
• *Writing Lab* **CD-ROM**, Response to Literature

For the Teacher
• *Writers at Work* **Videotape**, Response to Literature
• *Resource Pro* **CD-ROM**

WRITING AND GRAMMAR WEBSITE

The Interactive Writing and Grammar Website provides a wide array of support for students, teachers and parents. Writing support includes:

• Interactive revision checkers
• Scoring rubrics with complete models

phwg.phschool.com

LITERATURE CONNECTIONS

Related Selections from *Prentice Hall Literature: Timeless Voices, Timeless Themes*, Gold:
"In These Girls, Hope Is a Muscle," Steve Gietschier, SE p. 285

Chapter
13 Response to Literature

Lesson Objectives

1. To understand the characteristics of a written response to literature.

2. To choose and narrow a topic for a written response to literature.

3. To consider audience and purpose in developing a writing topic.

4. To apply strategies for gathering and organizing details.

5. To draft a response to literature with an introduction, body, and conclusion.

6. To evaluate and revise the overall structure of a draft of a response to literature.

7. To write strong topic sentences for paragraphs.

8. To revise sentences for clarity.

9. To add evaluative modifiers.

10. To benefit from the peer review process in the revision of a written response to literature.

11. To edit, proofread, and publish a written response to literature.

Critical Viewing

Infer Students may say that the painting presents reading as an activity that encourages contentment, relaxation, or pleasant solitude.

Marshian Boy, Christian Pierre, Private Collection

▲ **Critical Viewing**
What message does this painting convey about reading?
[Infer]

Response to Literature in Everyday Life

Have you ever read a poem, play, or story that you couldn't put out of your mind? A character may have appealed to you or appalled you, the ending may have surprised or disappointed you, or you may simply have enjoyed the craft of a specific author. To extend your reading experience, you may have discussed your ideas with a friend or family member, or you may have compared responses with classmates at school.

In addition to reacting to the fiction you read, you may also find yourself analyzing the effectiveness of an advertisement, the persuasiveness of a speech, the realism of a movie script, or the clarity of another type of writing. In all cases, you are using the same set of critical response skills—the ones you'll learn and refine in this chapter.

280 • Response to Literature

⏱ TIME AND RESOURCE MANAGER

Resources
Technology: Writers at Work videotape

In-Depth Coverage	Accelerated Pace
• Cover pp. 280–281 in class. • Show Response to Literature section of the Writers at Work videotape. • Read literary review (pp. 282–285) in class, and use it with students to brainstorm for topics for responses to literature. • Discuss examples of written responses to literature, such as book reviews and personal essays.	• Discuss definitions and types of written responses to literature in class. • Assign Model From Literature (pp. 282–285) for independent reading.

What Is a Response-to-Literature Essay?

When you write a **response-to-literature essay**, you express the *what, how,* and *why* behind a piece of literature's effect on you as a reader. An effective response-to-literature essay

- analyzes the content of a literary work, its related ideas, or the work's effect on the reader.
- focuses on a single aspect of the work or gives an overall view of it.
- relies on evidence from the literary work to support the opinions the writer presents.
- uses a logical organization to convey ideas clearly.

To see the criteria on which your response-to-literature essay may be judged, preview the Rubric for Self-Assessment on page 299.

Types of Responses to Literature

There are many ways to share your response to literature. Here are some of the most common:

- **Literary interpretations** show how literary elements combine to create a general effect in a work of literature.
- **Critical reviews** present an evaluation of a piece of writing, citing evidence in the work to support the reviewer's opinions.
- **Character studies** analyze the actions, beliefs, behaviors, or motivations of one character in a literary work.
- **Comparisons of works of literature** compare two or more works of literature. These may discuss two works by one author, compare the work of two writers, or examine one literary element in several pieces of literature.

PREVIEW
Student Work
IN PROGRESS

In this chapter, you will follow the work of Andrea Montgomery, a student at Omaha Northwest High School in Omaha, Nebraska. You will see how Andrea used writing process strategies to evaluate the success of the poem "The Raven," by Edgar Allan Poe.

Writers in
ACTION

As a book reviewer whose work appears in a magazine, Lawrence Chua believes a book reviewer's job is to be aware of the power of literature:

"We pay attention to the way that we're reading, how we're processing the information that's on the page, how we're understanding it, what that's doing to us, what emotions that might provoke in us, what rage, anxiety, despair, . . . love, that might provoke in us, and why the text does that."

PREPARE and ENGAGE

Interest GRABBER On an overhead projector, display "in Just-Spring" by E. E. Cummings (*Timeless Voices, Timeless Themes,* Bronze level, page 404). Ask students to tell why they like or do not like the poem. Get a range of responses, from "I like the funny words, such as *puddle-wonderful"* to "It's too confusing without capitals and punctuation, and the spacing looks dumb." Tell students that in this chapter, they will give their opinion of a longer, more detailed literary work of their choice.

Activate Prior Knowledge

Go around the classroom and have each student name a written work he or she remembers and still thinks about. (Written works may vary in form and might include an article, a comic book, a novel, or a poem.) Have students explain briefly why they like the work. This activity will allow students to realize that they already possess the skills they need to write a response to a literary work.

☑ ONGOING ASSESSMENT: Diagnose

Use one of the following options to diagnose students' current level of proficiency in writing responses to literature.

Option 1 Ask each student to select the strongest example of his or her written responses to literature from last year. Review these samples to determine which students will need extra support in developing a written response to literature.	**Option 2** Ask each student to choose a literary work that he or she liked or disliked and to write one or two sentences explaining their reactions. If students have difficulty articulating their reasons, you may need to devote more time to the gathering evidence and elaboration phases of the writing process.

Reading\Writing Connection

Reading: Evaluate an Opinion

Readers almost always have personal reactions to the things they read. Point out to students that no person's opinion is more correct than anyone else's. However, critics must support their opinions with specific examples from the work, with their own knowledge or experience, or with references to a writer's other works.

Teaching From the Model

Use the Model From Literature to show how Elster uses different kinds of evidence to back up his opinion that *The Miracle of Language* is a good book.

Critical Viewing

Analyze Students may mention the fact that public libraries make literature available to readers regardless of their racial, political, religious, or economic backgrounds.

13.1 Model From Literature

Charles H. Elster is the author of many books on the development and correct use of the English language. He has also written extensively on using vocabulary effectively in speaking and writing. In this newspaper review, he praises the knowledge and experience of a colleague, Richard Lederer, and his book, The Miracle of Language.

Reading Strategy: Evaluate an Opinion Book reviews present the opinion of the reviewer who writes them. Whether the critic thinks the book is a wild success or a terrible bore, the review must include facts and examples from the writing to support an opinion. First, identify the opinion Elster presents. Then, in order to evaluate whether you agree with him, look for the evidence he cites to support his ideas. This way, you'll know whether his review is valuable to you.

▲ **Critical Viewing** In what ways do public libraries enhance the opportunities for response-to-literature activities? **[Analyze]**

Lederer's "Miracle" Is His Well of Wit and Wisdom With Words

Review by Charles Harrington Elster

Introduce yourself to Richard Lederer and you will in turn be introduced to what he calls "the most glorious of all human inventions, incomparably the finest of our achievements"—the English language. It is sure to be an enlightening association, for in the hands of this master teacher turned best-selling author, words are not just linguistic widgets and language is a lot more than a subject or object.

In the opening paragraph, Elster piques the reader's curiosity about the author of the book and identifies the writer's expertise: language.

282 • Response to Literature

To Lederer, language is "like the air we breathe"—invisible, ubiquitous and essential. It is also paradoxical, both a loyal friend and a cantankerous colleague. And, like love, it is tantalizing and mysterious, fraught with passion and adventure. In short, language is a miracle, says Lederer, one that defines who and what we are.

"The birth of language," he writes, "is the dawn of humanity; in our beginning was the word. We have always been endowed with language because before we had words we were not human beings."

In his previous books—*Anguished English, Get Thee to a Punnery, Crazy English* and *The Play of Words*—Lederer took us on giddy joyrides, delighting us with curiosities, trivia and sidesplitting solecisms. In *The Miracle of Language*, however, Lederer's love affair with language has mellowed into pure and eloquent devotion. This book has a more serious tone and intent, for its author has learned much from his linguistic journeys and has profound lessons to impart. . . .

The book begins with the miraculous stories of Helen Keller, Richard Wright, Malcolm X and Anne Frank, whose lives were transformed and liberated by language. Then, with wit and insight, Lederer dishes up a salmagundi of linguistic subjects. Like a master chef concocting a gourmet meal, he offers one delectable tidbit after another, until the reader is pleasantly stuffed with his robust enthusiasm for the savor and nourishment of words.

"Words," says Lederer, "are living, changing reflections of human attitudes, not dead and petrified artifacts. As long as we human beings remain alive, we shall shape, stretch and re-create our language."

There are chapters on linguistic prejudice, the power of short words, the richness of the English vocabulary, and a lovely paean to the epistolary art—the writing of letters. There are also encomi-

The writer provides a direct quotation to introduce the writer's ideas to an audience of newspaper readers.

Elster compares this book with others Lederer has written, identifying The Miracle of Language *as a more serious work that imparts "profound lessons."*

Elster explains the organization of the book, providing details and elaboration of each topic and lesson that Lederer addresses.

Model From Literature • 283

Engage Students Through Literature

Use this Model From Literature as one way to help students generate topics for responses to literature.

1. Work through the text and marginal notes with the whole class.

2. Point out the reviewer's opinions, along with evidence he uses to back them up. For example:
   - "enlightening association"—examples of Lederer's ideas that enlightened Elster
   - "master teacher"—quotations from the book to show that Lederer knows his subject
   - "pure and eloquent"—quotes from the book that Elster considers eloquent
   - "profound lessons"—examples of lessons from the book

3. Invite students to identify and reflect on literary works that have evoked a strong response (either positive or negative) in them.

Customize for
Less Advanced Students

This review contains many challenging vocabulary words, including (but not limited to) *widgets, ubiquitous, cantankerous, fraught, solecisms, salmagundi, concocting, paean, epistolary, encomiums, neologizer, adipose, pleonasm, banal, wag.* Have partners work together to find synonyms for these words. Then they can reread the review, inserting the easier words. Examples include "invisible, ~~ubiquitous~~ (everywhere) and essential" and "~~fraught with~~ (full of) passion."

☑ **ONGOING ASSESSMENT: Monitor and Reinforce**

If some students have difficulty with the vocabulary in the Model From Literature, use one of the following options.

Option 1 If students read the model independently, have them list any unfamiliar words they encounter. Then go over pronunciations and definitions with the class.	**Option 2** If the model is read aloud in class, define unfamiliar words as they come up. Elster uses many formidable words, such as *salmagundi* and *encomiums*, with which students may need help.

Language Highlight

Doublespeak George Orwell's novel *1984* (1948), describes England as a totalitarian society in which "telescreens" in every home spy on the inhabitants, and the main character's job is to rewrite history. Newspeak is a language Orwell invented for his novel. *Doublespeak* and *doublethink* are terms that refer to intentionally indirect speech and thought that cloud true meaning, as in calling garbage collectors "removal engineers."

Integrating Vocabulary Skills

Redundancy A redundant phrase, such as "daily journal," says the same thing twice. All journals are daily, according to the definition of the word *journal*. Therefore, the word *daily* is unnecessary. *Au jus* mean "with juice," so the word *with* in "roast beef with au jus" is redundant. Similarly, *du jour* means "of the day," so "soup du jour of the day" is silly.

ums to Samuel Johnson (who paved the way for the modern dictionary), Ambrose Bierce, T. S. Eliot, Mark Twain ("who gave a young nation a voice to sing of itself"), Emily Dickinson, Lewis Carroll and William Shakespeare, "our all-time champion neologizer," who invented an astounding 10 percent of his vocabulary and many of our most familiar words and phrases.

And there are warnings: In a chapter on the legacy of George Orwell, Lederer explores the dangers of Doublespeak, that sinister language that tells us workers are "reclassified," "deselected" or "nonretained" when they are fired; new taxes are "revenue enhancement"; and that the latest thing in nuclear missiles is the "Peacekeeper." Orwell, says Lederer, "alerted us that when words are used to lie rather than to tell the truth, the house of language grows dark and the human spirit withers."

In "The Department of Redundancy Department" (where members of William Safire's "Squad Squad" file duplicate copies of their complaints), Lederer unleashes his cutting wit on the "adipose tissue . . . of our linguistic waistline." We are "adrift in a sea of American overspeak," he says, in which redundancies and pleonasm are "the junk food of our language."

If you don't believe that, consult the nearest menu, where you will likely find "roast beef with au jus" and "soup du jour of the day." "Be sure to record these in your daily journal," Lederer writes.

Lederer rails against such absurdities as "at this point in time," "consensus of opinion," "foreign imports," "new innovations," "past experience," "advance warnings" and the unspeakably banal "free gift."

"I am surrounded by an army of recurrently repetitive redundancies," he writes. "In fact, I am completely surrounded. Even more than that, I am completely surrounded on all sides."

Lederer lights the way to sanity with three cheerful chapters in celebration of books and libraries—miraculous places where, as one student put it, "it's hard to avoid reading."

Lederer also is a great champion of librarians, those unsung

As the critic describes the book, he includes more quotations to support the lessons Lederer includes.

In this paragraph and the three that follow, Elster celebrates Lederer's "cutting wit" and provides examples to offer enthusiasm and support for Lederer's work.

Elster's review covers a wider range of subjects to provide an overall and comprehensive look at the work.

heroes on the front lines of literacy who, in an "average day," put up with some truly outrageous requests: "Ya got any good books here?" "Where are your hysterical novels?" "I want a book with no chapters."

With *The Miracle of Language*, Lederer, America's foremost wag of words, has also become a sage. If you retain just one lesson from this wise and engaging book, may it be this:

"The manner in which you utter words, write words and receive words throughout your life determines how effectively and resourcefully you carry on the business of being a member of the human race. . . . As people perceive that all about them things fall apart—education, the environment, the moral fabric—they are concerned to preserve and enlarge the hallmark of their human-ness, and that hallmark is their language."

Writing Application: Support Your Opinion
As you draft your response-to-literature essay, support your ideas and opinions with evidence from the work that prove your points.

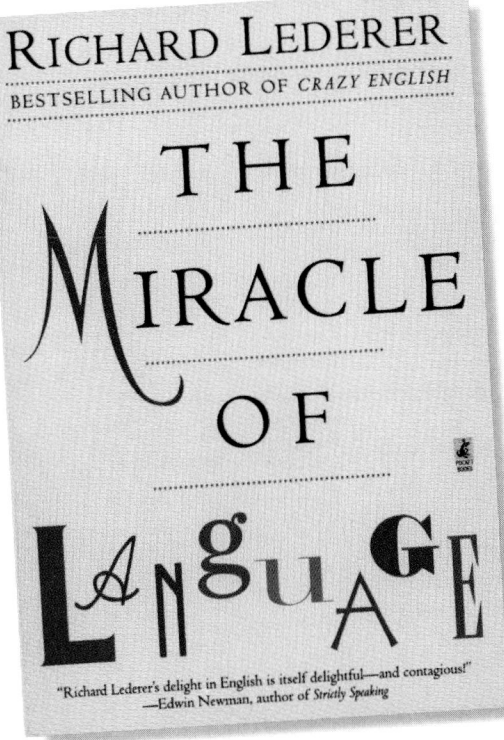

RICHARD LEDERER
BESTSELLING AUTHOR OF *CRAZY ENGLISH*

THE
MIRACLE
OF
LANGUAGE

"Richard Lederer's delight in English is itself delightful—and contagious!"
—Edwin Newman, author of *Strictly Speaking*

To conclude the review, Elster sum-marizes a key point from the book, clear-ly encouraging his audience to read the The Miracle of Language.

◀ **Critical Viewing**
What information on the cover of Lederer's book might encour-age readers to read the work? **[Interpret]**

LITERATURE

For another example of a response to litera-ture, see "In These Girls, Hope Is a Muscle," a book review by Steve Gietschier in *Prentice Hall Literature: Timeless Voices, Timeless Themes*, Gold.

Model From Literature • 285

Responding to Literature

Students might compare and contrast these two book reviews. Lederer's book deals with ideas, so Elster's review focuses on those ideas. Blais's book is about people, so Gietschier's review focuses on the human aspect of a basketball team. Both reviewers use details from the books to support their opinions.

Customize for
ESL Students

If the Model From Literature is too hard for some students, work with them as a group, using "In These Girls, Hope Is a Muscle" as the model for responding to literature.

Reading\Writing Connection
Writing: Support Your Opinion

Make sure that students understand the importance of supporting ideas and opinions with evidence. Explain to them that it will make their arguments stronger and more convincing.

Critical Viewing

Interpret Students may suggest that the phrases "best selling author" and "delightful—and contagious" create interest and positive feelings.

Prewriting: Class Book Awards

Teaching Resources: Writing Support Transparency 13-A

1. Go around the room and have each student name a book, story, or author he or she liked. As each student answers, call for a show of hands of others who read and liked the work.

2. Keep a tally on the chalkboard of the works that get the greatest number of positive responses.

3. You might want to organize students into small groups according to the books they like. Students can discuss their group's book and why they liked it. This discussion may generate ideas for topics.

Customize for
ESL Students

If students are having difficulty finding a work to respond to, suggest that they focus on authors from their home cultures, such as Isabel Allende, Leslie Marmon Silko, Tomás Rivera, Langston Hughes, Gish Jen, Naomi Shihab Nye, Yoshiko Uchida, and others.

13.2 Prewriting

Choosing Your Topic

Choose a selection to which you had a strong response. Use one or more of the following strategies to select a topic on which to write:

Strategies for Generating Topics

1. **Class Book Awards** Conduct a class survey to discover which books are favorites. You can narrow the focus of your survey by asking about books with the most interesting characters, the most suspenseful plot, or the most descriptive writing. Compare your own favorites against the list of winners, and choose a topic to develop.

2. **Sentence Starters** Sometimes, starting with an open-ended sentence can stimulate memories and opinions about literature. Complete the sentences below, and develop each idea for five minutes. Review your work to choose a topic for your essay.
   • A poem that moved me was . . .
   • One piece of writing that helped me understand life better was . . .
   • The most exciting ending I remember was . . .
   • I wish something had happened differently in . . .

Writing Lab
CD-ROM

For more help finding a topic, explore the activities and suggestions in the Choosing a Topic section of the Response to Literature lesson.

Student Work
IN PROGRESS

Name: *Andrea Montgomery*
Omaha Northwest High School
Omaha, NE

Using Sentence Starters to Find a Topic

When Andrea completed this sentence starter, she realized she had a poet whose work she could address in a response-to-literature essay.

A poem that had a strong effect on me was "The Raven." I read "The Tell-Tale Heart" by Poe in middle school. It was scary, but not like Stephen King. I like the way Poe writes. I think he has an interesting style. The rhymes seem to pull you into the eerie settings.

286 • Response to Literature

⏱ TIME AND RESOURCE MANAGER

Resources
Print: Writing Support Transparencies 13 A–D, Writing Support Activity Book 13-1
Technology: Writing Lab CD-ROM, Response to Literature

In-Depth Coverage	Accelerated Pace
• Cover pp. 286–290 in class. • Guide students through the strategies for generating topics. • Have students use hexagonal writing to narrow their topics.	• Have students read pp. 286–290 independently. • Ask students to submit topic proposals for your review.

TOPIC BANK

If you are having trouble finding a topic, review the following possibilities:

1. **Response to a Biography** Biographers often choose subjects who have lived a life worth examining. Consider the biographies you have enjoyed, and write a response in which you explain what readers can learn from the subject's experiences, philosophy, or actions.

2. **Letter to an Author** Write a letter to an author explaining your reaction to a particular work. In your letter, use specific evidence to back up your opinions, but take the opportunity to ask questions that your own analysis has left you unable to answer.

Responding to Fine Art

3. *Mexican Market* conveys a strong impression of its subject. Like art, literature can show you places you've never been. Consider the stories you know that are especially successful at creating a fictional setting or conveying a real-life exotic one to readers who may never have visited it. In an essay, evaluate the setting of the work you selected.

Mexican Market (detail), Jane Scott, Schalkwijk

Responding to Literature

4. Read Toni Cade Bambara's story "Blues Ain't No Mockin Bird," which shows the conflict between the media and a person's right to privacy. Then, in an essay, explain how the author develops this conflict and identify your own position on this issue. You can find the story in *Prentice Hall Literature: Timeless Voices, Timeless Themes*, Gold.

Cooperative Writing Opportunity

5. **Comparison of Short Stories** Work with a group to identify several stories that are related by theme, by setting, or by conflict. Split the task of analyzing each story according to the link that you identify. Present your essays in a booklet. To put your responses in context, include an introduction that presents the comparisons you have found.

Prewriting • 287

Responding to Fine Art
Mexican Market by Jane Scott
Teaching Resources: Writing Support Transparency 13-B

1. Display the transparency and invite students to discuss it. The following questions may be used to prompt discussion:
   • How many different objects can you identify in the photograph? What is notable about the people in the market? What words could you use to describe the mood or atmosphere this photo evokes?

2. Urge students to brainstorm topics suggested by the art. Here are some possibilities:
   • A poem, story, or play featuring an urban setting
   • A work of fiction or nonfiction containing vivid descriptions of things, people, and places

3. Students may include these topics in their data banks and add ideas of their own.

Responding to Literature

In Bambara's story, the filmmakers don't understand Granny, and they never will: they think everyone is eager to be in a movie. Granny understands them, though. She knows that they are so busy feeling important that they are rude and unable to put themselves in another person's place. Granny is busy living her life and taking care of her family—things that are really important.

Spotlight on the Humanities

For additional topic suggestions, refer students to the Spotlight on the Humanities on page 304.

☑ ONGOING ASSESSMENT: Monitor and Reinforce

If some students are having difficulty coming up with topics, use one of the following options.

Option 1 Suggest that students choose ideas from the Topic Bank. If many students have difficulty, work with the whole class on one idea selected from the Topic Bank or on ideas suggested by students.	**Option 2** If Topic Bank ideas seem too difficult, suggest that students try one of the assignments from the Topic Bank for Heterogeneous Classes in the Teaching Resources.

⏱ TIME SAVERS!

📄 **Writing Support Transparencies**
Use the transparencies for Chapter 13 to introduce or execute these strategies.

Prewriting: Using Hexagonal Writing

Teaching Resources: Writing Support Transparency 13-C; Writing Support Activity Book 13-1

1. Display the transparency.

2. Use Andrea's hexagonal writing to demonstrate how she identified the aspect of "The Raven" that interested her most.

3. Give students copies of the blank organizer for them to use as they narrow their topics.

Customize for
Less Advanced Students

Point out that the student model shows only one possible way of responding to a written work. Moreover, students may respond more readily to another genre besides poetry, such as humor, mystery, or science fiction. Help them find a text they like rather than one they find intimidating.

288

13.2

Narrowing Your Topic

To present an effective response that is clear to your readers, narrow your focus by finding a single point to address.

Use Hexagonal Writing to Narrow a Topic

By studying your topic from six basic angles, you can focus your response. Follow the directions below to complete each section of a hexagon like the one shown below. When the hexagon is finished, review your notes to focus your topic.

Plot Summarize the selection.

Personal Allusions Jot down experiences from your own life that the selection suggests to you.

Theme Identify the theme or generalization about life that the selection presents.

Analysis Provide evidence from the selection to support the theme you have identified.

Literary Allusions Jot down other works of literature that have a similar theme.

Evaluate Give your opinion of the work.

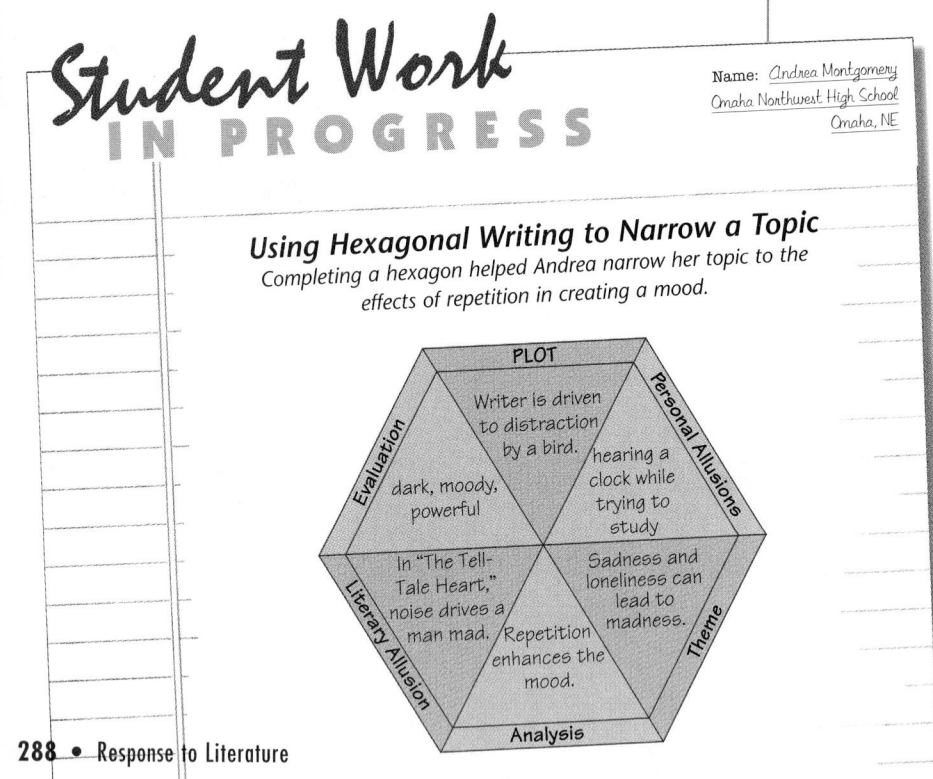

Student Work IN PROGRESS

Name: *Andrea Montgomery*
Omaha Northwest High School
Omaha, NE

Using Hexagonal Writing to Narrow a Topic
Completing a hexagon helped Andrea narrow her topic to the effects of repetition in creating a mood.

PLOT — Writer is driven to distraction by a bird.
Evaluation — dark, moody, powerful
Personal Allusions — hearing a clock while trying to study
Theme — Sadness and loneliness can lead to madness.
Analysis — Repetition enhances the mood.
Literary Allusion — In "The Tell-Tale Heart," noise drives a man mad.

288 • Response to Literature

13.3 Drafting

Shaping Your Writing

Develop a Thesis Statement

Your draft should have a clear statement of the main idea or thesis you intend to develop. Review your prewriting notes, looking for a single idea that brings together the ideas you've generated and the support you've gathered, Write this as a single sentence. Use this sentence, your thesis statement, to direct the writing of your response to literature.

SAMPLE THESIS STATEMENTS

- Daphne du Maurier's "The Birds" presents a gripping series of events to illustrate the unpredictability of nature.

- In "One Ordinary Day, With Peanuts," by Shirley Jackson, the main character is motivated by a wish to be kind to strangers.

- Even though it was written more than two thousand years ago, Homer's epic the Odyssey presents a hero that today's audiences can respect.

Organize to Support Your Ideas

Presenting your ideas in an organized way helps you guide your readers in following your thoughts and ideas.

Introduction After an inspired lead that grabs your audience's attention and links to your main ideas, your introduction should meet three more expectations:

- Identify the title and author of the work.
- State your thesis.
- Offer a brief summary of the work you are discussing.

Your response to literature should be evaluative or analytical, so avoid devoting too much attention to your summary. The length and level of this summary should be appropriate to your intended audience's needs.

Body Paragraphs Your development of a thesis is the main part of your essay. To build your thesis, offer several supporting ideas. Introduce each key idea in a new paragraph, and then use the details that you have gathered from the selection to support each idea.

Conclusion Your conclusion should restate your main ideas or make a final point. You can also present something new, such as your recommendation or opinion.

▲ Critical Viewing
What elements of this photograph would complement the frightening tone of a story such as Daphne du Maurier's "The Birds"? [Connect]

Drafting • 291

Step-by-Step Teaching Guide

Drafting: Shaping Your Writing

1. The thesis statement of an essay or review is the main point the writer wants to prove or defend. Often it serves as the writer's opening sentence. Invite the students to compare a thesis statement to the foundation of a building. The foundation must be dug and set in place before the builders can add the walls and floors and roof. In the same way, a thesis statement gives rise to all of the ideas in the body of an essay.

2. Suggest that students think of the thesis statement as a one-sentence summary of their response to a work of literature. From this sentence, the reader should be able to get a good idea of what the essay will say.

3. Go over the sample thesis statements on the page with the whole class. Ask students to suggest the kinds of evidence the writers might provide to defend these statements. Even if they have not read the works, students should see that the first paper should describe the gripping events in "The Birds" and explain why they are surprising, the second should list the actions taken by Jackson's main character and explain why they show that he wants to be kind, and the third should discuss the character of Odysseus and demonstrate why he is admirable.

Critical Viewing

Connect Students may mention the menacing quality of the birds.

⏱ TIME AND RESOURCE MANAGER

Resources
Print: Writing Support Transparency 13-E
Technology: Writing Lab CD-ROM, Response to Literature

In-Depth Coverage	Accelerated Pace
• Cover pp. 291–292 in class. • Have students draft their essays in class.	• Assign pp. 291–292 for independent student review. • Students draft their essays independently.

⏱ TIME SAVERS!

 Writing Support Transparencies
Use the transparencies for Chapter 13 to teach these strategies.

Drafting: Providing Elaboration

Teaching Resources: Writing Support Transparency 13-E

1. Go over the three types of supporting references, and give examples of situations in which students might want to use each type. Quotations and examples often go hand in hand. Examples of rhymes or similes, for example, would be quotations of actual rhymes and similes used by the author. On the other hand, paraphrases of an author's words are an apt way to elaborate on ideas about a work's theme, characters, or conflicts.

2. Refer students back to the Model from Literature. Have them note how Elster uses all three types of supporting references in his review of Lederer's book.

Real-World Connection

In a courtroom, lawyers must provide evidence to convince the judge and jury of the truth of their arguments. A defense attorney cannot simply claim that his or her client is innocent; he or she must back up this claim with facts and supporting evidence. In the same way, writers cannot make unsubstantiated claims about literary works they are reviewing. They must defend their opinions with concrete details in order to be believed.

13.3

Providing Elaboration

In everyday conversation, you probably often say, "You know what I mean." When you find your listener doesn't understand the point you imply, you can offer more explanation. Writing is not as interactive as conversation; help your reader know what you mean by providing elaboration to develop your points.

Instead of asking readers to trust your analysis, include specific examples from the text that illustrate your ideas.

Include References to Support Your Thesis

Include citations from the literary work to support the points you are making. These can include quotations of a character's dialogue, an example of a specific literary element, or an excerpt from the work. Consider these specific suggestions:

- **Quotations** Include quotations to illustrate a character's attitude, a writer's word choice, or an essay's argument.
- **Examples** Insert an example of a specific literary element to enhance your analysis of a writer's style.
- **Paraphrases** To develop a writer's theme, discuss the conflict, analyze the character, or restate key ideas from the literature in your own words.

✏ Collaborative Writing Tip

If you meet to discuss your ideas with a partner, you may discover the points that need the most explanation. Use your experience to guide you as you draft.

Student Work
IN PROGRESS

Name: *Andrea Montgomery*
Omaha Northwest High School
Omaha, NE

Incorporating References From the Text

To make her essay more effective, Andrea included direct quotations from the text to make her points. In the excerpt shown here, references to the test are underlined.

motion of the poem faster. To do this, Poe uses sets of three words that sound similar. For example, in the second stanza, Poe plays off the ending *–ember* with "remember/December/ember" and the ending *-orrow* with "morrow/borrow/sorrow." To extend the movement of the rhythm, Poe also intertwines the rhymes of "floor/Lenore/evermore" to pull the stanza together. Throughout the poem, Poe provides this type of triple rhyme.

292 • Response to Literature

⏱ TIME SAVERS!

 **Writing Support Transparencies**
Use the transparencies for Chapter 13 to teach these strategies.

☑ ONGOING ASSESSMENT: Monitor and Reinforce

If some students seize up and find it difficult to begin drafting, try the follwing strategy.

Have students set aside all of their prewriting notes. Invite them to reflect on the experience of reading their chosen literary work. What especially interested, impressed, or struck them about the work? Have them write down their thoughts as quickly as possible in a "quick, loose draft." Urge students to write without stopping to evaluate their work. Later they can choose the best ideas from this draft to organize and shape into a clear response to literature.

13.4 *Revising*

Once you have completed your first draft, take the time to revise your work. Set aside time to read through your writing, looking at structure, paragraphing, sentences, and word choice. Improving and polishing these elements can make your writing more interesting, accurate, and effective.

Revising Your Overall Structure

Check for Unity

Because it is complex and multifaceted, literature often provokes mixed responses. However, to avoid generating confusion in your reader, be sure you have remained true to the narrowed focus you have planned. Review your draft to see that you have presented a single idea to your reader. Eliminate any paragraphs or details that do not contribute to this idea.

▶**REVISION STRATEGY**
Identifying Contradictory Information

To keep your writing streamlined, identify ideas that stray from your thesis statement. Review your draft, confirming that each paragraph contains information that supports your main idea. If you notice paragraphs, details, or examples that distract from your main idea, circle these elements. When you have reviewed you draft, evaluate the circled information.

Evaluate	Revise
• Are there several circled items that seem related?	• If you can devise a way to link the information to your analysis, revise to include it. You may want to add a single paragraph for these details. If you choose this path, add a transitional sentence to develop the contrast so your readers can follow your thinking.
• Are there some circled items that seem random?	• Eliminate the items that you cannot link to your thesis.

Writers in
ACTION

E. B. White's book The Elements of Style *serves as a useful reference for writers of all ability levels. In addition to setting the standard for clarity in writing, he describes an approach to writing and offers this advice:*

"Remember, it is no sign of weakness or defeat that your manuscript ends up in need of major surgery. This is a common occurrence in all writing, and among the best writers."

Step-by-Step Teaching Guide

Revising: Revising Your Overall Structure

Remind students that even though they may have many things to say, some details may not be relevant to the central focus of their responses to this piece of literature. No matter how much students like these details, they should leave them out.

More About the Writer

Associated with the *New Yorker* magazine for nearly sixty years until his death in 1985, E. B. White was widely admired as a wit and a prose stylist. He remains best known for a pair of classic novels for children, *Stuart Little* (1945) and *Charlotte's Web* (1952).

⏱ **TIME AND RESOURCE MANAGER**

Resources
Print: Writing Support Transparencies 13F–H, Writing Support Activity Book 13-2
Technology: Writing Lab CD-ROM, Response to Literature

In-Depth Coverage	Accelerated Pace
• Cover pp. 293–297 in class. • Discuss the revision process with students. Review subject-verb agreement and evaluative modifiers.	• Assign pp. 293–297 for independent student review. • Have students work independently to revise their writing.

1. One basic way to organize a strong paragraph is to begin it with the topic sentence and then to add supporting details in order of importance. A final sentence can provide transition to the next paragraph or restate the topic sentence. This is not the only way to organize a paragraph, but it is one good way to start.

2. Point out how Andrea Montgomery added details. *Rapping* and *tapping* are much more interesting than *words*.

13.4

Revising Your Paragraphs
Review Topical Paragraphs

The topical, or body, paragraphs of your essay should state, develop, and support a key idea. Ultimately, they should contribute to your thesis statement. Each topical paragraph has a topic sentence that states an idea. Other sentences in the paragraph should expand, elaborate, and support the idea. To tune up your topical paragraphs, highlight all the topic sentences in your draft, and then be sure that each idea is well supported.

▶ **REVISION STRATEGY**
Highlighting Topic Sentences

Use a highlighter to mark the topic sentences of each of your topical paragraphs. For each, review the sentences that support the main idea, and evaluate the effectiveness of the paragraph. When possible, add more explanation, refine word choice to clarify your ideas, or review the literature you are discussing to find an example that will strengthen your point.

Student Work
IN PROGRESS

Name: *Andrea Montgomery*
Omaha Northwest High School
Omaha, NE

Highlighting Topic Sentences

When Andrea highlighted the topic sentence of this paragraph, she saw several opportunities for revision. In addition to adding specific language from "The Raven," she planned to add a complete reference to make her ideas more clear.

Poe also repeats words to emphasize a point. For example, *Add reference from poem.* to let the reader feel the nervousness created by the bird's knocking, Poe repeats the words throughout "rapping" three times in the first stanza. He adds the word "tapping" to complete the repetition of the sound.

TIME SAVERS!

Writing Support Transparencies
Use the transparencies for Chapter 13 to teach these strategies.

Revising Your Sentences

Review Sentence Clarity

When you are adding quotations from literature into your own writing, the resulting sentences may be unclear. To be sure your points are clear, review each sentence in your draft. Make sure that each one is grammatically correct. A strategy for doing this is to circle all the subjects and verbs.

▶ **REVISION STRATEGY**
Circling Subjects and Verbs

To evaluate the sentences in your draft, circle the subjects and verbs in each sentence. Be sure that the subjects and the verbs in each sentence agree. Be especially wary of sentences whose subjects and verbs are separated by modifiers, phrases, or clauses.

SEPARATED BY A PHRASE: The *celebration*, usually attended by thousands, *attracts* intense media coverage.

SEPARATED BY A CLAUSE: The *revelers*, who have been here since dawn, *remain* peaceful despite their number.

⚙ Grammar and Style Tip

If you are not sure about subject-verb agreement in a sentence, take out all the modifiers and look again.

Grammar in Your Writing
Agreement in Inverted Sentences

In an **inverted sentence**, the verb precedes its subject. Despite this format, the subject and verb must still agree. In this example, the subject *seat* follows the verb *is*.

Example: Near the bookcase is the most comfortable seat in the library.

The words *there* and *here* at the beginning of a sentence often signal an inverted sentence. These words are not the subject of the sentence; instead, the subject appears after the verb. For example, in the first of the following sentences, the singular subject *article* takes the singular verb *is*. In the second sentence, the plural subject *articles* takes the plural verb *are*.

Example: Here is the best article on the topic.
Example: Here are the more useful articles on the topic.

Find It in Your Reading Review "Lederer's 'Miracle' Is His Well of Wit and Wisdom With Words" on pages 282–285. Locate at least three inverted sentences, and analyze the agreement between subject and verb.

Find It in Your Writing Review your draft to find inverted sentences. Confirm the correct subject-verb agreement, and revise as necessary.

For more on subject-verb agreement, see Chapter 25.

Revising: Revising Your Sentences

Briefly review subject-verb agreement. Singular subjects take singular verbs; plural subjects take plural verbs. Go over tricky collective nouns, such as *team, audience, group, herd,* and so on, each of which stands for more than one person or animal but takes a singular verb when used to refer to a group acting as a unit.

Grammar in Your Writing: Agreement in Inverted Sentences

Suggest that students mentally rearrange inverted sentences so the subject comes at the beginning. If they think of the first example sentence as "The most comfortable seat in the library is near the bookcase," the subject, *seat,* is easy to spot.

Find It in Your Reading

Sample answers from Elster's seventh paragraph:

"There are chapters on linguistic prejudice . . ." subject: *chapters;* verb: *are*

"There are also encomiums . . ." subject: *encomiums;* verb: *are*

"And there are warnings . . ." subject: *warnings;* verb: *are*

Find It in Your Writing

Have students exchange papers with partners and look for problems in subject-verb agreement in one another's inverted sentences.

☑ ONGOING ASSESSMENT: Prerequisite Skills

If students have difficulty with subject-verb agreement, you may find it helpful to refer them to the following materials to assure coverage of prerequisite knowledge.

In the Textbook	Print Resources	Technology
Basic Sentence Parts, pp. 422–433 Agreement, pp. 572–582	Grammar Exercise Workbook, pp. 41–42, 49–52, 139–144	Language Lab CD-ROM, Subject-Verb Agreement; On-Line Exercise Bank, Sections 20.1, 20.2, and 25.1

Revising: Revising Your Word Choice

Teaching Resources: Writing Support Transparency 13-G

1. If students need help finding modifiers that convey just enough praise or criticism, they can use a thesaurus. Point out the great difference in the impressions made by the sentences "The book was good" and "The book was compelling." Remind students of Mark Twain's rule: "Use the right word, not its second cousin."

2. As students go through their essays to revise their modifiers, have them consider whether any modifiers are actually needed. There may be situations in which it is effective to show the reader the work's characteristics by example or quotation. In these cases, students should be sure to choose telling examples that support the points they want to make.

13.4

Revising Your Word Choice
Add Evaluative Modifiers

Although all the modifiers in your draft should be powerful, the words you use to convey praise or criticism should be especially precise. These evaluative adjectives and adverbs will help you describe and clarify your opinions. Consider these suggestions as you revise your writing:

MILD PRAISE:	*accurate, adequate, factual, intelligent, solid*
HIGH PRAISE:	*brilliant, excellent, entertaining, honest, original*
MILD DISAPPROVAL:	*confusing, dull, inconsistent, predictable, unfocused*
STRONG DISAPPROVAL:	*biased, pointless, ugly, misguided*

▶ **REVISION STRATEGY**
Bracketing Modifiers

With a colored pen or pencil, bracket any modifiers you've used. Evaluate each one, deciding whether you might add a more precise word. Notice any words that convey positive or negative criticism. If you've chosen vague or overused words, consider replacing them with words that more precisely capture your response.

Student Work
IN PROGRESS

Name: *Andrea Montgomery*
Omaha Northwest High School
Omaha, NE

Color-Coding Modifiers
Andrea bracketed all the modifiers in her conclusion, changing several to make her evaluation more precise.

Stanza after stanza, Poe creates [~~an interesting~~] *a compelling* rhythm through repetition. . . . These examples show how [~~an easy~~] *a simple* concept such as repetition can give a poem depth and intrigue. Poe was a master of repetition, and "The Raven" is [~~a good~~] *an excellent* example of the ways he could apply it to achieve [~~many~~] *a variety of* results.

> Andrea inserted the words "compelling" and "excellent" to convey her high opinion of Poe's writing.

☑ ONGOING ASSESSMENT: Monitor and Reinforce

If students have difficulty identifying modifiers that need to be revised, use the following strategy.

Partners can take turns reading their drafts aloud. If particular statements do not sound as admiring or critical as the writer intended, they should be marked. As students revise these modifiers to make them more or less forceful, remind them to concentrate on being as precise as possible.

◄ **Critical Viewing**
How would you guide a peer review like this one to help you improve your writing? **[Connect]**

Peer Review

Plus and Minus Scoring

Gather a small group of classmates to help you evaluate your revised draft. Using the criteria in the chart below, ask your readers to score your work. You may want to customize the chart to target your own draft and your own concerns.

As you read the criteria in each category, ask your reviewers to give your draft a plus or minus score. Record their responses, and ask your reviewers to explain their evaluations. Take notes when necessary, or begin a discussion to clarify any suggestions your reviewers may offer. Then, use your classmates' responses to revise your draft.

PLUS AND MINUS CHART

CRITERIA	Group Members			COMMENTS
	1	2	3	
Interesting introduction: First two sentences hook readers				
Identifiable thesis				
Identifiable title and author				
First idea clearly stated and elaborated				
Second idea clearly stated and elaborated				
Successful conclusion				
Overall evaluation				

Revising: Peer Review

Teaching Resources: Writing Support Transparency 13-H; Writing Support Activity Book 13-2

1. Remind students that as peer reviewers, their own opinion of the work being reviewed is not relevant. They could dislike (or not understand) "The Raven" and still agree that Andrea Montgomery has written a good response. Their role is to help their classmates by giving their opinions about whether arguments are presented clearly and thoughtfully.

2. Reviewers should feel free to point out unclear arguments, unsupported assertions, or other passages that they find ineffective or puzzling. Caution students to treat their classmates' work with the same respect they would wish for their own work.

Critical Viewing

Connect Students may mention the importance of honesty, specificity, and respect in working together during peer reviews.

STANDARDIZED TEST PREPARATION WORKSHOP

Using Modifiers Standardized test often measure students' ability to complete sentences using modifiers correctly. Share the following example with students:

Read the passage and choose the letter of the word that best completes the sentence.

On Saturday, my father and I woke up early to go fishing. We ___ walked down the stairs on our way out so as not to wake up my mother.

A very quiet   **C** quieter

B quiet   **D** quietly

The correct choice is item **D**. An adverb is needed to modify the verb walked.

 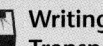
Writing Support Transparencies
Use the transparencies for Chapter 13 to teach these strategies.

Writing Support Activity Book
Use the graphic organizers for Chapter 13 to facilitate these strategies.

Have students highlight in their essays any words about whose spellings they are not 100 percent positive. Then they can use a dictionary to confirm correct spellings.

Grammar in Your Writing: Avoiding Common Homophone Errors

One of the most common homophone errors is the confusion of *its* and *it's*. Remind students that the former is a possessive pronoun, whereas the latter is a contraction of *it is*. One tip students can use as a memory aid is that possessive pronouns never have an apostrophe.

Find It in Your Writing

Have students circle any words that they are not sure of as they proofread.

13.5 Editing and Proofreading

An essay free of errors in spelling, grammar, and punctuation will help your readers enjoy your writing and devote more attention to considering the ideas you present. Check that your essay is free of errors.

Focusing on Spelling

Review your draft to be sure that each word is spelled correctly. One effective strategy for checking spelling is to read blocks of text from end to beginning. This helps you focus less on meaning and more on spelling. In addition, follow these suggestions:

- **Check Problem Words** As you develop a writing portfolio, build a list of words you often misspell. Keep this list handy, and check these words in your writing. Use a dictionary to confirm the spellings of any words you question.
- **Confirm Names** Your draft contains at least two proper nouns: the author and title of the work you address. Be sure that these and other names and places in your essay are spelled correctly.

🖉 Spelling Tip

The spell-check feature on your word-processing software will not catch a word that is spelled correctly but is used incorrectly; for example, it will not alert you to a discrepancy between *he* and *be*. Make sure that you check your final draft carefully.

Grammar in Your Writing
Avoiding Common Homophone Errors

A **homophone** is a word that sounds the same as another word but has a different meaning and a different spelling. Here are some common homophones to consider as you review your draft:

your/you're: *Your* is generally used as a possessive adjective; *you're* is a contraction of the words *you* and *are*.

right/write: *Right* is usually an adjective meaning "correct"; *write* is most often a verb meaning "to communicate using printed words."

Use a dictionary to clarify the spelling and meaning of homophones that present a problem to you.

Find It in Your Writing As you proofread your response to literature, check that you have not used a homophone instead of the word you intended.

To learn more about homophones, see Chapter 27.

⏱ TIME AND RESOURCE MANAGER

Resources
Print: Scoring Rubrics on Transparency, Chapter 13; Writing Assessment: Scoring Rubrics and Scoring Models for Response to Literature
Technology: Writing Lab CD-ROM, Response to Literature

In-Depth Coverage	Accelerated Pace
• Cover pp. 298–302 in class. • Distribute and review Proofreading Checklist and Correction Marks. • Have students edit and proofread their essays in class. **Option** Students can work on their own with the Editing and Evaluation sections of the Writing Lab CD-ROM.	• Assign pp. 298–302 for independent student review. • Have students edit and proofread their essays on their own. • Respond to individual editing needs.

13.6 Publishing and Presenting

Regardless of the strategy you choose, getting reactions from others will expand your insight into your response to literature. Consider these ideas for sharing your work:

Building Your Portfolio

1. **Library Display** Talk with your school librarian about establishing a Readers' Choice area where books are displayed next to students' written responses.
2. **Book Group** Bookstores and libraries often organize groups to discuss works of literature. Participate in a book group, and offer to read your essay as the starting point of a discussion on the literature you have analyzed.

Reflecting on Your Writing

Take a moment to reflect on the experience of writing your response to literature. Write your ideas, and add them to your writing portfolio. Use these questions to direct your thinking:

• What did you discover about the literature as you wrote?

• If you could start the writing process again, what might you do differently? Why?

 **Internet Tip**

To see model essays scored with this rubric, go to **www.phwg. phschool.com**

Rubric for Self-Assessment

Use the following criteria to evaluate your response to literature.

	Score 4	Score 3	Score 2	Score 1
Audience and Purpose	Presents sufficient background on the work(s); presents reactions forcefully	Presents background on the work(s); presents reactions clearly	Presents some background on the work(s); presents reactions at points	Presents little or no background on the work(s); presents few reactions
Organization	Presents points in logical order, smoothly connecting them to the overall focus	Presents points in logical order and connects them to the overall focus	Organizes points poorly in places; connects some points to an overall focus	Presents information in a scattered, disorganized manner
Elaboration	Supports evaluations with elaborated, well-chosen examples from the text	Supports evaluations with specific reasons and examples from the text	Supports some evaluations with reasons and examples from the text	Offers little support for evaluations; provides no reference to the text
Use of Language	Shows overall clarity and fluency; uses precise, evaluative words; makes few mechanical errors	Shows good sentence variety; uses some precise evaluative terms; makes some mechanical errors	Uses awkward or overly simple sentence structures and vague evaluative terms; makes many mechanical errors	Presents incomplete thoughts; makes mechanical errors that create confusion

Publishing and Presenting • **299**

☑ **ONGOING ASSESSMENT: Assess Mastery**

Use one of the following options to assess final drafts of students' responses to literature.

Self-Assessment Ask students to use the rubric provided to score their essays. Then have them write a paragraph reflecting on the most valuable thing they learned in completing this essay.

Teacher Assessment You may want to use the rubric and the scoring models provided in Writing Assessment, Response to Literature, to score the responses to literature.

Publishing and Presenting

1. Students may want to start a book review section in the school paper, or begin a literary magazine. Work with other teachers to support and encourage their efforts.

2. Students from your class and others can compile their reviews in a loose-leaf binder and give it to the school librarian to share with schoolmates who "can't find anything to read."

3. Students can send their reviews— with polite cover letters—to living writers whose work they have reviewed. They can mail their work to the books' publishers.

ASSESS

Assessment

Teaching Resources: Scoring Rubrics on Transparency 13; Formal Assessment, Chapter 13

1. Display the Scoring Rubric transparency and review the criteria with the class.

2. Before students proceed with self-assessment, you might review the final draft of the Student Work In Progress on pages 300–302. Invite students to score the final draft in one or more of the rubric categories. For example, how would they rate the essay's organization?

3. In addition to student self-assessment, you may wish to use the following assessment options.

• Score student essays yourself, using the rubric and scoring models from Writing Assessment.

• Review the Standardized Test Preparation Workshop on pages 306–307 and have students respond to a writing prompt within a time limit.

• Administer the Chapter 13 Test from Formal Assessment in Teaching Resources to assess students' grasp of concepts presented.

Teaching from the Final Draft

1. Help students recognize the elements of a thorough and thoughtful response to literature demonstrated by Andrea Montgomery's model. You might begin by making the following points.

   - Many of Andrea's classmates have read the poem and will find the subject interesting.

   - The writer's opinions are clearly presented and supported.

2. Have students look at the organization of the opening paragraphs. Ask students to identify Andrea's thesis statement (the final sentence of the first paragraph after the opening quotation). Point out that a thesis statement need not be the opening sentence of a paper.

3. Go through the margin notes. Have students try to apply similar standards to their own work. These notes will give them a good idea of what to look for.

4. Invite students to bring up questions about and criticisms of the model. For instance, some may feel that the summary on page 301 is too long. Ask students how they think the model might be improved.

Critical Viewing

Infer Students may mention the subject's coat, vest, shirt, tie, as well as the quality of the photographic reproduction.

Student Work
IN PROGRESS

FINAL DRAFT

◀ **Critical Viewing**
What details of this portrait of Edgar Allan Poe suggest the author lived in an earlier time? **[Infer]**

The Poetic Power of "The Raven"

**Andrea Montgomery,
Omaha Northwest High School
Omaha, Nebraska**

"Once upon a midnight dreary, while I pondered, weak and weary…"

This opening line is familiar and scary. The poem it begins, written by one of America's master writers of the mysterious, is "The Raven." Edgar Allan Poe's dark eighteen-stanza poem drags the reader into the strange and frightened mind of its speaker. Poe creates rhythm and rhyming patterns effectively in his poem. Using rhythm and repetition in a formalized way, he produces rhyming opportunities, emphasizes the issues his poem suggests, and builds the poem's dark mood.

Andrea sets the mood for her response to Poe's poem by quoting "The Raven" in her lead.

The thesis statement presents the writer's main idea: Poe uses rhythm and rhyming patterns effectively in his poem.

300 • Response to Literature

Even if the poem weren't so well written, its story might be powerful enough to keep a reader's interest. In "The Raven," a lonely student tries to ease his sorrow over a lost love by distracting himself in old books. Nearly asleep, or maybe even dreaming, he is interrupted by a gentle rapping on his door. He discovers the "visitor" to be a raven and starts a conversation with this eerie bird. Like other men Poe creates in his fiction, this speaker is driven mad. In this case, the bird responds "Nevermore" no matter what the speaker asks. In the end, the speaker, and probably the reader, is left exhausted and crushed by the exchange.

In this paragraph, Andrea summarizes the poem for her readers.

Poe uses the rhyming technique to create rhythm frequently in "The Raven." He produces rhythms and patterns that make the motion of the poem faster. To do this, Poe uses sets of three words that sound similar. For example, in the second stanza, Poe plays off the ending *-ember* with "remember/December/ember" and the ending *-orrow* with "morrow/borrow/sorrow." To extend the movement of the rhythm, Poe also intertwines the rhymes of "floor/Lenore/evermore" to pull the stanza together. Throughout the poem, Poe provides this type of triple rhyme.

To support her thesis, Andrea shows how rhyming patterns create rhythm.

Poe also repeats words to emphasize a point. For example, to let the reader feel the nervousness created by the bird's knocking, Poe repeats the word "rapping" three times in the first stanza. He adds the word "tapping" to complete the repetition of the sound.

In this paragraph, Andrea builds a second key idea: Repetition patterns emphasize Poe's point.

> While I nodded, nearly *napping*, suddenly there came
> a *tapping*,
> As of someone gently *rapping, rapping* at my chamber
> door.
> "'Tis some visitor," I muttered, "tapping at my chamber
> door—" (ll. 3–5)

Beyond this repetition that appears within stanzas, Poe repeats the words "nevermore," "nothing more," and the phrase "Quoth the Raven, 'Nevermore.'" This raises the anxiety or hopelessness that the speaker feels.

To emphasize the speaker's doubt and fear, Poe repeats words or phrases. For example, in stanza seventeen, the words "leave" and "take" are given special emphasis as the speaker begs the bird to leave.

> "Leave no black plume as a token of that lie thy soul hath
> spoken!
> Leave my loneliness unbroken!—quit the bust above my
> door!
> Take thy beak from out my heart, and take thy form
> from off my door!" (ll. 99–101)

To elaborate her ideas, Andrea includes an extended excerpt from the poem.

On careful examination of the poem, Poe's mastery of language, rhythm, and repetition reveals itself to be incredible. This poem is intricately woven and powerful in its attention to detail. If Poe had used repetition to achieve only one of the effects I describe, the poem would still be an amazing feat. However, Poe takes the technique of rhyming to achieve one more effect, pushing the poem to an even higher level of mastery.

Poe uses repetition to create a mood. For instance, in the beginning of the poem, the last line of most of the stanzas ends with the words, ". . . nothing more." The reader experiences the same fear that the narrator is trying to suppress. The well-known "Quoth the Raven, 'Nevermore'" is another example of the use of repetition to create mood. The word "nevermore" has a connotation of finality and ending. When repeated as often as it is, it brings that dark idea to the poem, conveying that feeling of the finality of death even more strongly.

Stanza after stanza, Poe creates a compelling rhythm through repetition. Stanza after stanza, he uses repetition to emphasize his ideas. Stanza after stanza, he creates a dark and gloomy mood. These examples show how a simple concept such as repetition can give a poem depth and intrigue. Poe was a master of repetition, and "The Raven" is an excellent example of the ways he could apply it to achieve a variety of results.

The Raven, 1845, Edmund Dulac

A functional paragraph give readers a chance to digest the information presented and to anticipate Andrea's last key point: Poe uses a repetition pattern to create his poem's mood.

Andrea borrows Poe's technique by introducing repetition in her conclusion. She restates the ideas she has developed and shows how repetition works to communicate effectively.

◄ **Critical Viewing** What artistic techniques allow the illustrator to convey a gloomy mood in this artwork? **[Analyze]**

Connected Assignment *Movie Review*

You can apply the same skills you use in writing a response to literature to a variety of reviews—among them movie reviews, art reviews, and television reviews. In each case, you decide what you think is effective about the work and what you feel was less successful. In a **movie review,** you refer to scenes or aspects of the film to support an overall opinion. You also provide enough summary information to give readers a taste of the film without giving away the ending.

The writing process skills introduced below will help you write your own review about a film you've seen.

▲ **Critical Viewing**
Why do you think movies are a popular form of entertainment? **[Hypothesize]**

Prewriting Consider the films you've seen recently. If possible, choose a film that is available on videotape so that you can view it more than once. As you watch, jot down your impressions. Then, note the pertinent facts such as cast members' names. Sift through your reactions, organizing them into positive and negative categories. Record your thoughts in a chart like the one shown here. Think about what recommendations or opinions about the film your notes suggest.

Pluses	Minuses
- great acting - moments of effective tension and excitement - extensive special effects	- too long - weak dialogue between certain characters - plot not fully developed

Drafting Let readers know exactly where you stand by stating your opinion of the film in your opening paragraph. Add a brief summary of the film's major events, but don't tell the whole story. Move through your opinion points as outlined in your chart, citing examples from the film to support your positions. Close by making your recommendation to readers.

Revising and Editing Read your review aloud. As you hear your work, decide whether it effectively communicates your opinion. To strengthen your review, clarify the opening and closing statements. Also, look at your evaluative language—insert precise adjectives to praise or criticize the work.

Publishing and Presenting When the final draft of your review is complete, submit it to the "Movie Review" section of your school newspaper.

Connected Assignment: Movie Review • **303**

▶ **Lesson Objectives**

• To evaluate a movie in a review.

Step-by-Step Teaching Guide

Movie Review

Teaching Resources: Writing Support Transparency 13-I; Writing Support Activity Book 13-3

1. Students can review a current movie, a recent one, or an older classic.

2. As in a response to literature, students should give their reactions to the plot, setting, characters, and writing style (which in this case is the film's dialogue). In addition, they need to consider casting, acting styles and abilities, cinematography (how the movie looks), costumes, special effects, and music.

3. Display the transparency to give students an idea of how to evaluate their chosen films. Give them copies of the blank organizer to complete.

4. If two students want to review the same movie, they can work together (as some professional movie critics do). They may both have the same response, or they may include one "thumbs-up" and one "thumbs-down."

5. After students have completed their reviews, urge them to look at movie guides in the public library and compare professional reviewers' responses of the movie to their own reactions.

Critical Viewing

Analyze Students may mention movies' ability to portray or capture a wide variety of human experiences, from the epic sweep of a battle scene to the intimacy of a private conversation.

Step-by-Step Teaching Guide

Analyzing Themes in Various Art Forms

1. Choose one of the Spotlight elements for class discussion, or have students work individually or in groups on the element of their choice. Give students the initiative to find the necessary books or pictures.

2. Interested students can research more about the life and work of Grace Albee.

3. You may want to bring in examples of Rockwell's work, including his advertising work.

4. Encourage students to find out more information about architects and skyscrapers in cities around the country.

Viewing and Representing

Activity Make sure students support their responses to the painting with details. Interested students may want to present their responses to the class.

Critical Viewing

Analyze Students may mention the puppy's energy and wide-eyed expression.

Spotlight on the Humanities

Analyzing Themes in Various Art Forms

Focus on Art: Grace Albee

After you see a good movie, chances are you like to share your response to it with others. Similarly, Grace Albee shared her response to urban and rural landscapes with the world through her artistic interpretations. Working as an artist until she was 93 years old, Grace Albee (1890–1985) is known for her black-and-white wood engravings that captured both urban and rural landscapes. Although she was a native of Rhode Island, she lived in Paris between the two World Wars and began sketching the French countryside. Her son was asked to sit for American painter Norman Rockwell in Paris, and Rockwell and Albee became friends. In 1932, she had her first one-person show in Paris and then returned to New York City, where she used Manhattan architecture as the subject of her work.

Art Connection Albee's friend Norman Rockwell (1894–1978) may be best known for his landmark covers for *The Saturday Evening Post*. His work appeared on the covers of the magazine from 1916 until 1969. Many of Rockwell's drawings were set in a small-town New England setting and captured the innocence and optimism of childhood.

Architecture Connection In the 1930's, Albee focused her work on the architecture of Manhattan. At that time, William Van Alen used his design skills to express pride in the car industry. As he planned New York's Chrysler Building, he incorporated radiator-cap gargoyles and abstract automobiles into its walls. He topped off the building with its infamous hubcap-inspired tower. Prior to the Empire State Building's completion in 1941, Van Alen's work was briefly the tallest building in the world, measuring 1,046 feet—119 feet taller than the Bank of Manhattan and even taller than the Eiffel Tower in Paris.

Response Writing Activity: Responding to Fine Art
Study the Norman Rockwell painting on this page, and write a response to it. Consider the mood Rockwell conveys and his ability to capture expressions. In your writing, explain your evaluation of his work.

Leapfrog, by Norman Rockwell, *Saturday Evening Post* cover, June 28, 1919. Photo Courtesy of The Norman Rockwell Museum at Stockbridge, MA

▲ Critical Viewing How does the dog at left add to the innocence and carefree attitude expressed in the illustration? **[Analyze]**

Media and Technology Skills

Comparing Your Responses to Others'

Activity: Evaluating Movie Ads and Reviews

As you scan the newspaper, a review quote leaps out from a movie advertisement: "THIS ONE STANDS OUT . . . " Intrigued, you go to see the film and hate it. Later, you look up the original review and find that it read, "Among the mass of formulaic junk coming out this year, *this one stands out* as one of the worst. . . ."

Improve your response to persuasion by evaluating advertisements, reviews, and previews before you accept their claims.

Learn About It Movie advertisements that quote reviews often take the reviewer's ideas out of their context in order to make them seem more favorable. In addition, previews are studio advertisements that can make even bad films look appealing.

Think About It Because each person creates his or her own interpretation of a film, there is no single, accurate response. In fact, a picture rated by one critic as one of the year's best might show up on another's ten-worst list. To navigate this area of subjective information, it may even be useful to read the reviews of several critics regularly to find one whose tastes are closest to your own.

Evaluate It Pick a film that you think you'd like to see, and consult several sources for review information. Use a chart like the one below to gather the information you find. Then, see the film and write your own brief review, providing reasons for your opinion.

> **Sources for Movie Evaluation**
>
> - Word of mouth (what you hear from friends and family)
> - Advertisements (TV, radio, newspaper, or magazine)
> - Theater or video previews
> - Reviews (in the newspaper and magazines or on TV and radio)

Comparing Sources of Movie Evaluation

Source	Information Provided
A newspaper ad that quotes from a review	
An original review	
The theater preview	
A friend's review	

Analyze It Review your results to decide which sources gave accurate, convincing, or reliable reviews and whether you agreed with the opinions stated. Then, summarize what you've learned from this exercise.

Lesson Objectives

- To write a response to literature in a test-taking situation.

Step-by-Step Teaching Guide

Responding to Literature-Based Prompts

1. Point out that writing prompts on standardized tests rarely if ever ask students merely to describe their responses to a text. Yet students' responses in a first reading can turn out to be useful in essays about some particular aspect or element in the work.

2. If necessary, draw students' attention to lines 2, 4, 7, 9, and 14, and invite them to explain their initial reactions (if any) to Lightman's use of line breaks.

3. Explain that students' ideas about the effects of these short lines — or of the pair of seven-line stanzas that comprise the poem — can be developed and organized into an effective response to the writing prompt.

Standardized Test Preparation Workshop

Responding to Literature-Based Prompts

Standardized tests frequently ask you to write a response to a work of literature included with the test booklet. You will be evaluated on your ability to do the following:

- Develop a clearly stated responsive position.
- Choose and present effective supporting details.
- Organize ideas in a logical way.
- Apply grammar, usage, and mechanics conventions.

Below is an example of a literature-based writing prompt. Use the suggestions on the next page to write a response. The clocks next to each stage suggest a plan for organizing your time.

Sample Writing Situation

Read the following poem by Alan P. Lightman.

In Computers

In the magnets of computers will
   be stored

Blend of sunset over wheat
   fields.
5 Low thunder of gazelle.
Light, sweet wind on high
   ground.
Vacuum stillness spreading from
   a thick snowfall.

10 Men will sit in rooms
upon the smooth, scrubbed earth
or stand in tunnels on the moon
and instruct themselves in how it
   was.
15 Nothing will be lost.
Nothing will be lost.

How does the poem's structure support its message? In an essay for your school's literary magazine, explain how the writer uses structure to support his message. Use examples from the poem to support your explanation.

Test Tips

- Read the literature provided with the prompt, noting your initial reactions. Then, read the prompt and focus a second reading on the elements it addresses.
- When writing a literary response for a test, make sure to cite the literary text accurately.

✎ TEST-TAKING TIP

Encourage students to jot notes during and after their second reading of a text. Point out that note-taking during a first reading would get in the way of comprehension and appreciation of the work. Yet after forming first impressions and reading the writing prompt, students can begin to flesh out their thoughts in brief written notes.

Prewriting

Allow about one quarter of your time for prewriting.

Think About the Poem Resist the urge to start writing immediately. Take a few minutes to really think about the poem and the prompt's directions. For example, this prompt discusses structure, so focus your prewriting work on details such as how words, lines, and stanzas are arranged on the page. When you're satisfied that your response is well reasoned, start looking for supporting details.

Drafting

Allow about half of your time for drafting.

Outline Ideas Develop and refine your thesis until you can state it in a single sentence. Then, prepare a quick outline. Write a brief summary, and plan to address details in order of their presentation.

Reflect and Elaborate Each time you read a poem, you'll see more in it. Look over the poem, the prompt, and your outlined ideas. As you write your response, add details that address the poet's word repetition and punctuation choices. Develop your points by stressing the way details support the poet's message.

Highlight Links This prompt calls for a cause-and-effect link between structure and content. Help readers see that link by using cause-and-effect transition words to highlight it. Words like *as a result* and *consequently* can clearly indicate the relationship between word position and meaning.

Revising, Editing, and Proofreading

Allow almost one quarter of your time for revising, editing, and proofreading.

Orient Readers As you review your work, make sure readers can follow your references to the poem. Note the line number of each detail you use so that readers can quickly and accurately locate it.

Check Your Attention to Audience Review the prompt to be sure you have adequately addressed your audience. If necessary, refine your word choice or add or delete details to better suit your readers' needs.

Be Accurate Don't rush your final read-through. You may replace one error with another. Think carefully about spelling and punctuation, but do not correct the spelling or punctuation of the poem itself. Use a caret [^] to show insertions, and cross out deleted text with a single line.

Customizing for *Less Advanced Students*

Review with students the difference between summarizing and responding to literature. Make sure they do not lapse into summarizing in their essays.

Customizing for *ESL Students*

Students learning English may be overwhelmed at the prospect of writing about poetry, since the genre relies so heavily upon the play of language. Review with them how to read poetry, as well as the literary concepts of rhyme, rhythm, and figurative language.

Time and Resource Manager

In-Depth Lesson Plan

	LESSON FOCUS	PRINT AND MEDIA RESOURCES
DAY 1	**Introduction to Writing for Assessment** Students learn key elements of writing for assessment (pp. 308–309).	*Writers at Work* Videotape *Writing Lab* CD-ROM, Practical and Technical Writing
DAY 2	**Prewriting** Students choose and narrow a topic (pp. 310–311).	**Teaching Resources** *Writing Support Transparency* 14-A
DAY 3	**Drafting** Students organize their ideas and write their first drafts (pp. 312–313).	**Teaching Resources** *Writing Support Transparency* 14-B
DAY 4	**Revising** Students revise their drafts in terms of overall structure, paragraphs, sentences, and word choice (pp. 314–315).	
DAY 5	**Editing and Proofreading; Publishing and Presenting** Students check their work for accuracy and correctness and present their final drafts (pp. 316–317).	**Teaching Resources** *Scoring Rubrics on Transparency,* Chapter 14; *Formal Assessment,* Chapter 14

Accelerated Lesson Plan

	LESSON FOCUS	PRINT AND MEDIA RESOURCES
DAY 1	**Prewriting to Drafting** Students review characteristics for writing for assessment, select topics, and write drafts.	*Writers at Work* Videotape *Writing Lab* CD-ROM, Practical and Technical Writing **Teaching Resources** *Writing Support Transparencies* 14-A–B
DAY 2	**Revising to Presenting** Students work individually or with peers to revise, edit, and proofread their work for presentation.	**Teaching Resources** *Scoring Rubrics on Transparency,* Chapter 14; *Formal Assessment,* Chapter 14

Options for Adapting Lesson Plans

HOMEWORK

Have students complete any stage of the lesson for homework.

TECHNOLOGY

Students can complete any stage of the lesson on computer. Have them print out their completed work.

FEATURES

Extend coverage with Connected Assignment (p. 319), Spotlight on the Humanities (p. 320), Media and Technology Skills (p. 321), and the Standardized Test Preparation Workshop (p. 322).

INTEGRATED SKILLS COVERAGE

Integrating Grammar
Homophones, SE p. 316

Speaking and Listening
Integrating Speaking Skills ATE p. 318

Language Highlight
ATE p. 313

Spelling
Integrating Spelling Skills ATE p. 315

Technology
Integrating Technology Skills ATE p. 315

Viewing and Representing
Critical Viewing, SE pp. 308, 315, 319, 320
Viewing and Representing ATE p. 320

BLOCK SCHEDULING

Pacing Suggestions
For 90-minute Blocks
• Have students complete the Prewriting and Drafting stages in a single period.
• Focus one class period on Revising and Editing and Publishing and Presenting. Allow at least 30 minutes for peer revision.

Resources for Varying Instruction
• *Writing Lab* **CD-ROM** If your students have access to hardware, a 90-minute block provides an ideal opportunity for students to work on computer.
• *Writers at Work* **videotape** Show the Writing for Assessment segment in class.

Professional Development Support
• *How to Manage Instruction in the Block* This Teaching Resource provides management and activity suggestions.

ASSESSMENT SUPPORT

Standardized Test Preparation SE p. 322; ATE p. 315
Standardized Test Preparation Workshop, pp. 27–28
Scoring Rubrics on Transparency, Ch. 14
Formal Assessment, Ch. 14
Writing Assessment and Portfolio Management

MEDIA AND TECHNOLOGY

For the Student
• *Writing Lab* **CD-ROM,** Practical and Technical Writing

For the Teacher
• *Writers at Work* **Videotape,** Writing for Assessment
• *Resource Pro* **CD-ROM**

MEETING INDIVIDUAL NEEDS

Less Advanced Students ATE p. 318 ; See also Ongoing Assessments ATE pp. 309, 311, 313, 317
ESL Students ATE p. 321
Visual Spatial Learners ATE p. 315
Verbal Linguistic Learners ATE p. 311
Gifted and Talented Students ATE pp. 312, 321

WRITING AND GRAMMAR WEBSITE

The Interactive Writing and Grammar Website provides a wide array of support for students, teachers, and parents. Writing support includes:

• Interactive revision checkers
• Scoring rubrics with complete models

phwg.phschool.com

Lesson Objectives

1. To recognize the elements of an effective response to an essay-test assessment.

2. To recognize four main types of essay questions.

3. To learn strategies for choosing an essay topic.

4. To learn a strategy for narrowing a response to an essay question.

5. To understand strategies for shaping a response.

6. To learn how to elaborate on a response with details and other specifics.

7. To learn strategies for revising the structure, paragraphs, sentences, and word choice in the essay.

8. To review strategies for catching errors in spelling, grammar, and punctuation.

9. To learn how to use graded tests to improve performance on future tests.

10. To understand specific writing strategies for open-book essay tests.

Critical Viewing

Analyze Students may say it helps you to confidently and succinctly answer the questions in the time allotted.

Chapter 14 Writing for Assessment

▲ Critical Viewing
How can preparation help you succeed on in-class tests? **[Analyze]**

Assessment in School

To make sure that you are learning and mastering the information and skills you are being taught in school, teachers frequently assess your knowledge. Tests, essays, oral reports, lab reports, performances, and research papers are different forms of assessment that evaluate your progress. Besides helping you to focus your learning and evaluate your own strengths and weaknesses, assessment gives you the chance to earn higher grades and show what you know. In this chapter, you will learn how to improve your performance skills for a common type of written assessment: the essay test.

308 • Writing for Assessment

⏱ TIME AND RESOURCE MANAGER

Resources
Technology: Writers at Work videotape

In-Depth Coverage	Accelerated Pace
• Cover pp. 308–309 in class. • Point out the elements of an effective essay-test response on p. 309. • Ask students to give additional examples of titles for the four types of essay questions listed on p. 309.	• Have students review the information on pp. 308–309 independently.

What Is Assessment?

By the time you've reached this stage of your school career, you should recognize essay tests as one of the most common forms of **writing for assessment.** In contrast to standardized tests that evaluate your critical thinking ability and writing skills, in-class exams require you to draw on the material you have studied in school. An effective essay-test response includes

- a direct response to the test question or prompt.
- a clearly worded and well-supported thesis statement or main idea.
- specific information about the topic, drawn from your reading or from class discussion.
- a clear organization.

To see criteria by which essay-test responses may be evaluated, preview the Rubric for Self-Assessment on page 317.

Types of Assessment

The topics you address in essay-tests depend on the classes you are studying. However, the format the essays take is often limited to a few familiar types of writing. In your academic classes, you can expect to encounter the following types of essays:

- **Explain a process** ("How a Script Becomes a Movie")
- **Defend a position** ("Why a Candidate Was Elected")
- **Compare and contrast** ("Tornadoes vs. Hurricanes")
- **Show cause and effect** ("Analyzing the Growing Popularity of E-mail")

PREVIEW

Student Work
IN PROGRESS

Megan Holbrook, a student at Buena High School in Ventura, California, wrote an essay-test response about a short story. In this chapter, you will see her work in progress, including strategies she used to draft and revise. At the end of the chapter, you can see the final essay that Megan wrote.

Writers in ACTION

The value of education has been celebrated by leaders in every generation. Education becomes an issue for campaigns, both local and national, with leaders offering their perspectives on the importance of learning. These words spoken by Booker T. Washington ring as true today as on the day he said them in 1895:

"There is no defense of security for any of us except in the highest intelligence and development of all."

Interest GRABBER Ask students to imagine that a tiny, personal cheerleader appears on each of their desks during essay tests. The cheerleader's job is to encourage students to do well. Ask students to come up with some themes for the cheers, such as "Don't panic," "Be confident in yourself," or "The right answers are in your head."

Activate Prior Knowledge

Pose this situation to students: Two ninth graders are trying out for the basketball team. One student has studied the rules of the game and practiced shooting baskets. The other student has watched one or two basketball games on TV. Which student has a better chance of making the team?

Ask students to apply this "study and practice" concept to taking essay tests. How can study and practice give students an advantage? (knowing better how to prepare for the test; understanding how to write more complete responses, or being able to use a limited amount of time effectively)

More About the Writer

Booker T. Washington (1856–1915) was the son of a slave. After the Civil War he worked his way through elementary school, high school, and college. He firmly believed that education and economic independence were necessary for African Americans to achieve social equality. He established the Tuskegee Institute in Alabama in 1881, still a leading African American school.

☑ ONGOING ASSESSMENT: Diagnose

Use one of the following options to diagnose students' current level of proficiency in writing for assessment.

Option 1 Ask each student to select the strongest example of his or her writing for assessment from last year. Hold conferences in which you review each student's sample. Use the conferences to determine which students will need extra support in developing skill at writing for assessment.

Option 2 Ask students to write for five minutes about their favorite hobby and why they enjoy it. If students have difficulty completing this exercise, you will need to devote more time on the process of organizing and evaluating information.

Prewriting: Choosing Your Topic

1. Write these essay-test topics on the chalkboard:

The Top Three World Leaders

Qualities of an Excellent Leader

My Personal Heroes

Ask students to imagine that an essay test requires them to write a response to one of these topics. Explain that you are going to lead students in selecting the best topic for each of them to write about.

2. Write this strategy on the chalk board: *Consider What You Know.* Ask students to think about the three topics and jot down answers to the following questions:

- Which topic would take the least response time?

- Which topic are you most familiar with?

- Write a few details for each topic. Which topic quickly brought to mind several ideas?

Direct students to write down the topic that seems easiest for them to write about.

3. Repeat this process for the remaining two strategies described. Use these questions:

Pinpoint Your Strengths

- Which are your best critical-thinking skills? (e.g., analyze, predict, explain, draw conclusions, speculate, compare and contrast, infer, evaluate)

- Which topic calls for your best skills?

Draft a Single Sentence

- Can you think of a main message (the main idea of the essay, written in just one sentence) for each topic?

- For which topic are you able to quickly write a main message that is clear and concise?

4. Have students choose the best topic of the three and add it to the Topic Bank. Direct students to repeat steps 1–3 above independently, this time selecting from the three topics (two existing topics and the one students added) in the Topic Bank.

14.1 # *Prewriting*

Choosing Your Topic

On some essay tests, a single writing topic is assigned. In other cases, you may have the opportunity to choose a topic from several that are offered. Time pressure requires that you make a commitment to one prompt early in the process. Follow these guidelines for choosing a topic:

Consider What You Know Examine which questions will take the least time. To stay focused, identify the topics you have reviewed most recently. Try jotting down a list of specific details for each topic. If you find you can list several ideas quickly for one prompt but only one idea for another, choose the one you can answer more comfortably.

Pinpoint Your Strengths The prompt for an essay question may ask you to address specific critical thinking skills in your writing; for example, you may need to *analyze*, to *predict*, or to *explain*. Find a question that connects with your strengths, and choose a prompt for which you can provide facts to support the type of response required.

Draft a Single Sentence Choose a topic for which you can develop a focus or main idea. For example, if a test prompt asks an open-ended question that requires you to select an important event, character, or theme, decide what you might discuss. In a single sentence, identify the main idea you would develop. Then, evaluate your ability to write an essay based on the sentence you've written.

TOPIC BANK

Following are some essay-test questions. If you plan to practice writing for assessment, choose one of these or ask your teacher to provide you with one.

1. **Role Models for Your Generation** Choose two Americans, living or deceased, as role models for today's youth. In a brief essay, compare and contrast the achievements and leadership qualities of these two heroes.

2. **Body Systems** The human body contains several major organ systems, including the skeletal system, the digestive system, the respiratory system, and the circulatory system. In an essay, explain how one of these organ systems works. Identify the organs involved, and describe the function the system performs.

⏱ TIME AND RESOURCE MANAGER

Resources
Print: Writing Support Transparency 14-A
Technology: Writing Lab CD-ROM: Practical and Technical Writing

In-Depth Coverage	Accelerated Pace
• Cover pp. 310–311 in class. • Work through the Step-by-Step Teaching Guides on pp. 310–311.	• Have students review the information on pp. 310–311 independently.

Narrowing Your Response
Circle Key Words to Identify Your Purpose

As you prepare to write your essay, circle key words and make any notes to help you interpret the directions. Note especially the verbs, nouns, and important phrases in the question. The chart below shows how the specific verbs you encounter direct the purpose of your writing.

Key Words	Essay Objectives
Analyze	Examine how various elements contribute to the whole
Describe	Give main features and examples of each
Compare and Contrast	Stress how two works or other items are alike and different
Discuss	Support a generalization with facts and examples
Explain	Clarify by probing reasons, causes, results, and effects
Defend	Support your position with examples from the text

Student Work
IN PROGRESS

Name: *Megan Holbrook*
Buena High School
Ventura, CA

Circling Key Words in Questions

Before she began writing, Megan circled the important verbs in the prompt she had chosen. By adding her own notes to paraphrase the question, she clarified the assignment.

Review the short stories we have studied in this unit. *List qualities of stories*

Consider the (criteria) you think are most important *Choose*

in a successful short story, and (identify the story) that *one story*

best meets these standards. (Explain) your response.
Show how one story meets these standards

Prewriting: Narrowing Your Response

Teaching Resources: Writing Support Transparency 14-A

1. Display the transparency and review the information Megan circled in the writing prompt.

2. Write the following questions on the chalkboard:

   A. How did the radio change American life?

   B. How does a radio work?

   C. How are radios and CD players different and alike?

   D. What are the main uses of the radio?

3. Explain that you've developed some essay-test questions based on radios. You're going to go through the essay questions on the chalkboard one by one. Then you'll ask students to respond by giving their ideas on the skill(s) they would have to use to answer each question. Refer students to the Key Words and Essay Objectives chart as a source for answers. (Answers: A. analyze or explain B. describe or explain C. compare and contrast D. discuss or explain)

Customize for
Verbal/Linguistic Learners

Point out the paraphrases in Megan's work in progress. Ask students to come up with additional paraphrases for "consider the criteria," "identify the story," and "explain your response."

☑ ONGOING ASSESSMENT: Monitor and Reinforce

If students are having difficulty remembering the specific terms (analyze, describe, explain) for writing modes, then try one of the following options.

Option 1 Point out that students can find clues to what is expected in their writing by underlining verbs, nouns, and other important words in the essay question.	**Option 2** Have students circle verbs in the essay question, then list them under the head *Follow Directions.* As they follow each verb's directions in writing their response, they can check it off their list. When all the verbs are checked, they'll know they've met all the expectations of the test question.

⏱ TIME SAVERS!

📄 **Writing Support Transparencies**
Use the transparency for Chapter 14 to teach these strategies.

1. Write the following essay topics on the chalkboard:

   How to Get Students to Do Their Homework

   Why Ninth Graders Should Rule the World

   A Story/Book Everyone Should Read

2. Assign each topic to one-third of the class. Ask all students to write a thesis statement—one sentence that defines the focus—for their topic. Invite students to share their statements with the class. (Sample statements might include: Exciting incentives will convince students to do their homework. Ninth graders see the world from the viewpoint of kids and adults. Everyone should read "Rosa Parks: My Story" because it shows how just one person can make a big difference.)

Customize for
Gifted/Talented Students

Direct students either to complete the essay outlined on page 312, or write an outline and essay on a different topic of their choice.

14.2 Drafting

Shaping Your Writing
Find a Focus

After you choose your topic, develop a focus for your essay. Consider the type of writing you are creating, and draft a statement that directly responds to the prompt. This sentence will shape an effective response. Use these suggestions:

- **Exposition** Develop a thesis statement to address the question. For problem-and-solution, cause-and-effect, or comparison-and-contrast essays, phrase your thesis statement to reflect the expectation of these types of writing.

- **Persuasion** Choose a position to argue, and identify the support you'll use to defend it.

- **Response to Literature** In a single sentence, identify your focus. For example, you may decide to evaluate a character, analyze a setting, or compare two works.

Plan a Structure

Quick Outline When you sketch an outline for your essay, divide it into three parts: introduction, body, and conclusion.

The **introduction** should state your thesis. The **body** of the essay should present at least two main points that support your thesis. The **conclusion** should restate the answer to the essay question and sum up the main points in the body. Look at this example:

⊙	**THESIS: The fire in the Triangle Shirtwaist Factory led to major reforms in fire safety standards.**
	INTRODUCTION: State thesis; summarize the fire.
	BODY 1 Reforms: Women's Trade Union League and Red Cross collaborate to urge city to fix fire safety standards
	BODY 2 Reforms: Labor union demonstrations lead to state legislation
◐	CONCLUSION: Tragedy leads to inspiration for safer working conditions

Fill in the Details Before you draft, collect the evidence, facts, and examples you'll need to prove your point. Jot down as many details as you can remember or generate.

312 • Writing for Assessment

🔵 Learn More

To review the unique qualities of each type of writing, review the appropriate chapters in Part One.

🕐 TIME AND RESOURCE MANAGER

Resources
Print: Writing Support Transparency 14-B
Technology: Writing Lab CD-ROM, Practical and Technical Writing

In-Depth Coverage	Accelerated Pace
• Cover pp. 312–313 in class. • Work through the Step-by-Step Teaching Guides on pp. 312–313. • Invite students to ask questions about any strategies they don't fully understand.	• Have students review the information on pp. 312–313 independently. • Assign the Customize for Gifted/Talented Students activity on p. 312.

Providing Elaboration

The proof of your knowledge is in the details you use. To demonstrate your mastery of the subject, include details from class discussions or readings to support your main idea.

Support Your Thesis With Specifics

Whatever your purpose, you need to include specific details to support your answer. Generally, these details must come from your memory or personal experience. Consider developing your ideas with these types of elaboration:

- **Facts, Dates, Names** Whenever you can, provide facts to make your response concrete. Instead of writing that an agreement was signed to end the war, name the treaty, indicate the date, and tell which leaders were involved in the negotiations.

- **Specific Examples** Provide examples that prove your point. For example, to illustrate that Robert Frost's poems are often set in rural areas, name and discuss several poems.

- **Explanations** It is not enough to say that a character changes. Elaborate by explaining the ways the character changes or showing what experiences cause the change.

- **Quotations or Paraphrases** You probably can't quote long passages from memory, but adding paraphrases or memorable quotations can bring your writing to life. For example, an essay on leadership could be strengthened by a few famous lines used by United States presidents to inspire the nation.

Student Work IN PROGRESS

Name: Megan Holbrook
Buena High School
Ventura, CA

Including Details to Support a Thesis
In this passage, Megan used insert marks neatly to make her examples and details more specific.

One meaningful change was the shift in Doodle's brother, from selfishness to love and sensitivity.

At first, he was embarrassed by Doodle's disability, and his effort to teach Doodle to walk

sprang from his own shame at having a disabled brother.

However, the scene in which Doodle walks on his sixth birthday brings out the

change in Doodle's brother. The narrator now understands that by teaching Doodle to walk he himself has been learning to love his brother. ~~the situation better.~~

Drafting • 313

Drafting: Providing Elaboration

Teaching Resources: Writing Support Transparency 14-B

1. Choose a story the entire class has recently read and enjoyed in *Timeless Voices, Timeless Themes,* such as "The Most Dangerous Game" or "The Birds." Have students turn to the story.

2. On the chalkboard, write the topic "A Story Everyone Should Read" as a column head. Under this head, write the following four categories:

   Facts, Dates, Names
   Specific Examples
   Explanations
   Quotations or Paraphrases

3. Category by category, ask students to provide verbal descriptions of items that could fit. As in an open-book test, students may refer to the story for answers and ideas.

4. Display the transparency to show students how Megan added details to her writing.

Language Highlight

Students shouldn't be surprised if providing elaboration in an essay test eats up time and strains their brain. The task is just living up to the meaning of the word *elaboration*. In ancient Latin, *elaboration* meant "hard or painstaking work." In sixteenth-century England, it meant "extreme detail." Students should remember: Provide plenty of elaboration to earn a grade that brings elation!

☑ ONGOING ASSESSMENT: Monitor and Reinforce

If students are concerned about providing elaboration on closed-book essay tests, try one of the following options.

Option 1 When students are asked to provide elaboration from memory, tell them not to panic! They should take a minute to freewrite about the topic. They'll be surprised at the facts, details, examples, and opinions they'll come up with.	**Option 2** Students may not remember all the details they've learned about an essay topic, but they will remember some. Tell them to focus on providing elaboration for these most familiar facts first. As they write, they may recall more details to add.

⏱ TIME SAVERS!

📠 **Writing Support Transparencies**
Use the transparency for Chapter 14 to teach these strategies.

1. Ask students to read the essay on page 318. Explain that the class will review the essay in light of each of the revising strategies on pages 314–315.

2. Read aloud the first revision strategy, Reviewing Question Against Answer. Ask students to reread the essay question (at the top right corner of page 318), then identify specifics in the finished essay that answer the question. (The writer listed the criteria and identified the story in paragraph 1; she explained her response in paragraphs 3, 4, and 5.)

3. Continue this process with each strategy. Student answers may include:

   • Confirm Coherence: The writer restates the two criteria in paragraph 1; she restates the criteria again in paragraphs 3 and 4; in paragraph 5, she connects the criteria to the introductory paragraph.

   • Check Introduction Against Conclusion: In the concluding paragraph, the writer restates the thesis and main points from paragraph 1.

   • Delete Irrelevant Ideas: The writer does not include irrelevant details (some students might think paragraph 2 is irrelevant, but it provides essential explanation for the reader); transitional and connecting words and phrases are provided, e.g., "To develop this idea," "However," "also," "because," "although."

   • Improve Diction: Examples of good diction include *criteria, interdependence, meaningful, selfishness to sensitivity, strong spirit,* and others.

   • Evaluate Informal Language: The writer used *greatly* instead of "a lot," *from a different perspective* instead of "a new way," etc.

While time is limited during an essay test, you should still leave yourself enough time to check your writing for accuracy and clarity.

Revising Your Overall Structure
Get the Big Picture

Your grade will be based in large part on your ability to answer the question presented. Review your response to be sure you have addressed each part of the question.

▶ **REVISION STRATEGY**
Reviewing the Question Against Your Answer

When you have finished writing, check to see that you have followed the instructions in the question. For example, if the question asks you to give examples of a specific literary technique in two of the works on a list, make sure that the examples in your discussion are drawn from two different works. If you are asked to explain at least two causes of the Vietnam War, check to see that your essay has covered at least two reasons.

Revising Your Paragraphs
Confirm the Coherence

While most writers take several drafts to move from inspiration to published work, the restrictions of an in-class essay test make such drastic revisions unlikely. However, if you change your thesis as you write, your essay-test response can be confusing to your reader. To be sure you present one idea coherently, look for transitional sentences that guide the flow of ideas, and compare your introduction with your conclusion.

▶ **REVISION STRATEGY**
Checking the Introduction Against the Conclusion

Compare the first paragraph of your essay with the last. The first paragraph should contain your focus or thesis in response to the essay question. The final paragraph should restate the thesis and sum up the main points.

If the main points in these paragraphs do not match, revise either paragraph to make the writing more coherent. If necessary, revise body paragraphs or add transitional sentences to bring the essay together.

Writing Lab CD-ROM

To review transitions that can improve the coherence of your response, see the Transitions Word Bin. You can find it in the Toolkit.

⏱ TIME AND RESOURCE MANAGER

Resources
Technology: Writing Lab CD-ROM, Practical and Technical Writing

In-Depth Coverage	Accelerated Pace
• Cover pp. 314–315 in class.	• Assign pp. 314–315 for independent student review. • Have students work independently to analyze how effectively the student writer used the revision process in completing her essay on p. 318. Ask students to provide a written analysis.

Revising Your Sentences

Double-Check for Relevance

In an essay test written under time limitations, every sentence is important, but details that do not contribute to the main ideas you are presenting can detract from your success. Review the sentences to be sure they are relevant to your thesis.

REVISION STRATEGY

Deleting Irrelevant Ideas

For each paragraph in your essay, identify the main idea you address. Read the supporting sentences, checking for any details that veer away from the main idea. Use transitional words or phrases like *at the same time, in contrast, eventually,* or *although* to tighten the paragraph. If you cannot link the details, delete them to strengthen your writing.

Revising Your Word Choice

Improve Your Diction

Examine your sentences for word choice, asking yourself whether you have selected words and phrases carefully in order to express exactly what you mean.

▲ Critical Viewing
Why do you think students often neglect the revising process during exams? [Relate]

REVISION STRATEGY

Evaluating Informal Language

An essay test is an opportunity for you to present information in a serious and thoughtful way. Review your draft to be sure the language you have chosen is appropriate to your purpose. Circle any words that are chatty and informal. To replace them, choose more refined, precise language. Look at these examples:

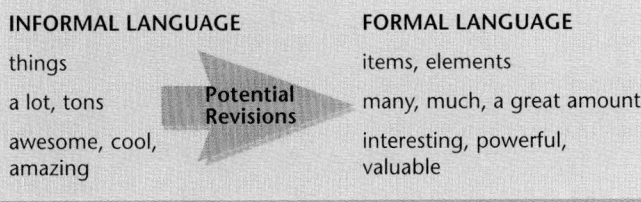

INFORMAL LANGUAGE	FORMAL LANGUAGE
things	items, elements
a lot, tons	many, much, a great amount
awesome, cool, amazing	interesting, powerful, valuable

Potential Revisions

Revising • 315

✏️ STANDARDIZED TEST PREPARATION WORKSHOP

Vocabulary Skills Standardized test questions often ask students to provide words that mean the same within a certain context. Ask students to choose a synonymous phrase for the underlined words below.

She was <u>in good spirits</u> after the operation.

A in a positive frame of mind

B seeing invisible beings

C very courageous

D jumping with joy

Item **A** is the correct choice. A person jumping with joy (choice D) is certainly in good spirits, but that choice does not fit the context of the sentence—a person who has had surgery.

Editing and Proofreading

1. Write the following items on the chalkboard:

   Sentence fragments

   Errors in end punctuation

   Messy handwriting

2. Explain that students should look for these potential problems as they edit and proofread their essays. Ask students to brainstorm for additional errors that they would need to check. (errors in spelling, grammar, internal punctuation, contractions, capitalization, and so on)

Grammar in Your Writing: Homophones

1. Write these words on the chalkboard:

   seen/scene

   right/write

   its/it's

   they're/their

   break/brake

   one/won

   piece/peace

2. Explain that the word pairs are homophones, words that sound alike but have different meanings and spellings.

3. Ask students if they can find any homophones in the essay on page 318. Have students report the words they find, then analyze if they were used correctly. (*two [to, too], you [ewe], their [there], for [fore, four], weak [week], muscle [mussel], scene [seen], been [bin], new [knew], one [won], lesson [lessen], see [sea], piece [peace].* All used correctly.)

Find It in Your Writing

You may want to have students exchange essays with a partner to check each other's work.

Editing and Proofreading

Focusing on Eliminating Errors

Because you must write quickly on a test, you may introduce some unintended errors in spelling, grammar, or punctuation. Review your draft, with special attention to these areas:

- **Sentence Construction** Be sure every sentence expresses a complete idea. Be especially aware of subordinate clauses punctuated as if they were sentences. In those cases, add information to complete the idea.

FRAGMENT:	Although the main theme of Pachelbel's *Canon* is not complex.
CORRECT:	Although the main theme of Pachelbel's *Canon* is not complex, the variations create depth.

- **Spelling** Review your work to catch any misspelled words. Neatly correct the errors you find.

- **Legibility** If you notice some words are written in a scrawl too difficult to read, neatly write them again.

Learn More

For more instruction on writing effective sentences, see Chapter 22.

Grammar in Your Writing
Homophones

Homophones are words that sound alike and are often confused. Check your essay for the proper usage of the following groups of homophones.

its, it's *Its* is a possessive pronoun showing ownership. *It's* is a contraction of the words *it is* or *it has*.

We need to find its proper place. Until then, it's going to create confusion.

their, there, they're *Their* is a possessive adjective showing ownership. *There* can be used to begin a sentence or to indicate place. *They're* is a contraction of the words *they are*.

They're going to post their ideas over there.

affect, effect *Affect* is almost always a verb meaning "to influence." *Effect* is usually a noun meaning "result."

The change will affect the system. We should study the effect closely.

Find It in Your Writing As you revise an essay-test response, be sure you've chosen the correct word of a homophone group to convey your ideas.

For more on homophones and other usage errors, see Chapter 27.

⏱ TIME AND RESOURCE MANAGER

Resources
Print: Scoring Rubrics on Transparency, Chapter 14; Writing Assessment: Scoring Rubric and Scoring Models on Writing for Assessment

In-Depth Coverage	Accelerated Pace
• Cover pp. 316–318 in class.	• Have students read pp. 316–318 independently.

14.5 Publishing and Presenting

Building Your Portfolio

After your test is graded, keep a copy of your essay in your portfolio. Consider these suggestions to make further use of it:

1. **Organize a Study Group** Compare your responses with those of your classmates. This will help all of you to review the material you have learned during the year.

2. **Prepare for Future Exams** Use your essay as a study tool. Review the grade you received and the scorer's comments to help you improve your performance on the next essay test you encounter.

Reflecting on Your Writing

Whether you address the strategies outlined in this chapter or consider your own experiences during a recent essay test, take a moment to reflect on your strengths and weaknesses in test situations. Write down your ideas, and include them in your portfolio. Use these questions to get started:

- What strategy presented in this chapter might best help you complete your next essay test?

- What do you find is the most challenging element of an essay test?

 **Internet Tip**

To see model essays scored with this rubric, go to **www.phwg.phschool.com**

Rubric for Self-Assessment

Use these criteria to evaluate your writing.

	Score 4	Score 3	Score 2	Score 1
Audience and Purpose	Uses appropriately formal diction; clearly addresses writing prompt	Uses mostly formal diction; adequately addresses prompt	Uses some informal diction; addresses writing prompt	Uses inappropriately informal diction; does not address writing prompt
Organization	Presents a clear, consistent organizational strategy	Presents a clear organizational strategy with few inconsistencies	Presents an inconsistent organizational strategy	Shows a lack of organizational strategy
Elaboration	Provides several ideas to support the thesis; elaborates each idea; links all information to thesis	Provides several ideas to support the thesis; elaborates most ideas with facts, details, or examples; links most information to thesis	Provides some ideas to support the thesis; does not elaborate some ideas; does not link some details to thesis	Provides no thesis; does not elaborate ideas
Use of Language	Uses excellent sentence and vocabulary variety; includes very few mechanical errors	Uses adequate sentence and vocabulary variety; includes few mechanical errors	Uses repetitive use of sentence structure and vocabulary; includes many mechanical errors	Demonstrates poor use of language; generates confusion; includes many mechanical errors

Publishing and Presenting • 317

Publishing and Presenting

1. Print out a model essay scored with the rubric on page 317 at www.phwg.phschool.com. Copy the model for each student.

2. Have students examine the scored model. Ask students to brainstorm for ways the student writer could use the scored essay to improve future test performance. For instance, the writer could use the scoring to identify strengths and weaknesses in writing skills.

3. Conclude the discussion by asking students to share the aspects of an essay test that they find most challenging. (Possible answers: the time limit, getting started, organizing ideas)

ASSESS

Assessment

Teaching Resources: Scoring Rubrics on Transparency 14; Formal Assessment, Chapter 14

1. Display the Scoring Rubric transparency and review the criteria in class.

2. Before students proceed with self-assessment, you may wish to review the final draft of the Student Work in Progress on page 318. Have students score the final draft in one or more of the rubric categories. For example, how would students score the piece in terms of audience and purpose?

3. In addition to student self-assessment, you may wish to use the following assessment options.

- score student essays yourself, using the rubric and scoring models from Writing Assessment.

- review the Standardized Test Preparation Workshop on pages 322–323 and have students respond to a persuasive writing prompt within a time limit.

- administer the Chapter 14 Test from Formal Assessment in Teaching Resources to assess students' grasp of concepts presented.

Teaching From the Final Draft

Lead a discussion about the final draft based on these questions:

- Which words from the prompt does Megan use in her introduction? *(stories we have studied in this unit, successful, criteria)*

- What are Megan's criteria for a successful short story? (presenting an important theme; providing a new perspective)

- What is the function of paragraph 2? (It provides a summary of the story.)

- According to Megan, how does the story meet her criteria? (It illustrates the theme of interdependence; it shows disabilities in a new way.)

- What details does Megan use to elaborate on her interpretation? (an event that shows the narrator's shift from selfishness to sensitivity; Doodle's courage in spite of all his falls)

- Which words from the prompt does Megan include in her conclusion? *(successful story; in the unit)*

Integrating Speaking Skills

Ask five students to read the essay aloud, one paragraph each. Even if students have already read the essay to themselves, reading it aloud or listening to it will enhance their understanding and appreciation of the writing.

Customize for
Less Advanced Students

Have pairs of students take turns reading the paragraphs of the final-draft essay to each other. Ask students to underline or write down any words or concepts they don't understand. Lead a small group discussion in which students can help each other arrive at the meanings for the unfamiliar terms.

Student Work
IN PROGRESS

14.6

FINAL DRAFT

> **Question:** Review the short stories we have studied in this unit. Consider the criteria you think are most important in a successful short story, and identify the story that best meets these standards. Explain your response.

The Lesson of "The Scarlet Ibis"

Megan Holbrook
Buena High School
Ventura, California

Among the stories we have studied in this unit, I have enjoyed some greatly and enjoyed others less. To me, a short story is most successful when it presents an important theme and makes readers think about their lives in a new way. According to these criteria, James Hurst's story "The Scarlet Ibis" was the most effective short story in the unit. It develops the theme of interdependence, and it helps readers look at disability from a different perspective.

The story is narrated by Doodle's older brother, who recalls the two boys' childhood. Doodle was born disabled, and doctors did not expect him to live. His lungs were weak, and he had poor muscle control. The brothers struggled to conquer Doodle's disability.

The story illustrates the theme of interdependence: When you help someone else, you enrich both your life and his. To develop this idea, the writer shows a meaningful shift in Doodle's brother from selfishness to sensitivity. At first, he was embarrassed by Doodle's disability. His effort to teach Doodle to walk sprang from his own shame at having a disabled brother. However, the scene in which Doodle walks on his sixth birthday brings out the change in Doodle's brother. The narrator now understands that by teaching Doodle to walk, he himself has been learning to love his brother. Through this scene, the reader sees how both boys are strengthened by their relationship.

The story also helps readers see disability in a new way. Even though Doodle was disabled, he had a strong spirit. Despite all the falls he took while learning to walk, he kept trying. This courage shows that a physical disability is not a mental one.

"The Scarlet Ibis" is the most successful story in the unit because it teaches a valuable lesson about interdependence and it encourages readers to see disability from a fresh perspective. Although the story wasn't action packed or filled with tension, it is one piece of literature I will remember for a long time.

The introduction uses language from the prompt and identifies Megan's criteria for evaluating short stories: the theme they convey and their ability to show a subject in a new way.

A summary provides background on the story's premise.

Megan gives her interpretation of the theme of "The Scarlet Ibis" and provides details from the story to support her analysis.

In a second support paragraph, Megan explains how the story shows disability in a new light.

The conclusion summarizes the response and provides a personal reflection on the story.

Connected Assignment *Open-Book Test*

In some classes, instead of completing a test with information you've gathered from memory, you are allowed to consult class texts during an exam. In such a situation, known as an **open-book test,** you may also be able to review your study notes or class notes. To study for an open-book test, you can focus more on identifying general themes than on memorizing specific details. During the test, you can gather supporting details from texts or notes as you write. To prepare for future open-book tests, consider these writing process tips:

Prewriting Plan your essay with a rough outline. Then, turn to your books and notes to gather details. Locate two to three supporting details for each point, as the example below shows. Capitalize on the open-book format by using quotations and statistics that wouldn't be available to you during a traditional test.

▲ Critical Viewing How is the process of writing an open-book test response different from writing a research paper? [Contrast]

> Thesis: Walt Whitman's poetry reflects a sympathetic attitude toward the workers of the country.
>
> A. "I Hear America Singing": (p. 413)
>   -mechanics, carpenters, masons, etc.
>
> B. From "Song of Myself," section 51: (p. 41)
>   -invites those who have done a "day's work" to join him...

Drafting Begin with an introduction stating your main idea. Elaborate on each point in a separate paragraph, drawing information and supporting details from the plan or from your books and notes. Close with a summary of the main points.

Revising and Editing Be sure the content of your draft is complete and accurate. Insert transitional words and phrases to stress connections between main points.

Publishing and Presenting After your essay has been graded, place it in your portfolio to demonstrate your ability to compile and organize information under time limitations.

Connected Assignment: Open-Book Test • 319

Critical Viewing

Contrast Students may say that writing a test response is more difficult because you need to provide a good amount of information in less space and time.

Step-by-Step Teaching Guide

Open-Book Test

1. Ask students to share their experiences taking open-book tests. Use the following questions to elicit discussion:

   - Can open-book tests be hard, even if you have the information at your fingertips? (Possible answer: Yes, because you must already be familiar with the information and know how to find it quickly.)

   - How can "narrowing your focus" be a good skill to have in open-book tests? (Possible answer: Even though you have access to all the information, you can't possibly use it all in one essay.)

   - Would you rather take a closed- or open-book test in English class? Math? Science?

2. Direct students to the writing process tips and point out that they can especially help in open-book essay tests.

Analyzing Ideas as Represented in Various Art Forms

Focus on Theater: *Annie*

You may think that the Great Depression is more suited for an essay-test question than for the setting of a successful Broadway musical. However, in 1977 the musical Annie opened in New York City. With music by Charles Strouse and lyrics by Martin Charnin, Annie was a huge hit. Despite its upbeat message, the play is set in New York City during the Depression. Songs like "We'd Like to Thank You, Herbert Hoover," and "We'll Get a New Deal for Christmas" set the play's historical context. Against this grim backdrop, Annie is the story of an optimistic orphan who conquers the odds and finds a home for herself and her dog, Sandy.

Art Connection In 1924, cartoon artist Harold Gray (1894–1968) created the legendary "Little Orphan Annie." The cartoon premiered in the *New York Daily News*. That same year, Daddy Warbucks was introduced as a character, and Annie's dog, Sandy, debuted in 1925. *Orphan Annie* went on to become a popular radio show in 1930 during the Great Depression, and listeners could order rings with secret compartments as well as decoder badges to help solve the program's mysteries.

Photography Connection In contrast to the upbeat mood of *Annie*, the photography of Berenice Abbott (1898–1991) captured grim images of Depression-era New York. Funded by the Federal Art Project, Abbott's photographs chronicled New York City between 1935 and 1939, revealing the faces of the unemployed and the stark realities of bread lines.

Assessment Writing Activity: Explain *Annie*'s Appeal
The Depression was one of the most difficult times in our nation's history. Millions of people lost nearly every possession they owned. In an essay, discuss why a comic strip about a lighthearted orphan would gain popularity in such a bleak time.

▲ **Critical Viewing** How do fictional characters like Annie and her dog help personalize a historic period such as the Great Depression for audiences? **[Analyze]**

Media and Technology Skills

Using Technology to Respond to a Variety of Test Formats

Activity: Practice With Computerized Test Banks

Computerized test-taking offers you some key advantages over traditional test formats. For essays, time-saving error-management tools allow you to spend more time on content without scrimping on presentation or accuracy. For short-answer exams, a computerized test bank can give you the chance to practice with specific test formats.

Learn About It The more comfortable you are with test formats, the better you are likely to perform at test time. To best prepare, find out what the tests will cover and how the questions will be structured—whether multiple-choice, essay, or another specific format. Then, study the material, and use computerized tutorials and sample tests to focus your study.

Practice With It As you prepare to practice, learn how the test bank works. Read directions, on-line files, or background materials. When practicing with test banks, create as authentic a test environment as possible—remove distractions, set a timer, consult only allowed references. Print out your results, and note any confusions you had with the test format.

Try It Locate a computerized test bank from school, the library, or the Web. While you work through a tutorial or sample test, familiarize yourself with program features. Note test-format questions or problems in a chart like the one here. Record your answers and solutions for future test-taking reference.

Tips and Techniques
- Use built-in clocks and calculators to track time and compute arithmetic without extra equipment.
- Apply text-editing features to speed up planning, aid text manipulation, and correct errors.
- Visit test publishers' Web sites for tips.
- Request large type or audio questioning if appropriate to your needs.
- Find out how to retrace your steps for review and revision purposes.

Test-Format Questions and Problems	Answers and Solutions
Should you guess?	
Can you skip a question and return to it?	
Is there a Help screen?	
What other features have you found to be helpful or important?	

Media and Technology Skills • 321

Step-by-Step Teaching Guide

Using Technology to Respond to a Variety of Test Formats

Teaching Resources: Writing Support Transparency 14-C; Writing Support Activity Book 14-1

1. Ask students to brainstorm some advantages computers can offer in taking essay tests. (Possible answers: Grammar and spell checks can save time and catch errors you might miss; you can get your ideas down faster and organize them easier; you don't have to worry about handwriting.)

2. Point out that a resource is available to students that lets them practice taking essay and other tests on the computer.

3. Arrange for students to explore computerized test banks.

4. Display the transparency and give students copies of the blank organizer for them to complete.

Customize for ESL Students

Arrange for students to explore computerized test banks in pairs. You might find it best to pair two students with the same home language. Or you might pair one English-language learner with a more advanced student.

Customize for Gifted/Talented Students

After students have explored computerized test banks, assign them to assist students who are not as advanced in using technology. Point out that the objective is for the less advanced student to learn and practice technology skills in the context of exploring computerized test banks. Caution the "teachers" not to do the work for the "learners."

Analyzing Mechanical Errors

1. Some students may want to mark up the sentences and passages. They can circle the errors they find, or edit the sentences for correct punctuation. They then can use this information to answer each question.

2. If students find that they consistently make errors with spelling, punctuation, or capitalization, encourage them to spend more time reviewing the rules of mechanics for the topic.

Standardized Test Preparation Workshop

Analyzing Mechanical Errors

When you edit and proofread your own writing, you correct the errors in mechanics you see. Using a multiple-choice format, standardized tests frequently measure your ability to recognize mechanical errors. In items like the ones you'll see in this workshop, you are asked to evaluate specific words, phrases, or sentences for errors. The following are some methods that will help you address these types of questions:

• Review your options. Errors in these types of questions will be limited to spelling, capitalization, and punctuation. Do not get bogged down in the factual accuracy of the passage.

• Be aware that some items will not contain mistakes.

The following sample test items will give you practice with errors in writing.

Test Tips

• If a sentence contains two or more items in a series, look for commas that separate these items.
• When reviewing capitalization, be sure all proper nouns are capitalized.

Sample Test Items	Answers and Explanations

Directions: Read the following passages, and decide which type of error, if any, appears in the underlined sections. Choose the letter for your answer.
 	
The group I joined visits retirement homes.
 	
<u>At first I was apprehinsive, but now I enjoy</u>
(1)
<u>the visits.</u>
 	
1 **A** Spelling error
     B Capitalization error
     C Punctuation error
     D No error
	The correct answer is *A*. *Apprehensive* is spelled incorrectly.

<u>After collecting paper, pencils paint and scis-</u>
(2)
<u>sors, we started to make the decorations.</u>
 	
2 **F** Spelling error
     G Capitalization error
     H Punctuation error
     J No error
	The correct answer is *H*. A comma is needed between *pencils* and *paint* and between *paint* and *scissors* to indicate items in a series.

 TEST-TAKING TIP

Encourage students to approach each question systematically. For example, they can first check a sentence or passage for capitalization errors, then punctuation errors, and so on.

Practice 1 **Directions:** Read the passages, and decide which type of error, if any, appears in each underlined section. Mark the letter for your answer.

<u>Hudson county</u> will hold its first spring
(1)
festival this weekend. Packed with crafts,

<u>food, games, rides, and other attractions:</u>
(2)
the fesitivities <u>offer something for every-</u>
              (3)
<u>one.</u> You'll find crafts created by local

<u>artists in our community.</u> In addition to
(4)
shopping and music, your family can

<u>enjoy Pony rides and a petting zoo.</u> Expect
(5)
to have fun: <u>it's going to be a great day!</u>
              (6)

1 **A** Spelling error
   B Capitalization error
   C Punctuation error
   D No error

2 **F** Spelling error
   G Capitalization error
   H Punctuation error
   J No error

3 **A** Spelling error
   B Capitalization error
   C Punctuation error
   D No error

4 **F** Spelling error
   G Capitalization error
   H Punctuation error
   J No error

5 **A** Spelling error
   B Capitalization error
   C Punctuation error
   D No error

6 **F** Spelling error
   G Capitalization error
   H Punctuation error
   J No error

There will be a <u>drama club meeting</u> after
                (7)
school today to discuss several open

issues. First, we'll entertain ideas for the

next play we would like to produce. If

you've just read a <u>great play in Literature</u>
                    (8)
<u>class</u> or you've heard about a drama that

<u>interests you come to the meeting.</u> We'll
(9)
debate our options and then announce the

results. Next, we'll talk about club officers.

<u>In order to keep things moving we need</u>
(10)
to appoint <u>Production Roles.</u> Get there
           (11)
<u>on time; we've got</u> big plans.
(12)

7 **A** Spelling error
   B Capitalization error
   C Punctuation error
   D No error

8 **F** Spelling error
   G Capitalization error
   H Punctuation error
   J No error

9 **A** Spelling error
   B Capitalization error
   C Punctuation error
   D No error

10 **F** Spelling error
   G Capitalization error
   H Punctuation error
   J No error

11 **A** Spelling error
   B Capitalization error
   C Punctuation error
   D No error

12 **F** Spelling error
   G Capitalization error
   H Punctuation error
   J No error

Answer Key

▶ **Practice 1**
1. B
2. H
3. A
4. J
5. B
6. J
7. D
8. G
9. C
10. H
11. B
12. J

In-Depth Lesson Plan

	LESSON FOCUS	PRINT AND MEDIA RESOURCES
DAY 1	**Introduction to Workplace Writing** Students learn key elements of workplace writing (pp. 324–325).	*Writers at Work* **Videotape,** Workplace Writing *Writing Lab* **CD-ROM,** Practical and Technical Writing **Teaching Resources** *Writing Support Transparency,* 15A
DAY 2	**Business Letter** Students study a model and learn how to write a business letter (pp. 326–327).	**Teaching Resources** *Writing Support Transparency,* 15A
DAY 3	**Meeting Minutes** Students learn how to take meeting minutes (pp. 328–329).	**Teaching Resources** *Writing Support Transparency,* 15B
DAY 4	**Forms and Applications** Students learn how to fill out model forms and applications (pp. 330–331).	**Teaching Resources** *Writing Support Transparencies,* 15C–D; *Writing Support Activity Book,* 15-1–2

Accelerated Lesson Plan

	LESSON FOCUS	PRINT AND MEDIA RESOURCES
DAY 1	**Introduction to Workplace Writing and Business Letters** Students learn key elements of business writing and how to write business letters.	*Writers at Work* **Videotape,** Workplace Writing *Writing Lab* **CD-ROM,** Practical and Technical Writing **Teaching Resources** *Writing Support Transparency,* 15A
DAY 2	**Meeting Minutes, Forms and Applications** Students learn how to take accurate meeting minutes and fill out forms and applications.	**Teaching Resources** *Writing Support Transparencies,* 15B–D; *Writing Support Activity Book,* 15-1–2

Options for Adapting Lesson Plans

HOMEWORK

Have students complete any stage of the lesson for homework.

TECHNOLOGY

Students can complete any stage of the lesson on computer. Have them print out their completed work.

FEATURES

Extend coverage with Connected Assignment (p. 332), Spotlight on the Humanities (p. 334), Media and Technology Skills (p. 335), and the Standardized Test Preparation Workshop (p. 336).

What Is Workplace Writing?

Workplace writing takes many forms—each appropriate to a specific situation. The way you write in the workplace will change, depending on the tasks you undertake and the places in which you work. Despite these differences, workplace writing usually results in a fact-based, written product that communicates specific information to readers in a structured format that most people recognize. Effective workplace writing

- communicates its information and message clearly, directly, and briefly.
- focuses on key topics and anticipates answers to questions readers may have.
- reflects thorough attention to accuracy and neatness.

Types of Workplace Writing

From the comments your teachers write on your report card to the application you complete to work in the public library, workplace writing is part of your life. There are several forms of workplace writing—both electronic and print. Each reflects particular audiences and purposes. These are several common formats:

- **Business letters** are created to communicate information or to address issues of almost any kind.
- **Meeting minutes** are generated to provide a written record of the decisions and plans discussed at a meeting. These notes benefit those attending and other interested parties.
- **Forms and applications** are completed to provide specific factual information necessary for a particular purpose, such as shopping on-line or obtaining a part-time job.

PREVIEW

Chapter Contents

In this chapter, you'll see several examples of workplace writing—such as a letter requesting information about a recycling program, the minutes of a student government meeting, an application for a personal savings account, and the forms typically used to introduce facsimiles (faxes) and to note phone messages. As you'll see, using the stages of the writing process can make these business forms more effective.

Writers in ACTION

Perhaps more than any other form of written communication, workplace writing involves specific and accepted traditions. These rules require practice to achieve success.

Popular children's writer Betsy Byers showed great insight into workplace writing when she made this comment:

"Writing is like baseball or piano playing. You have to practice if you want to be successful."

Workplace Writing • 325

Interest GRABBER Ask students to imagine that they have applied for a job testing software for new computer games. The job pays very well, and testing the games is a lot of fun. The company has asked each applicant to write a letter about why he or she should have the job. What qualities (such as neatness, clarity, persuasive language) should the letter contain to make the best impression?

Activate Prior Knowledge

Explain that people can usually tell at a glance if a letter is personal or formal. Ask students to think of the last time they received a letter by mail or e-mail. Invite students to share how they could tell what type of letter it was as soon as they opened it.

More About the Writer

When Betsy Byers says you "have to practice" to be a successful writer, she speaks from experience. Byers has written more than 50 books. Although Byers usually writes novels for young people, she has also written her share of business letters, meeting notes, and applications.

☑ ONGOING ASSESSMENT: Diagnose

Use the following option to diagnose students' current level of proficiency in workplace writing.

Have students draft a brief memo to an employer in which they request two days of vacation time. If students have difficulty drafting their memos, you may need to devote more time to writing business letters.

What Is a Business Letter?

Teaching Resources: Writing Support Transparency 15-A

1. Display the transparency.

2. Have volunteers identify each of the six parts of the business letter. As each part is identified, ask these corresponding questions:

   - Heading: What information does it convey? (writer's name, affiliation, address, date)

   - Inside address: What does it tell about the letter? (whom it will be sent to)

   - Salutation: What punctuation appears after it? (colon)

   - Body: What is the writer's purpose in this letter? (to ask for information)

   - Closing: What closing would you choose to end a business letter?

   - Signature: In what two ways is the signature presented?

Integrating Technology Skills

Some students may be familiar enough with word processing software to know that these programs offer features to help create different kinds of business letters and forms. These features often involve pre-formatted letters and forms that ensure the style of the letter or form is correct. Encourage students to familiarize themselves with these features.

15.1 Business Letter

What Is a Business Letter?

From a letter offering a job candidate a position to a letter requesting charitable donations, business letters are among the most common type of workplace writing. Whatever the subject, an effective business letter

- includes six parts: the heading, the inside address, the salutation or greeting, the body, the closing, and the signature.

- follows one of several acceptable forms: In *block format*, each part of the letter begins at the left margin; in *modified block format*, the heading, the closing, and the signature are indented to the center of the page.

- uses formal language to communicate respectfully, regardless of the letter's content.

The **heading** indicates the address and business affiliation of the writer. It also shows the date the letter was sent.

Model Business Letter

In this letter, Yolanda Dodson uses modified block format to request information.

The **inside address** indicates where the letter will be sent.

A **salutation** is punctuated by a colon. When the specific addressee is not known, use a general greeting such as "To whom it may concern:"

The **body** of the letter states the writer's purpose. In this case, the writer requests information.

The **closing** "Sincerely" is common, but "Yours truly" or "Respectfully yours" are also acceptable. To end the letter, the writer types her name and provides a **signature**.

Students for a Cleaner Planet
c/o Memorial High School
333 Veterans' Drive
Denver, Colorado 80211

January 25, 20 – –

Steven Wilson, Director
Resource Recovery Really Works
300 Oak Street
Denver, Colorado 80216

Dear Mr. Wilson:

Memorial High School would like to start a branch of your successful recycling program. We share your commitment to reclaiming as much reusable material as we can. Because your program has been successful in other neighborhoods, we're sure that it can work in our community. Our school includes grades 9–12 and has about 800 students.

Would you send us some information about your community recycling program? For example, we need to know what materials can be recycled and how we can implement the program.

At least fifty students have already expressed an interest in getting involved, so I know we'll have the people power to make the program work. Please help us get started.

Thank you in advance for your time and consideration.

Sincerely,

Yolanda Dodson

Yolanda Dodson

◈ STANDARDIZED TEST PREPARATION WORKSHOP

Grammar and Usage Standardized tests may ask students to evaluate workplace writing. Ask students which number in the following letter contains an error in the underlined text following it:

Dear (1) <u>Mr.</u> (2) <u>Harris;</u>

I enjoyed learning about your company when you visited our (3) <u>school</u>. Thank you for speaking at our Career Fair.

(4) <u>Sincerely,</u>
Maura Adams
Student Body President

Item **2** contains a punctuation error. The semicolon should be a colon.

TOPIC BANK

To write a business letter that communicates successfully, choose a real-life topic that interests you and focus on just one or two aspects of it. That way, you can keep your letter brief. If you're having trouble coming up with your own topic, consider these possibilities:

1. **Letter to an Author** Review the books you've enjoyed recently. Choose the one you liked best, and write a letter to the author. Express your pleasure in reading the work, and ask about the writer's plans for future books.

2. **Letter to a Workplace** Consider a career or job you might be interested in pursuing. Then, write a letter to a local professional to ask for an interview that will help you to learn more about what the job demands.

Prewriting If possible, identify the name and title of the person who will receive your letter. Then, jot down the information you want to convey. To make the best use of your reader's time and to increase the chances that your letter will generate a positive response, identify your most important point and plan to present it early in the letter.

Drafting As you draft, use a formal tone and provide any background information your reader will need.

Revising Because your letter must introduce and address an issue, check that the topic and main point are clear in the first paragraph. Review your draft to make the most efficient and effective use of details, adding those that are necessary and deleting those that are not.

Editing and Proofreading Carefully check your letter's format. Make absolutely certain that you've spelled the person's name correctly and that you have the right business name and address. Correct grammar, usage, and mechanics problems.

Publishing Write, type, or print your letter on standard business paper or send it by e-mail. Use a neutral color of paper, such as white or ivory. To mail your letter, fold it neatly into thirds and put it in a properly addressed matching envelope.

Business Letter • **327**

Customize for
Less Advanced Students

Invite students to work in pairs to choose a topic for their business letters. If they need another idea, try this: Think of the names of people you know who work in businesses. Write a letter to one of these people, explaining that you would like to know more about the kind of work he or she does. Include three questions in your letter.

Prewriting Tip

To help students decide what they want to say in their letters, ask them to identify no more than three "main messages" and write them down. For example:

- *I have good work habits.*
- *I want to work for your company.*
- *My long-term plans are for a career in . . .*

Next, have students arrange the three messages in order of importance, with the most important first:

- *I want to work for your company.*
- *I have good work habits.*
- *My long-term plans are for a career in . . .*

To write the body of the letter, students may simply flesh out this main message skeleton.

Customize for
Verbal/Linguistic Learners

After students have completed their final drafts of a business letter, have partners proofread them together. Partners can exchange letters and then read each aloud. What errors does the reader see? What errors does the listener hear? Have students correct their drafts.

☑ **ONGOING ASSESSMENT: Monitor and Reinforce**

Students may find it difficult to write in formal language without sounding stilted. These strategies may help them achieve the appropriate tone.

Option 1 Tell students to think of individuals they know who work in business, such as school officials, pharmacists, dentists, bank tellers. Have students choose one of these individuals to picture when writing their letters. Ask students to evaluate the formality of their language by asking themselves this question: Is this what I would say to this person in a formal meeting?

Option 2 After students write their first drafts, they can work in pairs. As one student reads his or her letter, the partner plays the role of the person to whom the letter is addressed. Does the letter sound appropriately formal in this setting? If the listener thinks so, the student has found the right level of formality.

⏱ **TIME SAVERS!**

 Writing Support Transparencies
Use the transparencies for Chapter 15 to teach these strategies.

What Are Meeting Minutes?

Teaching Resources: Writing Support Transparency 15-B

1. Review the model meeting minutes.

2. Ask students where in the minutes they could find answers to each of the following questions.

   • What did Clare and Kathleen disagree about? (Where: Old Business; yearbook donations)

   • Did Simon Weathers attend the meeting? (Where: Absent; no)

   • Which members have assignments to complete before the next meeting? (Where: Action Items; Roger, Dory, Brian)

Integrating Grammar Skills

Business letters use formal language, but they do not have to be boring. When students edit their work, encourage them to look for passive verbs and replace them with active verbs wherever possible.

15.2 Meeting Minutes

What Are Meeting Minutes?

When people hold a meeting to discuss issues of interest to them all, it's important to have a written record. Meeting minutes can provide the details. Effective meeting minutes

• provide a list of those who attended and identify the date, time, and place of the meeting.

• itemize the issues discussed and objectively summarize the views taken by those present.

• list action items and the people responsible for completing them.

> The title clearly identifies the group that is meeting, and the date helps all readers keep track of the progress of individual projects.

Model Meeting Minutes

As a member of his school's Student Council, Brian Pretkowski recorded these minutes of a meeting.

> In addition to a list of those who attended, the writer indicates an absent member to recognize him as a participant.

> Meeting minutes are typically organized into ongoing, or "old," business and new business. In each section, the writer titles the topic, briefly recounts the discussion, and lists the action items with the people responsible.

> Boldfaced type and underlining help organize the minutes and make it easier for readers to find the information they need.

Portland High School Student Council
Monthly Meeting: April 4, 20 – –

Attended: Luz Delgado, Roger Cash, Justin Healy, Clare Picone, Kathleen O'Rourke, Dory Marsh, Brian Pretkowski
Absent: Simon Weathers

Business Discussed:
• Minutes of last month's meeting were read by Justin Healy, who had recorded them. The minutes were approved as written.

Old Business:
• <u>Fund-raising for the Yearbook</u>: We are still exploring different ways to raise money for the yearbook. Clare strongly stated her feeling that we should not ask for student donations. Kathleen disagreed, pointing out that we can write a letter explaining that people will not be pressured to donate and that no donation is too small.

Action Item: Get advice from parents and teachers about donation issue. Report at next month's meeting. (Roger, Dory)

New Business:
• <u>Representative for School Board</u>: The School Board has created a spot for a student representative. They've asked the Council to select that member. Luz suggested that we invite all students to write an application letter telling why they would be good a representative. Brian felt that such a process would take too long and be too subjective. He suggested instead a lottery of interested students. We could set minimum qualifications, such as being in good academic standing. A motion was made and accepted to follow Brian's idea.

Action Item: Write letter announcing and explaining the lottery. (Brian) Photocopy letter. (Dory) Distribute letter.

Next Meeting: May 7, 20 – –

328 • Workplace Writing

⏱ TIME AND RESOURCE MANAGER

Resources
Print: Writing Support Transparency 15-B
Technology: Writing Lab CD-ROM, Practical and Technical Writing

In-Depth Coverage	Accelerated Pace
• Cover pp. 328–329 in class. • Set aside 15 minutes of classroom time to conduct a mock—or real—meeting. Ask students to take notes during the meeting, then write up their notes as minutes. • Have students compare their minutes and discuss the similarities and differences.	• Have students review the information on pp. 328–329 independently. • Allow students two weeks to attend a meeting independently and write up the minutes as directed on p. 329.

TOPIC BANK

To write effective meeting minutes, arrive at the meeting prepared to take notes. Focus on accuracy and objectivity. If you'd like to practice writing meeting notes and need some help to get started, consider these possibilities:

1. **Minutes of a Club Meeting** In schools and communities, people form clubs to share common interests, such as gardening, bowling, or reading. Attend the meeting of a club you belong to or ask permission to visit the meeting of another one. Record and write up minutes of the meeting.

2. **Minutes of a Public Meeting** In communities of many different sizes, citizens gather at public meetings to discuss issues such as education, library funding, and recreation. Contact city offices to learn of such meetings. Attend a meeting and record its minutes. To prepare, read local newspapers and the minutes of the previous meeting.

Prewriting Before you write up any minutes, attend a meeting. Record the names of participants, and take accurate notes about what happens. As each issue is addressed, identify the subject. Then, briefly summarize the views expressed. List actions to be taken, and name the people identified to follow up.

Drafting Use your notes to draft your meeting minutes. As you list and discuss each topic, present ideas objectively; record what was said, and do not take sides in any disputes. Use complete sentences, and identify any questions raised.

Revising Use a numbering system or bullets to organize topics, and use boldfaced type or underlining to help readers locate topics of interest. Revise to make the notes brief and to maintain a consistently objective tone.

Editing and Proofreading Check your final copy against your original notes. Be sure you have represented all discussions accurately and have spelled names correctly. Check that the formatting you have chosen is consistent.

Publishing Distribute your meeting notes before the next meeting. This courtesy gives participants a chance to review your notes with two goals in mind: First, club members will want to be sure they remember what decisions were made; second, they may need to be reminded of the actions they agreed to take.

Language Highlight

Just like school students today, young scholars in ancient Greece and Rome had to take notes and write rough drafts. They wrote their notes and drafts in *minuta scriptura,* or "small writing." Can students see where the word *minutes,* for meeting notes, came from?

Real-World Connection

People who take minutes in meetings must pay close attention to what is going on. They often must understand specialized words and terms too. Ask students whether they would enjoy a career in which they took minutes in one of these settings?

- courtroom
- surgical department in a hospital
- on-scene locations of a film crew
- company that invents new technologies

Model Form: Fax Cover Sheet

Teaching Resources: Writing Support Transparency 15-C; Writing Support Activity Book 15-1

1. Display the transparency. Ask students to refer to the model fax cover sheet to answer these questions:
   - Must the sheet include an explanatory note? (no)
   - Does the Fax Source Transmission Number belong to the sender or the recipient? (sender)
   - If the remarks do not fit on the cover sheet, where should they go? (into a formal business letter, which would be faxed following the cover sheet)
2. Give students copies of the blank form and have them practice filling it out.

Customize for
Intrapersonal Learners

Give each student a blank copy of your school's fax cover sheet (or a generic cover sheet). Ask students to work individually to complete the cover sheets. Post the cover sheets on a bulletin board so that students can view one another's work during free time.

15.3 Forms and Applications

What Are Forms and Applications?

In the fast-paced world of computer databases and printouts, forms and applications are everywhere—at school to help students join clubs, in the workplace to help people obtain jobs, and even in the home as people order from a catalog. Forms and applications are preprinted with blank spaces for specific information. To effectively complete these documents

- write legibly so that information can be read.
- read all the labels and instructions to make sure you're supplying the correct information.

Model Form: Fax (Facsimile) Cover Sheet

When people send a fax, they usually use a cover sheet to make the communication more formal. Cover sheets tell who sent the fax, who should receive it, and how many pages the complete fax contains. Most provide a space for a brief handwritten message. Look at this example:

> A company letterhead clearly identifies the sender of the fax.

> The sender completes information thoroughly, providing the recipient's fax number and the total number of pages.

> The remarks on a fax cover sheet should be brief and to the point. Longer or more in-depth comments should be included in a properly formatted business letter, which can be faxed along with the cover sheet.

Your Yearbook!
5 Harr Court • Columbus, Ohio 43229
phone 614.555.2637 • fax 614.555.2601
e-mail: jay@address.com

Fax

FACSIMILE COVER SHEET/TRANSMITTAL

DATE: *10/19/20--*

TO: *Luke Pelliccio – Photos by Pelliccio*

FAX NUMBER: *614-555-1200*

FAX SOURCE TRANSMISSION NUMBER: *614-555-2637*

FROM: *Elaine Rothman*

TOTAL NUMBER OF PAGES (including this cover sheet): *3*

REMARKS:

Luke - When will you be able to review the photos you took for Medford High? I need to set aside time for any reshoots that may be necessary. Let me know.
Thanks, Elaine

330 • Workplace Writing

⏱ TIME AND RESOURCE MANAGER

Resources
Print: Writing Support Transparencies 15-C–D; Writing Support Activity Book 15-1–2
Technology: Writing Lab CD-ROM, Practical and Technical Writing

In-Depth Coverage	Accelerated Pace
• Cover pp. 330–331 in class, pointing out the content in the side boxes. • Ask students to brainstorm for situations in which they have been asked to fill out a fax cover sheet, application, or other form.	• Have students review the information on pages 330–331 independently.

Model Application

Opening your first bank account is an exciting moment. In the model below, notice how one teenager completed the application for such an account.

GULFPORT SAVINGS BANK
Biloxi • Gulfport • Hurley

NAME(S): *Anthony Coratella*
Judith Coratella

ADDRESS: *171 Central Avenue*
Biloxi, MS 39531

TELEPHONE (HOME AND WORK):
Home: (228) 555-6035
Work: (Judith): (228) 555-3400 x51

TAX ID NUMBER(S):
Anthony: 999-00-9999
Judith: 888-00-8888

DATE(S) OF BIRTH:
(FOR CUSTODIAL ACCOUNT, INCLUDE MINORS)

Anthony: 7/5/89   Judith: 5/1/62

ACCOUNT NUMBER: *(for internal use)*

ACCOUNT TYPE:
☐ NOW   ☐ Statement Savings
☐ Money Market ☑ Passbook Savings
☐ Checking

ACCOUNT OWNERSHIP:
☐ Individual   ☐ Corporation
☑ Joint w/Survivorship ☐ Partnership/Firm
☐ Joint w/o Survivorship ☐ Custodial

SPECIAL INSTRUCTIONS:

Account # _____   Chex System ☐

CUSTOMER TAXPAYER IDENTIFICATION BACKUP WITHHOLDING CERTIFICATION
Under penalties of perjury, I certify that the number shown on this form is my correct Taxpayer Identification Number. I also certify that I am not subject to backup withholding either because I have not been notified that I am subject to backup withholding as a failure to report all interest and dividends, or because the Internal Revenue Service has notified me that I am no longer subject to backup withholding.
Signature *Judith Coratella*   Date *10/28/20--*

By signing this form, I/We agree to the rules and regulations regarding this account of Gulfport Savings Bank. I/We certify receipt of a Deposit Account Agreement, Schedule of Interest and Charges, Funds Availability Agreement, Electronic Funds Transfer Agreement and Truth-in-Savings Disclosures.

10/28/20--   *Judith Coratella*
DATE   SIGNATURE
10/28/20--   *Anthony Coratella*
DATE   SIGNATURE

DATE   SIGNATURE

Date Opened: *10/28/20--*   Initial Deposit: *$25* ☐ Check   Opened by: _____
                                             ☑ Cash

A writer includes only the specific information requested. In fact, some spaces are left blank as the directions request.

When there doesn't seem to be enough space, writers should write small but legibly or find out how to include requested information.

The writer neatly checks off the type of account desired. In this case, a bank employee can explain the different choices.

Noting one person's name inside parentheses helps readers know which information goes with each person listed on the form. Slashes also help separate this information when it is entered on the same line.

Knowing in advance that an adult's signature will be required avoids delays. Sometimes forms can be taken home and returned with the necessary signatures.

Forms and Applications • **331**

☑ ONGOING ASSESSMENT: Monitor and Reinforce

Legible handwriting is important on forms and applications. These strategies provide extra practice.

Option 1 Provide two blank forms for each student. Ask students to complete one form, then rewrite the information as neatly as possible on the second form.

Option 2 Have students copy by hand the information on the copyright page of a book. Ask them to print the information once using upper- and lowercase letters, then a second time using all capital letters. Which version is easier to read?

 TIME SAVERS!

 Writing Support Transparencies
Use the transparencies for Chapter 15 to teach these strategies.

 Writing Support Activity Book
Use the graphic organizers for Chapter 15 to facilitate these strategies.

Lesson Objectives

1. To write in a style appropriate to audience and purpose.
2. To produce legible work that shows accurate spelling and correct use of conventions.
3. To focus attention on the speaker's message.
4. To monitor speaker's message for clarity and ask relevant questions to clarify understanding.
5. To publish a correctly recorded telephone message to an audience.

Step-by-Step Teaching Guide

Phone Messages

Teaching Resources: Writing Support Transparency 15-E; Writing Support Activity Book 15-3

1. Ask the school office or local businesses to supply information about their telephone message policies and procedures. Examine any sample telephone message forms these workplaces utilize.
2. Suggest that students review strategies from Chapter 15.
3. Have student pairs take turns leaving and receiving mock phone calls. After students complete the activity, discuss which techniques they feel comfortable applying independently. Remind students that telephone etiquette takes some practice and encourage them to continue practicing.
4. Display a random selection of phone messages generated by the partner activity. If possible, have students show the messages to workers in the school office or local businesses. What feedback can these workers provide?

Connected Assignment
Phone Messages

Communicating effectively by telephone is an important workplace and life skill. Sometimes you'll be leaving phone messages and other times you'll be receiving them. In both cases, the goal is to ensure that the pertinent information gets to the intended person. Failed telephone communication can mean lost business or delays that prevent efficient business.

The tips below can help you leave and receive phone messages professionally.

Leaving Phone Messages

Before the Call Clarify the purpose of your call, using notes if necessary. This will prepare you whether you talk directly to the person or leave a message. Have any documents, such as order forms or your calendar, easily accessible.

Leaving the Message Speak slowly and clearly. Make sure you give your full name, and if you are representing a business, give the name of the company at the beginning of the call. State the reason for your call and how you can be reached. If time allows, repeat your name and phone number before hanging up. If you leave a message on a voice-mail, answering machine, or pager system, make sure to follow the directions of the system so that your message is correctly recorded.

Following Up If you're speaking to a person, ask him or her to read back your message for accuracy. Voice-mail systems may allow you to replay your message and even make revisions. If you don't receive a response to your message within an appropriate period of time, consider calling again.

▲ **Critical Viewing** How can a missed or inaccurate phone message hurt a business? [**Hypothesize**]

Critical Viewing

Hypothesize Students may say that missed or inaccurate phone messages can leave customers without information or materials that they need and can delay responses in ways that embarrass employees.

Receiving Phone Messages

Before the Call Be prepared for phone calls, especially if you are assigned to phone duty or are expecting a call. Keep paper along with working pens or pencils near your phone. If possible, use preprinted phone-message forms, which allow you to check off options rather than write out entire messages. Be prepared to tune out or remove distractions such as background noise.

During the Call Follow these tips to help you complete this important task efficiently:

1. Listen carefully in order to hear the facts correctly.
2. Write neatly to make the message easy to read. Writing that is too small is hard to read, and writing that is too large will not fit in the allotted spaces.
3. Ask the caller to repeat any information and spell out any names that you did not understand.
4. Read back telephone numbers to verify their accuracy.
5. Speak professionally and politely; when you are taking a message, you are representing someone else.

After the Call Reread your message for neatness and legibility. If necessary, rewrite it on a clean form or piece of paper. Make sure to note the time of the phone call and record your own name for any follow-up questions.

1. To evaluate media presentations.
2. To analyze ideas as represented in various media.
3. To recognize how visual and sound techniques convey messages.
4. To write a persuasive letter.

Step-by-Step Teaching Guide

Examining Ideas Represented in a Variety of the Arts

1. Choose one of the Spotlight elements for class discussion, or have students work individually or in groups on the element of their choice. Give students the initiative to find the necessary audiotapes, videotapes, or books.

2. Play audiorecordings of Tchaikovsky music for students. What moods does it evoke. Would students support his career?

3. Invite any students who have seen a ballet with Tchaikovsky music to describe the experience. Show a videotape of one ballet. How do the music and dance interact?

4. Have students research the ballet technique in *Swan Lake.* Ask students with ballet experience to comment. Then ask students to research contemporary dance of any kind. How do the steps and technique compare and contrast?

5. If students view *Funny Girl,* ask them whether they found the parody of *Swan Lake* humorous. Why or why not? How would they update such a scene for humor?

Spotlight on the Humanities

Examining Ideas Represented in a Variety of the Arts

Focus on Music:
Peter Ilich Tchaikovsky

If you were an artist looking to find a patron to support you financially as you established your career, you'd need to convince your benefactor that you were worthy of his or her time and money. In 1876, Peter Ilich Tchaikovsky (1840–1893) found a patron in Madam Nadejda von Meck who, through her financial support, sponsored one of the most prolific and creative periods of his life. Her patronage lasted for fourteen years, and Tchaikovsky was devastated when it ended. Considered the foremost Russian composer of the nineteenth century, Tchaikovsky wrote not only symphonies but also ballets and operas. Some of his best-known works are *The Nutcracker Suite* (1891–1892), his *Symphony No. 6 in B Minor* (1893), his *Violin Concerto in D Major* (1878), and the music for the ballet *The Sleeping Beauty* and the ballet *Swan Lake.*

Dance Connection Tchaikovsky composed the music for one of the most celebrated ballets of all time, *Swan Lake.* Originally presented in 1877, the first production of the ballet was not well received. The ballet was rechoreographed by Marius Petipa in 1895, and it became a hit. *Swan Lake* is known as one of the most technically challenging ballets since it includes multiple *fouettes,* or fast-spinning turns on one foot. In fact, the ballet requires the female lead to perform thirty-two consecutive *fouettes.*

Film Connection In the 1968 film *Funny Girl,* Tchaikovsky's ballet *Swan Lake* is the subject of hilarious parody by the famous Ziegfield actress Fanny Brice. In a show-stopping production of Tchaikovsky's work, Barbara Streisand as Fanny Brice turns an elegant swan into a wisecracking one. Streisand won an Academy Award for her performance.

Workplace Writing Activity: Grant Proposal Memo

Some organizations make grant money available to young artists. Write a letter stating your talent, your career aspirations, and your plans for future projects.

▲ **Critical Viewing**
What elements of a group dance might make it more difficult than a solo performance? **[Contrast]**

Viewing and Representing

Activity Invite students to present their grant proposal orally to a "jury" of classmates. Urge them to include sketches, graphics, or other visual material describing their goals, along with a question-answer session.

Critical Viewing

Contrast Students may say that dancers must synchronize their movements in order to present a cohesive flow in the dance. They must also avoid bumping into each other or dropping each other.

Media and Technology Skills

Using Technology for Aspects of Writing

Activity: Using Word Processing to Create Effective, Error-Free Writing

With basic word-processing tools, you can easily produce error-free workplace writing. Readers will appreciate your eye for detail and will also be able to attend to your message without distraction. Become familiar with word-processing error management, and make it a habit.

Learn About It Hire your computer as a peer editor by utilizing any of the following tools:

- **Grammar Check** Respond to grammar reminders—indicated by a mascot or by on-screen prompts. You can also activate these programs separately (look under Tools).

- **Spell Check** These programs may point out errors or wait for you to ask. To get help, highlight text or check the entire document. Click on the spell-check icon or select it under Tools.

- **Copy and Paste** Create and copy clipboards of text for documents containing repeated text. Paste in the clipboard text wherever you need it. This allows you to error-check a complex part of your writing or list of numbers only once, even if you use it many times. You can also make minor changes to a schedule, for example, without retyping the whole document.

- **Thesaurus** Use the thesaurus to vary your language and to avoid misusing words. Highlight a specific word, and activate your thesaurus under the Tools menu.

Apply It Trade word-processed writing products with a peer. Scan the basic options discussed above and in the sidebar. Check the writing product for errors, monitoring your efforts in a chart like the one shown here. To organize revisions, create an annotated table of contents for the Help chapter of your software's manual.

Tools Used ⟶	Errors Corrected
Spell Check	
Grammar Check	
Thesaurus	

Correction Tips

- Read manuals to learn about automatic correction features.
- Enter creative spellings (such as a club name) into your spell check to avoid error messages.
- Choose or create preset document formats for standard products such as business letters.
- Use word-count tools to limit length-specific documents.
- See your "symbols" menu for appropriate foreign language and other text alternatives.
- Create tables and charts to neatly and accurately present data.

Lesson Objectives

1. To proofread writing for appropriateness of conventions.
2. To evaluate writing for mechanics.
3. To demonstrate control over grammatical elements such as verb forms.

Step-by-Step Teaching Guide

Applying Verb Usage Rules

1. Stress with students the importance of following basic test-taking rules, no matter what the subject or format of the test is. First, read or listen to any and all directions carefully. This includes directions posted in the test-taking room or delivered orally by a test supervisor.

2. Tell students that often tests will contain example such as the one shown here. Remind students to read pertinent examples carefully before beginning a test.

3. Emphasize with students the importance of neatness in indicating answers. If students need to erase an answer, they should do so thoroughly enough to avoid confusion by examiners.

4. Familiarize students with cloze assignments such as the one shown here by offering them regularly.

Standardized Test Preparation Workshop

Applying Verb Usage Rules

Writing in the workplace should be error-free and follow the rules of grammar, usage, and mechanics. Standardized test questions often measure your ability to recognize errors in grammar, spelling, or punctuation. The following methods will help you address some commonly tested problems with correct verb usage:

- Identify the sequence of events in a passage. This will help you to determine whether a change in verb tense is necessary.

- Make sure the verb tense is logical throughout a passage; if there is no reason for a tense shift, do not introduce one.

The following sample test item will give you practice with questions that challenge you to identify verb-usage problems.

Test Tip

To make sure that verbs agree with their subjects, isolate the words in question by eliminating phrases or modifiers that come between them.

Sample Test Item	Answers and Explanations
Directions: Read the passage, and choose the word that belongs in the space. Choose the appropriate letter for your answer. After sending an e-mail to his co-worker, Chris realized that he (1) some important information. He immediately wrote another note and sent it out immediately. 1　A　forget 　B　forgot 　C　forgotten 　D　forgets	The correct answer is *B*. Since the entire passage is written in the past tense, *forgot* correctly indicates action in the past tense.

TEST-TAKING TIP

Tell students that they should adapt test-taking to their own strengths and weaknesses as much as possible. For example, if they find long or orally delivered directions difficult to remember they can jot down notes on their scrap paper. Writing a brief note can reinforce students' understanding of the specific tasks they have been asked to complete.

Practice 1 **Directions:** Read each passage, and choose the word or group of words that belongs in each space.

After ___(1)___ the museum, our class walked to the city park so we could spend an hour in the fresh air. Next time, I hope that we spend the whole day at the park. We ___(2)___ so many different kinds of birds, animals, and flowers. I especially enjoyed watching a duck with a train of ducklings in tow ___(3)___ in the pond. I've heard that there's a zoo and an ice-skating rink there, too. I never would ___(4)___ that there could be so much in one park.

1 A visited
   B visiting
   C was visiting
   D visit

2 F see
   G saw
   H seen
   J would see

3 A swims
   B swam
   C swum
   D swimming

4 F know
   G have known
   H knew
   J has known

My decision to write an article on immigration was inspired by my own heritage. My parents and grandparents ___(5)___ to this country as immigrants, and from them, I have gained insights to include in my writing. Through my family's stories, I have an awareness of the struggles immigrants ___(6)___ over the years. I also know the benefits and rewards that came to my family after they came to the United States. I am planning to research immigration through books and journals to find out more about its impact on this country. However, I ___(7)___ that the strength of my article will come from the firsthand knowledge I have gained from my family.

5 A moved
   B are moving
   C will move
   D move

6 F are facing
   G have faced
   H will face
   J could face

7 A thought
   B think
   C will think
   D would have thought

Jeffrey woke up at five-thirty in the morning to watch the sun rise and to paint the view. He thought that there ___(8)___ peaceful about early morning. He needed to use his time wisely, because in a few hours there would be people out walking and cars starting to move. He ___(9)___ for a clear day for almost a week, and it had finally arrived. It seemed like the rain from the previous days had left the air feeling clean and crisp. He noticed that the yellow and orange from the sun ___(10)___ with pink hues. He felt confident that this was going to be his best early-morning painting.

8 F will be something
   G is something
   H was something
   J have been something

9 A is waiting
   B had been waiting
   C could be waiting
   D would be waiting

10 F is lined
   G was lined
   H lined
   J have been lined

Answer Key

Practice 1

1. B
2. G
3. D
4. G
5. A
6. G
7. B
8. H
9. B
10. G

Customize for
Less Advanced Students

Work through items 1–4 with students orally. Have volunteers read aloud each sentence containing a numbered blank. Then ask students to take turns reading the sentence aloud with each of the four answer alternatives. Poll students on the correct answer. Encourage students to complete the same process silently when they respond to completion items such as these.

Customize for
More Advanced Students

Challenge students to name the verb forms given in the alternatives to one item. Then ask them to explain why the correct answer should be used in this particular grammatical context.

PART 2
GRAMMAR, USAGE, AND MECHANICS

▶ *Lesson Objectives*

1. To understand parts of speech and basic sentence patterns and to apply relevant concepts to their own writing.

2. To learn and apply key concepts governing usage of verbs.

3. To understand concepts of agreement relating to subjects and verbs and pronouns and antecedents, and to apply this understanding to their own writing.

4. To compose sentences of increasing sophistication and appropriateness.

5. To analyze works of literature as models of appropriate and effective English usage.

6. To recognize appropriate English usage in their own reading and writing.

7. To use "hands-on" strategies to reinforce understanding of grammar and usage concepts.

8. To master the conventions of capitalization, punctuation, and spelling, and to apply them accurately to their own writing.

PART

2

Grammar, Usage, and Mechanics

In Celebration, 1987, Sam Gilliam, National Museum of American Art, Washington, D.C.

Grammar, Usage, and Mechanics • **339**

In-Depth Lesson Plan

LESSON FOCUS	PRINT AND MEDIA RESOURCES
DAY 1 — **Nouns** Students learn and apply the concepts of common, proper, and compound nouns (pp. 340–345).	**Teaching Resources** *Grammar Exercise Workbook*, pp. 1–4; *Grammar Exercises Answers on Transparency*, Ch. 16; *Language Lab* **CD-ROM**, Nouns and Pronouns; *On-Line Exercise Bank*, Section 16.1
DAY 2 — **Pronouns** Students learn and apply the concepts of pronoun antecedents, personal pronouns, and reflexive and intensive pronouns (pp. 346–349).	**Teaching Resources** *Grammar Exercise Workbook*, pp. 5–12; *Grammar Exercises Answers on Transparency*, Ch. 16; *Language Lab* **CD-ROM**, Nouns and Pronouns; *On-Line Exercise Bank*, Section 16.2
DAY 3 — **Pronouns (continued)** Students learn and apply the concepts of demonstrative, relative, interrogative, and indefinite pronouns and do the Hands-On Grammar Activity (pp. 350–355).	**Teaching Resources** *Grammar Exercise Workbook*, pp. 5–12; *Grammar Exercises Answers on Transparency*, Ch. 16; *Hands-On Grammar Activity Book*, Chapter 16; *Language Lab* **CD-ROM**, Nouns and Pronouns; *On-Line Exercise Bank*, Section 16.2
DAY 4 — **Review and Assess** Students review chapter and demonstrate mastery of use of nouns and pronouns (pp. 356–358).	**Teaching Resources** *Formal Assessment*, Ch. 16; *On-Line Exercise Bank*, Section 16.1

Accelerated Lesson Plan

LESSON FOCUS	PRINT AND MEDIA RESOURCES
DAY 1 — **Nouns** Students cover concepts and usage of nouns as determined by Diagnostic Test (pp. 340–345).	**Teaching Resources** *Grammar Exercise Workbook*, pp.1–4; *Grammar Exercises Answers on Transparency*, Ch. 16; *Language Lab* **CD-ROM**, Nouns and Pronouns; *On-Line Exercise Bank*, Section 16.1
DAY 2 — **Pronouns** Students cover concepts and usage of pronouns as determined by Diagnostic Test (pp. 346–355).	**Teaching Resources** *Grammar Exercise Workbook*, pp. 5–12; *Grammar Exercises Answers on Transparency*, Ch. 16; *Hands-On Grammar Activity Book*, Chapter 16; *Language Lab* **CD-ROM**, Nouns and Pronouns; *On-Line Exercise Bank*, Section 16.2
DAY 3 — **Review and Assess** Students review chapter and demonstrate mastery of use of adjectives and adverbs (pp. 356–358).	**Teaching Resources** *Formal Assessment*, Ch. 16 *On-Line Exercise Bank*, Section 16.1

Options for Adapting Lesson Plans

HOMEWORK

Have students complete any section of the chapter for homework.

FEATURES

Extend coverage with the Grammar in Literature feature (p. 347), and the Standardized Test Preparation Workshop (p. 358).

TECHNOLOGY

Students can use the *On-Line Exercise Bank* to complete the exercises on computer. The Auto Check feature will grade their work.

INTEGRATED SKILLS COVERAGE

Grammar in Literature
SE p. 347

Reading
Find It in Your Reading, SE pp. 345, 354, 355

Writing
Find It in Your Writing, SE pp. 345, 354, 355
Writing Application, SE pp. 345, 355, 357

Language
Language Highlight, ATE p. 349

Spelling
Integrating Spelling Skills, ATE p. 343

Real-World Connection
ATE p. 352

Viewing and Representing
Critical Viewing, SE pp. 340, 343, 344, 346, 351

ASSESSMENT SUPPORT

Standardized Test Preparation SE p. 358; ATE pp. 348, 351
Standardized Test Preparation Workbook, pp. 31–32
Formal Assessment, Ch. 16

MEETING INDIVIDUAL NEEDS

Less Advanced Students ATE pp. 344, 351, 353; See also
Ongoing Assessments, ATE pp. 343, 347, 352
ESL Students ATE p. 348
More Advanced Students ATE p. 348

BLOCK SCHEDULING

Pacing Suggestions
For 90-minute Blocks
• Administer the Diagnostic Test to students to determine instructional coverage.
• Have students complete the necessary exercises in class. Use the Hands-on Grammar activity to provide a change of pace.

Resources for Varying Instruction
• *Language Lab* **CD-ROM** If your students have access to hardware, a 90-minute block provides an ideal opportunity for students to work on computer.

Professional Development Support
• *How to Manage Instruction in the Block* This Teaching Resource provides management and activity suggestions.

MEDIA AND TECHNOLOGY

For the Student
• *Language Lab* **CD-ROM**, Nouns and Pronouns
• *On-Line Exercise Bank,* Ch. 16

For the Teacher
• *Resource Pro* **CD-ROM**

WRITING AND GRAMMAR WEBSITE

The Interactive Writing and Grammar Website provides a wide array of support for students, teachers, and parents. Grammar support includes:
• *On-Line Exercise Bank* with Auto Check scoring
• Diagnostic and assessment support

phwg.phschool.com

LITERATURE CONNECTIONS

Grammar in Literature selections from *Prentice Hall Literature: Timeless Voices, Timeless Themes,* Gold:
from *The Cask of Amontillado,* Edgar Allen Poe, SE p. 347

▶ *Lesson Objectives*

1. To understand what nouns are and how they are used.
2. To identify compound nouns.
3. To understand the difference between common and proper nouns and how the difference affects capitalization.
4. To understand what pronouns are and how they are used.
5. To understand the relationship between pronouns and antecedents.
6. To identify personal pronouns.
7. To understand the functions of reflexive and intensive pronouns and to distinguish between them.
8. To learn how to use and identify demonstrative pronouns.
9. To learn how to use and identify relative pronouns.
10. To learn how to use and identify interrogative pronouns.
11. To learn how to use and identify indefinite pronouns.

Critical Viewing

Relate Students may name some of the following parts: head, antennae, legs, eyes, thorax, abdomen.

Chapter 16 Nouns and Pronouns

▲ **Critical Viewing**
Nouns can name parts of things as well as things themselves. How many parts can you name on this grasshopper? **[Relate]**

This chapter presents nouns and pronouns, which are the words we use to name people, places, things, and ideas. If you were to take a walk in the country and wanted to relate what you saw, you would use nouns: *tree, flowers, bees, ants, animals, leaves, stream, grass, sky, sun.* All these words are nouns. If you saw people during your walk, you would use nouns to identify them, too: *man, woman, children, gardener, Bob Smith, Clara.*

Sometimes you need a replacement for a noun—a word like *he* or *she, him* or *her, I* or *me.* These replacements are called pronouns, and they take the place of nouns in sentences.

In this chapter, you will study both nouns and pronouns.

340 • Nouns and Pronouns

☑ ONGOING ASSESSMENT: Diagnose

If students miss more than one item in each category, direct them to the relevant pages of the text and assign exercises for practice and review.

Nouns and Pronouns	Diagnostic Test Items	Teach	Practice	Section Review	Chapter Review
Skill Check A					
Nouns	A 1–5	pp. 342–344	Ex. 1–3	Ex. 4–7	Ex. 24–26
Skill Check B					
Pronouns and Antecedents	B 6–10	p. 346	Ex. 11–12	Ex. 17	Ex. 27
Skill Check C					
Reflexive and Intensive Pronouns	C 11–15	p. 349	Ex. 14	Ex. 20	Ex. 28–30

Diagnostic Test

Directions: Write all answers on a separate sheet of paper.

Skill Check A. Copy these sentences. Underline the common nouns, put two lines under compound nouns, and circle the proper nouns.

1. Because insects are so small, they must have creative ways to protect themselves, Sunday through Saturday, 365 days a year.
2. A saddleback caterpillar has sharp hairs that will break and release poison when they prick your skin.
3. An inchworm and a walking stick use camouflage.
4. Often insects like syrphus flies, which cannot defend themselves, mimic other insects that have better defenses.
5. One species, found in North America, looks like a type that tastes bad to birds.

Skill Check B. Copy the following sentences. Underline each pronoun, and draw an arrow to its antecedent.

6. Insects do not learn their behavior from their parents.
7. In fact, an adult usually dies before her young are born.
8. Consequently, an insect must rely on its instincts to survive.
9. The behavioral patterns are built deep in the nervous system, and they are apparent when stimulated.
10. Every insect reacts to its surroundings.

Skill Check C. Write the reflexive or intensive pronouns in these sentences, and label them.

11. If a cockroach sees a light, it will hide itself in a dark area.
12. If you're near a light at night, you may find yourself surrounded by moths.
13. People often find themselves bothered by mosquitos.
14. Animals themselves attract fleas by the warmth of their bodies.
15. Insects seem to think for themselves, but instinct rules.

Skill Check D. Write and label the demonstrative, interrogative, or relative pronoun in each sentence.

16. A female wasp that is ready to reproduce finds a place where she can build a nest.
17. She then seeks prey, which is usually a tarantula or caterpillar.
18. This is a tarantula captured by a wasp.
19. Those are the books with more facts about wasps.
20. Who borrowed one of the books?

Skill Check E. Write the indefinite pronoun from each sentence.

21. Insect behavior varies by species; most of it is ruled by instinct.
22. However, many do have some ability to learn.
23. A honeybee learns colors and specific landmarks, and it watches both as it returns to its hive.
24. Every species is different; each follows inherited patterns.
25. Behavioral patterns are characteristic of some species but not others, and they have been developed over time.

✓ ONGOING ASSESSMENT: Diagnose *continued*

Nouns and Pronouns	Diagnostic Test Items	Teach	Practice	Section Review	Chapter Review
Skill Check D					
Demonstrative, Relative, and Interrogative Pronouns	D 16–20	pp. 350–352	Ex. 15	Ex. 18, 20	Ex. 28, 30
Skill Check E					
Indefinite Pronouns	E 21–25	p. 353	Ex. 16	Ex. 19–20	Ex. 28, 30
Cumulative Reviews and Applications					Ex. 4–10 17–23	Ex. 24–32

Answer Key

Diagnostic Test

- Each item in the diagnostic test corresponds to a specific concept in the nouns and pronouns chapter. This will enable you to tailor instruction to the particular needs of your students. See "Ongoing Assessment: Diagnose" below for further details.

- Answers for the Diagnostic Test and all chapter exercises are available in *Grammar Exercises Answers on Transparencies* in your teaching resources.

Skill Check A

1. Because <u>insects</u> are so small, they must have creative <u>ways</u> to protect themselves, (Sunday) through (Saturday,) 365 <u>days</u> a <u>year</u>.
2. A saddleback <u>caterpillar</u> has sharp <u>hairs</u> that will break and release <u>poison</u> when they prick your <u>skin</u>.
3. An <u>inchworm</u> and a <u>walking stick</u> use <u>camouflage</u>.
4. Often <u>insects</u> like syrphus <u>flies</u>, which cannot defend themselves, mimic other <u>insects</u> that have better defenses.
5. One <u>species</u>, found in (North America), looks like a <u>type</u> that tastes bad to <u>birds</u>.

Skill Check B

6. their—Insects, their—Insects
7. her—adult
8. its—insect
9. they—patterns
10. its—insect

Skill Check C

11. itself—reflexive
12. yourself—reflexive
13. themselves—reflexive
14. themselves—intensive
15. themselves—reflexive

Skill Check D

16. that—relative
17. which—relative
18. This—demonstrative
19. Those—demonstrative
20. Who—interrogative

Skill Check E

21. most
22. many
23. both
24. Every, each
25. some, others

Write the following sentence on the chalkboard:

[Person] went to [place] to find a [thing] because [person] believed in [idea, action, condition, or quality].

Have students provide possible words to complete the sentence.

Activate Prior Knowledge

Have students provide examples of sentences with places, people, and things as subjects. Ask what is the name for these kinds of words. (noun)

TEACH

Step-by-Step Teaching Guide

Nouns

1. Point out that all the kinds of words that students have been discussing—people, places, things, ideas, actions, conditions, and qualities—are nouns.

2. Emphasize that nouns also can name things that cannot be seen or touched. Ask students to provide additional examples, such as *knowledge*, *patience*, and *fear*.

3. Have students note that collective nouns are different from plural nouns. Collective nouns name a group of things, but they are not always plural. A *family*, for example, is singular. Two *families* is plural.

Answer Key

Exercise 1

1. scientist—person, thorax—thing
2. insect—thing, identification—thing
3. scent—thing, laboratory—place
4. color—thing, botanist—person
5. appearance—thing, swamp—place
6. nest—thing, grocer—person
7. butterfly—thing, growth—thing
8. forest—place, abdomen—thing
9. shell—thing, country—place
10. technician—person, belief—thing

Section 16.1

Nouns

The word *noun* comes from the Latin word *nomen*, which means "name."

▶ **KEY CONCEPT** A **noun** is a word that names a person, place, or thing. Nouns name things that can be seen and touched as well as those that cannot be seen and touched. ■

Notice in the chart below that among the things nouns can name are ideas, actions, conditions, and qualities.

People			
Uncle Mike	Catherine	neighbor	boys

Places			
Canada	library	garden	city

Things		
Things You Can See and Touch	**Ideas and Actions**	**Conditions and Qualities**
cicada trees store mayfly	justice rebellion peace election	joy illness beauty bravery

Note About Collective Nouns: Nouns that name *groups* of people or things are known as *collective nouns*.

EXAMPLES: swarm   crowd   group
                committee   family   herd

▶ **Exercise 1** Identifying Nouns as People, Places, or Things
Write the two nouns in each group, and label each as a *person*, *place*, or *thing*.

1. scientist	thorax	eat
2. insect	flutter	identification
3. smelled	scent	laboratory
4. color	botanist	bright
5. immature	appearance	swamp
6. clear	nest	grocer
7. butterfly	growth	near
8. forest	undergo	abdomen
9. shell	country	exhausting
10. technician	belief	direct

Theme: Insects

In this section, you will learn about nouns. All the examples and exercises are about insects.

Cross-Curricular Connection: Science

▶ **More Practice**

Language Lab CD-ROM
• Nouns lesson
On-line Exercise Bank
• Section 16.1
Grammar Exercise Workbook
• pp. 1–2

⏱ TIME AND RESOURCE MANAGER

Resources
Print: Grammar Exercise Workbook, pp. 1–4
Technology: Language Lab CD-ROM, Nouns and Pronouns; On-Line Exercise Bank, Section 16.1

In-Depth Coverage	Accelerated Pace
• Work through all key concepts, pp. 342–344. • Assign and review Exercises 1–3.	• Assign pp. 342–344, for independent student review. • Assign Section Review Exercises 4–7, p. 345.

Compound Nouns

Nouns may not always be just one word. A name such as Uncle Mike is a noun. So, too, are other words that must stand together to name a person, place, or thing.

▶ **KEY CONCEPT** A **compound noun** is a noun that is made up of more than one word. ■

As the following chart shows, *compound nouns* are written in several different ways.

TYPES OF COMPOUND NOUNS		
Separated	**Hyphenated**	**Combined**
bubble bath station wagon	daughter-in-law hand-me-down	shipwreck handstand

Historically, most compound nouns begin as separate words. Over a long period of time, more and more people start to hyphenate the words. Finally, many compound nouns come to be written as one word. If you are not sure how to spell a compound noun, check a dictionary. If the compound noun you are looking for is not entered in the dictionary, you can safely spell it as separate words.

▶ **Exercise 2** **Recognizing Compound Nouns** List the ten compound nouns you find in the following paragraph.

EXAMPLE: Last weekend, Jane collected insects with her grandparents.

ANSWER: weekend; grandparents

Insects are fascinating animals. Each one has something unique about it. Any notebook belonging to a bug collector is full of interesting facts. Here are a few: The *Chrysiridia madagascarensis*, a moth, is full of vibrant colors. A railroad worm, the larval form of a beetle found in South America, makes its own light. A flea has a broad jump of over 33 centimeters. Honeybees do a dance to communicate where a specific flower is located, and the queen bee of bumblebees gives birth to every bee that lives in her beehive!

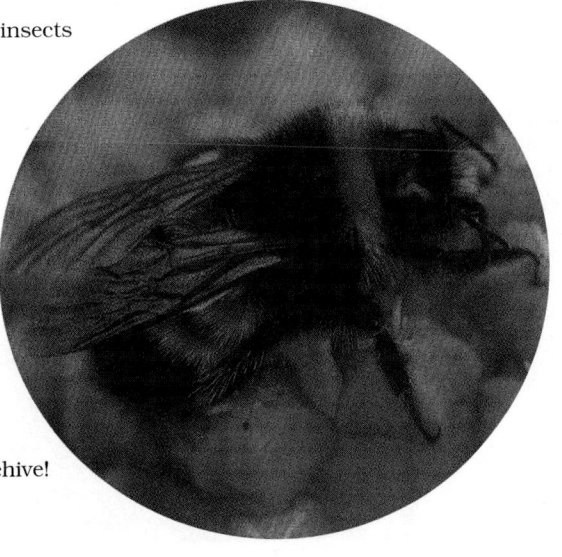

▼ **Critical Viewing** The name of this bee is a compound noun. What do you think it might be? [Deduce]

Nouns • 343

Common and Proper Nouns

1. After discussing the examples on the page, list the following types of proper nouns and their examples on the chalkboard:

   - days of the week (Tuesday, Friday)
   - months (April, December)
   - holidays (Easter, Deepavali)
   - buildings and structures (Sears Tower, Golden Gate Bridge)
   - titles of people (Senator Alfred Johnson)
   - titles of books, movies, and other works (*Star Wars, Moby Dick*)
   - geographic names (Lake Michigan, Africa)

2. Point out the words written are proper nouns because they refer to a *specific* person, place, or thing.

Customize for
Less Advanced Students

Some students may have difficulty understanding the difference between proper nouns and common nouns with words that can be used in both forms (*sergeant, earth, lake, river,* and so on). Provide several example sentence pairs:

I visited the Mississippi River.

I went swimming in a river.

His shoes were covered with earth from the garden.

The spacecraft returned to Earth.

Have students practice using these words as both common nouns and proper nouns by writing additional sentences for each word.

Answer Key

1. North America
2. India
3. Monday
4. Professor Jones
5. Venus
6. Chicago
7. Jurassic Period
8. National Bug Week
9. Mothers' Day
10. June

16.1

Common and Proper Nouns

All nouns can be divided into two groups: *common nouns* and *proper nouns.*

> **KEY CONCEPTS** A **common noun** names any one of a class of people, places, or things. A **proper noun** names a specific person, place, or thing. ∎

As you can see in the following chart, proper nouns always begin with a capital letter.

Common Nouns	Proper Nouns
writer	Mark Twain, Emily Dickinson
order	Odonata, Neuroptera
building	White House, Monticello

> **Exercise 3** Distinguishing Between Common and Proper Nouns Write the one proper noun in each group, adding the necessary capitalization.

EXAMPLE: planet   neptune   star
ANSWER: Neptune

1. insect	bumblebee	north america
2. reptile	india	ocean
3. thorax	professor	monday
4. wings	antennae	professor jones
5. venus	plant	fly
6. tarantula	chicago	condition
7. jurassic period	dinosaurs	jaw
8. syrphus fly	food	national bug week
9. dandelion	mothers' day	mothers
10. june	autumn	month

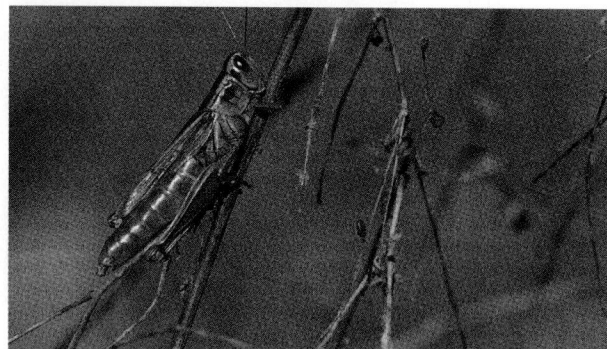

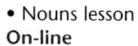

> **More Practice**
> Language Lab
> CD-ROM
> • Nouns lesson
> On-line
> Exercise Bank
> • Section 16.1
> Grammar Exercise
> Workbook
> • pp. 3–4

◀ Critical Viewing Would you use more common nouns or more proper nouns in a description of this picture? Why? **[Explain]**

Critical Viewing

Explain Students may say they would use more common nouns since scientific names may not be known.

Section 16.1 Section Review

GRAMMAR EXERCISES 4–10

Exercise 4 Identifying Nouns
Write the nouns in the following sentences.

1. Many insects die when winter comes.
2. However, some manage to survive by migration or hibernation.
3. Some hibernate as adults in a warm place, such as a barn or house.
4. Other insects hibernate in eggs, in cocoons, or as larvae.
5. The monarch is a kind of butterfly that migrates.

Exercise 5 Identifying Compound Nouns Write the compound nouns from the following sentences.

1. The life span of insects is different for each species.
2. An adult male mayfly never lives to see his offspring; he lives only a few hours.
3. A queen termite can live up to 50 years, although her lifestyle consists of populating the hive.
4. An individual dragonfly does not live long, but this species has survived about 150 million years.
5. The American cockroach survives because of its adaptability to change.

Exercise 6 Spelling Compound Nouns Correctly Use a dictionary to help you write compound nouns. On your paper, write the correct spelling from each of the following sets.

1. lifetime / life time / life-time
2. lifesize / life-size / life size
3. swandive / swan-dive / swan dive
4. often times / oftentimes / often-times
5. stonefly / stone-fly / stone fly

Exercise 7 Recognizing and Writing Proper and Common Nouns
Copy each sentence. Capitalize proper nouns, and underline common nouns.

1. During class, professor dominguez lectured about the order orthoptera.
2. Tree crickets are a species in this order.
3. Dragonflies and mayflies have noticeable wings, natasha pointed out.
4. We visited the beane museum to get a closer look at insect mouthparts.
5. Professor dominguez told us that beetles and grasshoppers have chewing mouthparts.

Exercise 8 Find It in Your Reading
Skim magazines or newspapers to find five examples each of proper and compound nouns and at least one collective noun. Bring your examples to class.

Exercise 9 Find It in Your Writing
Look through your portfolio, and select a piece of your writing. Identify at least one example of each type of noun (*common, proper, compound,* and *collective*).

Exercise 10 Writing Application
Write a comparison of two insects. Use at least three compound and five proper nouns. Underline the compound nouns, and circle the proper nouns.

Section Review • 345

Write the following paragraph on the chalkboard and read it aloud:

Sabrina unpacked Sabrina's computer. Sabrina plugged the computer in and turned the computer on. Sabrina heard the computer make a noise.

Ask what is strange about this paragraph. (The nouns *Sabrina* and *computer* are used over and over again.) Ask students what they would do to make it sound less strange (replace some of these nouns with *she, her,* and *it*).

Activate Prior Knowledge

Ask students if, when they talk about themselves, they use their own name or if they replace it with other words. (They replace their name with *I* or *me.*) Ask what these types of replacement words are called. (pronouns)

TEACH

Step-by-Step Teaching Guide

Pronouns

1. Emphasize that pronouns are used as stand-ins for nouns to avoid the clumsy repetition of nouns in a sentence.

2. Ask students to provide some examples of words that stand in for nouns. (*that, those, it, you, her,* and so on)

3. Discuss the examples of pronouns and their antecedents on the page. Help students write additional sentences with examples of the two more difficult concepts, pronouns standing for entire groups of words and antecedents that follow pronouns:

   Running a race is fun, but it is tiring too.

   After he graduated, Claudio got a job.

Critical Viewing

Apply Students may suggest: <u>It</u>—parade, <u>They</u>—the vehicles, <u>Them</u>—the crowd

---

Pronouns

You would probably never say, "Michael said Michael lost Michael's watch." Once you had clearly identified Michael as the person you were talking about, repeating the noun *Michael* would sound awkward. Instead, you would probably say, "Michael said he lost his watch." The words *he* and *his* are called *pronouns.* They stand for the noun *Michael.*

▶ **KEY CONCEPT** Pronouns are words that stand for nouns or for words that take the place of nouns. ■

Antecedents of Pronouns

Pronouns get their meaning from the words they stand for. These words are called *antecedents.*

▶ **KEY CONCEPT** Antecedents are nouns (or words that take the place of nouns) for which pronouns stand. ■

In the following examples, the arrows point from pronouns to their antecedents. In the first sentence, the pronouns *he* and *his* stand for the noun *Michael,* their antecedent. In the second, the pronouns *they* and *their* stand for the noun *Levines,* their antecedent. In the third, the pronoun *it* stands for an entire group of words that takes the place of a noun. This group of words is the antecedent of the pronoun *it.*

EXAMPLES: Michael said he lost his watch at the fair.

   When the Levines moved, *they* gave *their* pets to neighbors.

   Attending the Mardi Gras can be tiring, but *it* can be a lot of fun!

Antecedents do not always appear before their pronouns, however. Sometimes, an antecedent *follows* its pronoun.

EXAMPLE: Because of *its* carnival, Rottweil, Germany, is my favorite city.

There are several kinds of pronouns. Most of them have specific antecedents, but a few do not.

Theme: Carnivals

In this section, you will learn about pronouns. The examples and exercises are about celebrations from a variety of countries and cultures.

Cross-Curricular Connection: Social Studies

▲ **Critical Viewing** If you were to use the pronouns *it, they,* and *them* in referring to this photograph, what could be the antecedents of these pronouns? **[Apply]**

⏱ TIME AND RESOURCE MANAGER

Resources
Print: Grammar Exercise Workbook, pp. 5–12; Hands-on Grammar Activity Book, Chapter 16
Technology: Language Lab CD-ROM, Nouns and Pronouns; On-Line Exercise Bank, Section 16.2

In-Depth Coverage	Accelerated Pace
• Work through all key concepts, pp. 346–353. • Assign and review Exercises 11–16. • Do the Hands-on Grammar Activity, p. 354.	• Assign pp. 346–353, for independent student review. • Assign Section Review Exercises 17–20, p. 355.

GRAMMAR IN LITERATURE

from **The Cask of Amontillado**
Edgar Allan Poe

In the following excerpt, notice the underlined pronouns. The antecedent of each is italicized.

The thousand injuries of *Fortunato* I had borne as I best could, but when he ventured upon insult I vowed revenge. You, who so well know the nature of my soul, will not suppose, however, that I gave utterance to a threat. At length I would be avenged; this was a *point* definitely settled—but the very definitiveness with which it was resolved precluded the idea of risk.

Grammar in Literature

1. Have a volunteer read aloud the Poe excerpt. A cassette recording of the complete story is available in the Gold Level resources of *Timeless Voices, Timeless Themes.*

2. The language and phrasing in this excerpt may make it difficult for students to grasp the relationship between the pronouns and their antecedents. You can change the word order or paraphrase Poe's sentences to make these relationships clearer:

   I had tolerated *Fortunato's* insults as best I could, but when *he* . . .

More About the Writer

In "The Cask of Amontillado," the narrator uses a cask of sherry as bait to lure his unfortunate victim to his death. Ironically, Poe himself battled alcoholism throughout his adult life. Alcohol may have been a contributing factor in the mysterious circumstances that lead to his untimely death at the age of 40.

Exercise 11 Recognizing Antecedents Write the antecedent of each underlined pronoun.

1. Carnivals have varied their images over time.
2. Many carnivals developed from festivals in Europe that were held every year.
3. They included markets where merchants sold their wares.
4. Eventually, these carnivals adopted rides, games, shows, and exhibits that often included sideshows.
5. Another type of carnival is made up of merrymaking; it is celebrated just before a traditional time of fasting.
6. Rottweil, Germany, has its carnival in February or March.
7. There, the people dress themselves in fabulous costumes.
8. Rio de Janeiro, Brazil, also has a grand carnival; it is famous all over the world.
9. To prepare for it, samba dancers teach their skills in classes.
10. New Orleans, Louisiana, hosts Mardi Gras during February or March; thousands of people flock to it each year.

Exercise 12 Writing With Pronouns and Antecedents
Write a sentence or two using each of the following nouns, accompanied by a pronoun that uses the noun as an antecedent.

1. clowns
2. festival
3. dancer
4. New York City
5. fireworks

► **More Practice**
Language Lab CD-ROM
• Pronouns lesson
On-line Exercise Bank
• Section 16.2
Grammar Exercise Workbook
• pp. 5–6

Answer Key

Exercise 11
1. Carnivals
2. festivals
3. merchants
4. exhibits
5. type
6. Rottweil
7. people
8. carnival
9. dancers
10. Mardi Gras

Exercise 12
Possible sentences are given.
1. Clowns have lost their significance over time.
2. The festival has lost its surprise.
3. The dancer forgot her cue.
4. New York City has never forgotten its history.
5. The fireworks lost their flare as the show went on.

Pronouns • 347

☑ ONGOING ASSESSMENT: Monitor and Reinforce

If students miss more than three items in Exercise 12, refer them to the following for additional practice.

In the Textbook	Print Resources	Technology
Section Review, Ex. 17, p. 355	Grammar Exercise Workbook, pp. 5–6	Language Lab CD-ROM, Nouns and Pronouns; On-Line Exercise Bank, Section 16.2

Personal Pronouns

The most common pronouns are those that you use to refer to yourself and the people and things around you. These pronouns are called *personal pronouns.*

▶ **KEY CONCEPT** **Personal pronouns** refer to the person speaking (first person), the person spoken to (second person), or the person, place, or thing spoken about (third person). ■

PERSONAL PRONOUNS	Singular	Plural
First Person	I, me my, mine	we, us our, ours
Second Person	you your, yours	you your, yours
Third Person	he, him, his she, her, hers it, its	they, them their, theirs

▶ **Exercise 13** **Identifying Personal Pronouns and Their Antecedents** Write the personal pronouns and their antecedents. HINT: The antecedent may be in a previous sentence.

EXAMPLE: Liz handed her brother his coat.
ANSWERS: *her*, Liz; *his*, brother

1. Keiko and her family went to the carnival in the city this weekend.
2. Her father went straight toward the Ferris wheel.
3. He told them that the first Ferris wheel was built by George W.G. Ferris.
4. It was 250 feet in diameter and had 36 cabs that held 60 people each.
5. Keiko was astounded when she thought of 2,160 people on one Ferris wheel.

🪁 STANDARDIZED TEST PREPARATION WORKSHOP

Analogies Most standardized tests measure students' abilities to understand and complete analogies. Share the following sample question with students:

KITE: WIND::

A match: fire   D ink: pen

B plate: food   E painting: paint

C TV: electricity

The correct choice is item **C**. It is the only choice that reflects the relationship of the original pair of words: A kite requires wind to work, as a TV requires electricity.

Reflexive and Intensive Pronouns

The ending *-self* or *-selves* can be added to some personal pronouns to form *reflexive* and *intensive pronouns*.

> **KEY CONCEPTS** A **reflexive pronoun** ends in *-self* or *-selves* and indicates that someone or something performs an action to, for, or upon itself. Reflexive pronouns point back to a noun or pronoun earlier in the sentence. An **intensive pronoun** ends in *-self* or *-selves* and simply adds emphasis to a noun or pronoun in the same sentence. ■

The following chart lists the eight reflexive and intensive pronouns used in English.

REFLEXIVE AND INTENSIVE PRONOUNS		
	Singular	**Plural**
First Person	myself	ourselves
Second Person	yourself	yourselves
Third Person	himself, herself, itself	themselves

A reflexive pronoun is essential to the meaning of a sentence. In the examples below, *herself* tells who was helped to some turkey and *themselves* tells for whom the milk was poured.

REFLEXIVE: Joy helped *herself* to some turkey.

They poured *themselves* some milk.

An intensive pronoun, on the other hand, simply adds emphasis. If you omit an intensive pronoun, the sentence will still contain the same basic information.

INTENSIVE: The mayor *herself* attended the carnival.

An intensive pronoun usually comes directly after its antecedent, but not always.

INTENSIVE: Frank fixed the refrigerator *himself*.

Grammar and Style Tip

Don't use a pronoun that ends in *-self* or *-selves* in place of a personal pronoun.
Incorrect: Josh sent postcards from New Orleans to Les and myself.
Correct: Josh sent postcards from New Orleans to Les and me.

Reflexive and Intensive Pronouns

1. Point out that reflexive pronouns *reflect* back to the subject of the sentence since the subject receives the action of the verb as well as performs it.

2. Reflexive pronouns answer the question *Who?* or *For whom?* Demonstrate this with the examples on the page:

   Who helped herself to some turkey? (Joy)

   For whom did they pour some milk? ("for, they" = themselves)

3. Intensive pronouns are used to *intensify* a sentence by emphasizing the action of the subject. Have students note the difference in emphasis in the following sentences:

   The president himself delivered the message.

   The president delivered the message.

4. Ask students to write pairs of sentences that are identical except for the use of an intensive pronoun. Have them examine the difference in emphasis between the sentences.

Language Highlight

The pronoun gender must be consistent with antecedent gender. This can lead to problems in gender-neutral situations:

An astronaut trains for years before making <u>his</u> first voyage into space.

If an attendant arrives, ask <u>him</u> to bring more blankets.

Astronauts and attendants, of course, can be either male or female, so the use of the masculine pronoun his slights women. In the past, masculine pronouns were used in these types of situations. Today, however, they are clearly not appropriate. Two ways to rectify the situation are to pluralize (*Astronauts train for years before making their . . .*), or to use the *his or her/him and her* construction (*. . . ask him or her to bring . . .*). This can lead to awkward construction. Nonetheless, it is preferable to the commonly used but incorrect *their* referring to a singular subject, as in, *Does everyone have their homework?*

Step-by-Step Teaching Guide

Demonstrative Pronouns

1. Explain that when students use demonstrative pronouns, they are calling out, pointing to, or *demonstrating* something.

2. Say several sentences that contain demonstrative pronouns. Use hand gestures to illustrate the calling out function of each pronoun.

   That [point to book] is the book we will read next.

   There are many crayons, but this [point to crayon] is the red one.

3. Write the following sentences on the chalkboard and have students identify the antecedents for each demonstrative pronoun. Note that the antecedents for demonstrative pronouns are often found in adjoining sentences:

   Which sweater did I wash? This is it right here. (antecedent: sweater)

   That is a great idea. When did you think of buying him the magazine? (antecedent: buying him the magazine)

4. Point out that *this, that, these,* and *those* can also be used as adjectives. Students can identify these instances because the words will be followed by the nouns *(those rhinos, these zebras).*

Exercise 14 Distinguishing Between Reflexive and Intensive Pronouns Write the reflexive or intensive pronoun in each sentence. Then, label each *reflexive* or *intensive.*

EXAMPLE: The dancer spun herself in circles.
ANSWER: herself (reflexive)

1. Mardi Gras itself has become an event.
2. It was originally intended to allow people to enjoy themselves before a time of fasting.
3. If you yourself have ever attended one, you know it is a week-long celebration.
4. Participants dress themselves in colorful costumes.
5. The mayor himself enjoys the festivities.

Demonstrative, Relative, and Interrogative Pronouns

Another group of pronouns can be used to direct attention, relate ideas, or ask questions.

Demonstrative Pronouns *Demonstrative pronouns* help specify one of many different people, places, or things.

▶ **KEY CONCEPT** **Demonstrative pronouns** direct attention to specific people, places, or things. ■

The following chart lists the four demonstrative pronouns.

DEMONSTRATIVE PRONOUNS	
Singular	**Plural**
this, that	these, those

Demonstrative pronouns may come before or after their antecedents.

BEFORE: *This* is the person we want to hire.

AFTER: Of all the celebrations in the world, *that* is my favorite.

Relative Pronouns *Relative pronouns* relate clauses. (See Chapter 21 for more details about clauses.)

▶ **KEY CONCEPT** A **relative pronoun** begins a subordinate clause and connects it to another idea in the sentence. ∎

The chart below lists the five relative pronouns.

RELATIVE PRONOUNS				
that	which	who	whom	whose

The following examples show the way relative pronouns are used in sentences.

Independent Clause	Subordinate Clause
We planted a shrub	*that* attracts ladybugs.
I saw a cicada,	*which* was a surprise.
Louisa is the player	*who* pitched first.
Phil is the debater	*whom* the judges chose.
We visited Grandmother,	*whose* house is in New Orleans.

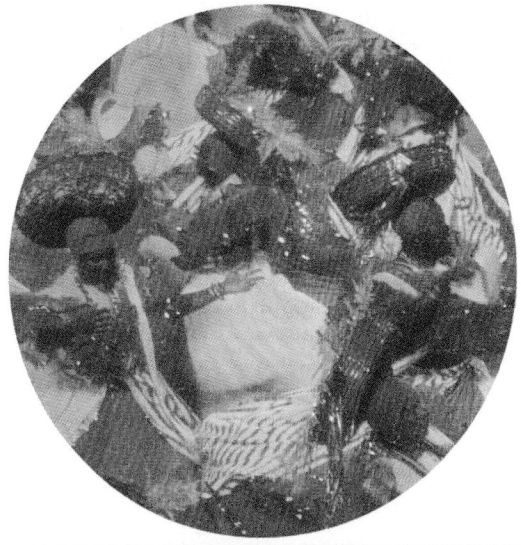

◀ **Critical Viewing**
Do you think this costume is designed more to reflect the meaning of Mardi Gras or the heritage of the individual wearing the costume? What do you think that heritage is? **[Deduce]**

Relative Pronouns

1. Relative pronouns *relate* whole groups of words to a noun or pronoun.

2. Review clauses. Explain that an independent clause can stand alone as sentence. A subordinate clause does not express a complete thought and cannot stand alone. The relative pronoun relates this clause to the main clause with which it is joined.

Customize for
Less Advanced Students

The decision to use *which* or *that* confuses people, even professional writers. The choice revolves around whether the clause is restrictive. A restrictive clause contains information that is essential to the meaning of a sentence. For example, *I ate the cupcake that was on the table.* A nonrestrictive clause contains information that is not essential to the meaning of a sentence. *I ate the cupcake, which my mother saved for me. That* is more often the correct choice. A simple rule works 99.9 percent of the time: *Which* is always preceded by a comma. *That* is not. *I ate the cupcake, that was on the table* simply looks wrong, and it is. Delete the comma, or change *that* to *which*.

Critical Viewing

Deduce Students' responses will vary, but make sure they support their answers with details from the photograph.

✦ STANDARDIZED TEST PREPARATION WORKSHOP

Grammar and Usage Many standardized tests require students to choose between pronouns to complete a sentence. To do so, students should identify the type of pronoun that is needed and the antecedent of the pronoun if specified. Have students choose the word that best completes the following sentence:

Darryl purchased the apple ___ was less bruised than the others.

A who

B he

C that

D himself

The correct answer is item **C**, the relative pronoun *that*. A relative pronoun is needed to introduce the subordinate clause *was less bruised than the others*. The clause modifies the antecedent *apple*.

Interrogative Pronouns

1. Students can identify if the pronoun *which*, *who*, or *whom* is being used as a relative or an interrogative pronoun by asking themselves the following question: Does the pronoun introduce a question, or does it introduce a subordinate clause?

2. Interrogative pronouns can stand in for a noun or group of words that are not yet identified, rather than specific antecedents. These nonidentified words would be provided in the answer to the question being asked.

    Q: <u>Who</u> will go with you to the park?
    A: <u>Jeremy</u> will go with me to the park.

    Q: <u>What</u> do you mean?
    A: I mean that <u>I don't need a jacket</u>.

3. Not every interrogative word is a pronoun. *When*, *why*, and *where*, for example, are adverbs.

Answer Key

Exercise 15

1. that (relative)
2. This (demonstrative)
3. which (relative)
4. these (demonstrative)
5. This (demonstrative)
6. Which (interrogative)
7. which (relative)
8. that (relative)
9. Who (interrogative)
10. who (relative)

Real-World Connection

Interrogative pronouns form a big part of the "5 Ws and H" that are at the core of a journalist's profession. Newspaper reporters are trained to introduce a story in the lead paragraph and then fill in the details that answer the questions *Who? What? When? Where? Why?* and *How?*

16.2

Interrogative Pronouns Most relative pronouns can also be used as *interrogative pronouns*.

▶ **KEY CONCEPT** An **interrogative pronoun** is used to begin a question. ■

The following chart lists the five interrogative pronouns.

INTERROGATIVE PRONOUNS				
what	which	who	whom	whose

An interrogative pronoun may or may not have a specific antecedent. In the following, only *which* has an antecedent.

EXAMPLES: *What* do you mean?

Which of the vegetables do you want?
Who will go with me to the park?

▶ **Exercise 15** Recognizing Demonstrative, Relative, and Interrogative Pronouns Write the pronoun in each sentence. Then, label each *demonstrative, relative,* or *interrogative*.

EXAMPLE: Alice chose the place that her family visited.
ANSWER: that (relative)

1. Mardi Gras is a carnival that is held before Lent begins.
2. This is the grand finale of a long carnival season.
3. Mardi Gras, which is a French tradition, was introduced to the United States in the early 1700's.
4. Several southern states started Mardi Gras as an annual tradition, and these still celebrate it today.
5. This is a holiday in a few states.
6. Which of the states has a famous celebration?
7. New Orleans, which is famous for its Mardi Gras celebration, starts activities early.
8. Societies that organize the event are called *krewes*.
9. Who comes to celebrate?
10. Tourists, who come from around the world, join locals to participate in Mardi Gras.

☑ ONGOING ASSESSMENT: Monitor and Reinforce

If students miss more than three items in Exercise 15, refer them to the following for additional practice.

In the Textbook	Print Resources	Technology
Section Review, Ex. 18, p. 355	Grammar Exercise Workbook, pp. 9–10	Language Lab CD-ROM, Nouns and Pronouns; On-Line Exercise Bank, Section 16.2

Indefinite Pronouns

Indefinite pronouns resemble interrogative pronouns in that they often lack specific antecedents.

SPECIFIC ANTECEDENT: *Some* of the tourists were late.

NO SPECIFIC ANTECEDENT: *Everyone* ate *something.*

KEY CONCEPT **Indefinite pronouns** refer to people, places, or things, often without specifying which ones. ■

The following chart lists the indefinite pronouns.

INDEFINITE PRONOUNS				
Singular			**Plural**	**Singular or Plural**
another	everyone	nothing	both	all
anybody	everything	one	few	any
anyone	little	other	many	more
anything	much	somebody	others	most
each	neither	someone	several	none
either	nobody	something		some
everybody	no one			

Exercise 16 **Identifying Indefinite Pronouns** Write the indefinite pronoun or pronouns in each sentence.

EXAMPLE: Most of us know something about carnivals.
ANSWER: Most; something

1. Before 1900, no one moved Ferris wheels from place to place.
2. Eventually, somebody working for the Eli Bridge Company started making portable Ferris wheels.
3. This someone was William E. Sullivan.
4. Many were sold to carnivals that wanted to travel.
5. Now, everyone could enjoy a ride on a Ferris wheel.
6. Most of the carnivals started selling popular carnival foods.
7. One could play games at most traveling carnivals.
8. A few may even win some prizes.
9. The carnivals had exhibits for anything considered spectacular.
10. Several had sideshows that featured natural wonders.

More Practice

Language Lab
CD-ROM
• Pronouns lesson
On-line
Exercise Bank
• Section 16.2
Grammar Exercise
Workbook
• pp. 9–10

Pronouns • **353**

Noun Classification Fold-up

Teaching Resources: Hands-on Grammar Activity Book, Chapter 16

1. Have students refer to their Hands-on Grammar Activity books or give them copies of the relevant pages for this activity.

2. Review with students how to properly construct the fold-ups.

3. After students have written the nouns that fit the label, have them use each noun in a sentence. Then challenge them to write two more nouns for each section.

Find It in Your Reading

Fortunato is a proper noun; the remaining nouns in the excerpt are common.

Find It in Your Writing

Have students underline or circle the nouns in their writing to help them identify the ones they need to add.

16.2

Hands-on Grammar

Noun Classification Fold-up

Cut a square for which the sides are at least six inches. Fold it in half diagonally to form a triangle. Fold the triangle in half. Unfold the square to reveal that you have created four triangular sections. Cut along each of the folds toward the center of the square, leaving a little bit of the fold uncut so that the triangles do not fall apart. Then, label the triangles as shown below.

Turn the square over, and label the other sides of the triangles as shown.

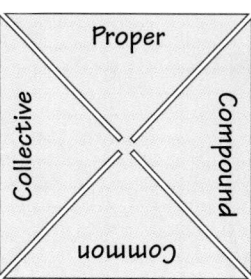
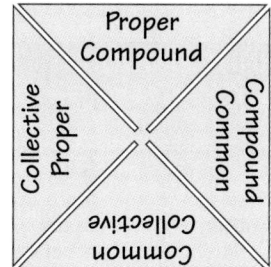

When you have finished labeling and cutting, fold one triangle over the other to show how nouns can fall into more than one category. For example, some nouns are common, but other nouns are both common and collective. Fold each triangle over the other to show combinations of noun types. On each triangle, write at least two nouns that fit the label for each section.

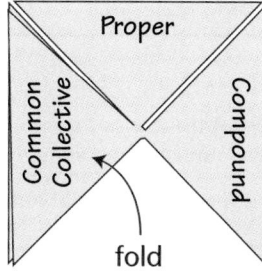

Find It in Your Reading Add nouns to each category as you find examples in your reading. You can begin by adding nouns from the excerpt from "The Cask of Amontillado" on page 347.

Find It in Your Writing Look through the writing in your portfolio to find examples that you can add to each section. If there is a particular type of noun that you cannot find, challenge yourself to add an example to a piece of writing.

354 • Nouns and Pronouns

⏱ TIME SAVERS!

✋ **Hands-on Grammar Book**
Use the Hands-on Grammar Activity sheet for Chapter 16 to facilitate this activity.

☑ ONGOING ASSESSMENT: Assess Mastery

Refer students to the following to assess their mastery of pronouns.

In the Textbook	Technology
Chapter Review, Ex. 27–30, pp. 356–357	On-Line Exercise Bank, Section 16.2

Section 16.2 Section Review

GRAMMAR EXERCISES 17–23

Exercise 17 **Recognizing Pronouns and Antecedents** Write the antecedent for each underlined pronoun. If it has no antecedent, write *none*. HINT: The antecedent may appear in a previous sentence in the exercise.

1. The merry-go-round is the oldest amusement ride <u>that</u> is still in use.
2. <u>It</u> has also been called a carousel, and <u>it</u> always has wooden animals fastened to <u>its</u> platform.
3. <u>They</u> are painted bright colors, and <u>anyone</u> may ride.
4. Mules were hooked to the old merry-go-round models, and <u>they</u> would pull the merry-go-round <u>themselves</u>.
5. Later on, <u>these</u> were replaced by electric or gas motors.

Exercise 18 **Recognizing Relative, Demonstrative, and Interrogative Pronouns** Write and label the relative, demonstrative, and interrogative pronouns from each numbered item.

(1) What is the history of carnival? (2) This is celebrated in many Roman Catholic countries. (3) Carnival has origins that are obscure. (4) It started in Italy—that is certain. (5) There are those who believe it was linked to ancient Roman festivals.

Exercise 19 **Recognizing Indefinite Pronouns** Write the indefinite pronoun in each sentence.

1. Many throughout the world know of the carnival in Rio de Janeiro, Brazil.
2. Most of the carnival centers on the samba, Brazilian dance music.
3. The carnival tradition is one rooted in the history of Brazil—rhythms from African slaves and cultural touches from Portugal.
4. Costumes are showy, and some include large headdresses.
5. Everyone spends his or her time dancing and enjoying the music.

Exercise 20 **Classifying Pronouns** On your paper, name the type of each underlined pronoun.

Veracruz, Mexico, celebrates (1) <u>its</u> carnival in February. (2) <u>It</u> started as the Festival of Masks, (3) <u>which</u> was approved by Maximilian (4) <u>himself</u> in 1866. (5) He gave permission to (6) <u>his</u> people to disguise (7) <u>themselves</u> in fancy masks and costumes. (8) <u>These</u> were worn as (9) <u>they</u> walked through the streets on (10) <u>their</u> way to the dance halls.

Exercise 21 **Find It in Your Reading** Read the excerpt from "The Cask of Amontillado" on page 347. How many personal pronouns are there in the excerpt? There are two other types of pronouns in the passage; identify and label them.

Exercise 22 **Find It in Your Writing** Review a selection in your writing portfolio, and identify the pronouns you use. Personal pronouns are probably the most common, but which do you use least? Why are they used less?

Exercise 23 **Writing Application** Write a descriptive paragraph about a celebration you attended. Use a variety of pronoun types. Identify each type you use.

Section Review
Each of these exercises correlates to a concept in the section on pronouns, pages 346–353. The exercises may be used for more practice, for reteaching, or for review of the Key Concepts presented.

Answer Key

Exercise 17
1. ride
2. merry-go-round, merry-go-round, merry-go-round
3. animals, none
4. mules, mules
5. mules

Exercise 18
1. What—interrogative
2. This—demonstrative
3. that—relative
4. that—relative
5. those—demonstrative

Exercise 19
1. Many
2. Most
3. one
4. some
5. Everyone

Exercise 20
1. its—personal
2. It—personal
3. which—relative
4. himself—intensive
5. He—personal
6. his—personal
7. themselves—reflexive
8. These—demonstrative
9. they—personal
10. their—personal

continued

Answer Key continued

Exercise 21

Find It in Your Reading
There are nine personal pronouns: *I, I, he, I, You, my, I, I, it. Who* in the third line and *that* in the fourth line are relative pronouns. *This,* in the fifth line, is demonstrative.

Exercise 22

Find It in Your Writing
Students will probably use demonstrative pronouns least. The kinds of sentences containing these pronouns are less frequent in all writing.

Exercise 23

Writing Application
Let groups of students work together to help one another identify the pronouns and check for correct usage.

TIME SAVERS!

Answers on Transparency Use the Grammar Exercises on Transparencies for Chapter 16 to have students correct their own or one another's exercises.

On-Line Exercise Bank Have students complete the exercises on computer. The Auto Check will grade their work for you!

CHAPTER REVIEW

Each of these exercises correlate to a concept in the chapter on nouns and pronouns, pages 340–355. The exercises may be used for more practice, for reteaching, or for review of the Key Concepts presented. Answers for all chapter exercises are available in *Grammar Exercises on Transparencies* in your teaching resources.

Answer Key

Exercise 24

1. Independence Day—proper, July—proper
2. Firetrucks—common, compound, bands—common, floats—common, parade—common, group—common, collective, people—common, collective
3. day—common, Declaration of Independence—proper
4. assembly—common, collective, document—common, Thomas Jefferson—proper
5. holidays—common, Memorial Day—proper, Labor Day—proper, summer—common

Exercise 25

Possible sentences are given.

1. The beads are from India.
2. George W. G. Ferris was the inventor of the Ferris wheel.
3. The excitement grew amongst the crowd.
4. Edgar Allan Poe is best known for his poem "The Raven."
5. The crowd cheered as the floats went by.

Exercise 26

Possible sentences are given.

I enjoy spending my time with Henry and Celine. We all go to the same school. Outside of school, we enjoy listening to Beethoven and watching movies from Hollywood. We also like the music of Bach. We saw *Pulp Fiction* last month.

Exercise 27

1. their—Chinese, its—dragon
2. their—people, their—babies
3. They—people
4. It—holiday
5. One—none

356

Chapter **16** *Chapter Review*

GRAMMAR EXERCISES 24–34

Exercise 24 **Classifying Nouns**
Write the nouns in each sentence, and label each *common, proper, compound,* or *collective.* Capitalize as appropriate. Some nouns fall into more than one category.

1. Independence Day is celebrated on July fourth.
2. Firetrucks, bands, and floats form a parade that is watched by a large group of people.
3. It commemorates the day the Declaration of Independence was signed.
4. The assembly that signed the document included Thomas Jefferson.
5. Two other holidays, Memorial Day and Labor Day, traditionally mark the beginning and end of summer.

Exercise 25 **Writing Sentences With Nouns** Use each of the following nouns in a sentence.

1. beads
2. George W.G. Ferris
3. excitement
4. Edgar Allan Poe
5. crowd

Exercise 26 **Revision Practice: Nouns** Revise the following paragraph, replacing the underlined common nouns with proper nouns. You may need to reorder, add, or eliminate some words as you revise. You may also add other details.

I enjoy spending time with <u>my</u> <u>friends</u>. We both go to the same school. Outside of school, we enjoy <u>music</u> and <u>movies</u>. We like the music of <u>that</u> <u>group</u>. We saw a <u>movie</u> last month.

Exercise 27 **Recognizing Pronouns and Antecedents** Write the pronouns from the following sentences, and identify the antecedent for each. If a pronoun does not have an antecedent, write *none.* HINT: Sometimes the antecedent will be in a previous sentence within the exercise.

1. The Chinese celebrate their New Year in February. A dragon (a person in a costume) makes its way through the streets.
2. In Peru, people hold little fiestas when their babies get their first haircuts.
3. In Japan, the people have a celebration to encourage being on time. They call it punctuality day or time-observance day.
4. Egypt has a holiday called Sham al-Nessim. It means "smelling of spring."
5. One plans to go outside on this day to enjoy the fragrance of the season.

Exercise 28 **Classifying Personal, Relative, and Demonstrative Pronouns** Label each of the following pronouns *personal, relative, demonstrative, reflexive/intensive, interrogative,* or *indefinite.*

1. I	12. this	23. who
2. whom	13. these	24. which
3. me	14. our	25. we
4. his	15. whose	26. those
5. it	16. their	27. them
6. ourselves	17. some	28. what
7. who	18. whose	29. no one
8. everyone	19. myself	30. which
9. much	20. several	
10. herself	21. each	
11. itself	22. whom	

Exercise 28

1. personal
2. relative/interrogative
3. personal
4. personal
5. personal
6. reflexive/intensive
7. relative/interrogative
8. indefinite
9. indefinite
10. reflexive/intensive
11. reflexive/intensive
12. demonstrative
13. demonstrative
14. personal
15. relative/interrogative
16. personal
17. indefinite
18. relative/interrogative
19. reflexive/intensive
20. indefinite
21. indefinite
22. relative/interrogative
23. relative/interrogative
24. relative/interrogative
25. personal
26. demonstrative
27. personal
28. interrogative
29. indefinite
30. relative/interrogative

Exercise 29 Writing Sentences With Reflexive and Intensive Pronouns

Write two sentences for each of the following pronouns. In the first sentence, use it as a reflexive pronoun. In the second sentence, use it as an intensive pronoun. Underline this pronoun in each of your sentences.

1. himself
2. yourself
3. themselves
4. yourselves
5. myself

Exercise 30 Identifying All Kinds of Pronouns

Copy the following paragraph onto your paper, and underline all the pronouns. Above each pronoun, label it *personal, reflexive, intensive, demonstrative, relative, interrogative,* or *indefinite.*

Last Tuesday, my family and I went to Mardi Gras. There were lots of people who were out to have a good time. We saw floats that were full of colors. Almost all were musical. Those riding them threw necklaces of beads. One fell at my feet. I wanted to pick it up for myself, but my brother grabbed it for himself. Who cares? I caught a doubloon, and that was a better prize. My brother himself offered to trade his beads for my coin.

Exercise 31 Supplying Pronouns

Supply a pronoun to fill each blank space. Identify the kind of pronoun you supply.

Celebrations are held at different times of year. ___?___ are held in the spring, ___?___ in the fall. There aren't many people ___?___ don't enjoy a celebration. A celebration is more than just a party. ___?___ is an acknowledgment of an event or an occasion.

Exercise 32 Revision Practice: Nouns and Pronouns

Revise the following passage by using pronouns to avoid repetition. Use a variety of types of pronouns.

While monarch butterflies are concentrated primarily in the Americas, monarch butterflies have spread around the world. Monarch butterflies have an extraordinary traveling capacity. The fact that they have an extraordinary traveling ability has given them the monarch butterfly's second name: wanderers. Monarchs are members of the order *Lepidoptera*. What do they look like? The butterfly is recognized by the distinctive reddish-brown color, black veins, and white spots of the butterfly's wings. In the fall, one might see a great crowd of monarchs during their migration south. I myself have seen the migration in Canada.

On their return trip in the spring, the monarchs stop to deposit eggs and then die. The eggs produce caterpillars. The caterpillars live on milkweeds. When the caterpillars are grown, the caterpillars attach themselves to a branch and spin a cocoon. The cocoon is where the butterfly develops. A few might remain where they hatch, but most continue the migration north once they reach maturity.

Exercise 33 Writing Application

Write a narrative paragraph about the adventures of two people at a fair. Use at least one of each kind of pronoun (personal, reflexive, intensive, demonstrative, relative, interrogative, and indefinite). Then, underline and label each pronoun.

Exercise 34 Writing Application

Write a paragraph describing a carnival or a festival you have attended or seen on television. Include at least one example of each type of noun and pronoun included in this chapter.

Chapter Review • 357

Answer Key continued

Exercise 34

Writing Application
When students have written their paragraphs and labeled the nouns and pronouns, have them go back and add any nouns or pronouns from the chapter that they did not include at first.

Exercise 29

Responses will vary. Samples are given.
1. He bought the CD for himself. He himself bought the CD.
2. Don't be so hard on yourself. You yourself know the answer.
3. They are driving themselves to the party. They themselves own the car.
4. You should make lunch for yourselves. You yourselves know what you like to eat.
5. I am taking myself home. I myself am president of the drama club.

Exercise 30

Last Tuesday, my—personal; family and I—personal; went to Mardi Gras. There were lots of people who—relative; were out to have a good time. We—personal; saw floats that—relative; were full of colors. Almost all—indefinite; were musical. Those —demonstrative; riding them—personal; threw necklaces of beads. One—indefinite; fell at my—personal; feet. I—personal; wanted to pick it—personal; up for myself—reflexive; but my—personal; brother grabbed it—personal; for himself—reflexive. Who—interrogative; cares? I—personal; caught a doubloon, and that—relative; was a better prize. My—personal; brother himself—intensive; offered to trade his—personal; beads for my—personal; coin.

Exercise 31

Responses will vary. Samples are given. Many—indefinite; some—indefinite; who—relative; It—personal

Exercise 32

Revisions will vary. Have students identify the kinds of pronouns they use in their revisions.

Exercise 33

Writing Application
Have volunteers read aloud their narratives. Ask the class to identify the pronouns they hear and the kinds of pronouns they are.

Lesson Objectives

1. To understand the relationships expressed between words in analogies.

2. To complete analogies in a test situation.

Step-by-Step Teaching Guide

Completing Analogies

1. Explain to students that most analogy questions can be answered by following a set of steps.

2. First, students should look for possible relationships between the original pair of words.

3. Students can then read the choices, looking for a similar relationship.

4. If students cannot immediately choose the correct choice, they should identify the relationships between the word pairs in each choice. This can help to clarify or further specify the relationship between the words in the original pairs.

Standardized Test Preparation Workshop

Completing Analogies

An analogy expresses a comparison between two pairs of words. The relationship between the words in the first pair is similar to the relationship between the words in the second pair. For example,

MONEY : VAULT ::
(A) orchestra : music
(B) airplane : hangar
(C) finger : hand
(D) tree : farm
(E) insect : ecosystem

To complete this analogy, you must first identify the relationship between the original pair, MONEY : VAULT. To help determine the relationship, create a sentence expressing the connection between the two words, such as *Money is kept in a vault.* The function of the noun *vault* is to store the noun *money.* Therefore, the correct answer will consist of two nouns that have a **function/purpose relationship.**

Only answer (B) expresses a relationship in which one noun, *hangar,* has a function—storing an object, which is the noun, *airplane.* Another relationship between words in analogies is **cause-effect** or **effect-cause.** See the following sample test item to learn more about this relationship.

Test Tips

- Make sure that your choice reflects or parallels the structure in the given word pair. If the relationship in the given word pair is cause-effect, then your answer choice should be exactly cause-effect and not effect-cause.
- Sometimes the relationship between two words is multiple. Always probe beneath the first relationship you recognize to see whether there is a less obvious but more important secondary relationship.

Sample Test Item	Answer and Explanation
Each question below consists of a related pair of words, followed by five pairs of words labeled *A* through *E.* Select the pair that best expresses a relationship similar to that expressed in the original pair. LIAR : MISTRUST :: A trivial : defend B deface : falsehood C knowledge : teacher D leader : respect E integrity : honesty	The correct answer is *D.* The noun *respect* is the effect of the noun *leader;* therefore, it expresses the same relationship as the original pair in which the noun *mistrust* is the effect of the noun *liar.* Answers *A, B,* and *E* do not express a **cause-and-effect relationship,** as the original pair does. Although answer *C* expresses a similar relationship, the first word is the effect and the second is the cause, so it can be eliminated.

🖋 TEST-TAKING TIP

Draw students' attention to the first Test Tip in their textbooks. Provide the following examples to illuminate this tip:

PIANO: INSTRUMENT::

A fork: eating   D violin: orchestra

B dessert: cake   E luggage: travel

C bike: vehicle

Two of the choices, **B** and **C**, reflect the relationship between the original pair (a *piano* is a **type** of instrument). But only item **C** reflects the **order** of the original pair. The remaining choices, while displaying similar relationships, do not match that of the original pair.

Answer Key

Practice 1 **Directions:** Each question below consists of a related pair of words or phrases, followed by five pairs of words or phrases labeled *A* through *E*. Select the pair that best expresses a relationship similar to that expressed in the original pair.

1. ENGINE : CAR ::
   - (A) radio : battery
   - (B) limb : tree
   - (C) sails : boat
   - (D) song : singer
   - (E) caboose : train

2. SKATES : ICE ::
   - (A) snow : storm
   - (B) skis : snow
   - (C) nail : saw
   - (D) auto : train
   - (E) slush : hail

3. ADMIRATION : AWARD ::
   - (A) outrage : crime
   - (B) hero : reward
   - (C) reprimand : embarrassment
   - (D) approval : speech
   - (E) competition : winner

4. WEAVER : RUG ::
   - (A) crop : farmer
   - (B) guitar : guitarist
   - (C) statue : sculptor
   - (D) artist : painting
   - (E) piano : tune

5. BOOKS : KNOWLEDGE ::
   - (A) television : entertainment
   - (B) teacher : school
   - (C) actor : stage
   - (D) store : books
   - (E) study : library

6. DICTIONARY : REFERENCE ::
   - (A) short story : epic
   - (B) textbook : table of contents
   - (C) paper : pen
   - (D) encyclopedia : almanac
   - (E) violin : music

7. PIPE : WATER ::
   - (A) tracks : train
   - (B) bones : skeleton
   - (C) sight : eyes
   - (D) boats : canals
   - (E) wire : electricity

8. HURRICANE : DESTRUCTION ::
   - (A) dancer : performance
   - (B) accident : injury
   - (C) concert : dancing
   - (D) floods : rain
   - (E) snow : ice

9. LIBRARY : BOOKS ::
   - (A) garage : car
   - (B) desks : school
   - (C) highway : trucks
   - (D) train : transportation
   - (E) beach : sand

10. DRYNESS : THIRST ::
    - (A) cold : snow
    - (B) hungry : food
    - (C) starvation : hunger
    - (D) tiredness : exercise
    - (E) thirst : water

1. C
2. B
3. C
4. D
5. A
6. E
7. E
8. B
9. A
10. C

In-Depth Lesson Plan

	LESSON FOCUS	PRINT AND MEDIA RESOURCES
DAY 1	**Action Verbs** Students learn the role played by and how to use action verbs and do the Hands-On Grammar Activity (pp. 362–365).	**Teaching Resources** *Grammar Exercise Workbook*, pp. 13–14; *Grammar Exercises Answers on Transparency*, Ch. 17; *Hands-On Grammar Activity Book*, Ch. 17 **Language Lab CD-ROM**, Parts of Speech; **On-Line Exercise Bank**, Section 17.1
DAY 2	**Linking Verbs** Students learn the role played by and practice using linking verbs (pp. 366–369).	**Teaching Resources** *Grammar Exercise Workbook*, pp. 15–16; *Grammar Exercises Answers on Transparency*, Ch. 17; **Language Lab CD-ROM**, Parts of Speech; **On-Line Exercise Bank**, Section 17.2
DAY 3	**Helping Verbs** Students learn the role played by and practice using helping verbs (pp. 370–373).	**Teaching Resources** *Grammar Exercise Workbook*, pp. 17–20; *Grammar Exercises Answers on Transparency*, Ch. 17; **Language Lab CD-ROM**, Parts of Speech; **On-Line Exercise Bank**, Section 17.3
DAY 4	**Review and Assess** Students review chapter and demonstrate mastery of verbs (pp. 374–377).	**Teaching Resources** *Formal Assessment*, Ch. 17 **On-Line Exercise Bank**, Section 17.1

Accelerated Lesson Plan

	LESSON FOCUS	PRINT AND MEDIA RESOURCES
DAY 1	**Verbs** Students cover concepts and usage of action, linking, and helping verbs as determined by Diagnostic Test (pp. 362–373).	**Teaching Resources** *Grammar Exercise Workbook*, pp. 13–20; *Grammar Exercises Answers on Transparency*, Ch. 17; *Hands-On Grammar Activity Book*, Ch. 17 **Language Lab CD-ROM**, Parts of Speech; **On-Line Exercise Bank**, Section 17.1–3
DAY 2	**Review and Assess** Students review chapter and demonstrate mastery of verbs (pp. 374–377).	**Teaching Resources** *Formal Assessment*, Ch. 17; *Grammar Exercises Answers on Transparency*, Ch. 17 **On-Line Exercise Bank**, Section 17.1

Options for Adapting Lesson Plans

HOMEWORK

Have students complete any section of the chapter for homework.

FEATURES

Extend coverage with the Grammar in Literature feature (pp. 362, 371), and the Standardized Test Preparation Workshop (p. 376).

TECHNOLOGY

Students can use the On-Line Exercise Bank to complete the exercises on computer. The Auto Check feature will grade their work.

INTEGRATED SKILLS COVERAGE

Grammar in Literature
SE pp. 362, 371

Reading
Find It in Your Reading, SE pp. 364, 365, 369, 373

Writing
Find It in Your Writing, SE pp. 364, 365, 369, 373
Writing Application, SE pp. 365, 369, 373, 375

Language
Language Highlight, ATE p. 368

Speaking and Listening
Integrating Listening Skills, ATE p. 370

Viewing and Representing
Critical Viewing, SE pp. 360, 363, 371

ASSESSMENT SUPPORT

Standardized Test Preparation SE p. 376; ATE pp. 364, 372
Standardized Test Preparation Workbook, pp. 33–34
Formal Assessment, Ch. 17

MEETING INDIVIDUAL NEEDS

See also Ongoing Assessments ATE pp. 363, 367, 368, 371
ESL Students ATE p. 363, 368
Logical/Mathematical Learners ATE p. 367

BLOCK SCHEDULING

Pacing Suggestions
For 90 minute Blocks
• Administer the Diagnostic Test to students to determine instructional coverage.
• Have students complete the necessary exercises in class. Use the Hands-on Grammar activity to provide a change of pace.

Resources for Varying Instruction
• *Language Lab* **CD-ROM** If your students have access to hardware, a 90 minute block provides an ideal opportunity for students to work on computer.

Professional Development Support
• *How to Manage Instruction in the Block* This Teaching Resource provides management and activity suggestions.

MEDIA AND TECHNOLOGY

For the Student
• *Language Lab* **CD-ROM,** Parts of Speech
• *On-Line Exercise Bank,* Ch. 17

For the Teacher
• *Resource Pro* **CD-ROM**

WRITING AND GRAMMAR WEBSITE

The Interactive Writing and Grammar Website provides a wide array of support for students, teachers, and parents. Grammar support includes:

• *On-Line Exercise Bank* with Auto Check scoring
• Diagnostic and assessment support

phwg.phschool.com

LITERATURE CONNECTIONS

Grammar in Literature selections from *Prentice Hall Literature: Timeless Voices, Timeless Themes,* Gold:
from *The Golden Kite, the Silver Wind,* Ray Bradbury, SE p. 362
from *Apollo 13,* Jim Lovell and Jeffrey Kluger, SE p. 371

► Lesson Objectives

1. To understand what action verbs are and how they are used.

2. To distinguish between verbs that show visible and mental action.

3. To distinguish between transitive and intransitive verbs.

4. To understand what linking verbs are and how they are used.

5. To identify forms of the linking verb *be*.

6. To identify other linking verbs.

7. To distinguish between action verbs and linking verbs.

8. To understand how helping verbs are added to other verbs to form verb phrases.

9. To recognize forms of *be* and other verbs used as helping verbs.

10. To understand how words in a verb phrase can be separated in a sentence.

Critical Viewing

Analyze Students' responses will vary. Make sure they support their responses with details from the photo.

▲ **Critical Viewing**
What verbs could you use to describe the action you see in this picture?
[Analyze]

The verb is perhaps the most important part of speech in English. Without it, there would be no sentences. A **verb** is a word that expresses time while showing an action, a condition, or the fact that something exists.

If you say, "Artists *paint* portraits," the verb *paint* shows an action. If you say, "Treasures *are* on display," the verb *are* shows a condition. If you say, "The king *was* there," the verb *was* expresses existence.

In this chapter, you will learn about *action verbs*, *linking verbs*, and *helping verbs*.

360 • Verbs

☑ ONGOING ASSESSMENT SYSTEM: Diagnose

If students miss more than one item in each category, direct them to the relevant pages of the text and assign exercises for practice and review.

Verbs	Diagnostic Test Items	Teach	Practice	Section Review	Chapter Review
Skill Check A					
Visible and Mental Action	A 1–5	p. 362	Ex. 1	Ex. 4	
Skill Check B					
Transitive and Intransitive Verbs	B 6–10	p. 363	Ex. 2	Ex. 5	Ex. 26
Skill Check C					
Linking Verbs	C 11–15	pp. 366–367	Ex. 9–10	Ex. 12	Ex. 27

Diagnostic Test

Directions: Write all answers on a separate sheet of paper.

Skill Check A. Identify the action verb in each sentence. Then, label each V (*visible action*) or M (*mental action*).

1. The earliest Chinese people lived in the Yellow River valley.
2. Written records go back about 3,500 years.
3. The Chinese believed in the importance of history.
4. Archaeologists wondered about the origin of the Chinese people.
5. They investigated ancient sites.

Skill Check B. Identify the action verb in each sentence. Then, label it *transitive* or *intransitive*.

6. The Shang dynasty once ruled the territory of present-day China.
7. Agriculture sustained the early Chinese.
8. The people worked hard on small patches of land.
9. They also raised pigs, dogs, sheep, and oxen.
10. The rulers lived in fine palaces.

Skill Check C. Write the following sentences. Underline the linking verb, and draw a double-headed arrow connecting the words linked by the verb.

11. The Shang was an aristocratic society.
12. The king became the head of a military nobility.
13. The rulers of each territory were his appointees.
14. The other classes may have been less influential.
15. The commoners remained the largest group.

Skill Check D. Write the verb in each sentence. Then, label it *linking* or *action*.

16. The Zhou dynasty remained powerful for a time.
17. Peasants grew millet, wheat, barley, and rice.
18. Men and women grew tired from long hours in the fields.
19. They turned over the harvest to the ruler.
20. This system appears unfair to people today.

Skill Check E. Write the verb phrase in each sentence. Include all helping verbs, but do not include any words that interrupt the verb phrase.

(21) The Qin dynasty had contributed much to the Chinese culture. (22) However, the accomplishments of the Qin dynasty must have been achieved at an enormous cost of wealth and human life. (23) Taxation and forced labor might have been responsible for the resentment of the dynasty. (24) The indignant population will always be remembered because they rebelled. (25) This power struggle could possibly have caused the fall of the dynasty.

Verbs • 361

✓ ONGOING ASSESSMENT SYSTEM: Diagnose *continued*

Verbs	Diagnostic Test Items	Teach	Practice	Section Review	Chapter Review
Skill Check D					
Linking Verbs or Action Verbs	D 16–20	p. 368	Ex. 11	Ex. 12–13	Ex. 28, 31
Skill Check E					
Helping Verbs and Verb Phrases	E 21–25	pp. 370–372	Ex. 17–19	Ex. 20–22	Ex. 29–30
Cumulative Reviews and Applications				Ex. 6–8, 14–16, 23–25	Ex. 32–33

Answer Key

Diagnostic Test

- Each item in the diagnostic test corresponds with concepts covered in this chapter. This will enable you to tailor instruction to the particular needs of your students. See "Ongoing Assessment System" below for further details.

- Answers for the Diagnostic Test and all chapter exercises are available in *Grammar Exercises Answers on Transparencies* in your teaching resources.

Skill Check A

1. lived—V
2. go—V
3. believed—M
4. wondered—M
5. investigated—V

Skill Check B

6. ruled—transitive
7. sustained—transitive
8. worked—intransitive
9. raised—transitive
10. lived—intransitive

Skill Check C

11. The Shang was an aristocratic society. (arrow from *Shang* to *society.*)
12. The king became the head of a military nobility. (arrow from *king* to *head.*)
13. The rulers of each territory were his appointees. (arrow from *rulers* to *appointees.*)
14. The other classes may have been less influential. (arrow from *classes* to *influential.*)
15. The commoners remained the largest group. (arrow from *commoners* to *group.*)

Skill Check D

16. remained—linking
17. grew—action
18. grew—linking
19. turned—action
20. appears—linking

Skill Check E

21. had contributed
22. must have been achieved
23. might have been
24. will be remembered
25. could have caused

Activate Prior Knowledge

Ask several students to explain how they will get home from school later today. Point out the action words in their responses (<u>ride</u> a bike, <u>catch</u> the bus, <u>walk</u> home).

TEACH

Step-by-Step Teaching Guide

Action Verbs

1. Explain to students that in a sentence with an action verb, the subject of the sentence performs a physical or mental activity.

2. Help students understand that action verbs need not express physical activity. Ask volunteers to provide additional examples of verbs that show mental action, or actions that cannot be seen. (Possible responses: wish, care, decide)

Step-by-Step Teaching Guide

Grammar in Literature

1. Read or have a volunteer read aloud the excerpt. As the excerpt is read, have students identify whether each verb is a mental or visible action verb.

2. For each verb, have students list on a sheet of paper another possible mental or visible action verb to go in the sentence.

Answer Key

Exercise 1

1. made—V
2. decorated—V
3. painted—V
4. remembered—M
5. hoped—M

362

Section 17.1 # Action Verbs

Action verbs tell what happens. S*it* and *throw*, for example, are action verbs.

> **KEY CONCEPT** An **action verb** is a verb that tells what action someone or something is performing. ■

EXAMPLES:
The <u>king</u> <u>rules</u>.
<u>Famine</u> <u>struck</u> the people.

The person or thing that performs the action is called the *subject* of the verb. The verb *rules* tells what the subject *king* does. The verb *struck* tells what the subject *Famine* did.

> **KEY CONCEPT** Action verbs show *mental* action as well as *visible* action. ■

VISIBLE ACTION: We *chose* two books about China.
MENTAL ACTION: They *remember* the film about China.

> **Exercise 1** **Recognizing Action Verbs** Identify the action verb in each sentence, and label it *V* (*visible*) or *M* (*mental*).

EXAMPLE: Sarah attended the concert.   attended (V)

1. Chinese artists of the Bronze Age made beautiful carvings.
2. Kings had tombs decorated extravagantly for themselves.
3. Artists painted the walls with scenes of daily life.
4. The Chinese remembered their ancestors.
5. They hoped for harmony between human beings and nature.

GRAMMAR IN LITERATURE

from **The Golden Kite, the Silver Wind**
Ray Bradbury

Notice in the following sentences how the verbs said, call, will whisper, and will know express the actions of the characters.

"Then," *said* the daughter, "*call* in your stonemasons and temple builders. I *will whisper* from behind the silken screen and you *will know* the words."

362 • Verbs

Theme: China

In this section, you will learn to recognize action verbs and to distinguish between those that are transitive and those that are intransitive. The examples and exercises in this section are about China.

Cross-Curricular Connection: Social Studies

⏱ TIME AND RESOURCE MANAGER

Resources
Print: Grammar Exercise Workbook, pp. 13–14; Hands on Grammar Activity Book, Chapter 17
Technology: Language Lab CD-ROM, Parts of Speech; On-Line Exercise Bank, Section 17.1

In-Depth Coverage	Accelerated Pace
• Work through all key concepts, pp. 362–363. • Assign and review Exercises 1–2. • Read and discuss Grammar in Literature, p. 362. • Do the Hands-on Grammar Activity, p. 364.	• Assign pp. 362–363, for independent student review. • Assign Section Review Exercises 3–8, p. 365.

▶ **Exercise 9** Recognizing Forms of *Be* Used as Linking **Verbs** Write each sentence on a separate sheet of paper, underlining the linking verb. Then, draw a double-headed arrow to show which words are linked by the verb.
1. The *Apollo 13* mission was successful.
2. It may be the most famous lunar-landing mission.
3. It would be difficult to name a more courageous crew.
4. Their names are James A. Lovell, Jr.; John L. Swigert, Jr.; and Fred Wallace Haise, Jr.
5. These men were aboard during an explosion on the module.

Other Linking Verbs

Verbs other than *be* may also be used as linking verbs.

▶ **KEY CONCEPT** Other verbs may be used in the same way as *be* to link two parts of a sentence. ■

OTHER LINKING VERBS					
appear	feel	look	seem	sound	taste
become	grow	remain	smell	stay	turn

In the examples below, you can see how these verbs act as linking verbs by helping words at the end of the sentences name or describe the place or thing at the beginning.

EXAMPLES: The situation on board *remained* serious.

The astronauts *grew* anxious.

▶ **Exercise 10** Identifying Other Linking Verbs Write each sentence, underlining the linking verb. Then, draw a double-headed arrow to show which words are linked by the verb.
1. The astronauts felt concerned after sensing the explosion.
2. After the system malfunction, the situation turned serious.
3. The tension in the module grew steadily.
4. The levels of oxygen, water, and power appeared lower.
5. Conditions became critical.
6. The moon landing seemed unlikely.
7. The lunar module remained a refuge for longer than expected.
8. The return to Earth looked impossible.
9. A minor mid-course correction became the only solution.
10. On Earth, Mission Control stayed positive.

Linking Verbs • 367

More Practice
Language Lab CD-ROM
• About the Eight Parts of Speech: Verbs lesson
On-line Exercise Bank
• Section 17.2
Grammar Exercise Workbook
• pp. 15–16

Answer Key

Exercise 9
1. was (arrow from *mission* to *successful*)
2. may be (arrow from *It* to *mission*)
3. would be (arrow from *It* to *difficult*)
4. are (arrow from *names* to *the group of names*)
5. were (arrow from *men* to *aboard*)

Step-by-Step Teaching Guide

Other Linking Verbs
1. Explain that other linking verbs are often used to connect a subject with an adjective that modifies the subject.
2. Demonstrate how these adjectives modify the subject by placing the adjectives from the example sentences in front of the subjects.
   The serious situation
   The anxious astronauts

Customizing for *Logical/Mathematical Learners*
Point out that the verb *be* used as a linking verb often functions like an equals sign in an equation. To demonstrate, write several sentence pairs on the board.
George Washington was our first president.
George Washington = our first president.

Answer Key

Exercise 10
1. felt (arrow from *astronauts* to *concerned*)
2. turned (arrow from *situation* to *serious*)
3. grew (arrow from *tension* to *steadily*)
4. appeared (arrow from *levels* to *lower*)
5. became (arrow from *conditions* to *critical*)
6. seemed (arrow from *landing* to *unlikely*)
7. remained (arrow from *module* to *refuge*)
8. looked (arrow from *return* to *impossible*)
9. became (arrow from *correction* to *solution*)
10. stayed (arrow from *Mission Control* to *positive*)

☐ ONGOING ASSESSMENT: Monitor and Reinforce
If students miss more than two items in Exercises 9 and 10, refer them to the following for additional practice.

In the Textbook	Print Resources	Technology
Section Review, Ex. 12, p. 369	Grammar Exercise Workbook, pp. 15–16	Language Lab CD-ROM, Parts of Speech On-Line Exercise Bank, Section 17.2

Language Highlight

New Words New verbs and other words often enter the language in works of literature. William Shakespeare, for example, is credited with introducing 1,500 words into the English language. The reason we say *rant and rave* today is that Shakespeare coined the verb *rant*. He adapted it from a Dutch word *ranten* that means, of course, "to rave." Other Shakespearean additions to our vocabulary include *leapfrog, go-between, cold-blooded,* and *eyeball.*

Answer Key

Exercise 11

1. seemed—linking
2. turned—action
3. occurred—action
4. felt—action
5. grew—linking

Linking Verb or Action Verb?

Most of the verbs in the chart on page 367 can be used as either linking verbs or action verbs. To determine whether a verb is being used as a linking verb or as an action verb in a sentence, you can substitute *am, are,* or *is* for the verb. If the substituted verb makes sense and connects two words, then the original verb is being used as a linking verb in that sentence. If the substituted verb makes the sentence illogical or fails to connect two words, then the original verb is an action verb.

▶ **KEY CONCEPT** A verb is functioning as a linking verb if *am, are,* or *is* can logically be substituted for the verb. ■

Linking Verbs	Action Verbs
The pears *taste* sweet.	I *taste the red pepper.*
The pears *are* sweet.	I *am* the red pepper.
(linking)	(not linking)
Apollo 13 appears ready.	*Apollo 13* appears suddenly.
Apollo 13 is ready.	*Apollo 13* is suddenly.
(linking)	(not linking)
The runner *grew* tired.	He *grew* a beard.
The runner *is* tired.	He *is* a beard.
(linking)	(not linking)

▶ **Exercise 11** Distinguishing Between Linking Verbs and Action Verbs Write the verb or verbs in each sentence. Then, label each *linking* or *action.*

EXAMPLE: Astronauts felt the heat through their suits.

ANSWER: felt   (action)

1. The *Apollo 13* mission seemed routine in its early stages.
2. An electrical surge turned a successful mission into a perilous one.
3. The surge occurred as a result of wires making contact.
4. The astronauts felt vibrations from the explosion.
5. They grew concerned about sparks igniting insulation.

368 • Verbs

Section 17.2 Section Review

GRAMMAR EXERCISES 12–16

Exercise 12 Identifying Linking Verbs Write each sentence, underlining the linking verb. Then, draw a double-headed arrow connecting the words linked by the verb.

1. The *Apollo 13* astronauts were often tired during their extensive screening.
2. Computer-based aids became necessary in the astronauts' training.
3. Knowledge of basic water survival would be crucial to the *Apollo 13* astronauts.
4. After the first year of training, they seemed well prepared.
5. The *Apollo 13* crew was completely ready for their mission.
6. Suddenly, a bright flame became visible.
7. The oxygen content of the air in the craft may have been low.
8. The craft smelled smoky.
9. The control center sounded chaotic to listeners.
10. Everyone felt relieved after the astronauts' safe return.

Exercise 13 Identifying Verbs as Linking or Action Verbs Write the verb in each sentence, and label it *linking* or *action*.

1. The space program looks for qualified candidates.
2. Physical and mental health requirements remain important.
3. Can astronauts grow a beard?
4. Astronauts seem ready for isolation and fear.
5. Most stay in the program.

6. Integrity, ability, and self-confidence appear essential.
7. The selection process looks rigorous.
8. The candidates grow anxious for a decision.
9. Many of the candidates appear at press conferences.
10. Some remain afterward for autograph signing.

Exercise 14 Find It in Your Reading In this excerpt from Jim Lovell and Jeffrey Kluger's *Apollo 13*, identify the linking verb that is part of a contraction. Which words does the verb link?

"Roger," Lousma responded, in the mandatory matter-of-factness of the Capcom, "we copy your venting."
"It's a gas of some sort," Lovell said.
"Can you tell us anything about it? Where is it coming from?"

Exercise 15 Find It in Your Writing Look through two or three pieces of writing in your portfolio. Find five examples of linking verbs. In each case, identify the words that are linked by the verbs.

Exercise 16 Writing Application Write a short explanation of why you would or would not want to take part in a space mission. Use at least one of the following verbs as both an action verb and as a linking verb: *look, appear, grow, stay.*

Section Review • 369

ASSESS and CLOSE

Section Review

Each of these exercises correlates with a concept covered on pages 366–368. The exercises may be used for more practice, for reteaching, or for review of the Key Concepts presented. Answers for all chapter exercises are available in *Grammar Exercises Answers on Transparencies* in your teaching resources.

Answer Key

Exercise 12

1. The *Apollo 13* astronauts <u>were</u> often tired during their extensive screening. (arrow from *astronauts* to *tired*)
2. Computer-based aids <u>became</u> necessary in the astronauts' training. (arrow from *aides* to *necessary*)
3. Knowledge of basic water survival <u>would be</u> crucial to *Apollo 13* astronauts. (arrow from *knowledge* to *crucial*)
4. After the first year of training, they <u>seemed</u> well prepared. (arrow from *they* to *prepared*)
5. The *Apollo 13* crew <u>was</u> completely ready for their mission. (arrow from *crew* to *ready*)
6. Suddenly, a bright flame <u>became</u> visible. (arrow from *flame* to *visible*)
7. The oxygen content of the air in the craft <u>may have been</u> low. (arrow from *content* to *low*)
8. The craft <u>smelled</u> smoky. (arrow from *craft* to *smoky*)
9. The control center <u>sounded</u> chaotic to listeners. (arrow from *center* to *chaotic*)
10. Everyone <u>felt</u> relieved after the astronauts' safe return. (arrow from *Everyone* to *relieved*)

Exercise 13

1. looks—action
2. remain—linking
3. grow—action
4. seem—linking
5. stay—action
6. appear—linking
7. looks—linking
8. grow—linking
9. appear—action
10. remain—action

continued

Answer Key continued

Exercise 14

Find It in Your Reading
The linking verb *is* ('s) links *It* and *gas.*

Exercise 15

Find It in Your Writing
If students cannot readily find examples in their own writing, then have them write five sentences that contain linking verbs.

Exercise 16

Writing Application
When students have finished, have volunteers read their explanations to the class.

Write the following sentences on the board:

I written about my family.

If there is enough time, I go to the ball park to buy tickets.

Ask students to correct the sentences by inserting an additional word in each one. Encourage them to discuss how they knew something was wrong with each sentence. (Possible responses: *had, have; will*)

Activate Prior Knowledge

Introduce helping verbs and verb phrases by having students explain how people express actions that they will perform in the future. Write *I rake the leaves* on the chalkboard. Ask:

- What is the verb in this sentence? *(rake)*

- How would you say this if you are going to rake the leaves later? *(I will rake the leaves.)*

- What is the verb phrase in the new sentence? *(will rake)*

TEACH

Step-by-Step Teaching Guide

Helping Verbs

1. Write several main verbs on the chalkboard, such as *play, decide, remember,* and *invite.* Have students suggest several verb phrases using these main verbs.

2. Ask students to write a sentence for each of the verb phrases they created. Then have students trade sentences with a partner and identify both the complete verb phrases and the helping verbs.

Integrating Listening Skills

Have partners take turns reading from a selection in the Gold Level *Timeless Voices, Timeless Themes.* As one student reads, the partner should jot down every helping verb he or she hears. After several sentences, pairs should pause and compare the verbs recorded with those that appear in the text. Students can then exchange roles.

Section 17.3 # Helping Verbs

Often, a single verb is formed from as many as four words. *Helping verbs* may be added to a verb such as *sung* to make a *verb phrase,* such as *had sung* or *should have been sung.*

▶**KEY CONCEPT** **Helping verbs** are verbs that can be added to another verb to make a single verb phrase. ■

Recognizing Helping Verbs

Learning the forms of *be* in the chart on page 366 and the other verbs that can be used as helping verbs will help you recognize helping verbs in sentences.

▶**KEY CONCEPT** Any of the many forms of *be* as well as some other verbs can be used as helping verbs. ■

HELPING VERBS OTHER THAN THE FORMS OF *BE*			
do	have	shall	can
does	has	should	could
did	had	will	may
	would	might	
		must	

Verb phrases are created by the addition of helping verbs to other verbs. The following chart lists six examples, but the possibilities are almost endless.

VERB PHRASES	
Helping Verbs	Verbs
am	talking
did	play
can	write
will be	studying
should have	seen
might have been	considered

Helping verbs are sometimes called *auxiliary verbs* or *auxiliaries* because they add meaning to other verbs. Notice how using helping verbs can change the meaning of a sentence.

WITHOUT HELPING VERBS: They *sing* in the morning.

WITH HELPING VERBS: They *will sing* in the morning.
They *might sing* in the morning.

Theme: Apollo 13

In this section, you will learn how to use helping verbs to form verb phrases. The examples and exercises in this section tell more about the mission of *Apollo 13.*

Cross-Curricular Connection: Social Studies

⏱ **TIME AND RESOURCE MANAGER**

Resources
Print: Grammar Exercise Workbook, pp. 19–20
Technology: Language Lab CD-ROM, Parts of Speech; On-Line Exercise Bank, Section 17.3

In-Depth Coverage	Accelerated Pace
• Work through all key concepts, pp. 370–372.	• Assign pp. 370–372 for independent student review.
• Assign and review Exercises 17–19.	• Assign Section Review Exercises 20–23, p. 373.
• Read and discuss Grammar in Literature, p. 371.	

GRAMMAR IN LITERATURE

from **Apollo 13**
Jim Lovell and Jeffrey Kluger

Notice how the helping verbs had been *and* might have *add meaning to the verbs* launched *and* metamorphosed *in the following sentences.*

. . . No one said anything out loud, no one declared anything officially, but the controllers began to recognize that the *Apollo 13*, which *had been* launched in triumph just over two days earlier, *might have* just metamorphosed from a brilliant mission of exploration to one of simple survival.

> **More Practice**
> **Language Lab CD-ROM**
> • About the Eight Parts of Speech: Verbs lesson
> **On-line Exercise Bank**
> • Section 17.3
> **Grammar Exercise Workbook**
> • pp. 19–20

> **Exercise 17** **Identifying Helping Verbs** Identify the helping verb(s) in each sentence.

EXAMPLE: Al will be watching the mission on television.

ANSWER: will be

1. Did you hear about the *Apollo 13* mission?
2. Many journalists have written about this historic flight.
3. People will be talking about the events of the *Apollo 13* mission for years to come.
4. On the way to the moon, *Apollo 13* must have experienced technical difficulties.
5. An electrical surge had occurred inside a fuel cell.
6. The following explosions might have been caused by the electrical surge.
7. The astronauts had been taught to enter the lunar module in case of emergency.
8. They could survive in the lunar module for 50 hours.
9. After 95 hours in the module, all supplies should have been exhausted.
10. The astronauts' courage has been admired by people throughout the world.

▶ Critical Viewing Use a verb phrase to describe this sight at the blastoff of *Apollo 13*. [Relate]

Helping Verbs • 371

> ☑ **ONGOING ASSESSMENT: Monitor and Reinforce**

If students miss more than two items in Exercise 17, refer them to the following for additional practice.

In the Textbook	Print Resources	Technology
Section Review, Ex. 20, p. 373	Grammar Exercise Workbook, pp. 19–20	Language Lab CD-ROM, Parts of Speech On-Line Exercise Bank, Section 17.3

Finding Helping Verbs in Sentences

1. Ask students to identify the words that make up the verb phrases in the following sentences.

   He had offered a good price for the bicycle. (had offered)

   Shelly can fly to Mississippi. (can fly)

2. Add interrupters to the sentences and repeat the question.

   He had not offered a good price for the bicycle. (had offered)

   Can Shelly fly to Mississippi? (can fly)

3. Point out that interrupted verb phrases are common in questions and negative statements. One way students can check their understanding of helping verbs in these cases is to change a negative sentence to a positive one, or answer a sentence that is a question.

   My mother was not happy with my report card.

   My mother was happy with my report card.

   Is Rika going to the party with us?

   Rika is going to the party with us.

Answer Key

Exercise 18

1. have been written
2. will be impressed
3. had been created
4. can be caused
5. would result
6. must keep
7. had been trained
8. did panic
9. will send
10. may have been

Exercise 19

Possible responses:

1. I have always admired the astronauts' courage.
2. Would you like to have a space adventure?
3. The astronauts did eat freeze-dried food.
4. Can you hear broadcasts from space?
5. Will you learn about the space program?

Finding Helping Verbs in Sentences

Verb phrases are often interrupted by other words.

KEY CONCEPT Other words may sometimes separate helping verbs from main verbs in sentences. ■

The following examples show the words of a verb phrase together as well as verb phrases interrupted by other words.

WORDS TOGETHER: They *will be flying* in the morning.
WORDS SEPARATED: They *will* definitely not *be going* with us.
                   Have you and the others *met* our friends?

Grammar and Style Tip

Even though an adverb might interrupt a verb phrase, it is not considered part of the verb phrase.

Exercise 18 **Identifying Verb Phrases** Write the verb phrase in each sentence. Include all helping verbs, but do not include any words that come between the helping verb and the main verb.

EXAMPLE: Most of this planet's galaxy has not been explored.
ANSWER: has been explored

(1) Differing accounts have sometimes been written of the events of the *Apollo 13* mission. (2) However, you will be impressed by the courage of the *Apollo 13* crew. (3) Had sparks been created by contact between two electrical wires? (4) A fire in space can be caused by any number of sources. (5) A fire would certainly result in limited supplies. (6) An astronaut in trouble must always keep a clear mind. (7) Fortunately, the *Apollo 13* crew had been trained to deal with emergencies. (8) The astronauts did not panic. (9) With correct propulsion adjustments, the moon's gravity will send a spacecraft back to Earth. (10) This voyage may have been the most successful failure in the annals of spaceflight.

Exercise 19 **Writing Sentences With Verb Phrases** Write sentences containing verb phrases, using the verbs and topics given below. Include these helping verbs: *have, will, did, can,* and *would.*
1. admire—astronauts' courage
2. like—space adventure
3. eat—freeze-dried food
4. hear—broadcasts from space
5. learn—space program

372 • Verbs

More Practice

Language Lab
CD-ROM
• About the Eight Parts of Speech: Verbs lesson
On-line
Exercise Bank
• Section 17.3
Grammar Exercise Workbook
• pp. 19–20

STANDARDIZED TEST PREPARATION WORKSHOP

Grammar and Usage Many standardized tests require students to identify the correct word for completing a sentence. Often, the answer choices include both verbs and verb phrases. Show the following example to students.

We don't have time to visit all of the museums. We _____ to the science museum tomorrow.

Choose the word or group of words that belong in the space.

A go   **B** will go

C had gone   **D** have gone

The correct answer is item **B**—the verb phrase made up of the helping verb *will* and the main verb *go.* The remaining items are the wrong tense.

Section 17.3 Section Review

GRAMMAR EXERCISES 20–25

Exercise 20 **Identifying Helping Verbs** Write the helping verb(s) in each sentence.

1. The *Apollo 13* mission may have been the most exciting in history.
2. The mission should have proceeded normally.
3. However, problems would arise from an electrical surge.
4. An electrical surge can cause an explosion and a fire.
5. The crew had quickly moved to the lunar module.
6. The crew's water-retaining strategy may have saved their lives.
7. During the mission, the crew was exposed to near-freezing temperatures.
8. The ship did return to Earth five days after the initial launch.
9. According to NASA, *Apollo 13* officially must be classed as a failure.
10. The mission will be viewed differently by those who know the full story.

Exercise 21 **Identifying Verb Phrases** Write all verb phrases, but do not include any words that come between the helping verb and the main verb.

1. NASA was diligently studying the causes of the crisis.
2. Such an event should never happen again.
3. Since *Apollo 13*, other missions have been sent to the moon.
4. By 1972, astronauts had landed on the moon six times.
5. They were wearing protective clothing.
6. Scientific instruments have always been carried on each flight.
7. A seismograph can easily detect small movements on the moon's surface.
8. Did astronauts always recover samples from the lunar surface?

9. Drills were sometimes used for collecting soil samples.
10. The *Apollo 14* lunar module would carry two astronauts.

Exercise 22 **Supplying Helping Verbs** Complete each sentence with an appropriate helping verb.

1. They ___?___ land near a crater.
2. The crater ___?___ originally been the target of *Apollo 13*.
3. During the *Apollo 15* mission, astronauts ___?___ driving a lunar rover.
4. Our knowledge of the moon ___?___ increased through these missions.
5. Much space technology ___?___ later applied to other fields.

Exercise 23 **Find It in Your Reading** In this excerpt from Jim Lovell and Jeffrey Kluger's *Apollo 13*, identify the verb phrases.

. . . If a tank of gas is suddenly reading empty and a cloud of gas is surrounding the spacecraft, it's a good bet the two are connected, especially if the whole mess had been preceded by a suspicious ship-shaking bang.

Exercise 24 **Find It in Your Writing** Identify the verb phrases in a recent piece of your writing. Underline the helping verb(s) in each verb phrase.

Exercise 25 **Writing Application** Write a description of one thing you would take with you on a voyage to the moon. Use at least three verb phrases in your sentences. Underline the helping verbs.

Section Review • 373

ASSESS and CLOSE

Section Review

Each of these exercises correlates with a concept covered in the section on helping verbs, pages 370–372. The exercises may be used for more practice, for reteaching, or for review of the Key Concepts presented. Answers for all chapter exercises are available in *Grammar Exercises Answers on Transparencies* in your teaching resources.

Answer Key

Exercise 20

1. may have
2. should have
3. would
4. can
5. had
6. may have
7. was
8. did
9. must be
10. will be

Exercise 21

1. was studying
2. should happen
3. have been sent
4. had landed
5. were wearing
6. have been carried
7. can detect
8. Did recover
9. were used
10. would carry

Exercise 22

Possible responses:

1. could
2. had
3. were
4. has
5. was

Exercise 23

Find It in Your Reading
is reading, is surrounding, are connected, had been preceded

Exercise 24

Find It in Your Writing
Have students work with a partner to check their responses. When students are done, have them share a sentence from their writing with the class.

continued

Answer Key continued

Exercise 25

Writing Application
When students have finished, have volunteers read their descriptions to the class. Have students identify the verb phrases.

Each of these exercises correlate to a concept covered in the chapter on verbs, pages 362–373. The exercises may be used for more practice, for reteaching, or for review of the Key Concepts presented.

Answer Key

Exercise 26

1. train—intransitive
2. examines—transitive
3. choose—intransitive
4. occurs—intransitive
5. use—transitive
6. vary—intransitive
7. simulate—transitive
8. program—transitive
9. provide—transitive
10. study—intransitive

Exercise 27

1. The few months before a flight seem long for the trainees. (arrow from *months* to *long*)
2. The crew members are well-prepared. (arrow from *members* to *well prepared*)
3. So far, the training has been enjoyable. (arrow from *training* to *enjoyable*)
4. Graduation will be very satisfying. (arrow from *Graduation* to *satisfying*)
5. The shuttle training will be a longer course. (arrow from *training* to *course*)
6. A mission specialist is extremely experienced. (arrow from *specialist* to *experienced*)
7. The longer flights are more complex. (arrow from *flights* to *complex*)
8. Some scientific experiments became models for extensive research. (arrow from *experiments* to *models*)
9. The pieces of equipment look very durable. (arrow from *pieces* to *durable*)
10. Teamwork is a major emphasis throughout the activities. (arrow from *Teamwork* to *emphasis*)

Exercise 28

1. grew—action
2. tasted—linking
3. seemed—linking
4. feels—linking
5. turned—linking
6. grew—linking
7. appeared—action
8. appeared—linking
9. sounded—action
10. sounded—linking
11. felt—action
12. looked—linking
13. looked—action
14. remained—linking
15. seemed—linking

GRAMMAR EXERCISES 26–33

Exercise 26 Distinguishing Between Transitive and Intransitive Verbs

Write the action verb in each sentence, and label it *transitive* or *intransitive*.

1. Astronauts train for years.
2. NASA examines the quality of each applicant.
3. Specialists never choose randomly.
4. Most flight training occurs immediately.
5. Trainees use simulators for training.
6. Abilities vary among the pilots.
7. Shuttle-mission simulators simulate nearly every element of flight.
8. Teams of instructors program computers with scripts of events.
9. Simulated spaceflights provide training and experience.
10. The pilots study in the training center.

Exercise 27 Recognizing Linking Verbs

Write each sentence, underlining the linking verb. Then, draw a double-headed arrow connecting words linked by the verb.

1. The few months before a flight seem long for the trainees.
2. The crew members are well prepared.
3. So far, the training has been enjoyable.
4. Graduation will be very satisfying.
5. The shuttle training will be a longer course.
6. A mission specialist is extremely experienced.
7. The longer flights are more complex.
8. Some scientific experiments became models for extensive research.
9. The pieces of equipment look very durable.
10. Teamwork is a major emphasis throughout the activities.

Exercise 28 Distinguishing Between Action and Linking Verbs

Identify the verb in each sentence, and label it *linking* or *action*.

1. Some experts grew special food for space missions.
2. The food tasted unusual.
3. Special clothing seemed necessary for space travel.
4. The clothing feels bulky and cumbersome.
5. In the days before the flight, the weather turned stormy.
6. The astronauts grew impatient.
7. On the first clear day, the crew appeared at the platform.
8. The countdown appeared routine.
9. Suddenly, an alarm sounded in the command module.
10. Over the radio, the crew sounded nervous.
11. The astronauts felt unusual heat in the module.
12. The situation looked critical.
13. Mission Control looked at the data from the computers.
14. The astronauts remained calm.
15. Canceling the mission seemed the right decision.

Exercise 29 Identifying Helping Verbs

Identify the helping verb(s) in each sentence.

1. Our class has been learning about the challenges of space travel.
2. We have read about many space-team members.
3. I should have watched the special report on the space shuttle.
4. It might have been seen around the world.

5. My family is considering a visit to the Johnson Space Center.
6. I might be allowed to sit in the zero-gravity simulator.
7. I will write my findings in a journal.
8. I could see one of the astronauts.
9. A career in the space program would be a challenge.
10. Maybe someday I will be considered a great astronaut.

Exercise 30 Identifying Verb Phrases Write the verb phrase in each sentence. Include all helping verbs, but do not include any words that interrupt the verb phrase.

(1) Most of the Earth has already been explored, (2) but space has not been completely explored yet. (3) Explorers have been faced with many obstacles. (4) They may sometimes spend years in preparation for a single mission. (5) They will look at every facet of the mission beforehand. (6) The astronauts will often have to depend on the expertise of others. (7) They have been trained for almost any emergency. (8) Even with all the training, they could not have been prepared for what occurred on the *Apollo 13* mission. (9) Given the conditions, the astronauts should not have survived the catastrophe. (10) Their quick thinking under pressure was essential to their rescue.

Exercise 31 Revision Practice: Action Verbs Review the following paragraph. Wherever possible and appropriate, change sentences with linking verbs to sentences with action verbs. You may need to reorder, add words, or combine some sentences.

(1) There are certain criteria for the selection of astronauts. (2) Clear thinking in stressful situations is one of them.

(3) Reliability and excellent communication are two other skills possessed by space-shuttle astronauts. (4) Specialists believe in the importance of these criteria for astronaut selection. (5) The number of astronauts on a mission is limited by NASA.

Exercise 32 Writing Application
Write a letter requesting information about a career in which you have an interest. Underline the verbs in each sentence. Label each verb *action* or *linking*. For each linking verb, draw a double-headed arrow connecting the words linked by the verb. Underline any helping verbs.

Exercise 33 CUMULATIVE REVIEW Nouns, Pronouns, and Verbs Identify each *common*, *proper*, and *compound* noun in the following sentences. Also, identify the *antecedent* for each underlined pronoun.

1. NASA has also launched many satellites.
2. They circle Earth in an orbit.
3. *Sputnik 1* was the first artificial satellite.
4. After *Sputnik*'s launch, the Soviet Union seemed the leader in space.
5. An artificial satellite may be classified according to the job it does.
6. Some of the satellites gather information about weather.
7. The information has been very useful to meteorologists.
8. Other satellites have made communication possible over long distances.
9. Pilots and sailors can easily find their exact position using navigational satellites.
10. You and I may also use them to find our location while on the highway.

Exercise 29
1. has been
2. have
3. should have
4. might have been
5. is
6. might be
7. will
8. could
9. would
10. will be

Exercise 30
1. has been explored
2. has been explored
3. have been faced
4. may spend
5. will look
6. will have
7. have been trained
8. could have been prepared
9. should have survived
10. was essential

Exercise 31
Answers will vary.
1. Certain criteria exist for the selection of astronauts.
2. One of them involves clear thinking in stressful situations.
3. Space-shuttle astronauts must demonstrate reliability and excellent communication skills.
4. no change
5. NASA limits the number of astronauts on a mission.

Exercise 32
Writing Application
Have students work with a partner to check their responses. You might have students rewrite their sentences using an action verb for each linking verb, and vice versa.
continued

Answer Key continued

Exercise 33
Cumulative Review
1. NASA, satellites
2. Earth, orbit; satellites
3. *Sputnik 1*, satellite
4. launch, Soviet Union, leader, space
5. satellite, job; satellite
6. satellites, information, weather; satellites
7. information, meteorologists
8. satellites, communication, distances
9. Pilots, sailors, position, satellites; Pilots, sailors
10. location, highway; You, I

TIME SAVERS!

Answers on Transparency Use the Grammar Exercises on Transparencies for Chapter 17 to have students correct their own or one another's exercises

On-Line Exercise Bank Have students complete the exercises on computer. The Auto Check feature will grade their work for you!

375

Step-by-Step Teaching Guide

Completing Sentences With Verbs

1. Explain to students that they should read the entire passage carefully to establish the time frame. This information will help them determine which choice makes sense.

2. In the sample passage, the phrase *in 1877* helps to determine that the event happened in the past. Choice C indicates an action that happened in the past.

3. Ask a volunteer to explain her or his reasoning for Question 2.

Standardized Test Preparation Workshop

Completing Sentences With Verbs

One way standardized test questions measure your ability to use verbs is to ask you to complete a sentence with the correct form of a verb. These types of questions include a passage with missing verbs and four word choices to complete the passage. Typically, the choices will be different forms or tenses of the same verb.

It is important to read the entire passage before making a choice. Determine whether the blank calls for a verb or verb phrase that shows action or one that is used for connecting ideas. Then, try to determine when the events in the passage occurred—in the past, present, or future. The following is a sample of these types of questions.

Test Tip

If you are unsure of an answer, silently "speak" the passage in your mind. Often, the verb that "sounds" best will be the correct choice.

Sample Test Items	Answers and Explanations

Directions Read the passage, and choose the letter of the word or group of words that belongs in each space.
 	
Alexander Graham Bell ___(1)___ the first telephone in 1877. People for a long time to come ___(2)___ his name.
 	
1 A patents
   B will patent
   C patented
   D has patented
	The sentence calls for a verb that shows that something happened in the past. Choice C, *patented*, is the only verb that shows an action that happened and was completed in the past. Therefore, C is the correct answer.

2 F have remembered
   G will remember
   H are remembering
   J do remember
	The sentence calls for a verb that shows that something will happen in the future. Therefore, choice G, *will remember*, best completes the sentence.

⬛ TEST-TAKING TIP

Remind students that they should reread the passage with their choice of verb to check their answer. Many times, more than one choice may seem correct, but students can avoid making unnecessary errors by checking their choice in the context of the passage.

> **Practice 1** **Directions:** Read the following passage. Choose the letter of the verb or verb phrase that belongs in each space.

By the time she was three, Joy was a prolific artist. She often ___(1)___ five or more pictures each day. She ___(2)___ never happier than when she was creating! It all ___(3)___ the day she ___(4)___ her art desk and a set of crayons. Although she ___(5)___ all sorts of crafts, her favorite was coloring.

1 **A** colored
  B colors
  C is coloring
  D will color

2 **F** will be
  G is
  H was
  J were

3 **A** begins
  B was beginning
  C will begin
  D began

4 **F** receives
  G received
  H will receive
  J has received

5 **A** loves
  B will love
  C will have loved
  D loving

> **Practice 2** **Directions:** Read the following passage. Choose the letter of the verb or verb phrase that belongs in each space.

___(1)___ now for dangerous weather tomorrow. The next time you ___(2)___ shopping, be sure you ___(3)___ emergency supplies on your list. You ___(4)___ lives with a simple, well-stocked emergency kit. For more information on preparing for weather emergencies, you ___(5)___ your local Red Cross or search the Internet for weather-related sites.

1 **A** Preparing
  B Prepared
  C Prepare
  D Will prepare

2 **F** go
  G went
  H will have gone
  J gone

3 **A** will include
  B includes
  C were including
  D have included

4 **F** can save
  G have saved
  H would have saved
  J were saving

5 **A** have contacted
  B will contact
  C should contact
  D will be contacting

Practice 1
1. A
2. H
3. D
4. G
5. A

Practice 2
1. C
2. F
3. D
4. F
5. C

In-Depth Lesson Plan

	LESSON FOCUS	PRINT AND MEDIA RESOURCES
DAY 1	**Adjectives** Students learn and apply the role of adjectives in modifying nouns, of nouns used as adjectives, and proper and compound adjectives (pp. 380–385).	**Teaching Resources** *Grammar Exercise Workbook,* pp. 21–24; *Grammar Exercises Answers on Transparency,* Ch. 18; *Language Lab* CD-ROM, Parts of Speech; *On-Line Exercise Bank,* Section 18.1
DAY 2	**Adjectives (continued)** Students learn and apply the concepts of pronouns used as adjectives and do the Hands-on Grammar Activity (pp. 386–389).	**Teaching Resources** *Grammar Exercise Workbook,* pp. 25–26; *Grammar Exercises Answers on Transparency,* Ch. 18; *Language Lab* CD-ROM, Parts of Speech; *On-Line Exercise Bank,* Section 18.1
DAY 3	**Adverbs** Students learn and apply the concepts of adverbs modifying verbs, adjectives and other adverbs (pp. 390–395).	**Teaching Resources** *Grammar Exercise Workbook,* pp. 27–32; *Grammar Exercises Answers on Transparency,* Ch. 18; *Language Lab* CD-ROM, Parts of Speech; *On-Line Exercise Bank,* Section 18.2
DAY 4	**Review and Assess** Students review chapter and demonstrate mastery of use of adjectives and adverbs (pp. 396–399).	**Teaching Resources** *Formal Assessment,* Ch. 18; *Grammar Exercises Answers on Transparency,* Ch. 18; *On-Line Exercise Bank,* Section 18

Accelerated Lesson Plan

	LESSON FOCUS	PRINT AND MEDIA RESOURCES
DAY 1	**Adjectives** Students cover concepts and usage of adjectives as determined by Diagnostic Test (pp. 380–389).	**Teaching Resources** *Grammar Exercise Workbook,* pp. 21–26; *Grammar Exercises Answers on Transparency,* Ch. 18; *Language Lab* CD-ROM, Parts of Speech; *On-Line Exercise Bank,* Section 18.1
DAY 2	**Adverbs** Students cover concepts and usage of adverbs as determined by Diagnostic Test (pp. 390–395).	**Teaching Resources** *Grammar Exercise Workbook,* pp. 27–32; *Grammar Exercises Answers on Transparency,* Ch. 18; *Language Lab* CD-ROM, Parts of Speech; *On-Line Exercise Bank,* Section 18.2
DAY 3	**Review and Assess** Students review chapter and demonstrate mastery of use of adjectives and adverbs (pp. 396–399).	**Teaching Resources** *Formal Assessment,* Ch. 18; *Grammar Exercises Answers on Transparency,* Ch. 18; *On-Line Exercise Bank,* Section 18

Options for Adapting Lesson Plans

HOMEWORK

Have students complete any section of the chapter for homework.

FEATURES

Extend coverage with the Grammar in Literature feature (pp. 381, 391), and the Standardized Test Preparation Workshop (p. 398).

TECHNOLOGY

Students can use the On-Line Exercise Bank to complete the exercises on computer. The Auto Check feature will grade their work.

INTEGRATED SKILLS COVERAGE

Grammar in Literature
SE pp. 381, 391

Reading
Responding to Literature, SE p. 381
Find It In Your Reading, SE pp. 388, 389, 395

Writing
Find It In Your Writing, SE pp. 388, 389, 395
Writing Application, SE pp. 389, 395, 397

Spelling
Integrating Spelling Skills ATE 394

Viewing and Representing
Critical Viewing, SE pp. 378, 381, 383, 385, 386, 390, 392

ASSESSMENT SUPPORT

Standardized Test Preparation SE p. 398; ATE pp. 385, 392
Standardized Test Preparation Workbook, pp. 35–36
Formal Assessment, Ch. 18

MEETING INDIVIDUAL NEEDS

Less Advanced Students See Ongoing Assessments ATE pp. 383, 384, 386, 387, 391, 393
ESL Students ATE p. 383
More Advanced Students ATE p. 394
Musical Learners ATE p. 381
Gifted/Talented Students ATE p. 384

BLOCK SCHEDULING

Pacing Sugestions
For 90-minute Blocks
• Administer the Diagnostic Test to students to determine instructional coverage.
• Have students complete the necessary exercises in class. Use the Hands-on Grammar activity to provide a change of pace.

Resources for Varying Instruction
• *Language Lab* **CD-ROM** If your students have access to hardware, a 90-minute block provides an ideal opportunity for students to work on computer.

Professional Development Support
• *How to manage Instruction in the Block* This teaching Resource provides management and activity suggestions.

MEDIA AND TECHNOLOGY

For the Student
• *Language Lab* **CD-ROM**, Parts of Speech
• *On-Line Exercise Bank,* Ch. 18

For the Teacher
• *Resource Pro* **CD-ROM**

WRITING AND GRAMMAR WEB SITE

The Interactive Writing and Grammar Website provides a wide array of support for students, teachers, and parents. Grammar support includes:

• *On-Line Exercise Bank* with Auto Check scoring
• Diagnostic and assessment support

phwg.phschool.com

LITERATURE CONNECTIONS

Grammar in Literature selections from *Prentice Hall Literature: Timeless Voices, Timeless Themes,* Gold:
from "The Long and Winding Road," John Lennon and Paul McCartney, SE p. 381
from "Tonight," Leonard Bernstein and Stephen Sondheim, SE p. 391

Lesson Objectives

1. To recognize adjectives and understand how they modify nouns and pronouns.
2. To distinguish between definite and indefinite articles.
3. To recognize adverbs and understand how they modify, verbs, adjectives, and adverbs.
4. To distinguish between adjectives and adverbs.
5. To use adjectives and adverbs appropriately to make writing vivid or precise.

Critical Viewing

Evaluate Students may agree that the liner's size, graceful lines, sleek appearance, and power all suggest majesty and grandeur.

Chapter 18 Adjectives and Adverbs

▲ Critical Viewing
Ocean liners like this one are often described as "majestic" or "grand." Do you think these adjectives are fitting? Why? **[Evaluate]**

Often a noun cannot express the exact meaning you have in mind. Imagine, for example, that a relative of a missing person reports, "She sailed off in a boat yesterday." "What kind of boat?" a Coast Guard officer might ask. If the relative were to answer, "She sailed off in a *white two-masted sailing* boat," the officer would have a clearer picture of the boat. Words that describe or explain nouns are called *adjectives*.

Adverbs, another part of speech, work in much the same way except that they describe or explain verbs, adjectives, and other adverbs. For example, the officer might have asked the relative, "Did the boat sail *north* or *south*?" These words are used as *adverbs*.

This chapter will examine both adjectives and adverbs. Together, these two parts of speech are known as *modifiers*. Used carefully, they can clarify and enliven your sentences.

☑ ONGOING ASSESSMENT: Diagnose

If students miss more than one item in each category, direct them to the relevant pages of the text and assign exercises for practice and review.

Adjectives and Adverbs	Diagnostic Test Items	Teach	Practice	Section Review	Chapter Review
Skill Check A					
Adjectives	A 1–5	pp. 380–382	Ex. 1–3	Ex. 11–12	Ex. 31
Skill Check B					
Articles	B 6–10	pp. 382–383	Ex. 4	Ex. 11, 13	Ex. 32
Types of Adjectives	B 6–10	pp. 384–388	Ex. 5–10	Ex. 13–15	Ex. 32–34

Diagnostic Test

Directions: Write all answers on a separate sheet of paper.

Skill Check A. List the adjectives, but not the articles, in these sentences.

1. Sir Samuel Cunard was a successful merchant and whaling-fleet owner.
2. The British shipowner sailed from Canada to England in 1838.
3. With several merchants, he formed a British and North American shipping company.
4. Later, this growing steamship company became known as the Cunard Line, Ltd.
5. The company dispatched the first steamship in 1840.

Skill Check B. Identify the underlined word as either a *definite* or *indefinite article*, or as a *demonstrative, interrogative, indefinite, compound,* or *proper adjective.*

6. Which ship was called <u>the</u> Britannia?
7. Its <u>fourteen-day</u>, eight-hour voyage from Liverpool to Boston was one of <u>many</u> milestones.
8. It marked the beginning of regular <u>steamship</u> service across the Atlantic.
9. The Britannia was followed across the ocean by <u>Cunard's</u> first iron ship, the Persia, in 1855.
10. In 1862, Cunard sailed his first <u>screw-propelled</u> ship, the China.

Skill Check C. List the adverbs in these sentences.

11. Public demand for transcontinental rail connections was originally inspired by two American statesmen.
12. This demand was further increased by the California Gold Rush of 1849.
13. The need for transcontinental lines was felt so urgently that construction began during the extremely costly Civil War.
14. The Union Pacific rails began in Omaha, Nebraska, and stretched westward.
15. The Central Pacific rails began in Sacramento, California, and later stretched eastward.

Skill Check D. Identify the underlined word as either an *adverb* or an *adjective.* If it is an adverb, identify the word it modifies as well as the part of speech of that word.

16. The <u>two</u> rails were joined at Promontory, Utah, in 1869.
17. Thus, the coast-to-coast connection for trains was <u>finally</u> completed.
18. It was <u>now</u> possible to cross the country in a matter of weeks instead of months.
19. Migration west was <u>greatly</u> accelerated by the transcontinental railroad.
20. Western cities <u>very</u> <u>soon</u> began to flourish due to the swifter arrival of eastern supplies.

Adjectives and Adverbs • 379

Write the following sentence on the board and ask students what is wrong with it:

The pretty walked to the park.

Students should recognize that a noun is missing after *pretty*. Explain to students that pretty is an *adjective*—a word that describes, or modifies, a noun. Without the noun, the reader cannot tell what is pretty.

Activate Prior Knowledge

Show students a work of fine art. (You may wish to select an art transparency from Writing Support Transparencies.) Ask students to describe the image, writing down any adjectives they use. Explain that these descriptive words are adjectives that provide additional details.

TEACH

Step-by-Step Teaching Guide

The Process of Modification

1. Point out the word *modify*. Explain that an adjective acts like the focusing adjustment on a camera lens. The noun *bread* creates an out-of-focus picture in a reader's mind. Adjectives such as *crusty* and *fresh* bring the image of the bread into focus by describing its texture and condition.

2. Emphasize that adjectives can modify, or describe, only nouns and pronouns. Students will learn about adverbs later in this chapter.

Answer Key

Exercise 1

Sample answers are shown.

WHAT KIND?
<u>blue</u> boat <u>gold</u> watch <u>tired</u> teacher
<u>black</u> hair <u>hot</u> weather

WHICH ONE?
<u>these</u> grapes <u>first</u> door
<u>last</u> train <u>any</u> choice <u>those</u> girls

HOW MANY?
<u>nine</u> answers <u>few</u> choices <u>three</u> boys
<u>several</u> questions <u>both</u> friends

HOW MUCH?
<u>little</u> time <u>no</u> food <u>ample</u> supplies
<u>more</u> space <u>enough</u> rain

Section 18.1

Adjectives

Whenever you are asked to describe something—your favorite animal, your best friend, or the longest trip you ever took—you are likely to give an answer that is filled with *adjectives*.

KEY CONCEPT An **adjective** is a word used to describe a noun or pronoun or to give a noun or pronoun a more specific meaning. ■

The process by which an adjective describes a word or makes it more specific is called *modification*.

The Process of Modification

To *modify* means to "change slightly." An adjective modifies meaning by answering any of four questions about a noun or pronoun.

KEY CONCEPT Adjectives answer the question *What kind? Which one? How many?* or *How much?* about the nouns and pronouns they modify. ■

The following are adjectives answering each of these questions:

What Kind?	
red boat	*silver* jewelry
sick passenger	*cool* water

Which One?	
third chance	*any* piece
this train	*those* apples

How Many?	
six cars	*several* reasons
both answers	*few* letters

How Much?	
enough space	*more* energy
no rain	*little* effort

Exercise 1 Coming Up With Examples of Adjectives
Come up with five additional adjective-noun pairs, answering each of the questions in the chart above.

Theme: Travel

In this section, you will learn about adjectives. The examples and exercises in this section are about various types of travel.

Cross-Curricular Connection: Social Studies

More Practice

Language Lab CD-ROM
• Parts-of-Speech lesson
On-line Exercise Bank
• Section 18.1
Grammar Exercise Workbook
• pp. 21–22

⏱ TIME AND RESOURCE MANAGER

Resources
Print: Grammar Exercise Workbook, pp. 21–26; Hands-on Grammar Activity Book, Ch. 18
Technology: Language Lab CD-ROM, Parts of Speech; On-Line Exercise Bank, Section 18.1

In-Depth Coverage	Accelerated Pace
• Work through all key concepts, pp. 380–387.	• Assign pp. 380–387 for independent student review.
• Assign and review Exercises 1–10.	• Assign Review Exercises 11 and 13.
• Read and discuss Grammar in Literature, p. 381.	

GRAMMAR IN LITERATURE

from The Long and Winding Road
John Lennon and Paul McCartney

Notice how the highlighted adjectives long, winding, wild, *and* windy *describe the road and the night in the song lyrics that follow. They answer the question* What kind?

The *long* and *winding* road that leads to your door,

Will never disappear,

I've seen that road before

It always leads me here,

Leads me to your door.

The *wild* and *windy* night the rain washed away,

Has left a pool of tears crying for the day.

▲ Critical Viewing
What three adjectives would you use to give a vivid description of the light in this photograph? **[Describe]**

An adjective usually comes before the noun it modifies. It may, however, come after the noun.

BEFORE THE NOUN: The *sick* child lay in bed.

AFTER THE NOUN: The child, *sick* with fever, lay in bed.

An adjective generally comes after a pronoun it modifies, usually directly after a linking verb such as *is, was, look,* or *seemed.* It may, however, come before the pronoun.

AFTER THE PRONOUN: She was *sick* for a week.

BEFORE THE PRONOUN: *Sick* in bed, he was very bored.

Adjectives • 381

Grammar in Literature

1. Copy this excerpt on the board, omitting the boldfaced adjectives. Have students read this edited version and discuss the impression it makes on them. Which version do they prefer? Why?

2. Ask students if they can find any other words in this excerpt that answer the questions *What kind? Which one? How much?* or *How many?* If students still don't know the answer, point out the words *the, that,* and *a.* Tell students that these are special categories of adjectives they will study in the next few pages of this chapter.

More About the Writers

The Beatles were a 1960's rock band consisting of British musicians John Lennon, Paul McCartney, George Harrison, and Ringo Starr. Lennon and McCartney wrote most of the band's material.

Responding to Literature

The complete text of "The Long and Winding Road" may be found in *Prentice Hall Literature: Timeless Voices, Timeless Themes,* p. 822. Have students identify all the adjectives (besides articles) in the song and list the question each one answers.

Critical Viewing

Describe Students may suggest such adjectives as *glowing, hazy, mysterious.*

Customize for
Musical Learners

Have students locate and listen to a few Beatles songs. You might recommend "Penny Lane," "Lucy in the Sky with Diamonds," and "She's Leaving Home." Have students analyze the use of adjectives in these songs. How many are there? Do students think there should be more? Fewer? Why? What effect do the adjectives have on the listeners?

Exercise 2

1. small workboats, what kind; early colonial times, what kind
2. first pleasure schooner, which one, what kind
3. large, luxurious yacht, what kind
4. American yacht clubs, what kind
5. six members, how many; America's first racing yacht, which one, what kind

Exercise 3

Revisions will vary.

1. 100-foot schooner
2. its fine lines; slimmer bow, yacht designs
3. its victory, international regatta, American yachting
4. America's Cup trophy, most famous prize, yacht racing
5. racing fleets, one-design crafts, rigorous specifications

Step-by-Step Teaching Guide

Articles

1. Ask students to volunteer definitions of the word *definite*. ("Sure"; "certain"; "fixed") Point out that *indefinite* means the opposite. *The* is called a definite article because it makes the reader sure of exactly which person, place, or thing it refers to. *A* and *an* are indefinite articles because they may refer to any one of a number of people, places, or things.

2. Have volunteers read aloud the examples in the chart at the top of page 383, so that all students can hear the difference in the sounds at the beginning of words. Give students several more words and have them call out *a* or *an* as the appropriate indefinite article for each. If students make mistakes, ask them to explain their answers. This practice will help them judge when to use each article.

18.1

> **Exercise 2** Identifying Adjectives and the Words They **Modify** Identify each adjective in the following sentences. Then, indicate the word each adjective modifies and the question that it answers (see the chart on page 382).
>
> 1. <u>Small</u> work boats were sailed extensively for pleasure in <u>early colonial</u> times.
> 2. The <u>first</u> <u>pleasure</u> schooner was built in 1816.
> 3. It was built specifically as a <u>large</u>, <u>luxurious</u> yacht.
> 4. <u>American</u> <u>yacht</u> clubs started around the 1840's.
> 5. <u>Six</u> members of the New York Yacht Club financed <u>America's</u> <u>first</u> <u>racing</u> yacht.

> **Exercise 3** Revising Adjective Placement In the paragraph below, identify all of the adjectives and the words they modify. Then, revise the paragraph, changing the placement of at least three adjectives.
>
> (1) The <u>100-foot</u> schooner *America* was finished in 1851. (2) Its fine lines and <u>slimmer</u> bow changed <u>yacht</u> designs. (3) Its victory in an <u>international</u> regatta in 1851 stimulated <u>American</u> yachting. (4) The <u>America's</u> <u>Cup</u> trophy, named for the *America*, became the most famous prize in <u>yacht</u> racing. (5) Competition for the America's Cup continues today with <u>racing</u> fleets of <u>one-design</u> crafts, each manufactured to meet <u>rigorous</u> specifications.

Articles

Three adjectives—*the*, *a*, and *an*—are called *articles*. *The* is called the *definite article*, *a* and *an* are called *indefinite articles*.

> **KEY CONCEPTS** The **definite article,** *the*, indicates that the noun it modifies refers to a specific person, place, or thing. The **indefinite articles,** *a* and *an*, indicate that the nouns they modify refer to any one of a class of people, places, or things. ■

Look at the examples below:

DEFINITE: *The* catcher wore *the* face mask.

IINDEFINITE: Give me *an* essay that you think I would enjoy.

Notice that *an* is used before a vowel sound; *a* is used before a consonant sound. The emphasis is on the sound, not the letter. The letter *h* is a consonant, but it may sound like a vowel. *O* and *u* are vowels, but they may sound like consonants.

> **More Practice**
>
> Language Lab CD-ROM
> • Parts-of-Speech lesson
> On-line Exercise Bank
> • Section 18.1
> Grammar Exercise Workbook
> • pp. 21–22

Consonant Sounds	Vowel Sounds
a *baseball*	an *apple*
a *history* lesson (*h* sound)	an *honest* man (no *h* sound)
a *one*-horse town (*w* sound)	an *only* child (*o* sound)
a *union* (*y* sound)	an *ugly* hat (*u* sound)

Exercise 4 **Completing Sentences With Definite and Indefinite Articles** Write the article needed to complete each sentence.

EXAMPLE: In (definite) 1800's, trains became popular modes of transportation.
ANSWER: the

1. (definite) first passenger train cars were 15 feet long and 17 feet wide.
2. They were built like (indefinite) stagecoach with railroad wheels.
3. Later, six wheels were placed on (definite) passenger cars.
4. Today, there are (indefinite) variety of passenger cars.
5. (definite) typical passenger car has (indefinite) aisle with seats on either side.

Nouns Used as Adjectives

Articles and descriptive words—such as *quick, red,* or *new*—are not the only kinds of words that can act as adjectives. In fact, nouns themselves may sometimes be used as adjectives before other nouns.

KEY CONCEPT A noun used as an adjective answers the question *What kind?* or *Which one?* about a noun that follows it. ∎

EXAMPLES: guitar — *guitar* music (*What kind* of music?)
evening — *evening* meal (*Which* meal?)

▼ Critical Viewing What adjectives could you use to describe a train that moves quickly? **[Analyze]**

💻 **Internet Tip**

Nouns used as adjectives make great search words and help to specify the information wanted. For example, just typing in *flares* will produce a variety of sites on flares. By typing in *road flares*, you will find only sites with that specific type of flare.

Adjectives • 383

ONGOING ASSESSMENT: Monitor and Reinforce

If students miss more than two items in Exercises 1–4, refer them to the following for additional practice.

In the Textbook	Print Resources	Technology
Section Review, Ex. 11, p. 389	Grammar Exercise Workbook, pp. 21–22	Language Lab CD-ROM, Parts of Speech; On-Line Exercise Bank, Section 18.1

Answer Key

Exercise 5
1. road, state
2. family, state
3. family
4. highway, visitor
5. road, travel

Exercise 6
Answers will vary.

Step-by-Step Teaching Guide

Proper Adjectives

1. Briefly review proper nouns with students. Personal names of people and places are proper nouns. So are months of the year (April), days of the week (Sunday), brand names (Kleenex), and certain periods in history (Reformation). Explain that the adjectival forms of these nouns are called *proper adjectives.*

2. Students can often recognize proper adjectives by the ending *-an* or *-ian.* Point to the examples on the page such as *Jeffersonian* and *Mexican* and challenge students to suggest others. (Possible examples: Egyptian, Elizabethan, Italian, Cambodian) Warn students that there are many proper adjectives that do not take these endings.

Customize for
Gifted/Talented Students

Have students write the letters *A* to *Z* down the left side of a sheet of paper. Challenge them to write a proper noun for each letter, and then its adjective form. As a last resort, students can use a dictionary for the hard letters.

> **Exercise 5** Identifying Nouns Used as Adjectives Write the noun or nouns that are used as adjectives in each sentence. Make sure each one modifies another noun.

(1) For a fun vacation, some families plan road trips to state monuments and historic sites. (2) This type of family vacation requires a careful review of state maps to plan a route that covers restaurants, motels, and the sites themselves.

(3) The first step is for family members to choose a destination. (4) Next, several different highway routes should be highlighted and studied for the best stops and visitor attractions. (5) Once a route is chosen, the road miles should be calculated, the travel time should be estimated, and a detailed itinerary should be made.

> **Exercise 6** Writing Sentences With Nouns Used as Adjectives Write sentences in which you use each of the following nouns as adjectives.

1. plane	3. beach	5. ground
2. automobile	4. airport	

Proper and Compound Adjectives

In addition to the types of adjectives already mentioned, there are *proper* and *compound* adjectives.

Proper Adjectives *Proper adjectives* can be simply proper nouns. Others are formed from proper nouns.

> **KEY CONCEPT** A **proper adjective** is a proper noun used as an adjective or an adjective formed from a proper noun. ∎

When proper nouns are used as adjectives, the form of the proper noun is not changed.

However, when an adjective is formed from a proper noun, the form of the proper noun is changed, as shown below.

EXAMPLES:	Alcott	*Alcott* novel (*What kind* of novel?)
	Chicago	*Chicago* storm (*What kind* of storm?)

EXAMPLES:	Jefferson	*Jeffersonian* democracy (*What kind* of democracy?)
	Mexico	*Mexican* art (*What kind* of art?)

Proper adjectives generally begin with a capital letter.

384 • Adjectives and Adverbs

More Practice

Language Lab
CD-ROM
• Parts-of-Speech lesson
On-line
Exercise Bank
• Section 18.1
Grammar Exercise
Workbook
• pp. 21–24

⚙ Grammar and Style Tip

Possessive nouns can act as adjectives. *England's,* for instance, may be considered a proper adjective when it shows ownership: *England's* waterways.

⏱ TIME SAVERS!

Answers on Transparency
Use the Grammar Exercises on Transparencies for Chapter 18 to have students correct their own or one another's exercises.

On-Line Exercise Bank
Have students complete the exercises on computer. The Auto Check feature will grade their work for you!

☑ ONGOING ASSESSMENT: Monitor and Reinforce

If students miss more than two items in Exercises 5–8, refer them to the following for additional practice.

In the Textbook	Print Resources	Technology
Section Review, Ex. 11–13, p. 389	Grammar Exercise Workbook, pp. 23–24	Language Lab CD-ROM, Parts of Speech; On-Line Exercise Bank, Section 18.1

Compound Adjectives Adjectives made up of more than one word are called *compound adjectives*.

▶ **KEY CONCEPT** A **compound adjective** is an adjective that is made up of more than one word. ■

Compound adjectives are usually written as hyphenated words. In a few cases, they are written as combined words. Consult a dictionary whenever you are in doubt about the spelling of a compound adjective.

EXAMPLES: *far-off* land   *farsighted* leader
hard-shell crabs   *hardhearted* neighbor

▶ **Exercise 7** Identifying Proper and Compound Adjectives
Write the proper and compound adjectives in each sentence.
(1) Late in 1577, Francis Drake left England to attempt a three-year circumnavigation of the globe. (2) After crossing the Atlantic Ocean, Drake sailed down the South American coast. (3) Drake lightened the expedition by disposing of two unfit ships and one high-spirited gentleman.
(4) Drake then sailed quickly through the Straits of Magellan and ran into a Pacific storm that sank one ship. (5) For the next five and a half months, his crew raided Spanish settlements at will, committing very little violence but taking many treasures.

▶ **Exercise 8** Revising to Include Proper and Compound Adjectives Revise the following paragraph so that it consists of sentences that each contain proper or compound adjectives.
(1) This summer, we took our vacation in London. (2) Our flight there took six hours. (3) Even though we traveled all night, our first day was packed with excitement. (4) We visited Buckingham Palace and ate in a restaurant where we sampled various foods that England has to offer. (5) In the days that followed, we visited famous sites throughout London.

▼ **Critical Viewing**
Describe this picture by telling what kind of ship it is, how many masts it has, how much wind there is, and what kind of ocean it is. What adjectives did you use in your description? **[Describe]**

Adjectives • **385**

Step-by-Step Teaching Guide

Compound Adjectives

1. Review compound words with students. Ask what all compound words have in common. (They are all made up of two words.) Explain that compound adjectives share this quality too.

2. Point out that many compound adjectives are hyphenated. Direct students' attention to some of the examples on the page. The hyphen shows that the two adjectives are linked and that together they modify the following noun.

3. Point out that every compound adjective consists of two adjectives, with the first one modifying the second and the combination modifying the noun.

      red-haired girl

      hot-fudge sundae

   Red describes the girl's hair, not the girl; *hot* describes the fudge, not the sundae. *Red-haired* describes the girl; *hot-fudge* describes the sundae.

Answer Key

▶ **Exercise 7**

1. three-year
2. South American
3. high-spirited
4. Pacific
5. Spanish

▶ **Exercise 8**

Answers will vary. Make sure that student sentences contain proper or compound adjectives.

Critical Viewing

Describe Students may suggest such adjectives as a *Spanish* ship, *three* masts, *westerly* wind, *vast* ocean.

✎ STANDARDIZED TEST PREPARATION WORKSHOP

Grammar and Usage Many tests require students to identify parts of speech in sentences. Distinguishing between adverbs and adjectives is a skill assessed using these sentences. Write the following item on the chalkboard:

What he liked the most about her was her <u>curly</u> *hair.*

What part of speech is the underlined word?

A noun   C adjective
B verb   D adverb

The correct answer is item **C**. *Curly* modifies the noun *hair* by answering the question *What kind?* Just because it ends in *-ly* does not make it an adverb.

Possessive Pronouns as Adjectives

1. Review pronouns. Have students list as many pronouns as they can on the chalkboard. Explain that just like nouns, pronouns can be used as adjectives. Demonstrate with a few phrases on the chalkboard, such as *my homework, its head,* and *her birthday.*

2. Ask students to define the word *possessive.* (showing ownership) Explain that possessive pronouns are considered adjectives because they show who or what a noun belongs to. *My homework* belongs to *me. Its head* belongs to *it.* Possessive nouns function the same way. *Seymour's spider* belongs to *Seymour.*

3. Review possessive nouns with students. Ask how to recognize a possessive noun. (It ends in either *'s* or *s'.*) Point out that no possessive pronoun has an apostrophe. Call attention to the spelling tip in the margin of page 11. Remembering that possessive pronouns have no apostrophes will help students avoid making mistakes with *it's* and *its.*

Answer Key

Exercise 9

1. his advice
2. your course
3. her friends'
4. Their boat
5. Our goal

Exercise 10 *(page 387)*

1. Each (indefinite)
2. Some (indefinite)
3. Those (demonstrative)
4. Many (indefinite)
5. What (interrogative)

Critical Viewing

Describe Students may suggest pronouns such as *its* sails or *this* craft.

18.1

Pronouns Used as Adjectives

The previous section presented descriptive adjectives, articles, nouns used as adjectives, proper adjectives, and compound adjectives. This section will discuss pronouns that can be used as adjectives.

▶ **KEY CONCEPT** A personal pronoun that can be used as an adjective answers the question *Which one?* about a noun that follows it. ∎

Possessive Pronouns as Adjectives Seven of the personal pronouns can be considered both pronouns and adjectives. *My, your, his, her, its, our,* and *their* can be thought of as pronouns because they have antecedents. They can also be thought of as adjectives because they modify nouns by answering the question *Which one?*

            antecedent   word modified
EXAMPLE: My daughter *Ellen* left *her* new *backpack* at school.

▶ **Exercise 9** Recognizing Personal Pronouns That Act as Adjectives Write the possessive pronouns or adjectives in each of the following sentences, followed by the word it modifies.

EXAMPLE: Yacht owners sail their boats long distances.
ANSWER: their boats

1. Have you asked a professional captain for his advice?
2. A professional can help you chart your course.
3. My sister enjoyed her friends' boat.
4. Their boat is large and has eight cabins.
5. Our goal is to have a small boat someday.

▶ **More Practice**

Language Lab
CD-ROM
• Parts-of-Speech lesson
On-line
Exercise Bank
• Section 18.1
Grammar Exercise
Workbook
• pp. 25–26

◀ Critical Viewing
What pronouns acting as adjectives might you use in describing this photograph? **[Describe]**

386 • Adjectives and Adverbs

☑ **ONGOING ASSESSMENT: Monitor and Reinforce**

If students have difficulty with Exercises 9–10, refer them to the following for additional practice.

In the Textbook	Print Resources	Technology
Section Review, Ex. 14–15, p. 389	Grammar Exercise Workbook, pp. 25–26	Language Lab CD-ROM, Parts of Speech; On-Line Exercise Bank, Section 18.1

▶ **KEY CONCEPT** A demonstrative, interrogative, or indefinite pronoun becomes an adjective if it answers the question *Which one? How many?* or *How much?* about a noun that follows it. ■

Demonstrative Adjectives All four of the demonstrative pronouns—*this, that, these,* and *those*—can be used as adjectives. When demonstrative pronouns are used as adjectives, they are called *demonstrative adjectives*. Remember that *demonstrate* means "point out."

PRONOUN: She sailed <u>these</u>.

ADJECTIVE: She sailed <u>these</u> boats.

Interrogative Adjectives Only three of the interrogative pronouns—*which, what,* and *whose*—can be used as adjectives. When used as adjectives, they are called *interrogative adjectives*. Remember that *interrogate* means "ask."

PRONOUN: *Which* did she see?
ADJECTIVE: *Which* ship did she see?

Indefinite Adjectives Many of the indefinite pronouns can also be used as adjectives. When used as adjectives, they are called *indefinite adjectives*. The chart below shows which ones can be used to modify singular nouns and which ones can be used to modify plural nouns.

EXAMPLES: *Each* boat had *several* sails.

They bought *more* rigging.

▶ **Exercise 10** Recognizing Other Pronouns Used as Adjectives Write the pronouns used as adjectives. Label each *demonstrative, interrogative, indefinite,* or *possessive*.

EXAMPLE: This is a safe sailing vessel.
ANSWER: This (demonstrative)

1. Each stateroom has a private breakfast room.
2. Some cruise ships stop in the Bahamas.
3. Those ships depart often from east-coast ports.
4. Many sail to Central and South America.
5. What kind of cruise would you like to take?

Adjectives • 387

💡 Spelling Tip

Its should not be confused with *it's*. *Its* is a possessive adjective: There is the dog's bowl and *its* bone. *It's* is a contraction of *it is* or *it has*: It's (*it is*) time for dinner. It's (*it has*) been a long day.

Step-by-Step Teaching Guide

Demonstrative Adjectives

1. Review the demonstrative pronouns with students. Write a few sample sentence pairs such as *I watched the gulls fly away. I watched those gulls fly away.* on the chalkboard and ask students to explain the difference in meaning. (Students should see that *those gulls* is more definite than *the gulls. Those* must refer to a very specific group of birds.)

2. When students are not sure if a demonstrative pronoun is being used as an adjective, have them look for a word it modifies. If it describes a noun or pronoun, then they know it is being used as an adjective.

Step-by-Step Teaching Guide

Interrogative Adjectives

1. Ask students what they think the word *interrogative* means. Explain that to interrogate is to question. Therefore, interrogative adjectives are question words.

2. When in doubt about how an interrogative pronoun is being used, students can rewrite the question in which it appears as a statement, then look for a noun or pronoun that *which, what,* or *whose* modifies. If they can find such a word, then they know the pronoun is being used as an adjective.

Step-by-Step Teaching Guide

Indefinite Adjectives

Discuss why plural indefinite adjectives can modify only plural nouns, and singular adjectives can modify only singular nouns. Help students see that *both, few, many,* and *several* all mean "more than one."

☑ ONGOING ASSESSMENT: Prerequisite Skills

If students have difficulty with demonstrative and interrogative adjectives, you may find it necessary to review the following to assure coverage of prerequisite knowledge.

In the Textbook	Print Resources	Technology
Nouns and Pronouns, pp. 346–355	Grammar Exercise Workbook, pp. 5–12	Language Lab CD-ROM, Nouns and Pronouns; On-Line Exercise Bank, Section 16.2

Adverb and Adjective Wheel

Teaching Resources: Hands-on Grammar Activity Book, Chapter 18

1. Have students refer to their Hands-on Grammar activity books, or give them copies of the relevant pages for this activity.

2. Have students follow the directions to prepare their wheels.

3. For variation, have students pair up and exchange their noun and verb wheels. Make sure that they keep their own "adjective or adverb" rectangle.

Find It in Your Reading

You may wish to suggest a text recently read in class.

Find It in Your Writing

Have students choose a sample of their own writing which dealt with description.

Hands-on Grammar

18.1

Adverb and Adjective Wheel

Cut two large equal-sized circles out of light-colored construction paper. Then, cut out two rectangles—one long and thin and one with a width that nearly matches the diameter of the circles.

Next, cut three slits out of the larger rectangle. The slits should be equally spaced apart, as shown in the diagram. Write verbs on one circle and nouns on the other circle. Write words that can function as either adjectives or adverbs on the thin rectangle, and write on the larger rectangle the words shown on the diagram.

Finally, use paper fasteners to attach the circles to the large rectangles. Do it so that the verbs and nouns show through the slits in the rectangle. Use tape and another piece of construction paper to attach the narrow rectangle to the other rectangle that you slide the narrow rectangle up and down.

With a group of classmates, experiment with different combinations of words. Notice how the words in the center can be used to modify either verbs or nouns and that the word being modified dictates the part of speech assumed by the modifier.

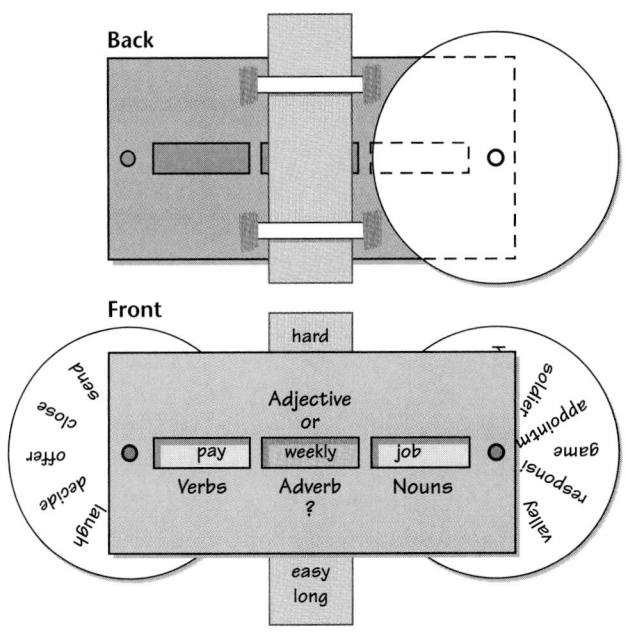

Find It in Your Reading Try this activitiy with words from one of your favorite literature selections.

Find It in Your Writing Try this activitiy with words from a piece of your own writing.

388 • Adjectives and Adverbs

☑ ONGOING ASSESSMENT: Assess Mastery

Use the following resources to assess students' mastery of adjectives.

In the Textbook	Technology
Chapter Review, Ex. 31–34, pp. 396–397 Standardized Test Preparation Workshop, pp. 398–399	Language Lab CD-ROM, Parts of Speech; On-Line Exercise Bank, Section 18.1

Section 18.1 Section Review

GRAMMAR EXERCISES 11–18

Exercise 11 Identifying Adjectives

List all adjectives, including articles, in the following sentences.

1. The wagon used by American pioneers was called the Prairie Schooner.
2. It was a common farm wagon.
3. The canvas top was supported by horseshoe-shaped wooden arches.
4. It had oval-shaped openings.
5. These openings allowed air to enter.

Exercise 12 Distinguishing Between Adjectives and Nouns

Identify each underlined word as an adjective or a noun used as an adjective.

1. recreational area
2. evening meal
3. fresh meat
4. wagon train
5. guitar music

Exercise 13 Identifying and Using Proper, Compound, Definite, and Indefinite Adjectives

Label each adjective proper, compound, definite, or indefinite. Then, use each one in a sentence.

stump-filled	muddy	American
the	underway	some
one-year-old	down	surprising
special	an	Atlantic
Jeffersonian	Irish	farsighted

Exercise 14 Identify Pronouns Used as Adjectives

Decide whether the underlined words, function as adjectives, pronouns, or both.

1. Have you heard of that Greek myth about Demeter and Persephone?
2. Demeter was Persephone's mother, and both were beautiful goddesses.
3. They lived on Mount Olympus with other gods and goddesses.
4. Demeter loved Persephone so dearly that she spent each second of every day with her.
5. Demeter, the goddess of the harvest, performed these duties with Persephone at her side.

Exercise 15 Identifying Possessive, Demonstrative, Interrogative, and Indefinite Adjectives

Copy the headings below. Place the words that follow in the correct category.

Demonstrative	Interrogative	Indefinite
whose	few	this	another
those	any	which	some

Exercise 16 Find It in Your Reading

Reread "The Long and Winding Road" on page 381. Write down and label all indefinite, demonstrative, interrogative, and possessive adjectives in the passage.

Exercise 17 Find It in Your Writing

Choose a paragraph from your portfolio. Underline the demonstrative adjectives, circle indefinite adjectives, and draw a box around interrogative adjectives.

Exercise 18 Writing Application

Imagine that you are traveling though the wilderness on the Oregon Trail. Write a week's worth of journal entries. In each day's entry, include at least one proper adjective, one compound adjective, and one noun used as an adjective.

Section Review • 389

Answer Key

Exercise 11

1. The, American
2. a, common, farm
3. The, canvas, horseshoe-shaped, wooden
4. oval-shaped
5. These

Exercise 12

1. adjective
2. noun
3. adjective
4. noun
5. noun

Exercise 13

stump-filled—compound adjective
the—definite article
one-year-old—compound adjective
special—adjective
Jeffersonian—proper adjective
muddy—adjective
some—indefinite adjective
down—adjective
an—indefinite article
Irish—proper adjective
American—proper adjective
underway—compound adjective
surprising—adjective
Atlantic—proper adjective
farsighted—compound adjective

Exercise 14

1. adjective
2. pronoun
3. adjective
4. adjective
5. adjective

continued

Answer Key continued

Exercise 15

Demonstrative: this, those
Interrogative: whose, which
Indefinite: few, another, any, some

Exercise 16

Find It in Your Reading
Indefinite: none
Demonstrative: that
Interrogative: none
Possessive: your, your

Exercise 17

Find It in Your Writing
If any category is blank, students can write a sentence that uses an adjective in that way.

Exercise 18

Writing Application
Challenge students to use at least one proper adjective, one indefinite adjective, two pronouns used as adjectives, a compound adjective, and two nouns used as adjectives.

Interest GRABBER Write several verbs on the chalkboard, such as *ate, overslept, painted*. Ask students to imagine people acting out these verbs. Then ask questions such as *Ate how? Overslept when? Painted in what manner?* (Possible responses: ate hungrily; overslept yesterday; painted neatly) Explain that the answers to these questions about verbs are called adverbs.

Activate Prior Knowledge

Ask students to list the parts of speech that adjectives modify. (nouns and pronouns) Have them list any other parts of speech they can think of. (verbs, adjectives, adverbs) Ask whether anyone knows the name of a word that can modify any of these three parts of speech. Introduce the word *adverb*.

TEACH

Step-by-Step Teaching Guide

Adverbs Modifying Verbs

1. Discuss the four questions that adverbs answer about verbs. Remind students of the questions adjectives answered.

2. Students probably recognize adverbs by the *-ly* suffix. Discuss *early* and *only*, which are not made from adjectives plus a suffix. Both can be used as an adjective or adverb.

   The *early* bird catches the worm. (adjective)

   The bus arrived *early*. (adverb)

   Hank is an *only* child. (adjective)

   Lois ate *only* one cupcake. (adverb)

Critical Viewing

Analyze Students may say that the moon shines brightly when it is full. This answer tells in what way the moon is shining.

Answer Key

Exercise 19

Responses will vary.

Section 18.2 *Adverbs*

Adverbs add meaning to three parts of speech:

> **KEY CONCEPT** An **adverb** is a word that modifies a verb, an adjective, or another adverb. ■

Adverbs Modifying Verbs

Adverbs can add meaning to verbs in many different ways:

> **KEY CONCEPT** An adverb modifying a verb answers the questions *Where? When? In what way?* or *To what extent?* ■

Adverbs can also be placed in many different positions. As shown in the chart, they can come after or before a verb or verb phrase or even between the words in a verb phrase.

ADVERBS MODIFYING VERBS

Where?	
fell *below*	move *aside*
went *there*	climbs *down*

When?	
arrived *today*	left *early*
should have spoken *before*	begins *then*

In What Way?	
happily *ran*	will end *abruptly*
danced *awkwardly*	had been sung *loudly*

To What Extent?	
partly understands	wash *completely*
have *not* completed	*hardly* would have known

Exercise 19 Coming Up With Examples of Adverbs Come up with five additional adverb/verb pairs answering each of the questions in the chart.

390 • Adjectives and Adverbs

Theme: The Night Sky

In this section, you will learn about adverbs. The examples and exercises in this section are about the night sky.

Cross-Curricular Connection: Science

▲ Critical Viewing Describe the moon by telling in what way or to what extent it shines. Which question did you answer? Which adverb(s) did you use? **[Analyze]**

⏱ TIME AND RESOURCE MANAGER

Resources
Print: Grammar Exercise Workbook, pp. 27–32
Technology: Language Lab CD-ROM, Parts of Speech; On-Line Exercise Bank, Section 18.2

In-Depth Coverage	Accelerated Pace
• Work through all key concepts, pp. 390–394.	• Assign pp. 390–394 for independent student
• Assign and review Exercises 19–23.	review.
• Read and discuss Grammar in Literature, p. 391.	• Assign Review Exercises 24–27.

GRAMMAR IN LITERATURE

from Tonight
Leonard Bernstein and Stephen Sondheim

Notice how the highlighted adverbs in the following excerpt from the song answer the questions When? *and* Where?

...Tonight, tonight,

It all began **tonight**.

I saw you and the world went **away**.

> **Exercise 20** **Identifying Adverbs That Modify Verbs** Make four columns with the headings shown below. Then, identify the adverb in each sentence, and place it in the correct column.

> *Where? When? In What Way? To What Extent?*

1. Ancient peoples often saw designs in the stars, called constellations.
2. They carefully named the constellations after various religious figures, animals, and objects.
3. Constellations are sometimes imagined to be groupings of bright stars.
4. Eighty-eight constellations are recognized today.
5. The names are derived mostly from Greek mythology.
6. Draco, the dragon, bravely defended the goddess Hera's apple tree.
7. Hercules subdued him quickly in a struggle to get apples.
8. Hera placed Draco overhead in the stars to remember him.
9. Draco is one of the constellations now.
10. The constellation Hercules is very near Draco.
11. Hercules originally was represented as a kneeling man with his foot on Draco.
12. Together, the constellations fully symbolize the Greek myth.
13. In another Greek myth, Leo the Lion ferociously devoured Peloponnesian villagers.
14. Hercules' weapons scarcely touched the lion.
15. If a weapon hit Leo, it bounced off him harmlessly.
16. Confidently, Hercules wrestled Leo.
17. Hercules brilliantly won the battle.
18. He then wrapped the lion's pelt about him for protection.
19. Leo went away to the heavens to commemorate the battle.
20. The constellation Leo is undeniably easy to see in the sky.

> **More Practice**
> Language Lab
> CD-ROM
> • Parts-of-Speech lesson
> On-line
> Exercise Bank
> • Section 18.2
> Grammar Exercise
> Workbook
> • pp. 27–28

Adverbs • 391

Step-by-Step Teaching Guide

Grammar in Literature

1. Have students identify the words that the two highlighted adverbs modify. (*Tonight* modifies *began; away* modifies *went.*)

2. Ask how students know that *tonight* and *away* are adverbs. (They modify verbs.)

More About the Writer

Pennsylvania native Stephen Sondheim wrote the lyrics to Leonard Bernstein's score for *West Side Story* early in his career. Sondheim, a talented composer, has won seven Tony awards for his beautiful musical scores and haunting lyrics. His *Sunday in the Park with George,* loosely based on the life of painter Georges Seurat, won the Pulitzer Prize for drama in 1985.

Responding to Literature

West Side Story includes both duet and quintet versions of the song "Tonight," each with different lyrics. The excerpt here is from the duet, which is sung in Act I. Have students locate and read the lyrics to either the duet or the quintet. Have them choose one verse, identify the adverbs, and note which question each one answers.

Answer Key

> **Exercise 20**

1. often—when
2. carefully–in what manner
3. sometimes—when
4. today—when
5. mostly—to what extent
6. bravely—in what manner
7. quickly—in what manner
8. overhead—where
9. now—when
10. very—to what extent
11. originally—when
12. fully—to what extent
13. ferociously—in what manner
14. scarcely—to what extent
15. harmlessly—in what manner
16. Confidently—in what manner
17. brilliantly—in what manner
18. then—when
19. away—where
20. undeniably—to what extent

> **ONGOING ASSESSMENT: Monitor and Reinforce**

If students more than three items in Exercise 19–20, refer them to the following for additional practice.

In the Textbook	Print Resources	Technology
Section Review, Ex. 24, p. 395	Grammar Exercise Workbook, pp. 27–28	Language Lab CD-ROM, Parts of Speech; On-Line Exercise Bank, Section 18.2

Adverbs Modifying Adjectives and Adverbs

1. Have a volunteer read the Key Concept statements aloud. Explain that since only certain adverbs can answer the question *To what extent?,* only certain adverbs can modify adjectives and adverbs. For example, *happily* cannot answer this question, but *almost* can. Have students suggest other examples of adverbs that can and cannot answer this question.

2. Go over the answers to Exercise 21 on the following page after everyone has completed it. List these common adverbs that modify other adverbs, such as *too, most, almost, rather,* and so on, on the chalkboard. Have students copy the list and keep it for reference.

Critical Viewing

Describe Students may suggest *brilliantly starry* night, *rapidly moving* lights.

18.2

Adverbs Modifying Adjectives and Adverbs

Many descriptions can be made more meaningful by adding an adverb to an adjective.

▶ **KEY CONCEPT** An adverb modifying an adjective answers only one question: *To what extent?* ■

When an adverb modifies an adjective, it usually comes directly before the adjective, as shown in the examples in the following chart.

ADVERBS MODIFYING ADJECTIVES	
very glad	*almost* ready
absolutely wrong	*entirely* grateful

Sometimes adverbs are used to sharpen the meaning of other adverbs.

▶ **KEY CONCEPT** An adverb modifying another adverb answers just one question: *To what extent?* ■

An adverb modifying another adverb generally comes directly before the adverb it modifies. In the following examples, *very* modifies *quickly, almost* modifies *over, not* modifies *completely,* and *only* modifies *just.*

ADVERBS MODIFYING ADVERBS	
moved *very quickly*	*not completely* wrong
climbed *almost over*	*only just* recognizable

▼ Critical Viewing What pairs of adverbs and adjectives might you use in describing this photograph? **[Describe]**

392 • Adjectives and Adverbs

🔧 STANDARDIZED TEST PREPARATION WORKSHOP

Grammar and Usage Standardized tests often ask students to identify the correct form of a particular part of speech. Use the following example to demonstrate how to identify the correct form of an adjective.

Underline the word in parentheses that best completes the sentence.

Bea was a very (friend, friendly) person.

The word in parentheses has to modify the noun *person;* therefore students should choose the adjective *friendly,* not the noun *friend.*

Exercise 21 Recognizing Adverbs That Modify Adjectives and Adverbs Identify all of the adverbs. Then, indicate the word each adverb modifies.

1. A glow just barely appears on the northern horizon.
2. Lights move unexpectedly fast across the sky.
3. A glowing curtain of light forms more clearly.
4. It arches farther forward.
5. It swirls and dances somewhat closer to the Earth.
6. I watch very quietly in awe.
7. I have only just comprehended the beauty of the night sky.
8. It starts to move more quickly away from us.
9. The glow is almost completely gone.
10. The Northern Lights will never completely disappear from my memory.

Exercise 22 Revising to Eliminate Unnecessary Adverbs Adverbs serve an important purpose in your writing. However, it is important to avoid using adverbs that do not significantly add to meaning. Revise this passage, eliminating unnecessary adverbs or replacing them with adverbs that add meaning.

(1) Last night's sunset was really and tremendously beautiful. (2) It was truly one of the most exciting points of our trip. (3) The sky was filled with very brilliant, flaming reds and oranges. (4) As the sky grew darker, the colors gently faded. (5) Finally, the sunset gave way to an incredibly brilliant star-filled night.

Adjective or Adverb?

Some words can be either adverbs or adjectives, depending on how they are used.

KEY CONCEPT An adverb modifies a verb, an adjective, or another adverb; an adjective modifies a noun or a pronoun. ■

Notice in the examples below that the adverb modifies a verb, while the adjective, modifies a noun.

ADVERB: I awoke *early*.

ADJECTIVE: I had an *early* class.

The word *early* takes the same form whether used as an adjective or adverb. Most such words, however, have an adjective form and an adverb form.

> **More Practice**
>
> Language Lab CD-ROM
> • Parts-of-Speech lesson
> On-line Exercise Bank
> • Section 18.2
> Grammar Exercise Workbook
> • pp. 29–30

Exercise 21

1. just barely
2. unexpectedly fast
3. more clearly
4. farther forward
5. somewhat closer
6. very quietly
7. only just
8. more quickly
9. almost completely
10. never completely

Exercise 22

Answers will vary.

Step-by-Step Teaching Guide

Adverb or Adjective?

1. Have a volunteer read aloud the first sentence under the heading. Point out that *early* and *hard* are two examples of words that keep the same spelling whether they are used as adverbs or adjectives (as do many of the answers to Exercise 23).

2. Stress that the only certain way to recognize an adverb is to examine the parts of speech of the words in a sentence. In *Catriona sang a lovely song,* it is the song that was lovely. *Lovely* modifies the noun *song,* so it is an adjective. In *Catriona easily reached the high notes,* the word *easily* describes how she reached (verb) the notes. So it is an adverb.

Adverbs • 393

☑ ONGOING ASSESSMENT: Monitor and Reinforce		
If students miss more than two items in Exercises 21–23, refer them to the following for additional practice.		
In the Textbook	**Print Resources**	**Technology**
Section Review, Ex. 25–27, p. 395	Grammar Exercise Workbook, pp. 29–32	Language Lab CD-ROM, Parts of Speech; On-Line Exercise Bank, Section 18.2

Integrating Spelling Skills

Y to I Write a few adjectives ending in -*y* on the chalkboard, such as *happy, angry, busy,* and *wary.* Challenge students to change these adjectives into adverbs. Point out the pattern: Many adjectives ending in *y* change the *y* to an *i* when they become -*ly* adverbs. Warn students not to apply this rule to an adjective ending in *ly.* Adjectives ending in *ly* cannot be changed to adverbs.

Answer Key

Exercise 23

1. adjective
2. adjective
3. adjective
4. adverb
5. adjective
6. adverb
7. adverb
8. adverb
9. adverb
10. adverb
11. adverb
12. adverb
13. adverb
14. adjective
15. adjective, adjective

Customize for
More Advanced Students

Challenge students to go back over Exercise 23, identifying the word or words each adverb or adjective modifies and the question each modifier answers.

Adjectives	Adverbs With -*ly* Endings
gentle hands	handle *gently*
bright paint	painted *brightly*

Do not, however, think that all words ending in -*ly* are adverbs. Some are adjectives formed by adding -*ly* to a noun.

Nouns	Adjectives With -*ly* Endings
a head of *curls*	*curly* hair
a close *friend*	*friendly* neighbors

Never identify a word as an adverb simply because it ends in -*ly.* Check to see whether it modifies a verb, an adjective, or an adverb.

▶ **Exercise 23** Distinguishing Between Adverbs and Adjectives Identify each underlined word as an adverb or an adjective.

1. Often when you look out your window at night, you see the <u>kindly</u> face of the Man in the Moon.
2. You will also see in the <u>far</u> reaches of the sky the stars that form the many constellations.
3. Some people think that the idea of constellations is <u>silly</u>.
4. However, constellations serve <u>well</u> as memory devices for identifying stars.
5. When you're staring at 11,000 to 11,500 stars, you'll have a <u>hard</u> time telling which is which.
6. However, <u>once</u> you recognize the stars of the constellation Orion the Hunter, for example, you will find the stars of his hunting dogs near him.
7. Ancient cultures saw pictures in the stars <u>late</u> at night.
8. They looked <u>high</u> into the heavens and saw the Lion, the Bull, the Fish, and the Scorpion.
9. The Crane is a modern constellation found <u>deep</u> in the southern sky.
10. Al Nair, a bright star on the Crane's foot, is spinning <u>fast</u>— at least 236 kilometers per second!
11. Early efforts to catalog the stars date <u>back</u> roughly 6,000 years.
12. Some constellations are seen <u>low</u> on the horizon.
13. Other constellations are <u>much</u> higher.
14. Some are seen most clearly in <u>late</u> summer.
15. Whether the constellations seem <u>far</u> or <u>near</u> depends on the rotation of the Earth.

394 • Adjectives and Adverbs

More Practice
Language Lab CD-ROM
• Parts-of-Speech lesson
On-line Exercise Bank
• Section 18.2
Grammar Exercise Workbook
• pp. 31–32

⏱ TIME SAVERS!

Answers on Transparency Use the Grammar Exercises Answers on Transparencies for Chapter 18 to have students correct their own or one another's exercises.

On-Line Exercise Bank Have students complete the exercises on computer. The Auto Check feature will grade their work for you!

✓ ONGOING ASSESSMENT: Assess Mastery

Use the following resources to assess students' mastery of adverbs.

In the Textbook	Print Resources	Technology
Chapter Review, p. 397, Ex. 35–37 Standardized Test Preparation Workshop, pp. 398–399	Grammar Exercise Workbook, pp. 27–32	Language Lab CD-ROM, Parts of Speech; On-Line Exercise Bank, Section 18.2

Section Review

GRAMMAR EXERCISES 24–30

> **Exercise 24** **Identifying Adverbs**

Identify each adverb and tell which question it answers: *Where? When? In what way?* or *To what extent?*

1. The Maya were very accomplished astronomers.
2. Their primary interest was in carefully observing Zenial Passages.
3. A special event occurred when the sun directly crossed over the Mayan latitudes.
4. The sun travels annually to its summer solstice point, latitude $23\frac{1}{3}$ degrees north.
5. Mayan cities were always located south of this point.

> **Exercise 25** **Identifying Adverbs That Modify Adjectives** Identify all of the adverbs that modify adjectives in the following sentences.

1. The ghost story was thoroughly scary.
2. She looked extremely pale.
3. It was unusually dark tonight because of the rain clouds.
4. I was somewhat hopeful that she would sleep tonight.
5. My assumption was partially correct.

> **Exercise 26** **Recognizing Adverbs That Modify Other Adverbs** Identify all the adverbs that modify other adverbs in the following sentences.

1. The sun is almost completely hidden.
2. The red color of the sunset spreads quite rapidly across the sky.
3. The sky darkens surprisingly fast.
4. The first star is just barely visible.
5. I make my wish as the star glows more clearly now.

> **Exercise 27** **Distinguishing Between Adjectives and Adverbs**

Identify the underlined word as an adverb or an adjective.

1. Vincent van Gogh painted *Starry Night* <u>late</u> in his career.
2. It was a very <u>hard</u> time in his life, and he was not well.
3. Although Van Gogh often discussed his paintings with his brother, he apparently said <u>little</u> about *Starry Night.*
4. In the painting, cosmic gold fireworks seem to swirl <u>fast</u> against the sky.
5. In contrast to the raging night sky, the <u>little</u> village below seems peaceful.

> **Exercise 28** **Find It in Your**

Reading Read a recent newspaper article, and make a list of the modifiers in the first paragraph. Label each modifier *adverb* or *adjective*, and explain how each one contributes information to the sentence.

> **Exercise 29** **Find It in Your**

Writing Find five sentences in your portfolio that would be clearer if you added an adverb or replaced an adverb with a more specific one. Revise the sentences.

> **Exercise 30** **Writing Application**

Most constellations in the night sky have a story or myth about their creation. For example, Leo the Lion stands as a symbol of Hercules' power in Greek mythology. Create your own story about a constellation. Use at least ten adverbs and ten adjectives. Label them, identify the word they modify, and tell what question they answer.

Section Review • **395**

ASSESS and CLOSE

Section Review

Each of these exercises correlates to a concept taught in the section on adverbs, pages 390–394. The exercises may be used for more practice, for reteaching, or for review of the Key Concepts presented. Answers for all chapter exercises are available in *Grammar Exercises Answers on Transparencies* in your teaching resources.

Answer Key

Exercise 24

1. very, to what extent
2. carefully, in what manner
3. directly, in what manner
4. annually, when
5. always, when

Exercise 25

1. thoroughly
2. extremely
3. unusually
4. somewhat
5. partially

Exercise 26

1. almost
2. quite
3. surprisingly
4. just
5. more

Exercise 27

1. adverb
2. adjective
3. adverb
4. adverb
5. adjective

Exercise 28

Find It in Your Reading
Have students choose partners. Each pair should read the same article, list and identify the modifiers independently, and then compare their results. If partners disagree, have them work together to decide which is correct and why.

continued

Answer Key continued

Exercise 29

Find It in Your Writing
Students can also find five sentences that contain boring adjectives or adverbs and replace them with more vivid or descriptive modifiers.

Exercise 30

Writing Application
Have students underline the adjectives in their myths and double-underline the adverbs.

Each of these exercises correlates to a concept taught in the chapter on adjectives and adverbs, pages 378–395. The exercises may be used for more practice, for reteaching, or for review of the Key Concepts presented. Answers for all chapter exercises are available in *Grammar Exercises Answers on Transparencies* in your teaching resources.

Answer Key

Exercise 31

Revisions will vary.

1. handsome, mighty
2. beautiful, mean
3. rash, possessive
4. angry, deep
5. devastating, mystical
6. rising, blind
7. magnificent, powerful
8. jealous, lovely
9. hunter's, bright
10. mighty, starry

Exercise 32

Sentence 1: space, noun used as adjective; a, indefinite article

Sentence 2: the, definite article

Sentence 3: the, definite article; Greek, proper noun used as adjective; the, definite article

Sentence 4: the, definite article; seventeenth, adjective; an, indefinite article; a, indefinite article; moon, noun used as adjective

Sentence 5: space, noun used as adjective; his, possessive adjective; the, definite article; the, definite article; the, definite article; nineteenth, adjective

Exercise 33

1. proper; their
2. compound; Every, their
3. compound, compound; their
4. proper
5. proper; this

Exercise 34

1. many—indefinite
2. few—indefinite
3. Which—interrogative
4. some—indefinite
5. that—demonstrative; both—indefinite

GRAMMAR EXERCISES 31–39

> **Exercise 31** Identifying and Revising Adjectives List the two adjectives in each of the following sentences. Do not include articles. Then, revise five sentences, replacing the adjectives with more specific ones.

(1) In mythology, Orion was a handsome and mighty hunter. (2) Orion fell in love with beautiful Merope, but her mean father refused to let them marry. (3) In a rash decision, Orion attempted to steal Merope away from her possessive father. (4) The angry father put Orion into a deep sleep and blinded him.

(5) To find a cure for the devastating blindness, Orion consulted a mystical oracle. (6) The oracle told him to go to the East and let the rays of the rising sun fall on his blind eyes. (7) His sight restored, Orion served as the magnificent hunter of the powerful goddess Artemis. (8) Artemis got rid of him in a jealous rage because he fell in love with the lovely Aurora, goddess of the dawn. (9) After the hunter's departure, Artemis placed Orion in the heavens as a bright constellation. (10) The mighty Orion can still be seen in the starry sky.

> **Exercise 32** Recognizing Definite Articles, Indefinite Articles, and Nouns Used as Adjectives Identify each of the adjectives in the paragraph below as *definite article, indefinite article,* or *noun used as adjective.*

People dreamed of spaceflight for millennia before it became reality. Evidence of the dream exists in myth and fiction as far back as 4000 B.C. The Greek myth of Daedalus and Icarus also reflects the desire to fly. In the seventeenth century, an astronomer wrote about a moon voyage. Jules Verne depicted space travel in his

novel *From the Earth to the Moon* in the nineteenth century.

> **Exercise 33** Identifying Proper and Compound Adjectives and Pronouns Used as Adjectives Identify the underlined adjective in each sentence as *proper* or *compound.* Then, identify any pronouns used as adjectives.

1. The <u>Mayan</u> kings timed their rituals according to the movements of the stars and the Milky Way.
2. Every twenty years, Mayan rulers erected a stone tree that depicted themselves in costumes with religious symbols in their <u>headdress</u> feathers.
3. In their arms, they held a <u>so-called</u> ceremonial bar that represented a <u>double-headed</u> serpent.
4. This linked the ancient <u>Mesoamerican</u> ruler to the sky, the gods, and the essential ingredient, life.
5. The religious philosophy of this <u>Native American</u> tribe was ruled to a great degree by the stars.

> **Exercise 34** Identifying Nouns and Pronouns Used as Adjectives List the nouns and pronouns used as adjectives in the following sentences. Label each pronoun *demonstrative, interrogative,* or *indefinite.*

1. Reaching the moon has been the objective of many space missions.
2. The first few attempts by the United States and the Soviet Union to put a probe on the moon failed.
3. Which country would land on the moon first?
4. The Soviet Union launched a probe on September 12, 1959, that landed on the

moon some days later.

5. Since that date, moon shots have been made by both countries.

> **Exercise 35** **Identifying Adverbs and the Words They Modify** List the words modified by each underlined adverb. Label them *verb*, *adjective*, or *adverb*.

1. The United States and the Soviet Union <u>quickly</u> started developing programs to place people in Earth's orbit after the success of artificial satellites.
2. Both countries sent <u>carefully</u> monitored dogs and primates into orbit to study the effects of weightlessness on mammals.
3. The Soviet Union progressed <u>very</u> quickly and sent cosmonaut Yuri Gagarin into one full orbit of the Earth on April 12, 1961.
4. He orbited the Earth in one hour and 48 minutes before landing <u>safely</u>.
5. The United States was <u>nearly</u> ready to launch its own astronaut into space.

> **Exercise 36** **Writing Sentences With Adjectives and Adverbs** Write sentences containing the adjectives and adverbs indicated below.

1. early (adverb)
2. early (adjective)
3. far (adverb)
4. far (adjective)
5. high (adverb)
6. high (adjective)
7. low (adverb)
8. low (adjective)
9. fast (adverb)
10. fast (adjective)

> **Exercise 37** **Revising to Add Adjectives and Adverbs** Revise the following passage, adding or replacing adjectives and adverbs to make the descriptions more vivid and combining sentences to make the passage more concise. To ensure that your details are accurate, you may want to consult an encyclopedia.

(1) Apollo 13 was scheduled to land on the moon. (2) Two other moon landings had already been completed. (3) The ship took off on April 11, 1970. (4) It was commanded by James Lovell, who had been an astronaut for many years. (5) The other two astronauts were not in the military. (6) Their names were Fred Haise, Jr., and John Swigert, Jr.

(7) The mission encountered difficulties when a tank that provided oxygen to the astronauts ruptured. (8) It was unclear whether the astronauts would survive. (9) They made it back into the atmosphere. (10) The craft landed in the ocean.

> **Exercise 38** **Writing Application** Imagine that you are a witness to a car accident. Write a report for the police, giving them an exact description of the cars involved, their movements, and the mistakes made by the drivers. Use at least three adjectives, three adverbs, one compound adjective, and one noun and one pronoun used as adjectives.

> **Exercise 39** **CUMULATIVE REVIEW Nouns, Pronouns, Verbs, Adjectives, and Adverbs** Identify all of the nouns, pronouns, verbs, adjectives, and adverbs in the following passage.

(1) Space travel has always been a subject that fascinates me. (2) As a young child, I used to watch all of the space shuttle missions on television. (3) My parents were amazed that I could watch for hours without ever losing interest. (4) Because of my interest in space travel, I enrolled in astronomy courses in college. (5) At some point in the future, I hope to enroll in the space program myself and travel in a rocket.

> **Exercise 35**
1. started—verb
2. monitored—adjective
3. quickly—adverb
4. landed—verb
5. ready—adjective

> **Exercise 36**
Answers will vary. Sample sentences are given.
1. The clerk called her early the next morning.
2. She asked the hotel desk clerk for an early call.
3. We had far better get a taxi to take us there.
4. It's too far to walk from here to the museum.
5. The acrobat swung high above the circus floor on the trapeze.
6. The singer surprised us with his beautiful high notes.
7. The hiker bent his head low and trudged forward into the wind.
8. The toddlers sat in low chairs at their own little table.
9. She ran so fast that she got there almost before she left.
10. He clapped as the ice skater moved to fast music.

> **Exercise 37**
Answers will vary.

> **Exercise 38**
Writing Application
Students can practice their speaking/listening skills by reading their descriptions aloud to the class.

continued

Answer Key continued

> **Exercise 39**
Cumulative Review
1. space (adj), travel (noun), has been (verb), always (adv), subject (noun), that (pron), fascinates (verb), me (pron)
2. young (adj), child (noun), I (pron), used (verb), all (pron), space shuttle (adj), missions (noun), television (noun)
3. My (adj), parents (noun), were (verb), amazed (adj), that (pron), I (pron), could watch (verb), hours (noun), ever (adv), losing (verb), interest (noun)
4. my (pron), interest (noun), space (adj), travel (noun), I (pron), enrolled (verb), astronomy (adj), courses (noun), college (noun)
5. some (adj), point (noun), future (noun), I (pron), hope (verb), space (adj), program (noun), myself (pron), travel (verb), rocket (noun)

Using Adjectives and Adverbs

1. As students read each passage, have them identify the part of speech of the word being modified by the missing word. They can then analyze what part(s) of speech may modify this word.

2. Have them eliminate any choices that are the incorrect part of speech.

3. Once students have made their selections, remind them to check their answer by reading the sentence with the choice in place.

Standardized Test Preparation Workshop

Using Adjectives and Adverbs

Many standardized tests measure your knowledge of adjectives and adverbs. One type of question that draws upon your knowledge of modifiers involves inserting the correct modifier in a passage that is provided. The passage will include a blank where the modifier should appear, and you will be called on to choose one of several possible modifiers to complete the passage.

Carefully read the entire passage before answering these types of questions. Ask yourself what word or words in the sentence are being described. An adjective is used to tell *what kind*, *how much*, and *how many*, and an adverb will tell *when*, *where*, or *how* about a word in the sentence.

The following test item will give you practice with questions that test your ability to choose the correct modifier.

Test Tip

Identify the part of speech of the word being modified. Adverbs modify verbs, adjectives, or other adverbs, while adjectives modify nouns and pronouns.

Sample Test Item	Answer and Explanation
Directions: Read the passage, and choose the letter of the word or group of words that belongs in each space. Even before we entered the restaurant, we could hear the clanging of the kitchen utensils and the cavernous sound of the cook's (1) voice bawling out the day's orders. 1 A softly B soft C hearty D heartily	The correct answer is **C**. The passage needs a modifier for the noun voice; the modifiers heartily and softly are adverbs. A cavernous sound is not likely to be soft; therefore, the correct choice is the adjective *hearty*.

⟡ TEST-TAKING TIP

Tell students to be on guard for words that end in -*ly*. Remind them that not all words ending in -*ly* are adverbs. In a test-taking situation, some students may automatically choose a word ending in -*ly* when looking for an adverb. Tell students not to rush, but to read each passage and set of choices carefully to avoid making careless mistakes.

Answer Key

> **Practice 1** **Directions:** Read the passage, and choose the letter of the word or group of words that belongs in each space.

On summer evenings, the formerly __(1)__ grassy marshes burst alive with a cacophony of sound. My sister, Meredith loves the __(2)__, untamed sounds of the wild sea birds. We sit __(3)__ listening to their songs. Meredith tries __(4)__ to identify each bird's __(5)__ notes.

1 A restless
  B restful
  C stillness
  D still

2 F dissonant
  G dissonance
  H harmonious
  J harmony

3 A quiet
  B quieter
  C quietly
  D still

4 F hardly
  G hard
  H persistent
  J diligent

5 A uniquely
  B differently
  C silent
  D unique

> **Practice 2** **Directions:** Read the passage, and choose the letter of the word or group of words that belongs in each space

On some summer evenings, we enjoy taking a __(1)__ swim. I __(2)__ dive from the highest board arching my body __(3)__. My sister can __(4)__ perform flips off the board. The activity and heat make us __(5)__ tired, extremely relaxed, and ready for bed.

1 A refreshingly
  B refreshing
  C difficult
  D briefly

2 F bold
  G boldly
  H timid
  J timidly

3 A loosely
  B loose
  C perfect
  D perfectly

4 F actual
  G actually
  H true
  J real

5 A very
  B real
  C ready
  D hardly

Practice 1

1. D
2. F
3. C
4. G
5. D

Practice 2

1. B
2. G
3. D
4. G
5. A

In-Depth Lesson Plan

LESSON FOCUS	PRINT AND MEDIA RESOURCES
DAY 1 — **Prepositions** Students learn and apply concepts covering the use of prepositions and do the Hands-On Grammar activity (pp. 400–407).	**Teaching Resources** *Grammar Exercise Workbook*, pp. 33–36; *Grammar Exercises Answers on Transparency*, Ch. 19; *Language Lab* **CD-ROM**, Parts of Speech; *On-Line Exercise Bank*, Section 19.1
DAY 2 — **Conjunctions and Interjections** Students learn and apply concepts covering the use of conjunctions and interjections (pp. 408–413).	**Teaching Resources** *Grammar Exercise Workbook*, pp. 37–40; *Grammar Exercises Answers on Transparency*, Ch. 19; *Hands-on Grammar Activity Book*, Chapter 19; *Language Lab* **CD-ROM**, Parts of Speech; *On-Line Exercise Bank*, Section 19.2
DAY 3 — **Review and Assess** Students review chapter and demonstrate mastery of use of prepositions, conjunctions and interjections (pp. 414–415).	**Teaching Resources** *Formal Assessment*, Ch. 19; *Grammar Exercises Answers on Transparency*, Ch. 19; *On-Line Exercise Bank*, Section 19.1

Accelerated Lesson Plan

LESSON FOCUS	PRINT AND MEDIA RESOURCES
DAY 1 — **Prepositions, Conjunctions and Interjections** Students cover concepts and usage of prepositions, conjunctions and interjections as determined by Diagnostic Test (pp. 400–414).	**Teaching Resources** *Grammar Exercise Workbook*, pp. 33–40; *Grammar Exercises Answers on Transparency*, Ch. 19; *Hands-on Grammar Activity Book*, Chapter 19; *Language Lab* **CD-ROM**, Parts of Speech; *On-Line Exercise Bank*, Section 19.1–2
DAY 2 — **Review and Assess** Students review chapter and demonstrate mastery of use of prepositions, conjunctions and interjections (pp. 414–419).	**Teaching Resources** *Formal Assessment*, Ch. 19; *Grammar Exercises Answers on Transparency*, Ch. 19; *On-Line Exercise Bank*, Section 19.1

Options for Adapting Lesson Plans

HOMEWORK

Have students complete any section of the chapter for homework.

FEATURES

Extend coverage with the Grammar in Literature features (pp. 403, 410), and the Standardized Test Preparation Workshop (p. 416).

TECHNOLOGY

Students can use the On-Line Exercise Bank to complete the exercises on computer. The Auto Check feature will grade their work.

INTEGRATED SKILLS COVERAGE

Grammar in Literature
SE pp. 403, 410

Reading
Find It In Your Reading, SE pp. 406, 407, 413

Writing
Find It In Your Writing, SE pp. 406, 407, 413
Writing Application, SE pp. 407, 413, 415
Integrating Writing Skills, ATE pp. 404, 409

Language
Language Highlight ATE p. 412

Real-World Connection
ATE p. 403

Viewing and Representing
Critical Viewing, SE pp. 400, 403, 405, 409, 410, 412

ASSESSMENT SUPPORT

Standardized Test Preparation SE p. 416; ATE p. 405
Standardized Test Preparation Workbook, pp. 37–38
Formal Assessment, Ch. 19

MEETING INDIVIDUAL NEEDS

Less Advanced Students ATE p. 411; See also Ongoing
Assessments ATE pp. 403, 404
More Advanced Students ATE p. 405
Bodily/Kinesthetic Learners ATE p. 402
ESL Students ATE p. 406

BLOCK SCHEDULING

Pacing Suggestions
For 90-minute Blocks
• Administer the Diagnostic Test to students to determine instructional coverage
• Have students complete the necessary exercises in class. Use the Hands-on Grammar activity to provide a change of pace.

Resources for Varying Instruction
• **Language Lab** CD-ROM If your students have access to hardware, a 90-minute block provides an ideal opportunity for students to work on computer.

Professional Development Support
• **How to Manage Instruction in the Block** This teaching Resource provides management and activity suggestions.

MEDIA AND TECHNOLOGY

For the Student
• **Language Lab** CD-ROM Parts of Speech
• **On-Line Exercise Bank,** Ch. 19

For the Teacher
• **Resource Pro** CD-ROM

WRITING AND GRAMMAR WEBSITE

The Interactive Writing and Grammar Website provides a wide array of support for students, teachers, and parents. Grammar support includes:
• **On-Line Exercise Bank** with Auto Check scoring
• Diagnostic and assessment support

phwg.phschool.com

LITERATURE CONNECTIONS

Grammar in Literature selections from *Prentice Hall Literature: Timeless Voices, Timeless Themes,* Gold:
from "Slam, Dunk, & Hook," Yusef Komunyakaa, SE p. 403
from *To the Residents of A.D. 2029,* Bryan Woolley, SE p. 410

▶ **Lesson Objectives**

1. Recognize that a prepositional phrase consists of a preposition and a noun or pronoun.

2. Distinguish prepositions with their objects from adverbs.

3. Identify coordinating, subordinating, and correlative conjunctions.

4. Correctly recognize and use conjunctive adverbs.

5. Understand that interjections express feeling or emotion and function independently of a sentence.

Critical Viewing

Relate Responses may include *on* the basketball court, *in* a class, *below* the basket, *outside* the school, *near* the coach.

Chapter 19 Prepositions, Conjunctions, and Interjections

▲ **Critical Viewing**
What prepositions can you use to describe the relationships of the people in this picture to each other and to the objects around them? **[Relate]**

Three parts of speech act as relaters, joiners, and attention-getters in sentences. They are *prepositions, conjunctions,* and *interjections.*

Consider the following sentence: Basketball can be played outdoors, *but* it began as an indoor exercise for the winter months.

The conjunction *but* helps to join the two ideas in a way that clarifies their relationship.

In this chapter, you will learn more about these three parts of speech—prepositions, conjunctions, and interjections—and about the ways they connect and relate words in sentences.

✓ ONGOING ASSESSMENT: Diagnose

If students miss more than one item in each category, direct them to the relevant pages of the text and assign exercises for practice and review.

Prepositions, Conjunctions, and Interjections	Diagnostic Test Items	Teach	Practice	Section Review	Chapter Review
Skill Check A					
Identifying Prepositional Phrases	A 1–10	pp. 402–404	Ex. 1–2	Ex. 4–6	Ex. 20
Skill Check B					
Distinguishing Prepositions from Adverbs	B 11–15	p. 405	Ex. 3	Ex. 7	Ex. 21

Diagnostic Test

Directions: Write all answers on a separate sheet of paper.

Skill Check A Write the prepositional phrase(s) in each sentence. Underline each preposition.

1. James Naismith devised basketball in December 1891.
2. Basketball is a court game played by two teams, with five players on each team.
3. Putting a ball into a basket, and thus scoring points against the opposing team, is the object of the game.
4. Naismith hung two peach baskets at opposite ends of a room.
5. During the winter, his YMCA athletes played the game with a soccer ball.
6. Players threw the soccer ball into the assigned basket.
7. People quickly heard about the new game.
8. It was soon being played throughout the eastern United States.
9. Women also played the game before 1900.
10. The rules today are based on the rules of Naismith's game.

Skill Check B Label each underlined word *preposition* or *adverb*.

11. Basketball's popularity led to improvements in equipment.
12. Peach baskets were soon out, and metal hoops were used.
13. The use of a backboard behind the net began in 1895.
14. Improvement in playing skills did not lag behind.
15. The number of spectators increased throughout the country.

Skill Check C Write each conjunction, and label it *coordinating*, *correlative*, or *subordinating*.

16. In early games, following each point, the opposing centers would face each other at mid-court and jump for the ball.
17. The team with the ball would either pass it or dribble it until a player was about 10 feet from the basket.
18. Although the early game was slow-paced, it drew many fans.
19. Its popularity grew when rules were adopted to speed up play.
20. The ball had to be moved past mid-court within 10 seconds, and players could remain within the foul lanes for only 3 seconds.

Skill Check D Rewrite the first three sentences by adding a conjunctive adverb. Add an interjection to the last two sentences.

21. Several events in the 1930's spurred the growth of basketball; these events made the game more exciting for the players.
22. College games played in Madison Square Garden became highly successful; colleges began building their own arenas for basketball.
23. Stanford University players shot one-handed while jumping; one Stanford player could out-score an entire opposing team that shot two-handed while standing still.
24. Those basketball scores shot up!
25. Women have played basketball since 1890.

Prepositions, Conjunctions, and Interjections • 401

Answer Key

Skill Check A

1. in December 1891
2. by two teams; with five players; on each team
3. into a basket; against the opposing team; of the game
4. at opposite ends; of a room
5. During the winter; with a soccer ball
6. into the assigned basket
7. about the new game
8. throughout the eastern United States
9. before 1900
10. on the rules; of Naismith's game

Skill Check B

11. in—preposition
12. out—adverb
13. behind—preposition
14. behind—adverb
15. throughout—preposition

Skill Check C

16. and—coordinating
17. either . . . or—correlative; until—subordinating
18. Although—subordinating
19. when—subordinating
20. and—coordinating

Skill Check D

Responses may vary.

401

Interest GRABBER Ask a student to describe a certain play in a sports event, such as a pick-and-roll in basketball. As he or she talks, write the prepositions on the board. Point out the role prepositions play in describing action.

Activate Prior Knowledge

On the board, write the definition of a preposition and list a few examples. Then have students brainstorm with partners for a list of as many words as they can think of that fit this definition. Compile their answers and compare the list to the chart on page 402.

TEACH

Step-by-Step Teaching Guide

Prepositions

1. Tell students that prepositions perform the important task of relating words in a sentence. They help to show relationships between separate things, including location, direction, cause, and possession.

2. Write the following sentences on the chalkboard:

   She passed the ball <u>over</u> the defense.

   He was <u>underneath</u> the basket.

   She dribbled <u>into</u> the lane.

   The foul occurred <u>before</u> the shot.

3. Have students identify the preposition in each sentence. Then have them point out the two things that are related by the preposition and the type of relationship that is shown.

Customize for
Bodily/Kinesthetic Learners

Small groups of students can play a version of "hot potato." Use any object and have students pass it to each other until you call *stop*. The recipient has to describe its location (in my hands, in front of me, at my feet, on my head, and so on). This will give hands-on practice in using and analyzing prepositions.

Prepositions

Prepositions—such as *at, by, in, on,* and *with*—play an important role in English. They are used to relate words within a sentence.

▶ **KEY CONCEPT** A **preposition** is a word that relates a noun or pronoun that appears with it to another word in the sentence. ■

The following chart lists several of the most commonly used prepositions.

FREQUENTLY USED PREPOSITIONS

about	behind	down	off	till
above	below	during	on	to
across	beneath	except	onto	toward
after	beside	for	opposite	under
against	besides	from	out	underneath
along	between	in	outside	until
amid	beyond	inside	over	up
among	but	into	past	upon
around	by	like	since	with
at	concerning	near	through	within
before	despite	of	throughout	without

Although most prepositions are single words, some prepositions are made up of two or three words. These prepositions are called *compound prepositions.* Some compound prepositions are spelled without a space between them, such as *without, throughout, into, underneath,* and *outside.* The chart above lists some compound prepositions.

Other compound prepositions are spelled as separate words, as shown in the chart below.

COMPOUND PREPOSITIONS

according to	because of	in place of	next to
ahead of	by means of	in regard to	on account of
apart from	in addition to	in spite of	out of
aside from	in back of	instead of	owing to
as of	in front of	in view of	prior to

Theme: Basketball

In this section, you will learn about prepositions and prepositional phrases. The examples and exercises in this section are about basketball.

Cross-Curricular Connection: Physical Education

🖥 Internet Tip

Prepositions are sometimes used to narrow a topic on the Internet. For example, using *basketball at . . .* as a search word instead of just *basketball* would narrow the topic down to places where basketball is played.

⏱ TIME AND RESOURCE MANAGER

Resources
Print: Grammar Exercise Workbook, pp. 33–36; Hands-on Grammar Activity Book, Ch. 19
Technology: Language Lab CD-ROM, Parts of Speech; On-Line Exercise Bank, Section 19.1

In-Depth Coverage	Accelerated Pace
• Work through all key concepts, pp. 402–405. • Assign and review Exercises 1–3. • Read and discuss Grammar in Literature, p. 403. • Do the Hands-on Grammar Activity, p. 406.	• Assign pp. 402–403 for independent student review. • Assign Exercise 3.

GRAMMAR IN LITERATURE

from **Slam, Dunk, & Hook**
Yusef Komunyakaa

Notice the highlighted prepositions in the following excerpt.

Dribble, drive *to* the inside, feint,
& glide like a sparrow hawk.
Lay ups. Fast breaks.
We had moves we didn't know
We had. Our bodies spun
On swivels *of* bone and faith . . .

▲ **Critical Viewing**
What prepositions can you use to tell where you might stand in relation to a basketball net? **[Speculate]**

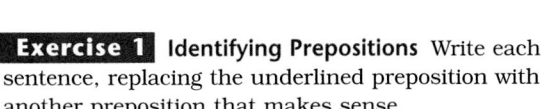

> **Exercise 1** **Identifying Prepositions** Write each sentence, replacing the underlined preposition with another preposition that makes sense.

EXAMPLE: The player stood <u>in</u> <u>front of</u> the coach.
ANSWER: The player stood <u>behind</u> the coach.

1. Does the basketball season generally come <u>before</u> the football season?
2. The standard length for a basketball court is 94 feet, and the width is 50 feet.
3. A basket attached to a backboard hangs <u>over</u> each end of the court.
4. Her free throw hit the backboard <u>above</u> the basket, and she failed to score.
5. Is the center considered the most important player <u>on</u> the team?
6. A player can advance the ball only <u>with</u> dribbling or <u>with</u> passing.
7. The forward dribbled the ball <u>over</u> the court and then passed it to a teammate.
8. The coach gives instructions to the players <u>during</u> the game.
9. An official may stand <u>along</u> the sideline.
10. Scorekeepers and timekeepers sit at a table <u>behind</u> the sideline.

> **More Practice**

Language Lab CD-ROM
• Prepositions, Conjunctions, and Interjections lesson
On-line Exercise Bank
• Section 19.1
Grammar Exercise Workbook
• pp. 33–34

Prepositions • 403

TEACH

Step-by-Step Teaching Guide

Grammar in Literature

1. Have a volunteer read aloud the excerpt from "Slam, Dunk, & Hook."

2. Point out that *inside*, which is usually a preposition or an adverb, is used as a noun in this case. In basketball, the inside, also known as the paint or the key, is an area near and under the basket.

Real-World Connection

Have students use sports articles from newspapers, magazines, or Web sites to compile a list of sports jargon or expressions. Have them use four in sentences with a preposition.
Example: *base line; He drove <u>along</u> the base line.*

Answer Key

> **Exercise 1**

Answers will vary. Samples are given.

1. Does the basketball season generally come <u>after</u> the football season?
2. The standard length <u>of</u> a basketball court is 94 feet, and the width is 50 feet.
3. A basket attached to a backboard hangs <u>at</u> each end of the court.
4. Her free throw hit the backboard <u>over</u> the basket, and she failed to score.
5. Is the center considered the most important player <u>of</u> the team?
6. A player can advance the ball only <u>by</u> dribbling or <u>by</u> passing.
7. The forward dribbled the ball <u>across</u> the court and then passed it to a teammate.
8. The coach gives instructions to the players <u>before</u> the game.
9. An official may stand <u>at</u> the sideline.
10. Scorekeepers and timekeepers sit at a table <u>outside</u> the sideline.

Critical Viewing

Speculate Most students will use prepositions such as *beneath, below, underneath,* and *in view of.*

403

Prepositional Phrases

1. Explain that prepositions are always part of a group of words called *prepositional phrases*. A prepositional phrase begins with a preposition and ends with a noun or pronoun, known as the *object* of the preposition.

2. Write the following prepositional phrases on the board for additional practice and have students identify the preposition and object of the preposition:

   to the *hoop*

   around the *basket*

   at the free throw *line*

   on a fast *break*

   for the *rebound*

3. Ask students why free throw and fast are not considered the objects of prepositions in the examples above. (They are adjectives; objects must be nouns or pronouns.) Remind students not to include modifiers when they identify the object of a preposition.

Integrating Writing Skills

Have students review a writing selection from their portfolios and identify at least three prepositional phrases. Have them underline the preposition and circle the object of the preposition in each.

Answer Key

▶ **Exercise 2**

1. into their own; in 1939
2. Since that time
3. for outstanding performances
4. after graduation; from college
5. at international games
6. for their leadership; on the court
7. In time; in popularity
8. of cheering fans
9. from June; through August
10. of the game; for fans

19.1

Prepositional Phrases

Prepositions are almost always followed by nouns or pronouns.

▶ **KEY CONCEPT** A **prepositional phrase** is a group of words that includes a preposition and a noun or pronoun. ■

The noun or pronoun generally found after a preposition is called the *object of the preposition*.

PREPOSITIONAL PHRASES	
Prepositions	**Objects of the Prepositions**
near	me
before	the storm
according to	her

Most *prepositional phrases* contain two or three words. However, they may be longer, depending on the number of words modifying the object and the length of the preposition.

EXAMPLES: *near* the tall, gently swaying *trees*
on account of the *rain*

▶ **Exercise 2** Identifying Prepositional Phrases Write the prepositional phrase or phrases in each sentence. The number at the end of each sentence tells how many prepositional phrases the sentence has.

EXAMPLE: Spectators in the stands cheered wildly. (1)
ANSWER: in the stands

1. College basketball tournaments came into their own in 1939. (2)
2. Since that time, players have been setting records. (1)
3. Players are often named all-American for outstanding performances. (1)
4. A few players join professional teams after graduation from college. (2)
5. Some teams win medals at international games. (1)
6. The best players are noted for their leadership on the court. (2)
7. In time, women's basketball grew in popularity. (1)
8. Thousands of cheering fans fill the stands. (1)
9. The regular season runs from June through August. (2)
10. The unpredictability of the game is very exciting for fans. (2)

404 • Prepositions, Conjunctions, and Interjections

⚙ Grammar and Style Tip

Whenever possible, avoid ending a sentence with a preposition. For example, *This is a good court to play on* can be rewritten *This is a good court for playing* or *This is a good court on which to play.*

▶ **More Practice**

Language Lab CD-ROM
• Prepositions, Conjunctions, and Interjections lesson
On-line Exercise Bank
• Section 19.1
Grammar Exercise Workbook
• pp. 35–36

☑ ONGOING ASSESSMENT: Monitor and Reinforce

If students miss more than two items in Exercise 1, 2, or 3, refer them to the following for additional practice.

In the Textbook	Print Resources	Technology
Section Review, Ex. 4–7, p. 407	Grammar Exercise Workbook, pp. 33–36	Language Lab CD-ROM, Parts of Speech; On-Line Exercise Bank, Section 19.1

Preposition or Adverb?

Many words that act as prepositions can also act as adverbs, depending on how they are used.

▶ **KEY CONCEPT** Remember that prepositions always have objects; adverbs do not. ■

If a word that can be used either as a preposition or as an adverb has an object, the word is acting as a preposition.

PREPOSITION: The ball flew *through* the net.
ADVERB: We were waved right *through*.
PREPOSITION: We play *behind* the school.
ADVERB: Leave your worries *behind* when you go on vacation.

For a word to act as a preposition, it must have an object and be part of a prepositional phrase. In the preceding examples, only the first and third sentences show prepositions with objects.

▲ **Critical Viewing**
Use *up* in two sentences about this picture. In the first sentence, use *up* as an adverb. In the second, use it as a preposition. **[Analyze]**

▶ **Exercise 3** **Distinguishing Between Prepositions and Adverbs** Label each underlined word *preposition* or *adverb*.

EXAMPLE: His sneakers had holes <u>underneath</u> in three places.
ANSWER: adverb

1. Have you ever seen a live college basketball game <u>before</u>?
2. A sign <u>outside</u> the arena said my two favorite teams were playing <u>inside</u>.
3. Come <u>along</u>; let's get to our seats before the game starts.
4. The teams came <u>out</u> to warm up <u>before</u> the game.
5. Two aggressive players fouled each other <u>throughout</u>.
6. At half time, one team was ahead <u>by</u> eight points.
7. A player threw the ball <u>in</u> <u>from</u> the sideline.
8. We walked <u>around</u> <u>during</u> half time.
9. <u>After</u> the game, the winners were given the championship trophy <u>inside</u> the locker room.
10. Despite losing <u>in</u> the playoffs, that team had a winning record <u>for</u> the season.

Preposition or Adverb?

1. Some words, such as *around, down, on, off, in, out, over,* and *up,* can function as either an adverb or a preposition. In order for a word to be a preposition, it must be followed by an object. If it is not, the word is an adverb.

2. To be sure that a word is an adverb, tell students to determine whether it answers one of the following questions: *Where? When? In what manner? To what extent?* If so, and if it has no object, it is an adverb.

3. Write the following sentences on the board, and ask students to identify each underlined word as a preposition or an adverb.

   The shot went <u>in</u>. (adverb)

   He went <u>in</u> the locker room. (preposition)

   The pass went <u>over</u> her head. (preposition)

   The game is <u>over</u>. (adverb)

Customize for
More Advanced Students

Have students write original pairs of sentences using the same word as a preposition and as an adverb. After they write three pairs, have students exchange papers and label the common word in each pair either *preposition* or *adverb*.

Critical Viewing

Analyze Students' responses may include *jump up* and *up the court.*

Answer Key

▶ **Exercise 3**

1. before—adverb
2. outside—preposition, inside—adverb
3. along—adverb
4. out—adverb, before—preposition
5. throughout—adverb
6. by—preposition
7. in—adverb, from—preposition
8. around—adverb, during—preposition
9. After—preposition, inside—preposition
10. in—preposition, for—preposition

◈ **STANDARDIZED TEST PREPARATION WORKSHOP**

Grammar and Usage Many standardized tests require students to identify the parts of speech of words in a sentence. Ask students to identify the underlined word that is not used as a preposition in the following sentences.

The team came <u>down</u> the court <u>for</u> the last shot. Taylor passed the ball <u>inside</u>. Conroy caught the pass and moved <u>to</u> the hoop.

A down   C inside
B for   D to

The correct answer is item **C**. All the other items have objects (court, shot, hoop), so they are prepositions.

405

Preposition Pet on a Leash

Teaching Resources: Hands-on Grammar Activity Book, Chapter 19

1. Give each student a copy of the Hands-on Grammar Activity sheet, Chapter 19.

2. Have students follow the directions for creating their houses and preposition pets.

3. For variation, have them write down their sentences and exchange them with a neighbor. Then, have the pairs rewrite each other's sentences, changing the preposition's function from preposition to adverb and vice versa.

Find It in Your Reading

Have students exchange papers and check each other's answers.

Find It in Your Writing

Have students circle all prepositions and identify their function.

Customizing for *ESL Students*

Give students two objects, such as a pen and a book, and have them model the relating function of prepositions as they use them in sentences. Have them say aloud each prepositional phrase as they illustrate it.

19.1

Hands-on Grammar

Preposition Pet on a Leash

To increase your understanding of prepositions, create and play Preposition Pet on a Leash.

First, build a house. Cut a piece of 8-1/2″ x 11″ paper into two 5-1/2″ x 8-1/2″ pieces. Fold each piece in half the short way and in half again, to make three parallel creases in the paper; then, unfold. On the creases, fold one of the pieces into an open triangle shape, and tape the overlapping edges to form a roof. Fold the other piece into an open rectangular box, and tape the edges where they meet to form the bottom of the house. Cut a small door (about 1-1/2″ high) in the middle of the taped edge. Then, tape the roof to the house at the open edges at each end. (See illustration.)

Now, make your pet and its leash. Cut out a small, simple dog or cat, about 1″ to 1-1/2″ long and high. Take a piece of string about 12″ long, and tape one end around the neck of your pet, to resemble a collar. Tape the other end to the door of your house. If you like, give your pet a name—Preppy, perhaps.

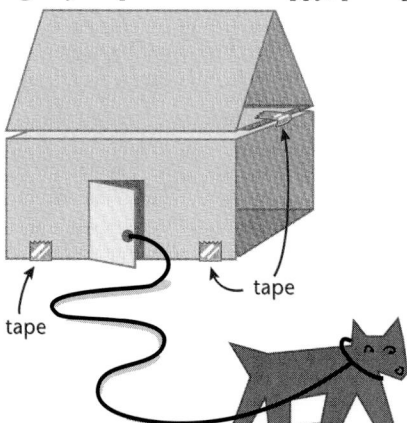

tape

tape

Finally, join with two or three of your "neighbors," and demonstrate where your pets can go on their leashes. Each person should take a turn moving his or her pet to different parts of the house, using prepositional phrases to explain where the pet is or is going. Then, take turns changing the prepositions to function as adverbs. Example: "Preppy goes *inside* the house." (preposition) "Preppy goes *inside* to eat." (adverb)

Find It in Your Reading Read a short newspaper or magazine article, and underline the prepositional phrases. Which prepositions are used most frequently? Circle any prepositions that are actually functioning as adverbs.

Find It in Your Writing Review a piece of your writing, and identify the prepositional phrases. See if there are places where you can add a prepositional phrase to clarify or expand on an idea.

406 • Prepositions, Conjunctions, and Interjections

⏱ TIME SAVERS!

✋ **Hand-on Grammar Book** Use the Hands-on Grammar activity sheet for Chapter 19 to facilitate this activity.

☑ ONGOING ASSESSMENT: Assess Mastery

Use the following resources to assess mastery of prepositions.

In the Textbook	Technology
Chapter Review, Ex. 20–21, 24, pp. 414–415	On-Line Exercise Bank, Section 19.1

Section 19.1 Section Review

GRAMMAR EXERCISES 4–10

Exercise 4 Recognizing **Prepositions** List the prepositions and the compound prepositions in each sentence.

1. Prior to the game, the coach gave all the members of his team a pep talk.
2. According to their coach, this season would be among the best.
3. The team entered the court through the doors next to the bleachers.
4. The first pass was thrown out of bounds by a player.
5. The game went into overtime because of a tied score.

Exercise 5 Identifying **Prepositional Phrases** Write the prepositional phrase or phrases in each sentence. The number at the end of each sentence tells how many prepositional phrases the sentence has.

1. John Robert Wooden was one of the greatest college basketball coaches. (1)
2. He was a three-time, all-American player at Purdue University before his coaching career. (2)
3. Wooden arrived at UCLA in 1948. (2)
4. He compiled 667 victories between the years 1946 and 1975. (1)
5. For his playing and coaching, Wooden was elected to the Basketball Hall of Fame. (3)

Exercise 6 Supplying Prepositions Rewrite the following paragraph, supplying appropriate prepositions to fill the blanks.

Basketball star Kareem Abdul-Jabbar was coached __?__ John Wooden. This all-time great played __?__ UCLA __?__ the 1960s. Kareem Abdul-Jabbar was an all-American __?__ three years and College Player __?__ the Year twice.

Exercise 7 Distinguishing Between **Prepositions and Adverbs** Label each underlined word *preposition* or *adverb.*

1. She turned the radio <u>on</u> to hear a program <u>about</u> basketball statistics.
2. The announcer listed MVPs <u>in</u> playoff games.
3. In the playoffs, the right forward made the last three-point shot as the buzzer went <u>off.</u>
4. The announcer said that the player hit the final shot just before time ran <u>out.</u>
5. <u>Throughout</u> the program, the announcer's love of the game came <u>through.</u>

Exercise 8 Find It in Your Reading In the excerpt from "Slam, Dunk, & Hook" on page 403, identify the complete prepositional phrase that each highlighted preposition begins.

Exercise 9 Find It in Your Writing In a recent piece of your own writing, identify the prepositional phrases. Are there places where you can add prepositional phrases to give more information?

Exercise 10 Writing Application Choose a sport that you enjoy playing or watching. Write an explanation of how to play the game. Include at least three prepositional phrases in your sentences. Underline each prepositional phrase.

Section Review • 407

Section Review

Each of these exercises correlates to a concept in the section on prepositions, pages 400–406. These exercises may be used for more practice, for reteaching, or for review of the Key Concepts presented. Answers for all chapter exercises are available in *Grammar Exercises Answers on Transparencies* in your teaching resources.

Answer Key

Exercise 4

1. Prior to, of
2. According to, among
3. through, next to
4. out of, by
5. into, because of

Exercise 5

1. of the greatest college basketball coaches
2. at Purdue University, before his coaching career
3. at UCLA, in 1948
4. between the years 1946 and 1975
5. For his playing and coaching, to the Basketball Hall of Fame

Exercise 6

Responses will vary. Sample answers given.

by, for, in, for, of

Exercise 7

1. on—adverb; about—preposition
2. in—preposition
3. off—adverb
4. out—adverb
5. Throughout—preposition, through—adverb

Exercise 8

Find It in Your Reading

to the inside, like a sparrow hawk, on swivels, of bone and faith

Exercise 9

Find It in Your Writing

If students find places where they can add prepositional phrases, they should do so.

continued

Answer Key continued

Exercise 10

Writing Application

Have students compare their explanations with those of classmates who chose the same sport.

on the board and have students fill in the blank with one word in as many ways as they can. Have students share some of the their answers. Tell them that these connecting words are called conjunctions.

He will eat ___ he comes home.

Activate Prior Knowledge

Write the words *coordinating* and *subordinating* on the board. Working in pairs, have students try to figure out what each word means. Encourage them to look for words or roots they recognize, such as *coordinate, sub,* or *insubordination.*

TEACH

Step-by-Step Teaching Guide

Coordinating and Correlative Conjunctions

1. Tell students that the common function of all coordinating conjunctions is to join similar kinds or groups of words. Write the following sentences on the chalkboard:

   Do you want the red dress or the green one?

   José is coming, but he will be late.

   Luisa and Victoria are here.

2. Like coordinating conjunctions, correlative conjunctions join equal elements in a sentence. However, correlative conjunctions always occur in pairs.

   Neither water nor air pollution will be tolerated.

   Both toxic waste and acid rain are damaging to the environment.

   Either we do nothing or we act to protect the environment.

3. Have students point out the correlative conjunctions and the words or groups of words they connect.

Section 19.2

Conjunctions and Interjections

The last two parts of speech discussed in this chapter are *conjunctions* and *interjections.* Of the two, conjunctions are more important because they link ideas. Interjections add emotion to a sentence, but do not link ideas.

Different Kinds of Conjunctions

Prepositions simply relate different words, but conjunctions make a direct connection between words.

▶ **KEY CONCEPT** A **conjunction** is a word used to connect other words or groups of words. ■

The three main kinds of conjunctions are *coordinating conjunctions, correlative conjunctions,* and *subordinating conjunctions.*

Coordinating Conjunctions *Coordinating conjunctions* connect similar kinds of words or similar groups of words.

COORDINATING CONJUNCTIONS						
and	but	for	nor	or	so	yet

EXAMPLES:

My sister *and* brother ran the program.

They wrote a short *yet* effective report.

The dog barked *but* wagged its tail.

Put the bags on the table *or* in the closet.

Bob left early, *so* I left with him.

Correlative Conjunctions *Correlative conjunctions* also connect similar words or groups of words. However, they always appear in pairs.

CORRELATIVE CONJUNCTIONS		
both . . . and	neither . . . nor	whether . . . or
either . . . or	not only . . . but also	

EXAMPLES:

He watched *both* lions *and* tigers.

Neither Don *nor* she will go.

Jean recycled bottles and cans *not only* consistently, *but also* carefully.

In this section, you will learn about three kinds of conjunctions and the use of interjections. The examples and exercises in this section are about the environment.

Cross-Curricular Connection: Science

⏱ TIME AND RESOURCE MANAGER

Resources
Print: Grammar Exercise Workbook, pp. 37–40
Technology: Language Lab CD-ROM, Parts of Speech; On-Line Exercise Bank, Section 19.2

In-Depth Coverage	Accelerated Pace
• Work through all key concepts, pp. 408–412. • Assign and review Exercises 11–13. • Read and discuss Grammar in Literature, p. 410.	• Assign pp. 408–410 for independent student review. • Assign Exercise 12.

Subordinating Conjunctions *Subordinating conjunctions* connect two complete ideas by making one of the ideas subordinate to the other. To *subordinate* means to "place below another in rank or importance."

FREQUENTLY USED SUBORDINATING CONJUNCTIONS		
after	before	till
although	even though	unless
as	if	until
as if	in order that	when
as long as	since	whenever
as soon as	so that	where
as though	than	wherever
because	though	while

Notice that the subordinating conjunction always comes just before the subordinate idea.

EXAMPLES:

We protect the wetlands *because* they are important to the ecosystem.
As soon as the volunteers arrived, the cleanup work began.

Subordinating Conjunction or Preposition? *After, before, since, till,* and *until* can be subordinating conjunctions or prepositions, depending on how they are used. In the first example below, *until* is a subordinating conjunction because it connects two complete ideas. In the second example, *until* is the first word in a prepositional phrase.

SUBORDINATING
CONJUNCTION:

Until you finish your wetland research, you are not ready to begin writing.

PREPOSITION:

Until recent decades, people were not often concerned about the environment.

◀ **Critical Viewing**
Explain the probable role of the wetlands in the survival of this egret. Use a sentence with a subordinating conjunction in your response. **[Infer]**

Conjunctions and Interjections • 409

Subordinating Conjunctions

1. Unlike coordinating and correlative conjunctions, which link similar kinds of words, subordinating conjunctions make one clause subordinate to, or dependent upon, the other.

   Before the meeting takes place, we need to research the issues.

   When we are ready, we intend to circulate a petition.

   As soon as people are aware of the issues, we can make a difference.

2. Have students identify the subordinate ideas in the sentences above. Point out that they cannot stand on their own as sentences.

3. Students may be confused by the fact that several subordinating conjunctions also can function as prepositions and adverbs. Provide these examples to model the way one word can function as subordinating conjunction, preposition, or adverb, depending upon its use in the sentence.

   Before you leave, please turn out the lights. (subordinating conjunction)

   Make sure you get there before noon. (preposition)

   I've seen that movie before. (adverb)

Critical Viewing

Infer Students may say that since the egret is an inhabitant of the wetlands, his survival depends on that of the wetlands.

Integrating Writing Skills

Remind students that subordinate clauses are always set off by a comma when they come at the beginning of a sentence (e.g., Until I read the article, I did not know much about the wetlands.) If they follow the main clause, they need no comma. Have them review a writing selection from their portfolio and check their use of subordinating conjunctions and clauses.

Grammar in Literature

1. Have a volunteer read the passage from "To the Residents of A.D. 2029."

2. Point out the use of correlative conjunctions in the passage. Read students the following alternative without correlative conjunctions and discuss how they add to the balance and grace of the writing:

> As a race we must retain our capacity for dreaming and then keep the possibility of doing. As a crowd of individuals we must retain our capacity for dreaming and then keep the possibility of doing.

(Students may say that the correlative conjunctions make the writing less repetitive and that they emphasize the contrast between the terms *race* and *crowds of individuals*.)

Answer Key

▶ **Exercise 11**

1. either . . . or—correlative
2. and—coordinating
3. both . . . and—correlative
4. not only . . . but also—correlative
5. When—subordinating
6. or—coordinating
7. because—subordinating
8. none
9. After—subordinating
10. Although—subordinating

GRAMMAR IN LITERATURE

from To the Residents of A.D. 2029
Bryan Woolley

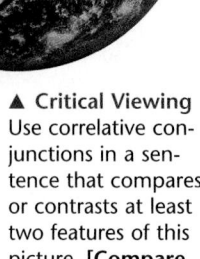

The correlative conjunctions in the following excerpt are highlighted.

Because of man's amazing record of making his dreams come true, I refuse to be pessimistic about the future, despite the frightening aspects of the present. As long as we—*both* as a race *and* as a crowd of individuals—retain our capacity for dreaming, we also keep the possibility of doing.

▲ **Critical Viewing** Use correlative conjunctions in a sentence that compares or contrasts at least two features of this picture. **[Compare and Contrast]**

▶ **Exercise 11** **Identifying Conjunctions** Write the conjunction(s) in each sentence. Then, label each *coordinating, correlative,* or *subordinating.* Write *none* if a sentence contains no conjunction.

EXAMPLE: In science, we studied both ecology and the environment.

ANSWER: both, and (correlative)

1. The term *environment* refers to the surroundings of either an individual organism or a community of organisms.
2. The word *surroundings* refers to all living and nonliving materials around an organism.
3. These materials include both food and water.
4. An organism is influenced not only by its immediate surroundings, but also by gravity.
5. When we use the word *environment,* we often think about the adverse effects of human activities.
6. Environmental groups work to prevent or lessen damage caused by human activities.
7. We study ecology because we want to analyze the interactions of organisms with their environment.
8. Since the 1970's, people have paid more attention to the environment.
9. After a ship struck the sandbar, an oil spill occurred.
10. Although volunteers arrived quickly, some wildlife could not be saved.

410 • Prepositions, Conjunctions, and Interjections

Conjunctive Adverbs

When an adverb is used to connect other words, it is called a *conjunctive adverb.*

> **KEY CONCEPT** A **conjunctive adverb** is an adverb that acts as a conjunction to connect complete ideas. ■

Conjunctive adverbs are often used as *transitions.* Transitions serve as bridges between different ideas.

FREQUENTLY USED CONJUNCTIVE ADVERBS

accordingly	finally	nevertheless
again	furthermore	otherwise
also	however	then
besides	indeed	therefore
consequently	moreover	thus

The following examples show how conjunctive adverbs can be used to make transitions between different ideas.

EXAMPLES: Maureen loves animals; *moreover,* she is a student of plant and animal life.
I arrived late; *moreover,* I forgot my books.

> **Exercise 12** **Recognizing and Supplying Conjunctive Adverbs** Read each sentence to see whether it contains a conjunctive adverb. If it does, write the conjunctive adverb. If it does not, rewrite the sentence to include a conjunctive adverb.

EXAMPLE: Gather your information; begin writing your report.

ANSWER: Gather your information; then, begin writing your report.

1. Human activities sometimes have damaging effects on the environment; therefore, society develops ways to prevent or lessen these damages.
2. Humans produce all kinds of waste; recycling is one way to reduce waste accumulation.
3. Recycling reduces the amount of waste; also, it conserves resources and cuts costs.
4. Beverage bottles can be reused for their original purpose; indeed, they can be used fifteen to twenty times before they break.
5. Some European countries encourage the reuse of beverage bottles; U.S. law does not permit the reuse of food or drink containers.

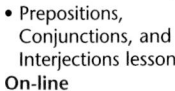

> **More Practice**
>
> Language Lab
> CD-ROM
> • Prepositions, Conjunctions, and Interjections lesson
> **On-line Exercise Bank**
> • Section 19.2
> **Grammar Exercise Workbook**
> • pp. 37–38

Conjunctions and Interjections • 411

411

19.2

Interjections

Interjections are used to express emotion.

▶ **KEY CONCEPT** An **interjection** is a word that expresses feeling or emotion; it functions independently of a sentence. ∎

Interjections—such as *aha, bravo, goodness, great, hurray, oh, oops, well, ugh,* or *whew*—express different feelings or emotions. Several different emotions are being expressed by the interjections below. Because an interjection is unrelated to any other words in the sentence, set it off from the other words by inserting an exclamation mark or a comma.

PAIN:	*Ouch!* That burns.
JOY:	*Wow!* This is great!
CONTEMPT:	*Oh,* go away.
HESITANCY:	Do you, *uh,* believe that?

Though common in speech, interjections should be used sparingly in writing.

▶ **Exercise 13** Supplying Interjections Write each sentence, adding an interjection that conveys the indicated emotion.

EXAMPLE:	(weariness) We worked hard cleaning the park.
ANSWER:	Whew! We worked hard cleaning the park.

1. (disappointment) Look at the garbage left on the ground.
2. (delight) The park certainly is cleaner since the town provided more garbage cans.
3. (happiness) Here comes the recycling truck at last.
4. (pain) I stumbled on that tree root.
5. (annoyance) I missed the trash can.
6. (uncertainty) Are you sure that plastic is recyclable?
7. (enthusiasm) That was a magnificent cleanup effort!
8. (disinterist) Could you bring back that petition another time?
9. (unintended mistake) I didn't mean to mix up the clear glass bottles with the green ones.
10. (discovery) Now I get it!

▼ **Critical Viewing**
What interjections can you use in response to this picture? **[Relate]**

☑ ONGOING ASSESSMENT: Assess Mastery

Use the following resources to assess mastery of conjunctions and interjections.

In the Textbook	Technology
Chapter Review, Ex. 22–24, pp. 414–415	On-Line Exercise Bank, Section 19.2

Section 19.2 Section Review

GRAMMAR EXERCISES 14–19

> **Exercise 14** Identifying
Conjunctions Write the conjunction(s) in each sentence. Then, label each *coordinating, correlative,* or *subordinating.* If there is no conjunction, write *none.*

1. Organisms live together in communities comprised of both plants and animals.
2. Communities may be very small or very large.
3. Biomes are extensive communities that occupy wide geographic areas.
4. Not only arctic tundras but also tropical jungles are considered biomes.
5. Some animals are found in only one layer of a biome, but most animals range through several layers.
6. In a biome, some species of animals are active during the day, whereas some are active at night.
7. Since they are active at different times, many organisms can occupy the same area.
8. If there are many species in a community, it is said to have a rich diversity.
9. After a disaster, a community will eventually restore itself.
10. Restoration occurs very slowly in the desert and the tundras because the climactic and soil conditions are not as rich or varied.

> **Exercise 15** Recognizing and
Supplying Conjunctive Adverbs Write the conjunctive adverbs in the following sentences. If a sentence has no conjunctive adverb, rewrite the sentence to include one.

1. Lichens and grasses are among the first species to invade a recovering area; they are called pioneers.

2. They are not the only pioneers; trees such as elm and aspen are, too.
3. These pioneers increase the organic content of the soil; moreover, they change the moisture conditions.
4. Some species release nitrogen into the soil; they fertilize the soil.
5. Many ecologists study ecosystems; accordingly, they determine how organisms retain and recycle minerals.

> **Exercise 16** Supplying
Interjections Supply an appropriate interjection for each sentence.

1. Those hot ashes burned me!
2. The fire ruined the animals' homes.
3. I wish the campers had put out their campfires.
4. Grass is already starting to grow after the forest fire.
5. I see new animals here already!

> **Exercise 17** Find It in Your
Reading Identify the subordinating conjunction in the excerpt from "To the Residents of A.D. 2029" on p. 410.

> **Exercise 18** Find It in Your
Writing Look through your writing portfolio. Find three coordinating conjunctions and two subordinating conjunctions in your own writing.

> **Exercise 19** Writing Application
Identify an area in your school or town that needs a cleanup. Create a poster persuading volunteers to join a cleanup project. Use at least three conjunctions and at least two interjections for emphasis.

Section Review • 413

Answer Key

> **Exercise 14**

1. both... and—correlative
2. or—coordinating
3. none
4. Not only... but also—correlative
5. but—coordinating
6. whereas—subordinating
7. Since—subordinating
8. If—subordinating
9. none
10. and—coordinating, because—subordinating, and—coordinating, or—coordinating

> **Exercise 15**

Answers will vary. Samples are given.

1. Lichens and grasses are among the first species to invade a recovering area; therefore, they are called pioneers.
2. They are not the only pioneers; in fact, trees such as elm and aspen are, too.
3. moreover
4. therefore
5. accordingly

> **Exercise 16**

Answers will vary. Samples are given.

1. Ouch!
2. Oh!
3. Darn, I wish the campers had put out their campfires.
4. Terrific!
5. Wow!

> **Exercise 17**

Find It in Your Reading
Pair students to have them exchange articles and discuss ways the subordinating conjunctions show relationships between ideas.

continued

Answer Key continued

> **Exercise 18**

Find It in Your Writing
Challenge students to try to rewrite the sentences using different kinds of conjunctions.

> **Exercise 19**

Writing Application
Suggest that students display their posters around the school.

Each of these exercises correlates with a concept in the chapter on prepositions, conjunctions, and interjections, pages 400–412. These exercises may be used for more practice, for reteaching, or for review of the Key Concepts presented.

Answer Key

Exercise 20

1. <u>of</u> paper, glass, and metals
2. <u>in spite of</u> the hassle
3. <u>to</u> a recycling bin
4. <u>after</u> using them
5. <u>from</u> the rest; <u>of</u> the trash

Exercise 21

1. down—adverb
2. Inside—preposition
3. off—adverb
4. After—preposition
5. near—preposition
6. out—adverb
7. down—adverb
8. outside—preposition
9. inside—adverb
10. in—preposition

Exercise 22

1. and—coordinating
2. After—subordinating
3. or—coordinating
4. Both . . . and—correlative
5. Not only . . . but also—correlative
6. either . . . or—correlative
7. When—subordinating
8. Although—subordinating
9. but—coordinating
10. and—coordinating

Chapter 19 Chapter Review

GRAMMAR EXERCISES 20–28

Exercise 20 Identifying Prepositions and Prepositional Phrases
Write the prepositional phrase or phrases in each sentence. Underline each preposition.

1. Recycling involves the recovery and reforming of paper, glass, and metals.
2. Recycling is worth doing in spite of the hassle.
3. Newspapers can go to a recycling bin.
4. People should separate recyclable containers after using them.
5. Recyclable glass should be separated from the rest of the trash.

Exercise 21 Distinguishing Between Prepositions and Adverbs
Label each underlined word *preposition* or *adverb*.

1. Metals are sold as scrap, which can be melted <u>down</u> and reformed.
2. <u>Inside</u> newer facilities, special equipment separates metals and glass.
3. Labels must be taken <u>off</u>.
4. <u>After</u> a short time, the landfill area for many communities may be used up.
5. This building site has a landfill <u>near</u> it.
6. Environmental engineers created a plan to prevent any hazardous materials from leaking <u>out</u>.
7. Programs that require homeowners to separate recyclable materials at home help keep collection costs <u>down</u>.
8. Some homeowners keep recycling bins <u>outside</u> the house.
9. Others prefer to keep them <u>inside</u>.
10. Transportation of waste materials is almost always included <u>in</u> the cost of recycling.

Exercise 22 Identifying Conjunctions Write the conjunction in each sentence. Then, label it *coordinating*, *correlative*, or *subordinating*.

1. Some animals speed the recycling of minerals by eating plants and other organisms.
2. After the plants have been eaten, minerals in the plants are returned to the soil in waste.
3. Scavengers break down large dead organisms faster than bacteria or fungi alone can.
4. Both bacteria and fungi eventually break down smaller organic matter into its mineral components.
5. Not only plant-eaters but also meat-eaters help recycle minerals.
6. Roots of plants may absorb minerals for reuse either from dead organisms or from soil.
7. When an ecosystem recycles minerals, it also recycles energy.
8. Although a plant-eater consumes grass and leaves, it absorbs only a small portion of a plant's energy.
9. Food passes through an animal's digestive tract, but some is not completely digested.
10. Most energy passes through animals and returns to the food chain.

Exercise 23 Recognizing Conjunctive Adverbs Write the conjunctive adverbs. If a sentence has no conjunctive adverb, rewrite the sentence to include one.

1. Ecologists observe that sometimes a species will dominate; consequently, another species will be eliminated.
2. One of the functions of herbivores is to control plant populations;

---

furthermore, parasites may serve as controls over the organisms they eat.
3. Larger animals may be affected by severe weather; predators and parasites may also control the population.
4. A forest in Minnesota destroyed by a fire may take hundreds of years to renew; one in Mexico destroyed by lava flow would take thousands of years.
5. Climate conditions in deserts and tundras are extreme; therefore, change occurs very slowly in these areas.

▶ Exercise 24   Identifying Prepositions, Conjunctions, and Interjections Write the prepositions, conjunctions, and interjections in the following sentences; then, label each one.

1. Plant material and food scraps can be recycled through composting.
2. In this form of recycling, dead plant materials are put in a pile until they decay.
3. Not only grass and leaves, but also materials such as coffee grinds are suitable for a compost pile.
4. The plant materials are layered above the ground.
5. Between each layer, a thin layer of soil may be added; moreover, watering will also speed decay.
6. If a container is used, it should have holes for air circulation.
7. Goodness! Turning over the compost pile is hard work, but the results are worth the effort.
8. Compost can be used either as fertilizer or as mulch on top of the soil.
9. When it is spread around plants, compost helps keep moisture in.
10. Wow! My plants are growing so fast since I started using compost!

▶ Exercise 25   Combining Sentences With Conjunctions Use a coordinating, correlative, or subordinating conjunction to combine each pair of sentences. Underline each conjunction you use.

1. Plastic bottles are shredded. They are re-formed into fiber for fiberfill.
2. Energy is used to reprocess waste material. Less energy is used for non-waste material.
3. Schools usually have recycling bins. Many office buildings also have them.
4. People don't recycle just paper, cans, and bottles. They recycle scrap wood and bricks, too.
5. Recycling isn't the whole solution to the problem of waste. Conservation is also not the whole solution.

▶ Exercise 26   Revising Sentences by Adding Prepositional Phrases Revise the following sentences, adding prepositional phrases according to the hints in parentheses.

1. We separated the trash (how).
2. (when), the recycling truck came.
3. Later, we went (where).
4. We bought a gift (recipient).
5. (where), we gave it (recipient).

▶ Exercise 27   Revising Sentences by Adding Interjections Add an appropriate interjection to each sentence.

1. If I recycle, electricity may not cost so much.
2. That bag of glass bottles for recycling was heavy.
3. I was hoping for that.
4. We finished that job on time!
5. I forgot to tell you.

▶ Exercise 28   Writing Application
Write a short descriptive paragraph about some scene or event in nature that you have observed. Include at least three prepositional phrases and three conjunctions, as well as one or more interjections. Underline each of these parts in your sentences.

Chapter Review • 415

Answer Key continued

Exercise 27

Answers will vary. Samples are given.

1. Great!
2. Whew!
3. Wow!
4. Hurray!
5. Oh,

Exercise 28

Writing Application
Suggest that students trade paragraphs with a partner, and write three questions about each other's work. Have them include at least one preposition, one conjunction, and one interjection in their questions.

Exercise 23

Answers will vary. Samples are given.

1. consequently
2. furthermore
3. Larger animals may be affected by severe weather; in addition, predators and parasites may also control the population.
4. A forest in Minnesota destroyed by a fire may take hundreds of years to renew; indeed, one in Mexico destroyed by lava flow would take thousands of years.
5. therefore

Exercise 24

1. preposition: through; conjunction: and
2. prepositions: in, of, in; conjunction: until
3. preposition: for; conjunctions: not only . . . but also, and
4. preposition: above
5. prepositions: between, of; conjunctive adverb: moreover
6. preposition: for; conjunction if
7. conjunction: but; interjection: Goodness!
8. prepositions: as, as, on, of; conjunction: either . . . or
9. prepositions: around conjunction: when
10. conjunction: since; interjection: Wow!

Exercise 25

Answers will vary. Samples are given.

1. Plastic bottles are shredded <u>and</u> re-formed into fiber for fiber fill.
2. Energy is used to reprocess waste material; <u>however,</u> less energy is used for non-waste material.
3. <u>Although</u> schools usually have recycling bins, many office buildings also have them.
4. People recycle <u>not only</u> paper, cans, and bottles but also scrap wood and bricks.
5. <u>Neither</u> recycling <u>nor</u> conservation is the whole solution to the problem of waste.

Exercise 26

Answers will vary. Samples are given.

1. We separated the trash into plastics and paper.
2. The recycling truck came before noon.
3. Later, we went to the recycling center.
4. We bought a gift for Paul on his birthday.
5. In the restaurant, we gave it to Paul.
continued

Lesson Objectives

1. To revise and edit passages according to standard grammar and usage.
2. To connect or clarify ideas using prepositional phrases, conjunctions, and interjections.

Step-by-Step Teaching Guide

Revising and Editing

1. Review each of the test tips in the textbook with students.

2. Make sure students understand how the different conjunctions, including correlative conjunctions, signal different relationships between ideas.

3. As students read a test passage, encourage them to look for repeated information that can be combined into one sentence, as well as sentences containing closely-related ideas that can be combined using conjunctions.

4. Have a volunteer explain why item D in the sample test item is the best revision to the original sentences.

Standardized Test Preparation Workshop

Revising and Editing

Standardized test questions evaluate your knowledge of standard grammar and usage. Testing your ability to connect ideas using prepositional phrases, conjunctions, and interjections is one way to do so. Before answering these types of questions, read the entire passage carefully. Note how using a prepositional phrase, a conjunction, or an interjection helps connect similar ideas, eliminate unnecessary words, or make meanings clearer. Finally, choose the letter of the best rewrite of the underlined sentences.

The following test item will give you practice with prepositions, conjunctions, and interjections.

Test Tips

Remember the following rules when answering these types of questions:
- Prepositional phrases relate a noun or pronoun to another word in the sentence.
- Conjunctions such as *and, but, or,* and *for* join closely related ideas.
- Interjections express feelings and emotions.

Sample Test Item

Directions: Read the following passage. Choose the letter of the best way to rewrite the underlined sections.

William Young was the first shoemaker to
(1)
make shoes designed for the left and right

feet. William Young lived in Philadelphia.

1 A William Young lived in Philadelphia and was the first shoemaker to make shoes designed for left and right feet.

  B The first shoemaker to make shoes designed for left and right feet was William Young. He lived in Philadelphia.

  C William Young made shoes designed for left and right feet. He was from Philadelphia.

  D William Young, of Philadelphia, was the first shoemaker to make shoes designed for left and right feet.

Answers and Explanations

The correct answer is *D*. The use of the prepositional phrase *of Philadelphia* combines the two sentences into one and eliminates unnecessary words.

416 • Prepositions, Conjunctions, and Interjections

⬦ TEST-TAKING TIP

Students always should compare each of the choices to the original passage to make sure that none of the information is missing or has changed. Once students have excluded choices that change the meaning of the original sentences, they can focus on identifying the best revision remaining.

Practice 1 **Directions:** Read the passage, and choose the letter of the best way to rewrite the underlined sections.

Franklin D. Roosevelt was elected
(1)
president in 1932. He served until his

death in 1945. In 1934, Roosevelt signed
                (2)
the Securities Exchange Act. In 1934,

he also signed the Communications Act.

1 A Franklin D. Roosevelt, elected president in 1932, served as president until his death in 1945.
   B Franklin D. Roosevelt was elected president in 1932 and served until his death in 1945.
   C Franklin D. Roosevelt was elected president in 1932, and he died in 1945.
   D President Franklin D. Roosevelt, who died in 1945, was elected president in 1932.

2 F Roosevelt signed the Securities Exchange Act in 1934; he signed the Communications Act in 1934.
   G Securities Exchange Act and also the Communications Act in 1934 were signed by Roosevelt.
   H In 1934, Roosevelt signed both the Securities Exchange Act and the Communications Act.
   J In 1934, Roosevelt signed the Securities Exchange Act, and he signed the Communications Act, as well.

Practice 2 **Directions:** Read the passage, and choose the letter of the best way to rewrite the underlined sections.

One program that provided economic
(1)
relief was the Works Progress

Administration (WPA). It was established

during the Great Depression. It was estab-
                                        (2)
lished to provide jobs. There were many

unemployed people at this time.

1 A One program that provided economic relief was the Works Progress Administration (WPA), and it was established during the Great Depression.
   B One program during the Great Depression that provided economic relief was the Works Progress Administration (WPA).
   C One program, the Works Progress Administration (WPA), was started during the Great Depression to provide economic relief.
   D One program that provided economic relief during the Great Depression was the Works Progress Administration (WPA).

2 F It was established to provide jobs, for there were many unemployed people at this time.
   G It was established to provide jobs for the many unemployed people at this time.
   H For the many unemployed people, it was established to provide jobs at this time.
   J It was established to provide jobs. Yes! There were many unemployed people at this time.

Answer Key

Cumulative Review

PARTS OF SPEECH

> **Exercise 1** **Identifying Nouns and Pronouns** List the nouns in the following sentences, labeling each *singular* or *plural* and *common* or *proper*. Also, label compound nouns as such. Then, list the pronouns and label each *personal, demonstrative, interrogative, reflexive, intensive, relative,* or *indefinite.*

1. Michael Romanov, elected czar in 1613, was the first of his family, the Romanovs, to rule Russia.
2. This was the time of new laws that favored noble landlords.
3. Alexis I succeeded his father in 1649.
4. During the reign of Alexis, there was a peasant revolt.
5. Then, it was his son, Fyodor III, who himself led the Russians into battle against the Ottoman Empire.
6. After Fyodor III died, who was to become czar?
7. First, his half-brother, Peter I, was named.
8. When his powerful sister, Sophia, attempted to assassinate Peter, she was herself forced to resign.
9. Under Peter I, Russia began to be a major European power.
10. Later, he declared Russia an empire and named himself emperor.

> **Exercise 2** **Identifying Verbs** Write the verbs in the following sentences. Label each *action* or *linking, visible* or *mental action,* and *transitive* or *intransitive.* Underline any helping verbs.

1. In 1697, Peter the Great led a diplomatic mission to western Europe.
2. When he returned, he wanted to transform Moscow and all of Russia.

3. He organized the Russian army, the government, and the social structure according to Western models.
4. Peter was using laws and decrees to force new developments.
5. Education, science, and industry were some areas that grew quickly.
6. Peter sent young Russians abroad, where they were taught crafts and trades.
7. The Great Northern War, which was fought against Sweden, continued for more than twenty years.
8. In 1703, Peter founded Saint Petersburg and made it his capital.
9. He modernized the administration and government; they were made much more efficient.
10. Also, the first Russian-language newspaper was published after the complex Russian alphabet was simplified.

> **Exercise 3** **Identifying Adjectives and Adverbs** Identify the underlined words in the following sentences as *adjective* or *adverb,* and write the word that each modifies.

1. Peter's second wife, Catherine I, ruled briefly after his death.
2. An extensive succession of rulers paraded rapidly through court over the next several years.
3. Anna Ivanovna ruled strictly and filled the court with her Prussian friends.
4. She was almost replaced by Ivan VI, but a palace conspiracy placed Elizabeth Petrovna on the throne.
5. The youngest daughter of Peter the Great, she soon started a national revival.
6. Her diplomatic victory was an end to a very lengthy war between Sweden and Russia.

Answer Key

Exercise 1

1. Michael Romanov—singular, compound, proper noun; czar—singular, common noun; his—personal; family—singular, common noun; Romanovs—plural, proper noun; Russia—singular, proper noun
2. this—demonstrative; time—singular, common noun; laws—plural, common noun; landlords—plural, compound noun
3. Alexis I—singular, proper noun; his—personal; father—singular, common noun; 1649—singular, common noun
4. reign—singular, common noun; Alexis—singular, proper noun; there—demonstrative; revolt—singular, common noun
5. it—personal; his—personal; son—singular, common noun; Fyodor III—singular, proper noun; who—relative; himself—intensive; Russians—plural, proper noun; Ottoman Empire—singular, compound, proper noun
6. Fyodor III—singular, proper noun; who—interrogative; czar—singular, common noun
7. his—personal; half-brother—singular, compound, common noun; Peter I—singular, proper noun
8. his—personal; sister—singular, common noun; Sophia—singular, proper noun; Peter—singular, proper noun, she—personal; herself—intensive
9. Peter I—singular, proper noun; Russia—singular, proper noun; power—singular, common noun
10. he—personal; Russia—singular, proper noun; empire—singular, common noun; himself—intensive; emperor—singular, common noun

Exercise 2

1. led—action, visible, transitive
2. returned—action, visible, intransitive; wanted—action, mental, transitive
3. organized—action, visible, transitive
4. was using—action, visible, transitive
5. were—linking; grew—action, visible, intransitive
6. sent—action, visible, transitive; were taught—action, visible, transitive

7. was fought—action, visible, intransitive; continued—action, visible, intransitive
8. founded—action, visible, transitive; made—action, visible, transitive
9. modernized—action, visible, transitive; were made—action, visible, intransitive
10. was published—action, visible, intransitive ; was simplified—action, visible, intransitive

Exercise 3

Check that students have identified all adjectives and adverbs correctly.
1. adjective: second wife; adverb: briefly ruled
2. adjectives: extensive succession, several years; adverbs: rapidly paraded; next several

3. adjectives: her Prussian friends; adverb: strictly ruled
4. adjective: palace conspiracy; almost was replaced
5. adjectives: youngest daughter, national revival; adverb: soon started
6. adjectives: diplomatic victory, lengthy war; adverb: very lengthy
7. adjective: German princess; adverb: swiftly was deposed
8. adjective: only successor; adverb: truly understood
9. adjective: unstable Peter III
10. adjective: French Enlightenment*
   *Students could also correctly classify French Enlightenment as a proper compound noun

7. After Peter III was swiftly deposed, his wife, a German princess, took the throne.
8. She was the only successor to Peter the Great who truly understood his reforms and continued them.
9. Catherine married the unstable Peter III in 1745.
10. Her interest in the French Enlightenment led her to apply some of the ideas to Russia.

Exercise 4 Classifying Prepositions, Conjunctions, and Interjections

Write and label each preposition, conjunction, and interjection. Then, identify each conjunction as *coordinating*, *correlative*, or *subordinating* or as a *conjunctive adverb*.

1. French literature influenced Catherine's political thinking; indeed, she corresponded frequently with the celebrated author Voltaire.
2. Yes, she even gave them financial support, although it may have been an attempt to create a favorable image.
3. Not only had she released the nobles from their military obligations, but she had also granted them many other privileges.
4. Catherine generously granted her supporters land, titles, and offices.
5. Whether or not her personal stance was against serfdom, she did much to expand its place in Russia.
6. State-owned serfs were transferred to private landowners, thus spreading serfdom to new territories.
7. Moreover, the legal control of the nobles over their serfs was increased.
8. A peasant revolt lasted for two years before it was quelled by the army.
9. Several major reforms were discussed, but Catherine's death stopped many of these plans.
10. Wow! Was Catherine the Great's rule long—thirty-four years!

Exercise 5 Revising by Adding Different Parts of Speech

Revise these sentences, following the instructions in parentheses.

1. Our neighbors came from Russia. (Change "Our neighbors" to two proper nouns.)
2. Our neighbors learned English __?__. (Change "Our neighbors" to a personal pronoun, and supply an adverb.)
3. We find them to be very __?__ people. (Change "We" to a common noun and a personal pronoun, and supply an adjective.)
4. They __?__ told us many stories __?__. (Supply a helping verb and a prepositional phrase.)
5. We have eaten Russian food, and it __?__ __?__. (Supply a linking verb and an adjective.)
6. We liked the thin cheese-filled pancakes called "blini." We found the caviar too salty. (Combine using a coordinating or a conjunctive adverb.)
7. My neighbors __?__ their friends in Moscow. (Supply an action verb.)
8. They __?__ send e-mail messages to them. (Supply an adverb.)
9. They installed the Russian alphabet in their computer. __?__ Isn't that amazing? (Supply an interjection.)
10. Russia is certainly far away. We would like to travel there some day. (Combine using a conjunctive adverb.)

Exercise 6 Writing Application

Write a brief description of what you would do as the king or queen of a country. Underline at least one noun, pronoun, verb, adjective, adverb, preposition, conjunction, and interjection. Then, label the part of speech of each as specifically as possible.

Exercise 4
1. indeed—subordinating conjunction; with—prep
2. Yes—interjection; although—subordinating conjunction
3. Not only . . . but also—correlative conjunction; from—prep
4. and—coordinating conjunction
5. Whether . . . or—correlative conjunction; against—prep; in—prep
6. to—prep; thus—conjunctive adverb; to—prep
7. Moreover—conjunctive adverb; of—prep; over—prep
8. for—prep; before—subordinating conjunction; by—prep
9. but—coordinating conjunction; of—prep
10. Wow—interjection

Exercise 5
Answers will vary. Samples are given.
1. Mischa and Ruth came from Russia.
2. They learned English quickly.
3. My Mom and I find them to be very friendly people.
4. They have told us many stories about their homeland.
5. We have eaten Russian food, and it tasted wonderful.
6. We liked the thin, cheese-filled pancakes called "blini," but we found the caviar too salty.
7. My neighbors visited their friends in Moscow.
8. They often send e-mail messages to them.
9. They installed the Russian alphabet in their computer. Hey! Isn't that amazing?
10. Russia is certainly far away; nevertheless, we would like to travel there someday.

Exercise 6
Writing Application
If students find that they do not have a particular part of speech in their descriptions, have them continue writing, making sure they include those parts of speech. When students are finished, have them exchange their descriptions with partners so that they can check each other's work.

In-Depth Lesson Plan

	LESSON FOCUS	PRINT AND MEDIA RESOURCES
DAY 1	**Complete Subjects and Predicates** Students learn and apply concepts covering subjects and predicates and do the Hands-on Grammar activity (pp. 422–427).	**Teaching Resources** *Grammar Exercise Workbook*, pp. 41–48; *Grammar Exercises Answers on Transparencies*, Chapter 20; *On-Line Exercise Bank*, Section 20.1
DAY 2	**Hard-to-Find Subjects** Students learn and apply concepts covering hard-to-find subjects (pp. 428–433).	**Teaching Resources** *Grammar Exercise Workbook*, pp.49–52; *Grammar Exercises Answers on Transparencies*, Chapter 20; *On-Line Exercise Bank*, Section 20.2
DAY 3	**Complements** Students learn and apply concepts covering direct and indirect objects and subject complements (pp. 434–443).	**Teaching Resources** *Grammar Exercise Workbook*, pp.53–64; *Grammar Exercises Answers on Transparencies*, Chapter 20; *On-Line Exercise Bank*, Section 20.3
DAY 4	**Review and Assess** Students review chapter and demonstrate mastery of use of basic sentence parts (pp. 444–447).	**Teaching Resources** *Formal Assessment*, Ch. 20; *Grammar Exercises Answers on Transparencies*, Chapter 20; *On-Line Exercise Bank*, Section 20.1

Accelerated Lesson Plan

	LESSON FOCUS	PRINT AND MEDIA RESOURCES
DAY 1	**Basic Sentence Parts** Students cover concepts and usage of subjects and predicates as determined by Diagnostic Test (pp. 422–441).	**Teaching Resources** *Grammar Exercise Workbook*, pp.41–64; *Grammar Exercises Answers on Transparencies*, Chapter 20; *On-Line Exercise Bank*, Section 20.1–3
DAY 2	**Review and Assess** Students review chapter and demonstrate mastery of use of basic sentence parts (pp. 444–447).	**Teaching Resources** *Formal Assessment*, Ch. 20; *Grammar Exercises Answers on Transparencies*, Chapter 20; *On-Line Exercise Bank*, Section 20.1

Options for Adapting Lesson Plans

HOMEWORK

Have students complete any section of the chapter for homework.

FEATURES

Extend coverage with the Grammar in Literature feature (pp. 432, 435) and the Standardized Test Preparation Workshop (p. 446).

TECHNOLOGY

Students can use the On-Line Exercise Bank to complete the exercises on computer. The Auto Check feature will grade their work.

INTEGRATED SKILLS COVERAGE

Grammar in Literature
SE pp. 432, 435

Reading
Find It in Your Reading SE pp. 426, 427, 433, 443

Writing
Find It in Your Writing SE pp. 426, 427, 433, 443
Writing Application SE pp. 427, 433, 443, 445

Spelling
SE p. 431

Speaking and Listening
Integrating Speaking and Listening ATE p. 439

Real-World Connection
ATE p. 437

Viewing and Representing
Critical Viewing SE pp. 420, 423, 424, 429, 436, 440

ASSESSMENT SUPPORT

Standardized Test Preparation SE p. 446; ATE pp. 429, 439

Standardized Test Preparation Workbook, pp. 39–40

Formal Assessment, Ch. 20

MEETING INDIVIDUAL NEEDS

Less Advanced Students See Ongoing Assessments ATE pp. 423, 424, 425, 431, 435, 437

Musical Learners ATE p. 430

BLOCK SCHEDULING

Pacing Suggestions
For 90-minute Blocks
• Administer the Diagnostic Test to students to determine instructional coverage.
• Have students complete the necessary exercises in class. Use the Hands-on Grammar activity to provide a change of pace.

Resources for Varying Instruction
• *Language Lab* CD-ROM If your students have access to hardware, a 90-minute block provides an ideal opportunity for students to work on computer.

Professional Development Support
• *How to Manage Instruction in the Block* This teaching resource provides management and activity suggestions.

MEDIA AND TECHNOLOGY

For the Student
• *On-Line Exercise Bank,* Ch. 20

For the Teacher
• *Resource Pro* CD-ROM

WRITING AND GRAMMAR WEBSITE

The Interactive Writing and Grammar Website provides a wide array of support for students, teachers, and parents. Grammar support includes:

• *On-Line Exercise Bank* with Auto Check scoring
• Diagnostic and assessment support

phwg.phschool.com

LITERATURE CONNECTIONS

Grammar in Literature selections from *Prentice Hall Literature: Timeless Voices, Timeless Themes,* Gold:
from "I Wandered Lonely as a Cloud," William Wordsworth, SE p. 432
from *I Had a Hammer,* Hank Aaron, SE p. 435

Lesson Objectives

1. To recognize and identify the complete subject of a sentence.
2. To recognize and identify the complete predicate of a sentence.
3. To distinguish between simple and complete subjects and predicates.
4. To recognize and identify compound subjects and verbs.
5. To find subjects in orders, directions, and questions.
6. To find subjects in sentences beginning with *Here* or *There*.
7. To find subjects in sentences with inverted word order.
8. To recognize and identify complements in subjects and predicates.
9. To recognize and identify direct and indirect objects.
10. To distinguish between direct and indirect objects and objects of prepositions.
11. To recognize predicate nominatives and predicate adjectives.
12. To recognize and identify object complements.

Critical Viewing

Speculate Students may suggest that medical researchers are inspired by the chance to effectively find cures for diseases such as cancer or AIDS.

Chapter 20 Basic Sentence Parts

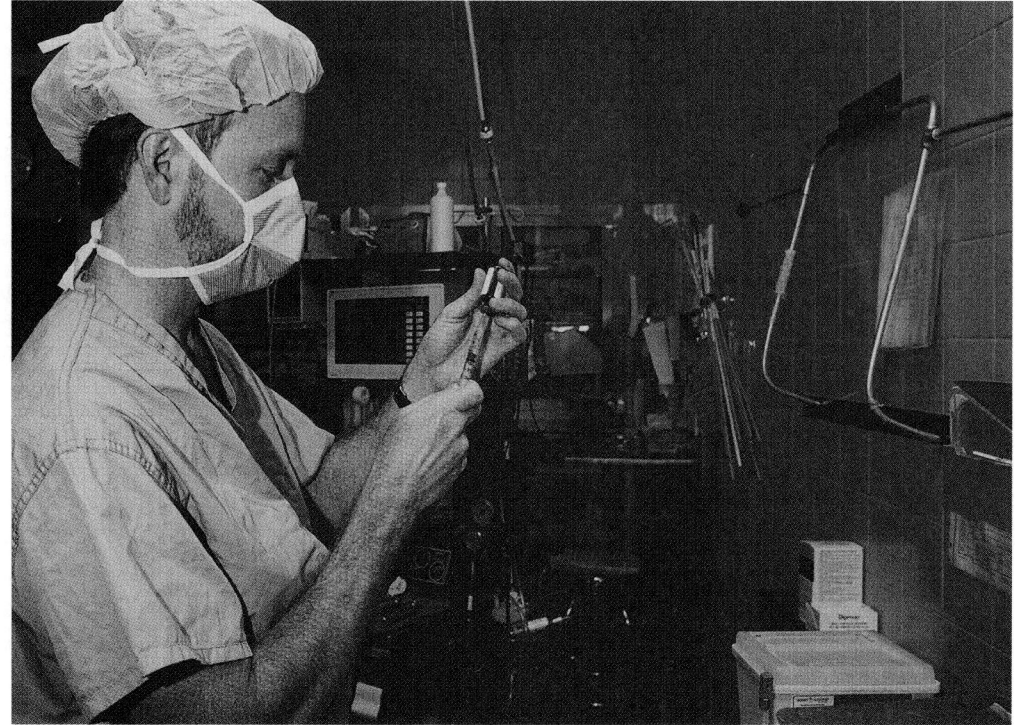

To work effectively in a career or job, one must use sentences to communicate with others. Nurses, doctors, architects, cooks—all must have good writing and speaking abilities. Effective writing and speaking depends on the ability to form sentences.

Every sentence in the English language, clearly written, follows certain basic patterns that can be described in grammatical terms. This chapter will explore some of the basic patterns, giving you a better understanding of the variety of expressions that you have at your command.

▲ **Critical Viewing** What do you think are some of the things that inspire medical researchers to choose their career? Answer in a complete sentence. **[Speculate]**

420 • Basic Sentence Parts

☑ ONGOING ASSESSMENT: Diagnose

If students miss more than one item in each category, direct them to the relevant pages of the text and assign exercises for practice and review.

Basic Sentence Parts	Diagnostic Test Items	Teach	Practice	Section Review	Chapter Review
Skill Check A					
Complete Subjects and Predicates	A 1–5	pp. 422–423	Ex. 1–2	Ex. 6–7	Ex. 41
Skill Check B					
Compound Subjects and Verbs	B 6–10	pp. 424–425	Ex. 3–5	Ex. 6–8	Ex. 42
Skill Check C					
Hard-to-Find Subjects	C 11–15	pp. 428–431	Ex. 12–13	Ex. 14–16	Ex. 43

Diagnostic Test

Directions: Write all answers on a separate sheet of paper.

Skill Check A. Write each sentence, drawing a vertical line between the complete subject and complete predicate. Then, underline each simple subject once and underline the verb twice.

1. High-school graduates have a great variety of career choices.
2. The amount of additional schooling for these careers varies.
3. Few careers accept less than a high-school diploma.
4. Educational programs in vocational schools, junior colleges, and universities help to prepare students for their professions.
5. Graduating from an institution of higher education shows determination and accomplishment.

Skill Check B. Make two columns on your paper, one labeled *subject* and one labeled *predicate*. Write the noun or nouns that make up each simple subject under the subject column and the verb or verbs under the predicate column.

6. Researchers and librarians work in information science.
7. These professionals seek, utilize, and even organize information.
8. Computer science, mathematics, and engineering are considered important areas of information science.
9. Libraries and archives store and catalog information.
10. Librarians and archivists must learn and use various research methods.

Skill Check C. Write the subject of the following directions, questions, and inverted-order sentences.

11. How much schooling does a physical therapist need?
12. Eventually, after college training, comes private practice.
13. There is the physical therapist's office.
14. Visit the physical therapist and practice your exercises.
15. Here are the exercises to strengthen your arm.

Skill Check D. Label each underlined word *direct object, indirect object,* or *object of the preposition.*

16. Most careers require some kind of higher <u>education</u>.
17. A teacher receives his or her <u>degree</u> in education.
18. His college granted <u>him</u> a degree in social work.
19. My friend received <u>information</u> about a management degree.
20. Mathematics courses are required for civil engineering <u>students</u>.

Skill Check E. Label each underlined word(s) *predicate nominative, predicate adjective,* or *objective complement.*

21. Generally, a nurse must be a <u>college graduate</u>.
22. Nurses are extremely <u>busy</u> with multiple responsibilities.
23. In addition, nurses must be both friends and <u>caregivers</u>.
24. The hospital appoints head nurses <u>leaders</u> of their departments.
25. Nurses must be <u>flexible</u> and must provide genuine care.

Basic Sentence Parts • 421

ONGOING ASSESSMENT: Diagnose *continued*					
Basic Sentence Parts	**Diagnostic Test Items**	**Teach**	**Practice**	**Section Review**	**Chapter Review**
Skill Check D					
Direct and Indirect Objects; Objects of Prepositions	D 16–20	pp. 434–438	Ex. 20–24	Ex. 24–32	Ex. 44
Skill Check E					
Predicate Nominatives and Adjectives	E 21–25	pp. 439–441	Ex. 25–28	Ex. 33–36	Ex. 45
Cumulative Reviews and Applications				Ex. 9–11, 17–19, 38–40	Ex. 46–49

Answer Key

Diagnostic Test

- Each item in the diagnostic test corresponds to a specific concept in the chapter on basic sentence parts. This will enable you to tailor instruction to the particular needs of your students. See "Ongoing Assessment: Diagnose" below for further details.
- Answers for the Diagnostic Test and all chapter exercises are available in *Grammar Exercises Answers on Transparencies* in your teaching resources.

Skill Check A

1. High school <u>graduates</u> | <u>have</u> a great variety of career choices.
2. The <u>amount</u> of additional schooling for these careers | <u>varies</u>.
3. Few <u>careers</u> | <u>accept</u> less than a high-school diploma.
4. Educational <u>programs</u> in vocational schools, junior colleges, and universities | <u>help to prepare</u> students for their professions.
5. <u>Graduating</u> from an institution of higher education | <u>shows</u> determination and accomplishment.

Skill Check B

6. subjects: Researchers, librarians; verb: work
7. subject: professionals; verbs: seek, utilize, organize
8. subjects: science, mathematics, engineering; verb: are considered
9. subjects: Libraries, archives; verbs: store, catalog
10. subjects: Librarians, archivists; verbs: learn, use

Skill Check C

11. therapist
12. practice
13. office
14. you
15. exercises

Skill Check D

16. object of the preposition
17. direct object
18. indirect object
19. direct object
20. object of the preposition

Skill Check E

21. predicate nominative
22. predicate adjective
23. predicate nominative
24. objective complement
25. predicate adjective

examples of two-word sentences, such as *He called. She snarled. Carl sang.* Draw a line between the subject and verb. Ask students to add further details to both sides of each line, making sentences such as *He called to tell her to come home.* Explain that the first two words, the subject and verb, are called the simple subject and the simple predicate.

Activate Prior Knowledge

Ask students to define the word *sentence.* Elicit from them that a sentence must include a subject and a verb. Ask them what function all the extra words in a sentence serve. Show students how all the other words in a sentence describe either the subject or the verb. Introduce the term *predicate.*

TEACH

Step-by-Step Teaching Guide

Complete Subjects and Predicates

1. Warn students that they will sometimes see words in between the subject and the verb. Such words may be part of the subject or part of the predicate. In these sentences, students should apply this rule: If a word modifies the verb, it is part of the predicate; if not, it is part of the subject.

My thoughts often drifted back to the last time we had met.

2. *Often* comes between the subject, *thoughts,* and the verb, *drifted.* Since it modifies *drifted,* it is part of the complete predicate.

Answer Key

Exercise 1

1. Nurses | teach preventive care and rehabilitation.
2. Most nurses | work in hospitals.
3. Other nurses | provide their services in health agencies, nursing homes, offices, schools, and industries.
4. Nurses | can be educators, administrators, or supervisors.
5. Most nursing | was done at home in the nineteenth century.

Section 20.1

Complete Subjects and Predicates

Every *sentence* has two main parts.

▶ **KEY CONCEPT** A **sentence** is a group of words with two main parts: a *complete subject* and a *complete predicate.* Together, these parts express a complete thought. ∎

The chart below shows the two main parts of three complete sentences. In each sentence, the *complete subject* includes a noun or pronoun that names the person, place, or thing that the sentence is about. Each *complete predicate* includes a verb that tells something about the complete subject.

Complete Subjects	Complete Predicates
Several pilots from various countries	have vanished in or near the Bermuda Triangle.
The Bermuda Triangle, the area in question,	lies between Florida, Bermuda, and Puerto Rico.
The U.S.S. *Cyclops*	disappeared there in 1918.

As you can see in the following examples, the complete subject or complete predicate can consist of several words or just one word.

EXAMPLES: He | read about many different careers.
         COMPLETE SUBJECT   COMPLETE PREDICATE

The nurse in the white uniform | arrived.
     COMPLETE SUBJECT   COMPLETE PREDICATE

▶ **Exercise 1** **Recognizing Complete Subjects and Predicates**
Write each sentence, drawing a vertical line between the complete subject and the complete predicate.

EXAMPLE: The tired nurse | completed her rounds.

1. Nurses teach preventive care and rehabilitation.
2. Most nurses work in hospitals.
3. Other nurses provide their services in health agencies, nursing homes, offices, schools, and industries.
4. Nurses can be educators, administrators, or supervisors.
5. Most nursing was done at home in the nineteenth century.

422 • **Basic Sentence Parts**

Theme: Helping Professions
....
In this section, you will learn about simple and compound subjects and predicates. The examples and exercises in this section are about professionals who help others.
....
Cross-Curricular Connection: Social Studies

▶ **More Practice**

On-line Exercise Bank
• Section 20.1
Grammar Exercise Workbook
• pp. 41–46

⏱ TIME AND RESOURCE MANAGER

Resources
Print: Grammar Exercise Workbook, pp. 41–48; Hands-on Grammar Activity Book, Chapter 20
Technology: On-Line Exercise Bank, Section 20.1

In-Depth Coverage	Accelerated Pace
• Work through all key concepts, pp. 422–425. • Assign and review Exercises 1–5.	• Assign pp. 422–425 for independent student review. • Assign Review Exercises 6–8.

Simple Subjects and Predicates

Every complete subject and complete predicate contains a word or group of words that is essential to the sentence.

KEY CONCEPTS The **simple subject** is the essential noun, pronoun, or group of words acting as a noun that cannot be left out of the complete subject. The **simple predicate** is the essential verb or verb phrase that cannot be left out of the complete predicate. ■

Notice that all the other words in the complete subject add details to the simple subject. Similarly, all of the other words in the complete predicate either modify the simple predicate or help it complete the meaning of the sentence.

SIMPLE SUBJECT	SIMPLE PREDICATE
EXAMPLES: Two of his *friends*	*studied* law enforcement.
COMPLETE SUBJECT	COMPLETE PREDICATE

SIMPLE SUBJECT	SIMPLE PREDICATE
Sick in bed, *she*	*had missed* her job interview.
COMPLETE SUBJECT	COMPLETE PREDICATE

Note About *Simple Subjects*: The simple subject is never the object of a preposition.

EXAMPLE: Most nations of the world have their own police.

In this example, *nations* is the simple subject of the sentence; *world* is the object of the preposition *of*.

Exercise 2 **Recognizing Simple Subjects and Predicates** Write each sentence, drawing a vertical line between the complete subject and complete predicate. Underline the simple subject once and the verb twice.

EXAMPLE: A <u>friend</u> of mine|<u>visited</u> the
           police barracks.

1. The police are government agents.
2. They protect citizens from unlawful acts.
3. The U.S. police establishment operates at several levels.
4. The Federal Bureau of Investigation (FBI) is the largest and most important department.
5. Two other federal departments are the Secret Service and the Customs Service.

▼ Critical Viewing
Using a complete sentence, name one one way in which law enforcement officers protect us. **[Relate]**

Complete Subjects and Predicates • 423

Simple Subjects and Predicates

1. Ask a volunteer to read the Key Concepts statement aloud. Emphasize *essential noun* and *pronoun*. Since a complete subject can contain several nouns or pronouns, students should always find the verb and then look back to see which noun is performing the action or is in the condition described by the verb.

2. Point out the note about the object of a preposition. Review prepositions and have students use the sentences on these two pages to practice identifying nouns and pronouns that are objects of prepositions. Point out that the object of a preposition always follows the preposition in the sentence:

   Most nurses work in hospitals.

   In is a preposition; *hospitals* is its object. It follows the preposition in the sentence.

Answer Key

Exercise 2

1. The <u>police</u> | <u>are</u> government agents.
2. <u>They</u> | <u>protect</u> citizens from unlawful acts.
3. The U.S. police <u>establishment</u> | <u>operates</u> at several levels.
4. The Federal <u>Bureau</u> of Investigation (FBI) | <u>is</u> the largest and most important department.
5. Two other federal <u>departments</u> | <u>are</u> the Secret Service and the Customs Service.

Critical Viewing

Relate Students may suggest that law enforcement officers protect us by patrolling the streets.

☑ **ONGOING ASSESSMENT SYSTEM: Prerequisite Skills**

If students have difficulty with subjects and predicates, you may find it necessary to review the following to assure coverage of prerequisite knowledge.

In the Textbook	Print Resources	Technology

Nouns and Pronouns,
    pp. 340–359
Verbs, pp. 360–377
	Grammar Exercise Workbook,
	    pp. 1–20
		Language Lab CD-ROM,
		    Nouns and Pronouns, Verbs;
		On-Line Exercise Bank,
		    Sections 16.1–17.3

Compound Subjects

1. Review conjunctions. Since a conjunction joins together two words, it makes them function as one part of speech. When compound subjects and verbs consist of more than two words, students should not use *and* or *or* between the items in the list. Instead, they should connect the words with commas.

2. Use sentence 1 in Exercise 3 to demonstrate that a compound subject made of singular nouns takes a plural verb. If the sentence were about either the therapist or the patient, the verb would be *plans*. Since the sentence is about both these subjects, it becomes a plural subject and the verb becomes *plan*.

Critical Viewing

Connect Students may say that both doctors and physical therapists have changed the methods in which computers are used by using them to test and analyze processes.

Answer Key

Exercise 3

1. therapist, patient
2. heat, light, water, massage
3. joints, pain
4. bath, compress
5. patient, therapist
6. therapy, therapy
7. tools, materials
8. doctors, therapists
9. victims, people
10. therapists, therapists

20.1

Compound Subjects

Some sentences have two or more subjects.

KEY CONCEPT A **compound subject** is two or more subjects that have the same verb and are joined by a conjunction such as *and* or *or*. ■

In each of the following examples, the parts of the compound subject are underlined once and the verb twice.

EXAMPLES: You and she took entrance tests yesterday.
Either the actor or the tailor will talk at our career day.
Snow, ice, and flooding made the roads treacherous.

Exercise 3 **Recognizing Compound Subjects** Write the nouns that make up each compound subject.

EXAMPLE: Carpenters and plumbers spoke to us about their trades on our career day.
ANSWER: carpenters, plumbers

1. The physical therapist and his patient plan exercises.
2. Heat, light, water, and massage are used to treat certain physical disabilities.
3. Stiff joints and pain are generally eased with heat.
4. A hot bath or a hot compress heats deep, sore tissues.
5. The patient and the therapist work together to help the patient relearn motor functions.
6. Physical therapy and occupational therapy help patients improve their motor abilities.
7. In occupational therapy, tools and hands-on materials are used rather than exercise aids.
8. Doctors and therapists help patients reestablish basic physical skills and contact with the world outside the hospital.
9. Stroke victims and people who have been seriously injured sometimes have to relearn basic skills, such as handling a spoon or fork.
10. Physical therapists and occupational therapists should feel proud of their work with patients.

▼ Critical Viewing
What are some of the ways in which computers have changed methods used by doctors and physical therapists? Answer using a compound subject. [Connect]

Answers on Transparency
Use the Grammar Exercises Answers on Transparencies for Chapter 20 to have students correct their own or one another's exercises.

On-Line Exercise Bank
Have students complete the exercises on computer. The Auto Check feature will grade their work for you!

☑ ONGOING ASSESSMENT: Monitor and Reinforce

If students miss more than two items in Exercises 1–5, refer them to the following for additional practice.

In the Textbook	Print Resources	Technology
Section Review, Ex. 6–8, p. 427	Grammar Exercise Workbook, pp. 41–48	On-Line Exercise Bank, Section 20.1

Compound Verbs

Just as a sentence can have a compound subject, it can also have a *compound verb*.

▶**KEY CONCEPT** A **compound verb** is two or more verbs that have the same subject and are joined by a conjunction such as *and* or *or*. ■

In the next examples, each subject is underlined once and the parts of the compound verb are underlined twice.

EXAMPLES: I neither want nor need your help on the test.
The little children hopped, skipped, and jumped around the playground.

Sometimes, a sentence has both a compound subject and a compound verb.

EXAMPLE: The boys and girls danced and listened to records for hours.

▶**Exercise 4** Recognizing Compound Verbs Write the verbs that make up each compound verb.
1. Some students go to college and study to become computer programmers.
2. Programmers write and encode application programs.
3. Operating systems programs run the user's input and output requests and process them.
4. Operating systems programs connect to a network and interpret data requests.
5. Applications programs tailor the computer's powers and perform specific tasks.

▶**Exercise 5** Combining Sentences With Compound Subjects and Verbs Combine each pair of sentences into one using a compound subject or a compound verb.
1. Computer programmers encode programs. They also test them.
2. Often, a programmer will discuss a line of code. The discussion will take place with his or her colleagues.
3. A computer programmer will uncover defects in design specifications. He or she will also fix them.
4. Design defects must be eliminated. System bugs must be eliminated, as well.
5. Programmers work long hours writing the code for a new application. They have a great sense of satisfaction when it works well.

▶**More Practice**
On-line
Exercise Bank
• Section 20.1
Grammar Exercise Workbook
• pp. 47–48

Step-by-Step Teaching Guide

Compound Verbs

1. Review compound subjects. Students' knowledge of compound subjects should make compound verbs easy to grasp. Instead of a multipart subject whose parts all share one verb, students will now study multipart verbs whose parts all share one subject.

2. Have students rewrite the first example sentence on the page as two sentences. (I do not want your help on the test. I do not need your help on the test.) Point out that this entails repeating the subject and helping verb. Using a compound verb eliminates this repetition.

Answer Key

Exercise 4

1. go and study
2. write and encode
3. run and process
4. connect and interpret
5. tailor and perform

Exercise 5

1. Computer programmers encode and test programs.
2. Often a programmer and his or her colleagues will discuss a line of code.
3. A computer programmer will uncover and fix defects in design specifications.
4. Both design defects and system bugs must be eliminated.
5. Programmers work long hours writing code for a new application and have a great sense of satisfaction when it works well.

☑ **ONGOING ASSESSMENT: Assess Mastery**

Use the following resources to assess student mastery of complete subjects and predicates, and compound subjects and verbs.

In the Textbook	Technology
Chapter Review, Ex. 41–42, p. 444 Standardized Test Preparation Workshop, pp. 446–447	On-Line Exercise Bank, Section 20.1

Simple Sentence Builders

Teaching Resources: Hands-on Grammar Activity Book, Chapter 20

1. Have students refer to their Hands-on Grammar activity books or give them copies of the relevant pages for this activity.

2. Make sure students use nouns and past tense verbs that are compatible.

3. As students build their sentences, have them write each one down.

4. To extend the activity, have students create more subject and verb squares.

Find It in Your Reading

Have students bring directions into class. Work as a class to find compound subjects and verbs.

Find It in Your Writing

If students cannot combine sentences, have them revise some sentences to include compound subjects and verbs.

20.1

Hands-on Grammar

Simple Sentence Builders

Make and use Simple Sentence Builders to see how a sentence can grow with compound subjects and verbs. To begin, take two sheets of paper in different colors, and cut twelve 2" x 2" squares from each sheet. Take a third sheet of paper, and cut five T shapes, with the stems 1" wide and 2" high and the top 3" across. Next, on each of the squares of one color, write a noun that will serve as a subject. Examples: *Tony, Juan, Lisa, my brother, my sisters, our friends, I, we, they, the team, the cat, the dogs*, and so on. On the other squares, write past tense verbs—a few with complements. Examples: *ran, sang, played, danced, chased the ball, ate lunch, slept until noon,* and so on. Then, write the word *and* on the stem of each T shape. Finally, turn the T shapes over, and draw a comma on the back of each one.

Now, begin building sentences. Take one subject square, and place it next to one verb square. Then, fit an *and* T over the subject and add another subject square to its left. Next, fit an *and* T over the verb, and add another verb square to its right. Then, fit a *comma* T over the second subject, and add a third subject square. To add a third verb, you must turn over the T shape so that a comma shows; then, add another *and* T and the new verb. (See illustrations.)

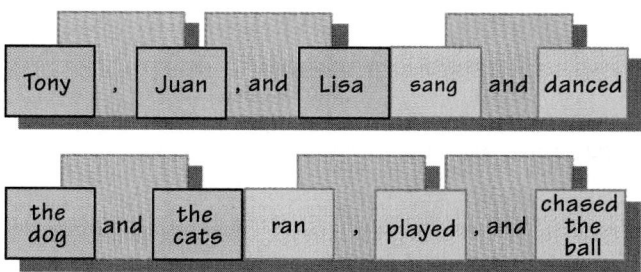

You might try variations using *but* on one of the T shapes:

Find It in Your Reading Read some directions for building, fixing, installing, or cooking something. Notice where compound subjects and verbs are used.

Find It in Your Writing Review a piece of your writing, and note where you have used simple sentences. See if you can combine any short, simple sentences by making compound subjects and verbs.

⏱ **TIME SAVERS!**

✋ **Hands-on Grammar Book**
Use the Hands-on Grammar activity sheet for Chapter 20 to facilitate this activity.

Section 20.1 Section Review

GRAMMAR EXERCISES 6–11

Exercise 6 Recognizing **Compound Subjects** Write the nouns that make up each compound subject.

1. Accounting and bookkeeping help people and businesses make economic decisions.
2. The figures in a bookkeeper's ledger follow basic accounting principles.
3. Businesses and other types of organizations use financial statements for their financial planning.
4. Investors and stock traders are supplied with accounting information to make decisions about companies.
5. Large corporations and small firms need the services of accountants.
6. Investors, creditors, and the general public have uses for financial reports.
7. Stockholders and other outsiders receive information about a company's financial standing from these reports.
8. The balance sheet and other important statements provide a way of examining a company's performance.
9. Financial accounting and tax accounting are the two major areas in the accounting field.
10. Tax accountants must keep up with the frequent changes in tax laws.

Exercise 7 Recognizing **Compound Verbs** Write the verbs that make up each compound verb.

1. Orthodontists diagnose and correct teeth and jaw abnormalities.
2. An orthodontist adjusts and corrects tooth positions by using braces.
3. Braces are attached to teeth and are tightened and retightened.
4. Over a period of time, an orthodontist examines braces and makes corrections.
5. Sometimes, they recommend additional time in braces or prescribe a retainer.

Exercise 8 Revising a Paragraph to **Combine Sentences** Revise this paragraph, combining the short sentences into longer ones with compound subjects or compound verbs.

Crusty snow covered the sidewalk. There were patches of ice on the sidewalk too. Suddenly. I slipped. I fell. I twisted my ankle. The doctor examined my injury. He gave me some advice. I was to soak my ankle. I was to rest it for several days. Eventually, the pain would subside. The swelling would also subside.

Exercise 9 Find It in Your Reading
Read a newspaper or magazine article. Find at least one sentence with a compound subject and one with a compound verb. Write the sentences, underlining the subjects once and the verbs twice.

Exercise 10 Find It in Your **Writing** Review a paper from your portfolio, and write down any sentences that contain compound subjects or verbs, underlining the compound subjects once and the compound verbs twice. See if there are places where you can combine two short sentences into one sentence with a compound subject or compound verb.

Exercise 11 Writing Application
Write a paragraph about where you hope to be ten years from now. You may include educational, career, or personal goals. Write at least two sentences that contain compound subjects and two that contain compound verbs.

Answer Key continued

Exercise 11

Writing Application
Students can talk with partners about their goals, and share suggestions about how to attain them.

ASSESS and CLOSE

Section Review

Each of these exercises correlates to the concepts taught in the section on compound subjects and verbs, pages 422–425. The exercises may be used for more practice, for reteaching, or for review of the Key Concepts presented. Answers for all chapter exercises are available in *Grammar Exercises on Transparencies* in your teaching resources.

Answer Key

Exercise 6

1. Accounting, bookkeeping
2. figures
3. Businesses, types
4. Investors, traders
5. corporations, firms
6. Investors, creditors, public
7. Stockholders, outsiders
8. sheet, statements
9. accounting, accounting
10. accountant

Exercise 7

1. diagnose, correct
2. adjusts, corrects
3. are attached, are tightened, (are) re-tightened
4. examines, makes
5. recommend, prescribe

Exercise 8

Crusty snow and patches of ice covered the sidewalk. Suddenly, I slipped and fell, twisting my ankle. The doctor examined my injury and gave me some advice. I was to soak and rest my ankle for several days. Eventually, the pain and the swelling would subside.

Exercise 9

Find It in Your Reading
Suggest that students rewrite both sentences, using simple subjects and verbs. (They will have at least four new sentences.) Have them compare the sentences to reinforce the idea that compounds make writing smoother.

Exercise 10

Find It in Your Writing
If students' paragraphs do not contain compound subjects or verbs, they should write the sentences to include compounds.

continued

Interest GRABBER Ask students where sentences with the understood *you* are most often found (in ads and commercials). Give examples such as *Go to this Web site, Click on the button,* or *Buy this product.* Have students provide other examples.

Activate Prior Knowledge

Remind students that the subject of a sentence is the person, place, or thing that performs the action or that is being described. This rule applies to all subjects, including those that are hard to find and those that are understood but don't appear in the sentence.

TEACH

Step-by-Step Teaching Guide

Subjects in Orders and Directions

1. Write a few short imperative sentences such as *Run for your lives!* on the chalkboard. Challenge students to identify the subjects. If they have difficulty finding the subject, ask them who is performing the action.

2. Explain that *you,* the person being ordered or directed in an imperative sentence, is the person who will perform the action specified in the verb. That is why *you* is always the subject of such a sentence.

Answer Key

Exercise 12

1. Ted, [you] plan on having different chores each season.
2. In the fall, [you] rake the leaves, and put them into a bag.
3. In the winter, [you] cover the tender plants to protect them from harsh weather conditions.
4. [You] Fertilize your soil and plant your beds of annual flowers in the spring.
5. When summer at last arrives, [you] remember to water the lawn and plants and keep your shrubs trimmed.

Section 20.2 *Hard-to-Find Subjects*

Basic methods for finding the subject and verb of a sentence were explained in Section 20.1. This section presents ways of finding subjects that are hard to find or that appear to be missing.

Subjects in Orders and Directions

In most sentences that give orders or directions, the subject is understood rather than actually stated.

▶ **KEY CONCEPT** In sentences that give orders or directions, the subject is understood to be *you.* ■

In the following chart, sentences are given with and without the understood *you.* In the second example, the subject is still understood to be *you* even though the sentence contains a *noun of direct address*—that is, the name of the person being addressed.

Orders or Directions	With Understood Words Added
Look at the bird perched on the branch.	[You] look at the bird perched on the branch.
Michael, come here.	Michael, [you] come here.

▶ **Exercise 12** Finding Subjects in Orders or Directions
Write each sentence, inserting the understood subject.

EXAMPLE: During the autumn, enjoy the scenery.
ANSWER: During the autumn, [you] enjoy the scenery.

1. Ted, plan on having different garden chores to do each season.
2. In the fall, rake the leaves and put them into special large leaf bags.
3. In the winter, cover the tender plants to protect them from harsh weather conditions.
4. Fertilize your soil and plant your beds of annual flowers in the spring.
5. When summer at last arrives, remember to water the lawn and plants and keep your shrubs trimmed.

Theme: Plants and Animals

In this section, you will learn to locate hard-to-find subjects. The examples and exercises in this section are about plants and animals.

Cross-Curricular Connection: Science

▶ **More Practice**

On-line Exercise Bank
• Section 20.2
Grammar Exercise Workbook
• pp. 49–50

⏱ TIME AND RESOURCE MANAGER

Resources
Print: Grammar Exercise Workbook, pp. 49–52
Technology: On-Line Exercise Bank, Section 20.2

In-Depth Coverage	Accelerated Pace
• Work through all key concepts, pp. 428–431. • Assign and review Exercises 12–13. • Read and discuss Grammar in Literature, p. 432.	• Assign pp. 428–431 for independent student review. • Assign Review Exercises 14–16.

Considering Your Audience and Purpose

After narrowing the focus of your response, consider the format your writing will take. For example, if you are writing to introduce the play *Romeo and Juliet* to an audience who has not studied it, include background information and a summary. In contrast, if you want to write a critical review of the play for an audience of classmates, you need not provide extensive introductory context for the play. Instead, include your opinions and support them with direct evidence from the text. Evaluate your audience and purpose to help you identify the level of information that will make your writing successful.

Analyze Your Audience

Use the questions that follow to help you develop an audience profile that identifies the readers you expect to reach. Note your answers, and use them to guide the level of language and detail you include in your essay.

Audience Profile:

☑ Have they read this work of literature?

☑ What will they be interested in?

☑ How much will they know about the subject?

☑ What kind of language should I use?

Analyze Your Purpose

Whether you are responding to the work of a well-known writer, providing an interpretation of a piece of literature that you have discovered, or writing to achieve another goal, include language and details that support your purpose. Consider these tips:

- **To praise:** Include concrete details to back up your enthusiasm for the work.

- **To analyze:** Support your interpretation with evidence from the text.

- **To show a personal response:** Make the connection between your ideas, opinions, or experience and the writing you are addressing.

Writing Lab CD-ROM

To help you evaluate your audience, use the Audience Profile activity in the Response to Literature lesson.

Prewriting: Considering Your Audience and Purpose

1. Ask students who their primary audience is. The audience should be more specific than their teachers or their classmates. For example, if they are responding to a book about a sport, is their audience people who already know about that sport or people who are not yet fans? Considerations such as these will help them decide how much technical detail to include.

2. Caution students not merely to retell the plot of a book or story. In a literary response such as a book review, a writer needs to give readers just enough plot information to whet their appetites and to understand comments about the book's characters or theme. A literary response should not reveal an ending or overwhelm readers with a catalog of details. Its purpose is not to summarize, but to discuss, analyze, and evaluate.

☑ ONGOING ASSESSMENT: Monitor and Reinforce

If some students lapse into the habit of writing only for teachers, try one of the following options.

Option 1 Suggest that students write to a specific audience of one—a relative, a friend, or a much younger acquaintance.	**Option 2** Have students write a brief profile of their intended audience, including their readers' level of education, skills, and background knowledge of the topic.

1. Repeated reading of a text can help students focus on exactly how to convey their impressions of a poem, story, or book. Have them set some time aside each day or evening to reread their literary work. If it is brief enough, they can reread the entire work; if not, they can read a chapter or two or skim various parts. Doing this throughout the writing process not only will help students recall details, but also will strengthen their impressions.

2. Good literature is usually composed of an effective blend of plot, characters, setting, and writing style. Often, however, one literary element stands out. For example, Poe's use of language is the focus of Andrea's response. Ask students to decide what aspect of their chosen work is most meaningful to them.

13.2

Gathering Details
Find Details to Support Your Position

To find evidence to support your points, gather details from the literature, such as examples, excerpts, and direct quotations. Identify the main ideas you want to convey, and then return to the literature with a research goal: to find the proof.

Using Index Cards Prepare a series of index cards with each main point written across the top. Underneath, put your notes on the details you gathered to support that point.

Student Work
IN PROGRESS

Name: *Andrea Montgomery*
Omaha Northwest High School
Omaha, NE

Using Index Cards to Gather Supporting Details
Andrea used index cards to find evidence for her essay.

What I want to prove:
repetition enhances mood

What I want to prove:
repetition reinforces theme

What I want to prove:
repetition is used for emphasis

How I can prove it:
quote lines that use "rapping" and "tapping"

Use these tips to gather details about literary elements:

- **Character** When you analyze a character, find evidence that shows the character's actions, beliefs, and motivations. Note other details, including the ways other characters respond to the character you discuss and any change you see.

- **Setting** To provide an interpretation of the setting, find words that describe time and place and note the mood or atmosphere the setting generates.

- **Diction** Locate examples of word choice by considering the vocabulary level and formality of the language. Also, evaluate the connotation or emotional meanings of the writer's words.

- **Sound Devices** When analyzing poetry, address rhyme, rhythm, and repetition. Note examples of figurative language—such as simile or metaphor—that create meaning.

INTEGRATED SKILLS COVERAGE

Integrating Grammar
Active Verbs ATE p. 328

Language Highlight
ATE p. 329

Technology
Integrating Technology Skills ATE p. 326

Real-World Connection
ATE p. 329

Viewing and Representing
Critical Viewing SE pp. 324, 332, 334

ASSESSMENT SUPPORT

Standardized Test Preparation SE p. 336; ATE p. 326
Standardized Test Preparation Workshop, pp. 29–30
Scoring Rubrics on Transparency, Ch. 15
Formal Assessment, Ch. 15
Writing Assessment and Portfolio Management

MEETING INDIVIDUAL NEEDS

Less Advanced Students ATE p. 327, 337; See also Ongoing Assessments ATE pp. 325, 327
ESL Students ATE pp. 331, 333
Visual/Spatial Learners ATE p. 335
Verbal/Linguistic Learners ATE p. 327
Intrapersonal Learners ATE p. 330, 333

BLOCK SCHEDULING

Pacing Suggestions
For 90-minute Blocks
• Have students complete the Prewriting and Drafting stages in a single period.
• Focus one class period on Revising and Editing and Publishing and Presenting. Allow at least 30 minutes for peer revision.

Resources for Varying Instruction
• *Writing Lab* **CD-ROM** If your students have access to hardware, a 90-minute block provides an ideal opportunity for students to work on computer.
• *Writers at Work* **Videotape** Show the Workplace Writing segment in class.

Professional Development Support
• *How to Manage Instruction in the Block* This Teaching Resource provides management and activity suggestions.

MEDIA AND TECHNOLOGY

For the Student
• *Writing Lab* **CD-ROM**, Practical and Technical Writing

For the Teacher
• *Writers at Work* **Videotape**, Workplace Writing
  Resource Pro **CD-ROM**

WRITING AND GRAMMAR WEBSITE

The Interactive Writing and Grammar Website provides a wide array of support for students, teachers, and parents. Writing support includes:
• Interactive revision checkers
• Scoring rubrics with complete models

phwg.phschool.com

Lesson Objectives

1. To understand the characteristics of effective workplace writing.
2. To recognize different types of workplace writing in both electronic and print forms.
3. To recognize the five parts of a business letter.
4. To identify acceptable forms and language for business letters.
5. To include key details, including meeting attendees, date, time, and place.
6. To summarize discussions objectively.
7. To identify and list action items.
8. To remember to write legibly when filling out forms.
9. To follow the directions correctly when completing forms.

Critical Viewing

Draw Conclusions Students may say that all businesses rely on the communication of important information. Writing and speaking effectively are skills central to good communication.

Chapter 15 Workplace Writing

▲ Critical Viewing
Why are skills such as the ability to write and speak effectively important in business? [Draw Conclusions]

Workplace Writing in Everyday Life

When you send a thank-you letter to a neighbor who participated in a school fund-raiser or when you complete an application for a local youth services job bank, you're using workplace writing skills. Workplace writing helps co-workers, classmates, businesses, and even governments communicate important information and work together across geographic distances. Effective workplace writing can lead to school success and job possibilities, notify a company of customer satisfaction or dissatisfaction, invite people to important events, and even communicate urgent messages to resolve community problems.

324 • Workplace Writing

⏱ TIME AND RESOURCE MANAGER

Resources
Print: Writing Support Transparency 15-A
Technology: Writers at Work videotape

In-Depth Coverage	Accelerated Pace
• Cover pp. 324–325 in class. • Point out the parts, format, and formal language used in the business letter example on p. 326. • Review the Topic Bank suggestions on p. 327 and use them to lead the students in brainstorming for some specific examples. • Have students work in pairs or small groups to write a business letter.	• Invite students to give examples of business letters they have received or read. Ask students to evaluate the effectiveness of the letters they describe. **Option** Bring in some examples of business letters, such as advertisements and school communications. Have students work independently to write a business letter.

Subjects in Questions

In most sentences, the subject comes before the verb. However, in some sentences, including many sentences that ask questions, the subject comes after the verb. Such sentences are said to be *inverted.*

KEY CONCEPT In questions, the subject often follows the verb. ■

Questions that are in inverted order will generally begin with a verb, with a helping verb, or with one of the following words: *how, what, when, where, which, who, whose,* or *why.* The following examples show all three types of inverted questions. The subjects are underlined once and the verbs or verb phrases, twice. In the last two examples, notice that the subject comes between the parts of a verb phrase.

VERB FIRST:	Are the sunflowers very tall?
HELPING VERB FIRST:	Have you collected the seeds?
ADVERB FIRST:	When will Anike roast them?

To find the subject in questions with inverted order, mentally rephrase the question as a statement. This will place the subject before the verb. Then, follow the same steps that you would follow to find any other subject and verb.

Questions	Reworded as Statements
Is dinner ready?	Dinner is ready.
Are you working here?	You are working here.
When will it snow?	It will snow when.

Note About *Questions*: Not all questions are in inverted order. Sometimes, questions beginning with an adjective or a pronoun are in the usual subject-verb order.

EXAMPLES: Whose flower garden is in bloom?
What is being planted next year?

▲ Critical Viewing
What is it about sunflowers like these that would make them an appealing subject for an artist? Use a sentence with an inverted subject and verb in your response. [Relate]

Subjects in Questions

1. Go over the Key Concept on this page. Have students make up questions for you to write on the chalkboard. Have other students practice finding the subjects in these questions.

2. Another way to find the subject of a question is to answer it. Have students try this with the example sentences on the page. They might answer the first sentence by saying *No, dinner won't be ready until seven.* Immediately, it becomes clear that *dinner* is the subject. This rule works with any question, including those that follow the usual subject-first order. The sample question *Which record is playing?* can be answered *"The Stars and Stripes Forever" is playing.* "The Stars and Stripes Forever" replaces the noun *record;* therefore *record* is the subject of the question.

Critical Viewing

Relate Students may respond:
Look at how beautiful the sunflowers are!

STANDARDIZED TEST PREPARATION WORKSHOP

Grammar and Usage Standardized tests often ask students to identify particular grammatical elements in sentences. Use this example to demonstrate identification of hard-to-find subjects.

One word is underlined in each of the following sentences. Which underlined word is *not* the subject of its sentence?

(A) *Laura* looked up from her book. (B) "Shut the *door*; you're letting in the cold air! (C) Who was *it* at the door? (D) Did the *packages* finally come?"

Students should choose item **B.** *Door* is the direct object of the verb *shut.* The subject of this sentence is the understood *you,* which would appear before the verb. The *you* in the contraction *you're* is also a subject, since this is a compound sentence.

Sentences Beginning with *Here* and *There*

1. Have a volunteer read the Key Concept aloud, and work through the explanation and examples with students. Emphasize that *here* and *there* are words that show location and direction; this is why they usually function as adverbs.

2. Explain that *here* and *there* are not nouns and cannot function as such. This is why they can never be the subject of a sentence. When students see sentences beginning with *here* or *there,* they should look for nouns in the sentence and decide which is the subject. In the second sample sentence, *palms* cannot be the subject, because it is the object of the preposition *of.* Therefore, the subject must be *photographs.*

Customize for
Musical Learners

Have students find song titles that begin with *Here* or *There.* Challenge them to identify the subject of each title.

Sentences Beginning With *Here* and *There*

Some inverted sentences begin with the word *here* or *there.*

> **KEY CONCEPT** The subject of a sentence is never *here* or *there.* ■

In sentences that begin with the word *here* or *there,* the subject will usually be found after the verb. In each of the following three examples, *here* and *there* are adverbs. Each of them answers the question *Where?* and modifies the verb in the sentence.

EXAMPLES: There <u>is</u> the aromatic eucalyptus <u>tree.</u>
Here <u>are</u> <u>photographs</u> of the beautiful, towering coconut palms.
There <u>goes</u> the tree <u>specialist</u> to fertilize our neighbor's Japanese maple.

Like inverted questions, sentences beginning with *here* or *there* can usually be rephrased mentally in order to place the subject in the normal position before the verb. All you need to do is make a logical sentence that does not begin with *here* or *there* out of the other words given in the sentence. Then, follow the same steps that you would for finding any subject in a sentence.

Sentences Beginning With *Here* or *There*	Reworded With Subjects Before Verbs
There <u>is</u> your <u>train</u> to Arizona.	Your <u>train</u> to Arizona <u>is</u> there.
Here <u>are</u> the <u>pictures</u> of the Grand Canyon.	The <u>pictures</u> of the Grand Canyon <u>are</u> here.
There <u>goes</u> the <u>senator.</u>	The <u>senator</u> <u>goes</u> there.

In some sentences, you may find that the word *there* is used just to get the sentence started. In these situations, *there* is not an adverb modifying the verb. Instead, it just fills out the sentence. When the word *there* is used simply to fill out a sentence, it is called an *expletive.*

EXAMPLES: There <u>were</u> a large <u>saguaro cactus</u> and a <u>barrel cactus</u> visible from our room.
There <u>are</u> many <u>types</u> of cactus.

▣ Internet Tip

For links to a wealth of information about plants and botanical gardens and arboretums around the country, go to the Web site of the Big Island Association of Nurserymen at **http://www. hawaiiplants.com/ links.htm#Botanical Gardens and Arboretums**

Sentences With Expletive *There*	Questions for Finding Subject
There <u>were</u> four misspelled <u>words</u> in the article.	*Question: What* were? *Answer:* words
There <u>are</u> two <u>reasons</u> for her resignation.	*Question: What* are? *Answer:* reasons

Rephrasing a sentence to place the subject first is not always possible when *there* is used as an expletive. The important thing to remember is that *there* will never be the subject. To find the subject in a sentence that cannot be rephrased, drop the word *there* and ask *Who?* or *What?* before the verb.

Note About *Inverted Sentences:* Some sentences beginning with *here* or *there* are not inverted but are in normal word order.

EXAMPLE: There <u>they</u> <u>are</u>.

Other Inverted Sentences

Occasionally, sentences are inverted to draw attention to the last words in the sentence.

▶**KEY CONCEPT** In some sentences, the subject is placed after the verb in order to give it greater emphasis. ■

In the following example, notice how the order of the words creates suspense by leading up to the subject *eagle*.

EXAMPLES: High on the cliff overlooking the rugged landscape <u>was</u> an <u>eagle</u>.
Bright <u>is</u> her <u>smile</u>, but heavy <u>is</u> her <u>heart</u>.
Soon after the sound of the drums <u>came</u> the <u>marchers</u>.

These sentences can be mentally rephrased in normal subject-verb order.

Inverted Word Order for Emphasis	Reworded With Subject Before Verb
High on the cliff overlooking the rugged landscape <u>was</u> an <u>eagle</u>.	An <u>eagle</u> <u>was</u> high on the cliff overlooking the rugged landscape.

 **Spelling Tip**

The words *there, their,* and *they're* are homophones—words that sound the same but are spelled differently and have different meanings. Remember that *there* is an adverb or an expletive, *their* is a possessive pronoun, and *they're* is a contraction of *they are*.

Other Inverted Sentences

1. Have volunteers read the sample sentences aloud and ask the class to give their reactions. (Students may suggest that these sentences sound fancy, literary, elegant, affected, or poetic.) Point out that the subject-verb pattern is fundamental to the English language. Students are so used to it that the inversion in these sentences makes them sound fresh. Many poets and other writers use inversion precisely for that reason.

2. If students have difficulty finding the subject of a sentence when it occurs after the verb, have them ask questions such as, "What is the action in this sentence? Who or what is performing the action?" These questions will lead students right to the simple subject and verb.

☑ **ONGOING ASSESSMENT: Monitor and Reinforce**

If students miss more than two items in Exercises 12–13, refer them to the following for additional practice.

In the Textbook	Print Resources	Technology
Section Review, Ex. 14–16, p. 433	Grammar Exercise Workbook, pp. 49–52	On-Line Exercise Bank, Section 20.2

Grammar in Literature

1. Have students copy the quotation, underline the complete subject, and double underline the complete predicate. (Students should underline *I* and double underline all other words.) Point out that all the words in a complete predicate do not always come together in a sentence. In this sentence, the subject appears in the middle of the predicate.

2. Have students look at the entire poem in *Timeless Voices, Timeless Themes,* page 789, and locate the subjects. They should divide the poem into these "sentences": lines 1–2 (subject: *I*); lines 3–6 (*I*); lines 7–10 (*They*); lines 11–12 (*I*); lines 13–14 (*waves*); lines 15–16 (*poet*); and lines 17–18 (*I*).

More About the Writer

William Wordsworth became poet laureate of England in 1843, at age 73. Most of Wordsworth's poetry deals with his extraordinary personal response to the natural world around him. Although his early poetry was considered rather new and radical, Wordsworth became more conservative as he grew older.

Answer Key

Exercise 13

1. sea
2. waters
3. penetration
4. penetration
5. percentage
6. more
7. sea
8. materials
9. characteristics
10. range
11. effects
12. fish
13. you
14. fishes
15. they

20.2

GRAMMAR IN
LITERATURE

from **I Wandered Lonely as a Cloud**
William Wordsworth

Notice in these lines from the poem that the subject I *follows the verb* saw. *This inverted order maintains the rhythm of the line.*

Ten thousand *saw I* at a glance,
Tossing their heads in sprightly dance.

Exercise 13 Finding Subjects in Questions and Inverted Sentences Write the simple subject of each sentence.

EXAMPLE: In her hand was a beautiful starfish.
ANSWER: starfish

1. Where in the world is the deep blue sea?
2. Beyond the edge of the continental shelf and below the level of light penetration are the ocean waters of the deep blue sea.
3. How far is the penetration of sunlight into ocean water?
4. There is not much penetration of sunlight below a few hundred meters.
5. What is the percentage of ocean water in the deep sea?
6. In the deep sea is more than 90 percent of the ocean volume.
7. Among the Earth's least-known environments is the deep sea.
8. Sinking below the lighted surface waters are organic materials.
9. What are some characteristics of the deep sea?
10. There is a range of 20 to more than 1,000 atmospheres of pressure in the deep sea.
11. There are various effects on the organisms in the deep sea caused by the lack of light.
12. Also present in the shallower parts are fish with very large eyes.
13. Have you ever seen the fish and invertebrates with their own light-making organs?
14. There are many deep-sea fishes with large mouths.
15. Why do they have such large mouths?

432 • Basic Sentence Parts

More Practice

On-line
Exercise Bank
• Section 20.2
Grammar Exercise
Workbook
• pp. 51–52

☑ **ONGOING ASSESSMENT SYSTEM: Assess Mastery**

Use the following resources to assess student mastery of finding hard-to-find subjects.

In the Textbook	Technology
Chapter Review, Ex. 43, p. 444 Standardized Test Preparation Workshop, pp. 446–447	On-Line Exercise Bank, Section 20.2

Section 20.2 Section Review

GRAMMAR EXERCISES 14–19

Exercise 14 Finding Subjects in Orders or Directions Write each sentence, inserting the understood subject.

1. If you're looking for a great vacation spot, consider the Grand Canyon.
2. To get the most out of your trip, pack binoculars.
3. Drive west on Highway 160 into Arizona.
4. From Highway 160, take the exit to Highway 89.
5. Enjoy the open roads.

Exercise 15 Finding Subjects in Questions and Inverted Sentences Write the subject of each sentence.

1. There are vast arid lands in the world.
2. Are there other types of deserts besides the hot, dry ones?
3. Yes, there are semiarid deserts and coastal deserts.
4. Lying about 25 degrees north and south of the equator are most of the world's deserts.
5. Can plants and animals survive with such little water?
6. There are certain plants and animals well adapted for survival in dry climates.
7. Among the more interesting animals are the tarantula and the gila monster, a type of lizard.
8. There are also many varieties of cactus with the ability to store water.
9. Probably most familiar is the giant saguaro, found in the southwestern United States and Mexico.
10. Low to the ground and widely spaced is typical desert vegetation.

Exercise 16 Revising Sentences to Invert Subjects and Verbs Revise these sentences, following the instructions.

You may have to add or omit some words.

1. Many plant adaptations are here in the desert. (begin with *Here in . . .*)
2. Spines, hairs, and thick leaves are included among the adaptations. (begin with *Included among . . .*)
3. Some seeds lie dormant for many years. (begin with *There are . . .*)
4. The seeds finally germinate. (change to a question.)
5. The new shoots come after a rare desert rainfall. (begin with *After a . . .*)

Exercise 17 Find It in Your Reading Read this excerpt from Emily Dickinson's "'Hope' is the thing with feathers—" and explain how the inverted subject and verb maintain the poem's rhythm.

> And sweetest—in the Gale—is heard—
> And sore must be the storm—
> That could abash the little Bird
> That kept so many warm—

Exercise 18 Find It in Your Writing In your writing, find two examples of inverted statements. Rewrite them so that the subject precedes the verb. If you don't find any, choose two statements and reword them so that they are inverted.

Exercise 19 Writing Application Write a three- or four-line description of something you are learning about in one of your other classes. In it, include the following types of sentences: a question, an inverted statement beginning with *there*, and a statement that is inverted to emphasize the subject.

Section Review • 433

ASSESS and CLOSE

Section Review

Each of these exercises correlates to the concepts taught in the section on hard-to-find subjects on pages 428–432. The exercises may be used for more practice, for reteaching, or for review of the Key Concepts presented. Answers for all chapter exercises are available in *Grammar Exercises Answers on Transparencies* in your teaching resources.

Answer Key

Exercise 14

1. If you're looking for a great vacation spot, (You) consider the Grand Canyon.
2. To get the most out of your trip, (You) pack binoculars.
3. (You) drive west on Highway 160 into Arizona.
4. From Highway 160, (you) take the exit Highway 89.
5. (You) enjoy the open roads.

Exercise 15

1. lands
2. types
3. deserts, deserts
4. most
5. plants, animals
6. plants, animals
7. tarantula, monster
8. varieties
9. saguaro
10. vegetation

Exercise 16

1. Here in the desert there are many plant adaptations.
2. Included among adaptations are spines, hairs and thick leaves.
3. There are seeds that lie dormant for many years.
4. Do the seeds finally germinate?
5. After a rare desert rainfall come new shoots.

Exercise 17

Find It in Your Reading
If students need help, have a volunteer read the second line with the subject first. How does the line's rhythm change?

continued

Answer Key continued

Exercise 18

Find It in Your Writing
Students can read their sentences aloud, for classmates to find the subjects.

Exercise 19

Writing Application
Challenge partners to find the subjects.

Activate Prior Knowledge

Ask students what a sentence needs in order to be a complete thought (a subject and a verb). Write the example *Oscar baked* on the chalkboard and ask if it is a complete sentence (yes). Ask a student to complete it (for example, *Oscar baked me some cookies*) Circle *some cookies* and explain that these words are the complement. They complete the thought.

TEACH

Step-by-Step Teaching Guide

The Direct Object

1. Point out the first seven letters of *transitive* (transit) and explain that just as a rapid transit system carries passengers from one place to another, a transitive verb carries an action from the subject who performs it to the object that receives it:

   Ling slammed the door.

   Ling performs the action; *door* receives the action. *Slammed* carries the action from subject to object.

2. Explain that a direct object is always a noun or a pronoun, or a word that functions as a noun or pronoun. A subject can perform an action only on a person, place, or thing, never on a verb, adverb, or adjective.

3. Emphasize "action verb" in the Key Concept. Explain that linking verbs never take direct objects, because they do not describe actions.

Complements

In addition to a verb, the complete predicate of a sentence often contains a *complement*.

▶ **KEY CONCEPT** A **complement** is a word or group of words that completes the meaning of the predicate of a sentence. ■

It is, of course, possible to have a complete sentence with just a subject and verb. However, most of the sentences you read and write will contain one or more complements that are needed to complete the meaning of the sentence.

Different kinds of complements will be presented here and in the next two sections. This section discusses one of the most important complements, the *direct object*.

Direct Objects

Direct objects are generally found after action verbs.

▶ **KEY CONCEPT** A **direct object** is a noun or pronoun that receives the action of a transitive action verb. ■

You can determine whether a word is a direct object by asking *Whom?* or *What?* after an action verb. In the following examples, the subjects are underlined once; the action verbs, twice; and the direct objects are boxed and labeled. Notice how each direct object answers the question *Whom?* or *What?*

                                        DO
EXAMPLES: The <u>hailstorm</u> <u><u>bombarded</u></u> the [picnickers.]
             Bombarded *whom? Answer:* picnickers
                                        DO
             The rugby <u>players</u> <u><u>are</u></u> <u><u>running</u></u> the [ball.]
             Are running *what? Answer:* ball

Not all action verbs have direct objects. Transitive action verbs do; intransitive action verbs do not. Because some action verbs can be either transitive or intransitive, knowing that a verb is an action verb will not tell you whether or not it has a direct object. You will always need to ask the question *Whom?* or *What?* after the verb to see whether there is a direct object.

                                        DO
EXAMPLES: Jenn <u><u>won</u></u> the [match.]
             Won *what? Answer:* match

             Jenn <u><u>won</u></u> yesterday.
             Won *what?* There is no answer, so there is no direct object.

 **Learn More**

For more about transitive and intransitive verbs, see Chapter 17.

⏱ TIME AND RESOURCE MANAGER

Resources
Print: Grammar and Exercise Workbook, pp. 53–64
Technology: On-Line Exercise Bank, Section 20.3

In-Depth Coverage	Accelerated Pace
• Work through all key concepts, pp. 434–441. • Assign and review Exercises 20–28. • Read and discuss Grammar in Literature, p. 435.	• Assign pp. 434–441 for independent student review. • Assign Review Exercises 29–37.

GRAMMAR IN LITERATURE

from **I Had a Hammer**

Hank Aaron

Notice how the direct objects ball *and* field *complete the meaning of the sentence in this excerpt.*

My father threw out the first *ball*, and then we took the *field* against the Dodgers. Their pitcher was Al Downing, a veteran lefthander whom I respected.

Note About *Direct Objects in Questions*: When a question is inverted, the direct object is sometimes located near the beginning of the sentence, before the verb. To find the direct object in an inverted question, reword the question as a statement.

QUESTION: Which bus <u>should</u> <u>I</u> <u>take</u>?   DO

REWORDED AS A STATEMENT: <u>I</u> <u>should</u> <u>take</u> which |bus.|

Like subjects and verbs, direct objects can be compound.

▶ **KEY CONCEPT** A **compound direct object** is two or more nouns or pronouns that receive the action of the same verb. ■

                                 DO   DO

EXAMPLE: <u>We</u> <u>photographed</u> the |players| and the |coach.|

If a sentence contains a *compound direct object*, asking the question *Whom?* or *What?* after the verb will lead to two or more answers.

▶ **Exercise 20** **Recognizing Direct Objects** Write the sentences, underlining the direct object or objects in each.

EXAMPLE: Most football players own a <u>football</u>.

(1) Football rivals baseball as the most popular athletic event for spectators in the United States. (2) Millions of people watch football games on the high-school, college, and professional levels. (3) Half-time shows, with marching bands and alumni or fan-club gatherings, usually accompany the games. (4) Football teams usually play eight to sixteen games in a season. (5) The best of the teams enter post-season playoffs.

▶ **More Practice**

On-line
Exercise Bank
• Section 20.1
Grammar Exercise Workbook
• pp. 53–54

Complements • 435

435

Direct Object or Object of a Preposition?

1. Review prepositions. Make a quick class list of common prepositions, such as *of, in, through,* and *under,* on the chalkboard. Have students add an object to each preposition to make a prepositional phrase, for example, *of the country, in the drawer, through the night, under the umbrella.* Explain that a prepositional phrase like these acts as one part of speech. Prepositional phrases describe nouns and verbs. They cannot receive the action of a verb.

2. Write the sample sentence *Soon, they moved into a new home* on the chalkboard. Point out that it does not answer the question *What?* or *Whom?* Ask students which question it does answer (Moved *where?*). Ask them which part of speech the phrase must be (adverb). Explain that because prepositional phrases are modifiers, they answer the same questions as adjectives and adverbs.

Answer Key

Exercise 21

1. game
2. turns
3. innings
4. men
5. none
6. ball
7. none
8. glove
9. gloves
10. ball

Critical Viewing

Speculate Students may say that the umpire will call the <u>play</u> safe.

20.3

Direct Object or Object of a Preposition? Do not confuse a direct object with the object of a preposition.

▶ KEY CONCEPT A direct object is never the noun or pronoun at the end of a prepositional phrase. ■

The first example below contains a direct object only. The second contains a direct object and a prepositional phrase. The third contains a prepositional phrase only.

EXAMPLES:
$\qquad$ DO
They bought a dilapidated Victorian mansion.
Bought what? *Answer:* mansion

$\qquad$ DO $\qquad$ PREP PHRASE
They restored the downstairs of the mansion.
Restored *what? Answer:* downstairs

$\qquad$ PREP PHRASE
Soon, they moved into the mansion.
Moved *what? Answer:* none

▶ Exercise 21 **Distinguishing Between Direct Objects and Objects of Prepositions** Write the direct object in each sentence. If a sentence does not have one, write *none.*

EXAMPLE: $\quad$ Baseball players have used metal bats for a long time.
ANSWER: $\quad$ bats

(1) Spectators love the popular game of baseball. (2) Two teams of nine players take turns on the field and at bat. (3) The teams play nine innings, with the home team batting last. (4) The team at bat sends its nine men to the plate, one at a time, in a specified sequence. (5) Each batter attempts to hit a ball. (6) The pitcher throws the ball at varying speeds and placement within the strike zone. (7) The batter runs to as many bases as possible without being tagged out. (8) Each player on the field wears a leather glove on one hand. (9) The players use the gloves to catch any balls hit toward them. (10) With the ungloved hand, they throw the ball to a teammate.

🔍 Learn More

For a list of prepositions and more on prepositional phrases, see Chapter 19.

▼ **Critical Viewing** How will the umpire call this play? Answer using a direct object. **[Speculate]**

Indirect Objects

In addition to a verb and direct object, the complete predicate of a sentence may contain an *indirect object.*

> **KEY CONCEPT** An **indirect object** is a noun or pronoun that appears with a direct object and names the person or thing that something is given to or done for. ■

A sentence cannot have an indirect object unless it has a direct object. You can tell whether a word is an indirect object by finding the direct object and asking *To or for whom?* or *To or for what?* after the action verb.

EXAMPLE:
$$\underset{\text{IO}}{\text{I bought my }\boxed{\text{brother}}\text{ a new pair of }\boxed{\text{skis.}}}$$
Bought *for whom?* *Answer:* brother

Like subjects, verbs, and direct objects, indirect objects can be compound.

EXAMPLE:
$$\text{We wrote }\underset{\text{IO}}{\boxed{\text{Sue}}}\text{ and }\underset{\text{IO}}{\boxed{\text{Al}}}\underset{\text{DO}}{\boxed{\text{letters}}}\text{ about our trip.}$$
Wrote *to whom?* *Answer:* Sue and Al

> **Exercise 22** **Recognizing Indirect Objects** Write the indirect object in each sentence.

EXAMPLE: He brought me his old bowling shoes.
ANSWER: me

1. Many colleges offer students bowling as an elective course.
2. The instructor teaches each class basic rules.
3. My father lent John and me his bowling balls.
4. My friend gave me a wrist brace to help keep my wrist straight as I bowled.
5. Mr. Neil taught us the history of bowling.

> **Exercise 23** **Supplying Indirect Objects** Supply an indirect object that logically completes each sentence.

EXAMPLE: I lent ___?___ my new racquet.
ANSWER: Philip

1. Philip told ___?___ the time of the match.
2. I gave ___?___ a call to remind her to come.
3. She asked ___?___ a question about the tickets.
4. I said that I had given ___?___, ___?___, and ___?___ the extra ones.
5. We all enjoyed the match and cheered loudly when the sponsor awarded ___?___ the first-place trophy.

> **More Practice**
>
> On-line
> Exercise Bank
> • Section 20.2
> **Grammar Exercise Workbook**
> • pp. 53–58

Complements • **437**

Step-by-Step Teaching Guide

Indirect Object or Object of a Preposition?

1. Read the Key Concept statement aloud and go over the example sentences with students. Point out that the meaning of the sentence is not affected by the presence or absence of the prepositions *to* and *for*.

2. Go over some of the sentences in Exercise 24 with the whole class. Point out that in sentences 1, 4, 8, and 10, the prepositional phrase functions similarly to an indirect object. It still answers the question *To/for whom?* or *To/for what?* The same is true of the example sentence at the top of the page. *Conductor* in the second sentence is still the person to whom something is given. Conversely, when sentences 2, 7, and 9 are rewritten to include the prepositions *to* or *for,* the words *schools, gymnasts,* and *Soviet Union* still function similarly to indirect objects.

Answer Key

Exercise 24

1. Gymnastics coaches teach gymnasts physical tumbling and acrobatic skills.
2. Gymnasts offer gymnastic demonstrations to local schools.
3. none
4. His inventions gave the sport more than 30 pieces of apparatus.
5. none
6. none
7. Judges give relatively unbiased scores to gymnasts by using specific guidelines.
8. In 1774, Johann Bernhard Basedow taught students physical exercises at his school.
9. Gymnast Olga Korbut earned considerable popularity for the Soviet Union in the international games.
10. The performances of Nadia Comaneci gained Romania widespread recognition in the 1976 games.

Indirect Object or Object of a Preposition? Do not confuse indirect objects with objects of prepositions.

> **KEY CONCEPT** An indirect object never immediately follows a preposition in a sentence. ■

In the first of the following examples, *conductor* is an indirect object. In the second, however, *conductor* is the object of the preposition *to.*

	IO	DO
INDIRECT OBJECT:	I gave the conductor our tickets.	

	DO	OBJ of PREP
OBJECT OF A PREPOSITION:	I gave our tickets to the conductor.	

> **Exercise 24** **Distinguishing Between Indirect Objects and Objects of Prepositions** In the following sentences, change each indirect object into a prepositional phrase. Change each prepositional phrase, if possible, into an indirect object. If you can't change a prepositional phrase into an indirect object, write *none.*

EXAMPLE: Janet taught a gymnastic routine to you.

ANSWER: Janet taught you a gymnastic routine.

1. Gymnastics coaches teach physical tumbling and acrobatic skills to gymnasts.
2. Gymnasts sometimes offer local schools gymnastic demonstrations.
3. Dr. Dudley Allen Sargent introduced the sport of gymnastics to the United States.
4. His inventions gave more than thirty pieces of apparatus to the sport.
5. Six gymnasts make up the teams for international competitions.
6. Rhythmic routines are performed individually or in group performances for six gymnasts.
7. Judges give gymnasts relatively unbiased scores by using specific guidelines.
8. In 1774, Johann Bernhard Basedow taught physical exercises to students at his school.
9. Gymnast Olga Korbut earned the Soviet Union considerable popularity in the international games.
10. The performances of Nadia Comaneci gained widespread recognition for Romania in the 1976 games.

> **More Practice**
>
> On-line
> Exercise Bank
> • Section 20.3
> **Grammar Exercise Workbook**
> • pp. 57–60

Subject Complements

The last two sections were about complements that help complete the meaning of sentences with transitive action verbs. Sentences with linking verbs contain a different kind of complement: a *subject complement.*

▶ **KEY CONCEPT** A **subject complement** is a noun, pronoun, or adjective that appears with a linking verb and tells something about the subject of the sentence. ■

A subject complement will almost always be found *after* a linking verb. The two kinds of subject complements are known as *predicate nominatives* and *predicate adjectives.*

Predicate Nominative The word *nominative* comes from the same Latin word (meaning "name") that the words *noun* and *pronoun* come from.

▶ **KEY CONCEPT** A **predicate nominative** is a noun or pronoun that appears with a linking verb and renames, identifies, or explains the subject of the sentence. ■

In a sentence with a predicate nominative, the linking verb acts as an equal sign between the subject and the predicate nominative. They refer to the same person or thing.

In the examples, subjects are underlined once, linking verbs twice, and predicate nominatives are boxed and labeled.

EXAMPLES: The <u>winner</u> of the tournament <u><u>is</u></u> our [team]. (PN)
Team renames *winner.*

The new <u>captain</u> of the team <u><u>will be</u></u> [Sue]. (PN)
Sue renames *captain.*

Their first <u>choice</u> <u><u>was</u></u> [you]. (PN)
You identifies *choice.*

▶ **KEY CONCEPT** A **compound predicate nominative** is two or more nouns or pronouns that appear with a linking verb and rename the subject of the sentence. ■

EXAMPLE: The <u>co-captains</u> <u><u>are</u></u> [you] (PN) and [Chris]. (PN)
You and *Chris* identify *co-captains.*

📖 Journal Tip

This section contains information on a variety of sports. In your journal, jot down some notes about those that interest you. Then, review them later to find a topic for an essay or research report—perhaps on the development of a particular sport.

The Predicate Nominative

1. Review linking verbs. Remind students that linking verbs show no action; therefore, they cannot take direct objects. Instead, they describe a state or condition of the subject. This state or condition can be defined by a noun or pronoun that follows the linking verb. This word is called the predicate nominative.

2. Explain to students that subject pronouns are nominative; object pronouns are objective. This information will help students remember always to use subject pronouns after linking verbs.

Integrating Speaking Skills

Colloquial English In casual conversation, Americans often use object pronouns as predicate nominatives. "That's him over there" is much more common than "That is he." Although this usage is technically incorrect, students are accustomed to hearing it. Use Step 2 above to explain why it is incorrect and caution students to use subject pronouns as predicate nominatives in formal writing and in formal speeches.

⬦ STANDARDIZED TEST PREPARATION WORKSHOP

Sentence Construction Standardized tests often measure students' ability to identify complete and correctly punctuated sentences. Share the following test item with students:

Choose the letter of the best way to write each underlined section.

<u>My sister left for college. Yesterday.
She will be studying there. She will study
English literature.</u>

A My sister left for college yesterday, so she will be studying English literature.

B Yesterday, my sister left for college, studying English literature.

C Yesterday, my sister left for college, where she will study English literature.

D Correct as is.

Item **C** is the correct choice. It is the only choice that creates a complete sentence and does not change the meaning of the original sentences and fragments.

Exercise 25

1. exertion
2. birth
3. skill
4. game
5. business

Exercise 26

1. good
2. easy
3. crawl stroke
4. breaststroke, butterfly stroke
5. graceful

Step-by-Step Teaching Guide

The Predicate Adjective

1. Review adjectives with students. Adjectives modify either nouns or pronouns. A predicate adjective describes the subject of a sentence after a linking verb. A compound predicate adjective, as the name implies, is two or more adjectives used to describe the subject of the sentence.

2. Provide the following examples for students:

> PA
> The <u>sandpaper</u> <u>feels</u> rough.
>
> PA   PA
> The <u>wind</u> <u>was</u> fierce and cold yesterday.

Critical Viewing

Assess Students may suggest such predicate adjectives in their responses as,

> The swimmer appears <u>strong</u> and <u>successful</u>.   PA
> PA

20.3

Exercise 25 Recognizing Predicate Nominatives Write the predicate nominative(s) in each sentence.

1. A sport is physical exertion for recreation or competition.
2. From a historical standpoint, the ancient Olympic Games were the birth of organized sports.
3. About 5,000 years ago, wrestling was essentially a survival skill.
4. Rugby is a game accidentally invented by students at Cambridge.
5. Professional sports in the twentieth century were a profitable business, often involving highly paid athletes.

Predicate Adjective The other kind of subject complement is called a *predicate adjective*.

KEY CONCEPT A **predicate adjective** is an adjective that appears with a linking verb and describes the subject of the sentence. ■

> PA
EXAMPLES: The <u>swimmer</u> <u>was</u> |fast.|
> *Fast* describes *swimmer.*

A compound predicate adjective is two or more adjectives that appear with a linking verb and describe the subject of the sentence.

> PA   PA
EXAMPLE: The <u>uniforms</u> <u>are</u> |green| and |white|

Exercise 26 Recognizing Predicate Adjectives Write the predicate adjective(s) in each sentence.

EXAMPLE: Jean seemed tired after her swimming lesson.

ANSWER: tired

1. Swimming is good for strengthening muscles.
2. The popular crawl stroke appears easy.
3. The backstroke is similar to the crawl stroke.
4. Leg and arm movements are simultaneous in the breast stroke and the butterfly stroke.
5. The butterfly stroke appears graceful.

Grammar and Style Tip

Use vivid subject complements to add interest as well as information to a description of your subject.

▼ **Critical Viewing** How strong and how skilled do you think this swimmer is? Use predicate adjectives in your response. **[Assess]**

☑ **ONGOING ASSESSMENT: Monitor and Reinforce**

If students miss more than two items in Exercise 20–28, refer them to the following for additional practice.

In the Textbook	Print Resources	Technology
Section Review, Ex. 29–37, pp. 442–443	Grammar Exercise Workbook, pp. 53–64	On-Line Exercise Bank, Section 20.3

Objective Complements

Indirect objects generally come before direct objects. Complements called *objective complements* generally come after direct objects and give additional information about them.

KEY CONCEPT An **objective complement** is an adjective or noun that appears with a direct object and describes or renames it. ■

To find an objective complement, say the verb and the direct objective, and then ask *What?*

EXAMPLES:
$$\text{DO} \quad \text{OC}$$
She painted her room green.
Painted room *what?* Answer: green

$$\text{DO} \quad \text{OC}$$
The coach appointed David captain of the team.
Appointed David *what?* captain

Exercise 27 **Recognizing Objective Complements** Write the objective complement in each sentence.
EXAMPLE: The race made him weak.
ANSWER: weak

1. Track and field participants call the competitions *meets.*
2. The track coach made Brian a sprinter in the track meet.
3. He also called Brian his best distance runner.
4. The sprint made Brian tired.
5. The coach classifies Sue a high jumper.
6. Sue made 6 feet the new school record in the high jump.
7. The judges considered Sue a qualifier for the finals.
8. Qualifying in the event made Sue happy.
9. The schedule made the last track meet on a Saturday.
10. The newspaper named Joe Klepak Coach of the Year.

Exercise 28 **Writing Sentences With Objective Complements** Write sentences with objective complements, using the verbs and direct objects given below.
1. consider swimming
2. called the captain
3. is making me
4. classifies the sport
5. dubbed the mascot

More Practice
On-line
Exercise Bank
• Section 20.3
Grammar Exercise Workbook
• pp. 59–64

Complements • 441

Objective Complement

1. Read the Key Concept aloud. Go over the examples with students. Explain that like other complements, the object complement is a modifier. It describes and gives further details about the object.
2. Help students understand the difference between an indirect object and an object complement:

   I gave the usher the ticket.
   I called the usher Gracie.
3. In the first sentence, the indirect object *usher* names the person to whom something is given. In the second sentence, the complement *Gracie* renames *usher,* which is the direct object of the verb *called.*
4. Work through the first few sentences of Exercise 27 with the class. Have students take turns writing the sentences on the chalkboard and labeling the subject, verb, direct object, and complement. After each sentence, have the class decide whether each part of speech is correctly labeled, and explain any corrections they think are required.

Answer Key

Exercise 27
1. meets
2. sprinter
3. runner
4. tired
5. jumper
6. record
7. qualifier
8. happy
9. meet
10. Coach

Exercise 28
Answers will vary. Samples given below.
1. She considered swimming wonderful.
2. He called the captain terrific.
3. She is making me sad.
4. He classifies the sport bad.
5. He dubbed the mascot Smarty.

Answer Key

Exercise 29

1. basketball
2. ball
3. points
4. basketball
5. championships

Exercise 30

1. none
2. players
3. none
4. game
5. *mintonette*

Exercise 31

Answers will vary. Samples are given.

1. me
2. her
3. them
4. me
5. us

Exercise 32

1. Stefan told Jason the rules of ice hockey.
2. none
3. Using a hockey stick, a hockey player passes his teammate the puck.
4. Hockey coaches can give their team a time out.
5. Canada and Russia have given the game of hockey many active players.

442

GRAMMAR EXERCISES 29–40

Exercise 29 **Recognizing Direct Objects** Write the direct object in each sentence.

1. A YMCA instructor invented basketball in 1891.
2. In basketball, players put a ball through a basket to make points.
3. The winning team scores the most points.
4. Spectators first watched basketball in the nineteenth century.
5. Most states now hold championships in basketball.

Exercise 30 **Distinguishing Between Direct Objects and Objects of Prepositions** Write the direct object in each sentence. If a sentence does not have one, write *none*.

1. Volleyball is played by hitting a ball back and forth over a net.
2. Each team has six players.
3. In beach volleyball, teams consist of two players.
4. William G. Morgan invented the game in 1895 as a recreational pastime.
5. The game was originally called *mintonette*.

Exercise 31 **Supplying Indirect Objects** Supply a logical indirect object in each sentence.

1. Pam told ___?___ the highlights of the basketball game.
2. At the beginning of the game, the center tipped ___?___ the jump ball.
3. A foul gave ___?___ a chance to score.

4. In the last 30 seconds of the game, the guard passed ___?___ the ball and he made a three-pointer.
5. As a result, the home team gave ___?___ another victory.

Exercise 32 **Distinguishing Between Indirect Objects and Objects of Prepositions** In the following sentences, change each indirect object into a prepositional phrase. Change each prepositional phrase, if possible, into an indirect object. If you can't, write *none*.

1. Stefan told the rules of ice hockey to Jason.
2. The players wear ice skates for the game.
3. Using a hockey stick, a hockey player passes the puck to his teammate.
4. Hockey coaches can give a timeout to their team.
5. Canada and Russia have given many active players to the game of hockey.

Exercise 33 **Revising to Combine Sentences Using Direct and Indirect Objects** Revise this paragraph, combining short sentences into longer ones with compound direct or indirect objects.

Sam told Jill the events of his soccer game. He also told Simran. Sam made three goals for his team. He had three assists, as well. He passed the right wing ball, and Jill scored a goal. The ball several times. In addition, he passed the left wing the ball several times. One midfielder had a number of shots on goal. He also had a number of corner kicks.

442 • Basic Sentence Parts

Exercise 33

Sam told Jill and Simran the events of the soccer game. He made three goals and assists for his team. He passed both the right wing and the left wing the ball several times and Jill scored a goal. One midfielder had a number of shots on goal and corner kicks.

Exercise 34 Recognizing
Predicate Nominatives Write the predicate nominative in each sentence.

1. Lugeing and bobsledding are forms of tobogganing.
2. Bobsledding is a fast and dangerous winter sport.
3. The luge is a small sled used for one- and two-man and one-woman competitions.
4. Eugenio Monti was a great bobsledder between 1957 and 1968.
5. St. Moritz was the home of the first bobsled event in 1888.

Exercise 35 Recognizing
Predicate Adjectives Write the predicate adjective(s) in each sentence.

1. Tobogganing became popular in the northern United States and Canada in the 1930's.
2. Tobogganing remains well received as a sport today.
3. The toboggan sled is runnerless.
4. The sport of tobogganing is recreational and exciting.
5. Cresta tobogganers, or tobogganers in the Cresta Valley at Saint Moritz, are adventurous.

Exercise 36 Supplying Objective
Complements Complete each sentence with one or more objective complements as indicated.

1. Weight lifting makes participants ___?___ .
2. It makes muscles ___?___ and ___?___ .
3. Powerful weight lifters leave spectators ___?___ .
4. Being unable to lift the desired weight leaves the lifter ___?___ .
5. In recent decades, people have come to consider weight lifting a ___?___ .

Exercise 37 Writing Sentences
With Subject Complements Use each subject and verb to write a sentence. Add words to form the kind of complement indicated in parentheses.

1. game seemed (predicate adjective)
2. parents were (predicate nominative)
3. team remained (predicate nominative)
4. captain named (objective complement)
5. Matt felt (predicate adjective)

Exercise 38 Find It in Your
Reading Read this excerpt from *I Had a Hammer*. Write it on your paper. Underline the subjects once; underline the verbs twice; and box and label direct objects, indirect objects, and objects of prepositions.

" . . . Their pitcher was Al Downing, a veteran lefthander whom I respected. Downing always had an idea of what he was doing when he was on the mound, and he usually pitched me outside with sliders and screwballs."

Exercise 39 Find It in Your
Writing Look through your portfolio for one example of each of the following: direct object, indirect object, object of a preposition, predicate nominative, predicate adjective, and objective complement. Write the sentences and label each complement.

Exercise 40 Writing Application
Write an account of a sports event you recently participated in or witnessed; or you can make up an event. In it, include at least one of each of the following: direct object, indirect object, object of a preposition, predicate nominative, predicate adjective, and objective complement. Write down the sentences, and label each complement.

Section Review • 443

CHAPTER REVIEW

Each of these exercises correlates to the concepts taught in the chapter on basic sentence parts, pages 422–447. The exercises may be used for more practice, for reteaching, or for review of the Key Concepts presented. Answers for all chapter exercises are available in *Grammar Exercises Answers on Transparencies* in your teaching resources.

Answer Key

Exercise 41

1. subject: Badminton; predicate: is a sport for two or four players
2. subject: It; predicate: is a backyard recreational or competitive indoor sport
3. subject: Badminton; predicate: dates back to the 1800's
4. subject: The first badminton club; predicate: was formed in 1878 in New York City
5. subject: Long-handled rackets; predicate: are used to hit a shuttlecock over a net
6. subject: Badminton rackets; predicate: are lightweight and much smaller than those in tennis
7. subject: A player; predicate: has to serve the shuttlecock into play in order to score
8. subject: A server; predicate: scores against his or her opponent
9. subject: A fault; predicate: results in a loss of serve
10. subject: Fifteen points; predicate: wins a game in doubles

Exercise 42

1. subjects: people, people; verbs: travel, compete, recreate
2. verbs: organize, enjoy
3. subjects: races, riders; verbs: influenced, dominated
4. subjects: French, Spanish, Italians
5. verbs: competed, turned, moved

Exercise 43

1. players
2. members
3. teams
4. impression
5. [You]

Chapter 20 Chapter Review

GRAMMAR EXERCISES 41–49

Exercise 41 **Recognizing Simple and Complete Subjects and Predicates**
Make two columns. Write each complete subject in the first column and each complete predicate in the second column. Then, underline the simple subject once and the verb twice.

1. Badminton is a sport for two or four players.
2. It is a backyard recreational or competitive indoor sport.
3. Badminton dates back to the 1800's.
4. The first badminton club was formed in 1878 in New York City.
5. Long-handled rackets are used to hit a shuttlecock over a net.
6. Badminton rackets are lightweight and much smaller than those in tennis.
7. A player has to serve the shuttlecock into play in order to score.
8. A server scores against his or her opponent.
9. A fault results in a loss of serve.
10. Fifteen points wins a game in doubles.

Exercise 42 **Recognizing Compound Subjects and Verbs** Write the subjects that make up each compound subject and the verbs that make up each compound verb.

1. Young people and old people travel, compete, and relax on bicycles.
2. Cycling clubs organize and enjoy weekly bicycle rides.
3. After World War II, European road races and riders influenced competitive cycling and dominated the sport.
4. The French, Spanish, and Italians often succeed at competitive cycling.
5. Many American cyclists competed internationally, turned professional, and then moved to Europe to compete.

444 • Basic Sentence Parts

Exercise 43 **Identifying Hard-to-Find Subjects** Write the subject of each sentence. Use brackets to indicate understood subjects.

1. There are two or four players in a game of racquetball.
2. Among my teammates are two health-club members.
3. There were sixteen teams in our recent tournament.
4. What is your impression of racquetball as a sport?
5. Come to the club some weekend, and join us.

Exercise 44 **Distinguishing Among Direct Objects, Indirect Objects, and Objects of Prepositions** In three separate columns on your paper, write each direct object, indirect object, and object of a preposition in the following sentences.

1. Upon kicking a teammate the soccer ball, a player sometimes bumps an opponent by accident.
2. Therefore, soccer players use shinguards for protection.
3. Players wear shinguards under their socks.
4. They do not cause the players difficulty.
5. They have protected many soccer players from extensive injuries.
6. The coach bought the entire team new shinguards before the start of the season.
7. The coach explained the drill to the new players.
8. They ran toward the goal while watching for the ball.
9. The midfielder passed the right wing the ball.
10. The goalkeeper stopped a shot by an opposing striker.

Exercise 44

	Direct Object	Indirect Object	Object of Preposition
1.	opponent	teammate	ball, accident
2.	shinguards		protection
3.	shinguards		socks
4.	difficulty	players	
5.	players		injuries
6.	shinguards	team	start, season
7.	drill		players
8.			goal, ball
9.	ball	right wing	
10.	shot		striker

> **Exercise 45** Recognizing **Predicate Nominatives and Predicate Adjectives** Write the predicate nominative(s) and predicate adjective(s) in each sentence.

1. Snowmobiling has become popular in North America.
2. Snowmobile clubs are organizations for maintaining snowmobiling trails.
3. Organized races are exciting for professional snowmobile racers.
4. The snowmobiles are machines capable of speeds in excess of 118 mph.
5. To some people, snowmobiles are a noisy nuisance.

> **Exercise 46** Distinguishing **Sentence Parts** Read the paragraph, and identify each underlined word as a subject, verb, direct object, indirect object, object of a preposition, predicate nominative, predicate adjective, or objective complement.

Jane's team won the basketball (1) game in overtime last night. At the end of regulation time, the score was (2) even—52–52. (3) They had been (4) behind, but because Jane (5) scored a three-point shot as the clock ran out, they tied the (6) game. Her teammates were (7) relieved that she (8) had made the (9) shot. The thought of an overtime (10) game made (11) them extremely (12) nervous, but it was better than losing. When the clock started, Jane's (13) team scored five quick (14) points. The team, as always, had become a united (15) group.

> **Exercise 47** Revision Practice Revise the following paragraph, combining short sentences where possible, making compound subjects, compound verbs, direct objects, indirect objects, and subject or objective complements.

Jeremy is learning tennis this summer. His sister Keesha is, too. For the children's birthdays, their parents bought them rackets. They also bought them sweatbands, shorts, and socks. The gifts made Jeremy and Keesha very happy. They also made Jeremy and Keesha eager to start tennis lessons. Mr. Ellison at the local sports club is an excellent tennis teacher. He is also a former professional player. Mr. Ellison is teaching Keesha a number of important techniques. He's teaching them to Jeremy, as well. Jeremy says he considers tennis one of his two favorite sports. His other favorite sport is snowboarding.

> **Exercise 48** Supplying All Basic **Sentence Parts** Write each sentence on your paper, supplying the missing part as indicated in parentheses by the following abbreviations.

DO (direct object)
IO (indirect object)
PN (predicate nominative)
PA (predicate adjective)
OC (objective complement))

1. Randy organized neighborhood (DO).
2. He made (DO) (OC) of the team.
3. The other players were (PN) and (PN).
4. We were (PA) because we played well.
5. Later, he gave (DO) a post-game party.
6. The snacks were (PN), (PN), and (PN).
7. Al gave (IO) some (DO).
8. We considered the event a (OC).
9. My father gave (IO) a (DO) home.
10. I felt (PA) after the long day.

> **Exercise 49** Writing Application Describe your favorite sport in a five-sentence paragraph that you might write to a friend in a foreign country who is not very familiar with your sport. Underline each of your subjects once and your verbs twice. Label each complement.

> **Exercise 45**

1. popular (PA)
2. organizations (PN)
3. exciting (PA)
4. machines (PN)
5. nuisance (PN)

> **Exercise 46**

1. DO
2. PA
3. subject
4. PA
5. verb
6. DO
7. PA
8. verb
9. DO
10. OP
11. DO
12. OC
13. subject
14. DO
15. PN

> **Exercise 47**

Jeremy and his sister Keesha are learning tennis this summer. For the kids' birthdays, their parents bought them racquets, sweatbands, shorts and socks. The gifts made Jeremy and Keesha very happy and eager to start tennis lessons. Mr. Ellison at the local sports club is an excellent tennis teacher and a former professional player. Mr. Ellison is teaching Keesha and Jeremy a number of important techniques. Jeremy says he considers tennis and snowboarding his two favorite sports.

> **Exercise 48**

Answers will vary. Samples are given.

1. Randy organized neighborhood sports.
2. He made the neighbors members of the team.
3. The other players were friends and classmates.
4. We were happy because we played well.
5. Later, he gave the team a post-game party.
6. The snacks were pizza, chips, and dip.
7. Al gave Sam some snacks.
8. We considered the event a success.
9. My father gave Al a ride home.
10. I felt tired after the long day.

> **Exercise 49**

Students will respond by writing a 5 sentence paragraph.

Lesson Objectives

1. To recognize appropriate sentence construction.
2. To identify subjects and verbs.
3. To recognize appropriate use of punctuation.

Recognizing Appropriate Sentence Construction

1. Explain to students that they will be confronted with questions that require them to assimilate a great deal of information.

2. Students should read through the given passage to determine its overall meaning. Students should also begin to get a sense of how the sentences and fragments can be combined to form complete, correctly punctuated sentences.

Standardized Test Preparation Workshop

Recognizing Appropriate Sentence Construction

Knowing how to use the basic parts of a sentence correctly is the foundation for good writing. Every sentence must contain a subject (the *who* or *what* that performs the action) and a verb (the action the subject is performing) and express a complete thought. If one of these parts is missing, the sentence is incomplete.

Standardized tests measure your ability to identify complete sentences. When answering these test questions, check each group of words for a subject and a verb, and then determine whether it expresses a complete thought. Also, make sure that the sentence is not really two sentences pushed together incorrectly.

The following question will give you practice with the format used for testing your knowledge of basic sentence parts.

Test Tips

- Remember that a verb can either follow or come before its subject. Also, a form of *be* can act as the main verb of a sentence.
- Watch out for answer choices that are really two sentences run together with no punctuation or with just a comma separating them.

Sample Test Item	Answers and Explanations
Directions: Choose the letter of the best way to write each underlined section. If the underlined section needs no change, choose "Correct as is." Documentaries are nonfiction films. Which (1) have gained in popularity. They tell of real people. And of real events.	
1 A Documentaries are nonfiction films that tell of real, popular people and events. **B** Documentaries, which have gained in popularity, are nonfiction films that tell of real people and events. **C** Documentaries are nonfiction films that tell of real people and events, which have gained in popularity. **D** Correct as is	The correct answer is *B*. This choice successfully eliminates the fragment, *Which have gained in popularity,* by making it a subordinate clause modifying *Documentaries.* This choice also combines a short sentence and a fragment by forming a compound object of the preposition *of* and turns the resulting sentence into a subordinate clause modifying *films.* Choice A changes the meaning of the original. Choice C makes it seem as though it is the real people and events, rather than the documentaries, that have gained in popularity.

TEST-TAKING TIP

Remind students about the importance of reading each choice carefully. If students find even a single error in any of the choices, they can immediately eliminate it. If a choice looks correct grammatically, make sure students check for proper punctuation. Punctuation may be one element that students overlook in a test-taking situation.

▶ **Practice 1** **Directions:** Choose the letter of the best way to write each underlined section. If the underlined section needs no change, choose "Correct as is."

Eduardo knew it would be his last time at
(1)
bat. When he got up slowly. When he came

out of the dugout. Positioning himself at the
(2)
plate and watched. The first ball sped by

him. The second ball sped by him. Then, he
(3)
heard the crack of the bat, he heard it

against the ball.

1 **A** Eduardo knew it was his last time at back, so he got up slowly and came out of the dugout.

   B Being his last time at bat, Eduardo got up slowly and came out of the dugout.

   C When he got up slowly and came out of the dugout, Eduardo knew it would be his last time at bat.

   D Correct as is

2 **F** He positioned himself at the plate and watched the first ball and the second ball speed by him.

   G Positioning himself, the first ball and the second ball sped by him.

   H Positioning himself at the plate, he watched the first ball and the second ball, which sped by him.

   J Correct as is

3 **A** Then, he heard the crack of the bat, which was against the ball.

   B Then, he heard the crack of the bat against the ball.

   C Then, he heard the crack of the bat and knew it was against the ball.

   D Correct as is

▶ **Practice 2** **Directions:** Choose the letter of the best way to write each underlined section. If the underlined section needs no change, choose "Correct as is."

The case was covered heavily in the papers.
(1)
Also a lot on TV, too. Now, a question
                              (2)
lingered in everyone's mind: Would the

defendant get a fair trial? The judge assured
                                    (3)
the parties in the case. He considered the

jurors were honest people.

1 **A** The case was covered heavily in the papers, and it was covered on TV, too.

   B In the papers. and on TV as well, the case was covered heavily.

   C The case was covered heavily in the papers and on TV.

   D Correct as is

2 **F** Everyone was wondering, now, whether or not the defendant would get a fair trial.

   G Everyone was asking this lingering question: Would the defendant get a fair trial?

   H There was a question lingering in everyone's mind now: Would the defendant get a fair trial?

   J Correct as is

3 **A** The judge assured the parties in the case that he considered the jurors honest people.

   B The judge assured the parties in the case and said that the jurors were honest people.

   C The judge told the parties in the case they could consider the jurors honest.

   D Correct as is

Practice 1
1. C
2. F
3. B

Practice 2
1. C
2. J
3. A

Chapter 21 Time and Resource Manager

In-Depth Lesson Plan

LESSON FOCUS	PRINT AND MEDIA RESOURCES
DAY 1 **Phrases** Students learn and apply the concepts of prepositional, adverb, and appositive phrases (pp. 448–455).	**Teaching Resources** *Grammar Exercise Workbook*, pp. 65–66; *Grammar Exercise Answers on Transparencies*, Ch. 21; **On-Line** *Exercise Bank*, Section 21.1
DAY 2 **Phrases (continued)** Students learn and apply the concepts of participles and participial phrases, gerunds and gerund phrases, infinitives and infinitive phrases, and do the Hands-on Grammar activity (pp. 456–467).	**Teaching Resources** *Grammar Exercise Workbook*, pp. 65–66; *Grammar Exercise Answers on Transparencies*, Ch. 21; **On-Line** *Exercise Bank*, Section 21.1
DAY 3 **Clauses** Students learn and apply the concepts of independent, subordinate, and adjective, adverb, and noun clauses (pp. 468–485).	**Teaching Resources** *Grammar Exercise Workbook*, pp. 83–90; *Grammar Exercise Answers on Transparencies*, Ch. 21; **On-Line** *Exercise Bank*, Section 21.2
DAY 4 **Review and Assess** Students review chapter and demonstrate mastery of use of phrases and clauses (pp. 486–489).	**Teaching Resources** *Formal Assessment*, Ch. 21; *Grammar Exercise Answers on Transparencies*, Ch. 21; **On-Line** *Exercise Bank*, Section 21.1

Accelerated Lesson Plan

LESSON FOCUS	PRINT AND MEDIA RESOURCES
DAY 1 **Phrases** Students cover concepts and usage of phrases as determined by Diagnostic Test (pp. 448–467).	**Teaching Resources** *Grammar Exercise Workbook*, pp. 65–66; *Grammar Exercise Answers on Transparencies*, Ch. 21; **On-Line** *Exercise Bank*, Section 21.1
DAY 2 **Clauses** Students cover concepts and usage of clauses as determined by Diagnostic Test (pp. 468–485).	**Teaching Resources** *Grammar Exercise Workbook*, pp. 83–90; *Grammar Exercise Answers on Transparencies*, Ch. 21; **On-Line** *Exercise Bank*, Section 21.2
DAY 3 **Review and Assess** Students review chapter and demonstrate mastery of use of phrases and clauses (pp. 486–489).	**Teaching Resources** *Formal Assessment*, Ch. 21; *Grammar Exercise Answers on Transparencies*, Ch. 21; **On-Line** *Exercise Bank*, Section 21.1

Options for Adapting Lesson Plans

HOMEWORK
Have students complete any section of the chapter for homework.

FEATURES
Extend coverage with the Grammar in Literature feature (pp. 461, 476) and the Standardized Test Preparation Workshop (p. 488).

TECHNOLOGY
Students can use the On-Line Exercise Bank to complete the exercises on computer. The Auto Check feature will grade their work.

INTEGRATED SKILLS COVERAGE

Grammar in Literature
SE pp. 461, 476

Reading
Find It in Your Reading SE pp. 466, 467, 485

Writing
Find It In Your Writing SE pp. 466, 467, 485
Writing Application SE pp. 467, 485, 487
Integrating Writing Skills ATE p. 454

Language
Language Highlight ATE p. 463

Speaking and Listening
Integrating Speaking and Listening Skills ATE p. 460

Real-World Connection
ATE pp. 453, 474

Viewing and Representing
Critical Viewing SE pp. 448, 451, 452, 454, 455, 459, 462, 464, 470, 471, 472, 474, 476, 478, 480, 481, 484

ASSESSMENT SUPPORT

Standardized Test Preparation SE p. 488; ATE pp. 459, 470
Standardized Test Preparation Workbook, pp. 41–42
Formal Assessment, Ch. 21

MEETING INDIVIDUAL NEEDS

Less Advanced Students ATE pp. 470, 483; See also Ongoing Assessments ATE pp. 451, 452, 455, 457, 460, 463, 466, 469, 479, 480, 481, 482
ESL Students ATE p. 456
Visual/Spatial Learners ATE p. 453
Verbal/Linguistic Learners ATE p. 464
Gifted/Talented Students ATE p. 477

BLOCK SCHEDULING

Pacing Suggestions
For 90-minute Blocks
• Administer the Diagnostic Test to students to determine instructional coverage.
• Have students complete the necessary exercises in class. Use the Hands-on Grammar activity to provide a change of pace.

Resources for Varying Instruction
• *Language Lab* CD-ROM If your students have access to hardware, a 90-minute block provides an ideal opportunity for students to work on computer.

Professional Development Support
• *How to Manage Instruction in the Block* This teaching resource provides management and activity suggestions.

MEDIA AND TECHNOLOGY

For the Student
• *On-Line Exercise Bank,* Ch. 21

For the Teacher
• *Resource Pro* CD-ROM

WRITING AND GRAMMAR WEBSITE

The Interactive Writing and Grammar Website provides a wide array of support for students, teachers, and parents. Grammar support includes:

• *On-Line Exercise Bank* with Auto Check scoring
• Diagnostic and assessment support

phwg.phschool.com

LITERATURE CONNECTIONS

Grammar in Literature selections from *Prentice Hall Literature: Timeless Voices, Timeless Themes,* Gold:

from "There Is a Longing . . .," Chief Dan George, SE p. 461

from *Talk,* retold by Harold Courlander and George Herzog, SE p. 476

► *Lesson Objectives*

1. To recognize prepositional phrases in sentences and distinguish between adjective phrases and adverb phrases.

2. To identify appositives and appositive phrases and the words they rename.

3. To recognize participles and participial phrases in sentences.

4. To identify gerunds and gerund phrases in sentences.

5. To identify infinitives and infinitive phrases in sentences.

6. To recognize clauses as phrases with a subject and verb.

7. To distinguish between independent and subordinate clauses.

8. To classify sentences by structure and by function.

Critical Viewing

Analyze In the picture, the Apache warrior is wearing a feathered headdress, holding a spear and standing next to his decorated tepee. Students may suggest that an Apache warrior with a spear in his hands stands by his tepee with the deer painted on its side.

Chapter 21 Phrases and Clauses

▲ **Critical Viewing**
Use a phrase to add details to this sentence about the picture: An Apache warrior stands by his tepee. **[Analyze]**

Knowing when and how to use the parts of speech and the basic parts of a sentence will enable you to begin building strong sentences. This chapter will help you expand on your sentences by introducing two additional elements, the *phrase* and the *clause*. A **phrase** is a group of words, without a subject and verb, that functions in a sentence as one part of speech. A **clause** is a group of words with its own subject and verb. Some clauses can stand by themselves as complete sentences; others can only be parts of sentences.

The Native American tepee pictured above was put together carefully so that it would be strong. In the same way, you tie words together to create strong sentences. Phrases and clauses allow you to form effective sentences in which ideas are clear and concise. Whether writing about Native Americans or travel to Africa, phrases and clauses provide important details that add meaning to your sentences.

448 • Phrases and Clauses

☑ **ONGOING ASSESSMENT: Diagnose**

If students miss more than one item in each category, direct them to the relevant pages of the text and assign exercises for practice and review.

Phrases and Clauses	Diagnostic Test Items	Teach	Practice	Section Review	Chapter Review	Cumulative Review and Applications
Skill Check A						
Adjective and Adverb Phrases	A 1–5	pp. 450–453	Ex. 1–4	Ex. 19	Ex. 46	Ex. 22, 24
Skill Check B						
Appositive Phrases	B 6–10	pp. 459–455	Ex. 5–8	Ex. 19	Ex. 47	Ex. 22–23

Diagnostic Test

Directions: Write all answers on a separate sheet of paper.

Skill Check A. Write the prepositional phrase(s) from each sentence. Label them *adverb* or *adjective*.

1. Arrowheads are made of stone, bone, or metal.
2. They are fastened to the end of an arrow shaft.
3. A notch at the top of the arrow shaft is cut.
4. The arrowhead is then secured in the arrow shaft with sinew.
5. Finally, the arrow shaft is fitted with feathers.

Skill Check B. Write the appositive phrases from each sentence. Then, label the underlined phrase *infinitive* or *prepositional*.

6. Flint, a rock that chips easily, is used to make arrowheads.
7. The process results in a sharp point, the arrowhead, chipped to the perfect shape.
8. A special process of making percussion fractures, chipping off smaller pieces by applied pressure, is then used to sharpen the edge.
9. The arrow, a simple yet effective weapon, enabled Native Americans of earlier times to protect themselves and to hunt for animals.
10. The arrowhead was even able to pierce the thick hide of their most common prey, the buffalo.

Skill Check C. Label the underlined word(s) in each sentence *present participle*, *past participle*, *gerund*, or *verb*.

11. For many Native American tribes, hunting buffalo was important for all aspects of life.
12. Dried brush from buffalo plains was often used as fuel for fire.
13. Hides were wrapped around wooden frames to make tepees and war shields as well as a covering for boats.
14. Some tribes followed the herd of buffalo as they were grazing.
15. Ceremonies were performed, honoring the buffalo.

Skill Check D. Copy the following sentences. Label each sentence *simple*, *complex*, *compound*, or *compound-complex*. Underline the subordinate clauses, and label them *adjective* or *adverb*.

16. Southwestern tribes hold a festival when the first corn of the year is harvested.
17. During this week of festivities, whatever debts or injuries a person has at the time are forgiven.
18. The Utes, an Indian tribe from the Utah area, celebrate the Bear Dance every spring.
19. The dance grounds are made to resemble a bear's den, and one opening faces the East.
20. A woman asks a man to dance by brushing him with her shawl, but if the man tries to avoid dancing, he is put back into line by the "Catman," who is chosen to keep order!

Answer Key

Diagnostic Test

- Each item in the diagnostic test corresponds to a specific concept in the phrases and clauses chapter. This will enable you to tailor instruction to the particular needs of your students. See "Ongoing Assessment: Diagnose" below for further details.

- Answers for the Diagnostic Test and all chapter exercises are available in *Grammar Exercises Answers on Transparencies* in your teaching resources.

Skill Check A

1. of stone, bone, or metal—adverb
2. to the end—adverb; of an arrow shaft—adverb
3. at the top—adjective; of the arrow shaft—adjective
4. in the arrow shaft—adverb; with sinew—adverb
5. with feathers—adverb

Skill Check B

6. a rock that chips easily; infinitive
7. the arrowhead; prepositional
8. chipping off smaller pieces by applied pressure; infinitive
9. a simple yet effective weapon; infinitive
10. the buffalo; infinitive

Skill Check C

11. gerund
12. past participle
13. verb; gerund
14. verb
15. present participle

Skill Check D

16. Southwestern tribes hold a festival when the first corn of the year is harvested. complex; adverb
17. During this week of festivities, whatever debts or injuries a person has at the time are forgiven. complex; noun, adverb
18. The Utes, an Indian tribe from the Utah area, celebrate the Bear Dance every spring. simple
19. The dance grounds are made to resemble a bear's den, and one opening faces the East. compound
20. A woman asks a man to dance by brushing him with her shawl, but if the man tries to avoid dancing, he is put back into line by the "Catman," who is chosen to keep order! compound-complex; adverb, adjective

ONGOING ASSESSMENT: Diagnose *continued*						
Phrases and Clauses	Diagnostic Test Items	Teach	Practice	Section Review	Chapter Review	Cumulative Review and Applications
Skill Check C						
Gerunds, Gerund Phrases, Infinitives, and Infinitive Phrases	C 11–15	pp. 456–465	Ex. 9–18	Ex. 20	Ex. 48	Ex. 24, 55–56
Skill Check D						
Sentences Classified by Structure	D 16–20	pp. 482–483	Ex. 41	Ex. 38, 39	Ex. 53–54	Ex. 40–42, 55–56

Have students brainstorm a menu for a home-cooked meal and describe it to a friend who wants to know the ingredients used. Students should respond in complete sentences using the form: *We had salad with ____.* Then have students identify the adjective phrase and the noun it modifies.

Activate Prior Knowledge

Have partners take turns writing questions that ask *Which one?* or *What kind?* and answers that use adjective clauses. For example: Q: Which bird sings? A: The bird *in the cage* sings.

TEACH

Step-by-Step Teaching Guide

Adjective Phrases

1. Emphasize the basic principle of adjective phrases: An adjective phrase is a prepositional phrase that modifies either a noun or a pronoun.

2. Remind students that like adjectives, adjective phrases answer the question *What kind?* or *Which one?* but they do so in phrases of several words.

3. Write the following sentences on the board and have students identify the noun or nouns and the adjective phrase or phrases that modify them.

   The <u>doll</u> <u>in her hand</u> was plastic.

   The <u>sweater</u> <u>in the shop</u> was wool.

4. More than one adjective phrase can modify the same noun. Write the following sentences on the board and have students identify the noun and then the adjective phrases that modify the noun.

   The <u>book</u> <u>of poetry</u> <u>on the desk</u> was old.

   The <u>party</u> <u>at my house</u> <u>for my birthday</u> took place yesterday.

Phrases

This section will explore the ways several different kinds of phrases can be used to add variety and meaning to sentences. There are several types of phrases, among them *prepositional, appositive, participial, gerund,* and *infinitive* phrases.

Prepositional Phrases

A *prepositional phrase,* such as *by the lake* or *out of gas,* is made up of a preposition and a noun or pronoun, called the object of the preposition. Prepositions may also have compound objects, such as *for Maria and me* and *to the kitchen, hallway, or living room.* (See Section 19.1 to review prepositions.) Prepositional phrases function either as adjectives by modifying nouns and pronouns or as adverbs by modifying verbs, adjectives, and adverbs.

Adjective Phrases

When acting as an adjective, a prepositional phrase is called an *adjective phrase.*

▶ **KEY CONCEPT** An **adjective phrase** is a prepositional phrase that modifies a noun or pronoun by telling *what kind* or *which one.* ∎

EXAMPLES: The tepee *of buffalo hide* was sturdy.

   The decoration *on the hide* was painted carefully.

   The opening *in the front* was narrow.

At other times, more than one adjective phrase may be used to modify the same noun.

EXAMPLE: The drawing *of a warrior on the tepee* was painted in red.

Theme: Native Americans

In this section, you will learn how phrases are used to modify nouns, pronouns, verbs, adjectives, and adverbs. The examples and exercises in this section are about Native Americans.

Cross-Curricular Connection: Social Studies

⏱ TIME AND RESOURCE MANAGER

Resources
Print: Grammar Exercise Workbook, pp. 65–66; Hands-on Grammar Activity Book, Chapter 21
Technology: On-Line Exercise Bank, Section 21.1

In-Depth Coverage	Accelerated Pace
• Work through all key concepts, pp. 450–454. • Assign and review Exercises 1–4.	• Assign pp. 450–454 for independent student review. • Assign Exercise 5. • Assign Review Exercises 19–20.

Exercise 1 Identifying Adjective Phrases Write each sentence, underlining the adjective phrase or phrases in each. Then, draw an arrow from each phrase to the word it modifies.

EXAMPLE: Native American tribes in the Northwest were numerous.

1. There are several different kinds of Native American tribes in North America.
2. The culture of each tribe varies.
3. The tribes of western Louisiana and eastern Texas are the Caddo.
4. Farming provided their main source of food.
5. Also important was the annual hunt for buffalo.

Exercise 2 Writing Sentences With Adjective Phrases
Using the following prepositional phrases, write sentences of your own. Use each prepositional phrase as an adjective phrase.

EXAMPLE: of farming
ANSWER: Native Americans taught their ways *of farming* to colonists.

1. of the culture
2. about Native American tribes
3. for fishing
4. from buffalo
5. in the Utah area

More Practice

On-line
Exercise Bank
• Section 21.1
Grammar Exercise Workbook
• pp. 41–43

▼ Critical Viewing
These totems in Stanley Park, Vancouver, were made by Native Americans. Describe the totems with two sentences. Use an adjective phrase in one and an adverb phrase in the other. [Describe]

Phrases • 451

Adverb Phrases

1. Students may find distinguishing between adjective and adverb phrases confusing. Remind them that adjective phrases modify nouns and pronouns; adverb phrases modify verbs, adjectives, and adverbs.

2. Write the following sentences on the board and have students identify the adjective and the adverb phrase.

    Juanita lived in the brick house. (adverb phrase: in the brick house *modifies the verb* lived)

    The house of brick was where Juanita lived. (adjective phrase: it modifies the noun house)

3. Remind students that adverb phrases always answer the question *Where? When? In what manner?* or *To what extent?* Have students practice writing simple sentences using adverb phrases that answer these questions.

Critical Viewing

Describe Students may say that the Native American represented in the art work is carrying a staff in his hands and is wearing a feathered headdress on his head.

Answer Key

Exercise 3 *(page 453)*

1. The Pawnee divided themselves into four different tribes. [arrow to *divided*]
2. Most of them lived in earth lodges. [arrow to *lived*]
3. One tribe, the Skidi Pawnee, died out in the early 1800's. [arrow to *died*]
4. Religion was very important to this tribe. [arrow to *important*]
5. In their religion, they paid homage to the morning star. [arrow to *paid*]

Exercise 4 *(page 453)*

Answers will vary. Samples are given.

1. The Pawnee lived *in different sections of the United States.*
2. They danced *during the festival.*
3. They celebrated *after the hunt.*
4. They pounded the corn repeatedly *with a hard stone.*
5. They ate well *from farming and fishing.*

21.1

Adverb Phrases

When a prepositional phrase functions as an adverb, it is called an *adverb phrase.*

▶ **KEY CONCEPT** An **adverb phrase** is a prepositional phrase that modifies a verb, an adjective, or an adverb by pointing out *where, when, in what way,* or *to what extent.* ■

MODIFYING A VERB: Abstract animal figures were carved *in totem poles.* (carved *where?*)

Southwestern art dates back *before Columbus.* (dates back *when?*)

MODIFYING AN ADJECTIVE: The forest was quiet *before dawn.* (quiet *when?*)

They are happiest *at the play-ground.* (happiest *where?*)

MODIFYING AN ADVERB: He arrived late *for lunch.* (late *to what extent?*)

While an adjective phrase almost always comes directly after the word it modifies, an adverb phrase may be separated from the word it modifies.

EXAMPLE: Put the package *in the closet.* (put *where?*)

Two or more adverb phrases may also be used to modify the same word.

EXAMPLE: *On Saturdays,* my cousin studies *at the Native American Art Museum.* (studies *when?* studies *where?*)

▲ Critical Viewing
Use the prepositional phrases *in his hands* and *on his head* as adverb phrases to describe the dancer in this Native American artwork. **[Describe]**

☑ ONGOING ASSESSMENT: Monitor and Reinforce

If students miss more than two items in Exercise 1, 2, or 3, refer them to the following for additional practice.

In the Textbook	Print Resources	Technology
Section Review, Ex. 19, p. 467	Grammar Exercise Workbook, pp. 65–66	On-Line Exercise Bank, Section 21.1

Exercise 3 Identifying Adverb Phrases Write each sentence, underlining the adverb phrase or phrases in each. Then, draw an arrow from each phrase to the word it modifies.

EXAMPLE: Native American tribes divided *for different reasons.*

1. The Pawnee divided themselves into four different tribes.
2. Most of them lived in earth lodges.
3. One tribe, the Skidi Pawnee, died out in the early 1800's.
4. Religion was very important to this tribe.
5. In their religion, they paid homage to the morning star.

Exercise 4 Writing Sentences With Adverb Phrases Using the following prepositional phrases, write sentences of your own. Use each prepositional phrase as an adverb phrase.
1. in different sections of the United States
2. during the festival
3. after the hunt
4. with a hard stone
5. from farming and fishing

Appositives and Appositive Phrases

Appositives and *appositive phrases* are used to develop the meaning of nouns and certain pronouns.

Appositives

KEY CONCEPT An **appositive** is a noun or pronoun placed near another noun or pronoun to identify, rename, or explain it. ■

Notice in the following example that the appositive is set off by commas, which indicates that it is not essential to the meaning of the sentence and can be removed.

EXAMPLE: A tribe of the Northeast, the *Iroquois*, made pottery, baskets, beadwork, and quill work.

In the example below, the appositive is not set off by commas because it is needed to complete the meaning of the sentence.

EXAMPLE: The Native American writer *N. Scott Momaday* won a Pulitzer Prize for his novel *House of Dawn.*

More Practice
On-line
Exercise Bank
• Section 21.1
Grammar Exercise
Workbook
• pp. 41–43

Phrases • 453

Appositives

1. Appositives are nouns or pronouns that help to clarify or describe other nouns or pronouns in a sentence.

2. Use the catchy expression *appositives are positives* to help students remember that appositives are often easy to spot in sentences because they are punctuated by a pair of commas. Write the following sentence on the board and have students come up and underline the appositive.

    The pet, *a bulldog*, waited for his owner to return.

3. Explain that some appositives are not set off by commas because the information they contain is essential to the meaning of the sentence.

    The pet bulldog waited for his owner to return.

4. Have students write four sentences that use appositives, only two of which require commas. Ask students to cross out the appositives in the sentences that use commas, then decide if the sentences still make sense. If the sentences are illogical, explain that commas may not have been needed.

Customize for
Visual/Spatial Learners

Have students draw or design a simple floor plan of one floor of your school. Ask them to write one complete sentence that uses an adverb phrase for each room on the plan. Each sentence should describe what activity is performed in that room. For example, *We study in the library.*

Real-World Connection

Sportscasters and on-air commentators make frequent use of adverb phrases to provide accurate descriptions of actions. "He runs toward the fifty-yard line." "She swims to the finish!" Encourage students to listen for adverb phrases the next time they watch or listen to sports on the television or radio.

Appositive Phrases

1. Appositive phrases are similar to appositives, but they have their own modifiers and—unlike appositives—are generally punctuated with commas or dashes.

2. Students may have trouble distinguishing between appositives and appositive phrases. Write sentences on the board that clearly illustrate the difference between the two.

   My friend, _Sylvia_, lives down the street. (appositive)

   Sylvia, _the ballerina in the school play_, lives down the street. (appositive phrase)

Critical Viewing

Speculate Students may suggest that the container, a decorated buffalo bull's horn, contained food.

Integrating Writing Skills

Appositives work by renaming something in a way that makes it more specific. The United States Constitution opens with an appositive clause: _We, the people._ The appositive _the people_ makes clear that the authors of this important government document are the citizens. Ask students to review one selection from their recent writings to find opportunities to use appositives to explain or specify what is being said.

21.1

Appositive Phrases

When an appositive has its own modifiers, it forms an _appositive phrase._

▶ **KEY CONCEPT** An **appositive phrase** is a noun or pronoun with modifiers, placed next to a noun or pronoun to add information and details. ■

The modifiers added to make an appositive phrase can be adjectives, adjective phrases, or other groups of words acting as adjectives. Notice the construction of the appositive phrases in the following chart. Also, note how they are used to add important information to the sentence.

APPOSITIVE PHRASES
Unmarried Hopi girls often wore their hair in twisted buns, _the design of squash blossoms._
The horrible smoke, _a blend of burnt rubber and industrial fumes,_ made her choke.
The dog, _a large Saint Bernard,_ crushed the flowers in the garden.

Although many appositives and appositive phrases follow the subject, they can accompany almost any noun or pronoun used in a sentence. Following are some examples:

EXAMPLES: Her toy is a Kachina doll, _a doll made by Pueblo Indians._

The man took his daughter, _a talented artist,_ to see Native American paintings.

Appositives and appositive phrases also make it possible for a writer to combine sentences with similar ideas.

TWO SENTENCES: Navajo is a tribe in the West. They developed silver-working skills for making jewelry.

COMBINED: The Navajos, _a tribe in the West,_ developed silver-working skills for making jewelry.

Appositives can be compound.

EXAMPLE: Symbols of wealth, _copper_ and _horses,_ were important to Northwestern tribes.

▲ **Critical Viewing** This horn was used by Native Americans as a container. Use an appositive or appositive phrase in a sentence that tells what the container might have held. [Speculate]

> **Exercise 5** **Identifying Appositive Phrases** Write the appositive phrase in each sentence. Then, write the word or words each appositive phrase renames.

1. Sugar cane, a plant with a strong stem, was used to make armor for Creek warriors.
2. Clubs, slings, lances, and bows and arrows—the usual weapons of war—were made of cane, rock, and other materials found in the area.
3. A war post, a cane stock painted red and hung with feathers and arrows, signified the start of a war party.
4. Those who wanted to enlist would hit the post as hard as they could with a war club, a piece of cane painted red.
5. Then, warriors would put themselves through a purification rite, a physically strenuous ceremony.

> **Exercise 6** **Combining Sentences Using Appositive Phrases** Combine the two sentences by making the information in one into an appositive phrase.

EXAMPLE: A headdress was placed upon the warrior's head. The headdress was rows of feathers fastened together.

COMBINED: A headdress, with rows of feathers fastened together, was placed upon the warrior's head.

1. Feathers were used not only for headdresses but for acts of bravery. These feathers were called honor feathers.
2. Markings on the feathers identified the brave deed. The markings were cuts or adornments.
3. A small piece of colored feather appeared at the end of one feather. This feather represented a warrior riding into battle without weapons.
4. A feather with a split meant that the warrior had been wounded. The split was a tear down the center of the feather.
5. Counting *coup* was the bravest deed a warrior could perform. Counting *coup* was using a stick to touch a live enemy in battle and not killing him.

> **More Practice**
>
> On-line
> Exercise Bank
> • Section 21.1
> Grammar Exercise
> Workbook
> • pp. 41–43

◄ **Critical Viewing** Use "a beaded band decorated with feathers" as an appositive phrase in a sentence about the picture. **[Describe]**

Phrases • 455

> **Exercise 5**

1. a plant with a strong stem— sugar cane
2. the usual weapons of war— clubs, slings, lances, and bows and arrows
3. a cane stalk painted red and hung with feathers and arrows— post
4. a piece of cane painted red— club
5. a physically strenuous ceremony—rite

> **Exercise 6**

1. Feathers, called honor feathers, were not only used for headdresses but for acts of bravery.
2. Markings on the feathers, cuts or adornments, identified the brave deed.
3. A small piece of colored feather, representing a warrior riding into battle without weapons, appeared at the end of one feather.
4. A feather with a split, a tear down the center of the feather, meant the warrior had been wounded.
5. Counting coup, a ritual whereby a stick was used to touch a live enemy during battle and not kill him, was the bravest deed a warrior could perform.

Critical Viewing

Describe Students may say that the headdress, a beaded band decorated with feathers, is worn by the chief of a tribe.

ONGOING ASSESSMENT: Monitor and Reinforce

If students miss more than one item in Exercises 5 and 6, refer them to the following for additional practice.

In the Textbook	Print Resources	Technology
Section Review, Ex. 17, p. 467	Grammar Exercise Workbook, pp. 67–68	On-Line Exercise Bank, Section 21.1

Participles and Participial Phrases

1. Explain that one easy way to remember *participles* is that they are forms of verbs that act as adjectives.

2. Students may have trouble distinguishing between past and present participles. Most participles are easy to identify, because, like verbs, they tend to have endings we associate with present and past tenses—*-ing* for present and *-ed* for past. Like some verbs, participles have irregular endings as well. Have students brainstorm some verbs that have irregular forms in the past tense. (*eat, run, sit, fly,* and so on)

Answer Key

Exercise 7

1. simplified—past
2. Attaining—present
3. respected—past
4. chosen—past
5. growing—present

Customize for ESL Students

All languages have irregular verbs. Students learned them in their home languages by hearing and using the words over and over. In time, they will learn English irregular verbs too.

21.1

Participles and Participial Phrases

Sometimes certain forms of verbs are used not as verbs but as other parts of speech. Verb forms used as other parts of speech are called *verbals.*

Verbals may be used alone or in phrases. Like verbs, they can have complements or be modified in different ways.

This section will cover the verbal known as the *participle.*

▶ **KEY CONCEPT** A **participle** is a form of a verb that can act as an adjective. ■

Participles fall into two groups: *present participles* and *past participles.* You can identify these two different kinds of participles by their endings. Present participles end in *-ing* (*dancing, playing, waiting*). Past participles generally end in *-ed* (*danced, played, waited*), but they may also have irregular endings such as *-nt* or *-en* (*burnt, spoken*). (See Section 23.1 for lists of irregular verb endings.)

Like adjectives, participles answer the questions *What kind?* or *Which one?* The following chart shows how these participles are used as adjectives in sentences.

PRESENT PARTICIPLES	PAST PARTICIPLES
A *whining* sound came from the man's horse.	The *ground* corn was used to make tortillas.
Competing, each tribe tried to show off its riches.	*Disgusted*, Len walked away without saying goodbye.

▶ **Exercise 7** **Identifying Participles** Underline the participle in each sentence. Then, label each as *present* or *past.*

EXAMPLE: The Pueblo tribe was a <u>dignified</u> tribe. (past)

1. The Pueblo Native Americans lived simplified lives.
2. Attaining wealth and high social status was not prized.
3. The good of the community and personal integrity were the most respected values.
4. Their chosen ideal was to live a good, pious life.
5. Everyone helped to teach values to the growing youth.

💡 Spelling Tip

Not all past participles end in *-ed.* Verbals that do not follow the pattern include *frozen, broken, chosen, sought, caught,* and others.

▶ **More Practice**

On-line Exercise Bank
• Section 21.1
Grammar Exercise Workbook
• pp. 44–45

⏱ TIME SAVERS!

Answers on Transparency Use the Grammar Exercises on Transparencies for Chapter 21 to have students correct their own or one another's exercises.

On-Line Exercise Bank Have students complete the exercises on computer. The Auto Check feature will grade their work for you!

Verb or Participle?

Because verbs often have endings such as *-ing* and *-ed*, you must be careful not to confuse them with participles acting as adjectives.

▶ **KEY CONCEPTS** A **verb** shows an action, a condition, or the fact that something exists. A **participle** acting as an adjective modifies a noun or pronoun. ■

The same word can be used as a verb and as a participle.

VERBS	PARTICIPLES
The train was *chugging* down the track.	The *chugging* train puffed down the track.
The directions *confused* her.	*Confused*, she could not follow the directions.

▶ **Exercise 8** **Distinguishing Between Verbs and Participles**
Identify each underlined word as a *verb* or *participle*. If the word is used as a participle, also write the word it modifies.

EXAMPLE: The Shoshone people <u>valued</u> the land and its usefulness.

ANSWER: verb

1. To the north of the Pueblo tribes lived <u>scattered</u> bands of people.
2. They were known as the Shoshone, and they <u>inhabited</u> the deserts of the West.
3. They <u>hunted</u> small game such as rabbits or lizards for food.
4. For clothes, they used scraps of skins from the <u>hunted</u> rabbits.
5. Using the resources they had, the Shoshone in this area made their homes of <u>dried</u> brush and desert plants.
6. They used <u>sharpened</u> sticks to dig out edible roots and insects for food.
7. Large gatherings were uncommon as the amount of food in one area <u>sustained</u> very few people.
8. Occasionally, tribes <u>gathered</u> for meetings or ceremonies, which were always simple in style.
9. <u>Dreamed</u> visions were often sung during these ceremonies.
10. Sometimes, the whole community <u>danced</u> to ask for protection for one or more of its members.

Phrases • 457

Step-by-Step Teaching Guide

Verb or Participle?

1. Like adjectives, participles answer the question *What kind?* or *Which one?* Verbs are words that imply actions or conditions of some kind.

2. If students confuse verbs and participles, have them write ten sentences using the following five words as participles and as verbs: *weeping, disoriented, winding, amazed, running.*

Sample answers:

P: The weeping child had a nightmare.

V: She was weeping all morning.

P: Disoriented, she ran from store to store.

V: The darkness disoriented her, and she got lost.

P: The winding road led to the dead end.

V: She is winding the spool with thread.

P: Amazed, she laughed at their good news.

V: He amazed them with his magic tricks.

P: The running faucet kept them awake.

V: The girl is running the race.

Answer Key

▶ **Exercise 8**

1. participle—bands
2. verb
3. verb
4. participle—rabbits
5. participle—brush
6. participle—sticks
7. verb
8. verb
9. participle—visions
10. verb

☑ **ONGOING ASSESSMENT: Prerequisite Skills**

If students are having difficulty distinguishing between verbs and participles, you may find it necessary to review the following to assure coverage of prerequisite knowledge.

In the Textbook	Print Resources	Technology
Verbs, pp. 362–375	Grammar Exercises Workbook, pp. 13–20	Language Lab CD-ROM, Using Verbs; On-Line Exercise Bank, Sections 17.1–17.3

Participial Phrases

1. Participial phrases are similar to participles, except that they are modified by an adverb or an adverb phrase.

2. Point out that like participles, participial phrases function as adjectives, and they include verbals in the present and past tenses.

3. Make a chart with students of definitions and examples of present participles, past participles, verbs, and participial phrases. Making frequent reference to the chart, ask students to assign words or phrases from sentences on the board to the different categories of the chart.

4. Explain that participial phrases are not always set off by commas. As students may recall from the lesson on appositives, punctuation depends on what is essential to the meaning of the sentence. Participial phrases that are essential to the meaning of the sentence are not punctuated with commas.

21.1

Participial Phrases

Because participles are forms of verbs, they can be expanded with modifiers and complements.

▶**KEY CONCEPT** A **participial phrase** is a participle modified by an adverb or adverb phrase or accompanied by a complement. The entire phrase acts as an adjective. ■

In the following chart, note how the participial phrases are constructed and which words they modify:

PARTICIPIAL PHRASES
Studying carefully, she learned much about Native American people.
Frightened by its sudden appearance, I yelled, "Snake!"
Her sister, *using a calm voice*, told us to stand still.

Placement A participial phrase can usually be placed either before or after the word it modifies.

EXAMPLES:　*Gleaming in the sun*, Aztec temples and towers were awesome.

Aztec temples and towers, *gleaming in the sun*, were awesome.

Punctuation The participial phrases you have seen so far have been set off by commas or dashes. However, when a participial phrase distinguishes one person, place, or thing from another, it is not set off by commas. In the following example, *wearing the war bonnet* is essential to the meaning of the sentence.

EXAMPLE:　The man *wearing the war bonnet* was a chief of the Sioux people.

► Exercise 9 Recognizing Participial Phrases Write the participial phrase in each sentence. Then, write the word or words it modifies.

EXAMPLE: Being a resourceful people, the Nootka used their surroundings to make many things.

ANSWER: Being a resourceful people (the Nootka)

1. Living in the Northwest, the Nootka and other tribes built their lives around fish and wood.
2. Hollowed out trees were turned into boats.
3. Fishing from these boats, the tribes brought in abundant amounts of salmon and halibut.
4. Some boats measuring 60 feet were even strong enough to bring in a whale.
5. Hunting whales with great skill, the Nootka tribe of Vancouver Island became well known for its catches.
6. Men, wearing armor carved from wood, had protection when fighting during their battles.
7. They made masks in the hope that their enemies, frightened by the horrible faces, would run away.
8. Fashioned to the form of the body, even everyday clothes were often made of bark.
9. Houses, built of wooden planks, often contained several families living together.
10. Door poles, fantastically carved and painted, held family symbols and emblems prized by the Nootka.

► More Practice

On-line
Exercise Bank
• Section 21.1
Grammar Exercise Workbook
• pp. 41–43

▼ Critical Viewing
Include one of these words—*reaching* or *caught*—as a participle in a participial phrase in a sentence about this picture. [Speculate]

1. Living in the Northwest (the Nootka and other tribes)
2. Hollowed out (trees)
3. Fishing from these boats (the tribes)
4. measuring 60 feet (Some boats)
5. Hunting whales with great skill (the Nootka tribe of Vancouver Island)
6. wearing armor carved from wood (Men)
7. frightened by the horrible faces (their enemies)
8. Fashioned to the form of the body (everyday clothes)
9. built of wooden planks (Houses)
10. fantastically carved and painted (Door poles)

Critical Viewing

Speculate Students may say that the fish, caught recently by the tribesmen, is being dried by the woman in the picture.

Phrases • **459**

◇ STANDARD TEST PREPARATION WORKSHOP

Grammar and Usage Many standardized tests require students to recognize correct punctuation in a passage. Ask students to choose the correct punctuation for the following sentence.

The dog, that barked all night, kept us awake.

A No change

B The dog that barked all night, kept us awake.

C The dog that barked all night kept us awake.

D The dog, that barked all night kept us awake.

The correct answer is item **C**, because the participial phrase *barked all night* is essential to the sentence and should not be set off by commas or punctuated in any way.

⏱ TIME SAVERS!

 **Answers on Transparency** Use the Grammar Exercises on Transparencies for Chapter 21 to have students correct their own or one another's exercises.

On-Line Exercise Bank Have students complete the exercises on computer. The Auto Check feature will grade their work for you!

Gerunds and Gerund Phrases

1. The two keys to identifying a gerund are simple. First, the word always ends in *-ing.* Second, the word is always a form of a verb that functions as a noun.

2. Have students use the following gerunds in sentences: *sailing, visiting, traveling, interrupting, advertising.* (Sample responses: Sailing is hard to do when there is no wind. Visiting the circus is fun. I enjoy traveling to new places. My sister has the bad habit of interrupting. Stores sell items through advertising.)

3. Since gerunds always function as nouns, they may appear in sentences as subject, indirect object, direct object, predicate nominative, object of preposition, or appositive. Review these terms with students in the examples in the chart on the page.

Integrating Speaking and Listening Skills

Dropping the final *g* from gerunds and other words that end in *ing* is a common speaking error. Let partners choose paragraphs from *Timeless Voices, Timeless Themes* that contain *-ing* words—such as the first paragraph of "The Scarlet Ibis"—and read them aloud to each other, really stressing the final *g*'s.

Answer Key

Exercise 10

1. prospering (subject)
2. Fishing and hunting (subject)
3. working (predicate nominative)
4. entertaining (object of preposition)
5. Dancing (subject)

21.1

Gerunds and Gerund Phrases

Many of the nouns you use are actually forms of verbs called *gerunds.*

▶ **KEY CONCEPT** A **gerund** is a form of a verb that acts as a noun. ∎

Gerunds always end in *-ing* and function as nouns—subject, indirect object, direct object, predicate nominative, object of a preposition, or appositive. The following chart shows how a gerund may be used.

GERUNDS	
Subject:	*Writing* by the Aztecs was often recorded on paper made of cactus.
Direct Object:	On their vacation, the Rezendes discovered *canoeing.*
Indirect Object:	His performance gives *acting* a bad reputation.
Predicate Nominative:	One relaxing exercise is *swimming.*
Object of a Preposition:	The Aztecs obtained much of their food by *fishing.*
Appositive:	I have a new hobby, *cooking.*

▶ **Exercise 10** **Identifying Gerunds** Write the gerund in each sentence, and identify its function in the sentence.

EXAMPLE: Displaying one's social status was important to some Native American tribes.

ANSWER: Displaying (subject)

1. For some tribes, prospering was easy on the west coast.
2. Fishing and hunting for berries there took little time.
3. This meant time spent working was reduced.
4. There was more free time for entertaining.
5. Dancing was less important than the wealth of a person or tribe.

▶ **More Practice**

On-line
Exercise Bank
• Section 21.1
Grammar Exercise
Workbook
• pp. 46–47

☑ **ONGOING ASSESSMENT: Prerequisite Skill**

If students have difficulty with gerunds and gerund phrases, you may find it necessary to review the following to assure coverage of prerequisite knowledge.

In the Textbook	Print Resources	Technology
Nouns, pp. 342–344 Basic Sentence Parts, pp. 422–427	Grammar Exercise Workbook, pp. 1–4, 41–46	Language Lab CD-ROM, Using Nouns; On-Line Exercise Bank, Sections 16.1 and 20.1

GRAMMAR IN LITERATURE

from **There Is a Longing . . .**
Chief Dan George

In the following excerpt, the gerunds are highlighted in blue italics.

. . . There is a *longing* among
the young of my nation to secure for
    themselves
and their people the skills that will
provide them with a sense of worth and
purpose. They will be our new warriors.
Their *training* will be much longer and
more demanding than it was in olden days. . . .

Verb, Participle, or Gerund?

Sometimes distinguishing between verbs, participles, and gerunds can be difficult.

The following examples of a verb, a participle, and a gerund demonstrate their differences.

VERB: Small Dove is weaving cloth.

PARTICIPLE: Small Dove, weaving cloth, uses the Incan method.

GERUND: Weaving is a Native American art.

▶ **Exercise 11** **Distinguishing Between Verbs, Participles, and Gerunds** Identify each underlined word as a *verb*, *participle*, or *gerund*.

1. People of the Crow tribe once made a living by <u>farming</u>.
2. When horses were introduced, the tribe changed to <u>hunting</u> for a living.
3. <u>Making</u> tepees from the skins of the animals they hunted, the Crow were more comfortable in <u>freezing</u> winter temperatures than they had been.
4. The tribe was <u>growing</u> in size and <u>staying</u> in one place longer.
5. Since the advantages of <u>hunting</u> far outweighed the advantages of <u>farming</u>, the Crow became mostly a <u>hunting</u> tribe.

Grammar in Literature

1. Have a volunteer read aloud the excerpt from "There Is a Longing . . ." A cassette recording of the complete speech is available in the Gold Level resources of *Timeless Voices, Timeless Themes*.

2. After discussing the author's use of the gerunds *longing* and *training*, ask students if there is a mistake in their textbook: Shouldn't *demanding* be highlighted also? (No. Here *demanding* is an adjective that modifies *training*.)

Answer Key

▶ **Exercise 11**

1. gerund
2. gerund
3. participle
4. verb, verb
5. gerund, gerund, participle

Gerund Phrases

1. A gerund phrase is simply the *-ing* word along with the words that go with it.

2. Go over the sentences in the Gerund Phrases box, discussing how and why the italicized words are closely connected. For example, *loud* and *irregular* describe the snoring. *In stone* tells where the carving was done.

3. Explain that gerund phrases with personal pronouns always require the possessive form of the personal pronoun. Remind students that because gerunds always function as nouns, the possessive form must be used. They would say *his book,* not *him book; their house,* not *them house.*

4. Refer to the examples in the middle of the page. Possessive pronouns refer to ownership. It is not exactly the case that a smirker owns his smirking, but it is his smirking, not anyone else's.

Answer Key

Exercise 12

1. planting crops (object of preposition)
2. fighting the Sioux (object of preposition)
3. hunting buffalo (object of preposition)
4. decorating clothing and other costumes (object of preposition)
5. Trading with Native Americans (subject)

Critical Viewing

Analyze Students may say that the weaving in the belt resembles a spider's web. They may also suggest that the Caddo's decorating included insect-like designs.

21.1

Gerund Phrases

A gerund, like a participle, may be part of a phrase.

▶ **KEY CONCEPT** A **gerund phrase** is a gerund with modifiers or a complement, all acting together as a noun. ■

GERUND PHRASES

Carving in stone was how the Aztecs made their calendars.
The Aztecs were skilled at *building in dense forests.*
Denise's greatest accomplishment was *weaving a blanket.*
They ran into the tepee without *removing muddy moccasins.*
Vicky's morning routine includes *showering leisurely.*
The loud, irregular snoring annoyed him.

In the first sentence, the gerund *carving* is modified by an adjective phrase. In the next sentence, the gerund is modified by a prepositional phrase. In the third and fourth sentences, the gerund is modified by direct objects. In the fifth, *showering* is modified by the adverb *leisurely.* And in the last sentence, *snoring* is modified by the adjectives *loud* and *irregular.*

Note About *Gerunds* and *Possessive Pronouns*: Always use the possessive form of a personal pronoun before a gerund.

INCORRECT: Mr. Avery disliked *him smirking.*
CORRECT: Mr. Avery disliked *his smirking.*

▶ **Exercise 12** **Identifying Gerund Phrases** Write the gerund phrases in each sentence, and identify their functions.

EXAMPLE: By invading Native American territory, the Europeans caused great hardship.
ANSWER: invading Native American territory (object of a preposition)

1. The Wampanoags taught their planting methods to the Pilgrims.
2. For the Chippewa, advanced weapons helped when fighting the Sioux, causing the Sioux to be pushed farther west.
3. The Sioux became a tribe who lived by hunting buffalo.
4. Beads brought by the Europeans were used in decorating clothing and other costumes.
5. Trading with Native Americans allowed Europeans to survive.

▼ **Critical Viewing** Notice the geometric designs the Caddo used to decorate these artifacts. Write two sentences telling what the designs make you think of. Use gerunds or gerund phrases in each sentence. **[Analyze]**

Infinitives and Infinitive Phrases

A third kind of verbal, in addition to the participle and the gerund, is the *infinitive*.

▶ **KEY CONCEPT** An **infinitive** is a form of a verb that generally appears with the word *to* and acts as a noun, adjective, or adverb. ■

The following chart shows the different functions that an infinitive can have in a sentence.

INFINITIVES	
Subject:	*To decorate* requires gold, tropical feathers, and rare furs.
Direct Object:	Alone and frightened, she wanted *to survive.*
Predicate Nominative:	The purpose of pictures was *to record* an idea.
Object of a Preposition:	He had no choice except *to relent.*
Appositive:	His goal, *to travel*, was never realized.
Adjective:	The director of the camp is the person *to notify.*
Adverbs:	Cortés plotted *to take over* the Aztec Empire.
	Afraid *to speak*, he looked at his shoes.

▶ **Exercise 13** **Identifying Infinitives** Write the infinitive in each sentence. Then, tell how each functions in the sentence.
1. Native Americans had a variety of ways to travel.
2. To walk on top of the snow is the purpose of snowshoes.
3. If a woman wanted to carry many objects at a time, she may have used a carrying basket.
4. It was made especially to fit on her shoulders and head.
5. Those who planned to travel by water used boats made of wood, bark, or animal skins.

Infinitives and Infinitive Phrases

1. Infinitives are easy to identify: *to* plus a verb. For example, *to hop, to skip, to jump.*
2. Have volunteers read each entry in the chart, supplying additional examples.

Answer Key

▶ **Exercise 13**
1. to travel—adjective
2. to walk—subject
3. to carry—direct object
4. to fit—adverb
5. to travel—direct object

Language Highlight

Infinitives Perhaps the most famous infinitives in the English language appear in William Shakespeare's play, *The Tragedy of Hamlet,* in which the phrase, "To be, or not to be, that is the question," is invoked. The infinitive form anticipates a future condition. Encourage students to look in their own writing for infinitives that suggest action to come.

▶ **More Practice**
On-line
Exercise Bank
• Section 21.1
Grammar Exercise Workbook
• pp. 48–49

Phrases • 463

☑ **ONGOING ASSESSMENT: Monitor and Reinforce**

If students miss more than two items in Exercise 15 or 16, refer them to the following for additional practice.

In the Textbook	Print Resources	Technology
Section Review, Ex. 20, p. 467	Grammar Exercise Workbook, pp. 79–82	On-Line Exercise Bank, Section 21.1

⏱ **TIME SAVERS!**

🔲 **Answers on Transparency** Use the Grammar Exercises on Transparencies for Chapter 21 to have students correct their own or one another's exercises.

🖥 **On-Line Exercise Bank** Have students complete the exercises on computer. The Auto Check feature will grade their work for you!

Prepositional Phrase or Infinitive?

The only possible pitfall is confusing an infinitive with a prepositional phrase that begins with *to*. There is a simple rule students can use to tell them apart. In a prepositional phrase, *to* is always followed by an object: *He walked to the store. I went to bed.*

Answer Key

> **Exercise 14**

1. to area—prepositional phrase
2. to make—infinitive
3. to cover—infinitive
4. to their knees—prepositional phrase
5. to one side—prepositional phrase
6. to keep—infinitive
7. to the forest—prepositional phrase
8. to make—infinitive
9. to protect—infinitive
10. To the Native Americans—prepositional phrase

Customizing for *Verbal/Linguistic Learners*

Ask students to write ten sentences that each include an infinitive and a *to* prepositional phrase. Then they can trade papers with a partner to label each I or P.

Critical Viewing

Compare and Contrast Students' responses will vary.

21.1

Prepositional Phrase or Infinitive?

You should take care not to confuse a prepositional phrase beginning with *to* with an infinitive.

▶ **KEY CONCEPT** A **prepositional phrase** always ends with a noun or pronoun. An infinitive always ends with a verb. ■

Notice the difference in the following examples.

PREPOSITIONAL PHRASE	INFINITIVE
We went *to the movies* last week.	I didn't want the movie *to end.*

▶ **Exercise 14** Distinguishing Between Prepositional **Phrases and Infinitives** Write each phrase beginning with *to* in the sentences below. Then, label each *prepositional phrase* or *infinitive.*

1. Clothing of different tribes varied from area to area.
2. Plains tribes used tubes of bone to make a hair-pipe breastplate.
3. Breechcloths, cloths hung around the waist to cover the lower body, were used by several different tribes.
4. Women in the California area wore grass skirts to their knees.
5. Chiefs of the Southeast wore robes of feathers to one side.
6. Many Native Americans living in colder climates made their clothing out of fur to keep themselves warm.
7. Many tribes went to the forest for materials.
8. Those that lived in the Northwest often used bark and reed to make their clothing.
9. Moccasins were worn to protect feet.
10. To the Native Americans living in warmer climates, clothing was not always an important part of survival.

◀ **Critical Viewing** Compare the way these Native Americans dance with the way you and your friends dance. Use at least three infinitives. **[Compare and Contrast]**

Infinitive Phrases

Like other verbals, infinitives can be used to form phrases.

KEY CONCEPT An **infinitive phrase** is an infinitive with modifiers, complements, or a subject all acting together as a noun, adjective, or adverb. ■

NOUN: Professional dancers need *to practice daily.*

ADJECTIVE: Aztecs had a complex system *to irrigate the land.*

ADVERB: The Aztecs used these floating islands *to grow crops.*

Sometimes infinitives do not include the word *to*. After the verbs *dare, hear, help, let, make, please, see,* and *watch, to* will usually be understood.

EXAMPLE: Slave labor helped *build* many Aztec buildings.

Exercise 15 **Identifying Infinitive Phrases** Write the infinitive phrases in the following passage. Then, identify their function.

To dance in a powwow was to participate in a formal ceremony. Starting in the 1920's, ceremonial tribal boundaries loosened and tribes came together to participate. Dancing styles became competitive, and groups practiced many hours to show their very best. Today, people come more to celebrate dancing than to observe a formal ceremony. Powwow dancers like to use brighter colors, more motions, and new styles of dance. Their observance has spread across the United States where tribes people prepare to dance. The desire of participants and visitors is to take part in a modern-day powwow. Before visiting a powwow, one might take a course to study the culture or etiquette. Of course, the dancers and singers have certain behaviors to perform. However, powwow etiquette makes visitors behave in a certain way, too.

Exercise 16 **Writing Sentences With Infinitives** Write a sentence for each infinitive phrase, using the infinitive phrase as the part of speech indicated
1. to succeed in school (subject)
2. to call home (direct object)
3. to leave on vacation (adverb modifying adjective *happy*)
4. to travel to another state (predicate noun)
5. to go to the ceremony (appositive)

More Practice

On-line
Exercise Bank
• Section 21.1
Grammar Exercise
Workbook
• pp. 48–49

Phrases • 465

"Where to?" Wheel

Teaching Resources: Hands-on Grammar Activity Book, Chapter 21

1. Give students copies of the Hands-on Grammar Activity Book, Chapter 21.

2. Have them follow the directions to prepare the wheel.

3. For variation, suggest additional sentence pairs for the students to use with their wheels.

4. You may wish to extend their activity by having the students work in groups, with each group member adding one or two phrases to the wheel.

Find It in Your Reading

Have students work with partners to check each other's work.

Find It in Your Writing

Have students do this activity with a sample of their own writing.

21.1

Hands-on Grammar

"Where to?" Wheel

There are two kinds of phrases that begin with the word *to.* Infinitives and infinitive phrases begin with the word *to* and are followed by a verb. Some prepositional phrases also begin with the word *to* followed by a noun or pronoun. The phrase wheel illustrated below will help you to determine which is an infinitive and which is a prepositional phrase.

Cut out a wheel, and put a variety of phrases beginning with *to* around the wheel. Make a window frame with two windows, as shown. Make sure that the words on your wheel will show through the windows. One side of the frame tests for prepositional phrases by completing the sentence *They drove.* The other side of the frame tests for infinitives by completing the phrase *He wanted.* You will have to turn the frame upside down to read the infinitive side.

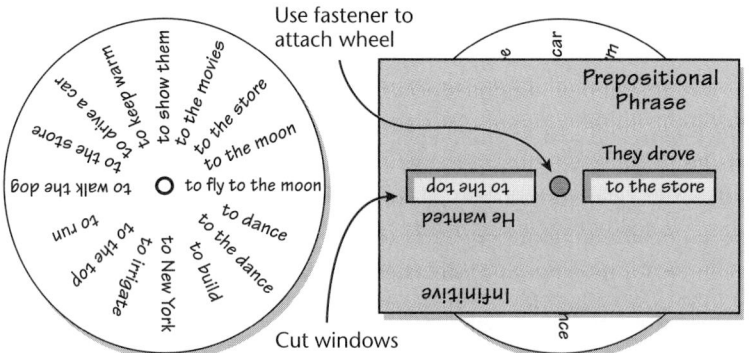

Find It in Your Reading In a short story or a textbook, find examples of phrases beginning with the word *to.* Make a second wheel to test to see whether the phrases are infinitives or prepositional phrases. (You can use the same window frames; just replace the wheel.)

Find It in Your Writing Look through a piece of your writing to find examples of prepositional phrases and infinitive phrases. Find at least three examples of each. If you cannot find any, challenge yourself to add details to your writing by adding three of each.

✋ **Hands-on Grammar Book** Use the Hands-on Grammar activity sheet for Chapter 21 to facilitate this activity.

☑ ONGOING ASSESSMENT: Assess Mastery

Use the following resources to assess student mastery of phrases.

In the Textbook	Technology
Chapter Review, Ex. 46–48, p. 486 Standardized Test Preparation Workshop, pp. 488–489	On-Line Exercise Bank, Section 21.1

Section 21.1 *Section Review*

GRAMMAR EXERCISES 17–22

▶ **Exercise 17** **Identifying Adjective and Adverb Phrases** Write the phrase(s) from each sentence. Label prepositional phrases either *adjective* or *adverb*. Indicate the word it modifies. For appositive phrases, indicate the word that is renamed.

1. Tribes from the Northeast were called the Woodland tribes.
2. One of these, the Powhatan tribe, lived in the Virginia area.
3. They seemed unfriendly, but when the English settlers came to the American continent, the Powhatans saved them more than once.
4. The Native Americans taught the settlers to survive on American foods—corn, succotash, and baked beans.
5. Another tribe, the Delaware, was a group of extremely peaceful people.

▶ **Exercise 18** **Identifying Verbals** Write the verbal phrases in the following sentences. Label them *participial*, *infinitive*, or *gerund*. Identify the word or words the verbals modify or the way each is used in the sentence.

1. Five tribes came together to form the Iroquois nation.
2. This united league was known as "The Tree of Peace."
3. In Iroquoian culture, to live peacefully under one roof was expected.
4. The Tree of Peace, based on the same idea, showed that many people could live under one sky in peace.
5. Governing the nation were fifty men from each of the five tribes.

▶ **Exercise 19** **Combining Sentence Phrases** Combine the following pairs of sentences into one sentence using an appositive or an appositive phrase.

1. The Iroquois were divided into the Mohawk, Seneca, Onondaga, Oneida, and Cayuga nations. Each Iroquois nation had its own council.
2. The Council of Fifty made important decisions. The council was made up of fifty men from the five tribes.
3. Mothers of the clan chose the council members. The council members were the decision makers of the tribe.
4. The council was formed to prevent fighting among the nations. It was called the League of the Iroquois.
5. The most powerful people in the Eastern Woodlands were the Iroquois. The Iroquois lived in what is now New York State.

▶ **Exercise 20** **Find It In Your Reading** Read the excerpt from "The Man to Send Rain Clouds." Identify each underlined phrase, and tell how it is used.

The priest approached the grave slowly, <u>wondering how</u> they had managed <u>to dig into the frozen ground</u>; and then he remembered that this was New Mexico, and saw the pile of cold loose sand <u>beside the hole</u>.

▶ **Exercise 21** **Find It in Your Writing** Look through your writing portfolio. Find examples of sentences with prepositional phrases, participial phrases, or infinitive phrases. Underline the phrases, and tell how they are used.

▶ **Exercise 22** **Writing Application** Write an article on Native American crafts for your school paper. Make sure that prepositional, appositive, and verbal phrases are used correctly.

Section Review • **467**

ASSESS and CLOSE

Section Review

Each of these exercises correlates to a concept in the section on phrases, pages 450–465. These exercises may be used for more practice, for reteaching, or for review of the Key Concepts presented. Answers for all chapter exercises are available in *Grammar Exercises on Transparencies* in your teaching resources.

Answer Key

▶ **Exercise 17**

1. from the Northeast—adjective; Tribes
2. the Powhatan tribe—renames *One;* in the Virginia area—adverb; lived
3. to the American continent—adverb; came
4. on American foods—adverb; survive; corn, succotash, and baked beans—renames American foods
5. The Delaware—renames tribe; of extremely peaceful people—adjective; group

▶ **Exercise 18**

1. to form the Iroquois nation—infinitive; adverb
2. united—participial; *league*
3. to live peacefully under one roof—infinitive; subject
4. based on the same idea—participial; *The Tree of Peace*
5. Governing the nation—gerund; subject

▶ **Exercise 19**

Answers may vary.

1. Each Iroquois nation—the Mohawk, Seneca, Onondaga, Oneida and Cayuga—had its own council.
2. The Council of Fifty, fifty men from the five tribes, made important decisions.
3. Mothers of the clan chose the council members, decision makers of the tribe.
4. The council, the League of the Iroquois, was formed to prevent fighting among the nations.
5. The most powerful people in the Eastern Woodlands, what is now New York State, were the Iroquois.

continued

Answer Key continued

▶ **Exercise 20**

Find It in Your Reading

wondering how: participial phrase, adjective; *to dig into the frozen ground:* infinitive, direct object; *beside the hole:* prepositional phrase, modifies *pile*

Go over the phrases as a class, explaining any that students labeled differently.

▶ **Exercise 21**

Find It in Your Writing

Have students exchange papers with a partner, who can identify the appositives.

▶ **Exercise 22**

Writing Application

Interested students may want to work together to adapt their separate articles into one group article to submit to the school paper.

because it is made of 2,000 toothpicks (subordinate)

which stuck to the bottom of his sneaker (subordinate)

his favorite sandwich is peanut butter and crushed cornflakes (independent)

Activate Prior Knowledge

Ask partners to choose a piece of writing from one of their portfolios and highlight the subordinate clauses in one color and the independent clauses in another color. Have volunteers share some of their examples with the class.

TEACH

Step-by-Step Teaching Guide

Independent and Subordinate Clauses

1. Explain that clauses are groups of related words that have a subject and verb. Caution students to look carefully at clauses; just because they have a subject and verb does not mean that they are sentences. *When I went to school* has a subject *(I)* and a verb *(went),* but it is not a sentence.

2. Ask students to define the words *independent* and *subordinate.* Then explain to the students that, as they might expect, independent clauses have subjects and verbs that enable the clauses to stand alone as sentences, while subordinate clauses cannot stand by themselves as complete sentences.

Answer Key

Exercise 23

1. independent
2. independent
3. subordinate
4. independent
5. subordinate

Section 21.2

Clauses

Clauses, like phrases, are groups of related words, but unlike phrases, they have a subject and a verb.

▶ **KEY CONCEPT** A **clause** is a group of words with its own subject and verb. ■

Independent and Subordinate Clauses

There are two basic kinds of clauses: *independent clauses* and *subordinate clauses.*

▶ **KEY CONCEPT** An **independent clause** can stand by itself as a complete sentence. ■

All complete sentences must contain at least one independent clause. *My aunt visited Africa for two weeks* is an independent clause. *Flora went to South Africa, and her sister went to Egypt* is one independent clause added to another.

▶ **KEY CONCEPT** A **subordinate clause** cannot stand by itself as a complete sentence; it can only be part of a sentence. ■

Note how each subordinate clause works with an independent clause to form a complete idea in the following examples:

EXAMPLES: We visited Kenya, *which is a country in Africa,* for two weeks.
Because he woke up late, he missed the flight.
They have decided *that you should study more.*

There are three different kinds of subordinate clauses: *adjective, adverb,* and *noun.*

▶ **Exercise 23** Identifying Independent and Subordinate Clauses Identify each clause as *independent* if the clause can stand alone or *subordinate* if the clause cannot stand alone.
1. weavers of this tribe make beautiful cloth
2. each one has a different pattern
3. because one is mostly yellow
4. it is called "Gold Dust"
5. when Ghana elected its first president

Theme: Africa

In this section, you will learn about clauses and how to classify sentences by structure. The examples and exercises in this section are about the continent of Africa.

Cross-Curricular Connection: Social Studies

🕐 TIME AND RESOURCE MANAGER

Resources
Print: Grammar Exercise Workbook, pp. 83–90
Technology: On-Line Exercise Bank; Section 21.2

In-Depth Coverage	Accelerated Pace
• Work through all key concepts, pp. 468–481.	• Assign pp. 468–481 for independent student review.
• Assign and review Exercises 25–32.	
• Read and discuss Grammar in Literature, p. 476.	• Assign Review Ex. 40.

Adjective Clauses

Adjective clauses modify nouns or pronouns in ways often not possible with one-word adjectives or adjective phrases.

KEY CONCEPT An **adjective clause** is a subordinate clause that modifies a noun or pronoun by telling *what kind* or *which one*. ■

Adjective clauses usually begin with a relative pronoun, such as *that, which, who, whom,* or *whose*. Sometimes, they may begin with a relative adverb, such as *before, since, when, where,* or *why.*

ADJECTIVE CLAUSES

Ghana, *which means "land of gold,"* lies just north of the equator in Africa.

It was called "Gold Coast" by European traders *who found gold in abundance in this area.*

In the year *since I last saw you,* I have been to Africa twice.

The sun never shines on days *when I can enjoy it.*

Adjective clauses are set off by commas only when they are not essential to the meaning of a sentence.

Exercise 24 **Identifying Adjective Clauses** Write the adjective clause in each sentence. Then, circle the relative pronoun or relative adverb in each.

EXAMPLE: The ports where major trading occurs are the biggest cities of Ghana.
(where) major trading occurs

1. Algeria, which is a country in Africa, is a diverse combination of land, people, and culture.
2. Early invaders settled in Tell, which is north of the Atlas mountain range.
3. The high plateaus that run south of the Atlas Mountains are used for cattle grazing.
4. Members of the Ouled Nail tribe, who are known for their distinctive silver jewelry, live in this area.
5. Men of the Tuareg tribe, whose history is full of caravan raids, wear veils.

More Practice

On-line
Exercise Bank
• Section 21.2
Grammar Exercise Workbook
• pp. 53–54

Adjective Clauses

1. Students may have difficulty distinguishing between adjective clauses and adjective phrases. An adjective phrase is a prepositional phrase of two or more words that describes a noun. An adjective clause always has a subject and a verb.
2. Explain that adjective clauses are subordinate clauses that modify nouns or pronouns and usually begin with a relative pronoun, such as *that, which, who, whom,* and *whose.*
3. Ask students which of the following are independent and which are subordinate clauses.

   that is a flying saucer (independent)

   that I saw last night (subordinate)

   which has a long green tail (subordinate)

   which lizard do you prefer (independent)

   whose picture is on the dollar bill (independent)

   whose dollar is this (independent)

Answer Key

Exercise 24

1. (which) is a country in Africa
2. (which) is north of the Atlas mountain range
3. (that) run south of the Atlas mountains
4. (who) are known for their distinctive silver jewelry
5. (whose) history is full of caravan raids

☑ ONGOING ASSESSMENT: Monitor and Reinforce

If students miss more than two items in Exercises 25–28, refer them to the following for additional practice.

In the Textbook	Print Resources	Technology
Section Review, Ex. 40, p. 485 Chapter Review, Ex. 50	Grammar Exercise Workbook, pp. 83–84	On-Line Exercise Bank, Section 21.2

⏱ TIME SAVERS!

Answers on Transparency Use the Grammar Exercises on Transparencies for Chapter 21 to have students correct their own or one another's exercises.

On-Line Exercise Bank Have students complete the exercises on computer. The Auto Check feature will grade their work for you!

Step-by-Step Teaching Guide

Modifying Nouns and Pronouns

1. Have students write five adjective clauses in their notebooks beginning with the words *who, which, that, whom*. Then ask them to write sentences using these adjective clauses to modify subjects and direct objects.

2. Students may have difficulty distinguishing between subjects and direct objects. A subject is generally the person or thing doing the action in a sentence. A direct object tends to be acted on.

Customize for
Less Advanced Students

Students may have difficulty recognizing that adjective clauses are *always* incomplete sentences that require more information to become complete. One way to guide students to recognize these clauses as subordinate is to have them ask if the clause completely answers the question *What kind?* or *Which one?* If the clause requires more information to answer the question, then it is a subordinate clause.

Critical Viewing

Infer The women, who were just in the fields, are now carrying the picked grain back to their village.

Answer Key

Exercise 25

1. South of the Atlas Mountains lies the Sahara Desert, which comprises 85% of Algeria.
2. The people, who are approximately 80% Arab, are mostly Muslim, and still speak their traditional dialect.
3. The majority of the other 20%, who are given the name Berber, also speak their own language.
4. They both speak different languages, which does not stop them from having similar lifestyles.
5. Both races work to produce coffee, which is the major crop of their area.

Modifying Nouns and Pronouns Adjective clauses, like single-word adjectives or adjective phrases, may modify any noun or pronoun in a sentence. The following examples suggest only a few of the many possibilities:

MODIFYING A SUBJECT: The city *where I would like to live* is Nairobi.

MODIFYING A DIRECT OBJECT: We ate cookies *that were made from rice*.

An adjective clause must closely follow the word it modifies. If it does not, the meaning of the sentence may be unclear.

INCORRECT: The person on the boat *who went* is my cousin.

CORRECT: The person *who went on the boat* is my cousin.

Combining Sentences Adjective clauses often allow you to combine information from two sentences into one sentence. They not only add detail to sentences but also indicate the relationship between ideas.

TWO SENTENCES: Ghana has a varied landscape. It is most densely populated along the coast.

COMBINED: Ghana, *whose landscape is varied*, is most densely populated along the coast.

▼ **Critical Viewing** Use adjective phrases in sentences to describe these women from Ghana carrying grain on their heads. **[Infer]**

> **Exercise 25** Combining Sentences With Adjective Clauses
> Combine each pair of sentences by making one an adjective clause.
> 1. South of the Atlas Mountains lies the Sahara. It comprises 85 percent of Algeria.
> 2. The people are mostly Muslim and still speak their traditional dialect. They are approximately 80 percent Arab.
> 3. The majority of the other 20 percent also speak their own language. This group is given the name Berber.
> 4. They both speak different languages. This does not stop them from having similar lifestyles.
> 5. Both races work to produce coffee. Coffee is the major crop of their area.

◆ STANDARDIZED TEST PREPARATION WORKSHOP

Revising and Editing Some standardized test questions measure students' ability to revise and edit sentences based upon their knowledge of phrases and clauses. Share the following example with students:

Choose the letter that best combines all four phrases and clauses to form a complete sentence.

(1) before he could take a break
(2) Sam was tired
(3) but he had much more work to do
(4) Sam was hungry

A Sam was tired before he could take a break but he had much more work to do and he was hungry.

B Sam was tired and hungry, but he had much more work to do before he could a break.

C Before he could take a break, Sam had much more work to do.

D Sam, tired and hungry, before he could a break.

The correct choice is item **B**. It is the only complete sentence that does not change the meaning of the phrases and clauses.

► **Exercise 26** Writing Sentences With Adjective Clauses

Use each of the adjective clauses below to write a complete sentence on a separate sheet of paper.

1. who explored the river
2. which is where I want to live
3. when I am older
4. since he was last in Morocco
5. whose handwriting this is
6. whom I wanted to see
7. when they need someone to row
8. that lies in the valley below
9. that you can find in Nigeria
10. before you were born

► **More Practice**

On-line
Exercise Bank
• Section 21.2
Grammar Exercise Workbook
• pp. 53–54

Relative Pronouns A relative pronoun has two functions in a sentence with an adjective clause. First, it connects the adjective clause to the word the clause modifies. Second, it acts within the clause as a subject, direct object, object of a preposition, or adjective.

RELATIVE PRONOUNS				
who	*whom*	*whose*	*which*	*that*

◄ **Critical Viewing**
In this village in Ghana, residents spread grain out to dry in the sun. Compare the clothing of the people in the picture using relative pronouns in your sentences. **[Compare and Contrast]**

Clauses • 471

Integrating Grammar Skills

Combining Sentences with Adjective Clauses One reason why adjective clauses are useful and important is that they use fewer words to express an idea. Because they serve as connective links between two separate ideas, adjective clauses offer a quick and clear way to say two things at one time. Encourage students to use them whenever possible, since they sharpen ideas and make writing more polished.

Critical Viewing

Compare and Contrast Students' responses will vary.

► *Step-by-Step Teaching Guide*

Relative Pronouns

1. Students think of pronouns as words that substitute for or take the place of the names of people, places, and things: *I, me, we, you, he, she, they, them, its,* and so on. In *Consuelo rode her bike, her* is used instead of *Consuelo's.*

2. Relative pronouns, however, do not substitute for nouns. They identify or refer back to a noun. In *Consuelo is the person who rides a bike, who* connects the action (riding a bike) to the person doing the action (Consuelo). *Who* is not a replacement word.

Exercise 27

1. (whose) people make their living mostly by farming (adjective)
2. (which) makes up two-thirds of Ghana's exports (subject)
3. (whom) the big factories have attracted (direct object)
4. (that) has also attracted many people (subject)
5. for (whom) disease was a problem (object of a preposition)

Critical Viewing

Analyze Students' responses will vary.

21.2

▶ **KEY CONCEPT** **Relative pronouns** connect adjective clauses to the words they modify and act as subjects, direct objects, objects of prepositions, or adjectives in the clauses. ■

You can tell how a relative pronoun is being used within a clause by separating the clause from the rest of the sentence and then finding the subject and verb in the clause.

USED AS A SUBJECT IN A CLAUSE:	The city (that) *is the largest* is Accra.
USED AS A DIRECT OBJECT IN A CLAUSE:	The movie (that) *you recommended* is no longer playing.
USED AS AN OBJECT OF A PREPOSITION IN A CLAUSE:	The person *of* (whom) *you spoke* is my friend.

Note About *Understood Words*: Sometimes a relative pronoun is left out of an adjective clause. The missing word, nevertheless, is understood and still functions in the sentence.

EXAMPLES: The flowers [*that*] *she bought* made him sneeze.
The relatives [*whom*] *they visited* were cousins.

▶ **Exercise 27** **Recognizing the Uses of Relative Pronouns**
Write the adjective clause in each sentence, and circle the relative pronoun. Then, label the use of the relative pronoun within the clause as *subject, direct object, object of a preposition,* or *adjective.*

EXAMPLE: Ghana's western frontier, which borders the Ivory Coast, is a stretch of warm, tropical forests.

ANSWER: (which) borders the Ivory Coast (subject)

Ghana, whose people make their living mostly by farming, produces the most cocoa in the world. This product, which makes up two thirds of Ghana's exports, provides more jobs for Ghana's people than any other. However, many people, whom the big factories have attracted, have been migrating to the cities. Tema is a major port that has also attracted many people. Fortunately, the people of big cities, for whom disease was a problem, have been improving sanitation. Disease is no longer as widespread.

▼ **Critical Viewing** Use the relative pronouns *that, which,* and *who* to describe this African forest. **[Analyze]**

☑ **ONGOING ASSESSMENT: Prerequisite Skills**

If students have difficulty with relative pronouns, you may find it necessary to review the following to assure coverage of prerequisite knowledge.

In the Textbook	Print Resources	Technology
Pronouns, pp. 346–355	Grammar Exercise Workbook, pp. 5–12	Language Lab CD-ROM, Pronouns; On-Line Exercise Bank, Section 16.2

Relative Adverbs Like a relative pronoun, a *relative adverb* connects clauses while playing a role within the adjective clause.

▶ **KEY CONCEPT** **Relative adverbs**—*where* and *when*—connect adjective clauses to the words they modify and act as adverbs in the clauses. ■

Unlike the relative pronoun, the relative adverb has only one use within the clause. It acts only as an adverb.

EXAMPLE: The settlers cleared a plot of land (where) they could build.

▶ **Exercise 28** **Recognizing the Use of Relative Adverbs**
Write the adjective clause in each sentence, and circle the relative adverb. Then, tell what word the relative adverb modifies.

EXAMPLE: The land where Ghana's forests lie is full of valuable resources.

ANSWER: (where) Ghana's forests lie (land)

1. The Yoruba people choose to live along the banks of the Niger River, where the soil is fertile.
2. Do you remember the time when we went to the museum?
3. The rooms in the museum where they keep the artifacts are very carefully guarded.
4. I was thinking about the visit when we saw the African masks.
5. The exhibit hall where you can see dioramas is my favorite.

▶ **Exercise 29** **Writing Sentences With Adjective Clauses**
Use each of the adjective clauses to modify a noun in a complete sentence. Write your sentences on a separate sheet of paper.
1. that is the most annoying
2. of which I am a part
3. when we arrived
4. who makes me laugh
5. that he wanted

▶ **More Practice**

On-line
Exercise Bank
• Section 21.2
Grammar Exercise
Workbook
• pp. 53–54

Clauses • 473

Relative Adverbs

1. Make a T chart for relative adjectives and post it for students' reference.

Relative Adjectives	Relative Adverbs
that	where
who	when
whom	
whose	
which	

2. Explain that relative adverbs are like relative adjectives. They connect adjective clauses to the words they modify. But they are different because a relative adverb has only one use in the clause, which is to act as an adverb.

Answer Key

▶ **Exercise 28**

1. (where) the soil is fertile, fertile
2. (when) we went to the museum, went
3. (where) they keep the artifacts, keep
4. (when) we saw the African masks, saw
5. (where) you can see dioramas, see

▶ **Exercise 29**

Answers will vary. Samples are given.

1. The part of the day that is the most annoying is the morning, because it is difficult to wake up.
2. The team of which I am a part practices on Monday.
3. The look on their faces when we arrived made us laugh.
4. The friend who makes me laugh lives next door.
5. The book that he wanted was on the top shelf.

☑ **ONGOING ASSESSMENT: Monitor and Reinforce**

If students miss more than two items in Exercises 29–31, refer them to the following for additional practice.

In the Textbook	Print Resources	Technology
Section Review, Ex. 40, p. 485	Grammar Exercise Workbook, pp. 85–86	On-Line Exercise Bank, Section 21.2

Adverb Clauses

1. Subordinate clauses (clauses with a subject and verb that cannot stand alone as sentences) can also act as adverbs. That is, they can modify verbs, adjectives, adverbs, or verbals.

2. Have volunteers create sentences that begin with some of the subordinating conjunctions in the box. (Subordinating conjunctions need not occur at the beginning of a sentence, but this placement makes them easier to see.) Write the sentences on the board, then circle the verb the conjunctions refer to.

3. Now have students rearrange the sentences so that the adverb clauses do not begin the sentences.

Real-World Connection

Adverb clauses are especially useful in instructions telling how, when, or where to do something. In recipes, it is important to peel potatoes *before you boil them* and to put on the icing *after the cake has cooled.* In carpentry, you use a *level so that the shelves will not slant.* Drivers should get gas *whenever the needle points to E.*

Critical Viewing

Compare and Contrast Students may say that although the African grasslands boast giraffes and elephants, they see dogs and cats when they look out their windows.

Adverb Clauses

In addition to acting as adjectives, subordinate clauses can act as adverbs.

▶ **KEY CONCEPT** An **adverb clause** is a subordinate clause that modifies a verb, an adjective, an adverb, or a verbal by telling *where, when, in what way, to what extent, under what condition,* or *why.* ■

▶ **KEY CONCEPT** All adverb clauses begin with subordinating conjunctions. ■

The chart lists some of the most commonly used subordinating conjunctions. (See Section 19.2 for a more complete list and a review of subordinating conjunctions.)

SUBORDINATING CONJUNCTIONS		
after	even though	unless
although	if	until
as	in order that	when
as if	since	whenever
as long as	so that	where
because	than	wherever
before	though	while

▼ **Critical Viewing** Compare this scene in the African grasslands to what you see out the window of your house or apartment. Use two subordinate clauses in your response. **[Compare and Contrast]**

1. (Because) Africa's grasslands provide a wide grazing range
2. (because) they hunt the plant-eaters
3. (until) they have eaten most of the vegetation
4. (wherever) they find more plants
5. (when) they are threatened
6. (unless) they are very hungry
7. (although) they usually eat what other animals have caught
8. (as long as) it can scavenge
9. (after) the other animal is finished
10. (before) they approach another animal's catch

ADVERB CLAUSES

Wherever they need to go, Vai people carry their possessions on their heads.

I will help you with your history *whenever you ask*.

He ran *as if he had twisted an ankle*.

She ran more rapidly *than I did*.

If you visit the Uge people, they may give you kola nuts as a sign of welcome.

Jeanette wanted to stay *because the band was good*.

Adverb clauses answer the same questions adverbs answer. The first clause above tells *where*, the second tells *when*, and so on. The last two clauses are special in that they answer questions that simple adverbs cannot: *Under what condition?* and *Why?*

Exercise 30 Identifying Adverb Clauses Write the adverb clause in each sentence. Then, circle the subordinating conjunction in each.

EXAMPLE: Because Africa has both coast regions and deserts, its animal life is widely varied.

ANSWER: (Because) Africa has both coast regions and deserts

1. Because Africa's grasslands provide a wide grazing range, many large plant-eating animals are able to survive there.
2. Meat-eaters, such as lions, jackals, and hyenas, live in the grasslands because they hunt the plant-eaters.
3. Elephants, giraffes, zebras, hippopotamuses, and antelopes stay in one area until they have eaten most of the vegetation.
4. They then graze wherever they find more plants.
5. Elephants gather in a herd when threatened by a predator.
6. Lions won't attack a herd unless they are very hungry.
7. Jackals can hunt, although they usually eat what other animals have caught.
8. A jackal eats well as long as it can scavenge from other animals.
9. They eat after the other animal is finished.
10. Jackals check the area before they approach another animal's catch.

More Practice

On-line
Exercise Bank
• Section 21.2
Grammar Exercise
Workbook
• p. 55

TIME SAVERS!

Answers on Transparency
Use the Grammar Exercises on Transparencies for Chapter 21 to have students correct their own or one another's exercises.

On-Line Exercise Bank
Have students complete the exercises on computer. The Auto Check feature will grade their work for you!

Grammar In Literature

1. Have a volunteer read aloud the sentence from "Talk."

2. Ask the class how the highlighted adverb clause affects our understanding of the sentence. What does the adverb clause tell about the man, or about the dog?

3. Have students identify the subject and verb of the sentence *(the man, became),* then ask them to identify what the adverb clause modifies. (It tells why the man became angry.)

4. Finally, ask students what they think about the man's response to the dog. In what way is his reaction brought on by the dog's behavior? What does this tell about the way the adverb clause functions in the sentence?

Critical Viewing

Compare and Contrast Answers will vary.

Answer Key

Exercise 31 *(page 477)*

Answers will vary. Samples are given.

1. The Ashanti folktale teaches a lesson while it tells a joke.
2. I laughed after the joke was told.
3. We read it when the letter arrived.
4. Since I enjoy them, I will probably read more folktales.
5. Reading the tale was fun because it made us giggle.
6. We did not go to the lake because it was too far.
7. Whenever I see him, Mark looks gloomy.
8. Susan planned to stay until her friends left.
9. We wanted to stop so that we could get a drink of water.
10. You will enjoy the story if you sit still and listen.

21.2

GRAMMAR IN
LITERATURE

from **Talk**
**an Ashanti folk tale retold by Harold Courlander
and George Herzog**

The highlighted adverb clause adds information to the sentence. The clause modifies the verb became *and answers the question* Why?

The man became angry, *because his dog had never talked before,* and he didn't like his tone besides.

Modification of Different Words An adverb clause can modify a verb, an adjective, or an adverb.

MODIFYING
A VERB: They will be caught *unless they can run faster..*

MODIFYING
AN ADJECTIVE: The cheetah is swift *because his legs are built for speed.*

MODIFYING
AN ADVERB: The storm struck sooner *than the forecasters expected.*

◄ Critical Viewing Compare the landscape in this picture with the landscape in the part of the country where you live. Use at least two adverb clauses in your comparison. **[Compare and Contrast]**

476 • Phrases and Clauses

Placement in Sentences Adverb clauses can be placed at the beginning, in the middle, or at the end of a sentence. When the clause is at the beginning or in the middle of a sentence, it is set off by commas.

EXAMPLES: *When it rains*, the river often floods.

The river, *when it rains*, often floods.

The river often floods *when it rains*.

Sometimes the position of an adverb clause can affect the meaning of the sentence. To be safe, you should generally place the clause as close as possible to the word it modifies. Notice in the following examples how the placement of the adverb clause changes the word that the clause modifies.

EXAMPLES: *After the meeting ended*, they decided to stay.

They decided to stay *after the meeting ended*.

▶ **Exercise 31** Revising Sentences With Adverb Clauses
Supply an adverb clause to complete each sentence below. Introduce the adverb clause with the subordinating conjunction shown in parentheses. You can put your adverb clause at the beginning or at the end of the sentence, whichever is more appropriate.
1. The Ashanti folk tale teaches a lesson. (while)
2. I laughed. (after)
3. We read it. (when)
4. I will probably read more folk tales. (since)
5. Reading the tale was fun. (because)
6. We did not go to the lake. (because)
7. Mark looks gloomy. (whenever)
8. Susan planned to stay. (until)
9. We wanted to stop. (so that)
10. You will enjoy the story. (if)

▶ **More Practice**

Language Lab CD-ROM
• Varying Sentence Structure lesson
On-line Exercise Bank
• Section 21.2
Grammar Exercise Workbook
• p. 55

Placement in Sentences

1. Students can easily see that no matter where *when it rains* appears, the meaning of the sentence does not change. (They may, however, think that the second example sounds pretentious or "phony.") Just as students vary sentence length in their writing, encourage them to use different placement of clauses to add variety and interest.

2. Students may not see the difference between the *after the meeting* sentences. In the first example, it was not until the meeting ended that they made a decision. In the second example, they made a decision at some unspecified time that they would not leave when the meeting ended.

Customize for *Gifted/Talented Students*

Have students write ten sentences that use adverb clauses at the beginning, middle, and end. Students can exchange papers with a partner to punctuate the sentences correctly, paying special attention to the rule that adverb clauses in the beginning and middle of sentences usually are punctuated with commas.

Phrases • 477

Step-by-Step Teaching Guide

Adverb Clauses Used to Combine Sentences

1. Explain that, as with adjective clauses, adverb clauses can be used to combine two sentences into one.

2. When combining, clauses again can be placed at the beginning or end of a sentence: *The cat broke the vase while we were outside.*

Answer Key

Answers may vary. Samples are given.

1. Although Africa does have dry regions, it also has enormous rain forests.
2. Because the rain forests offer rich vegetation, monkeys, bats, and flying squirrels find those areas hospitable.
3. Since gorillas live in the deep jungle, they roam without fear of any predator but man.
4. These giants can grow as tall as man although they weigh much more.
5. At night a male gorilla will stay on the ground while the females and young sleep in a tree.

Critical Viewing

Infer Students may suggest that the gorilla is making the face because he notices a predator approaching.

Adverb Clauses Used to Combine Sentences

Adverb Clauses Used to Combine Sentences Like adjective clauses, adverb clauses often can be used to combine information from two sentences into one sentence.

TWO SENTENCES: We were outside. The cat broke the vase.
COMBINED: *While we were outside*, the cat broke the vase.

▶ **Exercise 32** Combining Sentences Using Adverb Clauses
Combine each pair of sentences by changing one into an adverb clause.

EXAMPLE: Africa enjoys varied weather patterns. Its coastline and many inland areas receive an abundance of rain.

ANSWER: Because Africa enjoys varied weather patterns, its coastline and inland areas receive an abundance of rain.

1. Africa does have dry regions. It also has enormous rain forests.
2. The rain forests offer rich vegetation. Monkeys, bats, and flying squirrels find the forests hospitable.
3. Gorillas live in the deep jungle. They roam without fear of any predators but humans.
4. These giants can grow as tall as humans. They weigh much more.
5. At night, a male gorilla will stay on the ground. The females and young sleep in trees.

▼ **Critical Viewing** Come up with several adverb clauses used in sentences to explain why the gorilla is making that face. **[Infer]**

478 • Phrases and Clauses

Elliptical Adverb Clauses When adverb clauses begin-ning with *as* or *than* are used to express comparisons, words are sometimes left out. Such adverb clauses are called *elliptical clauses.*

▶ **KEY CONCEPT** An **elliptical clause** is a clause in which the verb or the subject and verb are understood but not actually stated. ∎

The missing words in an elliptical clause still function in the sentence. In the following examples, the missing words have been added in brackets.

VERB UNDERSTOOD: I respect him more *than she* [*does*].

SUBJECT AND VERB   I respect him more *than* [*I respect*] *her.*
UNDERSTOOD:

When writing elliptical clauses, you should mentally add the missing words to ensure that the sentence retains its meaning.

▶ **Exercise 33** Recognizing Elliptical Adverb Clauses Write each sentence, adding the missing words in any elliptical clause. Then, underline the complete adverb clause in each sentence, and circle any words you have added.

EXAMPLE: Currently, Africa has more native languages spoken than the United States.
Currently, Africa has more native languages spoken <u>than the United States (*does*)</u>.

1. More than 700 different dialects developed in Africa by tribes of people who lived more apart than together.
2. Although similar, these languages have significant differences.
3. Strong boundaries were created by climate as much as by geographical features.
4. Their languages were as varied as their cultures.
5. When studying a group, anthropologists consider geo-graphic features as well as cultural.

> **More Practice**
>
> Language Lab
> CD-ROM
> • Varying Sentence
>   Structure lesson
> On-line
> Exercise Bank
> • Section 21.2
> Grammar Exercise
> Workbook
> • p. 55

Clauses • **479**

Elliptical Adverb Clauses

1. Elliptical clauses are not as difficult as they appear. Students use them in speaking every day: "I'm taller than you," "You're not as tall as Susannah."

2. The mistake students are likely to make is using the wrong pronoun. That is why they need to add (mentally or in writing) the missing words.

Answer Key

▶ **Exercise 33**

1. Over 700 different dialects developed in Africa by groups of people who lived more apart than (they lived) together.
2. Although (they are) similar, these languages have significant differences.
3. Strong boundaries were created by climate as much as (they were) by geographical features.
4. Their languages were as varied as their cultures (were).
5. When (they are) studying a group, anthropologists consider geographic features as well as cultural.

☑ **ONGOING ASSESSMENT: Monitor and Reinforce**

If students miss more than two items in Exercise 33, refer them to the following for additional practice.

In the Textbook	Print Resources	Technology
Section Review, Ex. 38, p. 485	Grammar Exercise Workbook, pp. 87–88	On-Line Exercise Bank, Section 21.2

479

Noun Clauses

1. Explain to students that noun clauses are subordinate clauses that act as nouns.

2. Students may look at the examples in the chart and be frustrated because they cannot find a noun in the italicized parts of the subject, indirect object and predicate nominative sentences. Remind them that the clauses are acting *as* nouns. This will be clearer if they put a person's name (a proper noun) in the sentences.

   ~~Whomever you bring~~ Peter will be welcome.

   The teacher gave ~~whoever presented an oral report~~ Peter extra credit.

Critical Viewing

Speculate Students may say that whoever carries such large plates of fruit on his or her head must have great balance.

21.2

Noun Clauses

In addition to acting as adjectives and adverbs, subordinate clauses can also act as nouns.

▶ **KEY CONCEPT** A **noun clause** is a subordinate clause that acts as a noun. ■

The following chart shows noun clauses functioning as several different parts of sentences.

NOUN CLAUSES	
Subject:	*Whomever you bring* will be welcome.
Direct Object:	The nomads can find *whatever water is in the desert.*
Indirect Object:	The teacher gave *whoever presented an oral report* extra credit.
Predicate Nominative:	The big question is *whether he will be allowed to play on the team.*
Object of a Preposition:	They store their food in plastic or in *whatever containers they have.*

◀ Critical Viewing
What do you think of this Ghanian woman's abilities? Use a noun clause beginning with *whoever* to respond. **[Speculate]**

> **Exercise 34** Identifying Noun Clauses Write the noun clause in each sentence. Then, label the clause *subject*, *direct object*, *predicate nominative*, or *object of a preposition*.

EXAMPLE: We know that some organisms cause health problems.

ANSWER: that some organisms cause health problems (direct object)

1. Our biology book says that many parasites breed in tropical regions.
2. Whatever animal is infested with a hookworm will also become severely anemic.
3. A hookworm causes severe problems for whatever animal it infects.
4. Mosquitoes transmit malaria to whomever they bite.
5. Locusts fly in large swarms and devour whatever crops lie in their way.
6. Whatever area contains tsetse flies is dangerous for cattle.
7. Tsetse flies carry sleeping sickness and can quickly take the lives of whatever herd they infest.
8. Scientists say that they will soon breed disease-resistant cattle.
9. One organization gives a research grant to whoever works on this project.
10. This work is what will save the cattle of Africa.

> **Exercise 35** Writing Sentences With Noun Clauses
Use each clause below in a complete sentence. Identify whether the noun clause functions as a *subject*, a *direct object*, an *indirect object*, a *predicate nominative*, or the *object of a preposition*.
1. what they discovered
2. whoever travels farthest
3. what the name of the country is
4. that I could travel in the boat
5. whomever arrives last
6. that traveling by boat is best
7. what is in the boat
8. how long it will take
9. who is interested
10. how to get from here to there

▲ **Critical Viewing**
Use a noun clause in a sentence to explain the importance of this fishing boat to the Ghanian people who are repairing it. **[Draw Conclusions]**

> **More Practice**
On-line Exercise Bank
• Section 21.2
Grammar Exercise Workbook
• p. 56

Phrases • 481

Answer Key

> **Exercise 34**
1. that many parasites breed in tropical regions (direct object)
2. Whatever animal is infested with a hookworm (subject)
3. whatever animal it infects (object of a preposition)
4. whomever they bite (object of a preposition)
5. whatever crops lie in their way (direct object)
6. Whatever area contains tsetse flies (subject)
7. whatever herd they infest (object of a preposition)
8. that they will soon breed resistant cattle (direct object)
9. whoever works on this project (object of preposition)
10. what will save the cattle of Africa (predicative nominative)

> **Exercise 35**
Answers will vary. Samples are given.
1. The scientists revealed what they discovered. (direct object)
2. Whoever travels farthest is the winner. (subject)
3. I don't remember what the name of the country is. (direct object)
4. I knew that I could travel in the boat. (direct object)
5. Whomever arrives last is the loser. (subject)
6. I think that traveling by boat is best. (direct object)
7. What is in the boat is a mystery. (subject)
8. I know how long it will take to get home. (direct object)
9. I know who is interested in the trip. (direct object)
10. She does not know how people get from here to there. (direct object)

Critical Viewing

Draw Conclusions Students may suggest that whoever does not own a fishing boat cannot make a proper living.

☑ ONGOING ASSESSMENT: Monitor and Reinforce

If students miss more than two items in Exercises 36–37, refer them to the following for additional practice.

In the Textbook	Print Resources	Technology
Section Review, Ex. 40, p. 485	Grammar Exercise Workbook, pp. 89–90	On-Line Exercise Bank, Section 21.2

Sentences Classified by Structure

1. Before students can understand the differences among sentences, they need to remember the definitions of a clause and a phrase. A *clause* is a group of words with a subject and a verb. (They should remember independent and subordinate clauses. An independent clause can stand by itself; it is a "sentence." A subordinate clause cannot stand by itself.) A *phrase* is a group of words without a subject or a verb that functions as one part of speech. This distinction should be fresh in their minds, as this chapter focuses on clauses and phrases. If they have trouble remembering which is which, they can write the definitions in their notebook for reference.

2. Sentences are the basis of all writing. Go over pages 38 and 39 slowly with the whole class.

3. Then identify sentences 1, 3, 5, and 6 in Exercise 36 together, explaining how the four sentences differ.

4. Finally, suggest that partners complete Exercise 36 together. If they cannot agree on any of the sentences, urge them to consult with another pair.

21.2

Sentences Classified by Structure

All sentences can be classified in two ways. First, they can be classified by structure—that is, by the number and types of clauses they contain. Second, they can be classified by function—that is, by whether they state ideas, ask questions, give orders, or express surprise.

The Four Structures of Sentences

There are two kinds of clauses: *independent* and *subordinate*. These can be used to form four basic sentence structures: *simple, compound, complex,* and *compound-complex*.

▶ **KEY CONCEPT** A **simple sentence** consists of a single independent clause. ■

Although a *simple sentence* is just one independent clause with one subject and one verb, the subject, verb, or both may be compound. A simple sentence may also have modifying phrases and complements. However, it cannot have a subordinate clause.

In the following simple sentences, the subjects are underlined once and the verbs twice.

ONE SUBJECT AND VERB:	The snow melted.
COMPOUND SUBJECT:	Diamonds and manganese are mined in Ghana.
COMPOUND VERB:	The tree rotted and died.
COMPOUND SUBJECT AND VERB:	Neither the driver nor the skier heard or saw the other boat.
WITH PHRASES AND COMPLEMENT:	Loading everything on a boat, the Lozi move from flooding land to higher ground every year.

▶ **KEY CONCEPT** A **compound sentence** consists of two or more independent clauses. ■

The clauses in a compound sentence can be joined by a comma and a coordinating conjunction (*and, but, for, nor, or, so, yet*) or by a semicolon (;). Like a simple sentence, a compound sentence contains no subordinate clauses.

EXAMPLES:　A Sotho bride carries a beaded doll at her wedding, and she keeps the same doll for a year.
Stan read the book Friday; he wrote his essay today.

> **KEY CONCEPT** A **complex sentence** consists of one independent clause and one or more subordinate clauses. ■

The independent clause in a complex sentence is often called the *main clause* to distinguish it from the subordinate clause or clauses. The subject and verb in the independent clause are called the *subject of the sentence* and the *main verb.* The second example shows that a subordinate clause may fall between the parts of a main clause.

EXAMPLES:

MAIN CLAUSE   SUBORD CLAUSE
No one answered the phone when she called us.

MAIN   SUBORD CLAUSE   CLAUSE
The doll that the bride carries doesn't have arms.

> **KEY CONCEPT** In complex sentences with noun clauses, the subject of the main clause may sometimes be the subordinate clause itself. ■

EXAMPLE:

SUBORD CLAUSE   MAIN CLAUSE
That I wanted to go bothered them.

> **KEY CONCEPT** A **compound-complex sentence** consists of two or more independent clauses and one or more subordinate clauses. ■

EXAMPLES:

IND CLAUSE
After a year, the first child is born, and the

IND CLAUSE
baby receives the same name

SUBORD. CLAUSE
that the doll was given

SUBORD. CLAUSE
when the bride was married.

SUBORD. CLAUSE   IND CLAUSE
When the lights went out, we felt extremely

IND CLAUSE
uneasy, but we always knew

SUBORD. CLAUSE
that morning would eventually come.

Critical Viewing

Apply Students may suggest that the musician smiles as she plays the drums.

Answer Key

Exercise 36

1. simple
2. simple
3. compound-complex
4. complex
5. compound-complex
6. compound-complex
7. simple
8. complex
9. complex
10. complex

Exercise 37

Answers will vary. Samples are given.

1. Neither the man nor the woman heard or saw the intruder.
2. She cooked the food and he cleaned the house.
3. When she saw the diamond ring, she cried.
4. After she went jogging, she went home to rest because she was tired.
5. When the dog got sick, we felt bad, but we always believed that he would get better.

> **Exercise 36** Identifying the Structure of Sentences

Identify each sentence as *simple, compound, complex,* or *compound-complex.*

1. South Africa is the southernmost country of Africa.
2. It is the most powerful and the wealthiest country of the region.
3. Gold and diamonds are mined in both South Africa and Namibia, yet it was South Africa where the biggest diamond in the world was found.
4. Although it is not as wealthy as South Africa, Mozambique is the site of the second biggest port in all of Africa.
5. Its capital, Maputo, is the city where the port is located; it is linked by rail with South Africa, Swaziland, and Zimbabwe.
6. Even though most people think of Africa as a desert, Zimbabwe has a hot, tropical climate, so mangoes, passion fruit, pineapples, and avocados grow well.
7. In fact, only a small percentage of southern Africa is desert.
8. However, because soil quality is poor, farms only thrive in places that receive more than 20 inches of rain annually.
9. One of the many surprising facts about west Africa is that the Sahara was not always a desert.
10. Rock paintings show that as recently as several thousand years ago, people hunted hippopotamuses in the region's rivers and chased buffalo on its wide, grassy plains.

> **Exercise 37** Writing Sentences With Different Structures

Use the following instructions to write five sentences of your own.

1. Write a simple sentence with a compound subject and verb.
2. Write a compound sentence with two independent clauses joined by *and.*
3. Write a complex sentence with one independent and one subordinate clause.
4. Write a complex sentence with one independent clause and two subordinate clauses.
5. Write a compound-complex sentence.

More Practice

On-line
Exercise Bank
• Section 21.2
Grammar Exercise
Workbook
• p. 57

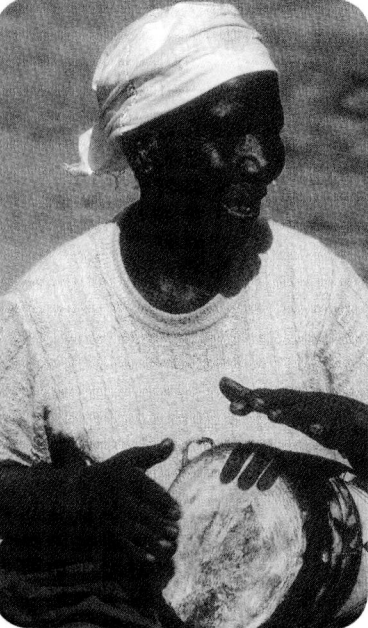

▲ Critical Viewing
In a complex sentence, describe this picture. Begin with the simple sentence "The musician smiles." **[Apply]**

⏱ TIME SAVERS!

Answers on Transparency
Use the Grammar Exercises on Transparencies for Chapter 21 to have students correct their own or one another's exercises.

On-Line Exercise Bank
Have students complete the exercises on computer. The Auto Check feature will grade their work for you!

Section 21.2 Section Review

GRAMMAR EXERCISES 38–43

> **Exercise 38** Recognizing Adjective, Adverb, and Noun Clauses
Write the adjective, adverb, or noun clause from each sentence. Label each correctly.

1. The Zaire River, which is also known as the Congo, runs almost the whole length of the country.
2. Because it has many tributaries, it is an important source of transportation.
3. The river drains a vast area of rain forests so its levels are always high.
4. The climate of Zaire is hot and humid; it lies on the equator.
5. Besides whatever cooking and cleaning African women do, they also work in the fields and sell crops in the market.

> **Exercise 39** Identifying Sentence Structure
Label each sentence in the following paragraph *simple, complex, compound,* or *compound-complex.*

(1) The Sahel is a region defined by location, climate, and vegetation. (2) The Sahel, which extends across Africa, separates the Sahara to the north from the tropical rain forests to the south. (3) For centuries, the region was a busy crossroads and a meeting place for different cultures. (4) Today, the area contains more than a dozen independent countries; each one has its own vision of the past, present, and future.

> **Exercise 40** Combining Sentences With Clauses
Change the second sentence in each of the following into an adjective, an adverb, or a noun clause. Then, make the clause part of the first sentence.

1. The book is no longer in print. You wanted a book on Zaire.

2. We left on vacation. First we took the dogs to the kennel.
3. Chinua Achebe is a Nigerian writer. I read his book *Arrow of God.*
4. This museum was built in 1896. This is the museum in our travel guide.
5. The plane trip to Zimbabwe was long. It was longer than I could believe.

> **Exercise 41** Find It in Your Reading
Read the following lines from "Talk," an Ashanti folk tale. Identify the two sentence structures that are used.

Once, not far from the city of Accra on the Gulf of Guinea, a country man went out to his garden to dig up some yams to take to market. While he was digging, one of the yams [spoke] to him.

> **Exercise 42** Find It in Your Writing
In a piece of your own writing, find an example of each type of sentence structure. If you cannot find an example of complex or compound-complex sentences, challenge yourself to use adjective and adverb clauses to combine sentences.

> **Exercise 43** Writing Application
Write a brief description of a dry climate. Use at least three of the following clauses, and identify the type of each clause you use. Then, identify each of the sentence structures you have made.

that is hot and dry
where there isn't much rain
whatever rain falls
since the last rainfall
when the temperature rises
where the temperature rises
who can farm the land

Each of these exercises correlates to a concept in the chapter on phrases and clauses, pages 450–485. These exercises may be used for more practice, for reteaching, or for review of the Key Concepts presented.

Answer Key

Exercise 44

1. phrase
2. clause
3. phrase
4. clause
5. phrase

Exercise 45

1. prepositional
2. prepositional
3. prepositional
4. prepositional
5. appositive

Exercise 46

1. verb phrase
2. participle
3. infinitive
4. participle
5. gerund

Exercise 47

1. independent
2. subordinate
3. subordinate
4. independent
5. subordinate

Exercise 48

1. Which is a stew eaten by Ethiopians; adjective; Beg wot
2. Although the stew itself is filling; adverb; served
3. What can be done to improve growing conditions; noun; direct object
4. Whatever grazing animals a farmer has; noun; direct object
5. Which is approximately twice the size of California; adjective modifying *Nigeria*

Chapter 21 Chapter Review

GRAMMAR EXERCISES 44–54

> **Exercise 44** Recognizing Phrases and Clauses Label each underlined part *phrase* or *clause*.

(1) In West Africa, (2) where many languages are heard, most people can speak English or French (3) as well as their native tongue. Portuguese is spoken in Cape Verde and Bissau, (4) while Spanish is the official language of Equatorial Guinea. The colonial language is still used (5) for official matters.

> **Exercise 45** Classifying Phrases Identify each numbered phrase as *prepositional, participial,* or *appositive.*

The Sphinx guards the ancient pyramids (1) in Egypt. These pyramids were built (2) as royal tombs (3) for the ancient rulers (4) of Egypt, (5) the pharaohs.

> **Exercise 46** Recognizing Verbals Identify the underlined word or phrase in each sentence as *gerund* (or *gerund phrase*), *participle* (or *participial phrase*), *infinitive* (or *infinitive phrase*), *verb* (or *verb phrase*).

1. The Wagenia fishermen have constructed catwalks above the Congo River to look for trapped fish.
2. The handcrafted traps are woven from bamboo stalks and are 10 feet wide at the mouth and 15 feet long.
3. It can be dangerous to place the traps in the rapids of the river.
4. The young boys of the tribe have the tiring job of cleaning the traps.
5. Dancing is a festival tradition in southern Mali.

> **Exercise 47** Recognizing Independent and Subordinate Clauses Label each of the following *independent* or *subordinate* clause.

1. the President of Senegal lives in a mansion in Dakar
2. which is the capital of Senegal
3. even though it won its independence in 1960
4. President Senghor ruled for 20 years
5. until it became a true democracy

> **Exercise 48** Classifying Clauses Identify the subordinate clause in each sentence. Label the clause *adjective, adverb,* or *noun.* If the clause is used as an adjective or adverb, tell which word it modifies. If it is a noun clause, tell whether it is used as a *subject,* a *predicate nominative,* a *direct object,* an *indirect object,* or the object.

1. *Beg wot,* which is a stew eaten by Ethiopians, is cooked with meat, tomatoes, and hot peppers.
2. Although the stew itself is filling, it is often served with a doughy bread called *injera.*
3. Agricultural groups study what can be done to improve growing conditions.
4. Pastures in Morocco feed whatever grazing animals a farmer has.
5. Of the coastal nations of West Africa, Nigeria, which is approximately twice the size of California, has the most varied climate and vegetation.

> **Exercise 49** Combining Sentences With Adverb Clauses Combine each pair of sentences by changing one into an adverb clause.

Exercise 49

Answers will vary. Samples are given.

1. When he travels from north to south in Nigeria, George will encounter coastal swamps, tropical rain forests, savannas, and desert scrub.
2. Nigeria has fertile land in the south, where cocoa is grown.
3. Because the climate in Ethiopia is dry, farmers sometimes lose their crops.
4. Because the soil is poor, few crops grow well.
5. Although Nigeria is smaller areawise, it has a larger population than Morocco.

1. George will encounter coastal swamps, tropical rain forests, savanna, and desert scrub. He travels from north to south in Nigeria.
2. Nigeria has fertile land in the south. Cocoa is grown in the south.
3. The climate in Ethiopia is dry. Farmers sometimes lose their crops.
4. Few crops grow well. The soil is poor.
5. Nigeria has a larger population than Morocco. Nigeria is smaller areawise.

Exercise 50 Identifying Relative Pronouns and Adverbs Write the relative pronoun or relative adverb from each sentence. Label each *relative pronoun* or *relative adverb*.

1. Variations in climate affect the places where people live.
2. Historically, the most powerful groups were the ones who took control of the most valuable land.
3. Weaker groups were left with the land that the dominant groups didn't want.
4. Rainfall, which is vital to farming, varies widely across the country.
5. Farmers try to predict the time when rain is most likely to fall.

Exercise 51 Recognizing Structures of Sentences Label the following sentences *simple, complex, compound,* or *compound-complex.*

1. Morocco has many valuable resources.
2. In fact, about one third of the country's exports are minerals, and it is the leading exporter of phosphates.
3. The majority of these exports leave the country through its main port, Casablanca; however, most of the imports coming through Casablanca are from France, as France is the country's major trading partner.
4. Moroccan people are skilled at handcrafting products, which include carpets, jewelry, and leather goods.

5. Also important is the manufacturing of consumer goods such as textiles and footwear.

Exercise 52 Revising to Vary Sentence Structure Revise the following paragraph. Combine some of the simple sentences into compound and complex sentences.

Morocco is a country in northwestern Africa. The Mediterranean Sea is to the north. The Atlantic Ocean is to the west. The capital of Morocco is Rabat. Rabat is located on the Atlantic Coast. A staple in the diet of most Moroccans is a dish called *couscous.* It consists of steamed wheat served with vegetables and meat. The national drink in Morocco is mint tea. Mint tea is served in small glasses without handles.

Exercise 53 Writing Application Write a brief comparison of two different climates. Use at least one adjective clause, one adverb clause, one noun clause, one appositive phrase, one gerund phrase, and one participial phrase.

Exercise 54 CUMULATIVE REVIEW Parts of Speech and Basic Sentence Parts On your paper, write whether the underlined word or group of words in each sentence is a *subject, verb, direct object, predicate noun,* or *predicate adjective.* Then, make separate lists of the nouns, the verbs, the adjectives, and the adverbs.

The Republic of Mozambique <u>stretches</u> for 1,535 miles along Africa's southeast coast. <u>Maputo</u>, the capital city, has <u>a population</u> of a million. Most <u>people</u> <u>speak</u> Portuguese or a Bantu language. Twenty-five rivers <u>cross</u> the country; the Zambezi is the <u>largest</u>. Mozambique is generally <u>flat</u>.

Exercise 50
1. where—relative adverb
2. who—relative pronoun
3. that—relative pronoun
4. which—relative pronoun
5. when—relative adverb

Exercise 51
1. simple
2. compound
3. compound-complex
4. complex
5. simple

Exercise 52
Morocco, a country in northwestern Africa, has the Mediterranean Sea to the north and the Atlantic Ocean to the west. Rabat, which is located on the Atlantic coast, is the capital of Morocco. Couscous, a staple in the diet of most Moroccans, is a dish which consists of steamed wheat served with vegetables and meat. The national drink in Morocco is mint tea, which is served in small glasses without handles.

Exercise 53
Writing Application
Have students label their clauses and phrases, then have them work with a partner to double-check.

Exercise 54
Cumulative Review
1. verb
2. subject
3. direct object
4. subject
5. verb
6. verb
7. predicate adjective
8. predicate adjective

⏱ TIME SAVERS!

🔦 Answers on Transparency Use the Grammar Exercises on Transparencies for Chapter 21 to have students correct their own or one another's exercises.

💻 On-Line Exercise Bank Have students complete the exercises on computer. The Auto Check feature will grade their work for you!

Revising and Editing

1. Remind students that questions of this nature will require them to use their knowledge of phrases and clauses as well as punctuation. Students should be prepared to know which kinds of phrases and clauses require certain punctuation.

2. Encourage students to underline or circle any repeated information in the passages they read. This will help them determine how the sentences can be combined without changing the original meaning.

3. Then have students circle or underline any parts of speech in the passages, such as conjunctions, that might help them combine the sentences.

4. Have students identify the repeated information in the sample test item. Students should see that *the hallway was dark* and *the hallway was narrow* can be combined to *form the hallway was dark and narrow*. In addition, students should see that the conjunction *but* can be used to combine the sentences.

Standardized Test Preparation Workshop

Recognizing Appropriate Sentence Construction

Knowledge of grammar is tested on standardized tests. Questions that measure your ability to use phrases and clauses show your understanding of basic sentence construction and style. A phrase is a group of words that acts as a unit without a subject and a verb; a clause is a group of words that contains a subject and verb. When faced with revising and editing questions such as these, first read each sample to get an idea of the author's purpose. Note any similarities or ways they can be combined without changing meaning. Then, choose a rewrite that uses a phrase or clause to combine similar ideas without changing the meaning or the author's message.

The following items will give you practice with the format of questions that test rules of standard grammar.

Test Tip

Although an answer choice may make sense, it may not be the best way to rewrite the original. You may need to add punctuation or change words to make the most sense.

Sample Test Item	Answer and Explanation

Directions: Read the following phrases and clauses. Choose the letter that best combines all four to form a complete sentence.
 	
(1) Alma lit a candle
(2) but instead of a flashlight
(3) the hallway was dark
(4) the hallway was narrow
 	
  A But instead of a flashlight Alma lit a candle in the narrow, dark hallway.
 	
  B The hallway was dark and narrow, but instead of a flashlight, Alma lit a candle.
 	
  C Alma lit a candle instead of a flashlight because the hallway was dark and narrow.
 	
  D The dark and narrow hallway made Alma light a candle instead of a flashlight.
	The correct answer is **B.** This is the best combination of the three sentences because it is grammatically correct without changing the meaning.

488 • Phrases and Clauses

TEST-TAKING TIP

Remind students that questions like the ones here involve constructing sentences from phrases and clauses. Therefore, students always should compare each of the choices to the original information to make sure that the meaning has not been changed. One helpful strategy is for students to read the choices in order to immediately identify any that can be eliminated.

Practice 1 **Directions:** Read the following phrases and clauses. Choose the letter that best combines all four to form a complete sentence.

(1) as Jula jumped into the ocean
(2) the ocean was beautiful
(3) a dolphin swam by
(4) the ocean was balmy

1 A A dolphin swam by the balmy, beautiful ocean as Jula jumped into it.
   B The balmy ocean was beautiful when Jula jumped in and a dolphin swam by.
   C As Jula jumped into the beautiful, balmy ocean, a dolphin swam by.
   D The ocean was balmy and beautiful as Jula jumped into it and a dolphin swam by.

(1) the children laughed
(2) the clown was silly
(3) at the clown
(4) when he ripped his pants

2 A The children laughed at the silly clown when he ripped his pants.
   B When he ripped his pants the children laughed at the clown who was silly.
   C The clown ripped his pants and he was silly when the children laughed.
   D The children laughed at the clown when he was silly when he ripped his pants.

Practice 2 **Directions:** Read the following phrases and clauses. Choose the letter that best combines all four to form a complete sentence.

(1) to shoot hoops
(2) until the end of the day
(3) the day was long
(4) the child couldn't wait

1 A Until the long day ended, the child couldn't wait to shoot hoops.
   B To shoot hoops, the child would have to wait until the end of the long day.
   C The end of the day was long and the child couldn't wait to shoot hoops.
   D The child couldn't wait until the end of the long day to shoot hoops.

(1) leapt out of nowhere
(2) when the cat
(3) William jumped and
(4) and William screamed

2 A William jumped and screamed when the cat leapt out of nowhere.
   B When the cat leapt out of nowhere, William jumped and William screamed.
   C The cat leapt out of nowhere and William screamed, then William jumped.
   D William jumped when the cat leapt out of nowhere and screamed.

Answer Key

Practice 1
1. C
2. A

Practice 2
1. D
2. A

In-Depth Lesson Plan

	LESSON FOCUS	PRINT AND MEDIA RESOURCES
DAY 1	**Four Types of Sentences** Students learn and apply the concepts of the four different types of sentences (pp. 490–494).	**Teaching Resources** *Grammar Exercise Workbook*, pp. 93–94; *Grammar Excercises Answers on Transparency*, Chapter 22; **Language Lab** CD-ROM, Sentence Errors; **On-Line Exercise Bank**, Section 22.1
DAY 2	**Sentence Combining** Students learn and apply the concepts of creating compound and complex sentences (pp. 495–499).	**Teaching Resources** *Grammar Exercise Workbook*, pp. 95–96; *Grammar Excercises Answers on Transparency*, Chapter 22; **Language Lab** CD-ROM, Sentence Errors; **On-Line Exercise Bank**, Section 22.2
DAY 3	**Varying Sentences** Students learn and apply concepts of varying sentence length and beginnings and using inverted word order (pp. 500–503).	**Teaching Resources** *Grammar Exercise Workbook*, pp. 97–98; *Grammar Excercises Answers on Transparency*, Chapter 22; **Language Lab** CD-ROM, Sentence Errors; **On-Line Exercise Bank**, Section 22.3
DAY 4	**Avoiding Sentence Errors** Students learn and apply concepts for avoiding sentence errors such as fragments and run-on sentences (pp. 504– 517).	**Teaching Resources** *Grammar Exercise Workbook*, pp. 101–112; *Grammar Excercises Answers on Transparency*, Chapter 22; **On-Line Exercise Bank**, Section 22.4
DAY 5	**Review and Assess** Students review chapter and demonstrate mastery of using effective sentences (pp. 518–522).	**Teaching Resources** *Formal Assessment*, Ch. 22; *Standardized Test Prep Workshop*, Ch. 22; **On-Line Exercise Bank**, Section 22.1

Accelerated Lesson Plan

	LESSON FOCUS	PRINT AND MEDIA RESOURCES
DAY 1	**Effective Sentences** Students cover concepts and usage of sentence types, combining, and varied length as determined by Diagnostic Test (pp. 490–503).	**Teaching Resources** *Grammar Exercise Workbook*, pp. 93–98; *Grammar Excercises Answers on Transparency*, Chapter 22, **Language Lab** CD-ROM, Sentence Errors; **On-Line Exercise Bank**, Section 22.1–3
DAY 2	**Avoiding Sentence Errors** Students cover concepts and usage of avoiding sentence errors as determined by Diagnostic Test (pp. 504–517).	**Teaching Resources** *Grammar Exercise Workbook*, pp. 101–112; *Grammar Excercises Answers on Transparency*, Chapter 22; *Hands-on Grammar Activity Book*, Chapter 22; **On-Line Exercise Bank**, Section 22.4
DAY 3	**Review and Assess** Students review chapter and demonstrate mastery of using effective sentences (pp. 518–522).	**Teaching Resources** *Formal Assessment*, Ch. 22; *Standardized Test Prep Workshop*, Ch. 22; On-Line Exercise Bank, Section 22.1

Options for Adapting Lesson Plans

HOMEWORK

Have students complete any section of the chapter for homework.

FEATURES

Extend coverage with the Grammar in Literature feature (pp. 493, 512) and the Standardized Test Preparation Workshop (p. 520).

TECHNOLOGY

Students can use the On-Line Exercise Bank to complete the exercises on computer. The Auto Check feature will grade their work.

INTEGRATED SKILLS COVERAGE
TEKS CORRELATIONS

Grammar in Literature
SE pp. 493, 512

Reading
Find It in Your Reading SE p. 494, 499, 503, 516, 517

Writing
Find It in Your Writing SE p. 494, 499, 503, 516, 517
Writing Application SE pp. 494, 499, 503, 517, 519

Language
Language Highlight ATE p. 492

Speaking and Listening
Integrating Speaking and Listening Skills ATE p. 493

Real-World Connection
ATE p. 513

Viewing and Representing
Critical Viewing SE pp. 490, 492, 495, 498, 500, 507, 508, 510, 513, 514

ASSESSMENT SUPPORT

Standardized Test Preparation SE p. 520; ATE p. 509
Standardized Test Preparation Workbook, pp. 43–44
Formal Assessment, Ch. 22

MEETING INDIVIDUAL NEEDS

Less Advanced Students ATE p. 514; See also Ongoing Assessments ATE pp. 496, 497, 498, 501, 506, 508, 510, 513, 515, 516
ESL Students ATE p. 510
Gifted/Talented Students ATE p. 501
Musical Learners ATE p. 507

BLOCK SCHEDULING

Pacing Suggestions
For 90-minute Blocks
• Administer the Diagnostic Test to students to determine instructional coverage.
• Have students complete the necessary exercises in class. Use the Hands-on Grammar activity to provide a change of pace.

Resources for Varying Instruction
• *Language Lab* CD-ROM If your students have access to hardware, a 90-minute block provides an ideal opportunity for students to work on computer.

Professional Development Support
• *How to Manage Instruction in the Block* This teaching resource provides management and activity suggestions.

MEDIA AND TECHNOLOGY

For the Student
• *Language Lab* CD-ROM, Effective Sentences
• *On-Line Exercise Bank*, Ch. 22

For the Teacher
• *Resource Pro* CD-ROM

WRITING AND GRAMMAR WEBSITE

The Interactive Writing and Grammar Website provides a wide array of support for students, teachers, and parents. Grammar support includes:

• *On-Line Exercise Bank* with Auto Check scoring
• Diagnostic and assessment support

phwg.phschool.com

LITERATURE CONNECTIONS

Grammar in Literature selections from *Prentice Hall Literature: Timeless Voices, Timeless Themes,* Gold:
from *The Most Dangerous Game,* Richard Connell, SE p. 493
from "Rules of the Game," Amy Tan, SE p. 512

► Lesson Objectives

1. To distinguish among the four types of sentences.
2. To create compound sentences by combining phrases and clauses.
3. To create short sentences from long ones.
4. To write in complete sentences.
5. To identify and correct run-on sentences.
6. To identify and correct misplaced modifiers.
7. To compose increasingly more involved sentences.

Critical Viewing

Respond Students may suggest such sentences as *The tiger is resting, What is the tiger thinking?, Don't feed the tiger,* and *What a fierce tiger!*

Chapter 22 Effective Sentences

Both domestic and wild cats have various forms of communication. The position and movement of the tail indicates mood. Roars, purrs, and squeals help cats share information about their surroundings.

Humans, on the other hand, use sentences to communicate in writing and in speaking. We use sentences every day—to ask questions, make statements, express emotion, or share information. In writing, putting words together to form effective sentences is the first step in clear communication.

▲ **Critical Viewing**
Write sentences about this tiger in which you make a statement, ask a question, give an order, or express an exclamation.
[Respond]

490 • Effective Sentences

☑ ONGOING ASSESSMENT: Diagnose

If students miss more than one item in each category, direct them to the relevant pages of the text and assign exercises for practice and review.

Effective Sentences	Diagnostic Test Items	Teach	Practice	Section Review	Chapter Review
Skill Check A					
The Four Types of Sentences	A 1–5	pp. 492–493	Ex. 1	Ex. 2–4	Ex. 41
Skill Check B					
Combining Sentences	B 6–10	pp. 495–498	Ex. 8–11	Ex. 12–14	Ex. 42–43
Skill Check C					
Varying Sentences and Sentence Beginnings	C 11–15	pp. 500–502	Ex. 18–20	Ex. 21–23	Ex. 44

Diagnostic Test

Directions: Write all answers on a separate sheet of paper.

Skill Check A. Label each sentence *declarative*, *interrogative*, *imperative*, or *exclamatory*.

1. Have you ever seen a Bengal cat?
2. The word *Bengal* brings to mind tigers.
3. Think about a wildcat as a pet.
4. Do you know that house cats are domesticated wildcats?
5. What an incredible temperament that cat has!

Skill Check B. Combine the following sentences using the method indicated in parentheses.

6. Bengal cats were bred to help increase the number of endangered wildcats. Many wildcats were sold in pet shops. (join with subordinating conjunction)
7. The female is an Asian leopard. The male is a domestic cat. (join with a comma and coordinating conjunction)
8. The Bengal cat growls. The traditional domestic cat hisses. (join with subordinating conjunction)
9. The Bengal cat plays fetch. It walks in a harness. It retrieves objects. (use a compound verb)
10. Bengal cats have friendly, inquisitive, and affectionate personalities. This is true if they are treated kindly and with respect. (turn one sentence into a phrase)

Skill Check C. Rewrite the following sentences to be more direct or to vary their beginnings as shown in parentheses.

11. Bengal cats may be spotted like a leopard, with black or brown spots accenting a light coat of the color tan, orange, rust, or gold.
12. The coat of the Bengal cat is different from that of tabbies since it has chocolate-brown or brick-red spots. (participial phrase)
13. If the Bengal cat has a gray coat with black spots, it could be referred to as a charcoal-spotted cat.
14. A beautiful Bengal, the seal lynx point snow, is a cat that is white as snow and has bright blue eyes like a Siamese cat.
15. The seal sepia snow cat is unusual, with yellow eyes and a dark brown coat. (prepositional phrase)

Skill Check D. Label each of the following items *fragment*, *run-on*, or *misplaced modifier*. Then, rewrite the item so that it is correct.

16. Talking about the coloring of the coat, the beautiful patterns were described by her.
17. The spotted variety.
18. A rosetted Bengal is spotted, what makes the spots different is that they have two colors.
19. Like the spots on a jaguar.
20. I saw the most beautiful cat the other day at Joe's house with golden glitter in its fur.

Effective Sentences • 491

Answer Key

Diagnostic Test

- Each item in the diagnostic test corresponds to a specific concept in the chapter on effective sentences. This will enable you to tailor instruction to the particular needs of your students. See "Ongoing Assessment: Diagnose" below for further details.
- Answers for the Diagnostic Test and all chapter exercises are available in *Grammar Exercises Answers on Transparencies*.

Skill Check A

1. interrogative 4. interrogative
2. declarative 5. exclamatory
3. imperative

Skill Check B

Answers will vary. Samples are given.

6. Bengal cats were bred to help increase the number of endangered wildcats, even though many wildcats were sold in pet shops.
7. The female is an Asian leopard, and the male is a domestic cat.
8. The Bengal cat growls while the traditional domestic cat hisses.
9. The Bengal cat plays fetch, walks in a harness, and retrieves objects.
10. Treated kindly and with respect, Bengal cats have friendly, inquisitive, and affectionate personalities.

Skill Check C

11. The spots on a tan, orange, rust, or gold Bengal cat may be black or brown.
12. Differing from a tabby's coat, a Bengal's coat has chocolate-brown or brick-red spots.
13. A charcoal-spotted Bengal cat has a gray coat with black spots.
14. The beautiful seal lynx point snow Bengal is pure white with bright blue eyes like those of a Siamese cat.
15. With yellow eyes and dark brown coat, the seal sepia snow cat is unusual.

Skill Check D

Rewritten sentences will vary.

16. misplaced modifier
17. fragment
18. run-on
19. fragment
20. misplaced modifier

ONGOING ASSESSMENT: Diagnose *continued*					
Effective Sentences	Diagnostic Test Items	Teach	Practice	Section Review	Chapter Review
Skill Check D					
Avoiding Sentence Errors	D 16–20	pp. 504–516	Ex. 27–34	Ex. 35–37	Ex. 45, 46
Cumulative Reviews and Applications				Ex. 2–7, 12–17, 21–26, 35–40	Ex. 41–47

Activate Prior Knowledge

Write the words *declarative, imperative, interrogative,* and *exclamatory* on the chalkboard. Ask students to assign one of the words to each sentence in the Interest Grabber.

TEACH

Step-by-Step Teaching Guide

Classifying the Four Functions of a Sentence

1. Declarative and imperative sentences can both be statements. The difference is that an imperative sentences tells someone (usually the understood *you*) to do something.

2. Imperative and exclamatory sentences can both end with exclamation points, in which case they are both exclamations. Again, the difference is that the imperative statement is exclaiming to the understood *you.*

Critical Viewing

Connect Students may suggest sentences such as *What a shame the lynx is endangered!* and *Please help the lynx.*

Language Highlight

The word *emperor* is derived from the Latin *imperator,* which is the past participle of the verb *imperare* (to command).

Section 22.1

The Four Functions of a Sentence

Sentences can be classified according to what they do—that is, whether they state ideas, ask questions, give orders, or express strong emotions. The four types of sentences in English are *declarative, interrogative, imperative,* and *exclamatory.*

Declarative sentences are the most common type. They are used to "declare," or state, facts.

▶ **KEY CONCEPT** A **declarative sentence** states an idea and ends with a period. ■

DECLARATIVE: In many Asian countries, wildcats are common. The leopard has a beautiful pattern of brown spots edged in black.

To *interrogate* means "to ask." An *interrogative sentence* is a question.

▶ **KEY CONCEPT** An **interrogative sentence** asks a question and ends with a question mark. ■

INTERROGATIVE: Whose Bengal cat is this?
In what country do tigers live?

The word *imperative* is related to the word *emperor,* a person who gives commands. *Imperative* sentences are like emperors: They give commands.

▶ **KEY CONCEPT** An **imperative sentence** gives an order or a direction and ends with either a period or an exclamation mark. ■

Most imperative sentences start with a verb. In this type of imperative sentence, the subject is understood to be *you.*

IMPERATIVE: Follow the directions carefully.
Watch out for lions while on the safari!

Notice the punctuation in the examples on the next page. In the first sentence, the period suggests that a mild command is being given in an ordinary tone of voice. The exclamation mark at the end of the second sentence suggests a strong command, one given in a loud voice.

To *exclaim* means to "shout out." *Exclamatory sentences* are used to "shout out" emotions, such as happiness, fear, or anger.

492 • Effective Sentences

Theme: Wild and Domestic Cats

In this section, you will learn to classify sentences according to their function. The examples and exercises are about different types of wild and domestic cats.

Cross-Curricular Connection: Science

▼ **Critical Viewing** Write an exclamatory sentence and an imperative sentence you might use in talking with someone about an endangered animal, such as this lynx. **[Connect]**

⏱ **TIME AND RESOURCE MANAGER**

Resources
Print: Grammar Exercise Workbook, pp. 93–94
Technology: Language Lab CD-ROM, Sentence Errors; On-Line Exercise Bank, Section 22.1

In-Depth Coverage	Accelerated Pace
• Work through all key concepts, pp. 492–493. • Assign and review Exercise 1. • Read and discuss Grammar in Literature, p. 493.	• Assign pp. 492–493 for independent student review. • Assign Section Review Exercise 4.

GRAMMAR IN LITERATURE

from **The Most Dangerous Game**
Richard Connell

The following passage illustrates three of the four types of sentences.

"Don't talk rot, Whitney," said Rainsford. "You're a big-game hunter, not a philosopher. Who cares how a jaguar feels?"

"Perhaps the jaguar does," observed Whitney.

▶ **KEY CONCEPT** An **exclamatory sentence** conveys strong emotion and ends with an exclamation mark. ■

EXCLAMATORY: She's not telling the truth!
                        This is an outrage!

▶ **Exercise 1** Identifying the Four Types of Sentences Read each of the following sentences carefully, and identify it as *declarative, interrogative, imperative,* or *exclamatory.* Then, write the appropriate punctuation mark for each sentence.

EXAMPLE: Have you ever seen a lynx
ANSWER: interrogative (?)

1. The lynx is a wildcat that measures up to three feet in length
2. What color is the lynx
3. It has a brownish-gray coat with a black, bobbed tail and black ear tufts
4. It is so adorable
5. Look for the lynx in dense forests
6. What is the purpose of camouflage
7. Lynxes are successful hunters because their prey cannot differentiate between them and the dense forest
8. Have you ever wondered why the lynx is endangered
9. What a sad thing that is
10. Read this article if you want to learn more

▶ **More Practice**
Language Lab CD-ROM
• Effective Sentences lesson
On-line Exercise Bank
• Section 22.1
Grammar Exercise Workbook
• pp. 93–94

Grammar in Literature

1. Ask a volunteer to read aloud the literature excerpt. Have students identify the type of each sentence and explain their answers. Tell them to ignore the words "said Rainsford" and "observed Whitney." (imperative, declarative, interrogative, declarative)

2. Challenge students to rewrite some of the sentences in the excerpt as sentences of different types.

   "You are talking rot, Whitney," said Rainsford.

   "Are you a big-game hunter or a philosopher?"

Answer Key

▶ **Exercise 1**

1. declarative (.)
2. interrogative (?)
3. declarative (.)
4. exclamatory (!)
5. imperative (.)
6. interrogative (?)
7. declarative (.)
8. interrogative (?)
9. exclamatory (!)
10. imperative (.)

Integrating Speaking and Listening Skills

When spoken aloud, each type of sentence described on pp. 492–493 requires a different tone of voice to help get the meaning across. For example, an interrogative sentence will end in a rising tone to signal that a question is being asked. Have students record examples of each type of sentence based on voice cues from the readers.

Section Review

Each of these exercises correlates with one of the concepts in the section on the four functions of a sentence, pages 492–493. These exercises may be used for more practice, for reteaching, or for review of the Key Concepts presented. Answers for all chapter exercises are available in *Grammar Exercises Answers on Transparencies* in your teaching resources.

Answer Key

► Exercise 2

1. declarative
2. imperative
3. declarative
4. interrogative
5. declarative
6. imperative
7. interrogative
8. imperative
9. exclamatory
10. declarative

► Exercise 3

Answers will vary. Samples are given.

1. Go to the La Brea tar pits.
2. Have you found another fossil?
3. The short tail of the saber-toothed tiger indicates that it did not chase its prey.
4. The saber-toothed tiger was very dangerous!
5. In Berkeley, you can see representations of these ferocious animals.

► Exercise 4

1. Do you know what a saber is? interrogative
2. A saber is a large sword with a blade that is slightly curved. declarative
3. Don't call that animal a tiger. imperative
4. Why is it not a tiger? interrogative
5. These ice age animals were unlike any wildcats that live today. declarative
6. Their weight allowed them to attack mastodons and mammoths. declarative
7. What a powerful animal it was! exclamatory
8. How could the cats eat their prey without sharp teeth? interrogative

---

Section 22.1 Section Review

GRAMMAR EXERCISES 2–7

► Exercise 2 Identify the Four Types of Sentences Read each sentence carefully, and label it *declarative, interrogative, imperative,* or *exclamatory.*

1. Saber-toothed tigers get their name from their large, sharp teeth.
2. Study the saber-toothed tiger if you are interested in extinct cats.
3. Evidence of these animals has appeared in two different eras.
4. Do you know why they had such big teeth?
5. Researchers have proposed that they used them to attack prey.
6. Watch out for the saber-toothed tiger!
7. Could they break their teeth by using them that way?
8. Look for a broken tooth in the fossil record.
9. I can't find one!
10. Saber-toothed tigers also used their teeth to tear the flesh off their prey.

► Exercise 3 Revising to Vary Sentence Type Rewrite the following sentences to fit the type indicated in italics.

EXAMPLE: Saber-toothed tigers once lived in California. *interrogative*

ANSWER: Did saber-toothed tigers once live in California?

1. Have you ever gone to the La Brea tar pits? *imperative*
2. You found another fossil! *interrogative*
3. Does the short tail of the saber-toothed tiger indicate that it did not chase its prey? *declarative*
4. How dangerous was the saber-toothed tiger? *exclamatory*
5. Go to Berkeley to see representations of these ferocious animals. *declarative*

494 • Effective Sentences

► Exercise 4 Punctuating the Four Types of Sentences Copy the following sentences onto your paper. Add the appropriate punctuation mark for each sentence, and identify its type.

1. Do you know what a saber is
2. A saber is a large sword with a blade that is slightly curved
3. Don't call that animal a tiger
4. Why is it not a tiger
5. These ice age animals were unlike any wildcats that live today
6. Their weight allowed them to attack mastodons and mammoths
7. What a powerful animal it was
8. How could the cats eat their prey without sharp teeth
9. Look at those strong muscles in its head, neck, and shoulders
10. We're so lucky they aren't alive today

► Exercise 5 Find It in Your Reading
The excerpt from "The Most Dangerous Game" on page 493 contains three of the four sentence types. Add an example of the fourth kind of sentence to continue the conversation.

► Exercise 6 Find It in Your Writing
Look through your portfolio for examples of each of the four types of sentences. If you can't find all four kinds, challenge yourself to add the missing types to a piece of your writing.

► Exercise 7 Writing Application
Write a short essay comparing wildcats and domestic cats. Discuss their similarities and their differences. Include all four types of sentences.

---

9. Look at those strong muscles in its head, neck, and shoulders. imperative
10. We're so lucky they aren't alive today! exclamatory

► Exercise 5

Find It in Your Reading
Students should add an exclamatory sentence, such as, "I never knew you were so sentimental!" cried Rainsford, laughing.

► Exercise 6

Find It in Your Writing
Students can trade papers with a partner to check for correct punctuation.

► Exercise 7

Writing Application
Students may want to use library and/or Internet resources to find information for their essays.

Section 22.2 *Sentence Combining*

If you use too many short sentences, your writing may seem choppy and disconnected. One way to avoid the excessive use of short sentences and to achieve sentence variety is to combine sentences—to express two or more related ideas or pieces of information in a single sentence.

EXAMPLE:	We went to the zoo.
	We saw tigers.
COMBINED SENTENCES:	We went to the zoo and saw tigers.
	We saw tigers at the zoo.
	We saw tigers when we went to the zoo.

> **KEY CONCEPT** Sentences can be combined by using a compound subject, a compound verb, or a compound object. ■

TWO SENTENCES:	Moira enjoyed watching the lions.
	Jon enjoyed watching the lions.
COMPOUND SUBJECT:	Moira and Jon enjoyed watching the lions.
TWO SENTENCES:	Lisa played the game.
	Lisa won a prize.
COMPOUND VERB:	Lisa played the game and won a prize.
TWO SENTENCES:	Scott saw the cheetah.
	Scott saw the hyena.
COMPOUND OBJECT:	Scott saw the cheetah and the hyena.

> **Exercise 8** **Combining Sentences Using Compound Subjects, Verbs, and Objects** Combine each pair of sentences in the way that makes the most sense. Identify what you have done to combine them.

EXAMPLE:	Lions eat gazelles. Lions eat warthogs.
ANSWER:	Lions eat gazelles and warthogs. (compound object)

1. Thomas heard the roar of the lion. Micah heard the roar of the lion.
2. Lions are social animals. Lions live in groups called prides.
3. As many as twelve females live in a pride. Their cubs live in a pride.
4. The lionesses stalk prey. The lionesses hunt for food.
5. Cubs get milk from their mother. Cubs get milk from other female lions.

Theme: Wild and Domestic Cats

In this section, you will learn to combine sentences. The examples and exercises tell more about wild and domestic cats.

Cross-Curricular Connection: Science

▲ **Critical Viewing** In a single sentence describing this tiger, mention at least two of its features. **[Analyze]**

TIME AND RESOURCE MANAGER

Resources
Print: Grammar Exercise Workbook, pp. 95–96
Technology: Language Lab CD-ROM, Sentence Errors; On-Line Exercise Bank, Section 22.2

In-Depth Coverage	Accelerated Pace
• Work through all key concepts, pp. 495–498. • Assign and review Exercises 8–11.	• Assign pp.495–498 for independent student review. • Assign Section Review Exercises 13–14.

Joining Clauses

1. Independent clauses should be combined only if they relate to the same topic. Discuss the examples in which the second sentence in each pair discusses the same topic as the first. Remind students that a sentence should express a complete thought. It should not discuss two completely different thoughts.

2. A semicolon indicates a halt in a sentence, not just a pause for breath. A semicolon marks the end of a complete thought and a shift, but not a total change, in subject or mood. A semicolon can be used instead of a comma and a conjunction such as *and* or *but*.

Answer Key

Exercise 9

1. The tiger is the largest species in the cat family; it can weigh up to eight hundred pounds.
2. The eye of the tiger is specialized to help the tiger see in dim light, so it is able to hunt at night.
3. Tigers live in areas that are thick with grasses and trees; this natural cover allows them to hide and ambush their prey.
4. Tigers are solitary animals, but they will keep their young with them until the young reach the age of two or three.
5. At this age, young tigers can find their own food, and they can find and mark their own territory.

22.2

> **KEY CONCEPT** Sentences can be combined by joining two independent clauses to create a compound sentence. ∎

Use a compound sentence when combining ideas that are related but independent. Compound sentences are created by joining two independent clauses with a comma and a coordinating conjunction (such as *and, but, or, yet,* or *so*) or with a semicolon.

EXAMPLE: The antelope was on the lookout for enemies. It did not notice the lion hiding in the high grass nearby.

COMPOUND SENTENCE: The antelope was on the lookout for enemies, but it did not notice the lion hiding in the high grass nearby.

EXAMPLE: The lion waited patiently. Its prey kept moving closer.

COMPOUND SENTENCE: The lion waited patiently; its prey kept moving closer.

> **Exercise 9** **Creating Compound Sentences** Combine each pair of sentences according to the method indicated in parentheses.

EXAMPLE: The tiger is a cat. It is not likely that anyone would want one as a pet. (comma and conjunction)

ANSWER: The tiger is a cat, but it is not likely that anyone would want one as a pet.

1. The tiger is the largest species in the cat family. It can weigh up to 800 pounds. (semicolon)
2. The eye of the tiger is specialized to help it see in dim light. It is able to hunt at night. (comma and conjunction)
3. Tigers live in areas that are thick with grasses and trees. This natural cover allows them to hide and ambush their prey. (semicolon)
4. Tigers are solitary animals. They will keep their young with them until the young reach the age of two or three. (comma and conjunction)
5. At this age, young tigers can find their own food. They are able to find and mark their own territory. (comma and conjunction)

> **More Practice**
>
> Language Lab CD-ROM
> • Effective Sentences lesson
> On-line Exercise Bank
> • Section 22.2
> Grammar Exercise Workbook
> • pp. 95–96

☑ ONGOING ASSESSMENT SYSTEM: Prerequisite Skills

If students have difficulty with compound subjects and verbs, you may find it necessary to review the following to assure coverage of prerequisite knowledge.

In the Textbook	Print Resources	Technology
Basic Sentence Parts, pp. 422–425	Grammar Exercise Workbook, pp. 47–48	On-Line Exercise Bank, Section 20.1

Subordinate Clauses

1. Review with students the definition of a clause: a group of words with a subject and a verb. This means that a clause can be a sentence: *I* [subject] *dropped* [verb] *the ball.* A subordinate clause is not a sentence: *when I* [subject] *dropped* [verb] *the ball.*

2. The word *subordinate* means "helper." A subordinate clause helps the independent clause to which it is joined by clarifying or describing its subject and verb.

KEY CONCEPT Sentences can be combined by changing one into a subordinate clause to create a complex sentence. ■

Use a complex sentence when you are combining sentences to show the relationship between ideas in which one depends on the other. The subordinating conjunction will help readers understand the relationship.

EXAMPLE:	We were frightened. We thought the lion we saw on safari was hungry.
COMBINED WITH A SUBORDINATE CLAUSE:	We were frightened because we thought the lion we saw on safari was hungry.

Exercise 10 Combining Sentences Using Subordinate Clauses Combine each pair of sentences using the subordinating conjunction that is given in parentheses.

EXAMPLE:	The tiger is an endangered species. It has been overexploited as a resource. (because)
ANSWER:	The tiger is an endangered species because it has been overexploited as a resource.

1. There are eight species of tigers. Three of them are extinct. (although)
2. People see pictures of these magnificent creatures. They don't realize they are endangered. (when)
3. The resources required to sustain the life of the tigers are diminishing. Tigers have few places to live and little food to eat. (so that)
4. Poachers diminish the tiger population. They can get high prices for tiger parts. (since)
5. Forty years ago there were four thousand South China tigers living in the wild. Today there are fewer than thirty. (while)
6. The government mistakenly declared the South China tiger a pest in the 1950's. Thousands of the animals were slaughtered. (after)
7. The Chinese government has become actively involved in efforts to preserve the South China tiger. The government wants to prevent the animal's extinction. (because)
8. The South China tiger is the most critically endangered tiger. Other subspecies are also threatened. (although)
9. Efforts were made to halt the hunting of Siberian tigers. There were fewer than fifty of these huge beasts surviving in the wild. (until)
10. Strong pressure has been brought to protect tigers. More people have learned of their peril. (as)

Sentence Combining • 497

Answer Key

Exercise 10

1. There are eight species of tigers although three of them are extinct.
2. People don't realize these magnificent creatures are endangered when they see pictures of them.
3. The resources required to sustain the lives of tigers are diminishing, so that tigers have few places to live and little food to eat.
4. Poachers diminish the tiger population since they can get high prices for tiger parts.
5. Forty years ago there were 4,000 South China tigers living in the wild while today there are fewer than thirty.
6. After the government mistakenly declared the South China tiger a pest in the 1950's, thousands of the animals were slaughtered.
7. The Chinese government has become actively involved in efforts to preserve the South China tiger because the government wants to prevent the animal's extinction.
8. The South China tiger is the most critically endangered tiger although other subspecies are also threatened.
9. Until efforts were made to halt hunting of Siberian tigers, there were fewer than fifty of these huge beasts surviving in the wild.
10. Strong pressure has been brought to protect tigers as more people have learned of their peril.

☑ ONGOING ASSESSMENT SYSTEM: Monitor and Reinforce

If students miss more than two items in Exercises 8–11, refer them to the following for additional practice.

In the Textbook	Print Resources	Technology
Section Review, Ex. 12–14, p. 499	Grammar Exercise Workbook, pp. 95–96	Language Lab CD-ROM, Sentence Errors; On-Line Exercise Bank, Section 22.2

Step-by-Step Teaching Guide

Combining Sentences Using Phrases

1. Review the definition of a phrase: a group of words *without* a subject and a verb, which functions as a part of speech.

2. In the first combined example sentence, *against the Cougars* modifies the verb *plays,* so the phrase functions as an adverb. In the second combined example, *the only undefeated team in the league* renames the noun *Cougars,* so the phrase functions as an appositive.

Answer Key

Answers will vary. Samples are given.

1. The cheetah moves stealthily through the tall grass.
2. It watches its prey, a gazelle.
3. The cheetah runs quickly after the gazelle.
4. The cheetah tires quickly, unable to chase the gazelle very far.
5. Relieved to have escaped, the gazelle stops running and catches its breath.

Critical Viewing

Analyze Students may suggest sentences such as *Slinking furtively over the ground, the cheetah soundlessly approaches its prey.*

▶ **KEY CONCEPT** Sentences can be combined by changing one of them into a phrase. ∎

EXAMPLE:	My team plays tomorrow. We play the Cougars.
COMBINED WITH PREPOSITIONAL PHRASE:	My team plays *against the Cougars* tomorrow.
EXAMPLE:	My team will play against the Cougars. They are the only undefeated team in the league.
COMBINED WITH: APPOSITIVE PHRASE:	My team will play against the Cougars, *the only undefeated team in the league.*
EXAMPLE:	The Cougars scored quickly. The Cougars jumped out to a two-goal lead.
COMBINED WITH PARTICIPIAL PHRASE:	*Scoring quickly,* the Cougars jumped out to a two-goal lead.

▶ **Exercise 11** Combining Sentences Using Phrases
Combine each pair of sentences by turning one sentence into a phrase that adds detail to the other.

EXAMPLE:	The cheetah has a tawny-colored coat. It has round, black spots.
ANSWER:	The cheetah has a tawny-colored coat with round, black spots.

1. The cheetah moves stealthily. It moves through the tall grass.
2. It watches its prey. Its prey is a gazelle.
3. The cheetah runs quickly. It runs after the gazelle.
4. The cheetah tires quickly. It is unable to chase the gazelle very far.
5. The gazelle is relieved to have escaped. The gazelle stops running and catches its breath.

◀ Critical Viewing Think of a sentence that combines several details about the way this cheetah moves. **[Analyze]**

ⓘ Learn More

To review information about different types of phrases, see Chapter 21.

Section 22.2 Section Review

GRAMMAR EXERCISES 12–17

Exercise 12 **Combining Sentence Parts** Combine each pair of sentences by creating a compound subject, verb, or object.

1. Lions are majestic animals. Tigers are majestic animals.
2. The male lion is a strong fighter. The male lion is called King of the Jungle.
3. Lions hunt zebras. Lions hunt antelopes.
4. Lions inhabit grassland. Lions inhabit thinly forested areas.
5. Lion cubs are born with spots. Lion cubs lose the spots by their third month.

Exercise 13 **Combining Clauses and Phrases** Combine each pair of sentences by creating a compound sentence, forming a complex sentence, or changing one sentence into a phrase.

1. I have often visited the zoo. The zoo is in San Diego.
2. I visit the zoo. My first stop is the tiger habitat.
3. Tigers are cats. They do not purr.
4. Instead, tigers have a variety of roars. They communicate with these roars.
5. A tiger's tail serves two purposes. The tail is long and flexible.
6. The tail aids balance during running. It also expresses emotion.
7. A tiger with its tail upright and moving slowly is friendly. A tiger with its tail lowered and twitching is angry.
8. The natural habitat of the Bengal tiger and Indochinese tiger has declined. It has declined because of overhunting.
9. The Sumatran tiger is similar to the Bengal tiger. It is smaller and its stripes are closer together.
10. I plan to study tigers in college. I hope to work at the San Diego Zoo someday.

Exercise 14 **Revising a Paragraph by Combining Sentences** Revise the paragraph below by combining some of the short sentences to form longer ones.

(1) Cheetahs live on the grassy plains and in the dense bush. (2) The plains and bush are in Africa. (3) Cheetahs once lived in southern and central Asia. (4) Their habitat has shrunk. (5) Many of their former lands have been taken over by farms. (6) Their wooded homelands have been replaced by manufacturing plants. (7) Cheetahs are known for their beauty. (8) Cheetahs are known for their speed. (9) Cheetahs can run up to 60 miles per hour. (10) They can capture even the fastest prey.

Exercise 15 **Find It in Your Reading** Several ideas have been combined in this sentence from "The Most Dangerous Game." Write the ideas that have been combined as separate sentences.

He struggled up to the surface and tried to cry out, but the wash from the speeding yacht slapped him in the face and the salt water in his open mouth made him gag and strangle.

Exercise 16 **Find It in Your Writing** Look in your portfolio for examples of short, choppy sentences. Combine some of these to form longer sentences.

Exercise 17 **Writing Application** Write a short essay telling why endangered animals should or should not be protected. Combine clauses and phrases to form longer, more interesting sentences.

ASSESS and CLOSE

Section Review

Each of these exercises correlates to one of the concepts in the section on sentence combining, pages 495–498. The exercises may be used for more practice, for reteaching, or for review of the Key Concepts presented. Answers for all chapter exercises are available in *Grammar Exercises Answers on Transparencies* in your teaching resources.

Answer Key

Exercise 12

1. Lions and tigers are majestic animals.
2. The male lion is a strong fighter and is called King of the Jungle.
3. Lions hunt zebras and antelopes.
4. Lions inhabit grassland and thinly forested areas.
5. Lion cubs are born with spots but lose them by their third month.

Exercise 13

Answers will vary. Samples are given.

1. I have often visited the zoo in San Diego.
2. When I visit the zoo, my first stop is the tiger habitat.
3. Tigers are cats, but they do not purr.
4. Instead, tigers have a variety of roars that they use to communicate.
5. A tiger's tail, which is long and flexible, serves two purposes.
6. The tail aids balance during running, and it also expresses emotion.
7. A tiger with its tail upright and moving slowly is friendly, but a tiger with its tail lowered and twitching is angry.
8. The natural habitat of the Bengal tiger and Indochinese tiger has declined because of overhunting.
9. The Sumatran tiger is similar to the Bengal tiger except that it is smaller and its stripes are closer together.
10. I plan to study tigers in college, and I hope to work at the San Diego Zoo someday.

continued

Answer Key continued

Exercise 14

Answers will vary.

Exercise 15

Find It in Your Reading
He struggled up to the surface. He tried to cry out. The wash from the speeding yacht slapped him in the face. The salt water in his open mouth made him gag and strangle.

Exercise 16

Find It in Your Writing
Suggest that students combine sentences in several ways, such as with a semicolon and with a comma and coordinating conjunction.

Exercise 17

Writing Application
Students may want to visit the Websites of organizations working to protect endangered animals to learn more about conservationists' efforts.

Interest GRABBER Play for students the Listening to Literature audiocassette of Martin Luther King's "I Have a Dream" speech. It is effective for many reasons: King's passion; the soaring spiritual references combined with down-to-earth images of innocent children. It also works because of King's mixture of sentence types: long ones, punctuated with short ones, such as "I have a dream today" and "this is our hope."

Activate Prior Knowledge

Have students look at King's speech in *Prentice Hall Literature's Timeless Voices, Timeless Themes.* Ask them to identify simple, compound, and complex sentences.

TEACH

Step-by-Step Teaching Guide

Vary Sentence Length

1. Tell students that one helpful method for making simpler sentences is to underline or circle the different ideas expressed in a sentence.

2. If students find that a sentence has two or more distinct ideas, then they can consider breaking it down into shorter, simpler sentences.

Critical Viewing

Analyze, Make a Judgment
Students may mention the reason the man is riding his bike, how he feels, the color of the sky, and time of day. The first two ideas would belong in one sentence, and the last two in another.

Section 22.3 # Varying Sentences

Varying the length and form of your sentences can make them more interesting. It can help to create a rhythm, to achieve an effect, or to emphasize the connections between ideas. There are several ways you can create variety in your sentences:

Vary Sentence Length

You have already learned that you can combine several short, choppy sentences to create a longer, more fluid and stylistically mature sentence. However, too many long sentences one after another can be as uninteresting as too many short sentences. When you want to emphasize a point or surprise a reader, insert a short, direct sentence to interrupt the flow of several long sentences. You can also break some longer sentences that contain two or more ideas into shorter sentences to achieve variety.

Some sentences contain only one idea and can't be broken up. It may be possible, however, to state the idea in a shorter sentence. Other sentences contain two or more ideas and might be shortened by breaking up the ideas.

ONE LONG
SENTENCE: Although bicycles have evolved into several forms from the original three-wheeled transportation machine, the originators could not have fathomed the daredevil stunts that people would attempt on mountain bikes, and even much of the population is not aware of the adventure, the adrenaline rush, and the extreme athleticism that are all part of a trip through the mountains.

TWO
SENTENCES: Although bicycles have evolved into several forms from the original three-wheeled transportation machine, the originators could not have fathomed the daredevil stunts that people would attempt on mountain bikes. Even much of the population is not aware of the adventure, the adrenaline rush, and the extreme athleticism that are all a part of a trip through the mountains.

Theme: Bicycles and Cyclists

In this section, you will learn ways to vary sentence length and beginnings to make your writing more interesting. The examples and exercises are about bicycles and cyclists.

Cross-Curricular Connection: Physical Education

▼ **Critical Viewing** Think of three or four ideas that this picture brings to mind. Which ideas should go in separate sentences? Which should be combined in one sentence? **[Make a Judgment]**

⏱ TIME AND RESOURCE MANAGER

Resources
Print: Grammar Exercise Workbook, pp. 97–98
Technology: Language Lab CD-ROM, Sentence Errors; On-Line Exercise Bank, Section 22.3

In-Depth Coverage	Accelerated Pace
• Work through all key concepts, pp. 500–502. • Assign and review Exercises 18–20.	• Assign pp. 500–502 for independent student review. • Assign Section Review Exercise 22.

▶ **Exercise 18** **Making Simpler Sentences** Rewrite the following sentences. Break each one into two sentences or rewrite the sentence in a simpler, more direct way.

EXAMPLE: The casual observer may think of the unicycle as a circus toy, but it is a complex machine that requires great coordination and skill, as you will learn if you ever try one.

ANSWER: The unicycle looks like a simple circus toy. However, if you ever try one, you will see that it requires great coordination and skill.

1. The height of the frame of the giraffe unicycle, also known as the tall unicycle, gives it its name, and it ranges in height from five to eight feet.
2. The biverticycle has two wheels stacked vertically to improve the balance and momentum in turning the wheels and to propel the cycle forward, but it can be considered a unicycle because only one of its wheels touches the ground when the trained professional rides the cycle.
3. In order to learn to ride the biverticycle, it is necessary to train new muscle and nerve reactions because the movement is a backward pedaling motion, which is not the same as the movements required on a normal unicycle.
4. The triverticycle has three wheels, as the name implies, and is easier to ride than the biverticycle because you pedal in a forward direction.
5. Although it may not seem practical, unicycles having up to four or five vertically stacked wheels have been built for entertainment and sport, although the potential hazards of these cycles have not made these cycles popular.

Vary Sentence Beginnings

Another way to create sentence variety is to avoid starting each sentence in the same way. You can start sentences with different parts of speech.

START WITH A NOUN:	Bicycles are difficult to make.
START WITH AN ADVERB:	Naturally, bicycles are difficult to make.
START WITH A PARTICIPLE:	Having tried to make several bicycles, I know they are very difficult to make.
START WITH A PREPOSITIONAL PHRASE:	For the average person, bicycles are very difficult to make.
START WITH AN INFINITIVE PHRASE:	To win the race is his goal.

▶ **More Practice**

Language Lab CD-ROM
• Effective Sentences lesson
On-line Exercise Bank
• Section 22.3
Grammar Exercise Workbook
• pp. 97–98

💡 **Spelling Tip**

If you are having difficulty spelling a word, try to think of another form of the word that might indicate the correct spelling. For example, if you are trying to spell *bicycle,* you may want to spell it like it sounds, *bicicle.* However, by thinking of the word *cycle,* the correct spelling, *bicycle,* becomes clear.

Varying Sentences • 501

Answer Key

▶ **Exercise 18**

Answers will vary. Samples are given.

1. The giraffe unicycle is also known as the tall unicycle. Its frame ranges in height from five to eight feet.
2. The biverticycle has two wheels stacked vertically, but because only one wheel touches the ground during riding, it is considered a unicycle.
3. A biverticycle exercises different muscles from those exercised by a normal unicycle: the rider pedals backward. Therefore, one must train first.
4. Since you pedal it in a forward direction, the three-wheeled triverticle is easier to ride than the biverticycle.
5. Four- and five-wheeled vertical unicycles have been built for entertainment and sport. However, the potential hazards of these cycles have prevented them from becoming popular.

Step-by-Step Teaching Guide

Vary Sentence Beginnings

1. Ask students why they think it's important to vary the beginning of sentences when they write. (It makes the text more interesting to read.)
2. Remind students that they should vary sentence beginnings in ways that do not change the intended meaning of the sentences in question.

Customize for Gifted/Talented Students

The prefixes *uni-, bi-,* and *tri-* mean "one," "two," and "three." Challenge students to work as a group to list all the words they can think of with these prefixes.

☑ **ONGOING ASSESSMENT SYSTEM: Monitor and Reinforce**

If students miss more than two items in Exercises 18–20, refer them to the following for additional practice.

In the Textbook	Print Resources	Technology
Section Review, Ex. 21–23, p. 503	Grammar Exercise Workbook, pp. 97–100	On-Line Exercise Bank, Section 22.3

Answers will vary. Samples are given.

1. To cycling enthusiasts, the initials BMX stand for Bicycle Motocross.
2. Typically, this sport is different from MMX, Motorcycle Motocross, because BMX depends on the power of the rider's legs instead of the power of the engine.
3. From a simple beginning, BMX has grown into a sport with many components.
4. Done on ramps like those used in skateboarding, Vert Riding is an exciting sport.
5. BMX riders use ramps, ledges, and rails in their sport.
6. Doing stunts while on a normal flat surface is called flatland.
7. Clearly, dirt jumping is one of the preferred aspects of BMX.
8. Unsurprisingly, dirt jumping consists of riding over dirt trails and jumps.
9. In John's opinion, BMX is the sport most similar to MMX.
10. To succeed in this sport, much strength and skill are required.

Step-by-Step Teaching Guide

Invert Subject-Verb Order

Explain to students that this variation will not always be the best choice. Occasionally, inverting subject-verb order will create an awkward construction.

22.3

▶ **Exercise 19** Varying Sentence Beginnings Rewrite the following sentences so that they begin with the part of speech indicated in parentheses.
  1. The initials *BMX* stand for "Bicycle Motocross" to cycling enthusiasts. (prepositional phrase)
  2. This sport is different from MMX, Motorcycle Motocross, because BMX depends on the power of a rider's legs instead of the power of an engine. (adverb)
  3. BMX has grown from a simple beginning into a sport with many components. (prepositional phrase)
  4. Vert riding is an exciting sport done on ramps known as half-pipes or quarter-pipes, similar to those used in skateboarding. (participial phrase)
  5. In their sport, BMX riders use ramps, ledges, and rails. (noun)
  6. Flatland is the sport of doing stunts while on a normal, flat surface. (gerund phrase)
  7. Dirt jumping is one of the preferred aspects of BMX. (adverb)
  8. Dirt jumping consists of riding over dirt trails and jumps. (adverb)
  9. Jon knows this sport is the most similar to MMX. (prepositional phrase)
  10. Much strength and skill are required to succeed in this sport. (infinitive phrase)

Invert Subject-Verb Order

You can also vary sentence beginnings by reversing the traditional subject-verb order.

SUBJECT-   The bus is here.
VERB ORDER: The ship sailed into the bay.

INVERTED   Here is the bus.
ORDER: Into the bay sailed the ship.

▶ **Exercise 20** Inverting Sentences Invert the following sentences by reversing the order of the subject and verb. Rearrange other words as needed.
  1. The recumbent bicycle is driven by human power.
  2. A recumbent bicycle races at a top speed of 65 miles per hour.
  3. A picture of the bicycle is here.
  4. Recumbent bicycles sit close to the ground.
  5. A rider's abdomen is toned and strengthened by recumbent riding.

Language Lab
CD-ROM
• Effective Sentences lesson
On-Line Exercise Bank
• Section 22.3
Grammar Exercise Workbook
• pp. 99-100

⏱ TIME SAVERS!

Answers on Transparency
Use the Grammar Exercises on Transparencies for Chapter 22 to have students correct their own or one another's exercises.

On-Line Exercise Bank
Have students complete the exercises on computer. The Auto Check feature will grade their work for you!

Answer Key

1. Driven by human power is the recumbent bicycle.
2. At a top speed of sixty-five miles per hour races a recumbent bicycle.
3. Here is a picture of the bicycle.
4. Close to the ground sit recumbent bicycles.
5. Toned and strengthened by recumbent riding is a rider's abdomen.

Section 22.3 Section Review

GRAMMAR EXERCISES 21–26

Exercise 21 Revising to Simplify Long Sentences Rewrite each sentence, either breaking it into two sentences that each contain one idea or forming a simpler, more direct sentence.

1. Discipline, professionalism, and commitment have been the key elements in helping Steve Larsen, who excelled in mountain biking after fifteen years of road racing, to achieve a success that is uncommon for the ordinary man.
2. Steve wore the Stars-and-Stripes jersey as a member of the World Championship Team and as a U.S. National Champion, raising his ranking and establishing himself as a hero in mountain-biking history.
3. Although mechanical problems prevented Steve from finishing first in many races, his success through determination and willpower is encouraging for others who wish to follow that same course.
4. Unless you are an avid mountain biker who knows much about bikes, the various components of a bike, such as ergonomic shift levers, brake levers with quick index-barrel adjusters, and chain rings, will be foreign to you.
5. Perhaps the most important equipment that a person can wear while mountain biking is a helmet that is lightweight, provides superior protection, and allows good visibility.

Exercise 22 Revising Sentences by Varying Beginnings and Inverting Subject-Verb Order Rewrite the sentences following the direction in parentheses.

1. In the 1996 Olympics in Atlanta, Georgia, the gold medalist was an Italian woman, Paola Pezzo. (start with a noun)
2. She was victorious in the championship race by a significant margin. (invert)
3. She was later honored by her country with a victory parade. (invert)
4. She maintained her dominance with a win in the European mountain bike championship. (start with preposition)
5. As part of her training, Paola typically takes a four-hour bike ride early each morning. (start with adverb)

Exercise 23 Revising Sentences in Several Ways Revise the paragraph below by varying sentence beginnings and word order.

(1) A tandem bicycle is there in the store window. (2) Two riders sit one behind the other on a tandem bike. (3) The riders must keep pace with each other for best performance. (4) It is not easy to stay perfectly synchronized. (5) Riders sometimes lose their balance.

Exercise 24 Find It in Your Reading Look through a book by one of your favorite authors. How does the author vary his or her sentences?

Exercise 25 Find It in Your Writing Look through your portfolio for examples of long sentences. Rewrite them by using shorter, more direct sentences. Also, try to vary the sentence beginnings.

Exercise 26 Writing Application Write a short narrative describing the first time that you rode a bicycle. Include short and long sentences, and invert some sentences to provide more interest.

Section Review

Each of these exercises correlates to one of the concepts in the section on varying sentences, pages 500–502. The exercises may be used for more practice, for reteaching, or for review of the Key Concepts presented.

Answer Key

Exercise 21

Answers will vary. Samples are given.

1. Mountain biker Steve Larsen excelled because of his discipline, professionalism, and commitment.
2. Steve is a national champion, a member of the World Championship Team, and a hero in mountain-biking history.
3. Mechanical problems prevented Steve from winning many races. However, his determination and willpower encourage other bikers.
4. Unless you are an avid and knowledgeable mountain biker, many components of a bike will be foreign to you.
5. A lightweight protective biking helmet may be your most important piece of mountain biking equipment.

Exercise 22

1. Paola Pezzo was a gold medalist in the 1996 Olympics in Atlanta, Georgia.
2. By a significant margin was she victorious in the championship.
3. With a victory parade was she later honored by her countrymen.
4. With a win in the European mountain bike championship, she maintained her dominance.
5. Typically, Paola takes a four-hour bike ride early each morning as part of her training.

continued

Answer Key continued

Exercise 23

1. There in the store window is a tandem bicycle.
2. On a tandem bike, two riders sit one behind the other.
3. For best performance, the riders must keep pace with each other.
4. Staying perfectly synchronized is not easy.
5. Sometimes riders lose their balance.

Exercise 24

Find It in Your Reading
Students can read aloud short sections, and the class can discuss various writers' styles.

Exercise 25

Find It in Your Writing
Ask students whether the shorter sentences are an improvement, or if they liked the longer sentences better. Why?

Exercise 26

Writing Application
Have students read aloud some of their paragraphs and compare bike-riding experiences.

⏱ TIME SAVERS!

Answers on Transparency
Use the Grammar Exercises on Transparencies for Chapter 22 to have students correct their own or one another's exercises.

On-Line Exercise Bank
Have students complete the exercises on computer. The Auto Check feature will grade their work for you!

Eating the leaves at the top of a tree, she saw two giraffes.

Giraffes, zebras, and hippos.

Giraffes have long necks, they have the same number of neck bones as other animals.

Activate Prior Knowledge

Review the definition of a sentence with students. Remind them that a sentence must have a subject and a verb and it must express a complete thought. Any group of words that does not fit this definition is a fragment.

TEACH

Step-by-Step Teaching Guide

Recognizing Fragments

1. Challenge students to find the subject and verb in each fragment. They should realize that one or both elements is missing in each case, which is why these are fragments.

2. Write the following fragments and sentence on the chalkboard:

   After the concert. (F)

   She played beautifully.

   If Jamie doesn't get here soon. (F)

3. Have them identify the two fragments and then rewrite them as complete sentences.

Section 22.4

Avoiding Sentence Errors

Fragments, run-on sentences, and misplaced modifiers can all confuse your readers. Being aware of these common writing problems can help you avoid them.

Recognizing Fragments

Some groups of words, even though they have a capital letter at the beginning and a period at the end, are not complete sentences. They are *fragments.*

▶ **KEY CONCEPT** A **fragment** is a group of words that does not express a complete thought but is punctuated as if it were a sentence. ■

FRAGMENTS

In the early evening.
Felt happy and relaxed.
The sign in the rehearsal hall.
The violinist performing the concerto.
When she first touched the drums.

Reading the words aloud can often help you tell if a group of words expresses a complete thought. In the following chart, words have been added to the preceding fragments to make complete sentences. Read each italicized fragment; then, read the complete sentence. Can you hear the difference?

COMPLETED SENTENCES

The opera began *in the early evening.*
I *felt happy and relaxed.*
The sign in the rehearsal hall indicated the audition results.
The violinist was *performing the concerto.*
When she first touched the drums, her family wondered why they had consented to let her play.

Each of the preceding examples needed one or more new parts. The first needed both a subject and a verb. The second needed only a subject. The third became complete when a verb and complement were added. The fourth became complete when a helping verb was added. The final example needed an independent clause to go with the subordinate clause.

Theme: Musical Instruments

In this section, you will learn to recognize and correct certain types of sentence errors. The examples and exercises are about different types of musical instruments.

Cross-Curricular Connection: Music

⏱ TIME AND RESOURCE MANAGER

Resources
Print: Grammar Exercises Workbook, pp. 101–112; Hands-on Grammar Activity Book, Chapter 22
Technology: Language Lab CD-ROM, Sentence Errors; On-Line Exercise Bank, Section 22.4

In-Depth Coverage	Accelerated Pace
• Work through all key concepts, pp. 504–515. • Assign and review Exercises 27–34. • Read and discuss Grammar in Literature, p. 512. • Do the Hands-on Grammar activity, p. 516.	• Assign pp. 504–575 for independent student review. • Assign Review Exercises 35–37.

Exercise 27 Recognizing Sentence Fragments Write *F* if an item below is a fragment and *S* if it is a complete sentence.

EXAMPLE: Musicians sounding their instruments.

ANSWER: F

1. An array of finely tuned instruments.
2. Will play any instrument in the band.
3. In the concert hall on the stage.
4. Stringed, woodwind, brass, and percussion instruments.
5. That's loud.
6. Wanting to play the harp.
7. To play the violin takes many years of practice.
8. Performers playing electronic instruments such as synthesizers or electric guitars.
9. Achieved popularity in the 1970's and 1980's.
10. After you finish reading, I will practice the cello.

Correcting Phrase Fragments

A phrase by itself is a fragment. It cannot stand alone because it does not have a subject and verb.

KEY CONCEPT A phrase should not be capitalized or punctuated as if it were a sentence. ■

Three types of phrases—prepositional, participial, and infinitive—are often mistaken for sentences. A *phrase fragment* can be changed into a sentence in either of two ways. The first way is to try adding the fragment to a nearby sentence.

FRAGMENT:	The orchestra began rehearsing. *At 8:00 in the morning.*
ADDED TO NEARBY SENTENCE:	The orchestra began rehearsing *at 8:00 in the morning.*

In the next example, the participial phrase fragment can easily be corrected by attaching it to the beginning of the sentence that follows it.

FRAGMENT:	*Arriving at the airport.* The members of the choir were exhausted from the long flight.
ADDED TO NEARBY SENTENCE:	Arriving at the airport, the members of the choir were exhausted from the long flight.

Sometimes, however, you may not be able to correct a phrase fragment by adding it to a nearby sentence. In this case, you will need to correct the fragment by adding to the phrase whatever is needed to make it a complete sentence. Often, this method requires adding a subject and a verb.

Avoiding Sentence Errors • 505

> **More Practice**
> Language Lab
> CD-ROM
> • Effective Sentences lesson
> **On-line**
> **Exercise Bank**
> • Section 22.4
> **Grammar Exercise**
> **Workbook**
> • pp. 101–102

Step-by-Step Teaching Guide

Correcting Phrase Fragments

Remind students that all phrases are fragments. This is because they do not have subjects and verbs. Phrases add details to sentences. They often function as adverbs and adjectives, describing the subject or the verb of the sentence.

⏱ **TIME SAVERS!**

🎞 **Answers on Transparency**
Use the Grammar Exercises on Transparencies for Chapter 22 to have students correct their own or one another's exercises.

💻 **On-Line Exercise Bank**
Have students complete the exercises on computer. The Auto Check feature will grade their work for you!

Answers will vary. Samples are given.

1. Flutes, oboes, clarinets, and saxophones are included in the woodwind section of the band.
2. Chris got interested in percussion by hearing someone playing the ocarina.
3. After hearing the harmonica, the dog howled.
4. Pressing the keys of the clarinet in certain combinations is called fingering.
5. It's easy to break the reed of an oboe, so be careful.
6. Get advice from your teacher before buying a flute.
7. Miguel is trying to learn how to play the oboe.
8. Being more difficult to play than the bassoon, the contrabassoon isn't too popular.
9. Dave plays the saxophone in the jazz band.
10. Tom wants our band to include the bagpipes since that's his instrument.

Exercise 29

Answers will vary. Samples are given.

After practicing in my garage for nearly four months, our band was ready to make its public debut. We entered a "battle of the bands" competition at the high school. We were the third band to perform, following two well-known groups. From our place backstage, we listened to the loud applause the first two groups received, which just added to our nervousness. Walking on stage, I tripped over one of our amps and caused the electricity to short out. We didn't win, but we did make a lasting impression on the audience.

22.4

CHANGING PHRASE FRAGMENTS INTO SENTENCES

Phrase Fragments	Complete Sentence
Near the historic park.	The band played a tribute *near the historic park.*
Touching his hand.	*Touching his hand,* she asked for her father's advice.
To play well.	Sam learned *to play well.*

> **Exercise 28** Changing Phrase Fragments Into Sentences
Turn each phrase fragment into a sentence. You may use the phrase at the beginning, at the end, or in any other position in a sentence. Check to be sure that each of your sentences contains a subject and verb.

EXAMPLE: In the morning after breakfast.
ANSWER: Sheri practices in the morning after breakfast.

1. In the woodwind section of the band.
2. Playing the ocarina.
3. After hearing the harmonica.
4. Pressing the keys of the clarinet.
5. To break the reed.
6. Before buying a flute.
7. Trying to learn how to play the oboe.
8. Being more difficult to play than the bassoon.
9. Plays the saxophone in the jazz band.
10. To include the bagpipes.

> **Exercise 29** Revising to Correct Phrase Fragments
Rewrite the following paragraph, connecting phrase fragments to nearby sentences or adding needed sentence parts.

After practicing in my garage for nearly four months. Our band was ready to make its public debut. Entered a "battle of the bands" competition at the high school. We were the third band to perform. Following two well-known groups. From our place backstage. We listened to the loud applause the first two groups received. Just added to our nervousness. Walking on stage, I tripped over one of our amps and caused the electricity to short out. Didn't win but did make a lasting impression on the audience.

506 • Effective Sentences

> **More Practice**

Language Lab CD-ROM
• Effective Sentences lesson
On-line Exercise Bank
• Section 22.4
Grammar Exercise Workbook
• pp. 103–104

⏱ TIME SAVERS!

🗒 **Answers on Transparency**
Use the Grammar Exercises on Transparencies for Chapter 22 to have students correct their own or one another's exercise

🖥 **On-Line Exercise Bank**
Have students complete the exercises on computer. The Auto Check feature will grade their work for you!

✓ ONGOING ASSESSMENT SYSTEM: Prerequisite Skills

If students have difficulty with phrase and clause fragments, you may find it necessary to review the following to assure coverage of prerequisite knowledge.

In the Textbook	Print Resources	Technology
Phrases and Clauses, pp. 448–489	Grammar Exercise Workbook, pp. 101–104	On-Line Exercise Bank, Section 22.4

Correcting Clause Fragments

All clauses have subjects and verbs, but some cannot stand alone as sentences.

▶ **KEY CONCEPT** A subordinate clause should not be capitalized and punctuated as if it were a sentence. ■

Subordinate clauses do not express complete thoughts. Although a subordinate adjective or adverb clause has a subject and a verb, it cannot stand by itself as a sentence. (See Sections 19.2 and 21.2 for more information about subordinate clauses and the words they begin with.)

Like phrase fragments, *clause fragments* can usually be corrected in one of two ways: by attaching the fragment to a nearby sentence or by adding whatever words are needed to make the fragment into a sentence.

Notice how the following clause fragments are corrected by using the first method.

FRAGMENT:	The class enjoyed the lyrics. *That I recited to them as part of my oral report.*
ADDED TO NEARBY SENTENCE:	The class enjoyed the lyrics *that I recited to them as part of my oral report.*
FRAGMENT:	I'll play the piano. *As long as you play, too.*
ADDED TO NEARBY SENTENCE:	I'll play the piano *as long as you play, too.*

To change a clause fragment into a sentence by the second method, you must add an independent clause to the fragment.

CHANGING CLAUSE FRAGMENTS INTO SENTENCES

Clause Fragments	Complete Sentence
That you described.	I found the zither *that you described.*
	The zither *that you described* has been found.
When he knocked.	I opened the door *when he knocked.*
	When he knocked, I opened the door.

▲ **Critical Viewing**
Add three different independent clauses to the clause fragment "When I heard the drums beating" to create complete sentences. **[Connect]**

Avoiding Sentence Errors • 507

Correcting Clause Fragments

One way to correct a clause fragment is to drop the words that make it a subordinate clause. It then becomes an independent clause and can stand alone as a sentence.

Fragment	*Sentence*
That you sang.	*You sang.*
When he knocked.	*He knocked.*

Critical Viewing

Connect Students may suggest such sentences as *When I heard the drums beating, I jumped up and I grabbed Jana's hand, and we began to dance wildly.*

Customize for *Musical Learners*

Have students listen to any of the musical instruments described or mentioned in this section of the chapter, then write brief descriptions of the impression this instrument made on them. Remind students to avoid sentence fragments and run-on sentences.

Exercise 30

Answers will vary. Samples are given.

1. Before you go to the Caribbean, you should read about some of the islands.
2. You'll hear a lot of good music since steel drum bands are popular there.
3. These are the mallets that they use to strike the instruments.
4. You can join the band if you can play the tambourine.
5. Although the beat is steady, the tune is catchy.
6. Since he knows how to play the conga, he can teach the rest of us.
7. When the musician plays her solo, the audience falls silent.
8. We teased him because he had never heard of the guiro.
9. Since another drum was needed, we saved money to buy one.
10. After I heard the beat, I knew I loved calypso music.
11. Whenever I think of the Caribbean, I think of steel drum music.
12. We couldn't keep from dancing while the band was playing.
13. Our parents waited up until we returned from the concert.
14. No one like to dance as much as she does.
15. We plan to go to the band's next concert, provided tickets are available.

Critical Viewing

Compare Students may say that like some run-on sentences, songs played without interruption are not properly separated.

22.4

> **Exercise 30** Changing Clause Fragments Into Sentences

Turn each of the clause fragments into a sentence. Make sure that each sentence contains an independent clause.

EXAMPLE: That she wanted to use.

ANSWER: I lent her the drum set that she wanted to use.

1. Before you go to the Caribbean.
2. Since steel-drum bands are popular there.
3. That they use to strike the instruments.
4. If you can play the tambourine.
5. Although the beat is steady.
6. Since he knows how to play the conga.
7. When the musician plays her solo.
8. Because he had never heard of the guiro.
9. Since another drum was needed.
10. After I heard the beat.
11. Whenever I think of the Caribbean.
12. While the band was playing.
13. Until we returned from the concert.
14. As much as she does.
15. Provided that tickets are available.

▼ **Critical Viewing** Imagine that this band played song after song, without taking a break. In what ways would that be similar to a run-on sentence? **[Compare]**

508 • Effective Sentences

☑ **ONGOING ASSESSMENT: Monitor and Reinforce**

If students miss more than two items in Exercises 28–30, refer them to the following for additional practice.

In the Textbook	Print Resources	Technology
Section Review, Ex. 35, p. 517	Grammar Exercise Workbook, pp. 105–106	Language Lab CD-ROM, Sentence Errors; On-Line Exercise Bank, Section 22.4

Run-on Sentences

A fragment is an incomplete sentence. A *run-on* is two or more sentences that are punctuated as one.

▶ **KEY CONCEPT** A **run-on** is two or more complete sentences that are not properly joined or separated. ∎

Run-ons are usually the result of haste. Learn to check your sentences carefully to see where one sentence ends and the next one begins.

Two Kinds of Run-ons

There are two kinds of run-ons. One kind is made up of two or more sentences run together without any punctuation between them. This type of run-on is called a *fused sentence*. The other type of run-on consists of two or more sentences separated only by a comma (instead of a comma and a conjunction or a semicolon). This is called a *comma splice*.

RUN-ONS	
With No Punctuation	**With Only a Comma**
I use our library often the reference section is my favorite part.	The keyboard makes sound when the keys are depressed, the harpsichord, piano, and organ are keyboard instruments.

▶ **Exercise 31** Recognizing Run-ons On your paper, write *S* if an item is a sentence and *RO* if it is a run-on. Indicate whether each run-on is a *fused sentence* or a *comma splice*.

1. Percussion instruments produce sound when struck or shaken, some examples are drums, rattles, and bells.
2. The marimba is a percussion instrument with wooden bars arranged like the keys on a piano, mallets are used to strike the bars and produce sound.
3. If you are near a beach, you can collect driftwood to make your own marimba.
4. Gather several pieces of driftwood test each one for sound quality by striking it in the center.
5. To make the marimba, place the driftwood pieces in order by tone, then attach the pieces side by side over two long support pieces.

▶ **More Practice**

Language Lab CD-ROM
• Effective Sentences lesson

On-line Exercise Bank
• Section 22.4

Grammar Exercise Workbook
• pp. 105–106

Avoiding Sentence Errors • **509**

STANDARDIZED TEST PREPARATION WORKSHOP

Grammar and Usage Standardized tests often ask students to choose an incorrect item from a group. Ask students which of the following sentences is incorrect:

A Overnight, the snow had fallen, covering the town in a white blanket.

B Jerome listened to the radio, waiting for the magic words.

C "Schools are closed today!"

D He ran to the closet for his coat, hat, gloves, and boots, he got his sled too.

Item **D** is a run-on. All the other sentences are correct.

Using End Marks

Have volunteers read aloud the key concept statements on these two pages. Have students try different methods of correcting each example sentence and discuss the results. Explain that most run-on sentences can be corrected by any of the three methods shown.

Critical Viewing

Compare Students may say that rests and pauses help separate distinct musical motifs and passages, just as end marks help separate complete thoughts in writing.

Customize for
ESL Students

ESL students may not be sure about breaks between sentences. They may have difficulty identifying where one thought ends and another begins, or they may be confused about related punctuation rules. Have ESL students work with students who can identify run-ons. Have these students read examples on this page so that ESL students can listen for the natural break that signals the end of a sentence.

22.4

Three Ways to Correct Run-on Sentences

There are three easy ways to correct a run-on:

Using End Marks End marks are periods, question marks, and exclamation marks.

▶ **KEY CONCEPT** Use an end mark to separate a run-on into two sentences. ■

Properly used, an end mark splits a run-on into two shorter but complete sentences. Be sure to use an end mark that is appropriate to the function of the first sentence.

RUN-ON:	Though he began losing his hearing early in his career the composer Ludwig van Beethoven continued to write music he completed some of his most famous works after he was totally deaf.
CORRECTED SENTENCES:	Though he began losing his hearing early in his career, the composer Ludwig van Beethoven continued to write music. He completed some of his most famous works after he was totally deaf.
RUN-ON:	Have you heard of the kettledrum, I thought kettles were for the kitchen.
CORRECTED SENTENCES:	Have you heard of the kettledrum? I thought kettles were for the kitchen.

▼ Critical Viewing
How are rests and pauses in a musical composition like end marks that separate complete thoughts in writing? [Compare]

510 • Effective Sentences

☑ ONGOING ASSESSMENT: Assess Mastery

Use the following resources to assess student mastery of how to correct run-on sentences.

In the Textbook	Technology
Chapter Review, Ex. 45, p. 519 Standardized Test Preparation Workshop, pp. 520–521	On-Line Exercise Bank, Section 22.4

Using Commas and Coordinating Conjunctions

Sometimes, the two parts of a run-on are related and should stay in the same sentence. In that case, the run-on can be changed into a compound sentence.

KEY CONCEPT Use a comma and a coordinating conjunction to combine two independent clauses into a compound sentence. ■

The five coordinating conjunctions used most often are *and, but, or, for,* and *nor.* To separate the two clauses properly, it is necessary to use both a comma and a coordinating conjunction. A comma by itself is not enough.

RUN-ON: My mother and father practice the viola with the Cleveland Orchestra on Saturday, I stay home to practice the violin.

CORRECTED SENTENCE: My mother and father practice the viola with the Cleveland Orchestra on Saturday, and I stay home to practice the violin.

RUN-ON: I want to go to the symphony, I haven't any money.

CORRECTED SENTENCE: I want to go to the symphony, but I haven't any money.

Using Semicolons You can sometimes use a semicolon to punctuate the two parts of a run-on.

KEY CONCEPT Use a semicolon to connect two closely related ideas. ■

Do not overuse the semicolon. Remember, semicolons should be used only when the ideas in both parts of the sentence are closely related.

RUN-ON: The first performance begins at 6:30, the second show doesn't start until 9:15.

CORRECTED SENTENCE: The first performance begins at 6:30; the second show doesn't start until 9:15.

RUN-ON: The oboist sounded an A, the rest of the orchestra tuned their instruments to that note.

CORRECTED SENTENCE: The oboist sounded an A; the rest of the orchestra tuned their instruments to that note.

Step-by-Step Teaching Guide

Using Commas and Coordinating Conjunctions

1. Tell students that the comma indicates a pause between the two complete thoughts in a compound sentence.

2. Remind students to pay attention to the relationship between the two complete thoughts. This relationship will indicate the coordinating conjunction they should use to create the compound sentence.

Step-by-Step Teaching Guide

Using Semicolons

1. Students may be reluctant to use semicolons. They know that two sentences are separated by a period. Separating them with a semicolon seems incorrect. Also, they do not see semicolons frequently in their reading.

2. Urge students to be alert to semicolons in their reading and to pause and see how and why the semicolon works in those instances.

Grammar in Literature

1. Have a volunteer read aloud the excerpt from "Rules of the Game."

2. Point out that Tan varies her sentence length; she includes one short sentence and one very long one in this paragraph. Ask students to comment on Tan's style.

More About the Author

This excerpt is from a novel called *The Joy Luck Club,* in which Tan tells the stories of four Chinese women who came to the United States, and the stories of their four daughters, all torn between their Chinese heritage and the American culture around them. "Rules of the Game" is the story of Waverly, one of the daughters, who rebels against her mother's desire to make her a junior chess champion.

Answer Key

Exercise 32

Answers will vary. Samples are given.

1. Maracas are rattles with a round or oval shape. Centuries ago they were made from hollow gourds filled with seeds.

2. Ana spends hours playing the maracas in a band, so her wrists get tired from shaking the instruments.

3. The maracas are a common instrument in Latin American bands. Orchestras use them to add a Caribbean flavor to the music.

4. Ruben could hardly wait to play percussion in the *Jeremiah Symphony;* the maracas would be used as drumsticks.

5. Would you know which ancient instrument was found in Peru, and would you be able to play it?

6. If you know how to play the recorder, you can probably play the kena. They have similar mouthpieces and fingering, and they are both woodwind instruments.

7. Although the kena is now made of cane, in ancient times it was made from human or animal bones, clay, or hollowed-out gourds. Some were even made of silver or gold.

512

22.4

GRAMMAR IN
LITERATURE

from **Rules of the Game**
Amy Tan

In the following excerpt, the author has used a semicolon to join two clauses; without the semicolon, the sentence would be a run-on.

. . . My brother Winston chose wisely as well. His present turned out to be a box of intricate plastic parts; the instructions on the box proclaimed that when they were properly assembled he would have an authentic miniature replica of a World War II submarine.

▶ **Exercise 32** **Revising to Eliminate Run-on Sentences** On a separate sheet of paper, revise the sentences below to eliminate run-on sentences. Use any of the methods described in this section. Use each method at least two times in the exercise.

EXAMPLE: Play the maracas, they are easier than most instruments.

ANSWER: Play the maracas. They are easier than most instruments.

1. Maracas are rattles with a round or oval shape, centuries ago they were made from hollow gourds filled with seeds.
2. Ana spends hours playing the maracas in a band her wrists get tired from shaking the instruments.
3. The maracas are a common instrument in Latin American bands, they are used to add Caribbean flavor to the music.
4. Ruben could hardly wait to play percussion in the *Jeremiah Symphony* the maracas would be used as drumsticks.
5. Would you know which ancient instrument was found in Peru, would you be able to play it?
6. If you know how to play the recorder, you could probably play the kena they have similar mouthpieces and fingering they are both woodwind instruments.
7. Although the kena is now made of cane, in ancient times it was made from human or animal bones, clay, or hollowed-out gourds, some were even made of silver or gold.
8. Don't try to use the barimbau as a bow to play the violin, it is intended to be played as an instrument on its own.
9. A stick that taps the string produces the sound, a small wicker basket rattle, known as a caxixi, keeps the rhythm.
10. This instrument from Brazil has a hollowed-out gourd at the base of the bow it alters the pitch of the sound.

8. Don't try to use the barimbau as a bow to play the violin; it is intended to be played as an instrument on its own.
9. A stick that taps the string produces the sound. A small wicker basket rattle, known as a caxixi, is used to keep the rhythm.
10. This instrument from Brazil has a hollowed-out gourd at the base of the bow; it alters the pitch of the sound.

Misplaced Modifiers

A phrase or clause that acts as an adjective or adverb should be placed close to the word it modifies. Otherwise, the meaning of the sentence may be unclear.

▶ **KEY CONCEPT** A modifier should be placed as close as possible to the word it modifies in order to avoid confusion. ■

Recognize Misplaced Modifiers

A modifier placed too far away from the word it modifies is called a *misplaced modifier*. Because they are misplaced, such phrases and clauses seem to modify the wrong word in a sentence.

MISPLACED MODIFIER:	We rented a recorder from the music store *with an instruction booklet.*

The misplaced modifier is the phrase *with an instruction booklet*. In the sentence, it sounds as though this music store is the only one that has an instruction booklet. The sentence needs to be reworded slightly to place the modifier closer to *recorder*.

CORRECTED SENTENCE:	At the music store, we rented a recorder *with an instruction booklet.*

Below is a somewhat different type of misplaced modifier.

MISPLACED MODIFIER:	*Walking toward the house,* the tree on the lawn looked beautiful to Elizabeth.

In this sentence, *walking toward the house* should modify a person. Instead, it incorrectly modifies *tree*. The sentence needs to be rewritten to indicate who is actually doing the walking.

CORRECTED SENTENCE:	*Walking toward the house,* Elizabeth admired the beautiful tree on the lawn.

▲ **Critical Viewing**
What happens if you misplace your fingers while playing a recorder? What happens when you misplace a modifier in a sentence you have written? [**Speculate**]

Avoiding Sentence Errors • 513

Misplaced Modifiers

1. Readers usually assume that a modifier refers to the noun closest to it. Therefore, a modifier should usually be placed next to the noun it describes.

2. Ask students to tell why the modifiers on this page are misplaced. (It is the recorder, not the store, that has an instruction booklet. Elizabeth, not the tree, was walking.)

Critical Viewing

Speculate Students may say that misplacing your fingers while playing the recorder causes harsh or misplaced notes; sentences with misplaced modifiers are likewise jarring.

Real-World Connection

Misplaced modifiers can be found in newspaper and magazine headlines, often with humorous results.

Have students bring in any examples of misplaced modifiers they find. Ask them how they would correct each example.

1. MM
2. MM
3. MM
4. C
5. MM

Customize for
Less Advanced Students

Give students extra practice by having them rewrite sentences 1, 2, 3, and 5 in Exercise 33 to make them correct. Have partners go over the new sentences together and make sure they are correct.

Critical Viewing

Connect Students should say that the boy comes next.

Step-by-Step Teaching Guide

Revise Sentences with Misplaced Modifiers

1. Emphasize again that modifiers should always be placed as close as possible to the words they modify.
2. Students should always read a sentence, identify the word being modified, and then rearrange the sentence as needed to be sure that it is clear and correct.

22.4

▶ **Exercise 33** Recognizing Misplaced Modifiers Read each sentence carefully, and check the placement of the modifiers. If the sentence is correct, write *C* on your paper. If the sentence contains a misplaced modifier, write *MM*.

EXAMPLE: Vivaldi taught the violin after he discovered that he had a breathing disorder at a music seminary for young orphan girls.

ANSWER: MM

1. The violin is held between the shoulder and the chin, a small four-stringed instrument.
2. In its primitive form, pig bladders, tortoise shells, and wooden boxes were used to enhance the resonance of the violin.
3. Carved to imitate a tortoise shell, ancient forms of the violin include the lyre.
4. The zither, with a polygonal shaped drum, is another ancient form of the violin.
5. Playing the rote, the instrument was held against a person's left shoulder.

Revise Sentences With Misplaced Modifiers

Among the most common misplaced modifiers are prepositional phrases, participial phrases, and adjective clauses. All are corrected in the same way—by placing the modifier as close as possible to the word it modifies.

First, consider a misplaced prepositional phrase. This error usually occurs in a sentence with two or more prepositional phrases in a row.

MISPLACED: Lydia played the trombone in the band *with great enthusiasm*.

The misplaced modifier should be moved to make it clear that it modifies *played*.

CORRECTED: *With great enthusiasm*, Lydia played the trombone in the band.

A participial phrase is sometimes used at the beginning of a sentence. When such a phrase is used this way, it must be followed immediately by a word that it can logically modify.

▲ **Critical Viewing** In a sentence that begins *Holding the bow gently,* should the next words be *the boy* or *the violin* in order to avoid a misplaced modifier? **[Connect]**

▶ **KEY CONCEPT** When a participial phrase introduces a sentence, place the word it modifies directly after the introductory phrase. ■

MISPLACED: *Flying over the mountains*, the electrical storm endangered our plane.

It seems as if the storm is flying over the mountains. Rewrite the sentence to put the word *plane* next to the modifier.

CORRECTED: *Flying over the mountains*, our plane was endangered by an electrical storm.

An adjective clause should also go near the word it modifies. The clause below seems to modify *practicing*, not *piccolo*.

MISPLACED: I played the piccolo after several months of

practicing *that my grandfather gave me.*

CORRECTED: After several months of practicing, I played the

piccolo *that my grandfather gave me.*

▶ **Exercise 34** Revising Sentences to Eliminate Misplaced Modifiers On your paper, revise the following sentences. Eliminate the misplaced modifiers. In each rewritten sentence, underline the modifier that had been misplaced and draw an arrow from the modifier to the word it modifies.

1. The harp had already been purchased by someone else that Chelsea wanted.
2. Reaching the concert hall, Chelsea's harp was already on the stage.
3. Anyone could buy a harp at the auction without pedals.
4. Told to keep playing, the fingers and shoulders of the harpist ached.
5. He played the harp in the orchestra with great enthusiasm.
6. The angular harp was prevalent in Egypt, having a separate top that is attached to a resonator.
7. The five-foot-high harp is a part of the orchestra with a range of six-and-a-half octaves.
8. Wagner and Tchaikovsky used the pedal harp to add color to their orchestral pieces, who are renowned composers.
9. Hae Jin received a new harp from her dad with a pillar that gives better structure and a higher pitch.
10. Stretching from top to bottom, the harp has a strong frame within which there are strings.

▶ **More Practice**
Language Lab
CD-ROM
• Effective Sentences lesson
On-line
Exercise Bank
• Section 22.4
Grammar Exercise Workbook
• pp. 109–112

Answer Key

Exercise 34

Answers will vary. Samples are given.

1. The harp <u>that Chelsea wanted</u> had already been purchased by someone else. [arrow to *harp*]
2. Chelsea saw that her harp was already on stage <u>when she reached the concert hall</u>. [arrow to *saw*]
3. Anyone could buy a harp <u>without pedals</u> at the auction. [arrow to *harp*]
4. The fingers and shoulders of the harpist ached, but she <u>was told to keep playing</u>. [arrow to *she*]
5. <u>With great enthusiasm,</u> he played the harp in the orchestra. [arrow to *he*]
6. <u>With its separate top, attached to a resonator,</u> the angular harp was prevalent in Egypt. [arrow to *harp*]
7. <u>With a range of six-and-a-half octaves,</u> the five-foot-high harp is a part of the orchestra. [arrow to *harp*]
8. <u>Renowned composers</u> Wagner and Tchaikovsky used the pedal harp to add color to their orchestral pieces. [arrow to *Wagner, Tchaikovsky*]
9. The new harp that Hae Jin received from her dad has a <u>pillar that gives better structure and a higher pitch</u>. [arrow to *harp*]
10. The harp has a strong frame within which there are strings <u>stretching from top to bottom</u>. [arrow to *strings*]

☑ **ONGOING ASSESSMENT: Monitor and Reinforce**

If students miss more than two items in Exercises 32–33, refer them to the following for additional practice.

In the Textbook	Print Resources	Technology
Section Review, Ex. 37, p. 517	Grammar Exercise Workbook, pp. 109–112	Language Lab CD-ROM, Sentence Errors; On-Line Exercise Bank, Section 22.4

🕐 **TIME SAVERS!**

📽 **Answers on Transparency** Use the Grammar Exercises on Transparencies for Chapter 22 to have students correct their own or one another's exercises.

🖥 **On-Line Exercise Bank** Have students complete the exercises on computer. The Auto Check feature will grade their work for you!

515

Movable Modifiers

Teaching Resources: Hands-on Grammar Activity Book, Chapter 22

1. Have students refer to their Hands-on Grammar activity books or give them copies of relevant pages for this activity.
2. Review the directions for constructing the sentence strips.
3. Once students have worked through the activity, you may want to assign more modifier phrases and sentences to the class.

Find It in Your Reading

Have students list the sentences they find. Have them draw one line under each modifying phrase and two lines under each sentence that is modified.

Find It in Your Writing

You may want to divide the class into pairs and have students look for misplaced modifiers in each other's compositions. They should then work together to correct the sentences.

22.4

Hands-on Grammar

Movable Modifiers

Phrases used as modifiers can create confusion if they are misplaced in a sentence. To avoid confusion, place the phrase as close as possible to the word it modifies. To practice putting misplaced modifiers in their proper place in sentences, do the following activity.

Take several paper clips and pairs of self-sticking removable notes. You will also need several long, thin strips of paper on which to write sentences. Put each paper clip inside two notes, so that its clip side remains free (see the diagram below). Stick the notes together around the paper clip.

On one of the notes, write a phrase such as *filled with water and ice*. On one of the strips of paper, write a sentence such as: *A glass sat on the windowsill.* Attach the clipped phrase to the sentence strip. Slide the clip along the sentence until you have placed the phrase in its proper location. In this case, the phrase should go between the words *glass* and *sat*, so that the complete sentence reads: *A glass filled with water and ice sat on the windowsill.* What confusion might result if you placed the phrase after the word *windowsill*, instead?

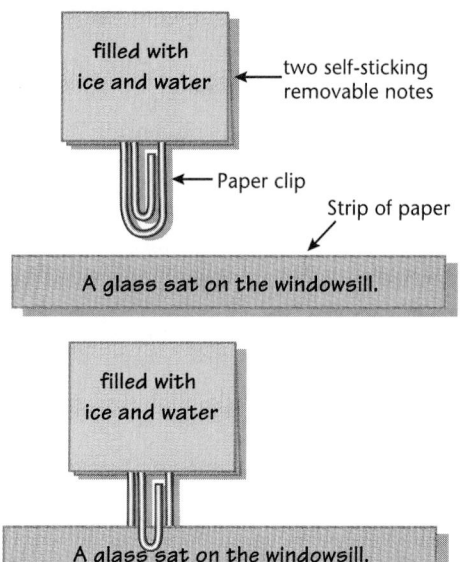

Write several more sentences and phrases of your own on the remaining strips of paper and pairs of removable notes, and test your friends. You can also use this activity to help correct the sentences in Exercise 34 on page 515.

Find It in Your Reading Select a paragraph from a story in your literature book that contains sentences with phrase modifiers. Discuss with a partner why the modifiers are correctly placed.

Find It in Your Writing Look for misplaced modifiers in your own compositions. Then, use this activity to determine the correct location for each modifier.

⏱ TIME SAVERS!

✋ **Hands-on Grammar**
Use the Hands-on Grammar Activity Sheet for Chapter 22 to facilitate this activity.

☑ ONGOING ASSESSMENT: Assess Mastery

Refer students to the following to assess their mastery of avoiding sentence errors.

In the Textbook	Technology
Chapter Review, Ex. 45, p. 519 Standardized Test Preparation Workshop, pp. 520–521	On-Line Exercise Bank, Section 22.4

Section 22.4 *Section Review*

GRAMMAR EXERCISES 35–40

> **Exercise 35** **Revising Fragments to Form Sentences** Change each of the following fragments into a sentence. Check to see that each of your sentences contains an independent clause.

1. Playing the piano.
2. To understand why there are three pedals.
3. Since it takes much practice.
4. Of ivory and ebony.
5. Called a pianoforte.

> **Exercise 36** **Revising to Eliminate Run-on Sentences** On your paper, revise each of the following sentences to eliminate run-ons.

1. Before the appearance of the lute, there was an instrument called an *oud*, it was brought to Spain by the Moors around 711.
2. Europeans changed the oud by adding more strings and frets, the oud evolved into the lute.
3. The lute was probably the most popular instrument during the Renaissance there is more music for the lute than for any other instrument.
4. The lute reached its golden age in the 1500's, lute composers and performers were popular and well paid.
5. By the 1800's, the lute was replaced by the guitar it is believed to have been invented by the people of Malaga.

> **Exercise 37** **Revising a Paragraph to Eliminate Sentence Errors** Revise the following paragraph, correcting any fragments, run-ons, or misplaced modifiers.

To make every piece of music distinct. Composers use the qualities of emotional expression, rhythm, harmony, and form, the combination of these qualities gives music its style. Through the nineteenth century, musical styles adopted the names of the era from which they came, these eras include Medieval, Renaissance, Baroque, Classical, Romantic, and Impressionist. Much of the music was cultivated by the Roman Catholic Church during the Middle Ages. To use in its worship services. Plain song was promoted by church leaders, which was also known as Gregorian Chant. The Renaissance period in music produced fuller and richer sounds, which lasted from about 1450 to 1600. Composers of the Romantic Era believed music should be imaginative, developing their own personal style.

> **Exercise 38** **Find It in Your Reading** In this sentence from "Rules of the Game," identify how the writer has avoided creating a run-on sentence.

I learned about opening moves and why it's important to control the center early on; the shortest distance between two points is straight down the middle.

> **Exercise 39** **Find It in Your Writing** Review the compositions in your writing portfolio to see if they contain fragments, run-ons, or misplaced modifiers. Rewrite the sentences, correcting, the errors.

> **Exercise 40** **Writing Application** Write a description of music or instruments you have seen or heard. Avoid fragments, run-ons, and misplaced modifiers in your description.

Section Review • 517

ASSESS and CLOSE

Section Review

Each of these exercises correlates to one of the concepts in the section on avoiding sentence errors, pages 504–515. The exercises may be used for more practice, for reteaching, or for review of the Key Concepts presented. Answers for all chapter exercises are available in *Grammar Exercises Answers on Transparencies* in your teaching resources.

Answer Key

> **Exercise 35**

Answers will vary. Samples are given.

1. I love playing the piano.
2. It's easy to understand why there are three pedals.
3. Since it takes much practice to learn, the piano can be called a difficult instrument.
4. The piano keys are made of ivory and ebony.
5. One early piano was called the pianoforte.

> **Exercise 36**

Answers will vary. Samples are given.

1. Before the appearance of the lute, there was an instrument called an *oud*. It was brought to Spain by the Moors around 711.
2. Europeans changed the oud by adding more strings and frets; eventually, the oud evolved into the lute.
3. The lute was probably the most popular instrument during the Renaissance; there is more music for the lute than for any other instrument.
4. The lute reached its golden age in the 1500's, and composers and performers were popular and well paid.
5. By the 1800's, the lute was replaced by the guitar. The guitar is believed to have been invented by the people of Malaga.

> **Exercise 37**

Sample rewrite: To make every piece of music distinct, composers use the qualities of emotional expression, rhythm, harmony, and form. The combination of these qualities gives music its style. Through the nineteenth century, musical styles

continued

Answer Key continued

adopted the names of the era from which they came. These eras include Medieval, Renaissance, Baroque, Classical, Romantic, and Impressionist. Much of the music was cultivated by the Roman Catholic Church from the Middle Ages to use in its worship services. Plain song, which was also known as Gregorian Chant, was promoted by church leaders. The Renaissance period in music, which lasted from about 1450 to 1600, produced fuller and richer sounds. Composers of the Romantic Era believed music should be imaginative, and they developed their own personal style.

> **Exercise 38**

Find It in Your Reading
The semicolon between the two parts of the sentence prevent it from being a run-on.

> **Exercise 39**

Find It in Your Writing
Students can explain to partners the reasons for their revisions.

> **Exercise 40**

Writing Application
Encourage students to read their descriptions aloud and play the music for the class.

CHAPTER REVIEW

Each of these exercises correlates to one of the concepts in the chapter on effective sentences, pages 490–517. The exercises may be used for more practice, for reteaching, or for review of the Key Concepts presented. Answers for all chapter exercises are available in *Grammar Exercises Answers on Transparencies* in your teaching resources.

Answer Key

Exercise 41

Sample sentences are given.

1. imperative; Have you ever heard the balalaika, a Central Asian lute?
2. interrogative; The body of the balalaika is triangular.
3. interrogative; How fascinating it is to play or hear a balalaika!
4. exclamatory; Don't you love the sound of the balalaika?
5. declarative; Be careful with the balalaika.

Exercise 42

Answers will vary. Samples are given.

1. The tabor is a drum that is played alone or played together with the pipe. compound verb
2. The pipe has a ridge around the bottom and a mouthpiece like the recorder. compound object
3. Pipes and drums are simple instruments. compound subject
4. The player must be very coordinated and have a sense of rhythm and melody. compound verb
5. The drum is carried by a strap over the shoulder and is struck with a mallet. compound verb

Exercise 43

Answers will vary. Samples are given.

1. The bagpipe, which traces its history to ancient times, was mentioned in the Bible.
2. Sheepherders easily made bagpipes from reed pipes and sheepskin or goatskin.
3. The Roman emperor Nero learned how to play the bagpipes.
4. Early bagpipes had a single drone; through the years, they acquired a second and then a third pipe.

Chapter 22 — Chapter Review

GRAMMAR EXERCISES 41–47

Exercise 41 **Identifying the Four Types of Sentences** Identify the type of each sentence. Then, change each sentence into the type indicated in italics.

1. Listen to the balalaika, a Central Asian lute. *interrogative*
2. Did you know that the body of the balalaika is triangular? *declarative*
3. A balalaika is how fascinating to play or hear? *exclamatory*
4. I love the balalaika's sound! *interrogative*
5. A balalaika is delicate, and it requires careful handling. *imperative*

Exercise 42 **Combining Sentences Using Compound Subjects, Verbs, and Objects** Combine each pair of sentences in the way that makes the most sense. Identify what you have done to combine them.

1. The tabor is a drum that is played alone. The tabor is played together with the pipe.
2. The pipe has a ridge around the bottom. The pipe has a mouthpiece like the recorder.
3. The pipe is a simple instrument. The drum is a simple instrument.
4. The player must be very coordinated. The player must have a sense of rhythm and melody.
5. The drum is carried by a strap over the shoulder. The drum is struck with a mallet.

Exercise 43 **Combining Short Sentences** Combine each pair of sentences. Use any of the methods you have learned in this chapter.

1. The bagpipe traces its history to ancient times. It was mentioned in the Bible.

518 • **Effective Sentences**

2. It was easy for sheepherders to make bagpipes. They used sheepskin or goatskin and a pipe of reed.
3. The bagpipes were brought to Rome. The Emperor Nero learned how to play them.
4. The bagpipes' sound began with a single drone. Through the years, it acquired a second and third pipe.
5. During the Renaissance, bagpipes grew in popularity. After the Renaissance, their popularity continued to grow.
6. Students learning to play the bagpipes should follow some preliminary steps. They can get started.
7. They should find a set of bagpipes, an instructor, and instruction materials. They know all of the resources available.
8. Students learn through books and tapes. They must remember that mistakes will go uncorrected.
9. Some universities and communities offer courses in bagpipe playing. The members of the community can learn.
10. Most important, a student should practice consistently. Practice makes perfect.
11. The crumhorn is a unique instrument of European origin. The word means "curved horn" in German.
12. The crumhorn is a double-reed instrument. It produces sound by the vibration of the reeds.
13. The fingering system of the crumhorn is similar to the fingering system of the clarinet. The clarinet is also a reed instrument.
14. A crumhorn can have a range of one octave or a few notes more. Its range depends on when it was constructed.
15. The curve of the crumhorn is only decorative. It has nothing to do with the quality of the sound.

---

5. The bagpipe, which was popular during the Renaissance, grew even more popular afterward.
6. Students can start learning to play the bagpipes by following some preliminary steps.
7. Students should find a set of bagpipes, instruction materials, and an instructor; they should know all of the resources available.
8. Students who learn through books and tapes must remember that mistakes will go uncorrected.
9. Some universities and communities offer members of the community courses in bagpipe playing.
10. Most important, a student should practice consistently; practice makes perfect.
11. The crumhorn, which means "curved horn" in German, is a unique instrument of European origin.
12. The vibration of the double reed produces the crumhorn's sound.
13. The fingering system of the crumhorn is similar to that of the clarinet, another reed instrument.
14. The octave-plus range of the crumhorn varies according to when it was made.
15. The decorative curve of the crumhorn has nothing to do with the quality of the instrument's sound.

Exercise 44 **Varying Sentence Length and Beginnings** Rewrite each sentence. Break the sentence into two sentences, rewrite it in a simpler, more direct way, or vary the beginning of the sentence.

1. Archaeologists have made many fascinating discoveries in caves of ancient people, and one fascinating finding is a flute that is thousands of years old.
2. The oldest musical instrument ever unearthed is a flute, and it shows evidence of being played with four notes that match the first four notes of the modern scale.
3. The flute is actually a bone segment from a prehistoric animal, and was found inside a cave by Dr. Ivan Turk of the Slovenian Academy of Sciences.
4. The alignment of the holes on the instrument of bone indicates that it is a flute that produces whole- and half-tone scales which are the basis of a seven-note scale.
5. Ancient humans could obviously appreciate the merits and beauty of music, as this flute shows.

Exercise 45 **Revising to Eliminate Sentence Errors** Label each item *fragment*, *run-on*, or *misplaced modifier*. Then, rewrite it correctly.

1. The Renaissance awakened the senses, the resulting music of the Renaissance is smooth and expressive.
2. Through their music and playing, a universal search for truth and knowledge was conducted by Renaissance musicians.
3. Present-day major and minor scales are a characteristic of the Baroque style with their accompanying melodic and harmonic sounds.
4. The Baroque Era of ornamental music was followed by the Classical Era. Which featured established standards of form and complexity.

5. Romantic music stressed the importance of emotional expression over structure this idea created a musical style that is exotic and expressive.

Exercise 46 **Revision Practice: Writing Effective Sentences** Rewrite the following paragraph, combining sentences or revising sentences as needed. Correct all errors in sentence structure.

In the old Irish and Scottish kingdoms, the harp was an aristocratic instrument reserved for the courts only kings and chiefs had the privilege of hearing its music. Modern harps use gut or nylon strings. The Gaelic harp used bronze wire. The harpist played the harp. He could cause the listeners to weep in sorrow or beam with joy. Depending on the song that he interpreted. It was not uncommon for the king to sleep through a performance, this behavior was often induced by the harp. Creates a relaxing and meditative atmosphere. This beautifully carved, triangular instrument was popular entertainment which did not originally have pedals. Images of a harp are depicted on tablets from Mesopotamia with three strings. There is a statue of a musician holding an angled harp in the British Museum in London made of wood. On the wall of a tomb at Thebes. There is a depiction of a musician holding a harp. Although harpists would like to believe that King David played the harp, there are indications that he played the lyre in portraits.

Exercise 47 **Writing Application** Invent an imaginary musical instrument. Write a description of your instrument. Include how it is played and when it is used. Combine some simple sentences, and vary your sentence beginnings. Proofread carefully to be sure you have no fragments, run-ons, or misplaced modifiers.

Exercise 44

Answers will vary. Samples are given.

1. One fascinating discovery made by archaeologists is a flute thousands of years old.
2. The oldest musical instrument ever found is a flute. It could apparently play the first four notes of the modern scale.
3. The flute is made of a bone from a prehistoric animal. Slovenian scientist Dr. Ivan Turk found it inside a cave.
4. The holes on the bone flute show that it can produce whole- and half-tone scales, which are the basis of a seven-note scale.
5. Obviously, ancient humans could appreciate the merits and beauty of music.

Exercise 45

1. run-on; The Renaissance awakened the senses; the resulting music is smooth and expressive.
2. misplaced modifier; Through their music and playing, Renaissance musicians conducted a universal search for truth and knowledge.
3. misplaced modifier; Present-day major and minor scales, with their accompanying melodic and harmonic sounds, are a characteristic of the Baroque style.
4. fragment; The Baroque era of ornamental music was followed by the Classical era, which featured established standards of form and complexity.
5. run-on; Romantic music stressed the importance of emotional expression over structure. This idea created a musical style that is exotic and expressive.

continued

Answer Key continued

Exercise 46

Sample rewrite: In the old Irish and Scottish kingdoms, the harp was an instrument reserved for the royal courts. Only kings and chiefs had the privilege of hearing its music. While the Gaelic harp used bronze wire, modern harps use gut or nylon strings. The playing of the harpist could cause listeners to weep in sorrow or beam with joy, depending on the song that he interpreted. Because the harp creates a relaxing and meditative atmosphere, it was not uncommon for the king to sleep through a performance. Originally, this popular, beautifully carved, triangular instrument did not have pedals. Images of a harp with three strings are depicted on tablets from Mesopotamia. In the British Museum, there is a wooden statue of a musician holding an angled harp. On the wall of a tomb at Thebes, there is a depiction of a musician holding a harp. Although harpists would like to believe that King David played the harp, portraits indicate that he played the lyre.

Exercise 47

Writing Application
Students may want to include a drawing of their instrument.

⏱ TIME SAVERS!

📺 Answers on Transparency Use the Grammar Exercises on Transparencies for Chapter 22 to have students correct their own or one another's exercises.

💻 On-Line Exercise Bank Have students complete the exercises on computer. The Auto Check feature will grade their work for you!

Revising and Editing Sentences

1. Explain to students that they should read the passage carefully and note each idea that it expresses. This will help them be sure that their edited version includes all important information.

2. In the sample passage, the ideas expressed are *too early for Patrick to get out of bed* and *crack of dawn*. The only choice that expresses both of these ideas is **A**.

Standardized Test Preparation Workshop

Revising and Editing Sentences

Whether writing an e-mail or an essay for a test, using sentences correctly and effectively is critical to creating logical, clear communication. Because this skill is so important, standardized tests often evaluate your ability to write effectively. When choosing the most effective sentence from the list of answer choices, use the following strategies:

- Avoid choosing run-on sentences in which two or more complete sentences are written as a single sentence.

- Identify and avoid any sentence fragments in your choices. Fragments do not express a complete thought.

- Determine whether you can combine several short sentences into one longer one.

- Make sure your choice presents all of the important information without changing the meaning of the original.

Test Tip

Read each answer silently to yourself to help you pick out fragments or run-ons. Then, choose the sentence that is correct and that will best fit the passage.

Sample Test Item	Answer and Explanation
Carla has written a short story for English class. You have been asked to read the story and think about suggestions for improving it. When you finish reading this passage, answer the multiple-choice question that follows. 1 It was too early in the morning for 2 Patrick to get out of bed. It was the crack 3 of dawn.	

1 What is the BEST way to combine the sentences in lines 1–3? (*"It . . . dawn."*)
 	
  A It was the crack of dawn, which was too early for Patrick to get out of bed.
 	
  B It was the crack of dawn, and Patrick got out of bed early.
 	
  C Patrick got out of bed at dawn.
 	
  D At the crack of dawn, early in the morning, Patrick got out of bed.
	The correct answer is *A*. Choice *A* correctly combines the important elements of both sentences to form one complete sentence.

520 • Effective Sentences

✎ TEST-TAKING TIP

When dealing with questions that test their ability to revise and edit sentences, students should carefully compare their edited sentences with the original sentences to be sure the information they have included is accurate and complete. Students may want to highlight key words and phrases in each choice.

Practice 1 *Desirée has written an essay for English class and has asked you to review it for her. When you finish reading the passage below, answer the multiple-choice questions that follow.*

1 The young bird would leave the nest soon.
2 I waited for that moment eagerly. The bird
3 was gray. The brisk wind was wintry.
4 Colder than an underground cave at
5 night. "How can a little bird be so
6 determined?" I asked myself this question.
7 "When it is so cold?"

1 What is the BEST way to combine the sentences in lines 1–3? (*"The . . . gray."*)

A It would be an eager moment when the young bird would leave the nest.

B I eagerly awaited the moment when the young, gray bird would leave the nest.

C I waited eagerly for that moment as the young bird left its nest.

D The young, gray bird waited eagerly to leave the nest.

2 What is the BEST way to rewrite the sentences in lines 3–4? (*"The . . night."*)

A The brisk, wintry wind made it feel like an underground cave.

B At night the brisk wind was like winter. Colder than an underground cave.

C The wintry wind was colder than an underground cave at night.

D The wintry wind blew cold. Like an underground cave at night.

3 What is the BEST way to combine the sentences in lines 5–7? (*"How . . . cold?"*)

A "How can a little bird be so determined?" I asked myself coldly.

B I asked myself this question: "How can a little, cold bird be so determined?"

C "How can a little bird be so determined when it is so cold?" I asked myself.

D "How cold is the determined little bird?" I asked myself.

Practice 2 *Daniel has written a report for a social studies course. You have been asked to review it. When you finish reading the passage below, answer the multiple-choice questions that follow.*

1 Photographing wildlife isn't as romantic
2 as it sounds. Especially when the climate
3 is hot and humid. Like in parts of Africa
4 or South America. A wildlife photographer
5 is also exposed to poisonous plants. Of
6 all sorts. Some are plants that will leave
7 him or her itching for days.

1 What is the BEST way to rewrite the sentences in lines 1–4? (*"Photographing . . . America."*)

A Photographing wildlife isn't as romantic as it sounds, especially in a hot, humid climate, like that in parts of Africa or South America.

B In certain parts of Africa or South America, photographing wildlife isn't as romantic as it sounds. Especially when the climate is hot and humid.

C Photographing wildlife isn't as romantic as it sounds in humid parts of Africa or South America.

D Photographing wildlife in parts of Africa and South America can be romantic even though the climate is hot and humid.

2 What is the BEST way to combine the sentences in lines 4–7? (*"A . . . days."*)

A Poisonous plants of all sorts can leave a wildlife photographer itching that he or she is exposed to for days.

B A wildlife photographer is exposed to all sorts of poisonous plants, some of which will leave him or her itching for days.

C Poisonous plants will leave a wildlife photographer itching for days.

D A wildlife photographer is exposed to all sorts of poisonous plants, some will leave him or her itching.

Answer Key

Practice 1
1. B
2. C
3. C

Practice 2
1. A
2. B

CUMULATIVE REVIEW

Answer Key

Exercise A

1. Russia's <u>throne</u> <u>passed</u> to Nicholas I after the Decembrist revolt.
2. A <u>monarchy</u> or a <u>republic</u> <u>was</u> the hope of the officers behind the revolt.
3. <u>Nicholas</u> <u>suppressed</u> the revolt, but the <u>unrest</u> <u>increased</u>.
4. There <u>was</u> a secret police <u>organization</u>.
5. <u>Did</u> <u>it</u> <u>enforce</u> censorship of all publications?

Exercise B

1. obedient—predicate adjective
2. schoolbooks—direct object; materials—objective complement
3. people—indirect object; ideas—direct object
4. threat—predicate nominative
5. one—predicate nominative

Exercise C

Answers will vary. Samples are given.

1. <u>Nicholas</u> <u>sought</u> to expand his empire and <u>looked</u> south, southwest and east.
2. The <u>Caucasus</u> and <u>Central</u> <u>Asia</u> <u>were</u> (two) of Nicholas's targets.
3. A <u>war</u> with Ivan <u>ended</u> in 1828 and <u>Russia</u> <u>acquired</u> part of Armenia and the city of Yerevan.
4. A Russian naval <u>fleet</u> <u>joined</u> British vessels and French ships to battle the Turkish fleet.
5. The <u>Treaty of Adrianople</u> <u>granted</u> Nicholas power over the Caucasus and a protectorate Moldavia and Walachia.
6. <u>Did</u> <u>this</u> <u>end</u> the Pusso-Turkish war?
7. In 1830 in Poland <u>began</u> a major <u>revolt</u> against Russia.
8. <u>Great Britain</u>, <u>France</u>, <u>Prussia</u>, and <u>Austria</u> <u>considered</u> Russia's growing power a threat.
9. In 1833, Russian <u>troops</u> <u>entered</u> Turkey and <u>planned</u> to capture Constantinople.
10. Soon after, <u>Russia</u> <u>fought</u> the Crimean War and <u>was</u> (defeated).

Cumulative Review

USAGE

Exercise A **Recognizing Subjects and Predicates** Copy the following sentences, underlining each simple subject once and each simple predicate twice.

1. Russia's throne passed to Nicholas I after the Decembrist revolt.
2. A monarchy or a republic was the hope of the officers behind the revolt.
3. Nicholas suppressed the revolt, but the unrest increased.
4. There was a secret police organization.
5. Did it enforce censorship of all publications?

Exercise B **Recognizing Complements** Write the complements in the sentences below and label each *direct object, indirect object, objective complement, predicate nominative,* or *predicate adjective.*

1. The new police forces were obedient to the wishes of the emperor.
2. Nicholas considered schoolbooks dangerous materials.
3. In his mind, education gave the people revolutionary ideas.
4. University professors were a threat to the security of his throne.
5. Fyodor Dostoyevsky was one of many writers arrested.

Exercise C **Revising Sentences** Rewrite the following sentences according to the directions in parentheses. In your new sentences, underline each simple subject once and each simple predicate twice. Circle each subject complement.

1. Nicholas sought to expand his empire. He looked south, southwest, and east. (combine by creating a compound predicate)

2. The Causasus area was one of Nicholas's targets. He also wanted to expand to Central Asia. (combine by creating a compound subject)
3. A war with Iran ended in 1828. Russia acquired part of Armenia and the city of Yerevan. (combine by creating a compound sentence)
4. A Russian naval fleet joined British vessels to battle the Turkish fleet. French ships also fought the Turks. (combine by creating a compound direct object)
5. With the Treaty of Adrianople, Nicholas received power over the Caucasus. The treaty also granted a protectorate over Moldavia and Walachia. (combine by creating an indirect object and a compound direct object)
6. This ended the Russo-Turkish War. (rewrite by creating an interrogative)
7. In 1830 in Poland, a major revolt against Russia began. (rewrite by inverting subject-verb order)
8. Europe considered Russia's growing power a threat. These European countries included Great Britain, France, Prussia, and Austria. (rewrite with a compound subject, a direct object, and an objective complement)
9. In 1833, Russian troops entered Turkey. They planned to capture Constantinople. (rewrite with a compound verb)
10. Soon after, Russia fought the Crimean War. Russia was defeated. (combine with a compound verb)

Exercise D **Identifying Phrases** Label each phrase in the following sentences *prepositional phrase, appositive phrase, participial phrase, gerund phrase,* or *infinitive phrase.*

1. Alexander II, son of Nicholas I and

nephew of Alexander I, assumed the throne in 1855.
2. Signing the Treaty of Paris gave Russia peace in 1856.
3. Although he initiated great judicial reforms, Alexander II declined to establish a constitution.
4. Revolutionary movements increased, adopting a variety of policies and goals.
5. In 1881, one revolutionary group, the Narodnaya Volya, throwing a bomb into his carriage, assassinated Alexander II.

Exercise E Identifying Clauses

Label each clause in the following sentences *adjective clause, adverb clause,* or *noun clause.*

1. Alexander III, who was reacting to his father's assassination, ended most of the liberal reforms.
2. He tried to impose the Russian language on whoever was a racial minority.
3. Different minorities were forced to live in specific areas, where they were assigned to professions.
4. Unless they accepted these "Russification" programs, many were sternly repressed.
5. In reaction, revolutionary propaganda spread among factory workers who supported Marxist theories.

Exercise F Revising Sentences

With Phrases and Clauses Rewrite the following sentences according to the instructions in parentheses. Underline the required structure. Then, label the structure of your new sentence *simple, complex, compound,* or *compound-complex.*

1. In 1894, Nicholas II married Alexandra. She was born a German princess with the name Alix of Hesse-Darmstadt. (combine by creating an appositive phrase)

2. Alexandra had four daughters and one son. The son, Alexis, suffered from hemophilia. (combine by creating a sentence with a adjective clause)
3. Nicholas and Alexandra made many attempts to cure Alexis. This made them open to many doctors and religious fanatics. (combine by creating a gerund phrase)
4. A Siberian monk, Grigory Yefimovich Rasputin, seemed to help Alexis. They were open to his attempts and advice. (combine by creating a noun clause)
5. Rasputin himself appointed many of the government's officials. That was because Nicholas and Alexandra trusted and relied on him. (combine by creating an adverb clause)
6. The royal family's association with Rasputin roused suspicion. The monarchy was alienated from the Russian people. (combine by creating a participial phrase)
7. Rasputin was murdered in 1916 by a group of aristocrats. This was an attempt to stem the revolutionary tide. (combine by creating an infinitive phrase)
8. There had already been a revolution. That was 1905. (combine by creating a prepositional phrase)
9. A revolutionary priest led the people. His name was Georgy Apollonovich Gapon. They marched to the Winter Palace with their demands. (combine by creating an appositive phrase)
10. The people were fired on. This day became known as Bloody Sunday. Strikes and riots began throughout Russia. (combine by creating an adjective clause and an adverb clause)

Exercise G Writing Application

Write a short description of a historical figure or family that you have learned about. Underline each simple subject once and each simple verb twice. Then, circle at least three phrases and three clauses.

Cumulative Review • 523

Answer Key continued

Exercise G

Writing Application
If students cannot find at least three phrases and three clauses in their descriptions, have them revise their work to include more examples.

Exercise D
1. son of Nicholas I and nephew of Alexander I—appositive phrase; in 1855—prepositional phrase
2. Signing the Treaty of Paris—gerund phrase; in 1856—prepositional phrase
3. to establish a constitution—infinitive phrase
4. adopting a variety of policies and goals—participial phrase
5. In 1881—prepositional phrase; The Naroduaya Voiza—appositive phrase; Throwing a bomb—participial phrase; into his carriage—prepositional phrase

Exercise E
1. adjective clause
2. noun clause
3. adverb clause
4. adverb clause
5. adjective clause

Exercise F
Answers will vary. Samples are given.

1. In 1894, Nicholas married Alexandra, <u>a German princess born with the name Alix of Hesse-Darmstadt</u>. (complex)
2. Alexandra had four daughters and one son, Alex, <u>who suffered from hemophilia</u>. (complex)
3. <u>Their making many attempts to cure Alexis</u> made Nicholas and Alexandra open to many doctors and religious fanatics. (complex)
4. They thought <u>that the attempts and advice of a Siberian monk, Grigory Vefimovich Raspatin, seemed to help Alexis</u>. (complex)
5. Rasputin himself appointed many of the government officials <u>as Nicholas and Alexandra trusted and relied on him</u>. (complex)
6. The royal family's association with Rasputin roused suspicion, <u>alienating them from the Russian people</u>. (simple)
7. Rasputin was murdered in 1916 by a group of aristocrats <u>to stem the revolutionary tide</u>. (simple)
8. There had already been a revolution <u>in 1905</u>. (simple)
9. A revolutionary priest, <u>Georgy Apollonovich Gapon</u>, led the people who marched to the Winter Palace with their demands. (complex)
10. <u>After people were fired on</u>, this day became known as Bloody Sunday, <u>during which strikes and riots began throughout Russia</u>. (complex)

continued

523

Time and Resource Manager

In-Depth Lesson Plan

	LESSON FOCUS	PRINT AND MEDIA RESOURCES
DAY 1	**Verb Tenses and Principal Parts of Verbs** Students learn and apply the concepts of verb tense and the principal parts of regular and irregular verbs (pp. 524–532).	**Teaching Resources** *Grammar Exercise Workbook,* pp. 113–116; *Grammar Exercises Answers on Transparencies,* Chapter 23; *Language Lab* **CD-ROM,** Using Verbs; *On-Line Exercise Bank,* Section 23.1
DAY 2	**Conjugating Tenses** Students learn and apply the concepts of conjugating tenses (pp. 533–539).	**Teaching Resources** *Grammar Exercise Workbook,* pp. 117–126; *Grammar Exercises Answers on Transparencies,* Chapter 23; *Language Lab* **CD-ROM,** Using Verbs; *On-Line Exercise Bank,* Section 23.1
DAY 3	**Active and Passive Voice** Students learn and apply the concepts of active and passive voice and do the Hands-on Grammar activity (pp. 540–545).	**Teaching Resources** *Grammar Exercise Workbook,* pp. 127–130; *Grammar Exercises Answers on Transparencies,* Chapter 23; *Hands-on Grammar Activity Book,* Chapter 23; *Language Lab* **CD-ROM,** Using Verbs; *On-Line Exercise Bank,* Section 23.2
DAY 4	**Review and Assess** Students review chapter and demonstrate mastery of using verbs (pp. 546–549).	**Teaching Resources** *Formal Assessment,* Ch. 23; *Grammar Exercises Answers on Transparencies,* Chapter 23; *Language Lab* **CD-ROM,** Using Verbs; *On-Line Exercise Bank,* Section 23.1

Accelerated Lesson Plan

	LESSON FOCUS	PRINT AND MEDIA RESOURCES
DAY 1	**Verb Tenses and Parts** Students cover concepts and usage of verb tenses, principal parts, and regular and irregular verbs as determined by Diagnostic Test (pp. 526–532).	**Teaching Resources** *Grammar Exercise Workbook,* pp. 113–126; *Grammar Exercises Answers on Transparencies,* Chapter 23; *Language Lab* **CD-ROM,** Using Verbs; *On-Line Exercise Bank,* Section 23.1
DAY 2	**Verb Conjugation and Voice** Students cover concepts and usage of verb conjugation and active and passive voice as determined by Diagnostic Test (pp. 533–545).	**Teaching Resources** *Grammar Exercise Workbook,* pp. 113–130; *Grammar Exercises Answers on Transparencies,* Chapter 23; *Hands-on Grammar Activity Book,* Chapter 23; *Language Lab* **CD-ROM,** Using Verbs; *On-Line Exercise Bank,* Section 23.1–2
DAY 3	**Review and Assess** Students review chapter and demonstrate mastery of using verbs (pp. 546–549).	**Teaching Resources** *Formal Assessment,* Ch. 23; *Grammar Exercises Answers on Transparencies,* Chapter 23; *Language Lab* **CD-ROM,** Using Verbs; *On-Line Exercise Bank,* Section 23.1

Options for Adapting Lesson Plans

HOMEWORK

Have students complete any section of the chapter for homework.

FEATURES

Extend coverage with the Grammar in Literature feature (pp. 527, 542) and the Standardized Test Preparation Workshop (p. 548).

TECHNOLOGY

Students can use the On-Line Exercise Bank to complete the exercises on computer. The Auto Check feature will grade their work.

INTEGRATED SKILLS COVERAGE

Grammar in Literature
SE pp. 527, 542

Reading
Find It in Your Reading SE pp. 539, 544, 545

Writing
Find It in Your Writing SE pp. 539, 544, 545
Writing Application SE pp. 539, 545, 547

Language
Language Highlight ATE 531, 536

Vocabulary
Integrating Vocabulary Skills ATE 534

Viewing and Representing
Critical Viewing SE pp. 524, 527, 528, 530, 535, 537, 541, 543

ASSESSMENT SUPPORT

Standardized Test Preparation SE p. 548; ATE pp. 531, 536
Standardized Test Preparation Workbook, pp. 45–46
Formal Assessment, Ch. 23

MEETING INDIVIDUAL NEEDS

Less Advanced Students ATE p. 530; See also Ongoing Assessments ATE pp. 524, 529, 532, 533, 535, 537, 542, 544
ESL Students ATE pp. 527, 530, 532
More Advanced Students ATE pp. 531, 532
Verbal/Linguistic Learners ATE p. 531
Visual/Spatial Learners ATE p. 534

BLOCK SCHEDULING

Pacing Suggestions
For 90-minute Blocks
• Administer the Diagnostic Test to students to determine instructional coverage.
• Have students complete the necessary exercises in class. Use the Hands-on Grammar activity to provide a change of pace.

Resources for Varying Instruction
• *Language Lab* **CD-ROM** If your students have access to hardware, a 90-minute block provides an ideal opportunity for students to work on computer.

Professional Development Support
• *How to Manage Instruction in the Block* This teaching resource provides management and activity suggestions.

MEDIA AND TECHNOLOGY

For the Student
• *Language Lab* **CD-ROM**, Using Verbs
• *On-Line Exercise Bank,* Ch. 23

For the Teacher
• *Resource Pro* **CD-ROM**

WRITING AND GRAMMAR WEBSITE

The Interactive Writing and Grammar Website provides a wide array of support for students, teachers, and parents. Grammar support includes:

• *On-Line Exercise Bank* with Auto Check scoring
• Diagnostic and assessment support

phwg.phschool.com

LITERATURE CONNECTIONS

Grammar in Literature selections from *Prentice Hall Literature: Timeless Voices, Timeless Themes,* Gold:
from *On Summer,* Lorraine Hansberry, SE p. 527
from "Caucasian Mummies Mystify Chinese," Keay Davidson, SE p. 542

Lesson Objectives

1. To learn the six tenses of verbs.
2. To distinguish between the basic and progressive forms of each tense.
3. To learn the four principal parts of verbs.
4. To distinguish between regular and irregular verbs.
5. To conjugate verbs in the six tenses.
6. To use verbs appropriately and consistently in writing.
7. To distinguish between active voice and passive voice.
8. To use voice correctly in writing.

Critical Viewing

Connect, Contrast Students may say that the tenses vary in that the past tense either adds *-d* or *-ed* to the present tense or changes the present tense in irregular ways.

Chapter 23 Verb Usage

Using verbs correctly is one of the most important language skills to acquire. Most native speakers of English usually choose the right verb when they speak, but some verbs cause trouble. For example, someone might say, "A new season begun" instead of "A new season began" or "A new season has begun."

Just as seasons change, verbs also change their forms and tenses to suit different meanings. Because there are many chances to misuse verbs, you should take special care to learn the various forms of verbs. This chapter explains how verbs are formed, how they are used to indicate time, and how verbs are used to show who is performing an action.

▲ **Critical Viewing**
Think of the present and past tense forms of three different verbs that describe actions that occur on Thanksgiving Day. How do the two tenses vary in form? **[Connect, Contrast]**

☑ ONGOING ASSESSMENT: Diagnose

If students miss more than one item in each category, direct them to the relevant pages of the text and assign exercises for practice and review.

Verb Usage	Diagnostic Test Items	Teach	Practice	Section Review	Chapter Review
Skill Check A					
Verb Tenses and Forms	A 1–10	pp. 526–537	Ex. 1–9	Ex. 10–16	Ex. 29–35
Skill Check B					
Irregular Verbs	B 11–20	pp. 530–532	Ex. 4	Ex. 12	Ex. 30

Diagnostic Test

Directions: Write all answers on a separate sheet of paper.

Skill Check A. Identify the tense of each verb. Then, tell whether the form is *basic* or *progressive*.

1. Thanksgiving Day is a holiday celebrated in the fall.
2. As usual, it will fall on the fourth Thursday in November in the United States.
3. Canadians have been celebrating Thanksgiving Day on the second Monday in October.
4. Most people will be gathering with family and friends.
5. A holiday feast has become a tradition.
6. Thanksgiving Day has been celebrated in New England every year since the Pilgrims and Native Americans began the tradition in the 1600's.
7. The Pilgrims were giving thanks for the survival of their colony.
8. However, the idea had originated with the harvest festivals of ancient times.
9. Children in Pilgrim costumes often march in Thanksgiving Day parades.
10. Such costumes have included bonnets or hats, dark clothes, and shoes with large buckles.

Skill Check B. Choose the correct form of the verb in parentheses.

11. Two years after the feast of the Pilgrims and Native Americans, a drought (striked, struck).
12. The people might have (lose, lost) their crops.
13. Instead, the rains (came, come) during their prayers.
14. From these events, the custom of setting a special day of Thanksgiving annually after the harvest (arose, arisen).
15. Many Thanksgiving celebrations have (began, begun) with a horn-shaped basket overflowing with fruits and vegetables.
16. You may have (call, called) this basket a *cornucopia*.
17. For centuries, many European communities have (choose, chosen) to decorate with cornucopias.
18. The tradition of a Thanksgiving feast has (took, taken) hold in the United States.
19. Turkey, stuffing, cranberry sauce, squash, mashed potatoes, sweet potatoes, and pumpkin pie have (become, became) traditional Thanksgiving Day foods.
20. Most of these foods are (grew, grown) in North America today.

Skill Check C. Identify each verb as *active* or *passive*.

21. Teams in the National Football League established traditions of playing football games on Thanksgiving Day afternoon.
22. The televised games are watched by millions of fans.
23. Retailers sponsor large parades.
24. The annual Thanksgiving Day parade in New York has been enjoyed by all.
25. Floats in the parade are accompanied by gigantic balloons.

Answer Key

Diagnostic Test

Each section in the diagnostic test corresponds to a specific concept in the chapter on verb usage. This will enable you to tailor instruction to the particular needs of your students. See "Ongoing Assessment: Diagnose" below for further details.

Skill Check A

1. present basic
2. future basic
3. present perfect progressive
4. future progressive
5. present perfect basic
6. present perfect basic, past basic
7. past progressive
8. past perfect basic
9. present basic
10. present perfect basic

Skill Check B

11. struck
12. lost
13. came
14. arose
15. begun
16. called
17. chosen
18. taken
19. become
20. grown

Skill Check C

21. established—active
22. are watched—passive
23. sponsor—active
24. has been enjoyed—passive
25. are accompanied—passive

ONGOING ASSESSMENT: Diagnose continued

Verb Usage	Diagnostic Test Items	Teach	Practice	Section Review	Chapter Review
Skill Check C					
Active and Passive Voice	C 21–25	pp. 540–544	Ex. 20–22	Ex. 23–25	Ex. 34, 35
Cumulative Reviews and Applications				Ex. 10–19 Ex. 23–28	Ex. 29–37

⏱ TIME SAVERS!

Answers on Transparency Use the Grammar Exercises Answers on Transparencies for Chapter 23 to have students correct their own or one another's exercises.

On-Line Exercise Bank Have students complete the exercises on computer. The Auto Check feature will grade their work for you!

Verb Tenses

In this section, you will learn to recognize and use the six tenses of verbs. The examples and exercises are about the seasons of the year and seasonal activities.

Cross-Curricular Connection: Social Studies

Interest GRABBER Ask each student to think of one thing he or she did this morning. Write the past-tense verbs from their answers on the chalkboard (such as *showered, brushed, dressed, yawned, ate*). Ask students to rephrase their sentences to describe what they will do tomorrow. List these future-tense verbs next to the past-tense ones. Repeat the activity for present tense. Explain that these different forms of verbs are called tenses.

Activate Prior Knowledge

Have volunteers use the verb *happen* to define the words *past, present*, and *future* (what has happened, what is happening, what will happen). Underline the helping verbs. Explain that the forms of *be* and *have* indicate different verb tenses and verb forms.

TEACH

Step-by-Step Teaching Guide

Recognizing the Six Tenses of Verbs

1. Go over the charts on these two pages with the whole class. Point out that both the basic and progressive forms of the perfect tenses always include a form of the helping verb *have*. All progressive forms also include a form of the helping verb *be*.

2. Point out that all future-tense verbs are formed with the helping verb *will*. *Will* sometimes appears by itself, but another verb is always understood to go with it:

   Will you sit down? I will.

   The complete verb in the question is *will sit*. *Sit* is understood in the answer: The meaning of the sentence is *I will sit*.

3. Emphasize the difference in meaning between basic and progressive forms. The basic form describes events with a definite beginning and end. The progressive ending *-ing*, on the other hand, indicates continuous action. The helping verbs specify when this action takes place; in the past, present, or future.

In speaking and writing, you often need to indicate when something happens—now, yesterday, or tomorrow. In English, the different tenses of verbs are used to show when something occurs.

▶ **KEY CONCEPT** A **tense** is a form of a verb that shows the time of an action or a condition. ■

Recognizing the Six Tenses of Verbs

Verbs have six tenses that indicate whether something is happening now, was happening at some time in the past, or will be happening at some time in the future. Each of these tenses can be expressed in two different forms:

▶ **KEY CONCEPT** Each tense has a basic and a progressive form. ■

The following chart gives examples of the six tenses in their basic forms:

BASIC FORMS OF THE SIX TENSES	
Present	She *skis* for a hobby.
Past	She *skied* every day last year.
Future	She *will ski* again this year.
Present Perfect	She *has skied* at many different resorts.
Past Perfect	She *had skied* when she was only three years old.
Future Perfect	She *will have skied* ten times this season by Valentine's Day.

The basic forms are identified simply by their tense names. The progressive forms, however, are identified by their tense names plus the word *progressive*.

The next chart gives examples of the six tenses in their *progressive form*. Note that all these forms end in *-ing*.

🖋 Spelling Tip

When you are spelling words that end in *-ing* and the vowel in the root has a short sound, add a double letter before the *-ing*. For example, *swimming* has a double *m* before the *-ing*.

⏱ TIME AND RESOURCE MANAGER

Resources
Print: Grammar Exercise Workbook, pp. 113–126
Technology: Language Lab CD-ROM, Using Verbs; On-Line Exercise Bank, Section 23.1

In-Depth Coverage	Accelerated Pace
• Work through all key concepts, pp. 526–537. • Assign and review Exercises 1–9. • Read and discuss Grammar in Literature, p. 527.	• Assign pp. 536–547 for independent student review. • Assign Section Review Exercises 10–16.

PROGRESSIVE FORMS OF THE SIX TENSES

Present Progressive	She *is skiing* down a mountain now.
Past Progressive	She *was skiing* yesterday morning.
Future Progressive	She *will be skiing* again very soon.
Present Perfect Progressive	She *has been skiing* for years.
Past Perfect Progressive	She *had been skiing* when she broke her leg.
Future Perfect Progressive	She *will have been skiing* for a decade by the end of this year.

As you can see, the forms of a verb change in order to show present, past, and future time.

GRAMMAR IN LITERATURE

from On Summer
Lorraine Hansberry

Several past tense verbs in the following excerpt are shown in blue italics, and a past perfect tense verb is shown in red italics.

It also *seemed* to me, esthetically speaking, that nature *had got* inexcusably carried away on the summer question and let the whole thing get to be rather much. By duration alone, for instance, a summer's day *seemed* maddeningly excessive; an utter overstatement. Except for those few hours at either end of it, objects always *appeared* in too sharp a relief against backgrounds; shadows too pronounced and light too blinding. It always gave me the feeling of walking around in a motion picture which *had been* too artsily-craftsily exposed.

▼ **Critical Viewing** Use tenses of the same verb in three sentences about making a sand castle—yesterday, today, and tomorrow. How does the verb change from sentence to sentence? **[Connect, Contrast]**

Verb Tenses • 527

Grammar in Literature

1. Have students identify the tense of each verb in the excerpt (*seemed*, past; *had got*, past perfect; [had] *let*, past [perfect]; *seemed*, past; *appeared*, past; *gave*, past; *had been exposed*, past perfect). Ask whether these verbs are basic or progressive and have students explain their answers (basic; none of the verbs ends in *-ing*).

2. Ask students why they think Hansberry uses past and past-perfect verb tenses in her description. (Possible responses: Past tense, because she is writing about her memories of the past; perfect tense, because she is writing about her general impression of summers over the period of several years.)

More About the Writer

African American writer Lorraine Hansberry is best known for her hit play *A Raisin in the Sun*, which tells the story of an urban family about to become the first African Americans in a white suburb.

Critical Viewing

Connect, Contrast Students may say that the verbs in their sentences changed from the past to the present to the future tense.

Customize for *ESL Students*

Have partners read the literature excerpt. Students should read it on their own, noting any words they don't understand. Afterward, partners can compare their lists and teach each other any words that one partner knows and the other doesn't. Then they can work together to define the other words. Encourage them to use context clues before they check a dictionary. You may want to give students some help with *artsily-craftsily*.

23.1

> **Exercise 1** **Recognizing Tenses and Forms of Verbs** Write the verb or verb phrase in each sentence. Then, identify the tense and form of each verb. Be careful to avoid choosing words that look like verbs but are acting as other parts of speech. In the first sentence, for example, *skiing* is a gerund that acts like a noun.

EXAMPLE: He has been skiing in Colorado.

ANSWER: has been skiing (present perfect progressive)

1. Skiing has become a very popular winter sport.
2. By the twenty-first century, people had skied for thousands of years.
3. Millions of people worldwide are skiing for recreation.
4. This article describes the two types of recreational skiing, alpine and nordic.
5. Alpine, or downhill, skiing developed in the late 1800's as a way of moving down snow-covered slopes.
6. In alpine skiing, people have been using lifts as transportation to the top of a slope.
7. Before alpine skiing, some skiers will have tried nordic, or cross-country, skiing.
8. Most nordic skiers will ski on flat trails prepared for their convenience.
9. Many people have taken lessons from professionals.
10. By the end of the day, many people will have been skiing for hours.

> **More Practice**
> Language Lab
> CD-ROM
> • Verb Usage lesson
> On-line
> Exercise Bank
> • Section 23.1
> Grammar Exercise
> Workbook
> • pp. 113–114

▶ **Critical Viewing** Think of two sentences—one with a basic form verb and one with a progressive form verb—to describe actions of the person in this picture. **[Analyze]**

528 • Verb Usage

The Four Principal Parts of Verbs

Tenses are formed from *principal parts* and helping verbs.

▶ **KEY CONCEPT** A verb has four **principal parts**: the *present*, the *present participle*, the *past*, and the *past participle*. ■

The chart below lists the principal parts of two verbs:

FOUR PRINCIPAL PARTS			
Present	Present Participle	Past	Past Participle
walk	walking	walked	(have) walked
run	running	ran	(have) run

The first principal part is used to form the present and future tenses. To form the present, an *-s* or *-es* is added whenever the subject is *he, she, it,* or a singular noun (*she walks, Paul runs*). To form the future tense, the helping verb *will* is added (*she will walk, Paul will run*).

The second principal part is used with various helping verbs to produce all six of the progressive forms (*she is walking, Paul was walking,* and so on).

The third principal part is used to form the past tense (*she walked, Paul ran*).

The fourth principal part is used with helping verbs for the three perfect tenses (*she has walked, Paul had run, we will have run*).

▶ **Exercise 2** Recognizing Principal Parts Identify the principal part used to form each verb in Exercise 1 on page 528. The example sentence from Exercise 1 is provided as a model below.

EXAMPLE: He has been skiing in Colorado.
ANSWER: present participle (skiing)

▶ **Exercise 3** Writing Sentences with Principal Parts of Verbs
For each numbered item, write a sentence using the subject and the principle. part of the verb indicated. Then identify the tense of the verb in the sentence you have written.
1. We, past participle of talk
2. Mike, present participle of wait
3. People, present of laugh
4. I, past of stop
5. You, present participle of help

Verb Tenses • 529

☑ ONGOING ASSESSMENT: Monitor and Reinforce

If students miss more than two items in Exercise 1, 2 or 3, refer them to the following for additional practice.

In the Textbook	Print Resources	Technology
Section Review, Ex. 10–11, p. 538	Grammar Exercise Workbook, pp. 113–114	Language Lab CD-ROM, Using Verbs; On-Line Exercise Bank, Section 23.1

Forming Regular and Irregular Verbs

1. Explain that regular verbs all follow the same spelling pattern; they all change their form in the same way. Each irregular verb changes form in its own way.

2. Encourage students to study the chart of irregular verbs on the next two pages and memorize as many as they can. Students should already be familiar with many of these verbs. Most are common and students will want to use them in writing and conversation.

Customize for
Less Advanced and ESL Students

Language users usually look for patterns or rules that apply to groups. Stress that this does not work for irregular verbs. *Cry/cried* but *fly/flew; think/thought* but *drink/drank*. Urge students to use the dictionary when they are unsure, and reassure them that after a while they will remember how to form tenses of irregular verbs.

Critical Viewing

Analyze Students may suggest sentences such as "The catcher holds up his mitt" and "The batter is hoping to hit a home run."

23.1

Forming Regular and Irregular Verbs

The way the past and the past participle of a verb are formed determines whether the verb is *regular* or *irregular*.

Regular Verbs Most of the verbs in the English language, such as the verb *walk*, are regular.

▶ **KEY CONCEPT** The past and past participle of a **regular verb** are formed by adding *-ed* or *-d* to the present form. ■

The past and past participle of regular verbs have the same form. In the following chart, *has* is in parentheses in front of the past participle to remind you that this verb form is a past participle only if it is used with a helping verb.

Notice that the final consonant is sometimes doubled to form the present participle (*skipping*) as well as the past and the past participle (*skipped*). Notice also that the final *e* may be dropped in forming the present participle (*typing*).

PRINCIPAL PARTS OF REGULAR VERBS			
Present	**Present Participle**	**Past**	**Past Participle**
play	(is) playing	played	(has) played
skip	(is) skipping	skipped	(has) skipped
type	(is) typing	typed	(has) typed

▲ Critical Viewing Think of a sentence with a basic form verb to describe the catcher's actions in this picture. Think of a sentence with a progressive form verb to describe the batter's actions. **[Analyze]**

530 • Verb Usage

Irregular Verbs Although most verbs are regular, a number of very common verbs, such as *run*, are irregular.

▶ **KEY CONCEPT** The past and past participle of an **irregular verb** are not formed by adding *-ed* or *-d* to the present form. ■

The past and past participle of irregular verbs are formed in various ways. Some common irregular verbs are shown in the charts that follow. The third problem is spelling. Just as with regular verbs, the final consonant is sometimes doubled to form the present participle (for example, *sitting*).

Whenever you are in doubt about the principal parts of an irregular verb, use a dictionary to check.

IRREGULAR VERBS WITH THE SAME PAST AND PAST PARTICIPLE			
Present	Present Participle	Past	Past Participle
bind	binding	bound	(have) bound
bring	bringing	brought	(have) brought
build	building	built	(have) built
buy	buying	bought	(have) bought
catch	catching	caught	(have) caught
fight	fighting	fought	(have) fought
find	finding	found	(have) found
get	getting	got	(have) got or (have) gotten
hold	holding	held	(have) held
keep	keeping	kept	(have) kept
lay	laying	laid	(have) laid
lead	leading	led	(have) led
leave	leaving	left	(have) left
lose	losing	lost	(have) lost
pay	paying	paid	(have) paid
say	saying	said	(have) said
send	sending	sent	(have) sent
sit	sitting	sat	(have) sat
sleep	sleeping	slept	(have) slept
spend	spending	spent	(have) spent
spin	spinning	spun	(have) spun
stand	standing	stood	(have) stood
stick	sticking	stuck	(have) stuck
swing	swinging	swung	(have) swung
teach	teaching	taught	(have) taught
win	winning	won	(have) won
wind	winding	wound	(have) wound

Customize for
Verbal/Linguistic Learners

Ask volunteers to give the four principal parts of the verb *shrink* (*shrink, shrinking, shrank, shrunk*) and write them on the chalkboard. Write the movie title *Honey, I Shrunk the Kids* on the chalkboard. Ask students to identify the mistake in the title. (*Shrunk* should be *Shrank*, since there is no helping verb.) Explain that with an irregular verb like *shrink*, it is easy to make mistakes like this.

Language Highlight

British Verb Forms Although the English spoken in America and Great Britain share the same ancestry, there are some surprising differences. For example, students may be interested to know that, in Britain, the past tense form of the verb *spell* is *spelt*, not *spelled*. This would actually make a regular verb, in American English, an irregular verb.

Customize for
More Advanced Students

Challenge students to use a dictionary or other reference source to find other examples of verbs that are regular in American English, but irregular in British English.

◆ STANDARDIZED TEST PREPARATION WORKSHOP

Using Verbs Standardized tests often measure students' ability to determine the correct tense of a verb needed to complete a sentence. Share the following sample item with students and have them choose the letter of the word or group of words that best completes the sentence:

Carla told me that she ___ to Brazil with her parents three times last year.

A is flying   **C** will be flying

B will have flown   **D** flew

Because the action of the sentence takes place in the past, item **D** is the correct choice. All the other choices are in the wrong tense.

Customize for ESL Students

Highlight the two irregular verbs *lie* and *lay* in the charts on this page and the previous one. (Tell students that this *lie* means to lie down, not to tell a lie.) Write the four principal parts of these easily confused verbs on the chalkboard and explain the difference in meaning. *Lie* is an intransitive verb. *Lay* is always a transitive verb that requires a direct object. Since the past principle part of *lie* and the present principal part of *lay* are spelled alike, students will have to determine meaning from the context of the sentence:

I lay down.

I lay the letter down.

In the first sentence, *lay* is the past principal part of *lie*, because there is no direct object. In the second sentence, *lay* is the present principal part of *lay*, because there is a direct object (the letter).

Answer Key

Exercise 4

1. began
2. grew
3. given
4. became, won
5. sought

Customize for More Advanced Students

Challenge students to rewrite the sentences in Exercise 4 so that they use the other verb in parentheses. Students should note that for three sentences they cannot do this, and explain why. (Sentences 2, 4, and 5. *Growed*, *winned*, and *seeked* are not words.)

IRREGULAR VERBS THAT CHANGE IN OTHER WAYS

Present	Present Participle	Past	Past Participle
began	beginning	began	(have) begun
break	breaking	broke	(have) broken
choose	choosing	chose	(have) chosen
come	coming	came	(have) come
do	doing	did	(have) done
draw	drawing	drew	(have) drawn
drive	driving	drove	(have) driven
eat	eating	ate	(have) eaten
fall	falling	fell	(have) fallen
freeze	freezing	froze	(have) frozen
go	going	went	(have) gone
grow	growing	grew	(have) grown
know	knowing	knew	(have) known
lie	lying	lay	(have) lain
ring	ringing	rang	(have) rung
rise	rising	rose	(have) risen
run	running	ran	(have) run
see	seeing	saw	(have) seen
shake	shaking	shook	(have) shaken
sing	singing	sang	(have) sung
sink	sinking	sank	(have) sunk
speak	speaking	spoke	(have) spoken
steal	stealing	stole	(have) stolen
swim	swimming	swam	(have) swum
take	taking	took	(have) taken
write	writing	wrote	(have) written

Exercise 4 Using the Correct Forms of Irregular Verbs

Choose the correct form of the verb in parentheses.

EXAMPLE: Baseball has (became, become) my best sport.
ANSWER: become

1. No one knows for sure when baseball (began, begun), but legend claims it was around 1839.
2. Baseball (growed, grew) in popularity, and many people saw the sport as a source of financial profit.
3. Until 1869, the National Association of Baseball Players had not (gave, given) players any form of payment for playing.
4. In 1869, the Cincinnati Red Stockings (become, became) the first professional baseball team. They (winned, won) 60 games without a loss in their first year.
5. Soon, major cities across the United States (seeked, sought) to form their own baseball teams.

532 • Verb Usage

More Practice

Language Lab
CD-ROM
• Verb Usage lesson
On-line
Exercise Bank
• Section 23.1
Grammar Exercise
Workbook
• pp. 115–116

⏱ TIME SAVERS!

Answers on Transparency
Use the Grammar Exercises Answers on Transparencies for Chapter 23 to have students correct their own or one another's exercises.

On-Line Exercise Bank
Have students complete the exercises on computer. The Auto Check feature will grade their work for you!

☐ ONGOING ASSESSMENT: Prerequisite Skills

If students have difficulty with irregular verbs, you may find it necessary to review the following to assure coverage of prerequisite knowledge.

In the Textbook	Print Resources	Technology
Verbs, pp. 360–377	Grammar Exercise Workbook, pp. 13–20	On-Line Exercise Bank, Section 17.1 and 17.2

Conjugating the Tenses

With the principal parts of verbs and helping verbs, you can form all of the tenses. One way to become familiar with the variety of verb forms is through *conjugation*.

> ▶ **KEY CONCEPT** A **conjugation** is a complete list of the singular and plural forms of a verb in a particular tense. ■

For each tense, singular and plural forms correspond to the first-, second-, and third-person forms of personal pronouns.

The following charts conjugate the verb *see*. To conjugate the six tenses in their basic form, you need only three of the principal parts: the present (*see*), the past (*saw*), and the past participle (*seen*). To conjugate the six tenses in their progressive form, you need the present participle and a form of the verb *be*.

CONJUGATION OF THE BASIC FORMS OF *SEE*		
Person	**Singular**	**Plural**
Present		
First person	I see	we see
Second person	you see	you see
Third person	he, she, it sees	they see
Past		
First person	I saw	we saw
Second person	you saw	you saw
Third person	he, she, it saw	they saw
Future		
First person	I will see	we will see
Second person	you will see	you will see
Third person	he, she, it will see	they will see
Present Perfect		
First person	I have seen	we have seen
Second person	you have seen	you have seen
Third person	he, she, it has seen	they have seen
Past Perfect		
First person	I had seen	we had seen
Second person	you had seen	you had seen
Third person	he, she, it had seen	they had seen
Future Perfect		
First person	I will have seen	we will have seen
Second person	you will have seen	you will have seen
Third person	he, she it will have seen	they will have seen

Verb Tenses • 533

Step-by-Step Teaching Guide

Conjugating the Tenses

1. Use the present tense of the verb *see* to demonstrate the present tense of verbs. Explain that in the present tense, this verb is regular. All pronouns except the third-person singular *he/she/it* take the first principal part of the verb, which is *see*. In the third-person singular, you simply add *-s* to the first principal part: *he/she/it sees*. Almost every verb in English follows this pattern, including most of the irregular verbs in the charts on pages 531 and 532.

2. Introduce the few verbs that are irregular in the present tense. The verbs *be* and *have* are highly irregular. *Do* and *go* take the ending *-es* in the third-person singular: *he does, she goes*. Verbs whose present principal part ends in *y* (such as *fly, cry, try, pry*) change the *y* to *i* and then add *-es* for the third-person singular: *he cries, she tries, it flies*.

3. In order to conjugate the perfect tenses, students need to know the principal parts of the verb *have*. In order to conjugate the progressive tenses, they also need to know the principal parts of the verb *be*. These are the two least-regular verbs in the English language. Urge students to memorize these verbs in all their tenses. Students can find the verb *be* conjugated on page 534.

✓ ONGOING ASSESSMENT: Assess Mastery

Use the following resources to assess student mastery of irregular verbs.

In the Textbook	Print Resources	Technology
Chapter Review, Ex. 29–36, pp. 546–547 Standardized Test Preparation Workshop, pp. 548–549	Grammar Exercise Workbook, pp. 113–116	Language Lab CD-ROM, Using Verbs; On-Line Exercise Bank, Section 23.1

Integrating Vocabulary Skills

Define and Conjugate Challenge students to discover five interesting verbs such as *covet*, *swindle*, *perambulate*, *aggrandize*, or *imbibe* in their vocabulary books or the dictionary. Partners can take turns challenging each other to define and conjugate these verbs. Students can use prior knowledge, context clues, and so on to help them arrive at correct definitions. Partners can check their work together in dictionaries. This activity will give them good practice in conjugation as well as new words they can use to impress friends and family.

Customize for
Visual/Spatial Learners

Write the following words on index cards: *I, you, he/she/it, we, they, am, are, is, was, were, be, been, being, have, has*. Have partners arrange them in as many grammatically correct ways as possible and list their combinations (*I am, she has been*, and so on). Then pairs can check and compare their lists.

More Practice
Language Lab
CD-ROM
• Verb Usage lesson
On-line
Exercise Bank
• Section 23.1
Grammar Exercise
Workbook
• pp. 117–118

CONJUGATION OF THE BASIC FORMS OF *SEE*		
Person	**Singular**	**Plural**
Present		
First person Second person Third person	I see you see he, she, it sees	we see you see they see
Past		
First person Second person Third person	I saw you saw he, she, it saw	we saw you saw they saw
Future		
First person Second person Third person	I will see you will see he, she, it will see	we will see you will see they will see
Present Perfect		
First person Second person Third person	I have seen you have seen he, she, it has seen	we have seen you have seen they have seen
Past Perfect		
First person Second person Third person	I had seen you had seen he, she, it had seen	we had seen you had seen they had seen
Future Perfect		
First person Second person Third person	I will have seen you will have seen he, she it will have seen	we will have seen you will have seen they will have seen

Note About *Be*: The verb *be* is highly irregular. The following conjugation of the first two tenses lists the forms.

PRESENT: I am   we are
           you are   you are
           he, she, it is   they are

PAST: I was   we were
           you were   you were
           he, she, it was   they were

> **Exercise 5** Conjugating Basic Forms of Verbs Conjugate
the basic forms of the five verbs below as shown in the example.

EXAMPLE: spend (conjugated with *we*)

Present: we spend   Present perfect: we have spent
Past: we spent   Past perfect: we had spent
Future: we will spend   Future perfect: we will have spent

1. move (conjugated with *I*)
2. see (conjugated with *you*)
3. teach (conjugated with *he*)
4. start (conjugated with *they*)
5. go (conjugated with *we*)

> **Exercise 6** Conjugating Progressive Forms of Verbs
Conjugate the progressive forms of the five verbs below as
shown in the example.

EXAMPLE: spend (conjugated with *we*)

Present progressive: we are spending
Past progressive: we were spending
Future progressive: we will be spending
Present perfect progressive: we have been spending
Past perfect progressive: we had been spending
Future perfect progressive: we will have been spending

1. play (conjugated with *I*)
2. watch (conjugated with *you*)
3. hit (conjugated with *he*)
4. leave (conjugated with *they*)
5. know (conjugated with *we*)

> **Exercise 7** Supplying the Correct Tense Write the
indicated form for each verb in parentheses.
1. Present perfect progressive—We (swim)
   by moving our hands and feet in or
   on the water.
2. Past—Human beings (develop) a variety
   of body movements to move them
   through water.
3. Future progressive—Many people (go) to
   their local swimming pool this summer
   to swim.
4. Past perfect—Before today, currents
   (make) swimming in the inlet hazardous.
5. Present progressive—Wherever you
   (travel) this summer, you will find
   a place to swim.

▼ **Critical Viewing**
Describe the action
in this picture using
sentences with
present progressive
verbs. [Describe]

Verb Tenses • 535

Answer Key

> **Exercise 5**

1. I move, I moved, I will move, I
   have moved, I had moved, I will
   have moved
2. you see, you saw, you will see,
   you have seen, you had seen,
   you will have seen
3. he teaches, he taught, he will
   teach, he has taught, he had
   taught, he will have taught
4. they start, they started, they will
   start, they have started, they had
   started, they will have started
5. we go, we went, we will go, we
   have gone, we had gone, we will
   have gone

> **Exercise 6**

1. I am playing, I was playing, I will
   be playing, I have been playing, I
   had been playing, I will have
   been playing
2. you are watching, you were
   watching, you will be watching,
   you have been watching, you
   had been watching, you will
   have been watching
3. he is hitting, he was hitting, he
   will be hitting, he has been
   hitting, he had been hitting, he
   will have been hitting
4. they are leaving, they were
   leaving, they will be leaving,
   they have been leaving, they had
   been leaving, they will have
   been leaving
5. we are growing, we were
   growing, we will be growing, we
   have been growing, we had
   been growing, we will have been
   growing

> **Exercise 7**

1. have been swimming
2. developed
3. will be going
4. had made
5. are traveling

Critical Viewing

Describe Students' descriptions will
vary. Make sure they use present
progressive verbs, such as *are playing*.

☑ **ONGOING ASSESSMENT: Monitor and Reinforce**

If students miss more than two items in Exercise 5, 6, or 7 refer them to the following for additional
practice.

In the Textbook	Print Resources	Technology
Section Review, Ex. 13, p. 538	Grammar Exercise Workbook, pp. 117–118	Language Lab CD-ROM, Using Verbs; On-Line Exercise Bank, Section 23.1

Expressing Time with Verb Tenses

1. Ask students to give examples of when they would use past, present, and future forms of verbs. (Students should explain that present describes what is happening now, past describes what happened before, and future describes what will happen next.) Explain that this basic pattern applies to perfect and progressive forms as well as to basic ones.

2. Use the sample sentences in the chart under *Past* and *Present Perfect* to demonstrate the difference between these two tenses.

Language Highlight

Be Everyone learns to talk by hearing others talk. If students hear incorrect grammatical usage from family, friends, and, especially, the media, they will invariably repeat it. You cannot repeat too often that uses of *be* such as "I be going to the movies" and "She be my sister" are incorrect.

Answer Key

Exercise 8

Answers may vary.

1. correct
2. rented, bought
3. reached, felt
4. cast, hooked
5. cheered

23.1

Expressing Time With Verb Tenses

You know that the tense of a verb indicates the time of the action or the state of being expressed by the verb. The chart below shows the different uses of the various verb tenses:

TENSES AND THEIR USES		
Tense	**Uses**	**Examples**
Present	Present action or condition	It is below freezing.
	Continuing action or condition	He is enjoying winter.
Past	Completed action or condition	We tried ice fishing.
	Continuous completed action or condition	The weather was being agreeable.
Present Perfect	Completed action or condition	She has been on skates before.
	Action or condition continuing to present	They have fished for hours.
	Action continuing to present	We have been waiting for them.
Past Perfect	Action or condition completed before another	I had been there before Thanksgiving.
	Continuing action interrupted by another	We had been eating when you called.
Future	Future action or condition	You will catch something soon.
	Continuing future action or condition	He will be wearing a parka.
Future Perfect	Future action or condition completed before another	By noon, he will have caught some fish.
	Continuing future action completed before another	By then, we will have been fishing for four hours.

Exercise 8 **Revise to Create Consistent Verb Tense** Revise this paragraph so that it is written in a consistent tense.

(1) My brother took me fishing last weekend. (2) We rent a small motorboat and buy some bait. (3) By the time we will reach our favorite fishing spot, I feel very excited. (4) Almost as soon as I cast my line over the side of the boat, I hook a fish. (5) As I brought the fish into the boat, my brother is cheering at my good luck.

536 • Verb Usage

⬧ STANDARDIZED TEST PREPARATION WORKSHOP

Grammar and Usage Standardized tests often ask students to choose the correct form of a word. Have students choose the correct verb or verb phrase to complete the following sentence:

As I _____ up to the plate, I remembered the last time I faced this pitcher.

A step

B stepped

C have stepped

D had stepped

Choice **A** describes an action that is taking place in the present. **B** describes an action with a definite beginning and end. The fact that *remembered* and *faced* are past-tense verbs should also help students see that **B** is correct. Choices **C** and **D** express indefinite, and perhaps continuing, events in the past.

Exercise 9 Identifying the Uses of Tense Identify the tense as well as the use of each underlined verb in the following sentences.

EXAMPLE: He has gone sailing every summer.

ANSWER: present perfect (action continuing to present)

1. Sailing attracts people to lakes and rivers all over the world.
2. Many have enjoyed the excitement and the challenge of the sport.
3. That boat was sailing directly into the wind.
4. The crew had checked the sails before leaving the dock.
5. They have always maintained the boats well.
6. Sailboat races often will cover a triangular course.
7. To maneuver the boat, the crew will be changing the position of the rudder and the sails.
8. You will have learned about trimming and tacking by the end of the day.
9. Windsurfing, another water sport, is also gaining in popularity.
10. In this sport, a sail has been attached to a surfboard.

More Practice
Language Lab
CD-ROM
• Verb Usage lesson
On-line
Exercise Bank
• Section 23.1
Grammar Exercise
Workbook
• pp. 119–126

◄ **Critical Viewing**
Based on the picture, describe an action that began before and is continuing to the present. What verb did you use? What is its tense? **[Connect]**

Verb Tenses • 537

Answer Key

Exercise 9
1. present, present action
2. present perfect, action continuing to present
3. past progressive, continuous completed action
4. past perfect, action completed before another
5. present perfect, action continuing to present
6. future, future action
7. future progressive, continuing future action
8. future perfect, future action completed before another
9. present progressive, continuing action
10. present perfect, completed action

Critical Viewing

Describe Students may say that the boats *have been sailing* (sailing, present perfect).

ONGOING ASSESSMENT: Assess Mastery

Use the following resources to assess student mastery of verb tenses and forms.

In the Textbook	Technology
Chapter Review, Ex. 29–33, pp. 546–547 Standardized Test Preparation Workshop, pp. 548–549	On-Line Exercise Bank, Section 23.1

 **TIME SAVERS!**

Answers on Transparency Use the Grammar Exercises Answers on Transparencies for Chapter 23 to have students correct their own or one another's exercises.

On-Line Exercise Bank Have students complete the exercises on computer. The Auto Check feature will grade their work for you!

537

Section Review

Each of these exercises correlates to a concept taught in the section on verb tenses, pages 528–537. The exercises may be used for more practice, for reteaching, or for review of the Key Concepts presented. Answers for all chapter exercises are available in *Grammar Exercises Answers on Transparencies* in your teaching resources.

Answer Key

Exercise 10

1. past progressive
2. present
3. past perfect progressive
4. future
5. future perfect
6. present progressive
7. future progressive
8. present perfect
9. present perfect progressive
10. present perfect progressive, present

Exercise 11

1. present participle
2. present
3. present participle
4. present
5. past participle
6. present participle
7. present participle
8. past participle
9. present participle
10. present participle, present

Exercise 12

1. begun
2. threw
3. stolen
4. broken
5. struck
6. drove
7. eaten
8. drawn
9. chosen
10. did

23.1 Section Review

GRAMMAR EXERCISES 10–19

Exercise 10 **Recognizing Tenses and Forms of Verbs** Identify the tense and form of the verb or verbs in each sentence.

1. We were studying the reasons for the change of season.
2. The position of the Earth in orbit around the sun determines the season.
3. The sun had been shining for more hours per day during the summer season.
4. The seasons will change because of the tilt of the Earth's axis.
5. This tilt will have caused the North Pole to be closer to the sun for half of the year.
6. The hemisphere toward the sun is receiving the sun's rays more directly.
7. In summer, the Northern Hemisphere will be tilting toward the sun.
8. In winter, the Northern Hemisphere has tilted away from the sun.
9. Mars has been orbiting the sun in a similar way.
10. Knowing this, we have been assuming for many years that Mars' seasons are similar to Earth's.

Exercise 11 **Recognizing Principal Parts** Identify the principal part used to form each verb in Exercise 9.

Exercise 12 **Using the Correct Forms of Irregular Verbs** Choose the correct form of the verb in parentheses.

1. Baseball fans are happy when spring training has (began, begun).
2. The mayor (throwed, threw) out the first ball to start the game.
3. That player has (stole, stolen) more bases than any other player.
4. The pitcher has also (broke, broken)

538 • Verb Usage

the record for scoreless innings.
5. He just (striked, struck) out another batter.
6. Finally, a batter (drove, driven) a ball into the outfield.
7. We have always (ate, eaten) peanuts at baseball games.
8. The playoff game has (drew, drawn) a large crowd.
9. Have you (chose, chosen) your favorite team?
10. We already (did, done) that.

Exercise 13 **Conjugating the Basic Forms of Verbs** Use the person indicated to conjugate the basic forms of the verbs in each of the six tenses.

1. open (conjugated with *I*)
2. move (conjugated with *you*)
3. know (conjugated with *he*)
4. begin (conjugated with *we*)
5. fall (conjugated with *they*)

Exercise 14 **Conjugating the Progressive Forms of Verbs** Use the person indicated to conjugate the progressive forms of the verbs in each of the six tenses.

1. go (conjugated with *I*)
2. teach (conjugated with *you*)
3. spin (conjugated with *he*)
4. shake (conjugated with *we*)
5. swim (conjugated with *they*)

Exercise 15 **Identifying Uses of Tenses** Identify the tense of each underlined verb, and explain how it indicates time.

1. An equinox <u>occurs</u> when both hemispheres are the same distance from the sun.
2. This <u>will happen</u> about March 21 and

Exercise 13

1. I open, I opened, I will open, I have opened, I had opened, I will have opened
2. you move, you moved, you will move, you have moved, you had moved, you will have moved
3. he knows, he knew, he will know, he has known, he had known
4. we begin, we began, we will begin, we have begun, we had begun, we will have begun
5. they fall, they fell, they will fall, they have fallen, they had fallen, they will have fallen

September 23 each year.

3. In March, spring <u>will have started</u> in the Northern Hemisphere when the vernal equinox occurs.

4. When the autumnal equinox occurs in September, autumn <u>has begun</u> in the Northern Hemisphere.

5. The sun <u>appeared</u> directly over the Earth's equator during the equinox.

6. When this <u>has happened</u>, the lengths of day and night are equal over almost all the Earth, except at the poles.

7. A solstice <u>has occurred</u> when the distance from either pole to the sun is at its greatest.

8. On about June 21, the sun <u>is standing</u> at its northernmost position; this is the summer solstice in the Northern Hemisphere.

9. The Southern Hemisphere's winter solstice <u>will have occurred</u> at the same time.

10. Whichever hemisphere tilts toward the sun on the solstice <u>will have</u> the longest day and the shortest night.

▶ Exercise 16 Revising Sentences by Changing the Verb Tense Rewrite

each sentence, changing the tense of the underlined verb as indicated in parentheses. You do not need to change the tense of other verbs in the sentence.

1. The change in the length of daylight accompanying the seasons <u>differed</u> at different latitudes. (present)

2. In this article, you <u>discover</u> that summer near the poles is six months of daylight and winter is six months of darkness. (future)

3. Those who <u>live</u> at the equator will experience the hottest climate. (future progressive)

4. Some people <u>have thought</u> that the days near the summer solstice are the hottest days of the year; however, they are not. (past progressive)

5. Scientists <u>are discovering</u> that temperature depends not only on the amount of heat the atmosphere receives but also the amount it loses. (past)

6. The atmosphere <u>loses</u> heat through absorption into the ground or through reflection. (future perfect)

7. The temperature of the ocean <u>changed</u> much more slowly than the atmosphere's temperature. (present perfect)

8. The atmosphere <u>warmed</u> up quickly in the spring and summer but was still losing much heat to the oceans. (past perfect)

9. The oceans <u>had absorbed</u> enough heat to reach equilibrium with the temperature of the atmosphere. (present perfect progressive)

10. Some people <u>were using</u> temperature to determine the season instead of looking at the calendar! (past perfect progressive)

▶ Exercise 17 Find It in Your

Reading In the excerpt from "On Summer" on page 527, identify the tense of each of the verbs in the last sentence and tell whether the verb is regular or irregular.

▶ Exercise 18 Find It in Your

Writing Choose a paragraph from a piece of your own writing. Identify the tenses of the verbs, and tell whether they are basic or progressive.

▶ Exercise 19 Writing Application

Write a short essay about your favorite season and some activities you particularly enjoy doing at that time. Underline the verbs you use, and identify the tense and form of each verb.

Section Review • 539

Answer Key continued

Exercise 18

Find It in Your Writing
If a tense (present, past, or future) is not represented in the paragraph, have students write an additional sentence using that tense.

Exercise 19

Writing Application
Tell students to be sure to use the present, past, and future tenses in their essays.

Exercise 14 *(page 538)*

1. I am going, I was going, I will be going, I have been going, I had been going, I will have been going

2. you are teaching, you were teaching, you will be teaching, you have been teaching, you had been teaching, you will have been teaching

3. he is spinning, he was spinning, he will be spinning, he has been spinning, he had been spinning, he will have been spinning

4. we are shaking, we were shaking, we will be shaking, we have been shaking, we had been shaking, we will have been shaking

5. they are swimming, they were swimming, they will be swimming, they have been swimming, they had been swimming, they will have been swimming

Exercise 15 *(page 538)*

1. present, present action
2. future, future action or condition
3. future perfect, future action completed before another
4. present perfect, completed action
5. past, completed action
6. present perfect, completed action
7. present perfect, completed action
8. present, continuing action
9. future perfect, future action completed before another
10. future, future action

Exercise 16

1. differs
2. will discover
3. will be living
4. were thinking
5. discovered
6. will have lost
7. has changed
8. had warmed
9. have been absorbing
10. had been using

Exercise 17

Find It in Your Reading

gave—past, irregular

had been exposed—past perfect, regular

continued

Interest GRABBER Share the following quotation from Ernest Hemingway's novel *The Sun Also Rises*:

. . . it made him [Robert] bitter. He took it out in boxing, and he came out of Princeton with a painful self-consciousness . . . and was married by the first girl who was nice to him.

Ask students to describe the difference between the first two verbs and the third verb in the last sentence of this quotation. (In the first two, Robert performs the action; in the last one, the girl performs it on him.) Introduce the terms *active voice* and *passive voice*.

Activate Prior Knowledge

Ask a student to tell the difference between the words *active* and *passive*. (Active means "taking action"; passive means "letting someone or something else act.") Explain to students that they are going to learn how these two terms are used in grammar to affect subjects and verbs.

TEACH

Step-by-Step Teaching Guide

Active and Passive Voice

1. Explain that *active* and *passive* describe the subject of a sentence. If the subject takes action, the verb is in the active voice. If the subject is acted on, the verb is in the passive voice.

2. Point out the preposition *by* in sentences 3, 5, and 7 of Exercise 20 on page 541. Tell students that when they see this preposition immediately following a past-tense verb, they will know that the verb is in the passive voice.

3. Passive-voice sentences without *by* are not always easy to identify. When students are in doubt, have them ask themselves *Who or what is performing the action*? If no word in the sentence answers this question, the sentence is passive:

   Stories have been told throughout recorded history.

   No word in the sentence answers the question *Who or what told stories?* Therefore, the sentence is passive.

Section 23.2

Active and Passive Voice

In addition to indicating time, most verbs can indicate whether the subject is performing an action or having an action performed upon it. Two different voices of verbs are used to show how an action is performed.

▶ **KEY CONCEPT** **Voice** is the form of a verb that shows whether the subject is performing the action. ■

Linking verbs do not show voice. Only action verbs show voice. The voice may be either *active* or *passive*.

Recognizing Active and Passive Voice

Any action verb, with or without a direct object, can be in the *active* voice.

▶ **KEY CONCEPT** A verb is **active** if its subject performs the action. ■

In the two examples below, the subjects are the performers.

ACTIVE VOICE: Laura *found* a dinosaur bone.
The archaeologist *called* yesterday.

Most action verbs can also be used in the *passive* voice.

▶ **KEY CONCEPTS** A verb is **passive** if its action is performed upon the subject. ■

A passive verb is made from a form of *be* plus the past participle of a transitive verb. ■

In a sentence with a passive verb, the performer of the action may or may not be named. In the first example below, Laura is still the performer. The word *Laura*, however, is no longer the subject but the object of the preposition *by*. In the second example, the person who will be calling tomorrow is not identified.

PASSIVE VOICE: A dinosaur bone *was found* by Laura.
The archaeologist *will be called* tomorrow.

540 • Verb Usage

Theme: Anthropology

In this section, you will learn to recognize and use verbs in active and passive voice. The examples and exercises are about anthropology and archaeology.

Cross-Curricular Connection: Social Studies

⚙ **Grammar and Style Tip**

To make your writing more interesting, use a balance of active and passive voice.

⏱ **TIME AND RESOURCE MANAGER**

Resources
Print: Grammar Exercise Workbook, pp. 127–130; Hands-on Grammar Activity Book, Chapter 23
Technology: Language Lab CD-ROM, Using Verbs; On-Line Exercise Bank, Section 23.2

In-Depth Coverage	Accelerated Pace
• Work through all key concepts, pp. 540–542 • Assign and review Exercises 20–22 • Read and discuss *Hands-on Grammar*, p. 544	• Assign pp. 540–542 for independent student review • Assign Section Review Exercises 23–25

> **Exercise 20** Distinguishing Between the Active and
Passive Voice Write the verb phrase in each sentence. Then,
label each verb as *active* or *passive.*

1. The study of all aspects of human life and culture is called anthropology.
2. Anthropologists examine such things as people's lives and their interactions with their environments.
3. Human diversity has been explored by anthropologists.
4. They investigate the common interests of people.
5. Some common questions about humans are asked by anthropologists.
6. Have people developed differently in different environments?
7. Societies from the ancient past to the present have been studied by anthropologists.
8. The work of anthropologists has uncovered clues to our past.
9. As a result, we will learn much about the present-day needs of people.
10. Better ways of life for the future may also be found.

Using Voice Correctly

To write well, you need to know when to use the active voice and when to use the passive voice. There are no firm rules, but here are some suggestions:

> **KEY CONCEPT** Use the active voice whenever possible. ■

Good writing is crisp and direct. Sentences with active verbs are less wordy and more direct than those with passive verbs.

ACTIVE VOICE: The scientist *opened* the package.
PASSIVE VOICE: The package *was opened* by the scientist.

> **More Practice**
> Language Lab
> CD-ROM
> • Verb Usage lesson
> On-line
> Exercise Bank
> • Section 23.2
> Grammar Exercise
> Workbook
> • pp. 127–128

◀ **Critical Viewing**
Use the verbs *found*
and *were found* in
two sentences about
the Egyptian hiero-
glyphics in this pho-
tograph. Which sen-
tence is in the active
voice and which is in
the passive voice?
[Connect]

Active and Passive Voice • 541

Grammar in Literature

1. Read the passage aloud to students.

2. Ask students why they think Keay Davidson used passive, then active voice in the sentence beginning "Sixteen… " (Possible responses: The mummies gain prominence in the sentence because of the passive voice. The active voice is appropriate for *has granted* because it shortens an extremely long sentence.)

23.2

GRAMMAR IN LITERATURE

from **Caucasian Mummies Mystify Chinese**
Keay Davidson

A passive voice verb phrase *in this passage is in blue italics. An* active voice verb phrase *is in red italics.*

A former Stanford scientist is analyzing the mummies' DNA in hopes of answering haunting questions: Who are they? Where did they come from? And what on earth were these European-looking men, women and children doing in China's parched out-back 2,000 years before Jesus, when Europe was largely a dark forest? Sixteen years after the first mummies *were found*, the Chinese government *has granted* Western researchers their first close look at these faces from prehistory: a baby in colorful swaddling clothes; a 20-year-old girl with braided hair, found buried in a curled-up position with her hands by her chest, as if dozing; a man with a pigtail, scarlet-colored clothes and red, blue, and amber leg wrappings. . . .

> **KEY CONCEPT** Use the passive voice when you want to emphasize the receiver of an action rather than the performer of an action. ■

EXAMPLE: My best friend was awarded a medal by the archaeological society.

> **KEY CONCEPT** Use the passive voice to point out the receiver of an action whenever the performer is not important or not easily identified. ■

EXAMPLE: The mysterious find was made at midnight. At noon, the doors to the tomb were unlocked, and the archaeologists entered it.

✦ Spelling Tip

Many words have letters that are not pronounced. *Archaeology,* for instance, has a silent *a.* Be sure to include it when you write the word!

542 • Verb Usage

☑ **ONGOING ASSESSMENT: Monitor and Reinforce**

If students miss more than two items in Exercises 20–22, refer them to the following for additional practice.

In the Textbook	Print Resources	Technology
Section Review, Ex. 23–25, p. 545	Grammar Exercise Workbook, pp. 127–130	Language Lab CD-ROM, Using Verbs; On-Line Exercise Bank, Section 23.2

Exercise 21 **Using the Passive Voice** Explain why the passive voice is appropriate in each of the following sentences.

EXAMPLE: Anthropologist Dr. Black was taught by my uncle.
ANSWER: passive voice (emphasizing receiver of action)

1. The work of anthropologists has been divided into different specialties.
2. Cultural anthropology, linguistic anthropology, archaeology, and physical anthropology were made areas of specialization in the United States.
3. Special training is required of all anthropologists.
4. Different research techniques are used by many scientists.
5. In the United States, courses are taught covering all of the subfields.

Exercise 22 **Revising a Paragraph to Eliminate Unnecessary Use of the Passive Voice** Rewrite the following paragraph, changing at least five uses of the passive voice to the active voice. Explain why you chose to revise or leave each use of passive voice.

EXAMPLE: Anthropology *is being studied* by many students.
ANSWER: Many students are studying anthropology. (shorter and more direct)

(1) Archaeology is also studied by anthropologists. (2) The study of past human societies and culture is focused on by archaeologists. (3) Various artifacts have been studied by archaeologists. (4) The remains of items made by past humans—such as tools, pottery, and buildings—are referred to as artifacts. (5) Fossils, or hardened remains of plant and animal life, have also been looked at by archaeologists. (6) Past environments are also examined by archaeologists to understand how natural forces shaped the development of human culture. (7) Such factors as climate and the amount of food available at that time are referred to as past environments. (8) Cultures existing before the development of writing have been studied by some archaeologists. (9) This period is known as prehistory. (10) The study of the periods prior to the first development of agriculture is called paleoanthropology. (11) This period took place thousands of years ago. (12) More recent cultures have been studied in historical archaeology. (13) The material remains of the past as well as written documents have been examined by archaeologists. (14) Archaeology is only one of the fields of interest to anthropologists. (15) All of their findings are used in understanding human life today.

More Practice
Language Lab
CD-ROM
• Verb Usage lesson
On-line
Exercise Bank
• Section 23.2
Grammar Exercise
Workbook
• pp. 129–130

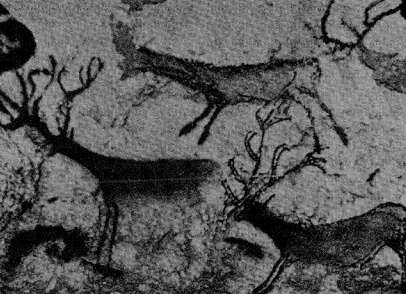

▲ **Critical Viewing** Use the active voice to describe what the animals in the cave painting are doing. Use the passive voice to describe the artwork itself. **[Analyze, Connect]**

Active and Passive Voice • 543

Answer Key

Exercise 21
1. performer of action is unidentified
2. emphasizing receiver of action
3. emphasizing receiver of action
4. emphasizing receiver of action
5. performer of action is unidentified

Exercise 22
Answers will vary. Samples are given.
1. Anthropologists also study archaeology. (shorter and more direct)
2. Archaeologists focus on the study. . . . (emphasizes archaeology, which is subject of whole paragraph)
3. Archaeologists have studied various artifacts. (emphasizes archaeology, which is subject of whole paragraph)
4. leave as is (emphasizes receiver of action)
5. Archaeologists have also looked at fossils. . . . (emphasizes archaeology, which is subject of whole paragraph)
6. Archaeologists have also examined past environments. . . . (emphasizes archaeology, which is subject of whole paragraph)
7. leave as is (performer of action is unknown)
8. Archaeologists have studied cultures. . . . (emphasizes archaeology, which is subject of whole paragraph)
9. leave as is (performer of action is unknown)
10. leave as is (performer of action unknown)
11. already in active voice
12. leave as is (emphasizes receiver of action)
13. Archaeologists have examined the material remains. . . . (emphasizes archaeology, which is subject of whole paragraph)
14. linking verb, has no voice
15. leave as is (performer of action unknown)

Critical Viewing
Analyze, Connect Students may suggest such sentences as "The animals in the cave painting are running" and "The cave paintings were discovered fifty years ago."

543

Active Arrows and Passive Points

Teaching Resources: Hands-on Grammar Activity Book, Chapter 23

1. Have students refer to their Hands-on Grammar activity books or give them copies of relevant pages for this activity.

2. Make sure students create sentences containing both active and passive verbs.

3. Have students write down each version for each sentence they create. Have them evaluate both versions to determine which one is more acceptable.

Find It in Your Reading

Have students change the active-voice sentences they find to passive voice, and vice-versa. Have them discuss how this change affects the sentences.

Find It in Your Writing

You may want to have students complete this activity in pairs so they can evaluate each other's work.

23.2

Hands-on Grammar

Active Arrows and Passive Points

You should write most sentences in the active voice unless you want to emphasize the receiver of an action or you are not indicating the performer of an action. To practice revising sentences by changing them from passive to active voice, do the following activity:

Cut out several arrows, similar to the ones shown below. On the side of an arrow pointing to the right, write a past tense form of a verb. Examples: *addressed, bought, drew, knew, saw.*

Flip the arrow over so that it points to the left. Write the same verb in the passive voice. (Remember that a passive voice verb includes a form of *be* and a past participle.) Examples: *has been addressed, was bought, are drawn, was known, has been seen.* Fold the flat end of the arrow, and write the word *by* on it, to be hidden or revealed as needed.

Next, take two equal piles of index cards. On each card in one pile, write a performer of an action—*a boy, an anthropologist, a scientist, my brother.* On each card in the other pile, write a noun that can receive the action—*a house, a pyramid, a fossil, the portrait.*

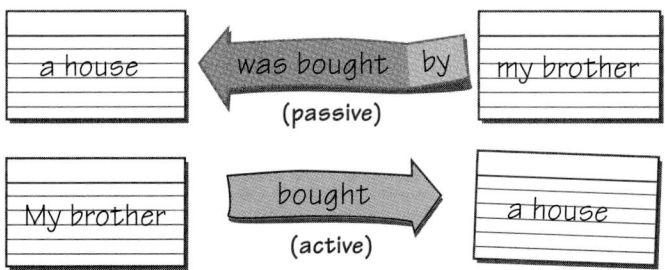

Working alone or with a partner, place a receiver and a performer card words up, with a space between them. Choose an arrow to fill the space. Point the arrow toward the receiver of the action. Read this passive voice sentence. Then, flip the arrow over, and shift the two index cards to create a new active voice sentence. Your second sentence should be shorter and more direct. Experiment by creating some sentences in your fold under the word *by* and do *not* state the performer of the action. Note that these sentences must stay in the passive voice.

Find It in Your Reading Select a paragraph from a story in your literature book that contains sentences with both active and passive voice verbs. Discuss with a partner why the writer chose each voice.

Find It in Your Writing Use this activity to evaluate the voice of several sentences in your own writing. If you discover some passive voice sentences, consider whether you should revise them to be in the active voice.

544 • Verb Usage

⏱ TIME SAVERS!

Hands-on Grammar Book
Use the Hands-on Grammar activity sheet for Chapter 23 to facilitate this activity.

☑ ONGOING ASSESSMENT: Assess Mastery

Use the following resources to assess student mastery of active and passive voice.

In the Textbook	Technology
Chapter Review, Ex. 35, p. 547	On-Line Exercise Bank, Section 23.2

Section 23.2 Section Review

GRAMMAR EXERCISES 23–28

Exercise 23 Distinguishing Between the Active and Passive Voice
Write the verb phrase in each sentence. Then, identify each verb as *active* or *passive*.

1. Archaeologists have uncovered artifacts from a great span of time.
2. They have identified different time periods and different cultures.
3. They specialize in these different areas and also in particular study methods.
4. The ancient civilizations of the Middle East or Europe are studied by some.
5. Later historical time periods are also explored by archaeologists.
6. Many other fields important to archaeological study have been examined by archaeology students.
7. Physical anthropology, geology, ecology, and climatology are all included in the archaeologist's study.
8. Archaeologists have studied with three goals in mind: chronology, reconstruction, and explanation.
9. Explanations of scientific theories have been proposed by archaeologists.
10. These theories explain what the people who lived in the past thought and did.

Exercise 24 Using the Passive Voice Explain why the passive voice is appropriate in each of the following sentences.

1. Chronological data relating to the spread of ideas have been studied by archaeologists.
2. Ideas were spread from one region to another over time.
3. This information about past cultures has been analyzed by archaeologists.
4. Information from various archaeological sites has been used.
5. Assembling a sequence or pattern has been made easier.

Exercise 25 Revising to Eliminate Unnecessary Use of the Passive Voice
Revise the following paragraph, changing at least three uses of the passive voice to the active. Explain why you chose to revise or leave each use of passive voice.

(1) The appearance of people and life in the past has been reconstructed by archaeologists. (2) How well the material remains have been documented by archaeologists will determine the accuracy of the reconstruction. (3) Environmental remains have been found as well. (4) Animal body parts have been included in the environmental remains that archaeologists have found. (5) Environmental remains also include parts of plants, which would also be found by the archaeologist.

Exercise 26 Find It in Your Reading In the excerpt from "Caucasian Mummies Mystify Chinese" on page 542, identify the voice of all the verbs that are not highlighted.

Exercise 27 Find It in Your Writing Look through your writing portfolio. Find at least three examples of passive verbs. Could any of the sentences be improved by changing the verbs to the active voice?

Exercise 28 Writing Application Write a description of a job that you find interesting. Be sure to identify the actions people perform in that job. Label each verb *active* or *passive*.

ASSESS and CLOSE

Section Review

Each of these exercises correlates to a concept taught in the section on active and passive voice, pages 540–544. The exercises may be used for more practice, for reteaching, or for review of the Key Concepts presented.

Answer Key

Exercise 23

1. have uncovered—active
2. have identified—active
3. specialize—active
4. are studied—passive
5. are explored—passive
6. have been examined—passive
7. are included—passive
8. have studied—active
9. have been proposed—passive
10. explain—active

Exercise 24

1. emphasis on receiver of action
2. performer of action unknown
3. emphasis on receiver of action
4. performer of action unknown
5. performer of action unknown

Exercise 25

Answers will vary. Samples are given.

1. Archaeologists have reconstructed the appearance of people (emphasis on performer of action)
2. How well they have documented the material remains (shorter and more direct)
3. leave as is (emphasis on receiver of action)
4. leave as is (emphasis on receiver of action)
5. Archaeologists also find environmental remains (emphasis on performer of action)

continued

Answer Key continued

Exercise 26

Find It in Your Reading
is analyzing—active
are—active
did come—active
were doing—active
was—active

Exercise 27

Find It in Your Writing
If students say that the active voice would be an improvement, have them write new sentences.

Exercise 28

Writing Application
Have students exchange descriptions with partners and check each other's labeling for accuracy.

⏱ TIME SAVERS!

Answers on Transparency Use the Grammar Exercises on Transparencies for Chapter 23 to have students correct their own or another's exercises.

On-Line Exercise Bank Have students complete the exercises on computer. The Auto Check feature will grade their work for you!

Answer Key

Exercise 29

1. present
2. future progressive
3. future
4. past perfect
5. present perfect progressive
6. past progressive
7. present progressive
8. future
9. future perfect
10. present perfect

Exercise 30

1. find, finding, found, (have) found
2. look, looking, looked, (have) looked
3. search, searching, searched, (have) searched
4. lie, lying, lay, (have) lain
5. build, building, built, (have) built

Exercise 31

1. I dig, I dug, I will dig, I have dug, I had dug, I will have dug
2. you look, you looked, you will look, you have looked, you had looked, you will have looked
3. he searches, he searched, he will search, he has searched, he had searched, he will have searched
4. they bury, they buried, they will bury, the have buried, they had buried, they will have buried
5. we see, we saw, we will see, we have seen, we had seen, we will have seen

Exercise 32

1. I am digging, I was digging, I will be digging, I have been digging, I had been digging, I will have been digging
2. you are looking, you were looking, you will be looking, you have been looking, you had been looking, you will have been looking

---

Chapter

23 Chapter Review

GRAMMAR EXERCISES 29–37

> **Exercise 29** **Recognizing Tenses and Forms of Verbs** Identify the tense and form of each verb.

1. In order to excavate, archaeologists locate a potential site.
2. They will be searching the site for artifacts and other remains.
3. Archaeologists will work carefully on one small area at a time.
4. Someone had removed the artifacts, altering the site forever.
5. Because of this, archaeologists have been trying not to damage sites.
6. Archaeologists were surveying and sampling the terrain.
7. What is waiting for them below the surface?
8. The archaeologists will find some sites very easily.
9. A careful search will have uncovered most sites.
10. Of course, simple accident has led to some sites.

> **Exercise 30** **Forming the Principal Parts of Regular and Irregular Verbs** On your paper, make four headings: *Present, Present Participle, Past,* and *Past Participle.* Then, list the principal parts for each verb under the appropriate headings.

1. find
2. look
3. search
4. lie
5. build

> **Exercise 31** **Conjugating the Basic Forms of Verbs** Conjugate the basic forms of the following verbs in the present, past, future, present perfect, past perfect, and future perfect tenses.

1. dig (conjugated with *I*)
2. look (conjugated with *you*)
3. search (conjugated with *he*)
4. bury (conjugated with *they*)
5. see (conjugated with *we*)

> **Exercise 32** **Conjugating the Progressive Forms of Verbs** Conjugate the progressive forms of the verbs in Exercise 30 in the six tenses.

> **Exercise 33** **Identifying the Uses of Tense** Identify the tense of the underlined verb in each sentence, and explain how the verb is being used to indicate time.

1. Archaeologist Howard Carter <u>knew</u> that Tutankhamen's tomb existed.
2. He <u>had discovered</u> information from other sites that led him to the tomb.
3. Searching for some archaeological sites <u>will take</u> years.
4. It <u>was</u> seven years before Carter found the tomb in 1922.
5. He <u>had searched</u> through much rubble in the Valley of the Kings before finding the tomb.
6. Archaeologists <u>have been depending</u> on their systematic survey methods to help them carry out their work.
7. To find the sites, the archaeologists <u>will have relied</u> on high-technology tools and techniques.
8. Airplanes <u>carry</u> radar and photographic equipment, called airborne technology.
9. This technology <u>has allowed</u> archaeologists to learn, without digging, about what lies beneath the ground.
10. They <u>will be locating</u> general areas of interest, such as ancient buildings.

---

3. he is searching, he was searching, he will be searching, he has been searching, he had been searching, he will have been searching
4. they are burying, they were burying, they will be burying, they have been burying, they had been burying, they will have been burying
5. we are seeing, we were seeing, we will be seeing, we have been seeing, we had been seeing, we will have been seeing

Exercise 33

1. past, completed action
2. past perfect, action completed before another
3. future, action will occur in the future
4. past, completed action
5. past perfect, action completed before another
6. present perfect progressive, action continuing
7. future perfect, future action completed before another
8. present, present action
9. present perfect, completed action
10. future progressive, continuing future action

Exercise 34 Supplying the Correct Tense

Write the indicated form for each verb in parentheses.

1. Present—Archaeologists often (use) ground surveys to find places to dig.
2. Future progressive—When doing a ground survey, the archaeologists (walk) great distances.
3. Present progressive—They (look) for clues, such as fragments of pottery.
4. Present perfect—By using ground radar, magnetic-field recording, and metal detectors, they also (locate) remains that are buried.
5. Future progressive—Archaeologists (use) computers to map sites and the landscapes around sites.
6. Future—Two- and three-dimensional maps (help) in planning excavations.
7. Past—Archaeologists Rene Million and George Cowgill (spend) years mapping Teotihuacan, what is now Mexico City.
8. Past perfect—By around A.D. 600, this city (become) one of the largest human settlements in the world.
9. Future perfect—When done, the researchers (map) the city's ceremonial areas and also apartment complexes.
10. Past—Million and Cowgill (find) evidence that merchants lived in these areas.

Exercise 35 Revising to Eliminate Unnecessary Use of Passive Voice

Revise most sentences below, changing them from passive to active voice. If you decide to leave a sentence in passive voice, explain why.

1. The age of the site has been determined by archaeologists.
2. The use of two methods is required by archaeologists for accurate dating.
3. The date of finds in relation to other finds is established by relative dating.
4. Absolute dating also is used by archaeologists to determine the year in which an item was deposited.
5. Absolute dating is sometimes called chronometric dating by archaeologists.
6. Absolute dates are obtained by archaeologists after much research.
7. Authorities on prehistoric periods are carefully studied by them.
8. A variety of well-established and experimental methods may be used.
9. Historical documents of people have been found to confirm the date.
10. Pottery made by the Minoan inhabitants was studied by Sir Arthur Evans, in the early 1900's.

Exercise 36 Revision Practice: Verb Usage

Rewrite the sentences in the following paragraph, correcting any errors in verb forms or tense and any unnecessary use of the passive voice. Some sentences may be correct.

(1) Our class had took a field trip to the art museum to see an exhibit of Egyptian artifacts. (2) Examples of clothing, furniture, jewelry, and pottery were saw by us. (3) Some valuable treasures from the tomb of King Tutankhamen were on display. (4) He had die at about the age of 18. (5) In the four rooms of the tomb, many beautiful gold-covered items has been find by archaeologist Howard Carter. (6) When Carter finds the tomb, a magnificent gold mask covered the face of the mummy. (7) Chests, thrones, jewelry, and swords were also uncovered by Carter. (8) Long before Carter discovered the tomb, artists covered its walls with bright decorations and paintings. (9) These were show scenes in the life of the young pharaoh. (10) The paintings also indicate to experts today that women in ancient Egypt wear makeup and jewelry.

Exercise 37 Writing Application

Write a short essay on a period of history that interests you, describing the people of the time and their activities. Include at least two irregular verbs, one progressive form of a verb, and one sentence using the passive voice.

Exercise 34
1. use
2. will be walking
3. are looking
4. have located
5. will be using
6. will help
7. spent
8. had become
9. will have mapped
10. found

Exercise 35
Answers will vary. Samples are given.
1. Archaeologists have determined the age of the site.
2. Archaeologists must use two methods for accurate dating.
3. Relative dating establishes the date of finds in relation to other finds.
4. Archaeologists also use absolute dating to determine the year in which an item was deposited.
5. leave as is—emphasize receiver of action
6. Archaeologists obtain absolute dates after much research.
7. They carefully study authorities on prehistoric periods.
8. leave as is—performer of action unknown
9. leave as is—performer of action unknown
10. In the early 1900's Sir Arthur Evans studied pottery made by the Minoan inhabitants.
continued

Answer Key continued

Exercise 36
Answers will vary. Samples are given.
(1) Our class took a field trip to the art museum to see an exhibit of Egyptian artifacts. (2) We saw examples of clothing, furniture, jewelry, and pottery. (3) leave as is (4) He died at about 18. (5) In the four rooms of the tomb, the archaeologist Howard Carter found many beautiful gold-covered items. (6) When Carter found the tomb, a magnificent gold mask covered the face of the mummy. (7) Carter also uncovered chests, thrones, jewelry, and swords. (8) leave as is (9) These showed scenes in the life of the young pharoah. (10) The paintings also indicate to today's experts that women in ancient Egypt wore makeup and jewelry.

Exercise 37
Writing Application
Students can combine their essays, in chronological order, into a class book.

Using Verbs

1. Explain to students that they should read the entire passage for word and context clues that will help them choose the correct tenses.

2. In the sample passage, *yesterday* indicates that the events described took place in the past. This helps students narrow their choices to past-tense verbs.

3. In the sample passage, *when* indicates that an action was going on when another action took place. Therefore, the only possible choices for completing the sentence are items D and A.

Standardized Test Preparation Workshop

Standard English Usage: Using Verbs

Your knowledge of verb usage is frequently measured on standardized tests. Your ability to determine the correct tense of a verb—present, present perfect, past, past perfect, future, and future perfect and their progressive forms—is tested when you must choose a verb or verb phrase to complete a sentence. When choosing a verb, first read the sentence silently to yourself, and determine when it is taking place. Then, choose a verb that indicates the same point in time or tense of the sentence.

The following test items will give you practice with the format of questions that test verb usage.

Test Tip

Read the sentence silently to yourself several times. Each time, substitute answer choice in place of the blank. Eliminate those choices that sound awkward or change the meaning of the sentence.

Sample Test Item	Answers and Explanations

Directions: Read the passage, and choose the letter of the word or group of words that belongs in each space.
 	
Yesterday, I __(1)__ in the shower when I __(2)__ the phone.
 	
1 A sing
  B will have been singing
  C had sung
  D was singing
	The correct answer is *D*. The passage hints at a continuing action that took place at the time of another past event. Therefore, the past progressive form *was singing* is the correct choice for completing the sentence.

2 F heard
  G had heard
  H had been hearing
  J was hearing
	The correct answer is *F*. The passage indicates an action that occurred in the past. Therefore, the past tense verb *heard* is the correct choice for completing the sentence.

548 • Verb Usage

TEST-TAKING TIP

When dealing with questions that test students' knowledge of tenses, it might help them to read the incomplete sentences several times, looking for clues to when the events of the sentence take place. Narrowing down the time frame to past, present, or future enables students to limit the possible answers.

> **Practice 1** **Directions:** Read the passage, and choose the letter of the word or group of words that belongs in each space.

When she __(1)__ the old house, the first thing that Bonnie __(2)__ was a dusty photograph of a rock-and-roll band from the 1950's. Then, she __(3)__ over a stack of old records. Who knows how long they __(4)__ been there? "What __(5)__ next?" Bonnie asked herself, "a Hula-Hoop?"

1 A enter
   B was entered
   C entered
   D entering

2 F encounter
   G encountered
   H is encountering
   J hadn't encountered

3 A stumbled
   B was stumbling
   C stumble
   D will stumble

4 F were
   G might
   H might have
   J might of

5 A were
   B will
   C would
   D will be

> **Practice 2** **Directions:** Read the passage, and choose the letter of the word or group of words that belongs in each space.

The person I met __(1)__ a scrawny little boy. He __(2)__, at most, twelve years old. A single, tough, curly lock of hair __(3)__ from his forehead, like a corkscrew. This gave him the look that is often __(4)__ a Saturday-morning cartoon. You could tell from the sly grin on his face that he was capable __(5)__ havoc.

1 A was
   B would be
   C is
   D had been

2 F may
   G had
   H may have been
   J has been

3 A sprang
   B sprunged
   C will spring
   D sprung

4 F find
   G found in
   H founded
   J finding

5 A of raised
   B of raising
   C raising
   D will rise

Practice 1

1. C
2. G
3. A
4. H
5. D

Practice 2

1. A
2. H
3. D
4. G
5. B

In-Depth Lesson Plan

LESSON FOCUS	PRINT AND MEDIA RESOURCES
DAY 1 — **Pronoun Case** Students learn and apply the concepts of pronoun case (pp. 550–558).	**Teaching Resources** *Grammar Exercise Workbook*, pp. 131–136; *Grammar Exercises Answers on Transparency*, Chapter 24; *Language Lab* **CD-ROM**, Nouns and Pronouns; *On-Line Exercise Bank*, Section 24.1
DAY 2 — **Solving Pronoun Problems** Students learn and apply concepts of solving such pronoun problems as use of *who, whom,* and *whose* correctly and do the Hands-on Grammar activity (pp. 559–564).	**Teaching Resources** *Grammar Exercise Workbook*, pp.137–138; *Grammar Exercises Answers on Transparency*, Chapter 24; *Hands-on Grammar Activity Book*, Chapter 24; *Language Lab* **CD-ROM**, Nouns and Pronouns; *On-Line Exercise Bank*, Section 24.2
DAY 3 — **Review and Assess** Students review chapter and demonstrate mastery of use of pronouns (pp. 565–569).	**Teaching Resources** *Formal Assessment*, Ch. 24; *On-Line Exercise Bank*, Section 24.1

Accelerated Lesson Plan

LESSON FOCUS	PRINT AND MEDIA RESOURCES
DAY 1 — **Pronoun Usage** Students cover concepts and usage of pronouns as determined by Diagnostic Test (pp. 550–564).	**Teaching Resources** *Grammar Exercise Workbook*, pp.131–138; *Grammar Exercises Answers on Transparency*, Chapter 24; *Hands-on Grammar Activity Book*, Chapter 24; *Language Lab* **CD-ROM**, Nouns and Pronouns; *On-Line Exercise Bank*, Section 24.1-2
DAY 2 — **Review and Assess** Students review chapter and demonstrate mastery of use of pronouns (pp. 566–569).	**Teaching Resources** *Formal Assessment*, Ch. 24; *On-Line Exercise Bank*, Section 24.1

Options for Adapting Lesson Plans

HOMEWORK

Have students complete any section of the chapter for homework.

FEATURES

Extend coverage with the Grammar in Literature feature (p. 559) and the Standardized Test Preparation Workshop (p. 568).

TECHNOLOGY

Students can use the On-Line Exercise Bank to complete the exercises on computer. The Auto Check feature will grade their work.

INTEGRATED SKILLS COVERAGE

Grammar in Literature
SE p. 559

Reading
Find It in Your Reading SE pp. 558, 564, 565

Writing
Find It in Your Writing SE pp. 558, 564, 565
Writing Application SE pp. 558, 565, 567

Language
Language Highlight ATE p. 556

Viewing and Representing
Critical Viewing SE pp. 550, 554, 556, 560, 563

ASSESSMENT SUPPORT

Standardized Test Preparation SE p. 568; ATE p. 568
Standardized Test Preparation Workbook, Ch. 24
Formal Assessment, Ch. 24

MEETING INDIVIDUAL NEEDS

Less Advanced Students ATE p. 555; See also Ongoing
Assessments ATE pp. 554, 557, 562, 564
More Advanced Students ATE pp. 556, 561

BLOCK SCHEDULING

Pacing Suggestions
For 90-minute Blocks
• Administer the Diagnostic Test to students to determine instructional coverage.
• Have students complete the necessary exercises in class. Use the Hands-on Grammar activity to provide a change of pace.

Resources for Varying Instruction
• *Language Lab* CD-ROM If your students have access to hardware, a 90-minute block provides an ideal opportunity for students to work on computer.

Professional Development Support
• *How to Manage Instruction in the Block* This teaching resource provides management and activity suggestions.

MEDIA AND TECHNOLOGY

For the Student
• *Language Lab* CD-ROM, Nouns and Pronouns
• *On-Line Exercise Bank,* Ch. 24

For the Teacher
• *Resource Pro* CD-ROM

WRITING AND GRAMMAR WEBSITE

The Interactive Writing and Grammar Website provides a wide array of support for students, teachers, and parents. Grammar support includes:

• *On-Line Exercise Bank* with Auto Check scoring
• Diagnostic and assessment support

phwg.phschool.com

LITERATURE CONNECTIONS

Grammar in Literature selections from *Prentice Hall Literature: Timeless Voices, Timeless Themes,* Gold:
from *The Tragedy of Romeo and Juliet,* William Shakespeare, SE p. 559

▶ Lesson Objectives

1. To learn the three cases of pronouns.
2. To relate the case of a pronoun to its function in a sentence.
3. To use the pronouns *who, whom,* and *whose* correctly.
4. To use pronouns correctly in elliptical clauses.

Critical Viewing

Analyze Students may say that he is washing his car, so it must instill pride in him.

Chapter 24 Pronoun Usage

Cars come in many shapes and forms. Some cars are built for speed; others are built to travel over rough roads. The form of a car usually indicates its function, or purpose. This chapter will explain the different forms of pronouns and their functions in sentences.

At one time in the history of the English language, the form of nouns and pronouns was changed to indicate how they were being used in a sentence. Today, the form of nouns changes only to show possession. In modern English, however, the form of pronouns still changes to show how they are being used in a sentence.

▲ Critical Viewing
What details in this photograph shows pride of possession? Answer using personal pronouns *he, his, him, it.* [**Analyze**]

550 • Pronoun Usage

☑ ONGOING ASSESSMENT: Diagnose

If students miss more than one item in each category, direct them to the relevant pages of the text and assign exercises for practice and review.

Pronoun Usage	Diagnostic Test Items	Teach	Practice	Section Review	Chapter Review
Skill Checks A–C					
Pronoun Case	A 1–5 B 6–10 C 11–15	pp. 552–557	Ex. 1–7	Ex. 8–13	Ex. 23–25
Skill Check D					
Who, Whom, and *Whose*	D 16–20	pp. 559–562	Ex. 14–15	Ex. 17–18	Ex. 27

Diagnostic Test

Directions: Write all answers on a separate sheet of paper.

Skill Check A. Identify the underlined pronoun in each sentence as *nominative, objective,* or *possessive.*

1. You and I have consumer protection rights because of the efforts of government organizations, individuals, and businesses.
2. Consumers should know the laws protecting their rights.
3. Some consumers are unaware of the laws that protect them.
4. Mrs. Larson bought a shirt that she later wanted to return.
5. The salesperson helped her to choose another one.

Skill Check B. Choose the correct case of the pronoun to complete each sentence.

6. The saleswoman helped my brother Paul and (I, me).
7. We seemed like good customers to (she, her).
8. Other customers thought (they, them) might buy the same car.
9. Paul and (I, me) did purchase the car.
10. To drive the car legally, it is required of (we, us) that we buy insurance.

Skill Check C. Supply a pronoun to complete each sentence.

11. Insurance agent Jane spoke to Paul about ___?___ new car.
12. "I want to know if this is___?___," Jane asked.
13. Paul told her that it was also ___?___.
14. "If it is ___?___ also," Jane said, "the cost of insurance will go up."
15. Paul told the agent that the car was ___?___.

Skill Check D. Write *who, whom, whose,* or *who's* to complete each of the following sentences.

16. From ___?___ did you get that product?
17. I want to meet the salesperson ___?___ sold this to you.
18. ___?___ name should I ask for when I call the company?
19. ___?___ the best person to call for a refund?
20. It is she ___?___ you should contact.

Skill Check E. Choose the correct pronoun in the elliptical clause. Then, write any words or phrases that are understood to come before or after the noun.

21. I worked longer last night than (he, him) ___?___.
22. He feels that he is as skilled as (I, me) ___?___.
23. Helen has a more flexible schedule than (us, we) ___?___.
24. However, we work longer hours than (she, her) ___?___.
25. The supervisor knows me better than (she, her) ___?___.

- Each section in the diagnostic test corresponds to a specific section in the chapter. This will enable you to tailor instruction to the particular needs of your students. See "Ongoing Assessment: Diagnose" below for further details.
- Answers for the Diagnostic Test and all chapter exercises are available in *Grammar Exercises Answers on Transparencies* in your teaching resources.

Skill Check A
1. nominative
2. possessive
3. objective
4. nominative
5. objective

Skill Check B
6. me
7. her
8. they
9. I
10. us

Skill Check C
11. our
12. his or hers or yours
13. mine or his
14. his or hers or yours
15. ours

Skill Check D
16. whom
17. who
18. Whose
19. Who's
20. whom

Skill Check E
21. he did or he worked
22. I am
23. we have or we do
24. she does or she works
25. she knows her

ONGOING ASSESSMENT: Diagnose *continued*

Pronoun Usage	Diagnostic Test Items	Teach	Practice	Section Review	Chapter Review
Skill Check E					
Elliptical Clauses	E 21–25	pp. 562–563	Ex. 16–17	Ex. 19	Ex. 27
Cumulative Reviews and Applications				Ex. 11–12, 17–22	Ex 23–28

PREPARE and ENGAGE

Interest GRABBER Ask students to define the word *pronoun.* (A word that takes the place of a noun) Call on students to list as many pronouns as they can. Write their answers on the board in three columns, one for each case. Challenge students to explain the groupings you have used. Explain that in this section, they will learn about the three different forms, or cases, of pronouns.

Activate Prior Knowledge

Ask students to explain the difference between the subject and the direct object of a sentence. (The subject performs the action; the direct object receives it.) Explain that any noun can appear unchanged as either subject or object: Pronouns, however, exist in different forms, one for subjects and one for objects.

TEACH

Step-by-Step Teaching Guide

The Three Cases

1. Go over the two charts on this page with students. Paraphrase the uses in the first chart if students do not understand all the terms.
2. Challenge each student to write a sentence showing a nominative pronoun. Repeat this for the other two cases. Have students read their sentences aloud and discuss and correct any errors.
3. Point out that the pronouns *you* and *it* are the only ones that are the same in both the nominative and objective cases. All the other pronouns change their spelling in all three cases.

Section 24.1

Identifying Case

The case of a pronoun reflects its function.

KEY CONCEPT **Case** is the form of a noun or a pronoun that indicates its use in a sentence. ■

In this section, you will learn how to recognize the three cases of pronouns and when to use them in sentences.

Theme: Employment

In this section, you will learn about the nominative, objective, and possessive cases of pronouns. The examples and exercises in this section are about working in a store.

Cross-Curricular Connection: Social Studies

The Three Cases

Both nouns and pronouns have three cases. The chart below shows the uses of each of these three cases.

KEY CONCEPT The three cases are the *nominative*, the *objective*, and the *possessive*. ■

Case	Use in Sentence
Nominative	Subject or predicate nominative
Objective	Direct object, indirect object, object of a preposition, or object of a verbal
Possessive	To show ownership

Using the correct case of nouns is seldom a problem because the form changes only in the possessive case.

Personal pronouns, on the other hand, often require a change in form for all three cases. The chart below shows the various forms of the personal pronouns in the three cases.

Nominative	Objective	Possessive
I	me	my, mine
you	you	your, yours
he, she, it	him, her, it	his, her, hers, its
we	us	our, ours
they	them	their, theirs

Learn More

To review what you have already learned about pronouns, turn to Chapter 16.

TIME AND RESOURCE MANAGER

Resources
Print: Grammar Exercise Workbook, pp. 131–136
Technology: Language Lab CD-ROM, Nouns and Pronouns; On-Line Exercise Bank, Section 24.1

In-Depth Coverage	Accelerated Pace
• Work through all key concepts, pp. 552–557. • Assign and review Exercises 1–7.	• Assign pp. 552–557 for independent student review. • Assign Review Exercise 10.

▶ **Exercise 1** **Identifying Case** Write the case of each underlined pronoun.

EXAMPLE: The manager gave <u>me</u> the good news about the job.

ANSWER: me (objective)

1. After waiting ten minutes, <u>we</u> finally spoke to the manager.
2. My friend gave him <u>our</u> résumés.
3. He asked <u>us</u> to fill out applications.
4. Later in the week, he called <u>me</u> for an interview.
5. The other associates said that <u>they</u> would help me learn the job.
6. There are a variety of duties involved in <u>my</u> job.
7. The trainer and <u>I</u> worked all day on Friday.
8. She taught <u>me</u> how to interact with customers.
9. I must always be ready to answer <u>their</u> questions.
10. They ask for a certain item, and I give it to <u>them</u>.

Using the Nominative Case

There are two major uses of pronouns in the nominative case:

▶ **KEY CONCEPT** Use the nominative case for the subject of a verb. ■

EXAMPLES: *I* do most of the advertising.
            You know we are friends.

Informal usage is appropriate for casual conversations, but you should use the nominative case after linking verbs in formal writing.

If the pronoun is part of a compound subject, remove the other subject to check that you have used the nominative case.

COMPOUND SUBJECT: Janie and I do most of the advertising.
                    (*I* do most of the advertising.)

▶ **KEY CONCEPT** Use the nominative case for a predicate nominative. ■

A predicate nominative is the noun or pronoun that appears after a linking verb and identifies or renames the subject.

EXAMPLE: Who's there? It is *I.*

▶ **More Practice**

Language Lab CD-ROM
• Pronoun Case lesson
On-line Exercise Bank
• Section 24.1
Grammar Exercise Workbook
• pp. 131–132

Answer Key

▶ **Exercise 1**

1. nominative
2. possessive
3. objective
4. objective
5. nominative, objective
6. possessive
7. nominative
8. objective
9. possessive
10. objective

Step-by-Step Teaching Guide

Using the Nominative Case

1. Remind students that pronouns are more general than nouns. The pronoun *him,* for instance, can refer to any male person or animal.

2. When students use pronouns in their sentences, they must always be sure that the reader will know to whom each pronoun refers. When a pronoun is the subject of a sentence, the antecedent will have to appear in a previous sentence.

    *I handed **Carl** the leash. **He** was so excited to be given the responsibility of taking the dog out!*

    The nominative pronoun *he* must agree in gender and number with the antecedent *Carl.*

TIME SAVERS!

▣ **Answers on Transparency** Use the Grammar Exercises on Transparencies for Chapter 24 to have students correct their own or one another's exercises.

▣ **On-Line Exercise Bank** Have students complete the exercises on computer. The Auto Check feature will grade their work for you!

Answer Key

Exercise 2

1. he; predicate nominative
2. she; predicate nominative
3. I; subject
4. he; subject
5. they; predicate nominative

Exercise 3

Sample answers are given.

1. We; subject
2. we; predicate nominative
3. She; subject
4. I; subject
5. he; predicate nominative

Exercise 4

Answers will vary. Samples are given.

1. Dana and I went shopping yesterday.
2. The two people carrying stacks of clothes to the fitting rooms were we.
3. He and they soon left for the food court to rest their feet.
4. The ones who bought the most were she and I.
5. You and they can go shopping with us next time.

Critical Viewing

Infer Students may say that she checks the fruit.

Exercise 2 Identifying Pronouns in the Nominative Case Choose the pronoun in the nominative case. Then, write the use of the pronoun.

EXAMPLE: Greg and (me, I) will start our new job.

ANSWER: I (subject)

1. The manager for two years has been (he, him).
2. The new members of the store's staff are Greg and (she, her).
3. Mary and (I, me) will work the morning shift tomorrow.
4. The manager and (he, him) will work the evening shift.
5. It is (them, they) who will clean up at closing.

Exercise 3 Supplying Pronouns in the Nominative Case Write a nominative case pronoun to complete each sentence. Then, write the use of the pronoun.

EXAMPLE: Alma and ___?___ will do the shopping.

ANSWER: I (subject)

1. ___?___ are hoping to close the store quickly tonight.
2. It is ___?___ who must restock the shelves right away.
3. ___?___ is the associate I enjoy working with the most.
4. You know that ___?___ am a fast worker.
5. The fastest worker, however, is ___?___.

Exercise 4 Writing Sentences Using the Nominative Case Pronouns Write sentences about a shopping trip, using nominative case pronouns according to the instructions below.
1. Use a person's name and *I* as a compound subject.
2. Use *we* as a predicate pronoun.
3. Use *he and they* as a compound subject.
4. Use *he* (or *she*) *and I* as a compound predicate pronoun.
5. Use *you and they* as a compound subject.

▲ **Critical Viewing** What does this woman do as part of her market job? Answer using a nominative case pronoun. **[Infer]**

More Practice

Language Lab CD-ROM
• Pronoun Case lesson
On-line Exercise Bank
• Section 24.1
Grammar Exercise Workbook
• pp. 133–134

⏱ TIME SAVERS!

Answers on Transparency Use the Grammar Exercises on Transparencies for Chapter 24 to have students correct their own or one another's exercises.

On-Line Exercise Bank Have students complete the exercises on computer. The Auto Check feature will grade their work for you!

☑ ONGOING ASSESSMENT: Monitor and Reinforce

If students miss more than two items in Exercises 1–4, refer them to the following for additional practice:

In the Textbook	Print Resources	Technology
Section Review, Ex. 8–9, p. 558	Grammar Exercise Workbook, pp. 131–134	Language Lab CD-ROM, Nouns and Pronouns; On-Line Exercise Bank, Section 24.1

Using the Objective Case

The *objective case* is used when a pronoun functions as the object of a verb, the object of a preposition, or the object in a verbal phrase.

KEY CONCEPT Use the objective case for the object of a verb or preposition and as the object in most verbal phrases. ■

The chart below provides examples of objective pronouns used as direct objects, indirect objects, objects of prepositions, and objects of participles, gerunds, and infinitives.

OBJECTIVE PRONOUNS	
Use	**Examples**
Direct Object	I sold *them* yesterday. Our manager praised *her*.
Indirect Object	Give *him* the new product. Alice gave *us* the paychecks.
Object of Preposition	Between *us*, there are no unserved customers. Stock the shelves beside *them*.
Object of Participle	Racing *her*, I stock the shelves in minutes. The girl chasing *them* was her employer.
Object of Gerund	The manager likes helping *me* with difficult customers. Warning *them* was my primary concern.
Object of Infinitive	To tell *her* clearly, he had to shout. He wants to ask *me* about the warranty.

Identifying Objective Pronouns in Compounds If an objective pronoun is part of a compound, make sure that you have selected the correct form by removing the other part of the compound.

EXAMPLES: Mr. Rodriguez promoted Carlos and *her*.
Mr. Rodriguez promoted *her*. (*Her* is a direct object.)

Tom gave my sister and *me* five dollars.
Tom gave *me* five dollars. (*Me* is an indirect object.)

This matter is between you and *me*.
(*Me* is the object of the preposition *between*.)

Speaking and Listening Tip

When using compound pronouns as objects, people often make the mistake of using the nominative case, as in these incorrect examples: *It's between you and I. Beth told Tom and she.* To accustom yourself to using compound objective pronouns correctly, pair up with a classmate and practice reading aloud the examples on this page and in Exercise 5 on page 556.

Using the Objective Case
1. Summarize the difference between nominative and objective pronouns for students. Nominative pronouns take the action or are in the state or condition described in the sentence. Objective pronouns are acted upon.
2. Students can think of nominative pronouns as being active-voice pronouns, and objective pronouns as being passive-voice pronouns.

Customize for *Less Advanced Students*

Use this chapter for a review of pronoun-antecedent agreement. Remind students that each pronoun must agree in gender and number with the noun it modifies. Have students identify the antecedents (stated or understood) of the pronouns in Exercises 1–3.

▶ **Exercise 5** Identifying Pronouns in the Objective Case

Choose the pronoun in the objective case. Then, write the use of the pronoun.

EXAMPLE: The manager asked only (us, we) workers for a conference.

ANSWER: us (direct object)

1. This secret is just between you and (I, me).
2. The manager gave both Greg and (I, me) a raise.
3. Between the other associates and (we, us), there is a big difference.
4. The man training (they, them) is the manager.
5. We are training (them, they) to be more effective in customer service.

▶ **Exercise 6** Using Pronouns in the Objective Case Write an objective pronoun to complete each sentence. Then, write the use of the pronoun.

EXAMPLE: My parents gave ____?____ a watch for my birthday.

ANSWER: me (indirect object)

1. We gave ____?____ advice on how to handle customer-service problems.
2. Ask for the manager or ____?____ if you cannot handle a customer.
3. Training ____?____ did not take long.
4. The associates gave ____?____ a good example to follow.
5. I congratulated ____?____ for their improved job performance.

▶ **Critical Viewing** What is the role of the young man, and what might his purpose be in showing the jacket? Include two objective pronouns in your response. [Speculate]

Using the Possessive Case

The *possessive case* of personal pronouns shows possession before nouns and gerunds. It can also be used alone.

▶**KEY CONCEPT** Use the possessive case before nouns to show ownership. ■

EXAMPLES: *My* shoes do not fit properly.
The store owner visited *our* class.
Their purchase came as a surprise.

▶**KEY CONCEPT** Use the possessive case before gerunds. ■

EXAMPLES: *Your* complaining bothers all of us.
We did not like *his* chattering during work.

▶**KEY CONCEPT** Use certain possessive pronouns by themselves to indicate possession. ■

EXAMPLES: That book is *hers*, not *his*.
Is this money *yours* or *theirs*?

Sometimes, possessive pronouns cause problems because they are incorrectly spelled with an apostrophe. Spellings such as *your's*, *our's*, *their's*, and *her's* are incorrect. In addition, do not confuse a possessive pronoun with a contraction.

POSSESSIVE PRONOUN: The monkey wanted to get out of *its* cage.

CONTRACTION: The store is closed today but *it's* open tomorrow.

▶**Exercise 7** Using Pronouns in the Possessive Case Supply a possessive pronoun to complete each sentence.

EXAMPLE: Doing a job well is often ___?___ own reward.
ANSWER: its

1. I spoke to Ralph about ___?___ offering me a job.
2. I asked him if the job was ___?___.
3. Marty works with Shelly on ___?___ shared register.
4. Everybody comes in to ___?___ store at once.
5. The store is at ___?___ fullest near lunchtime.
6. The staff members do most of ___?___ work in the afternoon.
7. Together, ___?___ line serves the most customers.
8. ___?___ paying attention to each customer is important.
9. ___?___ brother wants to work with us.
10. I asked Ralph if ___?___ store had another opening.

Spelling Tip

The pronoun *their* is spelled differently from the adverb *there*. *Their* is a possessive pronoun, and *there* indicates a location or acts as a sentence opener. Remember also that *theirs* is a pronoun and *there's* is the contraction of *there is*.

▶**More Practice**

Language Lab
CD-ROM
• Pronoun Case lesson
On-line
Exercise Bank
• Section 24.1
Grammar Exercise
Workbook
• pp. 133–136

Identifying Case • 557

Step-by-Step Teaching Guide

Using the Possessive Case

1. Explain the difference between my/your/her/our/their and mine/yours/hers/ours/theirs. The first set of pronouns appear before the nouns or pronouns to which they refer.

   That is **my** chair.
   He is **our** shortstop.
   This is **their** house.

2. The second set of pronouns always follow the nouns to which they refer.

   The chair is **mine**.
   That shortstop is **ours**.
   This house is **theirs**.

3. Point out that *his* is the only pronoun that does not change its spelling for these two different uses.

   The chair is **his**.
   This is **his** chair.

4. Emphasize the rule that no possessive pronoun is spelled with an apostrophe. Remembering this rule will help students avoid the common error of using *it's* for *its*.

Answer Key

Exercise 7

Some answers may vary.

1. his
2. mine
3. their
4. our
5. its
6. their
7. our
8. Our
9. His
10. our

☑ ONGOING ASSESSMENT SYSTEM: Monitor and Reinforce

If students miss more than two items in Exercises 5–7, refer them to the following for additional practice:

In the Textbook	Print Resources	Technology
Section Review, Ex. 8–9, p. 558	Grammar Exercise Workbook, pp. 133–136	Language Lab CD-ROM, Nouns and Pronouns; On-Line Exercise Bank, Section 24.1

⏱ TIME SAVERS!

Answers on Transparency
Use the Grammar Exercises on Transparencies for Chapter 24 to have students correct their own or one another's exercises.

On-Line Exercise Bank
Have students complete the exercises on computer. The Auto Check feature will grade their work for you!

Section Review

Each of these exercises correlates to a concept taught in the section on using pronouns, pages 552–557. The exercises may be used for more practice, for reteaching, or for review of the Key Concepts presented. Answers for all chapter exercises are available in *Grammar Exercises Answers on Transparencies* in your teaching resources.

Answer Key

Exercise 8

1. us; objective
2. them; objective
3. Their, possessive
4. I, nominative
5. she; nominative
6. him; objective
7. Our, possessive
8. me; objective
9. My, possessive
10. us; objective

Exercise 9

1. they
2. his
3. he
4. Our
5. them

Exercise 10

Revisions will vary. Sample is given.

He hired Verna and Max to work in the movie theater. Several of their classmates work at the theater. Karen sells movie tickets. Customers often ask her if the movie has already begun. Kenny works at the concession stand. He enjoys selling snacks and beverages.

Exercise 11

Find It in Your Reading
I; nominative (twice)
we; nominative
your; possessive
you; nominative (3 times)
me; objective
it; nominative

Exercise 12

Find It in Your Writing
Check students' work to be sure they have used the correct pronoun case in each sentence. Challenge them to identify the case of each pronoun in their sentences.

GRAMMAR EXERCISES 8–13

Exercise 8 Choosing Pronouns in the Correct Case Choose the pronoun that is in the correct case to complete each sentence. Identify the case of the pronoun you choose.

1. School fund-raisers taught (we, us) how to sell products to the public.
2. When promoting a product to customers, a salesperson should provide an incentive for (they, them) to buy.
3. (Them, Their) buying often depends on how they react to the seller.
4. This year, my teammates and (I, me) are selling team-spirit banners.
5. The treasurer is (she, her).
6. We will deliver Mr. Barouski's purchase to (he, him).
7. (Our, Us) delivering saves him from having to pick up his order.
8. This fund-raiser is important to my teammates and (I, me).
9. (Me, My) learning to interact with the public is an important part of the experience.
10. Customers know that the sale helps (we, us) earn money for the team.

Exercise 9 Supplying Pronouns
Supply a pronoun to fill in each blank.

The business of selling things has been practiced for thousands of years. Prehistoric people traded for the things that ___(1)___ needed. If one man was a good hunter, he might have traded some of ___(2)___ catch for clothing or tools. The bargaining skills that ___(3)___ would use would involve some techniques used in selling. Many historical documents that reveal how people lived are actually sales orders. ___(4)___ looking at what people bought and sold helps us to learn what was important or necessary to ___(5)___.

Exercise 10 Revision Practice: Pronouns Revise the following passage by replacing some nouns with pronouns in the appropriate case.

The theater manager hired Verna and Max to work in the movie theater. Several of Verna and Max's classmates work at the theater. Karen sells movie tickets. Customers often ask Karen if the movie has already begun. Kenny works at the concession stand. Kenny enjoys selling snacks and beverages.

Exercise 11 Find It in Your Reading Identify the case of each pronoun in the following excerpt from Edgar Allan Poe's "The Cask of Amontillado."

"Come," I said, with decision, "we will go back; your health is precious. You are rich, respected, admired, beloved; you are happy, as once I was. You are a man to be missed. For me it is no matter."

Exercise 12 Find It in Your Writing Using the chart on page 552, find at least one example in your own writing of each pronoun in each case. On a separate sheet of paper, write the sentences in which you have used the pronouns.

Exercise 13 Writing Application Write a brief dialogue between a salesperson and a customer. In your dialogue, use a possessive pronoun with a gerund, a subjective case pronoun as a predicate nominative, and an objective case pronoun in a verbal phrase.

Exercise 13

Writing Application
Students may want to work with partners on their dialogues, each writing the speeches for one character. Partners should discuss and agree on case of all pronouns in their dialogues.

Section 24.2 *Special Problems With Pronouns*

In this section, you will study the proper uses of *who* and *whom* and the related forms *whoever* and *whomever*. You will also study the use of pronouns in clauses where some words are omitted but understood.

Using *Who*, *Whom*, and *Whose* Correctly

▶ **KEY CONCEPT** *Who* and *whoever* are nominative. *Whom* and *whomever* are objective. *Whose* and *whosever* are possessive. ∎

Case	Pronoun	Use in Sentence
Nominative	who, whoever	Subject or predicate nominative
Objective	whom, whomever	Direct object, object of a verbal, or object of a preposition
Possessive	whose, whosever	To show ownership

Note About *Whose*: Do not confuse the contraction *who's*, which means *who is*, with the possessive pronoun *whose*.

POSSESSIVE PRONOUN: Whose short story won the contest?

CONTRACTION: Who's our first singer tonight?

GRAMMAR IN LITERATURE

from The Tragedy of Romeo and Juliet
William Shakespeare

In the following excerpt, the prince questions a young nobleman about the start of a street fight. The nominative case is highlighted in blue italics. The objective case is highlighted in red italics.

PRINCE.   Benvolio, *who* began this bloody fray?

BENVOLIO.   Tybalt, here slain, *whom* Romeo's hand did slay.

Theme: William Shakespeare

In this section, you will learn correct uses of *who* and *whom* and of pronouns in elliptical clauses. The examples and exercises in this section are about William Shakespeare.

Cross-Curricular Connection: Literature

PREPARE and ENGAGE

✷ Interest GRABBER   Write the pronouns *who's* and *whose* on the chalkboard. Challenge students to use each of the pronouns in a sentence. Tell them that in this section of the chapter, they will learn the correct usage of all the forms of the pronoun *who*.

Activate Prior Knowledge

Ask students to name the nouns the pronoun *who* can replace. (It has to replace the name of a person.) Remind students to use the pronouns *what, which, this, these, that,* and *those* to refer to things.

TEACH

Step-by-Step Teaching Guide

Using *Who, Whom,* and *Whose* Correctly

1. Go over the chart with students. Challenge them to use each of the six pronouns correctly in a sentence. Write their sentences on the chalkboard, discussing and correcting any errors. Point out that the pronoun *whosever* has very limited use, and may sound stilted; students should avoid it in their writing.

2. Remind students again that no possessive pronoun is spelled with an apostrophe. This includes the pronoun *whose*.

Step-by-Step Teaching Guide

Grammar in Literature

Call on students to explain the use of pronouns in this excerpt from Shakespeare. Challenge them to substitute pronouns for each of the nouns in the excerpt. Have students explain their answers.

⏱ TIME AND RESOURCE MANAGER

Resources
Print: Grammar Exercise Workbook, pp. 137–138; Hands-on Grammar Activity Book, Chapter 24
Technology: Language Lab CD-ROM, Nouns and Pronouns; On-Line Exercise Bank, Section 24.2

In-Depth Coverage	Accelerated Pace
• Work through all key concepts, pp. 559–564. • Assign and review Exercises 14–17. • Do the Hands-on Grammar Activity, p. 564.	• Assign pp. 559–564 for independent student review. • Assign Review Exercises 18–20.

Using *Who* and *Whom*

1. Point out the linking verb in the example under the second key concept. Remind students that a pronoun after a linking verb should always be in the nominative case. Students are probably accustomed to hearing object pronouns after linking verbs. Remind them that this usage is incorrect; linking verbs always take nominative pronouns.

2. Point out the examples on page 561. Explain that in English, it is never a good idea to end a sentence with a preposition. Since every preposition has an object, ending a sentence with a preposition breaks up the prepositional phrase.

Critical Viewing

Analyze Students may say they can learn *who* the author is and for *whom* the play was written.

24.2

Using the Nominative Case: *Who*

The nominative case is used for subjects and for predicate nominatives.

▶ **KEY CONCEPT** Use *who* for the subject. ■

EXAMPLES: *Who* is the main character in *Romeo and Juliet*?
(*Who* is the subject of the sentence.)

I know *who* is the main character in the play.
(*Who* is the subject of the subordinate clause.)

▶ **KEY CONCEPT** Use *who* for a predicate nominative. ■

EXAMPLE: The villain is *who*?
(*Who* is a predicate nominative because it renames *villain*.)

Using the Objective Case: *Whom*

The objective case of personal pronouns is used for direct objects of verbs, the objects of a verbal, and objects of prepositions.

▶ **KEY CONCEPT** Use *whom* and *whomever* for the direct object of a verb or the object of a verbal. ■

In the following example, *whom* is the object of the verb *ask*. *She* is the subject performing the action and *whom* is the one receiving the action; therefore, *whom* is an object.

EXAMPLE: *Whom* did she ask to the dance?

Pronouns in the objective case also occur in the subordinate clauses of complex sentences.

EXAMPLES: She did not know *whom* he chose.
You can select *whomever* you wish.

▼ **Critical Viewing**
What details can you learn from the cover of this play script? Use *who* and *whom* in your response.
[Analyze]

THE
MOST EX-
cellent and lamentable
Tragedie, of Romeo
and *Iuliet*.

Newly corrected, augmented, and amended:

As it hath bene sundry times publiquely acted, by the right Honourable the Lord Chamberlaine his Seruants.

LONDON
Printed by Thomas Creede, for Cuthbert Burby, and are to be sold at his shop neare the Exchange.
1 5 9 9.

Note About *Checking for the Correct Use of* Who *or* Whom
To see if the correct pronouns have been used, first isolate the subordinate clause (*whom he chose, whomever you wish*). Next, put the clauses in normal word order: *he chose whom, you wish whomever.* It now becomes clear that the subjects are *he* and *you* and that the direct objects are correctly *whom* and *whomever.*

▶ **KEY CONCEPT** Use *whom* for the object of a preposition. ■

A common error is to use the nominative case in sentences in which the pronoun is separated from the preposition for which it is the object. It is best to rewrite or restate such sentences so that the pronoun immediately follows the preposition.

INCORRECT:	*Who* did Romeo receive the message from? I spoke to the actor *who* we had lunch with.
BETTER:	*Whom* did Romeo receive the message from? I spoke to the actor with *whom* we had lunch.
BEST:	From *whom* did Romeo receive the message? I spoke to the actor *with whom we had lunch.*
PRONOUN IMMEDIATELY FOLLOWS THE PREPOSITION:	From *whom* did Romeo receive the message?

▶ **Exercise 14** Using *Who* and *Whom* Correctly Choose the correct pronoun from each pair in parentheses.

EXAMPLE: With (who, whom) are you going to the play?
ANSWER: whom

1. (Who, Whom) knows the characters of Shakespeare's play *Romeo and Juliet*?
2. From (who, whom) did you hear about the play *Romeo and Juliet*?
3. (Who, Whom) is Romeo's love for most of the play?
4. At (whose, who's) party did the star-crossed lovers meet?
5. The Capulets expected Juliet to marry (who, whom)?
6. (Whose, Who's) Juliet's choice?
7. With (who, whom) did the lovers confide?
8. (Who, Whom) will Tybalt insist on fighting?
9. (Who, Whom) spoke to the Montagues and Capulets about their feud?
10. Escalus, the prince of Verona, punished (who, whom) for the death of Tybalt?

▶ **More Practice**
Language Lab CD-ROM
• Pronoun Case lesson
On-line Exercise Bank
• Section 24.1
Grammar Exercise Workbook
• pp. 137–138

Special Problems With Pronouns • 561

Customize for More Advanced Students
Have students choose partners to review a brief scene from *Romeo and Juliet*. Partners should choose any relatively brief conversation between two characters. Students can identify all the pronouns in their chosen dialogue, identifying their cases, and explaining why each case is appropriate for each pronoun.

Answer Key

▶ **Exercise 14**
1. who
2. whom
3. Who
4. whose
5. whom
6. Who's
7. whom
8. Who
9. Who
10. whom

◆ STANDARDIZED TEST PREPARATION WORKSHOP

Grammar and Usage Standardized tests often ask students to identify the grammatically correct version of a sentence. Share the following example with students:

Which of the following sentences is correct?

A She asked Jean and I to come to her party.
B Her asked Jean and me to come to her party.

C She asked Jean and me to come to her party.
D She asked Jean and me to come to she's party.

Students should identify item **C** as the correct version. The other versions all contain usage errors in pronoun cases.

⊘ TIME SAVERS!

🔲 **Answers on Transparency** Use the Grammar Exercises on Transparencies for Chapter 24 to have students correct their own or one another's exercises.

🖥 **On-Line Exercise Bank** Have students complete the exercises on computer. The Auto Check feature will grade their work for you!

Answer Key

Exercise 15

In 1594, William Shakespeare belonged to a company of actors who presented a variety of plays. These actors, who were called the Lord Chamberlain's Men, were very popular. Not everyone with whom Shakespeare worked admired him. Some critics who wrote for the newspapers of the time wrote poor reviews of his work. As time passed, people began to wonder whether a common actor could be the one by whom the plays were written. Today, few scholars doubt that Shakespeare is the one to whom the plays should be credited.

Step-by-Step Teaching Guide

Using Pronouns Correctly in Elliptical Clauses

1. Ask students if they know what the word *elliptical* means. Explain that it comes from a Greek word meaning *defective* or *lacking*—missing something. An elliptical clause is a clause that is missing some words. These words are not written, but they are understood by the reader or listener.

2. Point out the example at the bottom of the page. Emphasize that students must be careful in their choice of pronouns, since a pronoun in the wrong case can change the meaning of the sentence. Students can try writing out the sentence with the missing words included so that they will be sure to include the correct pronoun. Once they are sure, however, the extra words should be deleted.

continued

24.2

Exercise 15 Proofreading for the Correct Usage of *Who* and *Whom* Copy the following passage onto a separate sheet of paper. Change any incorrect uses of *who* and *whom*. Leave correct uses as is.

In 1594, William Shakespeare belonged to a company of actors whom presented a variety of plays. These actors, who were called The Lord Chamberlain's Men, were very popular. Not everyone who Shakespeare worked with admired him. Some critics who wrote for the newspapers of the time wrote poor reviews of his work. As time passed, people began to wonder whether a common actor could be the one by who the plays were written. Today, few scholars doubt that Shakespeare is the one to whom the plays should be credited.

Using Pronouns Correctly in Elliptical Clauses

In an *elliptical clause*, some words are omitted because they are understood. Sentences with elliptical clauses are often used to draw comparisons. *Fran is smarter than he,* or *Tom is as happy as I.* In selecting the case of the pronoun, you must know what the unstated words are.

KEY CONCEPT In elliptical clauses beginning with *than* or *as*, use the form of the pronoun that you would use if the clause were fully stated. ■

The case of the pronoun depends upon whether the omitted words belong before or after the pronoun.

WORDS LEFT OUT AFTER PRONOUN:	Jo is as talented as *he.* Jo is as talented as he [is].
WORDS LEFT OUT BEFORE PRONOUN:	We gave Scott the same choices as *her.* We gave Scott the same choices as [we gave] her.

If the words left out come *after* the pronoun, use a nominative pronoun. If the words left out come *before* the pronoun, use an objective pronoun because the pronoun will be an object.

Often, the entire meaning of the sentence depends on the case of the pronoun, as in the following examples.

WITH A NOMINATIVE PRONOUN:	We liked him better than *she.* We liked him better than she [did].
WITH AN OBJECTIVE PRONOUN:	We liked him better than *her.* We liked him better than [we liked] her.

562 • Pronoun Usage

More Practice

Language Lab CD-ROM
• Pronoun Case lesson
On-line Exercise Bank
• Section 24.1
Grammar Exercise Workbook
• pp. 137–138

Internet Tip

To find a wealth of information and links about Shakespeare, visit the Shakespeare Resources page of the Internet School Library Media Center at:

http://falcon.jmu.edu/~ramseyil/shakes.htm

☑ ONGOING ASSESSMENT: Monitor and Reinforce

If students miss more than two items in Exercises 14–15, refer them to the following for additional practice:

In the Textbook	Print Resources	Technology
Section Review, Ex. 18–19, p. 565	Grammar Exercise Workbook, pp. 137–138	Language Lab CD-ROM, Nouns and Pronouns; On-Line Exercise Bank, Section 24.2

Step-by-Step Teaching Guide continued

▶ **Exercise 16** Identifying the Correct Pronoun in Elliptical **Clauses** Rewrite each sentence, choosing one of the pronouns in parentheses and correctly completing the elliptical clause.

EXAMPLE: We studied Shakespeare more than (he, him).

ANSWER: We studied Shakespeare more than *he* did.

1. Beth has more experience with Shakespeare than (I, me).
2. She feels that I know as much as (she, her).
3. The director gave her the part of Juliet because she fit the role better than (I, me).
4. The actor who plays Romeo is as talented as (she, her).
5. They gave more advice to her than to (me, I).

▶ **Exercise 17** Supplying Pronouns in Elliptical Clauses Rewrite each sentence, supplying an appropriate pronoun and completing the elliptical clause.

EXAMPLE: Joanne reads plays more often than ___?___.

ANSWER: Joanne reads plays more often than I do.

1. My teacher knows much more about Shakespeare than ___?___.
2. When we were taught his plays, our teacher was as excited as ___?___.
3. His enthusiasm led us to enjoy the plays as much as ___?___.
4. We have also read works by Christopher Marlowe, but I like Shakespeare better than ___?___.
5. Although I thought I was the biggest Shakespeare fan in the class, Sarah enjoyed reading *Hamlet* more than ___?___.
6. Luisa, who learned to play madrigals on her guitar, was an even greater Shakespeare fan than ___?___.
7. The teacher said that Luisa knew more about Elizabethan music than ___?___.
8. Elizabeth I favored the songs of the madrigalists, and members of her court liked them as much as ___?___.
9. Playing the lute and singing these cheerful part songs gave as much pleasure to the queen as ___?___.
10. Luisa has heard more songs performed in Shakespearean plays than ___?___.

▼ **Critical Viewing**
Using a least one elliptical clause, compare two kinds of guitars or guitar music. **[Compare and Contrast]**

Special Problems With Pronouns • 563

3. Emphasize that an elliptical clause should never have its "missing" words included. These words are left out deliberately, because they are not needed. The case of the pronoun in the elliptical clause makes the meaning of the whole perfectly clear; including the "missing" words would make the sentence redundant.

Answer Key

Critical Viewing

Compare and Contrast Students' responses will vary. Make sure they use pronouns correctly.

Who/Whom Pickup

Teaching Resources: Hands-on Grammar Activity Book, Chapter 24

1. Have students refer to their Hands-on Grammar activity books or give them copies of the relevant pages.

2. Review with students the directions for making the cards.

3. You may wish to extend the activity by having students write more sentences to use in the game.

Find It in Your Reading

Have students bring the examples they chose into class.

Find It in Your Writing

If students do not find more than a few examples, have them revise their writing to include more examples of *who* and *whom*.

24.2

Hands-on Grammar

Who/Whom Pickup

To learn when to use the nominative *who* or the objective *whom*, get together with three or four classmates, and play Who/Whom Pickup. To begin, cut out sixteen 2" x 2" squares from one piece of heavy paper and sixteen 2" x 3" rectangles from another piece, preferably of a different color. On eight of the square cards, print *WHO*, and on the other eight, print *WHOM*. Then, mix them up and stack them neatly upside down on a desk or table. Next, write a short statement on each rectangular card; for example: *Joe drove Michelle to the game. We talked to Mara and Al. Lucy wrote about Shakespeare. Mr. Ames visited Dr. Frye.* Make sure that the subjects and objects are people. When you have sixteen sentences, mix them up and stack them neatly upside down next to the WHO/WHOM pile. (See illustrations.)

To play, the first person picks up a rectangle from each stack. He or she must then turn the statement into a question, using either *who* or *whom*, depending on the word drawn. If *who* is drawn, it must substitute for the subject of the sentence. If *whom* is drawn, it must substitute for an object. Write down your questions as you go along.

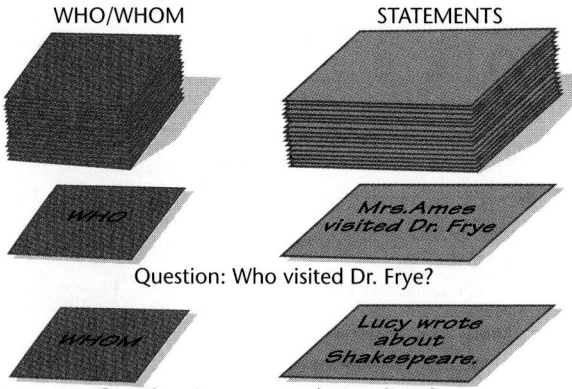

WHO/WHOM   STATEMENTS

Question: Who visited Dr. Frye?

Question: Lucy wrote about whom? or
About whom did Lucy write?

Take turns until all the cards have been drawn. Then, trade sentence cards with another group, and play another round. Pay close attention to when you use the nominative *who* and the objective *whom*.

Find It in Your Reading Read a passage of biographical writing in a book or a magazine, and look for uses of *who* and *whom*. See if you can determine if each one is used correctly or if the author used *who* informally when he or she should have used *whom*.

Find It in Your Writing Look through one or more pieces of writing in your portfolio to see if you have used *who* and *whom* correctly. Revise any that are in the wrong case.

⏱ TIME SAVERS!

✋ **Hands-on Grammar Book**
Use the Hands-on Grammar activity sheet for Chapter 24 to facilitate this activity.

☑ ONGOING ASSESSMENT: Assess Mastery

Use the following resources to assess student mastery of special problems with pronouns.

In the Textbook	Technology
Chapter Review, Ex. 24–29, pp. 566–567 Standardized Test Preparation Workshop, pp. 568–569	Language Lab CD-ROM, Nouns and Pronouns; On-Line Exercise Bank, Section 24.2

Section 24.2 Section Review

GRAMMAR EXERCISES 18–23

> **Exercise 18** Supplying *Who* and *Whom* Supply *who* or *whom* to complete each sentence.

1. Can you tell us ___?___ Shakespeare's most popular characters are?
2. We listen to opinions from all ___?___ will give them.
3. The character of Hamlet, ___?___ you like, is a favorite of mine.
4. It is he to ___?___ Shakespeare gave the most lines of any role in all his plays.
5. Hamlet's father is the ghost ___?___ haunts the castle.

> **Exercise 19** Proofreading Practice: *Who* and *Whom* Copy the following passage onto a separate sheet of paper. With different-colored pens, correct any errors in the usage of *who* and *whom*.

I know <u>whom</u> the villain is in Othello. He is an officer <u>who</u>, we see, will scheme to destroy Othello's marriage and career. Desdemona is the woman to <u>whom</u> Othello is married. <u>Whomever</u> meets her is charmed by her love for her husband. Roderigo, <u>who's</u> jealous of Othello, schemes with Iago. Because of their trickery, Othello becomes insanely jealous of <u>whoever</u> goes near Desdemona. In the end, Cassio knows <u>whose</u> schemes brought ruin to the characters of the play. In Shakespeare's tragedies, only one character is left alive to <u>whom</u> everyone can go for the whole story.

> **Exercise 20** Completing Elliptical Clauses Write the pronoun and the understood words to complete the elliptical clause in each of the following sentences.

1. In the play *Henry IV*, Falstaff, compar-

ing himself with others in the play, believes that he is more witty than ___?___ .
2. However, Prince Hal, who will become King Henry V, is just as clever as ___?___ .
3. Falstaff talks bravely to everyone but runs away from danger faster than ___?___ .
4. Falstaff plays dead on the battlefield while his friends fight because his own life is more important to him than ___?___ .
5. Nonetheless, we didn't like the other characters as much as ___?___ .

> **Exercise 21** Find It in Your Reading Identify the cases of *who* as used in the following excerpt from *The Tragedy of Romeo and Juliet*.

Of Tybalt deaf to peace, but that he tilts / With piercing steel at bold Mercutio's breast; / Who, all as hot, turns deadly point to point, / And, with a martial scorn, with one hand beats / Cold death aside and with the other sends / It back to Tybalt, whose dexterity / Retorts it. . . .

> **Exercise 22** Find It in Your Writing Find three examples in your own writing of *who* and *whom*. Copy the sentences onto a separate sheet of paper. If you cannot find examples, compose sentences that include these pronouns.

> **Exercise 23** Writing Application Write a scene between two characters in a play. Include at least one elliptical clause, one *who*, one *whom*, and the possessive pronoun *whose*.

ASSESS and CLOSE

Section Review

Each of these exercises correlates to a concept taught in the section on using pronouns, pages 559–563. The exercises may be used for more practice, for reteaching, or for review of the Key Concepts presented. Answers for all chapter exercises are available in *Grammar Exercises Answers on Transparencies* in your teaching resources.

Answer Key

> **Exercise 18**

1. who
2. who
3. whom
4. whom
5. who

> **Exercise 19**

I know who the villain is in *Othello*. He is an officer who, we see, will scheme to destroy Othello's marriage and career. Desdemona is the woman to whom Othello is married. Whoever meets her is charmed by her love for her husband. Roderigo, who is jealous of Othello, schemes with Iago. Because of their trickery, Othello becomes insanely jealous of whomever goes near Desdemona. In the end, Cassio knows whose schemes brought ruin to the characters of the play. In Shakespeare's tragedies, only one character is left alive to whom everyone can go for the whole story.

> **Exercise 20**

1. they are
2. he is
3. they do
4. theirs are
5. we liked him

continued

Answer Key continued

> **Exercise 21**

Find It in Your Reading
Who, nominative
whose, possessive

> **Exercise 22**

Find It in Your Writing
Check students' sentences to be sure they have used *who* and *whom* correctly.

> **Exercise 23**

Writing Application
Check students' dialogues to be sure they have used pronouns correctly.

> ⏱ **TIME SAVERS!**

📄 **Answers on Transparency** Use the Grammar Exercises on Transparencies for Chapter 24 to have students correct their own or one another's exercises.

💻 **On-Line Exercise Bank** Have students complete the exercises on computer. The Auto Check feature will grade their work for you!

Each of these exercises correlates to a concept taught in the chapter on using pronouns, pages 550–564. The exercises may be used for more practice, for reteaching, or for review of the Key Concepts presented. Answers for all chapter exercises are available in *Grammar Exercises Answers on Transparencies* in your teaching resources.

Answer Key

Exercise 24

1. you, nominative
2. his, possessive
3. he, nominative; them, objective; they, nominative (twice)
4. his, possessive; him, objective (twice); she, nominative
5. his, possessive (twice); she, nominative (twice); him, objective
6. his, possessive; she, nominative; him, objective
7. her, objective
8. their, possessive
9. he, nominative; his, possessive
10. her, possessive (twice); it, objective; its, possessive

Exercise 25

1. their, possessive
2. We, nominative
3. her, objective
4. he, nominative
5. him, objective
6. her, objective
7. who, nominative
8. she, nominative
9. him, objective
10. me, objective

Exercise 26

In the play *Twelfth Night,* a ship veers off <u>its</u> course and sinks. A brother and a sister each thinks that the other has drowned, and they mourn their loss. The sister, Viola, disguises herself as a man. She becomes a servant to Duke Orsino, <u>whose</u> love for Olivia causes his unhappy mood. Viola tells the Duke the story of a sister, but the story is really <u>hers</u>. As a reader, <u>your</u> confusion is multiplied when her brother, Sebastian, appears in the same town and everyone confuses him with his sister.

566

GRAMMAR EXERCISES 24–29

Exercise 24 Identifying Pronoun Case Write each pronoun and its case as used in the following sentences.

1. Have you read Shakespeare's play *King Lear*?
2. King Lear decides to divide the kingdom among his three daughters.
3. He gives them portions according to how much they tell him they love him.
4. In a flowery speech, his daughter Goneril tells him that she loves him more than words can express.
5. Regan, his other daughter, professes she loves him so much that she is not happy unless in his presence.
6. Cordelia, his favorite and honest daughter, explains that she loves him as a daughter and cannot speak empty praise.
7. King Lear becomes angry and banishes her from the kingdom.
8. Goneril and Regan are given the kingdom and treat their father cruelly.
9. Lear goes mad and holds a mock trial in which he accuses his daughters of being evil monsters.
10. Hearing of her father's plight, Cordelia raises an army to take the kingdom from her sisters and give it back to its rightful ruler.

Exercise 25 Supplying Pronouns Supply a pronoun to complete each sentence. Identify the case of the pronoun you use.

1. In high school, many students read a Shakespearean play in ___?___ English classes.
2. ___?___ might read *Julius Caesar* or *A Midsummer Night's Dream* in my sophomore year.

3. In the play *As You Like It*, Rosalind is a leading female character, and Shakespeare gave ___?___ a substantial number of lines.
4. She falls in love with Orlando and pines for him when ___?___ flees to the forest to escape his evil older brother Oliver.
5. Disguised as a boy, Rosalind meets Orlando in the forest and has a conversation with ___?___.
6. When Orlando speaks *about* Rosalind, he doesn't realize he is speaking *to* ___?___.
7. It is Rosalind ___?___ gives advice to Orlando.
8. Although he doesn't know it is ___?___, he says he will take her advice.
9. At the play's end, all is settled for Rosalind and ___?___.
10. My teacher asked Julie and ___?___ to read the dialogue.

Exercise 26 Proofreading Practice: Possessive Pronouns Proofread the following paragraph. Correct all errors in the usage of possessive pronouns. Not every sentence will need to be corrected.

In the play *Twelfth Night*, a ship veers off it's course and sinks. A brother and a sister each thinks that the other has drowned, and they mourn their loss. The sister, Viola, disguises herself as a man. She becomes a servant to Duke Orsino, who's love for Olivia causes his unhappy mood. Viola tells the Duke the story of a sister, but the story is really her's. As a reader, you're confusion is multiplied when her brother, Sebastian, appears in the same town and everyone confuses him with his sister.

> **Exercise 27** **Completing Elliptical Clauses** Choose the correct pronoun to complete each sentence. Then, label each pronoun *nominative* or *objective*.

1. My sister likes Shakespeare less than (I, me).
2. Our last teacher gave me a higher grade in our Shakespeare class than (she, her).
3. Our *Complete Works of Shakespeare* is less valuable to her than (I, me).
4. Compared with other playwrights, Shakespeare is more skilled than (they, them).
5. In *Much Ado About Nothing*, Beatrice is fooled by her cousin, who is more clever than (she, her).
6. Benedick is also fooled by the Prince, who is more clever than (he, him).
7. The prince is not a major character; we found Benedick more interesting than (he, him).
8. When she's nearby, Beatrice's cousin calls her hardhearted and lets her think Benedick is more deserving of love than (she, her).
9. At the end of the play, it is clear that no one is more in love than (they, them).
10. I don't like any other characters as much as (they, them).

> **Exercise 28** **Writing Application**
Write an original sentence following the directions in each item below.

1. Write a sentence with a nominative pronoun used as a predicate nominative.
2. Write a sentence with a nominative pronoun used as a subject and one possessive pronoun.
3. Write a sentence with an objective pronoun used as an indirect object.
4. Write a sentence with an objective pronoun used as a direct object.
5. Write a sentence with an objective pronoun used as an object of a preposition and two possessive pronouns.

> **Exercise 29** **CUMULATIVE REVIEW Effective Sentences, Verb Usage, and Pronoun Usage** Revise the following passage, correcting sentence errors and errors in verb and pronoun usage. When appropriate, replace nouns with pronouns in the correct case and combine sentences when possible to eliminate repetition. You may choose to rearrange the order of some words.

William Shakespeare is the playwright whom is giving us some of the best plays in the English language. There are people who study Shakespeare's plays, they study the plays to learn more about Shakespeare.

We know whom Shakespeare's parents were, and that he has lived in Stratford-Upon-Avon as a boy.

Who did Shakespeare marry? Shakespeare married Anne Hathaway in 1582. Shakespeare had three children. Names of the three children Susanna, Hamnet, and Judith.

Shakespeare appeared in London in the 1590's and begun a career as an actor who packed the theater every night with enthusiastic audiences who cheered his performances, and they returned to see him often. Although other actors were as popular as Shakespeare, none have stayed as famous as him. It is the works that Shakespeare was writing that established Shakespeare's long-lasting fame.

Shakespeare was an unrivaled playwright who's works had remained popular for centuries. Shakespeare died in April of 1616, but in his works he left a great legacy, which people continue to read and perform.

I say this to whoever wants to savor greatness: Read the plays and poems of William Shakespeare. They will bring you as much pleasure as they do my friends and I.

> **Exercise 27**
1. I, nominative
2. her, objective
3. me, objective
4. they, nominative
5. she, nominative
6. he, nominative
7. him, objective
8. she, nominative
9. they, nominative
10. them, objective

> **Exercise 28**
Writing Application
Students' sentences will vary.

> **Exercise 29**
Cumulative Review
   William Shakespeare is the playwright who gave us some of the best plays in the English language. There are people who study his plays. They study the plays to learn more about him.
   We know who his parents were, and that he lived in Stratford-upon-Avon as a boy. Whom did Shakespeare marry? He married Anne Hathaway in 1582. They had three children. Their names were Susanna, Hamnet, and Judith.
   Shakespeare appeared in London in the 1590s and began a career as an actor who packed the theater every night. Although other actors were as popular as he, none have remained as famous. His written work has established his long-lasting fame.
   Shakespeare was an incredible playwright. His works have remained popular for centuries. He died in April of 1616, but his legacy survives in us.
   I say this to whomever wants to savor greatness: Read the plays and poems of William Shakespeare. They will bring you as much pleasure as they do my friends and me.

567

Pronoun Usage

1. Review with students when to use each pronoun case. It may be helpful for students to make a chart in their notebooks that organizes this information.

2. Tell students to read each test item carefully and to try to determine the part of speech required to complete the sentence. Students can then look for the appropriate pronoun case in the available choices.

Standardized Test Preparation Workshop

Standard English Usage: Pronoun Usage

Standardized tests measure your knowledge of the rules of standard grammar, such as correct pronoun usage. Questions test your ability to use the three cases of personal pronouns correctly. When answering these questions, determine what type of pronoun is needed in the sentence—nominative case pronouns are used as subjects or predicate pronouns; objective case pronouns are used as direct objects, indirect objects, or objects of prepositions; and possessive case pronouns are used to show ownership. The following test item will give you practice with the format of questions that test your knowledge of pronoun usage.

Test Tip

Remember that a pronoun is used in place of the noun in a sentence to avoid repetition.

Sample Test Item	Answers and Explanations
Directions: Read the passage, and choose the letter of the word or group of words that belongs in each space. The afternoon was great for Malcolm and ___(1)___. Malcolm's father treated ___(2)___ to a show.	

1 A I
   B we
   C him
   D me
	The correct answer is *D*. The pronoun is part of a compound object of the preposition *for*; therefore, an objective pronoun is needed. Choices *A, B,* and *C* are subjective pronouns, which makes *me* the only correct choice.

2 A him and I
   B he and I
   C him and me
   D me and he
	The correct answer is *C*. The pronouns needed must function as the compound direct object of the verb *treated*. The only pair in which both pronouns are objective is *him and me*. Each of the other choices contains at least one subjective pronoun.

🎸 TEST-TAKING TIP

Remind students that they can avoid careless mistakes by substituting their choices for each item in the blank.

▶ **Practice 1** **Directions:** Read the passage, and choose the letter of the word or group of words that belongs in each space.

At the restaurant, ___(1)___ saw Anisa and Lily. They invited us to sit at ___(2)___ table. So, ___(3)___ joined ___(4)___. After lunch, there was enough food left over for ___(5)___ wanted to take home a doggie bag.

1 A Malcolm and me
  B me and Malcolm
  C Malcolm and I
  D Malcolm's and mine

2 F their
  G there
  H they're
  J there's

3 A him, his dad, and I
  B him, his dad, and me
  C he, his' dad, and me
  D he, his dad, and I

4 F their
  G them
  H they
  J theirs

5 A whom
  B whomever
  C who
  D whoever

▶ **Practice 2** **Directions:** Read the passage, and choose the letter of the word or group of words that belongs in each space.

Malcolm said, "I wonder ___(1)___ making all that noise." I said, "Some kids are having a party over there; it must be ___(2)___." Two of ___(3)___ were looking out the window." ___(4)___ do you think ___(5)___ expecting?" Anisa asked.

1 A whom's
  B who's
  C whose
  D who

2 F they
  G them
  H their
  J theirs

3 A them
  B there
  C they
  D their

4 F Whose
  G Who
  H Whoever
  J Whom

5 A their
  B there
  C they're
  D they

Practice 1
1. C
2. F
3. D
4. G
5. B

Practice 2
1. B
2. F
3. A
4. G
5. C

In-Depth Lesson Plan

	LESSON FOCUS	PRINT AND MEDIA RESOURCES
DAY 1	**Subject and Verb Agreement** Students learn and apply agreement concepts covering singular and plural subjects and compound subjects (pp. 572–575).	**Teaching Resources** *Grammar Exercise Workbook*, pp. 139–150; *Language Lab* **CD-ROM**, Subject-Verb Agreement; *On-Line Exercise Bank*, Section 25.1
DAY 2	**Subject and Verb Agreement** (continued) Students learn and apply concepts covering confusing subjects and do the Hands-on Grammar activity (pp. 576–583).	**Teaching Resources** *Grammar Exercise Workbook*, pp. 139–150; *Language Lab* **CD-ROM**, Subject-Verb Agreement; *On-Line Exercise Bank*, Section 25.1
DAY 3	**Pronoun and Antecedent Agreement** Students learn and apply agreement concepts covering personal pronouns and antecedents, reflexive and indefinite pronouns, and special pronoun agreement problems (pp. 584–591).	**Teaching Resources** *Grammar Exercise Workbook*, pp. 145–150; *Language Lab* **CD-ROM**, Pronoun-Antecedent Agreement; *On-Line Exercise Bank*, Section 25.2
DAY 4	**Review and Assess** Students review chapter and demonstrate mastery of use of agreement concepts (pp. 592–595).	**Teaching Resources** *Formal Assessment*, Ch. 25; *On-Line Exercise Bank*, Sections 25.1–2

Accelerated Lesson Plan

	LESSON FOCUS	PRINT AND MEDIA RESOURCES
DAY 1	**Subject and Verb Agreement** Students cover subject and verb agreement concepts as determined by Diagnostic Test (pp. 572–583).	**Teaching Resources** *Grammar Exercise Workbook*, pp. 139–150; *Language Lab* **CD-ROM**, Subject-Verb Agreements; *On-Line Exercise Bank*, Section 25.1
DAY 2	**Pronoun and Antecedent Agreement** Students cover pronoun and antecedent concepts as determined by Diagnostic Test (pp. 584–591).	**Teaching Resources** *Grammar Exercise Workbook*, pp. 145–150; *Language Lab* **CD-ROM**, Pronoun-Antecedent Agreement; *On-Line Exercise Bank*, Section 25.2
DAY 3	**Review and Assess** Students review chapter and demonstrate mastery of use of agreement concepts (pp. 592–595).	**Teaching Resources** *Formal Assessment*, Ch. 25; *On-Line Exercise Bank*, Sections 25.1–2

Options for Adapting Lesson Plans

HOMEWORK

Have students complete any section of the chapter for homework.

FEATURES

Extend coverage with the Grammar in Literature feature (pp. 578, 589), and the Standardized Test Preparation Workshop (p. 594).

TECHNOLOGY

Students can use the On-Line Exercise Bank to complete the exercises on computer. The Auto Check feature will grade their work.

INTEGRATED SKILLS COVERAGE

Grammar in Literature
SE pp. 578, 589

Reading
Find It In Your Reading, SE pp. 581, 583, 591

Writing
Find It In Your Writing, SE pp. 581, 583, 591
Writing Application, SE pp. 583, 591, 593
Integrating Writing Skills, ATE pp. 577, 581, 588

Language
Language Highlight ATE p. 585

Technology
Integrating Technology Skills ATE p. 575

Viewing and Representing
Critical Viewing, SE pp. 570, 573, 574, 580, 585, 587, 588, 590

ASSESSMENT SUPPORT

Standardized Test Preparation SE pp. 594; ATE p. 575, 586
Standardized Test Preparation Workbook, pp. 49–50
Formal Assessment, Ch. 25

MEETING INDIVIDUAL NEEDS

Less Advanced Students ATE pp. 576, 587; See also Ongoing
Assessments ATE pp. 573, 574, 577, 579, 581, 585, 589, 590
ESL Students ATE p. 578
More Advanced Students ATE pp. 577, 586
Linguistic Learners ATE p. 580

BLOCK SCHEDULING

Pacing Suggestions
For 90-minute Blocks
• Administer the Diagnostic Test to students to determine instructional coverage.
• Have students complete the necessary exercises in class. Use the Hands-on Grammar activity to provide a change of pace.

Resources for Varying Instruction
• *Language Lab* **CD-ROM** If your students have access to hardware, a 90-minute block provides an ideal opportunity for students to work on computer.

Professional Development Support
• *How to Manage Instruction in the Block* This teaching Resource provides management and activity suggestions.

MEDIA AND TECHNOLOGY

For the Student
• *Language Lab* **CD-ROM**, Subject-Verb Agreement, Pronoun-Antecedent Agreement
• *On-Line Exercise Bank*, Ch. 25

For the Teacher
• *Resource Pro* **CD-ROM**

WRITING AND GRAMMAR WEBSITE

The Interactive Writing and Grammar Website provides a wide array of support for students, teachers, and parents. Grammar support includes:

• *On-Line Exercise Bank* with Auto Check scoring
• Diagnostic and assessment support

phwg.phschool.com

LITERATURE CONNECTIONS

Grammar in Literature selections from *Prentice Hall Literature: Timeless Voices, Timeless Themes,* Gold:
from "Glory and Hope," Nelson Mandella, SE p. 578
from *The Road Ahead,* Bill Gates, SE p. 589

► *Lesson Objectives*

1. To identify the number of a subject, including singular and plural subjects, compound subjects, confusing subjects, collective nouns, and indefinite pronouns.

2. To recognize and correct vague, ambiguous, and distant pronoun references.

3. To demonstrate control over grammatical elements such as subject-verb agreement and pronoun-antecedent agreement.

4. To use writing as a study tool to clarify and remember information.

5. To use technology for aspects of creating, revising and editing.

6. To proofread writing for appropriateness of content, style, and conventions.

7. To evaluate writing for both mechanics and content.

8. To analyze the characteristics of texts, including their structure and word choice.

Critical Viewing

Analyze Plural nouns might include columns, stairs, arches, windows. Singular nouns may include building, government, dome.

Chapter 25 Agreement

When you speak, you automatically use words that agree with other words. You might say, for example, "She *speaks* faster than they *speak*." You know you must add an *-s* to *speak* when the subject is *she* to make the verb agree with the subject.

Agreement is the match—the "fit"—between words or grammatical forms. Because grammatical agreement is not always obvious, you need to study some sentences more closely than others. In this chapter, you will learn to make a verb agree with its subject and to make a pronoun agree with its antecedent.

▲ **Critical Viewing**
Which parts of this picture would you name with plural nouns? Which parts would you name with singular nouns? [Analyze]

☑ **ONGOING ASSESSMENT: Diagnose**

If students miss more than one item in any category, direct them to the relevant pages of the text and assign exercises for practice and review.

Agreement	Diagnostic Test Items	Teach	Practice	Section Review	Chapter Review
Skill Check A					
Singular and Plural Subjects	A 1–2	pp. 572–573	Ex. 1–3	Ex. 8–10	Ex. 30–31
Compound Subjects	A 3–5	pp. 574–575	Ex. 4	Ex. 8–10	Ex. 30–31
Confusing Subjects	A 6–15	pp. 576–580	Ex. 5–7	Ex. 9–12	Ex. 30–31
Skill Check B					
Personal Pronouns and Antecedents	B 16–18	pp. 584–586	Ex. 18–20	Ex. 24	Ex. 32
Indefinite Pronouns	B 19–20	pp. 587–588	Ex. 21	Ex. 25–26	Ex. 32

Diagnostic Test

Directions: Write all answers on a separate sheet of paper.

Skill Check A. Choose the verb in parentheses that agrees with the subject in each of the following sentences.

1. In most democracies, the people (enjoys, enjoy) basic rights.
2. Freedom of speech, along with other ideals, (is, are) treasured.
3. Neither dictatorships nor most monarchies (grants, grant) broad freedoms to their people.
4. In some countries, either secret police or the military (enforces, enforce) the law.
5. The people and their government (needs, need) to work together for the common good.
6. Dear to the hearts of many (is, are) the concept of liberty.
7. Today in the world, there (is, are) many changes taking place.
8. Among the changes (is, are) a struggle for a free society.
9. Collapsing communist governments (is, are) one reason for the changes.
10. A group of Russians (wants, want) to return to communism.
11. Politics (is, are) difficult in many former communist countries.
12. Each of the countries (deals, deal) with different conditions.
13. Roger Manser's *Failed Transitions* (describes, describe) problems in the Eastern European economy after the fall of communism.
14. Fifty years (was, were) a long time to wait for freedom.
15. More than half the world's population (is, are) still waiting.

Skill Check B. Choose the pronoun in parentheses that agrees with the antecedent in each of the following sentences.

16. Many say our culture takes (its, their) freedom for granted.
17. The development of democracy has changed the way in which people around the world conduct (his or her, their) lives.
18. Neither Thomas Jefferson nor Benjamin Franklin could have judged the impact (his, their) work would someday have.
19. Every person enjoying democracy today may owe some of (his or her, their) opportunities to America's founders.
20. Each of us should be grateful for (his or her, our) freedom.

Skill Check C. Revise the following sentences to correct problems in pronoun reference.

21. Even in a corrupt democracy, the government may prevent your progress.
22. Officials may demand bribes from ordinary citizens in exchange for basic services. This practice makes them rich.
23. When opposing forces unseat a corrupt leader, most citizens are relieved. Then, they have a big job ahead.
24. In the newspaper article, it said that a free election was held.
25. You hear about these changes in the news every day.

Agreement • 571

Answer Key

Diagnostic Test

Each item in the diagnostic test corresponds to a specific section in this chapter. This will enable you to tailor instruction to the particular needs of your students. See "Ongoing Assessment: Diagnose" below for further details.

Skill Check A

1. enjoy	9. are
2. is	10. wants
3. grant	11. is
4. enforces	12. deals
5. need	13. describes
6. is	14. was
7. are	15. is
8. is	

Skill Check B

16. its	19. his or her
17. their	20. our
18. his	

Skill Check C

21. Even in a corrupt democracy, the government may prevent a person's progress.
22. Officials may demand bribes from ordinary citizens in exchange for basic services. This practice makes the officials rich.
23. When opposing forces unseat a corrupt leader, most citizens are relieved. Then the citizens have a big job ahead.
24. The newspaper article said that a free election was held.
25. These changes are reported in the news every day.

⏱ TIME SAVERS!

Answers on Transparency
Use the Grammar Exercises Answers on Transparencies for Chapter 25 to have students correct their own or one another's exercises.

On-Line Exercise Bank
Have students complete the exercises on computer. The Auto Check feature will grade their work for you!

✓ ONGOING ASSESSMENT: Diagnose *continued*

Agreement	Diagnostic Test Items	Teach	Practice	Section Review	Chapter Review
Skill Check C					
Special Problems in Pronoun Agreement	C 21–25	pp. 588–590	Ex. 22–23	Ex. 25–26	Ex. 32
Cumulative Reviews and Applications				Ex. 13–17 Ex. 25–29	Ex. 33–36

Use the Hands-on Grammar activity on page 581 to introduce students to the concept of subject-verb agreement. Materials and procedures are specified in the Step-by-Step Guide on that page of this Teacher's Edition. Materials for this activity are also available in the *Hands-on Grammar Activity Book.*

Activate Prior Knowledge

Have students work in pairs. Each student makes a list of two singular and two plural nouns. The students trade lists, then write four sentences, using each noun as a subject. Have students exchange sentences and check for subject-verb agreement.

TEACH

Step-by-Step Teaching Guide

Agreement with Singular Plural Subjects

1. Emphasize to students this basic principle of subject-verb agreement: If the subject is singular, the verb form must be singular. If the subject is plural, the verb form must be plural.

2. Remind students that the subject of a sentence tells whom or what the subject is about. It is always a noun, a pronoun, or a construct that functions as a noun.

3. Point out that except for the verb *be,* the verb form changes to indicate number only in the present (and present perfect) tense and only with a third person subject. Put these examples on the board, underlining the verb forms:

   Singular: Brian <u>takes</u> algebra.

   Plural: Annie and Marty also <u>take</u> algebra.

   Singular: Rhonda <u>is planning</u> a vacation.

   Plural: Our neighbors <u>are planning</u> a vacation.

4. Often a phrase or clause intervenes between the subject and the verb, and a noun—not the subject—is closer to the verb than the subject is. The temptation is to make the verb agree with the closer noun.

continued

572

Subject *and* Verb Agreement

For a subject and verb to agree, both must be singular or both must be plural. In this section, you will learn how to distinguish between singular and plural subjects, how to make verbs agree with compound subjects, and how to deal with special agreement problems caused by confusing subjects.

Singular and Plural Subjects

When making a verb agree with its subject, you identify the subject and determine whether it is singular or plural.

▶ **KEY CONCEPT** A singular subject must have a singular verb. A plural subject must have a plural verb. ■

SINGULAR SUBJECT AND VERB:	<u>Hungary</u> *is* a small European country.
PLURAL SUBJECT AND VERB:	<u>Hungarians</u> *vote* in free elections.

▶ **Exercise 1** Making Verbs Agree With Their Subjects
Choose the verb in parentheses that agrees with the subject of each sentence.
  1. Before 1940, most Hungarians (was, were) farmers.
  2. Today, many people (works, work) in industry.
  3. When thinking of the past, my uncle (remembers, remember) the restrictions of Communist party rule.
  4. Since the fall of the communist government, a great change (has, have) occurred.
  5. Today, the citizens (elects, elect) their leaders.

▶ **KEY CONCEPT** A phrase or clause that interrupts a subject and its verb does not affect subject-verb agreement. ■

EXAMPLES:	<u>Citizens</u> of the country *vote.*
	The <u>legislature</u>, which has 386 members, *is called* the National Assembly.

In the first example, the plural subject *citizens* takes the plural verb *vote.* Even though the singular noun *country* is closer to the verb, it is the object of a preposition and does not affect the agreement of the subject and the verb. In the second example, the singular subject *legislature* takes the singular verb *is.* The clause that interrupts the subject and verb does not affect the agreement.

In this section, you will learn about subject and verb agreement. The examples and exercises in this section are about governments.

Cross-Curricular Connection: Social Studies

▶ **More Practice**

Language Lab CD-ROM
• Special Problems in Agreement lesson
On-line Exercise Bank
• Section 25.1
Grammar Exercise Workbook
• pp. 82–84

⏱ TIME AND RESOURCE MANAGER

Resources
Print: Grammar Exercise Workbook, pp.139–150; Hands-on Grammar Activity Book, Chapter 25
Technology: Language Lab CD-ROM, Subject-Verb Agreement, On-Line Exercise Bank, Section 25.1

In-Depth Coverage	Accelerated Pace
• Work through all key concepts, pp. 572–580. • Assign and review Exercises 1–7. • Read and discuss Grammar in Literature, p. 578. • Do the Hands-on Grammar Activity, p. 581.	• Assign pp. 572–575, for independent student review. • Assign Review Exercises 8–14.

Step-by-Step Teaching Guide
continued

Remind students that the verb must agree with the subject, not the closer noun. Give this example:

A news reporter, along with two camera operators, is [not are] covering the story.

Critical Viewing

Describe Answers will vary, but might include dome, spires, or other architectural features. Have students exchange papers with a partner and check to make sure that subjects and verbs agree and are properly labelled.

Answer Key

Exercise 1 (page 572)

1. were
2. work
3. remembers
4. has
5. elect

Exercise 2

1. guarantees
2. holds
3. is
4. attract
5. seem

Exercise 3

1. is
2. sit
3. correct
4. were
5. has

> **Exercise 2** **Making Separated Subjects and Verbs Agree**

Choose the verb in parentheses that agrees with the subject of each sentence.
1. In Hungary, a system of multiple parties (guarantees, guarantee) electoral choice.
2. The legislative body, representing local and national interests, (holds, hold) office for four years.
3. Hungary's Supreme Court, the final court of appeals, (comprises, comprise) two citizens and one judge.
4. Members of the Socialist Workers' party no longer (attracts, attract) much popular appeal.
5. Citizens, exercising their right to vote, currently (seems, seem) to prefer the more conservative political party.

> **Exercise 3** **Correcting Subject and Verb Agreement**

Revise the following paragraph, correcting all errors in subject and verb agreement.

(1) Hungary's capital city, Budapest, are really three separate cities combined to form one. (2) Obuda and Buda sits on the west bank of the Danube River. (3) The city of Pest stands majestically on the east bank. (4) The three cities was merged into one in the late nineteenth century. (5) Budapest, now one of Europe's busiest capitals, have become an industrial and commercial center.

▲ Critical Viewing
Describe three features of this building. Write the subject and verb you use in each sentence. Label each *singular* or *plural*. **[Describe]**

Subject and Verb Agreement • **573**

✓ ONGOING ASSESSMENT: Prerequisite Skills

If students have difficulty with subject-verb agreement, you may find it necessary to review the following to assure coverage of prerequisite knowledge.

In the Textbook	Print Resources	Technology
Nouns and Pronouns, pp. 340–359 Basic Sentence Parts, pp. 422–437	Grammar Exercise Workbook, pp. 1–4, 41–48	Language Lab CD-ROM, Sections 16.1 and 20.1

⏱ TIME SAVERS!

Answers on Transparency Use the Grammar Exercises Answers on Transparencies for Chapter 25 to have students correct their own or one another's exercises.

On-Line Exercise Bank Have students complete the exercises on computer. The Auto Check feature will grade their work for you!

Compound Subjects

1. Students can find it confusing to determine whether to use a singular or a plural verb form with a compound subject. Write this formula on the board to summarize the rules:

Compound Subject	Verb
singular and singular	= plural
singular or singular	= singular
plural and plural	= plural
plural or singular	= singular
singular or plural	= plural

2. Have students apply this formula to the examples on this page.

3. Have them write the formula in their notebooks so they can refer to it as they do Exercise 4.

Critical Viewing

Connect Answers may or may not relate to the fall of the Berlin wall, but should all agree with the plural subject *Berliners*.

25.1

Compound Subjects

A compound subject consists of two or more subjects, usually connected by *or* or *and*, that have the same verb. A number of different rules apply to compound subjects.

Subjects Joined by *and* Only one rule applies to compound subjects connected by *and:* Whether the parts of the compound subject are all singular, all plural, or mixed, the verb is usually plural.

▶ **KEY CONCEPT** A compound subject joined by *and* is generally plural and must have a plural verb. ∎

TWO SINGULAR SUBJECTS:	The <u>chancellor</u> and his <u>cabinet</u> *are going* to meet.
TWO PLURAL SUBJECTS:	The <u>ministers</u> and their <u>assistants</u> *discuss* a new bill.
A SINGULAR AND A PLURAL SUBJECT:	The <u>chancellor</u> and the <u>cabinet members</u> *go* over the agenda.

There are two exceptions to the preceding rule. If the parts of the compound subject are the same thing or are thought of as one item, then a singular verb is needed. A singular verb is also needed if the word *every* or the word *each* precedes a compound subject.

EXAMPLES: <u>Germany's capital</u> and <u>largest city</u> *is* Berlin.

<u>Give</u> and <u>take</u> *is* a rule of negotiations.

Each <u>issue</u> and <u>proposal</u> *is* discussed.

Singular Subjects Joined by *or* or *nor* When both parts of a compound subject connected by *or* or *nor* are singular, a singular verb is required.

▶ **KEY CONCEPT** Two or more singular subjects joined by *or* or *nor* must have a singular verb. ∎

EXAMPLE: <u>Schroeder</u> or <u>Kohl</u> *was going* to win.

In the preceding example, the conjunction *or* connects two singular subjects that act as a singular compound subject. Either Schroeder or Kohl would be the winner, not both.

▼ **Critical Viewing** In 1989, Berliners destroyed the wall that had divided their city for twenty-eight years. Identify three other verbs besides *tore* that agree in number with *Berliners*. **[Connect]**

☑ **ONGOING ASSESSMENT: Monitor and Reinforce**

If students miss more than two items in Exercises 1, 2 or 3, refer them to the following for additional practice.

In the Textbook	Print Resources	Technology
Section Review, Ex. 8, p. 582	Grammar Exercise Workbook, pp. 141–142	Language Lab CD-ROM, Subject-Verb Agreement; On-Line Exercise Bank, Section 25.1

Plural Subjects Joined by *or* or *nor* When both parts of a compound subject connected by *or* or *nor* are plural, a plural verb is required.

▶ **KEY CONCEPT** Two or more plural subjects joined by *or* or *nor* must have a plural verb. ■

EXAMPLE: The <u>liberals</u> or the <u>conservatives</u> *are going* to win.

Subjects of Mixed Number Joined by *or* or *nor* If one part of a compound subject is singular and the other is plural, the verb agrees with the subject that is closer to it.

▶ **KEY CONCEPT** If a singular subject is joined to a plural subject by *or* or *nor*, the subject closest to the verb determines whether the verb is singular or plural. ■

EXAMPLES: Either <u>Schroeder</u> or the <u>ministers</u> *are going* to speak.
Either the <u>ministers</u> or <u>Schroeder</u> *is going* to speak.

▶ **Exercise 4**   **Making Verbs Agree With Compound Subjects**
Choose the verb in parentheses that agrees with the subject in each sentence.

EXAMPLE: Neither East Germany nor West Germany (was, were) interested in remaining divided.
ANSWER: was

1. East Germany and West Germany (is, are) now reunited under a federal republic.
2. Neither the Berlin Wall nor many other aspects of division (exists, exist) any longer.
3. East Germany and West Germany (is, are) united.
4. In the current German government, the president and the chancellor (works, work) as partners.
5. Neither the president nor the Parliament (selects, select) ministers for the chancellor's cabinet.
6. In the Parliament, either the upper house or the lower house (passes, pass) laws.
7. Either one political party or a coalition (governs, govern) the country.
8. The six parties and each candidate (participates, participate) actively in the political process.
9. Often, labor issues or the environment (forms, form) the basis for some political platforms.
10. Each state and major city (has, have) some Social Democrats and some Christian Democrats.

⊙ **Technology Tip**

When writing with a word-processing program, use the "Search" feature to locate places in a document where you have used *and, or,* or *nor.* If you have used these conjunctions to join the parts of a compound subject, check these sentences carefully for subject-verb agreement.

▶ **More Practice**

Language Lab
CD-ROM
• Special Problems in Agreement lesson
On-line
Exercise Bank
• Section 25.1
Grammar Exercise Workbook
• pp. 82–84

Integrating Technology Skills

E-mail, which is frequently used for quick and casual communication, tends to be filled with grammatical errors. If students have e-mail accounts, have them check some of their old messages for errors in subject-verb agreement. Ask them to underline the subject and circle the verb in each sentence, correcting those that do not agree in number and person.

Answer Key

▶ **Exercise 4**

1. are
2. exist
3. are
4. work
5. selects
6. passes
7. governs
8. participate
9. forms
10. has

Subject and Verb Agreement • 575

✎ **STANDARDIZED TEST PREPARATION WORKSHOP**

Grammar and Usage Many standardized tests require students to recognize correct usage within the context of a passage. Use the following example to demonstrate.

Neither the prime minister nor the cabinet members <u>favors</u> the new bill.

Is the underlined word used correctly? If not, decide the correct usage.

A No change   **C** favor
B is favoring   **D** has favored

The correct answer is **C**, because this is the form of the verb that agrees with the nearer subject, *members.*

⏱ **TIME SAVERS!**

🖥 **Answers on Transparency**
Use the Grammar Exercises Answers on Transparencies for Chapter 25 to have students correct their own or one another's exercises.

💻 **On-Line Exercise Bank**
Have students complete the exercises on computer. The Auto Check feature will grade their work for you!

Confusing Subjects

1. Give students several examples of inverted sentences:

   Beyond the stars <u>waits</u> a mysterious <u>destiny</u>.

   Where <u>are</u> the <u>heroes?</u>

   There <u>is</u> a <u>ship</u> on the horizon.

2. Point out to students that it's usually fairly easy to find the subject in an inverted sentence if they simply read the sentence in normal order:

   A mysterious destiny waits beyond the stars.

   The heroes are where.

   A ship is there on the horizon.

3. A common mistake is to use *Here's* or *There's* regardless of the subject. Remind students to use *Here are* or *There are* with plural subjects.

4. Remind students when using the indefinite pronouns that may be singular or plural to look at the context to determine whether to use a singular or plural verb form.

Customize for
Less Advanced Students

For students who have difficulty with sentences beginning with *There*, suggest that they try rewording the sentence without *There*:

Only one government is in Germany

Several parties are in the government.

This strategy will help students focus on the true subject of the sentence.

Answer Key

▶ **Exercise 5**

1. are
2. is
3. is
4. are
5. Does

25.1

Confusing Subjects

Some subjects create special agreement problems:

Inverted Sentences Foremost among the confusing subjects are hard-to-find subjects that come after their verbs. A sentence in which the subject comes after the verb is said to be inverted. Subject and verb order is usually inverted in questions.

▶ **KEY CONCEPT** A verb that comes before its subject must still agree with the subject in number. ■

EXAMPLES: On the wall *are* <u>slogans</u>. (<u>Slogans</u> *are* on the wall.)
             Is the <u>message</u> clear? (The <u>message</u> *is* clear.)

In the first example, the plural verb *are* agrees with the plural subject *slogans*. In the second example, a question, the singular verb *is* agrees with the singular subject *message*. Check the verb by mentally rewording the sentence so that the subject comes at the beginning.

The words *there* and *here* at the beginning of a sentence often signal an inverted sentence. The words *there* and *here* never function as the subjects of sentences.

EXAMPLES: There *is* only one <u>government</u> in Germany.
             There *are* several <u>parties</u> in the government.

The subject in the first of the preceding examples is *government*. It is singular and takes the singular verb *is*. The plural subject *parties* in the second sentence takes the plural verb *are*.

Note About *There's* and *Here's*: The contractions *there's* (*there is*) and *here's* (*here is*) contain singular verbs. They should not be used with plural subjects.

CORRECT: Here's the <u>minister</u> now.
            Here *are* the <u>ministers</u> now.

▶ **Exercise 5** Making Subjects and Verbs Agree in Inverted Sentences For each sentence, choose the verb in parentheses that agrees with the subject.
1. Making up Germany's Parliament (is, are) two houses.
2. There (is, are) an election held every four years to select members of the Bundestag.
3. Chosen as chancellor (is, are) the leader of the strongest party.
4. In the Bundestag (is, are) 662 deputies.
5. (Does, do) the chancellor vote?

▶ **More Practice**

Language Lab CD-ROM
• Special Problems in Agreement lesson
On-line Exercise Bank
• Section 25.1
Grammar Exercise Workbook
• pp. 82–84

Subjects of Linking Verbs Subjects with linking verbs may also cause agreement problems. Do not be misled by a predicate nominative.

▶**KEY CONCEPT** A linking verb must agree with its subject, regardless of the number of the predicate nominative. ■

EXAMPLES: Economic <u>conditions</u> *are* one cause for concern.
One <u>cause</u> for concern *is* economic conditions.

In the first example, the verb *are* agrees with the plural subject *conditions* even though the predicate nominative *cause* is singular. In the second example, the subject is now *cause*, which requires the singular verb *is*, and *conditions* becomes the predicate nominative.

Collective Nouns Collective nouns—such as *assembly*, *audience*, *class*, *club*, and *committee*—name groups of people or things. A collective noun is considered singular if it refers to the group acting as a unit. The noun is considered plural if it refers to the members of the group acting as individuals.

▶**KEY CONCEPT** A collective noun takes a singular verb when the group it names acts as a single unit. A collective noun takes a plural verb when the group it names act as individuals with different points of view. ■

EXAMPLES: Singular: The <u>committee</u> *votes* on the issue.
Plural: The <u>committee</u> *have split* their votes.

Plural-Looking Nouns Some nouns that end in *-s* appear to be plural but are actually singular in meaning. Some of these nouns name branches of knowledge, such as *civics*, *economics*, *physics*, *mathematics*, and *social studies.* Others are singular because, like collective nouns, they name single units: *molasses* (one kind of syrup), *mumps* (one disease), *news* (one body of information), and so on.

▶**KEY CONCEPT** Nouns that are plural in form but singular in meaning take singular verbs. ■

EXAMPLES: <u>Social studies</u> *has become* my favorite subject.
<u>Measles</u> *is* a dangerous disease for unborn babies.

⚙ **Grammar and Style Tip**

Use inverted sentences to vary the sentence patterns in your writing. When used after several sentences in subject-verb order, an inverted sentence creates a mental pause for emphasis or thought.

Integrating Writing Skills

Remind students that inverting the order of subject and verb can add emphasis to a sentence or bring a welcome variation in sentence patterns. Ask students to review one selection from their recent writings to find opportunities to invert the order of a sentence to vary their sentence patterns or to create emphasis.

Customize for
More Advanced Students

Ask students to list as many additional "plural-looking" singular nouns as they can. Write them on the chalkboard and, as a class, identify them as singular or plural. (Students might add *politics, linguistics, ethics, ballistics, series,* and *rickets* as nouns that are singular. Other nouns ending in *-s* that refer to one item but are plural in meaning include *scissors, pants, pliers, eyeglasses, binoculars,* and *tweezers.*

☑ **ONGOING ASSESSMENT: Monitor and Reinforce**

If students have difficulty with key concepts on pp. 576–577, refer them to the following for additional practice.

In the Textbook	Print Resources	Technology
Section Review, Ex. 9–11, p. 582	Grammar Exercise Workbook, pp. 143–144	Language Lab CD-ROM, Subject-Verb Agreement; On-Line Exercise Bank, Section 25.1

Grammar in Literature

1. Read or have a prepared student read the passage by Nelson Mandela aloud. A cassette recording of the complete speech is available in the Gold level resources of *Prentice Hall Literature: Timeless Voices, Timeless Themes.*

2. After discussing the annotation about "all of us," ask students what form of the verb would be used if Mandela had begun a sentence with "All of the country." *(The singular would be used.)*

More About the Speaker

Considered a living testament to the strength of the human spirit, Nelson Mandela emerged from a twenty-seven-year term as a political prisoner to become the first black president of South Africa. A life-long opponent of apartheid, the legal discrimination against blacks in South Africa, Mandela saw the unjust system end in 1991. He shared the Nobel Peace Prize in 1993, and the next year was elected president. This excerpt is from his inaugural address.

Customize for
ESL Students

Students are sometimes confused when *each, either,* and *neither* are followed by a prepositional phrase containing a plural. To help them remember that these pronouns are always singular, tell them to mentally add *one: each one, either one, neither one.*

25.1

GRAMMAR IN
LITERATURE

from Glory and Hope
Nelson Mandela

In the following passage, the indefinite pronoun all *refers to a group acting as individuals. Therefore, it takes the plural verb* do.

Your majesties, your royal highnesses, distinguished guests, comrades and friends: Today, *all* of us *do*, by our presence here, and by our celebrations in other parts of our country and the world, confer glory and hope to newborn liberty.

Our daily deeds as ordinary South Africans must produce an actual South African reality that will reinforce humanity's belief in justice, strengthen its confidence in the nobility of the human soul and sustain all our hopes for a glorious life for all.

Indefinite Pronouns Some indefinite pronouns are always singular, some are always plural, and some may be either singular or plural.

ALWAYS SINGULAR:	anybody, anyone, anything, each, either, every, everybody, everyone, everything, neither, nobody, no one, nothing, somebody, someone, something
ALWAYS PLURAL:	both, few, many, others, several
SINGULAR OR PLURAL:	all, any, more, most, none, some

▶ **KEY CONCEPT** Singular indefinite pronouns take singular verbs. Plural indefinite pronouns take plural verbs. ■

Do not be misled by a prepositional phrase that interrupts the subject and verb. The interrupting phrase does not affect subject-verb agreement.

SINGULAR: <u>Either</u> of your plans *is* acceptable to me.
PLURAL: <u>Few</u> of the representatives *are* here.

578 • Agreement

💡 Spelling Tip

To remember that *neither* is an exception to the *i before e* rule, recognize the word *either* in *neither.* You are not likely to begin *either* with an *i*, and remembering the connection between the words will help you spell *neither* correctly.

> **KEY CONCEPT** The pronouns *all, any, more, most, none,* and *some* take a singular verb if they refer to singular words and a plural verb if they refer to plural words. ■

SINGULAR: <u>Most</u> of South Africa *was* proud.
PLURAL: <u>Most</u> of the South Africans *were* proud.

Exercise 6 Making Verbs Agree With Indefinite Pronouns
Choose the verb in parentheses that agrees with the indefinite pronoun in each sentence.
1. Everyone in Kenya (learns, learn) about the country's history.
2. Few (recalls, recall) when the British took over their country.
3. Most of Kenya's best land (was, were) controlled by British settlers during the late 1890's.
4. Many (was, were) unhappy with British rule of their country.
5. Some still (remembers, remember) the day Kenya gained its independence.

Titles of Creative Works and Names of Organizations Plural words in the title of a creative work or in the name of an organization do not affect subject-verb agreement when the title or name is the subject of a verb.

> **KEY CONCEPT** A title or the name of an organization is singular and must have a singular verb. ■

EXAMPLES: <u>Hard Times</u> *is* a novel by Charles Dickens.
<u>Sunflowers</u> *is* Van Gogh's most famous painting.
<u>DiCuffa Brothers</u> *makes* the best pizza.

Amounts and Measurements Most amounts and measurements, although they appear to be plural, actually express single units or ideas.

> **KEY CONCEPT** A noun expressing an amount or a measurement is usually singular and requires a singular verb. ■

EXAMPLES: <u>Fifty cents</u> *is* more than enough.
<u>Twenty feet</u> *was* the length of the voting line.
Usually, only <u>one third</u> of the country *votes*.
<u>Half</u> the votes *were* counted.

In the first three examples, the subjects take singular verbs. *Fifty cents* equals one sum of money; *twenty feet* is one measurement; and *one third* is one part of a total country. In the last example, however, the subject *half* refers to many individual items and is therefore plural.

> **More Practice**
> **Language Lab CD-ROM**
> • Special Problems in Agreement lesson
> **On-line Exercise Bank**
> • Section 25.1
> **Grammar Exercise Workbook**
> • pp. 82–84

⟳ Learn More

For practice with subject-verb agreement in a standardized test format, use the Standardized Test Preparation Workshop on pages 594–595.

Subject and Verb Agreement • **579**

Step-by-Step Teaching Guide

Agreement with Indefinite Pronouns

1. Point out to students that certain singular indefinite pronouns are frequently used in connection with a plural word. This use often causes agreement problems. Give them these examples:

   Each of the countries . . .

   Either of the countries . . .

   Both of these examples may suggest that more than one country is being discussed, causing the speaker or writer to use a plural verb form. However, the pronouns *each* and *either* both refer to just one item, so a singular verb form is correct:

   Each of the countries *has* a delegate.

   Either of the countries *provides* assistance.

2. You might tell students that many of these indefinite pronouns can be used as indefinite adjectives. Point out the differences:

   some money (adjective)

   some of the money (pronoun)

   many girls (adjective)

   many of the girls (pronoun)

   If students are trying to determine what verb form to use with an indefinite pronoun that can be either singular or plural, you might suggest that they try using the pronoun as an adjective to get the right sense—either singular or plural.

✓ **ONGOING ASSESSMENT: Monitor and Reinforce**

If students have difficulty with key concepts on pp. 579–580, refer them to the following for additional practice.

In the Textbook	Print Resources	Technology
Section Review, Ex. 12–13, p. 582	Grammar Exercise Workbook, pp. 143–144	Language Lab CD-ROM, Subject-Verb Agreement; On-Line Exercise Bank, Section 25.1

25.1

▶ **Exercise 7** Making Verbs Agree With Confusing Subjects

Choose the item in parentheses that agrees with the subject of each sentence.

1. Only after years of protest and sanctions (was, were) apartheid abolished in South Africa.
2. Almost every country, including the United States, (was, were) critical of South Africa's racial policies.
3. A television audience of millions (was, were) thrilled to watch Nelson Mandela's inauguration.
4. There (is, are) now reasons for hope throughout the country.
5. More than three fourths of the population (consists, consist) of blacks; the remaining quarter (comprises, comprise) whites, Asians, and people of mixed race.
6. Human rights for all South Africans (is, are) the focus of the new government.
7. (Isn't, Aren't) economics also a great concern?
8. Anybody from one of the poorer areas (hopes, hope) conditions will improve.
9. Watching South Africa's progress (is, are) leaders of many other nations.
10. Catherine Bradley's *Causes and Consequences* (discusses, discuss) problems in the new South Africa.

▼ **Critical Viewing**
Describe the flags. What verb did you use with *flags*? With *stripes*? **[Describe]**

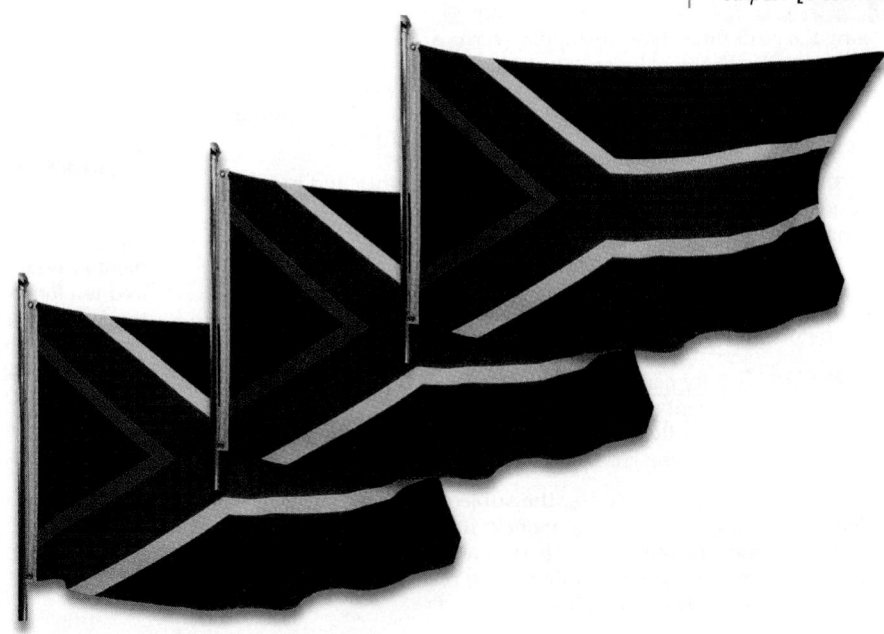

580 • Agreement

Hands-on Grammar

Subject-Verb Agreement Color Match

Cut three strips of paper of equal length. Draw a blue line across the center of one. Draw a red line across the center of the other. Fold the strip into thirds, as shown in the illustration. Then, write a sentence with a singular subject, a singular verb form, and a phrase across the blue line. Write the subject in the first fold, the verb in the second, and the remaining words in the third fold. Write the same sentence on the strip with the red line, but use a plural subject and plural verb form. Next, cut each strip on the folds. Finally, try to line up the parts of the sentence. You will find that you can't create a color match between a singular subject and a plural verb form.

The Minister	attends	every session

The Ministers	attend	every session

The Ministers	attends	every session

Find It in Your Reading Do this activity with a sentence from the Grammar in Literature passage from "Glory and Hope," on page 578. If the sentence has too many phrases, just use the subject and verb.

Find It in Your Writing Review a recent piece of writing in your portfolio. Use this activity with several sentences from the piece.

Subject and Verb Agreement • 581

Subject-Verb Agreement Color Match

Teaching Resources: Hands-on Grammar Activity Book, Chapter 25

1. If you wish to do this activity in class, be prepared with colored pencils (red and blue) and scissors. Give each student a copy of *Hands-on Grammar Activity Book,* Chapter 25.

2. Have them follow the directions to prepare the strips.

3. For a variation, suggest that students write a phrase or clause that modifies the subject on strip 2. When they arrange the strips in 1, 2, 3 order, they need to be sure that the verb agrees with the subject, not a noun in the modifying phrase or clause.

4. You may wish to expand this activity by having students work in pairs to use one of the generated sentences as the first sentence in a short piece of writing. Have students share and compare their work.

Integrating Writing Skills

In addition to this activity, you may wish to expand the potential of students' portfolios as a database of sentences for review and reteaching. For example, you might ask students to select sentences from their work to change the subject from plural to singular, to combine sentences to create a compound subject, or to invert the order of subject and verb.

☑ ONGOING ASSESSMENT: Assess Mastery

Use the following resources to assess student mastery of subject-verb agreement.

In the Textbook	Technology
Chapter Review, Ex. 30–31, p. 592 Standardized Test Preparation Workshop, pp. 594–595	On-Line Exercise Bank, Section 25.1

⏱ TIME SAVERS!

Hands-on Grammar Book
Use the Hands-on Grammar activity sheet for Chapter 25 to facilitate this activity.

Section Review

Each of these exercises correlates to a concept in the section on subject-verb agreement, pages 572–581. These exercises may be used for more practice, for reteaching, or for review of the Key Concepts presented.

Answer Key

Exercise 8

1. exists
2. are
3. include
4. possesses
5. are
6. is
7. are
8. comes
9. are
10. is

Exercise 9

1. Toward the end of a political convention *come* the nominations.
2. Then *begins* the campaign.
3. correct
4. Yes, there *are* numerous personal appearances by the candidates.
5. *Are* there many ads on television?
6. correct
7. Neither Congress nor the president *has* absolute authority.
8. correct
9. Either the citizens or the press *monitors* the government.
10. Neither police nor soldiers *rule.*

Exercise 10

1. are
2. are
3. is
4. has
5. determines

Exercise 11

Not everyone *knows* how laws are established. However, each of us *realizes* the importance of laws. A committee votes (correct) on whether to send the bill further. In the House or Senate, many *debate* aspects of the bill. Politics always *plays* a role.

Exercise 12

1. has
2. is
3. was
4. was
5. provides

Section 25.1 Section Review

GRAMMAR EXERCISES 8–17

Exercise 8 Choosing Verbs That Agree Choose the verb in parentheses that agrees with the subject of each sentence.

1. Democracy (exists, exist) when the people direct the nation's activities.
2. Free systems of government (is, are) common in Western nations.
3. Concepts of democracy (includes, include) the election of representatives.
4. An individual in a free system (possesses, possess) many basic rights.
5. Freedom of speech and freedom of the press (is, are) protected.
6. There (is, are) no letup in the ads.
7. When (is, are) the voting and the counting of ballots?
8. In November (comes, come) the vote.
9. There (is, are) predictions of the winner immediately after the polls close.
10. However, only after several hours (is, are) there an official count.

Exercise 9 Revising Sentences for Subject-Verb Agreement Read each sentence. If it is correct, write *correct.* If the verb does not agree with the subject, rewrite the sentence correctly.

1. Toward the end of a political convention comes the nominations.
2. Then begin the campaign.
3. During the fall, is each candidate's campaign in full swing?
4. Yes, there is numerous personal appearances by the candidates.
5. Is there many ads on television?
6. Unreasonable search and seizure is forbidden under the law.
7. Neither Congress nor the President have absolute authority.
8. The President and each elected member of Congress swear to uphold the Constitution.
9. Either the citizens or the press monitor the government.
10. Neither police nor soldiers rules.

Exercise 10 Choosing the Correct Linking Verb Choose the verb in parentheses that agrees with the subject of each sentence.

1. Our courts (is, are) a large system.
2. Criminal and civil cases (is, are) the responsibility of the district courts.
3. The responsibility of the Supreme Court (is, are) appeals from the district courts.
4. The Court (has, have) nine justices.
5. In the Supreme Court, the majority (determines, determine) the decision.

Exercise 11 Revising Sentences With Difficult Subjects Revise the paragraph, correcting errors in subject-verb agreement.

Not everybody know how laws are established. However, each of us realize the importance of laws. A committee votes on whether to send the bill further. In the House or Senate, many debates aspects of the bill. Politics always play a role.

Exercise 12 Choosing Verbs That Agree With Titles, Names, and Amounts and Measurements Choose the verb in parentheses that agrees with the subject of each sentence.

1. Since 1790, the United States (has, have) taken a census of the population.

2. Ten years (is, are) the interval between censuses.
3. For the first census, $45,000 (was, were) paid by the government.
4. About 2.5 percent of the population (was, were) undercounted in 1970.
5. Deirdre Gaquin's *Places, Towns, and Townships* (provides, provide) census data for businesses.

Exercise 13 **Revising Sentences for Subject Verb Agreement** Rewrite each sentence, revising it according to the instructions given in brackets. Change the verb form as needed. Not all verbs will change.

1. Local government is important in the daily lives of Americans. [Change *government* to *governments*.]
2. The importance of the township differs from state to state. [Change *the township* to *townships*.]
3. Waste removal is regulated. [Add *and water supply* after *Waste removal*.]
4. There is usually a zoning law. [Change *a zoning law* to *zoning laws*.]
5. The town council votes on the laws. (Begin the sentence with *Members of*.]
6. Neither the council nor the mayor acts alone. [Add *members* after *council*.]
7. About 40 percent of the budget goes to schools. [Change *budget* to *budgets*.]
8. Policies interest most citizens. [Change *policies* to *politics*.]
9. Each of the states has county governments. [Change *Each* to *All but one*.]
10. *The Future of Us All* examines local politics. [Change *The Future of Us All* to *City Trenches*.]

Exercise 14 **Revising a Paragraph for Subject Verb Agreement** Copy the paragraph on a separate sheet of paper. Revise to correct all errors in subject-verb agreement. Not all verbs will change.

(1) Are lower taxes an important issue to you? (2) This question, and others like it,

are often asked by pollsters. (3) Does any of your friends think about big issues? (4) Have your mother or father ever been polled? (5) There's many issues in which a large percentage of the population take an interest. (6) The public's views on an issue forms public opinion. (7) Every pollster and politician try to keep abreast of public opinion. (8) The results of a poll, along with the margin for error, are often reported in the press. (9) Here's one of many books on polls: Susan Herbst's *Numbered Voices*. (10) It tells how politics have been shaped by opinion polls.

Exercise 15 **Find It in Your Reading** Read the following lines from Nelson Mandela's "Glory and Hope." Then, on your paper, write each subject and its verb, and identify whether each is singular or plural.

> Each time one of us touches the soil of this land, we feel a sense of personal renewal. The national mood changes as the seasons change.
>
> We are moved by a sense of joy and exhilaration when the grass turns green and the flowers bloom.

Exercise 16 **Find It in Your Writing** Review a draft from your portfolio written in the present tense. Underline each subject once and its verb twice. Make sure your subjects and verb forms agree.

Exercise 17 **Writing Application** Summarize the plot of a novel or a movie that you enjoyed. Describe the events in the present tense. Then, carefully check the agreement of your subjects and verbs.

Section Review • 583

Write the following sentences on the board, asking students if they can provide the missing pronoun.

Eric or Elaine will bring laptop.

(Students may recognize the problem: neither his nor her quite works. One solution would be to substitute the indefinite article a for the possessive pronoun. Another would be to rewrite the sentence entirely.)

Activate Prior Knowledge

Have students work in pairs, with each student making a list of ten nouns (proper and common, singular and plural). Then ask students to trade lists and write a pronoun that might replace each noun.

crowd	it
bicycle	it
hallway	it
Steven	he
cameras	they

Step-by-Step Teaching Guide

1. Explain to students this basic principle of pronoun and antecedent agreement: a pronoun must always agree with its antecedent in number and gender. For example, if the antecedent is feminine and singular (*Ms. Jones*), the pronoun used to replace it must also be feminine and singular (*she, her, hers*, or *herself*).

2. Have each student write down two feminine nouns, two masculine nouns, and two neuter nouns. They may be either singular or plural. Then have them trade lists with a partner and write a sentence for each noun. Each sentence must include the noun and a pronoun to replace it.

   Ms. Jones *is known for* her *challenging math tests.*

continued

Pronoun and Antecedent Agreement

Antecedents are the nouns (or the words that take the place of nouns) to which pronouns refer. The word *antecedent* comes from a Latin word meaning "to go before." In English, an antecedent usually precedes its pronoun. This section will explain how pronouns agree with their antecedents.

Agreement Between Personal Pronouns and Antecedents

The following rule of pronoun and antecedent agreement is the basis for almost all the other rules:

▶ **KEY CONCEPTS** A personal pronoun must agree with its antecedent in number and gender. ■

The grammatical number of a noun or pronoun indicates whether it is singular or plural.

Some pronouns and nouns also indicate one of three genders: masculine, feminine, or neuter. Nouns referring to males, such as *uncle* and *boy*, are masculine. Nouns referring to females, such as *actress* and *mother*, are feminine. Nouns that do not refer to either males or females, such as *stone* and *freedom*, are neuter. Only pronouns in the third-person singular indicate gender.

GENDER OF THIRD-PERSON SINGULAR PRONOUNS		
Masculine	Feminine	Neuter
he, him, his, himself	she, her, hers, herself	it, its, itself

In the following example, the pronoun and antecedent agree completely. Both the antecedent *Charlene* and the pronoun *her* are singular and feminine.

EXAMPLE: *Charlene* accessed *her* friend's Home Page.

Agreement in Number Making personal pronouns agree with their antecedents in number is usually a problem only when the antecedent is a compound.

▶ **KEY CONCEPT** Use a singular personal pronoun to refer to two or more singular antecedents joined by *or* or *nor*. ■

EXAMPLE: Neither *Keith nor Rob* remembers *his* password.

584 • Agreement

Theme: Technology and Communications
In this section, you will learn about pronoun and antecedent agreement. The examples and exercises are about communications and technology.

Cross-Curricular Connection: Science

⏱ TIME AND RESOURCE MANAGER

Resources
Print: Grammar Exercise Workbook, pp. 145–150
Technology: Language Lab CD-ROM, Pronouns and Antecedents; On-Line Exercise Bank, Section 25.2

In-Depth Coverage	Accelerated Pace
• Work through all key concepts, pp. 584–589.	• Assign pp. 584–589, for independent student review.
• Assign and review Exercises 18–21.	
• Read and discuss Grammar in Literature, p. 589.	• Assign Review Exercises 24–26, p. 591.

▷ **KEY CONCEPT** Use a plural personal pronoun to refer to two or more antecedents joined by *and*. ■

EXAMPLE: *Gene and Rita* have checked *their* e-mail.

Agreement in Person Errors in agreement between personal pronouns and their antecedents often involve a shift in person.

▷ **KEY CONCEPT** When dealing with pronoun-antecedent agreement, take care not to shift person. ■

SHIFT IN PERSON: Becca is studying programming, a course *you* need for a degree in computer science.

CORRECT: Becca is studying programming, a course *she* needs for a degree in computer science.

Note About Generic Masculine Pronouns: Historically, a masculine pronoun (*he, his, him, himself*) has been used to refer to a singular antecedent whose gender is not specified. Such use of the masculine pronoun is said to be generic, meaning it covers both the masculine and feminine genders. Today, however, many writers prefer to use both the masculine and feminine pronouns (*he or she, him or her, his or her, himself or herself*) instead of the generic masculine form. When using both forms becomes awkward, it is best to rewrite the sentence.

▷ **KEY CONCEPT** When gender is not specified, use the masculine and feminine pronouns or rewrite the sentence. ■

EXAMPLES: A *student* should keep *his or her* password a secret.
Students should keep *their* passwords a secret.

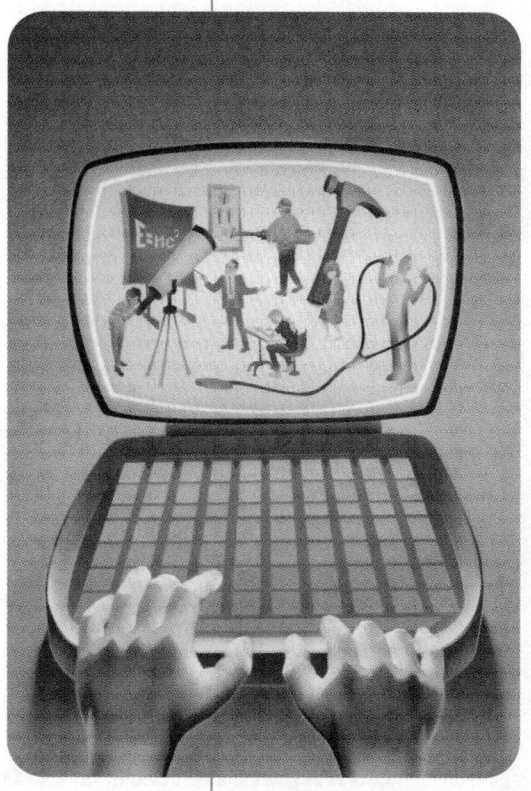

▲ **Critical Viewing**
In what ways has technology changed the way people communicate? **[Analyze]**

3. When they finish, have students give their sentences to their partners. Then, have them underline the pronoun and antecedent in each of the six sentences. If any of the pronouns do not agree in number and gender with their antecedents, have students make corrections so that they do.

Critical Viewing

Analyze Students may readily identify several technologies that have increased the convenience, frequency, and speed with which people communicate: e-mail, cell phones, video technology.

Language Highlight

The historical custom of using *his* and *him* for antecedents of unspecified gender is common to many languages besides English. Modern writers are becoming less comfortable with this custom but are well aware of the awkwardness of the *his or her* solution, especially when it is used repeatedly. The quest for a "gender-neutral pronoun" has a long history in English. There is evidence in some eighteenth century dialects that *you* once expressed *he, she*, or *it*. Among attempts to invent new pronouns are: *hiser* (combining *his* and *her*) and *thon* (combining *that* and *one*).

Pronoun and Antecedent Agreement • 585

☑ **ONGOING ASSESSMENT: Prerequisite Skills**

If students have difficulty with pronoun and antecedent agreement, you may find it necessary to review the following to assure coverage of prerequisite knowledge.

In the Textbook	Print Resources	Technology
Nouns and Pronouns, pp. 340–359	Grammar Exercise Workbook, pp. 5–12	Language Lab CD-ROM, Nouns and Pronouns; On-Line Exercise Bank 16.2

⏱ **TIME SAVERS!**

🗂 **Answers on Transparency** Use the Grammar Exercises Answers on Transparencies for Chapter 25 to have students correct their own or one another's exercises.

🖥 **On-Line Exercise Bank** Have students complete the exercises on computer. The Auto Check feature will grade their work for you!

Customize for
More Advanced Students

Ask students to rewrite exercise items 4, 6, and 8, making the subjects plural and changing the verbs and personal pronouns as necessary.

Topic Bank

The thematic emphasis on technology and communications provides students with a number of research and writing possibilities. Among many options, students may wish to explore the following:

• comparing and contrasting personal computers and mainframe computers

• a biographical sketch of one of the developers of personal computers

• the origins of the first personal computer

• how-to instructions for creating graphics on a computer

25.2

> **Exercise 18** Making Personal Pronouns Agree With Their Antecedents Write an appropriate personal pronoun to complete each sentence.

EXAMPLE: Personal computers are in the process of expanding ___?___ capabilities.

ANSWER: their

1. One computer pioneer is Alan Kay. ___?___ is noted for ___?___ role in the development of the PC (personal computer).
2. Before Kay introduced graphics and animation, ___?___ had not been seen before on PCs.
3. The PCs of today have much more memory than ___?___ predecessors.
4. In the 1970's, the average person did not have a computer in ___?___ home.
5. However, once the microprocessor was invented, ___?___ hastened the development of the PC.
6. When the fully assembled PC went on the market, ___?___ became a sales phenomenon.
7. At first, neither computer developers nor manufacturers realized what ___?___ had.
8. These days, a PC usually comes with several programs as part of ___?___ initial package.
9. Diana Adams, who sees ___?___ as a modern woman, takes a laptop computer with ___?___ wherever ___?___ goes.
10. However, you and I don't even have to leave home. ___?___ can access the world through ___?___ PCs.

Using Reflexive Pronouns

A reflexive pronoun ends in *-self* or *-selves* and points back to a noun or pronoun near the beginning of the sentence, as in "*David* taught *himself* to use the Internet."

> **KEY CONCEPT** A reflexive pronoun must have an antecedent in the sentence in which it appears. ■

POOR USE: Todd helped Jen and *myself* to search the Internet.

CORRECT: Todd helped Jen and *me* to search the Internet.

CORRECT: Jen searched the Internet *herself*.

> **More Practice**

Language Lab
CD-ROM
• Pronoun Antecedent Agreement lesson
**On-line
Exercise Bank**
• Section 25.2
Grammar Exercise Workbook
• pp. 85–87

◈ STANDARDIZED TEST PREPARATION WORKSHOP

Grammar and Usage Many standardized tests require students to identify errors in sentences. Problems with pronoun-antecedent agreement are among the errors included in these sentences. Following is a sample test item. Write the item on the board and ask students to identify the error.

<u>Each</u> of the companies <u>has had</u> to
   A   B
<u>expand</u> <u>their</u> production <u>facilities</u>.
  C   D   E

Students should recognize that the error is item **D**. The antecedent *Each* is singular, requiring the singular possessive pronoun *its*.

> **Exercise 19** Correcting Misuse of Reflexive Pronouns
Correct the sentences that misuse a reflexive pronoun. If a sentence is correct, write C.
  1. The assignment directed Sean and myself to find information on a space shuttle.
  2. Sean said that himself and I should try the Internet.
  3. The results of our Internet searches were a surprise to both the teacher and ourselves.
  4. I came up with 102,700 sites myself.
  5. Won't it be an effort for yourself to check all those sites?

> **Exercise 20** Supplying Reflexive Pronouns Supply a reflexive pronoun to complete each sentence.
  1. I can do that ___?___.
  2. Sean said he would search the Internet ___?___.
  3. We were proud of ___?___.
  4. They created a Web site ___?___.
  5. Do you want to check the sites ___?___?

Agreement With Indefinite Pronouns

When you write a sentence with a personal pronoun that has an indefinite pronoun as its antecedent, you must always make sure that the two pronouns agree.

> **KEY CONCEPTS** Use a singular pronoun to refer to a singular indefinite pronoun. Use a plural pronoun to refer to a plural indefinite pronoun. ■

SINGULAR: *One* of the boys will print *his* document.
PLURAL: *All* of the boys will print *their* documents.

If no gender is specified, you can use *his*, *his or her*, or you can reword the sentence, as in the following examples:

EXAMPLES: *Everyone* saved *his or her* document.
            All the students saved *their* documents.

With an indefinite pronoun that can be either singular or plural, agreement depends on the word to which the indefinite pronoun refers. In the first example below, *some* refers to part of the *document*, a singular noun. In the second example, *some* refers to part of the *students*, a plural noun.

EXAMPLES: *Some* of the document lost *its* formatting.
            Some of the students printed *their* documents.

▼ **Critical Viewing**
Antennae is the plural form of *antenna*. Write a sentence with the word *antenna*. Then, use the same verb in a sentence with *antennae*. How does the verb change? **[Analyze]**

Pronoun and Antecedent Agreement • 587

☑ **ONGOING ASSESSMENT: Monitor and Reinforce**

If students miss more than two items in Exercises 18–20, refer them to the following for additional practice.

In the Textbook	Print Resources	Technology
Section Review, Ex. 24, p. 591	Grammar Exercise Workbook, pp. 147–148	Language Lab CD-ROM, Pronouns and Antecedents; On-Line Exercise Bank, Section 25.2

1. their
2. its
3. it
4. them
5. they
6. his or her
7. their
8. their
9. he or she
10. our

Step-by-Step Teaching Guide

Three Special Problems in Pronoun Agreement

1. Emphasize that pronouns must have clearly stated or clearly understood antecedents. Pronouns like *they, you, it,* and *this* should refer to a specific antecedent, not to a vague or general idea.

2. Caution students also not to use a pronoun that could refer to two or more antecedents. This problem is known as ambiguous reference.

Critical Viewing

Relate Sample response: Each of these items helps me with my studies. "Helps" used because all the things shown contribute positively; the singular was used because "each" is singular.

Integrating Writing Skills

Vague use of *they, it,* and *you* is a common problem in student writing. Have students select a recent piece of writing from their portfolios, highlight or circle each appearance of *they, it,* or *you,* and then check that each pronoun refers to a single, obvious antecedent.

25.2

► **Exercise 21** Making Personal Pronouns Agree With Indefinite Pronouns On your paper, write a pronoun or pronouns to complete each sentence correctly.

EXAMPLE: Each of the students must have ___?___ own password.

ANSWER: his or her

1. Software companies have profited greatly from ___?___ word-processing programs.
2. Each of the editing features is valued for ___?___ ability to help people save time.
3. For example, some text in a document can be cut; then, ___?___ can be moved or copied as needed.
4. Few who do word processing make full use of the technology available to ___?___ .
5. Many are comfortable with basic computer tools, but ___?___ don't want to figure out how to create tables.
6. Anyone who practices for a short time will find ___?___ job easier.
7. Others improve ___?___ computer skills by taking classes.
8. Practice and classes—both are helpful in ___?___ own way.
9. Once somebody masters word processing, ___?___ may want to go on to learn about charts and graphs.
10. Shouldn't every one of us explore ___?___ computer programs thoroughly?

Three Special Problems in Pronoun Agreement

When you use personal pronouns, make sure that they have antecedents that are clearly defined. Problems can occur when the antecedent is unstated or unclear or when the personal pronoun refers to the wrong antecedent.

► **KEY CONCEPT** A personal pronoun requires an antecedent that is either stated or clearly understood. ■

POOR: The *program* was easy, but *they* didn't explain it clearly.

CORRECT: The *program* was easy, but *it* wasn't explained clearly.

▲ **Critical Viewing**
Use an indefinite pronoun in a sentence that describes the picture. What verb did you use? Why? **[Relate]**

► **More Practice**
Language Lab CD-ROM
• Pronoun Antecedent Agreement lesson
On-line Exercise Bank
• Section 25.2
Grammar Exercise Workbook
• pp. 85–87

GRAMMAR IN LITERATURE

from **The Road Ahead**
Bill Gates

Bill Gates uses both the masculine and feminine pronouns (his or her) *to refer to the indefinite antecedent* anybody.

Before the invention of writing 5,000 years ago, the only form of communication was the spoken word and the listener had to be in the presence of the speaker or miss his message. Once the message could be written, it could be stored and read later by *anybody*, at *his* or *her* convenience. I'm writing these words at home on a summer evening, but I have no idea where or when you'll read them. One of the benefits the communications revolution will bring to all of us is more control over our schedules.

In the preceding example, there is no antecedent for the pronoun *they*. The sentence can be corrected by replacing *they* with a noun or a personal pronoun that agrees with the antecedent *program*.

KEY CONCEPT A personal pronoun should always refer to a single, obvious antecedent. ∎

If a pronoun can refer to more than one antecedent, the sentence should be rewritten.

POOR: I saw the *procedure* in the *manual*, but now I can't find *it*.

CORRECT: I saw the *procedure* in the *manual*, but now I can't find the *procedure*.
I can't find the *procedure* I saw in the *manual*.

POOR: When the *technician* adjusted the sound, the *musician* was pleased. Even so, *he* wasn't satisfied.

CORRECT: When the *technician* adjusted the sound, the *musician* was pleased. Even so, the *technician* wasn't satisfied.
When the *technician* adjusted the sound, *he* wasn't satisfied. Even so, the *musician* was pleased.

Learn More

To get practice with pronoun-antecedent agreement in a standardized test format, use the Standardized Test Preparation Workshop on pages 594–595.

Pronoun and Antecedent Agreement • 589

Grammar in Literature
1. Read, or have a prepared student read, the passage from *The Road Ahead* aloud.
2. After discussing the annotation and Gates's use of *his or her,* note to students that the writer chose not to use *his or her* in the preceding sentence ("speaker . . . his *message*").
   Ask students how they might avoid the use of *his* in this situation. (*They might rewrite the sentence using plurals for* listener *and* speaker, *which would allow them to use the plural pronoun* their.)
3. Ask students if the writer's use of *you* in the third sentence is appropriate. (*It is appropriate, because Gates is directly addressing his readers.*)

More About the Writer
Bill Gates was nineteen years old when he founded a computer software company with his friend Paul Allen in 1975. Today Microsoft is the world's largest software company, and Bill Gates is reported to be the richest man in the world. His book, *The Road Ahead,* examines the future of computer technology.

ONGOING ASSESSMENT: Monitor and Reinforce

If students miss more than two items in Exercises 21–23 refer them to the following for additional practice.

In the Textbook	Print Resources	Technology
Section Review, Ex. 25, p. 591	Grammar Exercise Workbook, pp. 149–150	Language Lab CD-ROM, Pronouns and Antecedents; On-Line Exercise Bank, Section 25.2

TIME SAVERS!

Answers on Transparency Use the Grammar Exercises Answers on Transparencies for Chapter 25 to have students correct their own or one another's exercises.

On-Line Exercise Bank Have students complete the exercises on computer. The Auto Check feature will grade their work for you!

25.2

▶ **KEY CONCEPT** Use the personal pronoun *you* only when the reference is truly to the reader or the listener. ■

POOR: In a sound studio, *you* see high-tech equipment.

CORRECT: In a sound studio, *one* sees high-tech equipment.
In a sound studio, *there is* high-tech equipment.

▶ **Exercise 22** Recognizing Proper Pronoun Usage Identify the sentence that better follows the conventions of English usage of pronouns. Explain your choices.

1. (A) The concert was being held in the park, and we finally found it. (B) We finally found the park where the concert was being held.
2. (A) The sound was good, but they didn't play long enough. (B) The sound was good, but the musicians didn't play long enough.
3. (A) Everyone brought their own chair. (B) Everyone brought his or her own chair.
4. (A) The crowd was huge, but you could hear the music. (B) The crowd was huge, but everyone could hear the music.
5. (A) Next year, you should go to the concert. (B) Next year, he or she should go to the concert.

▶ **Exercise 23** Correcting Special Problems in Pronoun Agreement Revise the following paragraph, correcting all errors in pronoun and antecedent agreement.

(1) In sound recording, they convert acoustic energy into sound. (2) It can then be either stored or reproduced for later use. (3) Thomas Edison made improvements in recording in the late 1800's, when they invented a reproduction of audible sound. (4) Record players, which were the next great innovation, used an amplifier to magnify it. (5) In current recordings, you have the sound waves go into a microphone. (6) The microphone converts them into a signal that is recorded on tape. (7) If the engineer needs to, he or she can edit it. (8) You use laser technology to create compact discs. (9) Sound is written and read digitally without physical contact with them. (10) Motion picture recordings are called *optical* because they use a beam of light to create them.

▲ **Critical Viewing** In what ways has communication changed during the last fifty years? **[Analyze]**

▶ **More Practice**
Language Lab CD-ROM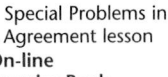
• Special Problems in Agreement lesson
On-line Exercise Bank
• Section 25.2
Grammar Exercise Workbook
• pp. 85–87

☑ **ONGOING ASSESSMENT: Assess Mastery**

Use the following resources to assess student mastery of pronoun-antecedent agreement.

In the Textbook	Technology
Chapter Review, Ex. 32–34, pp. 592–593	On-Line Exercise Bank, Section 25.2

Section 25.2 *Section Review*

GRAMMAR EXERCISES 24–29

▶ **Exercise 24** Correcting Errors in Pronoun-Antecedent Agreement In the following sentences, most of the pronouns do not agree with their antecedents. Identify pronouns that do not agree. Then, write the correct form. If the sentence is correct, write *C*.

1. Anyone who has e-mail probably corresponds with their friends often.
2. Both Marissa and Tashina check their mailboxes every day.
3. Neither likes to open their mailbox to find that no one has written to them.
4. However, each of the girls always has messages waiting for them.
5. One feature of an e-mail program is their ability to store messages.

▶ **Exercise 25** Correcting Special Problems in Pronoun-Antecedent Agreement Rewrite the following paragraph, correcting the errors in pronoun and antecedent agreement. Not all sentences have errors.

(1) There is a little gray thing attached to every computer. (2) It is a device that is needed to operate it. (3) They call it a mouse. (4) A mouse is a small, gray object that you roll along a hard, flat surface. (5) The connecting wire looks like its tail. (6) You use a mouse to control the movement of the pointer on the screen. (7) As it moves, the pointer on the screen moves in the same direction. (8) Mice have at least one button and sometimes three. (9) They have different uses, depending on which program is running. (10) Some newer ones include a scroll wheel for scrolling through long documents quickly and easily.

▶ **Exercise 26** Revision Practice: Pronoun Antecedent Agreement Revise the following paragraph, correcting errors in pronoun and antecedent agreement.

(1) There are homes in America in which they don't watch much TV. (2) Instead, each family member spends their time on other activities. (3) This is much better for you. (4) One health expert reports that when someone stares at TV, they don't use their imagination. (5) National TV-Turnoff Week is sponsored by TV-Free America, and millions of Americans participate in it.

▶ **Exercise 27** Find It in Your Reading Reread the excerpt from Bill Gates's *The Road Ahead* on page 589. Find at least three personal pronouns, and write them down along with their antecedents.

▶ **Exercise 28** Find It in Your Writing Select a writing sample from your portfolio. On your draft, draw a circle around each pronoun and underline its antecedent. Finally, check to be sure that the pronouns and the antecedents agree.

▶ **Exercise 29** Writing Application Write an e-mail message in which you describe an event you attended with a friend. Make sure that each pronoun has a clear antecedent and that the pronouns and antecedents agree.

ASSESS and CLOSE

Section Review

Each of these exercises correlates to a concept in the section on pronoun-antecedent agreement, pages 584–590. These exercises may be used for more practice, for reteaching, or for review of the Key Concepts presented. Some of the exercises, such as number 25, may have questions with more than one correct answer.

Answer Key

▶ **Exercise 24**

1. his or her
2. C
3. her, her
4. her
5. its

▶ **Exercise 25**

(1) There is a little gray thing attached to every computer. (2) The little gray thing is a device that is needed to operate the computer. (3) It is called a mouse. (4) A mouse is a small, gray object that is rolled along a hard, flat surface. (5) The connecting wire looks like its tail. (6) A mouse is used to control the movement of the pointer on the screen. (7) As the mouse moves, the pointer on the screen moves in the same direction. (8) Mice have at least one button and sometimes three. (9) The buttons have different uses, depending on which program is running. (10) Some newer mice include a scroll wheel for scrolling through long documents quickly and easily.

continued

Answer Key continued

▶ **Exercise 26**

(1) There are homes in America in which no one watches much TV. (2) Instead, each family member spends his or her time on other activities. (3) Doing other activities is much better for them than watching TV. (4) One health expert reports that when people stare at TV, they don't use their imagination. (5) National TV-Turnoff Week is sponsored by TV-Free America, and millions of Americans participate in the event.

▶ **Exercise 27**

1. his; speaker
2. it; message
3. his or her; anybody

▶ **Exercise 28**

When they finish this activity, have students exchange papers with a partner and check one another's agreement.

▶ **Exercise 29**

Students should send e-mail to one another and check each other's agreement.

⏱ **TIME SAVERS!**

▸ **Answers on Transparency** Use the Grammar Exercises Answers on Transparencies for Chapter 25 to have students correct their own or one another's exercises.

💻 **On-Line Exercise Bank** Have students complete the exercises on computer. The Auto Check feature will grade their work for you!

CHAPTER REVIEW

Each of these exercises correlates to a section of this chapter, pages 570–591. These exercises may be used for more practice, for reteaching, or for review of the Key Concepts presented. Some of the exercises, such as number 32, may have questions with more than one correct answer.

Answer Key

1. Does
2. is
3. was
4. are
5. features
6. has
7. is
8. was
9. were
10. was

1. After the regular baseball season come the long-awaited championship games.
2. The World Series brings baseball fever to its highest pitch.
3. The cheering fans are a thrilling sight.
4. Excited indeed are all baseball lovers across the country.
5. The early games of the series start the buildup to the final game.
6. Seven is the maximum number of series games.
7. However, there have been some series won in either four or five games.
8. Each team tries hard to come out on top.
9. *The October Heroes* describes great World Series games.
10. Baseball statistics are located at www.baseballstats.com.

Chapter
25 **Chapter Review**

GRAMMAR EXERCISES 30–36

▶ **Exercise 30** **Choosing Verbs That Agree With Subjects** Choose the verb that agrees with the subject in each sentence.

1. (Do, Does) your group of friends enjoy movies?
2. One of my favorite old films (is, are) *The Wizard of Oz.*
3. *The Wizard of Oz,* as well as *Return to Oz,* (was, were) based on a novel by Frank Baum.
4. Very popular today (is, are) action films.
5. Almost every one of them (features, feature) dazzling special effects.
6. Sophisticated electronics (has, have) made the visual effects possible.
7. Acoustics (is, are) the science that has given us the frighteningly realistic sound effects.
8. *Tarzan and the Amazons* (was, were) made with simple special effects in 1945.
9. Back then, only a small percentage of films (was, were) shot in color.
10. Black and white (was, were) more common.

▶ **Exercise 31** **Revising for Subject-Verb Agreement** Rewrite each sentence, revising it according to the instructions given in brackets. Change the verb form as needed. Not all verbs will change.

1. After the regular baseball season comes the long-awaited event. [Change *event* to *championship games.*]
2. The World Series contests bring baseball fever to its highest pitch. [Delete *contests.*]
3. The cheering crowd is a thrilling sight. [Change *crowd* to *fans.*]
4. Excited indeed is every baseball lover

592 • Agreement

across the country. [Change *every baseball lover* to *all baseball lovers.*]
5. The early part of the series starts the buildup to the final game. [Change *part* to *games.*]
6. The maximum number of series games is seven. [Change the word order, making *seven* the subject of the sentence.]
7. However, there have been series won in only four or five games. [Insert *some* before *series.*]
8. Both teams try hard to come out on top. [Change *Both teams* to *Each team.*]
9. Donald Honig's book *The October Heroes* describes great World Series games. [Delete *Donald Honig's book.*]
10. A Web site giving baseball statistics is located at www.baseballstats.com. [Delete *A Web site giving.*]

▶ **Exercise 32** **Revising for Pronoun-Antecedent Agreement** Revise the following paragraph, correcting all errors in pronoun and antecedent agreement.

(1) In the Hawaiian Islands, they have some of the best scuba diving in the world. (2) If yourself and your friends want a truly exciting experience, you should try it. (3) Each of the diving sites around the island of Oahu has their own special attractions. (4) The guides always take the divers to the places they like best. (5) A person diving in Maunalua Bay, for example, will see exotic fish that they won't see anywhere else. (6) A reef on the south shore contains a shipwreck, but a diver must be experienced to explore it. (7) Anyone who sees the orange cup corals at Ulua Cave won't believe their eyes. (8) Some divers might think that an occasional shark or octopus is dangerous, but usually they're not. (9) All the instruc-

---

(1) Some of the best scuba diving in the world can be found in the Hawaiian Islands. (2) If you and your friends want a truly exciting experience, try scuba diving in Hawaii. (3) Each of the diving sites around the island of Oahu has its own special attractions. (4) The guides always take the divers to the places the guides like best. (5) People diving in Maunalua Bay, for example, will see exotic fish that they won't see anywhere else. (6) A reef on the south shore contains a shipwreck, but a diver must be experienced to explore the shipwreck. (7) Anyone who sees the orange cup corals at the Ulua Cave won't believe his or her eyes. (8) Some divers might think that an occasional shark or octopus is dangerous, but usually it is not. (9) All the instructional manuals say that an individual must be physically fit to scuba dive. (10) If my sister and I were invited to go scuba diving in the Hawaiian Islands, we'd jump at the chance.

tional manuals say that you must be physically fit to scuba dive. (10) If my sister and myself were invited to go diving in the Hawaiian Islands, we'd jump at the chance.

Exercise 33 Revising Sentences to Eliminate Errors in Agreement
Revise the following sentences, correcting any errors in agreement. Not every sentence has an error.

1. The U.S. communications industry conveys information in their various forms.
2. In addition to TV and radio, you have publishing and the Internet.
3. Either television or the Internet are the source of news for most people, although both newspapers and radio are still important.
4. Each of the recent technological advances help provide information even faster.
5. However, often the advances mean that you have to buy expensive new equipment to access it.
6. Not all bits of information is beneficial.
7. For example, everyone must guard themselves against false advertising.
8. Almost every qualified person can find work in the communications industry.
9. However, they must have the right training.
10 *Cybercareers* (Massie and Morris), along with other books on communications jobs, are available in bookstores.

Exercise 34 Revising a Paragraph to Eliminate Errors in Agreement
Revise the following paragraph, correcting all errors in agreement.

(1) Almost every child has fun at the circus. (2) They burst with excitement when the sounds of the opening pageant begins. (3) As the elephants, horseback riders, and other performers parade around the ring, you hear the rousing music play. (4) After the marchers come the ringmaster into the center ring to introduce the acts. (5) Often there's acts going on in all three rings simultaneously. (6) The funniest act are the clowns. (7) In they come, running and tumbling, each wearing their own silly costume. (8) Sounds of laughter from the audience fills the big top. (9) One of the most breathtaking acts are the trapeze artists. (10) Flying through the air, he or she catches each other with amazing precision.

Exercise 35 Writing Application
Write a paragraph about either an aspect of your local or state government or a technological advance that interests you. Make sure that all your verbs agree with their subjects and that your pronouns agree with their antecedents.

Exercise 36 CUMULATIVE REVIEW
Sentence Errors   Revise the following paragraphs, correcting sentence errors and errors in verb and pronoun usage and agreement. Note that a numbered section may have one error, several errors, or no error.

(1) If one asks whomever has visited New York what they think of the statue in the harbor, the answer might be "Awesome." (2) Originally called Liberty Enlightening the World, it is now knowed as the Statue of Liberty. (3) It was a gift from France to we the American people. (4) The statue symbolizing freedom. (5) She holds a torch in her right hand. (6) in her left hand, she carries a book inscribed "July 4, 1776." (7) Broken chains symbolizing the defeat of tyranny lies at her feet. (8) The Statue of Liberty one of the largest statues in the world. (9) Its builded of copper sheets riveted to an iron frame. (10) Amazingly, 306 feet 8 inches are it's height from the base to the torch.

Answer Key continued

Exercise 35
Have students work in pairs and read each other's paragraphs to check for errors in agreement.

Exercise 36
Wording of some revisions may vary.

(1) If you ask someone who has visited New York what he or she thinks of the statue in the harbor, the answer might be "awesome." (2) Originally called Liberty Enlightening the World, it is now known as the Statue of Liberty. (3) It was a gift from France to us, the American people. (4) The statue symbolizes freedom. (5) Liberty holds a torch in her right hand. (6) In her left hand, she carries a book inscribed "July 4, 1776." (7) Broken chains symbolizing the defeat of tyranny lie at her feet. (8) The Statue of Liberty is one of the largest statues in the world. (9) It's built of copper sheets riveted to an iron frame. (10) Amazingly, 306 feet 8 inches is its height from the base to the torch.

Exercise 33
Wording of some revisions may vary.

(1) The U.S. communications industry conveys information in its various forms. (2) In addition to TV and radio, there are publishing and the Internet. (3) Either television or the Internet is the source of news for most people, although both newspapers and radio are still important. (4) Each of the recent technological advances helps provide information even faster. (5) However, often the advances mean that one has to buy expensive new equipment to access it. (6) Not all bits of information are beneficial. (7) For example, everyone must guard himself or herself against false advertising. (8) Almost every qualified person can find work in the communications industry. (9) However, he or she must have the right training. (10) *Cybercareers* (Massie and Morris), along with other books on communications jobs, is available in bookstores.

Exercise 34
Wording of some revisions may vary.

(1) Almost all children have fun at the circus. (2) They burst with excitement when the sounds of the opening pageant begin. (3) As the elephants, horseback riders, and other performers parade around the ring, the children hear the rousing music play. (4) After the marchers, the ringmaster comes into the center ring to introduce the acts. (5) Often there are acts going on in all three rings simultaneously. (6) The funniest act is the clowns. (7) In they come, running and tumbling, each wearing his or her own silly costume. (8) Sounds of laughter from the audience fill the big top. (9) One of the most breathtaking acts is the trapeze artists. (10) Flying through the air, they catch each other with amazing precision.

continued

⏱ TIME SAVERS!

📺 Answers on Transparency
Use the Grammar Exercises Answers on Transparencies for Chapter 25 to have students correct their own or one another's exercises.

💻 On-Line Exercise Bank
Have students complete the exercises on computer. The Auto Check feature will grade their work for you!

Step-by-Step Teaching Guide

Subject-Verb Agreement

1. Encourage students to read test instructions carefully. Not all standardized tests are graded in the same way. Some tests do not penalize students for incorrect answers, so that they may increase their scores with a judicious guess.

2. If students tend to get stuck on questions, suggest that they go quickly on to the next question and return to a difficult question later if time permits.

3. You may wish to provide students with standardized test answer sheets to practice the mechanics of marking in answers.

Standard English Usage: Subject-Verb Agreement

Knowledge of the rules of subject-verb agreement is one of the skills most frequently tested on standardized tests. When checking a test sentence for errors, first identify the subject. Next, identify the type of subject: singular, plural, or compound. Then, apply the rules of agreement to make sure that the verb in the sentence agrees with the subject.

The following questions will give you practice with different formats used for items that test knowledge of subject-verb agreement.

Test Tip

If you are having trouble with a sentence revision, eliminate any answer choices in which the subject and verb clearly do not agree.

Sample Test Item	Answers and Explanations
Identify which underlined words and phrases in the following sentence contain an error. Neither Zach nor Tim are interested in (A)　　　　(B)　　　　(C) attending Sunday's concert at the arena. 　　　　　　　(D) No error (E)	The correct answer is *C*. To arrive at this answer, identify the subject of the sentence (whom the sentence is about). The subject is *Zach nor Tim*. It is a compound subject made up of two singular subjects joined by *nor*. Such a subject takes a singular verb, in this case, *is*.
Choose the revised version of the following sentence that eliminates all errors in grammar, usage, and mechanics. Neither Zach nor Tim are interested in attending Sunday's concert at the arena. A　Neither Zach nor Tim is interested in attending Sunday's concert at the arena. B　Zach or Tim are not interested in attending Sunday's concert at the arena. C　Both Zach and Tim is not interested in attending Sunday's concert at the arena. D　Neither Zach and Tim are interested in attending Sunday's concert at the arena.	The correct answer is *A*. To arrive at this answer, identify the subject of the sentence (whom the sentence is about). The subject is *Zach nor Tim*. It is a compound subject made up of two singular subjects joined by *nor*. Such a subject takes a singular verb, in this case, *is*.

594 • Agreement

⬦ TEST-TAKING TIP

Remind students that, faced with a difficult problem of agreement, rephrasing the sentence may clarify the error. Rephrasing may involve moving an inverted subject, framing a question as a statement, or eliminating extra words. "Extra words" are words that may modify the subject, and can be important for meaning but are not necessary for determining agreement. For example: "Every one of the five or six people in the room (wants/want) to have dinner." is fairly complex, but eliminate all the words that modify "every one" and you end up with "Every one wants dinner."

▶ **Practice 1** Identify which underlined words and phrases in each of the
following sentences contain an error.

1. Evergreen trees never loses all their
         (A)   (B)
   leaves at one time but remain
          (C)
   green throughout the year. No error
      (D)   (E)

2. Like all evergreens, a pine or fir tree
          (A)   (B)
   reproduce by means of seeds
      (C)
   contained in its cones. No error
      (D)   (E)

3. Insects, such as the bee, avoid
        (A)   (B)
   the sticky sap of the evergreen.
       (C)   (D)
   No error
    (E)

4. Neither pine trees nor fir trees
        (A)   (B)
   thrives in a desert climate. No error
    (C)   (D)   (E)

5. Beyond those buildings is a
        (A)   (B)
   dense forest filled with evergreen
     (C)   (D)
   trees. No error
       (E)

▶ **Practice 2** Choose the revised version of each numbered sentence that
eliminates all errors in grammar, usage,
and mechanics.

1 The jack pine release its seeds when
heated in a fire, and this help renew the
forest.

  A The jack pines releases its seeds
    when heated by fire, and this helps
    renew the forest.
  B The jack pine releases its seeds
    when heated by fire, and this help
    renew the forest.
  C The jack pine release its seeds when
    heated by fire, and this help renews
    the forest.
  D The jack pine releases its seeds
    when heated by fire, and this helps
    renew the forest.

2 The Douglas fir, the spruce, and many
other types of evergreens thrives in cold
climates, such as that in New England.

  F The Douglas fir, the spruce, and
    many other types of evergreens thrive
    in cold climates, such as that in New
    England.
  G The Douglas fir, the spruce, or many
    other types of evergreens thrives in
    cold climates, such as that in New
    England.
  H Douglas firs, spruces, and many
    other types of evergreens thrives in
    cold climates, such as New England.
  J The Douglas fir, the spruce, and
    many other evergreens thrives in
    cold climates, such as New England.

Practice 1
1. B
2. C
3. E
4. C
5. E

Practice 2
1. D
2. F

Time and Resource Manager

In-Depth Lesson Plan

	LESSON FOCUS	PRINT AND MEDIA RESOURCES
DAY 1	**Degrees of Comparison** Students learn and apply concepts covering degrees to comparison (pp. 596–603).	**Teaching Resources** *Grammar Exercise Workbook,* pp. 151–154; *Grammar Exercises Answers on Transparency,* Ch. 26; *Language Lab* **CD-ROM,** Using Modifiers; *On-Line Exercise Bank,* Section 26.1
DAY 2	**Making Clear Comparisons** Students learn and apply concepts covering clear degrees of comparison and do the Hands-On Grammar activity (pp. 604–609).	**Teaching Resources** *Grammar Exercise Workbook,* pp. 155–158; *Grammar Exercises Answers on Transparency,* Ch. 26; *Hands-on Grammar Activity Book,* Chapter 26; *Language Lab* **CD-ROM,** Using Modifiers; *On-Line Exercise Bank,* Section 26.2
DAY 3	**Review and Assess** Students review chapter and demonstrate mastery of use of comparative degrees of modifiers (pp. 610–613).	**Teaching Resources** *Formal Assessment,* Ch. 26; *On-Line Exercise Bank,* Section 26.1

Accelerated Lesson Plan

	LESSON FOCUS	PRINT AND MEDIA RESOURCES
DAY 1	**Using Modifiers** Students cover concepts and usage of degrees of comparison in modifiers as determined by Diagnostic Test (pp. 596–609).	**Teaching Resources** *Grammar Exercise Workbook,* pp. 151–158; *Grammar Exercises Answers on Transparency,* Ch. 26; *Language Lab* **CD-ROM,** Using Modifiers; *On-Line Exercise Bank,* Section 26.1–2
DAY 2	**Review and Assess** Students review chapter and demonstrate mastery of use of comparative degrees of modifiers (pp. 610–613).	**Teaching Resources** *Formal Assessment,* Ch. 26; *On-Line Exercise Bank,* Section 26.1

Options for Adapting Lesson Plans

HOMEWORK

Have students complete any section of the chapter for homework.

FEATURES

Extend coverage with the Grammar in Literature feature (p. 601), and the Standardized Test Preparation Workshop (p. 612).

TECHNOLOGY

Students can use the On-Line Exercise Bank to complete the exercises on computer. The Auto Check feature will grade their work.

INTEGRATED SKILLS COVERAGE

Grammar in Literature
SE p. 601

Reading
Find It In Your Reading, SE pp. 603, 608, 609

Writing
Find It In Your Writing, SE pp. 603, 608, 609
Writing Application, SE pp. 603, 609, 611

Viewing and Representing
Critical Viewing, SE pp. 596, 599, 601, 602, 604

ASSESSMENT SUPPORT

Standardized Test Preparation SE p. 612; ATE pp. 602, 606
Standardized Test Preparation Workbook, pp. 51–52
Formal Assessment, Ch. 26

MEETING INDIVIDUAL NEEDS

Less Advanced Students ATE p. 602; See also Ongoing
Assessments ATE pp. 600, 601, 605, 607, 608
ESL Students ATE p. 600
More Advanced Students ATE p. 599

BLOCK SCHEDULING

Pacing Suggestions
For 90-minute Blocks
• Administer the Diagnostic Test to students to determine instructional coverage.
• Have students complete the necessary exercises in class. Use the Hands-on Grammar activity to provide a change of pace.

Resources for Varying Instruction
• *Language Lab* **CD-ROM** If your students have access to hardware, a 90-minute block provides an ideal opportunity for students to work on computer.

Professional Development Support
• **How to Manage Instruction In the Block** This Teaching Resource provides management and activity suggestions.

MEDIA AND TECHNOLOGY

For the Student
• *Language Lab* **CD-ROM**, Using Modifiers
• *On-Line Exercise Bank*, Ch. 26

For the Teacher
• *Resource Pro* **CD-ROM**

WRITING AND GRAMMAR WEBSITE

The Interactive Writing and Grammar Website provides a wide array of support for students, teachers and parents. Grammar support includes:
• *On-Line Exercise Bank* with Auto Check scoring
• Diagnostic and assessment support

phwg. phschool.com

LITERATURE CONNECTIONS

Grammar in Literature selections from *Prentice Hall Literature: Timeless Voices, Timeless Themes*, Gold:
from *Children in the Woods*, Barry Lopez, SE p. 601

► *Lesson Objectives*

1. To recognize and use the positive, comparative, and superlative forms of adjectives and adverbs.

2. To use adjectives and adverbs with *more* and *most*.

3. To use adjectives and adverbs with *less* and *least*.

4. To use comparative and superlative degrees correctly.

5. To make balanced comparisons.

6. To use *other* and *else* in comparisons.

Critical Viewing

Describe Students may say that the trees look much larger in their reflection. The mountains are greater in Alaska than in Texas.

Chapter 26 Using Modifiers

▲ Critical Viewing
Describe this Alaskan scenery using adjectives in comparative forms. **[Describe]**

On a hike through the forest, you may have to climb over some rocks. Some rocks are large, some are larger, and one is the largest rock you've ever seen. When comparing the size of rocks, we use modifying words to make our meaning more explicit. *Large, larger,* and *largest* help the reader understand these different sizes.

As you have learned, adjectives and adverbs modify other words. They are also used to make comparisons. You might say, for instance, that summer nights in a forest are *cool;* autumn nights, *cooler;* and winter nights, *coolest.* Notice that in using the word cool you change the form, depending on whether two or more things are being compared.

In this chapter, you will learn how to use adjectives and adverbs correctly in comparisons.

596 • Using Modifiers

☑ ONGOING ASSESSMENT: Diagnose

If students miss more than one item in each category, direct them to the relevant pages of the text and assign exercises for practice and review.

Using Modifiers	Diagnostic Test Items	Teach	Practice	Section Review	Chapter Review
Skill Check A					
Degrees of Comparison	A 1–10	p. 598	Ex. 1	Ex. 5	Ex. 21–22
Skill Check B					
Regular Forms	B 11–15	p. 599	Ex. 2	Ex. 6	Ex. 22

Diagnostic Test

Directions: Write all answers on a separate sheet of paper.

Skill Check A. In each line, one form of the adjective or adverb is missing. Write the missing word on your paper.

Positive	Comparative	Superlative
1. green	greener	
2. dense		densest
3.	shadier	shadiest
4. wet	wetter	
5. good		best
6.	more rapidly	most rapidly
7. leafy		leafiest
8. many	more	
9.	warmer	warmest
10. complex		most complex

Skill Check B. Select the correct form of the adjective or adverb in parentheses, and write it on your paper.

11. A forest is a (large, larger, largest) area of land where the main plants are trees.
12. Evergreen forests of cone-bearing trees are located in the regions (far, farther, farthest) north in North America.
13. In southern Canada and the eastern United States, where the weather is (warm, warmer, warmest), broadleaf forests are common.
14. In the fall, broadleaf trees—such as maples, beeches, oaks, and hickories—are (colorful, more colorful, most colorful) than cone-bearing trees, which stay green.
15. The (moist, moister, moistest) air of the west coast of North America provides an ideal climate for temperate rain forests.

Skill Check C. Write the appropriate comparative or superlative form of the modifier in parentheses.

16. The redwood is the (tall) tree in the forest.
17. It grows (fast) in wet climates than in dry climates.
18. Which of the two trees grows (good)?
19. The trees in Costa Rica are (far) from the United States than are the trees in Guatemala.
20. Central America has the (strange) trees in the world.

Skill Check D. Rewrite each sentence, correcting the unbalanced or illogical comparison.

21. Central America's rain forests are more numerous than North America.
22. The eye of a lizard is larger than a frog.
23. Southern Mexico's forests are more lush than any I've visited.
24. The expedition leader had traveled more miles than anyone I know.
25. This mountain is steepest than any in the area.

Answer Key

Diagnostic Test

Each item in the diagnostic test corresponds to a specific concept in the chapter on modifiers. This will enable you to tailor instruction to the particular needs of your students. See "Ongoing Assessment System" below for further details.

Skill Check A

1. greenest	6. rapidly
2. denser	7. leafier
3. shady	8. most
4. wettest	9. warm
5. better	10. more complex

Skill Check B

11. large
12. farthest
13. warm
14. more colorful
15. moist

Skill Check C

16. tallest
17. faster
18. better
19. farther
20. strangest

Skill Check D

21. Central America's rain forests are more numerous than North America's.
22. The eye of a lizard is larger than a frog's.
23. Southern Mexico's forests are more lush than any other I've visited.
24. The expedition leader had traveled more miles than anyone else I know.
25. This mountain is the steepest of all others in the area.

ONGOING ASSESSMENT: Diagnose *continued*

Using Modifiers	Diagnostic Test Items	Teach	Practice	Section Review	Chapter Review
Skill Check C					
Comparative and Superlative Degrees	C 16–20	p. 604	Ex. 11–12	Ex. 15–16	Ex. 26
Skill Check D					
Balanced Comparisons	D 21–25	pp. 606–607	Ex. 13–14	Ex. 17	Ex. 27
Cumulative Reviews and Applications				Ex. 5–10, 15–20	Ex. 28–30

TIME SAVERS!

Answers on Transparency
Use the Grammar Exercises on Transparencies for Chapter 26 to have students correct their own or one another's exercises.

On-Line Exercise Bank
Have students complete the exercises on computer. The Auto Check feature will grade their work for you!

Write the following words and sentences on the board. Ask students to choose one of the words to complete each sentence.

tastier scary smaller sharpest

Vampire bats aren't as (scary) as many people think.

They are only 3 inches long, (smaller) than a mouse.

They find animal blood (tastier) than human blood.

Their upper front teeth are the (sharpest) of all their teeth.

Activate Prior Knowledge

Ask students how they knew which word to add to each sentence. Ask why they didn't use *smaller* in the last sentence.

TEACH

Step-by-Step Teaching Guide

Recognizing Degrees of Comparison

1. Go over the three degrees of adjectives in the chart. Ask students to suggest other adjectives and provide the comparative and superlative forms.

2. Explain that the "positive" degree can describe a "negative" trait—such as ugly, lazy, unhappy, or painful.

Section 26.1 *Degrees of Comparison*

Often, instead of simply describing something, you may want to compare it with something else. There are three *degrees,* or forms, of adjectives and adverbs that are used to modify and make comparisons.

> **KEY CONCEPT** Most adjectives and adverbs have different forms to show degrees of comparison. ■

Recognizing Degrees of Comparison

In order to make comparisons, you need to know the three degrees of comparison.

> **KEY CONCEPT** The three degrees of comparison are the *positive,* the *comparative,* and the *superlative.* ■

EXAMPLES: cold   colder   coldest
            possible   more possible   most possible

The following chart lists the three degrees of some common adjectives and adverbs. As you can see, the *comparative* and *superlative* degrees of modifiers are formed in various ways. With the adjective *high,* for example, an *-er* is added for the comparative degree and an *-est* is added for the superlative, while *more* and *most* are used with the adjective *eager.*

ADJECTIVES		
Positive	Comparative	Superlative
high	higher	highest
eager	more eager	most eager
ADVERBS		
Positive	Comparative	Superlative
early	earlier	earliest
eagerly	more eagerly	most eagerly
well	better	best

Theme: Nature

In this section, you will learn how to form the comparative and superlative degrees of modifiers. The examples and exercises in this section are about the beauty of nature.

Cross-Curricular Connection: Science

🖉 Spelling Tip

When adding *-er* or *-est* to words ending in *y,* change the *y* to an *i.* For example, *dry* becomes *drier* and *driest,* and *sunny* becomes *sunnier* and *sunniest.*

🕐 TIME AND RESOURCE MANAGER

Resources
Print: Grammar Exercises Workbook, pp. 151–154
Technology: Language Lab CD-ROM, Using Modifiers; On-Line Exercise Bank, Section 26.1

In-Depth Coverage	Accelerated Pace
• Work through all key concepts, pp. 598–600. • Assign and review Exercises 1–4. • Read and discuss Grammar in Literature, p. 601.	• Assign pp. 598–602 for independent student review. • Assign Review Exercise 7.

▶ **Exercise 1** Recognizing Positive, Comparative, and Superlative Degrees Identify the degree of each underlined modifier.

EXAMPLE: That tree is the <u>tallest</u> tree in my yard.
ANSWER: superlative

1. Thousands of years ago, the only nonforested areas of the Earth were those where the land was the <u>driest</u>.
2. In areas where the environment was <u>more favorable</u>, forests extended from the equator to the far north.
3. Forests expanded by moving into formerly <u>icy</u> regions.
4. However, forests are <u>rapidly</u> declining, as clearing by humans and fire outpace the natural expansion of forest regions.
5. About 30 percent of the world is forested today, the <u>lowest</u> percentage ever.

Regular Forms

Modifiers are either regular or irregular. The comparative and superlative degrees of most regular adjectives and adverbs are formed using one of two rules. The first rule applies to modifiers with one or two syllables.

▶ **KEY CONCEPT** Use -er or more to form the comparative degree and -est or most to form the superlative degree of most one- and two-syllable modifiers. ■

The more common method for forming the comparative and superlative degrees of one- and two-syllable modifiers is to add -er and -est to the modifier rather than to use more and most.

EXAMPLES: green   greener   greenest
              dark   darker   darkest

More and most are used with one- and two-syllable modifiers when adding -er or -est would sound awkward. Notice that the words below would sound awkward with -er or -est.

EXAMPLES: crisp   more crisp   most crisp
              humid   more humid   most humid

To form the comparative and superlative degrees of adverbs that end with the suffix -ly, use more and most.

EXAMPLES: quickly   more quickly   most quickly
              smoothly   more smoothly   most smoothly

▲ **Critical Viewing** Describe the colors in this photograph using at least three superlatives. **[Describe]**

Degrees of Comparison • 599

Step-by-Step Teaching Guide

Regular Forms

1. Go over the rules on this page and the next. Give students the following further exceptions to the first rule:
   - Occasional doubling of a final consonant before adding the ending:
     sad, sadder, saddest
     wet, wetter, wettest
   - Dropping the final *e* before adding the ending:
     little, littler, littlest
   - Changing *y* to *i* before adding the ending:
     sleepy, sleepier, sleepiest
2. Adjectives ending in -*ing* or -*ful* always take *more* and *most* rather than the endings -*er* and -*est*.

Customize for
More Advanced Students

Challenge students to find a dozen one- or two-syllable adjectives and adverbs that take *more* and *most* rather than -*er* and -*est*.

Critical Viewing

Describe Students may say that the trees are the greenest they have ever seen; they are also the largest. The sky is the bluest in this picture than they could ever have imagined.

Answer Key

Exercise 2

1. taller, tallest
2. more beautiful, most beautiful
3. more ancient, most ancient
4. noisier, noisiest
5. more difficult, most difficult
6. more slowly, most slowly
7. newer, newest
8. shinier, shiniest
9. stronger, strongest
10. odder, oddest

Step-by-Step Teaching Guide

Irregular Forms

1. Go over the modifiers in the chart. Challenge students to use the different degrees of each modifier in sentences.

2. Use the following sentence to illustrate the difference between *farther* and *further:*

   I went to the library farther from my home to do further research on vampire bats.

3. Make sure students understand that when *little* refers to size rather than amount, it becomes *littler* and *littlest,* not *less* and *least.*

   She is a little kitten.

   The kitten is littler than the puppy.

   That kitten is the littlest of the litter.

   I'll have a seltzer with a little ice.

   I'd like less ice than that.

   One cube is the least ice you can have.

26.1

▶ **KEY CONCEPT** Use *more* and *most* to form the comparative and superlative degrees of all modifiers with three or more syllables. ■

EXAMPLE: popular   more popular   most popular

Note About Comparisons With Less and Least: *Less* and *least,* the opposite of *more* and *most,* can be used to form the comparative and superlative degrees of most modifiers.

EXAMPLES: favorable   less favorable   least favorable
           quickly   less quickly   least quickly

▶ **Exercise 2** Forming Regular Comparative and Superlative Degrees Write the comparative and the superlative form of each modifier.

1. tall   3. ancient   5. difficult   7. new   9. strong
2. beautiful 4. noisy   6. slowly   8. shiny   10. odd

Irregular Forms

▶ **KEY CONCEPT** Memorize the irregular comparative and superlative forms of certain adjectives and adverbs. ■

The most commonly used irregular modifiers are listed in the following chart. Notice that some modifiers differ only in the positive degree. For instance, the modifiers *bad*, *badly*, and *ill* all have the same comparative and superlative forms (*worse*, *worst*).

IRREGULAR MODIFIERS		
Positive	**Comparative**	**Superlative**
bad	worse	worst
badly	worse	worst
far (distance)	farther	farthest
far (extent)	further	furthest
good	better	best
ill	worse	worst
late	later	last or latest
little (amount)	less	least
many	more	most
much	more	most
well	better	best

☑ **ONGOING ASSESSMENT: Monitor and Reinforce**

If students miss more than two items in Exercise 1 or 2, refer them to the following for additional practice.

In the Textbook	Print Resources	Technology
Section Review, Ex. 5–6, p. 603	Grammar Exercise Workbook, pp. 151–152	Language Lab CD-ROM, Using Modifiers; On-Line Exercise Bank, Section 26.1

GRAMMAR IN LITERATURE

from Children in the Woods
Barry Lopez

The writer has used comparative and superlative modifiers. Most moving *is superlative,* heavily *and* wet *are positive,* older *is comparative.*

The most moving look I ever saw from a child in the woods was on a mud bar by the footprints of a heron. We were on our knees, making handprints beside the footprints. You could feel the creek vibrating in the silt and sand. The sun beat down heavily on our hair. Our shoes were soaking wet. The look said: I did not know until now that I needed someone much older to confirm this, the feeling I have of life here. I can now grow older, knowing it need never be lost.

⚙ Grammar and Style Tip

You can make comparisons to help your readers understand your exact meaning. The right forms of adjectives and adverbs will help you add color and depth to your writing.

> **Exercise 3** Forming Irregular Comparative and Superlative Degrees Write the comparative and the superlative degree of each modifier.

EXAMPLE: little
ANSWER: less, least

1. bad
2. good
3. far
4. much
5. well

▶ **Critical Viewing** Use the superlative degree of adjectives in sentences to compare the trees in this photograph of Alaskan scenery. **[Compare and Contrast]**

Degrees of Comparison • 601

Step-by-Step Teaching Guide

Grammar in Literature

1. Have a volunteer read aloud the excerpt.
2. Use the excerpt to give students extra practice with degrees of comparison. After they identify the degree of each modifier in the paragraph, have them write the other two degrees for each.

Answer Key

Exercise 3

1. worse, worst
2. better, best
3. farther, farthest
4. more, most
5. better, best

Critical Viewing

Compare and Contrast Students may say that the tree on the left is the tallest in the photograph.

☑ ONGOING ASSESSMENT: Prerequisite Skills

If students have difficulty with comparative and superlative degrees, you may find it necessary to review the following to assure coverage of prerequisite knowledge.

In the Textbook	Print Resources	Technology
Adjectives and Adverbs, pp. 378–399	Grammar Exercise Workbook, pp. 21–32	On-Line Exercise Bank, Sections 18.1 and 18.2

Answer Key

1. A woodland differs from a forest in that it consists of smaller, more widely separated trees.
2. Woodlands form a transition between moister conifer forests and drier grasslands or deserts.
3. Western forests and woodlands also have the widest variety of settings, which enhance their beauty: mountains, canyons and mesas, and cliffs and headlands.
4. The forests in the western United States boast the largest, tallest, and oldest trees in the world.
5. Fire can have the most devastating effect on a forest, but it is not always considered a tragedy.
6. Native Americans periodically set ground fires to clear out the underbrush to provide better forage conditions for big game.
7. Forests that have developed over the longest periods without catastrophic disturbance of either natural or human origin are known as old-growth forests.
8. Old-growth forests are more complex and more beautiful than many young forests.
9. Old-growth forests are important because they provide some of the best wildlife habitats, recreation areas, and commercial timber.
10. Because of their great commercial value, most old-growth forests have been eliminated except for those in national parks and wilderness areas.

Customize for
Less Advanced Students

Have students make a set of flashcards. On one side, each card should have one of the modifiers listed in the chart of irregular forms on page 600. On the other side, the card should show the other two degrees of that adjective. (Words such as *worse* will have more than two related words listed on the back.) Have partners use the flashcards to test each other on the irregular modifiers as often as necessary to learn them.

Critical Viewing

Compare and Contrast Students may say that their backyards have much less foliage than the Alaskan

602

26.1

▶ **Exercise 4** Using Comparative and Superlative Degrees **Correctly** Rewrite each sentence, replacing the modifier in italics with the comparative or superlative degree indicated in brackets. You may need to add *the* before some superlatives.

EXAMPLE: This year had *little* rainfall. [superlative]
ANSWER: This year had the least rainfall.

1. A woodland differs from a forest in that it consists of *small*, more widely separated trees. [comparative]
2. Woodlands form a transition between moist conifer forests and *dry* grasslands or deserts. [comparative]
3. Western forests and woodlands also have *wide* variety of settings, which enhances their beauty: mountains, canyons and mesas, and cliffs and headlands. [superlative]
4. The forests in the western United States boast *large, tall,* and *old* trees in the world. [superlative]
5. Fire can have a *devastating* effect on a forest, but it is not always considered a tragedy. [superlative]
6. Native Americans periodically set ground fires to clear out the underbrush to provide *good* forage conditions for big game. [comparative, irregular]
7. Forests that have developed over *long* periods without catastrophic disturbance of either natural or human origin are known as old-growth forests. [superlative]
8. Old-growth forests are *complex* and *beautiful* than many young forests. [comparative]
9. Old-growth forests are important because they provide some of the *good* wildlife habitats, recreation areas, and commercial timber. [superlative, irregular]
10. Because of their great commercial value, *many* old-growth forests have been eliminated, except for those in national parks and wilderness areas. [superlative, irregular]

More Practice

On-line
Exercise Bank
• Section 26.1
Grammar Exercise Workbook
• pp. 151–154

▶ **Critical Viewing** Compare this Alaskan forest to your own back yard or neighborhood. **[Compare and Contrast]**

602 • Using Modifiers

⟡ STANDARDIZED TEST PREPARATION WORKSHOP

Grammar and Usage Standardized tests often ask students to find a particular grammatical error among several choices. Ask students which of the following sentences contains an incorrect comparative adjective:

A Betty was much prettier than Veronica.

B I was more frightened in the forest than I had been when we were lost in the city.

C July was a humider month than August.

D I'm practicing to be a better catcher than Yogi Berra.

Students should choose item **C**. *More humid* is the correct comparative degree of the adjective *humid*.

Section 26.1 Section Review

GRAMMAR EXERCISES 5–10

> **Exercise 5** Identifying Positive, Comparative, and Superlative Degrees
Identify the degree of each underlined modifier.

1. Temperatures within the forest are often <u>cooler</u> than in nearby open areas.
2. The canopy blocks the sunlight, resulting in <u>lower</u> temperatures on the forest floor.
3. At night, however, the forest remains <u>warmer</u> than in open areas.
4. Plants in the forest are <u>less</u> subject to frost damage than those in the open.
5. Mature forest conifers often shed their <u>lowest</u> limbs.
6. The <u>warmest</u> rain forests produce their own rain beneath the forest canopy.
7. Mosses are everywhere in <u>damper</u> forests, forming plush carpets.
8. Each plant in the forest functions to its <u>best</u> ecological capabilities.
9. Some plant species have so <u>completely</u> adapted to life in the forest that they never occur outside it.
10. Mammals of the forest tend to be <u>darkly</u> pigmented.

> **Exercise 6** Forming Regular Comparative and Superlative Degrees
Write sentences using the comparative and the superlative form of each modifier.

1. shady
2. mossy
3. late
4. chilly
5. humid
6. rare
7. far
8. remote
9. dense
10. spectacular

> **Exercise 7** Supplying Comparative and Superlative Degrees Rewrite each sentence, replacing the modifier in italics with the degree indicated. You may need to add *the* before some superlatives.

1. All visitors to the forest should take precautions to ensure the *safe* visit possible. (superlative)
2. The *good* times for viewing birds and mammals are near dawn and dusk. (superlative)
3. The best place to see birds is in an area that is *much* open. (comparative)
4. One is *likely* to see animals by sitting quietly in one place for a time than by walking around. (comparative)
5. *Many* experts say not to feed or tease animals in the forest. (superlative)
6. It is *safe* not to approach baby animals. (comparative)
7. Cleaning up after meals is *effective* in discouraging bears. (superlative)
8. Insects can be *troublesome* pests in the forest. (superlative)
9. Learn to recognize the *unpleasant* plants and avoid them. (comparative)
10. When traveling in a forest, it is *good* to have a map and a compass. (comparative)

> **Exercise 8** Find It in Your Reading
Read a description in a travel magazine. Find five examples of modifiers used in the comparative and superlative degrees.

> **Exercise 9** Find It in Your Writing
Review your portfolio, and find examples of comparative and superlative modifiers. Make sure you have used them correctly.

> **Exercise 10** Writing Application
Write five sentences comparing places you have visited. In each sentence, include at least one modifying adjective or adverb. Underline the modifier, and identify it as positive, comparative, or superlative.

Section Review • 603

ASSESS and CLOSE

Section Review

Each of these exercises correlates to a concept taught in the section on degrees of comparison, pages 598–602. The exercises may be used for more practice, for reteaching, or for review of the Key Concepts presented. Answers for all chapter exercises are available in *Grammar Exercises Answers on Transparencies* in your teaching resources.

Answer Key

> **Exercise 5**

1. comparative
2. comparative
3. comparative
4. comparative
5. superlative
6. superlative
7. comparative
8. superlative
9. positive
10. positive

> **Exercise 6**

Students' sentences should contain the following words:

1. shadier, shadiest
2. mossier, mossiest
3. later, latest
4. chillier, chilliest
5. more humid, most humid
6. rarer, rarest
7. farther, farthest
8. more remote, most remote
9. denser, densest
10. more spectacular, most spectacular

> **Exercise 7**

1. safest
2. best
3. more
4. more likely
5. Most
6. safer
7. most effective
8. most troublesome
9. more unpleasant
10. better

> **Exercise 8**

Find It in Your Reading
Have students list the comparative forms of superlative modifiers they find and superlative forms of comparatives.

continued

Answer Key continued

> **Exercise 9**

Find It in Your Writing
Have students trade papers with a partner, to label the modifiers comparative or superlative.

> **Exercise 10**

Writing Application
If students need facts for their sentences, suggest that they use the Internet to gather details about the places they chose.

sentences on the board. Ask students why they don't make sense, or what is missing.

I like ice cream better. (Better than what? Than cookies? Than broccoli?)

That dog is the best. (The best what? Best pet? Best of its breed? Best dog in the whole world?)

My sister is smaller. (Smaller than what? Than you are? Than a school bus?)

Activate Prior Knowledge

Tell students that there is an old saying that you cannot compare apples and oranges. Ask students why you *can* compare them. (both fruit, both round, both sweet, and so on) Ask students to contrast them. (one red, one orange; eat apple skin, peel orange; and so on)

TEACH

Step-by-Step Teaching Guide

Using Comparative and Superlative Degrees

Write the prepositions *between* and *among* on the chalkboard. Ask students what the difference is. (*Between* is used when talking about two things; *among* when talking about three or more things.) This rule will help students remember the similar rule for comparatives and superlatives.

Integrating Vocabulary Skills

Each other and *one another* follow the same rule as *between* and *among*. *Each other* refers to two people: *Lonnie and Ronnie helped each other with grammar. One another* refers to three or more people: *Lonnie, Ronnie, and Bonnie quizzed one another on superlatives.*

Critical Viewing

Compare and Contrast Students may say that the actor on the right is closer to the audience than the others; she is also more expressive.

Section 26.2

Making Clear Comparisons

The problems you are likely to have with comparisons generally involve using the wrong degree, comparing unrelated things, or comparing something with itself.

Using Comparative and Superlative Degrees

There are two simple rules to keep in mind in order to use the correct degree of comparison:

▶ **KEY CONCEPTS** Use the comparative degree to compare two people, places, or things. Use the superlative degree to compare three or more people, places, or things. ∎

Notice in the following examples that it is not necessary to mention specific numbers when making a comparison.

COMPARATIVE: Steve is *more creative* than Michael.
The stage is *closer* to us than the exit.
My costume is *more colorful* than hers.

SUPERLATIVE: Sue is the *most creative* pupil in our class.
That door is the *closest* exit to our seats.
Of the costumes in the play, Teresa's is the *most colorful.*

Note About *Double Comparisons:* A double comparison is an error caused by using both -*er* and *more* to form the comparative degree or both -*est* and *most* to form the superlative. It can also be caused by adding any of these endings or words to an irregular modifier.

INCORRECT: Amy is *more smarter* than I.
Jim's acting is *worser* than Jon's.

CORRECT: Amy is *smarter* than I.
Jim's acting is *worse* than Jon's.

▶ **Critical Viewing** Compare and contrast the positions of the actors on the stage. **[Compare and Contrast]**

604 • Using Modifiers

Theme: Performing Arts

In this section, you will learn how to make clear and balanced comparisons. The examples and exercises in this section are about theater, dance, and opera.

Cross-Curricular Connection: Performing Arts

⏱ **TIME AND RESOURCE MANAGER**

Resources
Print: Grammar Exercises Workbook, pp. 155–158; Hands-on Grammar Activity Book, Chapter 26
Technology: Language Lab CD-ROM, Using Modifiers; On-line Exercise Bank, Section 26.2

In-Depth Coverage	Accelerated Pace
• Cover pp. 604–607 in class. • Assign and review Exercises 11–14. • Read and discuss Hands-on Grammar, p. 608.	• Assign pp. 604–607 for independent student review. • Assign Review Exercise 17.

▶ **Exercise 11** Using the Comparative and Superlative Degrees Correctly Choose the correct comparative or superlative form in parentheses to complete each sentence.

EXAMPLE: Acting is (more, most) complicated than it may appear on stage.

ANSWER: more

1. The history of the performing arts begins with one of the (more, most) ancient sources of Western civilization, the culture of ancient Greece.
2. Some of the (earlier, earliest) plays still performed were written by the Greeks more than 2,500 years ago.
3. Of the two types of plays written and performed by the Greeks, tragedies were (more, most) serious than comedies.
4. The (more, most) common subjects of Greek tragedy were the myths, which emphasized moral issues.
5. Present-day historians believe that (more, most) of a play was chanted, or sung.

▶ **Exercise 12** Supplying the Comparative and Superlative Degrees Write the appropriate comparative or superlative degree of the modifier in parentheses.

EXAMPLE: Of the two types of plays, tragedy is (intense).

ANSWER: more intense

1. While tragedy produced the (wide) variety of responses, comedy always invoked laughter.
2. The masks of Greek comedy were (ugly) and (silly) than those of tragedies.
3. Greek comedy employed a (great) amount of speech than tragedy, but the chorus was often sung.
4. Comedy deals with (humorous) subjects than tragedy, such as the quirks of daily living and trivial problems.
5. The Greek dramas that flourished in the 500's and 400's B.C. have had the (great) influence on Western drama.
6. When the Romans conquered Greece, they adapted Greek texts to depict even (glorious) tales of Rome.
7. During the Middle Ages, the (common) subjects of plays were saints and characters from the Bible.
8. The (great) and (influential) playwright was William Shakespeare, who wrote in the late 1500's and early 1600's.
9. Even though music and singing had been incorporated into plays in (early) times, people began writing plays in which the characters only sang.
10. In a (late) time period, the French planned stage productions using dancers who did not speak at all.

▶ **More Practice**

On-line
Exercise Bank
• Section 26.2
Grammar Exercise
Workbook
• pp. 155–158

Answer Key

▶ **Exercise 11**

1. most
2. earliest
3. more
4. most
5. most

▶ **Exercise 12**

1. widest
2. uglier and sillier
3. greater
4. more humorous
5. greatest
6. more glorious
7. most common
8. greatest, most influential
9. earlier
10. later

✓ **ONGOING ASSESSMENT: Monitor and Reinforce**

If students miss more than two items in Exercises 11–12, refer them to the following for additional practice.

In the Textbook	Print Resources	Technology
Section Review, Ex. 15–16, p. 609	Grammar Exercise Workbook, pp. 155–156	Language Lab CD-ROM, Using Modifiers; On-Line Exercise Bank, Section 26.2

⏱ **TIME SAVERS!**

🗂 **Answers on Transparency**
Use the Grammar Exercises on Transparencies for Chapter 26 to have students correct their own or one another's exercises.

💻 **On-Line Exercise Bank**
Have students complete the exercises on computer. The Auto Check feature will grade their work for you!

Step-by-Step Teaching Guide

Balanced Comparisons

1. Tell students to imagine that a sentence making a comparison between two things is like a scale. If the things being compared are not similar, the sentence is unbalanced.

2. Have students provide sentences in which two things are compared, making sure that the comparisons are balanced.

3. Another way to phrase balanced comparisons is by using *than that of* for singular nouns and *than those of* for plural nouns.

   An alligator's snout is broader than that of a crocodile.

   An alligator's teeth are shorter than those of a crocodile.

Answer Key

Exercise 13

1. Dance's origins go back even farther than theater's.
2. When a dance is performed more for the audience's pleasure than for the dancer's, it is considered theatrical dance.
3. Around 1400, the reigning princes of the Italian states used theatrical dance as a way to proclaim that their courts' brilliance and taste exceeded their neighbor's.
4. The first ballet that combined movement, music, décor, and special effects only vaguely resembled today's.
5. Even though the steps differed little, the earliest ballet steps were more polished and studied than ballroom dance's.
6. Early ballet's format varied slightly from opera's.
7. Later, ballet moved from the ballroom to the theater, and the professional's role replaced the court member's.
8. Dancing was considered an art of the gentleman, but women's importance as choreographers rivaled men's.
9. The choreographer's role may be more significant than the dancer's.
10. Women's roles in court ballets were minimal compared to men's until 1681.

Balanced Comparisons

Whenever you write a comparison, you must check the sentence to make sure that the things being compared are properly balanced. Otherwise, you may compare two or more items that cannot logically be compared.

▶ **KEY CONCEPT** Make sure that your sentences compare only items of a similar kind. ■

The following examples show unbalanced sentences. These sentences are illogical because they unintentionally compare dissimilar things. An audition cannot be compared to a person, and the blade of a sword cannot be compared to an entire sword.

UNBALANCED: *Joe's audition* was more dramatic than *Ken.*
CORRECT: *Joe's audition* was more dramatic than *Ken's.*

UNBALANCED: The *blade of a sword* is longer than a *dagger.*
CORRECT: The *blade of a sword* is longer than a *dagger's.*

▶ **Exercise 13** Revising to Eliminate Errors in Comparisons
Rewrite each sentence, correcting the unbalanced comparison.

EXAMPLE: Dancing's effect on an audience is just as significant as music.

ANSWER: Dancing's effect on an audience is just as significant as *music's.*

1. Dance's origins go back even farther than theater.
2. When a dance is performed more for the audience's pleasure than for the dancer, it is considered theatrical dance.
3. Around 1400, the reigning princes of the Italian states used theatrical dance as a way to proclaim that their courts' brilliance and taste exceeded their neighbor.
4. The first ballet that combined movement, music, décor, and special effects only vaguely resembled today.
5. Even though the steps differed little, the earliest ballet steps were more polished and studied than ballroom steps.
6. Early ballet's format varied slightly from opera.
7. Later, ballet moved from the ballroom to the theater, and the professional's role replaced the court member.
8. Dancing was considered an art of the gentleman, but women's importance as choreographers rivaled men.
9. The choreographer's role may be more significant than the dancer.
10. Women's roles in court ballets were minimal compared to men until 1681.

606 • Using Modifiers

💡 Spelling Tip

Many words in the English language have more than one acceptable spelling. *Theater* and *theatre* is an example. It is best to use the same spelling of a word consistently throughout any one piece of writing. The preferred spelling of a word is listed first in the dictionary entry. *Theater* is the preferred spelling.

◈ STANDARDIZED TEST PREPARATION WORKSHOP

Standard English Usage Standardized tests often measure students' ability to use modifiers correctly. Have students choose the letter of the word or group of words that best completes the following sentence:

Janice thinks that modern dance is ___ than classical ballet.

A interestinger
B interesting
C more interesting
D most interesting

Students should see that the comparative form is needed to complete the sentence. Item **C** is the only correct comparative form.

Other and *Else* in Comparisons

Another common error in making a comparison is to compare something with itself.

▶ **KEY CONCEPT** When comparing one of a group with the rest of the group, make sure that your sentence contains the word *other* or the word *else*. ■

Adding *other* or *else* in these situations will prevent comparing something with itself. For example, because Shakespeare was one English playwright, he cannot logically be compared to all English playwrights. He must be compared to all *other* English playwrights.

ILLOGICAL: Shakespeare was *greater than any* English playwright.

CORRECT: Shakespeare was *greater than any other* English playwright.

ILLOGICAL: I had more *lines than anyone* in the play.

CORRECT: I had more *lines than anyone* else in the play.

▶ **Exercise 14** Using *Other* and *Else* in Comparisons Rewrite each sentence, correcting the illogical comparison.

EXAMPLE: Beth is a better dancer than anyone in class.

ANSWER: Beth is a better dancer than anyone *else* in class.

1. Opera is different from any art form.
2. From the earliest times, civilized man has conveyed drama through music as much as any art form.
3. My knowledge of Greek drama is greater than any knowledge I have.
4. As opera evolved, Greek tragedy demonstrated a greater influence on opera than on any art form.
5. During the Middle Ages, theater became less musical because it cost more to train a singer than any performer.
6. King Louis XIV loved to participate in the court entertainment of dance and music more than anyone.
7. The "pre-operatic" theater was entertainment that was available to royal courts more than to anyone.
8. During the Renaissance, Italy, more than any country, claimed to be home to all the arts.
9. In the early operas, music was secondary to any characteristic of the play.
10. The opera *Euridice*, more than any opera, is considered to be the earliest that has survived intact.

▶ **More Practice**
On-line
Exercise Bank
• Section 26.2
Grammar Exercise Workbook
• pp. 155–158

Making Clear Comparisons • **607**

1. Explain to students that by using the words *other* or *else,* they will avoid writing sentences in which something is compared to itself.
2. Be sure that students understand the illogic of the second example sentence. The speaker had more lines than anyone except *himself,* in other words, than *anyone else.*

Answer Key

Exercise 14

1. Opera is different from any other art form.
2. From the earliest times, civilized man has conveyed drama through music as much as any other art form.
3. My knowledge of Greek drama is greater than any other knowledge I have.
4. As opera evolved, Greek tragedy demonstrated a greater influence on opera than on any other art form.
5. During the Middle Ages, theater became less musical because it cost more to train a singer than any other performer.
6. King Louis XIV loved to participate in the court entertainment of dance and music more than anyone else.
7. The "pre-operatic" theater was entertainment that was available to royal courts more than to anyone else.
8. During the Renaissance, Italy, more than any other country, claimed to be home to all the arts.
9. In the early operas, music was secondary to any other characteristic of the play.
10. The opera *Euridice,* more than any other opera, is considered to be the earliest that has survived intact.

☑ **ONGOING ASSESSMENT: Monitor and Reinforce**

If students miss more than two items in Exercise 13 or 14, refer them to the following for additional support.

In the Textbook	Print Resources	Technology
Section Review, Ex. 17, p. 609	Grammar Exercise Workbook, pp. 157–158	Language Lab CD-ROM, Using Modifiers; On-Line Exercise Bank, Section 26.2

Comparison-Star Standout

Teaching Resources: Hands-on Grammar Activity Book, Chapter 26

1. Have students refer to their Hands-on Grammar activity books, or give them copies of the relevant pages for this activity.

2. Carefully review with students the directions for assembling the star standouts.

3. Once students have worked through the activity, encourage them to write more names of groups to compare to, more names of people to compare to all others, and more comparisons.

Find It in Your Reading

Have students bring in their examples to share with the class.

Find It in Your Writing

If students cannot find adequate examples in their writing, have them write sentences with unbalanced and illogical comparisons. Then have them trade sentences with a partner to correct them.

26.2

Hands-on Grammar

Comparison-Star Standout

A common error in making a comparison is to compare something with itself. With this exercise, you will illustrate how one stands out from the group in a comparison.

1. Cut a 3" circle. Put slots in it as shown in the illustration. On the circle above the slots, write *all other.*

2. Cut a long strip of paper to feed through the slots in the circle. On it, write names of groups you will be comparing, such as *actors, writers, dancers, teachers, boys, girls,* and *students.* Space out the words so that they will show through the window.

3. Cut out seven stars. On each of the stars, write the person you want to compare with all the others.

4. Cut out seven strips of paper, each approximately 3" long and 1/2" wide. On each strip of paper, write the comparison. For example, *is more graceful than, is smarter than,* or *is nicer than.*

5. Fold each strip of paper up like an accordion. Attach one end to the star and the other end to the circle with pieces of tape.

6. Now, slide your strip of paper through the slots to make a balanced and logical comparison. For example, *George is more graceful than all the other dancers.*

7. Illustrate the following sentences:

Mrs. Dardis is nicer than all the other teachers.
Sam is smarter than all the other students.

Find It in Your Reading Find some comparisons in your reading that compare one person with a group. Illustrate your comparisons.

Find It in Your Writing Review a piece of your writing that has comparatives in it. Make sure that you have used balanced and logical comparisons and that you have not compared something with itself.

608 • Using Modifiers

⏱ TIME SAVERS!

✋ **Hands-on Grammar Book**
Use the Hands-on Grammar activity sheet for Chapter 26 to facilitate this activity

☑ ONGOING ASSESSMENT: Assess Mastery

Use the following resources to assess student mastery of using comparative and superlative degrees of modifiers.

In the Textbook	Technology
Chapter Review, Ex. 21–30, pp. 610–611 Standardized Test Preparation Workshop, pp. 612–613	On-Line Exercise Bank, Section 26.2

Section Review

GRAMMAR EXERCISES 15–20

Exercise 15 **Using Degrees of Modifiers Correctly** Choose the correct comparative or superlative form in parentheses to complete each sentence.

1. Many experts agree that Shakespeare wrote with (great, greater, greatest) wisdom than any other writer.
2. Shakespeare found the (more interesting, most interesting) stories for his plays in history books.
3. In *Macbeth*, a Scottish noble, whose (deep, deeper, deepest) desire is to be king, kills the ruling king.
4. Critics regard *The Tragedy of King Lear* as Shakespeare's (greater, greatest) work.
5. *Hamlet* kills his stepfather, who had (earlier, earliest) murdered Hamlet's father and taken his throne.

Exercise 16 **Supplying the Comparative and Superlative Degrees** Write the appropriate comparative or superlative degree of the modifier in parentheses.

1. Although Shakespeare died nearly 400 years ago, his plays are among those (often) read and performed.
2. Even the (bad) actor will learn to recognize at least one Shakespearean character.
3. Shakespeare's popularity as a playwright is unequaled by even the (good) modern-day writer.
4. His plays still command some of the (large) number of ticket sales.
5. The movie *West Side Story* is one of the (successful) modern versions of Shakespeare's *Romeo and Juliet.*

Exercise 17 **Revising to Eliminate Errors in Comparisons** Rewrite each sentence, correcting the unbalanced or illogical comparison.

1. In most of Shakespeare's tragedies, the hero's role is more significant than the heroine.
2. However, Juliet's role is equally as important as Romeo.
3. *Twelfth Night* is more musical than any Shakespeare play.
4. Lady Macbeth's character is colder and more cruel than Macbeth.
5. It is said that Shakespeare's comedies are more difficult to act than any of his plays.

Exercise 18 **Find It in Your Reading** Read the following from Romeo and Juliet. Explain why this is a logical comparison.

. . . That which we call a rose
By any other name would smell as sweet.

Exercise 19 **Find It in Your Writing** Look through your portfolio. Find examples of comparisons. Make sure that your comparisons are logical and balanced.

Exercise 20 **Writing Application** Write a logical and balanced comparison for each item below.

1. you and your father
2. a dog and a cat
3. an apple and an orange
4. two basketball teams
5. two flowers

Section Review • 609

ASSESS and CLOSE

Section Review
Each of these exercises correlates to a concept taught in the section on clear comparisons, pages 604–607. The exercises may be used for more practice, for reteaching, or for review of the Key Concepts presented.

Answer Key

Exercise 15

1. greater
2. most interesting
3. deepest
4. greatest
5. earlier

Exercise 16

1. most often
2. worst
3. best
4. largest
5. most successful

Exercise 17

1. In most of Shakespeare's tragedies, the hero's role is more significant than the heroine's.
2. However, Juliet's role is equally as important as Romeo's.
3. *Twelfth Night* is more musical than any other Shakespeare play.
4. Lady Macbeth's character is colder and more cruel than Macbeth's.
5. It is said that Shakespeare's comedies are more difficult to act than any of his other plays.

continued

Answer Key continued

Exercise 18

Find It in Your Reading
It is logical because it says "any other name," not "any name." It is not comparing a rose to a rose.

Exercise 19

Find It in Your Writing
Students should correct any unbalanced comparisons they find.

Exercise 20

Writing Application
Have each student read one sentence aloud. Ask the class to tell if it is balanced, and if not, why not.

TIME SAVERS!

Answers on Transparency Use the Grammar Exercises on Transparencies for Chapter 26 to have students correct their own or one another's exercises.

On-Line Exercise Bank Have students complete the exercises on computer. The Auto Check feature will grade their work for you!

Each of these exercises correlates to a concept taught in the chapter on using modifiers, pages 598–607. The exercises may be used for more practice, for reteaching, or for review of the Key Concepts presented. Answers for all chapter exercises are available in *Grammar Exercises on Transparencies* in your teaching resources.

Answer Key

Exercise 21

1. higher, highest
2. more slowly, most slowly
3. prettier, prettiest
4. better, best
5. later, latest
6. more frightening, most frightening
7. farther, farthest
8. shorter, shortest
9. more, most
10. likelier, likeliest

Exercise 22

1. superlative
2. positive
3. superlative
4. positive
5. superlative

Exercise 23

1. less
2. more
3. earliest
4. newer
5. most dynamic

Exercise 24

1. The same composers who have written the great operas have also written some of the most beautiful ballets.
2. In ballet, the music is often more memorable than the choreography.
3. Dance is more difficult to document than music.
4. The most significant development in dance was the use of *pointe.*
5. Perhaps the most influential individual of modern ballet was Sergei Diaghilev.

610

Chapter 26 Chapter Review

GRAMMAR EXERCISES 21–30

Exercise 21 Forming Comparative and Superlative Degrees
Write the comparative and the superlative forms of each modifier.

1. high
2. slowly
3. pretty
4. good
5. late
6. frightening
7. far
8. short
9. many
10. likely

Exercise 22 Recognizing Positive, Comparative, and Superlative Degrees
Identify the degree of each underlined modifier.

1. Some of the world's <u>most</u> talented composers have written the musical scores for ballets and operas.
2. Additionally, these composers also wrote <u>many</u> popular concertos and symphonies performed by orchestras around the world.
3. One of the <u>most</u> amazing musicians who ever lived was Wolfgang Amadeus Mozart.
4. Born in Austria in 1756, this <u>incredible</u> musician was playing solo concerts on the harpsichord when he was only five years old.
5. Even though he died when he was only thirty-five, Mozart composed the <u>finest</u> operas of the eighteenth century.

Exercise 23 Using the Comparative and Superlative Degrees Correctly Choose the correct comparative or superlative form in parentheses to complete each sentence.

1. A form of Western theatrical dancing that has (less, least) rigid rules than ballet is called modern dance.

2. Modern dance is (more, most) an attitude about dance than a technique.
3. Isadora Duncan, one of the (earlier, earliest) pioneers of modern dance, displayed an improvisational technique called "free dance."
4. As modern dance evolved into an expression of universal social themes, (newer, newest) techniques developed.
5. To Doris Humphrey, gravity caused the (more dynamic, most dynamic) movement.

Exercise 24 Supplying Comparative and Superlative Degrees
Rewrite each sentence, replacing the underlined modifier with the degree indicated in brackets.

1. The same composers who have written the great operas have also written some of the <u>beautiful</u> ballets. [superlative]
2. In ballet, the music is often <u>memorable</u> than the choreography. [comparative]
3. Dance is <u>difficult</u> to document than music. [comparative]
4. The <u>significant</u> development in dance was the use of *pointe.* [superlative]
5. Perhaps the <u>influential</u> individual of modern ballet was Sergei Diaghilev. [superlative]

Exercise 25 Revising to Eliminate Errors in Comparisons Revise each of the following sentences, correcting the illogical or unbalanced comparisons.

1. Jan Leighton performed in more theatrical, film, and television roles than anyone.
2. A bound volume of original work written by Mozart sold for $2.3 million more than Bach.

Exercise 25

1. Jan Leighton performed in more theatrical, film, and television roles than anyone else.
2. A bound volume of original work written by Mozart sold for $2.3 million more than a volume by Bach.
3. In February 1998, Luciano Pavarotti was applauded longer than any other singer.
4. The best approach to Shakespeare's comedies might be to think of them as children's plays rather than adults'.
5. In a few of Shakespeare's plays, the hero's role is more villainous than any other character's.

3. In February 1998, Luciano Pavarotti was applauded longer than any singer.
4. The best approach to Shakespeare's comedies might be to think of them as children's plays rather than adult.
5. In a few of Shakespeare's plays, the hero's role is more villainous than any character.

Exercise 26 Proofreading to Correct Errors With Modifiers Copy the following paragraph on a separate sheet of paper. Correct the errors in usage.

La Scala, in Milan, is considered the more beautiful opera house in Italy. Opening night is most eagerly awaited than any other performance night. It is possible that the cost of opening night tickets at La Scala is expensiver than the Metropolitan Opera House in New York City. The Met opens its season in September; La Scala opens latest, always on the seventh of December. On September 27, 1999, the tenor Placido Domingo sang in his eighteenth consecutive opening night performance—most than any singer up to that time, including Caruso! Although Domingo is a great singer, there are those who believe the good tenor is Franco Corelli.

Exercise 27 Writing Sentences With Comparatives and Superlatives Write sentences following the directions given.

1. Compare one president with all the rest using the word *better*.
2. Compare one city with all the rest.
3. Write a superlative using the word *bad*.
4. Describe your favorite singer using the word *most*.
5. Compare the humor on two television shows.
6. Compare a pine tree to a maple tree.
7. Write a superlative using the words *most difficult*.

8. Write a comparison using the words *smarter than*.
9. Write a sentence using the words *rained longer*.
10. Write a sentence using the words *more slowly*.

Exercise 28 CUMULATIVE REVIEW Revising Sentence Errors Revise the following paragraph, correcting sentence errors and errors in verb and pronoun usage and agreement. Note that a numbered section may have one error, several errors, or no error.

(1) Red roses on a white trellis blooms in my aunt's garden. (2) She and my uncle has been gardeners since I can remember. (3) When I was small, I loved the tall sunflowers I thought they were giants. (4) My aunt grows raspberries behind the garage that tasted delicious. (5) She was going to learn me to make jam. (6) My favorite time of the day was when the sun rised, and the colors is the most intense. (7) I will always remember how it's rays reflected off the water in the bird bath. (8) Each of my sisters had their favorite flowers. (9) Chelsea and me liked the daisies. (10) When I grow up, I will get me a garden.

Exercise 29 Writing Application Compare two pieces of music. Write five sentences, each one using modifiers to compare the two pieces. Use a *comparative* or *superlative* form of a modifier in each sentence.

Exercise 30 Writing Application Compare two dances that you can do or that you have observed. Write five sentences, each one using modifiers to compare some aspect of the two dances.

Answer Key continued

Writing Application
Invite students to bring in recordings of the music to play for the class, then read their comparisons.

Exercise 30

Writing Application
Students may want to demonstrate one or both of the dances and read their comparisons aloud.

Exercise 26

La Scala, in Milan, is considered the most beautiful opera house in Italy. Opening night is more eagerly awaited than any other performance night. It is possible that the cost of opening night tickets at La Scala is more expensive than the cost of tickets to opening night at the Metropolitan Opera House in New York City. The Met opens its season in September; La Scala opens later, always on the seventh of December. On September 27, 1999, the tenor Placido Domingo sang in his eighteenth consecutive opening night performance—more than any other singer up to that time, including Caruso! Although Domingo is a great singer, there are those who believe the best tenor is Franco Corelli.

Exercise 27

Answers will vary.

Exercise 28

Cumulative Review
(1) Red roses on a white trellis bloom in my aunt's garden. (2) She and my uncle have been gardeners as long as I can remember. (3) When I was small, I loved the tall sunflowers; I thought they were giants. (4) My aunt grows delicious raspberries behind the garage. (5) She was going to teach me to make jam. (6) My favorite time of day was sunrise, when the sun's colors were the most intense. (7) I will always remember how its rays reflected off the water in the bird bath. (8) Each of my sisters had her favorite flowers. (9) Chelsea and I liked the daisies. (10) When I grow up, I will have a garden.

continued

⏱ **TIME SAVERS!**

📋 **Answers on Transparency**
Use the Grammar Exercises on Transparencies for Chapter 26 to have students correct their own or one another's exercises.

🖥 **On-Line Exercise Bank**
Have students complete the exercises on computer. The Auto Check feature will grade their work for you!

Lesson Objectives

- To use the comparative and superlative forms of modifiers correctly.

Standard English Usage: Using Modifiers

1. Have volunteers read aloud the strategies in the textbook.

2. Encourage students to use a graphic organizer to arrange this information in order to help them remember these strategies.

3. Remind students to look for clues in the test items that will help them determine what form of comparison is required to best complete the given sentence.

4. Have students cover the "Answers and Explanations" column in their textbooks. Ask them to identify the clues in both sentences of the test item that will help them choose the correct form of comparison. Students should see that in item 1, *of all* indicates that the superlative form is required. In item 2, *than* indicates that a comparison between two things is being set up; therefore, the comparative form is required.

Standardized Test Preparation Workshop

Standard English Usage: Using Modifiers

Standardized test questions often measure your ability to use modifiers correctly. This may be done by testing your ability to choose the correct form of comparison to complete a sentence. Use the following strategies to help you determine which form to use in a sentence:

- If no comparison is being made, use the **positive form** of the modifier.
- If one thing or action is compared to another thing or action, use the **comparative form** of the modifier—ending in *-er* or preceded by *more.*
- If one thing or action is being compared to more than one other thing or action, use the **superlative form** of the modifier—ending in *-est* or preceded by *most.*
- Be aware that some modifiers have **special forms,** such as *good, bad, much,* and *many.*

Sample Test Items	Answers and Explanations

Directions: Read the passage, and choose the word or group of words that belongs in each space.
 	
Apple pie has always been considered the __(1)__ of all desserts. __(2)__ apples grow in this country than anywhere else in the world.
 	
1   A   Americanest
      B   more American
      C   most American
      D   mostest American
	The best answer is C. Apple pie is being compared to all other desserts, so a superlative is called for. The correct superlative formation is *most American.*

2   F   Most
      G   More
      H   Some
      J   Mostest
	The best answer is G. This is a comparative situation. Apple growth in this country is being compared to apple growth everywhere else in the world. The correct comparative formation is *more.*

612 • Using Modifiers

TEST-TAKING TIP

Tell students that following a plan of action in test situations can help them save valuable time. When confronted with test questions such as the ones found in their textbooks, they should first read the given sentence to determine the form of comparison needed to complete the sentence. They can then read through the choices, eliminating those that are not the correct form of comparison. Once students have made their choices, remind them to reread the original sentence with the choice in place. Most incorrect choices can be identified by placing them in the sentence in question.

> **Practice 1** **Directions:** Read the passage, and choose the word or group of words that belongs in each space.

Like many __(1)__ civilizations, India's first civilization grew up in a fertile river valley. It was the __(2)__ of the world's early civilizations. Archaeologists are still learning about this ancient civilization. They have excavated several __(3)__ cities as well as many __(4)__ towns. The cities of Harrappa and Mohenjo-Daro were the __(5)__.

1 **A** earliest
  B early
  C more early
  D most early

2 **F** larger
  G more large
  H largest
  J large

3 **A** larger
  B more large
  C largest
  D large

4 **F** smallest
  G smaller
  H more small
  J most small

5 **A** most important
  B more important
  C important
  D importantest

> **Practice 2** **Directions:** Read the passage, and choose the word or group of words that belongs in each space.

A revolution in agriculture during the 1700's created conditions that favored the Industrial Revolution. __(1)__ farms were combined to make __(2)__, __(3)__ ones. Increased food production improved people's diet and health, which contributed to rapid population growth. __(4)__ farming methods meant that __(5)__ people were needed to farm. Unemployed farmers formed a __(6)__ pool of available labor.

1 **A** Small
  B More small
  C Smaller
  D Smallest

2 **F** largest
  G most large
  H larger
  J more larger

3 **A** efficienter
  B more efficienter
  C most efficient
  D more efficient

4 **F** Better
  G More better
  H Best
  J More best

5 **A** littler
  B few
  C fewer
  D fewest

6 **F** largest
  G most large
  H larger
  J large

Time and Resource Manager

In-Depth Lesson Plan

	LESSON FOCUS	PRINT AND MEDIA RESOURCES
DAY 1	**Negative Sentences** Students learn and apply concepts for avoiding problems with negative sentences (pp. 616–619).	**Teaching Resources** *Grammar Exercise Workbook*, pp. 159–160; *Grammar Exercises Answers on Transparency*, Chapter 27; **On-Line Exercise Bank**, Section 27.1
DAY 2	**Common Usage Problems** Students learn and apply concepts for avoiding common usage problems and do the Hands-on Grammar activity (pp. 620–629).	**Teaching Resources** *Grammar Exercise Workbook*, pp. 161–162; *Grammar Exercises Answers on Transparency*, Chapter 27; *Hands-on Grammar Activity Book*, Chapter 27; **On-Line Exercise Bank**, Section 27.2
DAY 3	**Review and Assess** Students review chapter and demonstrate mastery of common usage problems (pp. 630–635).	**Teaching Resources** *Formal Assessment*, Chapter 27; *Grammar Exercises Answers on Transparency*, Chapter 27; **On-Line Exercise Bank**, Section 27.1

Accelerated Lesson Plan

	LESSON FOCUS	PRINT AND MEDIA RESOURCES
DAY 1	**Usage Problems** Students cover concepts for avoiding usage problems as determined by Diagnostic Test (pp. 616–629).	**Teaching Resources** *Grammar Exercise Workbook*, pp. 159–162; *Grammar Exercises Answers on Transparency*, Chapter 27; *Hands-on Grammar Activity Book*, Chapter 27; **On-Line Exercise Bank**, Section 27.1–2
DAY 2	**Review and Assess** Students review chapter and demonstrate mastery of common usage problems (pp. 630–635).	**Teaching Resources** *Formal Assessment*, Ch. 27; *Grammar Exercises Answers on Transparency*, Chapter 27; **On-Line Exercise Bank**, Section 27.1

Options for Adapting Lesson Plans

HOMEWORK

Have students complete any section of the chapter for homework.

FEATURES

Extend coverage with the Standardized Test Preparation Workshop (p. 632).

TECHNOLOGY

Students can use the On-Line Exercise Bank to complete the exercises on computer. The Auto Check feature will grade their work.

INTEGRATED SKILLS COVERAGE

Reading
Find It in Your Reading, SE p. 619, 628, 629

Writing
Find It in Your Writing, SE p. 619, 628, 629
Writing Application SE pp. 619, 629, 631, 635

Vocabulary
Integrating Vocabulary Skills ATE 623

Technology
Integrating Technology Skills ATE 625

Real-World Connection ATE 617

Viewing and Representing
Critical Viewing, SE pp. 614, 617, 618, 621, 623, 624, 626

ASSESSMENT SUPPORT

Standardized Test Preparation SE p. 632; ATE pp. 617, 626
Standardized Test Preparation Workbook, Ch. 27
Formal Assessment, Ch. 27

MEETING INDIVIDUAL NEEDS

Less Advanced Students ATE pp. 617, 622; See also Ongoing Assessments ATE pp. 614, 618, 627, 628
ESL Students ATE pp. 616, 623
Gifted/Talented Students ATE p. 624

BLOCK SCHEDULING

Pacing Suggestions
For 90-minute Blocks
• Administer the Diagnostic Test to students to determine instructional coverage
• Have students complete the necessary exercises in class. Use the Hands-on Grammar activity to provide a change of pace.

Resources for Varying Instruction
• *Language Lab* CD-ROM If your students have access to hardware, a 90-minute block provides an ideal opportunity for students to work on computer.

Professional Development Support
• *How to Manage Instruction in the Block* This teaching resource provides management and activity suggestions.

MEDIA AND TECHNOLOGY

For the Student
• *On-Line Exercise Bank,* Sections 27.1–2

For the Teacher
• *Resource Pro* CD-ROM

WRITING AND GRAMMAR WEBSITE

The Interactive Writing and Grammar Website provides a wide array of support for students, teachers, and parents. Grammar support includes:

• *On-Line Exercise Bank* with Auto Check scoring
• Diagnostic and assessment support

phwg.phschool.com

▶ *Lesson Objectives*

1. To recognize and correct double negatives.
2. To form negative sentences correctly.
3. To recognize and avoid common usage problems in grammar and spelling.

Critical Viewing
Distinguish Students may suggest sentences such as *The crab does not have four legs, The crab does not have fur,* or *The crab does not have an internal skeleton.*

Chapter 27 Miscellaneous Problems in Usage

▲ **Critical Viewing**
Use negative sentences to explain how this crab is different from a mammal such as a dog. **[Distinguish]**

In addition to the usage problems you have already studied, certain other words and expressions can sometimes cause problems for writers.

Consider this sentence: *There ain't no creatures who are more beautiful and fascinating then those living under the sea.* The sentence contains common usage errors. Written correctly, it could say: *There aren't any creatures that are more beautiful and fascinating than those living under the sea.*

This chapter discusses usage problems that have not been presented earlier. You will learn how to form negative sentences correctly, and you will examine a list of troublesome words and expressions.

614 • Miscellaneous Problems in Usage

✓ ONGOING ASSESSMENT: Diagnose

If students miss more than one item in each category, direct them to the relevant pages of the text and assign exercises for practice and review.

Problems in Usage	Diagnostic Test Items	Teach	Practice	Section Review	Chapter Review
Skill Check A					
Negative Sentences	A 1–10	pp. 616–618	Ex. 1–3	Ex. 4–6	Ex. 18–20
Skill Checks B and C					
Usage Problems	B 11–20 C 21–30	pp. 620–627	Ex. 10–12	Ex. 13–14	Ex. 21–23
Cumulative Reviews and Applications				Ex. 4–9, 13–17	Ex. 18–24

Diagnostic Test

Directions: Write all answers on a separate sheet of paper.

Skill Check A. Choose the word in parentheses that best completes each sentence.

1. Many people won't eat (no, any) fish, even if it is fresh.
2. Sardines don't eat (nothing, anything) except zooplankton.
3. The fish don't have (no, any) spines on their heads.
4. Unless it is between noon and sunset, sardines won't eat (nothing, anything).
5. Sardines do not eat their own eggs because they don't lay (no, any) eggs in the deep, cold water where they feed.
6. Although crabs are closely related to lobsters, they don't walk (nothing, anything) like the way lobsters do.
7. Crabs don't do (none, any) of their walking forward or backward; they walk sideways.
8. Don't go (nowhere, anywhere) near the pincers of an angry crab.
9. A crab don't have (no, any) skeleton inside its body.
10. A hermit crab doesn't have (no, any) shell.

Skill Check B. Choose the correct word to complete each sentence.

11. Hermit crabs (adopt, adapt) abandoned snail shells.
12. Hermit crabs use (they're, their, there) enlarged right claw to defend themselves.
13. Crabs have (too, to, two) sensory antennae.
14. Crabs can burrow (anywheres, anywhere) in the sandy bottom.
15. (Being as, Because) the lobster has an external skeleton like the crab, it must shed its shell to grow.
16. The lobster (don't, doesn't) eat during the day; it eats at night.
17. The (farther, further) from shore, the fewer lobsters you'll find.
18. If you look (in, into) the stomach of a lobster, you can find small invertebrates or algae.
19. (That there, That) lobster is tasty.
20. I have a friend in Australia (who, which) calls lobsters "crayfish."

Skill Check C. Rewrite each sentence, correcting any usage problems that you find. If the sentence is correct as is, write *correct*.

21. Buried in the mud or sand is where you can find ghost shrimp.
22. She never seen a ghost shrimp.
23. Ghost shrimp have a positive effect on the marine ecosystem.
24. Due to burrowing by the ghost shrimp, the amount of oxygen in the sediment increases.
25. Beside being an important resource under the sea, the ghost shrimp is used as bait by those who fish.
26. There are similarities between shrimp, lobsters, and crabs.
27. We set down at a seafood restaurant for a meal of shrimp.
28. We tasted the shrimp and decided they were cooked bad.
29. The reason the shrimp tasted funny was because of the sauce.
30. Since we had all ready paid for them, we ate the shrimp.

Answer Key

Diagnostic Test

Each item in the diagnostic test corresponds to a specific concept in the chapter on problems in usage. This will enable you to tailor instruction to the particular needs of your students. See "Ongoing Assessment: Diagnose" on page 614 for further details.

Skill Check A

1. any	6. anything
2. anything	7. any
3. any	8. anywhere
4. anything	9. any
5. any	10. any

Skill Check B

11. adopt	16. doesn't
12. their	17. farther
13. two	18. into
14. anywhere	19. That
15. Because	20. who

Skill Check C

21. You can find ghost shrimp buried in the mud or sand.
22. She had never seen a ghost shrimp.
23. correct
24. The amount of oxygen in the sediment increases due to burrowing by the ghost shrimp.
25. Besides being an important resource under the sea, the ghost shrimp is used by fishermen as bait.
26. correct
27. We sat down at a seafood restaurant for a meal of shrimp.
28. correct
29. correct
30. Since we had already paid for the shrimp, we ate them.

⏱ TIME SAVERS!

Answers on Transparency
Use the Grammar Exercises Answers on Transparencies for Chapter 27 to facilitate correction by students.

On-Line Exercise Bank
Have students complete the Diagnostic Test on computer. The Auto Check feature will grade their work for you!

Write the sentences *I don't know nothing about oysters* and *I don't know anything about oysters* on the chalkboard. Ask students which of the two is written in standard English. Ask a volunteer to explain what is wrong with the other sentence. Introduce the term *double negative*.

Activate Prior Knowledge

Write a few positive sentences on the chalkboard. Call on volunteers to come to the chalkboard and change these to negative sentences. Circle negative words students insert, such as *not* or *nothing*. If any students has created a double negative, ask volunteers to correct it and explain their reasoning.

TEACH

Step-by-Step Teaching Guide

Recognize Double Negatives

1. Use a few sample sentences with double negatives to demonstrate that two negatives equal one positive.

   SuAnn won't not go to the seashore.

   She doesn't know nothing about the ocean.

2. Explain that if SuAnn *won't not* go, that means she *will* go. If she *doesn't know nothing*, that means she *does know something*.

Answer Key

Exercise 1

1. any	4. any
2. anywhere	5. any
3. anywhere	

Customize for
ESL Students

Students who speak Spanish or French may have particular difficulty with the concept of the double negative, because in these and other languages, double negatives are used as single negatives are used in English.

Section 27.1 # Negative Sentences

Negative words, such as *not* or *never*, are used to deny or to refuse something. Only one negative word is necessary in a sentence to make the sentence negative.

Recognize Double Negatives

A *double negative* is the use of two negative words in a sentence when one is sufficient.

KEY CONCEPT Do not use double negatives in sentences. ■

The chart below provides examples of double negatives and the two ways that each might be corrected.

CORRECTING DOUBLE NEGATIVES	
Double Negatives	**Corrections**
Starfish *don't* bother *no one*.	Starfish *don't* bother *anyone*. Starfish bother *no one*.
I *haven't* seen *no* whales.	I *haven't* seen *any* whales. I have seen *no* whales.
Tom *never* said *nothing*.	Tom *never* said *anything*. Tom said *nothing*.

Exercise 1 Avoiding Double Negatives Choose the word in parentheses that best completes each sentence.

EXAMPLE: There aren't (no, any) biomes that occupy more of the Earth's surface than aquatic biomes.

ANSWER: any

1. Scientists can't classify (no, any) protists as exclusively animals or exclusively plants because protists have characteristics of both groups.
2. Brown algae are not found (nowhere, anywhere) on land; they are found in cold ocean waters.
3. Green algae won't live (nowhere, anywhere) that has a dry climate because they depend on water for survival.
4. There isn't (no, any) ice cream that does not contain red algae.
5. We could not see (none, any) of the single-celled golden algae, or diatoms, without a microscope.

Theme: Marine Life

In this section, you will learn to form negative sentences correctly. The examples and exercises in this section are about marine life, including algae, coral, and sharks.

Cross-Curricular Connection: Science

More Practice

Language Lab CD-ROM
• Problems With Modifiers
On-line Exercise Bank
• Section 27.1
Grammar Exercise Workbook
• pp. 159–160

⏱ TIME AND RESOURCE MANAGER

Resources
Print: Grammar Exercises Workbook, pp. 159–160
Technology: On-Line Exercise Bank, Section 27.1

In-Depth Coverage	Accelerated Pace
• Work through all key concepts, pp. 616–618. • Assign and review Exercises 1–3.	• Assign pp. 616–618 for independent student review. • Assign and review Exercise 5.

Form Negative Sentences Correctly

There are three common ways to form negative sentences:

Using One Negative Word The most common way to make a statement negative is to use one negative word, such as *never, no, nobody, none, not, nothing,* or *nowhere.*

▶ **KEY CONCEPT** Do not use two negative words in the same clause. ■

Using two negative words in the same clause will result in a double negative.

DOUBLE NEGATIVE: We *don't* want *no* help from you.

CORRECT: We *don't* want any help from you.
We want *no* help from you.

Using *But* in a Negative Sense When *but* means "only," it generally acts as a negative. Do not use it with another negative word.

DOUBLE NEGATIVE: There *wasn't but* one whale at the park.

CORRECT: There was *but* one whale at the park.

Using *Barely, Hardly,* and *Scarcely* All three of these words are negative.

▶ **KEY CONCEPT** Do not use *barely, hardly,* or *scarcely* with another negative. ■

DOUBLE NEGATIVE: The dull-gray coral *wasn't barely* visible in the dim light.

CORRECT: The dull-gray coral was *barely* visible in the dim light.

DOUBLE NEGATIVE: We *didn't scarcely* recognize the bright fluorescent coral in the ultraviolet light.

CORRECT: We *scarcely* recognized the bright fluorescent coral in the ultraviolet light.

DOUBLE NEGATIVE: I *couldn't hardly* believe the beauty of the coral when it was illuminated with ultraviolet light.

CORRECT: I could *hardly* believe the beauty of the coral when it was illuminated with ultraviolet light.

▲ **Critical Viewing** Write three sentences that discuss the variety of life in a coral reef using the words *barely, hardly,* and *scarcely.*

Negative Sentences • 617

Answer Key

▶ Exercise 2

1. anywhere
2. is
3. any
4. would
5. can

▶ Exercise 3

1. Unless they are disturbed, sharks will not attack anybody.
2. The whale shark, the largest fish, does not eat anything but plankton and small fish.
3. The great white shark doesn't usually attack any person unless it confuses the person for a sea lion or seal.
4. The skeptic would not believe anybody who told him that the great white shark can grow up to 25 feet long and weigh 7,300 pounds.
5. The bull shark will attack with hardly any provocation.
6. These animals often live in shallow inlets and rivers where they can hardly be seen because of the murky water.
7. Reports about the blue shark indicate that a swimmer could hardly count on being safe around these creatures.
8. Blue sharks can scarcely be seen from above or below because their skin is blue on top and white underneath.
9. There is nothing that you couldn't find in the stomach of a tiger shark; household objects have even been found.
10. Swimmers were given no chance (or: not given any chance) to survive the attack of the fierce-looking sand tiger sharks.

Critical Viewing

Speculate Students might say that they would not try to run away or that they would not open their eyes for fear of seeing the shark.

27.1

▶ **Exercise 2** Avoiding Problems With Negatives Fill in the blank to make each sentence negative without forming a double negative.

EXAMPLE: Jon ___?___ hardly believe he had caught such an odd-looking fish.

ANSWER: could

1. The anglerfish, camouflaged to look like the algae, could not be found ___?___ by the photographer.
2. The anglerfish lives on the ocean floor where there ___?___ barely any light.
3. When a frogfish enters a bed of algae, other fishes cannot see ___?___ trace of it.
4. The anglerfish ___?___ hardly be able to hunt for food without its dorsal fin, which glows in the dark.
5. The anglerfish ___?___ scarcely eat for days after consuming such a large meal.

▶ **Exercise 3** Revising to Eliminate Double Negatives On a separate sheet of paper, rewrite each sentence, correcting the double negative.

EXAMPLE: Sharks don't have no bones.

ANSWER: Sharks don't have any bones.

1. Unless they are disturbed, sharks will not attack nobody.
2. The whale shark, the largest fish, does not eat nothing but plankton and small fish.
3. The great white shark doesn't usually attack no person unless it confuses the person for a sea lion or seal.
4. The skeptic would not believe nobody who told him that the great white shark can grow up to 25 feet long and weigh 7,300 pounds.
5. The bull shark will attack with hardly no provocation.
6. These animals often live in shallow inlets and rivers where they can't hardly be seen because of the murky water.
7. Reports about the blue shark indicate that a swimmer couldn't hardly count on being safe around these creatures.
8. Blue sharks cannot scarcely be seen from above or below because their skin is blue on top and white underneath.
9. There isn't nothing that you couldn't find in the stomach of a tiger shark; household objects have even been found.
10. Swimmers were not given no chance to survive the attack of the fierce-looking sand tiger sharks.

▼ **Critical Viewing**
Imagine seeing this blue shark in the wild. Use negative sentences in a description of your encounter. **[Speculate]**

☑ ONGOING ASSESSMENT: Monitor and Reinforce

If students miss more than two items in Exercises 1–3, refer them to the following for additional practice.

In the Textbook	Print Resources	Technology
Section Review, Ex. 4–6, p. 619	Grammar Exercise Workbook, pp. 159–160	On-Line Exercise Bank, Section 27.1

Section 27.1 *Section Review*

GRAMMAR EXERCISES 4–9

Exercise 4 Avoiding Double Negatives Choose the word in parentheses that best completes each sentence.

1. The horseshoe crab is (nothing, anything) like a typical crab.
2. This marine animal hasn't (no, any) living relatives.
3. While it has positive medical uses, no one says (nothing, anything) positive about eating horseshoe-crab meat.
4. They may look frightening, but there isn't (nothing, anything) dangerous about horseshoe crabs.
5. They are not used (nowhere, anywhere) for fertilizer anymore.

Exercise 5 Revising Sentences to Correct Double Negatives Rewrite each sentence, correcting the double negative. If there is no double negative, write *correct*.

1. Without no shell, the octopus must rely on other resources for protection.
2. Prey can't scarcely tell the difference between an octopus's arm and a worm.
3. If not for large, complex eyes, the octopus wouldn't be able to locate nothing.
4. There is not hardly any other animal in the sea that has a nervous system as complex as that of the octopus.
5. They squeeze between rocks so that they are not easy targets for predators.
6. Because of their camouflage, a hidden octopus cannot barely be seen.
7. If an octopus is firmly attached to a rock, there isn't no way to pull it off.
8. An octopus will not never have fewer than eight legs because new legs grow in to replace lost ones.
9. Most octopuses cannot live no longer than about three years.
10. Many young octopuses cannot protect themselves and are eaten by fish.

Exercise 6 Revising a Paragraph to Avoid Problems With Negatives Revise the following, correcting any errors in double negatives.

The giant red mysid, a shrimplike animal, cannot be seen by nothing underwater. Although it appears as bright red to humans, it is not perceived that way by no underwater life. There isn't no mysid bigger than the giant red mysid. Where red mysids live, there aren't but low levels of oxygen. The animal defends itself by releasing a bioluminescent fluid. Attackers can't hardly see through the fluid and are unable to find their prey.

Exercise 7 Find It in Your Reading
Review newspaper and magazine articles to find examples of correct usage of negatives. Write down five examples in your notebook.

Exercise 8 Find It in Your Writing
Review several pieces of writing from your portfolio, checking for double negatives. If necessary, revise them to correct any problems with double negatives.

Exercise 9 Writing Application
Write a paragraph describing two people scuba-diving in a warm tropical sea. Use at least five of the following words. Be sure to avoid double negatives.

nothing	didn't	never
shouldn't	hardly	hadn't
not	couldn't	scarcely

Section Review • 619

ASSESS and CLOSE

Section Review
Each of these exercises correlates with a concept taught in the section on double negatives, pages 616–618. The exercises may be used for more practice, for reteaching or for review of the Key Concepts presented. Answers for all chapter exercises are available in *Grammar Exercises Answers on Transparencies* in your teaching resources.

Answer Key

Exercise 4

1. nothing
2. any
3. anything
4. anything
5. anywhere

Exercise 5

1. With no shell, the octopus must rely on other resources for protection.
2. Prey can scarcely tell the difference between an octopus's arm and a worm.
3. If not for large, complex eyes, the octopus wouldn't be able to locate anything.
4. There is hardly any other animal in the sea that has a nervous system as complex as that of the octopus.
5. correct
6. Because of their camouflage, a hidden octopus can barely be seen.
7. If an octopus is firmly attached to a rock, there isn't any way to pull it off.
8. An octopus will never have fewer than eight legs because new legs grow in to replace lost ones.
9. Most octopuses cannot live longer than about three years.
10. correct

Exercise 6

The giant red mysid, a shrimplike animal, cannot be seen by anything underwater. Although it appears as bright red to humans, it is not perceived that way by any underwater life. There is no mysid bigger than the giant red mysid. Where red mysids live, there are low levels of oxygen. The animal defends *continued*

Answer Key continued

itself by releasing a bioluminescent fluid. Attackers can hardly see through the fluid and are unable to find their prey.

Exercise 7

Find It in Your Reading
Have students bring in some articles for class discussion. Ask if anyone found an example of a double negative or another incorrect negative. Discuss and have students correct any mistakes they found.

Exercise 8

Find It in Your Writing
Have students correct any double negatives they find in their writing. Go over some examples with the class.

Exercise 9

Writing Application
Students may want to write their narratives with partners. They can write as if the adventure actually happened to both of them.

Tell students that the following sentences contain commonly misused words. Ask if they can find the errors.

Tiffany wants to adopt a homeless dog.

She will accept any breed except a pit bull.

She has already made her house all ready for the dog.

She hopes there will not be too many cute dogs at the pound to choose among.

The trick is that there are no errors—because teachers do not make grammar errors! Tell students that by the end of this section, they won't either.

Activate Prior Knowledge

Ask students to explain the importance of good grammar. Help them see that the purpose of language is communication, and that grammar is the set of rules by which we use language to communicate. If everyone follows the same rules, communication is much easier, clearer, and more easily understood. Explain that in these pages, students will learn to correct some common usage problems that may be getting in the way of their ability to communicate clearly.

TEACH

Step-by-Step Teaching Guide

Common Usage Problems

1. Go through the usage problems throughout this section with the whole class. Read, or have volunteers read, each of the forty-one explanations.

continued

Section 27.2

Common Usage Problems

This section provides a list of forty-one usage problems arranged in alphabetical order.

▶ **KEY CONCEPT** Study the items in this glossary, paying particular attention to similar meanings and spellings. ■

(1) accept, except *Accept* is a verb meaning "to receive." *Except* is a preposition meaning "other than."

VERB: I *accept* your gift gratefully.
PREPOSITION: Everyone *except* Craig was at the dance.

(2) adapt, adopt *Adapt* means "to change." *Adopt* means "to take as one's own."

EXAMPLES: The frogfish *adapts* its appearance to blend into its environment.
            The young man *adopted* his hero's style of dress.

(3) affect, effect *Affect* is almost always a verb meaning "to influence." *Effect*, usually a noun, means "result." Occasionally, *effect* is a verb meaning "to bring about" or "to cause."

VERB: The President's speech deeply *affected* me.
NOUN: Scientists study the *effects* of nuclear radiation.
VERB: The Student Council *effected* many changes.

(4) ain't *Ain't* was originally a contraction of *am not*. It is not considered standard English.

NONSTANDARD: Anglerfish *ain't* easy to find or identify.
CORRECT: Anglerfish *aren't* easy to find or identify.

(5) all ready, already The two words *all ready* are used as an adjective meaning "ready." *Already* is an adverb meaning "by or before this time" or "even now."

ADJECTIVE: I am *all ready* to go scuba-diving.
ADVERB: I have *already* checked my gear.

(6) all right, alright *Alright*, though it is seen more and more frequently in print, is not considered a correct spelling.

NONSTANDARD: That new album is *alright*.
CORRECT: He is feeling *all right* today.

(7) all together, altogether These two adverbs have different meanings. *All together* means "together as a group." *Altogether* means "completely" or "in all."

In this section, you will learn about forty-one common usage problems. The examples and exercises in this section are about marine animals such as octopuses, dolphins, and rays.

Cross-Curricular Connection: Science

 **Spelling Tip**

When you refer to many fish of the same species, use the word *fish*. If you want to refer to many fish of different species, use the word *fishes*.

⏱ TIME AND RESOURCE MANAGER

Resources
Print: Grammar Exercises Workbook, pp. 161–162; Hands-on-Grammar Activity Book, Chapter 27
Technology: On-Line Exercise Bank, Section 27.2

In-Depth Coverage	Accelerated Pace
• Work through all key concepts, pp. 620–625. • Assign and review Exercises 10–12. • Read and discuss the Hands-on Grammar Activity, p. 628.	• Assign pp. 620–625 for independent student review. • Assign and review Exercise 14.

EXAMPLES: Fish in a school travel *all together*.
             The old television set finally broke *altogether*.

(8) among, between *Among* and *between* are both prepositions. *Among* always implies three or more. *Between* is generally used only with two.

EXAMPLES: The fish swam *among* the coral.
             The surfers passed *between* two sharks.

(9) anywhere, everywhere, nowhere, somewhere None of these adverbs should ever end with an *-s*.

NONSTANDARD: The child lost the money *somewheres*.
CORRECT: The child lost the money *somewhere*.

(10) at Do not use *at* after *where*. Simply eliminate it.

NONSTANDARD: Can you tell me *where* to catch crabs *at*?
CORRECT: Can you tell me *where* to catch crabs?

(11) awhile, a while *Awhile* is used as an adverb and is never preceded by a preposition. *A while* is the word *while* used as a noun, and it is usually preceded by a preposition like *after*, *for*, or *in*.

ADVERB: Lie down *awhile* and rest.
NOUN: For *a while* he lay still without moving.

(12) bad, badly *Bad* is an adjective meaning "defective," "hurtful," or "ill." It cannot be used after an action verb. *Badly* cannot be used as an adjective, but it can be used as an adverb after an action verb.

ADJECTIVE: Fishing without a license is a *bad* idea.
             We felt *bad* after a long day in the cold.
ADVERB: Despite much practice, she played *badly*.

(13) because Do not use *because* after *the reason*. Say "The reason . . . is that" or reword the sentence altogether.

NONSTANDARD: *The reason* the fish were eaten is *because* they did not swim fast enough.
CORRECT: *The reason* the fish were eaten is *that* they did not swim fast enough.
              The fish were eaten *because* they did not swim fast enough.

(14) being as, being that Avoid using both expressions. Use *because* or *since* instead.

NONSTANDARD: *Being as* it was so late, we went home.
CORRECT: *Because* it was so late, we went home.

▲ Critical Viewing
Using the words *among* and *between*, write three sentences about the fish in this picture. **[Analyze]**

Step-by-Step Teaching Guide continued

2. *Ain't* can mean *is not, am not, are not, have not,* or *has not*. The context of a sentence with *ain't* will make its meaning clear. Students will see and hear many characters in literary and dramatic works say *ain't*. Although they can use this word when they are writing dialogue for certain characters in plays and stories, students should always substitute one of the standard English verb phrases in formal speech and expository writing.

3. The adverb *awhile* comes from the frequent use of the two words *a* and *while* as a pair. Remind students that *while* in this sense means "indefinite length of time."

4. The difference between *bad* and *badly* is the same as the difference between *good* and *well*. When students use any of these words, they should think about the part of speech the word modifies. If it is a noun or pronoun, students should use *bad* or *good*. If it is another part of speech, students should use *badly* or *well*.

continued

Critical Viewing

Analyze Students may say that there is a small fish swimming *between* two larger fish, that they would love to dive *among* the fish, and that there is little difference *among* most of the fish.

5. *Bring* is to *take* as *come* is to *go.* When something is brought to a person, it comes to him or her. When something is taken away, it leaves him or her. These two words should never be confused, because they are exact opposites in meaning.

6. Give paired examples to illustrate the difference between *less* and *fewer.*

> *On a diet, you eat fewer calories.*
>
> *On a diet, you eat less food.*
>
> *One dollar is less than five dollars.*
>
> *I have fewer five-dollar bills than one-dollar bills in my wallet.*

continued

Customize for
Less Advanced Students

Students may have difficulty understanding the difference between *bring* and *take.* To help them, have students act out "bringing" and "taking" objects to one another. For example, have one student ask another student to bring something near the first student to him or her. The student taking the object over should then say "I am taking ___ to you."

(15) beside, besides These two prepositions are different. *Beside* means "at the side of." *Besides* means "in addition to."

EXAMPLES: Mary saw a clownfish *beside* the anemone.
Other animals live in the coral reef *besides* coral.

(16) bring, take *Bring* means "to carry from a distant place to a nearer one." *Take* means "to carry from a near place to a more distant place."

EXAMPLES: *Bring* me the lobster platter, please.
They *take* their daily catches to the restaurants.

(17) different from, different than *Different from* is preferred.

LESS ACCEPTABLE: The frogfish is *different than* any other species of fish.

PREFERRED: The frogfish is *different from* any other species of fish.

(18) doesn't, don't Use *doesn't* instead of *don't* with all third-person singular pronouns and nouns.

NONSTANDARD: The machine *don't* work.
CORRECT: The machine *doesn't* work.

(19) done *Done* is the past participle of *do.* It should always follow a helping verb.

NONSTANDARD: He *done* his homework.
CORRECT: He *has done* his homework.

(20) due to *Due to* means "caused by" and should be used only when the words *caused by* can logically be substituted.

NONSTANDARD: *Due to* hunting and pollution, the monk seal has become endangered.
CORRECT: The near extinction of the monk seal is *due to* humans' hunting it and polluting its waters.

(21) farther, further *Farther* refers to distance. *Further* means "additional" or "to a greater degree or extent."

EXAMPLES: The *farther* from the surface of the ocean, the colder the water becomes.
I looked *further* into the sport of scuba diving.

(22) fewer, less Use *fewer* for things that can be counted. Use *less* for quantities that cannot be counted.

EXAMPLES: *fewer* calories, *fewer* dollars, *fewer* assignments
less sugar, *less* money, *less* homework

(23) gone, went *Gone* is the past participle of *go.* It should be used as a verb only with a helping verb. *Went* is the past tense of *go* and is never used with a helping verb.

NONSTANDARD: Craig and Louise *gone* to the movies.
You really *should have went* to the party.

CORRECT: Craig and Louise *went* to the movies.
You really *should have gone* to the party.

(24) in, into *In* refers to position. *Into* suggests motion.

EXAMPLES: The vampire squid lives *in* the deep sea.
The octopus can crawl *into* tiny spaces.

(25) just When you use *just* as an adverb meaning "no more than," place it right before the word it logically modifies.

LESS ACCEPTABLE: She *just* wants one piece of candy.
PREFERRED: She wants *just* one piece of candy.

(26) kind of, sort of Do not use in place of *rather* or *somewhat.*

NONSTANDARD: Siphonophores are *sort of* like jellyfish.
CORRECT: Siphonophores are *rather* like jellyfish.

(27) lay, lie *Lay* means "to put or set (something) down." Its principal parts—*lay, laying, laid,* and *laid*—are usually followed by a direct object. *Lie* means "to recline." Its principal parts—*lie, lying, lay,* and *lain*—are never followed by a direct object.

LAY: Please *lay* the basket on the counter.
Those turtles *are laying* their eggs on the beach.
Before she left, she *laid* the books on the table.
The masons have *laid* three rows of bricks.

LIE: If you are sick, you should *lie* down.
They are *lying* in the sunshine.
Last week, he *lay* in the hammock every evening.
The children have *lain* in bed long enough.

(28) learn, teach *Learn* means "to receive knowledge." *Teach* means "to give knowledge."

EXAMPLES: Dolphins can *learn* to follow commands.
The trainer *taught* the killer whale a new trick.

(29) leave, let *Leave* means "to allow to remain." *Let* means "to permit." Do not use one in place of the other.

NONSTANDARD: People should *let* animal habitats alone.
CORRECT: People should *leave* animal habitats alone.

NONSTANDARD: *Leave* me go!
CORRECT: *Let* me go!

▼ **Critical Viewing**
Write down your impressions of the octopus in the photograph below. Use the words *gone, went, in, into, lay,* and *lie.*
[Interpret]

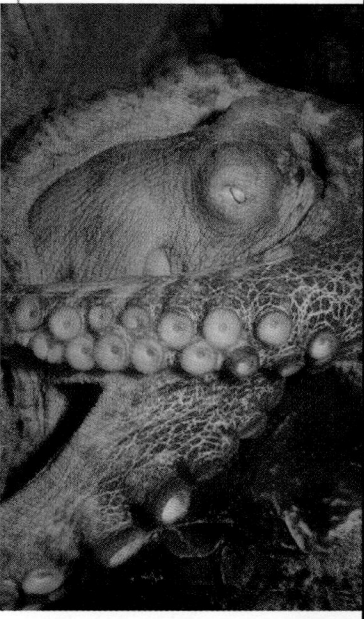

Common Usage Problems • **623**

Step-by-Step Teaching Guide continued

7. Point out that the verb *lie* also means "to tell an untruth." An additional source of confusion is that the two verbs are conjugated differently. To tell a falsehood: *lie, lying, lied.* To recline: *lie, lying, lay, lain.*

continued

Integrating Vocabulary Skills

Two other commonly confused words are *imply* and *infer. Imply* means to hint or to give the impression of something. The action "goes away from" the implier: *I implied by my hesitation that I didn't want to see that movie. Infer* means to arrive at a conclusion. The action "goes toward" the inferrer: *I inferred from her hesitation that she didn't want to see that movie.*

Customize for *ESL Students*

Many people learn a new language by imitating the way others speak it. This section may bewilder students learning English who have picked up such expressions as *ain't, where at,* or *kind of* for *somewhat* in the belief that they are correct English. Help students understand the difference between the standard of casual speech and that of formal writing.

Critical Viewing

Interpret Students may say such things as this: If you had *gone* to the aquarium with us, you would have seen the octopus swimming *in* the tank. Did you know they like to *lie* on the ocean floor and can squeeze *into* tiny spaces? The tour guide asked us not to *lay* our hands on the glass. Afterward, we *went* to lunch.

8. *Of* and *have* are confused because of pronunciation. The contraction *'ve* sounds like *of*.

continued

Customize for
Gifted/Talented Students

Have students choose one of the fish or other sea creatures mentioned in this section and do some research on it. Challenge them to write original paragraphs based on their research. Students' paragraphs should use any twelve of the words or phrases in this section correctly.

Critical Viewing

Analyze Students may respond that the color of the fish helps to camouflage them, protecting them from predators.

27.2

(30) like, as *Like* is a preposition meaning "similar to" or "such as." It should not be used in place of the conjunction *as*.

NONSTANDARD: She writes *like* she speaks— graciously.
CORRECT: She writes *as* she speaks— graciously.

(31) of, have Do not use the preposition *of* in place of the verb *have*.

NONSTANDARD: The octopus could *of* squirted its pursuer.
CORRECT: The octopus could *have* squirted its pursuer.

(32) only Because the position of *only* can affect the entire meaning of a sentence, be sure to place it before the word that should be modified.

EXAMPLES: *Only* Rita wanted to go bowling. (No one else wanted to go bowling.)
Rita *only* wanted to go bowling. (Rita did not want to do anything else.)

(33) set, sit *Set* means "to put (something) in a certain place." Its principal parts—*set, setting, set,* and *set*—are usually followed by a direct object. *Sit* means "to be seated." Its principal parts—*sit, sitting, sat,* and *sat*—are never followed by a direct object.

SET: *Set* the peaches on the table.
He should be *setting* the table now.
They *set* the television on the corner table.
We have *set* all the clocks to go off at seven.

SIT: I will *sit* in his place tonight.
You must have been *sitting* there for hours.
She *sat* in her office and thought.
We have *sat* in the front row for three weeks now.

(34) seen *Seen* is a past participle and can be used as a verb only with a helping verb.

NONSTANDARD: We *seen* the bright colors in the coral reef.
CORRECT: We *have seen* the bright colors in the coral reef.

(35) so *So* is a coordinating conjunction. It should not be used alone when you mean "so that."

LESS ACCEPTABLE: Sponges use filters *so* they can eat food.
PREFERRED: Sponges use filters *so that* they can eat food.

▲ **Critical Viewing** These and other fish living around coral reefs are extremely colorful. How does their color affect the way they relate to their environment? **[Analyze]**

(36) than, then *Than* is used in comparisons. Do not confuse it with the adverb *then*, which usually refers to time.

EXAMPLES: Some sharks are more aggressive *than* others.
We finished shopping and *then* ate lunch.

(37) that, which, who Use these relative pronouns correctly. *That* and *which* refer to things (*which* is set off by commas). *Who* refers only to people.

EXAMPLES: I saw the fish *that* you told me about.
Conch, which is a kind of shellfish, was served for dinner.
We thanked the waiter *who* helped us.

(38) that there, this here Avoid these nonstandard expressions. Simply leave out *here* and *there*.

NONSTANDARD: *That there* nudibranch is a beautiful creature.
This here sea slug is a nudibranch.
CORRECT: *That* nudibranch is a beautiful creature.
This sea slug is a nudibranch.

(39) their, there, they're *Their,* a possessive pronoun, always modifies a noun. *There* can be used either as an expletive at the beginning of a sentence or as an adverb. *They're* is a contraction for *they are.*

PRONOUN: Nag fish tie *their* bodies into knots.
EXPLETIVE: *There* are some reasons for doing this.
ADVERB: They can find food *there.*
CONTRACTION: *They're* trying to escape predators.

(40) to, too, two *To,* a preposition, begins a prepositional phrase or an infinitive. *Too,* an adverb, modifies adjectives and other adverbs; it can be used to mean "also" as well. *Two* is a number.

PREPOSITION: *to* the ocean floor
INFINITIVE: *to* swim
ADVERB: *too* tall, *too* quickly
NUMBER: *two* eggs, *two* fins

(41) when, where Do not use *when* or *where* directly after a linking verb, and do not use *where* in place of *that.*

NONSTANDARD: At night is *when* you can watch the fish feed.
Under the sea is *where* you find fish.
We read *where* taxes are rising.
CORRECT: At night is the time to watch fish feed.
Under the sea is the place for you to find fish.
We read that taxes are rising.

Common Usage Problems • 625

Step-by-Step Teaching Guide continued

9. The words in items 39 and 40 are no problem in speech. Listeners know which sound-alike word is meant. Mistakes that occur in writing are due to haste. Remind students to proofread their written work carefully for these kinds of errors.

continued

Integrating Technology Skills

Students should get into the habit of spell checking all writing they do on the computer. However, the computer will question only words it does not recognize. It will not question a real word, even if it is used incorrectly. Therefore, students should always proofread their writing for sense after they spell check.

Answer Key

Exercise 10

1. Because
2. takes
3. that
4. into
5. so that
6. too
7. Besides
8. a while
9. different from
10. that

Critical Viewing

Speculate Students may respond that *because* the lionfish has a fin like a mane, this may be why it is called a lionfish. Another reason may be *that* the lionfish can ferociously defend itself *so that* it acts like a lion in the wild. The lionfish may prey upon animals *different from* itself.

27.2

Exercise 10 Avoiding Usage Problems Choose the correct word to complete each sentence.

EXAMPLE: The (affects, effects) of predators on all undersea life are amazing.

ANSWER: effects

1. (Being that, Because) there are many undersea animals that are attacked by predators, many defense techniques have been developed.
2. In order to propel itself quickly to escape from predators, the octopus (brings, takes) water into its mantle cavity and quickly shoots a jet of water through a separate opening.
3. Another defense for the octopus is to squirt an inky fluid (that, which) causes the water to become cloudy and makes it very difficult for an attacker to see.
4. Lacking bones or a hard shell, the octopus can move (in, into) tight spaces between rocks to hide from its enemies.
5. The octopus can change its color to that of its surroundings (so, so that) it can hide from predators.
6. Rays use camouflage, (to, too, two), as a method of defense.
7. (Besides, Beside) being a color that blends into the ocean floor, a ray has poisonous spines on its tail.
8. A puffer fish can scare its enemies by inflating its body for (a while, awhile).
9. The porcupine fish, which is (different from, different than) the puffer, has sharp spines all over its body to discourage predators.
10. The reason the lionfish has venomous spines sticking out of its fins is (because, that) they help it to defend itself from enemies.

More Practice

On-line
Exercise Bank
• Section 27.2
Grammar Exercise Workbook
• pp. 161–162

▼ **Critical Viewing**
Why do you think this fish is called a lionfish? Using three problem words correctly, discuss how the lionfish got its name. **[Speculate]**

626 • Miscellaneous Problems in Usage

🎸 STANDARDIZED TEST PREPARATION WORKSHOP

Standard English Usage Standardized tests often measure students' mastery of standard usage. Share the following sample test item with students:

Choose the letter of the word or group of words that best completes the sentence.

My sister wants to go shopping, but she is having trouble deciding ___ a new shirt and a pair of sneakers.

A among   C whether

B between   D none of the above

The correct choice is item **B**. *Between* is used with two (*new shirt* and *pair of sneakers*).

Exercise 11 Revising Sentences to Eliminate Usage
Problems Rewrite each sentence, correcting any usage problems that you find. If the sentence is correct as is, write
correct.

1. Dolphins ain't fish; they are mammals.
2. If he had wanted, he could of gone diving with the dolphins.
3. The dolphin brain is kind of the same size as the human brain.
4. A dolphin does not breathe through its nose, but through a hole in the top of its head.
5. Scientists seen dolphins surface in order to breathe.
6. That there beak on the dolphin is called a *rostrum.*
7. Dolphins have grown thick layers of blubber under their skin due to the cold water in which they live.
8. Dolphins navigate by producing sounds and by listening to the echoes that come from their surroundings.
9. Dolphins have a language of there own.
10. Dolphins have an amazing ability to communicate their emotions by the sounds that they make.

Exercise 12 Revising a Paragraph to Eliminate Usage
Problems Revise the following paragraph. Correct any usage problems that you find.

   Their are animals living on coral reefs that have unique relationships with other species. They live this way in order to enhance there own lives or to help them to avoid the risks of undersea life. The clownfish, or anemone fish, and the sea anemone live together in a relationship called *obligate symbiosis.* This term means that the clownfish benefits from living between the poisonous tentacles of the anemone. However, the anemone doesn't gain nothing from the relationship. In order too survive among the stinging tentacles of the anemone, the body of the clownfish is coated with a protective mucus layer. Scientists believe that these fish have adapted this coating in order to survive better under the sea. This feature has a few benefits for the clownfish. First of all, the clownfish can lie its eggs between the many tentacles of the anemone. By doing this, it protects the eggs from any predators who would die from the sting of the anemone's tentacles. Second, the anemone provides a refuge and hiding place for clownfish that are escaping predator fish. Although the clownfish reaps many benefits from this relationship, the anemone is uneffected by the relationship.

More Practice
On-line
Exercise Bank
• Section 27.2
Grammar Exercise Workbook
• pp. 161–162

Common Usage Problems • **627**

Answer Key

Exercise 11

1. Dolphins aren't fish; they are mammals.
2. If he had wanted, he could have gone diving with the dolphins.
3. The dolphin brain is somewhat the same size as the human brain.
4. correct
5. Scientists have seen dolphins surface in order to breathe.
6. That beak on the dolphin is called a rostrum.
7. Dolphins have grown thick layers of blubber under their skin because of the cold water in which they live.
8. correct
9. Dolphins have a language of their own.
10. correct

Exercise 12

   There are animals living on coral reefs that have unique relationships with other species. They live this way in order to enhance their own lives or to help them avoid the risks of undersea life. The clownfish, or anemone fish, and the sea anemone live together in a relationship called obligate symbiosis. This term means that the clownfish benefits from living among the poisonous tentacles of the anemone. However, the anemone gains nothing (or: doesn't gain anything) from the relationship. In order to survive among the stinging tentacles of the anemone, the body of the clownfish is coated with a protective mucus layer. Scientists believe that these fish have adopted this coating in order to survive better under the sea. This feature has a few benefits for the clownfish. First of all, the clownfish can lay its eggs among the many tentacles of the anemone. By doing this, it protects the eggs from any predators that would die from the sting of the anemone's tentacles. Second, the anemone provides a refuge and hiding place for clownfish that are escaping predator fish. Although the clownfish reaps many benefits from this relationship, the anemone continues unaffected by the relationship.

ONGOING ASSESSMENT: Monitor and Reinforce

If students miss more than two items in Exercises 10–12, refer them to the following for additional practice.

In the Textbook	Print Resources	Technology
Section Review, Ex. 13–14, p. 629	Grammar Exercise Workbook, pp. 161–162	On-Line Exercise Bank, Section 27.2

627

Working on Usage Problems With Pictographs

Teaching Resources: Hands-on Grammar Activity Book, Chapter 27

1. Have students refer to their Hands-on Grammar activity books or give them copies of the relevant pages.

2. Review with students the directions for making the pictographs.

3. Help students understand what the function of a pictograph is. Students should be able to understand the meaning of each pictograph, so make sure they use appropriate illustrations.

Find It in Your Reading

Have students share their index cards with the class.

Find It in Your Writing

Encourage students to explain how they knew which word to use for each example they provide.

27.2

Hands-on Grammar

Working on Usage Problems With Pictographs

Work on common usage problems by forming pictographs—pictures that represent ideas or words. In the examples below, *further* and *farther* are illustrated with arrows showing that *farther* refers to distance and *further* means "to a greater extent." *Among* and *between* are illustrated with balls showing that *among* implies three or more, while *between* is generally used with two.

Each of the ten word pairs below represents a common usage problem. Using the Common Usage Problems glossary on pages 620–625, form pictographs for each word. Your pictures do not need to be elaborate, as long as they clearly illustrate what you have learned is the main difference between the proper usage of the two words. Use one index card for each word pair, and use the same side of the index card to illustrate both words.

After you have completed your pictographs, work with a partner to practice the correct usage of each word. Select your partner's cards at random, studying the pictographs and then coming up with sentences that use each word correctly. Refer to the Common Usage Problems glossary to check your answers.

1. all together, altogether
2. beside, besides
3. bring, take
4. learn, teach
5. than, then
6. in, into
7. lay, lie
8. fewer, less
9. set, sit
10. that, who

Find It in Your Reading In your literature or other textbooks, find examples of the words above used correctly in sentences. Write the example sentences on the backs of the appropriate index cards.

Find It in Your Writing Look through pieces of writing in your writing portfolio for examples of the words above used correctly in sentences. Write the example sentences on the back of the appropriate index cards. If you cannot find examples of any of the words, challenge yourself to write new sentences on the backs of the cards using the words correctly

628 • Miscellaneous Problems in Usage

TIME SAVERS!

Hands-on Grammar
Use the Hands-on Grammar activity sheet for Chapter 27 to facilitate this activity.

☑ ONGOING ASSESSMENT: Assess Mastery

Refer students to the following to assess their mastery of common usage problems.

In the Textbook	Technology
Chapter Review, Ex. 21–24, p. 631	On-Line Exercise Bank, Section 27.2

Section 27.2 *Section Review*

GRAMMAR EXERCISES 13–17

> **Exercise 13** Avoiding Usage
Problems Choose the correct word to complete each sentence.

1. (Being that, Being as, Because) ocean life varies according to depth, the ocean is divided into zones.
2. There is less oxygen and light (farther, further) down in the ocean.
3. The mesopelagic zone is lower (than, then) the surface layer of the ocean.
4. In the mesopelagic zone, there are (fewer, less) streamlined fish.
5. The fish in the mesopelagic zone go (into, in) the upper zone to feed at night because (farther, further) down (fewer, less) food is available.
6. The teeth of the mid-zone fish are often long and sharp, and (their, there, they're) jaws and stomachs are enlarged to accommodate larger fishes.
7. The bigscale fish is an example of a fish (who, that) lives in this zone.
8. The large scales and plates that cover its body make the bigscale fish (different from, different than) fishes (that, which) live in the most shallow zone.
9. A bigscale fish (don't, doesn't) chase its prey (so, so that) it can save energy.
10. The ctenophore is (kind of, somewhat) like the jellyfish.

> **Exercise 14** Revising to Eliminate
Usage Problems Rewrite each sentence, correcting any usage problems. If the sentence is correct as is, write *correct*.

1. The firefly squid is more advanced then the ctenophore because it has three organs who generate light.
2. Photophores are organs that produce light.
3. The firefly squid doesn't just glow for any reason.
4. They probably have this feature so predators would let them alone.

5. After studying the squid closely, scientists learned us that the firefly squid glows in order to attract other firefly squid.
6. Like humans use speech to communicate, firefly squid may use light to communicate.
7. The squid seen their prey because their glowing organs light up the darkness of the ocean.
8. In the darkness of the deep ocean is where photophores are useful.
9. Another animal that has photophores is the hatchet fish.
10. There are fish who have glowing organs on the undersides of their bodies and under there eyes.

> **Exercise 15** Find It in Your
Reading Read an article about fish in a science magazine. Identify five areas where problems in usage could have occurred, and explain how the writers avoided those problems.

> **Exercise 16** Find It in Your
Writing Choose one piece of writing in your portfolio. Check it carefully for the usage problems discussed in this chapter. If you find any usage problems, revise your writing to correct them.

> **Exercise 17** Writing Application
Write an original sentence for one of the words in each set listed below. Underline the word in your sentence, and check to be sure you have used it correctly.

awhile, a while	bring, take	their, there
farther, further	to, too, two	so, so that
sit, set	lie, lay	then, than

ASSESS and CLOSE

Section Review
Each of these exercises correlates with a concept taught in the section on common usage problems, pages 620–625. The exercises may be used for more practice, for reteaching or for review of the Key Concepts presented. Answers for all chapter exercises are available in *Grammar Exercises Answers on Transparencies* in your teaching resources.

Answer Key

> **Exercise 13**

1. Because
2. Farther
3. than
4. fewer
5. into, farther, less
6. their
7. that
8. different from, that
9. doesn't, so that
10. somewhat

> **Exercise 14**

1. The firefly squid is more advanced than the ctenophore because it has three organs that generate light.
2. correct
3. The firefly squid doesn't glow for just any reason.
4. They probably have this feature so that predators will let them alone.
5. After studying the squid closely, scientists taught us that the firefly squid glows in order to attract other firefly squid.
6. Just as humans use speech to communicate, firefly squid may use light to communicate.
7. The squid see their prey because their glowing organs light up the darkness of the ocean.
8. Photophores are useful in the deep darkness of the deep ocean.
9. correct
10. There are fish that have glowing organs on the undersides of the bodies and under their eyes.

> **Exercise 15**

Find It in Your Reading
Have students bring in their articles for class discussion. Ask if anyone found a usage problem. If so, have students share it with the class and correct it.

continued

Answer Key continued

> **Exercise 16**

Find It in Your Writing
Have students correct any errors they find in their writing.

> **Exercise 17**

Writing Application
Have students exchange papers and check each other's sentences for correct usage of the specified words. Have partners discuss any disagreements.

Each of these exercises correlates with a concept taught in the chapter on problems in usage, pages 616–625. The exercises may be used for more practice, for reteaching or for review of the Key Concepts presented. Answers for all chapter exercises are available in *Grammar Exercises Answers on Transparencies* in your teaching resources.

Answer Key

Exercise 18

1. any
2. is
3. any
4. any
5. anywhere

Exercise 19

1. There is but one animal that could have inspired the mysterious tales of mermaids.
2. If you hadn't ever seen a manatee before, you could be enchanted by its humanlike eyes.
3. Correct
4. Although mermaids are popular today as legends and in stories, the manatee is barely surviving.
5. There are but few places in the western Atlantic that manatees inhabit: coastal waters, river mouths, and freshwater inlets.
6. Manatees do not eat anything that is not vegetation.
7. She could scarcely believe that the manatee eats up to 100 pounds of food a day.
8. Correct
9. As coastal development continues there is not any place for the manatees to inhabit.
10. It did not do anything to help the population that an epidemic in 1996 killed more than 250 manatees.

Exercise 20

Deteriorating coral reefs are but one problem affecting ocean ecosystems. Hardly any of the coral reef is alive because it is made of skeletons of dead coral animals. Because living corals don't thrive without any sun, they attach to the top of the reef. Without very specific amounts of light, temperature, and oxygen, the coral reef cannot continue to sustain and support any life. If the problems of erosion and pollution continue. there won't be a suitable habitat for sea life. The stress of environmental changes forces shifts in habitat so that the algae don't live on the coral.

Thousands of fish would not have anywhere to live without the coral reef habitat. Beautiful white, sandy beaches wouldn't exist without any coral reef. There is nowhere that is better for diving because of the brilliant and beautiful marine life that lives among the coral reef. There are but a few parks that have been established to protect the fragile ecosystem of the coral reef.

GRAMMAR EXERCISES 18–25

> **Exercise 18** **Avoiding Problems With Negatives** Choose the word in parentheses that makes each sentence negative without forming a double negative.

1. There aren't (no, any) marine turtles larger than the Atlantic leatherback turtle.
2. There (is not, is) but one time the leatherback comes out of the water—to lay its eggs on the beach.
3. Leatherbacks do not lay (none, any) of their eggs on top of the sand; they lay their eggs in a shallow nest.
4. Of about 125 eggs that the female lays, scarcely (none, any) will survive to adulthood.
5. A leatherback that survives to adulthood will not go (anywhere, nowhere) to breed except the beach where it hatched.

> **Exercise 19** **Revising Sentences to Eliminate Problems With Negatives** Rewrite each sentence, correcting any problems with negatives. If there is no problem, write *correct*.

1. There isn't but one animal that could have inspired the mysterious tales of mermaids.
2. If you hadn't ever seen no manatee before, you could be enchanted by its humanlike eyes.
3. In the 1600's, mermaids were never depicted without a merman.
4. Although mermaids are popular today as legends and in stories, the manatee isn't barely surviving.
5. There aren't but few places in the western Atlantic that manatees inhabit: coastal waters, river mouths, and freshwater inlets.

6. Manatees do not eat nothing that is not vegetation.
7. She couldn't scarcely believe that the manatee eats up to 100 pounds of food a day.
8. There is nothing aggressive about the female manatee.
9. As coastal development continues, there is not no place for the manatees to inhabit.
10. It did not do nothing to help the population that an epidemic in 1996 killed more than 250 manatees.

> **Exercise 20** **Revising Paragraphs to Eliminate Problems With Negatives** Revise the following, correcting any errors in double negatives.

Deteriorating coral reefs aren't but one problem affecting ocean ecosystems. Hardly none of the coral reef is alive because it is made of skeletons of dead coral animals. Because living corals don't thrive without no sun, they attach to the top of the reef. Without very specific amounts of light, temperature, and oxygen, the coral reef cannot continue to sustain and support no life. If the problems of erosion and pollution continue, there won't barely be a suitable habitat for sea life. The stress of environmental changes forces shifts in habitat so that the algae don't live on the coral.

Thousands of fish would not have nowhere to live without the coral reef habitat. Beautiful white, sandy beaches wouldn't exist without no coral reef. There is nowhere that is better for diving because of the brilliant and beautiful marine life that lives among the coral reef. There aren't but a few parks that have been established to protect the fragile ecosystem of the coral reef.

Exercise 21 Avoiding Usage
Problems Choose the correct word to complete each sentence.

1. The reason whalers called the gray whale a "devil fish" is (because, that) it fought aggressively when attacked.
2. (Their, They're, There) known today by tourists as friendly whales.
3. At two different times, they could (have, of) become extinct.
4. However, (due to, because of) protection from humans, whales have fought their way back.
5. The gray whale in the Pacific migrates (further, farther) than any other whale.

Exercise 22 Revising Sentences
to Eliminate Usage Problems Rewrite each sentence, correcting any usage problems that you find. If the sentence is correct, write *correct.*

1. The reason the monk seal is called a living fossil is because there is evidence it lived 15 million years ago.
2. The monk seal altogether ceased to exist in the Caribbean.
3. The large tourist population, pollution, and hunting effect the monk seal population in the Mediterranean.
4. It is important to affect some changes in order to preserve the species.
5. There is fewer chance for recovery of the Mediterranean monk seal then the monk seals in the Hawaiian Islands.
6. Although the seal can weigh up to 400 pounds, swimmers have seen it escape a shark attack.
7. In order to have a cooler place to lay, monk seals dig down under the hot top layer of sand.
8. Monk seals eat lobsters, fishes living on coral reefs, eels, and octopuses two.
9. After a mother seal has a pup, she does not let it alone for six weeks.
10. She don't even leave the pup to feed herself.

Exercise 23 Revising a Paragraph
to Eliminate Usage Problems Rewrite the following paragraph, correcting all errors in usage.

Their are many marvelous creatures in the depths of the sea. There are many fishes who have had to adopt to survive deep beneath the ocean's surface. The dragonfish and the viperfish are to of these creatures. They usually do not chase no prey. They lay in wait for they're prey to come to them. That there is how they conserve energy. The teeth of both fish are long and sharp so they can spear prey that doesn't get into there mouths. The viperfish has a photophore as an extension of its dorsal fin who effects its hunting. The photophore acts like a lure. The dragonfish has a photophore among its two eyes. These here are ways in which these fascinating creatures survive between the other creatures in the sea.

Exercise 24 Writing Sentences to
Practice Correct Usage Write an original sentence for one of the words in each pair.

1. accept/except
2. beside/besides
3. farther/further
4. lay/lie
5. fewer/less
6. to/too
7. like/as
8. all ready/already
9. among/between
10. affect/effect

Exercise 25 Writing Application
Imagine that you are a sea creature. Write a paragraph describing your activities on a typical day. Correctly use at least five of the following words in your paragraph.

nothing	none	don't
barely	didn't	hardly
hasn't	can't	not

Answer Key continued

Exercise 25
Writing Application
Have students exchange paragraphs with a partner to check each other's work.

Exercise 21
1. that
2. They're
3. have
4. because of
5. farther

Exercise 22
1. The reason the monk seal is called a living fossil is that there is evidence it lived 15 million years ago.
2. correct
3. The large tourist population, pollution, and hunting affect the monk seal population in the Mediterranean.
4. It is important to effect some changes in order to preserve the species.
5. There is less chance for recovery of the Mediterranean monk seal than the monk seals in the Hawaiian Islands.
6. correct
7. In order to have a cooler place to lie, monk seals dig down under the hot top layer of sand.
8. Monk seals eat lobsters, fishes living on coral reefs, eels, and octopuses too.
9. After a mother seal has a pup, she does not leave it alone for six weeks.
10. She doesn't even leave the pup to feed herself.

Exercise 23
There are many marvelous creatures in the depths of sea. There are many fishes that have had to adapt to survive deep beneath the ocean's surface. The dragonfish and the viperfish are two of these creatures. They usually do not chase any prey. They lie in wait for their prey to come to them. That is how they conserve energy. The teeth of both fish are long and sharp so that they can spear prey that doesn't get into their mouths. The viperfish has a photophore as an extension of its dorsal fin that affects its hunting. The photophore acts as a lure. The dragonfish has a photophore between its two eyes. These are ways in which these fascinating creatures survive among the other creatures in the sea.

Exercise 24
Students' sentences will vary.
continued

▶ **Lesson Objectives**

1. To correct double negatives.
2. To select appropriate word choice.
3. To understand standard English usage.

Recognizing Standard English Usage

1. Explain to students that the best way to approach questions dealing with standard English usage is to read the sentence or passage carefully more than once.

2. Students should look for context clues that will help them determine the correct word needed to complete the sentences.

3. Students should then read through the choices, eliminating any choices they know are immediately incorrect.

4. Once students have made their choice, make sure they place their choice in the original sentence to double-check their work.

Standardized Test Preparation Workshop

Recognizing Standard English Usage

Your mastery of standard English usage is frequently tested on standardized tests. Some items test your ability to avoid or to correct double negatives. Others test your knowledge of appropriate word choice. You may face the following usage issues:

- words or word groups that look similar but have different meanings
- words or word groups with similar but different uses
- words used in informal English but not accepted as standard English

The following questions will give you practice with a format that is used to assess your usage knowledge.

Test Tip

When looking for the best word or group of words to complete a sentence, read the entire sentence silently to yourself, placing each choice in the sentence.

Sample Test Item

Directions: Read the passage, and choose the word or group of words that belongs in each space. Mark the letter for your answer.

While we were planning the school ski trip, we noticed that someone had _____ made the transportation arrangements.

1 A all ready

   B already

   C all together

   D altogether

Answers and Explanations

The correct answer is *B*. The word *already* completes the sentence according to the conventions of standard English usage and makes sense in the sentence. *Already* means "by or before this time" while *all ready* means "ready."

632 • Miscellaneous Problems in Usage

◆ **TEST-TAKING TIP**

Students should focus their attention on studying those common usage errors that they make repeatedly. Encourage students to develop memory aids to help them remember, for example, when to use *between* and when to use *among*. These memory aids will come in handy in test-taking situations.

Practice 1 **Directions:** Read the passage, and choose the word or group of words that belongs in each space.

I ___(1)___ never been to the ballet before. My family and I are ___(2)___ excited about going to see a performance of *The Nutcracker* ballet. My uncle gave the tickets to us. At first, we weren't sure we could ___(3)___ such a generous offer. ___(4)___ we decided to go and enjoy this famous ballet. I love the story, and I'm sure that the production will ___(5)___ my interpretation of it.

1 **A** have
  B ain't
  C am not
  D hardly

2 **F** real
  G really
  H allot
  J alot

3 **A** accept
  B excepted
  C except
  D accepting

4 **F** Than
  G Latter
  H Then
  J Irregardless

5 **A** affecting
  B affect
  C effect
  D effective

Practice 2 **Directions:** Read the passage, and choose the word or group of words that belongs in each space.

___(1)___ of the patterns for the wallpaper would have been nice, but this one was perfect. ___(2)___ the tiny flowers dotting the paper, a vivid green vine spreads across it. My friend and I visited many stores to find it. ___(3)___ decorating stores have so much to choose from it can be overwhelming. The ___(4)___ of us used the skills we learned in our decorating class, so there will not be ___(5)___ complaints after we complete our project.

1 **A** Every one
  B Anyone
  C Any one
  D Everyone

2 **F** Besides
  G Beside
  H Besides that
  J Being that

3 **A** These here
  B Those
  C Them
  D Them there

4 **F** to
  G too
  H two
  J one another

5 **A** no
  B none
  C all
  D any

Answer Key

Practice 1
1. A
2. G
3. A
4. H
5. B

Practice 2
1. C
2. F
3. B
4. H
5. D

Answer Key

Exercise A

1. they, nominative; converted, past, active
2. had been, past perfect, passive; it, objective
3. were, past, passive; its, possessive
4. protected, past, active
5. flourished, past, active; its, possessive
6. was, past, passive
7. they, nominative; had, past perfect, passive
8. they, nominative; dominated, past, active
9. they, nominative; it, objective
10. founded, past, active; its, possessive

Exercise B

1. most
2. became
3. complete
4. more
5. had
6. more, were, more
7. was, easily
8. was
9. was
10. were, immediately

Exercise C

The Aztecs are the people who dominated much of Mexico from the fourteenth to the sixteenth centuries. The Aztecs are better known for their elaborate empire. After the Toltec empire collapsed, many Aztec groups moved to central Mexico. They settled around Lake Texcoco. According to legend, they would see a cactus growing out of a rock in a marshy area. An eagle would be perched on the cactus, eating a snake. When they arrived at an island in the western part of Lake Texcoco, the priests knew they had found the best place. Unfortunately, the Aztecs occupied and farmed the swampy part of it. The Aztecs, overcoming a bad start, nevertheless thrived and became a great society. As they grew, they established a military and other civil organizations. In 1325 they founded the great city of Tenochtitlán. It was on the site of present-day Mexico City.

Cumulative Review

USAGE

▶ Exercise A Using Verbs and
Pronouns Choose the correct word or group of words that makes each sentence correct. For each verb or verb phrase, label its tense and voice. For each pronoun, identify its case.

1. When the Aztecs lived along the lake, (he, they) (convert, converted) the mud into productive gardens.
2. The city (had been, is) built on an island with bridges and causeways to connect (it, them) to the mainland.
3. Canals (were, are) dug to provide transportation for (its, the) people.
4. Strong dams (protect, protected) the city from floods.
5. The city (flourished, flourishes) due to (its, their) location and organization.
6. The great market (was, is) attracting up to 60,000 people each day.
7. Goods from lands (they, it) (has, had) conquered were exported by Aztecs.
8. Religious buildings—(they, it) consisted of pyramids with temples on top— (dominate, dominated) the city.
9. When the Spanish arrived, (he, they) compared (it, them) to Venice, Italy.
10. Hernán Cortés destroyed Tenochtitlán and (will found, founded) Mexico City on (its, his) ruins.

▶ Exercise B Making Words Agree
Choose the correct word or group of words to make each sentence correct.

1. The Aztecs had the (most, more) powerful military of any other group.
2. The Aztec city-states of Texcoco and Tlatelóco (become, became) allies.
3. The Aztecs had seized (most complete, complete) power within 100 years.
4. Kingships in conquered lands became (more, most) honorary than official.

5. By 1520, thirty-eight provinces (has, had) been established.
6. Some tribes remained (more, most) independent than others that (were, was) (more, most) closely controlled.
7. Because of internal divisions, Cortés (was, were) (easily, easier) able to defeat the empire.
8. The Aztec society (was, were) divided into slaves, commoners, and nobles.
9. The status of slaves (was, were) similar to that of indentured servants.
10. Slaves who escaped and reached the palace (was, were) (immediately, more immediately) freed.

▶ Exercise C Revising a Paragraph to
Eliminate Errors in Agreement Rewrite the following paragraph, correcting any errors in agreement.

The Aztecs is the people who dominated much of Mexico from the fourteenth to the sixteenth centuries. The Aztecs are better known for their elaborate empire. After the Toltec empire collapsing, many Aztec groups moved to central Mexico. He settled around Lake Texcoco. According to legend, they would seen a cactus growing out of a rock in a marshy area. An eagle would be perched on the cactus, eaten a snake. When they arrived at an island in the western part of Lake Texcoco, the priests knew they had found the most best place. Unfortunately, the Aztecs occupied and farm the swampy part of it. The Aztecs, overcoming a bad start, nevertheless thriving and becoming a great society. As they grew, it established a military and other civil organizations. In 1325, they founding the greater city of Tenochtitlán. They was on the site of present-day Mexico City.

> **Exercise D** **Using Modifiers** Choose the correct word or group of words that makes each sentence correct.

1. In the 1500's, Tenochtitlán was (more big, bigger) than (any, any other) city in the Aztec empire.
2. The city grew in size as the population of the city grew (more large, larger).
3. They built (long, longest) causeways to connect the city with the mainland.
4. Farmers filled in parts of the lake to create (more, most) farmland.
5. They anchored reed baskets filled with earth in the shallow lake, extending farmland (farther, farthest) out.
6. Because the crops were planted in baskets anchored in water, they grew (well, better) than on dry land.
7. One of the (most highest, highest) buildings was the emperor's palace.
8. The palace served as a (vast, vaster) storehouse for tribute.
9. It also housed a (fine, finer) library of history books and accounting records.
10. Aztecs adapted (many, more, most) ideas from the people they conquered.

> **Exercise E** **Revising Sentences to Eliminate Problems in Usage** Rewrite the following sentences, correcting negative sentences and other usage problems.

1. The slave class ain't the only distinction made in Aztec society.
2. Between the other classes, *tlalmaitl* were the lowest group of commoners.
3. They weren't but tenant farmers on other people's land.
4. That group of commoners was not allowed to own land anywheres.
5. Other commoners, the *maceualtin*, were given land already for them to build their houses.
6. The reason people were nobles was because they were born into the class.
7. Others, like warriors, were nobles due to the fact that they earned their rank.

8. Priests were another group which was included in the Aztec nobility.
9. Later civilizations didn't do nothing with the Aztec system of writings.
10. They're writing was a series of pictures on paper or animal hides.

> **Exercise F** **Revising a Paragraph to Eliminate Usage Errors** Revise the following paragraph to correct errors in usage. You may reorder words or combine sentences.

In Aztec religion, several gods are ruling over daily life. The moon goddess, that legend says had murdered his brother. The sun god. Tlaloc. The rain god, was worshiped, to. Quetzalcoatl was even most important. In the tenth century, they only was a god of the soil. The Toltecs farther associated Quetzalcoatl with the morning and evening star. Than the Aztecs made him a patron of the priests. According to they're beliefs, Quetzalcoatl was a god-king who had longest ago vowed to return from the east. Being that Quetzalcoatl was light-skinned and bearded, it was not hardly difficult for the king to believe that Cortés might been the returning god.

> **Exercise G** **Writing Application** Write a brief narrative of an imaginary trip in which you find a previously unknown civilization. Make your writing interesting by varying your sentence lengths and structures. Try to avoid sentence errors and common usage problems. Be sure that the words in your sentences follow the rules of agreement and that your modifiers are used correctly. Then, list your verbs and verb phrases, identifying their tense. Make a list of your pronouns, and label their case.

Cumulative Review • 635

Answer Key continued

> **Exercise G**

Writing Application
Have students read aloud their paragraphs to the class when they are done.

> **Exercise D**
1. bigger, any other
2. larger
3. long
4. more
5. farther
6. better
7. highest
8. vast
9. fine
10. many

> **Exercise E**
1. The slave class wasn't the only distinction made in Aztec society.
2. Among the other classes, tlalmaitl were the lowest group of commoners.
3. They were but tenant farmers on other people's land.
4. That group of commoners was not allowed to own land anywhere.
5. Other commoners, the maceualtin, were given land all ready for them to build their houses.
6. The reason people were nobles was that they were born into the class.
7. Others, like warriors, were nobles because of the fact that they earned their rank.
8. Priests were another group who was included in the Aztec nobility.
9. Later civilizations didn't do anything with the Aztec system of writings.
10. Their writing was a series of pictures on paper or animal hides.

> **Exercise F**
Revisions will vary. Sample is given.

In Aztec religion, several gods rule over daily life. According to legend, the moon goddess had murdered her brother Tlaloc, the sun god. The rain god was worshiped too. Quetzalcoatl was even more important. In the tenth century, there only was a god of the soil. The Toltecs further associated Quetzalcoatl with the morning and evening stars. Then the Aztecs made him a patron of the priests. According to their beliefs, Quetzalcoatl was a god-king who had long ago vowed to return from the east. Because Quetzalcoatl was light-skinned and bearded, it was not difficult for the king to believe that Cortés might have been the returning god.

continued

635

Time and Resource Manager

In-Depth Lesson Plan

	LESSON FOCUS	PRINT AND MEDIA RESOURCES
DAY 1	**Capitalization** Students learn and apply concepts of capitalization for words in sentences and proper nouns (pp. 636–643).	**Teaching Resources** *Grammar Exercise Workbook,* pp.163–164; *Grammar Exercises Answers on Transparency,* Ch. 28; *Language Lab* **CD-ROM,** *Capitalization and Punctuation;* **On-Line Exercise Bank,** Section 28
DAY 2	**Capitalization (continued)** Students do the Hands-on Grammar Activity and learn and apply concepts of capitalization for proper adjectives and titles (pp. 644–648).	**Teaching Resources** *Grammar Exercise Workbook,* pp.163–164; *Grammar Exercises Answers on Transparency,* Ch. 28; *Hands-on Grammar Activity Book,* Ch. 28; *Language Lab* **CD-ROM,** *Capitalization and Punctuation;* **On-Line Exercise Bank,** Section 28
DAY 3	**Review and Assess** Students review chapter and demonstrate mastery of use of capitalization (pp. 649–651).	**Teaching Resources** *Formal Assessment,* Ch. 28; *Grammar Exercises Answers on Transparency,* Ch. 28; **On-Line Exercise Bank,** Section 28

Accelerated Lesson Plan

	LESSON FOCUS	PRINT AND MEDIA RESOURCES
DAY 1	**Capitalization** Students cover concepts and usage of capitalization as determined by Diagnostic Test (pp. 636–648).	**Teaching Resources** *Grammar Exercise Workbook,* pp.163–164; *Grammar Exercises Answers on Transparency,* Ch. 28; *Hands-on Grammar Activity Book,* Chapter 28; *Language Lab* **CD-ROM,** *Capitalization and Punctuation;* **On-Line Exercise Bank,** Section 28
DAY 2	**Review and Assess** Students review chapter and demonstrate mastery of use of capitalization (pp. 649–651).	**Teaching Resources** *Formal Assessment,* Ch. 28; *Grammar Exercises Answers on Transparency,* Ch. 28; **On-Line Exercise Bank,** Section 28

Options for Adapting Lesson Plans

HOMEWORK

Have students complete any section of the chapter for homework.

FEATURES

Extend coverage with the Grammar in Literature feature (p. 639) and the Standardized Test Preparation Workshop (p. 651).

TECHNOLOGY

Students can use the On-Line Exercise Bank to complete the exercises on computer. The Auto Check feature will grade their work.

INTEGRATED SKILLS COVERAGE

Grammar in Literature
SE p. 639

Reading
Find It in Your Reading SE p. 644

Writing
Find It in Your Writing SE p. 644
Writing Application SE pp. 650

Workplace Skills
Integrating Workplace Skills ATE p. 646

Viewing and Representing
Critical Viewing SE pp. 636, 641, 643, 645, 647, 648

ASSESSMENT SUPPORT

Standardized Test Preparation SE p. 651; ATE pp. 642, 648
Standardized Test Preparation Workbook, pp. 55–56
Formal Assessment, Ch. 28

MEETING INDIVIDUAL NEEDS

Less Advanced Students; See Ongoing Assessments
ATE pp. 641, 645, 647

ESL Students ATE pp. 640, 647

Verbal/Linguistic Learners ATE p. 641

BLOCK SCHEDULING

Pacing Suggestions
For 90-minute Blocks
• Administer the Diagnostic Test to students to determine instructional coverage.
• Have students complete the necessary exercises in class. Use the Hands-on Grammar activity to provide a change of pace.

Resources for Varying Instruction
• *Language Lab* **CD-ROM** If your students have access to hardware, a 90-minute block provides an ideal opportunity for students to work on computer.

Professional Development Support
• **How to Manage Instruction in the Block** This teaching resource provides management and activity suggestions.

MEDIA AND TECHNOLOGY

For the Student
• *Language Lab* **CD-ROM**, Capitalization and Puctuation
• *On-Line Exercise Bank,* Section 28

For the Teacher
• *Resource Pro* **CD-ROM**

WRITING AND GRAMMAR WEBSITE

The Interactive Writing and Grammar Website provides a wide array of support for students, teachers, and parents. Grammar support includes:

• *On-Line Exercise Bank* with Auto Check scoring
• Diagnostic and assessment support

phwg.phschool.com

LITERATURE CONNECTIONS

Grammar in Literature selections from *Prentice Hall Literature: Timeless Voices, Timeless Themes,* Gold:
from "One Ordinary Day, With Peanuts," Shirley Jackson, SE p. 639

Chapter 28 Capitalization

Central Park

Capital letters are important signals in your writing. They show when a new sentence begins. They also indicate names of specific people, places, or things and show which words are most significant in a title.

If you visit New York City, many famous and exciting places will stand out in your mind—such as Central Park, the Empire State Building, the Statue of Liberty, and Yankee Stadium. They should also stand out in your writing by beginning with capital letters.

You have probably already mastered the major rules of capitalization. This chapter will help you review the rules you already know and give you a chance to master some new rules to help you communicate even more clearly.

▲ **Critical Viewing**
Name some of the people, places, or things in this photo that you would start with a capital letter. **[Identify]**

636 • Capitalization

Diagnostic Test

Directions: Write all answers on a separate sheet of paper.

Skill Check A. Copy the following sentences, adding the missing capitals.

1. there are many beautiful and exciting places to see in New York state!
2. Adirondack park is located in the northern corner of the state.
3. Whiteface mountain is the highest skiing peak in the east, and it is the only high peak in the adirondacks reachable by car.
4. in 1935, president Franklin D. Roosevelt opened the new state highway to the mountaintop.
5. The 1932 and 1980 winter olympic games were held at lake placid, located just south of whiteface mountain.

Skill Check B. Copy the following sentences, correcting any capitalization errors.

6. The Niagara river and niagara falls are located in Western New York.
7. More than 10 million visitors a year come to see the great Falls, which Native americans called the "Thunder of the waters."
8. There are five homes designed by the american Architect Frank Lloyd wright in the Western new York city of Buffalo.
9. To cross over to Central New York, you can rent a Houseboat and cruise the historic Erie canal.
10. The New York State capitol building is in Albany.

Skill Check C. Rewrite the following sentences, correcting all errors in capitalization.

11. For Bob smith, his first day at Washington high school had not begun well.
12. Bob had not wanted to move to New York and leave his old school in centerville, Indiana.
13. However, his Father had accepted a job at Saint John's university, and his mother had been offered a job as a reporter for *the new york times*, so they moved in august.
14. The bus this morning had been delayed in traffic on maple Street.
15. Bob's first class was history with mr. Harris.
16. finally, He found room 302 and took a seat.
17. mr. Harris was telling the class about the field trips they would be taking throughout the semester.
18. When Mr. Harris finished his lecture, the girl sitting next to bob smiled and extended her hand.
19. "I am Sarah carter," she said, "And this is my first day here."
20. perhaps tuesday, September 2, was going to be a good day after all.

Answer Key continued

13. However, his father had accepted a job at Saint John's University, and his mother had been offered a job as a reporter for the *New York Times,* so they moved in August.
14. The bus this morning had been delayed in traffic on Maple Street.
15. Bob's first class was history with Mr. Harris.
16. Finally, he found Room 302 and took a seat.
17. Mr. Harris was telling the class about the field trips they would be taking throughout the semester.
18. When Mr. Harris finished his lecture, the girl sitting next to Bob smiled and extended her hand.
19. "I am Sarah Carter," she said, "and this is my first day here."
20. Perhaps Tuesday, September 2, was going to be a good day after all.

Answer Key

Diagnostic Test

- Each item in the diagnostic test corresponds to a specific concept in the chapter on capitalization. This will enable you to tailor instruction to the particular needs of your students. See "Ongoing Assessment: Diagnose" on p. 636 for further details.

- Answers for the Diagnostic Test and all chapter exercises are available in *Grammar Exercises Answers on Transparencies* in your teaching resources.

Skill Check A

1. There are many beautiful and exciting places to see in New York State!
2. Adirondack Park is located in the northern corner of the state.
3. Whiteface Mountain is the highest skiing peak in the East, and it is the only high peak in the Adirondacks reachable by car.
4. In 1935, President Franklin D. Roosevelt opened the new state highway to the mountaintop.
5. The 1932 and 1980 Winter Olympic Games were held at Lake Placid, located just south of Whiteface Mountain.

Skill Check B

6. The Niagara River and Niagara Falls are located in western New York.
7. More than 10 million visitors a year come to see the great falls, which Native Americans called the "Thunder of the Waters."
8. There are five homes designed by the American architect Frank Lloyd Wright in the western New York city of Buffalo.
9. To cross over to central New York, you can rent a houseboat and cruise the historic Erie Canal.
10. The New York State Capitol Building is in Albany.

Skill Check C

11. For Bob Smith, his first day at Washington High School had not begun well.
12. Bob had not wanted to move to New York and leave his old school in Centerville, Indiana.

continued

Capitalizing Words in Sentences

One of the most important uses of capitals is to signal the beginning of each new sentence.

KEY CONCEPT Capitalize the first word in declarative, interrogative, imperative, and exclamatory sentences. ■

DECLARATIVE: The taxi stopped when I waved.
INTERROGATIVE: Do you know where we are going?
IMPERATIVE: Bring the travel brochures home tomorrow.
EXCLAMATORY: I would love to take a trip to New York City!

KEY CONCEPT Capitalize the first word in a quotation if the quotation is a complete sentence. ■

Each quotation below is a complete sentence. In the last example, note that the full quotation consists of two complete sentences. Each of the sentences begins with a capital letter.

EXAMPLES: She said, "The art museum is closed."
"The art museum is closed," she said.
"The art museum is closed," she said. "We will come back in the morning."

When a quotation consists of one complete sentence separated into two parts, only one capital letter is required.

EXAMPLE: "The art museum is closed," she said, "because they are setting up a new exhibit that opens tomorrow."

A fragment of a quotation contained within a larger sentence should not be capitalized.

EXAMPLE: June told us that the art exhibit was "better than the one last year."

Here is one more capitalization rule to keep in mind when writing sentences:

KEY CONCEPT Capitalize the first word after a colon only if the word begins a complete sentence. ■

EXAMPLES: We all had the same thought: How are we going to decide which attractions to visit?
We all agreed that the city has many worthwhile attractions: museums, theaters, parks, and zoos.

638 • Capitalization

▶ **Exercise 1** Using Capitalization Correctly in Sentences and Quotations Copy the following sentences on your paper, adding the missing capitals.

1. we have decided to take a family vacation in New York City this year.
2. our travel agent said, "it's one of the most exciting places in the world."
3. "you need to plan ahead," she said, "because there are many fascinating attractions to choose from."
4. there is one thing every visitor should know: the city is divided into five regions, and each has many educational and cultural attractions.
5. we spent all week reading about the many attractions we could visit while in the city: museums, art galleries, theaters, parks, historic landmarks, and many others.

GRAMMAR IN LITERATURE

from One Ordinary Day, With Peanuts

Shirley Jackson

The first word of each quote in this passage is capitalized. The first word of each sentence or fragment inside the quote is also capitalized to show where each new thought begins.

. . . They sat on the steps cracking peanuts in a comradely fashion, and Mr. Johnson said, "So you're moving?"

"Yep," said the boy.

"Where you going?"

"Vermont."

"Nice place. Plenty of snow there. Maple sugar, too; you like maple sugar?"

"Sure."

"Plenty of maple sugar in Vermont. You going to live on a farm?"

"Going to live with Grandpa."

▶ **More Practice**

Language Lab CD-ROM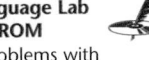
• Problems with Capitalization lesson

On-line Exercise Bank
• Section 28

Grammar Exercise Workbook
• pp. 163–164

Answer Key

▶ **Exercise 1**

1. We have decided to take a family vacation in New York City this year.
2. Our travel agent said, "It's one of the most exciting places in the world."
3. "We need to plan ahead," she said, "because there are many fascinating attractions to choose from."
4. There is one thing every visitor should know: The city is divided into five regions and each area has many educational and cultural attractions.
5. We spent all week reading about the many attractions we could visit while in the city: museums, art galleries, theaters, parks, historic landmarks, and many others.

Step-by-Step Teaching Guide

Grammar in Literature

1. Have two volunteers read aloud the excerpt, one being Mr. Johnson and one being the boy.
2. Go through the capital letters one by one. Ask why each is capitalized.

More About the Author

Shirley Jackson's most famous short story is "The Lottery" (1948), which matter-of-factly tells the story of a New England village with a ritual lottery, the "winner" of which is stoned to death. When the story was first published in *The New Yorker* magazine, it provoked the greatest response in the magazine's history; hundreds of readers were shocked and disturbed.

⏱ TIME SAVERS!

🔲 **Answers on Transparency**
Use the Grammar Exercises on Transparencies for Chapter 28 to have students correct their own or one another's exercises.

💻 **On-Line Exercise Bank**
Have students complete the exercises on computer. The Auto Check feature will grade their work for you!

Capitalizing Names of People, Geographical Names, and Other Special Places

1. Proper nouns name a specific place: *Let's meet at Golden Gate Park.* But *Let's meet at the park,* although it refers to a specific place, does not name it, so *park* is not capitalized.

2. Note that *the* in the Grand Canyon or the United States is not capitalized. An article should only be capitalized if it is the first word in a sentence or if it is part of the actual name.

Customize for
ESL Students

Have students write a proper noun from the country of their birth to go with each category on the geographical names table.

28

Capitalizing Proper Nouns

As you may recall, a proper noun names a specific person, place, or thing. All proper nouns are capitalized.

KEY CONCEPT Capitalize each part of a person's full name. ■

EXAMPLES: Diana T. Cheng   B. L. Baker

KEY CONCEPT Capitalize geographical names. ■

GEOGRAPHICAL NAMES	
Streets	Madison Avenue, Aborn Road
Towns and Cities	Evansdale, New York City, London
Counties	Macon County, Bergen County
States and Provinces	Vermont, Saskatchewan
Nations	United States of America, Japan
Continents	North America, Europe, Asia
Valleys and Deserts	Hudson Valley, the Sahara
Mountains	Sierra Nevadas, Adirondacks
Sections of a Country	the Great Plains, the Northeast
Islands	the Canary Islands, Maui
Scenic Spots	the Grand Canyon, Yellowstone National Park
Rivers and Falls	the Amazon River, the Tigris, Niagara Falls
Lakes and Bays	Lake Huron, Chesapeake Bay
Seas and Oceans	South China Sea, Atlantic Ocean

When a compass point names a specific area of a country, it is capitalized. It is not capitalized when it simply refers to a physical direction.

EXAMPLES: My family lives in the Northeast.
The wind came from the west.

KEY CONCEPT Capitalize the names of other special places. ■

EXAMPLES: the Statue of Liberty, John F. Kennedy Memorial, the Theater of Fine Arts, the Empire State Building, Room 114, the Madison Room, Conference Room B, the Milky Way, Earth, Venus, the Big Dipper

⏰ TIME AND RESOURCE MANAGER

Resources
Print: Grammar Exercises Workbook, pp. 165–166; Hands-on Grammar Activity Book, Chapter 28
Technology: Language Lab CD-ROM, Capitalization and Punctuation; On-Line Exercise Bank, Section 28

In-Depth Coverage	Accelerated Pace
• Work through all key concepts, pp. 640–645. • Assign and review Exercises 2–3. • Read and discuss Hands-on Grammar, p. 644.	• Assign pp. 640–645 for independent student review.

Capitalizing Names of Specific Events and Periods of Time

1. Have volunteers read the types of events and periods of time that should be capitalized.
2. Encourage students to provide at least one additional example for each row in the chart.

Customize for *Verbal/Linguistic Learners*

Have students write long sentences using as many kinds of proper nouns as possible. Be sure they punctuate correctly. For example: On Tuesday, July Fourth, also called Independence Day, everyone in Olathe, Kansas, will turn out for a parade down Elm Street, which begins at the statue of Sitting Bull, passes City Hall, and ends at Chipmunk Creek.

Critical Viewing

Connect Students should mention the person's name and the day of the week.

▶ **KEY CONCEPT** Capitalize the names of specific events and periods of time. ■

SPECIFIC EVENTS AND TIMES	
Historic Periods	the Renaissance, the Middle Ages, the Age of Enlightenment
Historic Events	the Revolutionary War, World War II
Documents	the Declaration of Independence, the Magna Carta
Days	Tuesday, Saturday
Months	April, November
Holidays	Fourth of July, Groundhog Day, Labor Day
Religious Days	Christmas, Easter, Passover, Ramadan
Special Events	Ashland Shakespeare Festival, Parade of Roses, New York City Marathon

Although they stand for specific times of the year, seasons are not capitalized.

EXAMPLES: We visited Manhattan last winter.
The spring is my favorite time of year.

▼ Critical Viewing
If you were writing a sentence about someone you know who was skating at this rink on a certain day, what words would you capitalize? **[Connect]**

The skating rink at Rockefeller Center is a famous tourist attraction.

Capitalization • 641

☑ ONGOING ASSESSMENT: Prerequisite Skills		
If students have difficulty with proper nouns, you may find it necessary to review the following to assure coverage of prerequisite knowledge.		
In the Textbook	**Print Resources**	**Technology**
Nouns and Pronouns, pp. 342–345	Grammar Exercise Workbook, pp. 3–4	Language Lab CD-ROM, Using Nouns, Using Pronouns; On-Line Exercise Bank, Section 16.1

Students have learned that titles of written works are italicized or put in quotation marks. Point out two exceptions. Titles of religious books and sections of them are not italicized or put in quotes: Bible, Exodus, Upanishads, I Ching, Koran, Book of the Dead, Talmud. Similarly, historical documents are not italicized: Constitution, Declaration of Independence, Bill of Rights, Magna Carta, Declaration of the Rights of Man.

28

KEY CONCEPT Capitalize the names of various organizations, government bodies, political parties, races, nationalities, and languages. ■

SPECIFIC GROUPS AND LANGUAGES	
Clubs, Organizations, Institutions, and Businesses	Kiwanis Club, Weld Chess Club, Red Cross, Fund for Animals, University of Washington
Government Bodies Political Parties	the Congress of the United States, the Department of Transportation the Republican party, the Democratic party, the Conservative party
Nationalities and Languages	Chinese, British English, Dutch, Swahili, Russian

KEY CONCEPT Capitalize references to religions, deities, and religious scriptures. ■

RELIGIOUS REFERENCES	
Christianity	God, the Lord, the Father, the Son, the Holy Spirit, the Bible, books of the Bible (that is, Genesis, Revelations, and so on).
Judaism	God, the Lord, the Father, the Prophets, the Torah, the Talmud, the Midrash
Islam	Allah, the Prophet, the Koran
Hinduism	Brahma, the Bhagavad Gita, the Vedas
Buddhism	the Buddha, Mahayana, Hinayana

The only exception to the rule for capitalizing religious terms occurs when you refer to a god or goddess of ancient mythology. In these cases, the word *god* is not capitalized.

EXAMPLES: the *god* Zeus, the *goddess* Hera

A number of other proper nouns not mentioned as yet also need capitalization. The following rule covers these.

More Practice

Language Lab CD-ROM
• Problems with Capitalization lesson
On-line Exercise Bank
• Section 28
Grammar Exercise Workbook
• pp. 165–166

STANDARDIZED TEST PREPARATION WORKSHOP

Capitalization Standardized tests often ask students to identify errors in capitalization. Ask students which of the following sentences contains an error in capitalization:

A Yankee Stadium is a famous New York City landmark.

B It is located in the borough of the bronx.

C It was opened in 1923.

D Great Yankee Players include Babe Ruth and Mickey Mantle.

In item **B**, *Bronx,* should be capitalized.

KEY CONCEPT Capitalize the names of other special proper nouns. ∎

OTHER SPECIAL PROPER NOUNS	
Awards	the Nobel Peace Prize, the John Newbery Medal
Air, Sea, Space, and Land Craft	the *Concorde*, the *Nautilus*, *Apollo I*, the Model T
Trademarks	Instaflash Film, Melody Records

When you use a trademark, all the words should be capitalized. If you are using only part of the trademark (the brand name), capitalize only the word that comes from the trademark.

TRADEMARK: Snapzit Instaphoto
BRAND NAME ALONE: Snapzit camera

Exercise 2 **Capitalizing Proper Nouns** Copy the following sentences, adding the missing capitals.

1. Jazz musicians in the 1920's nicknamed new york city the big apple.
2. The city is divided into five boroughs: manhattan, brooklyn, the bronx, queens, and staten island.
3. Each year, millions of tourists travel to this beautiful city in the northeast to visit its wide variety of attractions.
4. In the middle of manhattan is central park, the best known of the city's more than one hundred parks.
5. The brooklyn bridge has been linking brooklyn with manhattan since 1883.
6. Although the empire state building is no longer the world's tallest building, it is still one of the most famous.
7. On liberty island in new york harbor is the world-famous statue of liberty.
8. Manhattan is the home of a floating sea, air, and space museum that is on board the *intrepid*, a world war II aircraft carrier.
9. The oldest church building in new york, saint paul's chapel, stands on broadway across from city hall park.
10. A golden statue of the ancient greek god prometheus looks over the lower plaza at rockefeller center.

▼ **Critical Viewing** Write a sentence describing this bridge and the two places it connects. What words should you capitalize? [Connect]

The Brooklyn Bridge has a unique appearance.

Capitalization • **643**

Capitalizing Names of Other Special Proper Nouns

1. Have volunteers read each category in the chart.
2. Then have students provide additional examples.

Answer Key

Exercise 2

1. Jazz musicians in the 1920s nicknamed New York City the "Big Apple."
2. The city is divided into five boroughs: Manhattan, Brooklyn, the Bronx, Queens, and Staten Island.
3. Each year millions of tourists travel to this beautiful city in the Northeast to visit its wide variety of attractions.
4. In the middle of Manhattan is Central Park, the best known of the city's more than one hundred parks.
5. The Brooklyn Bridge has been linking Brooklyn with Manhattan since 1883.
6. Although the Empire State Building is no longer the world's tallest building, it is still one of the most famous.
7. On Liberty Island in New York Harbor is the world-famous Statue of Liberty.
8. Manhattan is the home of a floating sea, air, and space museum that is on board the *Intrepid*, a World War II aircraft carrier.
9. The oldest church building in New York, Saint Paul's Chapel, stands on Broadway across from City Hall Park.
10. A golden statue of the ancient Greek god Prometheus looks over the Lower Plaza at Rockefeller Center.

Critical Viewing

Connect Students may say that the Brooklyn Bridge connects Brooklyn and Manhattan.

Rule Reminder Reference Cards

Teaching Resources: Hands-on Grammar Activity Book, Chapter 28

1. Have students refer to their Hands-on Grammar activity books or give them copies of the relevant pages for this activity.

2. Carefully review with students the instructions for constructing the reference cards.

3. Remind students to add more cards in the appropriate category as they learn new rules.

Find It in Your Reading

Have students share any examples they find as they read.

Find It in Your Writing

Have students correct any mistakes they find. Encourage them to refer to their index cards as they review their writing.

28

Hands-on Grammar

Rule Reminder Reference Cards

This chapter includes dozens of important rules about capitalization that you will need to remember. Try this activity to devise your own "rule reminder reference."

Take stacks of index cards in two different colors. On each card of one color write a rule category, such as *Sentence Starters, Quotations, Proper Nouns, Proper Adjectives, Titles,* or *Abbreviations.* On the front of each card of the second color, write a rule from this chapter or that your teacher gives in class. The headings in the different charts in the chapter can help you select rules. On the back of each rule card, write sentences or lists to illustrate the rule.

Take a category card, and arrange under it any rule cards that fit that category. This will help you find the rule you want.

Now, punch a hole into the upper left corner of each card. Place a single loose-leaf ring through the holes to hold the stacks of cards together, or tie them with a piece of heavy string. You can now flip through your reference cards to find the category and rule you need. If you learn new rules, you can open the ring or string and insert a new rule card into its appropriate category. Then, refasten your stack of cards.

Store your rule reminder reference cards in your notebook.

Family
Capitalize titles showing family relationships unless they are preceded by a possessive noun or pronoun

Find It in Your Reading In your reading, find sentences with capitalized proper nouns, proper adjectives, and titles. You might write these sentences as examples on the back of your rule cards.

Find It in Your Writing Look through samples of your own writing to find sentences in which you have used both proper and common nouns to see if you have capitalized them properly. Also, look at any examples of quotations that you have used to see if they are capitalized correctly.

644 • Capitalization

✋ **Hands-on Grammar Book**
Use the Hands-on Grammar activity sheet for Chapter 28 to facilitate this activity.

Capitalizing Proper Adjectives

A proper adjective is a proper noun used as an adjective or an adjective formed from a proper noun.

KEY CONCEPT Capitalize most proper adjectives. ■

EXAMPLES: New York cabdriver
a Korean restaurant

Some proper adjectives, however, have been used so often that they have lost their capitals, such as *french fries* and *teddy bear.*

Here are a few exceptions that you should know concerning proper adjectives.

KEY CONCEPT Do not capitalize prefixes with proper adjectives unless the prefix refers to a nationality. ■

EXAMPLES: all-American   Sino-Russian
pre-Renaissance   Anglo-American
pro-Mexican

KEY CONCEPT In a hyphenated adjective, capitalize only the proper adjective. ■

EXAMPLE: French-speaking Canadians

Exercise 3 Capitalizing Proper Adjectives Copy the following sentences on your paper, adding needed capitals.

EXAMPLE: I am taking a chinese history course at NYU.
ANSWER: I am taking a Chinese history course at NYU.

1. Tourists love New York City's ethnic diversity. They can find everything from an egyptian mummy exhibit at the Metropolitan Museum of Art to an authentic mongolian, greek, or ethiopian meal at an ethnic restaurant.
2. During the 1650's, only about 1,000 people lived in the dutch colony of New Amsterdam on Manhattan Island.
3. During the 1800's and early 1900's, millions of european immigrants came to the city seeking a better life.
4. Since the mid-1900's, many african Americans from the southern states have moved to New York City.
5. Many spanish-speaking americans from caribbean and south american countries have also looked to New York City as a place to find a better life.

▲ **Critical Viewing**
What proper adjectives would you capitalize in a sentence describing immigrants from different countries viewing the Statue of Liberty? **[Describe]**

Capitalizing Proper Adjectives

1. Remind students that most proper adjectives require capitalization because they are formed from proper nouns.
2. Review with students the exceptions on this page. Tell them that they may come upon other exceptions in their reading and writing. Encourage them to record these exceptions when they find them.

Answer Key

Exercise 3

1. Tourists love New York City's ethnic diversity. They can find everything from an Egyptian mummy exhibit at the Metropolitan Museum of Art to an authentic Mongolian, Greek, or Ethiopian meal at an ethnic restaurant.
2. During the 1650's, only about 1,000 people lived in the Dutch colony of New Amsterdam on Manhattan Island.
3. During the 1800's and early 1900's, millions of European immigrants came to the city seeking a better life.
4. Since the mid-1900's, many African Americans from the southern states have moved to New York City.
5. Many Spanish-speaking Americans from Caribbean and South American countries have also looked to New York City as a place to find a better life.

☑ ONGOING ASSESSMENT: Monitor and Reinforce

If students miss more than two items in Exercises 1–3, refer them to the following resources for additional support.

In the Textbook	Print Resources	Technology
Chapter Review, Ex. 6, 8, p. 649	Grammar Exercise Workbook, pp. 163–166	Language Lab CD-ROM, Capitalization and Punctuation; On-Line Exercise Bank, Section 28

Capitalizing Titles

1. Reinforce the rule that most titles are only capitalized when followed by the person's name or used in direct address.

2. Share the following examples with students:

   Doctor Cooper is running late today.

   The doctor is running late today.

   Are you running late, Doctor?

Integrating Workplace Skills

Business letters to people at companies or organizations often include the addressee's title, which is capitalized to show respect:

   Mr. Paul Schmidt, Director

   National Translation Center

   Ms. Beatrice Collins, Editor in Chief

   Applegate Publishing Co.

28

Capitalizing Titles

▶**KEY CONCEPT** Capitalize titles of people and titles of works of art, literature, and music. ■

Titles of People Several rules apply to the titles of people. The first applies to titles used before names and in direct address.

▶**KEY CONCEPT** Capitalize a person's title when it is followed by the person's name or is used in direct address. ■

SOCIAL:	Sir, Madam or Madame, Lord, Lady
BUSINESS:	Professor, Doctor, Superintendent
RELIGIOUS:	Reverend, Bishop, Father, Pope, Sister, Rabbi
MILITARY:	Sergeant, Major, Lieutenant, Admiral, General
GOVERNMENT:	Mayor, Governor, President, Ambassador, Secretary of Defense

▶**KEY CONCEPT** Capitalize the titles of certain high government officials when the titles are not followed by a proper name or used in direct address. ■

The titles of some high government officials are almost always capitalized. These include the titles of the incumbent President and Chief Justice of the Supreme Court and the Queen of England. Notice in the following examples that these titles are often capitalized even when they do not refer to a particular person holding the office.

EXAMPLES: The visiting diplomats were presented to the Queen at a reception.
The Chief Justice is one of nine justices on the Supreme Court.
The President was vacationing at Camp David.

▶**KEY CONCEPT** Capitalize all important words in compound titles, but do not capitalize prefixes and suffixes. ■

EXAMPLES: Vice President
Commander in Chief

If a prefix or suffix is part of the title, it is not capitalized.

EXAMPLES: ex-Senator Smith
President-elect Jefferson

646 • Capitalization

More Practice

Language Lab
CD-ROM
• Problems with Capitalization lesson
On-line
Exercise Bank
• Section 28
Grammar Exercise
Workbook
• pp. 167–168

⏱ TIME AND RESOURCE MANAGER

Resources
Print: Grammar Exercises Workbook, pp. 167–168
Technology: Language Lab CD-ROM, Capitalization and Punctuation; On-Line Exercise Bank, Section 28

In-Depth Coverage	Accelerated Pace
• Work through all key concepts, pp. 646–648. • Assign and review Exercise 4–5.	• Assign pp. 646–648 for independent student review.

KEY CONCEPT Capitalize titles showing family relationships when they refer by themselves to a specific person or when they are used in direct address. ∎

EXAMPLES: Long ago, Grandfather Pleski took me to the Bronx Zoo.
I need a new jacket, Mother.
Did Father buy the tickets for the play?
Stan's grandmother once played the violin.

Titles of Things Titles are given not only to people but also to things such as written works and other works of art.

KEY CONCEPT Capitalize the first word and all other key words in the titles of books, periodicals, poems, stories, plays, paintings, and other works of art. ∎

All words in a title should be capitalized except articles (*a, an, the*) and prepositions and conjunctions with fewer than four letters. These words are capitalized only when they are the first and last word in a title.

EXAMPLES: *The Grapes of Wrath*
"There Is a Longing"
A Tour Through America's Museums

When capitalizing a subtitle, use the same rule that you use for titles. Notice in the following example that *A* is capitalized because it is the first word in the subtitle.

EXAMPLE: *Art History: A Look at Great Masterpieces*

◀ **Critical Viewing**
Write a title that includes a subtitle for a new book about the Bronx Zoo. What words should be capitalized in your title? [Connect]

Capitalizing Titles of Things

1. Tell students that titles of written works and works of art are capitalized because they are proper nouns.
2. Make sure students understand the rules for capitalizing articles, prepositions, and conjunctions in titles.

Customize for *ESL Students*

Many students may find the rules of capitalization confusing, because they vary greatly from one language to the next. For example, in French and Spanish, only the first word and any proper nouns in a title are capitalized. When in doubt, students should always capitalize the important words of titles in English.

Critical Viewing

Connect Students may come up with a title such as *The Bronx Zoo: Fun for Families.*

☑ ONGOING ASSESSMENT: Assess Mastery

Use the following resources to assess students' mastery of capitalization.

In the Textbook	Technology
Chapter Review, Ex. 6–9, pp. 15–16 Standardized Test Preparation Workshop, pp. 17–18	On-Line Exercise Bank, Section 28

Step-by-Step Teaching Guide

Capitalizing Titles of Courses

1. Explain to students that, as with titles of people, titles of courses are only capitalized when a specific course is named.

2. The only exception to this rule is language courses. These are always capitalized because they are proper nouns.

Answer Key

Exercise 4

1. Could you direct me, Sir, to Times Square?
2. We invited General Sadler to the play.
3. Last week, the President of the United States had a meeting at the United Nations headquarters in New York City.
4. While visiting in New York City, Reverend Casey was sure to stop at Saint Patrick's Cathedral.
5. Last summer, we visited Grandmother Johnson and several aunts in Idaho.

Exercise 5

1. *The Nutcracker*
2. *The Wall Street Journal*
3. *Porgy and Bess*
4. *The Sweet and Sour Animal Book*, *The Dream Keeper*
5. *The Sunshine Boys*

Critical Viewing

Analyze Students should say that *building* is only capitalized when it is part of the actual name of the building. If you were referring to the building in a generic sense, it would not be capitalized.

▶ **KEY CONCEPT** Capitalize titles of courses when the courses are language courses or when the courses are followed by a number. ■

EXAMPLES: French   Chemistry 1A   Economics 313

The capital letters are dropped when school subjects are discussed in a general way and no specific course is named. Languages, however, always receive capitals.

EXAMPLES: Last year, I studied chemistry and French.
After English class, I have to rush to biology.

▶ **Exercise 4** **Capitalizing Titles of People** Copy the following sentences, adding the missing capitals.
1. Could you direct me, sir, to Times Square?
2. We invited general Sadler to the play.
3. Last week, the president of the United States had a meeting at the United Nations headquarters in New York City.
4. While visiting in New York City, reverend Casey was sure to stop at Saint Patrick's Cathedral.
5. Last summer, we visited grandmother Johnson and several aunts in Idaho.

▶ **Exercise 5** **Capitalizing Titles of Things** Copy the titles that need capitalization in the following sentences, adding the missing capitals. Underline any titles that appear in italics.

EXAMPLE: Have you read the novel *the red pony* by Steinbeck?

ANSWER: The Red Pony

1. I went to Lincoln Center to see *the nutcracker* performed by the New York City Ballet.
2. *the wall street journal* is a respected newspaper that presents the news from the point of view of business people.
3. The New York City composer George Gershwin wrote the famous folk opera *porgy and bess*.
4. Langston Hughes, a famous poet of the Harlem Renaissance of the 1920's, also wrote the children's books *the sweet and sour animal book* and *the dream keeper*.
5. We saw a revival of Neil Simon's play *the sunshine boys* at a theater on Broadway.

The Federal Building (in front) is the spot where George Washington was inaugurated as President.

▲ **Critical Viewing** When would you capitalize the word *building* in a caption about this photo? When would you not need a capital letter? [Analyze]

⏱ TIME SAVERS!

▪ **Answers on Transparency** Use the Grammar Exercises on Transparencies for Chapter 28 to have students correct their own or one another's exercises.

▪ **On-Line Exercise Bank** Have students complete the exercises on computer. The Auto Check feature will grade their work for you!

✎ STANDARDIZED TEST PREPARATION WORKSHOP

Capitalization Standardized tests often measure students' ability to apply the rules of capitalization to a given passage. Share the following example with students:

Choose the letter of the underlined portion of the passage that contains an error in capitalization.

<u>In our french class</u> yesterday, <u>Mr. Masan</u> had us
   A   B

read a passage from one of <u>Victor Hugo's novels.</u>
                        C

<u>No error.</u>
 D

The correct answer is item **A**. *French* is a proper adjective and should be capitalized.

Chapter Review

GRAMMAR EXERCISES 6–12

Exercise 6 **Capitalizing Sentences and Proper Nouns Correctly** Copy the following sentences onto your paper, adding the missing capitals.

1. movies have made central park perhaps one of the best-known city parks in the world.
2. this park, designed by frederick law olmsted and calvert vaux, occupies 5 percent of the land area of manhattan.
3. central park was developed between 1856 and 1875, and it has many interesting features: the great lawn, the sheep meadow, belvedere castle, bethesda fountain, and wollman rink.
4. "let's skate at wollman rink in Central park," my brother suggested, "to try out our new skates."
5. "sure," I replied. "can we take the subway directly to the park?"

Exercise 7 **Capitalizing Titles Correctly** Copy the titles below onto your paper, and add capitals where necessary. Underline titles that are printed in italics.

1. book: *the empire state building: the making of a landmark*
2. play: *lost in yonkers*
3. magazine: *the new yorker*
4. song: "east side, west side"
5. movie: *manhattan murder mystery*
6. elected official: mayor edward koch
7. newspaper: the *new york daily news*
8. poem: "spring and all"
9. military title: lieutenant commander
10. clergy: reverend william d. morrison

Exercise 8 **Capitalizing Proper Nouns, Proper Adjectives, and Titles Correctly** Copy the following sentences onto your paper, adding the missing capitals. Underline any titles that appear in italics.

1. New York City served as the first american capital, and president george washington was inaugurated there.
2. Throughout history, many influential new yorkers have entertained and educated us and helped us create a better american way of life.
3. Have you read the short story "*rip van winkle,*" written by Washington Irving, who was born in New York city?
4. One of the most celebrated american poets, Walt Whitman, spent most of his life in brooklyn.
5. james baldwin—author of many essays, plays, and novels, including *go tell it on the mountain*—was born and raised in new york city.
6. The director Woody Allen has used the city for the setting of many of his films, such as *manhattan, broadway danny rose,* and *annie hall.*
7. Eleanor Roosevelt, the wife of present Franklin d. Roosevelt helped improve conditions for minorities and the poor.
8. Colin Powell, the son of caribbean immigrants, grew up in the south bronx.
9. general Powell became the first african American chairman of the joint chiefs of staff in 1989.
10. The retired general wrote a book about his life, *my american journey,* in 1995.

Exercise 9 **Proofreading to Correct Capitalization Errors of Sentences and Proper Nouns** Copy the following passage on a separate sheet of paper. Correct all errors in capitalization of proper nouns or first words in sentences.

When the Empire State building first opened in 1931, it was the tallest building in the World. The building contains 102 floors. located in the middle of manhattan, the Empire state Building was once the site of a mansion for millionaire john jacob

ASSESS and CLOSE

Chapter Review

Each of these exercises correlates to a concept taught in the chapter on capitalization, pages 636–648. The exercises may be used for more practice, for reteaching, or for review of the Key Concepts presented. Answers for all chapter exercises are available on *Grammar Exercises Answers on Transparencies* in your teaching resources.

Answer Key

Exercise 6

1. Movies; Central Park
2. This; Frederick Law Olmstead; Calvert Vaux; Manhattan
3. Central Park; Great Lawn; Sheep Meadow; Belvedere Castle; Bethesda Fountain; Wollman Rink.
4. Let's; Wollman Rink; Park
5. Sure; Can

Exercise 7

1. <u>The Empire State Building: The Making of a Landmark</u>
2. <u>Lost in Yonkers</u>
3. <u>The New Yorker</u>
4. "East Side, West Side"
5. <u>Manhattan Murder Mystery</u>
6. Mayor Edward Koch
7. The <u>New York Daily News</u>
8. "Spring and All"
9. no capitalization necessary
10. Reverend William D. Morrison

Exercise 8

1. New York City served as the first American capital and President George Washington was inaugurated there.
2. Throughout history, many influential New Yorkers have entertained and educated us and helped us create a better American way of life.
3. Have you read the short story "Rip Van Winkle," written by Washington Irving who was born in New York City?
4. One of the most celebrated American poets, Walt Whitman, spent most of his life in Brooklyn.
5. James Baldwin—author of many essays, plays, and novels, including <u>Go Tell It on the Mountain</u>—was born and raised in New York City.

continued

Answer Key continued

6. The director Woody Allen has used the city for the setting of many of his films, such as <u>Manhattan</u>, <u>Broadway Danny Rose</u>, and <u>Annie Hall</u>.
7. Eleanor Roosevelt, wife of President Franklin D. Roosevelt, helped improve conditions for minorities and the poor.
8. Colin Powell, the son of Caribbean immigrants, grew up in the South Bronx.
9. General Powell became the first African-American chairman of the Joint Chiefs of Staff in 1989.
10. The retired general wrote a book about his life, <u>My American Journey</u>, in 1995.

Exercise 9 (page 649)

Building; world; Located; Manhattan; State: John Jacob Astor; hotel; office building; today; More; Aunt; aunt; Uncle Bill; February; building; Some; We; romantic; New York

Exercise 10

1. Last summer, I spent two weeks with Grandmother Olsen in Riverdale, a neighborhood in the Bronx.
2. My grandmother and I visited places all around the city: historical buildings, parks, museums, as well as the Bronx Zoo and the New York Botanical Gardens.
3. We often consulted a travel guide, called <u>Seeing New York: The Best Places, and the Best Prices,</u> for information.
4. The Castle Clinton, in Battery Park, was actually built as a fort to defend the city in the War of 1812.
5. Theodore Roosevelt was born on East 20th Street. Grant's Tomb is near the Hudson River.
6. On a Saturday in August, Grandmother and I went to the Bronx Zoo. Our tour guide said it is "One of the finest and largest zoos in the United States."
7. I especially enjoyed riding the monorail through the Asian exhibit.
8. The New York Botanical Garden is right next to the zoo, and my grandmother and I spent a wonderful Sunday there.
9. "I love to see the roses," she said, "and I want you to see the beautiful Japanese cherry trees."
10. Both my dad and my aunt Susan attended Catholic elementary schools in New York and later studied engineering at Columbia University.

Exercise 11

York's; Chinatown; Manhattan; Canal Street; Chinese; Canton; Hunan; Szechwan; Chinese; history; Oriental art; traditional medicines; philosopher; Confucius; Confucius Plaza; Chinatown; Chinese Consolidated Benevolent Association of Chinatown; statue's; Chinese; English

Chapter Review Exercises cont'd.

astor. It was later replaced by a Hotel and then the giant Office Building that stands there Today. more than 15,000 people work inside the building, and 20,000 more visit it each day.

"It's a great place to work, said my aunt Gloria, "As long as you don't mind crowds and long elevator rides."

Not only does my Aunt work in the Empire State Building, but she and my uncle bill were also married there on valentine's day in 1980. Every year, a large group wedding ceremony is held on february 14 on the eightieth floor of the Building.

"some people think it is just a cold office building," Aunt gloria commented. "we think it is the most Romantic spot in new york City.

Exercise 10 Proofreading Sentences to Correct Errors in Capitalization Copy the following sentences onto your paper, adding missing capitals and correcting any errors in capitalization. Underline any titles that appear in italics.

1. last Summer, I spent two weeks with grandmother Olsen in riverdale, a Neighborhood in the bronx.
2. My Grandmother and I visited places all around the City: Historical buildings, parks, Museums, as well as the bronx zoo and the new york botanical garden.
3. We often consulted a travel guide, called *seeing new york: the best places, and the best prices,* for information.
4. The castle Clinton, in Battery park, was actually built as a Fort to defend the City in the war Of 1812.
5. Theodore Roosevelt was born on east 20th street. Grant's tomb is near the hudson river.

6. On a saturday in august, grandmother and I went to the Bronx zoo. Our Tour Guide said it is "One of the finest and largest zoos in the united states."
7. I especially enjoyed riding the Monorail through the asian exhibit.
8. The New York botanical garden is right next to the Zoo, and my Grandmother and i spent a wonderful sunday there.
9. "I love to see the Roses," she said, "And I wanted you to see the beautiful japanese cherry trees."
10. both my Dad and my Aunt Susan attended catholic elementary Schools in New york and later studied Engineering at columbia university.

Exercise 11 Proofreading Practice: Applying All the Rules of Capitalization Revise the paragraph below, adding and removing capitals as needed.

New york's chinatown is squeezed into a tiny area in lower manhattan. Starting on canal street, visitors can shop in hundreds of open storefront businesses or sample cuisine from many different chinese regions: Including canton, hunan, and szechwan. Students of chinese History will find rare and unusual books. Collectors of oriental Art will find many wonderful pieces. Those interested in Traditional Medicines will find these as well. A large statue of the Chinese Philosopher confucius stands before confucius plaza in chinatown. It was a gift of the chinese consolidated benevolent association of chinatown. The Statue's base is carved with wise sayings in chinese and english.

Exercise 12 Writing Application Think of a vacation trip you have taken with your family. Write a journal entry describing the people, places, and things you saw on one day of your trip. Include one or two quotes in your journal entry. Proofread carefully to make sure that you have used capital letters correctly.

Exercise 12

Writing Application
Have students exchange journal entries with partners to check each other's work.

Standardized Test Preparation Workshop

Lesson Objectives
• To proofread for errors in capitalization, spelling, and punctuation.

Proofreading for Errors in Capitalization, Spelling, and Punctuation

Many standardized tests measure your ability to proofread a passage and identify the type of error contained in a given section. The following items will allow you to practice this skill.

Test Tip

Although "No error" is sometimes the correct choice, do not choose this option too quickly. Always double-check to make sure you haven't missed an error.

Proofreading for Errors in Capitalization, Spelling, and Punctuation

1. Explain to students that they should approach each question carefully, first reading the passage for capitalization errors, then spelling errors, and then punctuation errors.

2. Tell students it may be helpful to circle or underline any errors they find as they read.

Answer Key

Practice 1
1. D
2. H
3. A
4. G

Sample Test Item	Answer and Explanation
Directions: Read the sentence, and decide which type of error, if any, appears in the underlined section. I asked <u>my Grandmother from Chicago</u> (1) to come over for dinner.	
1 A Spelling error B Capitalization error C Punctuation error D No error	The correct answer is *B*. Titles expressing family relationships, such as *grandmother,* are not capitalized when they follow a possessive pronoun, such as *my.*

Practice 1 **Directions:** Read the passage, and decide which type of error, if any, appears in each underlined section.

<u>After Grandma finished dinner,</u> I asked her
(1)
<u>a lot of questions,</u> for my history report.
(2)
I wanted <u>to no about her life in the Midwest</u>
(3)
<u>during the great depression.</u>
(4)

1 A Spelling error
  B Capitalization error
  C Punctuation error
  D No error

2 F Spelling error
  G Capitalization error
  H Punctuation error
  J No error

3 A Spelling error
  B Capitalization error
  C Punctuation error
  D No error

4 F Spelling error
  G Capitalization error
  H Punctuation error
  J No error

TEST-TAKING TIP

Students should pay extra-special attention to spelling errors, which involves carefully reading each word in a passage. Homophones can be extremely tricky, since the word may be spelled correctly. Students might miss these types of spelling errors if they do not use context clues to help determine the meaning of the word. Point out item 3 in Practice 1 as an example.

In-Depth Lesson Plan

LESSON FOCUS	PRINT AND MEDIA RESOURCES
DAY 1 — **End Marks and Commas** Students learn and apply concepts of punctuation covering end marks and commas and do the Hands-on Grammar activity (pp. 654–673).	**Teaching Resources** *Grammar Exercise Workbook*, pp. 169–178; *Grammar Exercises Answers on Transparency*, Ch. 29; *Hands-on Grammar Activity Book*, Chapter 29; *Language Lab* **CD-ROM**, Punctuation; *On-Line Exercise Bank*, Sections 29.1–2
DAY 2 — **Semicolons and Colons** Students learn and apply concepts of punctuation covering semicolons and colons (pp. 674–683).	**Teaching Resources** *Grammar Exercise Workbook*, pp. 179–182; *Grammar Exercises Answers on Transparency*, Ch. 29; *Language Lab* **CD-ROM**, Punctuation; *On-Line Exercise Bank*, Section 29.3
DAY 3 — **Quotation Marks, Dashes, Parentheses, and Hyphens** Students learn and apply concepts of punctuation covering quotation marks, dashes, parentheses and hyphens (pp. 684–711).	**Teaching Resources** *Grammar Exercise Workbook*, pp. 183–194; *Grammar Exercises Answers on Transparency*, Ch. 29; *Language Lab* **CD-ROM**, Punctuation; *On-Line Exercise Bank*, Sections 29.4–5
DAY 4 — **Apostrophes** Students learn and apply concepts of punctuation covering apostrophes (pp. 712–721).	**Teaching Resources** *Grammar Exercise Workbook*, pp. 195–200; *Grammar Exercises Answers on Transparency*, Ch. 29; *Language Lab* **CD-ROM**, Punctuation; *On-Line Exercise Bank*, Section 29.6
DAY 5 — **Review and Assess** Students review chapter and demonstrate mastery of use of punctuation (pp. 722–727).	**Teaching Resources** *Formal Assessment*, Ch. 29; *On-Line Exercise Bank*, Section 29.1

Accelerated Lesson Plan

LESSON FOCUS	PRINT AND MEDIA RESOURCES
DAY 1 — **End Marks and Commas** Students cover concepts and usage of end marks and commas as determined by Diagnostic Test (pp. 654–673).	**Teaching Resources** *Grammar Exercise Workbook*, pp. 169–178; *Grammar Exercises Answers on Transparency*, Ch. 29; *Hands-on Grammar Activity Book*, Chapter 29; *Language Lab* **CD-ROM**, Punctuation; *On-Line Exercise Bank*, Sections 29.1–2
DAY 2 — **Semicolons, Colons, and Quotation Marks** Students cover concepts and usage of semicolons, colons, and quotation marks as determined by Diagnostic Test (pp. 674–697).	**Teaching Resources** *Grammar Exercise Workbook*, pp. 179–188; *Grammar Exercises Answers on Transparency*, Ch. 29; *Language Lab* **CD-ROM**, Punctuation; *On-Line Exercise Bank*, Sections 29.3–4
DAY 3 — **Dashes, Parentheses, Hyphens, and Apostrophes** Students learn and apply concepts of punctuation covering dashes, parentheses, hyphens, and apostrophes (pp. 698–721).	**Teaching Resources** *Grammar Exercise Workbook*, pp.189–200; *Grammar Exercises Answers on Transparency*, Ch. 29; *Language Lab* **CD-ROM**, Punctuation; *On-Line Exercise Bank*, Sections 29.5–6
DAY 4 — **Review and Assess** Students review chapter and demonstrate mastery of use of punctuation (pp. 722–727).	**Teaching Resources** *Formal Assessment*, Ch. 29; *On-Line Exercise Bank*, Sections 29.1

Options for Adapting Lesson Plans

HOMEWORK

Have students complete any section of the chapter for homework

FEATURES

Extend coverage with the Grammar in Literature feature (p. 664), and the Standardized Test Preparation Workshop (p. 724).

TECHNOLOGY

Students can use the On-Line Exercise Bank to complete the exercises on computer. The Auto Check feature will grade their work.

INTEGRATED SKILLS COVERAGE

Grammar in Literature
SE p. 664

Reading
Find It in Your Reading, SE p. 657, 673, 683, 697, 711, 721

Writing
Find It In Your Writing, SE p. 657, 673, 683, 697, 711, 721
Writing Application, SE pp. 657, 673, 683, 697, 711, 721, 723, 727

Speaking and Listening
Integrating Speaking and Listening, ATE p. 663

Technology
Technology Tip, SE p. 691; ATE p. 704

Workplace Skills
Integrating Workplace Skills, ATE p. 713

Viewing and Representing
Critical Viewing, SE pp. 652, 654, 656, 659, 661, 665, 666, 668, 670, 675, 677, 678, 681, 685, 686, 688, 690, 693, 694, 696, 700, 703, 704, 707, 708, 715, 716, 719

ASSESSMENT SUPPORT

Standardized Test Preparation, SE p. 724; ATE p. 660
Standardized Test Preparation Workbook, pp. 57–58
Formal Assessment, Ch. 29

MEETING INDIVIDUAL NEEDS

Less Advanced Students, ATE pp. 654, 667, 676, 685, 689, 709; See also Ongoing Assessments, ATE pp. 652, 656, 662, 666, 668, 672, 677, 681, 682, 695, 696, 705, 708, 709, 710, 717, 719, 720
ESL Students, ATE pp. 655, 702, 712
More Advanced Students, ATE pp. 665, 674, 687, 700
Logical/Mathematical Learners, ATE p. 656
Visual/Spatial Learners, ATE p. 662

BLOCK SCHEDULING

Pacing Suggestions
For 90 minute Blocks
• Administer the Diagnostic Test to students to determine instructional coverage
• Have students complete the necessary exercises in class. Use the Hands-on Grammar activity to provide a change of pace.

Resources for Varying Instruction
• *Language Lab* **CD-ROM** If your students have access to hardware, a 90 minute block provides an ideal opportunity for students to work on computer.

Professional Development Support
• *How to Manage Instruction in the Block* This teaching resource provides management and activity suggestions.

MEDIA AND TECHNOLOGY

For the Student
• *Language Lab* **CD-ROM,** Punctuation
• *On-Line Exercise Bank,* Ch. 29

For the Teacher
• *Resource Pro* **CD-ROM**

WRITING AND GRAMMAR WEBSITE

The Interactive Writing and Grammar Website provides a wide array of support for students, teachers, and parents. Grammar support includes:

• On-Line Exercise Bank with Auto Check scoring
• Diagnostic and assessment support

phwg.phschool.com

LITERATURE CONNECTIONS

Grammar in Literature selections from *Prentice Hall Literature: Timeless Voices, Timeless Themes,* Gold:

from *Checkouts,* Cynthia Rylant, SE p. 664

Lesson Objectives

1. To demonstrate knowledge of correct use of periods, question marks, and exclamation marks.

2. To use commas correctly with compound sentences.

3. To use commas correctly between items in a series and between adjectives.

4. To use commas after introductory material.

5. To use commas with parenthetical expressions and nonessential expressions.

6. To use commas with dates and geographical names.

7. To recognize correct uses of a semicolon and a colon.

8. To recognize correct uses of quotation marks with direct quotations.

9. To identify indirect quotations.

10. To recognize correct use of quotation marks with other punctuation marks.

11. To identify correct use of quotation marks with dialogue.

12. To understand use of quotation marks, underlining, and italics.

13. To identify correct uses of the dash, parentheses, and the hyphen.

14. To identify correct uses of apostrophes.

Critical Viewing

Connect Students may say they allow a climber to rest.

Chapter 29 Punctuation

Hiking is a sport steeped in variety. Some hikes are short, while others are long; some wind through shady forests, while others trek through dry deserts. Certain tools, like a compass, help hikers navigate an overland course.

Writing sentences, like hiking, takes readers on a course through your ideas. Certain tools, like the punctuation marks you add, will help guide your readers.

When used accurately and effectively, punctuation marks help your readers follow your ideas. In this chapter, you will learn about the most important punctuation marks: commas, semicolons, colons, quotation marks, dashes, parentheses, apostrophes, and end marks.

▲ **Critical Viewing**
Why are pauses and stops important to a rock climber?
[Connect]

652 • Punctuation

	☑ ONGOING ASSESSMENT: Diagnose				

If students miss more than one item in each category, direct them to the relevant pages of the text and assign exercises for practice and review.

Punctuation	Diagnostic Test Items	Teach	Practice	Section Review	Chapter Review
Skill Check A					
Commas and End Marks	A 1–5	pp. 654–671	Ex. 1, 7–13	Ex. 2–6, 14–19	Ex. 66
Skill Check B					
Semicolons and Colons	B 6–10	pp. 674–682	Ex. 20–23	Ex. 24–29	Ex. 67
Skill Check C					
Quotation Marks, Underlining, Dashes, Parentheses, and Hyphens	C 11–15	pp. 684–710	Ex. 30–35, 42–47	Ex. 36–41, 48–53	Ex. 68–70

Diagnostic Test

Directions: Write all answers on a separate sheet of paper.

Skill Check A. Rewrite the following sentences, adding the appropriate commas and end marks.

1. Mountain climbing which is also called alpinism or mountaineering can be a life-threatening sport
2. Which steep dangerous mountains are considered the most important
3. The Himalayas attract the very best mountaineers who face high altitudes extreme cold and severe weather
4. Someone may ask you which peak is the highest in the Himalayas Surprise It is Mt Everest
5. Mt. Everest the highest peak in all the Himalayas and in all the world was first climbed by Sir Edmund Hillary and Tenzing Norgay

Skill Check B. Rewrite the following sentences, adding the appropriate semicolons and colons.

6. Mountaineers climbing on ice slopes must bring the appropriate tools climbing ropes, ice axes, and metal spikes or crampons.
7. They use the ropes in a rope harness that fits around the climbers' waists this protects them if they fall.
8. The job of a belayer is to stand at the bottom of a cliff, to keep tight the ropes connecting climbers, and to pull in the slack yet, surely, the most important role is to prevent the climbers from falling.
9. The *World Book Encyclopedia* explains "While advancing, the lead climber inserts pieces of gear into the snow, ice, or cracks in the rock, securing the rope to them with a snap link."
10. The lead climber belays the second climber the second climber reaches the top of the cliff the lead climber belays the third climber.

Skill Check C. Rewrite the following sentences, adding commas, quotation marks, underlining, dashes, hyphens, or parentheses. Divide any underlined words as if they were at the end of a line.

11. While hiking or <u>mountain</u> climbing, you might ask Are there any tips that I should keep in mind?
12. Yes answered George and I would <u>suggest</u> you read The Rock Climber's Handbook.
13. While I was hiking Brenda <u>continued</u> I saw a sign that read Please keep it cleaner than when you arrived.
14. Alpine style climbing you have to be half crazy to be a true fan of this! is said to be the purest and most <u>dangerous</u> way to climb a mountain.
15. Those who <u>participate</u> in mountaineering no matter how young or how old are usually serious climbers looking for new routes and new adventures.

10. The lead climber belays the second climber; the second climber reaches the top of the cliff; the lead climber belays the third climber.

Skill Check C

11. While hiking or mountain climbing, you might ask, "Are there any tips that I should keep in mind?"; moun-tain
12. "Yes," answered George, "and I would suggest you read <u>The Rock Climber's Handbook</u>."; sug-gest
13. "While I was hiking," Brenda continued, "I saw a sign that read: 'Please keep it cleaner than when you arrived.'"; con-tinued
14. Alpine-style climbing (You have to be half crazy to be a true fan of this!) is said to be the purest and most dangerous way to climb a mountain.; dan-gerous
15. Those who participate in mountaineering — no matter how young or how old—are usually serious climbers looking for new routes and new adventures.; par-ticipate

Diagnostic Test

- Each item in the diagnostic test corresponds to a specific concept in the chapter on punctuation. This will enable you to tailor instruction to the particular needs of your students. See "Ongoing Assessment System" on the bottom of page 656 for further details.

- Answers for the Diagnostic Test and all chapter exercises are available in *Grammar Exercises Answers on Transparencies* in your teaching resources.

Skill Check A

1. Mountain climbing, which is also called alpinism or mountaineering, can be a life threatening sport.
2. Which steep, dangerous mountains are considered the most important?
3. The Himalayas attract the very best mountaineers, who face high altitudes, extreme cold, and severe weather.
4. Someone may ask you which peak is the highest in the Himalayas. Surprise! It is Mt. Everest.
5. Mt. Everest, the highest peak in all the Himalayas and in all the world, was first climbed by Sir Edmund Hillary and Tenzing Norgay.

Skill Check B

6. Mountaineers climbing on ice slopes must bring the appropriate tools: climbing ropes, ice axes, and metal spikes or crampons.
7. They use the ropes in a rope harness that fits around the climbers' waists; this protects them if they fall.
8. The job of a belayer is to stand at the bottom of a cliff, to keep tight the ropes connecting climbers, and to pull in the slack; yet, surely, the most important role is to prevent climbers from falling.
9. The *World Book Encyclopedia* explains: "While advancing, the lead climber inserts pieces of gear into the snow, ice, or cracks in the rock, securing the rope to them with a snap link."

continued

Interest GRABBER Write the following on the board and ask students to read it aloud and add capitalization and punctuation.

Is this the art room my job is to put up these posters what a fantastic painting did you do this (Is this the art room? My job is to put up these posters. What a fantastic painting! Did you do this?)

Activate Prior Knowledge

Ask students why punctuation is important. (Without it, all the sentences run together and you can't understand them, as in the Interest Grabber.)

TEACH

Step-by-Step Teaching Guide

Basic Uses of End Marks

Most sentences end with a period. A period signals a statement or a command.

Customize for
Less Advanced Students

Some students may be confused by the text examples. All declarative sentences end with a period. Declarative sentences declare, or state, something—facts, opinions, indirect questions, most anything.

Critical Viewing

Speculate Students may respond with "Was it rough?" or "How was your climb?"

Section 29.1

End Marks

Just as every sentence must begin with a capital letter, so every sentence must end with an end mark. The three end marks are the period (.), the question mark (?), and the exclamation mark (!). These marks clearly indicate to a reader that you have arrived at the end of a thought. End marks also indicate the emotion or tone of a sentence so that the reader knows with what kind of expression it should be read. End marks can serve other important functions, as well. In this section, you will have the opportunity to review the more common uses of end marks and to study some of their other functions.

Basic Uses of End Marks

The period, the most common end mark, has three basic uses:

▶ **KEY CONCEPT** Use a period (.) to end a declarative sentence, a mild imperative, and an indirect question. ■

Declarative sentences include statements of fact and statements of opinion. Both types of statements require a period.

STATEMENT OF FACT: Some hikes can last for weeks.
STATEMENT OF OPINION: Hiking is the most exciting sport.

You should also place a period at the end of a mildly worded command called a *mild imperative*. You can recognize these sentences easily because they often begin with a verb and have an "understood you" as their subject.

MILD IMPERATIVE: Change your shoes quickly.

Indirect questions also require a period. An indirect question needs no answer; instead, it is a statement that refers to a question that might be or has been asked.

DIRECT QUESTION: Are the pants on sale?
INDIRECT QUESTION: I asked whether the pants were on sale.

A sentence that asks a direct question, one to which an answer might be made, is an interrogative sentence. The end mark used for interrogative sentences is the question mark.

654 • Punctuation

Theme: Mountain Climbing

In this section, you will learn about the end marks used to punctuate different types of sentences. The examples and exercises are about mountain climbing.

Cross-Curricular Connection:
Physical Education

▼ **Critical Viewing**
What questions might these climbers ask someone coming down the path that they are climbing? [Speculate]

TIME AND RESOURCE MANAGER

Resources
Print: Grammar Exercise Workbook, pp. 169–170
Technology: Language Lab CD-ROM, Punctuation; On-Line Exercise Bank, Section 29.1

In-Depth Coverage	Accelerated Pace
• Work through all key concepts, pp. 654–655. • Assign and review Exercise 1, p. 656.	• Assign pp. 654–655 for independent student review.

▶**KEY CONCEPT** Use a question mark (?) to end a direct question, an incomplete question, or a statement intended as a question. ■

A direct question demands an answer; it stands as a direct request. All direct questions must end with a question mark.

DIRECT QUESTIONS: Did you dress appropriately for the hike**?**
Which mountain are you planning to scale**?**

In some cases, only a portion of the question is written out and the rest is simply understood.

INCOMPLETE QUESTIONS: Where**?** What color**?** How much**?**

Sometimes, a question is phrased as if it were a declarative sentence. Use a question mark to show that the sentence is a question.

STATEMENTS INTENDED   You called me**?**
AS QUESTIONS: They have four dogs**?**

An exclamatory sentence shows strong emphasis or emotion. It expresses more feeling than other sentences do. An exclamation mark is used at the end of an exclamatory sentence to indicate the emphasis or emotion it expresses.

▶**KEY CONCEPT** Use an exclamation mark (!) to end an exclamatory sentence, a forceful imperative sentence, or an interjection expressing strong emotion. ■

EXCLAMATORY SENTENCE: The view from the top of the mountain is stunning**!**

A strongly worded imperative that demonstrates forcefulness or strong emotion will also take an exclamation mark.

STRONG IMPERATIVE: Get away from the cliff before you fall**!**

Occasionally (especially in conversations), one or two words are delivered emphatically. These strong interjections should also be followed by an exclamation mark.

STRONG INTERJECTIONS: Breathtaking**!** Ouch**!** Oh**!**

Sometimes, a strong interjection may appear before a short exclamatory sentence. If this occurs, you may use either a comma or an exclamation mark after the interjection.

WITH A COMMA: Goodness, that thunder was loud**!**
WITH AN
EXCLAMATION MARK: Goodness**!** That thunder was loud**!**

Question and Exclamation Marks

1. A question mark ends a direct question and a statement intended as a question.

2. To illustrate further the difference between a direct and indirect question, write the following sentences on the board and ask students to identify each as direct or indirect and supply the correct punctuation.

   She wants to know what you were saying (. indirect)

   What did you ask (? direct)

   Why do you think that (? direct)

   I want to know what got you going in that direction (. indirect)

3. An exclamation mark ends statements that show strong emotion. Both strong commands and exclamatory statements require an exclamation mark.

4. Write the following sentences on the board and ask students to tell why they require an exclamation mark.

   This meal is incredible! (strong emotion)

   Don't touch that! (strong imperative)

   Amazing! (strong interjection)

Customize for
ESL Students

Spanish questions and exclamations use question marks and exclamation marks at the beginning and end of a sentence. In English, only one end mark, is used.

655

Answer Key

Exercise 1

1. it.
2. climbed?
3. Yes. climbed.
4. 1913.
5. Asia.
6. world? Amazing!
7. peak.
8. mountains.
9. Where?
10. Himalayas.

Critical Viewing

Apply Possible answers: Wow! How high are those mountains? They are almost completely covered with snow.

Customize for
Logical/Mathematical Learners

Have students read several paragraphs of a magazine article and count periods, questions mark, and exclamation marks. They can show the results in a bar or circle graph.

29.1

> **Exercise 1** Using the Period, Question Mark, and Exclamation Mark Write the appropriate period, question mark, or exclamation mark with the word preceding it.

EXAMPLE: In mountain climbing, the objective is to reach the peak of a mountain by climbing its slopes

ANSWER: slopes.

1. Mountain climbing started in Europe, where people climbed peaks simply for the fun of it
2. Have all of the major mountain peaks been climbed
3. Yes With the exception of a few peaks in remote areas of the world, most major peaks have been climbed
4. Mount McKinley, the tallest peak in North America, was first climbed in 1913
5. In 1953, Sir Edmund Hillary of New Zealand and Tenzing Norgay of Nepal were the first to reach the summit of Mt. Everest in Asia
6. Can you believe that they were able to climb the tallest mountain in the world Amazing
7. Even today, mountaineers want to be the first to conquer the challenge of a new peak
8. However, the biggest attraction of competitive mountain climbing is finding new routes up challenging mountains
9. Where
10. I have never climbed anywhere more exhilarating and challenging than the Himalayas

▲ **Critical Viewing** Write three sentences about this picture. Use a different end mark for each sentence. [Apply]

> **More Practice**

On-line
Exercise Bank
• Section 29.1
Grammar Exercise Workbook
• pp. 169–170

656 • Punctuation

⏲ TIME SAVERS!

🖥 **Answers on Transparency** Use the Grammar Exercises on Transparencies for Chapter 29 to have students correct their own or one another's exercises.

💻 **On-Line Exercise Bank** Have students complete the exercises on computer. The Auto Check feature will grade their work for you!

☑ ONGOING ASSESSMENT: Monitor and Reinforce

If students miss more than two items in Exercise 1, refer them to the following for additional practice.

In the Textbook	Print Resources	Technology
Chapter Review, Ex. 66, p. 722	Grammar Exercise Workbook, Using End Marks, pp. 169–170	Language Lab CD-ROM, Punctuation; On-Line Exercise Bank, Section 29.1

Section 29.1 Section Review

GRAMMAR EXERCISES 2–6

> **Exercise 2** Punctuating the Ends
> **of Sentences** Write the end mark
required in each of the following sentences.

1. Backpacking is a popular type of hiking
2. Items that are packed must be as lightweight as possible
3. For crying out loud, you can't expect a backpacker to walk for 50 miles with 200 pounds on his back
4. By carrying clothes, food, and plenty of water, a backpacker can spend many days in remote areas where these supplies would normally be unavailable
5. Where Anyplace you want

> **Exercise 3** Identifying Uses of End
> **Marks** Write the correct end mark for
each of the following sentences. Then, label
each sentence *statement of fact, opinion, mild
imperative, direct question, indirect question,
incomplete question, statement intended as a
question, exclamatory sentence, strong imperative,* or *strong interjection.*

1. Besides backpacking, the sport of hiking has several other variations
2. You, as a competitor in orienteering, will compete in a course in the wilderness
3. Locate checkpoints along the course using only your map and compass
4. When you find all the checkpoints before the other teams, you win
5. Snowshoeing, another type of hiking, takes place in the snow
6. How can we learn more about the sport
7. If I tell you that the hiker wears large strung frames on her feet, does that bring an image to your mind
8. These frames distribute body weight over a larger area, so the hiker is better able to walk on top of the snow
9. Who is credited with the invention of this sport

10. Long before Europeans arrived, Native Americans were making frames of wood to walk on the snow

> **Exercise 4** Find It in Your Reading
> Read this excerpt from "Uphill" by
Christina Rosetti. Explain the pattern
formed by the end marks. Then, restate
each line that ends with a period as a
complete sentence.

> Does the road wind uphill all the way?
> Yes, to the very end.
> Will the day's journey take the whole
> long day?
> From morn to night, my friend.
>
> But is there for the night a resting
> place?
> A roof for when the slow dark hours
> begin.
> May not the darkness hide it from my
> face?
> You cannot miss that inn.

> **Exercise 5** Find It in Your Writing
> Select a piece of writing from your portfolio. Identify two sentences that express
strong emotion and that state an opinion.

> **Exercise 6** Writing Application
> Write three original sentences to fit each
situation below. Write each sentence according to the directions for each situation.

1. You missed your bus.
   a. statement of fact
   b. direct question
   c. explanation for being late
2. The cat walked through flour.
   a. humorous exclamation
   b. mild imperative
   c. statement of opinion

Section Review

Each of these exercises correlates to a concept in the section on end marks, pages 654–655. These exercises may be used for more practice, for reteaching, or for review of the Key Concepts presented. Answers for all chapter exercises are available in *Grammar Exercises on Transparencies* in your teaching resources.

Answer Key

> **Exercise 2**

1. .
2. .
3. !
4. .
5. ? .

> **Exercise 3**

1. . statement of fact
2. . mild imperative
3. . mild imperative
4. . statement of fact
5. . statement of fact
6. ? direct question
7. ? statement intended as a question
8. . statement of fact
9. ? direct question
10. . statement of fact

> **Exercise 4**

Find It in Your Reading
Have students check each other's answers.

> **Exercise 5**

Find It in Your Writing
Students should check that their sentences use correct punctuation.

> **Exercise 6**

Writing Application
Answers will vary. Samples are given.

1a. I missed my bus.
 b. Did I miss my bus?
 c. I was late because I missed my bus.
2a. My silly cat walked through the flour and left pawprints all over the rug!
 b. Don't walk through the flour.
 c. Cats are good pets that are worth the trouble.

Activate Prior Knowledge

Ask students to punctuate the following sentence.

Christopher when the class is over it is time to stop working. (Christopher, when the class is over, it is time to stop working.)

TEACH

Step-by-Step Teaching Guide

Commas With Compound Sentences

1. No punctuation mark creates more confusion than the comma. One rule to keep in mind is to use a comma only when there is a reason for using it.

2. Commas separate independent clauses of a compound sentence. But warn students that the shortcut of adding a comma before every coordinating conjunction will result in errors.

3. Use the prepositional-phrases sentence as an example. It is correct without a comma because there is only one subject: *they.* But a tiny change in the sentence makes all the difference.

   They ate lunch in the restaurant, and then they walked around the mall.

   Now the sentence is two independent clauses, each with it own subject *(they, they),* so the comma is needed.

Section 29.2

Commas

A comma represents a short pause. It tells the reader to hesitate before continuing the sentence. Commas also help set up relationships among parts of a sentence and make long sentences easier to read.

The comma is used more than any other internal punctuation mark. As a result, many errors are made in its use. Keep in mind two basic uses of the comma: (1) Commas can be used *to separate* similar items, and (2) one or more commas can be used *to set off* a single item at the beginning, middle, or end of a sentence. Do not use a comma unless there is a comma rule for it.

This section presents rules to help you use the comma correctly to separate basic elements and to set off added elements in sentences.

Commas With Compound Sentences

A compound sentence is two or more independent clauses joined by a coordinating conjunction (*and, but, for, nor, or, so,* and *yet*).

▶ **KEY CONCEPT** Use a comma before the conjunction to separate two independent clauses in a compound sentence. ■

EXAMPLES: Many families in developing countries produce their own food, but most families in the United States rely on the food industry for their food.

The food industry takes food from the place where it is grown, and it distributes the food where it is needed.

Always check to make sure that you have written two complete sentences joined by a coordinating conjunction before you insert a comma.

Sometimes, conjunctions merely join two words, phrases, or subordinate clauses. When they are used in one of these ways, no comma is required.

COMPOUND SUBJECT: Diana and Jill met for lunch at the mall.

COMPOUND VERB: The old friends chatted and laughed as they ate lunch.

TWO PREPOSITIONAL PHRASES: They ate lunch in the restaurant and then walked around the mall.

TWO SUBORDINATE CLAUSES: My brothers enjoy shopping trips only if they are relatively short and only if they are productive.

Theme: Stores
In this section, you will learn about the various uses of commas. The examples and exercises are about different kinds of stores.

Cross-Curricular Connection: Social Studies

⏱ TIME AND RESOURCE MANAGER

Resources
Print: Grammar Exercise Workbook, pp. 171–178; Hands-on Grammar Activity Book, Chapter 29
Technology: Language Lab CD-ROM, Punctuation; On-Line Exercise Bank, Section 29.2

In-Depth Coverage	Accelerated Pace
• Work through all key concepts, pp. 658–671 • Assign and review Exercises 7–13 • Do the Hands-on Grammar Activity, p. 672	• Assign pages 658–671 for independent student review • Assign Exercises 7–13

Exercise 7 Using Commas in Compound Sentences

Write each sentence, adding the necessary commas. If no comma is needed, write *correct*.

EXAMPLE: I try to save money but I still overspend.

ANSWER: I try to save money, but I still overspend.

1. The food industry includes the production and distribution of food as well as the people involved in this most important business.
2. About 3 million Americans work in farming or other related fields to produce basic foods for the food market.
3. Livestock farmers raise animals for beef yet not all our meat comes from this type of farming.
4. Private fishermen and large commercial fleets gather huge quantities of fish and shellfish.
5. Food is shipped to processing plants and it is then prepared and packaged for the market.
6. Fruits and vegetables are washed and sorted before they are sent to market.
7. Much food is put through a process called irradiation so that most of the bacteria on the food is killed by radiation.
8. Neither light nor moisture is good for food preservation so most food products are packaged immediately after they are processed.
9. Shipping companies transport the food from producers to consumers in refrigerated trucks for fresh food spoils quickly.
10. The finished food product can be sold in a variety of locations but in the United States the most common place is a supermarket or grocery store.

More Practice

Language Lab CD-ROM
• Commas lesson
On-line Exercise Bank
• Section 29.2
Grammar Exercise Workbook
• pp. 171–172

◀ **Critical Viewing** How would you express the contrast between the trees and the boxes? Would you need a comma to separate clauses? **[Describe]**

Answer Key

Exercise 7

1. correct
2. correct
3. Livestock farmers raise animals for beef, yet not all our meat comes from this type of farming.
4. correct
5. Food is shipped to processing plants, and it is then prepared and packaged for the market.
6. Correct
7. Correct
8. Neither light nor moisture is good for food preservation, so most food products are packaged immediately after they are processed.
9. Shipping companies transport the food from producers to consumers in refrigerated trucks, for fresh food spoils quickly.
10. The finished food product can be sold in a variety of locations, but in the United States the most common place is a supermarket or grocery store.

Critical Viewing

Describe Students may suggest that the trees are bare, and the boxes are full of fruit. A comma is needed to separate two independent clauses.

⏱ TIME SAVERS!

Answers on Transparency Use the Grammar Exercises on Transparencies for Chapter 29 to have students correct their own or one another's exercises.

On-Line Exercise Bank Have students complete the exercises on computer. The Auto Check feature will grade their work for you!

Side-by-Side Teaching Guide

Commas Between Items in a Series

1. Separating items in a series with commas is a natural way to distinguish among the items. Read the following example first as it is written, with a slight pause between the items in a series. Then read it with no pauses or changes in inflection.

   The sky was a mix of blue, pink, yellow, and orange.

2. Review the different situations in which commas are used. The common thread is a series of like items—words, phrases, or clauses.

3. Write the following sentences on the board for additional examples.

   Series of words: My favorite authors are Charles Dickens, Ernest Hemingway, Richard Wright, and Toni Morrison.

   Series of prepositional phrases: I look for books at bookstores, in the library, and on the Internet.

   Series of clauses: I have friends who collect books, who collect antiques, and who collect comic books.

4. If there is a conjunction between items in a series, no comma is needed. Write the following sentence on the board to reinforce this point:

   The breakfast choices are cereal and milk, bacon and eggs, muffins and jam, doughnuts, oatmeal, and pancakes.

29.2

Commas Between Items in a Series

Items in a series must be separated by commas. A series consists of three or more similar items. These items may be words, phrases, or clauses.

> **KEY CONCEPT** Use commas to separate three or more words, phrases, or clauses in a series. ■

The number of commas that should be used in a series is one fewer than the number of items in the series. For example, if you have a series of three items, you should use two commas; if you have a series of four items, you should use three commas; and so on.

SERIES OF WORDS:	Some farmers sell grain, dairy, and fruits directly to the processor.
SERIES OF PREPOSITIONAL PHRASES:	Other farmers belong to a marketing cooperative, to a terminal market, or to an auction market.
SERIES OF CLAUSES:	The bank filled quickly with people who transferred their accounts, who cashed checks, and who opened their safe-deposit boxes.

In the preceding examples, each series consists of three items; therefore, two commas are used in each of the series.

Some writers omit the last comma in a series except when it is needed to prevent confusion. In your own work, you will find that the full use of commas generally works better.

CONFUSING:	Endless streams of people, honking geese and police officers were all leaving the fair.
ALWAYS CLEAR:	Endless streams of people, honking geese, and police officers were all leaving the fair.

Two Exceptions

When each of the items in a series is joined to the next item by a conjunction, no commas are necessary.

EXAMPLE:	Supermarkets and grocery stores and restaurants all sell a variety of foods to consumers.

Commas are not necessary between pairs of items that are thought of as a single item.

EXAMPLE:	I asked for ham and eggs, coffee and cream, and bread and butter.

660 • Punctuation

◇ STANDARDIZED TEST PREPARATION WORKSHOP

Proofreading Standardized tests measure students' ability to identify errors in punctuation, spelling, and capitalization. Share the following example with students.

Choose the letter of the type of error, if any, that appears in the underlined section.

Yesterday, my mother asked me to go food shopping with her. I was glad because I wanted to get cereal, cookies and yogurt.

A Spelling error   **C** Punctuation error
B Capitalization error   **D** No error

The correct choice is item **C**. The end of the sentence contains items in a series, and there should be a comma after *cookies*.

660

Exercise 8 Proofreading for Commas With Items in a **Series** Copy each sentence that needs commas, adding the necessary commas. For sentences that need no commas, write *correct*.

EXAMPLE: I bought oregano parsley and garlic for the spaghetti sauce.

ANSWER: I bought oregano, parsley, and garlic for the spaghetti sauce.

1. In many developing countries, foods are sold to the general public in an open-market setting without being processed.
2. Markets are made up of individual merchants who set up shop under a tent on a blanket or behind a stand.
3. In the market, you can find shoes furniture dishes or fruits and vegetables.
4. In the Dominican Republic, food is also sold in street carts in supermarkets or in *colmados*.
5. *Colmados* are shops built onto a house or small business and run by one person.
6. There are usually two or three to a street, and they sell basic items, such as eggs soap salt and pepper and fresh meat.
7. Items are sold in bulk, such as flour butter sugar and bananas sold by the pound.
8. Food is not bought and stored in cupboards on shelves or in the refrigerator in the house. It is bought only when it is needed.
9. For this reason, the ability to buy in small amounts to be able to shop often and to serve the food quickly is very important.
10. Those who sell fruits and vegetables who clean shoes or who run errands may call out their services as they walk up and down the streets.

▶ **More Practice**

Language Lab
CD-ROM
• Commas lesson
On-line
Exercise Bank
• Section 29.2
Grammar Exercise
Workbook
• pp. 171–172

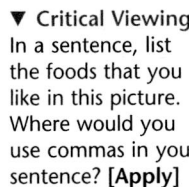

▼ **Critical Viewing**
In a sentence, list the foods that you like in this picture. Where would you use commas in your sentence? **[Apply]**

Answer Key

Exercise 8

1. correct
2. Markets are made up of individual merchants who set up shop under a tent, on a blanket, or behind a stand.
3. In the market, you can find shoes, furniture, dishes, or fruits and vegetables.
4. In the Dominican Republic, food is also sold in street carts, in supermarkets, or in *colmados*.
5. correct
6. There are usually two or three to a street, and they sell basic items, such as eggs, soap, salt and pepper, and fresh meat.
7. Items are sold in bulk, such as flour, butter, sugar, and bananas sold by the pound.
8. Food is not bought and stored in cupboards, on shelves, or in the refrigerator in the house. It is bought only when it is needed.
9. For this reason, the ability to buy in small amounts, to be able to shop often, and to serve the food quickly is very important.
10. Those who sell fruits and vegetables, who clean shoes, or who run errands may call out their services as they walk up and down the street.

Critical Viewing

Apply Students may suggest that they like pineapples, bananas, chicken, ham, fish, and avocados. Commas are used to separate a series of words.

⏱ **TIME SAVERS!**

📋 **Answers on Transparency** Use the Grammar Exercises on Transparencies for Chapter 29 to have students correct their own or one another's exercises.

💻 **On-Line Exercise Bank** Have students complete the exercises on computer. The Auto Check feature will grade their work for you!

661

Using Commas With Adjectives

1. A comma is used to separate only adjectives of equal rank. When adjectives are used in a specific sequence, no comma is needed.

2. One test of equal rank is if the adjectives can be used in reverse order.

   You sent a sweet, kind note. (You sent a kind, sweet note.)

3. A comma should never come between an adjective and the noun it modifies.

   It was a nasty, cold, blustery, snowy winter.

Answer Key

> **Exercise 9**

1. correct
2. attractive, colorful packaging
3. busy, powerful market
4. correct
5. correct

Customize for Visual/Spatial Learners

Ask students to look around the room and write three or four sentences that include series of adjectives.

29.2

Adjectives

Use commas to divide adjectives of equal rank. Such adjectives are called *coordinate adjectives*.

> **KEY CONCEPT** Use commas to separate adjectives of equal rank. ■

Two or more adjectives are considered equal in rank if the word *and* can be placed between the adjectives without changing the meaning of the sentence. Another test is to change the order of the adjectives. If the sentence still sounds correct, then the adjectives are of equal rank and a comma should be placed between them.

EXAMPLE: The dog's matted, filthy coat needed washing.

> **KEY CONCEPT** Do not use commas to separate adjectives that must stay in a specific order. ■

EXAMPLE: The tightly restricted food market is regulated by the government.

These adjectives must stay in the order in which they are written. Therefore, no comma is used to separate them.

Note About *Commas With Adjectives:* Do not use a comma to separate the last adjective in a series from the noun it modifies.

INCORRECT: The food-delivery truck followed a long, twisting, scenic, road.

CORRECT: The food-delivery truck followed a long, twisting, scenic road.

> **Exercise 9** Using Commas Between Adjectives Write the following phrases, and add any necessary commas. If no commas are needed, write *correct*.

EXAMPLE: a vivid beautiful scene
ANSWER: a vivid, beautiful scene

1. rented selling space
2. attractive colorful packaging
3. busy powerful market
4. many new marketplaces
5. cooperative grocery merchants

> **More Practice**
> Language Lab
> CD-ROM
> • Commas lesson
> **On-line**
> **Exercise Bank**
> • Section 29.2
> **Grammar Exercise**
> **Workbook**
> • pp. 171–172

⏱ TIME SAVERS!

▲ Answers on Transparency
Use the Grammar Exercises on Transparencies for Chapter 29 to have students correct their own or one another's exercises.

💻 On-Line Exercise Bank
Have students complete the exercises on computer. The Auto Check feature will grade their work for you!

☑ ONGOING ASSESSMENT: Monitor and Reinforce

If students have missed more than two items in Exercises 7–9, refer them to the following for additional practice.

In the Textbook	Print Resources	Technology
Chapter Review, Ex. 66, p. 722	Grammar Exercise Workbook, Using Commas, pp. 171–172	Language Lab CD-ROM, Punctuation; On-Line Exercise Bank, Section 29.2

Commas After Introductory Material

Commas are usually needed to set off introductory material from the rest of the sentence.

▶ **KEY CONCEPT** Use a comma after an introductory word, phrase, or clause. ∎

Following are examples of commas with introductory material.

KINDS OF INTRODUCTORY MATERIAL		
Words	**Introductory Words**	No, I will not order the magazine you want.
	Nouns of Direct Address	Cindy, could you search appliances on the Internet?
	Common Expressions	Of course, we can get that printed for you.
	Introductory Adverbs	Obviously, the student had tried. Hurriedly, she hid the present she had wrapped.
Phrases	**Prepositional Phrases (of four or more words)**	In the catalog next to the sink, you can find the shoes you are looking for.
	Participial Phrases	Jumping over the fence, the horse caught its back hoof.
	Infinitive Phrases	To buy things on the Internet, a credit card is often required.
Clauses	**Adverb Clauses**	When World War II ended, shopping centers became popular.

Commas After Introductory Material

1. Commas are used after three types of introductory material: words, phrases, and adverb clauses. Review the chart with students.

2. Read aloud the sentences for introductory words. Pause longer than usual at the commas.

3. Read the sentences aloud for introductory phrases and adverb clauses in the same manner.

4. A comma does not set off short introductory prepositional phrases.

   At dinnertime the family talks. (fewer than four words—no comma)

   During the evening meal, there is rarely a silent moment. (four-word introductory prepositional phrase—takes a comma)

Integrating Speaking and Listening Skills

Have one student read aloud a paragraph of a newspaper article while a partner writes it down, paying particular attention to the use of commas. Readers should read slowly and distinctly but take care not to exaggerate pauses.

Commas • 663

Grammar in Literature

1. Have a volunteer read aloud the excerpt from "Checkouts."
2. Ask students to examine each introductory comma in the passage and explain its use. (introductory word, prepositional phrase, clause, clause)

More About the Author

Cynthia Rylant (born 1954) was born in the West Virginia mountains. For a while she worked as a librarian, then she discovered that she could write. She likes writing about (and for) kids "because they have more possibilities. They can get away with more love, more anger, more fear than adult characters."

Answer Key

1. No,
2. In fact,
3. When retailers began to think of combining businesses,
4. With automobiles in mind,
5. For more than fifty years,
6. After World War II ended,
7. Suddenly,
8. To keep up with the growing trend of convenience,
9. By the end of the 1980's,
10. Attracting businesses of all kinds,

TIME SAVERS!

 **Answers on Transparency**
Use the Grammar Exercises on Transparencies for Chapter 29 to have students correct their own or one another's exercises.

On-Line Exercise Bank
Have students complete the exercises on computer. The Auto Check feature will grade their work for you!

29.2

GRAMMAR IN LITERATURE

from **Checkouts**
Cynthia Rylant

The introductory words and clauses are highlighted in blue italics. Each introductory element is followed by a comma.

Incredibly, it was another four weeks before they saw each other again. *As fate would have it,* her visits to the supermarket never coincided with his schedule to bag. *Each time she went to the store,* her eyes scanned the checkouts at once, her heart in her mouth. *And each hour he worked,* the bag boy kept one eye on the door, watching for the red-haired girl with the big orange bow.

▶ **Exercise 10** Using Commas After Introductory Material
For each of the following sentences, write the introductory material and the comma.

EXAMPLE: My friend do you know how malls are run?
ANSWER: My friend,

1. No shopping centers have not always been centers of American shopping.
2. In fact before 1945 very few shopping centers existed.
3. When retailers began to think of combining businesses they focused on the automotive industry.
4. With automobiles in mind the first modern shopping center was designed in Baltimore in 1896.
5. For fifty years the idea grew slowly.
6. After World War II ended America became obsessed with the shopping center.
7. Suddenly new shopping centers were springing up everywhere.
8. To keep up with the growing trend of convenience shopping centers were built with enclosed areas.
9. By the end of the 1980's there were about 35,000 shopping centers in the United States.
10. Attracting businesses of all kinds the shopping center industry is very profitable.

▶ **More Practice**
Language Lab
CD-ROM
• Commas lesson
On-line
Exercise Bank
• Section 29.2
Grammar Exercise Workbook
• pp. 173–174

Commas With Parenthetical and Nonessential Expressions

Commas are often used within a sentence to set off parenthetical and nonessential expressions.

Parenthetical Expressions

A parenthetical expression is a word or a phrase that is unrelated to the rest of the sentence and interrupts the general flow of the sentence. Study the following list of common parenthetical expressions.

NAMES OF PEOPLE BEING ADDRESSED:	Don, Judge Burke, my son,
CONJUNCTIVE ADVERBS:	also, besides, furthermore, however, indeed, instead, moreover, nevertheless, otherwise, therefore, thus
COMMON EXPRESSIONS:	by the way, I feel, in my opinion, in the first place, of course, on the other hand, you know
CONTRASTING EXPRESSIONS:	not that one, not there, not mine

For any parenthetical expressions, use the following rule:

▶ **KEY CONCEPT** Use commas to set off parenthetical expressions. ■

Two commas are used to enclose the entire parenthetical expression when the expression is located in the middle of the sentence.

NAMES OF PEOPLE BEING ADDRESSED:	We will go, Marge, as soon as your father arrives.
CONJUNCTIVE ADVERB:	The boys, therefore, decided to call a tow truck.
COMMON EXPRESSION:	The Internet, in my opinion, has made shopping easier than ever.
CONTRASTING EXPRESSIONS:	It was here, not there, that we found the camera we were looking for.

If one of these expressions is used at the end of a sentence, however, only one comma is necessary.

EXAMPLE:	We will go as soon as your father arrives, Marge.

▲ **Critical Viewing** Describe this mall, comparing it parenthetically to a mall or shopping center near you. **[Compare and Contrast]**

Parenthetical Expressions

1. Commas set off parenthetical expressions—words or phrases not essential to the meaning of a sentence. The best means of identifying parenthetical expressions is to omit them and read the sentence. The sentence retains its meaning.

2. Review the conjunctive adverbs that are set off by commas.

3. Common expressions such as *I think, of course,* and *you know* are set off by commas.

4. Read aloud the contrasting expressions and the sentence so students can see how these are set off from the rest of the sentence.

5. Write the following additional examples on the board and read them aloud, so students can hear where the commas go.

> *The job you did today, Carol, is really impressive.*
>
> *I think, therefore, that you can handle more responsibility.*
>
> *Today, in my opinion, you showed your real ability.*

Customize for
More Advanced Students

Ask students to work together to write a paragraph in which they use each example of a parenthetical expression shown on the page.

Critical Viewing

Compare and Contrast Students may suggest that the mall in the photograph is, in fact, much smaller than the mall in their neighborhood.

665

Exercise 11

1. correct
2. Each business pays rent plus a percentage of its profit, of course, to keep its location in the shopping center.
3. This extra percentage, called overage, makes up most of the profit of owning a shopping center.
4. The company in charge, therefore, hopes that each of the businesses will succeed.
5. correct
6. correct
7. The property, furthermore, must provide ample parking.
8. The owner rents the available spaces to stores that, as a group, will attract a large consumer pool.
9. After the center opens, it is the owner, not the individual businesses, that takes care of security and fire protection.
10. Sanitation and grounds care, moreover, are also provided by the shopping center firm.

Critical Viewing

Draw Conclusions Students may say, "This street, with its heavy pedestrian traffic and ample parking, ia a good location for a shopping center."

29.2

▶ **Exercise 11** **Setting Off Parenthetical Expressions** Copy each of the following sentences, inserting any commas necessary to set off parenthetical expressions. If no comma is needed, write *correct*.

EXAMPLE: The mall is so big in fact that there are three restaurants and a theater.
   The mall is so big, in fact, that there are three restaurants and a theater.

1. Most shopping centers are owned by one company and rented out to retail businesses.
2. Each business pays rent plus a percentage of its profit of course to keep its location in the shopping center.
3. This extra percentage called overage makes up most of the profit of owning a shopping center.
4. The company in charge therefore hopes that each of the businesses will succeed.
5. The location of a shopping center is chosen with great care.
6. It must be a place that is easily reached by shoppers.
7. The property furthermore must provide ample parking.
8. The owner rents the available spaces to stores that as a group will attract a large consumer pool.
9. After the center opens, it is the owner not the individual businesses that takes care of security and fire protection.
10. Sanitation and grounds care moreover are also provided by the shopping center firm.

More Practice
Language Lab CD-ROM
• Commas lesson
On-line Exercise Bank
• Section 29.2
Grammar Exercise Workbook
• pp. 173–174

▼ **Critical Viewing** What features make the location pictured a good location for a shopping center? Use the details you select to complete the following sentence: "This street, _____, is a good location for a shopping center." **[Draw Conclusions]**

ONGOING ASSESSMENT: Monitor and Reinforce

If students miss more than two items in Exercises 10–11, refer them to the following for additional practice.

In the Textbook	Print Resources	Technology
Chapter Review, Ex. 66, p. 722	Grammar Exercise Workbook, Using Commas, pp. 173–174	Language Lab CD-ROM, Punctuation; On-Line Exercise Bank, Section 29.2

Nonessential Expressions

Because commas are used only with nonessential expressions, writers must learn to distinguish between essential and nonessential material. (The terms *restrictive* and *nonrestrictive* are sometimes used to refer to the same type of expressions.)

An *essential expression* is a word, phrase, or clause that provides information that cannot be removed without changing the meaning of the sentence. It is restrictive.

Nonessential expressions provide additional, nonrestrictive, information in a sentence. You can remove nonessential material from a sentence, and the remaining sentence will still contain all the necessary information required by the reader.

Once you have decided whether or not an expression is essential, you can apply this rule.

▶ **KEY CONCEPT** Use commas to set off nonessential expressions. ■

An appositive, a participial phrase, or an adjective clause can be either essential or nonessential. In the following chart, note that essential material is not set off with commas. Nonessential items, however, are set off with two commas if they are in the middle of a sentence and with one comma if they are at the end.

ESSENTIAL AND NONESSENTIAL EXPRESSIONS

Appositive	Essential	My sister Joanne went to the Nicollet Mall in Minnesota.
	Nonessential	Joanne, my sister, went to the Nicollet Mall in Minnesota.
Participial Phrase	Essential	The teacher wearing a blue dress took the students to the mall.
	Nonessential	Mrs. Goff, wearing a blue dress, took the students to the mall.
Adjective Clause	Essential	The mall that we enjoyed the most had three levels and a swimming pool.
	Nonessential	The Pine-Woods Center, which was our favorite, had three levels and a swimming pool.

The examples in the chart show only expressions that are located in the middle of the sentence; each nonessential expression is set off with two commas. If the expression shifts to the beginning or the end of the sentence, use only one comma.

EXAMPLE: That evening, he met Joanne, my sister.

Essential and Nonessential Expressions

1. Commas set off the three types of nonessential expressions: appositives and appositive phrases, participial phrases, and adjective clauses. Nonessential expressions rename the noun they modify. They are nonessential because the sentence retains its meaning if they are omitted.

2. Appositives, participial phrases, and adjective clauses can be either essential or nonessential. Only a nonessential expression is set off by commas.

3. Write the following additional examples of nonessential expressions on the board and review them with students.

   Appositive: Sandy Koufax, the great Dodger pitcher, is in the Hall of Fame.

   Participial phrase: Koufax, throwing his fastball, was virtually unhittable.

   Adjective clause: His curveball, which many people think was his best pitch, was a wonder to behold!

Customize for *Less Advanced Students*

Work with students individually or in a small group to help them understand how nonessential expressions rename the noun. While providing additional and often helpful information, they can be removed from the sentence and not change its meaning.

29.2

Exercise 12 Distinguishing Between Essential and Nonessential Expressions If one of the following sentences contains an essential expression needing no additional commas, write *essential*. If the sentence contains a nonessential expression, copy the sentence, adding the necessary commas.

EXAMPLE: Shopping in the United States has changed since the 1800's.

ANSWER: essential

1. In small towns of the 1800's, the variety of clothing stores as well as food stores was limited.
2. Foods such as fruits and vegetables were grown on family farms.
3. Ice was sold by the iceman who traveled around in an ice wagon.
4. Small items such as household goods, tools, or fabrics were sold in the town's general store.
5. Specialists such as the blacksmith, the baker, and the tailor offered goods or services of other kinds.
6. Oftentimes, any special purchase like clothes or toys had to be ordered by catalog, and the consumer waited months for it to arrive.
7. Auctions which were held periodically would attract buyers for miles around.
8. Eventually, general stores grew into larger mercantile establishments department stores.
9. They started to carry items in the store that were available only by catalog before.
10. Specialty foods bakery and butcher products became available in one place called the supermarket.

> **More Practice**
>
> Language Lab
> CD-ROM
> • Commas lesson
> On-line
> Exercise Bank
> • Section 29.2
> Grammar Exercise
> Workbook
> • pp. 175–176

▼ **Critical Viewing**
If you described the place pictured as a store, would the fact that it sells pumpkins and flowers be essential or nonessential to the description? What if you described the place as a farmer's market? **[Apply]**

📝 ONGOING ASSESSMENT: Monitor and Reinforce

If students miss more than two items in Exercises 12–13, refer them to the following for additional practice.

In the Textbook	Print Resources	Technology
Chapter Review, Ex. 66, p. 722	Grammar Exercise Workbook, Using Commas, pp. 175–178	Language Lab CD-ROM, Punctuation; On-Line Exercise Bank, Section 29.2

Commas With Places, Dates, and Titles

The names of places are often made up of several parts. The name of a town may be followed by the name of a county, which in turn may be followed by the name of a state.

KEY CONCEPT When a geographical name is made up of two or more parts, use a comma after each item. ∎

EXAMPLE: I traveled from Taos, New Mexico, to Oklahoma City, Oklahoma.

Dates are also often made up of several parts, such as months, days, and years. Commas can help avoid confusion.

KEY CONCEPT When a date is made up of two or more parts, use a comma after each item except in the case of a month followed by a day. ∎

EXAMPLES: On Friday, April 17, we will have a special meeting.
The city's new subway system ran its first train on June 11, 1890.

You may omit the commas if the date contains only the month and the year.

EXAMPLE: February 1980 was one of the wettest months on record.

If the parts of a date have already been joined by prepositions, no comma is needed.

EXAMPLE: The city's new subway system ran its first train in June of 1890.

KEY CONCEPT When a name is followed by one or more titles, use a comma after the name and after each title. ∎

EXAMPLE: I noticed that Jeremy McGuire, Sr., works here.

A similar rule applies with some business abbreviations.

EXAMPLE: Bookwright, Inc., published a book about food technology.

Commas With Places, Dates, and Titles

1. Commas also separate the names of cities and countries.

   I drove from Rome, Italy, to Paris France.

2. Write these dates on the board, using a different color for the commas.

   Monday was sunny.

   May 4 was sunny.

   Monday, May 4, was sunny.

   Monday, May 4, 1998, was sunny.

Critical Viewing

Speculate Students may suggest orders, inventories, and deliveries.

Step-by-Step Teaching Guide

Other Uses of the Comma

1. There is an exception to the commas in numbers rule. Numbers in students' science textbooks are in the metric system. In that system, four-digit numbers do not contain a comma: 5742 meters.

2. In a series of numbers that already contain commas, use a semicolon to separate them.

   Tom, Dick, and Harry received the following votes: 16,311; 20,789; and 9,888.

3. Elliptical sentences often use a semicolon to separate the two (understood) independent clauses as was done in the example sentence at the bottom of the page. That would not eliminate the need for the comma after *countries*.

Other Uses of the Comma

▶ **KEY CONCEPT** Use a comma after each item in an address of two or more parts. ■

EXAMPLE: My new address is Katie Wedel, 243 Park Street, St. Louis, Missouri 63131.

When an address is written on an envelope, most of the commas are omitted. Notice in both cases that extra space, instead of a comma, is left between the state and the ZIP Code.

EXAMPLE: Katie Wedel
243 Park Street
St. Louis, Missouri 63131

▶ **KEY CONCEPT** Use a comma after the salutation in a personal letter and after the closing in all letters. ■

SALUTATIONS: Dear Rupert, Dear Aunt Dolly,
CLOSINGS: Sincerely, In appreciation,

▶ **KEY CONCEPT** With numbers of more than three digits, use a comma after every third digit starting from the right. ■

EXAMPLE: The company has sold 498,362,719 jelly beans.

Note About *Commas in Numbers:* Do not use commas in ZIP Codes, phone numbers, page numbers, serial numbers, years, or house numbers.

EXAMPLES: ZIP Code: 26413   Page number: 1047
Telephone number: (201) 236-7000

▶ **KEY CONCEPT** Use a comma to indicate the words left out of an elliptical sentence. ■

In the following example, the omitted word is clearly understood. The comma serves as a visual clue to the reader that an omission exists.

EXAMPLE: Developed countries buy food from the grocery store; undeveloped countries, the market.

Commas are also used to help show where direct quotations begin and end.

▲ **Critical Viewing** For what kinds of work-related writing might this store owner use commas? **[Speculate]**

KEY CONCEPT Use commas to set off a direct quotation from the rest of the sentence. ∎

Notice in the next examples that the placement of the commas depends on the location of the nonspoken words in the sentence.

EXAMPLES: The guest asked, "Do you know of any nearby supermarkets that are open all night?"
"If you don't mind a little drive," the host said, "you will find one about three miles down the road."
"Oh, that will be perfect," the guest replied.

Commas help readers by giving visual clues to avoid misreading.

KEY CONCEPT Use a comma to prevent a sentence from being misunderstood. ∎

UNCLEAR: Near the highway developers were building a shopping mall.
CLEAR: Near the highway, developers were building a shopping mall.

Exercise 13 **Using Commas in Other Situations** Copy the following sentences, adding the necessary commas. If no comma is needed, write *correct*.

EXAMPLE: Number (702) 555-4818 was billed for $2352.
ANSWER: Number (702) 555-4818 was billed for $2,352.

1. Thursday October 17 Bearnson and Sons Inc. delivered twenty boxes of soap.
2. On Friday of the same week, a check was sent for $1309.46 to Bearnson and Sons Inc. 1298 Ether Road Butler Idaho 83440.
3. She charged the amount to her credit card number 3565 3334 25 3676 on Monday October 21 2001.
4. The store next door was cited for the safety violation on page 1096 of the handbook; our store nothing.
5. John of Mayberry Street in Indianapolis is a friend of mine.

Learn More

To learn more about punctuating direct quotations, see 29.4, Quotation Marks With Direct Quotations

More Practice

Language Lab
CD-ROM
• Commas lesson
On-line
Exercise Bank
• Section 29.2
Grammar Exercise
Workbook
• pp. 177–178

Step-by-Step Teaching Guide

Commas With Direct Quotations

1. Review the use of commas to set off direct quotations. Before the quote, the comma is outside the quotation marks, and at the end it is inside the quotation marks.

2. Write the following examples on the board for additional practice and ask students to insert the commas.

   Franco said[,] "Let's do something that we can be proud of."

   "We could clean up the lot[,]" Shari suggested[,] "or we could help paint Ms. Rivers's house."

   "We should do both projects[,]" Meredith said.

Answer Key

Exercise 13

1. Thursday, October 17, Bearnson and Sons, Inc., delivered twenty boxes of soap.
2. On Friday of the same week, a check was sent for $1,309.46 to Bearnson and Sons, Inc., 1298 Ether Road, Butler, Idaho 83440.
3. She charged the amount to her credit card number 3565 3334 25 3676 on Monday, October 21, 2001.
4. The store next door was cited for the safety violation on page 1096 of the handbook; our store, nothing.
5. correct

⏱ TIME SAVERS!

Answers on Transparency
Use the Grammar Exercises on Transparencies for Chapter 29 to have students correct their own or one another's exercises.

On-Line Exercise Bank
Have students complete the exercises on computer. The Auto Check feature will grade their work for you!

Punctuation Spots

Teaching Resources: Hands-on Grammar Activity Book, Chapter 29

1. Have students refer to their Hands-on Grammar activity books or give them copies of the relevant pages.

2. Review the directions, making sure that students understand what to do.

3. Before students begin, ask them how they will be able to determine which appropriate end punctuation to use.

4. Once students have finished the activity, lead them in a discussion of how end punctuation and commas helps readers.

29.2

Hands-on Grammar

Punctuation Spots

To analyze how commas and end marks can affect meaning, do the following group activity. Photocopy a passage from your literature textbook. Keep one copy complete with punctuation. Then, use correction fluid or correction tape to eliminate the commas and end marks. Make three photocopies of the passage without commas or end marks, and distribute them to the group. Other group members should choose their own passages and eliminate the commas and end marks. Each member in a group of four should end up with three passages.

Use self-sticking dots from a stationery store to color-code the photocopies where you think commas and end marks should go. As a group, agree to use one color for periods, a second color for question marks, a third color for exclamation marks, and a fourth color for commas. Independently, mark the photocopies with the self-sticking dots. Then, compare your results with other group members, and discuss your choices. Finally, compare your color-coded versions to the originals.

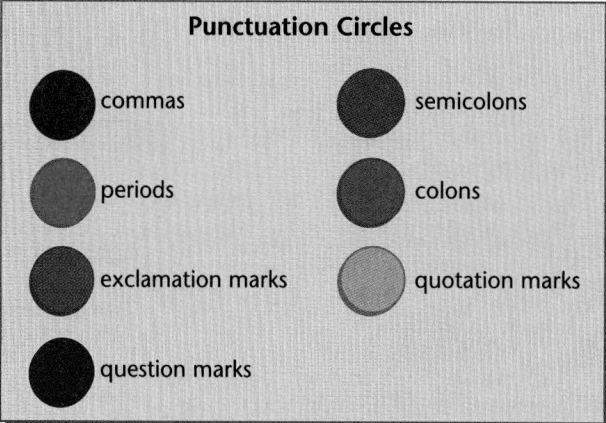

Punctuation Circles

- commas
- semicolons
- periods
- colons
- exclamation marks
- quotation marks
- question marks

Find It in Your Reading In a literature selection, find examples of commas used to separate items in a series, commas used to set off introductory material, and commas used to set off parenthetical expressions.

Find It in Your Writing Choose one piece of writing from your portfolio. Proofread it for the correct use of commas. If the writing sample you chose does not have any sentences that contain introductory phrases or clauses, challenge yourself to add at least two introductory elements, and punctuate them correctly.

672 • Punctuation

⏱ **TIME SAVERS!**

✋ **Hands-on Grammar Book**
Use the Hands-on Grammar activity sheet for Chapter 29 to facilitate this activity.

☑ **ONGOING ASSESSMENT: Assess Mastery**

Use the following resources to assess mastery of using commas.

In the Textbook	Technology
Chapter Review, Ex. 66, p. 722 Standardized Test Preparation Workshop, pp. 724–725	Language Lab CD-ROM, Punctuation; On-Line Exercise Bank, Section 29.2

Section 29.2 Section Review

GRAMMAR EXERCISES 14–19

> **Exercise 14** **Using Commas Correctly** Rewrite each sentence, inserting commas where necessary. If the sentence is written correctly, write *correct*.

1. The modern shopping mall was made possible by the automobile the growth of the suburbs and television advertising.
2. Some consist of one long or angled building usually of one story divided into several stores.
3. To get from store to store in an open mall a customer must go outdoors.
4. The enclosed mall is covered by a roof which can be eight stories tall.
5. This type of mall is large completely protected from the weather and temperature-controlled.
6. The Mall of America located in Bloomington Minnesota was the largest shopping mall in the United States when it was built in the 1990's.
7. Its nearest rival at the time the Del Amo Fashion Center in Torrance California was half its size.
8. Malls have become all-purpose entertainment centers where a person may shop or eat or go to the movies.
9. Shopping in cities presents problems lack of parking space for example that suburban malls do not have.
10. The mall has the best solution to the problem of scarce parking spaces: huge lots for all-day free parking.

> **Exercise 15** **Proofreading for Commas** On a separate sheet of paper, copy the following paragraph. Add or delete commas as needed.

Shopping in older cities like Bombay India is a bustling activity. Buildings are crowded into small, spaces and people seem to be everywhere.
Traders often specializing in one line of business sell their items, in small shops, that have fronts open to the streets. Going from shop, to shop you may ride in a rickshaw a hand-pulled cart. You will have to compete for space with people animals, automobiles other rickshaws and bicycles.

> **Exercise 16** **Using Commas in Special Situations** Rewrite the phrase, number, or situation for which a comma is needed. If no comma is needed, write *correct*.

1. Food production began around 8000 B.C.
2. "Shopping" explained the teacher "has existed since man started to trade."
3. The book was published by World Book Inc. 525 W. Monroe Chicago, IL 60661.
4. Look on page 2006 for the answer.
5. Last year 2,067,981 socks were sold.

> **Exercise 17** **Find It in Your Reading** Reread the excerpt from "Checkouts" by Cynthia Rylant on page 664. Identify the purpose of each comma.

> **Exercise 18** **Find It in Your Writing** Select a piece of writing from your portfolio. Find two examples of the use of commas to set off introductory material.

> **Exercise 19** **Writing Application** Follow each set of directions to form new sentences. Use commas correctly.

• Use the conjunction *but* to join two sentences.
• Write a sentence with a series of phrases.
• Write a sentence with an introductory phrase or clause.

Section Review • 673

ASSESS and CLOSE

Section Review
Each of these exercises correlates to a concept in the section on commas, pages 658–671. These exercises may be used for more practice, for reteaching, or for review of the Key Concepts presented. Answers for all chapter exercises are available in *Grammar Exercises Answers on Transparencies* in your teaching resources.

Answer Key

> **Exercise 14**

1. The modern shopping mall was made possible by the automobile, the growth of the suburbs, and television advertising.
2. correct
3. To get from store to store in an open mall, a customer must go outdoors.
4. The enclosed mall is covered by a roof, which can be eight stories tall.
5. This type of mall is large, completely protected from the weather, and temperature-controlled.
6. The Mall of America, located in Bloomington, Minnesota, was the largest shopping mall in the United States when it was built in the 1990's.
7. Its nearest rival at the time, the Del Amo Fashion Center in Torrance, California, was half its size.
8. correct
9. Shopping in cities presents problems, lack of parking space, for example, that suburban malls do not have.
10. correct

> **Exercise 15**

Shopping in older cities like Bombay, India, is a bustling activity. Buildings are crowded into small spaces, and people seem to be everywhere.
Traders, often specializing in one line of business, sell their items in small shops that have fronts open to the streets. Going from shop to shop, you may ride in a rickshaw, a hand-pulled cart. You will have to compete for space with people, animals, automobiles, other rickshaws, and bicycles.

continued

Answer Key continued

> **Exercise 16**

1. correct
2. "Shopping," explained the teacher, "has existed since man started to trade."
3. The book was published by World Book, Inc, 525 W. Monroe, Chicago, IL 60661.
4. correct
5. correct

> **Exercise 17**

Find It in Your Reading
to set off introductory word, prepositional phrase, clause, clause

> **Exercise 18**

Find It in Your Writing
Have students check to be sure their commas are correct, or correct them if necessary.

> **Exercise 19**

Writing Application
Let ESL and Less Advanced Students work with partners for this exercise. Students' sentences will vary.

Interest GRABBER Write the following sentences on the board and ask students to add necessary colons and semicolons.

The sign over the door said [:] Time Machine. Enter at Your Own Risk! Inside, the time machine had two buttons [:] "Past" and "Future." Buck chose the past [;] Chuck chose the future.

Activate Prior Knowledge

Ask students to tell in their own words why they used colons and semicolons in the Interest Grabber.

TEACH

Step-by-Step Teaching Guide

Use the Semicolon With Independent Clauses

1. A semicolon links two independent clauses not joined by coordinating conjunctions.

2. Review the examples. In each case, the ideas in the clauses are closely related. Using a semicolon to connect independent clauses is correct only when there is a close relationship between the clauses.

   Incorrect: The band rehearsed the entire program; the pizza was cold.

   Correct: The band rehearsed the entire program; the sound filled the arena.

3. Write an example of four independent clauses on the chalkboard.

   The leadoff hitter started the rally with a base hit to right; the second batter walked; the number-three hitter beat out an infield hit; the clean-up hitter whacked a grand slam out of the park.

continued

Customize for
More Advanced Students

Have students write a short, three- or four-paragraph essay about a topic of their choice in which at least one sentence in each paragraph uses a semicolon.

Section 29.3 Semicolons and Colons

The semicolon (;) is a punctuation mark that serves as the happy medium between the comma and the period. It signals to the reader to pause longer than for a comma but to pause without the finality of a period. The colon (:) is used primarily to point ahead to additional information. It directs the reader to look further.

The Semicolon

The semicolon is used to separate independent clauses that have a close relationship to each other. A semicolon is also used to separate independent clauses or items in a series that already contain a number of commas.

Use the Semicolon With Independent Clauses

▶ **KEY CONCEPT** Use a semicolon to join independent clauses that are not already joined by the conjunction *and, but, for, nor, or, so,* or *yet.* ■

EXAMPLE: The astronaut trainee sat in the spinning, swinging chair; she soon grew dizzy going in circles.

Do not use a semicolon to join unrelated independent clauses.

INCORRECT: Astronauts train for their missions; tomorrow, rain is expected.

CORRECT: The word *astronaut* is of Greek origin; it means "sailor among the stars."

Sometimes, the independent clauses will share a similar structure as well as a similar meaning. Occasionally, independent clauses may set up a contrast between one another.

EXAMPLES: With enthusiasm, he cast his line out into the lake; with pleasure, he later cooked his fish.

My sister excels at art; I can barely draw a straight line.

Semicolons can be used to join more than two independent clauses.

EXAMPLE: Alexei A. Leonov was the first human being to float freely in space; Edward H. White II was the first American to spacewalk; Valentina Tereshkova was the first woman in space.

674 • Punctuation

Theme: Space Travel

In this section, you will learn how to use semicolons and colons. The examples and exercises are about space travel.

Cross-Curricular Connection: Science

⏱ TIME AND RESOURCE MANAGER

Resources
Print: Grammar Exercise Workbook, pp. 179–182
Technology: Language Lab CD-ROM, Punctuation; On-Line Exercise Bank, Section 29.3

In-Depth Coverage	Accelerated Pace
• Work through all key concepts, pp. 674–682. • Assign and review Exercises 20–23.	• Assign pages 674–682 for independent student review. • Assign Exercises 20–23.

▶ **KEY CONCEPT** Use a semicolon to join independent clauses separated by either a conjunctive adverb or a transitional expression. ∎

The following list contains common conjunctive adverbs and transitional phrases.

CONJUNCTIVE ADVERBS:	also, besides, consequently, furthermore, however, indeed, instead, moreover, nevertheless, otherwise, therefore, thus
TRANSITIONAL EXPRESSIONS:	as a result, at this time, first, for instance, in fact, on the other hand, second, that is

Notice in the following examples that the semicolon is placed before the conjunctive adverb or the transitional expression. A comma follows the conjunctive adverb or the transitional expression because it serves as an introductory expression in the second independent clause.

CONJUNCTIVE ADVERB:	In 1967, the United States *Apollo* was scheduled to fly as the first manned *Apollo* spacecraft; however, the shuttle caught fire during a ground test, and the flight was cancelled.
TRANSITIONAL EXPRESSION:	We needed to get to the spare tire in the trunk; as a result, we had to unload the trunk.

Because words used as conjunctive adverbs and transitions can also interrupt one continuous sentence, use a semicolon only when there is an independent clause on each side of the conjunctive adverb or transitional expression.

INCORRECT:	The flight was; consequently, cancelled.
CORRECT:	The flight was, consequently, cancelled.

In these examples, *consequently* interrupts one continuous sentence; therefore, a semicolon would be incorrect.

▼ **Critical Viewing**
In what way does this picture illustrate the importance of the correct connection? **[Relate]**

4. Review the list of conjunctive adverbs and transitional expressions. In the examples on page 675, the independent clauses are connected by a semicolon because they are closely linked.

5. Use the following examples to reinforce the lesson:

One window on the nation's economy is the local retail mall; indeed, a full parking lot indicates booming business.

Retail sales are an important component of economic health; in fact, they are an early warning sign of which way the economy is headed.

6. Warn students that a conjunctive adverb or transitional expression does not automatically signal that a semicolon should be used. Semicolons are used only when there are two or more linked independent clauses.

Critical Viewing

Relate Students' responses will vary.

Semicolons and Colons • 675

Use the Semicolon to Avoid Confusion

Point out how a semicolon helps avoid confusion in sentences with items in a series and in sentences with appositives, participial phrases and adjective clauses. Review the text examples.

Customize for
Less Advanced Students

Sentences using semicolons tend to be wordier and denser than sentences students are comfortable reading and working with. Work individually or in small groups with students, helping them tackle smaller bits of the sentence at a time so they can see the construction and how commas are used for items in a series or nonessential expressions and semicolons are thus needed to separate the items to avoid confusion.

29.3

Use the Semicolon to Avoid Confusion

The semicolon can also be used to avoid confusion in sentences that contain other internal punctuation.

▶ **KEY CONCEPT** Consider the use of semicolons to avoid confusion when independent clauses already contain commas. ■

When a sentence consists of two independent clauses joined by a coordinating conjunction, the tendency is to place a comma before the conjunction. However, when one or both of the sentences also contain commas, a semicolon may be used before the conjunction to prevent confusion.

EXAMPLE: The astronauts who orbited the moon ten times in 1968 were William Anders, Frank Borman, and James Lovell; but they did not land on the moon.

▶ **KEY CONCEPT** Use a semicolon between items in a series if the items themselves contain commas. ■

EXAMPLE: Some of the women that the space program has trained include the Russian, Valentina Tereshkova, who orbited Earth in 1963; Sally K. Ride, the first American woman in space; and Christa McAuliffe, who was killed in a tragic accident seconds after liftoff in the shuttle *Challenger*.

You will use the semicolon in a series most commonly when the items contain either nonessential appositives, participial phrases, or adjective clauses.

APPOSITIVES: I sent notes to Mr. Nielson, my science teacher; Mrs. Jensen, my history instructor; and Mrs. Seltz, the librarian.

PARTICIPIAL PHRASES: I developed a fascination with space travel from television, watching live rocket launches; from school, learning about the science; and from movies, watching science-fiction adventures.

ADJECTIVE CLAUSES: The toy rocket that I bought has spare tires, which are brand new; a siren, which has just been installed; and a great engine, which has been newly tuned up.

Notice that commas are used to separate the nonessential material from the word or words they refer to or modify; the semicolons separate the complete items in the series.

▶ **More Practice**

Language Lab
CD-ROM
• Commas lesson
On-line
Exercise Bank
• Section 29.2
Grammar Exercise
Workbook
• pp. 179–180

▶ **Exercise 20** Using the Semicolon With Independent Clauses Decide where a semicolon is needed in each of the following sentences. Write the word that goes before the semicolon, write the semicolon, and write the word that goes after it.

EXAMPLE: Not all astronauts fly in space those who work on the Earth's surface for NASA are also considered astronauts.

ANSWER: space; those

1. Knowledge about space has not come easily since 1959 about 250 astronauts have flown in space.
2. For the first Mercury program, seven test pilots were chosen the group consisted of Air Force officers.
3. In 1962, nine more pilots were selected fourteen were chosen in 1963.
4. These pilots flew on two-person *Gemini* missions and *Apollo* flights to the moon this was the last time only Air Force officers were chosen as pilots.
5. The year 1965 marked the beginning of scientist astronauts a group of six men and five civilians was chosen.
6. All had received master's or doctor's degrees, and only two were jet pilots consequently, the rest received one year of military flight training.
7. In 1978, NASA changed the organization of the astronauts twenty mission specialists and fifteen new pilot astronauts was chosen.
8. This group included the first six women astronauts from the United States indeed, Russia had already sent a woman into space in 1963.
9. Many of the astronauts selected since the late 1970's have held advanced degrees this education was useful for mission specialists.
10. In 1983, Sally K. Ride, the first American woman to travel in space, orbited Earth on the space shuttle Challenger in 1990 NASA selected the first woman to become a pilot astronaut, a pilot who commands or controls a spacecraft.

▼ **Critical Viewing**
Which sentence in the exercise at left gives you a clue to the identity of this astronaut? **[Connect]**

Semicolons and Colons • **677**

✓ **ONGOING ASSESSMENT: Monitor and Reinforce**

If students miss more than two items in Exercises 20–21, refer them to the following for additional practice.

In the Textbook	Print Resources	Technology
Chapter Review, Ex. 67, p. 722	Grammar Exercise Workbook, Using Semicolons and Colons, pp. 179–180	Language Lab CD-ROM, Punctuation; On-Line Exercise Bank, Section 29.3

1. One who works in the space field may be called an astronaut, a space worker from the United States; or a cosmonaut, a space worker from the Commonwealth of Independent States.
2. Cosmonauts work and train at the Gagarin Center, also called *Star Town;* and the Baykonur Cosmodrome, where crews lift off into space.
3. Since 1961, more than 100 cosmonauts, which means "sailors of the universe," have traveled into space; four of them were killed during flight.
4. One cosmonaut, Vladimir Komarov, was killed when his parachute did not open; three others, members of the *Soyez II* crew, died when air leaked out of their capsule and asphyxiated them.
5. The former cosmonaut program consisted of two years of athletic activity, parachute jumping, and the use of chambers to push the physical limits of its trainees; but the modern-day program focuses on mental preparation and lasts 8–10 years.

Critical Viewing

Deduce Students may suggest that because the spacecraft is cramped and filled with scientific instruments, the cosmonauts must not only be technically trained, but must be able to get on well with others.

29.3

▶ **Exercise 21** **Using Semicolons With Internal Punctuation**
Copy each sentence, adding semicolons where they are needed to avoid confusion. Hint: Some commas may need to be replaced with a semicolon.

EXAMPLE: Cosmonauts work in space, handling equipment for space stations, satellites for communication, and experiments for scientific research.

ANSWER: Cosmonauts work in space, handling equipment for space stations; satellites for communication; and experiments for scientific research.

1. One who works in the space field may be called an astronaut, a space worker from the United States or a cosmonaut, a space worker from the Commonwealth of Independent States.
2. Cosmonauts work and train at the Gagarin Center, also called *Star Town* and the Baykonur Cosmodrome, where crews lift off into space.
3. Since 1961, more than one hundred cosmonauts, which means "sailors of the universe," have traveled into space four of them were killed during flight.
4. One cosmonaut, Vladimir Komarov, was killed when his parachute did not open three others, members of the *Soyez II* crew, died when air leaked out of their capsule and asphyxiated them.
5. The former cosmonaut program consisted of two years of athletic activity, parachute jumping, and the use of chambers to push the physical limits of its trainees, but the modern-day program focuses on mental preparation and lasts 8–10 years.

678 • Punctuation

▲ **Critical Viewing**
What qualities do you think these cosmonauts need to function well in a setting such as the one shown here? **[Deduce]**

▶ **More Practice**

Language Lab
CD-ROM
• Quotation Marks, Colons, and Semicolons lesson
On-line
Exercise Bank
• Section 29.3
Grammar Exercise
Workbook
• pp. 179–180

The Colon

The colon acts mainly as an introductory device. It is also used in several special situations.

Colons as Introductory Devices

KEY CONCEPT Use a colon before a list of items following an independent clause. ■

EXAMPLE: Astronaut trainees go through the following five phases of training: classroom work, flight training, survival training, mission training, and special training.

As shown in this example, the independent clause before a list often ends in a phrase such as *the following* or *the following items*. You should familiarize yourself with these phrases because they often indicate the need for a colon. Of course, you should not depend on these phrases alone to signal the need for a colon. The most important point to consider is whether or not an independent clause precedes the list. If it does, use a colon.

EXAMPLE: He had the right qualities to be an astronaut: fitness, courage, and commitment.

KEY CONCEPT Use a colon to introduce a quotation that is formal or lengthy or a quotation that does not contain a "he said/she said" expression. ■

Often, a formal quotation requiring a colon will consist of more than one sentence. However, your best guideline for inserting a colon should be the formality of the quotation. The more formal the quotation, the more likely you will need a colon.

Do not use a colon to introduce a casual quoted remark or dialogue, even if more than one sentence is used.

EXAMPLE: The speaker began with these words: "I have never been so honored in all my life."

Colons as Introductory Devices

1. The most frequent use of a colon is before a list of items following an independent clause.

2. Point out the frequent, but not consistent, use of key words such as *the following* to indicate this use of a colon.

   We planted the following vegetables today: lettuce, carrots, corn, and beans.

   Today we planted these vegetables: lettuce, carrots, corn, and beans.

3. Colons are used to introduce formal quotations or to set off quotes in a sentence where there is no other reference to the speaker. Point out again the commonsense approach of using a punctuation mark to avoid confusion.

4. Use the following additional examples if needed.

   Mr. Perez, with a genuinely shocked look, said: "This is the biggest surprise of my life."

   Ray stopped at the door and turned toward us: "I'm not participating in this scheme."

   continued

5. A colon introduces a sentence that summarizes or explains the preceding sentence.

Finally Sgt. Barnes tossed a plastic bag to me: I opened it to find the evidence we had been arguing about.

6. A colon is best used when a dramatic effect is intended.

The pitcher had the perfect response to the batter's delay getting into the batter's box: a fastball under the chin.

29.3

> **KEY CONCEPT** Use a colon to introduce a sentence that summarizes or explains the sentence before it. ■

Capitalize the first word after a colon if the word begins a complete sentence.

EXAMPLE: The technician provided her with one piece of advice: Check the water level often.

In this example, the colon points to the explanation contained in the next sentence.

Use a colon, instead of a comma, to introduce an appositive that follows an independent clause to give additional emphasis to the appositive.

> **KEY CONCEPT** Use a colon to introduce a formal appositive that follows an independent clause. ■

EXAMPLE: The Russian 1971 flight ended in an accident: a sudden loss of air in the cabin.

When you are using colons in sentences, always check to be sure that an independent clause comes before the colon.

INCORRECT: We decided to: see an old movie.
CORRECT: We decided to see an old movie: *The Right Stuff.*
INCORRECT: The lunar trips helped: collect lunar dust, bring back lunar rock, and set up scientific stations on the moon.
CORRECT: The lunar trips had three side-missions: to collect lunar dust, to bring back lunar rock, and to set up scientific stations on the moon.

Although an independent clause must precede a colon, it is not necessary that the words following the colon be an independent clause.

EXAMPLE: From the window, I looked out at the expanse of space and saw a familiar sight: Earth.

As you can see, the word *Earth* is an appositive for the words *familiar sight.* You could argue successfully that a comma would also be appropriate where the colon is inserted. However, the colon provides a slightly more dramatic, profound effect than that which would be achieved by the comma. As a writer, you will have the responsibility of deciding whether the comma or the colon more precisely fits the tone you are trying to establish in your writing.

ⓘ Learn More

For more information about capitalizing with colons, see Chapter 28.

Special Uses of the Colon The colon has several specialized functions that you will probably encounter in your reading and writing.

Many special situations require the use of a colon. Among them are references to time, volume and page numbers, chapters and verses in the Bible, book subtitles, business letter salutations, and labels that are used to introduce important ideas. Study the examples that are given in the following chart; it shows how the colon is used in each of these special situations.

▲ Critical Viewing
In a sentence using a colon, list words that describe the texture of the lunar surface (picted here). **[Apply]**

SPECIAL SITUATIONS REQUIRING COLONS	
Numerals Giving the Time	5:22 A.M. 7:49 P.M.
References to Periodicals (Volume Number: Page Number)	*Forbes* 4:8
Biblical References (Chapter Number: Verse Number)	Genesis 1:5
Subtitles for Books and Magazines	*Fixing Hamburger: One Hundred Ways to Prepare Delicious Meals*
Salutations in Business Letters	Dear Mr. Biggs: Ladies: Dear Sir:
Labels Used to Signal Important Ideas	WARNING: Cigarette smoking can be hazardous to your health. Note: This letter must be postmarked no later than the tenth of this month.

Special Uses of the Colon

1. Review the special uses of the colon chart.
2. Have students practice by writing sentences using each situation in the chart.

Critical Viewing

Apply Students may say that the lunar surface looks like fine dust: fluffy, smooth, and powdery.

☑ ONGOING ASSESSMENT: Monitor and Reinforce

If students miss more than two items in Exercises 22–23, refer them to the following for additional practice.

In the Textbook	Print Resources	Technology
Section Review, Ex. 25, p. 683	Grammar Exercise Workbook, pp. 181–182	Language Lab CD-ROM, Punctuation; On-Line Exercise Bank, Section 29.3

1. training: classroom
2. technology: rocket
3. classes: astronomy
4. possible: qualified
5. instructors: experienced

1. October 13, 2001
   6:35 P.M.
2. Dear Sirs:
   I am writing to tell you what I
   know about some moon trips.
3. On one trip to the moon, the
   astronauts read from Genesis
   1:1-10 over national television.
4. Upon landing in the Sea of
   Tranquility, these famous words
   came from the spacecraft:
   "Tranquility Base here . . . the
   Eagle has landed." Note: The
   prior landing destination proved
   unsuitable.
5. correct

29.3

> **Exercise 22** Using Colons as Introductory Devices Decide
where a colon is appropriate. On your paper, write the word
that comes before the colon, write the colon, and write the
word that comes after the colon with the correct capitalization.

EXAMPLE: NASA teaches classes that their trainees will
             need as astronauts aerodynamics, physics,
             physiology, and spacecraft-tracking techniques.

ANSWER: astronauts: aerodynamics

1. After one year at the Johnson Space Center, astronauts
   experience the first phase of specialized training classroom
   work.
2. In the early years of the space program, astronauts began
   the study of important space technology rocket engines,
   flight mechanics, and computer theory.
3. *Apollo* astronauts took additional classes astronomy, Earth
   geology, life sciences, and geology of the moon.
4. NASA also discusses what makes spaceflight possible
   qualified people, equipment, and funds.
5. NASA hires well-qualified instructors experienced astronauts, pilots, doctors, and university professors.

> **Exercise 23** Using Colons for Special Writing Situations
Copy each of the following items, adding the necessary colons.
If an item requires no colons, write *correct*.

EXAMPLE: For more information on astronauts, read *Liftoff*
             The Story of America's Adventure in Space.
             For more information on astronauts, read *Liftoff:*
             The Story of America's Adventure in Space.

1. October 13, 20--
   6 35 P.M.
2. Dear Sirs
   I am writing to tell you what I know about some moon
   trips.
3. On one trip to the moon, the astronauts read from Genesis
   1 1–10 over national television.
4. Upon landing in the Sea of Tranquillity, these famous
   words came from the spacecraft "Tranquillity Base here
   . . . the Eagle has landed." Note The prior landing destination proved unsuitable.
5. Sincerely yours,
   George Tuckett

682 • Punctuation

> **More Practice**
>
> **Language Lab**
> **CD-ROM**
> • Quotation Marks,
>   Colons, and
>   Semicolons lesson
> **On-line**
> **Exercise Bank**
> • Section 29.3
> **Grammar Exercise**
> **Workbook**
> • pp. 181–182

⏱ TIME SAVERS!

Answers on Transparency
Use the Grammar Exercises
on Transparencies for Chapter 29
to have students correct their
own or one another's exercises.

On-Line Exercise Bank
Have students complete the
exercises on computer. The Auto
Check feature will grade their
work for you!

☑ ONGOING ASSESSMENT: Assess Mastery

Use the following resources to assess mastery of using semicolons and colons.

In the Textbook	Print Resources	Technology
Chapter Review, Ex. 67, p. 722 Standardized Test Preparation Workshop, pp. 724–725	Grammar Exercise Workbook, pp. 179–182	Language Lab CD-ROM, Punctuation; On-Line Exercise Bank, Section 29.3

Section 29.3 Section Review

GRAMMAR EXERCISES 24–29

Exercise 24 Using Semicolons
Correctly Decide where a semicolon is needed in each of the following sentences. Write the word before the semicolon, write the semicolon, and write the word after the semicolon.

1. Astronaut trainees work hard to fill the requirements as a result, they are physically and mentally ready for the arduous tasks that lay before them.
2. Applicants are physically tested and interviewed for a period of one week trainees are selected from those who score the highest.
3. Those applying as pilot astronauts must also complete 1,000 hours in a top-level flight post, such as a command pilot in a high-performance jet aircraft following that, they must pass a spaceflight physical.
4. Pilot astronauts must be between 5'4" tall and 6'4" tall mission-specialist astronauts must be between 5' tall and 6'4" tall payload specialists have no height requirement.
5. To fit the requirements, an astronaut applicant must have the appropriate education, physical health and stature, and experience but, in most cases, an applicant may be of any age.

Exercise 25 Using Colons
Correctly Rewrite each item, adding colons where appropriate. Some items may require more than one colon. Write *correct* if an item needs no additional punctuation.

1. August 1, 1998
2. To whom it may concern
3. Meeting Friday, September 8, for Junior Space Camp
4. Place American Hills High School
5. Time 7 00 P.M.

Exercise 26 Proofreading for
Semicolons, Colons, and Capitalization
On a separate sheet of paper, write the following paragraph. Add any needed semicolons or colons. Correct any capitalization errors.

It is important for pilot astronauts to experience the next phase of training flight training. Flight training, done in a T-38 jet aircraft, is not as extensive as it once was astronauts used to have one year of military flight training before they could fly in space. Candidates practice maneuvering, reaching altitudes of above 5,000 feet, and they are taught to use the ejection seat. They also study other systems the aircraft's electrical system, life support, and ejection seat. Note mission specialists are also given flight training, but they do not pilot the jets during takeoffs or landings.

Exercise 27 Find It in Your
Reading On a notice on your school bulletin board, identify how colons and semicolons are used to transmit information.

Exercise 28 Find It in Your
Writing Select a piece of writing from your portfolio. Find examples of the use of colons and semicolons. If you are unable to locate such examples, challenge yourself to write two sentences using colons and semicolons.

Exercise 29 Writing Application
Write a brief letter to a local or national politician asking about the future of America's space exploration. Use at least two semicolons in your letter.

Section Review • 683

ASSESS and CLOSE

Section Review
Each of these exercises correlates to a concept in the section on semicolons and colons, pages 674–682. These exercises may be used for more practice, for reteaching, or for review of the Key Concepts presented. Answers for all chapter exercises are available in *Grammar Exercises Answers on Transparencies* in your teaching resources.

Answer Key

Exercise 24

1. requirements; as
2. week; trainees
3. aircraft; following
4. tall; mission
   tall; payload
5. experience; but

Exercise 25

1. August 1, 1998
2. To whom it may concern:
3. Meeting: Friday, September 8, for Junior Space Camp
4. Place: American Hills High School
5. Time: 7:00 P.M.

Exercise 26

(1) It is important for pilot astronauts to experience the next phase of training: flight training. (2) Flight training, done in a T-38 jet aircraft, is not as extensive as it once was; astronauts used to have one year of military flight training before they could fly in space. (3) Candidates practice maneuvering, reaching altitudes of above 5,000 feet; and they are taught to use the ejection seat. (4) They also study other systems: the aircraft's electrical system, life support, and ejection seat. (5) Note: Mission specialists are also given flight training, but they do not pilot the jets during takeoffs or landings.

Exercise 27

Find It in Your Reading
Have students share examples with the class.

Exercise 28

Find It in Your Writing
Students can trade papers with a partner to check each other's answers.

continued

Answer Key continued

Exercise 29

Writing Application
Students may want to combine their letters into one class letter and mail it to a politician.

Interest GRABBER

Write the following dialogue on the board and have volunteers come up and add quotation marks.

I have a new eating plan, said Wendy. My food has to match my clothes.

What do you mean? asked Leo.

Today I am wearing brown pants and a yellow sweater, Wendy explained. So for lunch I will have bacon and eggs.

Leo asked, What will you eat if you are wearing polka dots?

Wendy thought for a moment. I'll mix peas in my mashed potatoes! she announced.

Activate Prior Knowledge

Ask students to recall a conversation they had recently and attempt to reconstruct a part of it using quotations from each speaker.

TEACH

Step-by-Step Teaching Guide

Punctuating Direct Quotations

1. A direct quotation represents a person's or character's exact speech and requires quotation marks. An indirect quotation is a summary or gives the general meaning; it does not require quotation marks.

2. The initial letter of a fragment is capitalized only when it comes at the beginning of a sentence. Use the following additional examples.

   "Nobody goes there anymore. It's too crowded."—Yogi Berra (direct quotation)

   Among Yogi Berra's humorous sayings is the one about no one going to that place anymore because it is too crowded. (indirect quotation)

   "The Great Emancipator" was what some people called Abraham Lincoln.

   Abraham Lincoln was called "the Great Emancipator" by some people.

continued

Section 29.4

Quotation Marks With Direct Quotations

Writers try to provide concrete support for their ideas and arguments. Quoting an expert directly can provide support for your statements while making your writing more colorful.

Punctuating Direct Quotations

This section will take a close look at direct quotations to help clarify any uncertainties you may have regarding their punctuation.

▶ **KEY CONCEPT** A **direct quotation** represents a person's exact speech or thoughts and is enclosed in quotation marks (" "). ■

DIRECT QUOTATION: "I can make a steam carriage that will run 15 miles an hour on good, level railways."
—Oliver Evans

Sometimes, you will insert only a quoted phrase into a sentence. You must set this fragment off with quotation marks also. Notice in the following examples that the first word of a phrase or fragment is capitalized only when it falls at the beginning of a sentence or when it would be capitalized regardless of its position in a sentence.

EXAMPLES: In the early years of the locomotive, people often called it "the iron horse."
"The iron horse" is what people often called the locomotive in its early years.

▶ **KEY CONCEPT** An **indirect quotation** reports only the general meaning of what a person said or thought and does not require quotation marks. ■

INDIRECT QUOTATION: Oliver Evans, who had built a steam-powered scow with wheels in 1804, said that he could build a locomotive that could run 15 miles an hour on level track.

Theme: Trains

In this section, you will learn how to use quotation marks to set off direct quotations. The examples and exercises are about trains.

Cross-Curricular Connection: Social Studies

⏱ TIME AND RESOURCE MANAGER

Resources
Print: Grammar Exercise Workbook, pp. 183–188
Technology: Language Lab CD-ROM, Punctuation; On-Line Exercise Bank, Section 29.4

In-Depth Coverage	Accelerated Pace
• Work through all key concepts, pp. 684–696. • Assign and review Exercises 30–35.	• Assign pages 684–696 for independent student review. • Assign Exercises 30–35.

▶ **KEY CONCEPT** Use a comma or colon after an introductory expression. ■

INTRODUCTORY EXPRESSION:	A representative of the Smithsonian Institution wrote, "Railroad is one of the most important means of transportation."

If you do not use a "he said/she said" expression in your introduction to a quotation or if the introductory phrase takes a more formal tone, use a colon instead of a comma before the quotation.

EXAMPLES:	Walter Larson, mayor of Washington, Missouri, spoke with the reporter: "We are looking forward to the renovated station spurring additional visitors to our community."
	Solemnly, she stated: "I will resign as treasurer of this corporation."

▶ **KEY CONCEPT** Use a comma, a question mark, or an exclamation mark after a quotation followed by a concluding expression. ■

CONCLUDING EXPRESSION:	"Railroad is one of the most important means of transportation," wrote a representative of the Smithsonian Institution.

▶ **KEY CONCEPT** Use a comma after part of a quoted sentence followed by an interrupting expression. Use another comma after the expression. ■

INTERRUPTING EXPRESSION:	"Railroad," wrote a representative of the Smithsonian Institution, "is one of the most important means of transportation."

▶ **KEY CONCEPT** Use a comma, a question mark, or an exclamation mark after a quoted sentence that comes before an interrupting expression. Use a period after the expression. ■

EXAMPLE:	"Should we expect the train any time soon?" he asked. "It was an hour late yesterday."

▲ **Critical Viewing**
With a partner, role-play a conversation that might occur between two travelers on this platform. Write a few sentences of the dialogue you exchange, correctly punctuating with commas and quotation marks. **[Apply]**

🌼 **Grammar
and Style Tip**

When using a direct or an indirect quotation, give the speaker's name whenever possible to add credibility to your writing and to avoid plagiarizing others' works.

3. A comma or a colon is used between an introductory expression and a direct quotation. The purpose of the comma or colon is to set the quote off from the introductory expression. The quotation begins with a capital letter as if it were the beginning of a sentence.

4. A colon is used to set off a quotation from introductory material when a more formal tone is required.

5. Work through the different uses of a comma or end mark after quotations. A quoted sentence that is followed by an interrupting expression is set off with a comma. If the quotation ends the sentence, then it is concluded with the appropriate end mark placed inside the quotation marks.

6. When a quotation sentence is interrupted, the initial part is set off by a comma and the last part by an end mark. Both punctuation marks are placed inside the quotation marks.

Customize for
Less Advanced Students

Students with vision problems may have difficulty noting the position and usage of quotation marks, commas, and end marks. Write sample sentences on the board in large print and write the quotation marks, commas, and end marks in colored chalk to help them better see and understand the lesson.

Critical Viewing

Apply Have volunteers write their sentences on the board.

Exercise 30

1. Colonel Stevens stated: "The transportation by means of cars drawn by steam locomotives could be carried on at a considerably cheaper rate."
2. "I had read of your very ingenious proposition as to the railway communication," wrote his friend. "I fear, however, that they will be liable to serious objection."
3. "They would ultimately prove more expensive than a canal," the chancellor continued.
4. He spoke of the great strength that the rails would need to have to "sustain so heavy a weight."
5. "The wall on which they are placed," he explained, "must be at least four feet below the surface, to avoid frost."

Critical Viewing

Connect Have students share their work in class. Make sure that they fully understand the picture.

29.4

Exercise 30 **Indicating and Capitalizing Quotations** Copy the following sentences, making the necessary corrections in punctuation and capitalization. Quoted phrases are italicized.

EXAMPLE: in 1812 Colonel Stevens announced to the Legislature of New York *I could build a railroad at much less the cost of the proposed Erie Canal.*

ANSWER: In 1812, Colonel Stevens announced to the Legislature of New York, "I could build a railroad at much less the cost of the proposed Erie Canal."

1. colonel Stevens stated: *the transportation by means of cars drawn by steam locomotives could be carried on at a considerably cheaper rate.*
2. *I had read of your very ingenious proposition as to the railway communication* wrote his friend *I fear, however, that they will be liable to serious objection.*
3. *they would ultimately prove more expensive than a canal* the chancellor continued.
4. He spoke of the great strength that the rails would need to have to *sustain so heavy a weight.*
5. *the wall on which they are placed* he explained *must be at least four feet below the surface, to avoid frost.*

More Practice

Language Lab CD-ROM
• Quotation Marks, Colons, and Semicolons lesson
On-line Exercise Bank
• Section 29.4
Grammar Exercise Workbook
• pp. 183–184

▼ **Critical Viewing**
Find a quotation about progress that you would use as a caption for this picture. On a separate sheet of paper, write and punctuate the quotation, including the words that indicate the speaker. **[Connect]**

⏱ TIME SAVERS!

🗐 **Answers on Transparency** Use the Grammar Exercises on Transparencies for Chapter 29 to have students correct their own or one another's exercises.

🖥 **On-Line Exercise Bank** Have students complete the exercises on computer. The Auto Check feature will grade their work for you!

Other Punctuation Marks With Quotation Marks

Whether to place punctuation inside or outside the quotation marks presents a problem for some writers. Four basic rules, once learned, will help you avoid most of the confusion.

> **KEY CONCEPT** Always place a comma or a period inside the final quotation mark. ■

EXAMPLES: "You exhibited greater skill in today's lesson," the driving instructor announced.

"August 1829," the President of the Delaware and Hudson Canal Company wrote, "marked the first locomotive run upon this continent."

Note in the second example that the quotation is split but that this makes no difference in the placement of the comma. It still goes inside the quotation marks.

> **KEY CONCEPT** Always place a semicolon or colon outside the final quotation mark. ■

EXAMPLE: His history book reports, "John Stevens built the first steam locomotive in the United States"; however, it had many flaws.

> **KEY CONCEPT** Place a question mark or exclamation mark inside the final quotation mark if the end mark is part of the quotation. ■

EXAMPLE: Horatio Allen asked in a letter, "When was the exact date of the first locomotive trip in the United States?"

> **KEY CONCEPT** Place a question mark or exclamation mark outside the final quotation mark if the end mark is not part of the quotation. ■

EXAMPLE: Did you hear that speaker say, "We must reduce energy consumption"?

With question marks and exclamation marks, only one mark is needed. In the following, the quotation is a question and the sentence is a statement. No period, however, is needed.

EXAMPLE: My mother asked, "Did you feed the animals?"

⚙ Grammar and Style Tip

Use dialogue to improve characterization in short stories. The exact words a character speaks sometimes reveal more about a character than a description can.

Step-by-Step Teaching Guide

Other Punctuation Marks With Quotation Marks

1. Where to place punctuation marks relative to quotation marks follows simple rules. Commas and periods always go inside closing quotation marks. This is, by far, the most frequent occurrence.

2. Semicolons and colons always go outside the quotation marks. This is a rare occurrence.

3. Question marks and exclamation points follow a simple rule. If the end mark is part of the quote, it goes inside the quotation marks. If it is part of the sentence and not part of the quotation, it goes outside.

4. Use the following additional examples as needed.

   "Ask not what your country can do for you," President John F. Kennedy said, "ask what you can do for your country."

   In his commentary on Kennedy's speech, Louie asked, "What happened to the idealism of the 1960s?"

   Did Louie claim, "Reading this speech of John F. Kennedy's changed my life"?

Customize for *More Advanced Students*

Ask students to demonstrate their knowledge of quotation marks, commas, and end marks by writing sentences that display each variety shown on the page.

29.4

▶ **Exercise 31** Using Quotation Marks With Other **Punctuation Marks** Copy the following sentences, adding quotation marks and any needed commas, colons, semicolons, or end marks. *Note:* Italics included in some of the sentences are a clue to which text should be in quotations.

EXAMPLE: Marion de Lorme wrote a letter in 1641 to the Marquis about a *poor creature named Solomon de Cause;* Solomon had been locked up in Paris by the king for his *crazy* ideas about steam power.

ANSWER: Marion de Lorme wrote a letter in 1641 to the Marquis about a "poor creature named Solomon de Cause"; Solomon had been locked up in Paris by the king for his "crazy" ideas about steam power.

1. Solomon was sent away without being admitted to the king, but he was so persistent that the king *had him shut up as a madman!*
2. Nineteenth-century locomotives powered by steam were created by expanding on these basic ideas.
3. Was it really the Marquis of Worcester who first discovered the power of steam from observing *the motion of the lid of a teakettle of boiling water?*
4. Perhaps, but the author of The First Locomotives writes *it does seem far more likely that Solomon . . . would be the one to observe the effects of the steam upon the lid of a teakettle.*

▼ **Critical Viewing** Why might it be difficult to hear a speaker's exact words when traveling on this train? **[Speculate]**

Quotation Marks in Special Situations

Several special situations may occur when you write direct quotations. These include dialogues, quotations of more than one paragraph, and quotations within other quoted material.

First, consider the use of quotation marks when writing dialogue—a direct conversation between two or more people. Use quotation marks to enclose the directly quoted conversation, and begin a new paragraph for each change of speaker.

▶**KEY CONCEPT** When writing dialogue, begin a new paragraph with each change of speaker. ■

EXAMPLE: The station attendant shouted from behind the hood, "You're a quart low on oil, Mrs. Lowell. Would you like me to put some in for you?"
      "Yes, thank you," she replied.
      "What kind of oil do you use in the car?"
      She hesitated and then replied, "I believe the car takes multigrade."

▶**KEY CONCEPT** For quotations longer than a paragraph, put quotation marks at the beginning of each paragraph and at the end of the final paragraph. ■

EXAMPLE: "In July of 1831, the West Point Foundry Works of New York first put a steam vehicle on the road. They called it the De Witt Clinton, and to many it seemed like a steam locomotive without tracks.
      "This De Witt Clinton was not a lightweight vehicle. It weighed about six tons, and its wheels were about five feet across.
      "Two names associated with this project were John B. Jervis, the man who contracted for the vehicle to be built, and another man, known as Sir Matthew, who served as chief engineer of the project."

▶**KEY CONCEPT** Use single quotation marks for a quotation within a quotation. ■

EXAMPLE: The fund-raiser concluded, saying, "As we try to raise money for this worthy cause, let us not forget that old English proverb that says, 'Where there's a will there's a way.'"

Step-by-Step Teaching Guide

Quotation Marks in Special Situations

1. Dialogue requires a new paragraph every time there is a change of speaker. A change of paragraph alerts the reader that someone else is speaking.

2. Point out the use of quotation marks in multiple-paragraph quotes.

3. Quotations within quotations can be confusing. Point out the use of single and double quotation marks and the order in which they appear at the beginning and end of quotations. Also have students note that since the quotation in the text example ends the sentence, the period appears inside both the single and double quotation marks.

Customize for
Less Advanced Students

Students with vision problems may have difficulty noting the position and use of single and double quotation marks. Write sample sentences on the board in large print and write the quotation marks (and commas and end marks) in colored chalk to help them better see and understand the lesson.

689

"What is an electric railroad?" asked Peter.

"It is," replied Raajita, "an electrically powered railway system."

"Oh, would that include subways and streetcars?"

Raajita looked at him and explained, "Yes, they are a lot quieter than other trains; and they don't produce any smoke or exhaust."

Peter was doubtful. "Maybe, but how do they run?"

"Well, the encyclopedia says the world's fastest is France's TGV train and that it can reach up to 160 mph."

"There are magnetic levitation electrical trains," interrupted Desmond, "being designed by engineers right now."

"How do the two of you know so much about electric trains?" inquired Peter.

Desmond turned to him with a smile. "We have been to Europe," he explained. "Electric trains are common in Europe; but in the United States, less than 1 percent of inter-city track is electrified."

Critical Viewing

Apply Have students share their work in class.

29.4

Exercise 32 Punctuating and Capitalizing in Longer

Selections The following dialogue has no paragraphing, quotation marks, capitalization, or punctuation. Each number indicates a new speaker. Copy the dialogue, indicating paragraphs and adding the necessary quotation marks, capitalization, and punctuation.

1. what is an electric railroad asked peter
2. it is replied raajita an electrically powered railway system
3. oh, would that include subways and streetcars
4. raajita looked at him and explained yes, they are a lot quieter than other trains, and they don't produce any smoke or exhaust
5. peter was doubtful maybe, but how do they run
6. well, the encyclopedia says the world's fastest is france's tgv train and that it can reach up to 160 mph
7. there are magnetic-levitation electrical trains interrupted desmond being designed by engineers right now
8. how do the two of you know so much about electric trains inquired Raajita
9. desmond turned to him with a smile
10. we have been to europe, he explained electric trains are common in europe, but in the united states, less than 1 percent of inter-city track is electrified.

▲ **Critical Viewing**
Find an article about the "bullet train." Choose a fact or detail from the article and write it out as a direct quotation. Include in your sentence the author's name. **[Apply]**

More Practice

Language Lab
CD-ROM
• Quotation Marks, Colons, and Semicolons lesson
On-line
Exercise Bank
• Section 29.4
Grammar Exercise
Workbook
• pp. 185–186

⏱ TIME SAVERS!

Answers on Transparency
Use the Grammar Exercises on Transparencies for Chapter 29 to have students correct their own or one another's exercises.

On-Line Exercise Bank
Have students complete the exercises on computer. The Auto Check feature will grade their work for you!

Underlining and Other Uses of Quotation Marks

1. Underlining and quotation marks are used for titles. Underlining is done only when writing by hand or on a typewriter. On a computer, all underlining appears as italics.

2. Review the chart of works to be underlined. The rule is that longer works get underlined; shorter works, or parts of the longer works, get quotation marks.

Underlining and Other Uses of Quotation Marks

In printed material, italics and quotation marks are used to set some titles, names, and words apart from the rest of the text. In handwritten or typed material, italics are not available, so underlining is used instead. Quotation marks, on the other hand, are used in both printed and handwritten materials.

Underlining

▶ **KEY CONCEPT** Underline the titles of long written works and the titles of publications that are published as a single work. ■

Following are examples of titles you should underline.

TITLES OF WRITTEN WORKS THAT ARE UNDERLINED	
Titles of Books	Jane Eyre by Charlotte Brontë
Titles of Plays	A Raisin in the Sun by Lorraine Hansberry The Man Who Came to Dinner by Moss Hart
Titles of Periodicals (magazines, journals, pamphlets)	Eastern Railroad News Time Journal of American History TRAINS Magazine
Titles of Newspapers	The New York Times the Palm Beach Post the Chicago Sun-Times
Titles of Long Poems	Idylls of the King by Alfred, Lord Tennyson Beowulf

Note About *Newspaper Titles:* The portion of the title that should be underlined will vary from newspaper to newspaper. *The New York Times* should always be fully capitalized and underlined. Other papers, however, can usually be treated in one of two ways: *The Los Angeles Times* or the Los Angeles *Times.* Unless you know the true name of a paper, choose one of these two forms and use it consistently.

▶ **KEY CONCEPT** Underline the titles of movies, television and radio series, lengthy works of music, paintings, and sculpture. ■

💿 **Technology Tip**

Use the formatting tools of a word-processing program to italicize the titles of full-length works.

✓ ONGOING ASSESSMENT: Monitor and Reinforce

If students miss more than two items in Exercises 30–32, refer them to the following for additional practice.

In the Textbook	Print Resources	Technology
Chapter Review, Ex. 68, p. 722	Grammar Exercise Workbook, pp. 183–186	Language Lab CD-ROM, Punctuation; On-Line Exercise Bank, Section 29.4

Other Artistic Works That Are Underlined

1. Review the text chart with students. The same rule applies of underlining artistic works when handwriting them or typing them using a typewriter.

2. The only way to know if a foreign word has become part of the English language is to use the dictionary. If the word is not listed, or if it is written in italics in the dictionary, then it is still considered foreign.

29.4

OTHER ARTISTIC WORKS THAT ARE UNDERLINED	
Titles of Movies	The Caine Mutiny
Titles of Radio and Television Series	The Shadow Happy Days
Titles of Long Musical Compositions and Record Albums (any musical work made up of several parts, such as operas, musical comedies, symphonies, and ballets)	Bach's Christmas Oratorio The Beatles' Abbey Road Puccini's Tosca Haydn's Surprise Symphony Tchaikovsky's Swan Lake
Titles of Paintings and Sculpture	Dancers at the Bar (Degas) Indian on Horseback (Mestrovic)

▶ **KEY CONCEPT** Underline the names of individual air, sea, space, and land craft. ■

the Spirit of St. Louis   the S.S. Seagallant
the De Witt Clinton

▶ **KEY CONCEPT** Underline foreign words not yet accepted into English. ■

EXAMPLE: It is verboten to board the train without a ticket. (German: forbidden)

Since the process of accepting words and phrases into the English language is a continuous one, you cannot be certain whether a phrase is still considered foreign.

▶ **KEY CONCEPT** Underline numbers, symbols, letters, and words used to name themselves. ■

NUMBERS: When I say the number three, you start running.
SYMBOLS: Is that an ! at the end of that sentence?
LETTERS: Is that first letter a G or an S?
WORDS: She wrote the word fluid, but she meant fluent.

▶ **KEY CONCEPT** Underline words that you wish to stress. ■

EXAMPLE: We will need a minimum of six dollars for the trip.

Exercise 33 **Underlining Titles, Names, and Words** Write and underline titles, names, or words that require underlining. If a sentence needs no correction, write *correct*.

EXAMPLE: She graduated <u>magna cum laude</u>.

ANSWER: magna cum laude

1. He read the book Murder on the Orient Express.
2. The words all aboard signal the last boarding of the train.
3. They had to get some dinero before they could buy the TV.
4. Flimsies West and Hot Off the Rails Newsletter are both magazines about railroads.
5. In the former Soviet Union, President Mikhail Gorbachev introduced glasnost, beginning a major reform period.
6. You may read about a change in railroad legislation in The New York Times.
7. We won't get on this car but the next one.
8. The cast of Our Town took the subway to Times Square.
9. Although locomotives were built and tested up to the year 1829, the first locomotive to run for public use was the DeWitt Clinton in the year 1831.
10. The advances in technology from steam engines to the launching of Apollo 12 happened amazingly fast.

More Practice

On-line
Exercise Bank
• Section 29.4
Grammar Exercise
Workbook
• pp. 187–188

▼ Critical Viewing
Name three stories, novels, movies, or songs that this picture calls to mind. Which ones would be underlined or italicized in writing? **[Connect]**

Answer Key

Exercise 33

1. <u>Murder on the Orient Express</u>
2. <u>all aboard</u>
3. <u>dinero</u>
4. <u>Flimsies West</u>, <u>Hot Off the Rails Newsletter</u>
5. correct
6. <u>The New York Times</u>
7. We won't get on <u>this</u> car but the next one.
8. <u>Our Town</u>
9. <u>De Witt Clinton</u>
10. <u>Apollo 12</u>

Critical Viewing

Connect Answers will vary.

⏱ **TIME SAVERS!**

 **Answers on Transparency**
Use the Grammar Exercises on Transparencies for Chapter 29 to have students correct their own or one another's exercises.

🖥 **On-Line Exercise Bank**
Have students complete the exercises on computer. The Auto Check feature will grade their work for you!

Other Uses of Quotation Marks

1. Quotation marks are used for shorter works and works that appear as part of longer works.
2. Review the categories of written works that take quotation marks.
3. Titles of episodes in a TV series, individual songs, and parts of longer musical compositions also require quotation marks.

Critical Viewing

Analyze Students may suggest that visual clues and signals are important because the train is approaching a switching station.

29.4

Other Uses of Quotation Marks

Section 29.3 discussed the use of quotation marks (" ") with spoken words. Quotation marks also set off certain titles.

▶ **KEY CONCEPT** Use quotation marks around the titles of short written works. ■

Short works include short stories, chapters from books, short poems, essays, and articles.

SHORT STORY:	"The Jockey" by Carson McCullers
CHAPTER FROM A BOOK:	"Railroads in America"
SHORT POEM:	"Boy Breaking Glass" by Gwendolyn Brooks
ESSAY TITLES:	"Self-Reliance" by Ralph Waldo Emerson
ARTICLE TITLE:	"The Benefits of Train Travel"

▶ **KEY CONCEPT** Use quotation marks around the titles of episodes in a series, songs, and parts of long musical compositions. ■

EPISODE:	"The Iran File" from 60 Minutes
SONG TITLE:	"I've Been Working on the Railroad"
PART OF A LONG MUSICAL COMPOSITION:	"Spring" from The Four Seasons

Occasionally, you may refer to the title of one long work contained in a larger work. Singly, each title would require underlining; when used together, another rule applies.

Use quotation marks around the title of a work that is mentioned as part of a collection.

EXAMPLE: "Plato" from Great Books of the Western World

▶ **Critical Viewing** Explain how this picture illustrates the importance of understanding and following visual clues and signals. **[Analyze]**

694 • Punctuation

▶ **Exercise 34** **Using Quotation Marks With Titles** From each of the following sentences, copy the unpunctuated title and enclose it in quotation marks.

EXAMPLE: The story The Necklace has an interesting theme.
ANSWER: "The Necklace"

1. Streetcars Tie the City Together is an article about the importance of streetcars in the city.
2. Edgar Allan Poe wrote the famous story The Tell-Tale Heart.
3. A popular song about a train is The Chattanooga Express.
4. An important chapter to read from that book is Letters From Officials.
5. Robert Frost, one of my favorite poets, wrote Nothing Gold Can Stay.
6. The newspaper clipping was entitled Local Officials Celebrate New Train Station in Washington.
7. The story The Lottery speaks against blindly following the crowd.
8. Read The Inspector-General in *Prentice Hall Literature: Timeless Voices, Timeless Themes,* Gold.
9. Be sure to cover the chapter entitled The Industrial Revolution in your history books tonight.
10. They decided to sing Good Night, Ladies as the train left the station.

Titles Without Underlining or Quotation Marks

Some titles require neither underlining nor quotation marks. The first such classification consists of various religious works.

▶ **KEY CONCEPT** Do not underline or place in quotation marks the name of the Bible, its books, divisions, or versions or the names of other holy scriptures, such as the Koran. ■

EXAMPLE: He found a Bible in his hotel room.

Similarly, you should not underline or enclose in quotation marks certain government documents.

▶ **KEY CONCEPT** Do not underline or place in quotation marks the titles of government charters, alliances, treaties, acts, statutes, or reports. ■

EXAMPLES: the Declaration of Independence
the Civil Rights Act

▶ **More Practice**

Language Lab CD-ROM
• Quotation Marks, Colons, and Semicolons lesson

On-line Exercise Bank
• Section 29.4

Grammar Exercise Workbook
• pp. 187–188

Answer Key

Exercise 34

1. "Streetcars Tie the City Together"
2. "The Tell-Tale Heart"
3. "The Chattanooga Express"
4. "Letters From Officials"
5. "Nothing Gold Can Stay"
6. "Local Officials Celebrate New Train Station in Washington"
7. "The Lottery"
8. "The Inspector-General"
9. "The Industrial Revolution"
10. "Good-Night, Ladies"

Step-by-Step Teaching Guide

Titles Without Underlining or Quotation Marks

1. Holy scriptures and important government documents require neither underlining nor quotation marks.
2. Use the following additional examples if needed.

   Old Testament

   Book of Revelation

   Sherman Anti-Trust Act

   Treaty of Versailles

   Emancipation Proclamation

🗹 **ONGOING ASSESSMENT: Monitor and Reinforce**

If students miss more than two items in Exercises 33–35, refer them to the following for additional practice.

In the Textbook	Print Resources	Technology
Chapter Review, Ex. 69, p. 722	Grammar Exercise Workbook, pp. 187–188	Language Lab CD-ROM, Punctuation; On-Line Exercise Bank, Section 29.4

TIME SAVERS!

▦ **Answers on Transparency** Use the Grammar Exercises on Transparencies for Chapter 29 to have students correct their own or one another's exercises.

▯ **On-Line Exercise Bank** Have students complete the exercises on computer. The Auto Check feature will grade their work for you!

1. correct
2. correct
3. correct
4. correct
5. "Electric Railroad"; <u>World Book Encyclopedia</u>
6. <u>The Railroads: Opening the West</u>
7. <u>John Bull</u>
8. correct
9. <u>San Diego Times</u>
10. correct

Critical Viewing

Infer Students may say that train travel is more scenic.

29.4

> **Exercise 35** **Punctuating Different Types of Titles** Copy the titles, and enclose them in quotation marks or underline them. If neither quotation marks nor underlining is needed, write *correct*.

EXAMPLE: The Bill of Rights protects the rights of individuals.

ANSWER: correct

1. The Constitution was a collection of compromises.
2. The astronaut read from the first chapter of Genesis when he saw the Earth from space.
3. The family studied the Koran as they rode the train.
4. The Americans With Disabilities Act provides accommodations to those with disabilities.
5. They read Electric Railroad from the World Book Encyclopedia.
6. The Railroads: Opening the West would have several chapters about the history of railroads.
7. The English locomotive John Bull had four driving wheels of four feet in diameter.
8. There was a Bible in our hotel room.
9. The San Diego Times is a newspaper published in California.
10. All the leaders signed the Treaty of Versailles.

▲ **Critical Viewing** Based on details from this picture, why might some people prefer traveling by train to traveling by plane? **[Infer]**

> **More Practice**
>
> **Language Lab CD-ROM**
> • Quotation Marks, Colons, and Semicolons lesson
> **On-line Exercise Bank**
> • Section 29.4
> **Grammar Exercise Workbook**
> • pp. 185–186

Answers on Transparency Use the Grammar Exercises on Transparencies for Chapter 29 to have students correct their own or one another's exercises.

On-Line Exercise Bank Have students complete the exercises on computer. The Auto Check feature will grade their work for you!

☑ **ONGOING ASSESSMENT: Assess Mastery**

Use the following resources to assess mastery of using quotation marks and underlining.

In the Textbook	Print Resources	Technology
Chapter Review, Ex. 68–69, p. 722 Standardized Test Preparation Workshop, pp. 724–725	Grammar Exercise Workbook, pp. 183–188	Language Lab CD-ROM, Punctuation; On-Line Exercise Bank, Section 29.4

Section 29.4 Section Review

GRAMMAR EXERCISES 36–41

> **Exercise 36** **Punctuating Direct Quotations** Rewrite the following sentences, punctuating correctly.

1. John Edgar, a reporter, writes of a new program: this program offers train customers car-rental services at select stations throughout the country.
2. He is speaking of a new program many train stations have adopted with the facilities housing rental desks.
3. We have come together explains Executive Vice President Barbara J. Wylie to deliver a more seamless journey for our customers.
4. She continues it is the very kind of service that today's travelers expect.
5. You can read the paper to find out how this service works Upon arrival at participating stations, travelers may simply walk across the street to the car-rental location.

> **Exercise 37** **Using Punctuation in Direct Quotations** Rewrite the following dialogue, punctuating correctly. Each number indicates a new speaker..

1. Was it the Robert Fulton that was the first locomotive-engine that came from England and was afterward put on the road?
2. It certainly was he said and when it came great preparations were made for a large crowd of passengers
3. I read what happened on the day of the excursion Something [went] wrong with the Robert Fulton and the DeWitt Clinton took its place at the head of the train.
4. Of course the rest of the train Tom pointed out was too heavy for so small a machine
5. Some of the cars were pulled by the DeWitt, and the other popular mode of transportation pulled the rest of the amusing-looking cavalcade: horses.

> **Exercise 38** **Using Quotation Marks and Underlining** Rewrite the title(s) from each sentence. Add underlining or quotation marks where appropriate.

1. In 1832, the Baltimore and Ohio Railroad Company introduced a steam locomotive called the York.
2. For those who own passenger cars, the American Association of Private Railroad Car Owners is a good society to join.
3. We listened to Summer from The Four Seasons during the trip.
4. We pulled the information from Chapter 38: Additional Letters.
5. An informative paper designed for railroad fans is the Eastern Railroad News.

> **Exercise 39** **Find It in Your Reading** Explain the purpose of the quotation marks and underlining in the following passage.

"Space travel is humanity's greatest adventure," says Eugene F. Kranz, who describes the history and development of the space program in an article in the World Book Encyclopedia.

> **Exercise 40** **Find It in Your Writing** Choose a piece of writing from your portfolio. Find examples of direct quotations and indirect quotations.

> **Exercise 41** **Writing Application** Write a conversation between two or more people who are discussing travel plans. Use quotation marks correctly.

ASSESS and CLOSE

Section Review

Each of these exercises correlates to a concept in the section on quotation marks and underlining, pages 684–696. These exercises may be used for more practice, for reteaching, or for review of the Key Concepts presented. Answers for all chapter exercises are available in *Grammar Exercises Answers on Transparencies* in your teaching resources.

Answer Key

Exercise 36

1. John Edgar, a reporter, writes of a new program: "This program offers train customers car-rental services at select stations throughout the country."
2. He is speaking of a new program many train stations have adopted with the "facilities housing rental desks."
3. "We have come together," explains Executive Vice President Barbara J. Wylie, "to deliver a more seamless journey for our customers."
4. She continues, "It is the very kind of service that today's travelers expect."
5. You can read the paper to find out how this service works: "Upon arrival at participating stations, travelers may simply walk across the street to the car rental location."

Exercise 37

1. "Was it the Robert Fulton that was the first locomotive-engine that came from England and was afterward put on the road?"
2. "It certainly was," he said, "and when it came, great preparations were made for a large crowd of passengers."
3. I read what happened on the day of the excursion: "Something [went] wrong with the Robert Fulton and the De Witt Clinton took its place at the head of the train."
4. "Of course the rest of the train," said Tom, "was much too heavy for so small a machine!"

continued

Answer Key continued

5. Some of the cars were pulled by the De Witt, and the other popular mode of transportation pulled the rest of the "amusing-looking cavalcade": horses.

Exercise 38

1. York
2. correct
3. "Summer"; The Four Seasons
4. "Additional Letters"
5. Eastern Railroad News

Exercise 39

Find It in Your Reading
direct quotation, book title

Exercise 40

Find It in Your Writing
Have students check that they used quotation marks correctly.

Exercise 41

Writing Application
Students may want to work with partners, each student writing one person's dialogue.

PREPARE and ENGAGE

Interest GRABBER Write the following sentence on the board and ask students to punctuate it with appropriate dashes and hyphens.

Buster[—]the dumbest Labrador retriever in the world[—]managed to find and devour two[-]thirds of the meat we were planning to use for the chili.

Activate Prior Knowledge

Ask students to write sentences that use each of the punctuation marks covered in the section: dash(es), parentheses, and hyphens.

TEACH

Step-by-Step Teaching Guide

Dashes

1. The dash has multiple uses, and they are not always obvious. See that students examine the text charts and examples carefully and apply the knowledge.

2. A dash can indicate an abrupt change of thought, dramatically set off interrupting ideas, and set off a summary statement.

3. Use the following additional examples.

   Raise the corner—your bike is really cool—a little to the right. (abrupt change of thought)

   The pitch—a sharp breaking slider—had him totally fooled. (dramatically set off interrupting idea)

   Splitting wood, tossing hay bales, and wrestling with 1,200-pound horses—that's my workout routine. (set off a summary statement)

Section 29.5

Dashes, Parentheses, and Hyphens

Dashes

The dash, a long horizontal mark made above the writing line (—), functions to set off material in three basic ways:

▶ **KEY CONCEPT** Use dashes to indicate an abrupt change of thought, a dramatic interrupting idea, or a summary statement. ■

USES OF THE DASH	
To indicate an abrupt change of thought	I cannot believe what the barber did to my beautiful hair—oh, I don't even want to think about it!
To set off interrupting ideas dramatically	Oatmeal—which tastes delicious with honey and raisins—makes a nutritious breakfast when served with milk. The ruby-throated hummingbird—wow, what a beautiful bird—gets its name from the male's red throat.
To set off a summary statement	Vanilla, rocky road, strawberry, blackberry, and butter pecan—deciding which of these flavors to get took me a full five minutes. To eat twice its body weight in a day—this is the feeding goal of the hummingbird.

It may help you to know that words such as *all, these, this,* and *that* frequently begin a summary sentence preceded by a dash.

In certain circumstances, nonessential appositives and modifiers are also set off with dashes.

▶ **KEY CONCEPT** Use dashes to set off a nonessential appositive or modifier when it is long, when it is already punctuated, or when you want to be dramatic. ■

Only those appositives or modifiers that follow the rule need a dash. Notice how the examples in the following charts each meet at least one of the three criteria in the rule.

698 • Punctuation

Theme: Birds

In this section, you will learn about the various uses of dashes, parentheses, and hyphens. The examples and exercises are about birds.

Cross-Curricular Connection: Science

⏱ TIME AND RESOURCE MANAGER

Resources
Print: Grammar Exercise Workbook, pp. 189–194
Technology: Language Lab CD-ROM, Punctuation; On-Line Exercise Bank, Section 29.5

In-Depth Coverage	Accelerated Pace
• Work through all key concepts, pp. 698–710. • Assign and review Exercises 42–47.	• Assign pages 698–710 for independent student review. • Assign Exercises 42–47.

USING DASHES WITH NONESSENTIAL APPOSITIVES

Reasons for Use	Examples
Length	The ruby-throated hummingbird—a bird that lives in woods, orchards, and gardens but moves to the forests in the winter—eats nectar and small insects.
Internal Punctuation	Some of the stores in the mall—for example, The Bathing Beauties Bath Shop—never have any customers.
Strong Emphasis	The movies—three box-office blockbusters—were not among our favorites.

Nonessential modifiers are generally set off only when they have internal punctuation or when strong emphasis is desired.

USING DASHES WITH NONESSENTIAL MODIFIERS

Internal Punctuation	The ruby-throated hummingbird—which migrates to Central America for the winter—must build up a layer of body fat equal to half its body weight before migrating.
Strong Emphasis	Our new dog's hopeful expression—which he has mastered so well that even Lassie could take lessons from him—is so appealing that he is slowly winning me over.

Consider a final kind of sentence interrupter—a parenthetical expression. You may recall that a parenthetical expression consists of words or phrases that are inserted into a sentence but have no essential grammatical relationship to it. Parenthetical expressions are often enclosed by dashes.

Grammar and Style Tip

Do not overuse dashes; they will lose their impact if they appear too frequently in your writing.

Dashes With Nonessential Appositives and Modifiers

1. Review the uses of the dash with nonessential appositives and modifiers.

2. Help students see the logic in the rules. These nonessential elements are set off by dashes instead of commas for reasons of length, internal punctuation, and emphasis.

3. Use the following additional examples.

   The storm—60-mile-per-hour winds, a foot of snow, –40° windchill—created havoc. (appositive, length, and internal punctuation)

   Linda Pierce, school bus driver—who knows every inch of the road, every kid by name, and every trick kids are planning on pulling before they have even thought of pulling it—is the unsung hero of our town. (nonessential modifier, internal punctuation)

Dashes with Parenthetical Expressions

1. Dashes are used with parenthetical expressions for the same reasons they are used with nonessential appositives and modifiers: for reasons of length, internal punctuation, or dramatic emphasis. A dash is also used when the parenthetical expression is a question or exclamation.

2. Use the following additional examples.

   The parade of dignitaries we had here the last week—can you believe we had the governor, one senator, two congressional representatives, and the Chief Justice of the State Court of Appeals?—has been a cause of great excitement. (length, internal punctuation, question)

Customize for
More Advanced Students

Have students read news articles in newspapers, in magazines, and on Web sites and find sentences with a dash. Ask then to identify the reason for the dash in each sentence.

Critical Viewing

Describe Sentences will vary.

29.5

▶ **KEY CONCEPT** Use dashes to set off a parenthetical expression when it is long, already punctuated, or especially dramatic. ∎

Of course, not every parenthetical expression will take a dash. Short expressions hardly need dashes.

EXAMPLES: I will, I think, go.
Give it to me, Susan.

However, as with nonessential appositives, if the parenthetical expression is long or contains its own punctuation, you will often want to set it off with dashes.

EXAMPLE: This continual downpour—we had two inches Monday, one inch yesterday, and an inch already today—will certainly help the birds.

The use of dashes is especially likely if the parenthetical expression is a question or an exclamation.

EXAMPLE: After Mr. Mathers was caught stealing the exotic bird—did you have any idea?—he was taken to the police station and booked.

You can also enclose a parenthetical expression in dashes if you want the expression to stand out dramatically from the rest of the sentence.

EXAMPLE: Hummingbirds time their migration—a trip of over 1,850 miles, crossing 600 miles of the Gulf of Mexico—to arrive back at their North American homes just when their favorite nectar flowers bloom.

Although the dash has many uses, be careful not to overuse it. Using an occasional dash adds sentence variety and interest; putting dashes in too often will make your thoughts seem confused and disjointed. Therefore, always follow one of the rules when you use dashes. In all other situations, insert commas or, in some cases, parentheses for maximum effectiveness.

▼ Critical Viewing
Write a sentence about the hummingbird pictured here. Include the phrase "tiny and fast" as a parenthetical expression set off by dashes. [Describe]

> ▶ **Exercise 42** **Using the Dash** Copy the following sentences, adding one or two dashes in each.

EXAMPLE: Hummingbirds feed on the nectar from red flowers that is, most of the time.

ANSWER: Hummingbirds feed on the nectar from red flowers—that is, most of the time.

1. There are actually some flowers at least thirty-one varieties of blossoms that attract the ruby-throated hummingbird.
2. The fantastic agility of the hummingbird a hummingbird beats its wings ninety times per second lets it skip from flower to flower in the same movements an insect uses.
3. Flying from flower to flower, it can hover for long periods of time allowing it to gather nectar with its long beak and pollinate the flowers it feeds from.
4. Honeysuckle, petunias, nasturtiums, and lilacs all these flowers attract a hummingbird.
5. The hummingbird's main source of food nectar is supplemented with small insects and spiders.

Parentheses

Parentheses set off supplementary material not essential to the understanding of the sentence. Though not as dramatic as the dash, parentheses are the strongest separator you can use.

> ▶ **KEY CONCEPT** Use parentheses when the material is not essential or when it consists of one or more sentences. ■

Note that you can take out all the material in parentheses in the following example without altering the meaning.

EXAMPLE: The diet (seeds, nuts, berries, fruits, flowers, corn, and some insects) of the sulphur-crested cockatoo is especially varied for a bird.

Supplementary numbers may also be enclosed in parentheses.

> ▶ **KEY CONCEPT** Use parentheses to set off numerical explanations—such as dates of a person's birth and death—and around numbers and letters marking a series. ■

EXAMPLE: We established a memorial fund for Mary Tsai (1965–1981), which will be used to buy books.

▶ **More Practice**

Language Lab CD-ROM
• Section 29.4
Grammar Exercise Workbook
• pp. 189–190

Exercise 42

1. There are actually some flowers—at least thirty-one varieties of blossoms—that attract the ruby-throated hummingbird.
2. The fantastic agility of the hummingbird—a hummingbird beats its wings ninety times per second—lets it skip from flower to flower in the same movements an insect uses.
3. Flying from flower to flower—it can hover for long periods of time allowing it to gather nectar with its long beak—it pollinates the flowers it feeds from.
4. Honeysuckle, petunias, nasturtiums, and lilacs—all these flowers attract a hummingbird.
5. The hummingbird's main source of food—nectar—is supplemented with small insects and spiders.

Step-by-Step Teaching Guide

Parentheses

1. Parentheses are used to enclose incidental explanatory material and explanatory numbers.
2. Use the following additional examples to illustrate both usages:

    Leroy Bolton (the organization's founder and long-time president) presided over the meeting.

    Mozart (1756–1791) composed an astonishing amount of beautiful music in his short life.

Dashes, Parentheses, and Hyphens • **701**

TIME SAVERS!

▧ **Answers on Transparency** Use the Grammar Exercises on Transparencies for Chapter 29 to have students correct their own or one another's exercises.

▢ **On-Line Exercise Bank** Have students complete the exercises on computer. The Auto Check feature will grade their work for you!

Capitalizing and Punctuating With Parentheses

1. The rules for capitalizing and punctuating with parentheses may appear more complicated than they really are.

2. Here is a summary of the rules.

   • Capitalize and use an end mark only for interrupting questions or exclamations.

   • Punctuate within parentheses according to its place in the sentence.

3. Share with students the following additional examples:

   Walter asked the boy (What a generous gesture!) if he wanted to join the game.

   The boy (he was 11 years old) was thrilled to play with big kids.

   If more older boys did what Walter did (Did you tell his mother what Walter did?), it would really help.

Customize for *ESL Students*

Students may have trouble following the details of the rules of capitalizing and punctuating with parentheses. Have them work carefully through the rules. It may be helpful if they can grasp the general principles first, which will put the details in a logical context.

29.5

Capitalizing and Punctuating With Parentheses

Several guidelines will help you punctuate and capitalize the material in parentheses.

▶ **KEY CONCEPT** When a phrase or declarative sentence interrupts another sentence, do not use an initial capital or end mark inside the parentheses. ■

EXAMPLE: Cockatoos (my sister just bought one) look like parrots.

If the sentence is exclamatory or interrogative, however, the rule changes.

▶ **KEY CONCEPT** When a question or exclamation interrupts another sentence, use both an initial capital and an end mark inside the parentheses. ■

EXAMPLE: Cocky (That bird lived 82 years compared to the normal 50 in captivity!) lived in the London Zoo.

▶ **KEY CONCEPT** With any sentence that falls between two complete sentences, use both an initial capital and an end mark inside the parentheses. ■

EXAMPLE: We drove to the Ashland bird sanctuary. (It took more than fifteen hours.) The quality of the facility surpassed even our high expectations.

Be aware of punctuation that falls after a parenthetical phrase.

▶ **KEY CONCEPT** In a sentence that includes parentheses, place any punctuation belonging to the main sentence after the parenthesis. ■

Apply this rule for commas, semicolons, colons, and end marks.

EXAMPLES: The ocean water felt icy cold (about 45°)!

Nesting in a cliff or high niche (a dead eucalyptus tree with a hole in it is ideal), both the male and female cockatoos take care of the young.

▶ **More Practice**

Language Lab
CD-ROM
• Section 29.4
Grammar Exercise Workbook
• pp. 191–192

> **Exercise 43** **Using Parentheses** Copy the following sentences, adding the necessary parentheses.

EXAMPLE: The sulphur-crested cockatoo Have you ever seen one up close? is one of the most popular birds to keep as a pet.

ANSWER: The sulphur-crested cockatoo (Have you ever seen one up close?) is one of the most popular birds to keep as a pet.

1. The sulphur-crested cockatoo has been kept as a pet since the nineteenth century.
2. Its shrill voice heard mostly early in the morning or when it becomes alarmed can be trained to mimic the human voice.
3. Cockatoos that make the best pets are those that are bred in captivity. They are calmer and easier to train. Buying only birds that are captivity-bred also helps protect the birds of the wild.
4. A cockatoo will use the crest of feathers on its head to show strong emotion fear or aggression.
5. When buying a cockatoo, be sure to buy a large cage; cockatoos will grow to be over a foot 18–20 inches long.

▶ **Critical Viewing** Include a parenthetical comment in a statement about the bird in this picture. **[Apply]**

Dashes, Parentheses, and Hyphens • 703

Answer Key

▶ **Exercise 43**

1. The sulphur-crested cockatoo has been kept as a pet since the nineteenth (19th) century.
2. Its shrill voice (heard mostly early in the morning or when it becomes alarmed) can be trained to mimic the human voice.
3. Cockatoos that make the best pets are those that were bred in captivity. They are calmer and easier to train. (Buying only birds that are captivity-bred also helps protect the birds of the wild.) They are calmer and easier to train.
4. A cockatoo will use its crest of feathers on its head to show strong emotion (fear or aggression).
5. When buying a cockatoo, be sure to buy a large cage; cockatoos will grow to be over a foot (18–20 inches) long.

Critical Viewing

Apply Answers will vary.

29.5

▶ **Exercise 44** **Using Capitals and Punctuation With Parentheses** Copy each sentence that needs capitalization or punctuation, making the necessary changes. If no corrections are needed, write *correct*.

EXAMPLE: When I finished the assignment (what a tough one it was) I took a nap.

ANSWER: When I finished the assignment (What a tough one it was!), I took a nap.

1. Cockatoos are common in the wild throughout parts of Australia the eastern area and some islands close to the mainland.
2. In the North, these birds travel in small (at least two birds) groups.
3. In the South, they travel in huge flocks (Looking like a blanket of snow flying around) that can contain hundreds of birds.
4. Cockatoos spend the morning and evening looking for food. (Afternoons are spent entertaining themselves by pulling bark and leaves off trees.) They then return to their roosting grounds at nightfall.
5. Because they eat all the seeds until they are gone of course that is their natural diet they are sometimes a nuisance to farmers.

Hyphens

As a writer, you should appreciate the versatility of the hyphen, for this punctuation mark makes it possible not only to join but also to divide certain words. Unfortunately, the hyphen is often mistaken for its cousin, the dash, because the two share a similar appearance. However, you should note that the hyphen is distinctly shorter than the dash; in fact, typing the hyphen takes one mark (-), while the dash takes two (—). In books and other printed material, the hyphen is less than half as long as the dash.

The primary uses of the hyphen are to divide certain numbers and parts of words, to join some compound words, and to divide words at the ends of lines. This section will focus on the rules governing the appropriate use of the hyphen in these cases.

▼ **Critical Viewing** Identify several words of two or more syllables that describe this picture. Write each word, inserting hyphens between syllables. **[Analyze]**

With Numbers

When you write out numbers in words, some of them require hyphens.

▶**KEY CONCEPT** Use a hyphen when writing out two-word numbers from *twenty-one* through *ninety-nine*. ■

EXAMPLE: The average cockatoo is about thirty-two centimeters long.

Some fractions also require a hyphen.

▶**KEY CONCEPT** Use a hyphen with fractions used as adjectives. ■

EXAMPLE: The typical cockatoo diet is one-half seeds and nuts and one-half fruit.

In the preceding example, the fractions function as adjectives. If they were used as nouns, the hyphen would then be omitted.

EXAMPLE: Only *one third* of the birds in the parrot family are called parrots.

With Word Parts

Some word parts require the use of a hyphen.

▶**KEY CONCEPT** Use a hyphen after a prefix that is followed by a proper noun or adjective. ■

EXAMPLE: Eclectus parrots live on islands in the *east-Pacific* islands.

Certain prefixes and suffixes require the use of hyphens even when no proper noun or adjective is involved.

▶**KEY CONCEPT** Use a hyphen in words with the prefixes *all-*, *ex-*, and *self-* and in words with the suffix *-elect*. ■

EXAMPLES: all-powerful   self-addressed
ex-teacher   senator-elect

Hyphens With Numbers and Word Parts

1. Review the rules and examples for using hyphens.
2. Use the following additional examples for illustration.

> *Theodore Roosevelt was forty-two years old when he became the twenty-sixth president of the United States.*

> *Roosevelt was from New York, which has produced about one-sixth of all U.S. presidents.*

> *As ex-president, Roosevelt exerted influence over political affairs.*

Customize for
More Advanced Students

Have students read news articles in newspapers, in magazines, or on Websites and find sentences with a hyphen. Ask them to identify the reason for the hyphen in each sentence.

☑ ONGOING ASSESSMENT: Monitor and Reinforce

If students miss more than two items in Exercises 42–44, refer them to the following for additional practice.

In the Textbook	Print Resources	Technology
Chapter Review, Ex. 70, p. 723	Grammar Exercise Workbook, pp. 189–194	Language Lab CD-ROM, Punctuation; On-Line Exercise Bank, Section 29.5

Hyphens With Compound Words and for Clarity

1. Review the additional rules for using a hyphen.

2. There are no rules for compound words. Students must use the dictionary to find out of they are two words, one word, or hyphenated.

3. Use the following additional examples if needed.

   drive-in

   follow-up

   Venus's-flytrap

   down-to-earth

   green-eyed

   world-famous

   all-star

   re-collect versus recollect

   re-form versus reform

   re-cover versus recover

29.5

With Compound Words You must also use hyphens with some compound words.

▶ **KEY CONCEPT** Use a hyphen to connect two or more words that are used as one word unless the dictionary gives a contrary spelling. ■

EXAMPLES: merry-go-round   crow's-feet   sit-in

▶ **KEY CONCEPT** Use a hyphen to connect a compound modifier that comes before a noun. ■

EXAMPLE: Eclectus parrots were kept as pets by *forest-dwelling* natives.

If a compound modifier comes after the noun, however, the hyphen is dropped.

BEFORE: We got the bird food from an *all-night* pet store.

AFTER: A pet store open *all night* sold us the food.

If the compound modifier is hyphenated, the word remains hyphenated regardless of its position in the sentence.

EXAMPLES: We rode in a *jet-propelled* boat.

Our ski boat was *jet-propelled.*

▶ **KEY CONCEPT** Do not use hyphens with compound modifiers that include words ending in *-ly* or with compound proper adjectives or compound proper nouns acting as adjectives. ■

INCORRECT: The *badly-damaged* wing healed slowly.

CORRECT: The *badly damaged* wing healed slowly.

For Clarity

▶ **KEY CONCEPT** Use a hyphen within a word when a combination of letters might otherwise be confusing. ■

EXAMPLES: *co-op*   versus   *coop*
              re-create   versus   *recreate*

▶ **KEY CONCEPT** Use a hyphen between words to keep the reader from combining them erroneously. ■

EXAMPLES: *thirty-dollar tickets* versus *thirty dollar tickets*

◄ Critical Viewing
Why do you think
people like to teach
parrots to mimic
speech? [Speculate]

Exercise 45 Using Hyphens in Numbers, Word Parts, and
Words Rewrite the words that need hyphens, adding the necessary hyphens. Use a dictionary when in doubt. If no hyphen
is needed, write *correct*.

EXAMPLE: The male eclectus parrot is a bright yellow green
             color.
ANSWER: yellow-green

1. The female, in contrast, is a bright red and bluish purple
   color.
2. Because they are so different in color, at one time it was
   thought that they were two completely different species.
3. The male is considered to be a medium sized bird, and
   the female is slightly smaller.
4. When she is ready to lay eggs, a female parrot lays chewed
   up wood at the bottom of a hole in a tree for her nest.
5. The ever caring mother then stays with the eggs until
   they hatch.
6. For the twenty six days of incubation, the male makes
   frequent visits to the nest to feed the female.
7. The male's brightly colored feathers help him to hide in
   the treetops as he searches for food.
8. After hatching, fledglings spend 85 days in the nest,
   approximately one eleventh of the time required to reach
   adulthood.
9. The six week old female chicks are almost as multicolored
   as they will be as adults.
10. The male, in contrast, has a color that is still blue gray.

More Practice
Language Lab
CD-ROM
• Section 29.5
Grammar Exercise
Workbook
• pp. 193–194

707

Answer Key

Exercise 46

1. New Zealand, an island close to Australia, has short-winged birds.
2. They are strange-looking animals with stubby, coarse feathers that cannot be used to fly.
3. This bird, a night-walking bird, is called the brown kiwi.
4. The male is a light-brown kiwi that weighs around five pounds, while the female weighs about 20 percent more.
5. Kiwis have three-clawed feet that they use for finding food or for self-defense.
6. correct as is
7. correct as is
8. Full-fledged biologists know that the kiwi comes in four species.
9. A five-pound kiwi lays an egg that weighs over one pound.
10. correct as is

Critical Viewing

Describe Students may suggest blue-green water, shrub-like trees, or jagged-edged cliffs.

29.5

Exercise 46 **Using Hyphens to Avoid Ambiguity** Copy the sentences, adding hyphens to make each sentence clear. If no hyphens are required, write *correct as is.*

EXAMPLE: We had to relay the bricks in the garden wall.
ANSWER: We had to re-lay the bricks in the garden wall.

1. New Zealand, an island close to Australia, has short winged birds.
2. They are strange looking animals with stubby, course feathers that cannot be used to fly.
3. This bird, a night walking bird, is called the brown kiwi.
4. The male is a light brown kiwi that weighs around five pounds, while the female weighs about 20 percent more.
5. Kiwis have three clawed feet that they use for finding food or for self defense.
6. They have long bills decorated with small bill hairs whose sensitivity helps the kiwi find food.
7. At the base of its bill, the kiwi has long, threadlike feathers that help it find its way in the dark.
8. Full fledged biologists know that the kiwi comes in four species.
9. A five pound kiwi lays an egg that weighs over one pound.
10. The kiwi is the national symbol of New Zealand; “kiwis” is the worldwide symbol for New Zealanders.

More Practice

Language Lab CD-ROM
- Section 29.5

Grammar Exercise Workbook
- pp. 193–194

▼ **Critical Viewing** Choose three compound modifiers to describe three different nouns in this picture. Which modifiers require hyphens? **[Describe]**

TIME SAVERS!

Answers on Transparency Use the Grammar Exercises on Transparencies for Chapter 29 to have students correct their own or one another's exercises.

On-Line Exercise Bank Have students complete the exercises on computer. The Auto Check feature will grade their work for you!

ONGOING ASSESSMENT: Monitor and Reinforce

If students miss more than two items in Exercises 45–47, refer them to the following for additional practice.

In the Textbook	Print Resources	Technology
Chapter Review, Ex. 70, p. 723	Grammar Exercises Workbook, Hyphens, pp. 193–194	Language Lab CD-ROM, Punctuation; On-Line Exercise Bank, Section 29.5

Using Hyphens at the Ends of Lines

> **KEY CONCEPT** If a word must be divided, always divide it between syllables. ∎

EXAMPLE: The egg takes approximately twenty-six days to hatch.

Always place the hyphen at the end of the first line—never at the start of the next line.

INCORRECT: The cuckoo bird inhab
-its Africa.

CORRECT: The cuckoo bird inhabits Africa.

> **KEY CONCEPT** If a word contains word parts, it can almost always be divided between the prefix and the root or the root and the suffix. ∎

PREFIX: ex-tend   out-side   mis-fortune
SUFFIX: hope-less   incuba-tion fif-teen

If the suffix is composed of only two letters, however, do not divide the word between the root and suffix.

INCORRECT: walk-ed
CORRECT: walked

Be on the lookout for one-syllable words that sound like two-syllable words or look as if they are long enough to be two syllables. Do not divide them.

INCORRECT: lod-ge   clo-thes   thro-ugh
CORRECT: lodge   clothes   through

> **KEY CONCEPT** Do not divide a word so that a single letter stands alone. ∎

INCORRECT: stead-y   a-ble   e-vict
CORRECT: steady   able   evict

Using Hyphens at the Ends of Lines

1. Word processing helps eliminate the problem of how to hyphenate words at the end of a line. Students still need to know the rules.
2. The purpose of these rules is to create the least confusion for the reader. Make sure students understand that hyphenating words at the end of a line should be a rare occurrence in their writing. If done frequently, it is annoying and confusing to readers.

Customize for
Less Advanced Students

Since words need to be hyphenated at appropriate syllable breaks, review with students how to determine where the syllable breaks are in multisyllabic words. When in doubt, tell them to look for word parts that can be easily divisible. If they are unsure, they should use the dictionary.

Dividing Words

1. It is easier to remember rules when the logic for them is clear. Write a sentence on the chalkboard with a correctly hyphenated word and an incorrect example as shown in the text. Demonstrate to students how we all read scanning across the line. When we come to a word fragment, it slows us down.

2. Words usually can be divided between consonants: won-der-ful, wob-ble.

3. Warn students not to rely on pronunciation for syllabication. Is *elephant* hyphenated el-eph-ant or el-e-phant? Students have to use the dictionary. (It is el-e-phant.)

Answer Key

Exercise 47

1. correct
2. hilly
3. thicket
4. correct
5. correct

29.5

> **KEY CONCEPT** It is preferable not to divide proper nouns and proper adjectives. ∎

The following divisions have traditionally been considered undesirable or even incorrect.

INCORRECT: We recently hired Sylvia Rodriguez.

CORRECT: I just finished eating a South American banana.

> **KEY CONCEPT** Divide a hyphenated word only after the hyphen. ∎

If you use the word *apple-pie* as an adjective, you would hyphenate it. When dividing the word at the end of a line, divide it only at the hyphen.

INCORRECT: Everything appeared to be in apple-pie order.

CORRECT: Everything appeared to be in apple-
pie order.

> **KEY CONCEPT** Do not divide a word so that part of the word is on one page and the remainder is on the next page. ∎

> **Exercise 47** **Using Hyphens to Divide Words** If a word has been divided correctly, write *correct*. If not, divide the word correctly or write it as one word if it cannot be divided.

EXAMPLE: Have you ever thought why a peacock calls so loudly?

ANSWER: Have you ever thought
why a peacock calls so loudly?

1. The peafowl is a native of India, and many native Indians believe that their call is a sign of rain.
2. Blue peafowl live in hill-
y forest areas and tend to stay in groups.
3. During the day, they may sit in a thick-
et, but as the sun starts to set, they climb trees to roost.
4. As it climbs higher, the pea-
cock will screech loudly.
5. The peacock, the male of the peafowl species, re-
enacts the same routine every day.

⏱ TIME SAVERS!

📑 **Answers on Transparency**
Use the Grammar Exercises on Transparencies for Chapter 29 to have students correct their own or one another's exercises.

🖥 **On-Line Exercise Bank**
Have students complete the exercises on computer. The Auto Check feature will grade their work for you!

☑ ONGOING ASSESSMENT: Assess Mastery

Use the following resources to assess mastery of using dashes, parentheses, and hyphens.

In the Textbook	Technology
Chapter Review, Ex. 70,72, p. 723 Standardized Test Preparation Workshop, pp. 724–725	Language Lab CD-ROM, Punctuation; On-Line Exercise Bank, Section 29.5

Section 29.5 Section Review

GRAMMAR EXERCISES 48–53

> **Exercise 48** **Using Dashes**
> **Correctly** Rewrite the following sentences, adding dashes where appropriate.

1. Blue and yellow macaws which belong to the parrot family but are not actually called "parrots" live in South America.
2. Nuts, fruits, seeds, and berries these are the staple foods of the macaw diet.
3. Bonding between the pair is reinforced as the birds preen they groom each other's feathers.
4. When eggs are laid usually only two at a time the female incubates them.
5. Baby macaws always hatched in pairs are blind and featherless at hatching.

> **Exercise 49** **Using Hyphens Properly in Words and to Clarify**
> **Sentences** Rewrite the words that require hyphens. If no hyphen is needed, write *correct*.

1. The all powerful beak of a macaw is hinged to crush tough nuts that other birds are not able to eat.
2. From the top of the body to the tip of the tail, macaws can reach up to thirty three inches.
3. Nearly two thirds the length is accounted for in the tail.
4. Cuckoo birds create a coop with other species when raising their young.
5. A female cuckoo looks for an insect eating host species like the one she was raised in.

> **Exercise 50** **Revising With Dashes, Parentheses, and Hyphens**
> Rewrite the following paragraph, adding dashes, parentheses, and hyphens where necessary.

The Princess Parrot an endangered bird so rarely found that it is strictly protected by law lives mostly in central Australia. These birds live in a fair sized group twenty and stay in areas with eucalyptus trees or dry scrubland. Frequently moving, these birds are nomadic following the blossoming of the acacia plant. Princess parrots in flight communicate with a long, chattering note. These birds so surprisingly tame in the wild that you can approach them frequently without startling them fly high, fast, and seemingly without much effort.

> **Exercise 51** **Find It in Your Reading** Read the following excerpt from "The Scarlet Ibis" by James Hurst. On your paper, indicate why the parentheses and hyphen are used.

. . . But sometimes (like right now), as I sit in the cool, green-draped parlor, the grindstone begins to turn, and time with all its changes is ground away—and I remember Doodle.

> **Exercise 52** **Find It in Your Reading** Review a piece of writing from your portfolio. Challenge yourself to write two sentences using both a dash and parentheses.

> **Exercise 53** **Writing Application** Write a brief observation of a bird or other animal with which you are familiar. Include dashes to set off a nonessential phrase in the middle of a sentence; parentheses around an explanation within a sentence; and a hyphen in a word at the end of a line of writing.

Section Review • 711

ASSESS and CLOSE

Section Review

Each of these exercises correlates to a concept in the section on dashes, parentheses, and hyphens, pages 698–710. These exercises may be used for more practice, for reteaching, or for review of the Key Concepts presented. Answers for all chapter exercises are available in *Grammar Exercises Answers on Transparencies* in your teaching resources.

Answer Key

> **Exercise 48**

1. Blue and yellow macaws—which belong to the parrot family but are not actually called "parrots"—live in South America.
2. Nuts, fruits, seed, and berries—these are the staple foods of the macaw diet.
3. Bonding between the pair is reinforced as the birds preen—groom each other's feathers.
4. When eggs are laid—usually only two at a time—the female incubates them.
5. Baby macaws—always hatched in pairs—are blind and featherless at hatching.

> **Exercise 49**

1. all-powerful
2. thirty-three
3. correct
4. co-op
5. insect-eating

> **Exercise 50**

The Princess Parrot—an endangered bird so rarely found that it is strictly protected by law—lives mostly in central Australia. These birds live in a fair-sized group (twenty) and stay in areas with eucalyptus trees or dry scrubland. Frequently moving, these birds are nomadic—following the blossoming of the acacia plant. Princess parrots in flight communicate with a long chattering note. These birds—so surprisingly tame in the wild that you can approach them frequently without startling them—fly high, fast, and seemingly without much effort.

continued

Answer Key continued

> **Exercise 51**

Find It in Your Reading
parentheses: nonessential information; dash: dramatic effect

> **Exercise 52**

Find It in Your Writing
Students can trade papers with a partner to check.

> **Exercise 53**

Writing Application
Students can use reference books and/or the Internet to find information about their bird or animal. They may also want to illustrate their paragraph.

PREPARE and ENGAGE

 Interest GRABBER Write the following sentence on the chalkboard:

The dogs collar is too tight.

Ask students to identify the error. (need an apostrophe—dog's) Encourage students to discuss why apostrophes are important.

Activate Prior Knowledge

Ask students to name as many functions of the apostrophe as they can. If students cannot come up with general functions, then encourage them to provide examples of situations in which they use apostrophes.

Step-by-Step Teaching Guide

Apostrophes With Possessive Nouns

1. Students have to be careful not to confuse the plural, singular possessive, and plural possessive.

   The two <u>dogs</u> wanted to play fetch. (plural)

   The bigger <u>dog's</u> owner threw a ball. (singular possessive)

   Both <u>dogs'</u> owners waited for their pets to run back to them. (plural possessive)

2. Write the following irregular plural nouns on the board and ask students to form the possessive.

   children (children's)

   women (women's)

   people (people's)

   geese (geese's)

   fish (fish's)

   mice (mice's)

Customize for
ESL Students

The formation of possessives can vary widely in different languages. See that students understand the general rules and offer them extra drill and practice in more complicated formations of plurals ending in *-s,* compound nouns, and joint ownership.

Section 29.6 # Apostrophes

Apostrophes With Possessive Nouns

An apostrophe must be used with nouns to indicate ownership or relationship.

With Singular Nouns

First, consider possessives formed from singular nouns.

▶ **KEY CONCEPT** Add an apostrophe and *s* to show the possessive case of most singular nouns. ■

EXAMPLES: The government of India becomes *India's* government.
The sleeve of the *dress* becomes the *dress's* sleeve.

When a singular noun ends in *s,* as in the last example, you can still follow this style in most cases. However, if the apostrophe and *s* make the word difficult to pronounce, the apostrophe may be used alone.

EXAMPLES: Burns's poetry is not well known in India.
Burns' poetry is not well known in India.

With Plural Nouns

Showing possession with plural nouns ending in *s* or *es* calls for a different rule.

▶ **KEY CONCEPT** Add an apostrophe to show the possessive case of plural nouns ending in *s* or *es.* ■

EXAMPLE: The decision of the *representatives* becomes the *representatives'* decision.

▶ **KEY CONCEPT** Add an apostrophe and *s* to show the possessive case of plural nouns that do not end in *s* or *es.* ■

EXAMPLE: The books of the men becomes the *men's* books.

Theme: India

In this section, you will learn about the various uses of apostrophes. The examples and exercises are about India.

Cross-Curricular Connection: Social Studies

⏱ TIME AND RESOURCE MANAGER

Resources
Print: Grammar Exercise Workbook, pp. 195–200
Technology: Language Lab CD-ROM, Punctuation; On-Line Exercise Bank, Section 29.6

In-Depth Coverage	Accelerated Pace
• Work through all key concepts, pp. 712–720. • Assign and review Exercises 54–59.	• Assign pages 712–720 for independent student review. • Assign Exercises 54–59.

With Compound Nouns

▶ **KEY CONCEPT** Add an apostrophe and *s* (or just an apostrophe if the word is a plural ending in *s*) to the last word of a compound noun to form the possessive. ■

APOSTROPHES WITH COMPOUND NOUNS	
Businesses and Organizations	The House of the People's building the Lions Club's motto
Names With Titles	the Prime Minister's visit Edward VIII's abdication
Hyphenated Compound Nouns Used to Describe People	my father-in-law's glasses the secretary-treasurer's pen

With Expressions Involving Time and Amounts

If you use possessive expressions involving time amounts, you will need to use an apostrophe.

▶ **KEY CONCEPT** To form possessives involving time, amounts, or the word *sake*, use an apostrophe and *s* or just an apostrophe if the possessive is plural. ■

TIME:	a day's journey	six years' time
AMOUNT:	one quarter's worth	fifty cents' worth

To Show Joint and Individual Ownership

▶ **KEY CONCEPT** To show joint ownership, make the final noun possessive. ■

EXAMPLE: The president and the prime minister's term (They share one term.)

▶ **KEY CONCEPT** To show individual ownership, make each noun possessive. ■

EXAMPLE: The president's and the prime minister's term (Each has a different term.)

Step-by-Step Teaching Guide

Apostrophes With Compound Nouns, With Expressions Involving Time and Amounts, and to Show Joint and Individual Ownership

1. Write the following compound nouns on the board and ask students to form the possessive.

   vice-president (vice-president's)

   left fielder (left fielder's)

   Democratic Party (Democratic Party's)

   chief executive officer (chief executive officer's)

2. The rules for expressions involving time, amounts, and *sake* are straightforward. Review the examples with students. If necessary, use the following additional examples.

   three months' salary

   thirty-seven dollars' worth

   for the Dodgers' sake

3. Mistakes with possessives can result from confusion about the rule or from carelessness. Use the following additional examples if needed.

   the president and secretary of state's decision (joint decision)

   the president's and the secretary of state's decision (individual decisions)

Integrating Workplace Skills

Many workers write memos. Have students form the possessives of the following nouns.

Board of Trustees (Board of Trustees')

assistant vice-presidents (assistant vice-presidents')

Marketing Department (Marketing Department's)

trucks maintenance records trucks' maintenance records)

713

► **Exercise 54**

1. one's
2. husband's
3. parents'
4. society's
5. parents'

► **Exercise 55**

1. head of state's
2. heads of state's
3. Council of Ministers'
4. prime minister's
5. Sabhas's, Sabha's, president's, prime minister's

29.6

CHECKING THE USE OF APOSTROPHES		
Incorrect	**Explanation**	**Correction**
Jame's car	The owner is not *Jame*, but *James*.	James's
one boys' book	The owner is not *boys*, but *boy*.	boy's
two girl's lunches	The owner is not *girl*, but *girls*.	girls'

If you place the apostrophe correctly, the letters to the left of the apostrophe should spell out the owner's complete name.

► **Exercise 54** Using Apostrophes With Single-Word Possessive Nouns Copy the underlined nouns, putting them into the possessive form.

EXAMPLE: A <u>person</u> extended family is important in Indian society.
ANSWER: person's

1. In India, <u>one</u> personal life tends to be arranged around traditional extended families.
2. When a woman marries, she moves in with her <u>husband</u> family.
3. Parents usually arrange the marriages, but the couple may reject their <u>parents</u> decision.
4. According to <u>society</u> expectations, the couple will have a child within the first few years of a marriage.
5. Especially within small villages and farming communities, the <u>parents</u> preference is to have a male child.

► **Exercise 55** Using Apostrophes With Compound Nouns Write the underlined noun in the possessive form, as required by the sentence.

EXAMPLE: The <u>prime minister</u> power is significant.
ANSWER: prime minister's

1. It is the <u>head of state</u> job to appoint the prime minister.
2. All <u>heads of state</u> responsibilities include working with other government leaders to make laws.
3. The <u>Council of Ministers</u> appointment is made by the president on the advice of the prime minister.
4. The two houses of India's government are controlled by the <u>prime minister</u> political party.
5. <u>Lok Sabhas, Rajya Sabha, the president, and the prime minister</u> terms all last five years.

Learn More

To review possessive and compound nouns, see Chapter 16.

▶ **Exercise 56** Using Apostrophes to Show Joint and Individual Ownership Write the underlined words, changing them to show joint or individual ownership, as the instructions indicate.

EXAMPLE: Dravidians and Indo-Aryans ancestry lies in India. (individual)
ANSWER: Dravidians' and Indo-Aryans'

1. Western India and Pakistan mountains are the places where Dravidians established their ancient but advanced civilization. (joint)
2. Jammu and Kashmir people emigrated from central Asia. (individual)
3. In India, the forests and hills inhabitants are fewer than the cities' inhabitants. (individual)
4. Because of the people and cultures differences, languages in India number over 1,000. (individual)
5. For this reason, elementary schools and secondary schools requirements include studies in Hindi and English. (individual)
6. The national language of India is Hindi; this language or its dialect use is known by more than two fifths of the population. (joint)
7. Bureaucrats and businesspersons language is most often English. (joint)
8. English is widespread in the media as well as in colleges and universities courses. (individual)
9. Because non-Hindu speakers and politicians needs have varied, the government created many state boundaries based on language use. (individual)
10. Today, Bengal and Tamil Nadu official languages are different from that of the country of India. (individual)

▶ **More Practice**

Language Lab CD-ROM
• Types of Nouns lesson
On-line Exercise Bank
• Section 29.5
Grammar Exercise Workbook
• pp. 197–198

◀ **Critical Viewing** What do these women probably own jointly? **[Connect]**

▶ **Exercise 56**
1. Western India and Pakistan's
2. Jammu's and Kashmir's
3. forests' and hills'
4. people's and cultures'
5. elementary schools' and secondary schools'
6. language or its dialect's use
7. Bureaucrats and businessperson's
8. colleges' and universities'
9. speakers' and politicians'
10. Bengal's and Tamil Nadu's

Critical Viewing

Connect Students should say that the three women have joint ownership of the camel.

Apostrophes • 715

Apostrophes With Pronouns

1. Review the uses of apostrophes with indefinite pronouns. In two-word indefinite pronouns, only the last word receives the 's.

2. Possessive pronouns require no apostrophe since they already show ownership.

3. Point out these homophones: the possessive pronoun *whose* and the contraction *who's;* the possessive pronoun *its* and the contraction *it's.*

4. Use the following sentences as additional examples.

   Whose project is this? Its design is unique, and it's something I really like. I wonder who's responsible for it.

Critical Viewing

Apply Students may say *his* and *its.*

29.6

Apostrophes With Pronouns

Some pronouns showing ownership require an apostrophe.

> **KEY CONCEPT** Use an apostrophe and *s* with indefinite pronouns to show possession. ■

EXAMPLES: another's   nobody's   one's
anyone's   someone's   everybody's

If you form a two-word indefinite pronoun, add the apostrophe and *s* to the last word only.

EXAMPLE: nobody else's   one another's

Possessive personal pronouns do not need an apostrophe.

> **KEY CONCEPT** Do not use an apos--trophe with the possessive forms of personal pronouns. ■

With the words *yours, his, hers, theirs, its, ours,* and *whose,* no apostrophe is necessary. These already show ownership.

EXAMPLE: *Its* sacred writing makes the Vedas a guide to moral conduct for Hindus.

Pay special attention to the possessive forms *whose* and *its* since they are easily confused with the contractions *who's* and *it's.* Just remember, *whose* and *its* show possession.

PRONOUNS: *Whose* temple is this?
Its chimes rang out clearly.

Who's and *it's,* on the other hand, are contractions of the words *who is* and *it is.* They both require apostrophes to indicate the missing letters.

CONTRACTIONS: *Who's* taking notes for the meeting?
It's the main religion in India.

▲ **Critical Viewing** What possessive pronouns apply to this picture? **[Apply]**

Exercise 57 — Proofreading for Apostrophes With Pronouns

Rewrite any sentences in which pronouns are used incorrectly, making the necessary changes. If a sentence is already correct, write *correct*.

EXAMPLE: I think this book about yoga is your's.
ANSWER: yours.

1. Hindus believe in one spiritual force, Brahman, who's presence takes many forms.
2. The many gods and goddesses of Hindu beliefs are representations of his forms.
3. Several different cultures accept the basic beliefs of Hinduism as their's.
4. In India, almost everybody's life was once influenced by the caste system.
5. Ones' occupation and opportunities were affected by the caste system.
6. Although the caste system is now weakening, it was once a factor in everyones' existence.
7. Its power to separate people is not as great as it once was.
8. Although they are rooted in Hinduism, yoga and meditation are used by many whose beliefs are not Hindu.
9. Another belief, *ahimsa*, refers to nonviolence in everyone's life.
10. This is achieved largely through a popular practice of their's: yoga.

More Practice
Language Lab
CD-ROM
• Types of Nouns lesson
On-line
Exercise Bank
• Section 29.5
Grammar Exercise
Workbook
• pp. 197–198

▼ Critical Viewing
Write a sentence describing this scene. Include a pronoun showing ownership. [Describe]

Apostrophes • 717

Answer Key

Exercise 57
1. Hindus believe in one spiritual force, Brahman, whose presence takes many forms.
2. correct
3. Several different cultures accept the basic beliefs of Hinduism as theirs.
4. correct
5. One's occupation and opportunities were affected by the caste system.
6. Although the caste system is now weakening, it was once a factor in everyone's existence.
7. correct
8. correct
9. correct
10. This is achieved largely through a popular practice of theirs: yoga.

Critical Viewing
Describe Students' sentences will vary.

TIME SAVERS!

Answers on Transparency
Use the Grammar Exercises on Transparencies for Chapter 29 to have students correct their own or one another's exercises.

On-Line Exercise Bank
Have students complete the exercises on computer. The Auto Check feature will grade their work for you!

Apostrophes With Contractions

The meaning of a contraction is implied by its name. It is a word contracted in size by the removal of some letter or letters and the insertion of an apostrophe to indicate the missing letters. Use the following basic rule for contractions:

KEY CONCEPT Use an apostrophe in a contraction to indicate the position of the missing letter or letters. ■

Contractions With Verbs

Verbs often come in contracted form. Look at the chart, taking a moment to notice how often these verb contractions are used in common speech patterns.

COMMON CONTRACTIONS WITH VERBS		
Verbs with *not*	are not = aren't do not = don't	was not = wasn't were not = weren't
Pronouns with *will*	I will = I'll you will = you'll	she will = she'll they will = they'll
Pronouns and nouns with the verb *be*	I am = I'm you are = you're	who is = who's Mark is = Mark's
Pronouns with *would*	I would = I'd he would = he'd	we would = we'd they would = they'd

One special contraction changes letters as well as drops them: *Will not* becomes *won't* in contracted form.

Contractions With Years

In writing about years, insert an apostrophe in places where a number is left out.

EXAMPLE: Decathlon Champion of '05

Contractions With o', d', and l'

These letters followed by the apostrophe make up the abbreviated form of the words *of the* or *the*, as spelled in several different languages.

EXAMPLES: o'clock   d'Carlo
             O'Sullivan   l'Abbé

As you can see, these letters and apostrophes are combined most often with surnames.

Contractions With Dialogue

When writing dialogue, you will usually want to keep the flavor of the speaker's individual speaking style. Therefore, you should use any contractions the speaker might use. You may also want to include a regional dialect or a foreign accent. Because this often includes pronunciations with omitted letters, insert apostrophes to show those changes.

EXAMPLES: C'mon—aren't you comin' fishin'?
'Tis a fine spring morn we're havin'.
That li'l horse is afeelin' his oats!

As with most punctuation, overuse reduces the effectiveness and impact, so watch the overuse of the apostrophe with contractions—even in dialogue.

Exercise 58 Using Apostrophes With Contractions If a contraction is underlined in the following sentences, write the complete word or words from which the contraction is formed. If two words are underlined, write the contraction they would form.

EXAMPLE: Most Indian women wear a long piece of material that's draped around the body like a dress.
ANSWER: that is

1. From 6 o'clock, til dark, Indian women wear a wide variety of clothing.
2. Sometimes, they are influenced by their region, religion, or ethnic backgrounds.
3. However, most Indian women wear light, loose clothing that doesn't trap in the heat of the hot climate.
4. Women who are unmarried often wear *shalwar*, long flowing pants.
5. They're worn with a long blouse that is called a *kameez*.
6. I've seen many tribal women who'll wear long skirts.

> **More Practice**
> On-line
> Exercise Bank
> • Section 29.5
> Grammar Exercise
> Workbook
> • pp. 199–200

◀ Critical Viewing
What features of the clothing worn by the women in this picture make the clothing suitable for a hot climate? [Analyze]

Apostrophes • 719

Answer Key

Exercise 58
1. of the clock, until
2. they're
3. does not
4. who're
5. They are, that's
6. I have, who will

Critical Viewing

Analyze Students may say that the women's skirts and shawls are suitable for hot climates because they are made from light, flowing material. Moreover, the shawls cover the women's heads, thus shielding them from the sun.

✓ **ONGOING ASSESSMENT: Monitor and Reinforce**

If students miss more than two items in Exercises 54–58, refer them to the following for additional practice.

In the Textbook	Print Resources	Technology
Chapter Review, Ex. 71–72, p. 723	Grammar Exercise Workbook, pp. 195–200	Language Lab CD-ROM, Punctuation; On-Line Exercise Bank, Section 29.6

TIME SAVERS!

🗐 **Answers on Transparency** Use the Grammar Exercises on Transparencies for Chapter 29 to have students correct their own or one another's exercises.

🖥 **On-Line Exercise Bank** Have students complete the exercises on computer. The Auto Check feature will grade their work for you!

Special Uses of the Apostrophe

1. Review the special uses of an apostrophe and -s with numbers and letters. Point out the logic of the rule in that it allows these letters and numbers to be treated as nouns.

2. Use the following additional examples if needed.

    A frequent cause of spelling errors is the order of e's and i's when they appear together in a word.

    The year 2222 will feature four 2's.

Answer Key

Exercise 59

1. They had been living in India since the A.D. <u>100</u>'s.
2. While writing that down, please be sure to include two <u>0</u>'s in the date.
3. Make sure your capital <u>I</u>'s and lowercase <u>l</u>'s do not all look the same.
4. correct
5. They are called Parsis (that has two <u>s</u>'s in the word) in India.
6. correct
7. Maybe you feel some sentences deserve a few <u>?</u>'s.
8. Christianity came to India in the <u>1500</u>'s.
9. correct
10. correct

Special Uses of the Apostrophe

One final method for employing the apostrophe exists— using it to show the plural of numbers, symbols, letters, and words used to name themselves.

▶ **KEY CONCEPT** Use an apostrophe and *s* to write the plurals of numbers, symbols, letters, and words used to name themselves. ■

EXAMPLES: There are two *8*'s in that number.
You need two more *?*'s.
Her *b*'s and *d*'s all look the same.
A's and *an*'s cause confusion.

▶ **Exercise 59** Using the Apostrophe in Special Cases Copy the following sentences, adding an apostrophe and an *s* to numbers, symbols, letters, and words whenever necessary. Underline all items in italics. If no apostrophe or *s* is needed, write *correct*.

EXAMPLE: Many Indian Jews moved to Israel in *1950* and *1960*.

ANSWER: Many Indian Jews moved to Israel in the <u>1950</u>'s and <u>1960</u>'s.

1. They had been living in India since A.D. *100*.
2. While writing that down, please be sure to include two *0* in the date.
3. Make sure that your capital *I* and lowercase *l* do not all look the same.
4. The largest group of Zoroastrians in the world fled to India about 1,000 years ago.
5. They are called Parsis (that has two *s* in the word) in India.
6. They fled to India when Iran was converted to Islam.
7. Maybe you feel some sentences deserve a few *??*.
8. Christianity came to India in the *1500*.
9. The religion came with the Europeans and spread from its small communities to larger *ones*.
10. Christians in India live mostly in the southern states of Kerala and Tamil Nadu.

▶ **More Practice**
On-line
Exercise Bank
• Section 29.5
Grammar Exercise
Workbook
• pp. 199–200

☑ **ONGOING ASSESSMENT: Assess Mastery**

Use the following resources to assess mastery of using apostrophes.

In the Textbook	Technology
Chapter Review, Ex. 71–72, p. 723 Standardized Test Preparation Workshop, pp. 724–725	Language Lab CD-ROM, Punctuation; On-Line Exercise Bank, Section 29.6

Section 29.6 Section Review

GRAMMAR EXERCISES 60–65

Exercise 60 Using Apostrophes **With Possessive Nouns** Write the correct possessive for each underlined noun.

1. Also, the <u>Buddhist temples</u> walls are frequently covered in wall paintings.
2. They depict scenes from some <u>Buddhist men</u> stories.
3. Literature has a strong background in India; the <u>Nobel Prize Committee</u> selection in 1913 was Rabindranath Tagore.
4. Many of the famous <u>folk tales</u> beginnings came from India.
5. Music is also important in India; recently <u>film music</u> popularity has grown.

Exercise 61 Using Apostrophes **in Special Situations** Use apostrophes to form plurals where appropriate. If no corrections are needed in a sentence, write *correct.*

1. *India* is spelled with two *i.*
2. Since the 1950, the government has worked hard to increase the literacy rate.
3. The new Constitution of 50 provided education for children ages 6 to 14.
4. All Indian children receive the same education, learning to write their ABC and more.
5. However, by the time they reach their 10, only half of the children continue with their education.

Exercise 62 Proofreading for **Apostrophes** Rewrite the following passage, adding, deleting, or moving apostrophes as necessary.

Most villagers possession's are few in number. (Household items they can claim as their's include pots theyll use for cooking and carrying water.) The peoples' cooking takes place in a clay oven that burns coal. Even in the 90s people were still sleeping on string cots. The village and huts electric power frequently fails.

Exercise 63 Find It in Your **Reading** Copy the following paragraph on your paper, and explain why each apostrophe is used.

India was a British colony from the late 1700's until it became independent in 1947. Since then, the Indian government has been trying to develop the country's resources and improve people's standard of living.

Exercise 64 Find It in Your **Writing** Select a sample of dialogue from your writing portfolio. Identify where you have used contractions. If you have not used any contractions, challenge yourself to add at least two. Check that you have correctly placed the apostrophe in each contraction.

Exercise 65 Writing Application Write a paragraph describing your neighborhood to someone who lives in a faraway country, such as India. Use apostrophes in your paragraph to form plurals and to show ownership. Use at least three of these words and phrases in your paragraph:

1. friends' and neighbors'
2. 2's and 3's
3. teacher and students'
4. morning's
5. they're

Answer Key

Exercise 60

1. temples'
2. men's
3. Nobel Prize Committee's
4. folk tales'
5. film music's

Exercise 61

1. *i*'s
2. 1950's
3. '50
4. *ABC*'s
5. correct

Exercise 62

(1) Most villagers' possessions are few in number. (2) (Household items they can claim as theirs include pots they'll use for cooking and carrying water.) (3) The people's cooking takes place in a clay oven that burns coal. (4) Even in the '90's people were still sleeping on string cots. (5) The village's and huts' electric power frequently fails.

Exercise 63

Find It in Your Reading
1700's, numbers; country's, singular possessive noun; people's, plural possessive noun

Exercise 64

Find It in Your Writing
Students can trade papers with a partner to check.

Exercise 65

Writing Application
Students may want to mail or e-mail their paragraphs to friends or relatives in other cities.

721

Answer Key

▶ Exercise 66

1. The main foods of India are *pulses,* rice, wheat, and other grains.
2. What are *pulses?*
3. They are the seeds of pod vegetables like beans, chickpeas, and lentils.
4. Cooking in India is extremely varied; it's hard to believe that foods commonly eaten in one part of the country may be completely unknown in other parts.
5. Even so, almost all Indian food is heavily spiced. Amazing!
6. *Chapattis,* a thin bread, is a typical food in northern India.
7. It is usually eaten with *dal,* a porridge made with lentils, and a vegetable dish.
8. In the south, a common meal would consist of rice, *sambar,* and vegetables.
9. A West Bengal meal would include some type of fish, and rice would be eaten instead of *chapattis.*
10. However, most meals throughout the country would include yogurt, pickles, and fresh fruits.

▶ Exercise 67

1. Ellora; it
2. architecture; courtyards exteriors; and
3. stone; in
4. world; Gandhi
5. virtues: courage

▶ Exercise 68

1. "Generations to come," wrote Albert Einstein, "will scarce believe that such a one as [Gandhi] walked the earth in flesh and blood."
2. Revolutionary Ho Chi Minh said this: "I and others may be revolutionaries, but we are disciples of Mahatma Gandhi."

GRAMMAR EXERCISES 66–73

▶ Exercise 66 Using End Marks

Write the following sentences, adding end marks and commas where appropriate.

1. The main foods of India are *pulses,* rice, wheat and other grains
2. What are *pulses*
3. They are the seeds of pod vegetables like beans chickpeas and lentils
4. Cooking in India is extremely varied; it's hard to believe that foods commonly eaten in one part of the country may be completely unknown in other parts
5. Even so almost all Indian food is heavily spiced Amazing
6. *Chapattis* a thin bread is a typical food in northern India.
7. It is usually eaten with *dal* a porridge made with lentils and a vegetable dish.
8. In the south a common meal would consist of rice *sambar* and vegetables.
9. A West Bengal meal would include some type of fish and rice would be eaten instead of *chapattis.*
10. However most meals throughout the country would include yogurt pickles and fresh fruits.

▶ Exercise 67 Using Semicolons and Colons

Add semicolons and colons where appropriate in the following sentences. Write the word before the punctuation, the semicolon or colon, and the word after it.

1. Shiva, a Hindu god, is honored by a monument at Ellora it dates back to the late 700's.
2. We visited Hindu temples, noted for their architecture courtyards, known for their richly carved exteriors and palaces, famed for their tall towers that taper at the top.

3. Temples in south India have towers that are made of steplike layers of stone in fact, every layer has carvings in it that tell a story.
4. One man in India's history is known throughout the world Gandhi.
5. He was a strong leader who believed and acted upon basic virtues courage, nonviolence, and truth.

▶ Exercise 68 Using Quotation Marks and Related Punctuation

Rewrite the following sentences, adding the appropriate quotation marks, other punctuation, and capitalization.

1. Generations to come wrote Albert Einstein will scarce believe that such a one as [Gandhi] walked the earth in flesh and blood.
2. Revolutionary Ho Chi Minh said this I and others may be revolutionaries but we are disciples of Mahatma Gandhi.
3. Gandhi declared human dignity demands the courage to defend oneself he then lived to fulfill his words.
4. Gandhi impressed the world with his *nonviolent resistance philosophy* he continued to behave nonviolently until he was assassinated.
5. I would like people to compete with me in contentment he wrote of his happiness It is the richest treasure I own.

▶ Exercise 69 Using Underlining and Quotation Marks

Rewrite the italicized words, either underlining or adding quotation marks. If neither is appropriate, write *correct.*

1. the Vedas (sacred text of the Hindus)
2. the Ramayana (an epic poem from India)

---

3. Gandhi declared, "Human dignity demands the courage to defend oneself." He then lived to fulfill his words.
4. Gandhi impressed the world with his "non-violent resistance philosophy." He continued to behave nonviolently until he was assassinated.
5. "I would like people to compete with me in contentment," he wrote of his happiness. "It is the richest treasure I own."

▶ Exercise 69

1. correct
2. Ramayana
3. drone
4. correct
5. "Bhagavad-Gita"; Mahabharata

3. All danced when he called the word *drone.*
4. the *Constitution* of India
5. the *Bhagavad-Gita* from the *Mahabharata* (an epic poem from a collection of ancient poems)

> **Exercise 70** **Using Hyphens to Divide Words** Using hyphens, divide the following words correctly. If the word cannot be divided, write *correct.*

1. leader
2. nationalist
3. able

> **Exercise 71** **Using Apostrophes to Form Contractions** Write the contraction for the underlined words; if the word is already a contraction, write the words that form the contraction.

1. Most of India's people live in villages, but these <u>are not</u> villages such as we know.
2. The homes are small, and they usually <u>don't</u> have more than two rooms.
3. A typical house is made of mud and straw; <u>it'd</u> have a mud floor.
4. These houses <u>were not</u> the only kinds of houses; only the wealthy lived in houses of brick or concrete.
5. Small farms exist just outside of the villages, and <u>they're</u> worked by the families that own them.

> **Exercise 72** **Proofreading for All Punctuation Marks** Rewrite the following paragraph, adding the appropriate commas, semicolons, colons, capitals, dashes, hyphens, parentheses, quotation marks, and apostrophes.

   Just after India was separated from Pakistan in 1947 Hindu Muslim rioting broke out. Gandhi ideal was that Hindus and Muslims could live in peace in the same beautiful country India. In 1948 Gandhi at the age of seventy eight began a fast with the purpose of stopping the bloodshed. The fighting continued for five days but finally the leaders of the opposing sides promised to end the fighting. Gandhi after five days without eating broke his fast. Unfortunately twelve days later Gandhi was assassinated by a Hindu fanatic who opposed tolerance for all religions. The world was stunned by his untimely death and saddened by his loss several famous people wrote tributes to him Pearl S. Buck, Martin Luther King Jr., Ho Chi Minh, and others. Will Durant wrote not since buddha has India so reverenced any man. Martin Luther King Jr. said of him The intellectual and moral satisfaction that I failed to gain from [many great philosophers] I found in the nonviolent resistance philosophy of Gandhi. What is the secret of his success Gandhi advice goes out to us all Live as if you were to die tomorrow; learn as if you were to live forever.

> **Exercise 73** **Writing Application** Rewrite each of the following statements three different ways, as indicated in the directions beneath each. Use punctuation correctly.

1. Gandhi was a political and spiritual leader in India.
   a. as a question
   b. with a nonessential phrase or clause
   c. with a hyphen forming a compound adjective
2. He was married at the age of 13. This would be unusual in many countries.
   a. as an exclamation
   b. with a possessive
   c. as a compound sentence
3. Kasturba his wife was also 13 at the time of their marriage.
   a. with an introductory phrase
   b. with parentheses
   c. with dashes

Standardized Test Preparation Workshop

Proofreading

Many standardized tests include items that measure your ability to identify errors in punctuation, spelling, and capitalization. The following sample items will give you practice with these types of items in a standardized test format.

Sample Test Items

Answers and Explanations

Directions: Read the following passage. Identify the letter of the section that contains an error.
 	
In Russia in 1991, the communist govern-
    A   B
 	
ment collapsed and democracy was
                     C
 	
introduced. No error
   D   E
	The correct answer is *C*. There should be a comma between *collapsed* and *and* because *and* joins two independent clauses.

Directions: Read the following passage, and decide which type of error, if any, appears in the underlined section. Russia struggled through difficult transitions. The people suffered from inflation, a rise in unemployment, <u>and a shortage of</u> <u>they're basic material needs.</u> A Spelling error B Capitalization error C Punctuation error D No error	The correct answer is *A*. There is a spelling error in the underlined section. *Their* is incorrectly spelled as the contraction *they're*.

724 • Punctuation

Answer Key

Practice 1 **Directions:** Read the following passage. Identify the letter of the section that contains an error.

1 In everyday speech, the words *bug* and
                                    A
insect are used to refer to many different
                B
types of animals. In Science, however,
                              C
referring to a spider as a bug or an
        D
insect is highly inaccurate. No error.
                                  E

2 Insects are six-legged animals, such as
                                    A
ants; bees; butterflies; fleas; and
                B
grasshoppers. Spiders, mites, and ticks
                              C
—all of which have eight legs—are not
              D
insects. No error.
          E

3 People in central and western Asia
                    A
invented carpets more than a thousand

years ago. Most Oriental rugs are made
                              B
of sheeps wool, but the finest are made

of silk, which has a more supple texture
                              C
than wool. No error.
        D   E

Practice 2 **Directions:** Read the following passage, and decide which type of error, if any, appears in each underlined section.

Mountain lions range from a golden-brown

color to gray or black. Reaching up to
                              (1)
227 pounds, they are not only large, but

they are fast, to. They are found in the
              (2)
Mountains of several states. scientists
                              (3)
sometimes tag them to track their move-

ments and to evaluate populations.

1 **A** Spelling error
   B Capitalization error
   C Punctuation error
   D No error

2 **A** Spelling error
   B Capitalization error
   C Punctuation error
   D No error

3 **A** Spelling error
   B Capitalization error
   C Punctuation error
   D No error

CUMULATIVE REVIEW

Answer Key

Exercise A

1. Japanese literature is written in both Japanese and Chinese characters.
2. The development of Japanese literature is divided into five periods: the Yamato, Heian, Kamakura-muromachi, Edo, and Modern.
3. The first four are named after the government centers from that time.
4. There was no written literature in Japan before the eighth century A.D.
5. During the Yamato period, lyric poetry was collected by Yakamochi.
6. His book, The Anthology of a Myriad Leaves, features the work of the poet Kakinomoto Hitomaro.
7. In the late eighth century, the government moved to the present-day city of Kyoto.
8. Ki Tsurayuki compiled the Anthology of Ancient and Modern Poems in 905 A.D.
9. He also wrote the first Japanese literary diary about his journey from Tosa province to Kyoto.
10. Fairy tales, like "The Tale of the Bamboo Cutter," were popular in the early tenth century.
11. In 1010 Murasaki Shikibu wrote The Tale of Genji, considered the first important novel in world literature.
12. It tells the story of Prince Genji and his son Kaoru.
13. American scholar Edward Seidensticker translated Shikibu's book into English in 1976.
14. Another novel, The Pillow-Book, also contains stories about court society.
15. In 1928 it was first translated by English scholar Arthur Waley.

Exercise B

1. The Kamakura-Muromachi period was characterized by one thing: warfare.
2. Was this when the samurai, or warrior, became a dominant figure in Japanese society?
3. Yes. Buddhist priests who devoted themselves to lives of contemplation also emerged at this time.
4. The defeat of the Taira clan by

Cumulative Review

MECHANICS

▶ Exercise A Using Capitalization

Copy all the items in the following sentences that require capitalization, adding the missing capitals.

1. japanese literature is written in both japanese and chinese characters.
2. the development of japanese literature is divided into five periods: the yamato, heian, kamakura-muromachi, edo, and modern.
3. the first four are named after the government centers from that time.
4. there was no written literature in japan before the eighth century a.d.
5. during the yamato period, lyric poetry was collected by yakamochi.
6. his book, *the anthology of a myriad leaves*, features the work of the poet kakinomoto hitomaro.
7. in the late eighth century, the government moved to the present-day city of kyoto.
8. ki tsurayuki compiled the *anthology of ancient and modern poems* in 905 a.d.
9. he also wrote the first japanese literary diary about his journal from tosa province to kyoto.
10. fairy tales, like "the tale of the bamboo cutter," were popular in the early tenth century.
11. in 1010, murasaki shikibu wrote *the tale of genji*, considered the first important novel in world literature.
12. it tells the story of prince genji and his son kaoru.
13. american scholar edward seidensticker translated shikibu's book into english in 1976.
14. another novel, *the pillow-book*, also contains stories about court society.
15. in 1928, it was first translated by english scholar arthur waley.

▶ Exercise B Using End Marks, Commas, Semicolons, and Colons

Write the following sentences, inserting end marks, commas, semicolons, and colons where necessary.

1. The Kamakura-Muromachi period was characterized by one thing warfare
2. Was this when the samuri or warrior became a dominant figure in Japanese society
3. Yes Buddist priests who devoted themselves to lives of contemplation also emerged at this time
4. The defeat of the Taira clan by the Minamoto clan was an important subject in fact an anonymous author wrote *The Tales of the Taira Clan* in 1220
5. What was the *Diary of the Waning Moon* by a nun Abutsu about
6. It was a literary diary consisting of two parts prose and poetry
7. The otogizoshi collections of short stories by unknown authors emerged it became the major kind of fiction of this period
8. In the early fourteenth century a form of poetry with many regulations emerged the renga
9. Would poets work together to write this type of verse
10. The greatest masters of this form Sogi Shohaku and Socho composed "Three Poets at Minase" together

▶ Exercise C Proofreading for Capitalization

On a separate sheet of paper, copy the following passage. Correct capitalization errors.

The question of how the Unification of japan was first achieved is difficult to answer. Thanks to chinese and korean

---

the Minamoto clan was an important subject; in fact, an anonymous author wrote The Tales of the Taira Clan in 1220.
5. What was the Diary of the Waning Moon by a nun Abutsu about?
6. It was a literary diary consisting of two parts: prose and poetry.
7. The otogizoshi collections of short stories by unknown authors emerged; it became the major kind of fiction of this period.
8. In the early fourteenth century a form of poetry with many regulations emerged: the renga.
9. Would poets work together to write this type of verse?

10. The greatest masters of this form, Sogi Shohaku and Socho, composed "Three Poets at Minase" together.

Exercise C

The question of how the unification of Japan was first achieved is difficult to answer. Thanks to Chinese and Korean records, however, it is possible to get at least an approximate date. A memorial commemorating the achievements of King Kwang-gaeto describes the fighting that took place on the Korean peninsula from the end of the fourth century into the beginning of the fifth century. Special mention is made of a great army that succeeded in defeating the kingdoms of Kaya and Silla.

records, however, it is possible to get at least an approximate date. A Memorial commemorating the achievements of King Kwang-gaeto describes the fighting that took place on the Korean Peninsula from the end of the Fourth Century into the beginning of the fifth century. Special mention is made of a great Army that succeeded in defeating the kingdoms of kaya and silla.

> ### Exercise D Proofreading for
> **Punctuation** Write the following sentences, inserting end marks, commas, semicolons, colons, quotation marks, underlining, dashes, brackets, parentheses, hyphens, and apostrophes where necessary.

The Edo period produced a post wartime style of literature written by the new middle class Saikaku the most important figure of the time wrote the book Life of an Amorous Man which concerns a particular group the mercantile class. Many fiction writers imitated his style however none were able to equal his achievements Haiku a form of poetry with seventeen syllables per poem was perfected in this period indeed it has been called the greatest Japanese literary development

Did Bashō 1644 1694 a Zen Buddist priest write haiku Bashōs book Narrow Road Through the Deep North one poem begins Waterjar cracks: I lie awake Haiku writing said Rodrigo de Siquiera needs More than inspiration, it needs meditation. osa Buson who actually was a painter first was another great writer of haiku Buson during his time as a painter used the names Yahanti the Second Sha Cho-Koh and Shunsei Kobayashi Issa He came from a poor background furthermore he took most of his inspiration from that village life.

> ### Exercise E Proofreading Dialogue
> for Capitalization and Punctuation
> Write the following dialogue, inserting the proper capitalization, punctuation, and indentation.

Rebecca asked matt have you heard of any of the japanese literature that comes from the modern period asked nick i mean the period from 1867 to the present. yes i read the book the drifting cloud by futabatei shimei replied matt it is the first japanese novel that wasnt written in formal language. Really, what year was that book written wondered Rebecca.

well, said Matt it was translated in 1967 but had been written much earlier i believe in 1887 that was around the time of the society founded by the poet ozaki koyo i think ive heard of that but im not sure what that group did. the group of people in the society combined japanese traditions with western techniques chimed in nick for example higuchi ichiyo combines these two styles in her novel growing up oh yes added matt i have heard of the japanese being influenced by french german and english literature. nick said enthusiastically i really like the writing of mori ogai who was inspired by german writing. what did ogai write Everything said nick including poetry drama novels and biographies you should read his book the wild geese

> ### Exercise F Writing Application
> Write a brief first-person narrative that includes dialogue in which you and a friend discuss a book, movie, or television show that was made in a foreign country. Be sure to follow all the rules of capitalization and punctuation.

Exercise D

The Edo period produced a post-wartime style of literature written by the new middle class. Saikaku, the most important figure of the time, wrote the book Life of an Amorous Man which concerns a particular group: the mercantile class. Many fiction writers imitated his style; however, none were able to equal his achievements. Haiku, a form of poetry with seventeen syllables per poem, was perfected in this period; indeed, it has been called the greatest Japanese literary development.

Did Bashō (1644–1694), a Zen Buddhist priest, write haiku? In Bashō's book Narrow Road Through the Deep North, one poem begins "Waterjar cracks: I lie awake." "Haiku writing," said Rodrigo de Siquiera, "needs more than inspiration; it needs meditation." Osa Buson, who actually was a painter first, was another great writer of haiku. Buson, during his time as a painter, used the names Yahanti the Second, Sha Cho-Koh, and Shunsei Kobayashi Issa. He came from a poor background; furthermore, he took most of his inspiration from that village life.

Exercise E

Rebecca asked Matt, "Have you heard of any of the Japanese literature that comes from the modern period? I mean the period from 1867 to the present."

"Yes. I read the book The Drifting Cloud by Futabatei Shimei," replied Matt. "It is the first Japanese novel that wasn't written in formal language."

"Really, what year was that book written?" wondered Rebecca.

"Well," said Matt, "It was translated in 1967, but had been written much earlier, I believe in 1887."

"That was around the time of the society founded by the poet Ozaki Koyo."

"I think I've heard of that, but I'm not sure what that group did."

"A group of people in the society combined Japanese traditions with Western techniques," chimed in Nick. "For example, Higuchi Ichiyo combines these two styles in her novel Growing Up."

"Oh yes," added Matt, "I have heard of the Japanese being influenced by French, German, and English literature."

continued

Answer Key continued

Nick said enthusiastically, "I really like the writing of Mori Ogai, who was inspired by German writing."

"What did Ogai write?"

"Everything," said Nick, "including poetry, drama, novels, and biographies. You should read his book The Wild Geese."

Exercise F

Have students exchange their narratives with partners to check each other's work.

Sentence Diagraming Workshop

Diagraming is a visual means of helping you understand how all the different parts of a sentence relate to one another. Diagraming allows you to see a sentence not as a string of separate words, but as several groups of words arranged in a logical pattern.

Subjects, Verbs, and Modifiers

In a diagram, the subject and verb are placed on a horizontal line with the subject on the left and the verb on the right. A vertical line separates the subject from the predicate. The following examples show how to diagram a subject and verb.

EXAMPLE: Jonathan sneezed.

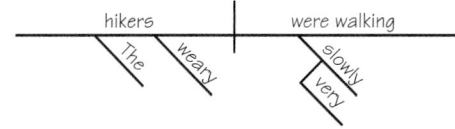

Adjective and adverbs are placed on slanted lines directly below the word they modify.

EXAMPLE: The weary hikers were walking very slowly.

A sentence whose subject is understood to be *you* is diagramed in the usual way. Often, however, the word *there* is used just to get the sentence started. When that is the case, the word *there* is an expletive. Interjections are also expletives. The following examples show how to diagram expletives.

EXAMPLES:

EXP
There was an accident.

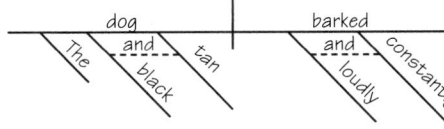

INT
Hooray, we won!

Exercise 1 Diagraming Subjects, Verbs, and Modifiers
Correctly diagram each sentence.
1. Sit down.
2. The weary runner suddenly sprinted ahead.
3. Your exceptionally studious friend thinks very quickly.
4. There was no test given today.
5. Goodness, Sandy sings very poorly.

Adding Conjunctions

Conjunctions that connect words are written on dotted lines drawn between the words that they connect. The following example shows where to place conjunctions that connect adjectives and adverbs.

EXAMPLE:

CONJ   CONJ
The black and tan dog barked loudly and constantly.

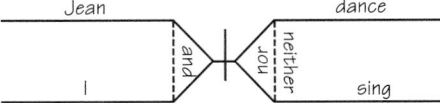

Conjunctions that connect compound subjects or compound verbs are also placed on dotted lines drawn between the words that they connect. Notice how the horizontal line must be split when a sentence has a compound subject or a compound verb.

CONJ CONJ   CONJ
EXAMPLE: Jean and I neither dance nor sing.

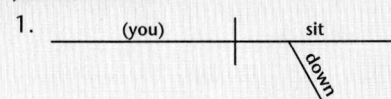

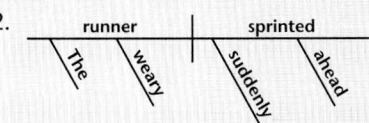

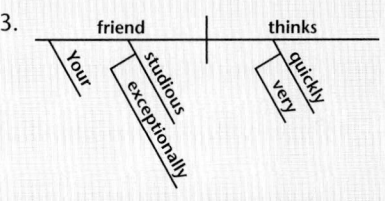

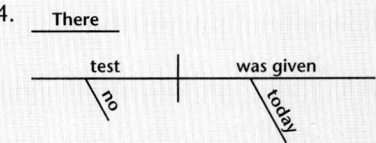

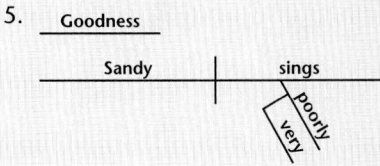

1.

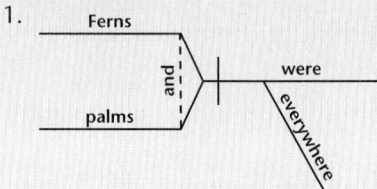

2.

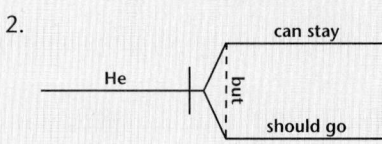

3.

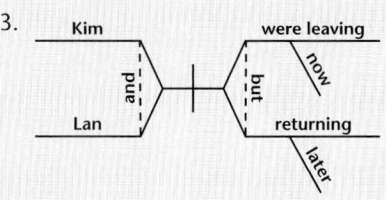

4.

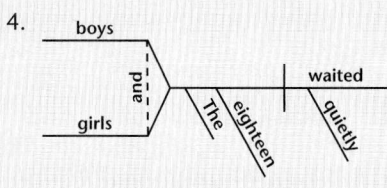

5.

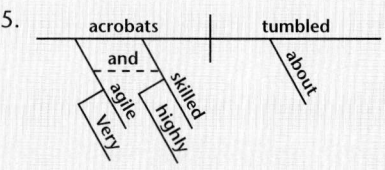

In sentences with compound subjects or verbs, a modifier is placed under the part of the sentence it modifies. If a word modifies both parts of a compound subject or verb, it is placed under the main line of the diagram.

EXAMPLE:

ADJ ADJ   ADJ   ADJ

My older sister and younger brother left early but

ADJ

arrived late.

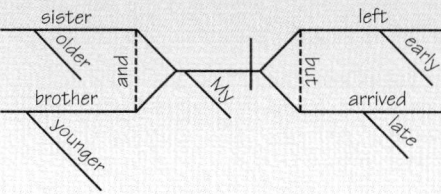

If each part of a compound verb has its own helping verb, each helping verb is placed on the line with its verb. If compound verbs share a helping verb, however, the helping verb is placed on the main line of the diagram.

EXAMPLE:

HV

Tomorrow I will either swim or fish.

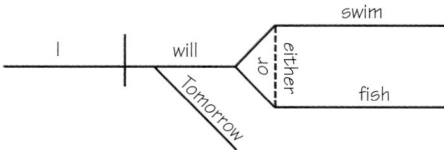

▶ **Exercise 2** Diagraming Sentences With Conjunctions

Correctly diagram each sentence.

1. Ferns and palms were everywhere.
2. He can stay, but she should go.
3. Kim and Lan were leaving now but returning later.
4. The eighteen boys and girls waited quietly.
5. Very agile and highly skilled acrobats tumbled about.

Complements

The following diagrams show how to add direct objects and indirect objects to sentence diagrams.

EXAMPLE:
    DO
Bill plays chess.

    IO   DO
I told Joan a story.

The next diagram shows where to place an objective complement.

EXAMPLES:
          DO   OC
Our class elected Beth Green treasurer.

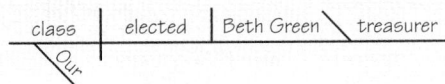

Predicate nominatives and predicate adjectives are diagramed in a similar way

EXAMPLE:
       PN
Sean is an actor.

      PA
He is talented.

Compound complements are diagramed by splitting the lines on which they are placed and adding on dotted lines any conjunctions that connect them.

EXAMPLE:
      IO   IO   DO   DO
We gave Ann and Ed some crackers and cheese.

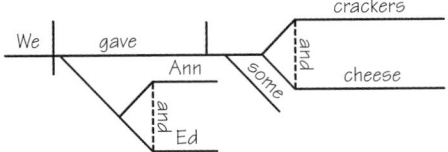

1.
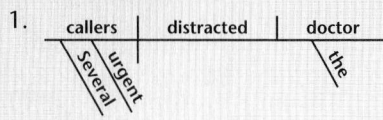

2.
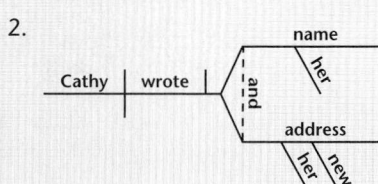

3.
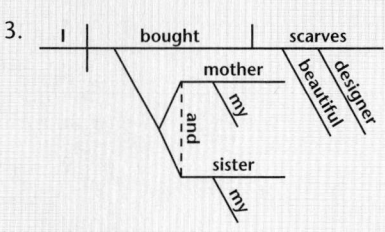

4.
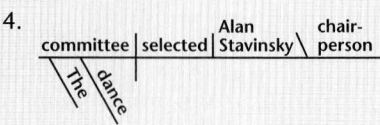

5.
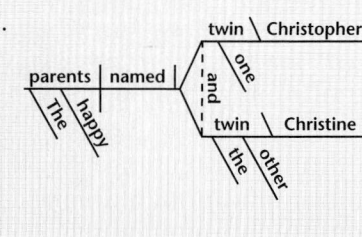

6.
That | is \ it

7.
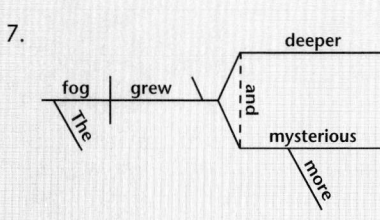

8.
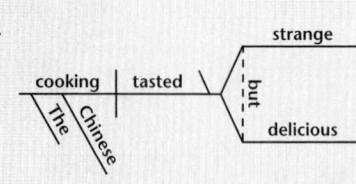

9.
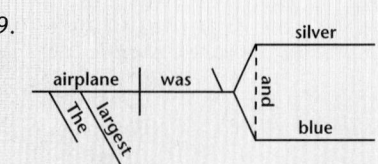

▶ **Exercise 3** Diagraming Complements Correctly diagram each sentence.
1. Several urgent callers distracted the doctor.
2. Cathy wrote her name and her new address.
3. I bought my mother and my sister beautiful designer scarves.
4. The dance committee selected Alan Stavinsky chairperson.
5. The happy parents named one twin Christopher and the other twin Christine.
6. That is it!
7. The fog grew deeper and more mysterious.
8. The Chinese cooking tasted strange but delicious.
9. The largest airplane was silver and blue.
10. The coin was very old but still shiny.

Prepositional Phrases

A prepositional phrase can act as either an adjective or an adverb in a sentence. In a diagram, an adjective phrase is placed directly below the noun or pronoun it modifies. An adverb phrase is placed directly below the verb, adjective, or adverb it modifies. The preposition is placed on a slanted line with its object on a horizontal line below the slanted line. Any adjectives that modify the object of the preposition are placed on slanted lines below the horizontal line.

EXAMPLE: The woman with the large hat went into the store.

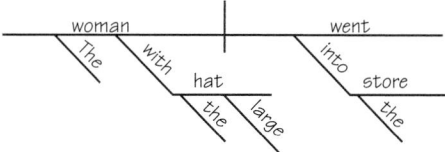

The first example on the next page shows how to diagram a prepositional phrase that modifies the object of another prepositional phrase. The other example shows how to diagram a prepositional phrase that modifies an adjective or an adverb.

10.
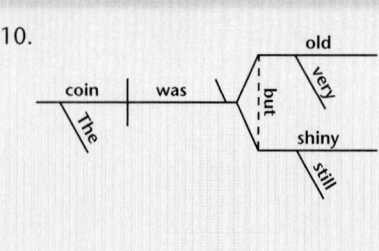

                                    PREP PHRASE
EXAMPLE: I ate pizza with mushrooms on it.

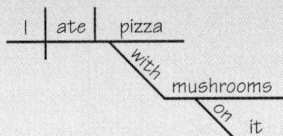

                                        PREP PHRASE
            The rain started yesterday after lunch.

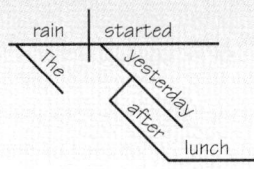

A prepositional phrase with a compound object is diagramed in the same way other compound sentence parts are diagramed. The diagram below is an example of a sentence containing a prepositional phrase with a compound object.

                                    PREP PHRASE
EXAMPLE: I eat whole-wheat bread with breakfast and lunch.

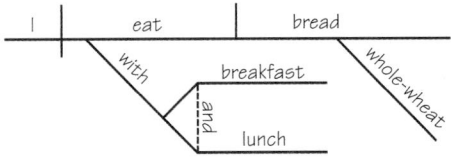

▶ **Exercise 4** **Diagraming Prepositional Phrases** Correctly diagram each sentence.

1. Mark is working at the radio station.
2. You may take the television to your room.
3. The boy on the bench played in the first half.
4. She runs for exercise.
5. The roof of the old house on the corner collapsed.

1.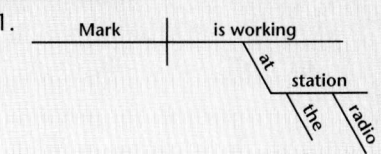

2.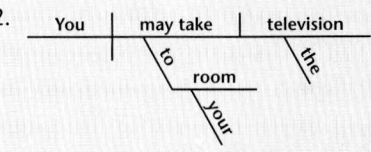

3.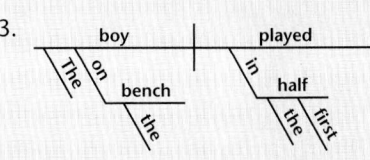

4.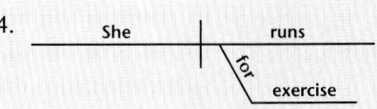

5.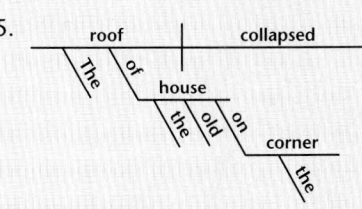

Sentence Diagraming Workshop • **733**

1.

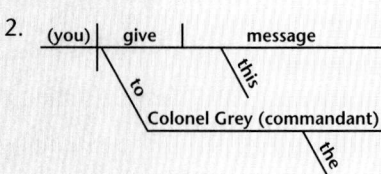

2.

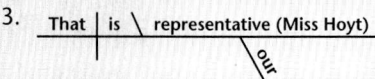

3.

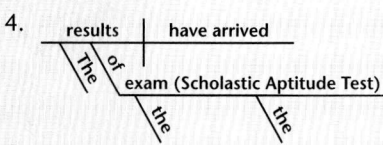

4.

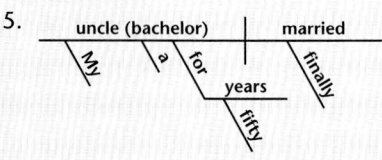

5.

Appositives and Appositive Phrases

To diagram an appositive, place it in parentheses beside the noun or pronoun it identifies, renames, or explains. Any adjectives or adjective phrases included in an appositive phrase are placed directly beneath the appositive.

APPOSITIVE PHRASE

EXAMPLE: Blue whales, the largest animals in the world, are rare.

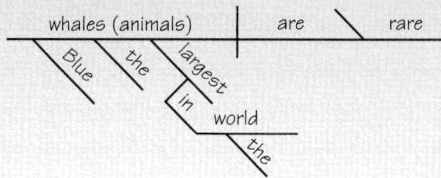

Exercise 5 Diagraming Appositives and Appositive **Phrases** Correctly diagram each sentence.

1. The governor announced the appointee, his wife!
2. Give to Colonel Gray, the commandant, this message.
3. That is our representative, Miss Hoyt.
4. The results of the exam, the Scholastic Aptitude Test, have arrived.
5. My uncle, a bachelor for fifty years, finally married.

Participles and Participial Phrases

Participles function as adjectives. Thus, in a diagram, they are placed directly beneath the nouns or pronouns they modify. Participles are placed partly on a slanted line and partly on a horizontal line extending from the slanted line. Any adverbs or adverb phrases included in a participial phrase are placed on slanted lines beneath the horizontal line. When a participle has a complement, it is placed on the horizontal line with the participle and separated from it by a short vertical line.

PARTICIPIAL PHRASE

EXAMPLE: Carefully following the instructions, Karen assembled the model airplane.

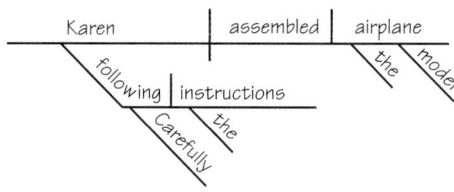

1.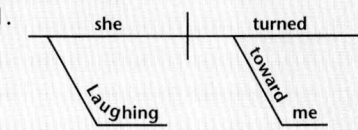

2.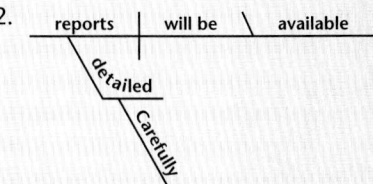

3.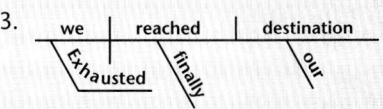

4.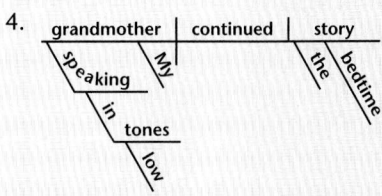

5.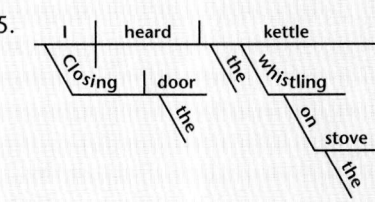

Exercise 6 Diagraming Participles and Participial Phrases
1. Laughing, she turned toward me.
2. Carefully detailed reports will be available.
3. Exhausted, we finally reached our destination.
4. My grandmother, speaking in low tones, continued the bedtime story.
5. Closing the door, I heard the kettle whistling on the stove.

Gerunds and Gerund Phrases

Because gerunds act as nouns, they can be subjects, complements, objects of prepositions, or appositives. When a gerund acts as a subject, direct object, or predicate nominative, it is placed on a pedestal above the main horizontal line of the diagram. Notice in the following diagram the stepped line on which all gerunds are written. Notice also that any modifiers and complements that are part of a gerund phrase are added to the diagram in the usual way.

GERUND PHRASE

EXAMPLE: We will not allow your reading comics in class.

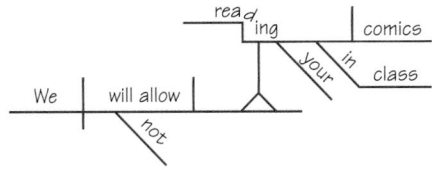

When a gerund acts as indirect object or an object of a preposition, it is placed on a line slanting down from the main horizontal line.

GERUND

EXAMPLE: His performance gives acting a bad name.

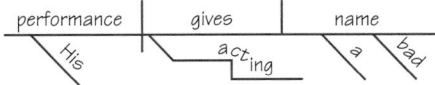

1.

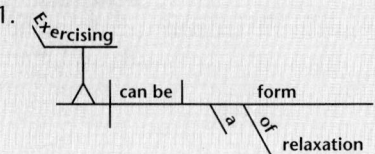

2.

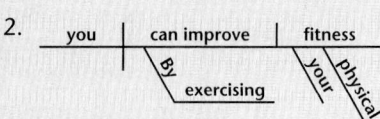

3.

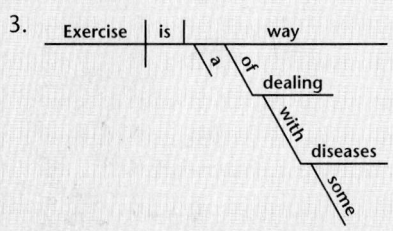

4.

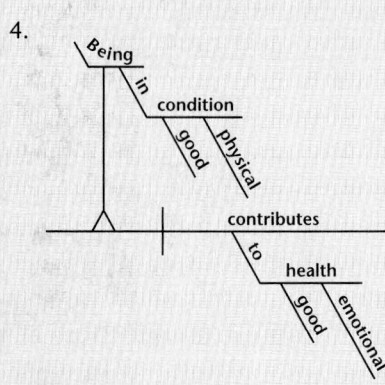

5.

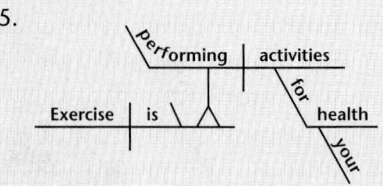

▶ **Exercise 7** Diagraming Gerunds and Gerund Phrases

Correctly diagram each sentence.

1. Exercising can be a form of relaxation.
2. By exercising, you can improve your physical fitness.
3. Exercise is a way of dealing with some diseases.
4. Being in good physical condition contributes to good emotional health.
5. Exercise is performing activities for your health.

Infinitives and Infinitive Phrases

Infinitives can act as nouns, adjectives, or adverbs. An infinitive acting as a noun is generally diagramed on a pedestal like a gerund, but the line on which the infinitive is written is simpler. Modifiers included in an infinitive phrase are added to a diagram in the usual way. Complements are also added in the usual way.

INFINITIVE PHRASE

EXAMPLE: To leave early was his goal.

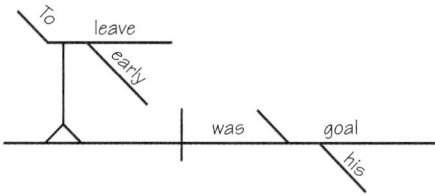

When an infinitive phrase has a subject, it is added to the left on a horizontal line.

INFINITIVE PHRASE

EXAMPLE: I want you to pay me the ten dollars.

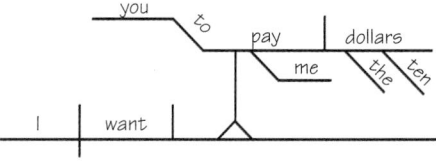

An infinitive used as an adjective or adverb is diagramed in much the same way as a prepositional phrase.

INFINITIVE

EXAMPLE: He will be happy to drive.

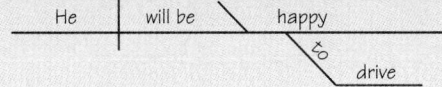

If an infinitive does not include the word *to*, add the word to the sentence diagram but place it in parentheses.

INFINITIVE PHRASE

EXAMPLE: They watched the ship sail into the harbor.

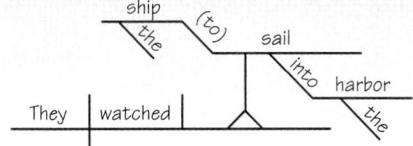

Exercise 8 Diagraming Infinitives and Infinitive Phrases

Correctly diagram each sentence.
  1. This is the road to take.
  2. Our goal is to drive across the continent.
  3. To pack the car is our next job.
  4. My father wants me to study German.
  5. We saw Bernstein conduct three symphonies.

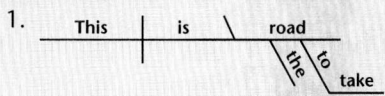

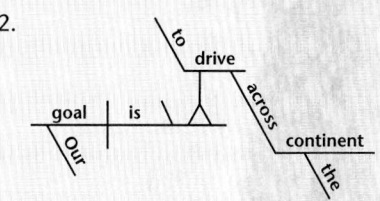

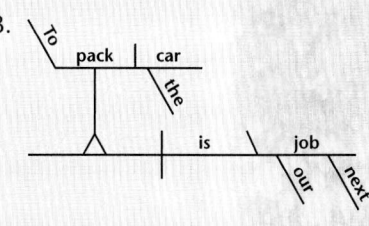

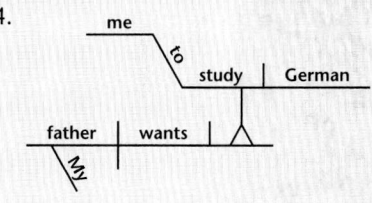

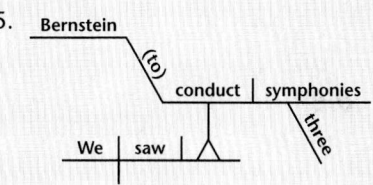

1.
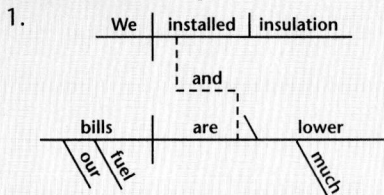

2.
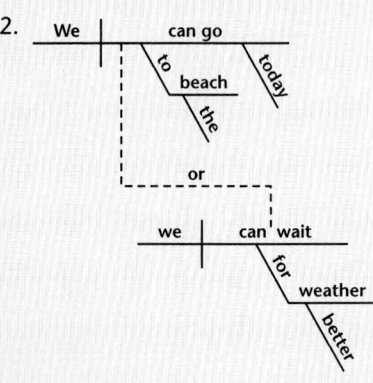

3.
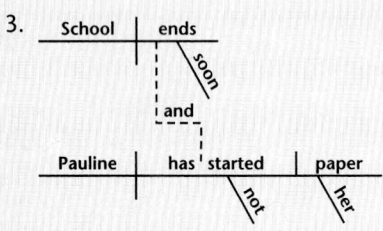

4.
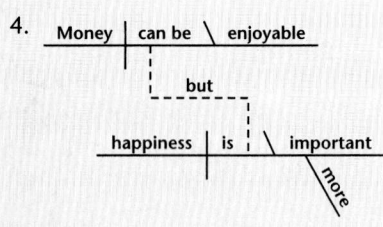

5.
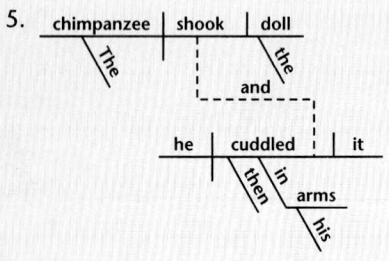

Compound Sentences

To diagram a compound sentence, simply diagram each of the independent clauses separately, join the verbs with a dotted line, and write the conjunction or semicolon on the dotted line.

INDEPENDENT CLAUSE

EXAMPLE: I found his books, and I returned them to him.

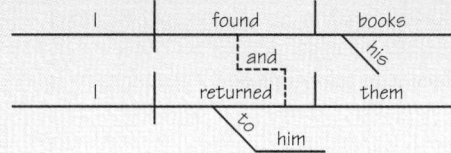

Exercise 9 Diagraming Compound Sentences Correctly diagram each sentence.
1. We installed insulation, and our fuel bills are much lower.
2. We can go to the beach today, or we can wait for better weather.
3. School ends soon, and Pauline has not started her paper.
4. Money can be enjoyable, but happiness is more important.
5. The chimpanzee shook the doll, and then he cuddled it in his arms.

Complex Sentences

Complex sentences contain an independent clause and one or more subordinate clauses. The subordinate clauses can be adjective clauses, adverb clauses, noun clauses, or any combination of these.

Adjective Clauses The line on which an adjective clause is placed goes beneath the main line, to which it is connected by a dotted line. The dotted line extends from the noun or pronoun being modified by the clause to the relative pronoun or relative adverb in the adjective clause. The position of the relative pronoun varies depending on its function in the adjective clause. In the following diagram, the relative pronoun is the direct object in the subordinate clause.

EXAMPLE: ADJECTIVE CLAUSE
The table lamps that you ordered have just arrived.

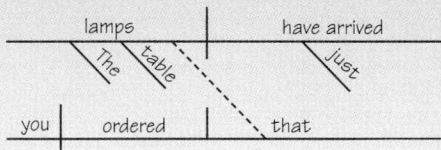

Sometimes, an adjective clause may be introduced by a relative pronoun acting as either an object of a preposition or as an adjective. The dotted line must be bent to connect the clauses properly. This is also true when the adjective clause is introduced by a relative adverb, as the following example illustrates.

EXAMPLE: ADJECTIVE CLAUSE
We visited a laboratory where testing was done.

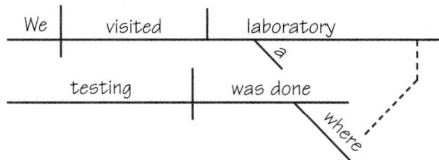

Adverb Clauses An adverb clause is diagramed in the same way as an adjective clause, except that the subordinate conjunction is written along the dotted line. This line extends from the verb, adjective, adverb, or verbal being modified by the clause to the verb in the adverb clause.

EXAMPLE: ADVERB CLAUSE
Gas will be rationed whenever a shortage occurs.

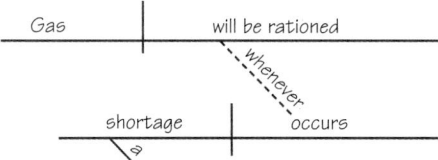

1.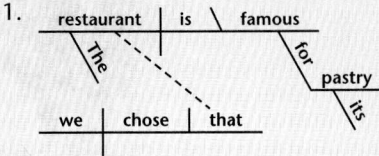

2.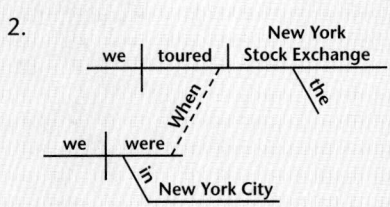

3.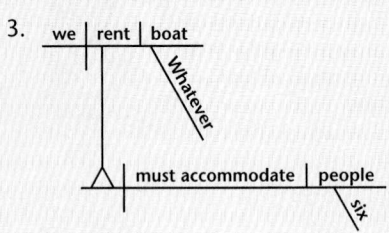

4.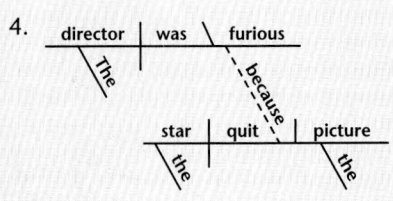

5.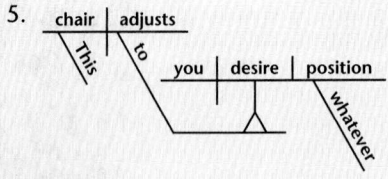

If the adverb clause is elliptical, the understood but unstated words are placed in the diagram in parentheses.

EXAMPLE: The tree in our yard is taller than the tree in yours.

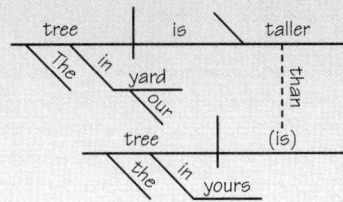

Noun Clauses To diagram a sentence containing a noun clause, first diagram the independent clause. Then, place the noun clause on a pedestal extending upward from the position the clause fills in the sentence. The noun clause in the following is acting as the subject of the sentence.

EXAMPLE: Whoever is responsible will pay for the damage.

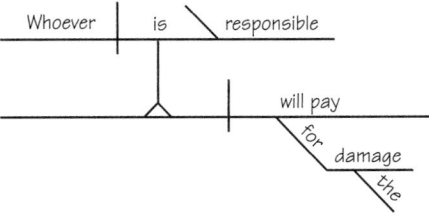

When the introductory word in a noun clause has no function in the clause, it is written alongside the pedestal.

EXAMPLE: I wonder whether we should wait for them.

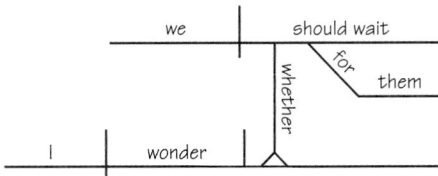

Exercise 10 Diagraming Complex Sentences Correctly diagram each sentence.
1. The restaurant that we chose is famous for its pastry.
2. When we were in New York City, we toured the New York Stock Exchange.
3. Whatever boat we rent must accommodate six people.
4. The director was furious because the star quit the picture.
5. This chair adjusts to whatever position you desire.

Compound-Complex Sentences

When diagraming a compound-complex sentence, begin by diagraming each of the independent clauses. Then, diagram each subordinate clause.

ADVERB CLAUSE   INDEPENDENT CLAUSE
EXAMPLE: Before the play began, the audience was restless

INDEPENDENT CLAUSE
and the actors were nervous.

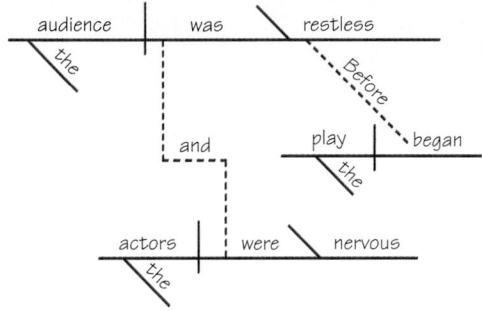

Exercise 11 Diagraming Compound-Complex Sentences
Correctly diagram each sentence
1. When their father returned, Jill set the table and Peter poured milk.
2. The letter that he received was short, but he read it very slowly.
3. We hoped that it would be sunny, but it was not.
4. After they reached the city, they bought a newspaper and Judy looked for a good restaurant.
5. The children gasped at their luck when they found the wallet, for they had been very worried.

1.
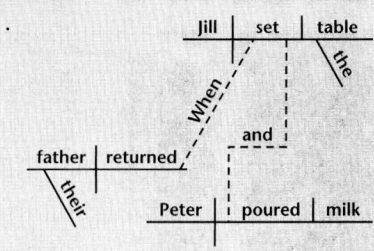

2.
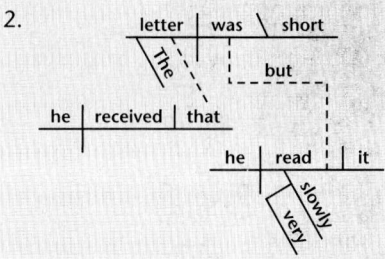

3.
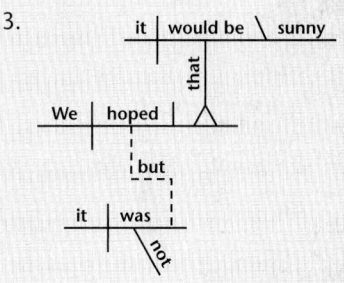

4.
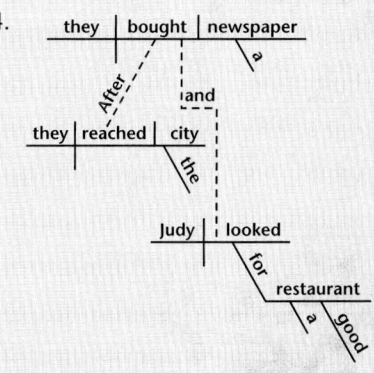

5.
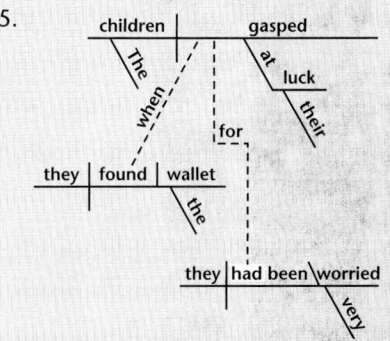

Lesson Objectives

1. To develop critical listening and effective speaking skills and apply them to various types of presentations.

2. To understand and evaluate visual images and messages in a variety of media.

3. To produce visual images, messages, and meanings that communicate with others.

4. To expand vocabulary through reading and listening and by developing skills in using context, word structure, word origins, and reference tools to determine word meanings.

5. To develop and apply reading strategies for a variety of purposes and texts.

6. To develop study and research skills and become familiar with reference tools and the resources of libraries and the Internet.

7. To develop skills in taking tests in various formats.

8. To learn and apply specific communication and procedural skills of the workplace, including problem-solving and managing time and money.

PART

3

Academic and Workplace Skills

Books II, 1993, Polly Kraft, Private Collection, Courtesy Fischbach Gallery, New York

Academic and Workplace Skills • **743**

Step-by-Step Teaching Guide

Responding to Fine Art

Books II by Polly Kraft

Use this work of art to start a discussion about the definition of academic and workplace skills.

1. Have students examine the painting on pages 742–743. You might use the following questions to prompt discussion:

   Where might this bookshelf be located? What kinds of writing would you expect to find?

2. Have students continue to suggest different places they would expect to find a bookshelf and the types of writing they would find in that place. For example, a lawyer's office would have bookshelves, and one might expect to find law journals, summaries of court cases, and other legal documents. Ask students why they think writing is important to so many types of work.

In-Depth Lesson Plan

	LESSON FOCUS	PRINT AND MEDIA RESOURCES
DAY 1	**Speaking Skills** Students learn and apply skills for preparing and giving a speech (pp. 744–748).	**Teaching Resources** *Academic and Workplace Skills Activity Book,* pp. 1–3
DAY 2	**Listening Skills** Students learn and apply listening skills (pp. 749–751).	**Teaching Resources** *Academic and Workplace Skills Activity Book,* pp. 1–3
DAY 3	**Viewing Skills** Students learn and apply such viewing skills as interpreting graphic organizers and critical viewing of information media (pp. 752–757).	**Teaching Resources** *Academic and Workplace Skills Activity Book,* pp. 4–7
DAY 4	**Representing Skills** Students learn and apply such representing skills as creating visual representations, using formatting and working with multimedia (pp. 758–763).	**Teaching Resources** *Academic and Workplace Skills Activity Book,* pp. 8–12

Accelerated Lesson Plan

	LESSON FOCUS	PRINT AND MEDIA RESOURCES
DAY 1	**Speaking and Listening Skills** Students learn and apply speaking and listening skills (pp. 744–751).	**Teaching Resources** *Academic and Workplace Skills Activity Book,* pp. 1–3
DAY 2	**Viewing and Representing Skills** Students learn and apply viewing and representing skills (pp. 752–763).	**Teaching Resources** *Academic and Workplace Skills Activity Book,* pp. 4–12

Options for Adapting Lesson Plans

HOMEWORK

Have students complete any stage of the lesson for homework.

TECHNOLOGY

Students can complete any stage of the lesson on computer. Have them print out their completed work.

FEATURES

Extend coverage with the Standardized Test Preparation Workshop (p. 764).

INTEGRATED SKILLS COVERAGE

Workplace Skills
Integrating Workplace Skills ATE p. 754

Technology
Integrating Technology Skills ATE p. 760

Viewing and Representing
Critical Viewing SE pp. 744, 746, 761
Integrating Viewing Skills, ATE p. 749

ASSESSMENT SUPPORT

Standardized Test Preparation, SE p. 764; ATE p. 750

Standardized Test Preparation Workbook, pp. 59–60

Formal Assessment, Ch. 30

MEETING INDIVIDUAL NEEDS

See Ongoing Assessments ATE pp. 745, 747, 751, 753, 757, 762, 763

ESL Students ATE p. 746

Logical/Mathematical Learners ATE p. 752

WRITING AND GRAMMAR WEBSITE

The Interactive Writing and Grammar Website provides a wide array of support for students, teachers and parents. Writing support includes:

• Interactive revision checkers
• Scoring rubrics with complete models

phwg.phschool.com

► Lesson Objectives

1. To use group discussions to express and hear ideas.
2. To identify the purpose of a speech.
3. To research a speech and make an outline.
4. To use presentation strategies for giving a speech.
5. To evaluate a speech.
6. To identify requirements of critical listening.
7. To identify and practice different types of listening.
8. To use different types of questions.
9. To interpret maps and graphs.
10. To identify and evaluate information in nonprint media.
11. To analyze bias caused by persuasive techniques.
12. To use critical-viewing strategies.
13. To interpret elements of fine art.
14. To use visual forms to better interpret large amounts of information.
15. To identify and work with multimedia presentations.

Critical Viewing

Analyze Students may say that some means of communication represented in the photograph are speech, print, telephone, and computer.

Chapter
30 Speaking, Listening, Viewing, and Representing

Communication travels between people in many forms. You convey information through speaking or through visual representations. You receive information by listening to others or by viewing visual representations. The more developed these four skills are—your speaking, listening, viewing, and representing skills—the more you will be able to communicate your ideas, as well as to comprehend the ideas of others. This chapter will help you increase your ability in these four areas of communication.

▲ **Critical Viewing**
Identify several different means of communication that you see in this photograph. **[Analyze]**

744 • Speaking, Listening, Viewing, and Representing

⏱ TIME AND RESOURCE MANAGER

Resources
Print: Academic and Workplace Skills Activity Book, pp. 1–3

In-Depth Coverage	Accelerated Pace
• Cover pp. 744–751 in class. • Discuss different types of speaking and listening skills. • Review Checklist for Evaluating a Speech, p. 748. **Option** Have students work individually or in groups on the Speaking and Listening section of the Writing Lab CD-ROM.	• Assign pp. 744–751 for independent student review. • Discuss definitions and types of speaking and listening skills.

Section 30.1
Speaking and Listening Skills

If you develop good speaking skills, you will be better prepared to contribute effectively in group discussions, to give formal presentations with more confidence, and to communicate your feelings and ideas to others more easily. If you improve your listening skills, it will become easier to focus your attention on classroom discussions and to identify important information more accurately.

Speaking in a Group Discussion

In a group discussion, you openly discuss ideas and topics in an informal setting. The group discussions in which you participate will involve, for the most part, your classmates and focus on the subjects you are studying. To get the most out of a group discussion, you need to participate in it.

▶ **KEY CONCEPT** Use group discussions to express and to listen to ideas in an informal setting. ■

Communicate Effectively The points you want to make, the order in which you want to make them, the words you will use to express them, and the examples that will support these points should all be thought of carefully before you speak. By thinking through your thoughts, your message will be clear.

Ask Questions Asking questions can help you in two ways. First, asking questions can help you improve your comprehension of another speaker's ideas. Second, asking questions may call attention to possible errors in another speaker's points.

Make Relevant Contributions Stay focused on the topic being discussed. Relate comments to your own experience and knowledge. When you contribute information or ideas, make clear how your contributions are connected to the topic.

▶ **Exercise 1** Holding a Group Discussion With three to five other students, hold a fifteen-minute group discussion about a topic you are studying in class. Review some related material from your textbooks to generate ideas and supporting information for your statements.

💿 Technology Tip

Search the Internet for more information on a topic you are studying. Use key words that are related to the topic. If you do not have good results with your first key word, try using other words related to it.

▶ **More Practice**

Academic and Workplace Skills Activity Book
• p. 1

Speaking, Listening, Viewing, and Representing • 745

☑ ONGOING ASSESSMENT: Diagnose

Use one of the following options to diagnose students' proficiency in speaking and listening skills.

| **Option 1** Observe as many students as possible in the group discussion exercise, their speaking skills, the questions they ask, their body language, and their listening skills. | **Option 2** Put students with common interests in a group and observe a structured group discussion on the topic of their choice. |

PREPARE and ENGAGE

☀ **Interest GRABBER** Ask students to recall a time they told a funny story to a group of people. Why did they tell that story? How did people react? Was the reaction what they hoped for? How did the reaction to their story make them feel?

Activate Prior Knowledge

Ask volunteers to tell a short, interesting anecdote or comment on a topic of their choice.

TEACH

Step-by-Step Teaching Guide

Speaking in a Group Discussion

1. Participating in a group discussion begins before having something to say. It really starts with a combination of how comfortable you feel in the group and your own level of confidence. Talk with students about confidence. Elicit that the general fear is of being rejected somehow, maybe made fun of. Ask students to think of ways they can make themselves more confident and, at the same time, make others feel more accepted and received in a group setting.

2. Focus on asking questions. Asking questions accomplishes several things. It allows you to understand what the speaker is saying. It focuses attention back on the speaker and makes him or her feel more welcomed and accepted. And it also provides an entry for a shy person into the conversation.

Answer Key

▶ **Exercise 1**

Answers will vary. Students should make active attempts to participate in the group discussion by making clear, supported statements relevant to the topic being discussed and by asking insightful questions.

Giving a Speech

Review the types of speeches. Write each type on the chalkboard and ask students to provide situations when it would be appropriate:

informative (class, club)

persuasive (political campaign, public issues)

entertaining (after-dinner speech)

extemporaneous (congratulatory toast)

Customize for
ESL Students

Students learning English may be especially reluctant to speak in front of a group. They fear—usually correctly—that they will use the wrong words and/or mispronounce them. Let students rehearse with fluent, friendly partners until they feel comfortable.

Answer Key

Exercise 2

Answers will vary. Samples are given.

Informative: Why leaves change color in the fall—science students; Planting a garden—gardeners

Persuasive: Why the voting age should be changed—voters; The need for more traffic lights—taxpayers, drivers

Entertaining: Ten ways to avoid cleaning your room—classmates; Why all kids hate broccoli—classmates

Extemporaneous: The best movie of the year—moviegoers; Why baseball is my favorite sport—sports enthusiasts

Critical Thinking

Infer Students may say that the student's conservative clothing and serious demeanor indicate that he may be making a persuasive speech, such as a campaign speech—because he may be running for student government.

30.1

Giving a Speech

Giving a presentation or speech before an audience is generally recognized as *public speaking.* To become an effective speaker and to deliver a good speech, you must become familiar with the different kinds of speeches, be well prepared, and deliver your speech smoothly and with confidence.

Recognizing Different Kinds of Speeches There are four main kinds of speeches: *expository speeches, persuasive speeches, entertaining speeches,* and *extemporaneous speeches.*

▶ **KEY CONCEPT** Consider the purpose of your speech and your audience before deciding what kind of speech you will give. ■

- Give an **informative** speech to explain an idea, a process, an object, or an event. In an informative speech, you may include technical language or terms to more accurately describe your topic.

- Give a **persuasive** speech to try to get your listeners to agree with your position or to take some action. In a persuasive speech, the language is usually formal English.

- Give an **entertaining** speech to offer your listeners something to enjoy or to amuse them. An entertaining speech may vary between informal and formal language.

- An **extemporaneous** speech is given to suit the occasion. It is an informal impromptu speech, because you do not rely on a prepared manuscript.

▶ **Exercise 2** Listing Kinds of Speeches
Give two topic examples for each kind of speech above. Then, speculate about who your audience might be for each kind of speech.

▶ Critical Viewing What kind of a speech do you think this student is making? What makes you think that? [Infer]

746 • Speaking, Listening, Viewing, and Representing

Learn More

To learn more about persuasive writing, read Chapters 7 and 8. To learn more about expository writing, read Chapters 9–11.

Preparing and Presenting a Speech If you are asked to deliver a speech, begin by thinking carefully about your topic. Choose a topic that you like or know well. Once you have completed this first step, you will need to prepare your speech so that you can present it to your audience.

▶ **KEY CONCEPT** To prepare your speech, research your topic, make an outline, and use numbered note cards. ■

Gather Information Use the library and other resources to gather reliable information and to find examples to support your ideas.

Make an Outline Organize your information in an outline of main ideas and major details. Use Roman numerals to list main ideas and capital letters for supporting details.

Use Numbered Note Cards Write the main ideas and major details on note cards that you can use when you deliver your speech. Include quotations and facts you want to remember. Use underlining and capital letters to make important information stand out.

▶ **KEY CONCEPT** When presenting your speech, use rhetorical forms of language and verbal and nonverbal strategies. ■

Use Rhetorical Language Repeat key words and phrases to identify your most important points. Use active verbs and colorful adjectives to keep your speech lively and interesting. Use parallel phrases or series of words to insert a sense of rhythm in your speech.

Use Verbal Strategies Vary the pitch and tone of your voice, as well as the rate at which you speak. Speak loudly enough, so the entire audience can hear your voice. Pronounce key words or phrases slower or louder for emphasis.

Use Nonverbal Strategies Maintain eye contact with members of the audience. Use gestures, facial expressions, and other movements to emphasize key points in your message.

▶ **Exercise 3** **Preparing and Presenting a Speech** Prepare an informative or persuasive speech on a topic in which you are interested. Use the steps in this section to prepare your speech and to present it to your classmates.

Outline
I. Main Idea
  A. Supporting detail
  B. Supporting detail
  C. Supporting detail

🗍 **Research Tip**

For more tips on how to deliver a speech effectively, use the card catalog in your library to find books on the subject. Start your search with the key words *Public Speaking.*

▶ **More Practice**

Academic and Workplace Skills Activity Book
• pp. 2–3

☑ **ONGOING ASSESSMENT: Monitor and Reinforce**

If some students are having difficulty using appropriate strategies, use one of the following options.

Option 1 Videotape students so they can see what they look like, whether they are fidgeting, slouching, and so on. Watch the tape with them and make a list of items for them to improve.

Option 2 Have students practice delivering their speech in front of a full-length mirror, observing their gestures, posture, and overall demeanor.

Preparing and Presenting a Speech

1. Make sure students pick focused (and appropriate) topics and that the overly ambitious have not chosen topics that will require too much research.

2. Organization is key to a successful speech. Tell students to have their main points, supporting details, and contrasting examples all lined up.

3. To write or not to write? Students who write out their speech may be tempted to read it to the class, which results in a stilted delivery. Well-prepared note cards coupled with good preparation, rehearsal, and even feedback from a sample audience is the better procedure. Students who are especially insecure may need a written text to refer to.

4. Parallel construction and repetitive emphasis on a main point are easily incorporated into speeches. Write the following example on the chalkboard and read it with the proper pace and emphasis:

   I looked under the bed. I looked in the closet. I looked in the dresser. I looked behind the curtains. There were no monsters. No monsters anywhere!

5. Model a stiff speaker, staring straight ahead. Elicit from students that a good speech depends on the speaker's confident manner. Encourage students to use whatever mind tricks they can to relax in front of the group. At the same time, tell them that an overly relaxed, slouched posture is inappropriate as well.

6. If in the middle of the speech students lose their place or forget what they want to say, they should stop, take a deep breath, apologize, and begin again from where they left off.

Answer Key

▶ **Exercise 3**

Students' speeches should reflect adequate research, and their presentations should use rhetorical language and verbal and nonverbal speaking strategies.

7

Evaluating a Speech

1. Review the items on the checklist. You might want to suggest an additional item, one that frequently is an issue with student speakers: Did the student project his or her voice? Was it easy to hear what he or she was saying? Did he or she mumble? Fill the speech with "uh," "er," "um"? Remind students that when they speak, they need to reach the back row. But don't shout!

2. To counterbalance the checklist, acknowledge that speaking in public is challenging for most people. We all should strive to do our best, but when listening to others, don't forget the difficulty of speaking in public and respect the effort speakers are making.

Answer Key

Exercise 4

Students' evaluations should be positive and helpful to the speaker and should answer all or most questions from the checklist.

30.1

Evaluating a Speech Evaluating a speech gives you the chance to judge another speaker's skills. It also gives you the opportunity to review and improve your own methods for preparing and presenting a speech.

▶ **KEY CONCEPT** When you evaluate a speech, you help the speaker and yourself. ■

The checklist below offers some criteria, or guidelines, for evaluating another person's speech as well as your own speeches.

CHECKLIST
FOR EVALUATING A SPEECH

☐ Did the speaker introduce the topic clearly, develop it well, and conclude it effectively?

☐ Did the speaker support each main idea with appropriate details?

☐ Did the speaker approach the platform confidently and establish eye contact with the audience?

☐ Did the speaker's facial expressions, gestures, and movements appropriately reinforce the words spoken?

☐ Did the speaker vary the pitch of his or her voice and the rate of his or her speaking?

☐ Did the speaker enunciate all words clearly?

▶ **Exercise 4** Evaluating a Speech Use the checklist above to help you make an evaluation of a speech given in class. List what you feel to be the areas at which the speaker excelled and those where he or she could have been more prepared. Give your evaluation to the speaker.

Using Critical Listening

Did you know that there is a difference between hearing and listening? Hearing happens naturally as sounds reach your ears. Listening, or critical listening, requires that you understand and interpret these sounds.

KEY CONCEPT Critical listening requires preparation, active involvement, and self-evaluation from the listener. ■

Learning the Listening Process Like all forms of communication, listening is interactive; the more you involve yourself in the listening process, the more you will understand.

Focus Your Attention Focus your attention on the speaker and his or her words. Block out all distractions—people, noises, and objects—that may redirect your attention. Before attending a formal speech or presentation, find out more about the subject that will be discussed.

Interpret the Information To interpret a speaker's message successfully, you need to identify and understand important information. Use the following suggestions to guide you:

- Listen for words and phrases that are emphasized or repeated.
- Pause momentarily from listening to silently repeat and to memorize important statements.
- Write down important statements, and summarize ideas.
- Watch for nonverbal signals—a change in the tone or pitch of the voice, gestures, and facial expressions—that may signal important information.
- Link the information currently being given into a meaningful pattern information with you already have.

Respond to the Speaker's Message Respond to the information you have heard by identifying the kind of speech, its overall message, its most interesting and useful points, and whether you agree or disagree with the speaker. If possible, ask questions to clarify your understanding.

Exercise 5 Using the Listening Process Apply the strategies described on this page to a lecture, speech, or classroom discussion. In writing, summarize the speaker's main points and respond to the message. Share your response with your classmates.

> **More Practice**
> Academic and
> Workplace Skills
> Activity Book
> • p. 4

Using Critical Listening

1. Critical listening is a key skill. When we listen with less than full attention, we miss much of what has been said. There is also a tendency to hear only what we want or expect to hear.

2. Focusing attention takes practice and some will power. It is hard to give full attention when our mind is full of distractions, pleasant or unpleasant. Suggest the following scenario to students: The person giving a speech could be you. How would you like it if you looked out at your audience and saw bored or distracted faces? Put yourself in the speaker's place and pay attention!

3. Taking notes is an excellent way for listeners to keep their mind on the speech. If not actual notes, encourage students to make mental notes, to identify main points and outstanding examples.

Integrating Viewing Skills

Have students practice critical listening by watching a TV news broadcast. Ask them to note both what is said and the nonverbal strategies of the anchorperson.

Answer Key

Exercise 5

Students' summaries should detail the speaker's main points and contain other related observations or a conclusion about the speaker's message.

Step-by-Step Teaching Guide

Using Different Types of Listening and Questions

1. Review the types of listening chart. Write the following situations on the chalkboard and ask students to volunteer the appropriate listening type:

   question-and-answer session (reflective)

   campaign speech (critical)

   talking on the bus with best friend (empathic)

   poetry reading (appreciative)

2. Review the different types of questions. Write the following questions on the chalkboard and ask students to identify the type of each question:

   How did you travel to Boston? (fact)

   What did you like about Boston? (open-ended)

   Did you visit Paul Revere's house? (closed)

Using Different Types of Listening You use different listening skills when you listen to a friend from those you use when you listen to a teacher or to a speech by one of your classmates. Different situations call for different types of listening. Learn more about the four main types of listening—*critical, empathic, appreciative,* and *reflective*—in the chart below.

Types of Listening		
Type	**How to Listen**	**Situations**
Critical	Listen for facts and supporting details to understand and evaluate the speaker's message.	Informative or persuasive essays, class discussions, announcements
Empathic	Imagine yourself in the other person's position, and try to understand what he or she is thinking.	Conversations with friends or family
Appreciative	Identify and analyze aesthetic or artistic elements, such as character development, rhyme, imagery, and descriptive language.	Oral presentations of a poem, dramatic performances
Reflective	Ask questions to get information, and use the speaker's responses to form new questions.	Class or group discussions

Using Different Types of Questions A speaker's ideas may not always be clear to you. The best way to clarify your understanding is by asking questions. You can ask a variety of questions, each with a different purpose. If you understand the different types of questions, you will be able to get the information you need.

- An **open-ended** question does not lead to a specific response. Use this question to open up a discussion: "What did you think of the piano recital?"

- A **closed** question leads to a specific response and must be answered with a yes or no: "Did you play a piece by Chopin at your recital?"

- A **factual** question is aimed at getting a particular piece of information and must be answered with facts: "How many years have you been playing the piano?"

750 • Speaking, Listening, Viewing, and Representing

STANDARDIZED TEST PREPARATION WORKSHOP

Question Types Students are often asked to identify and use different types of questions. Write the following examples on the chalkboard and have students match the questions with the question type:

1. Did you go to Fenway Park? **A.** closed
2. How do you like the Red Sox? **B.** fact
3. How many players are on a team? **C.** open

1A, 2C, 3B

> **Exercise 6** Using Different Types of Listening and Questions Identify at least one example of each type of listening and each type of question. Use examples from life, from television, from movies, or from descriptions in stories.

Evaluating Your Listening A good way to improve your listening is to evaluate it: to find out which listening skills work for you and which skills you need to improve. Use the following strategies to evaluate your listening skills.

Rephrase and Repeat Statements Test your understanding of a speaker's statements by rephrasing and then repeating them to the speaker. If the speaker agrees with your paraphrase, you know that you have understood him or her. If, however, the speaker disagrees with your paraphrase, ask the speaker for correction or clarification.

Compare and Contrast Interpretations Write your interpretation of a speaker's message, and then compare and contrast it with another student's interpretation. Use a Venn diagram to list the points with which you agree and disagree. Resolve these points of disagreement through discussion and, if necessary, by appealing to the speaker.

Research Points of Interest or Contention Use the library or other reference tools to acquire more information about the speaker's topic or to check questionable facts in his presentation.

> **More Practice**
> Academic and
> Workplace Skills
> Activity Book
> • p. 4

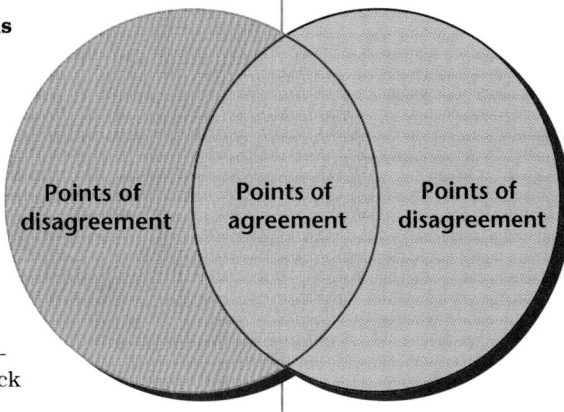

Points of disagreement | Points of agreement | Points of disagreement

> **Exercise 7** Evaluating Your Listening Skills Working with two other classmates, have one classmate read a speech or paper that he or she has recently written.
> 1. Tell the speaker to pause every paragraph or every few sentences, and take turns with your other classmate to rephrase and repeat the speaker's statements.
> 2. Have the speaker read the entire speech or paper while you and your classmate take notes. Then, compare and contrast your interpretations.
> 3. Write an evaluation of your listening skills. Identify areas of strength and areas in which you need to improve.

Evaluating Your Listening Skills

1. It is easy to fool ourselves about how well we are listening. One way of evaluating what was said is to compare notes with other listeners.

2. If possible, find a videotaped speech for which you can also obtain the text or transcript. Have students watch and listen to the speech and first evaluate what they think was said. Next, have students compare notes. Finally, distribute photocopies of the transcript and ask students to compare what they thought was said with the verbatim transcript.

☑ **ONGOING ASSESSMENT: Assess Mastery**

Use one of the following options to assess students' mastery of speaking and listening skills.

Self-Assessment Ask students to reflect on their speaking and listening skills, making sure they have identified areas they feel strong in and areas they would like to improve.	**Teacher Assessment** Review your notes on each exercise students have performed. Also consider their basic understanding of the subject matter as evidenced by their participation in class discussions.

Viewing Skills

1. Review the map of the Midwest and have students identify the type of map and information shown.

2. Review the map key. Have volunteers point out the national boundary, state capitals, and other cities.

Customize for
Logical/Mathematical Learners

Partners can challenge each other to find distances on the map in both miles and kilometers. (To measure rivers, yarn or dental floss works well.)

Section 30.2 *Viewing Skills*

Visual representation, or the use of images, is an important method of communicating. You see examples of this in television programs, magazines, billboards, textbooks, and works of art. In this section, you will learn how to use visual representations as sources of information.

Interpreting Maps and Graphs

Maps and graphs are useful tools to help readers clarify difficult, complicated information. Because these tools help you to understand information visually, they are sometimes called *visual aids*. To interpret these visual aids, you need to know the special features of each.

▶ **KEY CONCEPT** Interpret maps and graphs in order to obtain information visually. ■

Maps

A map can present much more information than simply the locations of cities and geographical formations. For example, maps can identify areas of population clusters, clarify battle activities in war, or report weather forecasts. To interpret a map, **(1)** determine the type and purpose of the map; **(2)** examine the symbols, distance, scale, and other data on the map; and **(3)** relate the information on the map to any written information accompanying it.

📖 **Research Tip**

To get a better idea of the kinds of information maps can show, go to the reference section of your library and browse through a few atlases.

⏱ TIME AND RESOURCE MANAGER

Resources
Print: Academic and Workplace Skills Activity Book, pp. 4–7

In-Depth Coverage	Accelerated Pace
• Cover pp. 752–757 in class. • Discuss different types of viewing skills in class.	• Assign pp. 752–757 for independent student review. • Discuss definitions and types of viewing skills.

Graphs

Graphs provide a visual way to compare several pieces of related information. Study the following three types of commonly used graphs.

Line Graph A **line graph** shows changes over a certain period of time. It features a line that connects points. The points, which may appear as dots on the graph, represent numbers or amounts of something. To interpret a line graph, **(1)** read the title of the graph and its labels to find out what type of information is represented and the time interval over which the data is being reported; **(2)** read each axis of the graph: the main vertical line and main horizontal line that make up the graph; **(3)** compare and contrast the data.

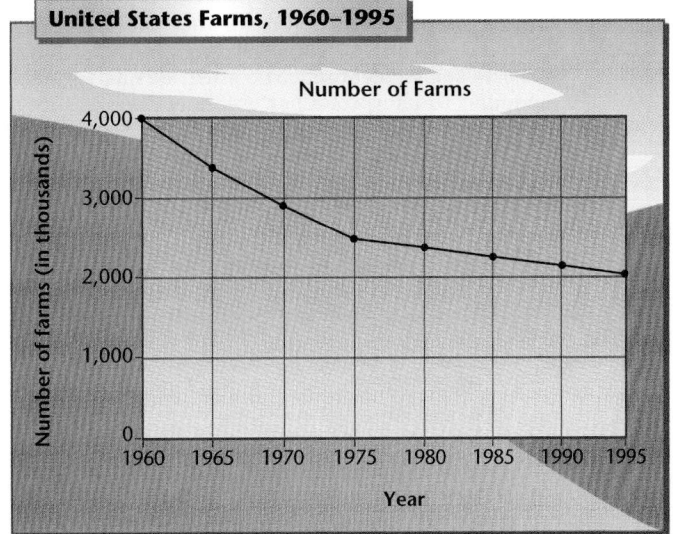

Pie Graph A **pie graph** shows the relationship of parts to each other and to a whole. To interpret a pie graph, **(1)** look at the numbers that go with the individual parts; **(2)** match the parts with the key; and **(3)** use the numbers and parts to make comparisons.

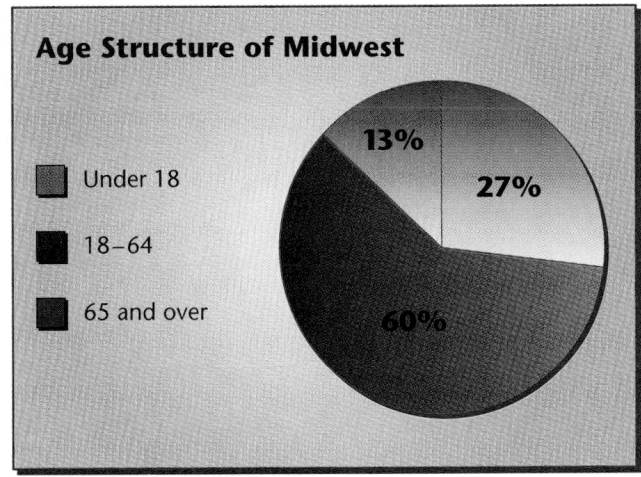

Graphs

1. Have students examine both graphs. Be sure that all can easily comprehend the information.

2. Point out that the numbers on the vertical axis of the line graph are "in thousands." This means that 1,000 equals 1,000 thousands, or 1 million.

3. To check comprehension of both graphs, ask the following questions:

    There were approximately 2,500,000 farms in what year? (1975)

    How many farms were there in 1960? (4 million)

    What percentage of people in the Midwest are under 18? (27%)

    What percentage of people in the Midwest are 18–64? (60%)

Viewing Skills • 753

☑ ONGOING ASSESSMENT: Monitor and Reinforce

If some students are having difficulty reading the graphs, use the following options.

Option 1 For the line graph, carefully explain that the vertical axis tells how many farms and the horizontal axis represents the year.	**Option 2** Help students understand that the whole pie graph equals everyone in the Midwest, that is, 100 percent of midwesterners. It does not tell the size of the population.

Bar Graph

1. See that students understand how the bar graph can compare and contrast information.

2. Review the graph. Explain that hydroelectric power is power from moving water and nuclear power comes from nuclear reactors that split atoms to make energy.

3. Ask students to speculate on what sources of power might make up the "Other" category. (Solar and wind power as well as energy from burning wood products are likely candidates.)

4. To check student comprehension, ask the following questions:

   What is the largest source of energy in the US? (petroleum)

   What percentage of energy comes from hydroelectric and nuclear power? (11%)

   Which two energy sources are tied at 24%? (natural gas and coal)

   What is the smallest source of energy? (other—3%)

Integrating Workplace Skills

Many businesses use graphs to analyze data. Have students work in small groups to make their own series of graphs showing easily available information. Some suggested topics: percentage of students in the class with last names beginning with A–E, F–J, and so on; comparing population figures for neighboring states or cities; percentage of students wearing various colored tops.

Answer Key

Exercise 8

Students' reports should show a clear understanding of the purpose of each visual aid they find and of the information contained in it.

30.2

Bar Graph A **bar graph** shows changes over a period of time or compares and contrasts information. A bar graph has a vertical axis and a horizontal axis. One axis shows the subjects being measured. The other axis lists numbers or amounts. To interpret a bar graph, **(1)** look at the "heights" or "lengths" of the bars to see what numbers they represent; **(2)** match the subject that goes with the bar to the number the bar reaches; and **(3)** compare and contrast the "heights" or "lengths" of bars.

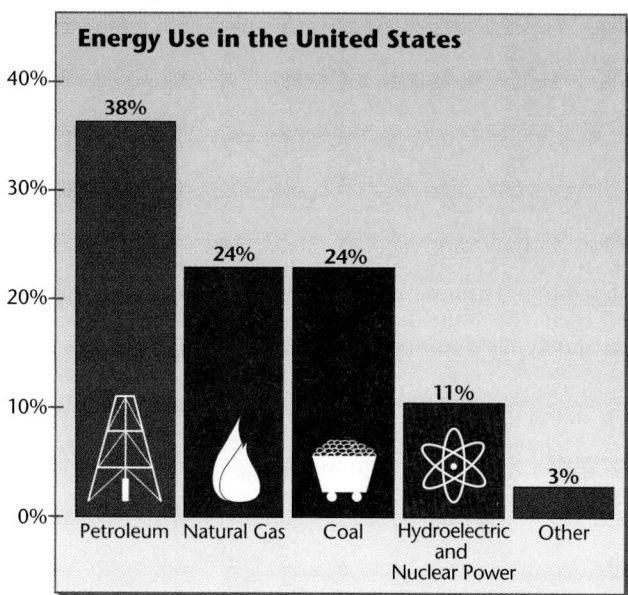

Energy Use in the United States

Exercise 8 **Reading Information Visually** Find an example from your textbooks or other sources of each type of visual aid (a map and a line, pie, and bar graph). Use the general guidelines and steps for interpretation to help you describe the visual aid and tell what kinds of information you can learn from each. Report your findings to your classmates.

More Practice

Academic and Workplace Skills Activity Book
• pp. 4–5

Viewing Information Media Critically

When you view information media critically, you think carefully about what you see and hear. Because the media distributes large amounts of information, it is important to learn the differences between various kinds of media as well as to evaluate the information being presented.

▶ **KEY CONCEPT** Learn to identify and evaluate the various kinds of information and images found in nonprint media. ■

Recognizing the Kinds of Information Media

Television, documentary films, and other media provide news and other information. The quality and importance of the information you get depends on the kind of program or film you are watching.

The following chart describes several forms of nonprint information media.

NONPRINT INFORMATION MEDIA			
Form of Medium	**Topic(s)**	**Coverage and Content**	**Point of View**
Television News Program	Current events or news	Brief summaries illustrated by video footage	Gives objective information
Documentary	One topic of social interest	Story shown through narration and video footage	Expresses controversial opinions
Interview	Topics of social interest	Conversations of questions and answers	Presents opinions of interviewer
Editorial	Current or controversial topics	Commentary by a single person supported by statistics or facts	Presents the opinions of a single individual
Commercial	Products, people, and ideas	Short message of images and slogans	Presents information to sell something

⟲ Learn More

Advertisements often use loaded language and images. To learn more about the techniques used in advertisements, read Chapter 8.

Viewing Information Media Critically

1. Discuss with students the importance of understanding the source of news and the point of view and any possible bias. See that they are sure about the difference between news programs that purport to present an objective view and editorials and columns that present an individual or collective point of view.

2. Extend the discussion to focus on news programs and objectivity. Ask students if they think they can believe everything they read or hear in a news article or news report. They should always read and listen critically, asking questions of what they read and hear and looking for possible bias that the writer or speaker may not even be aware of. For instance, do students think that articles about kids written by adults are always written objectively? If there were trouble at their school that was reported in the local paper or on local radio, would the information accurately reflect life at their school?

30.2

Evaluating Persuasive Techniques

1. Make sure that students have a solid grasp of the difference between fact—something provable—and opinion. Point out that facts are not always true. For example, the statement *New York City is the capital of the United States* is a factual statement because it is provable. It can be proved to be wrong in this case.

2. Write the following statements on the chalkboard and ask students to identify them as statements of fact or statements of opinion:

   Today is Thursday. (fact)

   Fridays are best. (opinion)

   Luigi's Pizza is on the corner. (fact)

   Luigi's Pizza is the best. (opinion)

3. Bias is often unconscious. Sometimes bias results from ignorance or being out of touch with a point of view. Ask students to consider the challenge older adults may have identifying with the needs and interests of kids, of how someone who is relatively well off can fail to understand the thinking and experience of someone who is homeless or poor. How well can people of vastly different backgrounds and experiences understand each other? Conclude with the idea that "objectivity" is not so easily arrived at. Point out that it behooves all of us to use critical judgment in analyzing information we get from different media. In short, think!

Answer Key

Exercise 9

Students' essays should identify the type of program viewed and summarize its contents. They should also identify the products, ideas, and so on, featured in the commercials. Their essays should mention something about the amount of information covered in the program and provide examples of persuasive techniques.

Evaluating Persuasive Techniques When you are reading or watching any form of media, you should be aware of persuasive techniques that are being used so that your understanding of the information is not distorted.

> **KEY CONCEPT** Be aware of persuasive techniques in media that may distort your understanding of actual events. ■

- **Facts and opinions** are two primary means of persuasion. A *fact* is a statement that can be proved to be true. An *opinion* is a viewpoint that cannot be proved to be true.

- **"Loaded" language and images** are words and visuals that appeal to your emotions in order to persuade you to think a certain way.

- **Bias** is a tendency to think from a particular point of view. As you view, consider whether the information is being presented objectively or with an intended viewpoint.

Evaluating Information From the Media Once you understand the different forms of media and their persuasive techniques, you are ready to evaluate the programs themselves.

> **KEY CONCEPT** Use critical viewing strategies to help you evaluate the media more effectively. ■

- As you watch a program, be aware of its form, its purpose, and its limitations.

- Separate facts from opinions. Be on the lookout for loaded language or sensational images that might cause you to react in a certain way. Listen for bias, and note any points of view that might be ignored.

- Check surprising or questionable information in other sources.

- View the complete program, and develop your own views about the issues, people, and information.

> **Exercise 9** **Analyzing Information Media** Watch a television program that provides information, such as a news program, a documentary, or an interview. Notice the commercials as well. Then, write an essay in which you identify the type of program and describe the topics covered. In addition, comment on what the commercials were selling. Finally, evaluate the information on each topic in the program and in the commercials using the strategies listed above.

Viewing Fine Art Critically

When you view fine art—such as a painting, drawing, photograph, or a sculpture—you use different standards for evaluation from those you use when viewing a program from the media—even if the work has a political or social message. The critical emphasis on bias, loaded words, and opinions gives way to an examination of line, shape, color, and motion.

▶ **KEY CONCEPT** To enrich your understanding and enjoyment of fine art, interpret the various elements of which the artwork is composed. ■

Interpreting Elements of Fine Art Consider the following questions as you observe a work of art:

Starry Night, Vincent van Gogh Museum of Modern Art

- What kind of work are you viewing: a painting, drawing, photograph, engraving, or collage?
- What are the subject and central focus of the piece of art?
- What technique does the artist use—color *versus* black and white, bold lines *versus* impressionistic ones (lines of short strokes), vivid *versus* muted colors?
- What mood, theme, or message does the work convey?
- Is your overall response to the work more positive or more negative? Why?

▶ **Exercise 10** **Interpreting Fine Art** Interpret the painting *Starry Night* by Vincent van Gogh by asking and answering the questions listed above. Write your answers to these questions in your notebook. Add any other observations.

▶ **More Practice**

Academic and Workplace Skills Activity Book
- pp. 7–8

Viewing Skills • **757**

ONGOING ASSESSMENT: Monitor and Reinforce

If some students are having difficulty viewing fine art, use the following options.

Option 1 Remind students that they don't have to like a piece of art to be able to understand the artist's technique and appreciate the effort and talent that went into its execution.

Option 2 Display works by realist painters such as Andrew or Jamie Wyeth and Edward Hopper or a playful artist such as Marc Chagall, and ask students to try to put themselves in the painting.

Step-by-Step Teaching Guide

Viewing Fine Art Critically

1. Talk about appreciating popular music, a subject most students will be more familiar with than fine art.

2. Ask students to name songs or bands they like. Then ask them to tell why they like them. Some students may be able to identify concrete reasons, such as the lyrics of a song, or a particular sound, or the playing of an instrumentalist. But also point out that aesthetic appreciation often comes from places inside us that we can't really explain. We hear it. We like it or don't like it.

3. Transition the discussion to fine art. There are two basic goals here. The first is to have students look at unfamiliar images with "fresh, open eyes." Too often people get intimidated by "fine art" and let social anxiety keep them from truly seeing what they are looking at.

4. Once students can look at fine art with fresh, open eyes and engage their aesthetic sense, they need to examine it critically, asking questions about, color, line, form, setting, and composition.

5. There is no correct response to art. The meaning of a painting is whatever it means to someone looking at it. Students may like or not like *Starry Night,* but all students should be able to describe their response.

Answer Key

Exercise 10

Answers will vary. Samples are given.

1. The work is a painting.
2. The subject is a starry night in the countryside surrounding a village.
3. The painting is colorful yet somber, mixing a sky with stars like fireworks with the subdued tones of night.
4. The mood is one of awe and exhilaration.
5. Overall response is positive, because the painting is interesting and invites the viewer to share the artist's appreciation of a beautiful night.

1. Discuss with students how using graphic organizers can help them understand and take notes on a text passage.

2. Show students examples of a concept map, Venn diagram, and flowchart. Ask students to volunteer any visual representations of their own they have used in the past and explain how they used them.

3. Remind students that aids like graphic organizers are tools to be used to accomplish the goals of understanding and retaining information. Be sure students don't spend so much time and energy making pretty visual representations that they fail to accomplish the goals of understanding and retention.

Section **30.3** *Representing Skills*

Visual representation, or the use of images, is an important method of communicating. You can design your own visual representations by using graphic organizers, multimedia presentations, and performances.

Creating Visual Representations

When you are reading, researching, studying, or presenting complicated ideas, you can use graphic organizers and other visual aids to give structure to the material. This makes the information easier to comprehend.

▶ **KEY CONCEPT** Large amounts of information or technical data can be absorbed more easily if you put them into visual form. ∎

Use these strategies to help you present information visually:

Use Text Descriptions In some types of writing, you will notice headings and subheadings that indicate various sections. A good way to organize this information visually is to design a graphic organizer, which is a tool that helps you organize information visually. For text with detailed descriptions, a drawing would help clarify the parts and details.

Look at Text Structure As you read, notice how the text is organized. Is it comparison-and-contrast, cause-and-effect, main-idea-and-details, or chronological order? If it is a comparison and contrast, you can use a Venn diagram or a comparison chart to show similarities and differences. If the text shows cause-and-effect relationships, you can use a flowchart to show the information visually. If the text uses many details to support a main idea, you can use an outline to organize the material. A good way to visualize chronological order is a timeline.

Chronology

Identify Your Purpose Think about what parts of the material you want to represent visually. Then, decide which type of graphic organizer will work best for your purposes. For example, you might want to show what two political systems have in common and how they differ, or you may want to chart three possible outcomes of an election. You might want to compare and contrast the percentages of people who have dogs, cats, or birds as pets.

758 • Speaking, Listening, Viewing, and Representing

Learn More

To learn more about graphic organizers, read "Using Graphic Organizers" in Chapter 32 "Reading."

⏱ TIME AND RESOURCE MANAGER

Resources
Print: Academic and Workplace Skills Activity Book, pp. 8–12

In-Depth Coverage	Accelerated Pace
• Cover pp. 758–763 in class. • Discuss different types of representing skills in class. • Have students create a flip chart like the one on p. 762.	• Assign pp. 758–763 for independent student review. • Discuss definitions and types of representing skills.

Charts, Graphs, and Tables For columns of numbers, survey statistics, and other complex information, you can prepare a chart, graph, or table. A chart can be any shape or color, and it can display any type of information, such as the heights of tall mountains. A graph, such as a bar or line graph, is a good way to show changes that take place over time, such as the daily outdoor temperature. Tables enable you to present scientific and numerical information in a clear and logical way.

Diagrams and Illustrations Diagrams and illustrations are line drawings that indicate the features of something. If you were describing the solar system, for example, you might make a diagram like the one below:

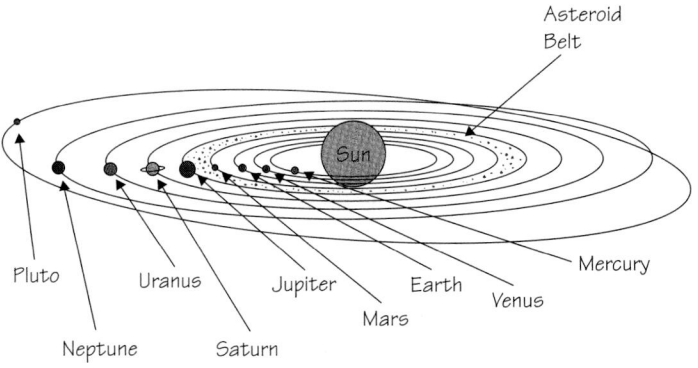

Maps If you want to know how to get somewhere or if you are studying the geography of several regions, a map can be quite useful. Maps can show almost any type of geographical information.

Exercise 11 **Creating Visual Representations** Use your knowledge of visual representations to complete one of the following activities:
1. Examine a chapter from one of your textbooks and prepare a chart, graph, or table to illustrate a portion of its information. Present your visual representation to the class, and explain why you chose to present the information in this way.
2. Make a map or diagram of your school or of an area of your town or city.

Technology Tip

You can get maps from the Internet by using the key word *Maps*. You can also get directions from any one location to another, as long as you have the two addresses. Print out some directions from a map Web site, and study the maps that accompany the directions.

More Practice

Academic and Workplace Skills Activity Book
• p. 9

Charts, Graphs, Tables, Diagrams, Illustrations, and Maps

1. Review how charts, graphs, tables, diagrams, illustrations, and maps can all help students organize information so they can better understand it and retrieve it for studying.

2. Remind students that everyone has his or her own particular learning style. Use the solar system diagram as an example. Someone who was more verbally than visually inclined might prefer to make up a sentence to remember the order of planets from the sun: Many Very Energetic Mice Jump Suddenly Up Near Panthers.

Answer Key

Exercise 11

Answers will vary.

1. Students' reasons for choosing one particular visual aid over another to present information should be logical, and the visual aid itself should demonstrate this.
2. Students' maps or diagrams should convey information accurately and be clearly labeled.

Using Formatting

1. Formatting has several applications. Discuss how while taking notes, students can use formatting to help highlight different ideas. For brochures and advertising, formatting applications can draw attention, order information, and direct the viewer's attention in a certain way.

2. Use the brochure featured in the text as an example. Point out how the type size and boldface letters guide the reader through the brochure; how the bullets and numbered list make reading easier.

Integrating Technology Skills

Make sure students know how to use all the formatting options available on the toolbar. Also, refer them to the Help option on the toolbar for additional assistance.

Answer Key

Exercise 12

Students' flyers should incorporate a variety of formatting techniques to highlight information at different levels of importance.

30.3

Using Formatting

You can enhance any written text by using the basic formatting features in your word-processing program. Formatting features include boldface, italics, capital letters, font sizes, and bullets, to name a few. Notice how this flyer uses formatting features to get its message across.

Here are some tips for using these features:

Capitals Use capital letters in heads to draw attention to important ideas and topics.

Boldface Use boldface type to emphasize key concepts or ideas on a page.

Italics Use italics to give special emphasis to a written line or word.

Numbered Lists Use a numbered list when you have steps that need to be followed in sequence.

Bulleted Lists For items that can be presented in any order, use a bulleted list.

Graphics Use graphics to attract a viewer's attention and to give an idea of what kind of information can be expected.

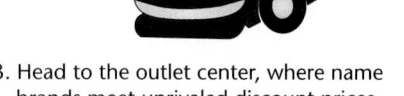

Go Now and Save With International Quality Tours!

If your vacation time and funds are limited, then you should check us out! Unlike lesser quality charter tours, we've got added value built into our prices.

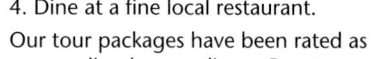

We've Got It ... Do They?
- transfers to and from airports
- complimentary breakfasts
- a dazzling array of side trips
- gratuities included in price

Here's a sample day's itinerary:

1. Visit the historic district, famous for its period architecture.
2. Break for lunch at the renowned Foods Around the World Hall, where you can sample international cuisine.
3. Head to the outlet center, where name brands meet unrivaled discount prices.
4. Dine at a fine local restaurant.

Our tour packages have been rated as outstanding by our clients. Because we offer great packages at great prices, you can enjoy a quality vacation without depleting your budget.

Exercise 12 Using Formatting to Summarize a Textbook Page Read a page from your textbook. Then, use the tips on formatting listed above to design a flyer that summarizes the textbook information. Give reasons for your formatting choices.

Working With Multimedia

An oral report becomes a multimedia presentation when the speaker illustrates the main points with media selections. If this type of presentation is well planned and executed, it can be effective and memorable.

KEY CONCEPT Multimedia presentations make use of a variety of media in order to explain information. Among the media used are text, slides, videos, music from audiotapes and CDs, maps, charts, and art. ■

Preparing a Multimedia Presentation First, prepare an outline of your report. Then, decide which parts of your report could best be illustrated through the use of media.

- Choose an appropriate form of media for your topic. For example, if you were discussing the music of Beethoven, a picture of the composer, video clips from movies based on his life, and music that he wrote would help enhance your presentation.

- As you deliver your report, incorporate the media at appropriate points. Do not show all the media at once.

- Check to be sure that the media you plan to present will be able to be seen and/or heard by everyone. A small photograph, for example, might not be clear to people in the back. It would be better to project the image using an overhead projector.

- Before the day of your presentation, rehearse with the equipment. Make sure that the use of visuals does not distract from your presentation. You should not be fumbling around with equipment during your presentation.

- Before your presentation, make sure that all your equipment (slide projectors, overhead projectors, microphones, cassette players, CD players) are in working condition.

- Always have an alternate plan in case something goes wrong with the equipment.

Exercise 13 **Preparing a Multimedia Presentation** Look through the writings in your portfolio. Find one piece to use as a multimedia presentation. Prepare an outline of your presentation, including the media you'd use and the order in which you would use it. Practice a few times, and then present it to your class.

Learn More

You will have to do research as you prepare your presentation. The steps you would follow to prepare the presentation are basically the same as the steps you would follow to prepare a research paper. To learn more about research methods, read Chapter 12.

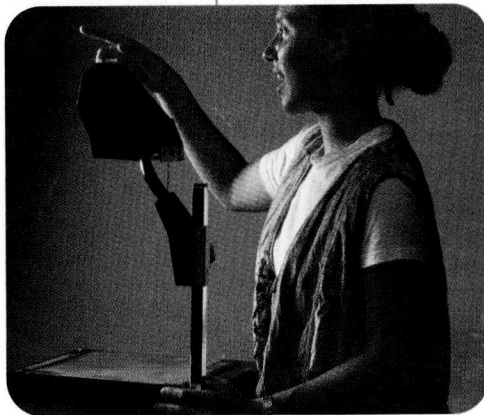

▲ **Critical Viewing** How can this student use this form of media to enhance her report? [Deduce]

More Practice

Academic and Workplace Skills Activity Book
• pp. 10–11

Representing Skills • 761

Working With Multimedia

1. Review the multimedia presentation guidelines. Students' ability to use this information will be dependent on the availability of resources. One way to model the process would be to contact a local public relations agency or business and ask if there is anyone who could come to class and provide a model multimedia presentation.

2. Remind students that different media are tools, not ends in themselves. The most successful presentations have a coherent message, presented in a clear, concise, and, if possible, entertaining manner. A lively, effective talk is much more persuasive than a slick multimedia presentation that does not have a coherent message.

3. A key to using multimedia is preparation. Video and audio examples need to be cued up and ready to go. No matter how much they add to the presentation, students will lose their audience if they fast-forward or fumble in search of an example.

4. Another source of failed presentations is malfunction. Everything needs to be tested in advance. Make sure that every piece of equipment is plugged in and turned on and that every slide is focused and right side up.

Answer Key

Exercise 13

Students should demonstrate an understanding of the purpose for using multimedia, and the multimedia they use should reinforce the oral portion of their presentation.

Critical Thinking

Deduce Students may say that the student can use the medium shown to share visuals with the class and make her report more informative.

Preparing a Flip Chart

1. Flip charts are the original low-tech media. A flip chart helps reinforce the main points and is useful for posting outlines and agendas. With a flip chart, speakers can reveal each page just when it is needed, so the audience is not distracted by reading something in advance, as they might be with material written on the chalkboard.

2. Some additional basic tips for making flip charts:
   - Pay careful attention to the printing. Lightly sketch each page in pencil, then do a finished copy in marker. Above all, the writing should be even on the page.
   - Use color. Alternate colors; use color to shade letters.
   - Pay attention to layout. The lettering needs to be large enough for everyone in the room to see. Leave enough white space so that the page is not cluttered.

Answer Key

Exercise 14

Flip charts should be neat, well constructed, and logically sequenced.

30.3

Preparing a Flip Chart

Flip charts are effective visual aids that help your audience remember the key points of your speech.

KEY CONCEPT Prepare a flip chart to help your audience follow the sequence of events in your story, the main points of your argument, or the steps to be followed in your directions. ■

Follow these steps to prepare and use a flip chart:

1. Determine the most important points in your presentation.
2. Obtain enough sheets of posterboard to allow one sheet per point.
3. Write each point on a separate sheet of posterboard. Be sure that the writing is large enough to be seen by all audience members. Keep it short—you can elaborate in your presentation. You can use charts, diagrams, and other visuals, but they must be clear.
4. Arrange the sheets in the order in which the points appear in your presentation.
5. Punch two or three holes in the top of each sheet of poster-board. Use shower curtain hooks or similar devices to attach the sheets and make them easy to flip.
6. Set the flip chart on an easel. If you are right-handed, stand on the left side of the chart. If you are left-handed, stand on the right side of the chart. This will make it easy for you to flip the pages and point out the important information on the chart.
7. Do not turn your back to your audience as you flip the pages. Face the audience at all times.

Exercise 14 **Preparing a Flip Chart** Prepare a flip chart of at least three pages. Follow the steps in the list above to make your chart. Be sure that each page of your flip chart is clear and concise. Remember that the purpose of a flip chart is to accompany and clarify your more elaborate presentation.

☑ ONGOING ASSESSMENT: Monitor and Reinforce

If some students are having difficulty creating a flip chart, use the following options.

Option 1 Help students organize their main points in an outline. Have them write their main points or the entire outline on a flip chart, one roman numeral per page.	**Option 2** Have students construct visual representations to support their presentations and copy each one on a flip chart page. If the visual presentations are fairly intricate, and resources are available, allow them to use blown-up photocopies to paste on flip chart pages.

Performing or Interpreting

A live performance is one of the oldest and most effective forms of communication.

KEY CONCEPT You can use a wide variety of techniques to convey the meaning of a text or song. ■

Preparing to Perform Whether you plan a performance of someone else's work or of an original piece of your own, keep the following tips in mind.

1. Write the text in a notebook or photocopy it. Then, highlight its most important words and ideas.
2. Read the text aloud several times, experimenting with the tone and pitch of your voice and with the emphasis you give to certain words and phrases.
3. Practice using different kinds of body language—such as hand gestures, posture, and facial expressions—to convey meaning.
4. Costumes, props, background setting, and music are all important elements that can contribute to the mood.
5. Rehearse until you feel comfortable enough to perform.

▶ **Exercise 15** **Giving an Oral Interpretation** Choose a poem or a story you'd like to interpret for an audience. Copy it and highlight its key ideas and words. Then, write a list of performance notes, planning the effect you'd like to create, the mood you'd like to set, and other details related to the performance.

**Technology Tip**

You might want to use the computer to make a copy of your text. If you do, you can highlight the most important words and ideas in various ways:

- You can use large type.
- You can use boldface type.
- You can use different colors for the type or for the background.

▶ **More Practice**

Academic and Workplace Skills Activity Book
- pp. 12–13

Reflecting on Your Speaking, Listening, Viewing, and Representing

Review the various concepts discussed in this chapter. Write a one-page reflection on these experiences. Begin your observations by responding to these questions:

- How has my understanding of being a good speaker and listener changed? In what ways can I improve each of these skills?
- What strategies have most improved my ability to view information critically?
- Which representing experiences did I find the most enjoyable?
- What have I learned about viewing and representing?

Share your insights with your classmates.

Representing Skills • 763

Performing or Interpreting

1. One key to live performance is the use of nonverbal strategies, particularly body language. Whether the performance is song, drama, dance, or speech, performers capture and hold audience interest with posture, gesture, facial expression, and eye contact.

2. Have students reflect on viewing and representing and share their reflections with the rest of the class.

☑ **ONGOING ASSESSMENT: Assess Mastery**

Use one of the following options to assess mastery of viewing and representing.

Self-Assessment Review students' reflections on viewing and representing, making sure they have identified areas they feel strong in and areas they would like to improve.	**Teacher Assessment** Review your notes on each exercise that students have performed. Also consider their basic understanding of the subject matter as evidenced by their participation in class discussions.

Interpreting Graphic Aids

1. Remind students that graphs must be read both horizontally (across) and vertically (up-and-down). In the graph shown, reading horizontally shows certain years, and reading vertically shows the number of families with radios. Reading the graph both horizontally and vertically shows the number of families with radios in certain years.

2. To answer the question, students need to find out how many families had radios in 1926 (about 5 million) and how many in 1924 (about 1 million). Subtracting 1 from 5 yields the answer to the first question, 4 million. B is the correct response.

3. To answer the second question, students should read the caption and reflect on their own life experience. Have a volunteer explain her or his reasoning.

Standardized Test Preparation Workshop

Interpreting Graphic Aids

Some standardized tests contain questions that test your ability to gather details, draw conclusions, and interpret from the information provided in maps, charts, graphs, and other graphic aids. The following sample items will help you become familiar with these types of questions.

Test Tip

As you examine each graphic aid, ask yourself what each part of the graphic means or represents in relation to the whole.

Sample Test Item

Directions: Read the passage and the chart, and answer the questions that follow.

The 1920's could be called the age of radio. Information was brought to a larger segment of the population. It brought different forms of entertainment to people and enabled them to learn of news as it happened.

1 Approximately, how many more families had radios in 1924 than in 1926?

   A 2 million

   B 4 million

   C 6 million

   D 1 million

2 How did radios change the lives of every-day people?

   F News and a variety of entertainment were brought into the home.

   G Information could be sent between households.

   H People could play tapes and albums.

   J It did not change lives.

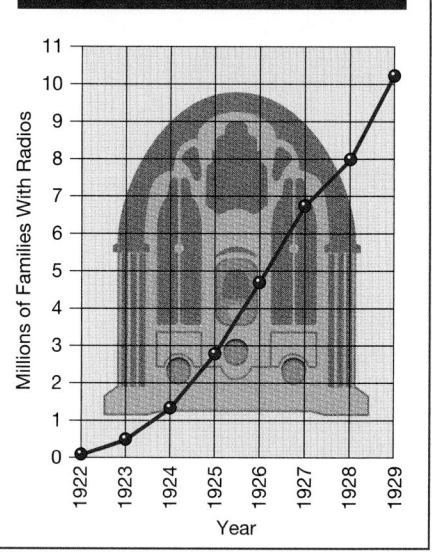

Families With Radios 1922–1929

Answers and Explanations

The correct answer for item 1 is *B*. Using the graph, you can determine that in 1924, a little more than a million homes had radios; in 1926, about 5 million homes had radios.

The correct answer for item 2 is *F*. News and a variety of entertainment were brought into the home for the first time.

✎ TEST-TAKING TIP

When answering multiple-choice questions involving graphic aids, it might help students to check their answers by reviewing the other possible responses. If students cannot justify them from the graph, they can be sure they have decided correctly.

Practice 1

1. B
2. J
3. C
4. H
5. B

> **Practice 1** **Directions:** Read the passage and the chart, and answer the questions that follow.

During the second half of the nineteenth century and the early 1900's, industrial areas in parts of Western Europe and the United States saw life expectancy rise. This was due to the many reforms that were passed during this time that made working conditions safer and working days shorter.

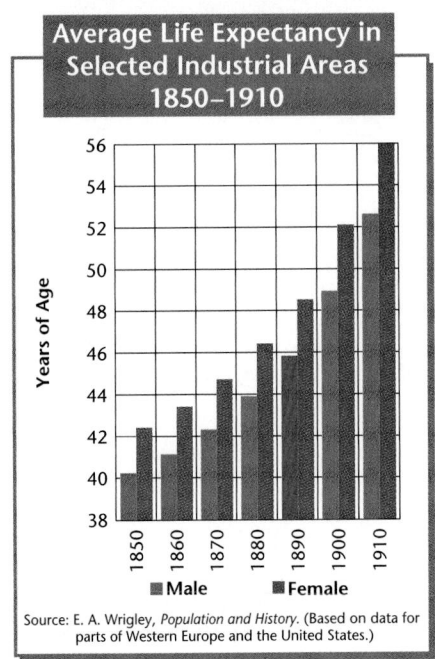

Average Life Expectancy in Selected Industrial Areas 1850–1910

Years of Age

■ Male   ■ Female

Source: E. A. Wrigley, *Population and History.* (Based on data for parts of Western Europe and the United States.)

1 What information does the chart's title provide?

A the life expectancy rate in 1850–1910

B the life expectancy in 1850–1910 in industrial areas

C years of age of those studied

D the country where the study was conducted

2 During which decade did women's life expectancy increase the most?

F 1850–1860

G 1870–1880

H 1890–1900

J 1900–1910

3 What is the difference in life expectancy in men's lives in 1850 and 1890?

A fifteen years

B ten years

C six years

D three years

4 Life expectancy grew during these years because of—

F better nutrition

G newly available health care

H working conditions and reforms

J reduction in industry

5 How did the difference in life expectancy of men and women change between the years 1850 and 1910?

A In 1850, the difference was four years; in 1910, the difference was ten years.

B In 1850, the difference was two years; in 1910, the difference was almost four years.

C In 1850, the difference was two years; in 1910, the difference was seven years.

D There was no difference.

Time and Resource Manager

In-Depth Lesson Plan

	LESSON FOCUS	PRINT AND MEDIA RESOURCES
DAY 1	**Developing Vocabulary** Students learn and apply concepts of vocabulary building including listening, reading, context clues, and related words (pp. 767–771).	**Teaching Resources** *Academic and Workplace Skills Activity Book*, pp. 13–16
DAY 2	**Studying Words** Students learn and apply the concepts of studying words in reference works and studying word roots and origins (pp. 772–778).	**Teaching Resources** *Academic and Workplace Skills Activity Book*, pp. 17–18.
DAY 3	**Spelling** Students learn and apply concepts of spelling (pp. 779–787).	**Teaching Resources** *Academic and Workplace Skills Activity Book*, pp. 23–29
DAY 4	**Review and Assess** Students review chapter and demonstrate mastery of use of vocabulary and spelling (pp. 788–789).	**Teaching Resources** *Formal Assessment*, Ch. 31

Accelerated Lesson Plan

	LESSON FOCUS	PRINT AND MEDIA RESOURCES
DAY 1	**Vocabulary Skills** Students learn and apply vocabulary building skills (pp. 767–778).	**Teaching Resources** *Academic and Workplace Skills Activity Book*, pp. 13–18
DAY 2	**Spelling** Students learn and apply concepts of spelling and demonstrate mastery of using context to determine word meaning (pp. 779–789).	**Teaching Resources** *Academic and Workplace Skills Activity Book*, pp. 23–29

Options for Adapting Lesson Plans

HOMEWORK

Have students complete any section of the chapter for homework.

FEATURES

Extend coverage with the Standardized Test Preparation Workshop (p. 788).

TECHNOLOGY

Students can use the On-Line Exercise Bank to complete the exercises on computer. The Auto Check feature will grade their work.

INTEGRATED SKILLS COVERAGE

Workplace Skills
Integrating Workplace Skills ATE p. 787

Viewing and Representing
Critical Viewing SE pp. 766, 771, 778, 781, 785, 786

ASSESSMENT SUPPORT

Standardized Test Preparation SE p. 788; ATE pp. 769, 771
Standardized Test Preparation Workbook, pp. 61–62
Formal Assessment, Ch. 31

MEETING INDIVIDUAL NEEDS

Less Advanced Students See Ongoing Assessments ATE pp. 767, 768, 773, 777, 780, 782, 785
ESL Students ATE pp. 768, 774, 781
Visual/Spatial Learners ATE p. 780
Interpersonal Learners ATE p. 774

BLOCK SCHEDULING

Pacing Suggestions
For 90-minute Blocks
- Administer the Diagnostic Test to students to determine instructional coverage.
- Have students complete the necessary exercises in class. Use the Hands-on Grammar activity to provide a change of pace.

Resources for Varying Instruction
- *Language Lab* CD-ROM If your students have access to hardware, a 90-minute block provides an ideal opportunity for students to work on computer.

Professional Development Support
- *How to Manage Instruction in the Block* This teaching resource provides management and activity suggestions.

MEDIA AND TECHNOLOGY

For the Student
- *Language Lab* CD-ROM Vocabulary, Spelling
- *On-Line Exercise Bank,* Ch. 31

For the Teacher
- *Resource Pro* CD-ROM

WRITING AND GRAMMAR WEBSITE

The Interactive Writing and Grammar Website provides a wide array of support for students, teachers, and parents. Grammar support includes:

- *On-Line Exercise Bank* with Auto Check scoring
- Diagnostic and assessment support

phwg.phschool.com

► *Lesson Objectives*

1. To understand the use of context in learning vocabulary.
2. To define synonyms, antonyms, and homophones.
3. To identify analogies.
4. To understand the value of a dictionary.
5. To identify the use for a thesaurus.
6. To define and use prefix, root, and suffix to learn words.
7. To make a spelling list of problem words.
8. To use memory aids to remember spelling of difficult words.
9. To learn rule for forming plural of most nouns.
10. To understand that adding a prefix does not change the spelling of the original word.
11. To learn how the addition of a suffix changes spelling.
12. To learn the rule for spelling *ie* and *ei* words.
13. To memorize words ending in *-cede, -ceed,* and *-sede.*
14. To practice proofreading writing for spelling errors.
15. To make a formal plan for studying spelling rules.

Critical Viewing

Compare Students may suggest such tools as "ink" and "plume." Today's tools should include the computer and ballpoint pens.

Chapter 31 Vocabulary and Spelling

The words you use and the way you present them can combine to create a powerful message. Your vocabulary includes all the words available to you in your speaking, reading, and writing. By increasing your vocabulary, you will understand more and communicate your ideas more precisely. Correct spelling is another key to clear communication.

This chapter will show you ways to learn and remember new words. It will also offer some practical suggestions and specific spelling rules to help you improve your spelling.

▲ **Critical Viewing**
Describe the tools for writing that you see in this picture. How do our tools differ? [Compare]

🕐 TIME AND RESOURCE MANAGER

Resources
Print: Academic and Workplace Skills Activity Book, pp. 13–16

In-Depth Coverage	Accelerated Pace
• Work through all key concepts, pp. 767–771. • Assign and review Exercises 1–5.	• Assign pp. 767–771 for independent student review.

Developing Your Vocabulary

Section 31.1

Words are the building blocks of communication. The more words you have at your command, the more elaborate and complete your communication can be.

To increase your vocabulary, you must have a desire to expand your knowledge of word meanings, as well as a commitment to learning new words. There are many methods and helpful techniques for building vocabulary.

Listening, Discussing, and Reading

Most of our everyday words and expressions we learned when we were small children. We learned by listening and by practicing.

▶**KEY CONCEPT** The most common ways to increase your vocabulary are listening, reading, and taking part in conversations. ■

Listen for and Use New Words Try to imagine what it must have been like when you were a baby. You had no language to communicate your wants and needs. You made a lot of noise, but everyone had to guess what you wanted. You quickly began to learn language. Before you could speak one word, you understood many. People spoke to you, and you listened very carefully to their words. Soon, you began to speak and, before long, you were stringing words into sentences and following grammar rules that you didn't even know existed.

Now, as then, listening is an excellent way to expand your vocabulary. When you talk to other people, listen and take notes in class, watch television, listen to the radio, or listen to literature on audiocassettes, notice the unfamiliar words. Jot the words down, and find out the meanings by using a dictionary or by asking someone. Whenever possible, try to use new words in conversation.

Wide Reading You will probably run into more unfamiliar words when you read than when you listen and discuss. People's written vocabulary is usually larger than their spoken vocabulary. You will encounter familiar words used in new ways, as well as brand-new words.

The more variety you have in your reading, the more variety you will have in your vocabulary. Try to expand your vocabulary by reading as widely as possible. Read textbooks, newspapers, magazines, novels, and articles on the Internet.

✓ ONGOING ASSESSMENT: Monitor and Reinforce

If some students are having difficulty increasing their vocabulary through conversation, use one of the following options.

Option 1 Have students work in small groups. Assign conversation topics.	**Option 2** Make sure ESL and less advanced students work in groups with peers who have wide vocabularies and are good mentors.

PREPARE and ENGAGE

Interest GRABBER Uh-oh! Pop quiz. Write the following words and definitions on the board. Mix up the words and definitions before you write them on the chalkboard. Let volunteers work in groups to discuss and try to match them.

howdah	a seat with a canopy for riding an elephant
riprap	a wall made of broken stones
gloaming	evening, dusk
katzenjammer	big confusion or mess
topiary	bushes trimmed in the shape of animals

Activate Prior Knowledge

Ask students how they find out the meanings of unfamiliar words. (if reading, use context clues; ask someone; use dictionary)

TEACH

Step-by-Step Teaching Guide

Increasing Your Vocabulary

1. Read a few paragraphs from a technical magazine or financial journal. Ask students to listen for words they do not know. Ask how they would go about finding their meanings.

2. If some students know the meanings of words you read let them share their knowledge. Explain that discussing word meanings with others is one way to increase vocabulary.

3. Have students give examples of when they found words they did not know in their reading. Ask what they did to find out what these words meant.

4. Have small groups of students discuss and define the following words or terms.

   euro

   currency conversion

   on-line

   dot com

767

Recognizing Context Clues

1. Have volunteers give examples of sentences containing difficult words and context clues for them.

2. Have students take turns making up sentences with context clues but leaving out an unfamiliar word. Have other students substitute words until they supply the missing word.

For example one student might say:

My pet ___ changes colors to match his surroundings. (chameleon)

Customize for
ESL Students

Students learning English may rely on using a dictionary to look up unfamiliar words. Here you want to change that strategy and have them develop the skill of reading on and using context clues to find the meaning of unfamiliar words. Understanding the usefulness of the clues will depend on their experience with English syntax, but encourage them to try the strategy on simple material to begin to develop skill and confidence.

Answer Key

Exercise 1

Answers will vary in wording. Samples are given.

1. inferred from little information
2. doubtful
3. firm, unmoving
4. small mechanical devices
5. untruthfulness

31.1

Recognizing Context Clues

By examining the meaning of a sentence, you can often find clues to the meaning of any unfamiliar words in it.

KEY CONCEPT A word's **context** is the sentence, the surrounding words, or the situation in which the word is used. ■

There are many types of context clues, including *description, example, restatement, comparison* or *contrast,* and *synonyms* or *antonyms.* Look at the following example:

EXAMPLE: The winning record of our team *intimidated* the other team so much that they didn't want to play against us.

CLUES: In this sentence, the *description* "winning record" suggests strength and skill. The words "didn't want to play against us" suggest the *contrast* between the ability of the two teams.

POSSIBLE
MEANING: *Intimidate* must mean "frighten."

The steps in the following chart explain how to use the context of a word to find clues to its meaning.

USING CONTEXT CLUES

1. Read the sentence, leaving out the unfamiliar word.
2. Find clues in the sentence that suggest the word's meaning.
3. Read the sentence again, substituting your possible meaning for the unfamiliar word.
4. Check your possible meaning by looking up the unfamiliar word in the dictionary. Write the word and its definition in your vocabulary notebook.

Exercise 1 Recognizing Context Clues Use context clues to determine the meaning of the underlined word in each sentence below. Check your answers in a dictionary.

1. After examining the evidence, Sherlock Holmes <u>surmised</u> that the criminal had escaped through the back door.
2. Because of his hesitation, I was <u>skeptical</u> that he really wanted to join our group.
3. My father remained <u>intransigent</u> and would not change his mind about buying me a new computer.
4. The store salesman showed us battery-operated staplers, labelmakers, and other such <u>gadgets</u>.
5. His <u>mendacity</u> was so well known in the town that no one believed him when he said he would never tell a lie again.

768 • Vocabulary and Spelling

🔲 Research Tip

Find a science book in the library. Locate three sentences in the book that provide context clues to help determine the meaning of a word. Add the new words to your notebook.

☑ ONGOING ASSESSMENT: Monitor and Reinforce

If some students are having difficulty using context clues, use one of the following options.

Option 1 Give students a heavily illustrated text and have them use context clues from the visuals to help them read.	**Option 2** Find or write exercises that use unfamiliar words with in-sentence clues, such as *Telling me twice to put on my seat belt is <u>redundant</u>.* As students gain experience and confidence, move them to next-sentence clues.

Step-by-Step Teaching Guide

Using Possible Sentences

1. Review the Possible Sentences strategy, reminding students that the key to using context clues is to be detectives and "solve the case of the unknown word."

2. Have students look in a textbook or newspaper to find an unknown word and test the Possible Sentences strategy.

Answer Key

Exercise 2

Answers will vary.

Using "Possible Sentences" You can have fun with unfamiliar words by using the Possible Sentences strategy outlined in the illustration below.

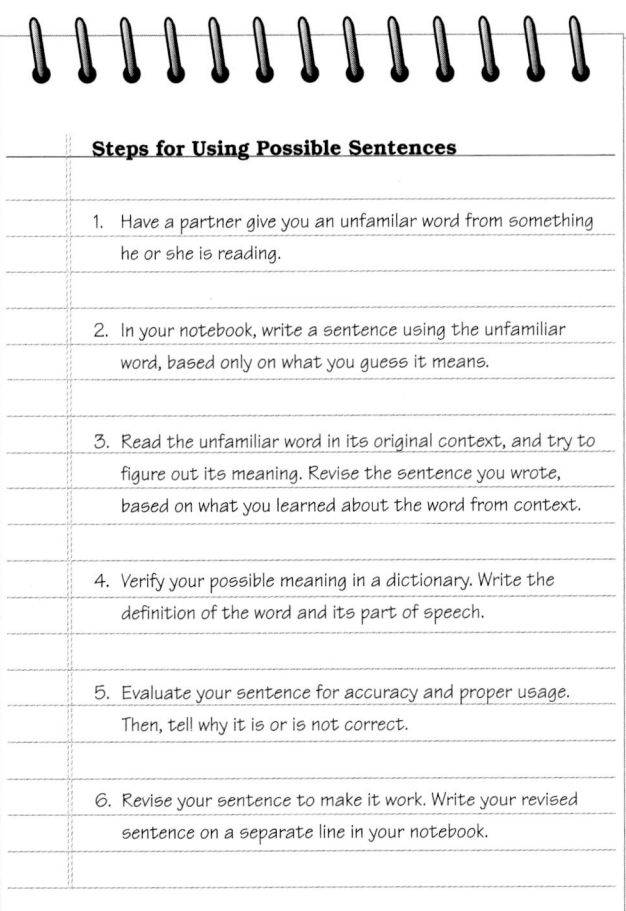

Steps for Using Possible Sentences

1. Have a partner give you an unfamilar word from something he or she is reading.

2. In your notebook, write a sentence using the unfamiliar word, based only on what you guess it means.

3. Read the unfamiliar word in its original context, and try to figure out its meaning. Revise the sentence you wrote, based on what you learned about the word from context.

4. Verify your possible meaning in a dictionary. Write the definition of the word and its part of speech.

5. Evaluate your sentence for accuracy and proper usage. Then, tell why it is or is not correct.

6. Revise your sentence to make it work. Write your revised sentence on a separate line in your notebook.

▶ **Exercise 2** **Using Possible Sentences** Using the steps mentioned above, apply the Possible Sentences strategy to increase your understanding of seven vocabulary words from your next reading assignment.

Developing Your Vocabulary • **769**

🖉 STANDARDIZED TEST PREPARATION WORKSHOP

Using Context Clues Standardized tests often measure students' ability to discern the meaning of a word using context clues. Have students read the following passage and choose the letter of the word(s) that best defines the underlined word:

Because the mayor spoke out so strongly on the issue, his office was <u>inundated</u> with phone calls from angry citizens.

A treated   **C** struck

B overwhelmed   **D** received

The correct choice is item **B**, because the office received *many* phone calls.

Denotation and Connotation

1. Explain to students that *denote* means to indicate or be a mark or symbol for. The symbol " denotes inches.
2. The word *connote* means to imply or suggest. In years past the word red connoted communist.

Answer Key

Exercise 3

Replacement words may vary. Reasonable responses are given.

1. Forgetful suggests overlooking unintentionally; negligent suggests marked by indifference.
2. Consoled suggests comforting in sorrow; reassured suggests restoring confidence.
3. Played suggests ordinary sounds; blared suggests loud or harsh sounds.
4. Shy suggests uncomfortable or retiring; fearful suggests frightened.
5. Clumsy suggests lacking in grace or skill; awkward suggests difficult or embarrassing.

Recognizing Related Words

1. Briefly review synonyms, antonyms, and homophones, making sure that students know the difference.
2. Write the following words on the board and ask students to come up with a synonym for each.

    disappear (vanish)

    merry (happy)

    intelligent (smart)

    gentle (kind)

3. Write the following words on the board and ask students to provide an antonym for each.

    smart (stupid)

    fancy (plain)

    fast (slow)

    expensive (cheap)

4. Write the following words on the board and ask students to provided a homophone for each:

    ware (wear)   *sea (see)*

    here (hear)   *fair (fare)*

31.1

Denotation and Connotation

Context can help you determine a word's exact meaning. Knowing the denotations and connotations of a word can help you discriminate between different shades of meaning.

> **KEY CONCEPT** The **denotation** of a word is its literal definition. Its **connotations** include the ideas, images, and feelings that are associated with the word. ∎

The denotation of the word *doctor* is "physician" or "surgeon"—a person licensed to practice any of the healing arts. The connotation of the word suggests prestige, success, and hard work. As you increase your vocabulary, be aware of both positive and negative connotations of words you use.

> **Exercise 3** Revising Sentences to Change Connotations
Read each sentence below. Then, revise each sentence by replacing the underlined word with a word that has a similar denotation but a different connotation.

1. The cashier was forgetful, often adding the sales tax twice.
2. The doctor's positive report consoled us.
3. The radio on the windowsill played endlessly.
4. Robert had trouble making friends because he was shy.
5. He made a clumsy attempt to apologize.

Recognizing Related Words

Three kinds of related words are *synonyms*, *antonyms*, and *homophones*. Examining the relationships between words will strengthen your understanding of their meanings and will help you remember new words.

> **KEY CONCEPTS** **Synonyms** are words that are similar in meaning. **Antonyms** are words that are opposite in meaning. **Homophones** are words that sound alike but have different meanings and spellings. ∎

> **Exercise 4** Recognizing Synonyms, Antonyms, and Homophones Identify each pair of words below as synonyms, antonyms, or homophones.

1. negative/positive
2. there/their
3. oppose/defend
4. careful/negligent
5. our/hour

Answer Key

Exercise 4

1. antonyms
2. homophones
3. antonyms
4. antonyms
5. homophones

Using Related Words in Analogies

Working with analogies, or word relationships, strengthens your vocabulary by increasing your understanding of connections between word meanings. It will also benefit you to practice analogies because they are typical items found in aptitude and achievement tests.

▶ **KEY CONCEPT** **Analogies** present a pair of words that have some relationship to each other. ■

Look at the following analogy, and see whether you can find the relationship between the given words:

EXAMPLE: SMALL : MINUTE :: large : tremendous

The relationship between the words appears to be that they are *synonyms*, but a closer look at the words reveals the finer relationship of *degree*. Just as the word *minute* means very small, *tremendous* means very large. Other common analogy relationships include *part to whole*, *defining characteristic*, *instrument*, and *kind*.

▶ **Exercise 5** **Working With Analogies** First, identify the analogy relationship expressed in the capitalized pair. Then, choose the lettered pair that best expresses this relationship

1. POODLE : DOG ::
   a. ram : bull
   b. Arabian : horse
   c. fox : wolf
2. PETAL : FLOWER ::
   a. bale : hay
   b. wood : axe
   c. branch : tree
3. HILL : MOUNTAIN ::
   a. tree : forest
   b. climber : rock
   c. pony : horse
4. BRUSH : ARTIST ::
   a. painting : color
   b. pen : author
   c. model : person
5. FIRE : HEAT ::
   a. ice : cold
   b. sun : moon
   c. volcano : eruption

 **Learn More**

To work with analogies in a standardized test format, see the Standardized Test Preparation Workshop on pages 358–359.

▼ Critical Viewing These students appear to be studying together. How does studying with a partner help you to learn? **[Infer]**

Developing Your Vocabulary • 771

Using Related Words in Analogies

1. The key to solving an analogy is recognizing how the first two words are related to each other— not to the answer choices.
2. Before students do Exercise 5, go over each capitalized pair and determine the relationship. (1. A poodle is a kind of dog. 2. A petal is part of a flower. 3. A hill is smaller than a mountain. 4. A brush is an instrument an artist uses. 5. Heat is a defining characteristic of fire.)

Answer Key

▶ **Exercise 5**

1. kind; b
2. part to whole; c
3. degree; c
4. instrument; b
5. defining characteristic; a

Critical Viewing

Infer Students may say that studying with a partner helps you to learn by having someone there to help check your work.

🔖 STANDARDIZED TEST PREPARATION WORKSHOP

Analogies Standardized tests often measure students' ability to complete questions involving analogies. Share the following example with students:

Identify the relationship expressed in the capitalized pair of words to choose the lettered pair that best expresses this relationship.

ICE : SKATING::

A rain : water   **C** road : driving

B conductor : playing   **D** reading : writing

The correct choice is item **C**. *Ice* is the surface on which one *skates*, just as a *road* is the surface on which one *drives*.

Using a Dictionary and a Thesaurus

1. Go over a few dictionary entries with students to review each part of the entry.

2. To see that students understand to remove a word ending before looking up a word, ask them what they would look up for the following words.

    multiplying

    skidded

    usually

3. See that students know both how to look up a word in a thesaurus and why they would do such a thing. Make sure they know to use synonyms to avoid overusing a word.

4. Write the following words on the board for extra practice and ask students to use a thesaurus to find synonyms:

    souvenir (memento)

    mistake (error)

    gift (present)

    elegance (stylishness)

Answer Key

> **Exercise 6**

1. to reveal secrets
2. advantage, purpose
3. wear
4. tree of the willow family
5. to ring slowly

Section 31.2

Studying Words Systematically

Using a Dictionary and a Thesaurus

A dictionary and a thesaurus can help you increase your vocabulary. Every time you come across an unfamiliar word, consult a dictionary to learn its meaning. Use a thesaurus to find new words that will better express your meaning.

KEY CONCEPT A **dictionary** gives the meaning, spelling, and proper pronunciation of words. ■

- Look up the base form of the word, the form without endings showing tense or number.
- Study the pronunciation of the word you look up. It is usually given in parentheses right after the word.
- Notice the different meanings that a single word can have.
- Notice the abbreviations that are used in the definitions to indicate the part of speech of the word.

KEY CONCEPT A **thesaurus** provides lists of words that are similar in meaning. ■

- Do not choose a word just because it sounds interesting. Choose the word that expresses the meaning you intend.
- To avoid errors, look up the word in a dictionary to check its precise meaning and to make sure it is properly used.

Exercise 6 Using a Dictionary Look up each word in a dictionary. Write the definition for the part of speech indicated in parentheses.

1. tattle (verb)
2. avail (noun)
3. fray (verb)
4. sallow (noun)
5. knell (verb)

Exercise 7 Using a Thesaurus Use a thesaurus to find a more precise word for the underlined word in each sentence.

1. The boy was happy when he won the raffle.
2. After the ten-mile hike, we were tired.
3. The speech that brought a standing ovation was good.
4. She felt afraid to walk home alone through the dark woods.
5. Because it was his first day on the job, he was a beginner.

Research Tip

Choose five words, and use a thesaurus to find a synonym for each of them. Then, use a dictionary to see whether there are any subtle differences between each word and its synonym.

⏱ TIME AND RESOURCE MANAGER

Resources
Print: Academic and Workplace Skills Activity Book, pp. 17–18

In-Depth Coverage	Accelerated Pace
• Work through all key concepts, pp. 772–774. • Assign and review Exercises 6–8.	• Assign pp. 772–774 for independent student review.

Remembering New Vocabulary

Even if you use a dictionary and thesaurus regularly, there still may be some word meanings that are harder for you to remember than others. Use these suggestions to reinforce your memory of new words once you have determined their meanings.

KEY CONCEPT Study and review new words a few times a week, using a variety of methods. ■

Using a Vocabulary Notebook Keep track of your new vocabulary in a separate section in your notebook. Use the following illustration to set up a notebook page for vocabulary words:

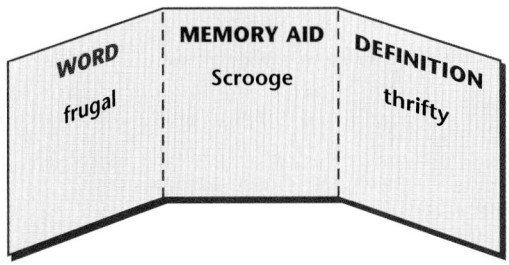

When studying, you can either cover the third column with another piece of paper or fold the paper back to hide the word's definition.

Using a Tape Recorder When reviewing your new words at home, you may find that a tape recorder is helpful. Saying, repeating, and hearing your new words can often make it easier to learn them.

Follow these steps when you study with a tape recorder:

1. Record a word on the tape.
2. Leave five seconds of space on the tape, and then give a definition followed by a sentence using the word. Leave another five-second pause before reading the next word.
3. Continue with the remainder of the words.
4. Study the words by replaying the entire tape and saying each definition aloud in the pause before the recorded definition plays and then again during the second pause.
5. Rerun the tape until you can give all the definitions.

Listening to your tape several times a week will help you make new words a permanent part of your vocabulary.

Step-by-Step Teaching Guide

Remembering New Vocabulary

1. Students can make a vocabulary section in their notebook by setting up a page in columns. Using bridges or other memory devices is fine unless they complicate the situation. Better than writing bridges is to use the word in a sentence and create a context for memorizing the word.

2. Use the word *frugal* as an example and write the following sentence on the board as a memory clue:

   Frugal people always look for bargains.

3. Review the instructions for using a tape recorder.

ONGOING ASSESSMENT: Monitor and Reinforce

If some students are having difficulty finding a workable method to study vocabulary, use one of the following options.

Option 1 Encourage students to start small, perhaps with three words a day. Reassure them that if they work at it, they will remember the words.	**Option 2** Work with students who need extra help. Have them write sentences that use the word in a way that both sets a context and has some personal meaning for them.

Step-by-Step Teaching Guide

Using Flashcards

1. Distribute index cards for students to use.

2. Encourage students to write sentences using the new word and the bridge word. For example, for the word *frugal* and the bridge word *Scrooge*, students might write: *Scrooge was frugal to the point of being stingy.*

3. If students have trouble using one definition or bridge word, encourage them to expand definitions or bridge words by listing several choices.

Answer Key

> **Exercise 8**

Students' responses will vary.

Customize for
Interpersonal Learners

Partners can quiz each other with their flashcards, thus doubling the number of words.

Customize for
ESL Students

Encourage students to include each word in their home language on the flashcards. For the tape recorder version, students can work with partners to be sure they pronounce the words correctly.

Using Flashcards Flashcards can also help you learn new words. On the front of an index card, write the word you want to learn. If it is difficult to pronounce, copy the phonetic spelling of the word from the dictionary, as shown below. On the lower right corner of the card, write in pencil a bridge word—a word or image that you associate with the meaning of the vocabulary word. When you no longer need this hint to remember the definition of the word, you can erase it. On the back of the card, write the definition of the word.

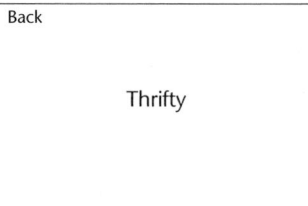

Use the following steps to drill yourself:

1. Flip through the cards, looking at both sides of each card, and try to associate the word with the definition.
2. Then, look at just the front side of each card, defining each word and using it in a sentence.
3. Place cards with words you cannot define in a review pile.
4. Repeat the first three steps with the cards in the review pile until you are able to define all the words.

Working With a Partner Reviewing vocabulary with a partner provides a chance for reinforcement as well as encouragement. In the first round, read the words from your partner's vocabulary notebook or flashcards and have your partner define them. If your partner is slow to respond, you should provide the bridge word if it is given. Repeat the words until your partner can correctly define all of them. During the second round, exchange roles with your partner, and have your partner read you the words from your vocabulary notebook or flashcards.

> **Exercise 8** **Using Different Study Methods** After reviewing vocabulary words using at least three of the methods explained here, decide which method works best for you. Then, choose a second method to add variety to your study. Explain the reasons for both choices.

Section 31.3 *Studying Word Parts and Origins*

When you analyze the parts of an unfamiliar word, you can find clues to its meaning. Many words have a *prefix*, a *root*, and a *suffix*.

Using Prefixes

One of the best ways to build your vocabulary is to learn how prefixes change the meanings of words.

▶ **KEY CONCEPT** A **prefix** is one or more syllables placed before the root. ■

You may want to memorize the prefixes in the chart below.

TEN COMMON PREFIXES		
Prefixes	**Meanings**	**Examples**
de-	away from, off	*de*face or to take away from the "face" or appearance of
dis-	away, apart	*dis*arm, or take the arms *away*
ex-	from, out	*ex*change, or change *from*
in-	not	*in*human, or *not* human
in-	in, into	*in*dent, or "bite" *into*
inter-	between	*inter*national, or *between* nations
mis-	wrong	*mis*understand, or understand *incorrectly*
re-	back, again	*re*new, or make new *again*
sub-	beneath, under	*sub*marine, or *beneath* the sea
un-	not	*un*happy, or *not* happy

▶ **Exercise 9** **Working With Prefixes** Using your knowledge of prefixes, figure out the meaning of each word below. Then, check your answers by looking up each word in a dictionary.
1. *re*kindle   3. *in*flame   5. *ex*clude
2. *mis*interpret   4. *inter*continental

▶ **Exercise 10** **Defining Prefixes and Prefix Origins** Using a dictionary, write the definition of each prefix and its origin. Then, provide an example for each prefix.
1. ad-   3. post-   5. com-
2. circum-   4. trans-

Studying Word Parts and Origins

1. Review that another way to figure out the meaning of an unfamiliar word is to analyze its parts. Many words in English come from ancient Greek and Latin, the languages of the Roman Empire.

2. Examine the common prefixes, asking students to come up with additional examples of words beginning with the prefixes shown.

3. Write the following words on the chalkboard and ask students to define them:
   antifreeze
   decode
   disrespect
   experiment
   incomplete
   misfire
   monologue
   recall
   substandard
   unforgiving

Answer Key

▶ **Exercise 9**

1. kindle again
2. to interpret wrongly
3. to set on fire
4. between or among continents
5. to close out of something

▶ **Exercise 10**

1. to, toward; Latin; administer
2. around, about; Latin; circumnavigate
3. after; Latin; postgraduate
4. across; Latin; transmit
5. with, together; Latin; compress

⏱ TIME AND RESOURCE MANAGER	
Resources **Print:** Academic and Workplace Skills Activity Book, pp. 19–22	
In-Depth Coverage	**Accelerated Pace**
• Work through all key concepts, pp. 775–778. • Assign and review Exercises 9–15.	• Assign pp. 775–778 for independent student review.

Recognizing Roots

1. Explore the use of roots as a way of finding out the meanings of unfamiliar words.

2. As you go through the chart of Ten Common Roots, ask students to suggest other words with the same root. (Possible answers: *induct, monograph, admit, position, impel, describe, respect, maintain, circumvent, inverse*)

Answer Key

Exercise 11

1. d
2. e
3. b
4. c
5. a

Exercise 12

1. to take or to seize
2. to say or to speak
3. to do or to make
4. to move
5. to see

31.3

Recognizing Roots

The root carries the basic meaning of a word. The same root can be used to form many different words.

KEY CONCEPT A **root** is the base of the word. ■

This chart lists ten common roots used in English words. Alternative spellings are shown in parentheses.

TEN COMMON ROOTS		
Roots	**Meanings**	**Examples**
-duc- (-duct-)	to lead	con*duc*t, or *lead* together
-graph-	to write	*graph*ic, or of *writing*
-mit- (-mis-)	to send	trans*mit*, or *send* across
-pon- (-pos-)	to put or place	com*pon*ent, or something *put* with something else
-puls- (-pel-)	to drive	re*puls*e, or *drive* back
-scrib- (-script-)	to write	in*scrib*e, or *write* into
-spec- (-spect-)	to see	in*spec*t, or *see* into
-ten- (-tain-)	to hold	con*tain*, or *hold* together
-ven- (-vent-)	to come	in*vent*, or *come* into
-vert- (-vers-)	to turn	re*vert*se, or *turn* back

Exercise 11 **Using Roots to Define Words** In your notebook, write each word, paying close attention to the word's root, shown in italics. Then, next to each word, write the letter of its meaning.

1. sub*script*
2. re*vert*
3. re*ten*tive
4. con*ven*tion
5. im*pos*e

a. to place a burden on
b. able to hold on to
c. a group meeting
d. a character written below another
e. to turn back to

Exercise 12 **Finding Common Roots** Look up each pair of words in a dictionary, paying close attention to each word's root, shown in italics. Then, write the basic meaning shared by each pair of words.

1. in*cap*acitate, *cap*tive
2. contra*dict*ion, *dict*ation
3. *fact*itious, *fac*ilitate
4. *mot*ion, *mov*ing
5. en*vis*ion, *vid*eo

Using Suffixes

Some suffixes—word endings—form plurals of nouns, such as the -s in *dogs*. Others show the tenses of verbs, such as the -*ed* in *wanted* or the -*ing* in *wanting*. The suffixes in this section form new words.

Ten common suffixes used to form new words are listed in the next chart.

▶ **KEY CONCEPT** A **suffix** is one or more syllables added at the end of a root, which can be used to form new words. ∎

TEN COMMON SUFFIXES		
Suffixes	**Meanings**	**Examples**
-able (-ible)	capable of being	sustain*able*, or *capable of being* sustained
-ance (-ence)	the act of	clear*ance*, or *the act of being* cleared
-ate	make or apply	activ*ate*, or *make* active
-ful	full of	scorn*ful*, or *full of* scorn
-ity	the state of being	inten*sity*, or *the state of being* intense
-less	without	hope*less*, or *without* hope
-ly	in a certain way	careless*ly*, or done *in a careless way*
-ment	the result of being	improve*ment*, or *the result of being* improved
-ness	the state of being	hopeless*ness*, or *the state of being* hopeless
-tion (ion, sion)	the act or state of being	admis*sion*, or *the act of being* admitted

Suffixes can indicate the word's part of speech. The following list shows the parts of speech indicated by the suffixes. Notice that -*ful* and -*ly* can each form two parts of speech.

NOUNS:	-ance	ADJECTIVES:	-able
	-ful		-ful
	-ity		-less
	-ment		-ly
	-ness		
	-tion		
VERB:	-ate	ADVERB:	-ly

ⓠ Learn More

To learn more about parts of speech, see Chapter 16, "Nouns and Pronouns," and Chapter 17, "Verbs."

Using Suffixes

1. Explain the difference between a base word and a word root. A base word is an English word to which prefixes and/or suffixes can be added: <u>read</u>, <u>reread</u>, <u>readable</u>. A root is a foreign word, almost always Latin or Greek, to which prefixes and/or suffixes can be added. A root is not usually an English word that can stand alone. *Autograph* is the prefix *auto-* ("self") attached to the Greek word for "write." *Telegrapher* is the prefix *tele-* ("away," "at a distance") , the Greek root *graph* ("write"), and the suffix -*er* ("a person who does something").

2. Review that suffixes have an additional use: They can tell the part of speech. Write the following words on the board and have students identify the part of speech.

   communicate (verb)

   communicably (adverb)

   communication (noun)

   communicable (adjective)

☑ **ONGOING ASSESSMENT: Monitor and Reinforce**

If some students are having difficulty using prefixes, roots, and suffixes to identify unknown words and their part of speech, use the following option.

Have students brainstorm a list of nouns, verbs, adjectives, and adverbs that end in the appropriate suffixes and copy them into their vocabulary notebooks.

Exercise 13

1. noun; the result of being contained
2. adjective; capable of being divided
3. adjective; full of bounty
4. noun; a person skilled in biology
5. verb; applying a motive to
6. noun; the state of being good
7. noun; the state of being common
8. adjective; without knowledge or wit
9. noun; state of being adapted
10. adjective; toward the north

Exercise 14

Answers will vary. Samples are given.

1. characteristic of, relating to; Greek; scenic
2. in a direction or course; Anglo-Saxon; eastward
3. science, doctrine, or theory; Anglo-Saxon; psychology
4. person who does or makes; Greek, tourist
5. characterized by; Latin; courteous

Exercise 15

1. Spanish, little fly
2. Greek, to measure the earth
3. acronym, self-contained underwater breathing apparatus
4. from taler, Bohemian
5. invented, left handed
6. French, kettle
7. Arabic, storehouse
8. invented by Gell-Mann 1964
9. Scottish, Gaelic, length of tartan
10. German, *Brezel,* having branches

Critical Viewing

Analyze Students may suggest adjectives such as *agreeable, cheerful,* and *eager.* (suffixes: *-able, -ful*)

31.3

> **Exercise 13** Determining Parts of Speech and Meaning
From Suffixes Using your knowledge of suffixes, write the part of speech and meaning of each word below. Then, check and correct your answer by looking up each word in a dictionary.

1. contain*ment*
2. divis*ible*
3. bounti*ful*
4. biolog*ist*
5. motiv*ate*
6. good*ness*
7. commun*ity*
8. wit*less*
9. adapta*tion*
10. norther*ly*

> **Exercise 14** Defining Suffixes and Suffix
Origins Using a dictionary, write the definition of each suffix and its origin. Then, provide an example of a word using each suffix.

1. -ic
2. -ward
3. -logy
4. -ist
5. -ous

Exploring Etymologies (Word Origins)

The **etymology** of a word is its origin and history.

> **KEY CONCEPT** Knowing the etymology of a word can help you understand its meaning. ■

Listed below are several ways in which words evolve:

- Words are borrowed from other languages.
- Words change meaning over time and through usage.
- Words are invented, or coined, to serve new purposes.
- Words are combined or shortened.
- Words are formed from acronyms, or the use of initials.

> **Exercise 15** Using a Dictionary to Learn About
Etymologies Find the word origins of each word below. Write the word origin, and then write a sentence using the word.

1. mosquito
2. geometry
3. scuba
4. dollar
5. southpaw
6. chowder
7. magazine
8. quark
9. plaid
10. pretzel

▲ **Critical Viewing**
What adjectives would you use to describe the attitudes of the girls in this picture? Which words have suffixes? What are the suffixes? **[Analyze]**

Improving Your Spelling

Keeping a Spelling Notebook

Make it a practice to keep a list of all the words that you regularly have trouble spelling. These words can be grouped into two categories. The first category contains the words that present special difficulty and have repeatedly caused you trouble. It is often best to memorize these spelling words.

The second category contains the words that you misspell because of error patterns, which will be further discussed in this section.

▶ **KEY CONCEPT** Make a personal spelling list of words that repeatedly cause you problems and your error patterns. ■

Identify Your Error Patterns Learn to identify the error patterns in your misspellings. The chart below lists common error patterns:

COMMON ERROR PATTERNS	
Error	**Example**
Doubling consonants	coming *not* comming
Adding syllables	athletic *not* athelectic
Deleting syllables	mathematics *not* mathmatics
Using apostrophes for plurals	ten boys *not* ten boy's
Dropping final *e*	management *not* managment
Retaining final *e*	debatable *not* debateable
Retaining final *y*	merriment *not* merryment
Blending sounds	length *not* lenth
Omitting silent letters	wealthy *not* welthy
Transposing letters	relevant *not* revelant
Separating combined words	classroom *not* class room
Confusing homophones	to/too/two
Confusing contractions and possessive pronouns	it's/its

EXAMPLES: believe   Never believe a lie.
necessary The word *necessary* causes problems.
calendar   A calendar shows the days of the week.
prairie   The air smells fresh on the prairie

Improving Your Spelling

1. Discuss good study habits. When we are working with information, it is in the front of our minds and we can't imagine not remembering it. Sometimes minutes, hours, or days later, it's a distant memory. The moral: Write it down.

2. Just as with vocabulary, the act of writing words helps imprint a pattern in the memory. See that students understand that for troublesome spelling words, there is no substitute for practice and memorization.

3. When students use a word processor, there is the tendency to use spell check and regard studying spelling as an unnecessary activity from the dinosaur age. Remind students that there are times when they actually have to write things by hand and spelling mistakes matter greatly. Impossible! Have them imagine that they are in an employment office filling out a job application (by hand). Who is going to spell check now? No matter what changes occur in technology, spelling still matters.

4. Examine the chart of Common Error Patterns with students. Have students study the chart carefully to identify any errors they commonly make.

5. Have students write words they identify into their spelling notebook.

⏱ TIME AND RESOURCE MANAGER

Resources
Print: Academic and Workplace Skills Activity Book, pp. 23–29

In-Depth Coverage	Accelerated Pace
• Work through all key concepts, pp. 779–787. • Assign and review Exercises 16–24.	• Assign pp. 779–787 for independent student review.

Exercise 16

1. omitting silent letters, vacuum
2. confusing homophones, Except
3. omitting silent letters, condemn
4. using apostrophes for plurals, girls
5. separating combined words, Someone

Step-by-Step Teaching Guide

Using Memory Aids

1. In terms of memory aids, the only rule is, "If it works, use it!" On the other hand, memory aids are shortcuts. It is possible to spend more time on the memory aid than on writing the word and memorizing it.

2. Review the examples of memory aids. Ask students to share any they have developed. If you have any of your own, contribute them as well. Students may feel self-conscious, especially if their memory aids tend to be goofy. So the sillier you are, the better for modeling purposes. Goofy example:

   A horse that says "Neigh!" is my neighbor.

Answer Key

Exercise 17

Possible answers are given:

1. one m, two rs, three os
2. There's a hand and a chief in handkerchief.
3. There's an extra and and an ordinary in extraordinary.
4. A capital letter has 2 as.
5. There's a law in lawyer.

Customize for
Visual/Spatial Learners

Urge students to form visual snapshots of troublesome words and recall them when they are needed.

> **Exercise 16** Identifying Error Patterns Each sentence below contains one or more incorrect spellings. Identify the error pattern of the misspelled word, and write the correct spelling. Then, look over the writing you have done in the past two weeks. Proofread your work for misspelled words, and identify your error patterns.

1. A completely empty space is called a vacum.
2. Accept for Rob, we all went out to lunch.
3. The group did not condem the person who was late.
4. There were three girl's sitting on the porch that morning.
5. Some one was in the car, but no one knew who it was.

Using Memory Aids

Most words can be easily learned through well-organized strategies and the use of rules, such as those listed in the following section. For some words, however, you may find that spelling success can best be achieved through the development and use of special memory aids or hints.

> **KEY CONCEPT** Use memory aids to remember the spelling of words that you find especially difficult to spell. ■

Some problem words lend themselves to the development of memory aids. With some words, for example, you can find a short, easy-to-spell word hidden within the more difficult word.

> **Exercise 17** Developing Memory Aids Perhaps the best memory aids are the ones you develop yourself. Create a memory aid for each word below. Then, choose five words in your spelling notebook, and find some memory aid for each. Enter the hints in your spelling notebook.

1. tomorrow
2. handkerchief
3. extraordinary
4. capital
5. lawyer

☑ ONGOING ASSESSMENT: Monitor and Reinforce

If some students are having difficulty with common spelling problems and using memory aids, use one of the following options.

Option 1 Ask students to use the word in five or ten different sentences that they write in their spelling notebook.	**Option 2** Encourage students to use their imaginations to form memory aids for particularly troubling words. If necessary, have students work in a group to come up with useful memory aids.

Following Spelling Rules

Although some words present spelling problems, the vast majority of English words follow some regular pattern. For example, you can learn rules for writing plurals, writing words with prefixes and suffixes, and choosing between *ie* and *ei*.

Plurals

The plural form of a noun is the form that means "more than one." The plural forms can be either *regular* or *irregular*.

▶ **KEY CONCEPT** The regular plural form of most nouns is formed by adding *-s* or *-es* to the singular. ■

Regular Plurals As a general rule, you can just add *-s* to form a regular plural. With certain regular plurals, however, you may have to choose whether to add *-s* or *-es*. Occasionally, you may also have to change a letter or two in the word

1. To form the plurals of words ending in *s, ss, x, z, sh*, or *ch*, add *-es* to the base word:

circus + -es = circuses	dress + -es = dresses
box + -es = boxes	waltz + -es = waltzes
dish + -es = dishes	church + -es = churches

2. To form the plurals of words ending in *y* or *o* preceded by a vowel, add *-s* to the base word:

journey + -s = journeys	holiday + -s = holidays
rodeo + -s = rodeos	patio + -s = patios

3. To form the plurals of words ending in *y* preceded by a consonant, change the *y* to *i* and add *-es*. For most words ending in *o* preceded by a consonant, add *-es*. For musical terms ending in *o*, simply add *-s*:

city + -ies = cities	enemy + -ies = enemies
echo + -es = echoes	tomato + -s = tomatoes
piano + -s = pianos	solo + -s = solos

4. To form the plurals of some words ending in *f* or *fe*, you might just add *-s* or you might have to change the *f* or *fe* to *v* and add *-es*. For words ending in *ff*, add *-s*:

leaf + -es = leaves	loaf + -es = loaves
wife + -es = wives	life + -es = lives
chief + -s = chiefs	proof + -s = proofs
staff + -s = staffs	cliff + -s = cliffs
staff + -s = staves (in music)	

▼ **Critical Viewing**
What steps should this student take to make sure that she has no spelling errors in her writing? **[Analyze]**

Following Spelling Rules

1. Explain to students that many words follow spelling rules. Knowing those rules can be very helpful. When they form plurals, some do not change. These are regular plurals.

2. Review the rules for regular plurals carefully.

3. For additional practice, write the following words on the board and ask students to write their plurals.

   crush (crushes)
   potato (potatoes)
   radio (radios)
   fly (flies)
   monkey (monkeys)
   roof (roofs)
   sheaf (sheaves)

Customize for
ESL Students

Help students persevere in the face of rules with so many exceptions. Remind them that the best way to learn is to choose representative words and use them in sentences to remember the rules that do apply. Any memory devices they can form to apply the rules will be useful.

Critical Viewing

Analyze Encourage students to suggest a variety of ways to avoid spelling errors, including partner checks, dictionary use, memory aids, and spell check.

Irregular Plurals

1. There is no rule for how some words form the plural. In some instances *(oxen, teeth, mice)*, the plural form is a distinctly different word. See that students understand the absence of any shortcuts here. The only solution is to study the irregular forms, use them, and memorize them.

2. Examine the chart of irregular plurals carefully.

3. Have students note the words that do not change form from singular to plural. Write the following words on the board as additions to the list:

   fish

   trout

   species

   Chinese, Japanese, Vietnamese

4. Have students write unfamiliar words, or rules they were unaware of, in their spelling notebooks.

Answer Key

Exercise 18

1. echoes
2. benches
3. foxes
4. mysteries
5. choruses
6. ashes
7. losses
8. vetoes
9. daughters-in-law
10. turkeys
11. proofs
12. alleys
13. bushes
14. potatoes
15. sopranos
16. sheep
17. peaches
18. scarves
19. altos
20. calves
21. geese
22. runners-up
23. tragedies
24. mosquitoes
25. knives

31.4

Irregular Plurals Irregular plurals are not formed according to the rules on the previous page. You can, however, find them in some dictionaries, listed right after the pronunciation of the word.

▶ **KEY CONCEPT** Consult a dictionary for irregular plurals.

The following chart lists some irregular plurals. ■

IRREGULAR PLURALS		
Singular Forms	**Ways of Forming Plurals**	**Plural Forms**
ox	add *-en*	oxen
child	add *-ren*	children
tooth, mouse, woman	change one or more letters	teeth, mice, women
radius, focus, alumnus	change *-us* to *-i*	radii, foci, alumni
alumna	change *-a* to *-ae*	alumnae
crisis, emphasis	change *-is* to *-es*	crises, emphases
medium, datum, curriculum	change *-um* to *-a*	media, data, curricula
phenomenon, criterion	change *-on* to *-a*	phenomena, criteria
deer, sheep	plural form same as singular	deer, sheep
	plural form only	scissors, slacks

Note About *Plurals of Compound Words*: Compound words written as single words follow the general rules for forming plurals (*cookbooks*, *footballs*, and *Englishmen*). To form the plurals of compound words written with hyphens or as separate words, make the modified word plural (*passers-by*, *all stars*, *suits of armor*, and *field mice*).

▶ **Exercise 18** **Spelling Plurals** Write the plural for each word below. Consult a dictionary when necessary.

1. echo	8. veto	14. tomato	21. goose
2. bench	9. daughter-	15. solo	22. runner-up
3. fox	in-law	16. sheep	23. tragedy
4. mystery	10. turkey	17. peach	24. mosquito
5. chorus	11. proof	18. scarf	25. knife
6. ash	12. alley	19. alto	
7. loss	13. bush	20. calf	

☑ **ONGOING ASSESSMENT: Monitor and Reinforce**

If some students are having difficulty forming plurals, use one of the following options.

Option 1 Have students use each example in a sentence first in the singular form, then the plural.	**Option 2** Hold a spelling bee (with suitable prizes) using the words on the two charts.

Prefixes and Suffixes

A **prefix** is one or more syllables added at the beginning of a word to form a new word. A **suffix** is one or more syllables added to the end of a word.

KEY CONCEPT Adding a prefix to a word does not affect the spelling of the original word. Adding a suffix often involves a spelling change in the word. ■

Prefixes When a prefix is added to the word, the spelling of the root remains the same.

EXAMPLES: dis- + appear = disappear
in- + sincere = insincere
mis- + inform = misinform

Exercise 19 **Spelling Words With Prefixes** Add one of the five prefixes below to each of the following words. Then, check each word in a dictionary.

in-   mis-   un-   dis-   com-

1. spell	6. mend	11. take	16. fort
2. satisfied	7. necessary	12. organic	17. mission
3. understand	8. form	13. guide	18. known
4. possess	9. pose	14. charge	19. cast
5. ability	10. dependent	15. lodge	20. like

Suffixes When adding suffixes to some words, a spelling change is required. The three charts that follow summarize the major kinds of spelling changes that can take place when a suffix is added.

SPELLING CHANGES IN WORDS ENDING IN *y*			
Word Endings	**Suffixes Added**	**Rules**	**Exceptions**
consonant + *y* (defy, happy)	most suffixes (*-ance, -ness*)	change *y* to *i* (defiance, happiness)	most suffixes beginning with *i*: *defy* becomes *defying*
vowel + *y* (employ, enjoy)	most suffixes (*-er, -ment*)	make no change (employer, enjoyment)	a few short words: *day* becomes *daily*:

Adding Prefixes

1. Point out that prefixes are good news in the spelling department because they do not change the spelling of the base word.

2. Review the textbook examples with students.

Answer Key

Exercise 19

1. misspell
2. dissatisfied
3. misunderstand
4. dispossess
5. inability, disability
6. commend
7. unnecessary
8. inform
9. dispose, compose
10. independent
11. mistake, intake
12. inorganic
13. misguide
14. discharge, mischarge
15. dislodge
16. comfort
17. commission
18. unknown
19. miscast, uncast
20. dislike, unlike

Step-by-Step Teaching Guide

Adding Suffixes

1. Advise students that adding a suffix can change how a word is spelled.

2. Have students examine the first chart carefully. Write the following words on the board for additional examples.

crazy   craziness

survey   surveyor

continued

3. Examine the charts carefully with students.

4. Write the following additional examples on the chalkboard and have students add suffixes:

love (lovable, loved, lover)

free (freely, freer, freed)

admit (admitted)

prefer (preferable)

31.4

SPELLING CHANGES IN WORDS ENDING IN *e*			
Word Endings	Suffixes Added	Rules	Exceptions
any word ending in *e* (believe, recognize)	suffix beginning with a vowel (*-able*)	drop the final *e* (believable, recognizable)	1. words ending in *ce* or *ge* with suffixes beginning in *a* or *o*: *trace* becomes *traceable*; *outrage* becomes *outrageous* 2. words ending in *ee*: *agree* becomes *agreeable*
any word ending in *e* (price, nice)	suffix beginning with a consonant (*-less, -ly*)	make no change (priceless, nicely)	a few special words: *true* becomes *truly*; *argue* becomes *argument*; *judge* becomes *judgment*

DOUBLING THE FINAL CONSONANT BEFORE SUFFIXES			
Word Endings	Suffixes Added	Rules	Exceptions
consonant + vowel + consonant in a stressed syllable (rob´, admit´)	suffix beginning with a vowel (*-er, -ed*)	double the final consonant (rob´ber, admit´ted)	1. words ending in *x* or *w*: *bow* becomes *bowing*; *wax* becomes *waxing* 2. words in which the stress changes after the suffix is added: *prefer´* becomes *pref´erence*
consonant + vowel + consonant in an unstressed syllable (an´gel, fi´nal)	suffix beginning with a vowel (*-ic, -ize*)	make no change (angel´ic, fi´nalize)	no major exceptions

▶ **Exercise 20** Spelling Words With Suffixes Write the new word formed by combining each of the following words and suffixes below. Check the spellings in a dictionary, and add the difficult words to your list.

1. accidental- + -ly
2. occur- + -ence
3. favor- + -able
4. imply- + -ing
5. survey- + -or
6. silly- + -ness
7. encourage- + -ment
8. amplify- + -er
9. rebel- + -ion
10. continue- + -ous

▶ **Exercise 21** Using Words With Suffixes in Sentences Make a new word to complete each sentence below by combining the words and suffixes in parentheses. Write each new word on your paper, spelled correctly. Check the spelling in a dictionary, and add the difficult words to your list.

1. The (shop- + er) had too many packages to carry.
2. I think a letter has been (omit- + ed) from this word.
3. Standing in a grocery store line with a (cry- + ing) child is very frustrating for parents.
4. This is a (beauty- + ful) butterfly specimen.
5. We learned a (value- + able) lesson while watching them swim.
6. The (amuse- + ment) park was very crowded because it was spring break.
7. To get the most benefit, one must exercise (day- + ly).
8. It is rash to make a (judge- + ment) too quickly.
9. When wet, ceramic tile can be very (slip- + ery).
10. Let's get together on Friday to (final- + ize) plans for the (confer- + ence).

Exercise 20
1. accidentally
2. occurrence
3. favorable
4. implying
5. surveyor
6. silliness
7. encouragement
8. amplifier
9. rebellion
10. continuous

Exercise 21
1. shopper
2. omitted
3. crying
4. beautiful
5. valuable
6. amusement
7. daily
8. judgment
9. slippery
10. finalize, conference

▶ Critical Viewing How can an interest in a subject like butterflies encourage you to learn the spelling of specialized vocabulary? **[Relate]**

Improving Your Spelling • 785

☑ **ONGOING ASSESSMENT: Monitor and Reinforce**

If some students are having difficulty remembering the exceptions to *ie* and *ei* words, use one of the following options.

Option 1 Have students use each of the words on the exceptions block in a sentence. Encourage them to write the word several times to reinforce the spelling.	**Option 2** Hold a spelling bee of difficult words, including *ie* and *ei* words.

31.4

Understanding Rules and Exceptions

Because English contains many words **borrowed from other languages**, most spelling rules have exceptions—words that do not follow the pattern and therefore must be memorized.

KEY CONCEPT For most words containing *ie* or *ei*, you can use the traditional rule: "Place *i* before *e* except after *c* or when sounded like *a*, as in *neighbor* or *weigh*." For its exceptions as well as the words ending in *-cede*, *-ceed*, and *-sede*, it is often best to memorize the correct spellings.

Spelling *ie* and *ei* Words The *ie* and *ei* rule applies for many of these words, but like most rules, it has exceptions.

Exceptions for *ie* Words: counterfeit, either, foreign, forfeit, heifer, height, leisure, neither, seismology, seize, seizure, sheik, sleight, sovereign, weird

Exercise 22 Spelling *ie* and *ei* Words Use *ie* or *ei* to complete the word from each sentence below.
1. Her ach _ _ vements in the modern art world are great.
2. He was warned to stay out of misch _ _ f.
3. She felt a moment of anx _ _ ty as she entered the room.
4. We were not sure we had suffic _ _ nt money.
5. They bel _ _ ve in freedom of action.

Words Ending in *-cede*, *-ceed*, and *-sede* The best way to handle words that end with these suffixes is to memorize the correct spelling.

Words ending in *-cede:* accede, concede, intercede, precede, recede, secede

Words ending in *-ceed:* exceed, proceed, succeed

Words ending in *-sede:* supersede

Exercise 23 Spelling Words Ending in *-cede, -ceed,* and *-sede* Write the incomplete word for each sentence, filling in the blanks with *-cede*, *-ceed*, or *-sede*.
1. Despite the setback, we must pro _ _ _ _ according to plan.
2. It is unlikely that he will suc _ _ _ _ in his efforts.
3. The country might se _ _ _ _ from the organization.
4. Clare will super _ _ _ _ Chuck as vice president.
5. I will gladly con _ _ _ _ that I was wrong.

Technology Tip

You can use the spell checker on your word processor to alert you when words are misspelled. Remember that if you have used a word incorrectly, a spell checker will not pick it up.

▼ Critical Viewing How does this picture illustrate one strategy for memorizing exceptions? [Connect]

Proofreading Carefully

One good strategy to use to improve your spelling skills is to proofread everything you write. By looking closely at the way you have spelled each word, you will become more conscious of the way words are supposed to look on the page.

KEY CONCEPT Proofread everything you write. ■

Following are some common proofreading strategies and tips:

- Proofread by slowly reading your work slowly.
- Proofread only one line at a time. Use a ruler or other device to focus on the line you are proofreading and to cover up the lines you are not proofreading.
- Read backward, from the last word to the first. This forces you to focus only on the words themselves.
- Consult a dictionary when you come across a word that you suspect is spelled incorrectly.
- Use peer proofreading. Exchange papers with a classmate, and check each other's paper for spelling errors.
- Always proofread more than once.

Exercise 24 Proofreading Carefully Each sentence below contains one incorrectly spelled word. Write the correct spelling of each misspelled word, using a dictionary when necessary.

1. We had a very pleasent picnic in the park.
2. The doctor advised her to get more exersise.
3. The prisonor denied that he had taken part in the crime.
4. The actor's performance was applauded by the critics.
5. The nurse said that he would accept the responsability.

Reflecting on Your Spelling and Vocabulary

Review your personal spelling list, the spelling rules in your notebook, and the methods you use to increase your vocabulary. See whether the spelling lists contain a pattern of the types of words with which you have difficulty. In a journal entry, ask yourself:

- Which words are easiest for me, and which words are hardest?
- What kinds of spelling errors do I typically make?
- Which method helped me to learn the greatest number of words?

Proofreading Carefully

1. Write the following on the board: *No Shortcuts!* Discuss that a writing assignment is not finished until it has been proofread and the errors identified and corrected.

2. The suggestions to read backward and use a ruler are useful approaches. Remind students that the challenge in proofreading is establishing distance from the work. They have just poured their heart and soul into it and are rightly proud of the effort. To spot errors they need to take a figurative step back from the work and look at it critically.

3. Have students set up a peer proofreading system for some (or all) written assignments.

Integrating Workplace Skills

Spelling errors have significance that goes beyond the classroom. Spelling errors on a job application might be interpreted in several ways. First, the employer would question the applicant's ability to spell. Second, errors raise questions about how carefully and completely he or she works. Third, they say to the employer that the applicant is either too lazy to proofread and correct errors or too ignorant to identify errors in the first place. None of these are favorable impressions.

Answer Key

Exercise 24

1. pleasant
2. exercise
3. prisoner
4. performance
5. responsibility

Step-by-Step Teaching Guide

Using Context

1. Review with students the strategies on page 768 that they can use to determine the meaning of a word from its context.

2. Draw students' attention to the Test Tip. Remind them to always determine the meaning of a word as it is used in the given passage, and not just to assume they know the meaning of the word.

Standardized Test Preparation Workshop

Using Context to Determine Word Meaning

The questions on standardized tests often require you to discern the meaning of a word using the context of a passage. Using the group of words surrounding an underlined term or phrase will help you determine the meaning of idioms, expressions, words with multiple meanings, figurative language, and specialized and technical terms.

Test Tip

You may recognize an underlined word but not know its definition. Some words have multiple meanings. Read the passage carefully, and choose a word that best defines the underlined word in the context of the passage.

Sample Test Item	Answers and Explanations
Directions: Read the passage. Then, read each question that follows the passage. Decide which is the best answer to each question. Martin Luther King, Jr., whose methods motivated many to demand equal rights in a peaceful manner, was an inspiration to all. His belief in civil disobedience urged activists to protest using nonviolent practices.	
1 In this passage, the word *inspiration* means— A politician B motivation to a high level of activity C the process of inhaling D figurehead	The correct answer for item 1 is *B*. Although both *B* and *C* are correct definitions of the word, the only meaning that applies using the context of the passage is "motivation to a high level of activity."
2 The term *civil disobedience* in this passage means— A passively refusing to obey B disobeying citizens C violent fighting D revolutionary acts	The correct answer for item 2 is *A*. The term *civil disobedience* is a specialized term used to refer to a political protest using nonviolent methods of resistance. The other words in the sentence—*activists, protest,* and *nonviolent practices*—hint at the meaning of the term.

788 • Vocabulary and Spelling

✎ TEST-TAKING TIP

If students come upon a completely unfamiliar word in a passage, have them reread the passage, underlining or circling any other words in the sentence that provide clues as to the meaning of the word. In the second sample item, for example, *civil disobedience* is defined within the same sentence by the phrase *nonviolent practices*.

Practice 1 **Directions:** Read the passage. Then, read each question that follows the passage. Decide which is the best answer to each question.

Many people are becoming Internet savvy, exhibiting their skills at mastering the Web. The Internet is also becoming a more reliable source of factual information. A Web-surfer can find information provided by reputable sources, such as government organizations and universities. Another reason the Internet has gained popularity is due to its rapid growth in e-commerce. Shopping online provides people with the ultimate convenience.

1 In this passage, the word *savvy* means—
   A incompetent
   B competent
   C users
   D nonusers

2 The word *reliable* in this passage means—
   F existing
   G available
   H dependable
   J relevant

3 In this passage, the term *Web-surfer* means—
   A someone who uses the Internet
   B a person who uses a surfboard
   C a person who knows a great deal about technology
   D a student

4 The word *reputable* in this passage means—
   F an approved Internet provider
   G well-known and of good reputation
   H purely academic
   J costly

Practice 2 **Directions:** Read the passage. Then, read each question that follows the passage. Decide which is the best answer to each question.

Experiments in the science classroom can be as simple as lighting a Bunsen burner or as difficult as understanding the physics of refracting light by causing it to deviate from a straight path. Using an observation journal to document your experiments will help you determine the efficacy of things previously untested.

1 In this passage, the term *Bunsen burner* means—
   A a set of matches
   B a laboratory burner used to pr0-duce a flame
   C a burner on an oven
   D a candle

2 The word *refracting* in this passage means—
   F resulting in
   G to bring back
   H bending
   J changing

3 In this passage, the term *deviate* means—
   A to change expression
   B to turn aside from a specified course
   C appearance from a specific view
   D to lose control

4 The word *document* in this passage means—
   F a written or printed paper
   G to draw diagrams
   H to record information
   J to observe

Practice 1
1. B
2. H
3. A
4. G

Practice 2
1. B
2. H
3. B
4. H

In-Depth Lesson Plan

	LESSON FOCUS	PRINT AND MEDIA RESOURCES
DAY 1	**Reading Methods** Students learn and apply methods and tools to improve reading (pp. 790–797).	**Teaching Resources** *Academic and Workplace Skills Activity Book,* pp. 30–34
DAY 2	**Reading Nonfiction** Students learn and apply concepts of critical nonfiction reading (pp. 798–803).	**Teaching Resources** *Academic and Workplace Skills Activity Book,* pp. 35–38
DAY 3	**Reading Literary Writing** Students learn and apply concepts of reading fiction, drama, and poetry (pp. 804–807).	**Teaching Resources** *Academic and Workplace Skills Activity Book,* pp. 39–42
DAY 4	**Reading Varied Sources** Students learn and apply concepts of reading varied media such as newspapers, diaries, journals, interviews, forms (pp. 808–811).	**Teaching Resources** *Academic and Workplace Skills Activity Book,* p. 43; *Formal Assessment,* Ch. 32

Accelerated Lesson Plan

	LESSON FOCUS	PRINT AND MEDIA RESOURCES
DAY 1	**Reading Methods** Students learn and apply methods and tools to improve reading (pp. 790–797).	**Teaching Resources** *Academic and Workplace Skills Activity Book,* pp. 30–34
DAY 2	**Reading Fiction, Nonfiction, and Varied Sources** Students learn and apply concepts of critical nonfiction reading; concepts of reading fiction, drama, and poetry; and concepts of reading varied media such as newspapers, diaries, journals, interviews, forms (pp. 798–811).	**Teaching Resources** *Academic and Workplace Skills Activity Book,* pp. 35–43; *Formal Assessment,* Ch. 32

Options for Adapting Lesson Plans

HOMEWORK

Have students complete any section of the chapter for homework.

FEATURES

Extend coverage with the Standardized Test Preparation Workshop (p. 810).

TECHNOLOGY

Students can use the On-Line Exercise Bank to complete the exercises on computer. The Auto Check feature will grade their work.

INTEGRATED SKILLS COVERAGE TEKS CORRELATIONS

Speaking and Listening
Integrating Speaking and Listening Skills ATE p. 803

Real-World Connection
ATE p. 797

Viewing and Representing
Critical Viewing, SE pp. 790, 794, 795, 800, 802, 807

ASSESSMENT SUPPORT

Standardized Test Preparation SE p. 810; ATE p. 800
Standardized Test Preparation Workbook, pp. 63–64
Formal Assessment, Ch. 32

MEETING INDIVIDUAL NEEDS

Less Advanced Students ATE p. 795; See also Ongoing Assessments ATE pp. 792, 793, 796, 799, 801, 803, 805, 806
ESL Students ATE p. 792
More Advanced Students ATE p. 805
Visual/Spatial Learners ATE p. 796

BLOCK SCHEDULING

Pacing Suggestions
For 90-minute Blocks
• Administer the Diagnostic Test to students to determine instructional coverage.
• Have students complete the necessary exercises in class. Use the Hands-on Grammar activity to provide a change of pace.

Resources for Varying Instruction
• *Language Lab* **CD-ROM** If your students have access to hardware, a 90-minute block provides an ideal opportunity for students to work on computer.

Professional Development Support
• *How to Manage Instruction in the Block* This teaching resource provides management and activity suggestions.

MEDIA AND TECHNOLOGY

For the Teacher
• *Resource Pro* **CD-ROM**

WRITING AND GRAMMAR WEBSITE

The Interactive Writing and Grammar Website provides a wide array of support for students, teachers, and parents. Grammar support includes:

• *On-Line Exercise Bank* with Auto Check scoring
• Diagnostic and assessment support

phwg.phschool.com

Chapter
32 Reading Skills

► *Lesson Objectives*

1. To effectively use special sections of a textbook to become familiar with text.
2. To choose appropriate reading style.
3. To use an outline to arrange important information.
4. To use the SQ4R method.
5. To use graphic organizers to understand relationships among ideas in text.
6. To use general reading strategies for comprehending nonfiction.
7. To identify author's purpose and reliability.
8. To identify forms of reasoning.
9. To identify different kinds of language.
10. To use a variety of reading strategies for better understanding of literature.
11. To identify central conflict in fiction.
12. To understand performance aspect while reading drama.
13. To understand images and details of poetry.

Your teachers in earlier years stressed learning to read; now, the stress is on reading to learn. Being a good reader of both fiction and nonfiction involves knowing how to approach the material and using the critical thinking skills of evaluating and judging. In this chapter, you will learn ways to improve your skills in reading books related both to your schoolwork and personal reading.

▲ **Critical Viewing**
What special sections of the textbook might these students be using to help them in their work? **[Analyze]**

Critical Viewing

Analyze Students might mention sections such as an index, glossary, table of contents, introduction, preface, appendix, or bibliography.

⏱ TIME AND RESOURCE MANAGER	
Resources **Print:** Academic and Workplace Skills Activity Book, pp. 30–32	
In-Depth Coverage	**Accelerated Pace**
• Work through all key concepts, pp. 791–797. • Assign and review Exercises 1–7.	• Assign pp. 791–797 for independent student review. • Assign Exercises 1–7.

Section 32.1 Reading Methods and Tools

To understand more fully the contents of a book, you have to be able to construct your own meaning of the material.

Using Sections in Textbooks

A good way to start improving your textbook reading skills is to become familiar with the parts of your textbook. The front and back of most textbooks include a number of sections.

KEY CONCEPT Use the special sections of the textbook to familiarize yourself with its contents. ■

Table of Contents In the front of the textbook, the table of contents shows the book's organization by listing the units and chapters and indicating the pages where they are located.

Preface or Introduction This information is located just after or just before the table of contents. The preface states the author's purpose in writing the book. The introduction gives an overview of the book's ideas.

Index The index, found in the back of the textbook, lists alphabetically the specific topics and terms covered in the textbook, along with the pages on which they can be found.

Glossary The glossary is a list of terms with definitions, located in the back of many textbooks. Generally, it includes specialized words taken directly from the textbook.

Appendix Located in the back of the textbook, the appendix contains a variety of information that the author considers useful in understanding the material in the book.

Bibliography The bibliography includes publication information about books and articles referred to by the author, as well as other related materials you might want to read.

> **Exercise 1** **Examining Your Textbooks** Examine two of your textbooks to become acquainted with their various sections. Answer the following questions for each book:
> 1. According to the table of contents, how many units and chapters does the textbook have?
> 2. What does the preface and the introduction each contain?
> 3. What are two pieces of information located in the index?
> 4. Does the textbook have a glossary? What are two pieces of information you can learn from it?
> 5. Does the textbook have an appendix or a bibliography? What kind of information does each contain?

> **More Practice**
> Academic and Workplace Skills Activity Book
> • p. 29

Answer Key

Exercise 1

Answers will vary. Students' responses should reflect an understanding of the use of each section—table of contents, preface or introduction, index, glossary, appendix, and bibliography.

PREPARE and ENGAGE

Interest GRABBER On an overhead projector, display a long, multiframe comic strip from the Sunday newspaper. Ask students how reading the comic is similar to reading a page in a textbook. If students insist that there are no similarities, point out that in both cases looking at pictures can help them understand the text. Moreover, both comic strips and textbooks are carefully organized works with identifiable beginnings, middles, and ends.

Activate Prior Knowledge

Ask students to describe a recent experience in which they had difficulty reading a book, story, or article. What strategies did they employ to get through it? How effective were these strategies? What additional strategies might they have used?

TEACH

Step-by-Step Teaching Guide

Using Sections in Textbooks

1. Have students locate each section of a textbook they are currently using.
2. Ask students to name situations for which they might need to consult one of the special sections of the book.
3. Review material in the appendix. Tell students that appendices might contain maps, important documents, and lists.
4. Have students refer to the title page in their texts. Explain that checking the publication date is a good way to see if the book is current. Though the names of the authors of textbooks may not be familiar to students, it is always a good idea to know who the author is and what his or her credentials are for writing the book.

Using Different Reading Styles

1. There is an obvious danger in recommending that students skim and scan. However, it may come as a surprise to those who practice the "once over lightly" approach that these techniques actually have a use. Help students understand that skimming is useful to see if the material is something they are interested in reading and that scanning is useful for finding specific information.

2. Ask students to provide examples of when skimming or scanning would be a useful reading style. Some examples:

   • Looking up a word in the dictionary—scanning

   • Flipping through a magazine for something interesting—skimming

   • Looking up a number in the phone book—scanning

3. Close reading is the hardest technique to develop. Tell students that they will learn more strategies in this chapter for improving their close reading.

Customize for
ESL Students

Unfamiliarity with a language can make skimming and scanning difficult to use. For scanning, have students write and keep a list of key words close by as they scan the book for those words. For skimming, remind them to use graphic cues as well as words.

Answer Key

Exercise 2

1. skimming
2. skimming
3. scanning
4. scanning
5. close reading
6. skimming
7. scanning
8. skimming
9. close reading
10. scanning

32.1

Using Different Reading Styles

You can also improve your reading skills through knowledge of different reading styles. The three types of reading styles are *skimming*, *scanning*, and *close reading*. Each style of reading has a different purpose. Before you begin reading any material, consider your purpose, and then decide which reading style is the most suitable.

▶ **KEY CONCEPT** Choose the style of reading suitable for your purpose and material. ■

Skimming When you **skim** a text, you look it over quickly to get a general idea of its contents. Look for highlighted or bold type, headings, and topic sentences. Use skimming to preview, review, and locate information.

Scanning When you **scan** a text, you look it over to find specific information. Look for words related to your topic or purpose for reading. Use scanning to research, review, and find information.

Close Reading When you **closely read** a text, you read it carefully to understand and remember its ideas, to find relationships between ideas, and to draw conclusions about what you read. Use close reading to organize, study, and remember information.

As you become familiar with the three styles of reading, you will learn to adjust your mind and eyes to the appropriate style for the material you are reading.

▶ **Exercise 2** Determining Which Style of Reading to Use
Decide which style or styles of reading you would use for each of the following purposes.

EXAMPLE: Finding an article in a magazine *(scanning)*

1. Seeing if a book will be suitable for pleasure reading
2. Surveying the questions at the end of a chapter
3. Finding a word in the glossary of a textbook
4. Locating a particular place on a map
5. Reading and taking notes for a chapter test
6. Checking the contents of a book by using the index
7. Locating the time a bus should arrive using a bus schedule
8. Previewing a chapter
9. Reading a short story for an assignment in English class
10. Finding statistics about the population in a book of facts

▶ **More Practice**

Academic and Workplace Skills Activity Book
• p. 30

☑ ONGOING ASSESSMENT: Monitor and Reinforce

If some students are having difficulty understanding the differences between skimming and scanning, try the following strategy.

Remind students that they use skimming and scanning all the time. When they peruse television listings to get an idea of what's on, they are skimming; when they are looking for the starting time of a particular show, they are scanning.

Using the SQ4R Method

You can also use the organization of a textbook to study individual assignments by mastering the following skills: Survey, Question, Read, Record, Recite, and Review. The SQ4R method will guide you as you read, and it will later help you recall information.

> **KEY CONCEPT** Use the SQ4R method to gain a better understanding of textbook material. ∎

The SQ4R method can help you to study textbook material more efficiently and increase your comprehension skills.

SQ4R: STEPS IN READING TEXTBOOKS	
Preparing for reading:	*Survey* for an overview of the material
Focusing your reading:	*Question* before you read each section *Read* to answer the questions *Record* by taking notes on the main ideas and major details
Remembering what you read:	*Recite* by reading your notes aloud *Review* on a regular basis

Surveying allows you to become acquainted with the material you will be reading. When you survey textbook material, look for these features: titles, headings, and subheadings; words in italics or bold print; introductions and summaries; pictures and captions; and questions at the end of a section or chapter. The survey should take no more than a few minutes.

Questioning is a good way to force yourself to think about the material before you read it. As you come to each heading and subheading, ask yourself what might be covered under each. Your ability to ask yourself questions can help you focus on the main ideas and major details as you read.

Reading is the time for comprehension and for finding the answers to the questions you posed in the previous step. In addition, you should determine the main ideas and major details of the material.

Recording involves taking notes on the main ideas and major details. Recording information is one of the best ways to remember what you have read. By organizing the ideas in your mind as you read and then writing them in outline form, you improve your chances of remembering the material.

Using the SQ4R Method

1. SQ4R may sound strange, but as you go through the steps together, students will see that it is composed of steps they already know. The key to SQ4R is performing these steps together in ways that will improve students' reading, comprehension, and retention skills.

2. Show students how surveying is a mixture of skimming and scanning. Its main purpose is to give the reader a sense of the lay of the land. How many pages is the assignment? What graphics are included? Are there questions they need to answer? We tend to be more patient and attentive readers when we know what's ahead of us.

3. Questioning is a focusing activity. It is especially helpful when students are not sure of the subject matter. If the text is about a person, readers can ask themselves questions such as: Why is this person important? When did he or she live? How did the person accomplish what he or she is famous for?

4. Reading, obviously, is the main event. Stress how students are better prepared for reading after they have done the two previous steps.

5. Remind students that reading takes concentration. Urge them to find quiet places to read. Reading in front of the TV may be cozy, but it is a serious distraction.

☑ ONGOING ASSESSMENT: Monitor and Reinforce

If some students are having difficulty understanding surveying, use one of the following options.

Option 1 Use an analogy to explain surveying: you walk into a room full of people, look around, check out who is there, note whom you want to talk to, and then approach someone.	**Option 2** Work with students as you survey a section or chapter of a textbook. Demonstrate how you check heads, subheads, graphics, any boldface words, and the length of the selection.

Using the SQ4R Method: Reciting and Reviewing

1. Ask students how they learn the words and melody to a song. Repeated listening and recitation are the key to remembering. In the same way, reciting (silently or out loud) is another way of imprinting information on the memory.

2. Prove the point with a little experiment. Divide the class into small groups. Provide students with song lyrics or a nursery rhyme to memorize. Give half the groups a ten-minute head start, instructing them to recite the words over and over. The other half hears the words only once. The group that had time to recite will remember better.

3. The key in reviewing is timing. Ask students what they think will happen if they do all the steps of SQ4R and then don't look at their notes for two weeks. Though they may remember more than they would if they hadn't used the steps, nonetheless they will forget certain bits of information. The key is to review notes almost immediately after writing them. Then repeat the process every few days, as well as immediately before a test.

Critical Viewing

Infer Students will probably say that the girl is using the recording step of SQ4R.

Answer Key

Answers will vary. Students' questions, notes, and outlines should indicate an understanding of each of the steps of the SQ4R method as well as of the progression of the steps.

794

32.1

Reciting reinforces what you have already learned, by listening to the material from the textbook and from your notes. There are a number of ways to carry out this step:

- Recite aloud the information you want to master.
- Mentally recite the information you want to remember.
- Read the summaries, outlines, or other notes into a tape recorder. Then, play back the tape several times.
- Pair up with a classmate for a question-and-answer session.

Reviewing will help ensure that you have retained what you have been studying. When you review, you should repeat some of the previous steps. For example, you might want to reread your notes and look again at the headings and subheadings of your textbook. *When* you review is almost as important as *how* you review. You should never allow so much time to elapse that the material seems unfamiliar to you. In order to master material, you will need to review it a number of times before taking a test on it.

▲ **Critical Viewing** Which step of the SQ4R method does this student appear to be using? **[Infer]**

> **Exercise 3** **Surveying and Questioning** Choose a chapter from one of your textbooks. Survey all the chapter headings and subheadings. Then, go back and turn each heading and subheading into a question.

> **Exercise 4** **Reading and Recording** Using the same textbook chapter you used for Exercise 3, Surveying and Questioning, read and take notes on the chapter. Write the main ideas and major details in an outline form.

> **Exercise 5** **Reciting and Reviewing** Using the outline you made for the textbook chapter in Reading and Recording, work with another student to ask and answer questions about the outlined material. Then, review the material by asking yourself and answering questions about the chapter headings and subheadings.

> **More Practice**
>
> Academic and Workplace Skills Activity Book
> • p. 31

Using Outlines

Making an outline for the material you read will help you to better understand the information. When you make an **outline**, you list the main ideas and supporting details of a topic.

▶ **KEY CONCEPT** Use an outline to arrange important information and ideas. ■

The examples below illustrate the organization of a topic outline and a sentence outline on the same topic:

TOPIC OUTLINE:

I. Habitat of wild boar ◀————————— Main Idea
   A. North Africa ⎫
   B. Southwest Asia ⎬————— Major details explaining I
   C. Central Asia ⎭
II. Physical appearance ◀————————— Main Idea
   A. Three feet high ⎫
   B. Four hundred pounds ⎬————— Major details explaining II
   C. Grayish black hide ⎭
      1. Short hair ⎫
      2. Bristly hide ⎬———— Minor details explaining C

SENTENCE OUTLINE:

I. The wild boar inhabits several continents.
   A. The wild boar lives in North Africa.
   B. It can also be found in Southwest Asia.
   C. It also lives in Central Asia.

▶ **Exercise 6** **Making Outlines** Using a section from your textbook, make a formal topic outline and a sentence outline of the material.

▼ Critical Viewing
Think of a topic for this photograph of wild boars in India. Add some details that you observe in the photograph. **[Analyze]**

Reading Methods and Tools • 795

Step-by-Step Teaching Guide

Using Outlines

1. Reading information is one thing, but remembering it is another. Ask students what they do to remember important information they read. It is human nature to believe that we will remember what we read. A few pages later, however, we forget much of what we have read. Writing down information is useful in two ways: we have something to look at later, and the act of writing helps us remember information.

2. Review the sentence and topic outlines in the text. Topic outlines work well for material with which students already feel comfortable. For new material, a sentence outline helps a reader express information more completely. In this case, a sentence outline helps students not only remember the information, but also understand it better in the first place.

Customize for
Less Advanced Students

Students may have trouble structuring an outline. Work with them to outline a section of a chapter that is especially well organized. As students fill in the outline, explain how its structure shows the relationship between a main idea and its supporting details.

Answer Key

Exercise 6

Answers will vary. Students' outlines should include Roman numerals, capital letters, and Arabic numerals; show proper indentations; and have at least two subcategories for every main idea.

Critical Viewing

Analyze Students might mention a topic such as the behavior of animal herds and note details such as numbers of boars of various ages and genders.

Using Graphic Organizers: Venn Diagram

1. Nonfiction writing often involves more than a simple narrative. Instead there are ideas, incidents, events, and people in all sorts of relationships to each other. Untangling those relationships is often the challenge for the reader. Graphic organizers can help sort out complex relationships among types of information in a text.

2. Explain how a Venn diagram illuminates comparison/contrast relationships. Then draw one on the board. Read the following text to students and fill in the Venn diagram with them.

   New York and California are both populous, powerful states that owe their importance to geography. Both are coastal states. New York is on the Atlantic coast; California is on the Pacific. New York was settled first by the Dutch. The Spanish first settled California. New York is the financial center of the country, whereas Hollywood makes California the film capital. Both states are music hubs. (New York: Atlantic, Dutch, financial. California: Pacific, Spanish, film. Both: populous, powerful, geography, music)

Customize for
Visual/Spatial Learners

Encourage students to create a Venn diagram and to sort items into the proper areas as they read.

32.1

Using Graphic Organizers

A graphic organizer is a good tool to use to summarize and review information, as well as to show relationships among ideas. Because the information is organized visually, the graphic organizer provides you with a quick overview of the subject. Before you make a graphic organizer, consider how the various parts of the subject are related. The format you choose depends on those relationships.

▶ KEY CONCEPT Use graphic organizers to help you understand relationships among ideas in the text. ■

Following is a summary of some of the graphic organizers you can use to increase your understanding of the text.

Venn Diagram Use this graphic organizer to compare and contrast two subjects. To make a Venn diagram, draw two overlapping circles. In the overlapping section of the circles, write the characteristics that the two subjects share. In the other sections of the circles, write their differences.

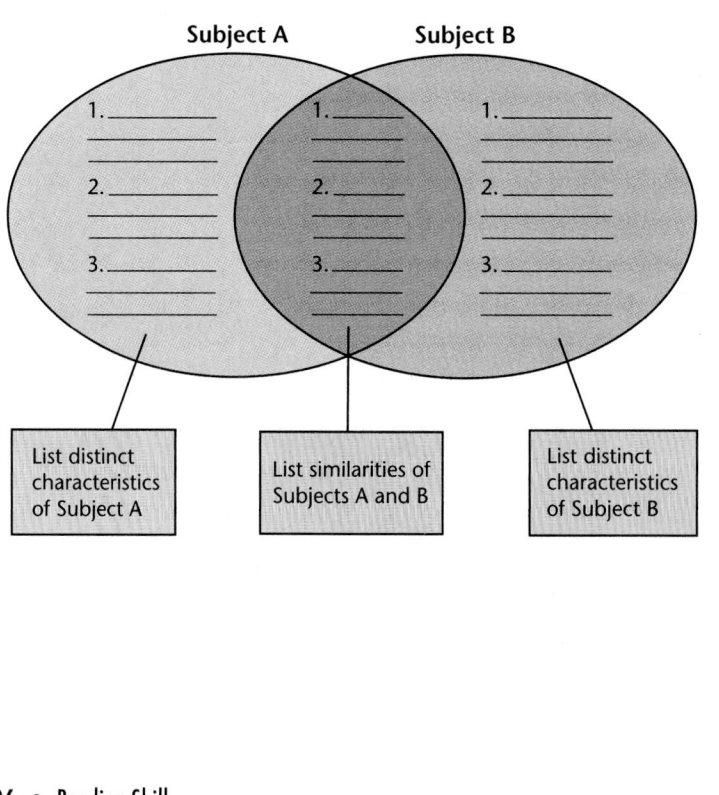

Subject A Subject B

List distinct characteristics of Subject A

List similarities of Subjects A and B

List distinct characteristics of Subject B

☑ ONGOING ASSESSMENT: Monitor and Reinforce

If some students are having difficulty understanding how to use a Venn diagram, try the following strategy.

Review the essentials of comparison and contrast. Insure that students understand that a	comparison shows shared characteristics and a contrast shows differences.

Web Diagram This graphic aid, sometimes called a cluster diagram in a slightly different format, is a useful tool for developing and organizing related ideas and supporting details. Begin your web diagram by writing your topic in the center of a sheet of paper. Circle that topic. Then, write any related ideas, and link them to the main topic with a line. Finally, write details that support each related idea.

Sequence Chart This graphic organizer, often used to review nonfiction, clarifies the sequence of a series of events from beginning to end. To make a sequence chart, write the initial event in sequence on a sheet of paper. Put a circle or square around it. Then, write each additional event in a square or circle, and use arrows to indicate how one event leads to the next.

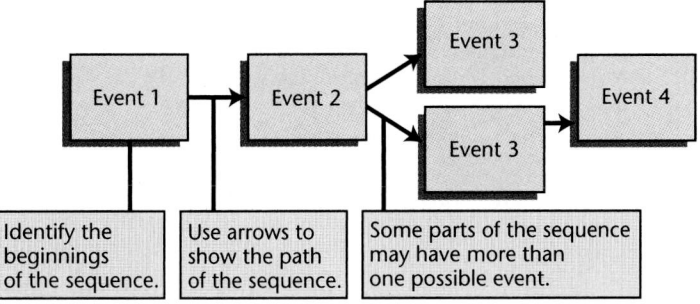

Topic

Related Idea / supporting detail

Related Idea / supporting detail / supporting detail

Related Idea / supporting detail / supporting detail / supporting detail

Event 1 → Event 2 → Event 3 / Event 3 → Event 4

| Identify the beginnings of the sequence. | Use arrows to show the path of the sequence. | Some parts of the sequence may have more than one possible event. |

▶ **Exercise 7** **Using Graphic Organizers** Read a chapter from one of your textbooks or a work of fiction. Then, use a Venn diagram, a web diagram, or a sequence chart to present this information.

▶ **More Practice**

Academic and Workplace Skills Activity Book
• p. 32

Reading Methods and Tools • **797**

Step-by-Step Teaching Guide

Using Graphic Organizers: Web Diagram and Sequence Chart

1. Main idea and supporting details is a basic organizational form used by many nonfiction writers. Examine the web diagram and discuss how it uses the same principles as an outline. In place of the roman numerals and capital letters, the web diagram uses lines.

2. Point out that web diagrams and outlines are tools for both readers and writers.

3. Ask students what kind of writing might have a sequence of events or steps in it. If necessary, help them recognize that history, how-to essays, and narratives all are built around a sequence. Insure that students understand the concept of chronology.

4. Students can practice making a sequence chart by charting their morning activities from waking up to arriving at school.

Real-World Connection

Search newspapers, newsmagazines, or Web sites for a story with a clear sequence of chronological events. Distribute copies of the story. Either as a whole-class or small-group activity, have students make a sequence chart of the events in the story.

Answer Key

▶ **Exercise 7**

Answers will vary. Students' graphic organizers should be accurately and neatly drawn, although their interpretations of shapes and spacing may vary, and include appropriate information based on the material.

Comprehending Nonfiction

1. Discuss two essential goals of reading nonfiction. First, students need to understand what the writer is saying. Then they need to evaluate what they have read. Point out that though these reading strategies are presented here in sequential order, in practice readers often use them simultaneously.

2. Students need to establish a more active purpose than "to complete an assignment." After surveying the material, students will have some idea what it is about. Remind them of SQ4R and explain that a few simple questions—"What is this about?" "When did it occur?"—will help them establish a purpose for reading.

3. Main points and details are the "bricks and mortar" of writing. When readers can identify main points and details, even boring or awkward writing becomes clear.

4. Remind students of the value of using graphic organizers. Understanding relationships between pieces of information is vital to unlocking the deeper meanings of a literary work.

5. Discuss how much more students absorb from reading when they are interested and actively involved with the process and the text. Point out that interpreting and responding are great ways to get involved. Invite them to think of reading as a dialogue in which they ask the author questions ("What does this mean?" "Why are you saying that?") and tell the author what they think ("This isn't clear," "I like the way you said that").

Reading Nonfiction Critically

When you read critically, you examine and question the writer's ideas, especially in light of his or her purpose. You also evaluate the information the writer includes as support, and you form a judgment about the content of the work.

Comprehending Nonfiction

When you read, the first thing you want to accomplish is comprehension in order to understand the main ideas of the material.

▶ **KEY CONCEPT** Use general reading strategies to learn more about the author's ideas in the text. ■

To help increase your ability to comprehend nonfiction, use these general strategies:

- **Establish a Purpose for Reading** Before you begin to read, decide why you are reading the material. Once you have established your purpose, look for information and other details in your reading that support this purpose.

- **Identify Main Points and Details** The main points are the most important ideas in the work. Details are the facts and examples used to support each main point.

- **Identify Relationships** As you read, determine the relationships between the ideas and events in the text. Some common relationships include sequence, part to whole, order of importance, cause and effect, comparison and contrast, and spatial order.

- **Interpret** State in your own words what you have read, to better understand the work.

- **Respond** Think about what the author has said and how you personally feel about the topic. Also, consider how you may apply this knowledge to your life.

▶ **Exercise 8** Using General Strategies for Reading Nonfiction Read a section from one of your textbooks, and use the strategies mentioned above to increase your understanding of the text. Then, answer the following questions:

1. What was your purpose for reading?
2. What main points and supporting details did you identify?
3. How was the material organized?
4. What is the importance of the information you read?
5. How might this information be applied to your own life?

▶ **More Practice**

Academic and Workplace Skills Activity Book
• p. 33

Answer Key

▶ **Exercise 8**

Answers will vary. Students' answers should show a clear understanding of the material they have read and its organizing premise.

⏱ TIME AND RESOURCE MANAGER

Resources
Print: Academic and Workplace Skills Activity Book, pp. 33–38

In-Depth Coverage	Accelerated Pace
• Work through all key concepts, pp. 798–803. • Assign and review Exercises 8–12.	• Assign pp. 798–803 for independent student review. • Assign Exercises 8–12.

Evaluating What You Read

Once you have a general understanding of the work, the next step is to evaluate the material, especially in light of the author's purpose and the reliability of the information given.

KEY CONCEPT Be an attentive reader so you can determine the purpose and reliability of the material you read. ■

Author's Purpose Part of being a critical reader is being able to determine why the author is writing. The chart below lists common purposes and clues to identifying them.

IDENTIFYING AUTHOR'S PURPOSE IN WRITING	
Purpose	**Informational Clues**
To inform	Series of factual statements that are verified by experimentation, records, or personal observation
To instruct	Sequential development of an idea or a process
To offer an opinion	Presentation of an issue with predominant point of view backed up by valid authority
To sell	Persuasive techniques, including facts and propaganda, designed to sell an idea or a product
To entertain	Narration of an event in a humorous manner; often used to lighten a serious topic

Inferences Sometimes, an author states his or her purpose in writing directly. More often, however, the purpose is implied. As you read, you must make inferences about the author's purpose from clues you find in the reading.

Exercise 9 Determining the Author's Purpose by Making Inferences Read the following sentences. Then, make an inference about the author's purpose. Explain your answer.

1. Today's session will guide you through the steps of how to build an oak cabinet with brass handles.
2. The temperature is 60 degrees Fahrenheit, and there is a light rain falling over the city.
3. Have you ever wondered why computers are so slow? Well, I have. Here are my solutions to solve this problem.
4. The political turmoil in the world reminds me of a funny joke my friend used to tell.
5. The X1-Viper snowboard has a rugged look and is designed from the latest technology that snowboarding has to offer.

Reading Nonfiction Critically • **799**

Step-by-Step Teaching Guide

Evaluating What You Read

1. Be sure that students understand that an author's purpose is different from a reader's purpose.
2. Examine the chart of author's purposes. Tell students that sometimes authors have more than one purpose in writing. For example, an advertising writer's main purpose is to sell something, but he or she also might wish to entertain, inform, instruct, or offer an opinion.
3. Identifying an author's purpose helps readers set up their own strategies. If we know that the writer's purpose is to sell, we are going to read much more critically, even skeptically, than if his or her purpose is to inform.
4. Write the following passage on the board and ask students to infer what the author is saying.

   Delegates arrived at the Constitutional Convention full of ideas, eager to talk. James Madison had been hard at work for months. He came with a vision of a new government for a new country. (Madison, in contrast to other delegates, had come ready with a blueprint for the Constitution.)

Answer Key

Exercise 9

Students' reasons for selecting a particular purpose will vary. The authors' purposes are as follows:

1. to instruct
2. to inform
3. to offer an opinion; to sell
4. to entertain
5. to inform; to sell

☑ **ONGOING ASSESSMENT: Monitor and Reinforce**
If some students are having difficulty understanding general reading strategies, use one of the following options.

Option 1 Model active reading. Read a passage and interpret and respond out loud as you read.	**Option 2** Pair students and have them set a purpose by asking at least four questions after having surveyed the material.

Evaluating What You Read: Fact and Opinion

1. Inform students that distinguishing fact from opinion is an important critical reading skill. A second vital skill is being able to verify whether a fact is true and whether an opinion is valid.

2. Write the following items on the chalkboard, and ask students to identify them as facts or opinions:

   World War II ended in 1945. (fact)

   The 1950s were a great era. (opinion)

3. Discuss the resources students have to determine if facts are true or false. Remind them that encyclopedias, almanacs, atlases, and on-line reference tools are useful for fact checking. Some facts can also be verified by using prior knowledge or common sense.

4. Validating opinion is trickier. Often the question is, who is a trustworthy authority? Suppose the author of the example about stress was a university scientist. Would he or she need to refer to expert opinion? Point out that this is a judgment for readers to make.

5. Finally, mention that unsupported opinions, though perhaps not technically *valid,* can have value. An essay about any number of subjects—sports, politics, music— can be full of unsupported opinions and still be interesting.

Answer Key

Exercise 10

1. opinion/invalid
2. opinion/valid
3. fact/true
4. fact/false
5. fact/true

Critical Viewing

Connect Students' responses will vary. William Shakespeare wrote *Hamlet.* (fact) Shakespeare's portrait was painted by a great artist. (opinion)

32.2

Fact and Opinion In order to decide whether the material you read is reliable, you have to be able to distinguish between fact and opinion statements. A *statement of fact* is one that can be verified, or proved true by written authority, personal observation, or experimentation. A *statement of opinion* cannot be proved true, but the opinion can be considered valid if it is supported by related facts.

FACT STATEMENT: The United States government has three branches. (True)

FACT STATEMENT: "The Raven" was written by the author Shirley Jackson. (False)

The first fact statement is *true* because it can be verified by written authority, an encyclopedia, almanac, or social studies textbook. On the other hand, the second statement is *false* because a literary or biographical dictionary tells us that Edgar Allan Poe—not Shirley Jackson—is the author of "The Raven."

OPINION STATEMENT: Scientists at the university feel that life was less stressful in past centuries since fewer people died of heart attacks, a stress-related disease. (Valid)

OPINION STATEMENT: Life was easier a century ago because people did not have cars. (Invalid)

The first opinion statement is valid because it gives supporting facts by an authority. The second opinion statement, however, is invalid since it isn't supported by any facts.

> **Exercise 10** Analyzing Fact and Opinion
> **Statements** Identify each statement as a *fact* or an *opinion.* Then, analyze whether each fact statement is *true* or *false* and whether each opinion statement is *valid* or *invalid.*

1. *The Wizard of Oz* is the best movie ever made.
2. Jan is a great swimmer; she has won six swim meets.
3. William Shakespeare wrote *A Midsummer Night's Dream.*
4. The World Trade Center is the tallest building in the world.
5. Hank Aaron broke Babe Ruth's record for total career home runs.

> **More Practice**
> Academic and Workplace Skills Activity Book
> • p. 34

▼ Critical Viewing
Tell a fact about William Shakespeare that can be validated. Then, give an opinion based on the picture. **[Connect]**

STANDARDIZED TEST PREPARATION WORKSHOP

Fact and Opinion Standardized test questions may require students to identify statements of fact and opinion. Ask students to tell whether each sentence below is fact or opinion.

1. Paris is the capital of France. (fact)
2. Paris is the best city in the world. (opinion)
3. The French Revolution began in 1789. (fact)
4. The French Revolution was more important than the American Revolution. (opinion)

Evaluating Forms of Reasoning

One way to improve your critical reading skills is by evaluating ideas to see if they are reasonable. Following is a list of three common forms of reasoning:

> **KEY CONCEPT** *Generalization, analogy,* and *cause and effect* are common forms of reasoning that can be used by an author to convey valid or invalid information. ■

A **generalization** is a statement made on the basis of a number of particular facts or cases.

VALID: There are seventy-four girls and sixty-six boys in Sue's ninth-grade class. Therefore, most of the students in Sue's ninth-grade class are girls.

HASTY: Sue's ninth-grade class has more girls than boys. Therefore, all ninth grades have more girls than boys.

The first example is a valid generalization because it is clearly supported by evidence. The second example, however, is a hasty generalization, because the author's statement is made about a whole group based on only one example.

RECOGNIZING VALID/HASTY GENERALIZATIONS

1. What facts or cases are being presented as evidence to support the general statement?
2. Are there any exceptions to the statement?
3. Are enough cases or examples being presented?

An **analogy** is a comparison between two things that are similar in some ways but are essentially unlike. An author will often use an analogy to convey an idea about one thing by showing its similarity to something more familiar.

COMPLETE: Like the human brain, a computer stores and processes information.

INCOMPLETE: A computer is like the human brain.

The first analogy is complete because it explains the functions of a computer by comparing them to the more familiar functions of the human brain. The second analogy is incomplete because a computer and the human brain are essentially dissimilar in structure and origin.

IDENTIFYING COMPLETE/INCOMPLETE ANALOGIES

1. How are the two things being compared essentially different?
2. How are the two things alike? Is the comparison logical?
3. What is the truth that the comparison tries to show?

Evaluating Forms of Reasoning

1. Generalizations are made by using specific evidence to form a larger statement or thought. Valid generalizations must be based on sufficient specific evidence; hasty generalizations are made without supporting evidence. Though the latter may turn out to be true, the generalization itself provides no assurance of that.

2. Write the following generalizations on the board and ask students to classify them as valid or hasty.

   In the last fifty years, Philadelphia's population has declined by hundreds of thousands of people. Today Philadelphia is a much smaller city than it was fifty years ago. (valid)

   Denver's population has grown for decades. In the future, Denver will become the biggest city in the United States. (hasty)

3. Analogy is a useful way to compare things. Tell students that an analogy is sometimes used to compare a writer's idea to something the reader is more familiar with.

4. Write the following additional example on the board and ask students to explain why it is a complete analogy.

   Standing in the crowded, slowly moving line at the checkout line and waiting to pay felt like being stuck in traffic on the expressway.

☑ ONGOING ASSESSMENT: Monitor and Reinforce

If some students are having difficulty understanding generalizations, use one of the following options.

Option 1 Have students repeat the example in the text by counting the number of boys and girls in the class and making a generalization of their own.	**Option 2** Ask students to name a good friend. Ask why they consider that person a good friend. Then help them form a valid generalization about friendship from the examples they have given.

Evaluating Forms of Reasoning: Cause and Effect

1. Cause and effect is frequently used in journalism as well as social science and science writing. Remind students that sometimes writers claim a cause-and-effect relationship is present when, in fact, none exists. It is the reader's job to determine whether the writer has made a valid claim.

2. Write the following examples on the board and ask students to determine whether each is a valid cause-and-effect sequence.

   The routine ground ball struck an uneven seam in the turf and bounced over the shortstop's head. (valid)

   I got an unlucky feeling, and then the shortstop missed the ball. (invalid)

Answer Key

Exercise 11

1. cause and effect/valid; food prices often determined by production costs
2. cause and effect/invalid; no support provided
3. generalization/invalid; ranking in one tournament does not foretell performance or ranking in future tournaments
4. cause and effect/invalid; clothing choice doesn't affect academic achievement
5. cause and effect or generalization/valid; the first and second events have causal relationship and are likely to occur regularly

Critical Viewing

Analyze Students might offer a generalization such as "new highways are often built to connect with, extend, or even replace existing highways."

32.2

A **cause-and-effect** sequence may be used by an author to conclude that one event has caused a second event because the first event happened immediately before the second. An author uses a *valid* cause-and-effect sequence when something is caused by one or more events that occurred before it. An author uses an *invalid* cause-and-effect sequence when the first event did not cause the second event.

VALID: Thunder occurs after each lightning flash because the lightning causes the air to heat and expand explosively.

INVALID: The lights went out because the lightning flashed.

DETERMINING CAUSE/EFFECT SEQUENCES

1. What evidence is there that the first event or situation could have caused the second?
2. What other events may have caused the second event?
3. Could the second event have occurred without the first?

> **Exercise 11** Analyzing Forms of Reasoning Identify the form of reasoning *(generalization, analogy, cause and effect)* found in each following statement. Then, identify whether each conclusion is *valid* or *invalid*, and explain your answer.

1. The cost of raising cattle has risen sharply; therefore, meat prices will go up this year.
2. The new highway that is being built will solve all of the city's traffic problems.
3. Sarah placed second in the tennis tournament, so she will place second in all tennis tournaments.
4. Wearing this shirt to the exam will help me get an *A*.
5. Students who spend all of their free time watching television instead of studying usually receive poor grades.

▶ Critical Viewing
Make a valid generalization about this picture. [Analyze]

Examining the Author's Language

Authors can use different kinds of language to make you think or feel a certain way about the ideas presented.

KEY CONCEPT *Denotative* and *connotative* words, and *jargon* are some of the ways authors use language to change the meaning of a fact or an event. ■

A **denotative word** refers to a word's literal or exact meaning and has a neutral tone. A **connotative word** suggests or implies meaning in a positive or negative tone. In the following example, words with strong connotations are italicized. Words that are not italicized do not carry strong connotations.

CONNOTATIVE: The *ill-planned* highway project has *dragged* on for six years at an *ever-escalating* annual expense of more than one million dollars.

DENOTATIVE: The *extensive* highway project has *continued* for several years at an annually *increasing* expense of one million dollars.

Jargon is language that appears to be scientific or technical but is vague and often meaningless. An author uses jargon to confuse or deceive the reader about the real meaning behind the words.

JARGON: Due to *business reversals* the company is forced to *eliminate your position.*

DIRECT LANGUAGE: Because the company has *lost money*, you will *lose your job.*

Exercise 12 Analyzing the Author's Language Read the following passage, and identify the following uses of language: *denotative words*, *negative* and *positive connotative words*, and *jargon.*

1. The decline in students' educational performance is the result of disturbing inadequacies in the way the educational process itself is constructed.
2. It is not our new school buildings or fancy enrichment programs that will restore the good old values of hard work and the three "R's" to our halls of learning.
3. "Back to Basics" must be the watchword of every school's educational policy.
4. If we pursue our goal with single-minded purpose, we can dispel the mists that cloud our vision like a wet blanket and concentrate on graduating students with a sound knowledge of basic educational skills.

More Practice

Academic and Workplace Skills Activity Book
• pp. 35–36

Reading Nonfiction Critically • **803**

Examining the Author's Language

1. Why don't writers just say what they mean? That is certainly a legitimate question for readers to ask. Of course, by using different kinds of language, writers create interest and avoid monotony.
2. Write the following additional examples on the board.

   Denotative: The tax increase had little support and was voted down.

   Connotative: The ill-fated tax increase was given a crushing defeat.
3. Explain that jargon is generally something writers should avoid, unless they are writing for a specific audience that uses it regularly. When students read, they need to do their best to decode the meaning of jargon.
4. There are two basic kinds of jargon. Technical jargon relates to an occupation, business, or activity. For example, *download* and *surf* are computer jargon. On the other hand, euphemistic jargon is used to cloud or distort meaning. Discuss how the example in the text version disguises the truth and obscures the company's responsibility for taking a person's job away.

Integrating Speaking and Listening Skills

Ask students to consider the language they use in conversation. Do they always say exactly what they mean? Point out that the use of connotative language, understatement, hyperbole, and sarcasm are fairly common in conversational speech.

Answer Key

Exercise 12

Answers will vary. Samples are given.

1. denotative, negative connotative
2. negative connotative, positive connotative, jargon
3. jargon, positive connotative
4. denotative, jargon, positive connotative

✓ ONGOING ASSESSMENT: Monitor and Reinforce

If some students are having difficulty understanding connotative and denotative language, use one of the following options.

Option 1 Model the difference, telling students something in both connotative and denotative language.	**Option 2** Ask students to describe something they really like. Provide a literal, denotative translation of what they have just said.

Reading Literary Writing: Reading Actively

1. Discuss the differences between reading fiction and nonfiction. We read nonfiction for information—to learn something. When we read fiction, we engage not only our brains, but also our imaginations and our feelings. We identify with characters, and we continue to read to find out what is going to happen to them.

2. Establishing a purpose is different for reading fiction and nonfiction. Before reading fiction, we might intend to become absorbed by interesting characters in a distant setting, for example. The personal connections we make during reading are a confirmation of our purpose.

3. When a story captivates us, reading can seem effortless. Still, it is useful to ask questions, to reread dense or profound passages, and to anticipate how the plot might develop.

4. Encourage students to extend their awareness of historical context to the setting in general. After students establish where and when the story takes place, they must be sensitive to any changes in setting.

Answer Key

Answers will vary. Students' summaries should show a clear understanding of the literature they have read.

Section 32.3

Reading Literary Writing

Literature is an imaginative form of writing that encompasses works by fiction writers, playwrights, and poets.

Reading Actively

Reading literary works involves using your judgment and imagination, and responding to the work on a personal level.

> **KEY CONCEPT** Use a variety of reading strategies to increase your understanding of literary works. ■

To increase your comprehension and add to your appreciation of prose, plays, and poetry, use these general strategies:

Establish a Purpose for Reading Before you begin to read, decide why you're reading the piece. Establishing a purpose for reading focuses your thoughts.

Ask Questions As you read, question what is happening in the text. Then, search the text for answers as you read further.

Reread or Read Ahead Reread a sentence, paragraph, or stanza to find the connections among the words or to connect the ideas in several sentences. Read ahead to find more information about difficult words or ideas.

Make Personal Connections Use your own experiences to help you get a better understanding of what you are reading. As you read, look for connections between people and events in your own life and those in the text.

Be Aware of the Historical Context When does the action occur? What are the manners, customs, and morals of the times? What mood does the historical context suggest?

Respond As you read, determine how you feel about the characters or speakers and the situations in which they are described. When you have finished reading, think about what the work means to you.

> **Exercise 13** Using Strategies to Comprehend Literature
> Read a short story, an act or scene from a play, a chapter of a novel, or a poem, and use the strategies mentioned above to increase your comprehension of the material. Then, write a summary describing what you learned.

> **More Practice**
> Academic and Workplace Skills Activity Book
> • pp. 37–38

⏱ TIME AND RESOURCE MANAGER

Resources
Print: Academic and Workplace Skills Activity Book, pp. 37–42

In-Depth Coverage	Accelerated Pace
• Work through all key concepts pp. 804–807. • Assign and review Exercises 13–17.	• Assign pp. 804–807 for independent student review. • Assign Exercises 13–17.

Reading Fiction

Short stories and novels are literature of the imagination in which the characters and events are made up by the author.

▶ **KEY CONCEPT** Short stories and novels usually focus on a central conflict that a character must face. ■

Determine the Point of View The point of view is the perspective from which the narrator tells a story. In *omniscient third-person point of view*, the narrator has complete knowledge of all the characters and tells what they feel and think. In *limited third-person point of view*, the narrator has knowledge of the thoughts and feelings of only one character and the world that the author creates is viewed from this character's perspective. In the *first-person point of view*, the narrator assumes the role of one character in the story and refers to himself or herself with the first-person pronoun "I."

Identify the Stages of Plot The plot is the sequence of events that make up the story. The *exposition* provides background information and sets the scene for the conflict. The conflict is a struggle between opposing people or forces that drives the action of the story. The introduction of the conflict marks the beginning of the rising action, in which the conflict intensifies until it reaches the high point, or climax, of the story. After the climax, the action falls to a resolution, which shows how the story turns out.

Describe the Characters A **character** is someone or something that takes part in the story. There are *major characters*, who play a significant role in the action, and *minor characters*, who play a less important role. In addition, a character can be *dynamic*, or experience change as the work progresses. If a character does not change, the character is said to be *static*.

Identify the Conflict Conflict is the struggle between opposing forces. There are two kinds of conflict: external and internal. An external conflict is a physical struggle between the character and an outside force. An internal conflict is a mental or emotional struggle that takes place within the character.

▶ **Exercise 14** **Reading Short Stories and Novels** Read a short story from your textbook, or choose one from your own collection. As you read, answer the following questions: What is the point of view in the story? What kind of characters are in the story? Do they experience an internal or external conflict? The next time you read a novel, ask these same questions.

Reading Literary Writing • 805

ONGOING ASSESSMENT: Monitor and Reinforce

If some students are having difficulty understanding reading strategies for comprehending literature, use one of the following options.

Option 1 Ask students to tell you about a recent TV show they liked. Point out the personal connections, historical context, and the responses in students' comments.	**Option 2** Have students tell each other about a book, movie, or TV show that takes place in an unusual place in the past or the future. Have them give as many details as possible about the setting.

Reading Fiction

1. Review the three types of point of view. The two types of third-person narrators are the most difficult to distinguish. A limited third-person narrator is unable to provide information about the thoughts and feelings of various characters. An omniscient narrator's knowledge has no apparent bounds.

2. Review the plot graphic. Ask students to test the plot of a story, TV show, or movie against the diagram. Most conventional stories follow this sequence of events.

3. Discuss how readers know who is the main character. Often it is fairly obvious: the main character is the subject of much of the book. Minor characters can be harder to figure out. Someone with a prominent role in the beginning can fade into the background, whereas another character may not appear until late in a story.

4. Explain that dynamic characters are changed by actions through which they pass in the plot. One point of a story with dynamic characters is to reveal the consequences of actions upon the characters. Point out that dynamic characters are more likely to be found in novels and dramas.

5. Many stories feature both external and internal conflict. Use as an example a novel that all (or most) students have read.

Customize for
More Advanced Students

Ask students to write a short essay about a character in a story they read recently. Challenge them to describe a dynamic character and to provide details about the character's changes.

Answer Key

▶ **Exercise 14**

Answers will vary. Students' responses should reflect a thorough understanding of the author's use of these literary elements.

Reading Literary Writing: Reading Drama

Explain that in reading any story, we use our imaginations to "see" the images described by the author. In reading a play we need to pay attention to the stage directions and the character descriptions in order to get the fullest sense of what is taking place. Point out to students that action in a story is described, whereas in a play it is acted out. That is why it is important to read the stage directions to find out exactly what gestures and actions are occurring.

Answer Key

> **Exercise 15**

Answers will vary. Students' choices of details noting the play's historical context, stage directions, and descriptions of characters and conflicts should all be supported by the text.

Reading Poetry

1. Students can feel challenged by poetry because they take reading cues only from work's structure. The key is to heed both structure and punctuation.

2. Explain that imagery sometimes functions differently in poetry and in prose. Freed from the burden of having to write complete sentences of description, poets can use imagery in especially concentrated, powerful ways.

3. Discuss with students how paraphrasing is useful for understanding a poem, but ultimately one's experience of a poem reaches beyond what is explicitly said.

Answer Key

> **Exercise 16**

Answers will vary. Students' answers should include identification of the poem's speaker, three images in the poem, and valid paraphrases of the poem's lines and stanzas.

806

32.3

Reading Drama

The story in a play is told mostly through dialogue and action. The stage directions indicate when and how the actors move and sometimes suggest sound and lighting effects.

> **KEY CONCEPT** When you read a drama, it is important to remember that it was written to be performed. ■

Read the Cast of Characters Before the first act or first scene of a play, you will see a list—often with descriptions of the characters that take part in the play. Reading this list can tell you the various relationships among the characters, as well as offer you some insight into their personalities.

Use Stage Directions to Envision the Play As you read the drama, use your imagination to mentally re-create the play. Use characters' descriptions of places and other characters, as well as the playwright's stage directions.

Summarize the Events After Acts or Scenes Dramas are often broken into acts or scenes. These natural breaks give you an opportunity to review the action that took place.

> **Exercise 15** Reading Drama Read the first act or first few scenes of a play. As you read, do the following: List three details describing the play's historical context. Name five stage directions that you feel contribute most to the play's action. Describe the main characters and the conflicts they face.

Reading Poetry

Poetry is a unique form that expresses meaning in few words. Poets achieve this concentration by selecting details and by using imaginative and sensory language.

> **KEY CONCEPT** A **poem** is a combination of images and details that work to create a total impression. ■

Identify and Understand the Speaker To identify and understand the speaker of the poem, ask yourself these questions: Who is the speaker? What does the speaker look like? In what situation or setting is the speaker placed? To whom is he or she speaking? What is the speaker's outlook on life?

Follow Punctuation The words of a poem are often put together and punctuated as sentences. As you read through a poem, be sure to follow the punctuation.

► **More Practice**

Academic and
Workplace Skills
Activity Book
• pp. 39–42

▌ **Speaking and Listening Tip**

One of the best ways to truly understand and appreciate a poem is to read it aloud. Listen to the sounds of the words and the rhythms of the lines. How does the poet use sound to enhance the poem's meaning?

☑ **ONGOING ASSESSMENT: Monitor and Reinforce**

If some students are having difficulty understanding strategies for reading drama, use one of the following options.

Option 1 Make sure students are reading the stage directions and character introductions. Often these appear in italics or another font, and readers may skip over them or skim them.	**Option 2** Go over the beginning of a popular play with students, showing them the important information that the playwright includes. Also show students stage directions within the text and between scenes.

Examine the Imagery Imagery is the descriptive language that writers use to create word pictures. These pictures, or images, are created through the details that describe sight, sound, smell, taste, and touch.

Paraphrase the Poem Paraphrasing, restating the speaker's experiences and feelings in your own words, is a helpful way to check your understanding of what you read. Before you paraphrase a poem, make sure you understand what is happening, who is speaking, and what ideas and images are being expressed.

▶ **Exercise 16** Reading Poetry Choose a poem from your textbook or from your personal reading. Read the poem accurately by paying close attention to the punctuation. As you read, identify the speaker, list three specific images, and paraphrase each stanza or every few lines in the poem.

Reading Myths and Folk Tales

Many folk songs, ballads, folk tales, legends, and myths originated in the oral tradition. A *myth* is a fictional tale that explains the actions of gods or the causes of natural phenomena. Myths have little historical truth and involve supernatural elements. Every culture has its collection of myths. *Folk tales* are entertaining stories about heroes or adventures.

Identify the Cultural Context Understanding the culture from which a myth or folk tale comes will help you to understand the ideas presented in it. Read any notes that accompany a story to find out more about the culture. While you read the story, look for details that tell you about the culture.

Predict Look for clues to help you make guesses about what will happen next. Revise your predictions as new details unfold, and check to see whether your predictions come true.

Recognize the Storyteller's Purpose Knowing why a myth or folk tale was told will help you understand why the characters in it behave in certain ways. It will also help you learn more about the culture itself.

▶ **Exercise 17** Reading Myths, Legends, and Folk Tales Read a myth or folk tale from your literature textbook, and answer the following questions.
1. List details of the story, and explain what they suggest about the culture presented in the piece.
2. What predictions did you make about events in the piece? Were you correct? Why or why not?
3. What is the purpose of this piece? What does the purpose suggest about the culture's values or beliefs?

▲ **Critical Viewing** Does this look like a good setting for reading a piece of literary writing? Why or why not? [Evaluate]

Reading Myths and Folk Tales

1. Explain to students that myths and folk tales are found in almost every culture throughout the world. These stories have many important cultural functions, ranging from explanations of natural phenomena to understanding one's place in the universe.
2. Remind students that a majority of these stories were meant to be spoken aloud. It wasn't until much later that many of these stories came to be written down.

Answer Key

Exercise 17

Answers will vary. Students' responses should reflect an accurate and sensitive close reading of a myth or folk tale.

Critical Viewing

Evaluate Many students may feel that an outdoor setting would be a relaxing or refreshing place to read a piece of literary writing.

Reading from Varied Sources

1. Have students construct a chart that lists each of the varied sources on pp. 808–809. Then have them write brief descriptions for each source. Finally, ask students to provide examples from their own past readings for each source.

2. If possible, bring in examples of these sources, such as diaries, letters, newspapers, interviews, and forms. You can use these examples to discuss the different kinds of information that can be found in each one.

Section 32.4 Reading From Varied Sources

Information is made available to you in a wide variety of formats, including books, magazines, Web pages, advertisements, newspapers, letters, and speeches. By familiarizing yourself with different types of sources, you will widen the range and type of information you can learn and use.

Read Diaries, Letters, and Journals

Diaries, letters, and journals are firsthand accounts of events or circumstances. They are often published after the writer's death with the permission of his or her family. Some may be written by people whose achievements make them interesting subjects. Others are written by people who lived in interesting times. Keep in mind when you read these primary sources that not all the information in them will be strictly factual. Much of it will reflect the writer's personal opinions.

Read Newspapers

Newspapers are a good source of information on current events and issues in your community, in the United States, and around the world. When you read a newspaper, notice whether the coverage is local, national, or global. Different sections of newspapers have different purposes. Editorial pages offer opinions of the topics they cover. Other sections give an unbiased account of the topics they cover. Read newspapers critically. Keep an eye out for bias or faulty logic.

Read Transcripts of Speeches and Interviews

A transcript is a written record of what was spoken. You can obtain transcripts of most famous speeches in library resources. Books and other references contain the printed record of what a speaker said. Interview transcripts are usually available through the media that produced the interview. Speeches and interviews offer one person's perspective on an issue, situation, or condition. These thoughts, unlike those set down in diaries or letters, are usually intended for publication. Like diaries and letters, speeches and interviews reflect on the person's opinions.

⏱ TIME AND RESOURCE MANAGER

Resources
Print: Academic and Workplace Skills Activity Book, p. 43

In-Depth Coverage	Accelerated Pace
• Cover pp. 808–809 in class. • Assign and review Exercise 18.	• Assign pp. 808–809 for independent student review. • Assign Exercise 18.

Answer Key

Exercise 18

Students should summarize, compare, and evaluate the three accounts, as well as note what special understanding they got from each source.

Read Forms and Applications

One of the most practical purposes for reading is to fill out forms and applications. Read these documents carefully. Understanding what information is being requested will help you fill out forms accurately. Filling out forms accurately leads to quicker results than if the form must be resubmitted again with new information.

Read Electronic Texts

Web pages, electronic advertising, and e-mail present text through an electronic medium. Whether you read text on screen or on a page, read critically. When you read a Web page, consider the source when you evaluate the reliability of the information. Look for evidence that the writer of the page has background in the subject area. Determine whether the page is sponsored by a company that wants to promote a particular point of view. The Internet can be a fine resource, but you must use it with a critical awareness.

Exercise 18 Reading Varied Sources Choose an event or time period from American history, such as the Civil War or the Depression. Find an account of the event or the period in at least three different sources described on these pages. Write a summary of the information you find in each. Then, in a brief evaluation, compare and contrast the information you found in each, as well as the unique perspective you gained from reading each source.

> **More Practice**
> Academic and
> Workplace Skills
> Activity Book
> • p. 43

Reflecting on Your Reading

After a week of practicing your reading skills, write a paragraph about the areas in which you found success and those in which you need to improve. Use the following questions as a starting point:

• Which sections of my textbooks did I find most useful?

• Which steps of the SQ4R method did I find most useful?

• Which graphic organizers have I recently used to organize ideas or explain a story's development?

• How have critical reading skills helped me to analyze and evaluate non-fiction material?

• Which strategies for reading fiction did I find the most useful? Which strategies did I find the most difficult to use?

Lesson Objectives

- To make inferences and predictions about a passage.

Step-by-Step Teaching Guide

Make Inferences and Predictions

1. Remind students that writers don't always explain everything directly. Sometimes, readers must "read between the lines" to look beyond the literal meaning of the words on the page. Consider the writer's tone, word choice, and details he or she includes.

2. Explain that a reader makes predictions by asking himself or herself questions while reading. Readers can make predictions based on information in the text and their own experiences.

Standardized Test Preparation Workshop

Make Inferences and Predictions

The reading sections of standardized tests often measure your ability to make inferences. You can make inferences, or draw logical conclusions, about what you have read about characters and stories, or you can make them about the author's purpose or point of view. Some questions require you to make a prediction or anticipate future actions or outcomes from the material you have read. Some tests will ask you to read a passage, think about it by responding to a question, and explain your response in writing.

The following sample items will help you prepare.

Test Tip

It is worthwhile noting the author's overall tone in a passage before answering any of the questions. The author's use of language can often help you conclude his or her intent.

Sample Test Item	Answers and Explanations
Directions: Read the passage. Then, answer the questions that follow the passage. from *Erewhon*, by Samuel Butler He had been asking me about my watch, and inquiring whether such dangerous inventions were tolerated in the country from which I came. I owned with some confusion that watches were not uncommon; but observing the gravity which came over his Majesty's face I presumed to say that they were fast dying out, and that we had few if any other mechanical contrivances of which he was likely to disapprove.	
1 What might you infer from the author's response to his Majesty's reaction? **A** He is trying to trick his Majesty. **B** He is trying to anger his Majesty. **C** He is trying to make his Majesty laugh. **D** He is trying to keep himself out of trouble by lying to his Majesty.	The answer for item 1 is *D*. We can infer, by the author's quick and untrue response, that he fears angering his Majesty.
Answer the following question. Base your answer on the passage from *Erewhon*. What is his Majesty's reaction to the author's explanation of his watch? Why do you think he responds this way?	The following is part of a possible response: His Majesty is suspicious of the watch, because he refers to it as "dangerous." He probably has never seen a watch before, and his ignorance is making him fearful.

810 • Reading Skills

 TEST-TAKING TIP

Encourage students to take notes while they read a given passage, or to underline or circle words and details that may help them make inferences and predictions.

Practice 1 **Directions:** Read the passage. Then, answer the questions that follow the passage.

from "The Mysterious Affair at Styles," by Agatha Christie

The papers, of course, had been full of the tragedy. Glaring headlines, sandwiched biographies of every member of the household, subtle innuendoes, the usual familiar tag about the police having a clue. Nothing was spared us. It was a slack time. The war was momentarily inactive, and the newspapers seized with avidity on this crime in fashionable life: "The Mysterious Affair at Styles" was the topic of the moment.

Naturally it was very annoying for the Cavendishes. The house was constantly besieged by reporters, who were consistently denied admission, but who continued to haunt the village and the grounds, where they lay in wait with cameras, for any unwary members of the household. We all lived in a blast of publicity. The Scotland Yard men came and went, examining, questioning, lynx-eyed and reserved of tongue. Towards what end they were working, we did not know. Had they any clue, or would the whole thing remain in the category of undiscovered crimes?

1 Why are the newspapers making "The Mysterious Affair at Styles" their lead story?
   A They are bored with the regular news.
   B The war is over.
   C The war has slowed down, and they need a good headline.
   D The Cavendishes were fashionable.

2 How would you describe the newspaper's coverage of "The Mysterious Affair at Styles"?
   F hard to read

G silly
H humorous
J thorough

3 Why are the Cavendishes annoyed?
   A They aren't getting enough attention.
   B The newspapers are lying.
   C They have lost their privacy.
   D They can't get into their house.

4 Which inference you can make about the Cavendish family?
   F They are wealthy.
   G They are actors.
   H They are mysterious.
   J They are royalty.

5 What word best describes the reporters?
   A ridiculous
   B persistent
   C relaxed
   D nervous

6 What does the last line of the passage lead you to believe?
   F Scotland Yard knows who committed the crime, but they are not divulging information.
   G It is inconclusive whether or not Scotland Yard knows who committed the crime.
   H Scotland Yard does not know who committed the crime.
   J Scotland Yard wants to put the crime in a category.

Practice 2 **Directions:** Answer the following question. Base your answer on "The Mysterious Affair at Styles."

What do you think the author's attitude toward the police and Scotland Yard is? Why? Use details from the passage to explain your answer.

Answer Key

Practice 1
1. C
2. J
3. C
4. F
5. B
6. G

Practice 2

Responses will vary. Make sure students support their explanations with details from the passage.

Time and Resource Manager

In-Depth Lesson Plan

	LESSON FOCUS	PRINT AND MEDIA RESOURCES
DAY 1	**Basic Study Skills** Students learn and apply basic study skills such as developing a study plan, keeping an assignment book, and taking notes (pp. 812–815).	**Teaching Resources** *Academic and Workplace Skills Activity Book,* pp. 44–45
DAY 2	**Reference Skills** Students learn and apply library reference skills (pp. 816–819).	**Teaching Resources** *Academic and Workplace Skills Activity Book,* pp. 46–52
DAY 3	**Reference Skills (continued)** Students learn and apply reference skills using periodicals, dictionaries, other reference works, and the Internet (pp. 820–826).	**Teaching Resources** *Academic and Workplace Skills Activity Book,* pp. 46–52
DAY 4	**Test-Taking Skills** Students learn such test-taking skills as answering objective, short-answer, and essay questions (pp. 827–832).	**Teaching Resources** *Academic and Workplace Skills Activity Book,* pp. 53–54; *Formal Assessment,* Ch. 33

Accelerated Lesson Plan

	LESSON FOCUS	PRINT AND MEDIA RESOURCES
DAY 1	**Basic Study Skills** Students learn and apply basic study skills such as developing a study plan, keeping an assignment book, and taking notes (pp. 812–815).	**Teaching Resources** *Academic and Workplace Skills Activity Book,* pp. 44–45
DAY 2	**Reference Skills** Students learn and apply library reference skills and skills in using periodicals, dictionaries, other reference works, and the Internet (pp. 816–826).	**Teaching Resources** *Academic and Workplace Skills Activity Book,* pp. 46–52
DAY 3	**Test-Taking Skills** Students learn such test-taking skills as answering objective, short-answer, and essay questions (pp. 827–832).	**Teaching Resources** *Academic and Workplace Skills Activity Book,* pp. 53–54; *Formal Assessment,* Ch. 33

Options for Adapting Lesson Plans

HOMEWORK

Have students complete any section of the chapter for homework.

FEATURES

Extend coverage with the the Standardized Test Preparation Workshop (p. 832).

TECHNOLOGY

Students can use the On-Line Exercise Bank to complete the exercises on computer. The Auto Check feature will grade their work.

INTEGRATED SKILLS COVERAGE

Technology
Integrating Technology Skills
ATE p. 824, 825

Viewing and Representing
Critical Viewing SE pp. 812, 814, 817, 825, 828

ASSESSMENT SUPPORT

Standardized Test Preparation SE p. 832; ATE p. 829
Standardized Test Preparation Workbook, pp. 65–66
Formal Assessment, Ch. 33

MEETING INDIVIDUAL NEEDS

Less Advanced Students ATE pp. 815, 817, 818, 826; See also
Ongoing Assessments ATE pp. 815,818, 823, 825, 828, 830
ESL Students ATE p. 821

BLOCK SCHEDULING

Pacing Suggestions
For 90-minute Blocks
• Have students complete the necessary exercises in class.

Resources for Varying Instruction
• *Language Lab* **CD-ROM** If your students have access to hardware, a 90-minute block provides an ideal opportunity for students to work on computer.

Professional Development Support
• *How to Manage Instruction in the Block* This teaching Resource provides management and activity suggestions.

MEDIA AND TECHNOLOGY

For the Teacher
• *Resource Pro* **CD-ROM**

WRITING AND GRAMMAR WEBSITE

The Interactive Writing and Grammar Website provides a wide array of support for students, teachers, and parents. Grammar support includes:
• *On-Line Exercise Bank* with Auto Check scoring
• Diagnostic and assessment support

phwg.phschool.com

▶ **Lesson Objectives**

1. To learn how to set up a study area and create a study schedule.

2. To practice using an assignment book.

3. To use a modified outline to take notes and to practice writing summaries.

4. To learn how to use the library catalog to find fiction books, nonfiction books, biographies, and reference books.

5. To learn the types and information contained in dictionaries.

6. To learn how to use an encyclopedia.

7. To learn to use an almanac.

8. To become familiar with atlases, gazetteers, and electronic map collections.

9. To practice using and judging the reliability of Websites.

10. To learn how to budget time for test preparation.

11. To understand different kinds of objective questions and strategies for answering them.

Critical Viewing

Deduce Most students will probably say that the boy is studying science.

Chapter 33 Study, Reference, and Test-Taking Skills

Studying, researching, taking tests—all are vital skills to develop as you progress through school. Most of these skills will also come in handy later in life as you train on the job or pursue your personal interests. In this chapter, you will learn how to make the most of your study time. You will also learn more about researching information in printed and electronic sources. Finally, you will receive valuable tips that can help improve your test scores.

▲ **Critical Viewing**
What subject do you think this student is studying? Why do you think so?
[Deduce]

⏱ **TIME AND RESOURCE MANAGER**	
Resources **Print:** Academic and Workplace Skills Activity Book, pp. 44–45	
In-Depth Coverage	**Accelerated Pace**
• Work through all key concepts, pp. 812–815. • Assign and review Exercises 1–4.	• Assign pp. 812–815 for independent student review. • Assign Exercises 1–4.

Basic Study Skills

Good study habits require time, organization, and practice. You need to schedule your study time in a suitable study area, keep track of assignments, and keep an organized notebook in which you take useful notes.

Developing a Study Plan

To study effectively, you need a space where there are no distractions, a space that you associate only with studying. It is also important to schedule set times in which to study. Plan your days so that you have enough time for studying, extra-curricular activities, chores, and relaxation.

KEY CONCEPT Establish a workable study area and regular periods for studying. ■

Plan a schedule that fits your personal needs. Vary the amount of time spent on each subject, depending on upcoming tests and long-term projects. Allow extra review time for those subjects that are challenging for you.

Study Schedule		
	7–8:00	8:00–9:00
Mon	Daily assignments	Study for math test tomorrow
Tues	Daily assignments	Work on research project / Review for Friday's science test
Wed	Review for Friday's science test / Daily assignments	More review for Friday's science test

Exercise 1 **Planning Your Study Schedule** Develop your own study schedule, using the sample as a model. Follow your schedule for a week. Then, evaluate it and make any needed changes. Keep a copy in your notebook.

▶ **More Practice**

Academic and Workplace Skills Activity Book
• p. 44

PREPARE and ENGAGE

Interest GRABBER Ask students to name favorite singers, athletes, and actors. What do they like about these people? What makes them noteworthy in their professions? Explain that all performers achieve success through hard work and practice. Even at the pinnacle of their professions, they work out, rehearse, practice, memorize lines. In short, they study.

Activate Prior Knowledge

Ask students to describe the conditions that produce their best studying. Where and how do they work?

TEACH

Step-by-Step Teaching Guide

Developing a Study Plan

1. Have students share their own tricks in adapting their home environments to carve out privacy and create effective study areas.

2. A first goal in creating a study schedule is to get students thinking in terms of time management and planning.

3. Ask students to recall the last two or three days and how they spent their study time. Review the text suggestions. Have students compare their study schedule with the text and make suggestions about what changes they could make.

Answer Key

Exercise 1

Students' schedules will vary but should follow the model.

Keeping an Assignment Book

1. Review the sample assignment book.

2. There is no "right" method for keeping an assignment book as long as all assignments are entered and students look at the book every day. Encourage students to explore what works best for them.

3. You might help students keep track of assignments by listing them each time in the same place on the board.

4. Encourage students to set up a buddy system for keeping track of assignments, especially after absences.

Answer Key

Exercise 2

Students' assignment books will vary but should follow the model.

33.1

Keeping an Assignment Book Instead of trusting your memory to recall homework and long-term projects, write them down in an assignment book that shows the due dates clearly.

▶ **KEY CONCEPT** Use an assignment book to record homework, long-range projects, and their due dates. ■

One simple way to set up your assignment book is to make four columns on each page. Use one column for subjects, one for detailed descriptions of assignments, one for dates the assignments are due, and one for checks when the assignments are completed. The sample below from an assignment book lists two short-term homework assignments and a long-term science project. Notice how the long-term project is divided into a series of steps.

▲ **Critical Viewing**
What subject do you think this student is working on? Give reasons for your answer. **[Speculate]**

Assignments - October 13			
Subject	Description	Date Due	Completed
Math	Exercise 4, p. 32	10/14	✓
English	Read Act 1, Romeo & Juliet	10/15	✓
Science	Science Fair Satellite Model	1/20	
	1. Do library research	11/2	✓
	2. Draw up plan with Jo	11/9	✓
	3. Submit plan to Mrs. S	11/9	✓
	4. Meet with Mrs. S	11/16	

▶ **Exercise 2** Setting Up an Assignment Book In a special section of your notebook or a separate notebook, set up an assignment book. Date each page and record assignments, using the sample above as a model.

Taking Notes

To understand and remember what you learn, it is important to take notes. Organize your notebook by school subject. Then, in the appropriate sections, take notes on what you learn in class as well as what you read in textbooks.

▶ **KEY CONCEPT** Use a modified outline to take notes while listening or reading. ■

One of the best ways to take notes quickly is to use a *modified outline form*, in which you list main ideas along the margin, indent to show major details, and indent further to show more supporting details.

MODIFIED OUTLINE

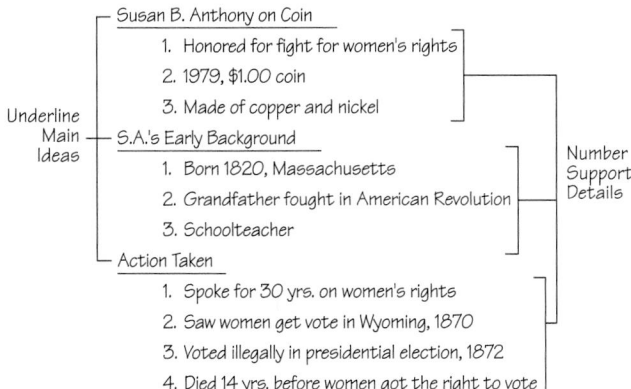

▶ **KEY CONCEPT** Write summaries of chapters or lectures to review what you have learned. ■

After reading a chapter or attending a class, summarize by identifying the main points and explaining how they are connected. Write your summary in your notebook, and use it to review at a later time.

▶ **Exercise 3** **Taking Notes in Outline Form** Choose a section in your mathematics textbook, and take notes on the important information. Use a modified outline form.

▶ **Exercise 4** **Making a Summary** Write a summary of a chapter or section of your social studies book.

▶ **More Practice**

Academic and Workplace Skills Activity Book
• pp. 44–45

Basic Study Skills • **815**

☑ **ONGOING ASSESSMENT: Monitor and Reinforce**

If some students are having difficulty mastering note-taking skills, use one of the following options.

| **Option 1** Work with students in creating outlines that list the main idea and supporting details in each paragraph. | **Option 2** Have students work in small groups and share ideas on how to take notes from class materials. |

Step-by-Step Teaching Guide

Taking Notes

1. Remind students that nobody can remember everything. Even the best students take notes.

2. Use an overhead to display examples of good and poor note taking. Lead a discussion of the specific pluses and minuses of each example.

3. Review the modified outline in the text and ask students for other ideas about taking notes. Some may jot down main ideas and important supporting information in the order in which they appear in the text. Suggest strategies such as going back over notes and using highlighters to code main ideas and supporting ideas.

4. Point out that summaries are useful for distilling the main ideas of a chapter or lecture.

5. Tell students that not everyone takes notes in *exactly* the same way. What counts is how effective the notes are in organizing information and helping students retain and retrieve it.

Customize for
Less Advanced Students

Students can have problems organizing information in order to take notes or summarize. Work with them on learning to recognize a main idea and supporting details. Use an essay that features strong topic sentences with main ideas and several supporting details. Show students how the main ideas and one or two details per paragraph can be put into an outline or summary.

Answer Key

▶ **Exercises 3 and 4**

Students' outlines and summaries will vary.

Using the Library: An Overview

1. Discuss how to find books in a library. Libraries use different systems to make it easy to locate books. Tell students that before computers, all libraries had card catalogs. Card catalogs are organized by author, title, and subject. Libraries also use a numbering system, which students will learn about on page 818.

2. Review each entry on the card in the text, making sure that students understand the relevance of each of them.

3. Explain to students that all catalog systems are based on alphabetical order. For quick practice, write the following author names on the board and ask students to alphabetize them by last name.

   Maya Angelou

   Julia Alvarez

   Hans Christian Andersen

   Isaac Asimov

   Jane Austen

   Chinua Achebe

   Margaret Atwood

   Sherwood Anderson

   (Achebe, Alvarez, Andersen, Anderson, Angelou, Asimov, Atwood, Austen)

Section 33.2

Reference Skills

You are living in what has been called the Information Age. To access the wealth of information available, you need to develop your reference skills. Just about every major form of printed reference now has its electronic equivalent on either CD-ROM, the Internet, or both. Many of the works, in both printed and electronic form, are available at school or public libraries.

Using the Library: An Overview

Most school and public libraries contain at least some of these resources: fiction and nonfiction books, audiocassettes and videocassettes, periodicals (newspapers, magazines, and scholarly journals), microfilm, vertical files of pamphlets and other small printed material, reference works in printed and electronic form, and computer access to the Internet.

▶ **KEY CONCEPT** Use the library catalog to find valuable information about the resources that a library contains. ■

The library catalog will be in one of these three forms:

Card Catalog This system lists books on index cards, with a separate *author card* and *title card* for each book. If the book is nonfiction, it also has at least one *subject card*. Cards are filed alphabetically in small drawers, with author cards alphabetized by last names and title cards alphabetized by the first words of the titles, excluding *A*, *An*, and *The*.

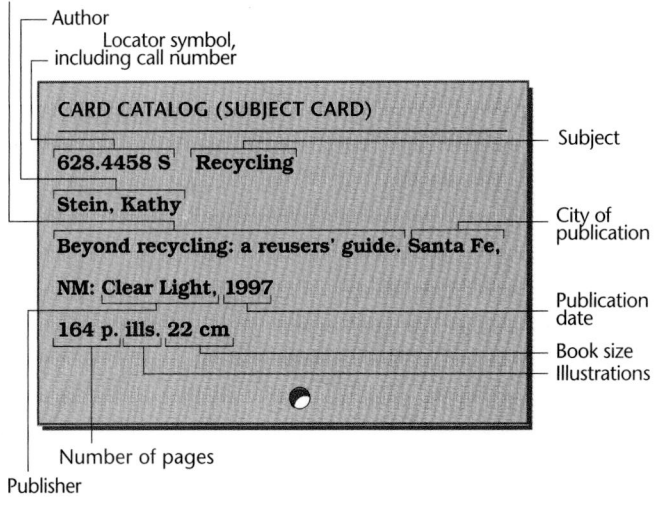

Full title
— Author
    Locator symbol,
— including call number

CARD CATALOG (SUBJECT CARD)
              — Subject
628.4458 S   **Recycling**
Stein, Kathy
             — City of publication
Beyond recycling: a reusers' guide. Santa Fe,
NM: Clear Light, 1997
             — Publication date
164 p. ills. 22 cm
             — Book size
             — Illustrations

Number of pages

Publisher

⏱ TIME AND RESOURCE MANAGER

Resources
Print: Academic and Workplace Skills Activity Book, pp. 46–52

In-Depth Coverage	Accelerated Pace
• Cover pp. 816–826 in class. • Assign and review Exercises 5–12.	• Assign pp. 816–826 for independent student review. • Assign Exercises 5–12.

Printed Catalog This catalog lists books in printed booklets, with each book listed alphabetically by author, by title, and—if nonfiction—by subject. Often, there are separate booklets for author, title, and subject listings.

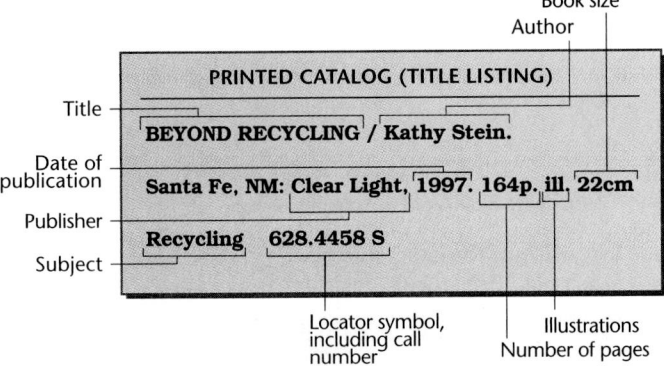

Book size
Author
Title
PRINTED CATALOG (TITLE LISTING)
BEYOND RECYCLING / Kathy Stein.
Date of publication
Santa Fe, NM: Clear Light, 1997. 164p. ill. 22cm
Publisher
Recycling   628.4458 S
Subject
Locator symbol, including call number
Illustrations
Number of pages

▼ Critical Viewing
What key words could this student type in to access the book listed in the printed catalog art at left? [Apply]

Electronic Catalog
An electronic catalog lists books in a CD-ROM or on-line database that you access from special computer terminals in the library. Usually, you can access an entry by typing in a title, key words in the title, an author's name, or, for nonfiction, an appropriate subject.

Exercise 5 **Using the Library Catalog** Visit your school or local library, and answer these questions.
1. What kind of catalog does the library use: card, printed, or electronic? Where is it located?
2. Who wrote *Little Women*? Is it fiction or nonfiction?
3. What are the titles, subjects, and call numbers of two books that your library carries by author Bill Bryson?
4. What are the titles, authors, and call numbers of three books about Mexico published since 1985?
5. What are the titles, authors, and call numbers of two nonfiction books about birds that are more than 100 pages long?

More Practice
Academic and Workplace Skills Activity Book
• p. 44

1. Many libraries have installed electronic catalogs. If your library has one, take students there and have them practice looking up books. If necessary, use a peer support system to have students who are familiar with the catalog help others learn how to use it.
2. If your library does not have an electronic catalog, review each entry on the text example. Explain that electronic catalogue systems have slightly different ways of operating. Usually there are on-screen directions, but in any case, students can always ask a librarian for help. That is what the librarian is there for.

Customize for
Less Advanced Students

Alphabetizing is a skill that is crucial to using a library catalog. Work with students as they practice alphabetizing to the third and fourth letter.

Critical Viewing

Apply Students might mention terms such as *recycling* or *Stein.*

Answer Key

Exercise 5

1. Answers will vary according to the libraries students visit.
2. Louisa May Alcott; fiction
3. Answers will vary.
4. Answers will vary.
5. Answers will vary.

Find Books on Library Shelves

1. Remind students that fiction books are arranged alphabetically according to the author's last name. Books by the same author are then arranged alphabetically by title.

2. It is not always clear from a title whether a book is fiction or nonfiction. If they are not sure, students should consult the catalog under the author or title entry.

3. Review the Dewey Decimal System. For additional practice, write the following numbers on the board and ask students to supply the category of the Dewey Decimal System.

    268 (religion)

    655 (technology)

    923 (history)

    481 (languages)

    742 (arts and leisure)

4. Scramble the following call numbers as you write them on the board and ask students to arrange them in the proper order for additional practice: *925.2, 925.23A, 925.3H, 925.31D, 925.9, 926.2, 928.1.*

continued

Customize for
Less Advanced Students

Some students may be unfamiliar with the terms for each category. *Philosophy* is the study of basic beliefs and ideas about life; the *social sciences* include history, economics (business), society (sociology), other cultures (anthropology), and psychology (how our minds and feelings work); the *sciences* are biology, physics, chemistry, and geology; *technology* is the study of how things work.

33.2

Finding Books on Library Shelves The library distinguishes between two kinds of books: *fiction* (made-up stories) and *nonfiction* (factual material). Nonfiction also includes two smaller groups that are often shelved separately: *biographies* and *reference books.*

▶ **KEY CONCEPT** Fiction and nonfiction books are shelved separately in the library, and each follows a special method of organization. ■

Most school and public libraries use the **Dewey Decimal System** to classify books. The Dewey Decimal System divides all knowledge into ten main classes, numbered from 000 to 999. The first digit on the left tells you the general subject.

This chart shows the number spans for the content areas.

MAIN CLASSES OF THE DEWEY DECIMAL SYSTEM	
Number	**Subject**
000–099	General Works (encyclopedias, periodicals, etc.)
100–199	Philosophy
200–299	Religion
300–399	Social Sciences
400–499	Languages
500–599	Science
600–699	Technology (applied science)
700–799	Arts and Leisure
800–899	Literature
900–999	History

Fiction Books In most libraries, fiction books (literature) are shelved in a special section and are alphabetized by authors' last names. In the library catalog and on its spine, a work of fiction may be labeled *F* or *FIC*, followed by one or more letters of the author's last name.

Nonfiction Books Nonfiction books are assigned different numbers and letters. These number-letter codes, called *call numbers,* are placed on the spine of each book, and the books are arranged in number-letter order on the shelves; for example, 619.1, 619.2, 619.31A, 619.31D, 619.32A. To find a nonfiction book, you look it up in the library catalog, find its call number, and then follow number-letter order to locate the book on the shelves.

Biographies Life stories of real people are technically 921 in the Dewey Decimal System. Sometimes, however, biographies are not assigned call numbers but instead are shelved in a special section alphabetized by the last names of their subjects (the people they are about). In the library catalog and on

818 • Study, Reference, and Test-Taking Skills

◉ **Technology Tip**

In electronic database searches, be sure to type carefully and spell everything correctly. One wrong letter often means inaccurate results.

🖉 **ONGOING ASSESSMENT: Monitor and Reinforce**

If some students are having difficulty using the Dewey Decimal System, use the following strategy.

Work with students individually. First, cover up the numbers and letters to the right of the decimal point and have students identify the section where the book will be located. Then have students work with the characters to the right of the decimal point individually—first the numbers and then the letters.

the book's spine, a biography may be labeled *B* or *BIO*, followed by one or more letters of the subject's last name; for example, *BIO Lin* may appear on a biography of Abraham Lincoln.

Reference Books These types of books may also be shelved in their own special section of a library. Frequently, the sources in the library's reference section are labeled *R* or *REF*. Because the book is nonfiction, a call number follows the abbreviation. Thus, if a book you look up in the card catalog has *REF* before its call number, go first to the library's reference section and then use the call number to locate the book on the shelves in that section.

Many college and research libraries use the **Library of Congress System.**

Library of Congress System

A	General Works	L	Education
B	Philosophy, Psychology, Religion	M	Music
		N	Fine Arts
C	History	P	Language and Literature
D	General History	Q	Science
E–F	American History	R	Medicine
G	Geography, Anthropology, Recreation	S	Agriculture
		T	Technology
H	Social Sciences	U	Military Science
J	Political Science	V	Naval Science
K	Law	Z	Bibliography and Library Science

► Exercise 6 Finding Books on Library Shelves

1. To find fiction by Louise Erdrich, would you look before or after fiction by Elizabeth Enright?
2. To find a nonfiction book with the call number 910.72M, would you look before or after a book with the call number 911.30B?
3. For a book with call number J523.4R, would you look in the reference, biography, or children's nonfiction section?
4. Arrange these works of fiction in the order in which you would find them on the library shelves: *Child of the Owl* by Laurence Yep, *White Fang* by Jack London, *The Left Hand of Darkness* by Ursula K. LeGuin, *Pedro Paramo* by Juan Rulfo, *Zeely* by Virginia Hamilton.
5. Arrange these call numbers in the order in which you would find them on the library shelves: 598.2P, 598.3A, 598.1L, 597.6Z, 599.1S. What would be the general subject matter of these books?

► **More Practice**

Academic and Workplace Skills Activity Book
• pp. 46–47

Step-by-Step Teaching continued

5. Have students put the following subjects of biographies in alphabetical order.

   John Hancock

   John Quincy Adams

   Alexander Hamilton

   John Adams

   Charles Francis Adams

   Thomas Jefferson

   Abigail Adams

   Henry Adams

   Samuel Adams

   (Abigail Adams, Charles Francis Adams, Henry Adams, John Adams, John Quincy Adams, Samuel Adams, Alexander Hamilton, John Hancock, Thomas Jefferson)

6. Reference books are shelved in a special section. Reference books stay in the library and cannot be borrowed.

7. Ask students to name different types of reference books. Encyclopedias, dictionaries, almanacs, and atlases are reference books.

Answer Key

Exercise 6

1. after
2. before
3. nonfiction
4. *Zeely, The Left Hand of Darkness, White Fang, Pedro Paramo, Child of the Owl*
5. 597.6Z, 598.1L, 598.2P, 598.3A, 599.1S; science

Using Periodicals, Periodical Indexes, and the Vertical File

1. Tell students that *periodical* is another word for magazine. Periodicals are issued at different periods of time—weekly, monthly or semi-monthly, for instance—hence the name.

2. Periodicals are good sources of information. A periodical index is a very handy tool. Instead of looking through stacks of magazines for an article on a topic, students can look up the topic in the periodical index and be directed to articles in different periodicals.

3. Most libraries keep back copies of periodicals in the reference section, and these copies do not circulate. Most libraries do have photocopying machines available. For long articles, it may be necessary to read the article in the library and take notes on relevant areas.

33.2

Using Periodicals, Periodical Indexes, and the Vertical File

Periodicals are printed materials, such as newspapers and magazines, that are published on a regular basis. To find all the articles on a particular subject in periodicals, you need to consult a *periodical index*. You can find the information contained in booklets or pamphlets in the *vertical file*.

> **KEY CONCEPT** Use periodicals to find current information, use periodical indexes to find articles in periodicals, and use the vertical file to find small printed materials. ■

Periodical Indexes When you want to find articles on a particular subject, you need to consult the periodical index. Periodical indexes, issued in printed or electronic form, are published or updated regularly. They cite articles that appeared during a specified period of time. Some periodical indexes cover articles from many periodicals; others cover articles from only one newspaper or magazine.

Citations in periodical indexes provide the information you need to find an article; namely, the title and date of the publication in which the article appears.

In *printed indexes*, citations are listed alphabetically by subject or author. The citations in printed indexes also may contain *abstracts*, or brief summaries, of the articles. In *electronic indexes*, citations appear in a database that you can search by subject, the author's name, or a key word or phrase. Some electronic indexes also provide the *full text*, or complete article, for some or all of the articles cited.

Below is a sample citation from a recent print edition of the *Readers' Guide to Periodical Literature:*

SAMPLE READERS' GUIDE ENTRY

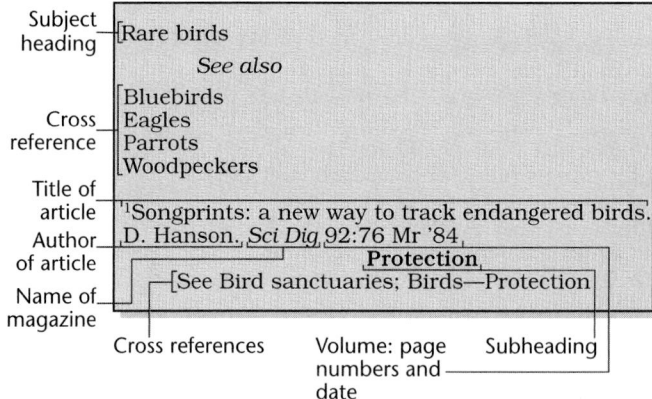

Technology Tip

Many leading newspapers and magazines have free Internet sites where you can read current editions of the material.

The Vertical File The vertical file is a special filing cabinet used to house small printed materials of various kinds, such as pamphlets, booklets, folded maps, newspaper and magazine clippings, and photographs. The materials are placed in files that are labeled and arranged alphabetically by subject.

> **Exercise 7** **Using Periodicals and Periodical Indexes** Visit your school or local library to answer these questions on periodicals and periodical indexes.
> 1. What newspapers does the library carry?
> 2. Give the titles of three newsmagazines the library carries. Find out how far back each goes and in what format(s) they are given.
> 3. Use a periodical index to find citations for articles on a subject you are studying in science or social studies. Then, find at least one of the articles in your library.

> **Exercise 8** **Exploring the Vertical File** Find out whether your school or library has a vertical file. If it does, survey and summarize the main kinds of materials that it contains.

Using Dictionaries

A dictionary tells you how words are pronounced, how they are used in a sentence, and, often, the word's history.

> **KEY CONCEPT** Dictionaries contain a wealth of information about words. ∎

Distinguishing Types of Dictionaries All dictionaries are not the same. Some dictionaries are for scholars; others are for general readers; still others are intended for people studying a special field.

THREE TYPES OF DICTIONARIES

Unabridged	Exhaustive study of the English language containing more than 250,000 words
Abridged	Compact edition containing listings of 55,000 to 160,000 words
Specialized	Edition limited to words of a particular field, such as foreign languages or mathematics

> **More Practice**
> Academic and
> Workplace Skills
> Activity Book
> • p. 47

Reference Skills • 821

Step-by-Step Teaching Guide

Using Dictionaries

An abridged dictionary should be sufficient for students' needs. Furthermore, abridged dictionaries are updated more often than are unabridged dictionaries. Often a newer, smaller dictionary is better than an older, bigger one.

Customize for ESL Students

Urge students to consult a bilingual dictionary whenever the need arises. If necessary, reassure students that this is not cheating. If you think student's finances will permit it, suggest that it might be a good idea to purchase a paperback bilingual dictionary and carry it in their backpacks at all times.

Answer Key

> **Exercises 7 and 8**

Students responses will vary according to various libraries' resources and students' interests.

Find Words in Dictionaries

1. To locate entries efficiently, students need to be able to use guide words. Write the following exercise on the chalkboard, asking students to match the guide words with the word on that page:

1. returnable/revere   a. revise
2. restorer/retaliate   b. reptile
3. repro/require   c. restrict
4. revere/reviver   d. reveal

(1 d; 2 c; 3 b; 4 a)

continued

33.2

Finding Words in Dictionaries A word listed in a dictionary, along with all the information about it, is called an *entry*.

In **printed dictionaries,** all the items are listed in strict **alphabetical order.** To speed your search for a word, use these features:

- **Thumb Index** This series of right-hand notches makes it easier to thumb alphabetically through the dictionary. Each notch, labeled *A, B,* and so on, shows the section of entries for words that start with that particular letter.

- **Guide Words** At the top of a dictionary page appear the first and last words covered on the page. All other entries on the page are for words that fall alphabetically between the two guide words. For instance, if the guide words are *need* and *neglect, needle* and *negative* will also be on the page; *necessary* will not be on that page.

In **electronic dictionaries,** you usually find a word's entry simply by typing the word and having the computer search the dictionary database.

Understanding Dictionary Entries In a dictionary, a word and all the information about it are called a *main entry.* The word itself is called an *entry word.*

1. Entry Word This may may be a single word, a compound word (two or more words acting as a single word), an abbreviation, a prefix or suffix, or the name of a person or place. Dots, spaces, or slashes in an entry word indicate the syllables. When you break a word at the end of a line, remember that you cannot leave a syllable of just one letter on a line by itself. Words with one syllable are never divided.

Ⓠ Learn More

For information on how dictionaries can help improve your vocabulary, see Chapter 32.

SAMPLE DICTIONARY ENTRY

① **liv·ery** (liv´ər ē) *n.,* pl. **-er·ies** [ME, allowance of food, gift of clothes to a servant, thing delivered <OFr *livree,* pp. of *livrer,* to deliver < L *liberare,* to LIBERATE] **1** an identifying uniform such as was formerly worn by feudal retainers or is now worn by servants or those in some particular group, trade, etc. **2** the people wearing such uniforms **3** characteristic dress or appearance **4** a) the keeping and feeding of horses for a fixed charge b) the keeping of horses, vehicles, or both, for hire ☆c) LIVERY STABLE ☆**5** a place where boats can be rented **6** [Historical] *Eng. Law* the legal delivery of property, esp. landed property, into the hands of the new owner.

② ③ ④ ⑤ ⑥ ⑦

2. Pronunciation Appearing right after the entry word, the pronunciation uses symbols to show how to say the word. The syllable that gets the most emphasis has a *primary stress*, usually shown by a heavy mark after the syllable ('). Words of more than one syllable may also have a *secondary stress*, usually shown by a shorter, lighter mark (').

3. Part-of-Speech Label A dictionary also tells you how a word can be used in a sentence—whether it functions as a noun, verb, or some other part of speech. This information is given in abbreviated form, usually after the pronunciation.

4. Plurals and Inflected Forms After the part-of-speech label, a dictionary may also show the plural forms of nouns and inflected forms of verbs—past tense and participle forms—if there is anything irregular about their spelling.

5. Etymology The origin and history of a word is called its *etymology*. The etymology usually appears in brackets, parentheses, or slashes near the start or end of the entry. Abbreviations (explained in the dictionary's key to abbreviations) are often used for languages.

6. Definition A definition is the meaning of a word. Definitions are numbered if there are more than one. Often, they include an example illustrating the use of the particular meaning in a phrase or sentence.

7. Usage Labels Such labels note how the word is generally used. Words labeled *Archaic (Arch.)*, *Obsolete (Obs.)*, *Poetic*, or *Rare* are not widely used today. Those labeled *Informal (Inf.)*, *Colloquial (Colloq.)*, or *Slang* are not considered part of formal English. Those labeled *Brit.* are used mainly in Britain, not in the United States.

8. Field Labels These labels indicate whether a word is used in a special way by people in a certain occupation or activity, such as *History (Hist.)*, *Mathematics (Math.)*, or *Chemistry (Chem.)*

9. Idioms and Derived Words The end of an entry may list and define idioms or expressions that contain the entry word. It may also list derived words, words formed from the entry word, and a part-of-speech label.

> **Exercise 9** **Working With a Dictionary** Use a dictionary to answer the following questions.
> 1. In what order would these entry words appear?
>   dolphin—knife—hand—length—mushroom
> 2. Which of these entry words would appear on a page with the guide words *contempt* and *continuation*?
>   contact—contemptuous—contest—continue—continuity
> 3. What two guide words appear on the page with *neutron*?
> 4. Which word is not spelled correctly?
>   lollipop—gasoline—kindergarden—judgment—license
> 5. Which word is spelled correctly?
>   inflamable—psychology—truely—nesessary—tomorow

⊚ Technology Tip

Abridged electronic dictionaries are now available in a format similar to pocket calculators. Foreign-language dictionaries in this format may be especially useful to travelers.

▶ **More Practice**

Academic and Workplace Skills Activity Book
• p. 48

Reference Skills • **823**

Step-by-Step Teaching continued

2. Review the pronunciation of *livery*. Dictionaries include a key of pronunciation symbols, usually at the bottom of each right-hand page.

3. Explain the etymology of *livery*. It comes from Middle English (ME). The < symbols trace the word even farther back—in this case to Old French, and originally to Latin.

4. If a word has a regular plural *(bird/birds)*, the plural will not be listed. *Livery* has an irregular plural, so its ending is given. The plural is *liveries*.

Answer Key

Exercise 9

1. dolphin; hand; knife; length; mushroom
2. contemptuous, contest
3. Answers will vary according to the dictionaries used by students.
4. kindergarden (kindergarten)
5. psychology

☑ **ONGOING ASSESSMENT: Monitor and Reinforce**

If some students are having difficulty using a dictionary, use one of the following options.

Option 1 Urge poor spellers to keep trying possible spellings of a word: *porpus, porpis, porpoise,* for example.	**Option 2** Students may not be able to decipher the small print because of a previously undetected vision problem. A trip to the school nurse may be called for.

Using Other Reference Works

1. Ask students to describe their experiences using an encyclopedia. What topics have they looked up? Why?

2. Encyclopedias are often good starting points for research. Any encyclopedia, for instance, will have an entry on Rosa Parks or baseball. An encyclopedia of African American women or sports would be a good next step, for instance, if a student were writing about Parks.

continued

Integrating Technology Skills

If resources are available, check to see whether or not students know how to use an electronic encyclopedia. They should know how to look up subjects, use highlighted words to cross-reference subject matter, print out articles, or copy and paste them onto a disk.

33.2

Using Other Reference Works

Periodical indexes and dictionaries are two examples of *reference works,* resources to which you refer for information instead of reading in their entirety. Most reference works—available in both printed and electronic form—are usually found in the reference section of the library.

> **KEY CONCEPT** Use articles in encyclopedias to get an overview of a variety of subjects. ■

Encyclopedias When you are investigating an unfamiliar subject, one of the best places to start is a general encyclopedia. A *general encyclopedia* is a collection of articles that provide basic information on a great many subjects. If you want to find more comprehensive and detailed articles in a particular subject area, use a *specialized encyclopedia.*

Printed encyclopedias list articles alphabetically by subject or, when the subject is a person, by last name. Encyclopedias usually span several volumes, with letters or words on each spine to show you which subjects that volume contains. In *electronic encyclopedias,* you can usually find articles by typing the subject or a key term and then having the computer search the encyclopedia database. You may also be able to browse an alphabetical list of subjects.

Biographical References These books provide brief histories of all kinds of famous people. Biographical references may offer short entries similar to those in dictionaries or longer articles more like those in encyclopedias.

Almanacs Annually issued handbooks, almanacs provide various lists and statistics on a host of subjects, including government, history, geography, weather, science, technology, industry, sports, and entertainment. To find a subject in a *printed almanac,* refer to the index, which may be at the front or back of the book. In an *electronic almanac,* you can usually find information by typing a subject or key word.

Atlases, Gazetteers, and Electronic Map Collections
Atlases and *electronic map collections* contain maps and geographical information based on them, such as cities, bodies of water, mountains, and landmarks. Some also supply statistics about population, climate, agricultural and industrial production, natural resources, and so on.

In *printed atlases,* use the index to learn on which map to look for a particular place. A *gazetteer* is a dictionary or index of place names. Often, it gives populations and sizes. You may find a gazetteer at the back of an atlas or a textbook. In *electronic atlases,* or map collections, you usually type the place name and have the computer search the database for the appropriate map.

Technology Tip

Electronic maps often have zoom and other features in which you simply click the mouse to enlarge or change the area shown.

◄ **Critical Viewing**
How do you think these students found the books they are reading? What methods may have been available to them? **[Speculate]**

Thesauruses A specialized dictionary, a thesaurus gives extensive lists of *synonyms*, or words with similar meanings. It may also list *antonyms*, or words with opposite meanings.

Many *printed thesauruses* arrange words alphabetically. Some arrange them thematically. For these thesauruses, you must look up the word in the index and then turn to the appropriate section to find its synonyms. In *electronic thesauruses*, you usually type in the word and have the computer search the database.

Exercise 10 **Using Other Reference Works** Use printed or electronic reference works to find answers to these questions. Indicate the type of reference you used.
1. Who was the first American woman to walk in space?
2. What did Europe's national borders look like in 1945?
3. List the title, editor, publisher, and publication date of an anthology that contains Sara Teasdale's poem "Barter."
4. Find a quotation about love from any work by William Shakespeare. Include the name of the work.
5. What are five synonyms for the verb *offer*?

Exercise 11 **Using All Types of Reference Works** Give at least two specific examples of something you would research in each of the following types of references.
1. atlas
2. almanac
3. thesaurus
4. dictionary
5. periodical index

More Practice

Academic and Workplace Skills Activity Book
• pp. 47–49

Reference Skills • 825

Step-by-Step Teaching Guide continued

3. Encourage students to recognize that almanacs are fun. Invite students to use an almanac to identify the deepest ocean, the fastest animal, the hottest temperature ever recorded, and the tallest volcano.
4. Explore the information contained in atlases and gazetteers. Encourage students to compare maps of their neighborhood, city, and state.

Integrating Technology

Check to see that all students know how to use the electronic thesaurus on the word processor.

Answer Key

Exercise 10
1. Sally Ride
2. Check students' work.
3. Answers will vary.
4. Possible answer: "Love is not love/Which alters when it alteration finds"; Sonnet 116
5. Possible answers: present, advance, award, bid, donate

Exercise 11

Sample answers:
1. States bordering Kansas; capital of Belgium
2. population of Mexico; rankings of oceans by volume
3. synonyms for inherit; antonyms for trust
4. plural form of roof; definitions of obscure
5. three recent magazine articles on the greenhouse effect; editorial endorsements by three major newspapers during 1992 presidential elections

---

✓ ONGOING ASSESSMENT: Monitor and Reinforce

If some students are having difficulty using an almanac, atlas, gazetteer, or thesaurus, use one of the following options.

Option 1 Help students identify how each reference work is organized. Most importantly, see that they know how to use an alphabetical index.

Option 2 Make sure that students can identify the best reference work to consult in a given situation. Both encyclopedias and almanacs contain maps, but an atlas is the better source to consult for geographical information, for instance.

Using the Internet

1. The World Wide Web offers virtually unlimited research possibilities, but it introduces problems such as determining the reliability of sources and monitoring student access to inappropriate information. Ask a knowledgeable volunteer to describe the simple process by which Websites are created. The message to other students should be clear: just because it's on the Web doesn't mean it's true.

2. See that all students know how to connect to the Web and use search engines to find information.

3. For practice, ask students to go to www.weather.com and find out the weather forecast for the next five days in your area.

Customizing for
Less Advanced Students

Though the computer and the Internet can be a big distraction for many students, it can also be a valuable vehicle for reaching and motivating otherwise uninterested students. Customize lessons and assignments so that they might use the computer and the Internet.

Answer Key

> **Exercise 12**

1. 10011
2. Michael Curtiz, director; Humphrey Bogart, Ingrid Bergman, Paul Henreid, Claude Rains, Conrad Veidt, Peter Lorre, Sydney Greenstreet
3. Answers will vary according to students' topics and web searches.
4. Answers will vary.
5. Answers will vary.

826

33.2

Using the Internet

The *Internet* is a worldwide network, or Web, of computers connected over phone and cable lines. When you go *on-line*, or hook up with the Internet, you have access to an almost unlimited number of Web sites where an amazing amount of information can be found. Each Web site has its own address, or *URL* (Universal Resource Locator). The site usually consists of several Web pages of text and graphics, and sometimes audio or video displays, which you can download and save on your computer.

> **KEY CONCEPT** You can use the Internet for all kinds of information, but judge Web sites for reliability. ∎

Here are some guidelines for finding reliable information on the Internet:

- If you know a reliable Web site and its address (URL), simply type the address into your Web browser. Often, television programs, commercials, magazines, newspapers, and radio stations provide Web site addresses where you can find more information about a show, product, company, and so on.

- Consult Internet coverage in library journals (like *Booklist* and *Library Journal*) to learn addresses of Web sites that provide useful and reliable information.

- If you don't know a specific Web site, you can do a general search for a key term on a search engine.

- Remember to bookmark or add to Favorites interesting and reliable sites you find searching the Web.

> **Exercise 12** **Using the Internet** On a library, school, or home computer, use the Internet to do this research.
> 1. Learn the ZIP Code for 1 Fifth Avenue, New York, NY.
> 2. Find the director and cast members of the movie *Casablanca*.
> 3. Choose a topic for a history paper. List names and URLs (addresses) of four Web sites that you think can help you.
> 4. Locate lyrics for a version of the ballad "Barbara Allen." Be sure to record the name and URL (address) of your source.
> 5. From a reliable source, find out about household problems posed by Indian meal moths. Record source information.

826 • Study, Reference, and Test-Taking Skills

⟳ Learn More

For more information on how to use the Internet, see the Internet Handbook section near the back of this book.

> **More Practice**

Academic and Workplace Skills Activity Book
• p. 50

Section 33.3 *Test-Taking Skills*

This section provides strategies that will improve your performance on tests and help you answer the different kinds of questions they may contain.

Answering Objective Questions

If you are familiar with the different kinds of objective questions that are frequently asked on tests, you may improve your performance on the tests.

▶ **KEY CONCEPT** Know the different kinds of objective questions and the strategies for answering them. ■

Multiple-Choice Questions This kind of question asks you to choose from four or five possible responses.

EXAMPLE: The opposite of energetic is ___.
a. frantic   c. busy
b. lethargic   d. certain

In the preceding example, the answer is *b*. Follow these strategies to answer multiple-choice questions:

- Try answering the question before looking at the choices. If your answer is one of the choices, select that choice.
- Eliminate the obviously incorrect answers, crossing them out if you are allowed to write on the test paper.
- Read all the choices before answering. For multiple-choice questions, there are often two possible answers but only one best answer.

Matching Questions Matching questions require that you match items in one group with items in another.

EXAMPLE: ___ 1. functional   a. aware
___ 2. remote   b. explanation
___ 3. interpretation c. hold back
___ 4. refrain   d. working
___ 5. cognizant   e. distant

In the preceding example, the answers are *d, e, b, c,* and *a.* Follow these strategies to answer matching questions:

- Count each group to see if items will be left over. Check the directions to see if items can be used more than once.
- Read all the items before you start matching.
- Match the items you know first.
- Match items about which you are less certain.

Test-Taking Skills • **827**

Test-Taking Skill: Answering Objective Questions

1. For true-or-false questions, the odds on guessing right are 50%, so unless there is a penalty for wrong answers, students should always answer the question even if they do not know the answer.

2. Remind students of the importance of reading the question carefully and of not jumping to conclusions in midsentence.

3. Fill-in questions are harder than true-or-false questions because there are no sample answers to choose from.

Answer Key

Exercise 13

Students' tests will vary in content but should contain five examples of each of the following types of questions: multiple-choice, matching, true-or-false, and fill-in.

Critical Viewing

Connect Students may say he is answering some form of objective questions. Advice will vary.

33.3

True-or-False Questions True-or-false questions require you to identify whether or not a statement is accurate.

EXAMPLE: ___ All citizens vote on Election Day.
___ High-school students always take three math courses.
___ Some schools have a foreign-language requirement.

In the preceding example, the answers are *F, F,* and *T.* Follow these strategies to answer true-or-false questions:

• If a statement seems true, be sure all of it is true.

• Pay special attention to the word *not,* which often changes the whole meaning of a statement.

• Look carefully at the words *all, always, never, no, none,* and *only.* They often make a statement false.

• Notice the words *generally, much, many, most, often, some,* and *usually.* They often make a statement true.

Fill-in Questions A fill-in question asks you to supply an answer in your own words. The answer may complete a statement or it may simply answer a question.

EXAMPLE: An ___?___ is a word that is the opposite of another word.

In the preceding example, the answer is *antonym.* Follow these strategies to answer fill-in questions:

• Read the question or incomplete statement carefully.

• If you are answering a question, change it into a statement by inserting your answer and see if that makes sense.

Exercise 13 **Answering Objective Questions** Using a subject you are studying in a class, prepare a short objective test on the material. Write five multiple-choice questions, five matching questions, five true-or-false questions, and five fill-in questions. Exchange tests with another student, and take the other student's test. Then, exchange again and grade the test.

▲ **Critical Viewing** What kind of test questions do you think this student is answering? What advice could you offer him for test taking? [**Connect**]

☑ **ONGOING ASSESSMENT: Monitor and Reinforce**

If some students are having difficulty answering objective questions, use the following strategy.

Poor test performance often results when students have little idea how to prepare for a test and lack resources such as class and text notes. Set up a workshop situation in which you teach a simple model lesson and work through the preparation of class and text notes. Follow up with a workshop on time management and studying and another on test-taking strategies. Walk students through the test, showing them how they are prepared to answer each question. You could repeat the process, the second time allowing them to take the test on their own. A successful showing will build confidence as well as a skill base to work from in the future.

Answering Analogies An analogy asks you to find pairs of words that express a similar relationship.

EXAMPLE: ELM : TREE ::
          a. whale : mammal   c. cart : horse
          b. painting : artist   d. cloud : rain

In the preceding example, the answer is *a*. The relationship between the pairs of words is *kind*. An elm is a *kind* of tree, and a whale is a *kind* of mammal.

COMMON ANALOGY RELATIONSHIPS

Relationship	Example
Synonym	joy : elation
Antonym	despair : hope
Quality	library : quiet
Degree (greater or lesser)	shout : speak
Part to whole	page : book
Kind	milk : beverage
Sequence	engagement : marriage
Proximity	shore : water
Device	telescope : astronomer

Exercise 14 **Answering Analogies** Choose the pair of words that has the same relationship as the first pair.

1. joy : elation ::
   A happiness : sadness   C wonder : amazement
   B curiosity : fear   D unrest : ease
2. page : book ::
   A sleeve : shirt   C page : paper
   B library : quiet   D hat : head
3. shout : speak ::
   A whisper : talk   C run : dash
   B shout : anger   D run : walk
4. despair : hope ::
   A hunger : eating   C love : hate
   B danger : peril   D shovel : gardener
5. milk : beverage ::
   A cow : horse   C orange : tree
   B carrot : vegetable   D vegetable : fruit

More Practice
Academic and Workplace Skills Activity Book
• pp. 51–52

Test-Taking Skills • 829

STANDARDIZED TEST PREPARATION WORKSHOP

Analogies Standardized test questions may require students to complete analogies. Write the following analogy on the board and ask students to choose the correct answer.

house : village ::

A teenager : grandparent
B carpenter : saw
C hamburger : hot dog
D store : shopping mall

The correct choice is item **D**. A house is part of a village, and a store is part of a shopping mall.

Answering Short-Answer and Essay Questions

1. To answer short-answer and essay questions students can use many of the strategies presented so far: staying calm and using common sense, and reading the question carefully to understand what is being asked, for instance.

2. Discuss what strategies students would use to answer short-answer and essay questions. An outline can be useful in writing essay questions. It enables students to plan their answers and allot their time.

3. Ideally, students should be fully prepared for a test. But in cases where students are not, talk about the strategy of emphasizing what they *do* know in longer essay questions. Since essays are usually graded on content, getting them half or two-thirds of the questions right is better than getting them all wrong. Students should write something, even if their essay does not fully answer the question.

Answer Key

> **Exercise 15**

Students' responses will vary.

830

33.3

Answering Short-Answer and Essay Questions

Some test questions require you to supply an answer, rather than just identifying a correct answer. Identify these questions when you preview the test. Allow time to write complete, accurate answers.

> **KEY CONCEPT** Allow time and space to respond to short-answer and essay questions. ■

Identify Key Words Whether you are responding to a short-answer question or an essay prompt, identify the key words in the test item. Look for words like *discuss, explain, identify,* and any numbers or restrictions. If the question asks for three causes, make sure you supply three.

Check Your Space On some tests, you will be given a certain number of lines on which to write your answer. Make sure you understand whether you are limited to that space or whether you can ask for more paper. If you are limited to a certain amount of space, use it for the most significant and relevant information.

Stick to the Point Do not put down everything you know about a topic. If the question asks you to identify three steps Jefferson took to limit government power, you will not get extra credit for including information about Jefferson's childhood. In fact, including unrelated information may cause you to lose points.

> **Exercise 15** Answering Essays Evaluate an essay answer that you wrote based on what you have learned.

> **More Practice**

Academic and Workplace Skills Activity Book
• pp. 51–52

Types of Standardized Tests

Besides the tests in your subject areas, you will be taking standardized tests. These may include state tests, high-school exit exams, and college board tests such as the SAT and the ACT. Following are descriptions of some of these tests:

PSAT The PSAT is the preliminary SAT. The PSAT is given nationwide and provides students with the opportunity to practice for the SAT. The PSAT has the same format as the SAT with the following exceptions: (1) The PSAT contains fewer sections than the SAT. (2) The PSAT contains items that test your knowledge of usage and mechanics; the SAT does not.

SAT The SAT is used by many colleges as one factor in admissions decisions. It is given nationwide, once a month from October through June except in February. If you are dissatisfied with your SAT scores, you may repeat the test; however, all previous scores will be reported to schools as well as the most recent scores. SAT's have a math portion and a verbal portion. The verbal portion contains the following sections:

1. **Sentence-completion questions** test your knowledge of vocabulary by asking you to fill in a blank within a sentence or passage with an appropriate word.
2. **Analogy questions** are like those on page 829.
3. **Critical-reading questions** are multiple-choice questions asked in response to a pair of related reading passages.
4. **Writing sections** will ask you to respond to a prompt.

ACT The ACT is another test used by colleges as one factor in admissions decisions. The questions—all multiple choice— focus on English, math, reading, and science reasoning. The English portion asks you to identify errors in grammar, usage, mechanics, logic, and organization. The reading portion presents four passages from different content areas, followed by questions that test your reading and reasoning skills.

⊘ Learn More

The Standardized Test Preparation Workshops that appear at the end of every chapter throughout this book provide instruction and practice in all of the types of items covered in these tests.

Types of Standardized Tests

1. Review with students the different types of standardized tests they will encounter.
2. Encourage students who have older siblings to talk to them about their experiences with these standardized tests. Have students share what they have learned with the class.

Reflecting on Your Study, Reference, and Test-Taking Skills

Answer the following questions that will help you think about what you have learned concerning your study, reference, and test-taking habits and skills.

- Which strategies seemed new or unusual? How can using these strategies help me improve my academic performance?

- Which strategies do I already use? Why do I find these most comfortable or useful?

Standardized Test Preparation Workshop

Constructing Meaning From Informational Texts

Standardized test questions usually include questions designed to evaluate your reading skills. This type of question will begin with a nonfiction passage for you to read. You will be given several questions that test your ability to construct meaning from the information provided in the passage. To succeed on the reading segment of standardized tests, you should be able to do the following:

• Identify facts and distinguish between facts and nonfacts, or opinions.

• Identify the stated or implied main idea of a section of the passage.

• Choose the best summary—a brief, clear restatement of the subject and main ideas.

Sample Test Item	Answer and Explanation
Directions: Read the passage. Then, read each question that follows the passage. Decide which is the best answer to each question. On April 15, 1755, Dr. Samuel Johnson—blind in one eye, impoverished, and incompletely educated—produced the first modern *Dictionary of the English Language.*	

1 Which of the following is an OPINION expressed in the passage?
 	
  A Dr. Johnson was impoverished.
 	
  B On April 15, 1755, Dr. Samuel Johnson produced the first modern *Dictionary of the English Language.*
 	
  C Dr. Johnson wanted to be remembered for his dictionary.
 	
  D Dr. Samuel Johnson was blind in one eye.
	Choices *A*, *B*, and *D* reflect provable facts stated in the passage. Although Dr. Johnson may have wanted to be remembered for his dictionary, as stated in choice *C*, the reader cannot know what was in the mind of another person, especially one long dead. Therefore, the correct answer is *C*.

832 • Study, Reference, and Test-Taking Skills

> **Practice 1**   **Directions:** Read the passage. Then, read each question that follows the passage. Decide which is the best answer to each question.

Amelia Lanier saw the need for women's rights three hundred years before any Western woman had even won the right to vote. She was a writer who saw beyond her times and dared to question the unfair treatment of women. In 1611, Lanier published a volume of poetry in which she questioned class privilege and called for women's social and religious equality with men.

1 Which of the following is a FACT expressed in the passage?
A Amelia Lanier disliked men.
B Amelia Lanier published inflammatory poetry.
C Amelia Lanier thought all women were unfairly treated.
D Amelia Lanier published a volume of poetry in 1611.

2 What is the main idea of the passage?
F Amelia Lanier was a woman ahead of her time.
G Amelia Lanier was an outstanding writer.
H Amelia Lanier was the first feminist.
J Amelia Lanier's poetry influenced the feminist movement.

3 Which of the following is the best summary of this passage?
A Amelia Lanier was a feminist who wrote poetry in the 1600's.
B Years before Western ideas of equality for women, Amelia Lanier was a visionary feminist who spoke out when few realized the need to do so.
C The poetry of Amelia Lanier sparked the contemporary women's movement.
D Women in the early 1600's were unfairly treated. Amelia Lanier sought to remedy the situation through her volume of poetry.

> **Practice 2**   **Directions:** Read the passage. Then, read each question that follows the passage. Decide which is the best answer to each question.

War was a daily fact in 1940's London. The German bombing, or "the Blitz," lasted from September 1940 until May 1941. German planes dropped bombs on London every night. Warning sirens and blackouts were everyday occurrences. Yet, amid the bombing, people continued to live in the city.

1 Which of the following is an OPINION expressed in the passage?
A German planes dropped bombs on London.
B Warning sirens and blackouts were everyday occurrences in London in 1940 and 1941.
C The citizens of London hated the Germans.
D The German bombing of London was referred to as "the Blitz."

2 What is the main idea of the passage?
F Amid the bombing, people continued to live in the city.
G Although war was a fact of life in 1940's London, people continued to live there.
H Germany waged war on Britain in 1940.
J German planes dropped bombs on London every night

3 Which of the following is the best summary of this passage?
A Amidst the nightly bombing raids by the Germans, people managed to live their lives during the "Blitz" of London in 1940 and 1941
B Germany declared war on London. Bombs were dropped every night for several months. Londoners had to endure sirens night after night.
C The 1940's were terrible years for the Germans and for the British they waged war against.
D War was a daily fact in 1940's London.

> **Practice 1**
>
> 1. D
> 2. F
> 3. B

> **Practice 2**
>
> 1. C
> 2. G
> 3. A

In-Depth Lesson Plan

	LESSON FOCUS	PRINT AND MEDIA RESOURCES
DAY 1	**Workplace Skills** Students learn and apply such workplace skills as working with people and teamwork (pp. 835–838).	**Teaching Resource** *Academic and Workplace Skills Activity Book,* pp. 55–60
DAY 2	**Workplace Competencies** Students learn and apply such workplace competencies as setting goals and problem solving (pp. 839–841).	**Teaching Resources** *Academic and Workplace Skills Activity Book,* pp. 55–60
DAY 3	**Workplace Competencies (continued)** Students learn and apply such workplace competencies as managing time and money and applying math and computer skills (pp. 842–845).	**Teaching Resources** *Academic and Workplace Skills Activity Book,* pp. 55–60

Accelerated Lesson Plan

	LESSON FOCUS	PRINT AND MEDIA RESOURCES
DAY 1	**Workplace Skills and Competencies** Students learn and apply workplace skills and competences (pp. 835–845).	**Teaching Resources** *Academic and Workplace Skills Activity Book,* pp. 55–60

Options for Adapting Lesson Plans

HOMEWORK

Have students complete any stage of the lesson for homework.

TECHNOLOGY

Students can complete any stage of the lesson on computer. Have them print out their completed work.

FEATURES

Extend coverage with the Standardized Test Preparation Workshop (p. 846).

INTEGRATED SKILLS COVERAGE

Viewing and Representing
Critical Viewing, SE pp. 834, 837, 839, 841, 844, 845

ASSESSMENT SUPPORT

Standardized Test Preparation SE p. 846; ATE p. 837

Texas Test Preparation Workshop, pp. 67–68

MEETING INDIVIDUAL NEEDS

See Ongoing Assessments ATE pp. 835, 836, 839, 841, 842, 844, 845

More Advanced Students ATE p. 840

ESL Students ATE p. 837

Verbal Linguistic Learners ATE p. 838

WRITING AND GRAMMAR WEBSITE

The Interactive Writing and Grammar Website provides a wide array of support for students, teachers, and parents. Writing support includes:

• Interactive revision checkers
• Scoring rubrics with complete models

phwg.phschool.com

► *Lesson Objectives*

1. Learn interviewing skills.
2. Practice teamwork skills.
3. Conduct an informal discussion group.
4. Set specific goals with an action plan.
5. Practice problem-solving and creative-thinking skills.
6. Practice time management skills.
7. Practice money management skills.
8. Use math skills in money management.
9. Enhance computer skills.

Critical Viewing

Support Students may say that with good communications skills, a trainee can learn more and a trainer can teach better.

▲ **Critical Viewing** How can effective writing, speaking, and listening skills improve a training session, such as the one shown here? **[Support]**

Many of the skills that contribute to school success also contribute to success in the workplace. Whether you interact with the public, pursue a field that involves the research and development of new products, or work in a labor-oriented job, your abilities to speak clearly, listen closely, read carefully, and interact effectively with people are keys to a productive career.

This chapter will help you to build new skills or to improve existing ones in a number of critical areas, such as communicating with others, setting and achieving goals, and solving problems efficiently. It will also offer suggestions on how to manage your time and money as well as how to apply math and computer skills in the workplace.

⏱ **TIME AND RESOURCE MANAGER**

Resources
Print: Academic and Workplace Skills Activity Book, pp. 55–60

In-Depth Coverage	Accelerated Pace
• Work through all key concepts, pp. 835–847. • Assign and review Exercises 1–10.	• Assign pp. 835–845 for independent student review.

Working With People

In school, you learn to work together with classmates and teachers. In the workplace, you will be expected to interact effectively with supervisors, co-workers, and clients. This section offers some practical suggestions to refine your communication skills in one-on-one and group situations.

Learn to Communicate One on One

On a formal interview or when interacting with peers, you will need to use communication skills.

Interviewing When you apply to a college, compete for a job, or show interest in a school committee, knowing how to interview can greatly increase your chances of success.

🔊 Speaking and Listening Tip

During an interview, work to maintain a positive impression. Be polite and confident, speak courteously, and listen carefully to the person conducting the interview.

TIPS FOR A SUCCESSFUL INTERVIEW

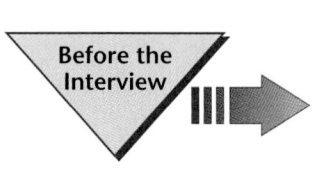

Before the Interview

1. Find out when, where, and with whom the interview is.
2. Prepare references and a copy of your résumé.
3. Learn about the company, group, or person with whom you have the interview.
4. Select a neat, appropriate outfit for the interview.

During the Interview

1. Smile and maintain eye contact.
2. Ask and answer questions politely and concisely.
3. Thank the interviewer, and ask when a decision will be made.

After the Interview

1. In a follow-up letter, restate your interest in the internship, job, or college, and extend your thanks.
2. When the deadline for a decision arrives, call to check the status.

Workplace Skills and Competencies • 835

☑ ONGOING ASSESSMENT: Monitor and Reinforce

If some students are having difficulty mastering interviewing skills, use one of the following options.

Option 1 Have students practice interviewing each other. Have them concentrate on telling about their background and skills and why they would be a good candidate for the job.	**Option 2** Have students write a practice letter to apply for a job and a follow-up letter after an interview.

 Interest GRABBER Present the following scenario. A new student comes to class. In the cafeteria he tries to make friends. He is dressed in a suit and tie. His shoes are shined. He looks at you directly in the eye. When introduced, he shakes hands vigorously with a firm grip.

Ask students what is wrong with the scenario. (The student's dress and behavior are out of place. He is acting as if he were at a job interview, not in a school cafeteria.) Ask what lessons can be learned from this mismatch, concentrating on the obvious fact that the world of work and interviews has different customs and rules from the everyday informal world of students.

Activate Prior Knowledge

Ask students how they would prepare for a job interview and what kind of reminders they would want to give themselves for how to act during the interview.

TEACH

Step-by-Step Teaching Guide

1. A sociology minilesson may help give students a context for learning and practicing interviewing skills. The world of work, especially the interviewing process, has its own customs relating to dress, attitude, and behavior. Help students understand the reason for these customs. Employers want to know that applicants, especially young ones, can adjust to the demands of the workplace; that they will be responsible and respectful of the job and their coworkers; and also that they can handle a boss telling them what to do.

2. Review the steps in the text and discuss how doing each step exhibits both responsibility and respect.

3. It is perfectly natural to be nervous. Most interviewers understand and try to put interviewees at ease. Students should try to relax and refrain from such habits as tapping their foot or cracking their knuckles. And no gum chewing!

Interacting Successfully

1. Ask students to recall a disagreeable conversation they had with someone. What was the source of the disagreement? Most likely it was a result of someone not following the guidelines for successful interaction. Ask students to try to recall the conversation in detail, to "replay the tape" and find instances where someone did not listen, interrupted, or expressed himself or herself in confrontational or disrespectful terms.

2. Ask students to imagine a conversation that involved serious differences of opinion that proceeded without anger or disrespect.

Answer Key

Exercise 1

Answers will vary.

Exercise 2

Answers will vary.

34

Interacting Successfully In school or at work, communication requires respectful interaction with people who have different priorities or opinions than you do. In fact, the people you encounter may have different personalities and working styles, too. In order to work successfully, strike a balance between communicating your own ideas and listening to those expressed by others. When you work on a project with a partner, speak to a teacher or supervisor, or deal with customers, the ability to compromise can often make everyone's job easier and more pleasant.

▶ **KEY CONCEPT** Effective interaction requires respect for and sensitivity to others. ■

Follow these guidelines for successful interaction:

- **Consider the other person's point of view.** Ask yourself how you would feel if you were in another's situation.
- **Listen without interrupting.**
- **Clarify by asking questions.**
- **Respect differences.** Recognize and accept that others may have different backgrounds, abilities, and opinions.
- **Express disagreement in nonconfrontational terms.** For example, rather than saying, "You're wrong," try saying, "I don't see it that way."
- **Be polite and professional.** A temper tantrum may be dramatic, but it is not an accepted behavior in the workplace. Whenever possible, avoid raising your voice. You can be more persuasive when you are in control of your emotions.

▶ **Exercise 1** Interviewing for a Job on the School Newspaper
With another classmate, role-play an interview for a job as a reporter for the school newspaper. The interviewer should ask questions that will prompt the interviewee to describe the reasons for wanting the job. Present your role-play to a group, and discuss what others can learn from the experience.

▶ **Exercise 2** Interacting in a Variety of Situations Working with another student, role-play the following situations:
1. Two classmates are collaborating on a project. They each participate in different activities, so coordinating their schedules is difficult. Role-play a conversation in which they arrive at two mutually agreeable times to work.
2. A bank teller must interact with an angry customer who has a problem with a bank statement. Role-play a conversation in which they try to solve the problem.

▶ **More Practice**

Academic and Workplace Skills Activity Book
• p. 55

☑ ONGOING ASSESSMENT: Monitor and Reinforce

If some students are having difficulty with interaction skills, use one of the following options.

Option 1 Ask students to make a list of things people say and do that annoy them. Then have them take a long, hard, honest look at the list and ask how often they are guilty of doing those things.	**Option 2** Ask students to recall a potentially difficult conversation that worked out well. Have them analyze what worked in that conversation and think about how to apply those successful techniques to other situations.

Learning Teamwork

To succeed in any team effort, such as organizing a fundraiser, studying for a test, or preparing a job-related presentation, group members must work together to achieve a common goal. Although personalities and opinions may differ, the shared goal should direct each member's focus.

Participating in Group Discussions The benefit of a group discussion is that it allows each person to access and consider a pool of ideas. For example, when embarking on a major project, businesses often ask members of different departments to share their knowledge and expertise to make the planning effective. This benefit is realized only if each member of the group participates,

▶ **KEY CONCEPT** Effective participation involves both contributing and allowing others to contribute. ∎

▲ **Critical Viewing** What problems might arise when people work in groups, as shown here? **[Hypothesize]**

Workplace Skills and Competencies • 837

Learning Teamwork

1. Ask volunteers to describe successful teamwork experiences. Have them analyze what went right, and write down those factors on the board. Compare the list with the tips in the text and note the overlaps and any significant additions.

2. The feeling of being part of a team is rarely present at the beginning of any endeavor. It results from the contributions of individuals and the group experience. Point out that the tips and factors you listed are the things that encourage teamwork. It is important for people to go into a group experience respectful of others, responsible, and with a positive attitude that some good can result from the effort.

3. The true test of teamwork is feeling a positive connection to teammates in a less than successful situation. Tell students that handling winning is easy. The real challenge for a team is how it handles a setback. Ask students to share any positive experiences of good teamwork in a losing or less than successful cause.

Customize for
ESL Students

Be aware of cultural differences in working through team and group experiences. If some students seem especially reticent, keep in mind that in some cultures, different customs and values can make participating in group experiences as taught here difficult. Some girls may come from cultures where speaking up and having opinions are discouraged. Work sensitively with students, encouraging them to do what they can, yet allowing for differences of culture and values.

Critical Viewing

Hypothesize Students may say that personalities can clash, that differences of opinion can arise, and that differences in temperament can make them hard to resolve.

🖉 STANDARDIZED TEST PREPARATION WORKSHOP

Reading Informational Texts Standardized tests often measure students' ability to read informational texts. Share the following example with students:

Read the text, and then answer the question that follows.

> **REBATE!**
>
> Purchase any computer from Sam's Computers and we will give you an instant rebate of $250! Limit one rebate per household.
>
> Offer good until March 15.

What is the most important information missing from this advertisement?

A the amount of the rebate

B the store's location

C the computer's speed

D none of the above

The correct choice is item **B**. Where the store is located should be included in the advertisement.

Step-by-Step Teaching Guide

Taking on Group Roles

1. Ask students who are members of organizations to relate experiences of meetings, positive or negative. Tell students that organizations all over the world, large and small, hold meetings. Well-run meetings get things accomplished and allow people to participate in the process. Poorly run meetings get little accomplished and often frustrate and bore people.

2. Give some thought to the students' groupings in the discussion activity. Be sure that each group has a mix of "talkers" and "listeners" and try to get each to do more of the opposite than usual.

3. One key to group discussion is paying careful attention to what the speaker is saying. Encourage students to show interest through eye contact, alert body language, and relevant questions.

4. Circulate around the room as students conduct their informal discussion groups. You can read body language as well as observe who is talking to gauge student involvement.

Customize for
Verbal/Linguistic Learners

Ask students who tend to have a lot to say to concentrate on listening to and responding to what other students say. Have them take notes. Encourage them to be better listeners.

Answer Key

Exercise 3

Answers will vary.

Exercise 4

Answers will vary.

Taking on Group Roles Group discussions held at meetings can be improved by a systematic sharing of responsibilities. In a group that meets regularly, these roles and responsibilities should rotate among the members.

KEY CONCEPT Members of a group assume distinct, yet important, roles to realize a common goal. ∎

These roles and responsibilities make meetings run smoothly:

Facilitator: Guides the discussion and makes sure that everyone has a chance to be heard
Note-taker: Records the discussion and prepares the notes for distribution
Timekeeper: Watches the time and keeps the discussion on schedule
Participants: Contribute ideas, help problem-solve, and participate in the discussion

Tips for Effective Participation Whether you are involved in a regularly scheduled meeting or are attending a single-session group discussion, consider these tips:

• Bring relevant documents or ideas to the meeting.
• Use an agenda, a prepared list of subjects to address.
• Share your perspective, and encourage others to provide their points of view.
• Focus your attention on the topic.
• Follow up on any decisions or plans the group makes.

Exercise 3 Conducting an Informal Group Discussion
Working with a group of four or five students, hold an informal discussion to identify three objects you'd want to save in a scrapbook. Then, evaluate how successfully the group encouraged participation and interaction from all members.

Exercise 4 Using Group Roles With a group of four or five students, hold a meeting using the following suggested agenda. Before beginning, set a time limit for each part of the discussion, and assign group roles. After the discussion, explain how the group roles affected the interaction.

TOPIC: Raising money for a class trip
Part 1: Brainstorm for ideas
Part 2: Narrow the number of ideas down to three or four
Part 3: Analyze ideas by listing pros and cons
Part 4: Reach agreement on a single idea

Learn More

For instructions on writing minutes or notes of a meeting, see pages 328–329 in the "Workplace Writing" chapter.

Moving Toward Your Goals

Goals—attainable, measurable outcomes—may take a short or a long time to fulfill. They may focus on improving your grades or your tennis serve, on becoming class president or a clerk at a local convenience store. As you set goals for various parts of your life, they may conflict with one another, leaving you to decide which one is most important to you.

Personal and Professional Goals

Personal goals focus on your lifestyle and how you want to develop as a person. For example, you decide to learn more about a favorite hobby or to be kinder to others. *Professional goals* focus on your career; for example, you may want to learn a new computer program or complete an important project within a set budget. While personal and professional goals are different, they often affect each other. Therefore, you may need to identify the ones you consider most important.

Setting and Achieving Goals To set a goal, clearly define the outcome so that you know what you are working toward. This first step is followed by the equally important step of achieving the goal, which requires a plan with a set time limit.

KEY CONCEPT Goals should be specific and should include a set time limit for completion. ■

By following the steps on the timeline below, you can develop an action plan that will help you realize your goals.

TIMELINE FOR MEETING GOALS

| Write down the goal in detail. | Set a reasonable time frame to complete each step. | Adjust the steps as needed. |
| | Break the goal down into specific steps. | Adjust your progress on a regular basis. |

GOAL

Exercise 5 **Developing an Action Plan** Using the steps above, develop an action plan for achieving a school-related goal. Outline the steps you will need to take to achieve your goal, and set a daily or weekly time limit for each one. Discuss your plan with your teacher, a family member, or a classmate. Then, follow your action plan. At the end of each interval, evaluate your progress, and adjust your plan as needed.

▲ **Critical Viewing**
Identify an attainable goal for an athlete beginning to learn tennis. **[Apply]**

More Practice
Academic and Workplace Skills Activity Book
• p. 56

Workplace Skills and Competencies • 839

Personal and Professional Goals

1. Engage students in a general discussion about goals and the process of goal setting. One problem is setting realistic goals. Get students to understand the difference between goals and dreams.

2. Review the distinction between personal and professional goals. Ask students to identify a few goals for each category.

3. Ask students to analyze the goals on their list in terms of how realistic and achievable they are and choose one for the class exercise that they think has a good chance of success.

4. Guide students through setting an action plan. See that they understand how crucial it is to set reasonable time frames and adjust steps as needed.

Answer Key

Exercise 5
Answers will vary.

Critical Viewing

Apply Students may say that one attainable goal for a beginner at tennis might be to serve the ball without missing it.

ONGOING ASSESSMENT: Monitor and Reinforce

If some students are having difficulty with setting goals, use one of the following options.

| **Option 1** Have students work in pairs to review goals for scope and practicality. | **Option 2** Establish groups in which students help each other choose goals that set up their action plans, monitor progress, make adjustments, and provide support. |

Solving Problems

1. Problem solving is something everyone gets better at with practice. The real skill is making intuitive knowledge conscious and applying it to new and different problems.

2. Ask students to describe situations in which they successfully solved a problem. Then ask them to tell about situations when they were baffled and got nowhere in solving the problem. Ask students to speculate on the difference between the successful and unsuccessful situations. In the successful situation, students probably started with a positive attitude and maybe a little bit of experience in dealing with the problem. As they progressed, success bred success and increased confidence. In the failed attempt, they probably started with a less than confident attitude, which only got worse as success eluded them.

Customize for
More Advanced Students

Ask students to pay careful attention as classmates relate their stories of successful and unsuccessful problem solving. Have students add their own experiences to the mix and then formulate some generalizations about successful and unsuccessful problem solving.

34

Solving Problems and Thinking Creatively

Whether you are working to achieve personal or professional goals, be prepared for the problems that will undoubtedly arise. Many successful people view these bumps in the road as opportunities because problems challenge people to see a situation in a new light. Keep in mind that not every problem can be solved in exactly the way you would like. Sometimes, solving the problem means accepting a compromise, or finding a solution you hadn't originally considered.

Problem Solving Effectively Use the graphic organizer like the one below to help you analyze a problem. These tips also offer useful advice:

- Keep a positive attitude.
- Identify the reason or reasons that the problem exists. If you can identify several elements that caused the problem, address one element at a time.
- Evaluate the pros and cons of a variety of solutions.
- Be willing to accept a less-than-perfect solution.

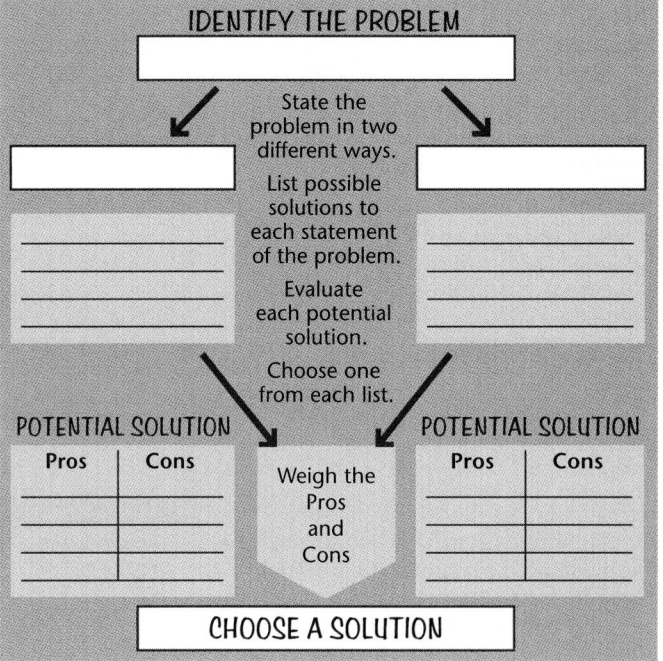

Learn More

For more instruction about problem-and-solution writing, see Chapter 11.

Thinking Creatively Sometimes, solving problems means thinking creatively—looking beyond the ordinary. When you are problem solving, think creatively by looking at the problem from several angles. The illustration below shows one method for approaching a problem from more than one angle. You may discover other techniques that help you come up with creative solutions.

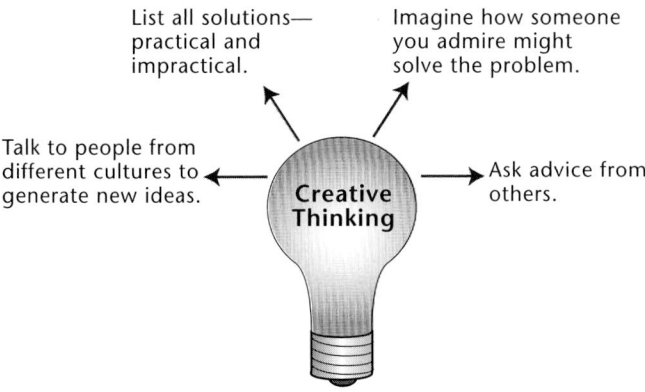

List all solutions—practical and impractical.

Imagine how someone you admire might solve the problem.

Talk to people from different cultures to generate new ideas.

Creative Thinking

Ask advice from others.

Exercise 6 **Applying Problem-Solving Skills** Use problem-solving skills to arrive at a potential solution for each of the following problems. In each case, write a brief explanation of how you arrived at the solution.

1. You spend at least fifteen minutes each morning looking for your house keys. Often, by the time you find them, you are late leaving the house.
2. You are nervous about speaking in front of a group, and you have a class presentation coming up in two weeks.

▶ **Critical Viewing** What are some of the benefits of problem-solving with a group? [Analyze]

Workplace Skills and Competencies • 841

Thinking Creatively

1. Ask students to discuss problems they or someone else solved creatively. What was their response to the creative solution? They may have thought or said, "That's brilliant!" or "What a great idea!"

2. Review the techniques in the text for thinking creatively. Point out that most creative thinkers do not think only in isolation but often arrive at solutions after much reading and discussion.

Answer Key

Exercise 6

Answers will vary. Samples are given.

1. If the house keys are always in the same place, you won't have to search for them. Ask permission to attach a hook to the wall near the door. As soon as you unlock the door and enter your home, you can hang your keys on the hook. The next time you need them, there they'll be!

2. Practice your speech in private, where no one can hear. Next, practice in front of someone whose opinion doesn't matter to you—dog, cat, baby brother. Then give the speech to your best friend, who will criticize in a kind way. Finally, give the speech to your mother, who loves you no matter what you do.

Critical Viewing

Analyze Students may say that group problem solving can generate ideas that people working by themselves would never have come up with.

☑ ONGOING ASSESSMENT: Monitor and Reinforce

If some students are having difficulty with problem solving, use one of the following options.

Option 1 Have students work in pairs to solve a problem, such as: You have a hard time talking with your parents about things that matter to you. How can you improve communications?

Option 2 Assign a solution to each of several small groups. Ask each group to come up with as many problems as they can that match the solution. Encourage the groups to share their conclusions.

Managing Time

1. Ask students if they have ever felt like they had too much to do in too little time. Or if they have a problem getting around to doing things that need getting done. These are common problems that can be helped with some time management skills.

2. Ask students to volunteer situations when they successfully handled several tasks in a short period of time. Sometimes, having lots to do can make people more productive; plenty of time can be a bad situation for getting a job done. Relate the traditional thought that unless you go about things with a sense of purpose, a task will take as long as the time available for it.

3. A key to time management and overcoming procrastination is the ability to "chunk" a task into smaller parts. It is a process related to the action plan for achieving goals: Break a task down into manageable bits, set a schedule, and accomplish the task a little at a time. Chunking is best summed up by the question and answer, How do you eat an elephant? One bite at a time!

4. Ask students to address their procrastination tendencies. Sometimes, doing the task is easier than avoiding it. It's always out there and on your conscience. When you get down to work and get things done, you feel good about yourself.

Answer Key

Exercise 7

Answers will vary.

34

Managing Time

In whatever career you choose, you will likely face a task that must be completed in a set amount of time. Between answering e-mails, phone calls, and dealing with unexpected problems, knowing how to use your time efficiently can mean the difference between success and failure.

Keeping Weekly and Daily Schedules Proper time management takes planning and the ability to decide which of your goals and activities is most important.

▶ **KEY CONCEPT** To manage your time, keep a schedule of activities and plan for upcoming events. ∎

The following strategies will help you accomplish what you must with minimal scrambling.

- Write down activities and goals for the week. Decide which projects are most important, and devote more time to them.
- Break big tasks into manageable steps.
- Make a daily to-do list.

WEEKLY SCHEDULE

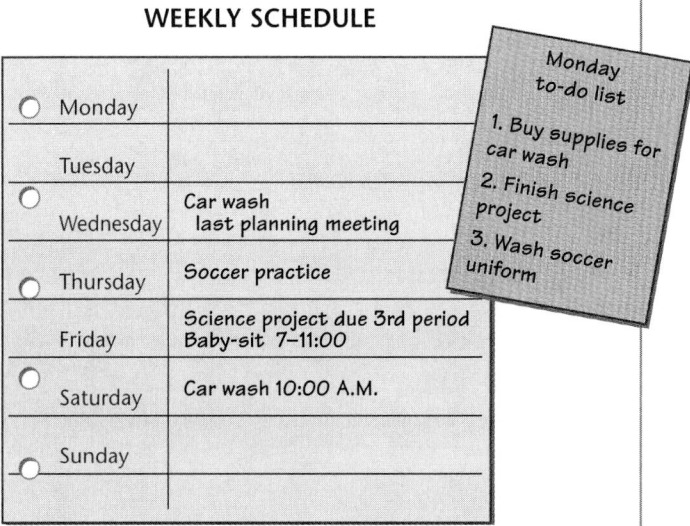

○	Monday	
	Tuesday	
○	Wednesday	Car wash last planning meeting
○	Thursday	Soccer practice
	Friday	Science project due 3rd period Baby-sit 7–11:00
○	Saturday	Car wash 10:00 A.M.
○	Sunday	

Monday to-do list
1. Buy supplies for car wash
2. Finish science project
3. Wash soccer uniform

▶ **Exercise 7** **Managing Your Time** In your notebook or in a weekly planner, record your schedule for a week. Include a daily to-do list. Break large projects or tasks into smaller activities or steps. After a week, identify one positive aspect of such a system.

Some Web sites offer on-line opportunities for managing your time. Locate such resources on-line, and use them to keep an electronic calendar.

✓ **ONGOING ASSESSMENT: Monitor and Reinforce**

If some students are having difficulty with time management skills, use one of the following options.

Option 1 Ask students to take a task they have to do and break it down into smaller tasks, then create a time schedule for accomplishing each subtask.	**Option 2** Have partners help each other break down and schedule tasks as well as provide mutual support.

Managing Money

In order to keep spending in line, a budget, or a spending plan, can be effective. From the chief financial officer in charge of a company's budget to the office manager who orders supplies, many employees are expected to record and manage expenses. This may present difficult choices about cutting spending or increasing income.

▶ **KEY CONCEPT** To manage money, keep track of spending, set financial goals, and save money to meet them. ∎

Developing a Budget In order for a budget to be successful, the money coming in should exceed the money going out. To outline a budget, show credits or money earned in black. Show debts or outgoing money in red. In the example below, income can cover the expenses identified.

Freshman Dance Budget

	Regular Income	Regular Expenses	Projected Expenses
Total Ticket Sales	1,000.00		
From Sponsors	250.00		
Raffle Prize			150.00
Disc Jockey		200.00	
Lights/Balloons		115.00	
Total	$1,250.00	$315.00	$150.00

▶ **Exercise 8** **Managing a Budget** Plan one month's budget for a hiking club with thirty members who each pay $1.00 a week in dues. Once a month, the club holds a bake sale. The supplies for the sale cost $20.00, and the sale brings in $130.00. Each month, the club sponsors a bus for $75.00 to take the members to a hiking site. Insurance for the trip costs $25.00. The club is saving to purchase a $100.00 tree for the school in June. Use your budget to answer these questions:
1. How many months will it take to save money for the tree?
2. Make two suggestions: one for reducing expenses and one for increasing income.

▶ **More Practice**

Academic and Workplace Skills Activity Book
• pp. 57–58

Managing Money

1. Basic money management means planning spending and trying to save. Students will no doubt bring up credit cards as a solution to spending what they don't have. While credit cards are easy to obtain, make sure students know about the normal 18 percent interest rate on credit cards.

2. Discuss establishing and maintaining a good credit rating. Tell students that credit bureaus monitor all credit transactions. When someone is late paying the phone company or misses a credit card payment, the credit bureau knows. Then when that person applies for a car loan or maybe a mortgage, the credit check shows him or her as being a bad risk. In short, no shortcuts. Get in over your head, spend money you don't have, and it can hurt you for years to come.

Answer Key

▶ **Exercise 8**

Monthly income:
    $120 dues; $130 bake sale = $250
Monthly expenses:
    $20 bake sale supplies; $75 bus; $25 insurance = $125
$250 – $120 =
    $130 monthly "profit"

1. It will take one month.
2. The groups could reduce expenses by buying less expensive ingredients for their baked goods or by hiring a bus company that charges less. It could increase income by increasing memberships or by sponsoring other fund-raising activities, such as a car wash.

Step-by-Step Teaching Guide

Applying Math Skills

1. The best buy depends on the buyer. Suppose that a quart of milk costs $1.50 and a half gallon (two quarts) costs $2.50. Obviously, the half gallon is a better buy. But if you don't drink a lot of milk, and it will get sour when the container is still half full, then a quart is a better buy for you.

2. Similarly, a bargain or a sale is good if you actually want or need the item. "Kitty Delight Cat Food: 10¢ a Can" is a bargain. But if your cat Binky hates Kitty Delight, then you've wasted money.

3. Students also need to know how to determine net profit from a job. If a job pays $6.00 an hour, they need to know what their net will be after taxes and any expenses for transportation, meals, and possibly uniforms.

Answer Key

Exercise 9

Baby-sitting pays $4 an hour. Dog feeding and walking pays $8 an hour. Dog walking might seem the better choice, unless you're allergic to dogs or crazy about children.

Critical Viewing

Analyze Students may say that as long as people punch a calculator's keys accurately, it can perform math functions faster and more accurately than most people working with pencil and paper.

Applying Math Skills

When it comes to applying the skills you have learned in class to the workplace, you will discover that math has many common applications and that a working knowledge of computers can give you an edge in your chosen career.

KEY CONCEPT Math skills help you shop wisely, plan for a profit, and determine the value of your time. ■

Determining the Best Buy Math skills can help you calculate the best price for a product or service. For example, some "buy one, get one free" sales actually work out to cost more than if you bought the two items at their regular price at another store. By calculating the difference, you can make an educated decision and save money.

Planning for Profit Any job or project that requires materials, space, or people's time usually involves costs that must be balanced by the income generated by sales. To figure out the cost of each finished item or each service performed, determine your investment and divide that number by the quantity of items you are making. In order to make a profit, you must sell the item or service at a higher rate than it costs you.

Setting the Value of Your Time When you are looking for a job, the wage you are quoted (if a flat rate) may be misleading. To effectively evaluate an offer that doesn't include an hourly wage, divide the offer by the number of hours the job will take. Then, decide whether the offer presented seems fair to you.

Exercise 9 Using Math Skills to Evaluate Two Job Offers

A neighbor has offered you $40 to baby-sit his child on the weekends (Saturday and Sunday), five hours each day. Another neighbor has offered you $40 to feed and walk her dog five times a week, which takes approximately one hour each day.

1. Identify the amount of time you would need to invest in each job.
2. What other factors might influence your decision?
3. Which job would you accept? Explain your answer.

Internet Tip

Some Web sites offer math support on-line. Search for a Web site that can help you with budgeting and calculations.

▼ Critical Viewing
How can calculators help workers increase efficiency? **[Analyze]**

☑ ONGOING ASSESSMENT: Monitor and Reinforce

If some students are having difficulty with money management skills, use one of the following options.

Option 1 Check that students have the math skills they need. If they do not, remediation is in order.	**Option 2** Pair students with a math whiz for peer tutoring.

Applying Computer Skills

The more you learn about your computer, the more useful it can be. You should begin by learning to keyboard quickly and accurately. Then, study your computer's special formatting features. You may even want to learn specialized spreadsheet programs or graphics applications.

 **KEY CONCEPT** A working knowledge of your computer can enhance your work. ■

Practice your typing skills. Being an accurate and quick typist gives you more time to focus on other tasks. A good typing speed is 45 words per minute, but remember that accuracy is more important than speed.

Use the thesaurus and spell-check tools. With the click of a mouse, you can find just the right word or catch errors that you may have missed while proofreading.

Learn how to format. Use fonts, bullets, and other features to organize and emphasize information.

▲ **Critical Viewing**
What are two benefits of learning strong computer skills?
[Analyze]

Exercise 10 Examining Computer Skills Using a computer at home or in school, do the following activities:
1. Working with a partner who will time you, type a page from a textbook as quickly and accurately as you can for one minute. Then, count how many words you typed and review your work for accuracy.
2. Review the classified section of a newspaper to identify the computer skills and programs that are most frequently requested in job openings. Choose one application or skill that interests you, and learn more about it. Share your findings with classmates.

▶ **More Practice**
Academic and Workplace Skills Activity Book
• pp. 59–60

Reflecting on Your Workplace Skills and Competencies

Consider your own readiness for the workplace. In your journal or notebook, begin by answering the following questions:

• Consider the job you want to pursue. Which skills will it require?

• What are your strengths? What are your weaknesses?

Applying Computer Skills

1. Write *Computer Literacy* on the board, with *literacy* underscored. Discuss how it used to be that you needed to be able to read and write to do most jobs. Now you need to be able to read, write, and use a computer. It is that simple: Good jobs require computer skills.

2. Ask students who are reasonably competent with computers to explain how they learned.

3. These students will probably be the best teachers for students who have not yet mastered the basic skills discussed in the text. Set up peer tutoring, matching students' skills and compatibility.

4. Direct students to do Reflecting on Your Workplace Skills and Competencies and share the results with the class.

Answer Key

Exercise 10

Answers will vary.

Critical Viewing

Analyze Students may say that a job candidate with good computer skills is more desirable than one without, and that computer jobs often pay well.

✓ ONGOING ASSESSMENT: Assess Mastery

Use one of the following options to assess students' mastery of workplace skills and competencies.

Self-Assessment Ask students to rate their mastery of each of the skills in the chapter and provide reasons for the rating they give themselves.	**Teacher Assessment** Use both the chapter exercises and your own observations of students' awareness and abilities.

Reading Informational Texts

1. Point out that many examples of informational text are full of details that must be carefully attended to, whether to achieve a goal or to be at a specific place at a specific time and appropriately prepared. For the reader to gather all the necessary information, he or she must often read the text several times.

2. In the sample, the individuals named in three of the possible answers are or will be participants in the craft fair. However, only one of the answers, D, names the individuals responsible for organizing the fair—the students. D is the correct response.

Standardized Test Preparation Workshop

Reading Informational Texts

Some standardized tests assess your ability to read real-world texts, such as flyers, brochures, and advertisements. Often, this involves carefully following a sequence of steps or directions. The following sample test item will give you practice in answering these types of questions.

Test Tip

Note the sequence of the directions presented. If you consider the reasons that one step must follow another, you may be better prepared to answer a question.

Sample Test Item

Directions: Read the text, and then answer the questions that follow.

School Craft Fair

The school will be holding a craft fair
Saturday, November 30
to raise money for charity. The first meeting will be held Tuesday in Room 311 at 2:30 P.M. The agenda of that meeting is as follows:

- **elect student leaders**
- **discuss advertising**
- **sign up for crafters**
- **permits for use of school gym**
- **arrangements with school custodial staff**
- **written plan for approval by principal**

The meeting is open to all students interested in participating.

1 According to the announcement, who will be organizing the craft fair?

A vendors

B teachers

C principal

D students

Answer and Explanation

The correct answer for item 1 is *D*, students. Although vendors, teachers, and the principal will be involved, electing student leaders and inviting student participation indicates that the fair will be organized and run by students.

⬥ TEST-TAKING TIP

When answering questions about informational text, it might help students to recall that often they must use inference to arrive at the right answer. For example, in the sample test item, it does not say explicitly, "Students will organize the fair." The correct answer must be inferred from the information given—that students will be meeting to make certain decisions about the fair.

Answer Key

1. D
2. G
3. A
4. H
5. D
6. H

Practice 1 **Directions:** Read the passage, and then answer the questions that follow.

Finn had been struggling with reading *Romeo and Juliet*. After many attempts to read it on his own and some extra help, he was finally getting it, and he liked it. His teacher suggested that he have some fun with the story. She suggested using software that would make reading the play an interactive adventure. He then went to the computer room, where he read the following instructions on installing the software and navigating through the CD-ROM *The World of Romeo and Juliet*.

The World of Romeo and Juliet

1. Insert *The World of Romeo and Juliet* in the CD-ROM drive

2. Double-click on the D drive (CD-ROM)

3. Double-click on **Setup.exe** icon.

4. Follow the on-screen installation instructions.

5. WIN: Start menu/programs menu/ Romeo + Juliet.

The first screen will ask you to provide your name and class. After signing in, you can choose to be either a Capulet or a Montague. The program will then direct you in both audio and text. If you need help, click on Romeo's friend, the level-headed Benvolio. If you want to quit, click the red button on the lower left side of the screen. Your work will be saved automatically.

---

1 Which of the following did Finn do first?
  A install the CD-ROM
  B navigate through the program
  C go for extra help
  D read *Romeo and Juliet*

2 What icon must you click during the installation process?
  F screen instructions
  G **Setup.exe**
  H start menu
  J D-drive

3 What happens when you press the red button on the lower left side of the screen?
  A The program shuts down.
  B You are given helpful hints.
  C You are taken to a menu of lessons.
  D A score is provided.

4 How do you save your work?
  F Click on the Save button.
  G Respond to a prompt.
  H It is saved automatically.
  J Save it to the hard drive.

5 What step has to be completed first?
  A Sign in and give your class.
  B Click on the **Setup.exe** icon.
  C Double-click on the D-drive.
  D Insert the CD-ROM into the drive.

6 Which of the following best describes how to get help?
  F Click on the Help button on the keyboard.
  G Click on the Help icon.
  H Click on a graphic of a character from the play.
  J Click on the title of the CD-ROM.

Citing Sources and Preparing Manuscript

Preparing Manuscript

The presentation of your written work is important. Your work should be neat, clean, and easy to read. Follow your teacher's directions for placing your name and class, along with the title and date of your work, on the paper.

For handwritten work:

- Use cursive handwriting or manuscript printing, according to the style your teacher prefers. The penmanship reference below shows the accepted formation of letters in cursive writing.
- Write or print neatly.
- Write on one side of lined 8-1/2" x 11" paper with a clean edge. (Do not use pages torn from a spiral notebook.)
- Indent the first line of each paragraph.

- Leave a margin, as indicated by the guidelines on the lined paper. Write in a size appropriate for the lines provided. Do not write so large that the letters from one line bump into the ones above and below. Do not write so small that the writing is difficult to read.
- Write in blue or black ink.
- Number the pages in the upper right corner.
- You should not cross out words on your final draft. Recopy instead. If your paper is long, your teacher may allow you to make one or two small changes by neatly crossing out the text to be deleted and using a caret [^] to indicate replacement text. Alternatively, you might make one or two corrections neatly with correction fluid. If you find yourself making more than three corrections, consider recopying the work.

PENMANSHIP REFERENCE

For word-processed or typed documents:

- Choose a standard, easy-to-read font.
- Type or print on one side of unlined 8-1/2" x 11" paper.
- Set the margins for the side, top, and bottom of your paper at approximately one inch. Most word-processing programs have a default setting that is appropriate.
- Double-space the document.
- Indent the first line of each paragraph.
- Number the pages in the upper right corner. Many word-processing programs have a header feature that will do this for you automatically.

- If you discover one or two errors after you have typed or printed, use correction fluid if your teacher allows such corrections. If you have more than three errors in an electronic file, consider making the corrections to the file and reprinting the document. If you have typed a long document, your teacher may allow you to make a few corrections by hand. If you have several errors, however, consider retyping the document.

For research papers:

Follow your teacher's directions for formatting formal research papers. Most papers will have the following features:

- Title page
- Table of Contents or Outline
- Works-Cited List

Sybil Luddington:
Female Paul Revere

Megan Mahoney
Language Arts
3rd Period
March 26, 20- -

Table of Contents

.... 6
.... 10
.... 12

.... 15

Cited

Incorporating Ideas From Research

Below are three common methods of incorporating the ideas of other writers into your work. Choose the most appropriate style by analyzing your needs in each case. In all cases, you must credit your source.

- **Direct Quotation:** Use quotation marks to indicate the exact words.
- **Paraphrase:** To share ideas without a direct quotation, state the ideas in your own words. While you haven't copied word-for-word, you still need to credit your source.
- **Summary:** To provide information about a large body of work—such as a speech, an editorial, or a chapter of a book—identify the writer's main idea.

Avoiding Plagiarism

Whether you are presenting a formal research paper or an opinion paper on a current event, you must be careful to give credit for any ideas or opinions that are not your own. Presenting someone else's ideas, research, or opinion as your own—even if you have rephrased it in different words—is *plagiarism*, the equivalent of academic stealing, or fraud.

You can avoid plagiarism by synthesizing what you learn: Read from several sources and let the ideas of experts help you draw your own conclusions and form your own opinions. Ultimately, however, note your own reactions to the ideas presented.

When you choose to use someone else's ideas or work to support your view, credit the source of the material. Give bibliographic information to cite your sources of the following information:

- Statistics
- Direct quotations
- Indirectly quoted statements of opinions
- Conclusions presented by an expert
- Facts available in only one or two sources

Crediting Sources

When you credit a source, you acknowledge where you found your information and you give your readers the details necessary for locating the source themselves. Within the body of the paper, you provide a short citation, a footnote number linked to a footnote, or an endnote number linked to an endnote reference. These brief references show the page numbers on which you found the information. To make your paper more formal, prepare a reference list at the end of the paper to provide full bibliographic information on your sources. These are two common types of reference lists:

- A **bibliography** provides a listing of all the resources you consulted during your research.
- A **works-cited list** indicates the works you have referenced in your paper.

Choosing a Format for Documentation

The type of information you provide and the format in which you provide it depend on what your teacher prefers. These are the most commonly used style guides:

- **Modern Language Association (MLA) Style** This is the style used for most papers at the middle-school and high-school level and for most language arts papers.
- **American Psychological Association (APA) Style** This is used for most papers in the social sciences and for most college-level papers.
- *Chicago Manual of Style* (CMS) This is preferred by some teachers.

On the following pages, you'll find sample citation formats for the most commonly cited materials. Each format calls for standard bibliographic information. The difference is in the order of the material presented in each entry and the punctuation required.

MLA Style for Listing Sources

Book with one author	Pyles, Thomas. *The Origins and Development of the English Language.* 2nd ed. New York: Harcourt Brace Jovanovich, Inc., 1971.
Book with two or three authors	McCrum, Robert, William Cran, and Robert MacNeil. *The Story of English.* New York: Penguin Books, 1987.
Book with an editor	Truth, Sojourner. *Narrative of Sojourner Truth.* Ed. Margaret Washington. New York: Vintage Books, 1993.
Book with more than three authors or editors	Donald, Robert B., et al. *Writing Clear Essays.* Upper Saddle River, NJ: Prentice-Hall, Inc., 1996.
A single work from an anthology	Hawthorne, Nathaniel. "Young Goodman Brown." *Literature: An Introduction to Reading and Writing.* Ed. Edgar V. Roberts and Henry E. Jacobs. Upper Saddle River, NJ: Prentice-Hall, Inc., 1998. 376–385. [Indicate pages for the entire selection.]
Introduction in a published edition	Washington, Margaret. Introduction. *Narrative of Sojourner Truth.* By Sojourner Truth. New York: Vintage Books, 1993.
Signed article in a weekly magazine	Wallace, Charles. "A Vodacious Deal." *Time* 14 Feb. 2000:63.
Signed article in a monthly magazine	Gustaitis, Joseph. "The Sticky History of Chewing Gum." *American History* Oct. 1998: 30–38.
Unsigned editorial or story	"Selective Silence." Editorial. *Wall Street Journal* 11 Feb. 2000: A14. [If the editorial or story is signed, begin with the author's name.]
Signed pamphlet	[Treat the pamphlet as though it were a book.]
Pamphlet with no author, publisher, or date	*Are You at Risk of Heart Attack?* n.p. n.d. [n.p. n.d. indicates that there is no known publisher or date]
Filmstrips, slide programs, and videotape	*The Diary of Anne Frank.* Dir. George Stevens. Perf. Millie Perkins, Shelley Winters, Joseph Schildkraut, Lou Jacobi, and Richard Beymer. Twentieth Century Fox, 1959.
Radio or television program transcript	"The First Immortal Generation." *Rockham's Razor.* Host Robyn Williams. Guest Damien Broderick. National Public Radio. 23 May 1999. Transcript.
Internet	*National Association of Chewing Gum Manufacturers.* 19 Dec. 1999 <http://www.nacgm.org/consumer/funfacts.html> [Indicate the date you accessed the information. Content and addresses at Web sites change frequently.]
Newspaper	Thurow, Roger. "South Africans Who Fought for Sanctions Now Scrap for Investors." *Wall Street Journal* 11 Feb. 2000: A1+ [For a multipage article, write only the first page number on which it appears, followed by a plus sign.]
Personal interviews	Smith, Jane. Personal interview. 10 Feb. 2000.
CD (with multiple publishers)	Simms, James, ed. *Romeo and Juliet.* By William Shakespeare. CD-ROM. Oxford: Attica Cybernetics Ltd.; London: BBC Education; London: HarperCollins Publishers, 1995.
Article from an Encyclopedia	Askeland, Donald R. (1991). "Welding." *World Book Encyclopedia.* 1991 ed.

APA Style for Listing Sources

The list of citations for APA is referred to as a Reference List and not a bibliography.

Book with one author	Pyles, T. (1971). *The Origins and Development of the English Language* (2nd ed.). New York: Harcourt Brace Jovanovich, Inc.
Book with two or three authors	McCrum, R., Cran, W., & MacNeil, R. (1993). *The Story of English.* New York: Penguin Books.
Book with an editor	Truth, S. (1993). *Narrative of Sojourner Truth* (M. Washington, Ed.). New York: Vintage Books.
Book with more than three authors or editors	Donald, R. B., Morrow, B. R., Wargetz, L. G., & Werner, K. (1996). *Writing Clear Essays.* Upper Saddle River, New Jersey: Prentice-Hall, Inc. [With six or more authors, abbreviate second and following authors as "et al."]
A single work from an anthology	Hawthorne, N. (1998) Young Goodman Brown. In E. V. Roberts, & H. E. Jacobs (Eds.), *Literature: An Introduction to Reading and Writing* (pp. 376–385). Upper Saddle River, New Jersey: Prentice-Hall, Inc.
Introduction to a work included in a published edition	[No style is offered under this heading.]
Signed article in a weekly magazine	Wallace, C. (2000, February 20). A vodacious deal. *Time, 155,* 63. [The volume number appears in italics before the page number.]
Signed article in a monthly magazine	Gustaitis, J. (1998, October). The sticky history of chewing gum. *American History, 33,* 30–38.
Unsigned editorial or story	Selective Silence. (2000, February 11). *Wall Street Journal,* p. A14.
Signed pamphlet	Pearson Education. (2000). *LifeCare* (2nd ed.) [Pamphlet]. Smith, John: Author.
Pamphlet with no author, publisher, or date	[No style is offered under this heading.]
Filmstrips, slide programs, and videotape	Stevens, G. (Producer & Director). (1959). *The Diary of Anne Frank.* [Videotape]. (Available from Twentieth Century Fox) [If the producer and the director are two different people, list the producer first and then the director, with an ampersand (&) between them.]
Radio or television program transcript	Broderick, D. (1999, May 23). The First Immortal Generation. (R. Williams, Radio Host). *Rockham's Razor.* New York: National Public Radio.
Internet	National Association of Chewing Gum Manufacturers. Available: http://www.nacgm.org/consumer/funfacts.html [References to Websites should begin with the author's last name, if available. Indicate the site name and the available path or URL address.]
Newspaper	Thurow, R. (2000, February 11). South Africans who fought for sanctions now scrap for investors. *Wall Street Journal,* pp. A1, A4.
Personal Interview	[APA states that, since interviews (and other personal communications) do not provide "recoverable data," they should only be cited in text.]
CD (with multiple publishers)	[No style is offered under this heading.]
Article from an encyclopedia	Askeland, D. R. (1991). Welding. In *World Book Encyclopedia.* (Vol. 21 pp. 190–191). Chicago: World Book, Inc.

CMS Style for Listing Sources

Book with one author	Pyles, Thomas. *The Origins and Development of the English Language,* 2nd ed. New York: Harcourt Brace Jovanovich, Inc., 1971.
Book with two or three authors	McCrum, Robert, William Cran, and Robert MacNeil. *The Story of English.* New York: Penguin Books, 1987.
Book with an editor	Truth, Sojourner. *Narrative of Sojourner Truth.* Edited by Margaret Washington. New York: Vintage Books, 1993.
Book with more than three authors or editors	Donald, Robert B., et al. *Writing Clear Essays.* Upper Saddle River, New Jersey: Prentice-Hall, Inc., 1996.
A single work from an anthology	Hawthorne, Nathaniel. "Young Goodman Brown." In *Literature: An Introduction to Reading and Writing.* Ed. Edgar V. Roberts and Henry E. Jacobs. 376–385. Upper Saddle River, New Jersey: Prentice-Hall, Inc., 1998.
Introduction to a work included in a published edition	Washington, Margaret. Introduction to *Narrative of Sojourner Truth,* by Sojourner Truth. New York: Vintage Books, 1993 [According to CMS style, you should avoid this type of entry unless the introduction is of special importance to the work.]
Signed article in a weekly magazine	Wallace, Charles. "A Vodacious Deal." *Time,* 14 February 2000, 63.
Signed article in a monthly magazine	Gustaitis, Joseph. "The Sticky History of Chewing Gum." *American History,* October 1998, 30–38.
Unsigned editorial or story	*Wall Street Journal,* 11 February 2000. [CMS states that items from newspapers are seldom listed in a bibliography. Instead, the name of the paper and the relevant dates are listed.]
Signed pamphlet	[No style is offered under this heading.]
Pamphlet with no author, publisher, or date	[No style is offered under this heading.]
Filmstrips, slide programs, and videotape	Stevens, George. (director). *The Diary of Ann Frank.* 170 min. Beverly Hills, California: Twentieth Century Fox, 1994.
Radio or television program transcript	[No style is offered under this heading.]
Internet	[No style is offered under this heading.]
Newspaper	*Wall Street Journal,* 11 February 2000. [CMS states that items from newspapers are seldom listed in a bibliography. Instead, the name of the paper and the relevant dates are listed.]
Personal Interview	[CMS states that, since personal conversations are not available to the public, there is no reason to place them in the bibliography. However, the following format should be followed if they are listed.] Jane Smith, conversation with author, 10 February 2000.
CD (with multiple publishers)	Shakespeare, William. *Romeo and Juliet.* Oxford: Attica Cybernetics Ltd.; London: BBC Education; London: HarperCollins Publishers, 1995. CD-ROM.
Article from an encyclopedia	[According to CMS style, encyclopedias are not listed in bibliographies.]

Sample Works-Cited List (MLA)

Carwardine, Mark, Erich Hoyt, R. Ewan Fordyce, and
    Peter Gill. *The Nature Company Guides: Whales,*
    Dolphins, and Porpoises. New York: Time-Life
    Books, 1998.

Ellis, Richard. *Men and Whales.* New York: Knopf,
    1991

Whales in Danger. "Discovering Whales." 18 Oct. 1999
    <http://whales.magna.com.au/DISCOVER>

Sample Internal Citations (MLA)

It makes sense that baleen whales such as the
blue whale, the fin whale, the bowhead whale, the
humpback whale, and the sei whale (to name just
a few) grow to immense sizes (Carwardine 19–21).

Author's
last name

The blue whale has grooves running from under its
chin to partway along the length of its underbelly.
As in some other whales, these grooves expand
and allow even more food and water to be taken in
(Ellis 18–21).

page numbers
where
information
can be found

Internet Research Handbook

Introduction to the Internet

The Internet is a series of networks that are interconnected all over the world. The Internet allows users to have almost unlimited access to information stored on the networks. Dr. Berners-Lee, a physicist, created the Internet in the 1980's by writing a small computer program that allowed pages to be linked together using key words. The Internet was mostly text-based until 1992, when a computer program called the NCSA Mosaic (National Center for Supercomputing Applications at the University of Illinois) was created. This program was the first Web browser. The development of Web browsers greatly eased the ability of the user to navigate through all the pages stored on the Web. Very soon, the appearance of the Web was altered as well. More appealing visuals were added, and sound was also implemented. This change made the Web more user-friendly and more appealing to the general public.

Using the Internet for Research

Key Word Search

Before you begin a search, you should identify your specific topic. To make searching easier, narrow your subject to a key word or a group of key words. These are your search terms, and they should be as specific as possible. For example, if you are looking for the latest concert dates for your favorite musical group, you might use the band's name as a key word. However, if you were to enter the name of the group in the query box of the search engine, you might be presented with thousands of links to information about the group that is unrelated to your needs. You might locate such information as band member biographies, the group's history, fan reviews of concerts, and hundreds of sites with related names containing information that is irrelevant to your search. Because you used such a broad key word, you might need to navigate through all that information before you find a link or subheading for concert dates. In contrast, if you were to type in "Duplex Arena and [band name]" you would have a better chance of locating pages that contain this information.

How to Narrow Your Search

If you have a large group of key words and still don't know which ones to use, write out a list of all the words you are considering. Once you have completed the list, scrutinize it. Then, delete the words that are least important to your search, and highlight those that are most important.

These **key search connectors** can help you fine-tune your search:

- AND: narrows a search by retrieving documents that include both terms. For example: *baseball AND playoffs*
- OR: broadens a search by retrieving documents including any of the terms. For example: *playoffs OR championships*
- NOT: narrows a search by excluding documents containing certain words. For example: *baseball NOT history of*

Tips for an Effective Search

1. Keep in mind that search engines can be case-sensitive. If your first attempt at searching fails, check your search terms for misspellings and try again.

2. If you are entering a group of key words, present them in order, from the most important to the least important key word.

3. Avoid opening the link to every single page in your results list. Search engines present pages in descending order of relevancy. The most useful pages will be located at the top of the list. However, read the description of each link before you open the page.

4. When you use some search engines, you can find helpful tips for specializing your search. Take the opportunity to learn more about effective searching.

Other Ways to Search

Using On-line Reference Sites *How* you search should be tailored to *what* you are hoping to find. If you are looking for data and facts, use reference sites before you jump onto a simple search engine. For example, you can find reference sites to provide definitions of words, statistics about almost any subject, biographies, maps, and concise information on many topics. Some useful on-line reference sites:

    On-line libraries
    On-line periodicals
    Almanacs
    Encyclopedias

You can find these sources using subject searches.

Conducting Subject Searches As you prepare to go on-line, consider your subject and the best way to find information to suit your needs. If you are looking for general information on a topic and you want your search results to be extensive, consider the subject search indexes on most search engines. These indexes, in the form of category and subject lists, often appear on the first page of a search engine. When you click on a specific highlighted word, you will be presented with a new screen containing subcategories of the topic you chose. In the screen shots below, the category *Sports & Recreation* provided a second index for users to focus a search even further.

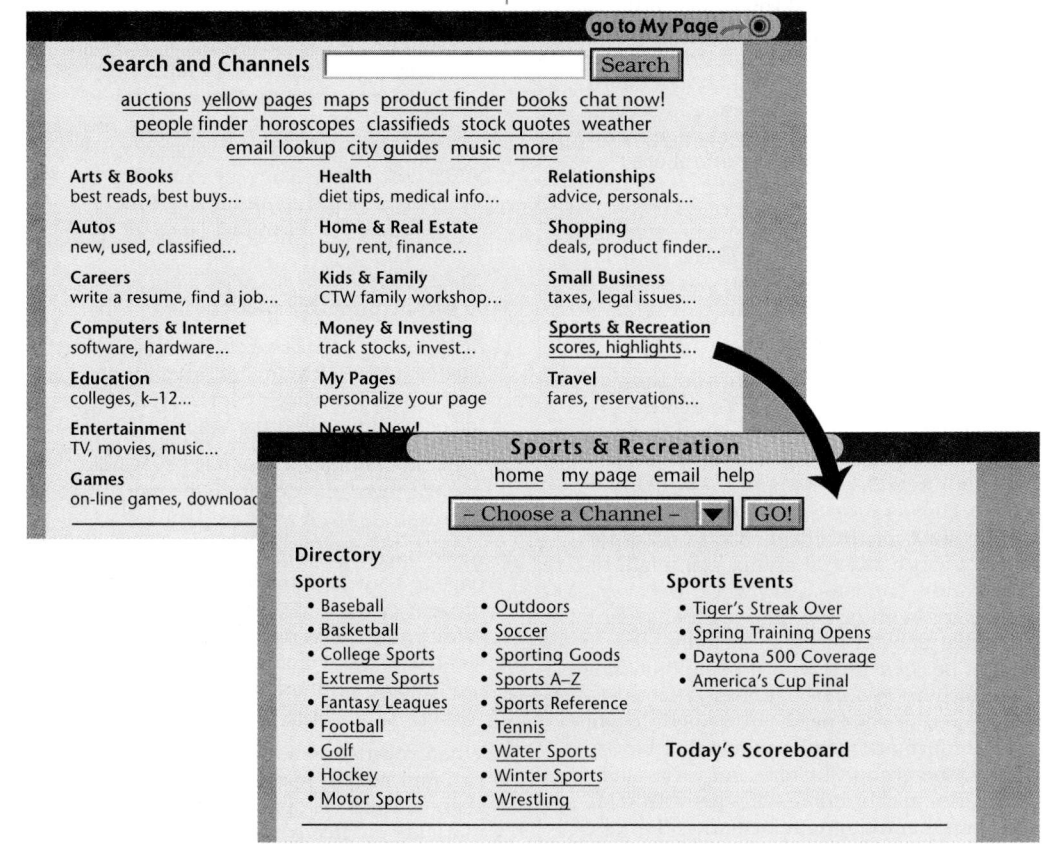

Evaluating the Reliability of Internet Resources

Just as you would evaluate the quality, bias, and validity of any other research material you locate, check the source of information you find on-line. Compare these two sites containing information on the poet and writer Langston Hughes:

Site A is a personal Web site constructed by a college student. It contains no bibliographic information or links to sites that he used. Included on the site are several poems by Langston Hughes and a student essay about the poet's use of symbolism. It has not been updated in more than six months.

Site B is a Web site constructed and maintained by the English Department of a major university. Information on Hughes is presented in a scholarly format, with a bibliography and credits for the writer. The site includes links to other sites and indicates new features that are added weekly.

For your own research, consider the information you find on Site B to be more reliable and accurate than that on Site A. Because it is maintained by experts in their field who are held accountable for their work, the university site will be a better research tool than the student-generated one.

Tips for Evaluating Internet Sources

1. Consider who constructed and now maintains the Web page. Determine whether this author is a reputable source. Often, the URL endings indicate a source.

   - Sites ending in *.edu* are maintained by educational institutions.
   - Sites ending in *.gov* are maintained by government agencies (federal, state, or local).
   - Sites ending in *.org* are normally maintained by nonprofit organizations and agencies.
   - Sites with a *.com* ending are commercially or personally maintained.

2. Skim the official and trademarked Web pages first. It is safe to assume that the information you draw from Web pages of reputable institutions, on-line encyclopedias, on-line versions of major daily newspapers, or government-owned sites produce information as reliable as the material you would find in print. In contrast, unbranded sites or those generated by individuals tend to borrow information from other sources without providing documentation. As information travels from one source to another, the information has likely been muddled, misinterpreted, edited, or revised.

3. You can still find valuable information in the less "official" sites. Check for the writer's credentials and then consider these factors:

   - Don't let official-looking graphics or presentations fool you.
   - Make sure the information is updated enough to suit your needs. Many Web pages will indicate how recently they have been updated.
   - If the information is borrowed, see whether you can trace it back to its original source.

Respecting Copyrighted Material

Because the Internet is a relatively new and quickly growing medium, issues of copyright and ownership arise almost daily. As laws begin to govern the use and reuse of material posted on-line, they may change the way that people can access or reprint material.

Text, photographs, music, and fine art printed on-line may not be reproduced without acknowledged permission of the copyright owner.

Glossary of Internet Terms

attached file: a file containing information, such as a text document or GIF image, that can be attached to an e-mail message; reports, pictures, or even spreadsheets can be transmitted to others by attaching these to messages as files

bandwidth: the amount of information, mainly compressed in bits per second (bps), that can be sent through a connection within a specific amount of time; depending on how fast your modem is, 15,000 bits (roughly one page of text) can be transferred per second

bit: a binary digit of computerized data, which is represented by a single digit that is either a 1 or a 0; a group of bits constitutes a byte

bookmark: a feature of your Web browser that allows you to place a "bookmark" on a Web page to which you wish to return at a later time

bulletin board system: a computer system that members access in order to join on-line discussion groups or to post announcements

case-sensitivity: the quality of a search engine that causes it to respond to upper- or lowercase letters in different ways

chat room: informal on-line gathering sites where people share conversations, experiences, or information on a specific topic; many chat rooms do not require users to provide their identity, so the reliability or safety of these sites is uncertain

cookie: a digitized piece of information that is sent to a Web browser by a Web server, intended to be saved on a computer; cookies gather information about the user, such as user preferences, or recent on-line purchases; a Web browser can be set to either accept or reject cookies

cyberspace: a term referring to the electronic environment connecting all computer network information with the people who use it

database: a large collection of data that have been formatted to fit a certain user-defined standard

digerati: a slang term to describe Internet experts; an offshoot of the term *literati*

download: to copy files, or open Web pages, onto your computer

e-mail: electronic mail, or the exchange of messages via the Internet; because it is speedier than traditional mail and offers easier global access, e-mail has grown in popularity; e-mail messages can be sent to a single person or in bulk to a group of people

error message: a displayed communication or printout that reports a problem with a program or Web page

FTP site (file transfer protocol): a password-protected server on the Internet that allows the transfer of information from one computer to another

GIF (Graphic Interchange Format): a form of graphics used on the Web

graphics: information displayed as pictures or images instead of text

hits: items retrieved by a key word search; the number tracking the volume of visits to a Web site

home page: the main Web page for an individual or an organization, containing links to subpages within

HTML (HyperText Markup Language): the coding text that is the foundation for creating Web pages

interactivity: a quality of some Web pages that encourages the frequent exchange of information between user and computer

Internet: a worldwide computer network that supports services such as the World Wide Web, e-mail, and file transfer

JPEG (Joint Photo Experts Group, the developers): a form of Web graphics especially suited to photographs

K: a term used to describe the size of a file or the capacity of a computer's memory or storage, as in 2K or 65K

key word: search term entered into the query box of a search engine to direct the results of the search

link: an icon or word on a Web page that, when clicked, transfers the user to another Web page or to a different document within the same page

login: the phrase or term users present as an account name in order to gain access to a Web site; a login is usually accompanied by a password

modem: a device that transfers data to a computer through a phone line. A computer's modem connects to a server, which then sends information in the form of digital signals. The modem converts these signals into waves, for the purpose of information reception. The speed of a modem affects how quickly a computer can receive and download information.

newsgroup: an on-line discussion group, where users can post and respond to messages; the most prevalent collection of newsgroups is found on USENET

newbie: jargon used to describe Internet novices

page: a computer file written in HTML that can be nearly any length; most pages are limited to 400 lines

query box: the blank box in a search engine where your search terms are input

relevance ranking: the act of displaying the results of a search in the order of their relevance to the search terms

search engines: tools that help you navigate databases to locate information; search engines respond to a key word search by providing the user with a directo-

ry of multiple Web pages about the key word or containing the key word.

server: a principal computer responsible for connecting other client computers to the Internet

signature: a preprogrammed section of text that is automatically added to an e-mail message

surfing: the process of reading Web pages and of moving from one Web site to another

URL (Uniform Resource Locator): a Web page's address; a URL can look like this:

http://www.phwg.phschool.com or
*http://www.senate.gov/~appropriations/
labor/testimony*

usenet: a worldwide system of discussion groups, or newsgroups

vanity pages: Web sites placed on-line by people to tell about themselves or their interests; vanity pages do not have any commercial or informational value

virus: a set of instructions, hidden in a computer system or transferred via e-mail or electronic files, that can cause problems with a computer's ability to perform normally

Web page: a document written in HTML that contains graphics, text, or sound files; a Web page can be found by its URL

Web site: a collection of Web pages that are linked together

WWW (World Wide Web): a term referring to the multitude of information systems found on the Internet; this includes FTP, Gopher, telnet, and http sites

W3: a group of Internet experts, including networking professionals, academics, scientists, and corporate interests, who maintain and develop technologies and standards for the Internet

zip: the minimizing of files through compression; this function makes for easier transmittal over networks; a receiver can then open the file by "unzipping" it

Commonly Overused Words

When you write, use the most precise word for your meaning, not the word that comes to mind first. Consult this thesaurus to find alternatives for some commonly overused words. Consult a full-length thesaurus to find alternatives to words that do not appear here. Keep in mind that the choices offered in a thesaurus do not all mean exactly the same thing. Review all the options, and choose the one that best expresses your meaning.

about approximately, nearly, almost, approaching, close to

absolutely unconditionally, perfectly, completely, ideally, purely

activity action, movement, operation, labor, exertion, enterprise, project, pursuit, endeavor, job, assignment, pastime, scheme, task

add attach, affix, join, unite, append, increase, amplify

affect adjust, influence, transform, moderate, incline, motivate, prompt

amazing overwhelming, astonishing, startling, unexpected, stunning, dazzling, remarkable

awesome impressive, stupendous, fabulous, astonishing, outstanding

bad defective, inadequate, poor, unsatisfactory, disagreeable, offensive, repulsive, corrupt, wicked, naughty, harmful, injurious, unfavorable

basic essential, necessary, indispensable, vital, fundamental, elementary

beautiful attractive, appealing, alluring, exqui-site, gorgeous, handsome, stunning

begin commence, found, initiate, introduce, launch, originate

better preferable, superior, worthier

big enormous, extensive, huge, immense, massive

boring commonplace, monotonous, tedious, tiresome

bring accompany, cause, convey, create, conduct, deliver, produce

cause origin, stimulus, inspiration, motive

certain unquestionable, incontrovertible, unmistakable, indubitable, assured, confident

change alter, transform, vary, replace, diversify

choose select, elect, nominate, prefer, identify

decent respectable, adequate, fair, suitable

definitely unquestionably, clearly, precisely, positively, inescapably

easy effortless, natural, comfortable, undemanding, pleasant, relaxed

effective impressive, striking, powerful, successful

emphasize underscore, feature, accentuate

end limit, boundary, finish, conclusion, finale, resolution

energy vitality, vigor, force, dynamism

enjoy savor, relish, revel, benefit

entire complete, inclusive, unbroken, integral

excellent superior, remarkable, splendid, unsurpassed, superb, magnificent

exciting thrilling, stirring, rousing, dramatic

far distant, remote

fast swift, quick, fleet, hasty, instant, accelerated

fill occupy, suffuse, pervade, saturate, inflate, stock

finish complete, conclude, cease, achieve, exhaust, deplete, consume

funny comical, ludicrous, amusing, droll, entertaining, bizarre, unusual, uncommon

get obtain, receive, acquire, procure, achieve

give bestow, donate, supply, deliver, distribute, impart

go proceed, progress, advance, move

good satisfactory, serviceable, functional, competent, virtuous, striking

great tremendous, superior, remarkable, eminent, proficient, expert

happy pleased, joyous, elated, jubilant, cheerful, delighted

hard arduous, formidable, complex, complicated, rigorous, harsh

help assist, aid, support, sustain, serve

hurt injure, harm, damage, wound, impair

important significant, substantial, weighty, meaningful, critical, vital, notable

interesting absorbing, appealing, entertaining, fascinating, thought-provoking

job task, work, business, undertaking, occupation, vocation, chore, duty, assignment

keep retain, control, possess

kind type, variety, sort, form

know comprehend, understand, realize, perceive, discern

like (adj) similar, equivalent, parallel

like (verb) enjoy, relish, appreciate

main primary, foremost, dominant

make build, construct, produce, assemble, fashion, manufacture

mean plan, intend, suggest, propose, indicate

more supplementary, additional, replenishment

new recent, modern, current, novel

next subsequently, thereafter, successively

nice pleasant, satisfying, gracious, charming

old aged, mature, experienced, used, worn, former, previous

open unobstructed, accessible

part section, portion, segment, detail, element, component

perfect flawless, faultless, ideal, consummate

plan scheme, design, system, plot

pleasant agreeable, gratifying, refreshing, welcome

prove demonstrate, confirm, validate, verify, corroborate

quick brisk, prompt, responsive, rapid, nimble, hasty

really truly, genuinely, extremely, undeniably

regular standard, routine, customary, habitual

see regard, behold, witness, gaze, realize, notice

small diminutive, miniature, minor, insignificant, slight, trivial

sometimes occasionally, intermittently, sporadically, periodically

take grasp, capture, choose, select, tolerate, endure

terrific extraordinary, magnificent, marvelous

think conceive, imagine, ponder, reflect, contemplate

try attempt, endeavor, venture, test

use employ, operate, utilize

very unusually, extremely, deeply, exceedingly, profoundly

want desire, crave, yearn, long

Commonly Misspelled Words

The list on these pages presents words that cause problems for many people. Some of these words are spelled according to set rules, but others follow no specific rules. As you review this list, check to see how many of the words give you trouble in your own writing. Then, read the instruction in the "Vocabulary and Spelling" chapter in the book for strategies and suggestions for improving your own spelling habits.

abbreviate	athletic	catastrophe	curious
absence	attendance	category	cylinder
absolutely	auxiliary	ceiling	deceive
abundance	awkward	cemetery	decision
accelerate	bandage	census	deductible
accidentally	banquet	certain	defendant
accumulate	bargain	changeable	deficient
accurate	barrel	characteristic	definitely
ache	battery	chauffeur	delinquent
achievement	beautiful	chief	dependent
acquaintance	beggar	clothes	descendant
adequate	beginning	coincidence	description
admittance	behavior	colonel	desert
advertisement	believe	column	desirable
aerial	benefit	commercial	dessert
affect	bicycle	commission	deteriorate
aggravate	biscuit	commitment	dining
aggressive	bookkeeper	committee	disappointed
agreeable	bought	competitor	disastrous
aisle	boulevard	concede	discipline
all right	brief	condemn	dissatisfied
allowance	brilliant	congratulate	distinguish
aluminum	bruise	connoisseur	effect
amateur	bulletin	conscience	eighth
analysis	buoyant	conscientious	eligible
analyze	bureau	conscious	embarrass
ancient	bury	contemporary	enthusiastic
anecdote	buses	continuous	entrepreneur
anniversary	business	controversy	envelope
anonymous	cafeteria	convenience	environment
answer	calendar	coolly	equipped
anticipate	campaign	cooperate	equivalent
anxiety	canceled	cordially	especially
apologize	candidate	correspondence	exaggerate
appall	capacity	counterfeit	exceed
appearance	capital	courageous	excellent
appreciate	capitol	courteous	exercise
appropriate	captain	courtesy	exhibition
architecture	career	criticism	existence
argument	carriage	criticize	experience
associate	cashier	curiosity	explanation

extension
extraordinary
familiar
fascinating
February
fiery
financial
fluorescent
foreign
forfeit
fourth
fragile
gauge
generally
genius
genuine
government
grammar
grievance
guarantee
guard
guidance
handkerchief
harass
height
humorous
hygiene
ignorant
illegible
immediately
immigrant
independence
independent
indispensable
individual
inflammable
intelligence
interfere
irrelevant
irritable
jewelry
judgment
knowledge
laboratory
lawyer
legible
legislature
leisure
liable

library
license
lieutenant
lightning
likable
liquefy
literature
loneliness
magnificent
maintenance
marriage
mathematics
maximum
meanness
mediocre
mileage
millionaire
minimum
minuscule
miscellaneous
mischievous
misspell
mortgage
naturally
necessary
negotiate
neighbor
neutral
nickel
niece
ninety
noticeable
nuclear
nuisance
obstacle
occasion
occasionally
occur
occurred
occurrence
omitted
opinion
opportunity
optimistic
outrageous
pamphlet
parallel
paralyze
parentheses

particularly
patience
permanent
permissible
perseverance
persistent
personally
perspiration
persuade
phenomenal
phenomenon
physician
pleasant
pneumonia
possess
possession
possibility
prairie
precede
preferable
prejudice
preparation
prerogative
previous
primitive
privilege
probably
procedure
proceed
prominent
pronunciation
psychology
publicly
pursue
questionnaire
realize
really
recede
receipt
receive
recognize
recommend
reference
referred
rehearse
relevant
reminiscence
renowned
repetition

restaurant
rhythm
ridiculous
sandwich
satellite
schedule
scissors
secretary
siege
solely
sponsor
subtle
subtlety
superintendent
supersede
surveillance
susceptible
tariff
temperamental
theater
threshold
truly
unmanageable
unwieldy
usage
usually
valuable
various
vegetable
voluntary
weight
weird
whale
wield
yield

Abbreviations Guide

Abbreviations, shortened versions of words or phrases, can be valuable tools in writing if you know when and how to use them. They can be very helpful in informal writing situations, such as taking notes or writing lists. However, only a few abbreviations can be used in formal writing. They are: *Mr., Mrs., Miss, Ms., Dr., A.M., P.M., A.D., B.C., M.A, B.A., Ph.D.,* and *M.D.*

The following pages provide the conventional abbreviations for a variety of words.

Abbreviations of Common Titles

Ambassador	Amb.	Lieutenant	Lt.
Attorney	Atty.	Major	Maj.
Brother	Br.	President	Pres.
Brigadier-General	Brig. Gen.	Professor	Prof.
Captain	Capt.	Representative	Rep.
Commander	Cmdr.	Reverend	Rev.
Colonel	Col.	Secretary	Sec.
Commissioner	Com.	Senator	Sen.
Corporal	Cpl.	Sergeant	Sgt.
Doctor	Dr.	Sister	Sr.
Father	Fr.	Superintendent	Supt.
Governor	Gov.	Treasurer	Treas.
Honorable	Hon.	Vice Admiral	Vice Adm.

Abbreviations of Academic Degrees

Bachelor of Arts	B.A. (or A.B.)	Esquire (lawyer)	Esq.
Bachelor of Science	B.S. (or S.B.)	Master of Arts	M.A. (or A.M.)
Doctor of Dental Surgery	D.D.S.	Master of Business Administration	M.B.A.
Doctor of Divinity	D.D.		
Doctor of Education	Ed.D.	Master of Fine Arts	M.F.A.
Doctor of Laws	LL.D.	Master of Science	M.S. (or S.M.)
Doctor of Medicine	M.D.	Registered Nurse	R.N.
Doctor of Philosophy	Ph.D.		

State	Traditional	Postal Service	State	Traditional	Postal Service
Alabama	Ala.	AL	Montana	Mont.	MT
Alaska	Alaska	AK	Nebraska	Nebr.	NB
Arizona	Ariz.	AZ	Nevada	Nev.	NV
Arkansas	Ark.	AR	New Hampshire	N.H.	NH
California	Calif.	CA	New Jersey	N.J.	NJ
Colorado	Colo.	CO	New Mexico	N.M.	NM
Connecticut	Conn.	CT	New York	N.Y.	NY
Delaware	Del.	DE	North Carolina	N.C.	NC
Florida	Fla.	FL	North Dakota	N.Dak.	ND
Georgia	Ga.	GA	Ohio	O.	OH
Hawaii	Hawaii	HI	Oklahoma	Okla.	OK
Idaho	Ida.	ID	Oregon	Ore.	OR
Illinois	Ill.	IL	Pennsylvania	Pa.	PA
Indiana	Ind.	IN	Rhode Island	R.I.	RI
Iowa	Iowa	IA	South Carolina	S.C.	SC
Kansas	Kans.	KS	South Dakota	S.Dak.	SD
Kentucky	Ky.	KY	Tennessee	Tenn.	TN
Louisiana	La.	LA	Texas	Tex.	TX
Maine	Me.	ME	Utah	Utah	UT
Maryland	Md.	MD	Vermont	Vt.	VT
Massachusetts	Mass.	MA	Virginia	Va.	VA
Michigan	Mich.	MI	Washington	Wash.	WA
Minnesota	Minn.	MN	West Virginia	W. Va	WV
Mississippi	Miss.	MS	Wisconsin	Wis.	WI

Common Geographical Abbreviations

Apartment	Apt.	National	Natl.
Avenue	Ave.	Peninsula	Pen.
Building	Bldg.	Park, Peak	Pk.
Block	Blk.	Province	Prov.
Boulevard .	Blvd.	Point	Pt.
County	Co.	Road	Rd.
District	Dist.	Route	Rte.
Drive	Dr.	Square	Sq.
Fort	Ft.	Street	St.
Island	Is.	Territory	Terr.
Mountain	Mt.		

Abbreviations of Traditional Measurements

inch(es)	in.	ounce(s)	oz.
foot, feet	ft.	pound(s)	lb.
yard(s)	yd.	pint(s)	pt.
mile(s)	mi.	quart(s)	qt.
teaspoon(s)	tsp.	gallon(s)	gal.
tablespoon(s)	tbsp.	Fahrenheit	F.

Abbreviations of Metric Measurements

millimeter(s)	mm	liter(s)	L
centimeter(s)	cm	kiloliter(s)	kL
meter(s)	m	milligram(s)	mg
kilometer(s)	km	centigram(s)	cg
milliliter(s)	mL	gram(s)	g
centiliter(s)	cL	Celsius	C

Other Commonly Used Abbreviations

and others	et al.	manager	mgr.
about (used with dates)	c., ca., circ.	manufacturing	mfg.
anonymous	anon.	market	mkt.
approximately	approx.	measure	meas.
associate, association	assoc., assn.	merchandise	mdse.
auxiliary	aux., auxil.	miles per hour	mph
bibliography	bibliog.	miscellaneous	misc.
boxes	bx(s).	money order	M.O.
bucket	bkt.	note well; take notice	N.B.
bulletin	bull.	number	no.
bushel	bu.	package	pkg.
capital letter	cap.	page	pg.
cash on delivery	C.O.D.	pages	pp.
department	dept.	pair(s)	pr(s).
discount	disc.	parenthesis	paren.
dozen(s)	doz.	Patent Office	pat. off.
each	ea.	piece(s)	pc(s).
edition, editor	ed.	poetical, poetry	poet.
equivalent	equiv.	private	pvt.
established	est.	proprietor	prop.
fiction	fict.	pseudonym	pseud.
for example	e.g.	published, publisher	pub.
free of charge	grat., gratis	received	recd.
General Post Office	G.P.O.	reference, referee	ref.
government	gov., govt.	revolutions per minute	rpm
graduate, graduated	grad.	rhetorical, rhetoric	rhet.
Greek, Grecian	Gr.	right	R.
headquarters	hdqrs.	scene	sc.
height	ht.	special, specific	spec.
hospital	hosp.	spelling, species	sp.
illustrated	ill., illus.	that is	i.e.
including, inclusive	incl.	treasury, treasurer	treas.
introduction, introductory	intro.	volume	vol.
italics	ital.	weekly	wkly
karat, carat	k., kt.	weight	wt.
left	L.		

Proofreading Symbols Reference

Proofreading symbols make it easier to show where changes are needed in a paper. When proofreading your own or a classmate's work, use these standard proofreading symbols.

insert	I proofred. *a*∧
delete	I<del>p</del> proofread.
close up space	I proof read.
delete and close up space	I proofreade.
begin new paragraph	¶ I proofread.
spell out	I proofread ⑩ papers. (sp)
lowercase	I Proofread. (lc)
capitalize	i proofread. (cap)
transpose letters	I proofraed. (tr)
transpose words	I only proofread her paper. (tr)
period	I will proofread⊙
comma	I will proofread∧and she will help.
colon	We will proofread for the following errors∧
semicolon	I will proofread∧she will help. ∧;
single quotation marks	She said, "I enjoyed the story∧The Invalid." ∨ ∨
double quotation marks	She said∧I enjoyed the story.∧
apostrophe	Did you borrow Sylvias book? ∨
question mark	Did you borrow Sylvia's book∧ ?/
exclamation point	You're kidding∧ !/
hyphen	on∧line /=/
parentheses	William Shakespeare∧1564–1616∧

Student Publications

To share your writing with a wider audience, consider submitting it to a local, state, or national publication for student writing. Following are several magazines and Web sites that accept and publish student work.

Periodicals

Creative Kids P.O. Box 8813, Waco TX 76714

Merlyn's Pen: The National Magazine of Student Writing P.O. Box 1058, East Greenwich, RI 02818

Skipping Stones P.O. Box 3939, Eugene, OR 97403

The McGuffey Writer McGuffey Foundation School, 5128 Westgate Drive, Oxford, OH 45056

Writing! General Learning Corporation, 900 Skokie Boulevard, Northbrook, IL 60062

On-line Publications

Kid Pub http://en-grade.com/kidpub

MidLink Magazine http://longwood.cs.ucf.edu/~MidLink/

Wild Guess Magazine http://members.tripod.com/~WildGuess/

Contests

Annual Poetry Contest National Federation of State Poetry Societies, 3520 State Route 56, Mechanicsburg, OH 43044

National Written & Illustrated By . . . Awards Contest for Students Landmark Editions, Inc., 1402 Kansas Avenue, Kansas City, MO 64127

Paul A. Witty Outstanding Literature Award International Reading Association, Special Interest Group for Reading for Gifted and Creative Students, c/o Texas Christian University, P.O. Box 32925, Fort Worth, TX 76129

Seventeen Magazine Fiction Contest Seventeen Magazine, 850 Third Avenue, New York, NY 10022

The Young Playwrights Festival National Playwriting Competition 321 East 44th Street, Suite 906, New York, NY 10036

Glossary

A

accent: the emphasis on a syllable, usually in poetry

action verb: a word that tells what action someone or something is performing (See linking verb.)

active voice: the voice of a verb whose subject performs an action (See passive voice.)

adjective: a word that modifies a noun or pronoun by telling *what kind* or *which one*

adjective clause: a subordinate clause that modifies a noun or pronoun

adjective phrase: a prepositional phrase that modifies a noun or pronoun

adverb: a word that modifies a verb, an adjective, or another adverb

adverb clause: a subordinate clause that modifies a verb, an adjective, an adverb, or a verbal by telling *where, when, in what way, to what extent, under what condition,* or *why*

adverb phrase: a prepositional phrase that modifies a verb, an adjective, or an adverb

allegory: a literary work with two or more levels of meaning—a literal level and one or more symbolic levels

alliteration: the repetition of initial consonant sounds in accented syllables

allusion: a reference to a well-known person, place, event, literary work, or work of art

annotated bibliography: a research writing product that provides a list of materials on a given topic, along with publication information, summaries, or evaluations

apostrophe: a punctuation mark used to form possessive nouns and contractions

appositive: a noun or pronoun placed after another noun or pronoun to identify, rename, or explain the preceding word

appositive phrase: a noun or pronoun with its modifiers, placed next to a noun or pronoun to identify, rename, or explain the preceding word

article: one of three commonly used adjectives: *a, an,* and *the*

assonance: the repetition of vowel sounds in stressed syllables containing dissimilar consonant sounds

audience: the reader(s) a writer intends to reach

autobiographical writing: narrative writing that tells a true story about an important period, experience, or relationship in the writer's life

B

ballad: a song that tells a story (often dealing with adventure or romance) or a poem imitating such a song

bias: the attitudes or beliefs that affect a writer's ability to present a subject objectively

bibliography: a list of the sources of a research paper, including full bibliographic references for each source the writer consulted while conducting research (See works-cited list.)

biography: narrative writing that tells the story of an important period, experience, or relationship in a person's life, as reported by another

blueprinting: a prewriting technique in which a writer sketches a map of a home, school, neighborhood, or other meaningful place in order to spark memories or associations for further development

body paragraph: a paragraph in an essay that develops, explains, or supports the key ideas of the writing

brainstorming: a prewriting technique in which a group jots down as many ideas as possible about a given topic

C

cause-and-effect writing: expository writing that examines the relationship between events, explaining how one event or situation causes another

case: the form of a noun or pronoun that indicates how it functions in a sentence

character: a person (though not necessarily a human being) who takes part in the action of a literary work

characterization: the act of creating and developing a character through narration, description, and dialogue

citation: in formal research papers, the acknowledgment of ideas found in outside sources

clause: a group of words that has a subject and a verb

classical invention: a prewriting technique in which writers gather details about a topic by analyzing the category and subcategories to which the topic belongs

climax: the high point of interest or suspense in a literary work

coherence: a quality of written work in which all the parts flow logically from one idea to the next

colon: a punctuation mark used before an extended quotation, explanation, example, or series and after the salutation in a formal letter

comma: a punctuation mark used to separate words or groups of words

comparison-and-contrast writing: expository writing that describes the similarities and differences between two or more subjects in order to achieve a specific purpose

complement: a word or group of words that completes the meaning of a verb

compound sentence: a sentence that contains two or more independent clauses with no subordinate clauses

conclusion: the final paragraphs of a work of writing in which the writer may restate a main idea, summarize the points of the writing, or provide a closing remark to end the work effectively (*See* introduction, body paragraph, topical paragraph, functional paragraph.)

conflict: a struggle between opposing forces

conjugation: a list of the singular and plural forms of a verb in a particular tense

conjunction: a word used to connect other words or groups of words

connotation: the emotional associations that a word calls to mind (*See* denotation.)

consonance: the repetition of final consonant sounds in stressed syllables containing dissimilar vowel sounds

contraction: a shortened form of a word or phrase that includes an apostrophe to indicate the position of the missing letter(s)

coordinating conjunctions: words such as *and, but, nor,* and *yet* that connect similar words or groups of words

correlative conjunctions: word pairs such as *neither . . . nor, both . . . and,* and *whether . . . or* used to connect similar words or groups of words

couplet: a pair of rhyming lines written in the same meter

cubing: a prewriting technique in which a writer analyzes a subject from six specified angles: description; association; application; analysis; comparison and contrast; and evaluation

D

declarative sentence: a statement punctuated with a period

demonstrative pronouns: words such as *this, that, these,* and *those* used to single out specific people, places, or things

denotation: the objective meaning of a word; its definition independent of other associations the word calls to mind (*See* connotation.)

depth-charging: a drafting technique in which a writer elaborates on a sentence by developing a key word or idea

description: language or writing that uses sensory details to capture a subject

dialect: the form of a language spoken by people in a particular region or group

dialogue: a direct conversation between characters or people

diary: a personal record of daily events, usually written in prose

diction: a writer's word choice

direct object: a noun or a pronoun that receives the action of a transitive verb

direct quotation: a drafting technique in which writers indicate the exact words of another by enclosing them in quotation marks

drafting: a stage of the writing process that follows prewriting and precedes revising in which a writer gets ideas on paper in a rough format

drama: a story written to be performed by actors

documentary: nonfiction film that analyzes news events or another focused subject by combining interviews, film footage, narration, and other audio/visual components

documented essay: research writing that includes a limited number of research sources, providing full documentation parenthetically within the text

E

elaboration: a drafting technique in which a writer extends his or her ideas through the use of facts, examples, descriptions, details, or quotations

epic: a long narrative poem about the adventures of a god or a hero

essay: a short nonfiction work about a particular subject

etymology: the history of a word, showing where it came from and how it has evolved into its present spelling and meaning

exclamation mark: a punctuation mark used to indicate strong emotion

exclamatory sentence: a statement that conveys strong emotion and ends with an exclamation mark

exposition: writing to inform, addressing analytic purposes such as problem and solution, comparison and contrast, how-to, and cause and effect

extensive writing: writing products generated for others and from others, meant to be shared with an audience and often done for school assignments (*See* reflexive writing.)

F

fact: a statement that can be proved true (*See* opinion.)

fiction: prose writing about imaginary characters and events

figurative language: writing or speech not meant to be interpreted literally

firsthand biography: narrative writing that tells the story of an important period, experience, or relationship in a person's life, reported by a writer who knows the subject personally

five *W*'s: a prewriting technique in which writers gather details about a topic by generating answers to the following questions: *Who? What? Where? When?* and *Why?*

fragment: an incomplete idea punctuated as a complete sentence

freewriting: a prewriting technique in which a writer jots down as many ideas on a topic as possible quickly

functional paragraph: a paragraph that performs a specific role in composition, such as to arouse or sustain interest, to indicate dialogue, to make a transition (*See* topical paragraph.)

G

generalization: a statement that presents a rule or idea based on particular facts

gerund: a noun formed from the present participle of a verb (ending in -*ing*)

gerund phrase: a group of words containing a gerund and its modifiers or complements that function as a noun

grammar: the study of the forms of words and the way they are arranged in phrases, clauses, and sentences

H

helping verb: a verb added to another verb to make a single verb phrase that indicates the time at which an action takes place or whether it actually happens, could happen, or should happen

hexagonal: a prewriting technique in which a

writer analyzes a subject from six angles: literal level, personal allusions, theme, literary devices, literary allusions, and evaluation

homophones: pairs of words that sound the same as each other yet have different meanings and different spellings, as *hear/here*

how-to writing: expository writing that explains a process by providing step-by-step directions

humanities: forms of artistic expression including, but not limited to, fine art, photography, theater, film, music, and dance

hyperbole: a deliberate exaggeration or over-statement

hyphen: a punctuation mark used to combine numbers and word parts, to join certain compound words, and to show that a word has been broken between syllables at the end of a line

I

I-Search report: a research paper in which the writer addresses the research experience in addition to presenting the information gathered

image: a word or phrase that appeals to one or more of the senses—sight, hearing, touch, taste, or smell

imagery: the descriptive language used to re-create sensory experiences, set a tone, suggest emotions, and guide readers' reactions

imperative sentence: a statement that gives an order or a direction and ends with either a period or an exclamation mark

indefinite pronoun: a word such as *anyone, each,* or *many* that refers to a person, place, or thing, without specifying which one

independent clause: a group of words that contains both a subject and a verb and that can stand by itself as a complete sentence

indirect quotation: reporting only the general meaning of what a person said or thought; quotation marks are not needed

infinitive: the form of a verb that comes after the word *to* and acts as a noun, adjective, or adverb

infinitive phrase: a phrase introduced by an infinitive that may be used as a noun, an adjective, or an adverb

interjection: a word or phrase that expresses feeling or emotion and functions independently of a sentence

interrogative pronoun: a word such as *which* and *who* that introduces a question

interrogative sentence: a question that is punctuated with a question mark

intransitive verb: an action verb that does not take a direct object (*See* transitive verb.)

interview: an information-gathering technique in which one or more people pose questions to one or more other people who provide opinions or facts on a topic

introduction: the opening paragraphs of a work of writing in which the writer may capture the readers' attention and present a thesis statement to be developed in the writing (*See* body paragraph, topical paragraph, functional paragraph, conclusion.)

invisible writing: a prewriting technique in which a writer freewrites without looking at the product until the exercise is complete; this can be accomplished at a word processor with the monitor turned off or with carbon paper and an empty ballpoint pen

irony: the general name given to literary techniques that involve surprising, interesting, or amusing contradictions

itemizing: a prewriting technique in which a writer creates a second, more focused, set of ideas based on an original listing activity. (*See* listing.)

J

jargon: the specialized words and phrases unique to a specific field

journal: a notebook or other organized writing system in which daily events and personal impressions are recorded

K

key word: the word or phrase that directs an Internet or database search

L

layering: a drafting technique in which a writer elaborates on a statement by identifying and then expanding upon a central idea or word

lead: the opening sentences of a work of writing meant to grab the reader's interest, accomplished through a variety of methods, including providing an intriguing quotation, a surprising or provocative question or fact, an anecdote, or a description

learning log: a record-keeping system in which a student notes information about new ideas

legend: a widely told story about the past that may or may not be based in fact

legibility: the neatness and readability of words

linking verb: a word that expresses its subject's state of being or condition (*See* action verb.)

listing: a prewriting technique in which a writer prepares a list of ideas related to a specific topic. (*See* itemizing.)

looping: a prewriting activity in which a writer generates follow-up freewriting based on the identification of a key word or central idea in an original freewriting exercise

lyric poem: a poem expressing the observations and feelings of a single speaker

M

main clause: a group of words that has a subject and a verb and can stand alone as a complete sentence

memoir: autobiographical writing that provides an account of a writer's relationship with a person, event, or place

metaphor: a figure of speech in which one thing is spoken of as though it were something else

meter: the rhythmic pattern of a poem

monologue: a speech or performance given entirely by one person or by one character

mood: the feeling created in the reader by a literary work or passage

multimedia presentation: a technique for sharing information with an audience by enhancing narration and explanation with media, including video images, slides, audiotape recordings, music, and fine art

N

narration: writing that tells a story

narrative poem: a poem that tells a story in verse

nominative case: the form of a noun or pronoun used as the subject of a verb, as a predicate nominative, or as the pronoun in a nominative absolute (*See* objective case, possessive case.)

noun: a word that names a person, place, or thing

noun clause: a subordinate clause that acts as a noun

novel: an extended work of fiction that often has a complicated plot, many major and minor characters, a unifying theme, and several settings

O

objective case: the form of a noun or pronoun used as the object of any verb, verbal, or preposition, or as the subject of an infinitive (*See* nominative case, possessive case.)

observation: a prewriting technique involving close visual study of an object; a writing product that reports such a study

ode: a long formal lyric poem with a serious theme

open-book test: a form of assessment in which students are permitted to use books and class notes to respond to test questions

opinion: beliefs that can be supported but not proved to be true (*See* fact.)

onomotopoeia: words such as *buzz* and *plop* that suggest the sounds they name

oral tradition: the body of songs, stories, and poems preserved by being passed from generation to generation by word of mouth

outline: a prewriting or study technique that allows writers or readers to organize the presentation and order of information

oxymoron: a figure of speech that fuses two contradictory or opposing ideas, such as "freezing fire" or "happy grief"

P

parable: a short, simple story from which a moral or religious lesson can be drawn

paradox: a statement that seems to be contradictory but that actually presents a truth

paragraph: a group of sentences that share a common topic or purpose and that focus on a single main idea or thought

parallelism: the placement of equal ideas in words, phrases, or clauses of similar types

paraphrase: restating an author's idea in different words, often to share information by making the meaning clear to readers

parentheses: punctuation marks used to set off asides and explanations when the material is not essential

participial phrase: a group of words made up of a participle and its modifiers and complements that acts as an adjective

participle: a form of a verb that can act as an adjective

passive voice: the voice of a verb whose subject receives an action (*See* active voice.)

peer review: a revising technique in which writers meet with other writers to share focused feedback on a draft

pentad: a prewriting technique in which a writer analyzes a subject from five specified points: actors, acts, scenes, agencies, and purposes

period: a punctuation mark used to end a declarative sentence, an indirect question, and most abbreviations

personal pronoun: a word such as *I, me, you, we, us, he, him, she, her, they,* and *them* that refers to the person speaking; the person spoken to; or the person, place, or thing spoken about

personification a figure of speech in which a nonhuman subject is given human characteristics

persuasion: writing or speaking that attempts to convince others to accept a position on an issue of concern to the writer

phrase: a group of words without a subject and verb that functions as one part of speech

plot: the sequence of events in narrative writing

plural: the form of a word that indicates more than one item is being mentioned

poetry: a category of writing in which the final product may make deliberate use of rhythm, rhyme, and figurative language in order to express deeper feelings than those conveyed in ordinary speech (*See* prose, drama.)

point of view: the perspective, or vantage point, from which a story is told

portfolio: an organized collection of writing projects, including writing ideas, works in progress, final drafts, and the writer's reflections on the work

possessive case: the form of a noun or pronoun used to show ownership (*See* objective case, nominative case.)

prefix: one or more syllables added to the beginning of a word root *(See* root, suffix.)

preposition: a word that relates a noun or pronoun that appears with it to another word in the sentence to indicate relations of time, place, causality, responsibility, and motivation

prepositional phrase: a group of words that includes a preposition and a noun or pronoun

presenting: a stage of the writing process in which a writer shares a final draft with an audience through speaking, listening, or representing activities

prewriting: a stage of the writing process in which writers explore, choose, and narrow a topic and then gather necessary details for drafting

problem-and-solution writing: expository writing that examines a problem and provides a realistic solution

pronoun: a word that stands for a noun or for another word that takes the place of a noun

prose: a category of written language in which the end product is developed through sentences and paragraphs (*See* poetry; drama.)

publishing: a stage of the writing process in which a writer shares the written version of a final draft with an audience

punctuation: the set of symbols used to convey specific directions to the reader

purpose: the specific goal or reason a writer chooses for a writing task

Q

question mark: a punctuation mark used to end an interrogative sentence or an incomplete question

quicklist: a prewriting technique in which a writer creates an impromptu, unresearched list of ideas related to a specific topic

quotation mark: a punctuation mark used to indicate the beginning and end of a person's exact speech or thoughts

R

ratiocination: a systematic approach to the revision process that involves color-coding elements of writing for evaluation

reflective essay: autobiographical writing in which a writer shares a personal experience and then provides insight about the event

reflexive pronoun: a word that ends in -*self* or -*selves* and names the person or thing receiving an action when that person or thing is the same as the one performing the action

reflexive writing: writing generated for oneself and from oneself, not necessarily meant to be shared, in which the writer makes all decisions regarding form and purpose (*See* extensive writing.)

refrain: a regularly repeated line or group of lines in a poem or song

relative pronoun: a pronoun such as *that, which, who, whom,* or *whose* that begins a

subordinate clause and connects it to another idea in the sentence

reporter's formula: a prewriting technique in which writers gather details about a topic by generating answers to the following questions: *Who? What? Where? When?* and *Why?*

research: a prewriting technique in which writers gather information from outside sources such as library reference materials, interviews, and the Internet

research writing: expository writing that presents and interprets information gathered through an extensive study of a subject

response to literature writing: persuasive, expository, or narrative writing that presents a writer's analysis of or reactions to a published work

revising: a stage of the writing process in which a writer reworks a rough draft to improve both form and content

rhyme: the repetition of sounds at the ends of words

rhyme scheme: the regular pattern of rhyming words in a poem or stanza

rhythm: the form or pattern of words or music in which accents or beats come at certain fixed intervals

root: the base of a word (*See* prefix, suffix.)

rubric: an assessment tool, generally organized in a grid, to indicate the range of success or failure according to specific criteria

run-on sentence: two or more complete sentences punctuated incorrectly as one

S

salutation: the greeting in a formal letter

satire: writing that ridicules or holds up to contempt the faults of individuals or of groups

SEE method: an elaboration technique in which a writer presents a statement, an extension, and an elaboration to develop an idea

semicolon: a punctuation mark used to join independent clauses that are not already joined by a conjunction

sentence: a group of words with a subject and a predicate that expresses a complete thought

setting: the time and place of the action of a piece of narrative writing

short story: a brief fictional narrative told in prose

simile: a figure of speech in which *like* or *as* is used to make a comparison between two basically unrelated ideas

sonnet: a fourteen-line lyric poem with a single theme

speaker: the imaginary voice assumed by the writer of a poem

stanza: a group of lines in a poem, seen as a unit

statistics: facts presented in numerical form, such as ratios, percentages, or summaries

subject: the word or group of words in a sentence that tells whom or what the sentence is about

subordinate clause: a group of words containing both a subject and a verb that cannot stand by itself as a complete sentence

subordinating conjunction: a word used to join two complete ideas by making one of the ideas dependent on the other

suffix: one or more syllables added to the end of a word root (*See* prefix, root.)

summary: a brief statement of the main ideas and supporting details presented in a piece of writing

symbol: something that is itself and also stands for something else

T

theme: the central idea, concern, or purpose in a piece of narrative writing, poetry, or drama

thesis statement: a statement of an essay's main idea; all information in the essay supports or elaborates this idea

tone: a writer's attitude toward the readers and toward the subject

topic sentence: a sentence that states the main idea of a paragraph

topic web: a prewriting technique in which a writer generates a graphic organizer to identify categories and subcategories of a topic

topical paragraph: a paragraph that develops, explains, and supports the topic sentence related to an essay's thesis statement

transition: words, phrases, or sentences that smooth writing by indicating the relationship among ideas

transitive verb: an action verb that takes a direct object (*See* intransitive verb.)

U

unity: a quality of written work in which all the parts fit together in a complete, self-contained whole

V

verbal: a word derived from the verb but used as a noun, adjective, or adverb (*See* gerund, infinitive, participle.)

verb: a word or group of words that expresses an action, a condition, or the fact that something exists while indicating the time of the action, condition, or fact

vignette: a brief narrative characterized by precise detail

voice: the distinctive qualities of a writer's style, including diction, attitude, sentence style, and ideas

W

works-cited list: a list of the sources of a research paper, including full bibliographic references for each source named in the body of the paper (*See* bibliography.)

Index

Note: **Bold numbers** show pages on which basic definitions appear.

A

a, an, the, **382**
Abbreviations
  academic degrees, **864**
  lists of common, **167**, **864–867**
  metric and standard measurements, **866**
  names of months, **167**
  names of states, **865**
  numerals of time, **167**
  titles, **167**, **864**
Accent, **870**
accept, except, **620**
ACT. *See* American College Testing Program
Action
  plan, 839
  in short story, **81**
  verbs, 362, 368, **870**
Active Voice, **870**. *See also* Verb Usage
Addresses, commas with, **670**
Adjective Clauses, 469–473, **870**
Adjective Phrases, 450–451, 676, **870**
Adjectives, **378**, **380–387**
  vs. adverbs, 393–394
  adverbs modifying, 392–393
  capitalizing proper, 645
  for comparisons, 601
  coordinate, **662**
  defined, **380–381**, **870**
  predicate, 440
  types of, **382–387**
Adverb Clauses, 143, 474–479, **870**
Adverb Phrases, 452–453, **870**
Adverbs, **378**, **390–394**, **870**
  for comparisons, 601
  conjunctive, **411**
  placement of, 217
  vs. prepositions, 405
  types of, **390**, **392**
  vs. verb phrase, 217
Advertisement, 156–175
  defined, **157**
  drafting, 163
  editing and proofreading, 167
  model from literature, 158
  prewriting, 159–162
  publishing and presenting, 168
  revising, 164–166
  rubric for self-assessment, 168
  types of, **157**
Advice Columns, 229
affect, effect, **316**, **620**
Agreement, Grammatical, 570–595
  See also Pronoun-Antecedent Agreement; Subject-Verb Agreement
Agreement, Points of, 751
ain't, arn't, **620**
ain't no, arn't any, **614**
all ready, already, **620**
all right, alright, **620**
all together, altogether, **620**
Allegories, **870**
Alliteration, **870**
Allusions, **870**
Almanacs, 824, 856
American College Testing Program (ACT), 831
American Psychological Association (APA), 852
among, between, **621**
Analogies
  answering, on tests, 829
  defined, **771**, **801**
  nouns in, on tests, 358–359
  and, **574**
Anecdotes, **49**, 140, 237
Annotated Bibliographies, **251**, **870**
Announcements, Public-Service, **157**
Antecedents, of pronouns, 346–347
  See also Pronoun-Antecedent Agreement
Anthologies, 119, 218
Antonyms, **770**
any, no, **616**
anywhere, everywhere, **621**
Apostrophes, 712–720, **870**
Appendixes, **791**
Application Forms, 325
  completing, **330–331**
  reading, **809**
model from literature, 158
Appositive Phrases, **215**, 453, **454–455**, **870**
Appositives
  defined, **453**, **870**
  nonessential, 699
  punctuating, 676, 680
Arguments, Supporting, 141
Arrows and Points Activity, 544
Art, Fine, **10**, 59, 757
  See also Humanities; Responding to Fine Art and Literature
Articles, Adjective
  defined, **870**
  types of, **382–383**
Articles, Published, 66, 203
as, like, **624**
Assessment. *See* Rubric for Self-Assessment; Writing for Assessment
Assignment Book, 814
Assonance, **870**
at, where, **621**
Atlases, 824
Attached Files, Electronic, **858**
Audiences
  addressing, directly for persuasion, 165
  analyzing persuasive essays for, 137
  for autobiographical writing, 56
  for comparison-and-contrast essays, 179, 182
  defined, **870**
  for description, 108
  identifying writer's, 178
  linking, with angle for advertisement, 162
  matching advertisement with target, 161
  matching research goals with, 258
  for problem-and-solution essays, 234
  profile of, 18
  questions to analyze profile of, 289
  tailoring narration language to, 80
  targeting, for cause-and-effect essays, 208

Audio Technology. *See* Media and Technology Skills
Audiotape, Autobiographical, 66
Authors
  identifying purpose of, 102–105, **799**
  language of, 803
  professional, 9
  strategies of, 9, 23, 49, 75, 101, 129, 157, 177, 203, 229, 251, 281, 309, 325
  See also Spotlight on the Humanities
Author's Forum, 90
Autobiographical Writing, 48–73
  defined, **49**, **870**
  drafting, 58–59
  editing and proofreading, 65
  model from literature, 50–53
  prewriting, 52–55
  publishing and presenting, 66
  revising, 60–64
  rubric for self-assessment, 66
  types of, **49**
awhile, a while, **621**

B

bad, badly, **621**
Ballads, 807, **870**
Bandwidth, Electronic, **858**
barely, hardly, scarcely, **617**
Basic Sentence Parts. *See* Sentence Parts, Basic
be, Forms of, **366**–370
because, **621**
being as, being that, **621**
beside, besides, **622**
between, among, **621**
Bias, 756, **870**
Biblical References, 681, 695
Bibliographies, **870**
  annotated, **251**
  conventions for writing, **269**
  textbook, **791**
Biographical References, 824
Biographies, **870**
  firsthand, **69**, **872**
  in library, 818
Bits, Electronic, **858**
Block Plan, **236**

Blocks, Paragraph, 41
Blueprinting, **870**
Body Paragraphs, **39**, 291, 312, **870**
Boldface, Word Processor, 760
Book Group, 299
Bookmarks, Electronic, **858**
Bracketing, 114, 296
  See also Circling; Color-Coding; Highlighting; Underlining
Brainstorming, 7, **870**
bring, take, **622**
Budget, Developing, 843
Building Your Portfolio
  action letter, 242
  advertisement bulletin board, 168
  advertisement mailings, 168
  article for school publication, 66
  book group, 299
  class anthology, 218
  comparison essay on-line, 192
  comparison photo montage, 192
  on computers, 29
  descriptive anthology, 119
  descriptive oral presentation, 119
  exam comments, 317
  library display, 299
  panel discussion, 270
  persuasive essay for action, 147
  persuasive essay for mailing, 147
  recording autobiographical audiotape, 66
  short-story author's forum, 90
  short-story illustrations, 90
  solutions handbook, 242
  study group comparisons, 317
  web posting, 218, 270
Bulleted Lists, Word Processor, 760
Bulletin Board Advertisement, 168
Bulletin Board System, Electronic, **858**
but, only, **617**

C

Calendar, Electronic, 842
Campaigns, Political, **157**
Capitalization, **636**–651
  within parentheses, 702, 704
  in word processing, 760

Card Catalogs, 745, 816–817
Case
  objective, **874**
  possessive, **875**
  pronoun, **552**–557
  pronoun and noun, **870**, **874**
Case-Sensitivity, Electronic, **858**
Catalogs, Electronic, 817
Cause-and-Effect Essay, 202–227
  for assessment, **309**
  defined, **203**
  drafting, 210–211
  editing and proofreading, 217
  model from literature, 204–205
  prewriting, 206–209
  publishing and presenting, 218
  revising, 212–216
  rubric for self-assessment, 218
  types of, **203**
Cause-and-Effect Relationships
  clarifying, 212
  in nonfiction, **802**
  on standardized tests, 226–227, 358–359
Cause-and-Effect Writing, **870**
-cede, -ceed, -sede, **785**–786
Character Studies, 81, **281**, 290
Characterization, 76–77, **871**
Characters, Action, **805**, 806, **870**
Charts, 138, 235, 263, **759**
Chat Rooms, Electronic, **858**
Chicago Manual of Style, The (CMS), 820, 852
Choosing a Form for Writing
  extensive, **14**
  focus on form, **14**
  modes, **14**
  reflexive, **14**
Choosing Your Topic Sources
  24-hour list, 256
  blueprinting, 54
  category brainstorming, 256
  class book awards, 286
  classroom interest poll, 159
  current events, 206
  discussion group, 134
  emotional thermometer, 206
  hot topics, 134
  initial draft sentence, 310
  invisible ink, 16
  itemized interest list, 78, 180

Index • **879**

newspaper scan, 232
notebook review, 134
observation, 106
previous knowledge and strengths, 310
products and services schedule, 159
related pairs, 180
sentence starters, 78, 232, 256, 286
song list, 54
trigger words and objects, 106
See also Topic Bank Ideas
Chronological Order, 210, 758
Chutes, for building conflict, **84**
Circling
action verbs, 63
key words, 311
main ideas, 164
repeated words, 25
subjects and verbs, 295
suspect words, 240
vague words, 88, 116, 216
See also Bracketing; Color-Coding; Highlighting; Underlining
Citations
APA, 852
CMS, 852
conventions for writing, **269**
defined, **871**
list, defined, **877**
listing, 268
MLA, 850, 851, 854
in periodical indexes, 820
styles of, 848–854
See also Bibliographies
Classical Inventions, **871**
Clauses, **448**, 468–484
adjective, **870**
adverb, 143, **870**
correcting fragment, **507–508**
defined, **448**, **871**
elliptical, 562–563
independent, **241**, 674–678, 679–680, **873**
main and noun, **874**
subordinate, **468**, **507–508**, **877**
types of, **468–484**
Clichés, 64
Climax, Literary, **871**

Clues, predicting, 807
Cluster Diagram, 17
Coherence, 37–**38**, 314, **871**
Collaborative Writing, **7**
See also Cooperative Writing Opportunities; Peer Review
Collective Nouns, **342**, **577**
Colon Marks, **679–682**, **871**
Color-Coding
causes and effects, 60, 212
clichés, 64
connections, 24
dull words, 166
general impressions, 112
generalizations, 238
main points, 141
modifiers, 296
run-on sentences, 114
short sentences, 214, 239
See also Bracketing; Circling; Highlighting; Underlining
Columns, Advice, **229**
Commas, **658–671**
in compound sentences, **241**
to correct run-on sentences, 511
defined, **871**
editing and proofreading, 65
to punctuate adverb clauses, 143
Commercials. *See* Infomercials
Common Nouns, **344**
Communication
comparing modes of, 125
effective, 745
exploring technology of, 45
one-on-one, 835
See also Listening; Media and Technology Skills; Reading; Representing; Viewing; Writing
Comparative Degrees, **598–602**, **604–605**
Compare-Contrast Writing, **871**
Comparison-and-Contrast Essay, 176–201
for assessment, **309**
defined, **177**
drafting, 184–185
editing and proofreading, 191
model from literature, 178–179
prewriting, 180–183
publishing and presenting, 192
revising, 186–190

rubric for self-assessment, 192
types of, **177**
Comparisons
balanced, 606
degrees of, **191**, **598–602**
identifying points of, 183
making clear, **604–607**
showing points of, 184
on standardized tests, 612–613
test prompts, 200–201
using *other* or *else* in, **607**
of works of literature, **281**
Complements, **434–441**, **871**
Compositions, **32–47**, **875**
Compound Adjectives, **385**
Compound Nouns, **343**, 712, 714
Compound Predicate Nominatives, **439–440**
Compound Prepositions, **402**
Compound Sentences. *See* Sentences
Compound Subjects, **424**, **574–575**
Compound Verbs, **425**
Compound Words, 706
Computers
applying skills for, 845
trouble-shooting problems with, 247
uses of, 11
See also Databases; E-mail; Internet; Test Banks; Word Processing
Concentration, vs. scanning on tests, 98–99
Conclusion Paragraphs, **871**
checking, with introductions, 314
citing expert's, 850
of composition, **39**
of writing, 291, 312
Conflict, **871**
in fiction, **805**
in short story, **81**
Conjugation, 533–535, **871**
Conjunctions
coordinating, **871**
correlative, **871**
defined, **400**, **408**
subordinating, **409**, **877**
types of, **408–411**

Conjunctive Adverbs, **411**
Connotation, **871**
  choosing words with positive, 166
  and denotation, **770**, **803**
  interpreting, 130–133
Considering Your Audience and Purpose. *See* Audiences; Purpose for Writing
Consonance, **871**
Consumer Reports, 177, **196–197**
Contests, for student work, 8, 869
Context
  clues of, 768
  historical, 804
  homophone errors in, 770
  of myths, 807
  on standardized tests, 788–789
Contractions, **718–719**, **871**
Contradictory Information, 293
Contrast, 140
Cookies, Electronic, **858**
Cooperative Writing Opportunities
  ad campaign, 159
  brochure on volunteerism, 135
  comparison of exercise programs, 181
  comparison of short stories, 287
  explained, 7
  group autobiography, 55
  short story with multiple authors, 79
  study-habit flyers, 233
  survey on extracurricular activities, 207
  technology-update research, 257
  travel brochure, 107
  See also Topic Bank Ideas
Coordinate Adjectives, **662**
Coordinating Conjunctions, **408**, 511, **871**
Copy/Paste, Word Processor, 335
Copyrighted Materials, Internet, 857
Correlative Conjunctions, **408**, **871**
Couplets, **871**
Creative Thinking, 841
Critical Viewing Skills
  analyze (Part 1), 7, 9, 37, 43, 69, 76, 88, 94, 112, 128, 130, 151, 156, 169, 170, 187, 193, 202, 228, 230, 245, 263, 267, 271, 275, 276, 282, 302, 303, 304, 308, 320
  analyze (Parts 2 and 3), 383, 390, 405, 448, 462, 472, 495, 498, 500, 528, 529, 543, 550, 570, 585, 587, 590, 621, 624, 648, 700, 704, 719, 744, 781, 790, 795, 802, 841, 844, 845
  apply, 346, 656, 661, 681, 685, 690, 703, 716, 817, 839
  assess, 440
  compare, 5, 508, 510, 766
  compare and contrast, 185, 410, 464, 471, 474, 476, 563, 601, 602, 604, 665
  connect, 32, 53, 56, 148, 218, 221, 291, 297, 492, 507, 514, 524, 527, 537, 541, 543, 574, 641, 643, 647, 652, 677, 686, 693, 715, 780, 800, 828
  contrast, 152, 178, 319, 334, 524, 527
  deduce, 343, 351, 678, 761, 812
  describe, 100, 111, 122, 246, 381, 385, 386, 392, 451, 452, 455, 535, 573, 580, 596, 599, 617, 645, 659, 708
  distinguish, 44, 124, 614
  draw conclusions, 324, 481, 666
  evaluate, 6, 48, 50–53, 163, 176, 190, 204, 213, 222, 378, 807
  explain, 344
  hypothesize, 74, 85, 145, 250, 264, 332, 837
  identify, 636
  infer, 120, 243, 280, 300, 363, 409, 470, 478, 554, 746, 771, 794
  interpret, 67, 484, 623, 778
  make a judgment, 108, 500
  relate, 193, 196, 315, 340, 371, 400, 412, 423, 675
  respond, 70, 91, 172, 198, 224, 490
  speculate, 4, 9, 403, 420, 436, 454, 459, 480, 513, 556, 618, 626, 654, 670, 688, 707, 814, 825
  support, 14, 35, 93, 139, 252, 834
  synthesize, 133
Critics, addressing, 142
Cross-Curricular Connections
  literature, 559
  music, 504
  physical education, 402, 434, 500, 654
  science, 342, 346, 366, 390, 408, 428, 492, 495, 584, 598, 616, 620, 674, 698
  social studies, 362, 370, 380, 422, 450, 468, 526, 540, 552, 572, 604, 638, 658, 684, 712
Cubing, 109, **160**, **871**
Cultural Context, 807
Cumulative Reviews
  Grammar Exercises, 726–727
  Parts of Speech, 418–419
  Phrases, Clauses, and Sentences, 522–523
  Usage, 634–635
Curricular Connections. *See* Cross-Curricular Connections
Cyberspace, Electronic, **858**

D

Dance. *See* Humanities
Dashes, **698–701**
Databases, Electronic, 260, 818, **858**
Dates (Calendar), punctuating, **669**
Declarative Sentences, **492**, **654**, **871**
Deductive Reasoning, **261**
Definite Articles, **382–383**
Degrees of Comparison, **598–602**, **604–607**
Demonstrative Adjectives, **387**
Demonstrative Pronouns, **350**, **871**
Denotation, **770**, **803**, **871**
Depth-Charging, **871**
Description, 100–127
  defined, **101**, **871**
    drafting, 110–111
    editing and proofreading, 118
    model from literature, 102–105

prewriting,106–109
publishing and presenting, 119
revising, 112–117
rubric for self-assessment, 119
types of, **101**
Design Elements, in ads, 158
Desktop Publishing, **11**
Dewey Decimal System, 818
Diagnostic Tests
Adjectives and Adverbs, 379
Agreement, 571
Basic Sentence Parts, 421
Capitalization, 637
Effective Sentences, 491
Miscellaneous Problems in
Usage, 615
Nouns and Pronouns, 341
Phrases and Clauses, 449
Prepositions, Conjunctions, and
Interjections, 401
Pronoun Usage, 551
Punctuation, 653
Using Modifiers, 597
Verb Usage, 525
Verbs, 361
Diagraming Sentences, 728–741
adjective clauses, 738–741
adverb clauses, 738–741
appositives and appositive
phrases, 734–735
complements, 731–732
complex sentences, 738–741
compound sentences, 738
compound-complex sentences,
741
conjunctions, 729–730
gerunds and gerund phrases,
735–736
infinitives and infinitive phrases,
736–737
modifiers, 728–730
noun clauses, 738–741
participles and participial phrases, 734–735
prepositional phrases, 732–733
subjects and verbs, 728–730
Diagrams, **759**
Dialects, **871**
Dialogues, **871**
forced vs. realistic, 85

paragraph conventions for, **40**
peer review, 117
punctuating, 65, **89**, 689, **719**
Diaries, **808**, **871**
Diction, **42**, 290, 315, **871**
Dictionaries, **772**, 821–823
different from, different than, **622**
Digerati, Electronic, **858**
Direct Objects, **434–436**, **872**
Direct Quotations. *See* Quotations
Discussions
group, 745, 837–838
to increase vocabulary, 767
panel, 270
Documentaries, **222–223**, **251**,
872
Documentation, **269**, 850–854
Documented Essays, **251**, **275**,
872
doesn't, don't, **622**
done, has done, **622**
don't anyone, **616**
Double Negatives, **616–618**
Downloads, Electronic, **858**
Drafting, **15**, **872**
Providing Elaboration
adding figurative language,
111
with anecdote, 140
describing situation, 140
including facts, 163
including references, 292
pointing to supports, 237
showing contrast, 140
showing vs. telling, 83
supporting generalizations
with specifics, 185
supporting thesis, 313
using examples and anecdotes,
237
using SEE method, 22
using sources, 263
using thought shots, 59
using TRI method, 211
Shaping Your Writing
block plan for, **236**
chronological order for, 210
to convey main point, 58
effective ad features for, 163
order of importance for, 110,
210

with organizational strategy,
261
with outline, 262
point-by-point plan for, **184**,
236
quick outline for, 312
spatial organization for, **110**
with strong lead, 21
subject-by-subject plan for, **184**
thesis statement for, 139, **261**,
291
with voice of storyteller, 82
See also Student Work in
Progress, Drafting
Drama, **94–95**, **806**, **872**
dramatic interpretations, presenting, 763
See also Humanities
due to, **622**

E

E-mail, Internet, **11**, **858**
-ed, -nt, -en, **456**
Editing and Proofreading, **15**
agreement, 118
errors, 26, 316
fact-checking, 146
grammar, 191
prepositional phrases on tests,
416–417
punctuation, 65, 89, 267
semicolons, 241
sentence clarity, 217
source documentation, 267
spelling, 167, 267, 298,
786–787
on standardized tests, 651
test revision prompts, 278–279
Editorials, **129**, 151
effect, affect, **316**, **620**
Effective Sentences, 490–521
combining, 495–498
errors of, 504–515
types of, defined, **492–493**
varying, 500–502
ei Words, spelling, **785–786**
either, neither, **578**
Elaboration, **872**
See also Providing Elaboration

Electronic Media. *See* Media and Technology Skills
Electronic Texts
dictionary, 823
encyclopedia, 824
reading, **809**
See also Internet
Elliptical Clauses, **479**, 562–563, **670**
else, other, **607**
Emotion, exclamation points to show, **65**
Emotional Thermometer, 206
Emphasis
creating paragraph, 40
underlining for, 692
Encyclopedias, 824, 856
End Marks, 654–656
to correct run-on sentences, **510**
defined, **875**
editing and proofreading, 65, 89
Endnotes, **269**
English
formal and informal, **43**
usage problems on tests, 632–633
Epics, **872**
-er, -est, -y, -i, **598**
Error Messages, Electronic, **858**
Errors
analyzing mechanical test, 322–323
avoiding sentence, 504–515
common homophone, **298**
correction tips on, 335
editing and proofreading, 316
patterns of spelling, **779**–780
proofreading, on tests, 724–725
Essays, **872**
action, for portfolio, 147
assessment, 308–323
cause-and-effect, 202–227
comparison-and-contrast, 176–201
documented, **251, 275, 872**
parts of, **312**
persuasive, 128–155
problem-and-solution, 228–249
reflective, **876**
reflective and personal, **49**

response-to-literature, 280–307
tests, 830
Essential Expressions, commas with, **667**–668
Etymologies, **872**
of words, **778**, 823
Evaluating Writing. *See* Peer Review; Reflecting on Your Writing; Rubrics for Self-Assessment
everywhere, anywhere, **621**
Evidence, Gathering. *See* Gathering Details
Exam Comments, 317
except, accept, **620**
Exclamation Marks, **872**
editing and proofreading, 89
sentences ending with, **492**–**493, 655**–656
to show emotion, **65**
Exclamatory Sentences. *See* Exclamation Marks
Exposition, **872**
See also Cause-and-Effect Essay; Comparison-and-Contrast Essay; Problem-and-Solution Essay
Expressive Writing. *See* Description; Journal; Narration; Poem
Extensive Writing, **872**

F

Facial Expressions, analyzing messages of, 125
Facilitators, Group Discussion, 838
Facts, **872**
checking, 146
citing, 850
vs. opinion, 50–53, **756, 800**
providing, 163
researching, 141
supporting main idea with, **35**
farther, further, **622**
fewer, less, **622**
Fiction, **872**
books in library, 818
reading, **805**
Field Labels, in dictionaries, 823
Figurative Language, **872**
types of, **111**

Film. *See* Humanities; Media and Technology Skills
Filmmakers, structure tips from, 60
Firsthand Biographies, 69, **872**
Five W's. *See who, what, where, when, why*
Flashcards, for vocabulary study, 774
Flip Charts, 762
Focus Groups, 166
Folk Tales, **807**
Footnotes, conventions for writing, **269**
Formal English, conventions of, **43**
Formatting, Word Processor, 760
Forms
of modifiers, 599–602
reading, **809**
workplace, 325, **330**
Fragments
defined, **872**
vs. sentences, **504**–508
Framing, to integrate references, 263
Freewriting, **872**
FTP Sites, Electronic, **858**
Function-Purpose Relationships. *See* Relationships
Functional Paragraphs, **40, 872**

G

Gathering Details
conducting research, 138
cubing, 109
hexagonal writing, 19
identifying points of comparison, 183
linking audience and angle, 162
locating sources, 260
reporter's formula, 19
scanning magazines, 162
for speeches, 747
for storytelling, 81
taking notes, 260
using index cards, 290
using organizer, 209
using T-chart, 138, 235
using timeline, 19, 57
Gazetteers, 824

Generalizations, 185, 238, **801**, **872**

Generating Topics. *See* Choosing Your Topic Sources

Genre, reading a wide variety of, 804–809

Geographical Abbreviations, **866**

Gerund Phrases, 460, **462**, **872**

Gerunds, **460–461**, **872**

GIF, Electronic. *See* Graphic Interchange Format

Glossaries, Textbook, **791**

Goals, personal and professional, **839**

gone, went, **623**

Government References, punctuating, 695

Grammar-Check, Word Processor, 335

Grammar Defined, **872**

Grammar, Hands-on. See Hands-on-Grammar

Grammar in Literature
  action verbs, 362
  active and passive voice verbs, 542
  adjectives, 381
  adverb clauses, 476
  adverbs, 391
  antecedents of pronouns, 347
  capitalization, 639
  comparative and superlative modifiers, 601
  correlative conjunctions, 410
  gerunds, 461
  helping verbs, 371
  indefinite pronouns, 578
  introductory commas, 664
  inverted subjects, 432
  masculine/feminine pronouns, 589
  nominative case of pronouns, 559
  prepositions, 403
  semicolon to correct run-on, 512
  types of sentences, 493
  verb tense, 527

Grammar in Your Writing
  active vs. passive voice, **87**
  adverb placement, **217**

agreement in inverted sentences, **295**

appositive phrases, **215**

avoiding homophone errors, **298**

conventions for, **3**

conventions for documentation, **269**

creating complex sentences, **239**

degrees of comparison, **191**

exclamation point, **65**

homophones, **316**

list of verb tenses, 189

punctuating adverb clauses, **143**

punctuating compound sentences, **241**

punctuating dialogue, **89**

relative pronouns, **62**

semicolons, **115**, **266**

using abbreviations, **167**

using conventions for titles, **146**

verb-indefinite pronoun agreement, **118**

Graphic Arts, interpreting, 764–765

Graphic Interchange Format (GIF), **858**

Graphic Organizers (Visual Representations),
  creating, 758-759
  charts, 758–759
  diagrams, 759
  formatting, 760
  graphs, 759
  illustrations, 759
  look at text structure to, 758
  maps, 759
  set a purpose for, 758
  tables, 759
  Venn diagram, 758
  interpreting, 759
  charts, 759, 797
  sequence chart, 797
  timeline, 758
  Venn diagram, 796
  web diagram, 797

Graphics
  electronic, **858**
  word processor, 760

Graphs, **759**
  for elaboration, 263

interpreting, 752–754
  types of, **753–754**

Group Discussions, 745, 837–838

H

Handwritten Work, style of, 848

Handbook, Solutions, 242

Hands-on-Grammar
  active arrows and passive points, 544
  adverb and adjective wheel, 388
  comparison star standout, 608
  movable modifiers, 516
  noun classification fold-up, 354
  pictographs of usage problems, 628
  Preposition Pet on a Leash, 406
  punctuation spots, 672
  rule reminder reference cards, 644
  simple sentence builders, 426
  subject-verb agreement color match, 581
  verb explorer, 364
  "Where to?" wheel, 466
  Who/Whom Pickup, 564

hardly, barely, scarcely, **617**

have, of, **624**

haven't any, **616**

he, him, **555**

he, his, him, himself, **585**

Health Articles, 203

Helping Verbs, **370–372**, **872**

her, she, **555**

here, there, 430

Hexagonal Writing, **873**
  for literature analysis, 19
  to narrow topic, 288

Highlighting
  to frame writing, 22
  performance script, 763
  sentences to evaluate structure, 212
  thesis statement, 264
  topic sentences, 238, 294
  verbs to identify active voice, 86
  See also Bracketing; Circling; Color-Coding; Underlining

himself, he, his, him, **585**

Historical Context, 804
Historical Essays, 177
History Papers, 203
Hits, Electronic, **858**
holy, wholly, **770**
Home Pages, Electronic, **858**
Homophones
  context and, **770**
  defined, **316, 873**
  errors, **298**
How-to Writing, **873**
HTML, Electronic. *See* HyperText
    Markup Language
Humanities, **873**
  art, 28, 198, 304
  dance, 124, 152, 246
  essays, 177
  film, 70, 276
  inspiration, 10
  music, 334
  myth, 96
  photography, 172
  theater, 320
  theatre, 44, 224
  See also Spotlight on
    Humanities; Topic Bank Ideas
Hyperbole, **873**
HyperText Markup Language
    (HTML), **858**
Hyphens, **704**–710, **873**

I

I, me, **555**
I-Search Report, **873**
-i, -y, -er, -est, **598**
Ideas
  description of, **101**
  evaluating, 252
  main, **33**–34, 204–205. *See also*
    Main Points
  supporting, 231, 255
  in writing process, **3**
Idioms, in dictionaries, 823
-ie Words, spelling, **785**–786
Illustrations, **35**, 90, **759**
Imagery, **873**
  in poetry, 807
Images, **873**
  for advertisement, 163
  creating visual, 758–759

"loaded", 756
  See also Photography
Imperative Sentences, **492, 654,
    873**
Impressions, General, 110, 112
in, into, **623**
Incidents, Autobiographical, **49**
Indefinite Adjectives, **387**
Indefinite Articles, **382**–383
Indefinite Pronouns, **353, 873**
  agreement with antecedents,
    587–588
  agreement with verbs, **118,
    578**–579
Independent Clauses, **468, 873**
  punctuating, **241, 674**–678,
    679–680
Index-Card Camera, **108**
Index Cards, 290, 644
Indexes
  for gathering information, 260
  periodical, 820–821
  textbook, **791**
Indirect Objects, **437**–438
Indirect Quotations. *See*
    Quotations
Inductive Reasoning, for organizing
    writing, **261**
Inferences
  of author's purpose, **799**
  making, on tests, 810–811
Infinitive Phrases, 463, **465, 873**
Infinitives, **463**–464, **873**
Influence Techniques. *See*
    Persuasive Techniques
Infomercials, **157**
Informal English, **43**
Information Media, 755–759
  analyzing, 756
  analyzing newscasts, 199
  and bias, 756
  commercial , 756
  documentary, 755
  editorial, 755
  examing media's influence on a
    perception of reality, 125
  facts and opinion in, 756
  interview, 755
  loaded language and images,
    756

newscasts, 755–756
  nonprint materials as, 755–756,
  purposes of, 755–756
  television news program, 755–
    756
  See also Media and Technology
    Skills
Informational Texts
  constructing meaning from,
    832–833
  on standardized tests, 846–847
-ing Words, **526**
Intensive Pronouns, 349–350
Interactivity, Electronic, **858**
Interjections, 400, **412, 873**
Internet, **11, 858**
  analyzing web pages and news-
    groups, 199
  budgeting sites on, 844
  consumer reports on, 197
  copyrighted materials on, 857
  dictionaries on, 823
  electronic calendar on, 842
  electronic databases on, 818
  library access on, 816, 817
  maps on, 263, 752, 759, 824
  narrowing topic with, 402
  newspapers and magazines on,
    820
  reliability of resources on, 857
  research using, 109
  search words, 383, 745
  Shakespeare resources on, 562
  subject searches, 856
  terms, **858**–859
  using, 826
  word search, 855
Internet Research Handbook,
    855–859
Interrogative Adjectives, **387**
Interrogative Pronouns, **352, 873**
Interrogative Sentences, **492, 873**
Interviews, **873**
  reading, **808**
  tips for, 835–836
Intransitive Verbs, **363, 873**
Introductions
  checking, against conclusion,
    314
  composition, **39, 873**

paragraph, 291, 312
textbook, **791**
Invisible Ink, 16
Invisible Writing, **873**
Irony, **873**
Irregular Forms, of modifiers, 599, 600–601
Irregular Verbs, **530**–532
Italics, Word Processor, 760
Itemizing, **873**
  to find topic, 78, 180
  See also Listing
its, it's, **316, 348, 387**

J

Jargon, **803, 873**
Journals, **873**
  idea, 4
  to narrow topic, 439
  reader's, 5
  reading, **808**
JPEG, Electronic, **859**
just (no more than), **623**

K

K Capacity, Electronic, **859**
Key Words, Electronic, **859, 874**
  See also Internet
kind of, sort of, **623**

L

Labels, Warning, 681
Ladders, for building conflict, **84**
Language
  body, 125
  evaluating author's, 803
  figurative, **111, 872**
  HTML, **858**
  informal, **315**
  "loaded", **756**
  persuasive, 145
  rhetorical, 747
  underlining foreign, 692
  variety in, 267
lay, lie, **623**
Layering, **874**
Lead, Composition, 21, 39, **874**
learn, teach, **623**

Learning Logs, 4, **874**
leave, let, **623**
Legends, **807, 874**
Legibility, **874**
  cursive *vs.* print, 848
  manuscript preparation, 848–854
less, fewer, **622**
Letters
  action, for portfolio, 242
  business, 325, **326**
  formal, **229**
  reading, **808**
Libraries
  finding on-line, 856
  using, 816–819
  using card catalog in, 745
  using reference section of, 752
Library Display, 299
Library of Congress System, 819
lie, lay, **623**
like, as, **624**
Linking Verbs, **366**–368, **577, 874**
Links, Electronic, **859**
Listening Skills, 744–745, 749–751
  analyzing news coverage, 199
  critical listening, 749–751
  comparing personal interpreta-
    tions with that of others, 125, 305, 751
  distinguish between fact and
    opinion, 125, 756
  eliminating barriers to listening,
    749
  examing media's influence on a
    perception of reality, 125
  evaluating objectivity, 199, 756
  evaluating speeches, 748
  for problems, 840–841
  generating criteria for evalua-
    tions, 748, 751
  identifying main idea and details,
    749
  interaction, 836
  monitoring listening, 749, 751
  preparing to listen, 749
  set a purpose for, 749
  taking notes, summarizing, and
    organizing, 749
  types of, **750**

  vocabulary development
    through, 767
Listing
  citations, 268–**269**
  defined, **874**
  to find topic, 78, 180
  sentence starters, 24
  verbs to evaluate tense, 188
  See also Itemizing
Literary Elements, listed, 290
Literary Interpretations, **281**
Literary Writing
  reading, **804**–807
  test prompts, 306–307
Literature, Grammar in. *See*
  Grammar in Literature
Literature Models. *See* Models
  From Literature
Literature, Responding to. *See*
  Responding to Fine Art and
  Literature
Login, Electronic, **859**
Logs, Learning, 4, **874**
Looping, 136, **874**
Lyric Poems, **874**

M

Magazines
  analyzing news coverage in, 199
  comparing photos to text in, 125
  scanning for details, 162
Mailings, advertisement, 168
Main Clauses, **874**
Main Ideas. *See* Ideas
Main Points, 58, 798
Manuscript, preparation of, 848–854
Maps
  for elaboration, 263
  electronic collections of, 824
  on Internet, 759
  interpreting, 752
Marks, Proofreading, list of com-
  mon, **868**
Masculine Pronouns, generic, 585
Math Skills, Workplace, 844
me, I, **555**
Measurements and Amounts,
  verb agreement with, **579**
Media and Technology Skills

analyzing news coverage, 199
building electronic portfolio, 29
comparing movie special
  effects, 225
creating a video postcard, 71
evaluating movie ads, 305
examining media's perception
  of reality, 125
exploring communication technology, 45
introduction to, 11
multimedia presentation, **874**
producing documentary video,
  277
producing short-story video, 97
recognizing persuasive techniques, 153
using computerized test banks,
  321
word processing, 173, 247, 335
Media, Information, 755–757
Memoirs, **49**, **874**
Memory Aids, spelling, 780
Memos, **229**
Messages, Phone, **332–333**
Metaphors, **111**, **874**
Meter, **874**
Minutes, Meeting, 325, **328**
Miscellaneous Problems in Usage,
  614–635
Misspelled Words, Commonly,
  862–863
Models From Literature
  Advertisement, 158–175
  Autobiographical Writing, 50–53
  Cause-and-Effect Essay, 204–205
  Comparison-and-Contrast Essay,
    178–179
  Description, 102–105
  Persuasive Essay, 130–133
  Problem-and-Solution Essay,
    230–231
  Research Report, 252–255
  Response to Literature, 282–285
  Short Story, 76–77
Modems, Electronic, **859**
Modern Language Association
  (MLA), 850–851, 854
Modification Process, defined, **380**
Modifiers, **378–399**
  activity for placing, 516

evaluating, 296
forms of, **191**, 599–602
misplaced, **513**–515
placement of, **217**
using, **596**–613
Money Management, 842
Monologues, **874**
Mood, **874**
Movie Reviews, 303
Movies. *See* Humanities; Media
  and Technology Skills
Multimedia Presentation, 761, **874**
  See also Media and Technology
    Skills
Music. *See* Humanities; Media
  and Technology Skills
Mysteries, Short Story, 75
Myths, **807**

N

Names, 669, 692
  See also Nouns
Narration, **874**
  See also Autobiographical
    Writing; Short Stories
Narrative Poem, **874**
Narrative Writing, test prompts,
  72–73
Narrators, types of, in storytelling,
  82
Narrowing Your Topic
  choosing focus, 182
  circling key words, 311
  conducting preliminary research,
    258
  cubing, **160**
  with hexagonal writing, 288
  with index-card camera, **108**
  with invisible writing, **56**
  listing and itemizing, 208
  looping, 136
  planning web or cluster diagram,
    17
  summarizing plot, 80
  with target diagram, **234**
  See also Topic Bank Ideas
Negative Sentences, 616–618
neither, either, **578**
never anything, **616**
never, no, none, not, **617**

Newbies, Internet, **859**
News. See Television Programs
Newsgroups, Electronic, **859**
Newspapers
  analyzing news coverage in, 199
  reading, **808**
  scanning for details in, 162
no, any, **616**
Nominative Case, **874**
  in pronoun usage, 552–554
  who, 560, 560–562
Nominatives, Predicate, 439–440
Nonessential Appositives, dashes
  with, 699
Nonessential Expressions, commas
  with, 667–668
Nonessential Material, parentheses
  with, 701
Nonessential Modifiers, dashes
  with, 699
Nonfiction
  books in library, 818
  strategies for reading, 798–803
Nonverbal Strategies, in speeches,
  747
nor, or, **574–575**
Note Cards
  for gathering information, 260
  for speeches, 747
Note Taking, 815
  for group discussions, 838
Notebooks
  idea, 4
  spelling, 779
  vocabulary, 773
Noun Classification, fold-up, 354
Noun Clauses, **480–481**, **874**
Nouns, **340**, **342–344**
  adjective clauses with, 470
  capitalizing proper, 640–643
  defined, **342**, **874**
  description of, in writing, **101**
  precise vs. vague, 88
  punctuating possessive, **712–715**
  that look like plurals, **577**
  types of, 342–344
  used as adjectives, **383–384**
Novels, **874**
  See also Fiction
nowhere, somewhere, **621**
-nt, -ed, -en, **456**

Numbered Lists, Word Processor, 760
Numbers
  commas in, 670, 671
  dashes with, 700
  hyphens with, 705
  underlining, 692

O

Objective Case, 874
  in pronoun usage, 552, 555–556
  whom, 560–562
Objective Complement, **441**
Objects, Direct, **434**–436, **872**
Objects, Indirect, **437**–438
Observation, **101**, **874**
Ode, **874**
of, have, **624**
On-line Essay, 192
On-line Publications, accepting student work, 8, 869
only, but, **617**
only, Placement of, **624**
Onomatopoeia, **874**
Open-Book Tests, 319, **874**
Opinions, **874**
  citing, 850
  evaluating, 282–285
  facts vs., 50–53, **756**, **800**
Opposition, addressing, 142
or, nor, **574–575**
Oral Presentations, 119
  See also Speeches
Oral Traditions, 807, **874–875**
Order of Importance, for writing, **110**, 210
Organizations, Names of, verb agreement with, **579**
Organizers
  cause-and-effect, 209
  graphic, **796–797**
Organizing Your Writing, **3**
  See also Shaping Your Writing
other, else, **607**
Outlines, **875**
  quick, 312
  for speeches, 747
  types of, **262**
  using, **795**

Overused Words, Commonly, **860–861**
Ownership, punctuating expressions of, **713**, 715
Oxymoron, **875**

P

Packaging. *See* Product Packaging
Pages, Electronic, **859**
Panel Discussion, 270
Papers, History, 203
Papers, Research. *See* Research Papers
Parables, **875**
Paradox, **875**
Paragraphs, **875**
  body, **39**, 291, 312, **870**
  developing topical, 211
  evaluating patterns in, 265
  introduction, 291, 312
  revising. *See* Revising Paragraphs
  topical, **877**
  types of, **40–41**
  writing effective, 32–47
  See also Conclusion Paragraphs
Parallelisms, **875**
Paraphrase, **875**
  crediting source of, 850
  for elaboration, **263**
  of poetry, 807
  to support thesis, 292, 313
Parentheses, **701–704**, 875
Parenthetical Expressions, punctuating, **665–666**, 700
Participial Phrases, 456, **458–459**
  defined, **875**
  punctuating, 676
Participles, **456–457**, 461, 875
Parts of Speech
  Cumulative Review on, 418–419
  identifying, on tests, 398–399
Passive Voice. *See* Verb Usage
Peer Review, **875**
  analytical reading for, 267
  encouraging specific, 117
  explained, 7
  of figurative language, 111
  focus groups for, 166
  for perspective, 25
  for plus and minus scoring, 297

pointing to passages for, 88
reading aloud for, 145, 216, 240
showing comparisons and contrasts for, 190
for vocabulary study, 774
of word choice, 64
Penmanship Reference, 848
Pentad, **875**
Performance, **763**
Periodicals
  finding on-line, 856
  in library, 820–821
  for publishing student work in, 8, 869
  punctuating references to, 681
Periods. *See* End Marks
Personal Essays, **49**
Personal Experience, reading and, 804
Personal Pronouns
  agreement with antecedents, **584**–586
  defined, **348**, **875**
Personification, **875**
Persuasion, **875**
  test prompts, 154–155, 174–175
  See also Advertisement; Persuasive Essays
Persuasive Essays, 128–155
  defined, **129**
  drafting, 139–140
  editing and proofeading, 146
  model from literature, 130–133
  prewriting,134–138
  publishing and presenting, 147
  revising, 141–145
  rubric for self-assessment, 147
  types of, **129**
Persuasive Techniques, 153, 756
  bias, 756
  evaluating, 756
  facts and opinions, 756
  loaded language and images, 756
  recognizing, 153
Phone Messages, **332–333**
Photo Montage, 192
Photography
  comparing messages of, 125
  See also Humanities; Images; Media and Technology Skills

Phrases, **448**, 450–465
  adjective, 676, **870**
  adverb, **870**
  appositive, **870**
  correcting fragment, **505**–506
  defined, **448**, **875**
  gerund, **872**
  participial, 676, **875**
  prepositional, **404**, **875**
  types of, **450–465**
Places, Names of, **669**
Plagiarism, 263, 685, 850
Planning Web, 17
Plots, **875**
  in fiction, **805**
  summarizing, 80
  tracking conflict in, 84
Plural Nouns, apostrophes with, 712
Plurals, **875**
  apostrophes with, **720**
  types of, for spelling, **781–782**
Poetry, **875**
  description in, 122–123
  lyric, **874**
  narrative, **874**
  ode, **874**
  reading, **806–807**
  sound devices in, 290
  sounds and rhythms of, 806
Point-by-Point Plan, for organizing writing, **236**
Point of View, **805**, **875**
Political Campaigns, **157**
Portfolios, 5, 27, **875**
  See also Building Your Portfolio
Position Papers
  assessment, **309**
  persuasive, **129**
Positive Degree, **598**–600
Possessive Case, **875**
  in pronoun usage, 552, 557
Possessive Nouns
  as adjectives, 384
  apostrophes with, **712–715**
Possessive Pronouns, as adjectives, **386**
"Possible Sentences" Strategy, 769
Predicates
  adjectives, 440
  complete, 422–425

nominatives, **439**
  simple, **423**
Prediction
  of clues in myths, 807
  on standardized tests, 810–811
Prefaces, Textbook, **791**
Prefixes, **775**, **783–785**, **875**
Prepositional Phrases, **404**, 450–453
  defined, **875**
  vs. infinitive, **464**
Prepositions, **400**, **402**–405
  defined, **402**, **875**
  vs. direct objects, **436**
  vs. indirect objects, **438**
  listed, 402
  vs. subordinating conjunctions, 409
Presentations
  evaluating, 748–749
  flip chart, 762
  interpretive, 763
  multimedia, 222, 761, **874**
  speech, 747–748
Presenting Compositions, **15**, **875**
Prewriting, **15**, **875**
  See also Audiences; Choosing Your Topic Sources; Gathering Details; Narrowing Your Topic; Purpose for Writing; Student Work in Progress; Prewriting
Print Media. *See* Magazines; Media and Technology Skills; Newspapers
Problem-and-Solution Essay, 228–249
  defined, **229**
  drafting, 236-237
  editing and proofreading, 241
  model from literature, 230–231
  prewriting, 232–235
  publishing and presenting, 242
  revising, 238–240
  rubric for self-assessment, 242
  types of, **229**
Problem-and-Solution Writing
  defined, **875**
  test prompts, 248–249
Problem-Solving Skills, 235, 840–841
Problems

miscellaneous usage, 614–635
  pronoun usage, 559–563
Process Essay, for assessment, **309**
Product Packaging
  for advertisement, 170–171
  as advertisements, **157**
Pronoun-Antecedent Agreement, **584**–590
Pronoun Usage, **550**–569
  test questions, 568–569
Pronouns, **340**, **346**–353
  adjective clauses with, 470
  agreement with antecedents, **584**–590
  apostrophes with, **716**–717
  clarity of, 191
  defined, **340**, **346**, **876**
  demonstrative, **871**
  and elliptical clauses, 562–563
  generic masculine, 585
  indefinite, **353**, **873**
  interrogative, **352**, **873**
  personal, **348**, **584**–586, **875**
  reflexive, **349**–350, **586**–587, **876**
  relative, **62**, **351**, **471**–472, **876**
  with special problems, 559–563
  types of, **346**–353
  used as adjectives, 386–387
Pronunciations, Dictionary, 823
Proofreading. *See* Editing and Proofreading
Proofreading Symbols
  list of common, **868**
  using, 26
Proper Adjectives, **384**, 645
Proper Nouns, **344**, 640–643
Proposals, **229**
Prose, **876**
Providing Elaboration
  adding figurative language, 111
  with anecdote, 140
  describing situation, 140
  including facts, 163
  including references, 292
  pointing to supports, 237
  showing contrast, 140
  showing vs. telling, 83
  supporting generalizations with specifics, 185
  supporting thesis, 313

using examples and anecdotes, 237
using SEE method, 22
using sources, 263
using thought shots, 59
using TRI method, 211
PSAT. *See* Scholastic Aptitude Test
Public-Service Announcements, **157**
Public Speaking, **746–748**
Publishers, of student work, 8, 869
Publishing, **15, 876**
Punctuation, **652–725**
 of adverb clauses, 143
 apostrophes in, **871**
 for clarity, **217**
 colons in, **871**
 commas, **658–671**
 of complex sentences, **239**
 of compound sentences, **241**
 defined, **876**
 of dialogue, **89**
 end marks, 510, **654–656, 875**
 exclamation points in, **65, 873**
 following, in poetry, 806
 hyphens in, **873**
 parentheses, **875**
 question marks, **876**
 quotation marks, **876**
 of quotations, **684–696**
 semicolons in, **115, 266, 674–678, 876**
 of titles, 146
Purpose for Reading, 798, 804
Purpose for Writing, **876**
 circling key words to assess, 311
 identifying and evaluating, 102
 identifying and supporting, 102–105
 identifying author's, 799
 matching audience with, 161
 recognizing, in myths, 807
Purposes for Writing
 autobiographies, 56
 cause-and-effect essays, 208
 comparison-and-contrast essays, 182
 description, 108
 identifying, 18, **758**
 persuasive essays, 137

problem-and-solution essays, 234
research reports, 259
response to literature, 289
short stories, 80

Q

Query Boxes, Electronic, **859**
Question-and-Answer Column, 245
Question Marks, **492, 655–656**
 defined, **876**
 editing and proofreading, 89
Questioning
 as active reading method, 804
 direct and indirect, **654–655**
 in group discussions, 745
 as study method, **793**
 types of, **750**
 vague vs. direct, 117
Questions
 direct objects in, 435
 subjects in, 429
 types of, on standardized tests, **126–127**
 types of test, **827–831**
 See also Standardized Test Preparation Workshops
Quicklist, **876**
Quotation Marks, **876**
 with direct quotations, **684–696**
 with other punctuation marks, 687–688
 in special situations, 689–690
 with titles, **694–695**
Quotations
 checking, 146
 colons with, 679
 commas with, 671
 direct, **263, 684–696, 850, 872**
 indirect, 684, **873**
 to support thesis, 292, 313
 underlining, 691–693

R

Radio, analyzing news coverage on, 199
Ratiocination, **876**
Readers' Guide to Periodical Literature, 820

Reading
 actively, **804**
 drama, **806**
 fiction, **805**
 to increase vocabulary, 767
 myths and folk tales, **807**
 poetry, **806–807**
 as study method, **793**
 varied sources, **808–809**
 visual information, 752–754
Reading Aloud
 for peer revision, 145, 216, 240, 267
 to revise dialogue, 85
Reading Skills, **790–811**
 active reading, 804
 author's language, 803
 author's purpose, 799
 close, 792
 connotation, 803
 denotation, 803
 determining style to use, 792
 for drama, 806
 evaluating text, 799
 fact and opinion, 800
 for fiction, 805
 graphic organizers, 796
  Venn diagram, 796
  web diagram, 797
  sequence chart, 797
 inferences, 799
 for myths and folk tales, 807
 outlines, using, 795, 815
 for poetry, 807
 reading nonfiction critically, 798
 scanning, 792
 sections in textbooks, using, 791
 skimming, 792
 SQ4R Method (survey, question, read, record, recite, review) 793–794
 types of, 792
 for varied sources, 808–809
Reading Styles, 792
Reading-Writing Connections
 distinguishing fact and opinion, **50–53**
 evaluating ideas, 252–255
 evaluating opinions, 282–285
 identifying and addressing audience, 178–179

identifying and developing main idea, 204–205
identifying and supporting purpose, 102–105
identifying indirect characterizations, 76–77
including facts and opinions, 53
incorporating design elements, 158
interpreting connotation, 130–133
supporting ideas, 230–231
supporting main idea, 255
supporting opinions, 285
Reasoning
  evaluating forms of, 801–802
  inductive and deductive, **261**
Reciting, as study method, **794**
Recording, as study method, **793**
Reference Books, Library, 819
Reference Skills, 812, 816–826
References
  electronic catalogs, 817
  incorporating, 292
  integrating, 263
  listing, 268–**269**
  on-line sites for, 856
  periodicals, 820
  periodical indexes, 820
  types of, 681, 695, 824, 848
Reflecting on Your Reading, 809
Reflecting on Your Speaking, Listening, Viewing, and Representing, 763
Reflecting on Your Spelling and Vocabulary, 787
Reflecting on Your Study, Reference, and Test-Taking Skills, 831
Reflecting on Your Workplace Skills and Competencies, 845
Reflecting on Your Writing, 26
  for advertisement, 168
  for assessment, 317
  for autobiographical writing, 66
  for cause-and-effect essays, 218
  for comparison-and-contrast essays, 192
  for description, 119
  as part of personal process, 8
  for persuasive essay, 147

for problem-and-solution essays, 242
for research report, 270
for response to literature, 299
for short story, 90
Reflective Essays, **49**, **876**
Reflexive Pronouns, **349**–350, **586**–587, **876**
Reflexive Writing, **876**
Refrain, **876**
Regular Forms, of modifiers, 599–600
Regular Verbs, **530**
Relationships
  function/purpose, 358–359
  identifying types of, **798**
Relationships, Cause-and-Effect
  clarifying, 212
  in nonfiction, **802**
  on standardized tests, 226–227, 358–359
Relative Adverbs, **473**
Relative Pronouns, **351**
  adjective clauses with, 471–472
  to combine sentences, **62**
  defined, **876**
Relevance, 315
Relevance Rankings, Electronic, **859**
Remembrance, as descriptive writing, **101**
Repetition, avoiding, 267
Rephrasing, statements for listening skill, 751
Reporter's Formula
  defined, **876**
  to obtain details, 19, 213
Reports
  consumer, 177, **196**–197
  I-Search, **873**
  lab, 203, 251
Representing Skills, 744, 758–763
Research
  analyzing, 267
  checking facts for, 141
  conducting, 138, 258
  defined, **876**
  incorporating ideas from, 850
  Internet handbook for, 855–859
  speaker's facts, 751

Research Papers, 250–279
  accessing prior knowledge for, 256–260
  defined, **251**
  drafting, 261–263
  editing and proofreading, 268
  model from literature, 252–255
  prewriting, 256–260
  publishing and presenting, 270
  revising, 264–267
  rubric for self-assessment, 270
  style of, 849
  types of, **251**
Research Writing, **876**
Resources. *See* References; Sources
Responding to Fine Art And Literature
  for advertisement, 159
  for autobiographical writing, 55
  for cause-and-effect essays, 207
  for comparison-and-contrast essays, 181
  for description, 107
  for persuasive essay, 135
  for problem-and-solution essays, 233
  for research report, 257
  for response to literature, 287
  for short story, 79
  See also Humanities; Spotlight on Humanities
Response to Literature, 280–307
  defined, **281**
  drafting, 291–292
  editing and proofreading, 298
  model from literature, 282–285
  prewriting, 286–290
  publishing and presenting, 299
  revising, 293–297
  rubric for self-assessment, 299
  types of, **281**
  writing, **876**
Reviewing Work. *See* Peer Review; Reflecting on Your Writing; Revising
Reviews
  critical, **281**
  movie, 303
Revising
  defined, **15**, **876**

prepositional phrases on tests, 416–417
on standardized tests, 278–279, 520–521
See also Peer Review; Student Work in Progress; Revising
Revising Overall Structure, Strategies for
checking for unity, 293
checking introduction against conclusion, 314
circling main ideas, 164
color-coding causes and effects, 212
color-coding main impression, 112
color-coding main points, 141
color-coding to improve unity, 60
highlighting to frame writing, 23
highlighting topic sentences, 238
improving introduction, 186
improving visual layout, 164
reviewing question against answer, 314
supporting arguments, 141
tracking thesis, 264
using chutes and ladders, **84**
Revising Paragraphs, Strategies for
addressing critics, 142
building snapshots, 113
color-coding connections, 24
color-coding generalizations, 238
confirming coherence, 314
exploding the moment, 61
highlighting topic sentences, 294
improving sentence power, 165
introducing functional, 265
making comparisons and contrasts clear, 187
making dialogue realistic, 85
reading with a partner, 85
refining or adding connecting sentences, 187
seeing patterns, 265
shortening sentences, 165
using reporter's formula, 213
Revising Sentences, Strategies for
circling subjects and verbs, 295
color-coding for sentence variety, 239

color-coding to evaluate length, 214
color-coding to identify run-ons, 114
combining to vary length, 62
deleting irrelevant ideas, 315
highlighting verbs to identify voice, 86
listing sentence starters, 24
listing verbs for tense, 188
shortening, to improve power, 165
underlining short, 266
using transition boxes to smooth writing, 144
Revising Word Choice, Strategies for
bracketing modifiers, 296
circling action verbs, 63
circling repeated words, 25
circling suspect words, 240
circling vague nouns, 88
circling vague verbs, 116
circling vague words, 216
color-coding dull words, 166
compiling synonym bank, 267
evaluating informal language, 315
identifying repeated words, 190
using persuasive language, 145
Rhetorical Language, 747
Rhyme
defined, **876**
scheme, **876**
Rhythm, **876**
Rhythms, in poetry, 806
right, write, **298**
Roles, group, 838
Roman Numeral Outline, 262
Roots, word, **776, 876**
Rubric for Self-Assessment, 26
of advertisement, 168
of assessment writing, 317
for autobiographical writing, 66
for cause-and-effect essays, 218
for comparison-and-contrast essays, 192
defined, **876**
for description, 119
for persuasive essay, 147

for problem-and-solution essays, 242
for research report, 270
for response to literature, 299
for short story, 90
Run-on Sentences
correcting, **509–512**
defined, **876**

S

Salutations, **876**
punctuating, **670,** 681
SAT. *See* Scholastic Aptitude Test
Satire, **876**
Scanning
vs. close reading, **792**
vs. concentrating on tests, 98–99
to gather details, 162
scarcely, barely, hardly, **617**
Schedules
study, 813
time, 842
Scholastic Aptitude Test (SAT), 831
preliminary of (PSAT), 830
Scoring, Plus and Minus, 297
Scripts, marking, 97
Search Engines, Electronic, "Search" Feature, in word processor, 575
-sede, -cede, -ceed, **785–786**
SEE Method, 22, **876**
seen, **624**
-self, selves, **349**
Semicolons, 674–678
in compound sentences, **115, 241, 266**
to correct run-on sentences, 511
defined, **876**
Sentence diagraming, 728–741
adjective clauses, 738–741
adverb clauses, 738–741
appositives and appositive phrases, 734–735
complements, 731–732
complex sentences, 738–741
compound sentences, 738
compound-complex sentences, 741
conjunctions, 729–730

gerunds and gerund phrases, 735–736

infinitives and infinitive phrases, 736–737

modifiers, 728–730

noun clauses, 738–741

participles and participial phrases, 734–735

prepositional phrases, 732–733

subjects and verbs, 728–730

Sentence Parts, Basic, 420–447

Sentences

capitalization in, 638–639

clarity of, 217, 295

combining short, 62, 214, **215**, 239

commas and compound, 658–659

completing, with verbs, 376–377

complex, **239**, **483**

compound, **241**, **482–483**, **871**

connecting, 187

construction of, on tests, 446–447, 488–489

declarative, **492**, **654**, **871**

defined, **422**, **876**

diagraming, 728–741

exclamatory, **493**, **872**

fluency of, **3**

fragmented, 316

imperative, **492**, **654**, **873**

interrogative, **492**, **873**

inverted, **295**, 431–432, **576**, 577

negative, 616–618

outline of, 262

paragraph style and variety of, **42**

punctuating adverb clauses in, 143

punctuating compound, 115, **266**

revising. *See* Revising Sentences

run-on, **876**

simple, **482**

starter, 24, 78, 232

strategy for "Possible", 769

structure of, **482–483**, 484

supporting, **35**

topic, **33–34**, 36, 238, **877**

See also Effective Sentences

Sequence Chart, **797**

Serial Commas, **660–662**

set, sit, **624**

Setting

defined, **877**

details of, 290

in short story, **81**

Shaping Your Writing

block plan for, **236**

chronological order for, 210

to convey main point, 58

effective ad features for, 163

order of importance for, 110, 210

with organizational strategy, **261**

with outline, 262

point-by-point plan for, **184**, 236

quick outline for, 312

spatial organization for, **110**

with strong lead, 21

subject-by-subject plan for, **184**

thesis statement for, 139, **261**, 291

with voice of storyteller, 82

she, her, **555**

Short Stories, 74–99

defined, **75**, **877**

drafting, 82-83

editing and proofreading, 89

fiction as, 805

model from literature, 76-77

prewriting,78-81

publishing and presenting, 90

revising 84-88

rubric for self-assessment, 90

showing vs. telling, 83

test questions, 98–99

types of, **75**

Signatures, Electronic, **859**

Similes, **111**, **877**

Singular Nouns, apostrophes with, 712, 714

sit, set, **624**

Sketches, Autobiographical, **49**

Slogans, Advertisement, 163

Snapshots, 113

so, that, **624**

Software, Computer. *See* Databases; Word Processing

Solutions, analyzing, 235, 840–841

somewhere, nowhere, **621**

Sonnets, **877**

sort of, kind of, **623**

Sound Devices, in poetry, 290, 806

Sound Effects. *See* Media and Technology Skills

Sources

citing, 848–854

crediting, 263, 850

locating, 260

types of, **263**

Spatial Organization, for writing, **110**

Speakers

defined, **877**

focusing on, 749

identifying, in poetry, 806

Speaking Skills 744–748

class participation and, 745

nonverbal strategies, 747

planning a speech, 747

preparation for, 747

preparing note cards for, 747

rhetorical language, 747

taking part in class discussions, 745, 883

types of speeches, 746

verbal strategies, 747

Special Effects, analyzing movie, 225

Specifics

replacing generalizations, 185

supporting thesis with, 313

Speeches, 726

audience and, 746, 748

delivering, 746–747

evaluating speeches, 748

giving and getting feedback, 747–748

nonverbal language, 747

persuasive, 129

planning a speech, 747

preparing note cards for, 747

preparing outline for, 747

providing main idea and details, 747

reading, **808**

researching, **747**

types of speech, 746

volume, pitch, and tone, 747

Spell Checker, Word Processor
  adding names to, 217
  described, 335
  limitations of, 298, 786
Spelling, 766, 779–789
  abbreviations, 167
  adverbs vs. pronouns errors of,
    557
  changed words ending in *y*, **598**
  homophone errors in, 298, 431
  list of problem words for, **862–
    863**
  preferred, 606
  rules for, **781–787**
  silent letters, 542
  species, 620
  tip for remembering, 501
  words ending in *ing*, **526**
Spotlight on the Humanities
  analyzing ideas in art, 198
  analyzing ideas in art forms, 320
  analyzing meaning in the arts, 10
  analyzing themes in art forms,
    304
  evaluating artistic performances,
    152
  evaluating persuasive art forms,
    172
  examining ideas and culture in
    art, 246
  examining ideas in art forms, 70
  examining ideas in arts, 334
  examining ideas in media, 276
  examining influence of art
    forms, 224
  examining relationships among
    art forms, 96
  exploring cultural themes, 28
  recognizing shared culture, 96
  recognizing themes, 44
  See also Humanities
Spotlight on the Humanities
    Activities
  analysis of *Annie's* appeal, 320
  art or music description, 124
  art review, 198
  film evaluation, 152
  fine art response, 304
  grant proposal memo, 334
  inspiration meaning, 10
  inspirational writers journal, 28

modern myth, 96
movie proposal, 70
photography analysis, 172
proposal essay, 246
quotations log, 44
report on Chicago Black Socks
  Scandal, 276
satire analysis, 224
SQ4R Method, **793–794**
Stage Directions, in drama, 806
Standardized Test Preparation
    Workshops
  analyzing mechanical errors,
    322–323
  applying verb usage rules, 336–
    337
  cause-and-effect prompts, 226–
    227
  choosing effective sentences,
    520–521
  comparison-and-contrast
    prompts, 200–201
  completing sentences with
    verbs, 376–377
  constructing meaning from
    text, 832–833
  inferences and predictions,
    810–811
  interpreting graphic arts, 764–
    765
  narrative writing prompts, 72–
    73
  nouns in analogies, 358–359
  organization and style questions,
    46–47
  persuasive passages, 174–175
  persuasive prompts, 154–155
  phrases and clauses, 488–489
  problem-and-solution prompts,
    248–249
  pronoun usage questions, 568–
    569
  proofreading, 651
  proofreading errors, 724–725
  questions about short stories,
    98–99
  reading informational texts,
    846–847
  recognizing sentence construc-
    tion, 446–447
  recognizing standard English

usage, 632–633
  responding to literature-based
    prompts, 306–307
  revising prepositional phrases,
    416–417
  revision prompts, 278–279
  subject-verb agreement, 594–
    595
  types of questions asked, **126–
    127**
  using adjectives and adverbs,
    398–399
  using context, 788–789
  using modifiers, 612–613
  using verbs, 548–549
  for the writer in you, 12–13
  writing skills prompts, 30–31
Stanzas, **877**
Statement, Extension, Elaboration
    (SEE) Method, 22, **876**
Stating, purpose for writing, 234
Statistics
  checking, 146
  citing, 850
  defined, **877**
  supporting main idea with, **35**
Storytelling
  elements of, **81**
  recognizing purpose for, 807
Structure
  overall. *See* Revising Overall
    Structure
  paragraph, **32–47**
Student Work in Progress,
    Drafting
  creating general impression, 110
  incorporating references, 292
  with Roman numeral outline,
    262
  showing vs. telling stories, 83
  with subject-by-subject organi-
    zation, 184
  with support points, 237
  supporting thesis, 313
  with thought shots, 59
  with topical paragraphs, 211
Student Work in Progress, Final
    Drafts of
  advertisement, 169
  assessment writing, 318
  autobiographical writing, 67–68

cause-and-effect essay, 218–221
comparison-and-contrast essay, 193–195
description, 119–121
persuasive essay, 148–150
problem-and-solution essay, 243–244
research report, 271–274
response to literature, 300–302
short story, 91–93
Student Work in Progress, Prewriting
blueprint to choose topic for, 54
cause-and-effect organizer for, 209
circling key words, 311
cubing details, 109
developing characters, 81
with emotional thermometer, 206
with hexagonal writing to narrow topic, 288
identifying points of comparison, 183
with index cards, 290
linking audience, angle, and details, 162
listing and itemizing to find topic, 78, 180
looping to narrow topic, 136
matching purpose with audience, 161, 256
with purpose-oriented research, 259
with sentence starters, 232, 286
with T-chart to gather details, 235
with T-chart to organize research, 138
with timeline to gather details, 57
with trigger words to choose topic, 106
See also Choosing Your Topic Sources
Student Work in Progress, Revising
to address critics, 142
with chutes and ladders technique, 184
circling verbs to enliven writing, 116
color-coding modifiers, 296
color-coding short sentences, 214
color-coding word choice, 166
evaluating action verbs, 63
evaluating vague words, 216
evaluating verb tense, 188
with exploding moments technique, 61
highlighting cause and effect sentences, 212
highlighting topic sentences, 294
highlighting verbs to identify voice, 86
to improve introduction, 186
refining word choice, 240
seeing paragraph patterns, 265
shortening sentences, 165
with snapshot technique, 113
to support arguments, 141
supporting generalizations, 238
using peer revision for word choice, 64
Study Group Comparisons, 317
Study Skills, 812–815
assignment book, 814
evaluating text, 799
note-taking, 815
outlining, 795, 815
sections in textbooks, using, 791
SQ4R Method (survey, question, read, record, recite, review) 793–794
study plan, 813
summarizing 815
Study, Reference, and Test-Taking Skills, 812–831
basic study skills, 813–815
reference skills, 815–826
reflecting on, 831
SQ4R Method (survey, question, read, record, recite, review) 793–794
test preparation on, 832–833
test-taking skills, 827–831
See also Note-taking; Reference; Standardized Test Preparation Workshop; Summaries
Studying, words, 772–778
Style Manuals, 268, 850–853
Styles
APA, 852
CMS, 853
handwritten, 848
MLA, 850, 851, 854
paragraph, 42–43
questions on tests, 126
research paper, 849
word-processing, 849
Style in Writing. See Audience and Purpose; Voice; Word Choice
Subject-Verb Agreement, 118, 572–580
for clarity, 217, 295
color match activity, 581
test prompts, 594–595
Subjects
complements, **439**–440
complete, 422–425
compound, **424**, **574**–575
confusing, 576–580
defined, **877**
hard-to-find, 428–432
of linking verbs, **577**
mixed, **575**
order of, with verbs, 502
plural, **572**, **575**
simple, **423**
singular, **572**, **574**
using on-line searches for, 856
Subordinate Clauses, **468**
correcting fragment, **507**–508
defined, **877**
Subordinating Conjunctions, **409**, **877**
Suffixes
defined, **877**
spelling, **783**–785
word, **777**–778
Summaries
citing research, 850
defined, **877**
of drama events, 806
for elaboration, **263**
and note-taking, 815
Superlative Degrees, of comparisons, **598**–602, **604**–605
Supports, Writing, 230, 237

Surfing, Electronic, **859**
Surveying, as study method, **793**
Syllables, dividing, **709**–710
Symbols, **877**
 underlining, 692
Symbols, Proofreading, list of
 common, **868**
Synonym Bank, for word choice,
 267
Synonyms, for context, **770**

T

T-Chart, 138, 235
Tables, **759**
Tables of Contents, Textbook,
 791
Tailoring, language for audiences,
 80
take, bring, **622**
Tape Recording
 for vocabulary study, 773
 See also Media and Technology
 Skills
Target Diagram, to narrow topic,
 234
Targeting, audiences, 208
teach, learn, **623**
Teamwork, learning, 837–838
Technology Skills
 and writing, 11, 29, 45, 173,
 247, 321, 335
 See Media and Technology Skills
Television Programs
 analyzing news on, 125, 199
 persuasive, 153
 See Media and Technology Skills
Tenses, verb. *See* Verb Usage
Test Banks, Computerized, 321
Test-Taking Skills, 812, 827–831
 See also Standardized Test
 Preparation Workshops
Tests, Open-Book, 319, **874**
Text, description and structure of,
 758
 See also Description; Revising
 Overall Structure, Strategies
 for
Text-Organizers, using to locate
 information,
 glossary, 791–792

graphic features, 792
 headings, 792
 tables of contents, 791–792
 textbook sections, 791
Textbooks
 appendix, 791
 chapter introduction and summary, 792–793
 glossary, 791–792
 index, 791–792
 pictures and captions, 792–793
 questions and exercises, 792–
 793
 tables of contents, 791–792
 titles, headings and subheadings,
 792–793
Texts, Informational, 832–833,
 846–847
than, then, **614, 625**
that there, this here, **625**
that, which, who, **625**
the, a, an, **382**
Theater. *See* Humanities
theater, theatre, **606**
their, there, they're, **316,** 431,
557, 625
Themes, composition, **877**
then, than, **614, 625**
there, here, 430
Thesaurus, **772,** 825
Thesaurus, Word Processor, 335
Thesis Statements
 composition, **39**
 defined, **877**
 developing, 139, 291
 proposing, **261**
 supporting, 139, 291, 292, 313
 tracking, 264
 unity with, 37
Thinking, Creative, 841
Thought Shots, for elaboration, 59
Thrillers, Short-Story, **75**
Time
 expressing, with verb tenses,
 536–537
 management, 842
 punctuating expressions of, **713**
 punctuating numerals of, 681
Timekeeping, for group discussions, 838
Timeline, 19, 57, 839

See also Chronological Order
Titles
 abbreviations of, **167, 864**
 capitalizing, 646–648
 commas with, **669**
 conventions for writing, **146**
 punctuating, 681
 underlining, 691–693
 using quotation marks around,
 694–695
 verb agreement with, **579**
 without quotation marks, 695
 See also Abbreviations
to, too, two, **625**
Tone, Writing, **42, 877**
Topic Bank Ideas
 account of a competition, 55
 advertisement for product, 159
 anecdote about humorous
 experience, 55
 biography response, 287
 comparison about athletes, 181
 comparison of U.S. regions, 181
 description of freedom, 107
 description of sporting event,
 107
 editorial about TV violence, 135
 essay about year-round schools,
 207
 essay on body systems, 310
 essay on funding girls' sports,
 135
 essay on recycling, 233
 essay on role models, 310
 essay on school spirit, 233
 letter to author, 287, 327
 letter to workplace, 327
 minutes of club meeting, 329
 minutes of public meeting, 329
 public-service announcement,
 159
 report on achievement, 257
 report on technology, 207
 report on TV accuracy, 257
 short story about a challenge, 79
 short story in unusual setting, 79
 See also Choosing Your Topic
 Sources; Narrowing Your
 Topic; Responding to Fine Art
 and Literature; Spotlight on
 the Humanities Activities

Topic Web, **877**
Topical Paragraphs, **40**
  defined, **877**
  developing, 211
Topics, Narrowing. *See*
  Narrowing Your Topic
Transition Boxes, to smooth writing, 144
Transitions
  defined, **877**
  list of connecting, 38, 187
  list of logical, 145
  paragraph, 40
Transitive Verbs, **363**, **877**
TRI Method, **36**, 211
Trigger Words, using, to choose
  topic, 106
Trouble-shooting, computer
  problems, 247
Twenty-four Hour List, for choosing topic, 256
two, to, too, **625**

U

Underlining
  to improve unity, 60
  quotations, 691–693
  short sentences, 266
  See also Bracketing; Circling;
    Color-Coding; Highlighting
Uniform Resource Locator (URL),
  859
Unity
  checking for, 293
  and coherence, 37–38
  defined, **877**
URL. *See* Uniform Resource
  Locator
Usage Problems
  miscellaneous, 614–635
  pronoun, 559–563
Usenet, electronic, **859**
Using Modifiers, **596–613**

V

Vanity Pages, electronic, **859**
Venn Diagram, 751, **796**
Verb Explorer, 364
Verb-Subject Agreement. *See*
  Subject-Verb Agreement

Verb Usage, **524**–549
  applying rules for, during tests,
    336–337
  tenses of, 188, 189, **526**–537
  test prompts of, 548–549
  voices of, 86, **87**, **540**–543
Verbal Strategies, in speeches,
  747
Verbals (Parts of Speech), **877**
  See also Gerunds; Infinitives;
    Participles
Verbs, **360**–377
  adverbs modifying, 390–391
  agreement with indefinite pro-
    nouns, 118, **578**–579
  compound, **425**
  defined, **360**, **877**
  evaluating action, 63
  helping, **872**
  highlighting, to identify voice, 86
  intransitive, **363**, **873**
  linking, **366**–368, 577, **874**
  order of, with subjects, 502
  vs. participles, **457**
  vs. participles or gerunds, 461
  precise vs. vague, 116
  principal parts of, **529**
  regular and irregular, 530–532
  transitive, **363**, **877**
  types of, **362**–372
Vertical File, Library, 820–821
Video Technology. *See* Media and
  Technology Skills
Viewing Skills, 744, 752–757
  analyzing news coverage, 199
  evaluating persuasive techniques,
    756
  examining media's influence on
    a perception of reality, 125
  fine art, analyzing elements, 757
  graphs, 753
    bar, 754
    line, 753
    pie, 753
  information media, 755–756
  link information to text, 754
  maps, 752
  photographs, 757
  See also Critical Viewing;
    Information Media;
    Responding to Fine Art

Vignettes, **101**, **877**
Viruses, Electronic, **859**
Visuals
  creating, 758–759
  for elaboration, 263
  See also Media and Technology
    Skills
Vocabulary, **766**–789
  remembering, 773–774
Voice, Writing
  defined, **3**, **877**
  types of, in narration, **82**
  See also Audience and Purpose;
    Verb Usage

W

W3, Internet Experts, **859**
A Walk Through the Writing
  Process. *See* Writing Process
Warning Labels, 681
Web Diagram, **797**
Web Postings, 218, 270
Web, World Wide (WWW), **859**
  See also Internet
Web Pages, Electronic, **859**
Web Sites, Electronic, electronic,
  859
went, gone, **623**
Westerns, Short Story, **75**
Wheels
  Adverb and Adjective, 388
  "Where to?", 466
when, where, **625**
where at, **621**
which, that, who, **625**
who, what, where, when, why, 19,
  213, **872**
who, whom, whose, **559**–562
wholly, holy, **770**
Word Choice
  revising. *See* Revising Word
    Choice
  in writing process, 3
  See also Words
Word Origins, **778**, 823
Word Processing, **11**
  creating ads with, 173
  documents, 849
  error management using, **335**
  formatting in, 760

for highlighting script, 763
organizing portfolio with, *29*
trouble-shooting problems with, 247
using "Search" feature, 575
Words
list of misspelled, **862–863**
list of overused, **860–861**
See also Word Choice
Working With Other Writers. *See* Cooperative Writing Opportunities
Workplace Skills and Competencies, 835–845
communicating one-on-one, 835
computer skills, 845
creative thinking, 841
goals, personal and professional, 839
group discussion, 837
group roles, 838
interaction, effective, 836
interviewing, 835
math skills, 844
money management, 843
problem-solving, effective, 840
teamwork, 837
time management, 842
working with people, 835
Workplace Writing, 324–337
applications, 330
business letter, 326
defined, **325**
forms, 330
meeting minutes, 328
types of, **325**
Works-Cited List
defined, **877**
World Wide Web (WWW), **859**
write, right, **298**
The Writer in You. *See* Writing Process
Writers. *See* Authors
Writing
types of, **14**, 21
using writing technologies, 11, 29, 45, 173, 247, 321, 335
See also Autobiographical Writing; Cause-and-Effect Essay; Comparison-and-Contrast

Essay; Narration; Persuasive Writing; Problem-and-Solution Essay; Research Report; Response to Literature; Short Story; Writing for Assessment
Writing Activities, Ideas for.
See Cooperative Writing Opportunities; Media and Technology Skills; Spotlight on the Humanities; Topic Bank Ideas
Writing Effective Paragraphs, **32**–47
Writing for Assessment, 308–323
defined, **309**
drafting, 312–313
editing and proofreading, 316
prewriting, 310–311
publishing and presenting, 317
revising, 314–315
rubric for self-assessment, 317
types of, **309**
Writing Process
overview of personal, 2–13
qualities of, **3**
responding to questions on, 30–31
summarized, **15**
using writing technologies, 11, 29
walk through, **14**–31
Writing Prompts. *See* Standardized Test Preparation Workshops
Writing-Reading Connections. *See* Reading-Writing Connections
WWW. See World Wide Web

Y

-y, -i, -er, -est, **598**
your, you're, **298**

Z

Zip Files, Electronic, **859**

Acknowledgments

Grateful acknowledgment is made to the following for permission to reprint copyrighted material:

Dover Publications, Inc.
"The Indomitable Spirit of Sojourner Truth" from Introduction to *Narrative of Sojourner Truth* by William Kaufman. Introduction copyright © 1997 by Dover Publications, Inc. Reprinted by permission.

Harcourt, Inc.
"Primer Lesson" from *Slabs of the Sunburnt West* by Carl Sandburg. Copyright © 1922 by Harcourt Brace & Company and renewed 1950 by Carl Sandburg.

The Barbara Hogenson Agency
"The Dancers" by Horton Foote. Copyright © Renewed 1982, 1983 by Horton Foote. Copyright © 1954, 1955 by Horton Foote. CAUTION: The reprinting of THE DANCERS included in this volume is reprinted by permission of the author and The Barbara Hogenson Agency. The amateur and stock performance rights in this play are controlled exclusively by Dramatists Play Services, Inc. 440 Park Avenue South, New York, NY 10016. No amateur or stock production of the play may be given without obtaining, in advance, the written permission of the Dramatists Play Service, Inc., and paying and requisite fee. Inquiries regarding all other rights should be addressed to Barbara Hogenson. The Barbara Hogenson Agency, 165 West End Avenue, Suite 19-C, New York, NY 10023.

Alan P. Lightman
"In Computers" from *Science 82* by Alan P. Lightman. Copyright © 1982 by Alan P. Lightman.

National Parks Magazine
"We Can Go Home Again" by Nevada Barr from *National Parks Magazine,* May/June 1999. Copyright © 1999 by the National Parks and Conservation Association. Reprinted by permission.

W.W. Norton & Company
"The Appalachian Tail" by Bruce Eason from *Flash Fiction* edited by James Thomas, Denise Thomas, and Tom Hazuka. Copyright © 1992 by James Thomas, Denise Thomas, and Tom Hazuka.

Post Eagle
"See Ya' at the Subway" from *Post Eagle* by Edwina Armstrong . Copyright © 1991 by Post Eagle.

Reader's Digest Association, Inc.
"The Shadowland of Dreams" by Alex Haley. Copyright © 1991 by The Reader's Digest Association, Inc.

The San Diego Union
"Lederer's Miracle is his Well of wit and wisdom with words" from The Miracle of Language, reprinted in *The San Diego Union,* December 15, 1991. Copyright © 1991 by The San Diego Union. Reprinted by permission of the author.

Simon & Schuster Inc.
From *Dinosaurs Rediscovered* by Don Lessen. Copyright © 1992 by Don Lessem.

Time/Warner
"Digital Video Daze" by Joshua Quittner from *Time* Magazine, 10/2/98. Copyright © 1998 by Time/Warner. "Murderous Mitch" by Tim Padgett from *Time* Magazine, 11/16/98. Copyright © 1998 by Time/Warner.

Note: Every effort has been made to locate the copyright owner of material reprinted in this book. Omissions brought to our attention will be corrected in subsequent editions.

Photo Credits

Cover: Corel Professional Photos CD-ROM™; Stamp Design ©United States Postal Service, All Rights Reserved.; **vi:** (top) Michael P. Gadomski/Photo Researchers, Inc.; (bottom) Corel Professional Photos CD-ROM™; **vii:** (top) Corel Professional Photos CD-ROM™; (bottom) ©1996, Bob Gage/FPG International Corp.; **ix:** ©The Stock Market/Mark Gamba; **x:** Nik Wheeler/CORBIS; **xi:** Nick Gunderson/Tony Stone Images; **xii:** Photofest; **xiii:** Al Campanie/ The Image Works; **xiv:** Pierre Berger/Photo Researchers, Inc.; **xv:** Courtesy Rebecca Graziano; **xvi:** *Gust of wind at Ejiri, in the province of Suruga.* From the series The Thirty-six Views of Fuji, Metropolitan Museum of Art, Rogers Fund, 1936. (JP 2553) © 1984/87 by The Metropolitan Museum of Art; **xvii:** ©StockFood America/Beery; **xviii:** Marshian Boy, Christian Pierre, Private Collection/SuperStock ; **xix:** (top)

David Young-Wolff/Tony Stone Images; (bottom) ©1996, Rob Gage/ FPG International Corp.; **xx:** (top) ©1993 Jack Vartoogian; (bottom) Corel Professional Photos CD-ROM™; **xxi:** (top) Corel Professional Photos CD-ROM™; (bottom) NASA; **xxii:** (top & bottom)) Corel Professional Photos CD-ROM™; **xxiii:** (top & bottom) Corel Professional Photos CD-ROM™; **xxiv:** Corel Professional Photos CD-ROM™; **xxv:** (top, middle, bottom) Corel Professional Photos CD-ROM™; **xxvi:** Andy Sacks/ Tony Stone Images; **xxvii:** (top) ©The Stock Market/Mug Shots; (bottom) Corel Professional Photos CD-ROM™; **1:** *Benjamin Comfort* (detail), Percy Ives, Detroit Historical Museum; **2:** ©1991 Arthur Tilley/FPG International Corp.; **4:** David Young-Wolff/PhotoEdit; **5:** ©The Stock Market/Jose L. Pelaez; **6:** Tony Freeman/PhotoEdit; **7:** Mary Kate Denny/PhotoEdit; **9:** (top)

Courtesy of the author; (bottom) Courtesy of Glo Simon; **10:** Ken Karp/ Omni-Photo Communications, Inc.; **14:** ©Jeff Greenberg/PhotoEdit/ PictureQuest; **28:** *Study for Old King Cole,* Maxfield Parrish, Art Resource, NY; **32:** ©StockFood America/ Grand; **35:** Ken Kerbs/ Monkmeyer; **37:** Corel Professional Photos CD-ROM™; **43:** Fotopic/Omni-Photo Communications, Inc.; **44:** Photofest; **48:** ©The Stock Market/Mark Gamba; **50:** ©FPG International Corp.; **53:** *Sardines and Olives,* Francis Livingston, Jerry Leff Associates, Inc.; **55:** *Travelling Carnival,* John Sloan, National Museum of American Art/Art Resource, NY; **56:** ©1999, Telegraph Colour Library/FPG International Corp.; **67:** ©1995, Gary Buss/FPG International Corp.; **69:** Esbin-Anderson/The Image Works; **70:** The Kobal Collection; **74:** Nik Wheeler/ CORBIS; **76:** CORBIS/Joel W. Rogers;

Acknowledgements/Photo Credits • 899

Photo Credits

79: *Basketball Superstars* by LeRoy Neiman Copyright © LeRoy Neiman, Inc. All Rights Reserved.; **85:** Laura Dwight/ CORBIS; **88:** ©The Stock Market/ John Henley; **91:** CORBIS; **93:** Amos Zezmer/Omni-Photo Communications, Inc.; **94:** FPG International Corp.; **96:** The Granger Collection, New York; **100:** Nick Gunderson/Tony Stone Images; **102 & 105:** CORBIS/ Bettmann; **107:** Vincent van Gogh, "The Bedroom of van Gogh at Arles", 1889. Oil on canvas. 57.5 x 74 cm. Musee d'Orsay, Paris, France. Erich Lessing/Art Resource, NY; **108:** (left) ©1993, S. Malmone/FPG International Corp.; (right) ©1991, Ron Thomas/FPG International Corp.; **111:** ©1999 Terry Qing/FPG International Corp.; **112:** Rudi Von Briel/ PhotoEdit; **120:** ©1993, Richard H. Smith/FPG International Corp.; **122:** Steve Warmowski/The Image Works; **124:** *Costume du Chinois pour Parade,* 1917, Pablo Picasso, Lauros-Giraudon/Art Resource, NY; **128:** *Trial by Jury,* 1964, Thomas Hart Benton, oil on canvas; 30" x 40" (76.0 x 1010.7cm), The Nelson-Atkins Museum of Art, Kansas City, Missouri, bequest of the artist. ©T.H. Benton and R.P. Benton Testamentary Trusts/Licensed by VAGA, New York, NY; **130:** (top) Michael P. Gadomski/Photo Researchers, Inc.;(bottom) Corel Professional Photos CD-ROM™; **132:** Corel Professional Photos CD-ROM™; **135:** *The Pond,* 1985, Adele Alsop, Courtesy of Schmidt Bingham Gallery, NYC. ; **139:** CORBIS/Bettmann; **145:** Ken Karp Photography; **148 & 150:** CORBIS/Bettmann; **151:** Pearson Education/PH College; **152:** Photofest; **156:** Artwork copyright 2000 by Phil Yeh www.ideaship. com; **158:** Michigan Opera Theatre; **163:** Al Campanie/The Image Works; **169:** Courtesy Megan Chill; **170:** Michelle Bridwell/PhotoEdit; **172:** ©Gordon Parks; **176:** Pierre Berger/Photo Researchers, Inc.; **178:** image© Copyright 1998 PhotoDisc, Inc.; **181:** *Love In Ice,* Veronica Ruiz de Velasco, Courtesy of the artist; **185:** (top) Janecek/Monkmeyer; (bottom) Leslye Borden/PhotoEdit; **187:** David W. Hamilton/The Image Bank; **190:** Bob Daemmrich/The Image Works; **193 & 195:** Michael Newman/ PhotoEdit; **196:** Spencer Grant/PhotoEdit; **198:** *St. John the Evangelist,* Apse Mosaic. Pisa Duomo, Cimabue, Scala/Art Resource, NY; **202:** NASA; **207:** *Two Lane Road Cut,* Woody Gwyn, Courtesy of the artist; **213:** Michael Newman/ PhotoEdit; **219–220:** David Young-Wolff/PhotoEdit; **221:** Courtesy Rebecca Graziano; **222:** Robert Brenner/PhotoEdit; **224:** Photofest; **228:** R. Crandall/ The Image Works; **230:** ©The Stock Market/Tom Bean; **233:** *Gust of wind at Ejiri, in the province of Suruga.* From the series The Thirty-six Views of Fuji, Metropolitan Museum of Art, Rogers Fund, 1936. (JP 2553) © 1984/87 by The Metropolitan Museum of Art; **243:** Michael S. Yamashita/CORBIS; **245:** image ©Copyright 1998 PhotoDisc, Inc.; **246:** ©Robbie Jack/CORBIS; **250:** *Icebergs,* Frederic Edwin Church, Art Resource, NY; **252:** Collection of The New-York Historical Society; **257:** *Three Studies of a Dancer in Fourth Position,* Charcoal and pastel with stumping, with touches of brush and black wash on greyish-tan laid paper with blue fibers (discolored from pinkish-blue). c. 1879/80, 48 x 61.5 cm. Bequest of Adele R. Levy, 1962.703. Photograph © 1999, The Art Institute of Chicago. All rights reserved.; **264:** Tony Freeman/ PhotoEdit; **267:** ©The Stock Market/ John Henley; **271:** ©StockFood America/Beery; **273:** Corel Professional Photos CD-ROM™; **274:** The Image Works; **275:** Tony Freeman/PhotoEdit; **276:** Photofest; **280:** *Marshian Boy,* Christian Pierre, Private Collection/SuperStock ; **282 & 284:** CORBIS; **287:** *Mexican Market* (detail), Jane Scott, Schalkwijk/Art Resource, NY; **291:** image©Copyright 1998 PhotoDisc, Inc.; **297:** Jeff Greenberg/The Picture Cube; **300:** Courtesy of the Library of Congress; **302:** *The Raven,* 1845, Edmund Dulac, The Granger Collection, New York; **303:** Bill Aron/PhotoEdit; **304:** Photo Courtesy of The Norman Rockwell Museum at Stockbridge; **308:** ©1996, Rob Gage/FPG International Corp.; **315:** Tony Freeman/PhotoEdit; **319:** David Young-Wolff/Tony Stone Images; **320:** Photofest; **324:** Corel Professional Photos CD-ROM™; **332:** Jeff Greenberg/PhotoEdit; **334:** ©1993 Jack Vartoogian; **338:** *In Celebration,* 1987, Sam Gilliam, National Museum of American Art, Washington, DC/Art Resource, NY; **363:** Corel Professional Photos CD-ROM™; **371:** NASA; **378–392:** Corel Professional Photos CD-ROM™; **402:** Pearson Education/ PH College; **405–411:** Corel Professional Photos CD-ROM™; **412:** NASA; **414 & 420:** Corel Professional Photos CD-ROM™; **423:** Mark D. Longwood/Pearson Education/PH College; **424:** Ken Karp/PH photo; **429–452:** Corel Professional Photos CD-ROM™; **454:** Silver Burdett Ginn; **455 & 459:** Corel Professional Photos CD-ROM™; **462:** Silver Burdett Ginn; **464:** Corel Professional Photos CD-ROM™; **470–510:** Corel Professional Photos CD-ROM™; **513:** Frank Siteman/ Omni-Photo Communications, Inc.; **514–543:** Corel Professional Photos CD-ROM™; **550:** Pearson Education/ PH College; **554:** image©Copyright 1998 PhotoDisc, Inc.; **556:** Michael Littlejohn/Pearson Education/PH College; **560:** Courtesy of the Library of Congress; **563:** M. Lopez/Pearson Education/PH School; **584–596:** Corel Professional Photos CD-ROM™; **599:** PH College; **599–601:** Corel Professional Photos CD-ROM™; **602:** PH College; **602–668:** Corel Professional Photos CD-ROM™; **675–681:** NASA; **685:** Corel Professional Photos CD-ROM™; **686:** Courtesy of the Library of Congress; **688–719:** Corel Professional Photos CD-ROM™; **742:** *Books II,* 1993, Polly Kraft, Private Collection, Courtesy Fischbach Gallery, New York; **744:** Elizabeth Crews/The Image Works; **746:** Richard Hutchings/ PhotoEdit; **757:** *Starry Night,* Vincent van Gogh, 1889, Oil on Canvas, 29 x 36 1/4 in. The Museum of Modern Art, New York. Acquired through the Lillie P. Bliss Bequest; **761:** Ken Karp/ PH Photo; **762:** Lane Yerkes; **766:** Corel Professional Photos CD-ROM™; **781:** ©The Stock Market/ Michal Heron; **785:** Corel Professional Photos CD-ROM™; **786:** ©1996, Bob Gage/FPG International Corp.; **790:** Will Faller; **794:** Ken Karp/PH Photo; **795:** Grace Davies/Omni-Photo Communications, Inc.; **800:** Courtesy of the Library of Congress; **802:** ©The Stock Market; **807:** Myrleen Ferguson/PhotoEdit; **812:** ©The Stock Market/Mug Shots; **814:** Will Hart; **817:** David Young-Wolff/PhotoEdit; **825:** Will Faller; **828:** Will Faller; **834:** David Aronson/Stock, Boston/ PictureQuest; **837:** Tony Freeman/PhotoEdit; **839:** David Young-Wolff/PhotoEdit; **841:** Dennis MacDonald/PhotoEdit/ PictureQuest; **844:** Corel Professional Photos CD-ROM™; **845:** Jeff Greenberg/ PhotoEdit